SOCIAL PSYCHOLOGY

Fifth Edition

ELLIOT ARONSON

University of California, Santa Cruz

TIMOTHY D. WILSON

University of Virginia

ROBIN M. AKERT

Wellesley College

PEARSON
Prentice Hall

Pearson Education International

If you purchased this book within the United States or Canada you should be aware that it has been wrongfully imported without the approval of the Publisher or the Author.

Senior Acquisitions Editor: Jeff Marshall
Editor-in-Chief: Leah Jewell
Editorial Assistant: Jill Liebowitz
Editor-in-Chief, Development: Rochelle Diogenes
Senior Development Editor: Roberta Meyer
Senior Media Editor: David Nusspickel
Executive Marketing Manager: Sheryl Adams
VP, Director of Production and Manufacturing: Barbara Kittle
Managing Editor: Joanne Riker
Assistant Managing Editor: Maureen Richardson
Production Editor: Nicole Girrbach
Manufacturing Buyer: Tricia Kenny
Creative Design Director: Leslie Osher

Senior Art Director: Ximena Tamvakopoulos
Designer: Wanda Espana
Cover Photo: Tony Wang Studios
Manager, Production/Formatting and Art: Guy Ruggiero
Illustrator (Interior): Maria Piper
Director, Image Resource Center: Melinda Reo
Manager, Rights and Permissions: Zina Arabia
Interior Image Specialist: Beth Brenzel
Photo Researcher: Barbara Salz
Image Permission Coordinator: LaShonda Morris
Manufacturing Manager: Nick Sklitsis
Composition: Pine Tree Composition, Inc.
Printer/Binder: Courier

Credits and acknowledgments borrowed from other sources and reproduced, with permission, in this textbook appear on appropriate page within text (or on pages 615–618).

Pearson Education LTD.
Pearson Education Australia PTY, Limited
Pearson Education Singapore, Pte. Ltd
Pearson Education North Asia Ltd
Pearson Education Canada, Ltd.
Pearson Educación de Mexico, S.A. de C.V.
Pearson Education -- Japan
Pearson Education Malaysia, Pte. Ltd
Pearson Education, Upper Saddle River, New Jersey

10 9 8 7 6 5 4 3 2 1
ISBN 0-13-132793-3

To my grandchildren: Jacob, Jason, Ruth, Eliana, Natalie, Rachel and Leo Aronson. My hope is that your wonderful capacity for empathy and compassion will help make the world a better place

E.A.

To my family, Deirdre Smith, Christopher and Leigh Wilson

T.D.W.

To my mentor, colleague, and friend, Dane Archer

R.M.A.

BRIEF CONTENTS

CONTENTS

CHAPTER 3　SOCIAL COGNITION: *How We Think about the Social World*　56

CHAPTER 7 ATTITUDES AND ATTITUDE CHANGE: *Influencing Thoughts and Feelings* 198

CHAPTER 8 CONFORMITY: *Influencing Behavior* 236

CHAPTER 10   INTERPERSONAL ATTRACTION:
From First Impressions to Close Relationships 316

CHAPTER 11 PROSOCIAL BEHAVIOR: *Why Do People Help?* 356

CHAPTER 12 AGGRESSION: *Why Do We Hurt Other People? Can We Prevent It?* 388

CHAPTER 13 PREJUDICE: *Causes and Cures* 428

SOCIAL PSYCHOLOGY IN ACTION 1   SOCIAL PSYCHOLOGY AND HEALTH 474

PREFACE

When we began writing this book, our overriding goal was to capture the excitement of social psychology. We have been pleased to hear, in many kind letters and e-mail messages from professors and students, that we succeeded. One of our favorites was from a student who said that the book was so interesting that she always saved it for last, to reward herself for finishing her other work. With that one student, at least, we succeeded in making our book an enjoyable, fascinating story, not a dry report of facts and figures.

There is always room for improvement, however, and our goal in this, the fifth edition, is to make the field of social psychology an even better read. When we teach the course, there is nothing more gratifying than seeing the sleepy students in the back row sit up with interest and say, "Wow, I didn't know that! Now *that's* interesting." We hope that students who read our book will have that very same reaction.

Social psychology comes alive for students when they understand the whole context of the field: how theories inspire research, why research is performed as it is, how further research triggers yet new avenues of study. We have tried to convey our own fascination with the research process in a down-to-earth, meaningful way and have presented the results of the scientific process in terms of the everyday experience of the reader. However, we did not want to "water down" our presentation of the field. In a world where human behavior can be endlessly surprising and where research results can be quite counterintuitive, students need a firm foundation on which to build their understanding of this challenging discipline. Here, in more detail, is how we present a rigorous, scientific approach to social psychology in a way that, we hope, engages and fascinates most students.

A STORYTELLING APPROACH

Social psychology is full of good stories, such as how the Holocaust inspired investigations into obedience to authority, how reactions to the marriage of the crown prince of Japan to Masako Owada, a career diplomat, illustrates cultural differences in the self-concept, and how Lance Armstrong's successful battle with cancer, and his incredible athletic feats (five consecutive victories in the Tour de France), illustrate social psychological approaches to health. By placing research in a real-world context, we make the material more familiar, understandable, and memorable.

Opening Vignettes

Each chapter begins with a real-life vignette that illustrates the concepts to come. We refer to this event at several points in the chapter, clarifying to students the relevance of the material they are learning. Examples of the opening vignettes include the tragic death of Amadou Diallo, who was shot forty-one times by four white police officers, as he reached for his wallet in the vestibule of his New York apartment building (Chapter 3, "Social Cognition: How We Think about the Social World"), some amazing acts of altruism at the sites of the terrorist attacks on September 11, 2001 (Chapter 11, "Prosocial Behavior: Why do People Help?"), and a murder trial in which an innocent man was sentenced to death because of faulty eyewitness testimony (Social Psychology in Action 3, "Social Psychology and the Law").

"Mini-Stories" in Each Chapter

Our storytelling approach is not limited to these opening vignettes. There are several "mini-stories" woven into each chapter that both illustrate specific concepts and bring the material to life. For each one, first, we describe an example of a real-life phenomenon that is designed to pique students' interest. These stories are taken from current events, literature, and our own lives. Second, we describe an experiment that attempts to explain the phenomenon. This experiment is typically described in some detail, because we believe that students should not only learn the major theories in social psychology but also understand and appreciate the methods used to test those theories. We often invite the students to pretend that they were participants in the experiment, to give them a better feel for what it was like and what was found. Here are a few examples of our "mini-stories" (if you thumb through the book, you will come across many others):

- In Chapter 4, on social perception, we introduce the concept of internal and external attributions by discussing public reaction to domestic doyene, Martha Stewart's 2003 indictment on nine counts of conspiracy, obstruction of justice and securities fraud by the federal government. In the initial days after her indictment, journalists (and the members of the public they interviewed) formed attributions to explain the mess in which this multimillionaire and CEO found herself. Her detractors made strong internal attributions: Her alleged stock-trading behavior was indicative of her personality, for example, her controlling nature, avarice, and over attention to detail. Her supporters made strong external attributions: It was nothing about her but aspects of her situation such as her gender and occupational success that caused her to be unfairly targeted by the Securities and Exchange Commission.

- In Chapter 8, on conformity, we discuss the tragic explosion of the Space Shuttle Challenger in 2003. A piece of insulating foam broke off the Shuttle as it launched and gashed the wing, allowing superheated gases to enter the Shuttle during re-entry. While pieces of foam had broken off in prior launches, this was not perceived as a problem by NASA but instead, as an acceptable "anomaly." When people are faced with an ambiguous situation, social influence leads them to conform to other people's judgments of the situation (Sherif, 1936). Recent research has found that the group members' judgments can converge to create a risky strategy (Levine, Higgins, & Choi, 2000). An independent investigating panel came to just this conclusion about the NASA managers in charge and NASA culture in general. As a group, they completely failed to label this ambiguous situation—the disintegrating foam—as a problem, but instead conformed to each other's perception of it as an odd but inconsequential event.

- In Chapter 9, on group processes, we introduce the topic of deindividuation with a description of a scene from Harper Lee's novel *To Kill a Mockingbird*. In this scene, we see a potential lynch mob through the eyes of the novel's protagonist, 8-year-old Scout. The mob has gathered to lynch Tom Robinson, a black man falsely accused of rape. The mob meets many of the conditions identified by social psychological research for deindividuation: It is dark, the men are dressed alike, and they have hats pulled over their ears. Then Scout unwittingly performs a brilliant social psychological intervention by singling out one of the men she recognizes, calling him by name, and asking after his son, who is her classmate. She succeeded in turning a faceless mob into a collection of individual citizens, thereby defusing a very dangerous situation.

- In Chapter 12, on aggression, we present an interesting historical observation: For hundreds of years, the Iroquois lived a peaceful existence, rarely, if ever, engaging in aggressive behavior. All of this changed in the seventeenth century when the newly arrived Europeans brought the Iroquois into direct competition with their neighbors, the Hurons. Within a short time, the Iroquois developed into fierce warriors. What does this say about the causes of aggression and its roots in culture? This story leads into a discussion of research on the cultural and economic roots of violence.

Social Psychological Methods: Another Good Story

It might seem that a storytelling approach would obscure the scientific basis of social psychology. On the contrary, we believe that part of what makes the story so interesting is explaining to students how to test hypotheses scientifically. In recent years, the trend has been for textbooks to include only short sections on research methodology and to provide only brief descriptions of the findings of individual studies. In this book, we integrate the science and methodology of the field into our story, in a variety of ways.

Separate Chapter on Methodology

Unlike most texts, we devote an entire chapter to methodology (Chapter 2). "But wait," you might say, "how can you maintain students' interest and attention with an entire chapter on such dry material?" The answer is by integrating this material into our storytelling approach. Even the "dry" topic of methodology can come alive by telling it like a story. We begin by presenting two pressing real-world problems related to violence and aggression: Does pornography promote violence against women? Why don't bystanders intervene more to help victims of violence? We then use actual research studies on these questions to illustrate the three major scientific methods (observational research, correlational research, and experimental research). Rather than a dry recitation of methodological principles, the scientific method unfolds like a story with a "hook" (What are the causes of real-world aggression and apathy toward violence?) and a moral (Such interesting, real-world questions can be addressed scientifically). We have been pleased by the reactions to this chapter in the previous editions.

Detailed Descriptions of Individual Studies

We describe prototypical studies in more detail than most texts. We discuss how a study was set up, what the research participants perceived and did, how the research design derives from theoretical issues, and the ways in which the findings support the initial hypotheses. We often ask readers to pretend that they were participants in order to understand the study from the participants' point of view. Whenever pertinent, we've also included anecdotal information about how a study was done or came to be; these brief stories allow readers insights into the heretofore hidden world of creating research. See, for example, the description of how Nisbett and Wilson (1977) designed one of their experiments on the accuracy of people's causal inferences on page 143 and the description of the origins of Aronson's jigsaw puzzle technique on pages 469–470.

Emphasis on Both Classic and Modern Research

We include a large number of charts and graphs detailing the results of individual experiments. The field of social psychology is expanding rapidly, and exciting new work is being done in all areas of the discipline. In this fifth edition, we have added a great deal of new material, describing dozens of major studies done within the past few years. We have added hundreds of references from the past few years. Thus the book provides thorough coverage of up-to-date, cutting-edge research.

In emphasizing what is new, many texts have a tendency to ignore what is old. We have tried to strike a balance between the latest research findings and classic research in social psychology. Some older studies (e.g., early work in dissonance, conformity, and attribution) deserve their status as classics and are important cornerstones of the discipline. For example, unlike several other current texts, we present detailed descriptions of the Schachter and Singer (1962) study on misattribution of emotion (Chapter 5), the Festinger and Carlsmith (1959) dissonance study (Chapter 6), and the Asch (1956) conformity studies (Chapter 8). We then bring the older theories up to date, following our discussions of the classics with modern approaches to the same topics, including culture, gender, self, and emotion (e.g., Cross & Gore, 2003; Fiske, 2003) in Chapter 5; self-esteem maintenance (e.g., Steele's self-affirmation theory and Higgins's self-discrepancy theory) in Chapter 6; the process of dissonance reduction in different cultures (e.g., Sakai, 1998; Stone, Wiegand, Cooper, & Aronson, 1997; Viswesvaran & Deshpande, 1996) in Chapter 6; and the role of accountability and accuracy in informational and normative conformity (e.g., Quinn & Schlenker, 2002; Barron and colleagues, 1996) in Chapter 8. This allows students to experience the continuity and depth of the field, rather than regarding it as a collection of studies published in the past few years.

SIGNIFICANT CHANGES TO THE FIFTH EDITION

To illustrate more concretely how the fifth edition has been updated, here is a sampling of new research that is covered:

- Chapter 3, "Social Cognition: How We Think about the Social World": This chapter has been updated to reflect the growing emphasis on automatic (nonconscious, involuntary, unintentional, and effortless) thinking versus controlled (conscious, voluntary, intentional, and effortful) thinking. The automatic versus controlled application of stereotypes is used as an illustration of these two modes of thinking, including a new opening vignette that discusses the case of Amadou Diallo, who was shot forty-one times by four white police officers as he reached for his wallet in the vestibule of his apartment building, and discussion of research studies by Payne (2001) and Correll et al. (2002). This possible case of automatic stereotyping is contrasted to cases in which people apply stereotypes more consciously and deliberately, as in the case of racial profiling. We give examples of the racial profiling of Middle Eastern-looking people after September 11, 2001. More than thirty new references have been added, including the work of Epley & Gilovich, 2001; Englich & Mussweiler, 2001; and Wegner, Fuller, & Sparrow, 2003.

- Chapter 4, "Social Perception: How We Come to Understand Other People": This chapter updates the discussion of the fundamental attribution error by increasing the prominence of the concept of the correspondence bias. The chapter highlights recent work on people's intuitive understanding of the correspondence bias, or the spotlight effect (e.g., Gilovich, Kruger, & Medvec, 2002). The section on culture and the correspondence bias has been revised and updated substantially to reflect current developments in this emerging research area, for example, the work of Miyamoto & Kitayama (2002), Choi and colleagues (2003), and Knowles and colleagues (2001).

- Chapter 5, "Self-Knowledge: How We Come to Understand Ourselves": This chapter begins with a new opening vignette, based on an episode from the TV show, "Friends." We have added dozens of new references, most from the past few years. There are updated discussions of such issues as culture, gender, and the self, and how parental praise influences intrinsic interest in children. As before, there is a balance between detailed discussions of classic findings (e.g., Schachter and Singer's work on emotion,

Lepper's work on intrinsic motivation) and modern, cutting edge approaches to these topics.

- Chapter 6, "Self-Justification and the Need to Maintain Self-Esteem": In addition to being brought completely up to date, one of the major additions to Chapter 6 is a discussion of the underlying reasons why people experience dissonance as painful. Highlighted in this discussion is the recent work of Greenberg, Solomon, Pyszczynski, and their colleagues (1997, 1999, 2001) on terror management, self esteem, and the fear of death.

- Chapter 7, "Attitudes and Attitude Change: Influencing Thoughts and Feelings": There is a new opening vignette for this chapter, that focuses on the history of cigarette advertising, including a discussion of how ads were tailored for women versus men. There is also a new section on implicit versus explicated attitudes, and updated discussions of all of the classic topics. For example, we discuss a recent study that found that advertisements that portray women in stereotypic ways can trigger stereotype threat (Davies, Spencer, Quinn, & Gerhardstein, 2002).

- Chapter 8, "Conformity: Influencing Behavior": This chapter begins with a new opening vignette, focusing on issues of conformity and obedience at the nation's public and private military academies. We review Shannon Faulkner's experience as the first woman to enter The Citadel, and focus on women cadets' recent allegations of rape by male cadets at the U.S. Air Force Academy. As before, this chapter contains detailed descriptions of some of social psychology's most famous and enduring research studies, such as the Sherif, Asch, and Milgram studies. It also discusses modern research on conformity and social norms, for example, the use of injunctive and descriptive norms to promote beneficial social behavior and the effects of social influence processes on women's and men's body image. The chapter includes a new section on propaganda. Building on Chapter 7 (Attitudes), this section discusses how propaganda (for example, in Nazi Germany) sways public opinion through informational and normative conformity.

- Chapter 9, "Group Processes: Influence in Social Groups": This chapter includes many new references and updates, including a revision of the section on gender and social roles and gender and leadership.

- Chapter 10, "Interpersonal Attraction: From First Impressions to Close Relationships": This chapter has been changed substantially, with the order of material reorganized and some material deleted to sharpen the focus on important elements. The chapter begins with a new vignette, focusing on the mate selection strategies operating among Nepalese vil-

lagers and Hindu and Muslim Indians living in Great Britain. This vignette presages the chapter's major emphasis on cross-cultural definitions of attraction and love. New material includes discussion of computer-mediated relationships and evolutionary approaches to love.

- Chapter 11, "Prosocial Behavior: Why Do People Help?": This chapter opens with a new vignette detailing some of the heroic acts by ordinary citizens on September 11th, 2001, such as people who lost their lives trying to save others at the World Trade Center. Each section is then updated with the addition of many references to recent research.

- Chapter 12, "Aggression: Why We Hurt Other People": This chapter has a new opening vignette, a discussion of the Columbine High School massacre in 1999, the reasons behind it, and how such tragedies can be avoided in the future (Aronson, 2000). Many other new research findings are discussed, such as the effects of violent video games on aggressive thoughts and feelings (Anderson & Dill, 2000); a broader discussion of domestic violence (Eisenstat & Bancroft, 1999); an expanded discussion of chemical and biochemical antecedents of violent behavior—including alcohol, testosterone, and serotonin (e.g., Dabbs, 2000; Lipsey, Wilson, Cohen, & Derzon, 1997); more on gender differences (e.g., Bettencourt & Miller, 1996); and more on discomfort leading to aggression (Anderson, Bushman, & Groom, 1997).

- Chapter 13, "Prejudice: Causes and Cures": This chapter now includes a discussion of the "racial divide" in America as exemplified by the differing reactions of black and white citizens to the verdict in the O. J. Simpson murder trial (e.g., Dershowitz, 1997), the most recent work on the distinction between subtle and blatant prejudice in the United States and Europe (e.g., Pettigrew, 1998), and an updating of the effect of cooperative learning on prejudice reduction (e.g., Johnson & Johnson, 2000; Slavin & Cooper, 1999; Walker & Crogan, 1998).

- Social Psychology in Action 1: "Social Psychology and Health": This chapter is updated with references to several recent studies. For example, we discuss the effects of stereotype threat on blood pressure, including a study by Blascovich, Spencer, Quinn, & Steele (2001).

- Social Psychology in Action 2: "Social Psychology and the Environment": This chapter has been reorganized with the addition of a new opening vignette. New, cutting edge research is discussed, including a recent prospective study on the effects of aircraft noise on children's cognitive performance (Hygge, Evans, & Bullinger, 2002).

- Social Psychology in Action 3: "Social Psychology and the Law": We have updated this module, including a discussion of new lie detection techniques. More than twenty-five new references are included.

INTEGRATED COVERAGE OF CULTURE AND GENDER

To understand behavior in a social context, we must consider such influences as culture and gender. Rather than adding a chapter on these important topics, we discuss them in every chapter, as they apply to the topic at hand. In many places, we discuss the wonderful diversity of humankind by presenting research on the differences between people of different cultures, races, or genders. We also discuss the commonalties people share by illustrating the applicability of many phenomena across culture, race, and gender. Here are examples:

- Chapter 1, "Introduction to Social Psychology": The issue of universality versus the cultural relativity of social psychological principles is introduced.

- Chapter 2, "Methodology: How Social Psychologists Do Research": The issue of how to generalize the results of studies across different types of people is discussed in the section on external validity. In addition, we include a section on cross-cultural research methods.

- Chapter 3, "Social Cognition: How We Think about the Social World": This chapter discusses gender differences and achievement in middle-school and high school, raising the question of whether these differences are due to the expectations about gender held by teachers and parents. There is also a section on the cultural determinants of schemas that discusses classic work by Bartlett.

- Chapter 4, "Social Perception: How We Come to Understand Other People": This chapter includes a good deal of material on culture and gender, including a discussion of the universality of facial expressions of emotion; cultural differences in other channels of nonverbal communication, such as eye contact, gaze, and personal space; gender differences in nonverbal communication (including a discussion of Eagly's social role theory); cultural variation in implicit personality theories; and cultural differences in attribution processes.

- Chapter 5, "Self-Knowledge: How We Come to Understand Ourselves": This chapter includes a major section on cultural differences in the definition of self that discusses research by Markus, Kitayama, Triandis, and others. There are major sec-

tions on gender differences in the definition of the self, discussing research by Cross and Madson and Gabriel and Gardner. We also discuss cultural differences in impression management.

- Chapter 6, "Self-Justification and the Need to Maintain Self-Esteem": This chapter includes a section on cultural differences in dissonance and dissonance reduction that discusses recent research in non-Western cultures.

- Chapter 7, "Attitudes and Attitude Change: Influencing Thoughts and Feelings": This chapter includes a section on culture and the basis of attitudes, including discussion of an experiment by Han and Shavitt (1994) that examined the effectiveness of different kinds of advertisements in Korea and the United States. In the context of a discussion of the effects of advertising, we discuss the ways in which the media can transmit cultural stereotypes about race and gender, and trigger stereotype threat.

- Chapter 8, "Conformity: Influencing Behavior": This chapter includes a discussion of the role of normative social influence in creating and maintaining cultural standards of beauty for both women and men. We highlight research on the strong normative pressures to be thin experienced by Japanese women, and how the need for social approval is much more predictive of eating disorders in Japanese women than in American women (e.g., Makai, Kambara, & Sasaki, 1998). We also discuss gender and cultural differences in conformity and a meta-analysis by Bond and Smith (1996) comparing conformity on the Asch line task in seventeen countries.

- Chapter 9, "Group Processes: Influence in Social Groups": We discuss research on gender and culture at several points in this chapter, including gender and cultural differences in social loafing, gender differences in leadership styles, and Brown's culture-value theory of group polarization. In addition, we discuss social roles and gender and include an exercise in which students are asked to deliberately violate a gender role and keep a journal of people's responses to them.

- Chapter 10, "Interpersonal Attraction: From First Impressions to Close Relationships": The role of culture comes up at several points in this chapter, including sections on cultural standards of beauty, cultural differences in the "what is beautiful is good" stereotype (Wheeler & Kim, 1997), and cultural differences in close relationships. We also discuss gender differences in the effects of physical attractiveness on liking and in reactions to the dissolution of relationships.

- Chapter 11, "Prosocial Behavior: Why Do People Help?": This chapter features a section on gender differences in prosocial behavior and a section on cultural differences in prosocial behavior.

- Chapter 12, "Aggression: Why We Hurt Other People": A major portion of this chapter is devoted to cultural differences in aggression, including a discussion of recent research by Richard Nisbett and Dov Cohen, and to differences in homicide rates in different countries. We also discuss research on gender differences in aggression and the effects of violent pornography on violence against women.

- Chapter 13, "Prejudice: Causes and Cures": An integral part of any discussion of prejudice is sex-role stereotyping. We have expanded our discussion of gender stereotypes, including a discussion of work by Alice Eagly, Kay Deaux, and Janet Swim. Issues about ingroups and outgroups and ways of reducing prejudice are also an integral part of this chapter.

- Social Psychology in Action modules on health, the environment, and the law: These modules include numerous sections relevant to culture and gender, such as a discussion of research on stereotype threat by Claude Steele and his colleagues, including studies on achievement in minority groups and men versus women. We also include a discussion of research on cultural differences in social support and in the Type A personality, a new discussion of the relationship between racism and stress, and a discussion of cultural differences in how density and crowding are perceived.

THE EVOLUTIONARY APPROACH

In recent years, social psychologists have become increasingly interested in an evolutionary perspective on many aspects of social behavior. Our approach is to integrate this perspective into the parts of chapters where it is relevant, rather than devoting a separate chapter to this topic. We present what we believe is a balanced approach, discussing evolutionary psychology as well as alternatives to it. Here are examples of places in which we discuss the evolutionary approach:

- Chapter 4, "Social Perception: How We Come to Understand Other People": We discuss the question of whether some facial expressions are universal, including Darwin's view that they are.

- Chapter 10, "Interpersonal Attraction: From First Impressions to Close Relationships": We present the evolutionary perspective on gender differences in romantic attraction and on why people fall in love.

- Chapter 11, "Prosocial Behavior: Why Do People Help?": Evolutionary psychology is presented as one of the major theories of why humans engage in prosocial behavior. We present evidence for and

against this perspective and contrast it to other approaches, such as social exchange theory.

- Chapter 12, "Aggression: Why We Hurt Other People": We include a section on whether aggression is inborn or learned, including a discussion of an evolutionary explanation of aggressive behavior.

- Chapter 13, "Prejudice: Causes and Cures": This chapter includes a discussion of research by David Buss on gender differences in nurturance.

THE APPLIED SIDE OF SOCIAL PSYCHOLOGY

One of the best ways to capture students' interest is to point out the real-world significance of the material they are studying. From the vignette that opens each chapter and runs throughout it to the discussions of historical events, current affairs, and our own lives that are embedded in the story line, the narrative is highlighted by real, familiar examples. Applications are an integral part of social psychology, however, and deserve their own treatment. In addition to an integrated coverage of applied topics in the body of the text, we include additional coverage in two ways.

Try it! ▸ Student Exercises

Interspersed throughout the fifth edition are Try It! exercises in which students are invited to apply the concepts they are learning to their everyday life. There are three such exercises in each chapter. They include detailed instructions about how to attempt to replicate actual social psychological experiments, such as Milgram's (1963) lost letter technique in Chapter 11 and Reno and colleagues' (1993) study on norms and littering in the second Social Psychology in Action module, "Social Psychology and the Environment." Other Try It! exercises reproduce self-report scales and invite the students to fill them out to see where they stand on these measures. Examples include Singelis's (1994) measure of people's interdependent and independent views of themselves in Chapter 5 and the Need for Cognition Scale in Chapter 7. Still others are quizzes that illustrate social psychological concepts, such as a Reasoning Quiz in Chapter 3 that illustrates judgmental heuristics, or demonstrations that explain how to use a particular concept in a student's everyday life, such as an exercise in Chapter 9 that instructs students to violate a sex-role norm and observe the consequences. Each exercise varies in format and time required. Additional Try It! exercises can be found on our companion Website: www.prenhall.com/aronson. The Try It! exercises are certain to generate a lot of student interest and make social psychological concepts more memorable and engaging.

CONNECTIONS •

In this new feature we highlight several sections, called "Connections," that are particularly relevant to interesting and important problems in everyday life. For example, there is a Connections section in Chapter 5 (Self-Understanding) on how parents should praise their children, based on recent research on intrinsic motivation. There is one in Chapter 7 (Attitudes) on the effectiveness of media campaigns to reduce drug use, one in Chapter 12 (Aggression) on how to curb bullying in schools, and one in Chapter 8 (Conformity) on how propaganda affects citizens' attitudes and behavior through informational and/or normative social influence processes. We believe that students will appreciate these links to important social issues.

Social Psychology in Action Chapters

Following Chapter 13 are three chapters devoted to applied topics in social psychology—one on health, one on the environment, and one on the law—under the umbrella of "Social Psychology in Action." You might wonder why these modules use a different naming and numbering system than the other chapters. The reason is that they are designed to be free-floating units that can be assigned at virtually any point in the text. Although we do occasionally refer to numbered chapters in these modules, they are constructed as much as possible to stand as independent units that could be relevant at many different points in a social psychology course.

In talking with many professors who teach social psychology, we have been struck by how differently they present applied material. Some prefer to assign this material at the end of the course, after they have covered the major concepts, theories, and research findings. Others prefer to integrate it with the more theoretical material when relevant. Our applied modules are designed to be used in either way. In fact, there are several ways in which the chapters in our book could be assigned. The box below presents two sample outlines that instructors have used successfully with our book. Surely there are others; we present these to illustrate the flexibility of the order in which the chapters and applied modules can be assigned.

SAMPLE OUTLINE I

- **I.** Introduction to Social Psychology
  - Chapter 1, Introduction
  - Chapter 2, Methodology
- **II.** Understanding Ourselves and the Social World
  - Chapter 3, Social Cognition
  - Chapter 4, Social Perception
  - Chapter 5, Self-Understanding
  - Chapter 6, Self-Justification
- **III.** Social Influence
  - Chapter 7, Attitudes and Attitude Change
  - Chapter 8, Conformity
  - Chapter 9, Group Processes
- **IV.** Social Interaction
  - Chapter 10, Interpersonal Attraction
  - Chapter 11, Prosocial Behavior
  - Chapter 12, Aggression
  - Chapter 13, Prejudice
- **V.** Applying Social Psychology
  - Social Psychology in Action I:
    - Social Psychology and Health
  - Social Psychology in Action II:
    - Social Psychology and the Environment
  - Social Psychology in Action III:
    - Social Psychology and the Law

SAMPLE OUTLINE II

- **I.** Introduction to Social Psychology
  - Chapter 1, Introduction
  - Chapter 2, Methodology
- **II.** Social Thinking
  - Chapter 5, Self-Understanding
  - Chapter 3, Social Cognition
  - Chapter 4, Social Perception
  - Chapter 6, Self-Justification
  - Social Psychology in Action I:
    - Social Psychology and Health
- **III.** Social Influence
  - Chapter 8, Conformity
  - Chapter 7, Attitudes and Attitude Change
  - Chapter 9, Group Processes
  - Social Psychology in Action III:
    - Social Psychology and the Law
- **IV.** Social Relations
  - Chapter 13, Prejudice
  - Chapter 12, Aggression
  - Chapter 10, Interpersonal Attraction
  - Chapter 11, Prosocial Behavior
  - Social Psychology in Action II:
    - Social Psychology and the Environment

ANCILLARY PACKAGE

A really good textbook should become part of the classroom experience, supporting and augmenting the professor's vision for the class. Social Psychology offers a number of supplements that will enrich both the professor's presentation of social psychology and the students' understanding of it.

NEW For 2004. Prentice Hall is pleased to announce the **American Psychological Society (APS)** reader series, *Current Directions in Psychological Science.* For classes starting in 2004, you can package the Current Directions in Social Psychology reader for *free* with this text.

This Reader contains selected articles from APS's journal *Current Directions in Psychological Science. Current Directions* was created as a means by which scientists could quickly and easily learn about new and significant research developments outside their major field of study. The journal's concise reviews span all of scientific psychology, and because of the journal's accessibility to audiences outside specialty areas, it is a natural fit for use in college courses. These Readers offer a rich resource that connects students and scholars directly to leading scientists working in psychology today.

The American Psychological Society is the only association dedicated solely to advancing psychology as a science-based discipline. APS members include the field's most respected researchers and educators representing the full range of topics within psychological science. The Society is widely recognized as a leading voice for the science of psychology in Washington, and is focused on increasing public understanding and use of the knowledge generated by psychological research.

Instructor's Supplements

- *NEW Instructor's Resource Binder.* This binder includes an exhaustive collection of teaching resources for both new and experienced instructors alike. Organized by chapter, this binder includes the Instructor's Resource Manual, the Test Item File, the Instructor's Resource CD-ROM, the computerized testing software, TestGen, and the color transparencies. All of these supplements are described below. Please contact your Prentice Hall rep to receive this item.

- *NEW Instructor's Resource Center on CD-ROM.* This valuable, time-saving supplement provides you with an electronic version of a variety of teaching resources all on one disk so that you may customize your lecture notes and media presentations. This CD-ROM includes PowerPoint slides, electronic versions of the artwork, electronic versions of the overhead transparencies, the electronic Instructor's Resource Manual, and the Test Item File.

- *Video.* A video is available that contains a series of clips that can be used as lecture openers or discussion lead-ins. Some of these clips are from classic psychology films. Others are from documentaries that are excellent illustrations of social psychological concepts. In still other clips, each of the authors of the text discusses some of his or her research. The Instructor's Manual includes notes that discuss the principles covered in each clip, providing discussion questions for students, and listing relevant references.

- *PowerPoints.* PowerPoints provide an active format for presenting concepts from each chapter. The PowerPoints files can be downloaded from the Social Psychology Website at www.prenhall.com/aronson or www.prenhall.com/psychology.

- *Color Transparencies.* Color transparencies of figures and tables from the text are available and can also be downloaded from the Social Psychology Website.

- *Instructor's Resource Manual.* Written by Melinda Blackman of California State University, Fullerton, the Instructor's Manual includes lecture ideas, teaching tips, suggested readings, chapter outlines, student projects and research assignments, Try It! exercises, critical thinking topics and discussion questions, and a media resource guide.

- *Test Bank.* Each of the two thousand questions in this test bank, compiled by Elissa Wurf of Lafayette College, is page-referenced to the text and categorized by topic and skill level. The test bank is also available to adopters in Windows and Macintosh computerized format.

- *Prentice Hall Test Generator.* One of the best-selling test-generating software programs on the market, Test Generator is available in Windows and Macintosh formats and contains a gradebook, on-line network testing, and many tools to help instructors edit and create tests.

- *On-Line Course Management.* For professors interested in using the Internet and on-line course management in their courses, Prentice Hall offers fully customizable on-line courses in WebCT, BlackBoard, and Course Compass to accompany this textbook. Contact your local Prentice Hall representative or visit www.prenhall.com/demo for more information.

- *Research Navigator.* Reliable, relevant, and resourceful. Prentice Hall's *Research Navigator*™ helps your students make the most out of your current research. Complete with extensive help on the research process and three exclusive databases full of relevant and reliable source material—including EBSCO's *ContentSelect* Academic Journal Database, the *New York Times* Search by Subject Archive, and the *Best of the Web* link library. Research Navigator is the one-stop research solution for your students.

Student Supplements

- *Student Study Guide.* The Student Study Guide, by Benjamin Le of Haverford College, contains chapter overviews, learning objectives and outlines, study questions, key terms, and practice tests.

- *Companion Website.* The Website www.prenhall.com/aronson, set up and maintained by Fred Whitford of Montana State University, includes additional Try It! exercises, updates on current events that are relevant to social psychological concepts, practice tests for each chapter, downloadable PowerPoint slides, and links to other sites.

- *Psychology Is Social.* The reader *Psychology Is Social: Readings and Conversations in Social Psychology,* edited by Edward Krupat of the Massachusetts College of Pharmacy and Allied Health Sciences, now in its fourth edition, exposes students to a wide spectrum of research and opinion, including articles by and interviews with highly acclaimed social psychologists. The selections, edited to maximize student comprehension, range from new to classic, popular to technical, and single-study to review and provide a glimpse into the minds of the thinkers who have shaped key areas of study in the field of social psychology.

- *How to Think like a Social Scientist.* This inexpensive primer by Thomas F. Pettigrew of the University of Santa Cruz is filled with examples drawn from the behavioral sciences and fosters critical thinking about psychology and the social sciences. It encourages readers to consider the nature of theory, comparisons and control, cause and change, sampling and selection, varying levels of analysis, and systems thinking in the social sciences.

- *Thinking Critically about Research on Sex and Gender.* Now in its second edition, this supplement, written by Paula J. Caplan of Brown University and Jeremy B. Caplan of Brandeis University, encourages students to evaluate the massive and diverse research that has appeared on this subject of sex and gender in recent decades. After demonstrating that much of the existing research is not as well established as one would think, the book provides readers with the critical tools necessary to assess the huge body of literature and to draw realistic and constructive conclusions.

- *Influence: Science and Practice.* This fascinating best-seller by Robert B. Cialdini of Arizona State University, now in its fourth edition, draws on evidence from research and the working world of influence professionals to examine the psychology of compliance. Focus is on the six basic psychological principles directing human behavior—reciprocation, consistency, social validation, liking, authority, and scarcity. This is must reading!

ACKNOWLEDGMENTS

Elliot Aronson is delighted to acknowledge the general contributions of his best friend (who also happens to be his wife), Vera Aronson. Vera, as usual, provided a great deal of inspiration for his ideas and acted as the sounding board for and supportive critic of many of his semi-formed notions, helping to mold them into more sensible analyses. He would also like to thank his son, Joshua Aronson, a brilliant young social psychologist in his own right, for the many stimulating conversations that contributed mightily to the final version of this book.

Tim Wilson would like to thank his graduate mentor, Richard E. Nisbett, who nurtured his interest in the field and showed him the continuity between social psychological research and everyday life. He thanks his graduate students, Sara Algoe, David Centerbar, Elizabeth Dunn, Debby Kermer, Jaime Kurtz, and Anna MacIntosh, who helped keep him a well-balanced professor—a researcher as well as a teacher and author. He thanks his parents, Elizabeth and Geoffrey Wilson, for their overall support. Most of all, he thanks his wife, Deirdre Smith, and his children, Christopher and Leigh, for their love, patience, and understanding, even when the hour was late and the computer was still on.

Robin Akert would like to thank her students and colleagues at Wellesley College for their support and encouragement. In particular, she is beholden to Professors Jonathan Cheek and Patricia Berman, and to Kristen Fay, Allison Bibbins Ward, and Linda DuFresne. Their advice, feedback, and senses of humor were vastly appreciated. She also wishes to thank her students in social psychology. Their intelligence, perspicacity, dedication and joie de vivre are her continuing sources of energy and motivation for this book. She is deeply grateful to her family, Michaela and Wayne Akert, and Linda and Jerry Wuichet; their inexhaustible enthusiasm and boundless support have sustained her on this project as on all the ones before it. Once again she thanks C. Issak for authorial inspiration. Finally, no words can express her gratitude and indebtedness to Dane Archer, mentor, colleague, and friend, who opened the world of social psychology to her and who has been her guide ever since.

No book can be written and published without the help of a great many people working with the authors behind the scenes, and our book is no exception. We would like to thank the many colleagues who read one or more chapters of this edition and of previous editions of the book.

Reviewers of the Fifth Edition

Bill Adler, Collin County Community College
Sowmya Anand, The Ohio State University

Danny Axsom, Virginia Polytechnic Institute and State University

Kathy L. Bell, University of North Carolina at Greensboro

Jennifer Bosson, The University of Oklahoma

Brad J. Bushman, Iowa State University

Russell D. Clark, III, University of North Texas

Eric Cooley, Western Oregon University

Mary Ellen Dello Stritto, Ball State University

Cindy Elrod, Georgia State University

Rebecca S. Fahrlander, University of Nebraska at Omaha

Timothy M. Franz, St. John Fisher College

Glenn Geher, State University of New York at New Paltz

Suzanne Kieffer, University of Houston

Steve Kilianski, Rutgers University

Elizabeth C. Lanthier, Northern Virginia Community College

Cynthia K.S. Reed, Tarrant County College

Darrin L. Rogers, The Ohio State University

Paul Silvia, University of North Carolina at Greensboro

Lori Stone, The University of Texas at Austin

William Douglas Woody, University of Northern Colorado

Reviewers of Past Editions

Jeffrey B. Adams, Saint Michael's College

John R. Aiello, Rutgers University

Charles A. Alexander, Rock Valley College

Art Aron, State University of New York, Stony Brook

Joan W. Baily, Jersey City State College

Norma Baker, Belmont University

John Bargh, New York University

William A. Barnard, University of Northern Colorado

Gordon Bear, Ramapo College

Susan E. Beers, Sweet Briar College

Leonard Berkowitz, University of Wisconsin—Madison

Ellen S. Berscheid, University of Minnesota

Thomas Blass, University of Maryland

C. George Boeree, Shippensburg University

Lisa M. Bohon, California State University, Sacramento

Peter J. Brady, Clark State Community College

Kelly A. Brennan, University of Texas, Austin

Richard W. Brislin, East-West Center of the University of Hawaii

Jeff Bryson, San Diego State University

Brad Bushman, Iowa State University

Thomas P. Cafferty, University of South Carolina, Columbia

Melissa A. Cahoon, Wright State University

Frank Calabrese, Community College of Philadelphia

Michael Caruso, University of Toledo

Nicholas Christenfeld, University of California, San Diego

Margaret S. Clark, Carnegie Mellon University

Susan D. Clayton, Allegheny College

Brian M. Cohen, University of Texas, San Antonio

Jack Cohen, Camden County College

Eric Cooley, Western Oregon State University

Steven G. Cole, Texas Christian University

Eric J. Cooley, Western Oregon State College

Diana Cordova, Yale University

Jack Croxton, State University of New York, Fredonia

Keith E. Davis, University of South Carolina, Columbia

Dorothee Dietrich, Hamline University

Susann Doyle, Gainesville College

Steve Duck, University of Iowa

Karen G. Duffy, State University of New York, Geneseo

Valerie Eastman, Drury College

Tami Eggleston, McKendree College

Steve L. Ellyson, Youngstown State University

Alan Feingold, Yale University

Phil Finney, Southeast Missouri State University

Susan Fiske, University of Massachusetts

Robin Franck, Southwestern College

William Rick Fry, Youngstown State University

Russell Geen, University of Missouri

Frederick X. Gibbons, Iowa State University

Cynthia Gilliland, Louisiana State University

Genaro Gonzalez, University of Texas

Beverly Gray, Youngstown State University

Gordon Hammerle, Adrian College

Judith Harackiewicz, University of Wisconsin—Madison

Elaine Hatfield, University of Hawaii, Manoa

Vicki S. Helgeson, Carnegie Mellon University

Joyce Hemphill, Cazenovia College

Tracy B. Henley, Mississippi State University

Ed Hirt, Indiana University

David E. Hyatt, University of Wisconsin—Oshkosh

Marita Inglehart, University of Michigan

Carl Kallgren, Behrend College, Pennsylvania State University, Erie

Bill Klein, Colby College

James D. Johnson, University of North Carolina, Wilmington

Lee Jussim, Rutgers University

Fredrick Koenig, Tulane University

Alan Lambert, Washington University, St. Louis

Emmett Lampkin, Kirkwook Community College

Patricia Laser, Bucks County Community College

G. Daniel Lassiter, Ohio University

John Malarkey, Wilmington College

Andrew Manion, St. Mary's University of Minnesota

Allen R. McConnell, Michigan State University

Joann M. Montepare, Tufts University

Richard Moreland, University of Pittsburgh

Carrie Nance, Stetson University

Todd D. Nelson, Michigan State University

Elaine Nocks, Furman University

Cheri Parks, Colorado Christian University

David Peterson, Mount Senario College

W. Gerrod Parrott, Georgetown University

Lee D. Ross, Stanford University
Alex Rothman, University of Minnesota
M. Susan Rowley, Champlain College
Delia Saenz, Arizona State University
Brad Sagarin, Northern Illinois University
Connie Schick, Bloomsburg University
Norbert Schwartz, University of Michigan
Richard C. Sherman, Miami University of Ohio
Randolph A. Smith, Ouachita Baptist University
Linda Solomon, Marymount Manhattan College
Janice Steil, Adelphi University
Jakob Steinberg, Fairleigh Dickinson University
Jonell Strough, West Virginia University
T. Gale Thompson, Bethany College
Scott Tindale, Loyola University of Chicago
David Trafimow, New Mexico State University
Gary L. Wells, Iowa State University
Paul L. Wienir, Western Michigan University
Kipling D. Williams, University of Toledo
Paul Windschitl, University of Iowa
Mike Witmer, Skagit Valley College

Gwen Wittenbaum, Michigan State University
William H. Zachry, University of Tennessee, Martin

We also thank the expert editorial staff of Prentice Hall for their expertise and professionalism, especially Jeff Marshall and Roberta Meyer. Finally, we thank Mary Falcon, but for whom we never would have begun this project.

Thank you for inviting us into your classroom. We welcome your suggestions, and we would be delighted to hear your comments about this book.

Elliot Aronson
elliot@cats.ucsc.edu

Tim Wilson
tdw@virginia.edu

Robin Akert
rakert@wellesley.edu

ABOUT THE AUTHORS

ELLIOT ARONSON

When I was a kid, we were the only Jewish family in a virulently anti-Semitic neighborhood. I had to go to Hebrew school every day, late in the afternoon. Being the only youngster in my neighborhood going to Hebrew school made me an easy target for some of the older neighborhood toughs. On my way home from Hebrew school, after dark, I was frequently waylaid and roughed up by roving gangs shouting anti-Semitic epithets.

I have a vivid memory of sitting on a curb after one of these beatings, nursing a bloody nose or a split lip, feeling very sorry for myself and wondering how these kids could hate me so much when they didn't even know me. I thought about whether those kids were taught to hate Jews or whether, somehow, they were born that way. I wondered if their hatred could be changed—if they got to know me better, would they hate me less? I speculated about my own character. What would I have done if the shoe were on the other foot—that is, if I were bigger and stronger than they, would I be capable of beating them up for no good reason?

I didn't realize it at the time, of course, but eventually I discovered that these were profound questions. And some thirty years later, as an experimental social psychologist, I had the great good fortune to be in a position to answer some of those questions and to invent techniques to reduce the kind of prejudice that had claimed me as a victim.

Elliot Aronson is one of the most renowned social psychologists in the world. In 2002 he was chosen as one of the 100 most eminent psychologists of the twentieth century. He is currently Professor Emeritus at the University of California at Santa Cruz and Distinguished Visiting Professor at Stanford University.

Dr. Aronson is the only person in the 110-year history of the American Psychological Association to have received all three of its major awards: for distinguished writing, distinguished teaching, and distinguished research. Many other professional societies have honored his research and teaching as well. These include: the American Association for the Advancement of Science, which gave him its highest honor, the Distinguished Scientific Research award; the American Council for the Advancement and Support of Education, which named him Professor of the Year of 1989; the Society for the Psychological Study of Social Issues, which awarded him the Gordon Allport prize for his contributions to the reduction of prejudice among racial and ethnic groups. In 1992, he was named a Fellow of the American Academy of Arts and Sciences. He has served as President of the Western Psychological Association as well as President of the Society of Personality and Social Psychology.

TIM WILSON

One day, when I was 8, a couple of older kids rode up on their bikes to share some big news: They had discovered an abandoned house down a country road. "It's really neat," they said. "We broke a window and nobody cared!" My friend and I hopped onto our bikes to investigate. We had no trouble finding the house—there it was, sitting off by itself, with a big, jagged hole in a first-floor window. We got off of our bikes and looked around. My friend found a baseball-sized rock lying on the ground and threw a perfect strike through another first-floor window. There was something exhilarating about the smash-and-tingle of shattering glass, especially when we knew there was nothing wrong with what we were doing. After all, the house was abandoned, wasn't it? We broke nearly every window in the house and then climbed through one of the first-floor windows to look around.

It was then that we realized something was terribly wrong. The house certainly did not look abandoned. There were pictures on the wall, nice furniture, books in shelves. We went home feeling frightened and confused. We soon learned that the house was the residence of an elderly couple who were away on vacation. Eventually my parents discovered what we had done and paid a substantial sum to repair the windows. For years, I pondered this incident: Why did I do such a terrible thing? Was I a bad kid? I didn't think so, and neither did my parents. How, then, could a good kid do such a bad thing? Even though the neighborhood kids said the house was abandoned, why couldn't my friend and I see the clear signs that someone lived there? How crucial was it that my friend was there and threw the first rock? Though I didn't know it at the time, these reflections touched on several classic social psychological issues, such as whether only bad people do bad things, whether the social situation can be powerful enough to make good people do bad things, and the way in which our expectations about an event can make it difficult to see it as it really is. Fortunately, my career as a vandal ended with this one incident. It did, however, mark the beginning of my fascination with basic questions about how people understand themselves and the social world—questions I continue to investigate to this day.

Tim Wilson did his undergraduate work at Williams College and Hampshire College and received his Ph.D. from the University of Michigan. Currently Sherrell J. Aston Professor of Psychology at the University of Virginia, he has published numerous articles in the areas of introspection, attitude change, self-knowledge, and affective forecasting, as well as the recent book, Strangers to Ourselves: Discovering the Adaptive Unconscious. *His research has received the support of the National Science Foundation and the National Institute for Mental Health. He has been associate editor of the Journal of Personality and Social Psychology and a member of the Social and Groups Processes Review Committee at the National Institute of Mental Health. He has been elected twice to the Executive Board of the Society for Experimental Social Psychology and is a Fellow in the American Psychological Society. Wilson has taught the Introduction to Social Psychology course at the University of Virginia for more than twenty years. He was recently awarded an All University Outstanding Teaching Award.*

ROBIN AKERT

One fall day, when I was about 16, I was walking with a friend along the shore of the San Francisco Bay. Deep in conversation, I glanced over my shoulder and saw a sailboat capsize. I pointed it out to my friend, who took only a perfunctory interest and went on talking. However, I kept watching as we walked, and I realized that the two sailors were in the water, clinging to the capsized boat. Again I said something to my friend, who replied, "Oh, they'll get it upright, don't worry."

But I was worried. Was this an emergency? My friend didn't think so. And I was no sailor; I knew nothing about boats. But I kept thinking, "That water is really cold. They can't stay in that water too long." I remember feeling very confused and unsure. What should I do? Should I do anything? Did they really need help?

We were near a restaurant with a big window overlooking the bay, and I decided to go in and see if anyone had done anything about the boat. Lots of people were watching but not doing anything. This confused me too. Very meekly, I asked the bartender to call for some kind of help. He just shrugged. I went back to the window and watched the two small figures in the water. Why was everyone so unconcerned? Was I crazy?

Years later, I reflected on how hard it was for me to do what I did next: I demanded that the bartender let me use his phone. In those days before "911," it was lucky that I knew there was a Coast Guard station on the bay, and I asked the operator for the number. I was relieved to hear the Guardsman take my message very seriously.

It had been an emergency. I watched as the Coast Guard cutter sped across the bay and pulled the two sailors out of the water. Maybe I saved their lives that day. What really stuck with me over the years was how other people behaved and how it made me feel. The other bystanders seemed unconcerned and did nothing to help. Their reactions made me doubt myself and made it harder for me to decide to take action. When I later studied social psychology in college, I realized that on the shore of the San Francisco Bay that day, I had experienced the "bystander effect" fully: The presence of other, apparently unconcerned bystanders had made it difficult for me to decide if the situation was an emergency and whether it was my responsibility to help.

Robin Akert graduated summa cum laude from the University of California at Santa Cruz, where she majored in psychology and sociology. She received her Ph.D. in experimental social psychology from Princeton University. She is currently a professor of psychology at Wellesley College, where she was awarded the Pinanski Prize for Excellence in Teaching early in her career. She publishes primarily in the area of nonverbal communication and recently received the AAUW American Fellowship in support of her research. She has taught the social psychology course at Wellesley College every semester for over twenty years.

SPECIAL TIPS FOR STUDENTS

The two quotes in the margin below, taken together, sum up everything you need to know to be a proficient student: Be an active, creative consumer of information, and make sure it sticks! How do you accomplish these two feats? Actually, it's not difficult at all. Like everything else in life, it just takes some work—some clever, well-planned, purposeful work. Here are some suggestions about how to do it.

GET TO KNOW THE TEXTBOOK

Believe it or not, in writing this book, we thought very carefully about the organization and structure of each chapter. Things are the way they appear for a reason, and that reason is to help you learn the material in the best way possible. Here are some tips on what to look for in each chapter.

Key terms are in boldface type in the text so that you'll notice them. We define the terms in the text, and that definition appears again in the margin. These marginal definitions are there to help you out if later in the chapter you forget what something means. The marginal definitions are quick and easy to find. You can also look up key terms in the alphabetical Glossary at the end of this textbook.

Make sure you notice the headings and subheadings. The headings are the skeleton that holds a chapter together. They link together like vertebrae. If you ever feel lost, look back to the last heading and the headings before that one—this will give you the "big picture" of where the chapter is going. It should also help you see the connections between sections.

The **summary at the end of each chapter** is a succinct shorthand presentation of the chapter information, with the key terms set in boldface. You should read it and make sure there are no surprises when you do so. If anything in the summary doesn't ring a bell, go back to the chapter and reread that section. Most important, remember that the summary is intentionally brief, whereas your understanding of the material should be full and complete. Use the summary as a study aid before your exams. When you read it over, everything should be familiar and you should have that wonderful feeling of knowing more than is in the summary (in which case you are ready to take the exam).

At the end of each chapter, we list **pertinent books and articles** that we think are particularly good. These reading recommendations are excellent resources for any papers you may be writing for your course. They are the first place to start in a bibliographic search for further information on the topic of your paper. As is always the case with literature searches, they will lead you to still other references. At the end of each chapter, we also list a few **novels and movies** that poignantly portray themes from that chapter.

Be sure to do the Try It! exercises. They will make concepts from social psychology concrete and help you see how they can be applied to your own life. Some of the Try It! exercises replicate social psychology experiments. Other Try It! exercises reproduce self-report scales so you can see where you stand in rela-

> There is then creative reading as well as creative writing.
> —Ralph Waldo Emerson, 1837

> I am a kind of burr; I shall stick.
> —William Shakespeare, 1604

tion to other people. Still other Try It! exercises are short quizzes that illustrate social psychological concepts.

Visit our Website at www.prenhall.com/aronson. You will be able to do more Try It! exercises, take interactive practice tests, and link to other sites.

JUST SAY NO
TO THE COUCH POTATO WITHIN

Because social psychology is about everyday life, you might lull yourself into believing that the material is all common sense. Don't be fooled. The material is more complicated than it might seem. Therefore, we want to emphasize that the best way to learn it is to work with it in an active, not passive, fashion. You can't just read a chapter once and expect it to stick with you. You have to go over the material, wrestle with it, make your own connections to it, question it, think about it, interact with it. Actively working with material makes it memorable and makes it your own. Since it's a safe bet that someone is going to ask you about this material later and you're going to have to pull it out of memory, do what you can to get it into memory now. Here are some techniques to use:

- Go ahead and be bold—use a highlighter! Go crazy—write in the margins! If you underline, highlight, circle, or draw little hieroglyphics next to important points, you will remember them better. We recall taking exams in college where we not only remembered the material but could actually see in our minds the textbook page it was written on and the little squiggles and stars we'd drawn in the margin.

- Read the textbook chapter before the applicable class lecture, not afterward. This way, you'll get more out of the lecture, which will introduce new material. The chapter will give you the big picture, as well as a lot of detail. The lecture will enhance that information and help you put it all together. If you don't read the chapter first, you may not understand some of the points made in the lecture or realize that they are important.

- Here's a good way to study material: Write out a difficult concept or a study (or say it out loud to yourself) in your own words, without looking at the book or your notes. Can you do it? How good was your version? Did you omit anything important? Did you get stuck at some point, unable to remember what comes next? If so, you now know that you need to go

over that information in more detail. You can also study with someone else, describing theories and studies to each other and seeing if you're making sense.

- If you have trouble remembering the results of an important study, try drawing your own version of a graph of the findings (you can use our data graphs for an idea of how to proceed). If all the various points in a theory are confusing you, try drawing your own flowchart of how it works. You will probably find that you remember the research results much better in pictorial form than in words and that the theory isn't so confusing (or missing a critical part) if you've outlined it. Draw information a few times and it will stay with you.

- Remember, the more you work with the material, the better you will learn and remember it. Write it in your own words, talk about it, explain it to others, or draw visual representations of it.

- Last but not least, remember that this material is a lot of fun. You haven't even started reading the book yet, but we think you're going to like it. In particular, you'll see how much social psychology has to tell you about your real, everyday life. As this course progresses, you might want to remind yourself to observe the events of your daily life with new eyes, the eyes of a social psychologist, and try to apply what you are learning to the behavior of your friends, acquaintances, strangers, and, yes, even yourself. Make sure you use the Try It! exercises and visit the Website. You will find out how much social psychology can help us understand our lives. When you read newspapers or magazines or watch the nightly news, think about what social psychology has to say about such events and behaviors—we believe you will find that your understanding of daily life is richer. If you notice a newspaper or magazine article that you think is an especially good example of "social psychology in action," please send it to us, with a full reference to where you found it and on what page. If we decide to use it in the next edition of this book, we'll list your name in the Acknowledgments.

We suspect that ten years from now you may not remember all the facts, theories, and names you learn now. Although we hope you will remember some of them, our main goal is for you to take with you into your future a great many of the broad social psychological concepts presented herein. If you open yourself to social psychology's magic, we believe it will enrich the way you look at the world and the way you live in it.

SOCIAL PSYCHOLOGY

CHAPTER

1

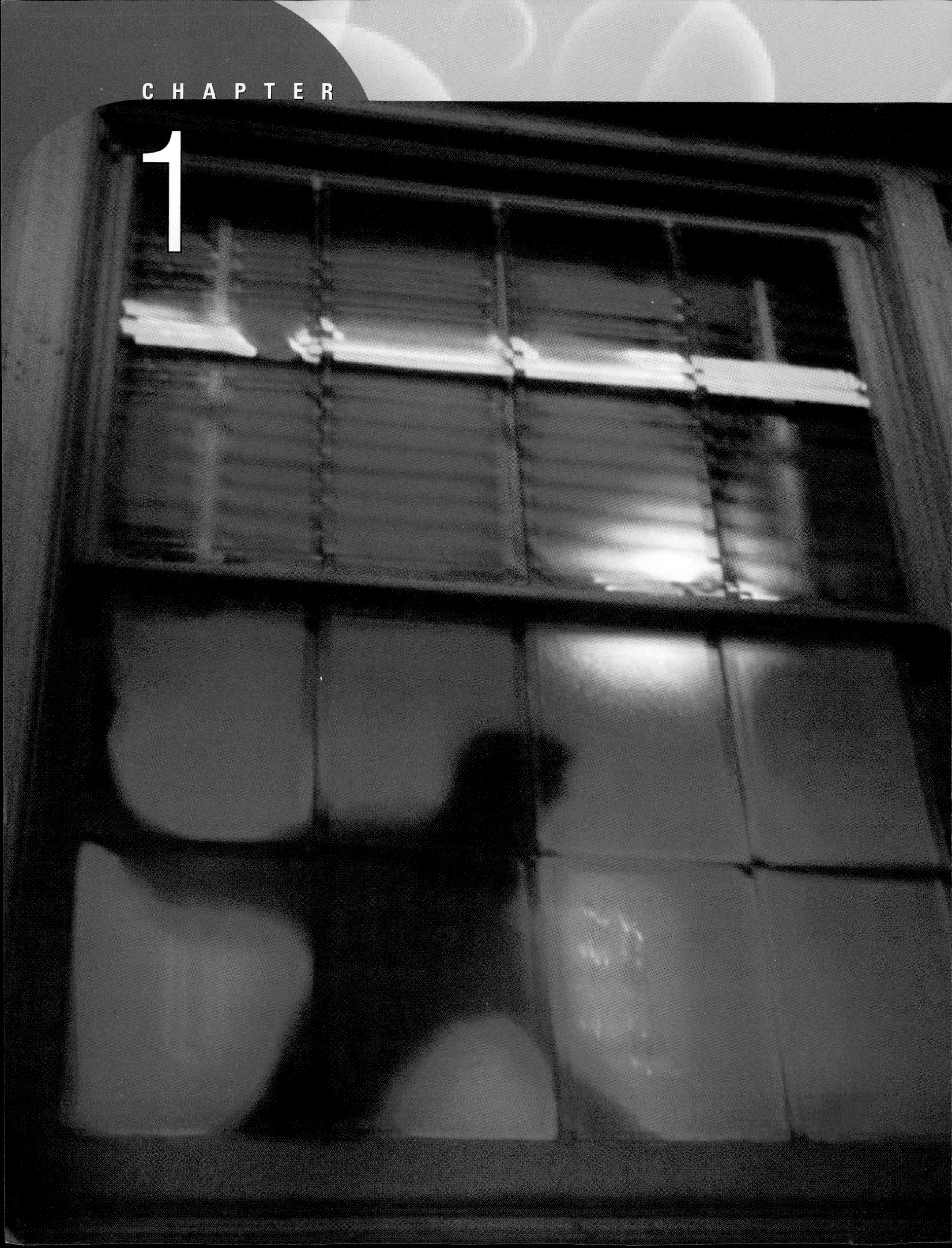

Introducing
Social Psychology

The task of the psychologist is to try to understand and predict human behavior. Different kinds of psychologists go about this in different ways, and in this book we will attempt to show you how social psychologists do it. Let's begin with a few examples of human behavior. Some of these might seem important; others might seem trivial; one or two might seem frightening. To a social psychologist, all of them are interesting. Our hope is that by the time you finish reading this book, you will find all of these examples as fascinating as we do. As you read these examples, try to think about how you would explain why what happened, happened.

- Just before dawn, the residents of a trendy neighborhood in Los Angeles heard desperate cries for help coming from a yellow house. "Please don't kill me!" screamed one woman. Other neighbors reported hearing tortured screams and cries for mercy. Yet not one neighbor bothered to investigate or help in any way. No one even called the police. One woman, who lived two houses away, went out onto her balcony when she heard the screams but went back into her house without doing anything. Twelve hours later, an acquaintance arrived at the yellow house and discovered that four people had been brutally murdered. A fifth person was critically wounded and spent those twelve hours lying in a bedroom, bleeding from her wounds, waiting in vain for just one neighbor to lift a finger and dial 911 (*New York Times,* July 3, 1981).

   Why do you think the neighbors failed to do anything after hearing the cries for help? Stop and think for a moment: What kinds of people are these neighbors? Would you like to have them as friends? If you had a small child, would you hire one of these neighbors as a baby-sitter?

- It is April 2003, just weeks after President George W. Bush ordered U.S. troops to invade Iraq. You are among a group of students in your campus lounge watching live coverage of the war on CNN. You haven't yet made up your mind over whether we should have gone to war, but as you watch the live footage and hear the reports about atrocities commit-ted by Sadam Hussein, you begin to feel that Bush was right. It was worth invading Iraq. You are about to express your new feeling about the war when Maria, an acquaintance, says, "I can't even believe this is happening! We had no business invading Iraq." "Right," says your friend Jessica. "Most of the world is against it." "Absolutely," your friend Steve chimes in. "Bush doesn't know what he's doing." What do you say? Do you conform to the unanimous opinion of your friends and say you oppose the war, or do you state your own opinion and risk their disapproval?

Would it surprise you to learn that when placed in a similar situation, most college students would go along with the majority opinion rather than appear to be odd?

- We have a friend whom we will call Oscar. Oscar is a middle-aged executive with a computer software company. As a student, Oscar had attended a large state university in the Midwest, where he was a member of a fraternity we will call Delta Nu. He remembers having gone through a severe and somewhat scary hazing ritual in order to become a member but believes it was worthwhile. Although he had been terribly frightened by the hazing, he loved his fraternity brothers and was proud to be a member of Delta Nu—easily the best of all fraternities. A few years ago, his son, Sam, was about to enroll in the same university; naturally, Oscar urged Sam to pledge Delta Nu: "It's a great fraternity—always attracts a wonderful bunch of fellows. You'll really love it." Sam did in fact pledge Delta Nu and was ac-cepted. Oscar was relieved to learn that Sam was not required to undergo a severe initiation in order to become a member; times had changed, and hazing was now forbidden. When Sam came home for Christmas break, Oscar asked him how he liked the fraternity. "It's all right, I guess," he said, "but most of my friends are outside the fraternity." Oscar was astonished.

How is it that Oscar had been so enamored of his fraternity brothers and Sam wasn't? Had the standards of old Delta Nu slipped? Was the fra-ternity now admitting a less desirable group of young men than in Oscar's day? Or was it just one of those inexplicable things? What do you think?

- In the mid-1970s, several hundred members of the Peoples Temple, a California-based religious cult, emigrated to Guyana under the guidance of their leader, Reverend Jim Jones. Their aim was to found a model in-terracial community, called Jonestown, based on "love, hard work, and spiritual enlightenment." In November 1978, Congressman Leo Ryan of

California flew to Jonestown to investigate reports that some of the members were being held against their will. He visited the commune and found that several residents wanted to return with him to the United States. Reverend Jones agreed they could leave, but as Ryan was boarding a plane, he and several other members of his party were shot and killed by a member of the Peoples Temple, apparently on Jones's orders. On hearing that several members of Ryan's party had escaped, Jones grew despondent and began to speak over the public address system about the beauty of dying and the certainty that everyone would meet again in another place. The residents lined up in a pavilion in front of a vat containing a mixture of Kool-Aid and cyanide. According to a survivor, almost all of the residents drank willingly of the deadly solution. At least eighty babies and infants were given the poison by their parents, who then drank it themselves. More than eight hundred people died, including Rev. Jones.

How is it that people can agree to kill themselves and their own children? Were they crazy? Were they under some kind of hypnotic spell? How would you explain their behavior?

We now have several questions about human social behavior—questions we find fascinating: Why did the Los Angeles residents ignore the screams coming from the yellow house when by dialing 911 or by shouting out the window they might have averted a tragedy? In the example of the invasion of Iraq, what are the factors that make most people conform to the opinion of others? Why did Oscar like his frat brothers so much more than Sam did? And how could large numbers of people be induced to kill their own children and themselves in Jonestown? In this chapter, we will consider what these examples have in common and why they are of interest to us. We will also suggest some reasonable explanations based on social psychological research.

WHAT IS SOCIAL PSYCHOLOGY?

At the very heart of social psychology is the phenomenon of **social influence:** We are all influenced by other people. When we think of social influence, the kinds of examples that readily come to mind are direct attempts at persuasion, whereby one person deliberately tries to change another person's behavior. This is what happens in an advertising campaign, when creative people use sophisticated techniques to persuade us to buy a particular brand of toothpaste, or during an election campaign, when similar techniques are used to get us to vote for a particular political candidate. Direct attempts at persuasion also occur when our friends try to get us to do something we don't really want to do ("Come on, have another beer—everyone is doing it") or when the schoolyard bully uses force or threats to get smaller kids to part with their lunch money or homework.

Social Influence

The effect that the words, actions, or mere presence of other people have on our thoughts, feelings, attitudes, or behavior

These direct attempts at social influence form a major part of social psychology and will be discussed in our chapters on conformity, attitudes, and group processes. To the social psychologist, however, social influence is broader than attempts by one person to change another person's behavior. For one thing, social influence extends beyond behavior—it includes our thoughts and feelings as well as our overt acts. In addition, social influence takes on many forms other than deliberate attempts at persuasion. We are often influenced merely by the presence of other people. Moreover, even when we are not in the physical presence of others, we are still influenced by them. Thus in a sense we carry our mothers, fathers, friends, and teachers around with us as we attempt to make decisions that would make them proud of us.

On a still subtler level, each of us is immersed in a social and cultural context. Social psychologists are interested in studying how and why our thoughts, feelings, and behaviors are shaped by the entire social environment. Taking all of these factors into account, we can define **social psychology** as the scientific study of the way in which people's thoughts, feelings, and behaviors are influenced by the real or imagined presence of other people (Allport, 1985). Of particular interest to social psychologists is what happens in the mind of an individual when various influences come into conflict with one another. This is frequently the case when young people (like many of our readers) go off to college and find themselves torn between the beliefs and values they learned at home and the beliefs and values their professors or peers are expressing. (See the Try It! exercise below.)

The Power of Social Interpretation

Other disciplines, like anthropology and sociology, are also interested in how people are influenced by their social environment. Social psychology is distinct, however, primarily because it is concerned not so much with social situations in any objective sense but rather with how people are influenced by their interpretation, or **construal**, of their social environment. To understand how people are influenced by their social world, social psychologists believe it is more important to understand how they perceive, comprehend, and interpret the social world than it is to understand the objective properties of the social world itself (Lewin, 1943).

An example will clarify. Imagine that Jason is a shy high school student who admires Debbie from afar. Suppose that as a budding social psychologist, you have the job of predicting whether or not Jason will ask Debbie to the senior prom. One way you might do this is to observe Debbie's objective behavior toward Jason. Does she pay attention to him and smile a lot? If so, the casual observer might decide that Jason will ask her out. As a social psychologist, however,

Social Psychology

The scientific study of the way in which people's thoughts, feelings, and behaviors are influenced by the real or imagined presence of other people

Construal

The way in which people perceive, comprehend, and interpret the social world

Try it!

Explicit and Implicit Values

Make a list of the explicit and implicit beliefs and values of your parents and close relatives. Then make a such a list for your favorite professors and your closest college friends. Note the similarities and differences in your lists. How do these differences affect you? Do you find yourself rejecting one set of values in favor of the other? Are you trying to make a compromise between the two? Are you attempting to form a whole new set of values that are your own?

Our thoughts, feelings and behaviors are influenced by our immediate surroundings as well as by our cultural and family background.

you are more interested in viewing Debbie's behavior through Jason's eyes—that is, in seeing how Jason interprets Debbie's behavior. If she smiles at him, does Jason construe her behavior as mere politeness, the kind of politeness she would extend to any of the dozens of nerds and losers in the senior class? Or does he view her smile as an encouraging sign, one that inspires him to gather the courage to ask her out? If she ignores him, does Jason figure that she's playing "hard to get"? Or does he take it as a sign that she's not interested in dating him? To predict Jason's behavior, it is not enough to know the details of Debbie's behavior; it is imperative to know how Jason *interprets* Debbie's behavior.

Given the importance placed on the way people interpret the social world, social psychologists pay special attention to the origins of these interpretations. For example, when construing their environment, are most people concerned with making an interpretation that places them in the most positive light (e.g., Jason believing "Debbie is going to the prom with Eric because she is just trying to make me jealous") or with making the most accurate interpretation, even if it is unflattering (e.g., "Painful as it may be, I must admit that Debbie would rather go to the prom with a sea slug than with me")? A great deal of research in social psychology has addressed these and other determinants of people's thoughts and behaviors. We will expand on these determinants later in this chapter.

Needless to say, the importance of construals extends far beyond the saga of Jason and Debbie. Consider what takes place in a murder trial. Even when the prosecution presents compelling evidence it believes will prove the defendant guilty, the verdict always hinges on precisely how each jury member construes that evidence. These construals rest on a variety of events and perceptions that often bear no objective relevant evidence. For instance, during cross-examination, did a key witness hesitate for a moment before answering, suggesting to some jurors that she might not be certain of her data? Or did some jurors consider the witness too remote, too arrogant, too certain of herself?

Another distinctive feature of social psychology is that it is an experimentally based science. As experimental scientists, we test our assumptions, guesses, and ideas about human social behavior empirically and systematically rather than by relying on folk wisdom, common sense, or the opinions and insights of philosophers, novelists, political pundits, grandmothers, and others wise in the ways of human beings. As you will see, doing systematic experiments in social psychology presents a great many challenges—primarily because we are attempting to predict the behavior of highly sophisticated organisms in a variety of complex situations.

As scientists, our goal is to find objective answers to a wide array of important questions: What are the factors that cause aggression? How might we reduce prejudice? What variables cause two people to like or love each other? Why do certain kinds of political advertisements work better than others? The specific ways in which experimental social psychologists meet these challenges will be illustrated throughout this book and discussed in detail in Chapter 2.

We will spend most of this introductory chapter expanding on the issues raised in the preceding paragraphs—of what social psychology is and how it is distinct from other, related disciplines. A good place to begin is with what social psychology is not.

How Else Can We Understand Social Influence?

Let's take another look at the examples at the beginning of this chapter. Why did people behave the way they did? One way to answer this question might be simply to ask them. For example, we could question the residents in Los Angeles about why they didn't call the police. We could ask Sam why he wasn't especially excited about his fraternity brothers. The problem with this approach is that people are not always aware of the origins of their own responses and feelings (Nisbett & Wilson, 1977b). It is unlikely that the neighbors know exactly why they went back to sleep without calling the police. It is unlikely that Sam could pinpoint why he liked his Delta Nu fraternity brothers less than his father had liked his.

Journalists, Instant Experts, and Social Critics   After the mass suicide at Jonestown, it was impossible to pick up a newspaper or turn on the TV without finding an explanation. These ranged from the (unfounded) assumption that Rev. Jones employed hypnotism and drugs to weaken the resistance of his followers to suspicion that the people who were attracted to his cult must have been disturbed and self-destructive in the first place. Such speculations, because they underestimate the power of the situation, are almost always wrong—or at the very least oversimplified.

Albanian Serbs attempting to escape the ravages of "ethnic cleansing" in 1999. One of the tasks of social psychological research is to find ways of reducing prejudice.

If we rely on commonsense explanations, then, we learn little from previous incidents. Jonestown was probably the first mass suicide involving Americans, but it wasn't the last. A few years ago in Waco, Texas, the followers of cult leader David Koresh barricaded themselves into a fortresslike compound to avoid arrest for the possession of illegal firearms and, when surrounded, apparently set fire to their own buildings. Eighty-six people died, including several children. Still more recently, thirty-nine members of an obscure cult called Heaven's Gate committed group suicide at a luxury estate in Rancho Santa Fe, California. The existing evidence makes it clear that the cult members died willingly and peacefully, believing that a huge alien spaceship, following closely behind the Hale-Bopp Comet, would pick up their souls and carry them into space (Purdham, 1997).

In the aftermath of both the Waco conflagration and the Heaven's Gate tragedy, the general population was just as confused as it had been following the Jonestown suicides. It is difficult for most people to grasp just how powerful a cult can be in affecting the hearts and minds of relatively normal people. Finding someone to blame became a national obsession. After the Heaven's Gate tragedy, many people blamed the victims themselves, accusing them of stupidity or derangement. But the evidence indicated that they were mentally healthy and for the most part uncommonly bright and well educated. After Waco, many pointed to the impatience of the FBI, the poor judgment of Attorney General Janet Reno, or the inadequate leadership of President Bill Clinton. Fixing blame may make us feel better by resolving our confusion, but it is no substitute for understanding the complexities of the situations that produced those events.

Don't get us wrong. We are not opposed to folk wisdom—far from it. We are convinced that a great deal can be learned about social behavior from journalists, social critics, and novelists—and in this book we quote from all these sources. There is, however, at least one problem with relying entirely on such sources: More often than not, they disagree with one another, and there is no easy way of determining which of them is correct.

Consider what folk wisdom has to say about the factors that influence how much we like other people. On the one hand, we know that "birds of a feather flock together." With a little effort, each of us could come up with lots of examples where indeed we liked and hung around with people who shared our backgrounds and interests. But then again, folk wisdom also tells us that "opposites attract." If we tried, we could also come up with examples where people with different backgrounds and interests did attract us. Which is it?

Similarly, are we to believe that "out of sight is out of mind" or that "absence makes the heart grow fonder," that "haste makes waste" or that "he who hesitates is lost"? And who is to say whether the Jonestown massacre occurred because

a. Reverend Jones succeeded in attracting the kinds of people who were psychologically depressed to begin with?

b. Only people with self-destructive tendencies join cults?

c. Jones was such a powerful, messianic, charismatic figure that virtually anyone—even strong, nondepressed individuals like you or us—would have succumbed to his influence?

d. People cut off from society are particularly vulnerable to social influence?

e. All of the above?

f. None of the above?

Philosophy   Throughout history, philosophy has been a major source of insight about human nature. Indeed, the creativity and analytical thinking of philoso-

Why did people obey Jim Jones'
suicide order?

phers are a major part of the foundation of contemporary psychology. This
has more than mere historical significance. In recent decades, psychologists
have looked to philosophers for insights into the nature of consciousness (e.g.,
Dennett, 1991) and how people form beliefs about the social world (e.g.,
Gilbert, 1991). Sometimes, however, even great thinkers find themselves in
disagreement with one another; when this occurs, how is one to know who
is right? Are there some situations where philosopher A might be right and
other conditions where philosopher B might be right? How would you determine this?

We social psychologists address many of the same questions that philosophers address, but we attempt to look at these questions scientifically—even
concerning that great human mystery, love. In 1663, the great Dutch philosopher Benedict Spinoza offered a highly original insight. He proposed that if
we love someone whom we formerly hated, that love will be greater than if hatred had not preceded it. Spinoza's proposition is beautifully worked out. His
logic is impeccable. But how can we be sure that it holds up? Does it always hold?
What are the conditions under which it does or doesn't hold? These are empirical questions for the social psychologist (Aronson, 1999; Aronson & Linder,
1965).

One of the tasks of the social psychologist is to make educated guesses
(called *hypotheses*) about the specific situations under which one outcome or the
other would occur. Just as a physicist performs experiments to test hypotheses
about the nature of the physical world, the social psychologist performs experiments to test hypotheses about the nature of the social world. The next task is to
design well-controlled experiments sophisticated enough to tease out the situations that would result in one or another outcome. This enriches our understanding of human nature and allows us to make accurate predictions once we
know the key aspects of the prevailing situation. We will discuss the scientific
methods social psychologists use in more detail in Chapter 2.

The major reason we have conflicting philosophical positions (just as we
have conflicting folk aphorisms) is that the world is a complicated place. Small
differences in the situation might not be easily discernible, yet these small differences might produce very different effects.

To elaborate on this point, let's return to our earlier discussion about the kinds of people we like and the relationship between absence and liking. We would suggest that there are some conditions under which birds of a feather do flock together and other conditions under which opposites do attract. Similarly, there are some conditions under which absence does make the heart grow fonder and others under which out of sight does mean out of mind. So both can be true. That statement helps—but is it good enough? Not really, for if you really want to understand human behavior, knowing that both can be true is not sufficient.

Social Psychology Compared with Personality Psychology

If you are like most people, when you read the examples that opened this chapter and started thinking about how those events might have come about, you probably wondered about the strengths, weaknesses, flaws, and personality traits that led the individuals involved to respond as they did. Why did the Los Angeles residents fail to call the police when they heard the cries for help? Most of us tend to assume that they possessed some personality flaw or quirk that made them reluctant to respond.

What character traits might these be? Some people are leaders and others are followers; some people are bold and others are timid; some people are public-spirited and others are selfish. Think back: How did you answer the question about whether you would want any of these people as a friend or a baby-sitter?

Asking—and trying to answer—questions like these is the work of personality psychologists. When trying to explain social behavior, personality psychologists generally focus on **individual differences**—the aspects of people's personalities that make them different from others. For example, to explain why the people at Jonestown ended their own lives and their children's by drinking poison, it seems natural to point to their personalities. Perhaps they were all "conformist types" or weak-willed; maybe they were even psychotic. The insights of personality psychologists increase our understanding of human behavior, but social psychologists are convinced that explaining behavior primarily through personality factors ignores a critical part of the story: the powerful role played by social influence. Remember that it was not just a handful of people who committed suicide at Jonestown but almost 100 percent of the people in the village. Though it is conceivable that they were all psychotic, it is highly improbable. If we want a deeper, richer, more thorough explanation of this tragic event, we need to understand what kind of power and influence a charismatic figure like Jim Jones possesses, the nature of the impact of living in a closed society cut off from other points of view, and a myriad of other factors that might have contributed to that tragic outcome.

These two different approaches can be illustrated by focusing on a couple of mundane examples. Consider my friend Rosa. She is the wife of one of my colleagues, and I see her frequently at faculty cocktail parties. At these cocktail parties, she generally looks rather uncomfortable. She usually stands off by herself and when approached has very little to say. Some people regard her as shy; others regard her as aloof, standoffish, even arrogant. It is easy to see why. But I have been a dinner guest at Rosa's home, and in that situation she is charming, gracious, and vivacious, a good listener and an interesting conversationalist. So which is it? Is Rosa a shy person, an arrogant person, or a charming and gracious person? Will the real Rosa please stand up? It's the wrong question; the real Rosa is both and neither. All of us are capable of both shy and gracious behavior. A much more interesting question is, What factors are different in these two social situations that have such a profound effect on her (our) behavior? That is a social psychological question. (See the Try It! exercise on page 12.)

Individual Differences
The aspects of people's personalities that make them different from other people

1. Think about one of your friends or acquaintances whom you regard as a shy person. For a moment, try not to think about him or her as "a shy person" but rather as someone who has difficulty relating to people in some situations but not in others.

2. Make a list of the social situations you think are most likely to bring out your friend's shy behavior.

3. Make a list of the social situations that might bring forth more outgoing behaviors on your friend's part. (For example, if someone showed a real interest in one of your friend's favorite hobbies or topics of conversation, it might bring out behaviors that could be classified as charming or vivacious.)

4. Set up a social environment in which this could be accomplished. Pay close attention to the effect that it has on your friend's behavior.

This is an important issue, so we'll give you one more example. Suppose you stop at a roadside restaurant for a cup of coffee and a piece of pie. The waitress comes over to take your order, but you are having a hard time deciding which kind of pie to order. While you are hesitating, the waitress impatiently taps her pen against her order book, rolls her eyes toward the ceiling, scowls at you, and finally snaps, "Hey, I haven't got all day, you know!" Like most people, you would probably think that the waitress is a nasty or unpleasant person; you might even complain about her to the manager.

But suppose you knew that the waitress is a single parent and was kept awake all night by the moaning of her youngest child, who has a painful terminal illness; that her car broke down on her way to work and she has no idea where she will find the money to have it repaired; that when she finally arrived at the restaurant, she learned that her co-worker was too drunk to work, requiring her to cover twice the usual number of tables; and that the short-order cook keeps screaming at her because she is not picking up the orders fast enough to please him. Given all that information, you might conclude that she is not necessarily a nasty person, just an ordinary person under enormous stress.

The key fact remains that without important information about a situation, when we are trying to understand someone's behavior in a complex situation, most people will find the reason for that behavior in the personality of the individual involved. And this fact—that we often fail to take the situation into account—is important to social psychologists, for it has a profound impact on how human beings relate to one another.

Social Psychology Compared with Other Social Sciences

Social psychology's focus on social behavior is shared by several other disciplines in the social sciences, including sociology, economics, and political science. Each of these examines the influence of social factors on human behavior, but important differences set social psychology apart, most notably in their level of analysis. Social psychology is a branch of psychology, rooted in the study of individuals, with an emphasis on internal psychological processes. *For the social psychologist, the level of analysis is the individual in the context of a social situation.* For example, to understand why people intentionally hurt one another, the social psychologist focuses on the specific psychological processes that trigger aggression in specific situations. To what extent is aggression preceded by frustration? Does frustration always precede aggression? If people are feeling frustrated, under what conditions will they vent their frustration with an overt, aggressive act? What factors might preclude an aggressive response by a frustrated individual? Besides frustration, what other factors might cause aggression? We will address these questions in Chapter 12.

Other social sciences are more concerned with broad social, economic, political, and historical factors that influence events in a given society. Sociology, for example, is concerned with such topics as social class, social structure, and social institutions. Of course, because society is made up of collections of people, some overlap is bound to exist between the domains of sociology and those of social psychology. The major difference is that sociology, rather than focusing on the psychology of the individual, looks toward society at large. So while sociologists are also interested in aggression, sociologists are more likely to be concerned with why a particular *society* or *group* within a society produces different levels and types of aggression in its members. Why, for example, is the murder rate in the United States so much higher than in Canada? Within the United States, why is the murder rate higher in some social classes than in others? How do changes in society relate to changes in aggressive behavior?

The people in this photo can be studied from a variety of perspectives: As individuals, as members of a family, a social class, an occupation, a culture, a region, and on and on.

The difference between social psychology and other social sciences in level of analysis reflects another difference between the disciplines: what they are trying to explain. *The goal of social psychology is to identify universal properties of human nature that make everyone susceptible to social influence, regardless of social class or culture.* The laws governing the relationship between frustration and aggression, for example, are hypothesized to be true of most people in most places, not just members of one social class, age group, or race. Social psychology is a young science that developed mostly in the United States; many of its findings have not yet been tested in other cultures to see if they are universal. Nonetheless, our goal as social psychologists is to discover such laws. And increasingly, as methods and theories developed by American social psychologists are adopted by European, Asian, African, Middle Eastern, and South American social psychologists, we are learning more about the extent to which these laws are universal. This type of cultural expansion is extremely valuable because it sharpens theories, either by demonstrating their universality or by leading us to discover additional variables whose incorporation will ultimately help us make more accurate predictions of human social behavior. We will encounter several examples of such cross-cultural research in subsequent chapters.

In sum, social psychology is located between its closest cousins, sociology and personality psychology (see Table 1.1, on page 14). Social psychology and sociology share an interest in the way the situation and the larger society influence behavior. But social psychologists focus more on the psychological makeup of individuals that renders people susceptible to social influence. And while social psychology and personality psychology both emphasize the psychology of the individual, rather than focusing on what makes people different from one another, social psychology emphasizes the psychological processes shared by most people that make them susceptible to social influence.

TABLE 1.1

Social Psychology Compared to Related Disciplines

SOCIOLOGY	SOCIAL PSYCHOLOGY	PERSONALITY PSYCHOLOGY
Provides general laws and theories about societies, not individuals.	Studies the psychological processes people have in common with one another that make them susceptible to social influence.	Studies the characteristics that make individuals unique and different from one another.

THE POWER OF SOCIAL INFLUENCE

When trying to convince people that their behavior is greatly influenced by the social environment, the social psychologist is up against a formidable barrier: All of us tend to explain people's behavior in terms of their personalities. This barrier is known as the **fundamental attribution error**—the tendency to explain our own and other people's behavior entirely in terms of personality traits, thereby underestimating the power of social influence.

Underestimating the Power of Social Influence

The head monkey at Paris puts on a traveller's cap, and all the monkeys in America do the same.

–Henry David Thoreau

When we underestimate the power of social influence, we gain a feeling of false security. For example, when trying to explain repugnant or bizarre behavior, such as the people of Jonestown, Waco, or Heaven's Gate taking their own lives or killing their own children, it is tempting and, in a strange way, comforting to write off the victims as flawed human beings. Doing so gives the rest of us the feeling that it could never happen to us. Ironically, this in turn increases our personal vulnerability to possibly destructive social influence by lulling us into lowering our guard. Moreover, by failing to fully appreciate the power of the situation, we tend to oversimplify complex situations; oversimplification decreases our understanding of the causes of a great deal of human behavior. Among other things, this oversimplification can lead us to blame the victim in situations where the individual was overpowered by social forces too difficult for most of us to resist, as in the Jonestown tragedy.

To take a more mundane example, imagine a situation in which people are playing a two-person game wherein each player must choose one of two strategies: They can play competitively and try to win as much money as possible and make sure their partner loses as much as possible, or they can play cooperatively and try to make sure both they and their partner win some money. We will discuss the details of this game in Chapter 9. For now, just consider that there are only two basic strategies to use when playing the game—competition or cooperation. How do you think your friends would play this game?

Few people find this question hard to answer; we all have a feeling for the relative competitiveness of our friends. "Well," you might say, "I am certain that my friend Jennifer, who is a hardnosed business major, would play this game more competitively than my friend Anna, who is a really caring, loving person." That is, we think of our friends' personalities and answer accordingly. We usually do not think much about the nature of the social situation when making our predictions.

But how accurate are such predictions? Should we think about the social situation? To find out, Lee Ross and Steven Samuels (1993) conducted the following experiment. First, they chose a group of students at Stanford University who

Fundamental Attribution Error

The tendency to overestimate the extent to which people's behavior is due to internal, dispositional factors and to underestimate the role of situational factors

were considered by the resident assistants in their dorm to be either especially cooperative or especially competitive. The researchers did this by describing the game to the resident assistants and asking them to think of students in their dormitories who would be most likely to adopt the competitive or cooperative strategy. As expected, the resident assistants easily identified students who fit each category.

Next, Ross and Samuels invited these students to play the game in a psychology experiment. There was one added twist: The researchers varied a seemingly minor aspect of the social situation—what the game was called. They told half the participants that the name was the Wall Street Game and half that it was the Community Game. Everything else about the game was identical. Thus people who were judged as either competitive or cooperative played a game that was called either the Wall Street Game or the Community Game, resulting in four conditions.

Again, most of us go through life assuming that what really counts is an individual's personality, not something so trivial as what a game is called. Some people seem competitive by nature and would thus relish the opportunity to go head to head with a fellow student. Others seem much more cooperative and would thus achieve the most satisfaction by making sure no one lost too much money and no one's feelings were hurt. Right? Not so fast! As seen in Figure 1.1 on page 16, even so trivial an aspect of the situation as the name of the game made a tremendous difference in how people behaved. When it was called the Wall Street Game, approximately two-thirds of the people responded competitively, whereas when it was called the Community Game, only a third of the people responded competitively. The name of the game sent a powerful message about how the players should behave. It alone conveyed strong social norms about what kind of behavior was appropriate in this situation. In Chapter 7, we will see that social norms can shape people's behaviors in powerful ways.

In this situation, a student's personality made no measurable difference in the student's behavior. The students labeled "competitive" were no more likely to adopt the competitive strategy than those who were labeled "cooperative." This pattern of results is one we will see throughout this book. Aspects of the social situation that may seem minor can have powerful effects, overwhelming the differences in people's personalities (Ross & Ward, 1996). This is not to say that personality differences do not exist or are unimportant; they do exist and frequently are of great importance. But we have learned that social and environ-

Suppose these students were asked to play a game for money. Would they play cooperatively or competitively? Do you think their characters or the situation will be most likely to influence them?

What influences how cooperative people will be—their personalities or the nature of the social situation?

Ross and Samuels (1993) found that college students' personalities, as rated by the resident assistants in their dormitories, did not determine how cooperative or competitive they were in a laboratory game. The name of the game—whether it was called the Wall Street Game or the Community Game—did, however, make a tremendous difference. Such seemingly minor aspects of the social situation can have powerful effects on people's behavior, overwhelming the differences in their personalities.

(Adapted from Ross & Samuels, 1993)

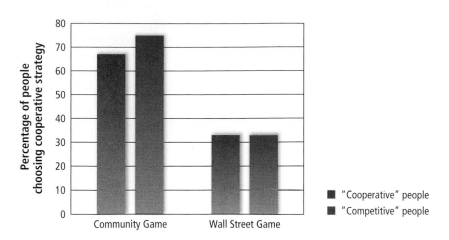

mental situations are so powerful that they have dramatic effects on almost everyone. This is the domain of the social psychologist.

The Subjectivity of the Social Situation

We have argued that the social situation often has profound effects on human behavior. But what exactly do we mean by the social situation? One strategy for defining it would be to specify the objective properties of the situation, such as how rewarding it is to people, and then document the behaviors that follow from these objective properties.

This was the approach taken by **behaviorism,** a school of psychology maintaining that to understand human behavior, one need only consider the reinforcing properties of the environment—that is, how positive and negative events in the environment are associated with specific behaviors. For example, dogs come when they are called because they have learned that compliance is followed by positive reinforcement (e.g., food or fondling); children will memorize their multiplication tables more quickly if you praise them, smile at them, and paste a gold star on their forehead following correct answers. Psychologists in this tradition, such as John Watson (1924) and B. F. Skinner (1938), suggested that all behavior could be understood by examining the rewards and punishments in the organism's environment and that there was no need to study such subjective states as thinking and feeling. Thus to understand the behavior of the Los Angeles residents who ignored their neighbor's predawn cries for help, a behaviorist would analyze the situation to see what specific, objective factors were inhibiting any attempts to help. What were the objective rewards and punishments implicit in taking a specific course of action? What were the rewards and punishments implicit in doing nothing?

Behaviorists chose not to deal with issues like cognition, thinking, and feeling because they considered these concepts too vague and mentalistic and not sufficiently anchored to observable behavior. Elegant in its simplicity, the behavioristic approach can account for a great deal of behavior. But because behaviorism does not deal with cognition, thinking, and feeling—phenomena vital to the human social experience—this approach has proved inadequate for a complete understanding of the social world. We have learned that social behavior cannot be fully understood by confining our observations to the physical properties of a situation. We need to look at the situation from the viewpoint of the people in it, to see how they construe the world around them (Griffin & Ross, 1991; Ross & Nisbett, 1991). For example, if a person approaches us, slaps us on the back, and asks us how we are feeling, is that rewarding or not? On the surface, it might

Behaviorism

A school of psychology maintaining that to understand human behavior, one need only consider the reinforcing properties of the environment—that is, how positive and negative events in the environment are associated with specific behaviors

seem like a reward. After all, isn't that person's interest in us a desirable thing? But in actuality, it is a complex situation that depends on our thoughts and feelings. We might construe the meaning differently, depending on whether the question is asked by a close friend who is deeply concerned about our health, a casual acquaintance simply passing the time of day, or an automobile salesperson attempting to ingratiate himself so that he might sell us a used car. This would be the case even if the question were worded the same and asked in the same tone of voice. For example, in responding to the salesperson's question, we would be unlikely to describe the pains we've been having in our kidney—something we might do in response to our closest friend's inquiry.

This emphasis on construal, the way people interpret the social situation, has its roots in an approach called **Gestalt psychology.** First proposed as a theory of how people perceive the physical world, Gestalt psychology holds that we should study the subjective way in which an object appears in people's minds (the gestalt, or whole), rather than the way in which the objective, physical attributes of the object combine. For example, one way to try to understand how people perceive a painting would be to break it down into its individual elements, such as the exact amounts of primary colors applied to the different parts of the canvas, the types of brush strokes used to apply the colors, and the different geometric shapes they form. We might then attempt to determine how these elements are combined by the perceiver to form an overall image of the painting. According to Gestalt psychologists, however, it is impossible to understand the way in which an object is perceived simply by studying these building blocks of perception. The whole is different from the sum of its parts. One must focus on the phenomenology of the perceiver—on how an object appears to people—instead of on the individual elements of the objective stimulus.

The Gestalt approach was formulated in Germany in the first part of the twentieth century by Kurt Koffka, Wolfgang Kohler, Max Wertheimer, and their students and colleagues. In the late 1930s, several of these psychologists emigrated to the United States to escape the Nazi regime and subsequently had such a major influence on American psychology that one astute observer remarked, "If I were required to name the one person who has had the greatest impact on the field, it would have to be Adolf Hitler" (Cartwright, 1979, p. 84).

Among the émigrés was Kurt Lewin, generally considered the founding father of modern experimental social psychology. As a young German-Jewish professor in the 1930s, Lewin experienced the anti-Semitism rampant in Nazi Germany. The experience profoundly affected his thinking, and once in the United States, Lewin's ideas helped shape American social psychology, directing it toward a deep interest in exploring the causes and cures of prejudice and ethnic stereotyping.

As a theorist, Lewin took the bold step of applying Gestalt principles beyond the perception of objects to social perception—how people perceive other people and their motives, intentions, and behaviors. Lewin was the first scientist to fully realize the importance of taking the perspective of the people in any social situation to see how they construe (perceive, interpret, and distort) this social environment. Social psychologists soon began to focus on the importance of considering subjective situations (how they are construed by people). These early social psychologists and their key statements are presented on the following pages.

Such construals can be rather simple, as in the example of the question "How are you feeling?" discussed earlier. Other construals might appear simple

In the 1930s a woman reads a government sponsored storefront sign urging the German people to boycott Jewish businesses. This was an early step that eventually led to the Holocaust.

Gestalt Psychology

A school of psychology stressing the importance of studying the subjective way in which an object appears in people's minds, rather than the objective, physical attributes of the object

Kurt Lewin: "If an individual sits in a room trusting that the ceiling will not come down, should only his 'subjective probability' be taken into account for predicting behavior or should we also consider the 'objective probability' of the ceiling's coming down as determined by engineers? To my mind, only the first has to be taken into account."

Fritz Heider: "Generally, a person reacts to what he thinks the other person is perceiving, feeling, and thinking, in addition to what the other person may be doing."

but are in reality remarkably complex. For example, suppose Maria gives Shawn a kiss on the cheek at the end of their first date. How will Shawn respond to the kiss? We would say that it depends on how he construes the situation: Does he interpret it as a first step—a sign of awakening romantic interest on Maria's part? Or does he see it as an aloof, sisterly expression—a signal that Maria wants to be friends but nothing more? Or does he see it as a sign that Maria is interested in him but wants to proceed slowly in their developing relationship?

Were Shawn to misconstrue the situation, he might commit a serious blunder; he might turn his back on what could have been the love of his life—or he might express passion inappropriately. In either case, we believe that the best strategy for understanding Shawn's reaction would be to find a way to determine Shawn's construal of Maria's behavior, rather than to dissect the objective nature of the kiss itself (its length, degree of pressure, etc.). But how are these construals formed? Stay tuned.

WHERE CONSTRUALS COME FROM: BASIC HUMAN MOTIVES

How will Shawn determine why Maria kissed him? If it is true that subjective and not objective situations influence people, then we need to understand how people arrive at their subjective impressions of the world. What are people trying to accomplish when they interpret the social world? Again, we could address this question from the perspective of people's personalities. What is it about Shawn, including his upbringing, family background, and unique experiences, that makes him view the world the way he does? As we have seen, such a focus on individual differences in people's personalities, though valuable, misses what is usually of far greater importance: the effects of the social situation on people. To understand these effects, we need to understand the fundamental laws of human nature, common to all, that explain why we construe the social world the way we do.

We human beings are complex organisms; at a given moment, various intersecting motives underlie our thoughts and behaviors. Over the years, social psychologists have found that two of these motives are of primary importance: the need to feel good about ourselves and *the need to be accurate*. There are times when each of these motives pulls us in the same direction. Often, though, these motives tug us in opposite directions—where to perceive the world accurately requires us to face up to the fact that we have behaved foolishly or immorally.

Leon Festinger, one of social psychology's most innovative theorists, was quick to realize that it is precisely when these two motives tug in opposite directions that we can gain our most valuable insights into the workings of the human heart and mind. An example will clarify. Imagine you are the president of the United States and your country is engaged in a difficult and costly war in Southeast Asia. You have poured hundreds of billions of dollars into that war, and it has consumed tens of thousands of American lives as well as a great many more lives of innocent Vietnamese civilians. The war seems to be at a stalemate; no end is in sight. You frequently wake up in the middle of the night bathed in the cold sweat of conflict: On the one hand, you deplore all the carnage that is going on; on the other hand, you don't want to go down in history as the first American president to lose a war.

Some of your advisers tell you that they can see the light at the end of the tunnel—that if you intensify the bombing, the enemy will soon capitulate and the war will be over. This would be a great outcome for you: Not only will you have succeeded in achieving your military and political aims, but history will consider you to have been a hero. Other advisers, however, believe that intensifying the bombing will only strengthen the enemy's resolve; they advise you to sue for peace (McNamara, 1995).

Which advisers are you likely to believe? As we shall see in Chapter 6, President Lyndon Johnson faced this dilemma exactly. Not surprisingly, he chose to believe the advisers who suggested that he escalate the war, for if he could succeed in winning the war, he would justify his prior behavior as commander in chief, whereas if he withdrew from Vietnam, he not only would go down in history as the first president to lose a war but also would have to justify the fact that all those lives and all that money had been spent in vain. This advice, however, proved erroneous. Increasing the bombing did strengthen the enemy's resolve, thereby prolonging the war. As this example illustrates, the need for self-justification can fly in the face of the need to be accurate—and can have catastrophic consequences.

The Self-Esteem Approach: The Need to Feel Good about Ourselves

Most people have a strong need to maintain reasonably high **self-esteem**—that is, to see themselves as good, competent, and decent (Aronson, 1992a, 1998; Baumeister, 1993; Harter, 1993; Kunda, 1990; Pyszczynski, Solomon, Greenberg, & Stewart-Fouts, 1995; Stone, 1998; Thibodeau & Aronson, 1992; Tice, 1993). The reason people view the world the way they do can often be traced to this underlying need to maintain a favorable image of themselves. Given the choice between distorting the world in order to feel good about themselves and representing the world accurately, people often take the first option.

Justifying Past Behavior Suppose that a couple gets divorced after ten years of a marriage made difficult by the husband's irrational jealousy. Rather than admitting the truth—that his jealousy and overpossessiveness drove her away—the husband blames the breakup of his marriage on the fact that his ex-wife was not responsive enough to his needs. His interpretation serves some purpose: It makes him feel better about himself. Acknowledging major deficiencies in ourselves is very difficult, even when the cost is seeing the world inaccurately. The consequence of this distortion, of course, is that learning from experience becomes very unlikely. In his next marriage, the husband is likely to run into the same problems.

We do not mean to imply that people totally distort reality, denying the existence of all information that reflects badly on them; such extreme behavior is rare outside of mental institutions. Yet it is often possible for normal people to put a slightly different spin on the existing facts, one that puts us in the best possible light. Consider Roger; everybody knows someone like Roger. He's the guy whose shoes are almost always untied and who frequently has coffee stains on the front of his shirt or mustard stains around his lips. Most observers might consider Roger a slob, but Roger might see himself as casual and noncompulsive.

The fact that people distort their interpretation of reality so that they might feel better about themselves is not surprising, even to the most casual observer of human behavior. The ways in which this motive operates, however, are often startling, but it can shed some light on otherwise mystifying behavior.

Suffering and Self-Justification Let's go back to one of our early scenarios: the case of Oscar and his son, Sam. Why was Sam less enamored of his fraternity brothers than Oscar had been when he was in college? Recall that Oscar quickly formed the hypothesis that perhaps his fraternity was not attracting the kinds of wonderful people who were there when he was in college. This might be true.

Leon Festinger: "The way I have always thought about it is that if the empirical world looks complicated, if people seem to react in bewilderingly different ways to similar forces, and if I cannot see the operation of universal underlying dynamics, then that is my fault. I have asked the wrong questions; I have, at a theoretical level, sliced up the world incorrectly. The underlying dynamics are there, and I have to find the theoretical apparatus that will enable me to reveal these uniformities."

Self-Esteem
People's evaluations of their own self-worth—that is, the extent to which they view themselves as good, competent, and decent

But we would assert that a far more compelling possibility involves the hazing it-self. Specifically, we would contend that a major factor that increased Oscar's lik-ing for his fraternity brothers was the unpleasant hazing ritual he underwent, a ritual Sam was able to avoid. That sounds a little strange. Why would something so unpleasant cause Oscar to like his fraternity? Didn't behavioristic psychology teach us that rewards, not punishments, make us like things associated with them? Quite so. But as we indicated earlier, in recent years social psychologists have discovered that this formulation is far too simple to account for human thinking and motivation. Unlike rats and pigeons, human beings have a need to justify their past behavior, and this need leads them to thoughts, feelings, and behaviors that don't always fit into the neat categories of the behaviorist.

Here's how it works. If Oscar goes through a severe hazing in order to be-come a member of the fraternity but later discovers unpleasant things about his fraternity brothers, he will feel like a fool: "Why did I go through all that pain and embarrassment in order to live in a house with a bunch of jerks? Only a moron would do a thing like that." To avoid feeling like a fool, he will try to justify his de-cision to undergo the hazing by distorting his interpretation of his fraternity ex-perience. In other words, he will try to put a positive spin on his experiences.

Suppose that having gone through all that hazing, Oscar moves into the fra-ternity house and begins to experience things that to an outside observer are not very positive: The fraternity dues make a significant dent in Oscar's budget; the frequent parties seem frivolous and take a toll on the amount of studying he can do, and consequently his grades begin to suffer; most of the meals served in the house are only a small step up from dog chow. Whereas an unmotivated ob-server—someone who didn't go through the hazing—might consider these ex-periences extremely negative, Oscar is motivated to see them differently; indeed, he considers them a small price to pay for the sense of brotherhood he feels to-ward his fraternity mates. He focuses on the good parts of living in the fraternity, and he distorts or dismisses the bad parts as inconsequential. The result of all this self-justification is bound to make Oscar more kindly disposed toward the fraternity than Sam was, because Sam, not having gone through the hazing, had no need to justify his behavior and thus no need to see his fraternity experiences in a positive light. The end result? Oscar loved his fraternity; Sam did not.

Does this sound far-fetched? How do we know that the people in the frater-nity were not objectively nicer when Oscar was a member than when Sam was a member? In a series of well-controlled laboratory experiments, social psycholo-

Doing silly or dangerous things as part of fraternity hazing, may be, well, silly or dangerous. At the same time, it does build cohesiveness.

gists have investigated the phenomenon of hazing, holding constant everything in the situation including the precise behavior of the fraternity members—except for the severity of the hazing students underwent in order to become members. These experiments demonstrated conclusively that the more unpleasant the procedure the participants underwent to get into a group, the better they liked the group—even though, objectively, the group members were the same people behaving in the same manner (Aronson & Mills, 1959; Gerard & Mathewson, 1966). We discuss this phenomenon more thoroughly in Chapter 6. The important points to remember here are (1) that human beings are motivated to maintain a positive picture of themselves, in part by justifying their past behavior, and (2) that under certain specifiable conditions, this leads them to do things that at first glance might seem surprising or paradoxical. For example, they might prefer people and things for whom they have suffered to people and things they associate with ease and pleasure.

Again, we want to emphasize that the results of this research tradition should not be taken to mean that behaviorist theories are dead wrong; those theories explain some behavior very well (see our discussion in Chapter 10 of the research on social exchange theory). In our view, however, behavioristic approaches are inadequate to account for a huge subset of important attitudes and behaviors. This will become much clearer as you read on; in future chapters, we will try to specify the precise conditions under which one or the other set of principles is more likely to apply.

The Social Cognition Approach: The Need to Be Accurate

As we've seen, even when people are bending the facts to see themselves in as favorable a way as they can, they do not completely distort reality. It would not be very adaptive to live in a fantasy world, believing that the car speeding toward us as we step off the curb is really a mirage or that our future spouse will be Denzel Washington or Gwyneth Paltrow, who will soon give up acting and arrive at our doorstep. In fact, human beings are quite skilled at thinking, contemplating, and deducing. One of the major hallmarks of being human is the ability to reason. As a species, we have highly developed logical and computational abilities that are truly amazing. In our lifetime alone, we have witnessed such extraordinary cognitive achievements as the invention and development of computers, the exploration of outer space, and the conquering of many human diseases.

Moreover, on a more common (but perhaps more important) level, it is impossible to observe the cognitive development of a child without being awestruck. Just think of the vast gains in knowledge and reasoning that occur in the first few years of life. In a relatively short time, we see our child transform from a squirming, helpless newborn who can do little but eat, cry, and sleep into a sophisticated, garrulous 4-year-old who can utter complex sentences, hatch diabolical plots to frustrate a younger sibling, and evoke both consternation and pride in parents.

Social Cognition   Given the amazing cognitive abilities of our species, it makes sense that social psychologists, when formulating theories of social behavior, would take into consideration the way in which human beings think about the world. We call this the cognitive approach to social psychology, or **social cognition** (Fiske & Taylor, 1991; Markus & Zajonc, 1985; Nisbett & Ross, 1980). Researchers who attempt to understand social behavior from the perspective of social cognition begin with the assumption that all people try to view the world as accurately as possible. Accordingly, human beings are viewed by researchers as amateur sleuths who are doing their best to understand and predict their social world.

But this is by no means easy, because we almost never know all the facts we need to accurately judge a given situation. Whether it is a relatively simple decision, such as which breakfast cereal offers the best combination of healthfulness

Social Cognition

How people think about themselves and the social world; more specifically, how people select, interpret, remember, and use social information to make judgments and decisions

and tastiness, or a slightly more complex decision, such as our desire to buy the best car we can for under $18,000, or a much more complex decision, such as choosing a marriage partner who will make us deliriously happy for the rest of our lives, it is almost never easy to gather all the relevant facts in advance. Moreover, we make countless decisions every day; even if there were a way to gather all the facts for each decision, we simply lack the time or the stamina to do so.

Does this sound a bit overblown? Aren't most decisions fairly easy? Let's take a closer look. We will begin by asking you a simple question: Which breakfast cereal is better for you, Lucky Charms or 100% Natural from Quaker? If you are like most of our students, you answered "100% Natural from Quaker." After all, everybody knows that Lucky Charms is a kid's cereal, full of sugar and cute little marshmallows, with a picture of a leprechaun on the box. 100% Natural has a picture of raw wheat on the box, the box is the color of natural wheat (light tan), and doesn't *natural* mean "good for you?" If that's the way you reasoned, you have fallen into a common cognitive trap—you have generalized from the cover to the product. A careful reading of the ingredients (in small print on the package) will reveal that although Lucky Charms has a bit more sugar in it than 100% Natural, the latter contains far more fat—so much so that *Consumer Reports* magazine ranked it a less healthful choice than Lucky Charms. Even in the simple world of cereals, things are not always what they seem.

Expectations about the Social World To add to the difficulty, sometimes our expectations about the social world interfere with perceiving it accurately. Our expectations can even change the *nature* of the social world. Imagine, for example, that you are an elementary school teacher dedicated to improving the lives of your students. At the beginning of the academic year, you review each student's standardized intelligence test scores. Early in your career, you were pretty sure, but not entirely sure, that these tests could gauge each child's true potential. But after several years of teaching, you have gradually become certain that these tests are accurate. Why the change? You have come to see that almost invariably, the kids who got high scores on these tests are the ones who did the best in your classroom, and the kids who got low scores performed poorly in class.

This scenario doesn't sound all that surprising, except for one key fact: You might be very wrong about the validity of the intelligence tests. It might be that the tests weren't very accurate but that you unintentionally treated the kids with high scores and the kids with low scores differently, making it look like the tests were accurate. This is exactly what Robert Rosenthal and Lenore Jacobson (1968) found in their investigation of a phenomenon called the *self-fulfilling prophecy*. They entered elementary school classrooms and administered a test. They then informed each teacher that according to the test, a few specific students were "bloomers" who were about to take off and perform extremely well. In actuality, the test showed no such thing; the children labeled as bloomers were chosen at random by drawing names out of a hat and thus were no different, on average, from any of the other kids. Lo and behold, on returning to the classroom at the end of the school year, Rosenthal and Jacobson found that the bloomers were performing extremely well. The mere fact that the teachers were led to expect these students to do well caused a reliable improvement in their performance. This striking phenomenon is no fluke; it has been replicated a number of times in a wide variety of schools (Rosenthal, 1995).

How did it come about? Though this outcome seems almost magical, it is embedded in an important aspect of human nature. If you were one of those teachers and were led to expect two or three specific students to perform well, you would be more likely to treat those students in special ways—paying more attention to them, listening to them with more respect, calling on them more frequently, encouraging them, and trying to teach them more difficult material. This, in turn, would almost certainly make these students feel happier, more respected, more motivated, and smarter, and—*voilà*—a self-fulfilling prophecy. Thus even when we are trying to perceive the social world as accurately as we can, there are many ways in which we can go wrong, ending up with the wrong impressions. We will see why—and the conditions under which social perception is accurate—in Chapters 3 and 4.

Additional Motives

We want to reiterate what we stated earlier: The two major sources of construals we have emphasized here—the need to maintain a positive view of ourselves (the self-esteem approach) and the need to view the world accurately (the social cognition approach)—are the most important of our social motives, but they are certainly not the only motives influencing people's thoughts and behaviors. Under various conditions, a variety of motives influence what we think, feel, and do. Biological drives such as hunger and thirst, of course, can be powerful motivators, especially under circumstances of extreme deprivation. At a more psychological level, we can be motivated by fear or by the promise of love, favors, and other rewards involving social exchange. These motives will be discussed at length in Chapters 10 and 11.

Still another significant motive is the need for control. Research has shown that people need to feel they exert some control over their environment (Langer, 1975; Taylor, 1989; Thompson, 1981). When people experience a loss of control, such that they believe they have little or no influence over whether good or bad things happen to them, there are a number of important consequences; we will discuss these further along in this book.

SOCIAL PSYCHOLOGY AND SOCIAL PROBLEMS

To recapitulate, social psychology can be defined as the scientific study of social influence. Social influence can best be understood by focusing on the major roots of human social behavior. It might have occurred to you to ask why we want to understand social influence in the first place. Who cares? And what difference does it make whether a behavior has its roots in the desire to be accurate or in the desire to bolster our self-esteem?

There are several answers to these questions. The most basic answer is simple: We are curious. Social psychologists are fascinated by human social behavior and want to understand it on the deepest possible level. In a sense, all of us are social psychologists. We all live in a social environment, and we are all more than mildly curious about such issues as how we become influenced, how we influence others, and why we fall in love with some people, dislike others, and are indifferent to still others.

Many social psychologists have another reason for studying the causes of social behavior: to contribute to the solution of social problems. From the very beginning of our young science, social psychologists have been keenly interested in such social challenges as reducing hostility and prejudice and increasing altruism and generosity. Contemporary social psychologists have continued this tradition and have broadened the issues of concern to include such endeavors as inducing people to conserve natural resources like water and energy (Dickerson, Thibodeau, Aronson, & Miller, 1992), educating people to practice safer sex in order to reduce the spread of AIDS (Aronson, 1997a, 1998; Stone, Aronson, Crain, Winslow, & Fried, 1994), understanding the relationship between viewing violence on television and the violent behavior of television watchers (Eron, Huesmann, Lefkowitz, & Walder, 1996), developing effective negotiation strategies for the reduction of international conflict (Kelman, 1997), finding ways to reduce racial prejudice (Aronson & Patnoe, 1997), and helping people adjust to life changes such as entering college or the death of a loved one (Harris, 1986).

Social psychology can help us study, and potentially solve, social problems, such as whether watching violent television shows produces aggressive and violent behavior in children and the means by which this may happen.

The ability to understand and explain complex and dysfunctional social behavior brings with it the challenge to change it. For example, when our government began to take the AIDS epidemic seriously, it mounted an advertising campaign that seemed intent on frightening people into practicing safer sex. This seems consistent with common sense: If you want people to do something they wouldn't ordinarily do, why not scare the daylights out of them?

This is not a stupid idea. As we shall see in subsequent chapters, there are many dysfunctional acts (e.g., cigarette smoking, drunk driving) for which the induction of fear can and does motivate people to take rational, appropriate action to preserve their health (Levy-Leboyer, 1988; Wilson, Purdon, & Wallston, 1988). But based on years of systematic research on persuasion, social psychologists were quick to realize that in the specific situation of AIDS, arousing fear would almost certainly not produce the desired effect for most people. The weight of the research evidence suggests that where sexual behavior is involved, the situation becomes murky. Specifically, most people do not want to be thinking about dying or contracting a horrible illness while they are getting ready to have sex. Such thoughts can, to say the least, interfere with the romantic aspect of the situation. Moreover, most people do not enjoy using condoms because they feel that interrupting the sexual act to put on a condom tends to destroy the mood. Given these considerations, when people have been exposed to frightening messages, instead of engaging in rational problem-solving behavior, most tend to reduce that fear by engaging in denial ("It can't happen to me," "Surely none of my friends have AIDS," etc.).

You may have figured out that the process of denial stems not from the desire to be accurate but from the need to maintain one's self-esteem. If people can succeed in convincing themselves that their sexual partners do not have AIDS, they can continue to enjoy unprotected sex while maintaining a reasonably good picture of themselves as rational beings. By understanding how this process works, social psychologists have been able to contribute important insights to AIDS education and prevention, as we shall see (Aronson, 1997a; Aronson, Fried, & Stone, 1991; Stone et al., 1994).

Throughout this book, we will examine many similar examples of the applications of social psychology. Likewise, throughout this book, we will also discuss some of the underlying human motives and the characteristics of the social situation that produce significant social behaviors, with the assumption that if we are interested in changing our own or other people's behavior, we must first know something about these fundamental causes. Although most of the studies discussed in these chapters are concerned with such fundamental causes, they also address critical social problems, including the effects of the mass media on attitudes and behavior (Chapter 7), violence and aggression (Chapter 12), and prejudice (Chapter 13). For the benefit of interested readers, we have also included three separate "modules" centering on the application of social psychology to contemporary issues involving health, the environment, and law. Your instructor may assign them at any time during the semester or may decide not to assign them at all, leaving that decision to your own curiosity.

SUMMARY

What Is Social Psychology?

We define **social psychology** as the scientific study of the way in which people's thoughts, feelings, and behaviors are influenced by the real or imagined presence of other people. People are constantly being influenced by other people.

The Power of Social Influence

Social influence is often powerful—usually outweighing **individual differences** in people's personalities as determinants of human behavior. To appreciate this fact, we must try to avoid falling into the **fundamental attribution error**—the tendency to explain our own and others' behavior entirely in terms of personality traits, thus underestimating the power of social influence.

Where Construals Come From: Basic Human Motives

To appreciate the power of social influence, we must understand how people form **construals** of their social environment. We are not computerlike organisms who respond directly and mechanically to environmental stimuli; rather, we are complex human beings who perceive, think about, and sometimes distort information from our environment. By emphasizing the way in which people construe the social world, social psychology has its roots more in the tradition of **Gestalt psychology** than in that of **behaviorism.**

Although human behavior is complex and nonmechanical, it is not unfathomable. A person's construals of the world are rooted primarily in two fundamental motives: the desire to maintain **self-esteem** and the desire to form an accurate picture of oneself and the social world (the **social cognition** approach). Accordingly, to understand how we are influenced by our social environments, we must understand the processes by which we do the perceiving, thinking, and distorting. Two major concepts in social psychology can thus be stated succinctly: (1) Social influence has a powerful impact on people, and (2) to understand the power of social influence, we must examine the motives that determine how people construe the social environment.

Social Psychology and Social Problems

Social psychological insights have been applied to a variety of practical problems in contemporary society such as prejudice reduction, the curbing of violence, and persuading people to live healthier lives.

Social psychology is an empirical science. Social psychologists attempt to find answers to key questions about social influence by designing and conducting research rather than by relying on common sense or the wisdom of the ages. In Chapter 2, we will discuss the scientific methods social psychologists use when conducting their research.

CRITICAL THINKING QUESTIONS

1. Both personality psychologists and social psychologists focus on the individual. But they concentrate on different aspects of individual behavior. How would you characterize the basic difference in the focus of these two disciplines?

2. Why are most people prone to commit the fundamental attribution error?

3. What are some of the negative consequences of our tendency to underestimate the power of the social situation?

for your own safety. Most of us assume that we would help in some way, though, such as by calling the police. It is because of this very assumption that people were shocked by an incident that occurred in the early 1960s. A woman named Kitty Genovese was brutally murdered in the alley of an apartment complex in Queens, New York. The attack lasted forty-five minutes. No fewer than thirty-eight of the apartment residents admitted later that they had rushed to their windows after hearing Genovese's screams for help. Not one attempted to help her—no one even bothered to telephone the police. For weeks after the crime, reporters, commentators, and critics of all kinds expressed their personal theories about why the bystanders had done nothing. Most agreed that living in a metropolis dehumanizes us and leads inevitably to apathy, indifference to human suffering, and lack of caring. New York and New Yorkers were to blame, concluded the observers; this kind of thing would not have happened in a small town, where people care more about each other (Rosenthal, 1964). Is this true? Did big-city life cause the bystanders to ignore Kitty Genovese's screams for help, or was there some other explanation? How can we find out?

SOCIAL PSYCHOLOGY: AN EMPIRICAL SCIENCE

> I love games. I think I could be very happy being a chess player or dealing with some other kinds of games. But I grew up in the Depression. It didn't seem one could survive on chess, and science is also a game. You have very strict ground rules in science, and your ideas have to check out with the empirical world. That's very tough and also very fascinating.
>
> —Leon Festinger, 1977

A fundamental principle of social psychology is that many social problems, like the causes of and reactions to violence, can be studied scientifically (Aronson, Wilson, & Brewer, 1998; Reis & Judd, 2000). Before we discuss how social psychological research is done, we begin with a warning: The results of some of the experiments you encounter will seem obvious, because social psychology concerns topics with which we are all intimately familiar—social behavior and social influence. This familiarity sets social psychology apart from other sciences. When you read about an experiment in particle physics, it is unlikely that the results will connect with your personal experiences. We don't know about you, but we have never thought, "Wow! That experiment on quarks was just like what happened to me while I was waiting for the bus yesterday," or "My grandmother always told me to watch out for positrons and antimatter." When reading about the results of a study on helping behavior or aggression, however, it is quite common to think, "Come on. I could have predicted that. That's the same thing that happened to me last Friday."

The thing to remember is that when we study human behavior, the results may appear to have been predictable—in retrospect. Indeed, there is a well-known human tendency called the **hindsight bias,** whereby people exaggerate how much they could have predicted an outcome *after* knowing that it occurred (Choi & Nisbett, 2000; Fischhoff, 1975; Sanna, Schwarz, & Stocker, 2002; Werth, Strack, &

Hindsight Bias

The tendency for people to exaggerate how much they could have predicted an outcome after knowing that it occurred

Foerster, 2002). Once we know the winner of a political election, for example, and begin to look for reasons why that candidate won. After the fact, the outcome seems inevitable and easily predictable, even if we were quite unsure who would win before the election. The same is true of findings in psychology experiments; it seems like we could have easily predicted the outcomes—once we know them. The trick is to predict what will happen in an experiment before you know how it turned out. To illustrate what we mean when we say that not all obvious findings are easy to predict, take the quiz in the Try It! exercise below.

Social psychology is a scientific discipline with a well-developed set of methods to answer questions about social behavior, such as the ones about violence

Try it!

Social Psychology Quiz: What's Your Prediction?

Answer the following questions, each of which is based on social psychological research.

1. Suppose an authority figure asks college students to administer near-lethal electric shocks to another student who has not harmed them in any way. What percentage of these students will agree to do it?

2. If you give children a reward for doing something they already enjoy doing, they will subsequently like that activity (a) more, (b) the same, or (c) less.

3. Who do you think would be happiest with their choice of a consumer product, such as an art poster, (a) people who spend several minutes thinking about why they like or dislike each poster or (b) people who choose a poster without analyzing the reasons for their feelings?

4. Repeated exposure to a stimulus, such as a person, a song, or a painting, will make you like it (a) more, (b) the same, or (c) less.

5. You ask an acquaintance to do you a favor—for example, to lend you $10—and he or she agrees. As a result of doing you this favor, the person will probably like you (a) more, (b) the same, or (c) less.

6. True or false: It is best for people's mental health to have a realistic view of the future, an accurate appraisal of their own abilities and traits, and an accurate view of how much control they have over their lives.

7. In the United States, female college students tend not to do as well on math tests as males do. Under which of the following circumstances will women do as well as men: (a) when they are told that there are no gender differences on the test, (b) when they are told that women tend to do better on a difficult math test (because under these circumstances, they rise to the challenge), or (c) when they are told that men outperform women under almost all circumstances?

8. Which statement about the effects of advertising is most true? (a) Subliminal messages implanted in advertisements are more effective than normal, everyday advertising; (b) normal TV ads for painkillers or laundry detergents are more effective than subliminal messages implanted in ads; (c) both types of advertising are equally effective; or (d) neither type of advertising is effective.

9. In public settings in the United States, (a) women touch men more, (b) men touch women more, or (c) there is no difference—men and women touch each other equally.

10. Which things in their past do people regret the most: (a) things they did that they wish they hadn't done, (b) things they didn't do that they wish they had done, or (c) it depends on how long ago the events occurred?

See page 54 for the answers.

with which we began this chapter. These methods are of three types: the *observational method*, the *correlational method*, and the *experimental method*. Any of these methods could be used to explore a specific research question; each is a powerful tool in some ways and a weak tool in others. Part of the creativity in conducting social psychological research involves choosing the right method, maximizing its strengths, and minimizing its weaknesses.

In this chapter, we will discuss these methods in detail. We, the authors of this book, are social psychologists who have done a great deal of research. We will therefore try to provide you with a firsthand look at both the joy and the difficulty of conducting social psychological studies. The joy comes in unraveling the clues about the causes of interesting and important social behaviors, just as a sleuth gradually unmasks the culprit in a murder mystery. Each of us finds it exhilarating that we have the tools to provide definitive answers to questions philosophers have debated for centuries. At the same time, as seasoned researchers, we have learned to temper this exhilaration with a heavy dose of humility, because the practical and ethical constraints involved in creating and conducting social psychological research are formidable.

FORMULATING HYPOTHESES AND THEORIES

Research begins with a hunch, or hypothesis, that the researcher wants to test. There is a lore in science that brilliant insights come all of a sudden, as when Archimedes shouted "Eureka! I have found it!" when the solution to a problem flashed into his mind. Though such insights do sometimes occur suddenly, science is a cumulative process, and people often generate hypotheses from previous theories and research.

Inspiration from Earlier Theories and Research

Many studies stem from a researcher's dissatisfaction with existing theories and explanations. After reading other people's work, a researcher might believe that he or she has a better way of explaining people's behavior (e.g., why they fail to help in an emergency). In the 1950s, for example, Leon Festinger was dissatisfied with the ability of a major theory of the day, behaviorism, to explain why people change their attitudes. He formulated a new approach—dissonance theory—that made specific predictions about when and how people would change their attitudes. As we will see in Chapter 6, other researchers were dissatisfied with Festinger's explanation of the results he obtained, and so they conducted further research to test other possible explanations. Social psychologists, like scientists in other disciplines, engage in a continual process of theory refinement: A theory is developed; specific hypotheses derived from that theory are tested; based on the results obtained, the theory is revised and new hypotheses are formulated.

Hypotheses Based on Personal Observations

Social psychology deals with phenomena we encounter in everyday life. Researchers often observe something in their lives or the lives of others that they find curious and interesting, stimulating them to construct a theory about why this phenomenon occurred—and to design a study to see if they are right.

Consider the murder of Kitty Genovese that we described earlier. As we noted, most people blamed her neighbors' failure to intervene on the apathy, indifference, and callousness that big-city life breeds. Two social psychologists who taught at universities in New York, however, had a different idea. Bibb Latané and John Darley got to talking one day about the Genovese murder. Here is how Latané describes it: "One evening after [a] downtown cocktail party, John Darley . . . came back with me to my 12th Street apartment for a drink. Our common complaint was the distressing tendency of acquaintances, on finding that we called ourselves social psychologists, to ask why New Yorkers were so apathetic" (Latané, 1987, p. 78). Instead of focusing on "what was wrong with New Yorkers," Latané and Darley thought it would be more interesting and more important to examine the social situation in which Genovese's neighbors found themselves: "We came up with the insight that perhaps what made the Genovese case so fascinating was itself what made it happen—namely, that not just one or two, but thirty-eight people had watched and done nothing" (Latané, 1987, p. 78).

The researchers had the hunch that, paradoxically, the more people who witness an emergency, the less likely it is that any given individual will intervene. Genovese's neighbors might have assumed that someone else had called the police, a phenomenon Latané and Darley (1968) referred to as the *diffusion of respon*sibility. Perhaps the bystanders would have been more likely to help had each thought he or she alone was witnessing the murder.

Once a researcher has a hypothesis, whether it comes from a theory, previous research, or an observation of everyday life, how can he or she tell if it is true? In science, idle speculation will not do; the researcher must collect data to test a hypothesis. Let's look at how the observational method, the correlational method, and the experimental method are used to explore research hypotheses such as Latané and Darley's (see Table 2.1).

This is the area where Kitty Genovese was attacked, in full view of her neighbors. Why didn't anyone call the police?

THE OBSERVATIONAL METHOD: DESCRIBING SOCIAL BEHAVIOR

There is a lot to be learned by being an astute observer of human behavior. If the goal is to describe what a particular group of people or type of behavior is like, the **observational method** is very helpful. This is the technique whereby a researcher observes people and records measurements or impressions of their behavior. The observational method may take many forms, depending on what the researchers are looking for, how involved or detached they are from the people they are observing, and how much they wish to quantify what they observe. One example is **ethnography,** the method by which researchers attempt to understand a group or culture by observing it from the inside, without imposing any preconceived notions they might have. The goal is to understand the richness and complexity of the group by observing it in action. Often this involves **participant observation,** whereby the researcher interacts with the people being

Observational Method

The technique whereby a researcher observes people and systematically records measurements or impressions of their behavior

Ethnography

The method by which researchers attempt to understand a group or culture by observing it from the inside, without imposing any preconceived notions they might have

Participant Observation

A form of the observational method in which the observer interacts with the people being observed but tries not to alter the situation in any way

TABLE 2.1		
A Summary of Research Methods		
METHOD	**FOCUS**	**QUESTION ANSWERED**
Observational	Description	What is the nature of the phenomenon?
Correlational	Prediction	From knowing X, can we predict Y?
Experimental	Causality	Is variable X a cause of variable Y?

"So! How is everybody today?"

observed but tries not to alter the situation in any way. Ethnography is the chief method of cultural anthropology, the study of human cultures and societies. As social psychology broadens its focus by studying social behavior in different cultures, ethnography is increasingly being used to describe different cultures and generate hypotheses about psychological principles (Fine & Elsbach, 2000; Squire, 2000; Uzzell, 2000).

Consider this example from the early years of social psychological research. In the early 1950s, a group of people in the Midwest predicted that the world would come to an end in a violent cataclysm on a specific date. They also announced that they would be rescued in time by a spaceship that would land in their leader's backyard. Assuming that the end of the world was not imminent, Leon Festinger and his colleagues thought it would be interesting to observe this group closely and chronicle how they reacted when their beliefs and prophecy were disconfirmed (Festinger, Riecken, & Schachter, 1956). In order to monitor the hour-to-hour conversations of this group, the social psychologists found it necessary to join the group and pretend that they too believed the world was about to end (see Chapter 6 for a description of Festinger and his colleagues' findings).

The key to ethnography is to avoid as much as possible imposing one's preconceived notions in order to understand the point of view of the people being studied. Sometimes, however, researchers have a specific hypothesis that they want to test using the observational method. An investigator might be interested, for example, in how much aggression children exhibit during school recesses. In this case, the observer would be systematically looking for particular behaviors that are concretely defined before the observation begins. For instance, aggression might be defined as hitting or shoving another child, taking a toy from another child without asking, and so on. The observer might stand at the edge of the playground and systematically record how often these behaviors occur. If the researcher were interested in exploring possible sex and age differences in social behavior, he or she would also note the child's gender and age. How do we know how accurate the observer is? In such studies, it is important to establish **interjudge reliability,** which is the level of agreement between two or more people who independently observe and code a set of data. By showing that two or more judges independently come up with the same observations, researchers ensure that the observations are not the subjective, distorted impressions of one individual.

Interjudge Reliability

The level of agreement between two or more people who independently observe and code a set of data; by showing that two or more judges independently come up with the same observations, researchers ensure that the observations are not the subjective, distorted impressions of one individual

Archival Analysis

A form of the observational method in which the researcher examines the accumulated documents, or archives, of a culture (e.g., diaries, novels, magazines, and newspapers)

Archival Analysis

The observational method is not limited to observations of real-life behavior. The researcher can also examine the accumulated documents, or archives, of a culture, a technique known as an **archival analysis** (Mullen, Rozell, & Johnson, 2001; Simonton, 1999). For example, diaries, novels, suicide notes, popular music lyrics, television shows, movies, magazine and newspaper articles, and advertising all tell us a great deal about how a society views itself. Much like our example of aggression, specific, well-defined categories are created and then applied to the archival source. (See The Try It! exercise on the next page.) Think back to the question of the relationship between pornography and violence. One problem with addressing this question is in defining what pornography is. Most of us have come across sexually explicit material at one time or another—for example, the centerfold photographs in magazines like *Playboy.* Does this constitute pornography? What about nudity in the movies or newspaper ads for

Try it!

Archival Analysis: Women, Men, and the Media

Try doing your own archival analysis to see how women and men are portrayed in the media. Choose three or four magazines that focus on different topics and audiences; for example, a news-magazine, a "women's" magazine such as *Cosmopolitan,* a "men's" magazine such as *GQ,* and a literary magazine such as the *New Yorker.* In each magazine, open the pages randomly until you find an advertisement that has at least one picture of a person in it. Repeat so that you look at two or three such ads in each magazine.

Make a note of how much of the image is devoted to the person's face and whether the person in the ad is a woman or a man. Specifically, place the picture of each person into one of these categories, depending on what part of the person you can see: (a) the entire body; (b) from the waist up, or (c) primarily the head and face. Were there differences in the way women and men are portrayed? If so, why do you think this is? Now turn to page 54 to see how actual research of this sort turned out.

lingerie that show scantily clad models? For decades, the nation as a whole has been struggling to define pornography; as Supreme Court Justice Potter Stewart put it, "I know it when I see it," but describing its exact content is not easy. What is being portrayed in American "adults only" literature and photographs?

Archival analysis is a good tool for answering this question, for it enables researchers to describe the content of documents present in the culture—in this case, the photographs and fictional stories that represent currently available pornography in the marketplace. One researcher, for example, studied the content of pornography in adults-only fiction paperback books sold at newsstands and regular bookstores (Smith, 1976). His data strikingly indicated that "the world of pornography is a male's world" (p. 21). The main character in the books was typically young, single, white, physically attractive, and heterosexual. Women's bodies were described in minute detail, whereas males' bodies received little attention. The most disturbing finding was that almost one-third of the sex episodes in the books involved the use of force (physical, mental, or blackmail) by a male to make a female engage in unwanted sex. Thus aggression against women was a major theme in these pornographic stories (Cowan & Campbell, 1994).

A second archival analysis focused on photographs posted on Internet newsgroups (Mehta, 2001). The researcher randomly selected nearly 10,000 images from thirty-two internet newsgroups that carried pornography and analyzed their content. Compared to an earlier archival study, he found fewer images portraying bondage but an increase in the percentage of images depicting children and adolescents.

Observational research, in the form of archival analysis, can tell us a great deal about society's values and beliefs. The fact that sexual violence against women is common in pornography suggests that these images and stories appeal to many readers (Dietz & Evans, 1982; Lowry, Love, & Kirby, 1981) and leads to some disturbing questions: Is pornography associated with sexually violent crimes against women that occur in our society? Do reading and looking at pornography cause some men to commit violent sexual acts? To answer these questions, research methods other than

Archival studies have found that women and men are portrayed differently in advertisements. What are the differences in this billboard ad for the movie "Once Upon a Time in Mexico"? To learn more about these differences, see the Try It! exercise above.

archival analysis must be used. Later in this chapter, we will see how researchers have used the correlational method and the experimental method to learn vital information about sexual violence against women.

Limits of the Observational Method

The observational method is useful if the researcher's goal is to describe social behavior, but it has some significant drawbacks. First, certain kinds of behavior are difficult to observe because they occur only rarely or only in private. For example, had Latané and Darley chosen the observational method to study the effects of the number of bystanders on people's willingness to help a victim, we might still be waiting for an answer. In order to determine how witnesses react to a violent crime, the researchers would have had to linger on street corners throughout the city, wait patiently for assaults to occur, and then keep careful track of the responses of any and all bystanders. Obviously, they would have had to wait a very long time before an assault happened to occur in their presence, and they would have found it difficult to gather data while a real-life emergency occurred at their feet.

Instead, Latané and Darley might have used an archival analysis—for example, by examining newspaper accounts of violent crimes and noting the number of bystanders and how many offered assistance to the victim. Yet here too, the researchers would have quickly run into problems: Did each journalist mention how many bystanders were present? Was the number accurate? Were all forms of assistance noted in the newspaper article? Clearly, these are messy data. As is always the case with archival analysis, the researcher is at the mercy of the original compiler of the material; the journalists had different aims when they wrote their articles and may not have included all the information researchers would later need.

Another limitation of the observational method is that it is confined to one particular group of people, one particular setting, and one particular type of activity—one doomsaying group in the Midwest or one type of pornography. This can be a problem if the goal is to generalize from what is observed to different populations, settings, and activities. For example, some studies have found that the depiction of violence and aggression in pornography is relatively common (Dietz & Evans, 1982), whereas other studies have found that it is relatively rare (Garcia & Milano, 1990; Scott & Cuvelier, 1993). This may be because Dietz and Evans looked at "hard core" pornography sold in adult bookstores in New York City, whereas the other studies looked at "softer" pornography in certain magazines and videos available at video rental stores. Which study best reflects the amount of violence in American pornography in general? It is difficult to tell.

THE CORRELATIONAL METHOD: PREDICTING SOCIAL BEHAVIOR

Social scientists usually want to do more than describe social behavior. A goal of social science is to understand relationships between variables and to be able to predict when different kinds of social behavior will occur. For example, what is the relationship between the amount of pornography people see and their likelihood of engaging in sexually violent acts? Is there a relationship between the amount of violence children see on television and their aggressiveness? To answer such questions, researchers frequently use a different approach—the correlational method.

With the **correlational method,** two variables are systematically measured, and the relationship between them—how much you can predict one from the other—is assessed. People's behavior and attitudes can be measured in a variety

Correlational Method

The technique whereby two or more variables are systematically measured and the relationship between them (i.e., how much one can be predicted from the other) is assessed

of ways. Just as with the observational method, researchers sometimes make direct observations of people's behavior. For example, using the correlational method, researchers might be interested in testing the relationship between children's aggressive behavior and how much violent television they watch. They might observe children on the playground also, but here the goal is to assess the relationship, or correlation, between the children's aggressiveness and other factors, like TV viewing habits, that the researchers also measure.

Researchers look at such relationships by calculating the **correlation coefficient,** a statistic that assesses how well you can predict one variable from another—for example, how well you can predict people's weight from their height. A positive correlation means that increases in the value of one variable are associated with increases in the value of the other variable. Height and weight are positively correlated; the taller people are, the more they tend to weigh. A negative correlation means that increases in the value of one variable are associated with decreases in the value of the other. If height and weight were negatively correlated in human beings, we would look very peculiar—short people, such as children, would look like penguins, whereas tall people, like NBA basketball players, would be all skin and bones! It is also possible, of course, for two variables to be completely unrelated, so that a researcher cannot predict one variable from the other.

Correlation coefficients are expressed as numbers that can range from −1.00 to +1.00. A correlation of 1.00 means that two variables are perfectly correlated in a positive direction; thus by knowing people's standing on one variable, the researcher can predict exactly where they stand on the other variable. In everyday life, of course, perfect correlations are rare. For example, one study found that the correlation between height and weight was .47 in a sample of men aged 18 to 24 (Freedman, Pisani, Purves, & Adhikari, 1991). This means that, on average, the taller people were heavier than the shorter people, but there were exceptions. A correlation of −1.00 means that two variables are perfectly correlated in a negative direction, whereas a correlation of 0 means that two variables are not correlated (see Figure 2.1).

Correlation Coefficient

A statistical technique that assesses how well you can predict one variable from another—for example, how well you can predict people's weight from their height

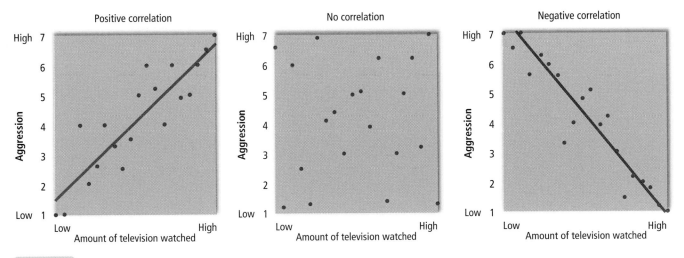

FIGURE 2.1

The correlation coefficient.

The diagrams show three possible correlations in a hypothetical study of watching violence on television and aggressive behavior in children. The diagram at the left shows a strong positive correlation: The more television people watch, the more aggressive they were. The diagram in the middle shows no correlation: The amount of television people watch is not related to how aggressive they were. The diagram at the right shows a strong negative correlation: The more television people watch, the less aggressive they were.

Surveys

The correlational method is often used in **surveys,** research in which a representative sample of people are asked (often anonymously) questions about their attitudes or behavior. Surveys are a convenient way to measure people's attitudes; for example, people can be telephoned and asked which candidate they will support in an upcoming election or how they feel about a variety of social issues. Researchers often apply the correlational method to survey results to predict how people's responses to one question predict their other responses. Political scientists, for example, might be interested in whether people's attitude toward a specific issue, such as gun control, predicts how they will vote. Psychologists often use surveys to help understand social behavior and attitudes—for example, by seeing whether the amount of pornography men say they read is correlated with their attitudes toward women.

Surveys have a number of advantages, one of which is allowing researchers to judge the relationship between variables that are difficult to observe, such as how often people engage in safer sex. When the variables of interest cannot easily be observed, researchers rely on surveys, on which people are questioned about their beliefs, attitudes, and behaviors. The researcher looks at the relationship between the questions asked on the survey, such as whether people who know a lot about how AIDS is transmitted are more likely than other people to engage in safer sex.

Another advantage of surveys is the ability to sample representative segments of the population. Answers to a survey are useful only if they reflect the responses of people in general—not just the people actually tested (called the *sample*). Survey researchers go to great lengths to ensure that the people they test are typical. They select samples that are representative of the population on a number of characteristics important to a given research question (e.g., age, educational background, religion, gender, income level). They also make sure to use a **random selection** of people from the population at large, which is a way of ensuring that a sample of people is representative of a population by giving everyone in the population an equal chance of being selected for the sample. As long as the sample is selected randomly, we can assume that the responses are a reasonable match to those of the population as a whole.

There are some famous cases in which people tried to generalize from samples that were not randomly selected—to their peril. In the fall of 1936, a weekly magazine called the *Literary Digest* conducted a large survey asking people which candidate they planned to vote for in the upcoming presidential election. The magazine obtained the names and addresses of its sample from telephone directories and automobile registration lists. The results of its survey of 2 million people indicated that the Republican candidate, Alf Landon, would win by a landslide. Of course, you know that there never was a President Landon; instead, Franklin Delano Roosevelt won every state in the Union but two. What went wrong with the *Literary Digest* poll? In the depths of the Great Depression, many people could not afford telephones or cars. Those who had them were doing well financially; most well-to-do voters were Republican and overwhelmingly favored Alf Landon. However, the majority of the voters were not well off—and overwhelmingly supported the Democratic candidate, Roosevelt. By using a list of names that excluded the less affluent members of the population, the *Literary Digest* surveyed a nonrepresentative sample. (The *Literary Digest* never recovered from this methodological disaster and went out of business shortly after publishing its poll.)

Modern surveys and political polls are not immune from such sampling errors. During the 1984 presidential race, telephone polls conducted by Ronald Reagan's campaign staff found that Reagan had a comfortable lead over Walter Mondale—except when the polls were conducted on Friday nights. After an ini-

Surveys

Research in which a representative sample of people are asked (often anonymously) questions about their attitudes or behavior

Random Selection

A way of ensuring that a sample of people is representative of a population by giving everyone in the population an equal chance of being selected for the sample

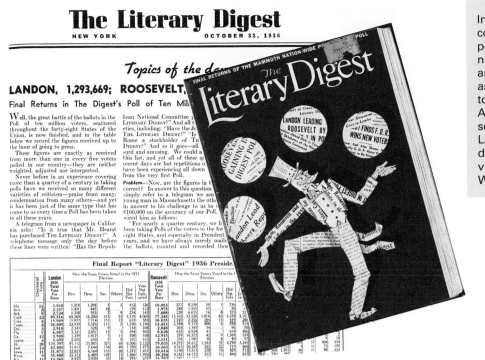

In 1936, The Literary Digest conducted one of the first political polls. Staffers randomly selected names from telephone directories and automobile registration lists and asked people for whom they planned to vote in the presidential election: Alf Landon or Franklin Roosevelt. As seen here, the poll indicated that Landon would win by a landslide. He didn't, of course; Roosevelt carried virtually every state in the Union. What went wrong with this poll?

tial panic, they figured out that because Democrats are poorer, on average, than Republicans, they were less likely to be out at the movies or eating at restaurants on Friday nights and so were more likely to be at home when the pollsters called. Despite such notable glitches, or perhaps because of them, surveys have improved enormously over the years and can now accurately detect correlations between many interesting social variables (Krosnick, 1999, Manza, Cook, & Page, 2002; Miller, 2002).

Another potential problem with survey data is the accuracy of the responses. Straightforward questions—regarding what people think about an issue or what they typically do—are relatively easy to answer. But asking survey participants to predict how they might behave in some hypothetical situation or to explain why they behaved as they did in the past is an invitation to inaccuracy (Schuman & Kalton, 1985; Schwarz, Groves, & Schuman, 1998). Often people simply don't know the answer—but they think they do. Richard Nisbett and Tim Wilson (1977b) demonstrated this "telling more than you can know" phenomenon in a number of studies in which people often made inaccurate reports about why they responded the way they did. Their reports about the causes of their responses pertained more to their theories and beliefs about what should have influenced them than to what actually influenced them. (We discuss these studies at greater length in Chapter 5.)

Limits of the Correlational Method: Correlation Does Not Equal Causation

The major shortcoming of the correlational method is that it tells us only that two variables are related, whereas the goal of the social psychologist is to identify the causes of social behavior. We want to be able to say that A causes B, not just that A is related to, or correlated with, B.

If a researcher finds that there is a correlation between two variables, it means that there are three possible causal relationships between these variables. For example, researchers have found a correlation between the amount of

A study conducted in the early 1990s found a correlation between the type of birth control women used and their likelihood of getting a sexually transmitted disease (STD). Surprisingly, women whose partners used condoms were more likely to have an STD than women who used diaphragms or contraceptive sponges. Does this mean the use of condoms caused the increase in STDs? Not necessarily—correlation does not imply causation. (See the text for some alternative explanations of this research finding.)

violent television children watch and how aggressive they are (similar to the pattern shown in the left-hand graph in Figure 2.1, though not quite as strong; see Eron, 1982). One explanation of this correlation is that watching TV violence causes kids to become more violent themselves. It is equally probable, however, that the reverse is true: that kids who are violent to begin with are more likely to watch violent TV. Or there might be no causal relationship between these two variables; instead, both TV watching and violent behavior could be caused by a third variable, such as having neglectful parents who do not pay much attention to their kids. (Experimental evidence does support one of these causal relationships; we will discuss which one in Chapter 12.) When using the correlational method, it is wrong to jump to the conclusion that one variable is causing the other to occur. *Correlation does not prove causation.*

Unfortunately, forgetting this adage is one of the most common methodological errors in the social sciences, as occurred in a study of birth control methods and sexually transmitted diseases (STDs) in women (Rosenberg, Davidson, Chen, Judson, & Douglas, 1992). The researchers examined the records of women who had visited a clinic, noting which method of birth control they used and whether they had an STD. Surprisingly, the researchers found that women who relied on condoms had significantly more STDs than women who used diaphragms or contraceptive sponges. This result was widely reported in the popular press, with the conclusion that the use of diaphragms and sponges caused a lower incidence of disease. Some reporters urged women whose partners used condoms to switch to other methods.

Can you see the problem with this conclusion? The fact that the incidence of disease was correlated with the type of contraception women used is open to a number of causal interpretations. Perhaps the women who used sponges and diaphragms had sex with fewer partners. (In fact, condom users were more likely to have had sex with multiple partners in the previous month.) Perhaps the partners of women who relied on condoms were more likely to have STDs than the partners of women who used sponges and diaphragms. There is simply no way of knowing. Thus the conclusion that the birth control methods protected against STDs cannot be drawn from this correlational study.

As another example of the difficulty of inferring causality from correlational designs, let's return to the question of whether pornography causes aggressive sexual acts against women, such as rape. One study examined the relationship between the amount of pornography sold in different states and the number of rapes reported in those states (Baron & Straus, 1984). To measure the amount of pornography, the researchers chose eight sexually explicit magazines (e.g., *Playboy, Hustler, Chic*) and gathered data on how many issues were sold in 1979 in each state. They compared this information to the incidence of rape in each state, using the FBI *Uniform Crime Reports* publication. (Since rape is an underreported crime, these data are undoubtedly conservative estimates of the actual number of rapes committed.)

The researchers' data revealed a positive correlation of .63 between pornography readership and rape. In addition, the researchers found that the amount of pornography sold was not as highly correlated with nonsexual violent crimes. They therefore ruled out the possible explanation that pornography leads to more violent crimes in general and not just to sexually violent crimes.

As suggestive as these findings are, they still do not establish that pornography was a cause of rape. Can you think of alternative explanations for this correlation? To their credit, the researchers took pains to acknowledge that causality was not proved in their study. As they noted, the findings could reflect differences between states in a hypermasculine culture pattern that led men both to purchase more pornographic magazines and to commit rape (Harris, 1994). Or it is possible that men who are aggressive toward women are more interested in violent pornography; that is, it is their aggression causing their attraction to pornography, and not the pornography causing their aggression (Malamuth et al., 2000).

Latané and Darley might also have used the correlational method to determine if the number of bystanders affects helping behavior. They could have surveyed victims and bystanders of crimes and then correlated the total number of bystanders at each crime scene with the number of bystanders who helped or tried to help the victims. Let's say that a negative correlation was found in these data: The greater the number of bystanders, the less likely it was that any one of them intervened. Would this be evidence that the number of bystanders caused helping behavior to occur or not? Unfortunately, no. Any number of unknown third variables could account for both the number of bystanders and the rate of helping. For example, the seriousness of the emergency could be such a third variable, in that serious or frightening emergencies, compared to minor mishaps, tend to draw large numbers of bystanders and make people less likely to intervene. Other examples of the difficulty of inferring causality from correlational studies are shown in the Try It! exercise on page 40.

THE EXPERIMENTAL METHOD: ANSWERING CAUSAL QUESTIONS

The only way to determine causal relationships is with the **experimental method.** Here, the researcher systematically orchestrates the event so that people experience it in one way (e.g., they witness an emergency along with other bystanders) or another way (e.g., they witness the same emergency but are the sole bystander). The experimental method is the method of choice in most social psychological research because it allows the experimenter to make causal inferences. The observational method helps us describe social behavior, and the correlational method helps us understand what aspects of social behavior are related. However, only a properly executed experiment allows us to draw conclusions about cause and effect. For this reason, the experimental method is the most commonly used research design in social psychology.

The experimental method always involves a direct intervention on the part of the researcher. By carefully changing only one aspect of the situation (e.g., group size), the researcher can see whether this aspect is the cause of the behavior in question (e.g., whether people help in an emergency). Sound simple? Actually, it isn't. Staging an experiment to test Latané and Darley's hypothesis about the effects of group size involves severe practical and ethical difficulties. What kind of emergency should be used? Ideally (from a scientific perspective), it should be as true to the Genovese case as possible. Accordingly, you would want to stage a murder that passersby could witness. In one condition, you could stage the murder so that only a few onlookers were present; in another condition, you could stage it so that a great many onlookers were present.

Obviously, no scientist in his or her right mind would stage a murder for unsuspecting bystanders. But how can we arrange a realistic situation that is upsetting enough to be similar to the Genovese case without it being too upsetting? In addition, how can we ensure that each bystander experiences the same emergency except for the variable whose effect we want to test—in this case, the number of bystanders?

> Theory is a good thing, but a good experiment lasts forever.
>
> —Peter Leonidovich Kapista

Experimental Method

The method in which the researcher randomly assigns participants to different conditions and ensures that these conditions are identical except for the independent variable (the one thought to have a causal effect on people's responses)

Try it!

Correlation and Causation: Knowing the Difference

It can be difficult to remember that when two variables are correlated, it doesn't necessarily mean that one caused the other; correlation does *not* allow us to make causal inferences. For each of the following examples, think about why the correlation was found. Even if it seems obvious which variable was causing the other, are there alternative explanations?

1. Recently, a politician extolled the virtues of the Boy Scouts and Girl Scouts. In his salute to the Scouts, the politician mentioned that few teenagers convicted of street crimes had been members of the Scouts. In other words, he was positing a negative correlation between activity in Scouting and frequency of criminal behavior. Why might this be?

2. A research study found that having a pet in childhood is correlated with a reduced likelihood of becoming a juvenile delinquent in adolescence. Why is this?

3. A recent study of soldiers stationed on army bases found that the number of tattoos a soldier had was correlated positively with becoming involved in a motorcycle accident. Why?

4. Officials in the Reagan administration took credit for a reduction in the crime rate because the crime rate went down after Reagan took office. That is, there was a negative correlation between the onset of the Reagan administration and the crime rate. What are some alternative explanations for this correlation?

5. Recently, it was reported that a correlation exists between people's tendency to eat breakfast and how long they live, such that people who skip breakfast die younger. Does eating Wheaties lead to a long life?

6. A few years ago, newspaper headlines announced, "Coffee Suspected as a Cause of Heart Attacks." Medical studies had found a correlation between the amount of coffee people drank and their likelihood of having a heart attack. Are there any alternative explanations?

7. A positive correlation exists between the viscosity of asphalt in city playgrounds and the crime rate. How can this be? When asphalt becomes viscous (softer), is some chemical released that drives potential criminals wild? When the crime rate goes up, do people flock to the playgrounds, such that the pounding of feet increases the viscosity of the asphalt? What explains this correlation?

8. A newsmagazine recently reported that the more time fathers spend with their children, the less likely the fathers are to sexually abuse these children. Why might this be?

9. According to a recent newspaper report, having sex at least once a week helps prevent the common cold. College students reported how often they had had sex in the previous month, and those who had made love at least once a week had higher levels of an antigen in their immune systems that helps ward off the cold virus. Does this prove that having sex prevents colds?

10. A recent survey found that people who watch public television have more sex than people who do not. "Who would have thought," the researchers reported, "that National Geographic Specials or Ken Burn's history of baseball could get people in the mood?" How would you explain this correlation?

See page 55 for the answers.

Let's see how Latané and Darley (1968) dealt with these problems. Imagine that you are a participant in their experiment. You arrive at the scheduled time and find yourself in a long corridor with doors to several small cubicles. An experimenter greets you and takes you into one of the cubicles, mentioning that five other students, seated in the other cubicles, will be participating with you.

The experimenter leaves after giving you a pair of headphones with an attached microphone. You put on the headphones, and soon you hear the experimenter explaining to everyone that he is interested in learning about the kinds of personal problems college students experience.

To ensure that people will discuss their problems openly, he explains, each participant will remain anonymous; each will stay in his or her separate room and communicate with the others only via the intercom system. Further, the experimenter says, he will not be listening to the discussion so that people will feel freer to be open and honest. Finally, the experimenter asks that participants take turns presenting their problems, each speaking for two minutes, after which each person will comment on what the others said. To make sure this procedure is followed, he says, only one person's microphone will be turned on at a time.

The group discussion begins. You listen as the first participant admits that he has found it difficult to adjust to college. With some embarrassment, he mentions that he sometimes has seizures, especially when under stress. When his two minutes are up, you hear the other four participants discuss their problems; then it is your turn. When you have finished, the first person speaks again. To your astonishment, he soon begins to experience one of the seizures he mentioned earlier:

> *I—er—um—I think I—I need—er—if—if could—er—er—somebody er—er—
> er—er—er—er—er—give me a little—er—give me a little help here because—er—
> I—er—I'm—er—er—h—h—having a—a—a real problem—er—right now and
> I—er—if somebody could help me out it would—it would—er—er s—s—sure be—
> sure be good . . . because—er—there—er—er—a cause I—er—I—uh—I've got
> a—a one of the—er—sei—er—er—things coming on and—and—and I could re-
> ally—er—use some help so if somebody would—er—give me a little h—help—
> uh—er—er—er—er c—could somebody—er—er—help—er—uh—uh—uh
> (choking sounds) . . . I'm gonna die—er—er—I'm . . . gonna die—er—help
> er—er—seizure—er (chokes, then quiet). (Darley & Latané, 1968, p. 379)*

What would you have done in this situation? If you were like most of the participants in the actual study, you would have remained in your cubicle, listening to your fellow student having a seizure, and done nothing about it. Does this surprise you? Latané and Darley kept track of the number of people who left their cubicle to find the victim or the experimenter before the end of the victim's seizure. Only 31 percent of the participants sought help in this way. Fully 69 percent of the students remained in their cubicles and did nothing—just as Kitty Genovese's neighbors had failed to offer assistance in any way.

Does this finding prove that the failure to help was due to the number of people who witnessed the seizure? How do we know that it wasn't due to some other factor? We know because Latané and Darley included two other conditions in their experiment. In these conditions, the procedure was identical to the one we described, with one crucial difference: The size of the discussion group was smaller, meaning that fewer people witnessed the seizure. In one condition, the participants were told that there were three other people in the discussion group besides themselves (the victim plus two others). In another condition, participants were told that there was only one other person in their discussion group (the victim). In this latter condition, each participant believed he or she was the only one who could hear the seizure.

Independent and Dependent Variables

The number of people witnessing the emergency was the **independent variable** in the Latané and Darley (1968) study, which is the variable a researcher changes or varies to see if it has an effect on some other variable. The **dependent variable**

Independent Variable

The variable a researcher changes or varies to see if it has an effect on some other variable

Dependent Variable

The variable a researcher measures to see if it is influenced by the independent variable; the researcher hypothesizes that the dependent variable will depend on the level of the independent variable

Independent Variable	Dependent Variable
The variable that is hypothesized to influence the dependent variable. Participants are treated identically except for this variable.	The response that is hypothesized to depend on the independent variable. All participants are measured on this variable.

Example: Darley and Latané (1968)	
The number of bystanders	**How many subjects helped?**
Participant + Victim	85%
Participant + Victim + Two others	62%
Participant + Victim + Four others	31%

FIGURE 2.2

Independent and dependent variables in experimental research.

is the variable a researcher measures to see if it is influenced by the independent variable; the researcher hypothesizes that the dependent variable will be influenced by the level of the independent variable. That is, the dependent variable is hypothesized to depend on the independent variable (see Figure 2.2). Latané and Darley found that their independent variable—the number of bystanders—did have an effect on the dependent variable—whether they tried to help. When the participants believed that four other people were witnesses to the seizure, only 31 percent offered assistance. When the participants believed that only two other people were aware of the seizure, helping behavior increased to 62 percent. When the participants believed that they were the only person listening to the seizure, nearly everyone helped (85 percent).

These results indicate that the number of bystanders strongly influences the rate of helping, but it does not mean that the size of the group is the only cause of people's decision to help. After all, when there were four bystanders, a third of the participants still helped; conversely, when participants thought they were the only witness, some of them failed to help. Obviously, other factors influence helping behavior—the bystanders' personalities, their prior experience with emergencies, and so on. Nonetheless, Latané and Darley succeeded in identifying one important determinant of whether people help—the number of bystanders that people think are present.

Internal Validity in Experiments

How can we be sure that the differences in help across conditions in the Latané and Darley seizure study were due to the different numbers of bystanders who witnessed the emergency? Could this effect have been caused by some other aspect of the situation? This is the beauty of the experimental method: We can be sure of the causal connection between the number of bystanders and helping because Latané and Darley made sure that everything about the situation was the same in the different conditions except the independent variable, the number of bystanders. Keeping everything but the independent variable the same in an experiment is referred to as *internal validity*. Latané and Darley were careful to maintain high internal validity by making sure that everyone witnessed the same emergency. They prerecorded the supposed other participants and the victim and played their voices over the intercom system.

You may have noticed, however, that there was a key difference between the conditions of the Latané and Darley experiment other than the number of bystanders: different people participated in the different conditions. Maybe the observed differences in helping were due to characteristics of the participants instead of the independent variable. The people in the sole witness condition might have differed in any number of ways from their counterparts in the other conditions, making them more likely to help. Maybe they were more likely to know something about epilepsy or to have experience helping in emergencies. If either of these possibilities is true, it would be difficult to conclude that it was the number of bystanders, rather than something about the participants' backgrounds, that led to differences in helping.

Fortunately, there is a technique that allows experimenters to minimize differences among participants as the cause of the results: **random assignment to condition.** This is the process whereby all participants have an equal chance of taking part in any condition of an experiment; through random assignment, researchers can be relatively certain that differences in the participants' personalities or backgrounds are distributed evenly across conditions. Because Latané and Darley's participants were randomly assigned to the conditions of their experiment, it is very unlikely that the ones who knew the most about epilepsy all ended up in one condition. Knowledge about epilepsy should be randomly (i.e., roughly evenly) dispersed across the three experimental conditions. This powerful technique is the most important part of the experimental method.

However, even with random assignment, there is always the (very small) possibility that different characteristics of people did not distribute themselves evenly across conditions. For example, if we randomly divide a group of forty people into two groups, it is possible that those who know the most about epilepsy will by chance end up more in one group than the other—just as it is possible to get more heads than tails when you flip a coin forty times. This is a possibility we take seriously in experimental science. The analyses of our data come with a **probability level (p-value),** which is a number, calculated with statistical techniques, that tells researchers how likely it is that the results of their experiment occurred by chance and not because of the independent variable. The convention in science, including social psychology, is to consider results *significant* (trustworthy) if the probability level is less than 5 in 100 that the results might be due to chance factors rather than the independent variables studied. For example, if we flipped a coin forty times and got forty heads, we would probably assume that this was very unlikely to have occurred by chance and that there was something wrong with the coin (we might check the other side to make sure it wasn't one of those trick coins with heads on both sides!). Similarly, if the results in two conditions of an experiment differ significantly from what we would expect by chance, we assume that the difference was caused by the independent variable (e.g., the number of bystanders present during the emergency). The *p*-value tells us how confident we can be that the difference was due to chance rather than the independent variable.

To summarize, the key to a good experiment is to maintain high **internal validity,** which we can now define as making sure that the independent variable, and *only* the independent variable, influences the dependent variable; this is accomplished by controlling all extraneous variables and by randomly assigning people to different experimental conditions (Campbell & Stanley, 1967). When internal validity is high, the experimenter is in a position to judge whether the independent variable causes the dependent variable. This is the hallmark of the experimental method that sets it apart from the observational and correlational methods: Only the experimental method can answer causal questions, such as whether exposure to pornography causes men to commit violent acts.

For example, researchers have tested whether pornography causes aggression by randomly assigning consenting participants to watch pornographic or nonpornographic films (the independent variable) and measuring the extent to which people acted aggressively toward women (the dependent variable). In a study by Donnerstein and Berkowitz (1981), males were angered by a female accomplice and then were randomly assigned to see one of three films: violent pornography (a rape scene), nonviolent pornography (sex without any violence), or a neutral film with no violence or sex (a talk show interview). The men were then given an opportunity to act aggressively toward the woman who had angered them by choosing the level of electric shock she would receive in an ostensibly unrelated learning experiment (the accomplice did not really receive shocks, but participants believed that she would). The men who had seen the violent pornography administered significantly more intense shocks to the woman

Random Assignment to Condition

A process ensuring that all participants have an equal chance of taking part in any condition of an experiment; through random assignment, researchers can be relatively certain that differences in the participants' personalities or backgrounds are distributed evenly across conditions

Probability Level (p-value)

A number calculated with statistical techniques that tells researchers how likely it is that the results of their experiment occurred by chance and not because of the independent variable or variables; the convention in science, including social psychology, is to consider results *significant* (trustworthy) if the probability level is less than 5 in 100 that the results might be due to chance factors and not the independent variables studied

Internal Validity

Making sure that nothing besides the independent variable can affect the dependent variable; this is accomplished by controlling all extraneous variables and by randomly assigning people to different experimental conditions

than the men who had seen the nonviolent pornography or the neutral film, suggesting that it is not pornography per se that leads to aggressive behavior but the violence depicted in some pornography (Mussweiler & Förster, 2000). We review this area of research more generally in Chapter 12.

External Validity in Experiments

For all the advantages of the experimental method, there are some drawbacks. By virtue of gaining enough control over the situation so as to randomly assign people to conditions and rule out the effects of extraneous variables, the situation can become somewhat artificial and distant from real life. For example, one could argue that Latané and Darley strayed far from the original inspiration for their study, the Kitty Genovese murder. What does witnessing a seizure while participating in a laboratory experiment in a college building have to do with a brutal murder in a densely populated urban neighborhood? How often in everyday life do we have discussions with other people through an intercom system? Did the fact that the participants knew they were in a psychology experiment influence their behavior?

These are important questions that concern **external validity,** which is the extent to which the results of a study can be generalized to other situations and other people. Note that two kinds of generalizability are at issue: (1) the extent to which we can generalize from the situation constructed by an experimenter to real-life situations (generalizability across *situations*) and (2) the extent to which we can generalize from the people who participated in the experiment to people in general (generalizability across *people*).

Generalizability across Situations   Research in social psychology is sometimes criticized for being conducted in artificial settings, such as psychological experiments at a university, that cannot be generalized to real life. To address this problem, social psychologists attempt to increase the generalizability of their results by making their studies as realistic as possible. But note that there are different ways in which an experiment can be realistic. By one definition—the similarity of an experimental situation to events that occur frequently in everyday life—it is clear that many experiments are decidedly unreal. In many experiments, people are placed in situations they would rarely, if ever, encounter in everyday life, such as occurred in Latané and Darley's group discussion of personal problems over an intercom system. The extent to which an experiment is similar to real-life situations is known as the **mundane realism** (Aronson & Carlsmith, 1968) of the experiment.

More important is the study's **psychological realism.** How similar are the psychological processes triggered in an experiment to psychological processes that occur in everyday life (Aronson, Wilson, & Brewer, 1998)? Even though Latané and Darley staged an emergency that in significant ways was unlike ones encountered in everyday life, was it psychologically similar to real-life emergencies? Were the same psychological processes triggered? Did the participants have the same types of perceptions and thoughts, make the same types of decisions, and choose the same types of behaviors that they would in a real-life situation? If so, then the study is high in psychological realism and we can generalize the results to everyday life.

Psychological realism is heightened if people feel involved in a real event. To accomplish this, experimenters often tell participants a **cover story**—a disguised version of the study's true purpose. Recall, for example that Latané and Darley told people that they were studying the personal problems of college students and then staged an emergency. It would have been a lot easier to say to people, "Look, we are interested in how people react to emergencies, so at some point

External Validity

The extent to which the results of a study can be generalized to other situations and to other people

Mundane Realism

The extent to which an experiment is similar to real-life situations

Psychological Realism

The extent to which the psychological processes triggered in an experiment are similar to psychological processes that occur in everyday life; psychological realism can be high in an experiment even if mundane realism is low

Cover Story

A description of the purpose of a study, given to participants, that is different from its true purpose, used to maintain psychological realism

Social psychologists have investigated the conditions under which people will help during emergencies. Experiments show that the more bystanders who witness an emergency, such as a violent crime, the lower the likelihood that any one person will help. An individual who overcomes the reluctance to help, however, and steps forward, can serve as a model to others, causing them to join in. Emergencies such as floods, for example, can bring a community together, as strangers work side by side to deal with the threat.

during this study we are going to stage an accident, and then we'll see how you respond." We think you'll agree that such a procedure would be very low in psychological realism. In real life, we never know when emergencies are going to occur, and we do not have time to plan our responses to them. If particants knew that an emergency was about to happen, the kinds of psychological processes triggered would have been quite different from those of a real emergency, reducing the psychological realism of the study.

Further, as discussed earlier, people don't always know why they do what they do or even what they will do until it happens. Consequently, describing an experimental situation to participants and then asking them to respond normally will produce responses that are, at best, suspect. For example, after describing the Latané and Darley seizure experiment to our students, we often ask them to predict how they would respond. Invariably, almost all of our students think they would have helped the victim, even when they know that in the condition where the group size was six, most people did not help. Unfortunately, we cannot depend on people's predictions about what they would do in a hypothetical situation; we can only find out what people will really do when we construct a situation that triggers the same psychological processes as occur in the real world.

Generalizability across People   Recall that social psychologists study the way in which people in general are susceptible to social influence. Latané and Darley's experiment documented an interesting, unexpected example of social influence, whereby the mere knowledge that others were present reduced the likelihood that people helped. But what have we learned about people in general? The participants in their study were fifty-two male and female students at New York University, who received course credit for participating in the experiment. Would the study have turned out the same way if a different population had been used? Would the number of bystanders have influenced helping behavior had the participants been middle-aged blue-collar workers instead of college students? Midwesterners instead of New Yorkers? Japanese instead of American?

The only way to be certain that the results of an experiment represent the behavior of a particular population is to ensure that the participants are randomly selected from that population. Ideally, samples in experiments should be randomly selected, just as they are in surveys. Unfortunately, it is impractical and expensive to select random samples for most social psychology experiments. It is difficult enough to convince a random sample of Americans to agree to answer a few questions over the telephone as part of a political poll, and such polls can cost thousands of dollars to conduct. Imagine the difficulty Latané and Darley would have had convincing a random sample of Americans to board a plane to New York to take part in their study, not to mention the cost of such an endeavor. Even trying to gather a random sample of students at New York University would not have been easy; each person contacted would have had to agree to to spend an hour in Latané and Darley's laboratory.

Of course, concerns about practicality and expense are not good excuses for doing poor science. Many researchers address this problem by studying basic psychological processes that make people susceptible to social influence, assuming that these processes are so fundamental that they are universally shared. In that case, participants for social psychology experiments don't really have to come from many different cultures. Of course, some social psychological processes are likely to be quite dependent on cultural factors, and in those cases, we'd need diverse samples of people. The question then is, how can researchers tell whether the processes they are studying are universal?

Replications   Suppose a researcher claims that her study is high in psychological realism, that it has captured psychological functioning as it occurs in everyday life, and that it doesn't matter that only college sophomores at one university participated because these psychological processes are universal. Should we take her word for it?

Not necessarily. The ultimate test of an experiment's external validity is **replication**—conducting the study over again with different subject populations or in different settings. If we think that Latané and Darley found the results they did only because their participants knew they were in a psychology experiment, then we should try to replicate their study in an experiment conducted outside of the laboratory. Do we think their results are limited to only certain kinds of emergencies? Then we should try to replicate the results with an emergency different from an epileptic seizure. Do we think that only New Yorkers would be so unhelpful? Then we should try to replicate it with southerners, Californians, or Germans. Only with such replications can we be certain about how generalizable the results are.

Often when many studies on one problem are conducted, the results are somewhat variable. Several studies might find an effect of the number of bystanders on helping behavior, for example, while a few do not. How can we make sense of this? Does the number of bystanders make a difference or not? Fortunately, there is a statistical technique called **meta-analysis** that averages the results of two or more studies to see if the effect of an independent variable is reliable. Earlier we discussed p-values, which tell us the probability that the findings of one study are due to chance or to the independent variable. A meta-analysis essentially does the same thing, except that it averages the results of many different studies. If, say, an independent variable is found to have an effect in only one of twenty studies, the meta-analysis will tell us that that one study was probably an exception and that on average, the independent variable is not influencing the dependent variable. If an independent variable is having an effect in most of the studies, the meta-analysis is likely to tell us that on average, it does influence the dependent variable.

Most of the findings you will read about in this book have been replicated in several different settings, with different populations; we know then that they are reliable phenomena, not limited to the laboratory or to college sophomores. For example, Anderson and Bushman (1997) compared laboratory studies on the causes of aggression with studies conducted in the real world. In both types of studies, violence in the media caused aggressive behavior. Similarly, Latané and

Replication

Repeating a study, often with different subject populations or in different settings

Meta-Analysis

A statistical technique that averages the results of two or more studies to see if the effect of an independent variable is reliable

Darley's original findings have been replicated in numerous studies. Increasing the number of bystanders inhibited helping behavior with many kinds of people, including children, college students, and future ministers (Darley & Batson, 1973; Latané & Nida, 1981); in both small towns and large cities (Latané & Dabbs, 1975); in a variety of settings, such as psychology laboratories, city streets, and subway trains (Harrison & Wells, 1991; Latané & Darley, 1970; Piliavin, Dovidio, Gaertner, & Clark, 1981; Piliavin & Piliavin, 1972); and with different kinds of emergencies, such as seizures, potential fires, fights, and accidents (Latané & Darley, 1968; Shotland & Straw, 1976; Staub, 1974), as well as with less serious events, such as having a flat tire (Hurley & Allen, 1974). Many of these replications took place in real-life settings (e.g., on a subway train) where people could not possibly have known that an experiment was being conducted. We will frequently point out similar replications of the major findings we discuss in this book.

Cross-Cultural Research

If American social psychologists conduct their research in America, with American participants, might their results be less than universal? Surely, many important psychological processes are shaped by the culture in which we grow up. To find out how culturally dependent a psychological process is, social psychologists conduct **cross-cultural research.**

For example, Charles Darwin (1872) argued that there is a basic set of human emotions (e.g., anger, happiness) that are expressed and understood throughout the world. Although a lively controversy has arisen as to whether Darwin was right (Russell, 1994), a lot of subsequent research has shown that people in different cultures express emotions on their faces in the same way, even in remote cultures having no contact with the rest of the world (Ekman, 1994; Ekman & Friesen, 1971; Frank & Stennett, 2000; Hejmadi, Davidson, & Rozin, 2000). And the effects of bystanders on helping behavior have been replicated in at least one other country, Israel (Schwartz & Gottlieb, 1976).

Clearly, however, our backgrounds shape our lives in fundamental ways. A goal of many cross-cultural studies is to explore the differences between us by examining how culture influences basic social psychological processes (Fiske, Kitayama, Markus, & Nisbett, 1998; Nisbett, 2003; Smith & Bond, 1999). Some findings in social psychology are culture-dependent, as we will see throughout this book. In Chapter 5, for example, we'll discuss cultural differences in the very way people define themselves. Whether we emphasize personal independence or social interdependence reflects our cultural values (Kitayama & Markus, 1994; Markus & Kitayama, 1991; Triandis, 1989). In Chapter 12, we will see that people's cultural and economic backgrounds have intriguing effects on how aggressive they are (Cohen, Nisbett, Bowdle, & Schwarz, 1996; Nisbett, 1993; Nisbett & Cohen, 1996).

Conducting cross-cultural research is not simply a matter of traveling to another culture, translating materials into the local language, and replicating a study there (Heine, Lehman, Peng, & Greenholtz, 2002; van de Vijver & Leung, 1997). Researchers always have to guard against imposing their own viewpoints and definitions, learned from their culture, onto another culture with which they are unfamiliar. They must also be sure that their independent and dependent variables are understood in the same way in different cultures (Bond, 1988; Lonner & Berry, 1986).

Suppose, for example, that you wanted to replicate the Latané and Darley (1968) seizure experiment in another culture. Clearly, you could not conduct the identical experiment somewhere else. The tape-recorded discussion of college life used by Latané and Darley was specific to the lives of New York University students in the 1960s and could not be used meaningfully elsewhere.

Cross-Cultural Research

Research conducted with members of different cultures, to see whether the psychological processes of interest are present in both cultures or whether they are specific to the culture in which people were raised

Some basic psychological processes are universal, whereas others are shaped by the culture in which we live. For example, are people's self-concepts shaped by cultural rules of how people must present themselves, such as the requirement by the Taliban regime in Afghanistan that women cover themselves from head to toe? Are people's ideas about their relationships to their family and social groups influenced by cultural practices, such as cradling one's child while at work, as this woman from Indonesia is doing? Cross cultural research is challenging, but necessary to explore how culture influences the basic ways in which people think about and interact with others.

What about more subtle aspects of the study, such as the way people viewed the person who had the seizure? Cultures vary considerably in how they define whether another person belongs to their social group; this factor figures significantly in how they behave toward that person (Gudykunst, 1988; Triandis, 1989). If people in one culture view the victim as a member of their social group but people in another culture perceive the victim as a member of a rival social group, you might find very different results in the two cultures—not because the psychological processes of helping behavior are different but because people interpreted the situation differently. It can be quite daunting to conduct a study that is interpreted and perceived similarly in dissimilar cultures. Cross-cultural researchers are sensitive to these issues, and as more and more cross-cultural research is conducted carefully, we will be able to determine which social psychological processes are universal and which are culture-bound.

The Basic Dilemma of the Social Psychologist

One of the best ways to increase external validity is by conducting **field experiments.** In a field experiment, researchers study behavior outside of the laboratory, in its natural setting. As in a laboratory experiment, the researcher controls the occurrence of an independent variable (e.g., group size) to see what effect it has on a dependent variable (e.g., helping behavior) and randomly assigns people to the different conditions. Thus a field experiment has the same design as a laboratory experiment except that it is conducted in a real-life setting, rather than in the relatively artificial setting of the laboratory. The participants in a field experiment are unaware that the events they experience are in fact an experiment. The external validity of such an experiment is high, since, after all, it is taking place in the real world, with real people who are more diverse than a typical college student sample.

Many such field studies have been conducted in social psychology. For example, Latané and Darley (1970) tested their hypothesis about group size and bystander intervention in a convenience store outside of New York City. Two "robbers" (with full knowledge and permission of the cashier and manager of the store) waited until there were either one or two other customers at the checkout counter. Then they asked the cashier to name the most expensive beer the store carried. The cashier answered the question and then said he would

Field Experiments

Experiments conducted in natural settings rather than in the laboratory

have to check in the back to see how much of that brand was in stock. While the cashier was gone, the robbers picked up a case of beer in the front of the store, declared, "They'll never miss this," put the beer in their car, and drove off.

Because the robbers were rather burly fellows, no one attempted to intervene directly to stop the theft. The question was, when the cashier returned, how many people would help by telling him that a theft had just occurred? The number of bystanders had the same inhibiting effect on helping behavior as in the laboratory seizure study: Significantly fewer people reported the theft when there was another customer-witness in the store than when they were alone.

It might have occurred to you to ask why researchers conduct laboratory studies at all, given that external validity is so much better with field experiments. Indeed, it seems to us that the perfect experiment in social psychology would be one that was conducted in a field setting, with a sample randomly selected from a population of interest and with extremely high internal validity (all extraneous variables controlled; people randomly assigned to the conditions). Sounds good, doesn't it? The only problem is that it is very difficult to satisfy all these conditions in one study—making such studies virtually impossible to conduct.

There is almost always a trade-off between internal and external validity—that is, between (1) having enough control over the situation to ensure that no extraneous variables are influencing the results and randomly assigning people to conditions and (2) making sure that the results can be generalized to everyday life. We have the most control in a laboratory setting, but the laboratory may be unlike real life. Real life can best be captured by doing a field experiment, but it is very difficult to control all extraneous variables in such studies. For example, the astute reader will have noticed that Latané and Darley's (1970) beer theft study differed from laboratory experiments in an important way: People could not be randomly assigned to the alone or in-pairs conditions. Were this the only study Latané and Darley had performed, we could not be sure whether the kinds of people who prefer to shop alone, as compared to the kinds of people who prefer to shop with a friend, differ in ways that might influence helping behavior. By randomly assigning people to conditions in their laboratory studies, Latané and Darley were able to rule out such alternative explanations.

The trade-off between internal and external validity has been referred to as the basic dilemma of the social psychologist (Aronson & Carlsmith, 1968). The way to resolve this dilemma is not to try to do it all in a single experiment. Most social psychologists opt first for internal validity, conducting laboratory experiments in which people are randomly assigned to different conditions and all extraneous variables are controlled; here there is little ambiguity about what is causing what. Other social psychologists prefer to maximize external validity by conducting field studies. And many social psychologists do both. Taken together, both types of studies meet the requirements of our perfect experiment. Through replication, a given research question can thus be studied with maximum internal and external validity. This approach has worked well in many areas of inquiry, in which lab and field studies have been conducted on the same problem and have yielded similar findings (Anderson, Lindsay, & Bushman, 1999).

BASIC VERSUS APPLIED RESEARCH

You may have wondered how people decide which specific topic to study. Why would a social psychologist decide to study helping behavior, cognitive dissonance theory, or the effects of pornography on aggression? Is he or she simply curious? Or does the social psychologist have a specific purpose in mind, such as trying to reduce sexual violence?

The goal in **basic research** is to find the best answer to the question of why people behave as they do, purely for reasons of intellectual curiosity. The researchers aren't trying to solve a specific social or psychological problem. In contrast, **applied research** is geared toward solving a particular social problem. Building a theory of behavior is usually secondary to solving the specific problem, such as alleviating racism, reducing sexual violence, or stemming the spread of AIDS.

In social psychology, the distinction between basic and applied research is fuzzy. Even though many researchers label themselves as either basic or applied scientists, the endeavors of one group are not independent of those of the other group. There are countless examples of advances in basic science that at the time had no known applied value but later proved to be the key to solving a significant applied problem. As we will see later in this book, for instance, basic research with dogs, rats, and fish on the effects of feeling in control of one's environment has led to the development of techniques to improve the health of elderly nursing home residents (Langer & Rodin, 1976; Richter, 1957; Schulz, 1976; Seligman, 1975).

Most social psychologists would agree that in order to solve a specific social problem, we must understand the psychological processes responsible for it Indeed, Kurt Lewin (1951), one of the founders of social psychology, coined a phrase that has become a motto for the field: "There is nothing so practical as a good theory." He meant that to solve such difficult social problems as urban violence or racial prejudice, one must first understand the underlying psychological dynamics of human nature and social interaction. Even when the goal is to discover the psychological processes underlying social behavior, the findings often have clear applied implications, as you'll see throughout this book. We also include at the end of the book three "Social Psychology in Action" modules that discuss how social psychology has been applied to important social problems.

> There is nothing so practical as a good theory.
> –Kurt Lewin, 1951

ETHICAL ISSUES IN SOCIAL PSYCHOLOGY

As you read this chapter, did it bother you to learn that researchers sometimes mislead people about the true purpose of their study or that in Latané and Darley's seizure study, people were put in a situation that might have been upsetting? This study illustrates that in their quest to create realistic, engaging situations, social psychologists frequently face an ethical dilemma. For scientific reasons, we want our experiments to resemble the real world as much as possible and to be as sound and well controlled as we can make them. But we also want to avoid causing our participants undue and unnecessary stress, discomfort, or unpleasantness. These two goals often conflict as the researcher goes about the business of creating and conducting experiments.

Researchers are concerned about the health and welfare of the individuals participating in their experiments. Researchers are also in the process of discovering important information about human social behavior—such as bystander intervention, prejudice, conformity, aggression, and obedience to authority. Many of these discoveries are bound to benefit society. Indeed, given the fact that social psychologists have developed powerful tools to investigate such issues scientifically, many scholars feel it would be immoral not to conduct these experiments. However, in order to gain insight into such critical issues, researchers must create vivid events that are involving for the participants. Some of these events might make the participants uncomfortable, such as witnessing someone having a seizure. What is required for good science and what is required for ethical science, then, can conflict. We can't resolve the dilemma by making pious claims that participants never experience discomfort in an experiment or by in-

Basic Research
Studies that are designed to find the best answer to the question of why people behave as they do and that are conducted purely for reasons of intellectual curiosity

Applied Research
Studies designed to solve a particular social problem

sisting that all is fair in science and forging blindly ahead. Clearly, some middle ground is called for.

The dilemma would be less problematic if researchers could obtain **informed consent** from their participants before their participation. To obtain informed consent, the researcher explains the nature of the experiment to participants before it begins and asks for their agreement to participate. If participants are made fully aware of the kinds of experiences they are about to undergo and state that they are willing to participate, the ethical dilemma is resolved. In many social psychology experiments, this sort of description is feasible—and where it is feasible, it is done. But sometimes it is impossible. Suppose Latané and Darley had told their participants that a seizure was about to be staged, that it wouldn't be a real emergency, and that the hypothesis stated they should offer help. Such a procedure would be bad science. In this kind of experiment, it's essential that the participant experience contrived events as if they were real; this is called a deception experiment. **Deception** in social psychological research involves misleading participants about the true purpose of a study or the events that transpire. (Note that not all research in social psychology involves deception.)

THE FAR SIDE By GARY LARSON

Sorry, your highness, but you're really not the dictator of Ithuvania, a small European republic. In fact, there is no Ithuvania. The hordes of admirers, the military parades, this office -- We faked it all as an experiment in human psychology. In fact, your highness, your real name is Edward Belcher, you're from Long Island, New York, and it's time to go home, Eddie.

Guidelines for Ethical Research

To ensure that the dignity and safety of research participants are protected, the American Psychological Association has published a list of ethical principles that govern all research in psychology (see Figure 2.3). In addition, all research conducted by psychologists must be reviewed by an institutional review board. Any aspect of the experimental procedure that this committee judges to be overly stressful or upsetting must be changed or deleted before the study can be conducted. When deception is used, the postexperimental interview, called the debriefing session, is crucial and must occur. **Debriefing** is the process of explaining to the participants, at the end of an experiment, the true purpose of the study and exactly what transpired. If any participants experienced discomfort, the researchers attempt to undo and alleviate it. During debriefing, too, the participants learn about the goals and purpose of the research. The best researchers question their participants carefully and listen to what they say, regardless of whether or not deception was used in the experiment. (For a detailed description of how debriefing interviews should be conducted, see Aronson, Ellsworth, Carlsmith, & Gonzales, 1990.)

In our experience, virtually all participants understand and appreciate the need for deception, as long as the time is taken in the postexperimental debriefing session to review the purpose of the research and to explain why alternative procedures could not be used. Several investigators have gone a step further and assessed the impact on people of participating in deception studies (e.g., Christensen, 1988; Epley & Huff, 1998; Finney, 1987; Gerdes, 1979; Sharpe, Adair, & Roese, 1992). These studies have consistently found that people do not object to the kinds of mild discomfort and deceptions typically used in social psychological research. In fact, some studies have found that most people who participated in deception experiments said they had learned more and enjoyed the experiments more than those who participated in nondeception experiments did (Smith & Richardson, 1983). For example, Latané and Darley (1970) reported that during their debriefing, the participants said that the deception was necessary and that they were willing to participate in similar studies in the future—even though they had experienced some stress and conflict during the study.

Informed Consent

Agreement to participate in an experiment, granted in full awareness of the nature of the experiment, which has been explained in advance

Deception

Misleading participants about the true purpose of a study or the events that will actually transpire

Debriefing

Explaining to participants, at the end of an experiment, the true purpose of the study and exactly what transpired

SELECTED ETHICAL PRINCIPLES OF PSYCHOLOGISTS IN THE CONDUCT OF RESEARCH

1. Psychologists seek to promote accuracy, honesty, and truthfulness in the science, teaching, and practice of psychology.
2. Psychologists respect the dignity and worth of all people, and the rights of individuals to privacy, confidentiality, and self-determination.
3. When psychologists conduct research . . . in person or via electronic transmission or other forms of communication, they obtain the informed consent of the individual.
4. When obtaining informed consent . . . psychologists inform participants about the purpose of the research, expected duration, and procedures, and their right to decline to participate and to withdraw from the research once participation has begun.
5. Psychologists have a primary obligation and take reasonable precautions to protect confidential information obtained through or stored in any medium.
6. Psychologists do not conduct a study involving deception unless they have determined that the use of deceptive techniques is justified by the study's significant prospective scientific, educational, or applied value and that effective nondeceptive alternative procedures are not feasible.
7. Psychologists explain any deception that is an integral feature of the design and conduct of an experiment to participants as early as is feasible.
8. Psychologists provide a prompt opportunity for participants to obtain appropriate information about the nature, results, and conclusions of the research, and they take reasonable steps to correct any misconceptions that participants may have.

FIGURE 2.3

Procedures for the protection of participants in psychological research.

(Adapted from American Psychological Association, 2003)

We do not mean to imply that all deception is beneficial. Nonetheless, if mild deception is used and time is spent after the study discussing the deception with participants and explaining why it was necessary, the evidence is that people will not be harmed.

SUMMARY

Social Psychology: An Empirical Science

The goal of social psychology is to answer questions about social behavior scientifically. Although some findings might appear obvious in retrospect, due to the **hindsight bias,** research must be conducted to determine how people are likely to behave and why they behave that way.

Formulating Hypotheses and Theories

The hypotheses social psychologists test come from many sources. Sometimes researchers are inspired by previous studies and theories; they have a different explanation that they want to test. Other times researchers come up with hypotheses from their own personal observations of social events, such as the Kitty Genovese murder in the early 1960s.

The Observational Method: Describing Social Behavior

The **observational method** primarily fulfills a descriptive function; it allows a researcher to observe and describe a social phenomenon. **Ethnography** is the observational method by which researchers attempt to understand a group or culture by observing it from the inside, without imposing any preconceived notions they might have. This often involves **participant observation,** whereby the researcher interacts with the people being observed. Other observational techniques attempt to test specific hypotheses, with the objectivity of the researcher's observations tested through **interjudge reliability.** In **archival analysis,** the researcher examines the accumulated documents or archives of a culture.

The Correlational Method: Predicting Social Behavior

The **correlational method** allows the researcher to determine if two or more variables are related—that is, whether one variable can be predicted from the other. The **correlation coefficient** is a statistical technique that reveals the extent to which one variable can be predicted from another. Correlations are often calculated from **surveys** conducted on a sample of a larger population chosen by **random selection.** This ensures that the responses of the sample are representative of those of the population. The major drawback of the correlational method is that it cannot determine causality. It is not possible to determine from a correlation whether A causes B, B causes A, or some other variable causes both A and B.

The Experimental Method: Answering Causal Questions

The **experimental method** is the preferred design in social psychology; it is the only design that allows the researcher to infer causality. Experiments can be conducted in the laboratory or in the field; **field experiments** are those conducted in natural settings. In experiments, researchers vary the level of an **independent variable,** which is the one hypothesized to have a causal effect on behavior. The **dependent variable** is the measured variable that is hypothesized to be caused or influenced by the independent variable. The researcher makes sure that participants are treated identically except for the independent variable and randomly assigns people to the experimental conditions. **Random assignment to condition,** the hallmark of true experimental design, minimizes the possibility that different types of people are unevenly distributed across conditions. A **probability level (*p*-value)** is calculated, telling the researcher how likely it is that the results are due to chance versus the independent variable.

Experiments are designed to be as high as possible in **internal validity** (making sure that nothing else besides the independent variable is influencing the results) and in **external validity** (making sure that the results can be generalized across people and situations). **Mundane realism** reflects the extent to which the experimental setting is similar to real-life settings. **Psychological realism** reflects the extent to which the experiment involves psychological responses like those occurring in real life. The best test of external validity is **replication**—repeating the experiment in different settings with different people to see if the results are the same. A statistical technique called **meta-analysis** allows researchers to see how reliable the effects of an independent variable are over many replications. Increasingly, social psychologists are exploring cultural differences in thought and social behavior by conducting **cross-cultural research.** Discoveries made about people in some cultures do not always generalize to people in other cultures.

Basic versus Applied Research

Researchers engage in both **basic research** and **applied research.** Though the line between these is often blurred, basic research aims to gain understanding of human social behavior without trying to solve a particular problem, whereas applied research aims to solve a specific problem, often one with social policy implications.

Ethical Issues in Social Psychology

A major concern in social psychological research is the ethical treatment of participants. The American Psychological Association's guidelines are followed carefully and include such procedures as obtaining **informed consent,** the ability to leave the experiment at any time, ensured anonymity and confidentiality, and debriefing following an experiment, particularly if **deception** (involving an intentionally misleading **cover story** about the purpose of the study or the independent or dependent variables) has been used.

CRITICAL THINKING QUESTIONS

1. Suppose you wanted to investigate the question of whether playing violent video games makes teenagers more aggressive. Describe how you would use the observational, correlational, and experimental method to examine this question. What are the advantages and disadvantages of each technique?

2. Suppose you read about a recent study that found a negative correlation between how mentally active older people are (how often they read the newspaper, play cards, do crossword puzzles, etc.) and how senile they were (how much memory loss they experienced). The more mentally active the people were, the less senile they were. The researchers concluded that staying mentally active helps people avoid senility. Is this a valid conclusion? What are some other interpretations of the correlation found in the study?

3. What is the basic dilemma of the social psychologist? Why is it a dilemma?

Answers, *Try it!* Page 29

1. In studies conducted by Stanley Milgram (1974), up to 65 percent of participants administered what they thought were near-lethal shocks to another subject. (In fact, no real shocks were administered.)

2. (c) Rewarding people for doing something they enjoy will typically make them like that activity less in the future (e.g., Lepper, 1995, 1996; Lepper, Greene, & Nisbett, 1973).

3. (b) Wilson et al. (1993) found that people who did not analyze their feelings were the most satisfied with their choice of posters when contacted a few weeks later.

4. (a) Under most circumstances, repeated exposure increases liking for a stimulus (Zajonc, 1968).

5. (a) More (Jecker & Landy, 1969).

6. False (Taylor & Brown, 1988, 1994).

7. (a) Research by Spencer, Steele, and Quinn (1997) and Steele (1997) found that when women think there are sex differences on a test, they do worse. When women were told that there were no gender differences in performance on the test, they did as well as men.

8. (b) There is no evidence that subliminal messages in advertising have any effect; considerable evidence shows that normal advertising is quite effective (Abraham & Lodish, 1990; Chaiken, Wood, & Eagly, 1996; Liebert & Sprafkin, 1988; Moore, 1982; Weir, 1984; Wilson, Houston, & Meyers, 1998).

9. (b) Men touch women more than vice versa (Henley, 1977).

10. (c) In the short run, people regret things they did that they wish they hadn't done more than things they didn't do that they wish they had done. In the long run, however, the opposite is true (Gilovich & Medvec, 1995a; Gilovich, Medvec, & Chen, 1995).

Answer, *Try it!* Page 33

1. Two teams of researchers (Archer, Iritani, Kimes & Barrios, 1983, and Akert, Chen & Panter, 1991) performed an archival analysis of portrait art and news and advertising photographs in print and television media. They coded the photographs according to the number of images that were devoted to the person's face. Their results? Over five centuries, across cultures, and in different forms of media, men are visually presented in a more close-up style (focusing on the head and face), while women are shown in a more long-shot style (focusing on the body). These researchers interpret their findings as indicating a subtle form of sex-role stereotyping: Men are being portrayed in a stronger style that emphasizes their intellectual achievements, whereas women are being portrayed in a weaker style that emphasizes their total physical appearance.

Answers, *Try it!* Page 40

1. The politician ignored possible third variables that could cause both Scout membership and crime, such as socioeconomic class. Traditionally, Scouting has been most popular in small towns and suburbs among middle-class youngsters; it has never been very attractive or even available to youths growing up in densely populated, urban, high-crime areas.

2. Families who can afford or are willing to have a pet might differ in any number of ways from families who neither can afford nor are willing to have one.

3. Did tattoos cause motorcycle accidents? Or for that matter, did motorcycle accidents cause tattoos? The researchers suggested that a third (unmeasured) variable was in fact the cause of both: A tendency to take risks and to be involved in flamboyant personal displays led to tattooing one's body and to driving a motorcycle recklessly.

4. By chance, the size of the cohort in the population that is most likely to commit crimes—teenagers—went down when Reagan took office.

5. Not necessarily. People who do not eat breakfast might differ from people who do in any number of ways that influence longevity—for example, in how obese they are, in how hard-driving and high-strung they are, or even in how late they sleep in the morning.

6. Coffee drinkers may be more likely to engage in other behaviors that put them at risk, such as smoking cigarettes or not exercising regularly.

7. Both the viscosity of asphalt and the crime rate go up when the temperature is high—for example, on a hot summer day or night.

8. The newsmagazine concluded that spending time with one's child reduces the urge to engage in sexual abuse (Adler, 1997). Can you think of alternative explanations? Perhaps child abuse leads to less time with children, due to feelings of guilt or fear of being caught. Or perhaps there is a third variable, such as an antisocial personality, that contributes to child abuse and less time spent with one's child.

9. No. Perhaps people with high levels of the antigen were healthier and thus more likely to have sex. Or maybe there is some unknown third variable that makes people healthier and more likely to have sex.

10. It is possible that watching public television makes people want to have more sex. It is equally possible, however, that some third variable, such as health or education, influences both television preferences and sexual behavior. It is even possible that having sex makes people want to watch more public television. Based on the correlation the researchers reported, there is no way of telling which of these explanations is true.

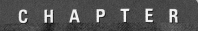

Social Cognition:
How We Think about the Social World

Early in the morning on February 4, 1999, four white police officers approached Amadou Diallo on a street in the Bronx, New York. Because the officers believed that Diallo, a black immigrant from West Africa, looked like sketches they had seen of a serial rapist, they ordered him to stop as he entered the vestibule of his apartment building. In fact, Diallo had no criminal record. He was working long hours as a street vendor and in his spare time was earning high school credits so that he could go to college. When the police approached Diallo, he reached for his wallet, probably so that he could show some identification. Alarmed by the sight of a black man reaching into his pocket, the four officers did not hesitate. They fired a total of forty-one shots at Diallo, killing him instantly.

Unfortunately, incidents such as this one are not rare. On the night of April 6, 2001, a Cincinnati police officer chased Timothy Thomas into an alley and demanded that he show him his hands. Before Thomas had a chance to comply, the officer shot and killed him. Thomas was unarmed.

Police officers often have to make extremely quick decisions and have little time to stop and analyze whether someone poses a threat. In both the Diallo and Thomas cases, however, many people wondered whether the officers' decisions to open fire so quickly were influenced by the victims' race. Thomas was the fifteenth African American killed by the Cincinnati police in the preceding six years; no whites were killed by the police during this time period (Singer, 2002). Would the officers have acted any differently if Diallo or Thomas were white? More generally, how do people size up their social worlds and decide how to act, in life-and-death situations such as these ones or in everyday situations people face all the time? The ways in which people analyze and think about the social world is the topic of this chapter.

As we discussed in Chapter 1, a central topic in social psychology is the study of **social cognition,** or the ways in which people think about themselves and the social world, including how they select, interpret, remember, and use social information. The assumption is that people are generally trying to form

Social Cognition

How people think about themselves and the social world, or more specifically, how people select, interpret, remember, and use social information to make judgments and decisions

accurate impressions of the world and do so much of the time. Because of the nature of social thinking, however, people sometimes form erroneous impressions—such as the police officers' assumption that Amadou Diallo was reaching for a gun.

To understand how people think about their social worlds and how accurate their impressions are likely to be, we need to distinguish between two different kinds of social cognition. One kind of thought is quick and automatic. The police officers did not pause and think about what might be in Diallo's pocket; when they saw him reach for something, they opened fire. They acted "without thinking"—that is, without consciously deliberating about what they saw and whether their assumptions were correct (Bargh & Ferguson, 2000; Ouellette & Wood, 1998; Sloman, 1996; Smith & De Coster, 1999).

Sometimes, of course, people do pause and think about themselves and their environments and think carefully about the right course of action. You may have spent hours deliberating over important decisions in your life, such as where to go to college, what to choose as your major, and whether to break up with your boyfriend or girlfriend. This is the second kind of social cognition—*controlled thinking*, which is more effortful and deliberate. Quite often the automatic and controlled modes of social cognition work very well together. Think of a plane that can fly on automatic pilot, that monitors hundreds of complex systems and adjusts instantly to changes in atmospheric conditions. The autopilot does just fine most of the time, though occasionally it is important for the human pilot to take over and fly the plane manually. Humans, too, have "automatic pilots" that monitor their environments, draw conclusions, and direct their behaviors. But we can also "override" this automatic type of thinking and analyze a situation slowly and deliberately. We will begin by examining the nature of automatic thinking.

> It is the mind which creates the world about us, and even though we stand side by side in the same meadow, my eyes will never see what is beheld by yours.
>
> —George Gissing, The Private Papers of Henry Ryecroft, 1903

ON AUTOMATIC PILOT: LOW-EFFORT THINKING

People often size up a new situation very quickly: they figure out who is there, what is happening, and what might happen next. Often these quick conclusions are correct. When you attended your first college class, for example, you probably made quick assumptions about who people were (the person standing at the lectern was the professor) and how to behave. We doubt that you confused the class with a fraternity party. And you probably reached these conclusions without even being aware that you were doing so.

Imagine a different approach: Every time you encounter a new situation you stop and think about it slowly and deliberately, like Rodin's statue *The Thinker*. When you are introduced to someone new, you have to excuse yourself for fif-

Rodin's famous sculpture, *The Thinker,* mimics controlled thinking, where people sit down and consider something slowly and deliberately. Even when we do not know it, however, we are engaging in automatic thinking, which is nonconscious, unintentional, involuntary, and effortless.

teen minutes while you analyze what you have learned and how much you like the person. When you drive down an unfamiliar road, you have to pull over and analyze its twists and turns before knowing how to proceed. Sounds exhausting, doesn't it? Instead, we form impressions of people quickly and effortlessly and navigate new roads without much conscious analysis of what we are doing. We do these things by engaging in an automatic analysis of our environments, based on our past experiences and knowledge of the world. **Automatic thinking** is thought that is nonconscious, unintentional, involuntary, and effortless. Although different kinds of automatic thinking meet these criteria to varying degrees (Bargh & Ferguson, 2000; Wegner & Bargh, 1998), for our purposes we can define automaticity as thinking that satisfies all or most of these criteria.

People as Everyday Theorists: Automatic Thinking with Schemas

Automatic thinking helps us understand new situations by relating them to our prior experiences. When we meet someone new, we don't start from scratch to figure out what he or she is like; we categorize the person as "an engineering student" or "like my cousin Helen." The same goes for places, objects, and situations. When we walk into a fast-food restaurant we've never visited, we know, without thinking, not to wait at a table for a waiter and a menu. We know that we have to go to the counter and order because our mental "script" automatically tells us that this is what we do in fast-food restaurants, and we assume that this one is no different.

More formally, people use **schemas,** which are mental structures that organize our knowledge about the social world. These mental structures influence the information we notice, think about, and remember (Bartlett, 1932; Markus, 1977; Taylor & Crocker, 1981). The term *schema* is very general; it encompasses our knowledge about many things—other people, ourselves, social roles (e.g., what a librarian or an engineer is like), and specific events (e.g., what usually happens when people eat a meal in a restaurant). In each case, our schemas contain our basic knowledge and impressions that we use to organize what we know about the social world and interpret new situations. For example, our schema about the members of the Animal House fraternity might be that they're loud, obnoxious partygoers with a propensity for projectile vomiting.

Automatic Thinking

Thinking that is nonconscious, unintentional, involuntary, and effortless

Schemas

Mental structures people use to organize their knowledge about the social world around themes or subjects and that influence the information people notice, think about, and remember

In a study by Correll et al. (2002), people played a video game in which they saw photographs of men who were holding a handgun or nonthreatening objects such as cell phones, such as the picture shown here. Half of the men were African American and half were white. Participants were instructed to press a button labeled "shoot" if the man had a gun and a button labeled "don't shoot" if he did not. Like a real police officer they had very little time to make up their minds (just over half a second). The most common mistake people made was to "shoot" an African American man who was not holding a gun, such as the man in this picture.

> Theory helps us to bear our ignorance of facts.
>
> –George Santayana, The Sense of Beauty, 1896

Stereotypes about Race and Weapons When applied to members of a social group such as a fraternity or gender or race, schemas are commonly referred to as *stereotypes*, which we will discuss in detail in Chapter 13. For now, we point out that the stereotypes can be applied rapidly and automatically when we encounter other people. For example, recent experiments have tested whether people's stereotypes about African Americans can influence their perception of whether a person is holding a weapon, as may have occurred in the Diallo tragedy. In one study, nonblack college students saw pairs of pictures in rapid succession on a computer screen (Payne, 2001). The first picture was always of a face, whereas the second picture depicted either a tool or a gun. Participants were told to pay attention only to the second picture and to press one key if it was a tool and another if it was a gun, as rapidly and as accurately as they could. In fact, they had only ½ second to identify the picture and press a key.

It just so happened that half of the faces in the first picture were of whites and half were of blacks. The question was, did the race of the face influence people's perception of whether they saw a gun or a tool in the second picture? Indeed it did; people were significantly more likely to misidentify a tool as a gun when it was preceded by a black face than when it was preceded by a white face, just as the policeman in the Bronx mistakenly thought that Amadou Diallo was reaching for a gun when he was simply reaching for his wallet.

In another study, people performed a task that was even closer to the dilemma faced by police officers (Correll, Park, Judd, & Wittenbrink, 2002). People played a video game in which they saw photographs of young men in realistic settings, such as in a park, at train station, and on a city sidewalk. Half of the men were African American and half were white. And half of the men in each group were holding a handgun and half were hold nonthreatening objects such as a cell phone, wallet, or camera. Participants were instructed to press a button labeled "shoot" if the man in the picture had a gun and a button labeled "don't shoot" if he did not. Like a real police officer, they had very little time to make up their minds (just over half a second). Participants won or lost points on each round of the game, modeled after the risks and benefits faced by officers in real life. Participants earned 5 points for not shooting someone who did not have a gun and 10 points for shooting someone who did have a gun. They lost 20 points if they shot someone who was not holding a gun and lost 40 points if they

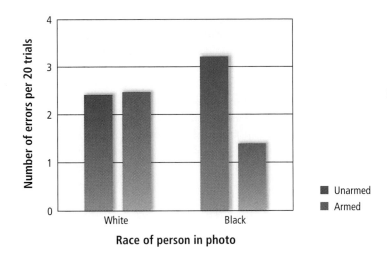

FIGURE 3.1

Errors made in "shooting" people in video game.

Participants played a video game in which they were supposed to "shoot" a man if he was holding a gun and withhold fire if he was not. People were influenced by the race of the men in the pictures. As seen in the figure, people were prone to make mistakes by shooting black men who were unarmed.

(Adapted from Correll, Park, Judd, & Wittenbrink, 2002)

failed to shoot someone who was holding a gun (which, in real life, would be the most life-threatening situation for a police officer).

The results? Participants were especially likely to pull the trigger when the people in the pictures were black, whether or not these people were holding a gun. This "shooter bias" meant that people made relatively few errors when a black person was in fact holding a gun but also that they made the most errors, shooting an unarmed person, when a black person was not holding a gun (see Figure 3.1). When the men in the picture were white, participants made about the same number of errors whether the men were armed or unarmed.

In both the Payne (2001) and Correll et al. (2002) studies, people had to respond so quickly that they had little time to control their responses or think about what they were doing. The errors they made were the result of automatic thinking that is rooted, perhaps, in the pervasive stereotypes in American culture about African Americans and violence. Correll and colleagues found that the people who were most likely to show the shooter bias were those who believed the strongest that there was a cultural stereotype linking African Americans to violence—even if they did not personally endorse this stereotype. The authors argue that knowledge of a cultural stereotype can influence people in insidious ways, even if the people are not themselves prejudiced.

In this chapter, we should keep in mind that stereotypes, such as the police officers' assumptions and beliefs about Amadou Diallo based on his race, are a special case of a more general phenomenon, people's organization of the world into schemas (Kunda, 1999). In addition to schemas about classes of people, for example, we have schemas about specific individuals (e.g., what Aunt Jane is like), social roles (how mothers are supposed to behave), and how people act in specific situations (e.g., at a party or in a restaurant). We turn now to properties of schemas more generally.

The Function of Schemas: Why Do We Have Them?   We've been focusing on the negative consequences of schemas, cases in which people "fill in the blanks" in erroneous ways (e.g., assuming that a black person is holding a gun when he is not). Schemas are typically very useful for helping us organize and make sense of the world and to fill in the gaps of our knowledge. Think for a moment what it would be like to have no schemas at all. What if everything you encountered was inexplicable, confusing, and unlike anything else you've ever known? Tragically, this is what happens to people who suffer from a neurological disorder called Korsakov's syndrome. People with this disorder lose the ability to form new memories and must approach every situation as if they were encountering it for the first time, even if they have actually experienced it many times before.

This can be so unsettling—even terrifying—that some people with Korsakov's syndrome go to great lengths to try to impose meaning on their experiences. The neurologist Oliver Sacks (1987) gives the following description of a Korsakov patient named Thompson:

> *He remembered nothing for more than a few seconds. He was continually disoriented. Abysses of amnesia continually opened beneath him, but he would bridge them, nimbly, by fluent confabulations and fictions of all kinds. For him they were not fictions, but how he suddenly saw, or interpreted, the world. Its radical flux and incoherence could not be tolerated, acknowledged, for an instant—there was, instead, this strange, delirious, quasi-coherence, as Mr. Thompson, with his ceaseless, unconscious, quick-fire inventions, continually improvised a world around him . . .* for such a patient must literally make himself (and his world) up every moment. (pp. 109–110; emphasis in original)

In short, having continuity, being able to relate new experiences to our past schemas, is so important that people who lose this ability invent schemas where none exist.

Schemas are particularly important when we encounter information that can be interpreted in a number of ways, because they help us reduce ambiguity. Consider a classic study by Harold Kelley (1950) in which students in different sections of a college economics class were told that a guest lecturer would be filling in that day. In order to create a schema about what the guest lecturer would be like, Kelley told the students that the economics department was interested in how different classes reacted to different instructors and that the students would thus receive a brief biographical note about the instructor before he arrived. The note contained information about the instructor's age, background, teaching experience, and personality. One version said, "People who know him consider him to be a very warm person, industrious, critical, practical, and determined." The other version was identical, except that the phrase "a very warm person" was replaced with "a rather cold person." The students received one of these personality descriptions at random.

The guest lecturer then conducted a class discussion for twenty minutes, after which the students rated their impressions of him. How funny was he? How sociable? How considerate? Given that there was some ambiguity in this situation—after all, the students had seen the instructor for only a brief time—Kelley hypothesized that they would use the schema provided by the biographical note to fill in the blanks. This is exactly what happened. The students who expected

People who know him consider him a very warm person, industrious, critical, practical, and determined.

People who know him consider him a rather cold person, industrious, critical, practical, and determined.

the instructor to be warm gave him significantly higher ratings than the students who expected him to be cold, even though all the students had observed the same teacher behaving in the same way. The students who expected the instructor to be warm were also more likely to ask him questions and to participate in the class discussion. Has this happened to you? Have your expectations about a professor influenced your impressions of him or her? Did you find, oddly enough, that the professor acted just as you'd expected? Ask a classmate who had a different expectation about the professor what he or she thought. Do the two of you have different perceptions of the instructor based on the different schemas you were using?

Of course, people are not totally blind to what is actually out there in the world. Sometimes what we see is relatively unambiguous and we do not need to use our schemas to help us interpret it. For example, in one of the classes in which Kelley conducted his study, the guest instructor happened to be obviously self-confident, even cocky. Given that cockiness is a relatively unambiguous trait, the students did not need to rely on their expectations to fill in the blanks. They rated the instructor as immodest in both the warm and cold conditions. However, when they rated this instructor's sense of humor, which was less clear-cut, the students relied on their schemas: The students in the warm condition thought he was funnier than the students in the cold condition did. The more ambiguous our information is, then, the more we use schemas to fill in the blanks.

It is important to note that there is nothing wrong with what the students in Kelley's study did. As long as people have reason to believe their schemas are accurate, it is perfectly reasonable to use them to resolve ambiguity. If a stranger comes up to you in a dark alley and says, "Take out your wallet," your schema about such encounters tells you that the person wants to steal your money, not admire pictures of your family. This schema helps you avert a serious and perhaps deadly misunderstanding. The danger comes when we automatically apply schemas that are *not* accurate, such as the police officers' assumption that Amadou Diallo was reaching for a gun.

> I know that often I would not see a thing unless I thought of it first.
>
> –Norman Maclean, A River Runs through It

Schemas as Memory Guides Human memory is reconstructive, and people often fill in the blanks with information that is consistent with their schemas. We don't remember exactly what occurred in a given setting, as if our minds were a film camera recording the precise images and sounds. Instead, we remember some information that was there (particularly information our schemas lead us to notice and pay attention to), and we remember other information that was never there but that we have unknowingly added later (Darley & Akert, 1991; Markus & Zajonc, 1985). For example, if you ask people what is the most famous line of dialogue in the classic Humphrey Bogart and Ingrid Bergman movie *Casablanca*, they will probably say, "Play it again, Sam." Similarly, if you ask them what is one of the most famous lines from the original (1966–1969) *Star Trek* television series, they will probably say, "Beam me up, Scotty." Here is a piece of trivia that might surprise you: Both of these lines of dialogue are reconstructions—the characters in the movie and the television series never said them.

Not surprisingly, memory reconstructions tend to be consistent with people's schemas. For example, participants in a study by Linda Carli (1999) read a story about a woman named Barbara and her relationship with a man named Jack. After dating for a while, Barbara and Jack went to a ski lodge for a weekend getaway. In one condition, the story ended with Jack proposing to Barbara; in the other, the story ended with Jack raping Barbara. Two weeks later, participants took a memory test in which they read several facts about Jack and Barbara and judged whether they had appeared in the story. In the marriage proposal condition, people were likely to misremember details that

> It is a capital mistake to theorize before you have all the evidence. It biases the judgment.
>
> –Sherlock Holmes (Sir Arthur Conan Doyle), 1898

Is this man an alcoholic or just down on his luck? Our judgments about other people can be influenced by schemas that are accessible in our memories. If you had just been talking to a friend about a relative who had an alcohol problem, you might be more likely to think that this man has an alcohol problem as well, because alcoholism is accessible in your memory.

were consistent with a proposal schema, such as "Jack wanted Barbara to meet his parents" and "Jack gave Barbara a dozen roses." Neither of these details had been in the story, but people in the proposal condition tended to think they were. Similarly, people in the rape condition were likely to misremember details that were consistent with a rape schema, such as "Jack liked to drink" and "Jack was unpopular with women." The fact that people filled in the blanks in their memory with schema-consistent details suggests that schemas become stronger and more resistant to change over time. We will explore the implications of this fact for changing prejudiced attitudes and stereotypes in Chapter 13.

Which Schemas Are Applied? Accessibility and Priming The social world is full of ambiguous information that is open to interpretation. Imagine, for example, that you are riding on a city bus and a man gets on and sits beside you. He mutters incoherently to himself, stares at everyone on the bus, and repeatedly rubs his face with his hands. How would you make sense of his behavior? You have several schemas you could use. Should you interpret his behavior with your "alcoholic" or "mentally ill person" schema? What dictates your choice?

The schema that comes to mind and guides your impressions of the man can be affected by **accessibility,** the extent to which schemas and concepts are at the forefront of the mind and are therefore likely to be used when we are making judgments about the social world (Ford & Thompson, 2000; Higgins, 1996a; Todorov & Bargh, 2002; Wyer & Srull, 1989). There are two kinds of accessibility. First, some schemas can be chronically accessible due to past experience (Chen & Andersen, 1999; Dijksterhuis & van Knippenberg, 1996; Higgins & Brendl, 1995; Rudman & Borgida, 1995). This means that these schemas are constantly active and ready to use to interpret ambiguous situations. For example, if there is a history of alcoholism in your family, traits describing an alcoholic are likely to be chronically accessible to you, increasing the likelihood that these traits will come to mind when you are thinking about the behavior of the man on the bus. If someone you know suffers from mental illness, however, then thoughts about how the mentally ill behave are more likely to be more accessible than thoughts about alcoholics, leading you to interpret the man's behavior very differently.

Second, schemas can become temporarily accessible for more arbitrary reasons (Bargh, 1996; Higgins & Bargh, 1987; Stapel & Koomen, 2000; Wyer & Srull, 1989). This means that a particular schema or trait is not always accessible but happens to be primed by something people have been thinking or doing before encountering an event. Suppose that right before the man on the bus sat down, you were reading *One Flew over the Cuckoo's Nest,* Ken Kesey's novel about

Accessibility

The extent to which schemas and concepts are at the forefront of people's minds and are therefore likely to be used when we are making judgments about the social world

patients in a mental hospital. Given that thoughts about mental patients were accessible in your mind, you would probably assume that the man was mentally ill. If, though, you had just looked out the window and seen an alcoholic leaning against a building drinking from a paper bag, you would probably assume that the man on the bus was drunk (see Figure 3.2). These are examples of **priming,** the process by which recent experiences increase the accessibility of a schema, trait, or concept. Reading Kesey's novel primes certain traits, such as those describing the mentally ill, making it more likely that these traits will be used to interpret a new event, such as the behavior of the man on the bus, even though this new event is completely unrelated to the one that originally primed the traits.

The following experiment illustrates the priming effect (Higgins, Rholes, & Jones, 1977). Research participants were told that they would take part in two unrelated studies. In the first, a perception study, they would have to identify different colors while at the same time memorizing a list of words. The second was a reading comprehension study in which they would be asked to read a paragraph about someone named Donald and then give their impressions of him. This paragraph is shown in Figure 3.3 on page 66. Take a moment to read it. What do you think of Donald?

You might have noticed that many of Donald's actions are ambiguous, interpretable in either a positive or a negative manner, such as the fact that he piloted

Priming

The process by which recent experiences increase the accessibility of a schema, trait, or concept

FIGURE 3.2

How we interpret an ambiguous situation: The role of accessibility and priming.

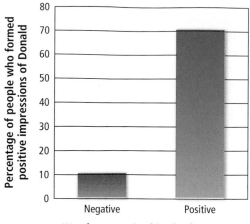

Description of Donald

Donald spent a great deal of time in his search of what he liked to call excitement. He had already climbed Mt. McKinley, shot the Colorado rapids in a kayak, driven in a demolition derby, and piloted a jet-powered boat—without knowing very much about boats. He had risked injury, and even death, a number of times. Now he was in search of new excitement. He was thinking, perhaps, he would do some skydiving or maybe cross the Atlantic in a sailboat. By the way he acted one could readily guess that Donald was well aware of his ability to do many things well. Other than business engagements, Donald's contacts with people were rather limited. He felt he didn't really need to rely on anyone. Once Donald made up his mind to do something it was as good as done no matter how long it might take or how difficult the going might be. Only rarely did he change his mind even when it might well have been better if he had.

FIGURE 3.3

Priming and accessibility.

In the second of a pair of studies, people were asked to read this paragraph about Donald and form an impression of him. In the first study, some of the participants had memorized words that could be used to interpret Donald in a negative way (e.g., *reckless, conceited*), while others had memorized words that could be used to interpret Donald in a positive way (e.g., *adventurous, self-confident*). As the graph shows, those who had memorized the negative words formed a much more negative impression of Donald than those who had memorized the positive words.

(Adapted from Higgins, Rholes, & Jones, 1977)

a boat without knowing much about it and that he wants to sail across the Atlantic. You might put a positive spin on these acts, deciding that Donald has an admirable sense of adventure. Or you could give the same behavior a negative spin, assuming that Donald is quite a reckless person.

How did the participants interpret Donald's behavior? As expected, it depended on whether positive or negative traits were primed and accessible. In the first study, the researchers divided people into two groups and gave them different words to memorize. People who had first memorized the words *adventurous, self-confident, independent,* and *persistent* later formed positive impressions of Donald, viewing him as a likable man who enjoyed new challenges. People who had first memorized *reckless, conceited, aloof,* and *stubborn* later formed negative impressions of Donald, viewing him as a stuck-up person who took needlessly dangerous chances.

But it was not just memorizing any positive or negative words that influenced people's impressions of Donald. In other conditions, research participants memorized words that were also positive or negative, such as *neat* or *disrespectful*. However, these traits didn't influence their impressions of Donald because the words did not apply to Donald's behavior. Thoughts, then, have to be both *accessible* and *applicable* before they will act as primes, exerting an influence on our impressions of the social world.

Priming is a good example of automatic thinking because it occurs quickly, unintentionally, and unconsciously. When judging others, people are usually not aware that they are applying concepts or schemas that they happened to be thinking about earlier. In fact, priming can occur even by flashing words at speeds that are too quick for people to recognize consciously. John Bargh and Paula Pietromonaco (1982) flashed words having to do with hostility (e.g., *hostile* and *unkind*) or neutral words (e.g., *water, between*) on a computer screen so quickly that people saw only a flash of light. People then read a paragraph describing a person who acted in ways that could or could not be interpreted as hostile (e.g., "A salesman knocked on the door, but Donald refused to let him enter"). Just as in the Higgins et al. (1977) study, people interpreted Donald's behavior in terms of the traits that had been primed; in this case, the people who saw the hostile words rated Donald as more hostile than people who saw the neutral words. Remarkably, this occurred even though people did not know they had seen the words, which supports the idea that priming is an automatic, nonconscious process. The Bargh and Pietromonaco study raises the specter of subliminal influence—whether it is possible to influence people's beliefs and attitudes with messages that they do not perceive consciously. We address this question in Chapter 7.

The Persistence of Schemas After They Are Discredited   Sometimes we hear something about an issue or another person that later turns out to be untrue. For example, a jury might hear something in court about a defendant that is false or labeled as inadmissible evidence. But even though the judge may instruct the jurors to disregard that information, because of the way schemas work, the jurors' beliefs can persist even after the evidence for them proves to be false. Schemas can take on a life of their own, even after the evidence for them has been completely discredited.

Imagine, for example, that you are a participant in a study in which you are given a stack of cards containing both real and fictitious suicide notes (Ross, Lepper, & Hubbard, 1975). You are told to guess which ones are real, supposedly to study the effects of physiological processes during decision making. After each guess, the experimenter tells you whether you are right or wrong. As the experiment progresses, you find out that you are pretty good at this task. In fact, you guess right on twenty-four of the twenty-five cards, which is much better than the performance of the average student.

At this point, the experimenter tells you that the study is over and explains that it was actually concerned with the effects of success and failure on physiological responses. You learn that you had been randomly assigned to a condition in which the experimenter *said* you were correct on twenty-four of the cards, regardless of how well you actually did. The experimenter then gives you a final questionnaire, which asks you how many answers you think you *really* got correct and how many times you think you would guess correctly on a second, equally difficult test with new cards. What would you say? Now pretend you were in the other condition of the study. Here everything is identical except you are told that you got only ten of the twenty-five answers correct, which is much worse than average. How would you respond to the questionnaire, once you found out that the feedback was bogus?

Depending on which condition you were in, you would have formed a schema that you were either very good or very poor at the task. What happens when the evidence for this schema is discredited? Ross and colleagues (1975) went to some pains to make sure that the participants understood that the feedback had been given randomly and had nothing to do with their actual performance. Even though the participants believed this, those who had received the "success" feedback still thought they had gotten more of the items correct and would do better on a second test than people who had received the "failure" feedback did. In addition, when asked how they would do on a new test, success participants said they would do better than failure participants did (see Figure 3.4 on page 68).

This result is called the **perseverance effect** because people's beliefs persevered even after the original evidence for them was discredited. When people received the feedback, they explained to themselves why they were doing so well or so poorly, recalling evidence that was consistent with their performance (e.g., "I am really very perceptive. After all, last week I was the only one who realized that Jennifer was depressed" or "Well, I'm not so good at this stuff; my friends always say I'm the last to know"). Even after learning that the feedback was false, these

Perseverance Effect
The finding that people's beliefs about themselves and the social world persist even after the evidence supporting these beliefs is discredited

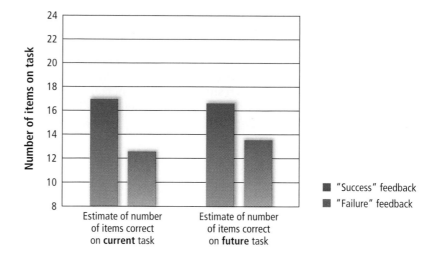

FIGURE 3.4

The perseverance effect.

People were told they had done very well (success feedback) or very poorly (failure feedback) on a test of their social sensitivity. They were then told that the feedback was bogus and had nothing to do with their actual performance. People's impressions that they were good or bad at the task persevered, even after learning that the feedback was bogus.

(Adapted from Ross, Lepper, & Hubbard, 1975)

thoughts were still fresh in people's minds, making them think they were particularly good or bad at the task (Anderson, 1995; Anderson & Lindsay, 1998; Davies, 1997; Sherman & Kim, 2002).

Making Our Schemas Come True: The Self-Fulfilling Prophecy   We've seen that when people encounter new evidence or have old evidence discredited, they tend not to revise their schemas as much as we might expect. People are not always passive recipients of information, however—they often act on their schemas in ways that change the extent to which these schemas are supported or contradicted. In fact, people can inadvertently make their schemas come true by the way they treat other people. This **self-fulfilling prophecy** operates as follows: People (1) have an expectation about what another person is like, which (2) influences how they act toward that person, which (3) causes that person to behave consistently with people's original expectations, making the expectations come true. Figure 3.5 illustrates the sad self-perpetuating cycle of a self-fulfilling prophecy.

Self-fulfilling prophecies can have some serious consequences. Consider these facts: In U.S. elementary schools, girls outperform boys on standardized tests of reading, writing, social studies, and math. By the middle school years, however, girls start to fall behind, and by high school, boys do better than girls on many kinds of standardized tests (Hedges & Nowell, 1995; Reis & Park, 2001; Stumpf & Stanley, 1998). On the Scholastic Assessment Test (SAT), used by many colleges to select students, males outscore females on the math and verbal sections (Mau & Lynn, 2001; Stumpf & Stanley, 1998). Although some people have argued that male and female brains process information differently (Geary, 1996; Kimura, 1987; Witelson, 1992), it is unlikely that differences in academic performance can be explained solely by any such biological differences, if they exist (Chipman, 1996; Feingold, 1996; Ghiselin, 1996; Hyde, 1997).

Then why do girls do worse than boys academically? Consider these pieces of the puzzle: If you ask teachers which of their current students are most academically gifted or who their most outstanding students have been over the years, an embarrassing truth leaks out—most of the students they mention are male. Many teachers, even if they are women themselves, believe that males are brighter and more likely to succeed academically than females (Jussim & Eccles, 1992). Parents hold similar beliefs about the talents of their children, and so do adolescents about their own talents (Catsambis, 1999; Raety, Vaenskae, Kasanen, & Kaerkkaeinen, 2002; Yee & Eccles, 1988).

> Prophecy is the most gratuitous form of error.
>
> *—George Eliot (Mary Ann Evans Cross), 1871*

Self-Fulfilling Prophecy

The case whereby people (1) have an expectation about what another person is like, which (2) influences how they act toward that person, which (3) causes that person to behave consistently with people's original expectations, making the expectations come true

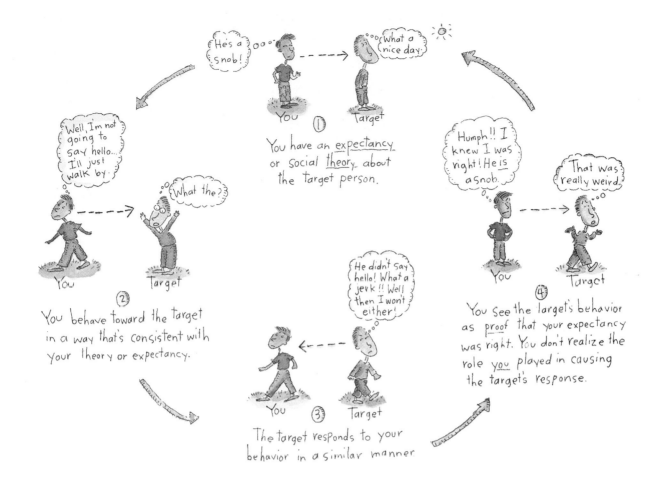

FIGURE 3.5

The self-fulfilling prophecy: A sad cycle in four acts.

Might girls do worse academically because of a self-fulfilling prophecy? Are teachers and parents treating boys and girls differently, in ways that make their expectations about gender and academic performance come true? First, let's be very clear: No one is suggesting that teachers or parents deliberately treat girls in ways that impede their performance. Nor are we suggesting that boys are always at an advantage in the classroom. Some researchers have recently suggested that teachers and parents treat boys in ways that stunt their emotional development by expecting them to act in "macho" ways, rather than expressing emotion in a more healthy manner (Kindlon & Thompson, 2000). We will focus on academic achievement, however, for there is compelling evidence that a self-fulfilling prophecy may be at work, meaning that teachers and parents unintentionally behave in ways that make their expectations about girls' achievement come true.

Consider this example, described by researchers after years spent observing teachers' behavior toward boys versus girls (Sadker & Sadker, 1994). A fifth-grade teacher is explaining a difficult problem and asks one of the girls to hold the math book so that everyone can see the problem. She then does something interesting: She turns her back to the girls (who are seated on her right) and explains the problem to the boys (who are seated on her left). Although she occasionally turns to the girls to read an example from the book, she directs virtually all of her attention to the boys, such that the girls can see only the back of her head. "The girl holding the math book had become a prop," Sadker and Sadker note. "The teacher . . . had unwittingly transformed the girls into spectators, an

Teachers can unintentionally make their expectations about their students come true by treating some students differently from others.

audience for the boys" (p. 3). The Sadkers document many such cases of teachers treating boys more favorably than girls.

Such anecdotes, while interesting, certainly do not prove that self-fulfilling prophecies are at work in our schools. It is necessary to conduct studies in which teachers' expectations are controlled experimentally. Robert Rosenthal and Lenore Jacobson (1968) did so in an elementary school in what has become one of the most famous studies in social psychology. They administered an IQ test to all of the students in the school and told the teachers that some of the students had scored so well that they were sure to "bloom" academically in the upcoming year. In fact, this was not necessarily true: The students identified as "bloomers" were chosen at random by the researchers. As we discussed in Chapter 2, the use of random assignment means that on average, the students designated as bloomers were no smarter or more likely to bloom than any of the other kids. The only way in which these students differed from their peers was in the minds of the teachers (neither the students nor their parents were told anything about the results of the test).

After creating the expectation in the teachers that certain students would do especially well, Rosenthal and Jacobson waited to see what would happen. They observed the classroom dynamics periodically, and at the end of the school year, they tested all of the children again with an actual IQ test. Did the prophecy come true? Indeed it did—the students in each class who had been labeled as bloomers showed significantly greater gains in their IQ scores than the other students did (see Figure 3.6). The teachers' expectations had become reality. Rosenthal and Jacobson's findings have since been replicated in a number of both experimental and correlational studies (Babad, 1993; Blank, 1993; Jussim, 1991; Madon, Jussim, & Eccles, 1997; Smith, Jussim, & Eccles, 1999).

Did the teachers in the Rosenthal and Jacobson (1968) study callously decide to give more attention and encouragement to the bloomers? Not at all. Most teachers are quite dedicated and would be upset to learn that they favored some students over others. Far from being a conscious, deliberate act, the self-fulfilling prophecy is instead an example of automatic thinking (Chen & Bargh, 1997). Interestingly, the teachers in the Rosenthal and Jacobson study reported that they spent slightly less time with the students who were labeled as bloomers. In subsequent studies, however, teachers have been found to treat bloomers (the students they expect to do better) differently in four general ways: (1) They create a warmer emotional climate for bloomers, giving them more personal attention, encouragement, and support; (2) they give bloomers more material to learn and material that is more difficult; (3) they give bloomers more and better feedback on their work; and (4) they give bloomers more opportunities to re-

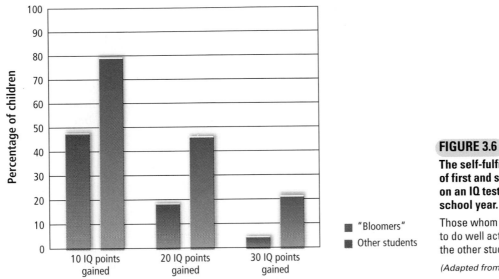

FIGURE 3.6

The self-fulfilling prophecy: Percentage of first and second graders who improved on an IQ test over the course of the school year.

Those whom the teachers expected to do well actually improved more than the other students.

(Adapted from Rosenthal & Jacobson, 1968)

spond in class and give them longer to respond (Brophy, 1983; Jussim, 1986; Rosenthal, 1994; Snyder, 1984).

Remember the teacher who taught math more to the boys than to the girls in her fifth-grade class? With her permission, she was being videotaped for a segment of the NBC television program *Dateline* on sexism in the schools. We can assume, then, that she was trying hard to treat the girls and the boys equally. Nonetheless, she favored the boys, which suggests how hard it can be to recognize that our expectations can strongly influence our behavior. (Recently, when one of us was discussing this incident in our social psychology course, we were startled to discover that a student in the class had appeared in the *Dateline* segment. We had fun watching a tape of the show and trying to pick her out of the class of fifth-grade students.)

A distressing implication of the fact that the self-fulfilling prophecy occurs automatically is that our schemas may be quite resistant to change. Suppose a teacher has the schema that boys are innately better at math than girls. "But Mr. Jones," we might reply, "how can you hold such a belief? There are plenty of girls who do very well in math." Mr. Jones would probably be unconvinced because he would have data to support his schema. "In my classes over the years," he might note, "nearly three times as many boys as girls have excelled at math." His error lies not with his characterization of the evidence but in his failure to realize his role in producing it. Robert Merton, an eminent sociologist, referred to this process as a "reign of error," whereby people can "cite the actual course of events as proof that [they were] right from the very beginning" (1948, p. 195).

Limits of Self-Fulfilling Prophecies   Does all of this mean that we are like putty in the hands of powerful people who have incorrect expectations about us? Suppose that Sarah is about to be interviewed for a job at a law firm by someone who has negative expectations about her qualifications, based, perhaps, on her gender, race, previous place of employment, or college. Will she be able to overcome these expectations and show the interviewer that she really is highly qualified for the job? Or, consistent with research on the self-fulfilling prophecy, will the interviewer mold Sarah's behavior in such a way that Sarah finds herself giving halting, inadequate answers to the questions?

Recent research confirms that self-fulfilling prophecies often occur but also demonstrates some of the conditions under which people's true nature will win out in social interaction (Madon et al., 2001). For example, self-fulfilling prophecies are most likely to occur when interviewers are distracted and do not have the ability to pay careful attention to the person they are interviewing (Biesanz, Neuberg, Smith, Asher, & Judice, 2001; Harris & Perkins, 1995). When interviewers are motivated to form an accurate impression and are not distracted, they are often able to put their expectations aside and see what the person is really like. Thus Sarah should hope that the lawyer interviewing her is not too busy or pressed for time. Otherwise, she might well fall prey to the interviewer's self-fulfilling prophecies. See the Try It! exercise below for a way to overcome your own self-fulfilling prophecies.

Cultural Determinants of Schemas   Have you ever met someone from another culture and been surprised at what he or she noticed and remembered about your country? If so, it may have been because the person was applying different schemas to what he or she saw. Tim Wilson had this experience when he was a teenager. One Sunday, a visitor from Iran came to his house for dinner. This man, Mr. Khetabdari, had arrived in the United States for the first time only a few days before. When he visited the Wilson house, Tim was idly watching a football game on television. As Mr. Khetabdari took off his coat and was introduced to the family, he glanced at the TV and recoiled with horror to the sight of the men in bizarre outfits slamming into each other. "Oh, what are they doing?" he asked. Mr. Khetabdari knew nothing about football and could not imagine why these oversized men were chasing each other while wearing strange clothes and helmets—or why Tim and his family were watching them do it. American football was so foreign to Mr. Khetabdari's schemas of the world that he was horrified by what he saw.

Clearly, an important source of our schemas is the culture in which we grow up. In fact, schemas are a very important way by which cultures exert their influ-

Try it!

Avoiding Self-Fulfilling Prophecies

1. Examine some of your own schemas and expectations about social groups, especially groups you don't particularly like. These might be members of a particular race or ethnic group, of a rival fraternity, of a political party, or people with a particular sexual orientation. Why don't you like members of this group? "Well," you might think, "one reason is that whenever I interact with these people, they seem cold and unfriendly." And you might be right. Perhaps they do respond to you in a cold and unfriendly fashion—not, however, because they are this way by nature but because they are responding to the way you have treated them.

2. Try this exercise to counteract the self-fulfilling prophecy: Find someone who is a member of a group you dislike and strike up a conversation with the person. For example, sit next to this person in one of your classes, or strike up a conversation at a party or gathering. Try to imagine that this individual is the friendliest, kindest, sweetest person you have ever met. Be as warm and charming as you can be. Don't go overboard—if, after never speaking to this person, you suddenly act like Mr. or Ms. Congeniality, you might arouse suspicion. The trick is to act as if you expect the person to be extremely pleasant and friendly.

3. Observe this person's reactions. Are you surprised by how friendly he or she responded to you? People you thought were inherently cold and unfriendly will probably behave in a warm and friendly manner themselves in response to the way you have treated them. If this doesn't work on your first encounter with the person, try it again on one or two later occasions. In all likelihood, you will find that friendliness really does breed friendliness (see Chapter 10).

ence—namely, by instilling mental structures that influence the very way we understand and interpret the world. In Chapter 5, we will see that people in different cultures have fundamentally different schemas about themselves and the social world, with some interesting consequences. For now, we point out that the schemas that our culture teaches us strongly influence what we notice and remember about the world.

One researcher, for example, interviewed a Scottish settler and a local Bantu herdsman in Swaziland, a small country in southeastern Africa (Bartlett, 1932). Both men had been present at a complicated cattle transaction that had occurred a year earlier. The Scottish man needed to consult his records to recall how many cattle were bought and sold and for how much. The Bantu man, promptly recited from memory every detail of the transaction, including from whom each ox and cow had been bought, the color of each animal, and the price of each transaction. The Bantu people's memory for cattle is so good that they do not bother to brand them; if a cow happens to wander away and get mixed up with a neighbor's herd, the owner simply goes over and takes it back, having no trouble distinguishing his cow from the dozens of others.

It is not the case that the Bantu have superior memories overall. Each of us has a superb memory in the areas that are important to us, areas for which we consequently have well-developed schemas. Cattle are a central part of the Bantu economy and culture, and therefore the Bantu have well-developed schemas about cattle. To an American, one cow might look like any other. This person undoubtedly has well-developed schemas and hence an excellent memory for things that are quite foreign to the Bantu, such as transactions on the New York Stock Exchange, pop music lyrics, or, for that matter, American football.

To summarize, we have seen that the amount of information we face every day is so vast that we have to reduce it to a manageable size. In addition, much of this information is ambiguous or difficult to decipher. One way we deal with this "blooming, buzzing, confusion," in William James's words, is to rely on schemas, which help us reduce the amount of information we need to take in and help us interpret ambiguous information. These schemas are applied quickly, effortlessly, and unintentionally; in short, they are one form of automatic thinking. Another form of automatic thinking is to apply specific rules and shortcuts when

The Bantu have an excellent memory for their cattle, possibly because they have much better schemas for cattle than people in other cultures do.

thinking about the social world. These shortcuts are, for the most part, extremely useful, but as we will see, they can sometimes lead to erroneous inferences about the world.

Mental Strategies and Shortcuts

Think back to your decision of where to apply to college. How did you narrow down your list from the schools you considered to the ones to which you actually applied? One strategy you might have taken would be to investigate thoroughly every one of the more than three thousand colleges and universities in the United States. You could have read every catalog from cover to cover, visited every campus, and interviewed as many faculty members, deans, and students as you could find. Getting tired yet? Such a strategy would, of course, be prohibitively time-consuming and costly. Instead of considering every college and university, most high school students narrow down their choice to a small number of options and find out what they can about these schools.

This example is like many decisions and judgments we make in everyday life. When deciding which job to accept, what car to buy, or whom to marry, we usually do not conduct a thorough search of every option ("OK, it's time for me to get married; I think I'll consult the Census Bureau's lists of unmarried adults in my town and begin my interviews tomorrow"). Instead, we use mental strategies and shortcuts that make the decisions easier, allowing us to get on with our lives without turning every decision into a major research project. These shortcuts do not always lead to the best decision. For example, if you had exhaustively studied every college and university in the United States, maybe you would have found one that you liked better than the one where you are now. Mental shortcuts are efficient, however, and usually lead to good decisions in a reasonable amount of time (Gigerenzer, 2000; Gilovich & Griffin, 2002; Nisbett & Ross, 1980).

What shortcuts do people use? One, as we have already seen, is to use schemas to understand new situations. Rather than starting from scratch when examining our options, we often apply our previous knowledge and schemas. We have many such schemas, about everything from colleges and universities (e.g., what Ivy League colleges and big midwestern universities are like) to other people (e.g., teachers' beliefs about the abilities of boys versus girls). When making specific kinds of judgments and decisions, however, we do not always have a ready-made schema to apply. At other times, there are too many schemas that could apply, and it is not clear which one to use. What do we do?

At times like these, people often use mental shortcuts called **judgmental heuristics.** The word *heuristic* comes from the Greek word meaning "discover"; in the field of social cognition, heuristics are the mental shortcuts people use to make judgments quickly and efficiently. Before discussing these heuristics, we should note that they do not guarantee that people will make accurate inferences about the world. Sometimes heuristics are inadequate for the job at hand or are misapplied, leading to faulty judgments. In fact, a good deal of research in social cognition has focused on just such mistakes in reasoning; we will document many such mental errors in this chapter, such as the case of teachers who mistakenly believed that boys were smarter than girls. As we discuss the mental strategies that sometimes lead to errors, however, keep in mind that people use heuristics for a reason: Most of the time, they are highly functional and serve us well.

How Easily Does It Come to Mind? The Availability Heuristic Suppose you are sitting in a restaurant with several friends one night when it becomes clear that the waiter made a mistake with one of the orders. Your friend Alphonse ordered the veggie burger with onion rings but instead got the veggie burger with fries. "Oh, well," he says, "I'll just eat the fries." This starts a discussion of whether he should have sent back his order, and some of the gang accuse Alphonse of not

Judgmental Heuristics

Mental shortcuts people use to make judgments quickly and efficiently being assertive enough. Suppose he turns to you and asks, "Do you think I'm an unassertive person?" How would you answer?

One way, as we have seen, would be to call on a ready-made schema that provides the answer. If you know Alphonse well and have already formed a picture of how assertive he is, you can recite your answer easily and quickly: "Don't worry, Alphonse, if I had to deal with a used-car salesman, you'd be the first person I'd call." Suppose, though, that you've never really thought about how assertive Alphonse is and have to think about your answer. In these situations, we often rely on how easily different examples come to mind. If it is easy to think of times Alphonse acted assertively (e.g., the time he stopped someone from butting in line in front of him at the movies), you will conclude that Alphonse is a pretty assertive guy. If it is easier to think of times Alphonse acted unassertively (e.g., the time he let a phone solicitor talk him into an expensive long-distance calling plan), you will conclude that he is pretty unassertive.

This mental rule of thumb is called the **availability heuristic,** which is basing a judgment on the ease with which you can bring something to mind (Dougherty, Gettys, & Ogden, 1999; Schwarz & Vaughn, 2002; Tversky & Kahneman, 1973). There are many situations in which the availability heuristic is a good strategy to use. If you can easily recall several instances when Alphonse stood up for himself, he probably is an assertive person; if you can easily recall several times when he was timid or meek, he probably is not. The trouble with the availability heuristic is that sometimes what is easiest to remember is not typical of the overall picture, leading to faulty conclusions.

When physicians are diagnosing diseases, for example, it might seem relatively straightforward for them to observe people's symptoms and figure out what disease, if any, they have. Sometimes, though, symptoms might be a sign of several different disorders. Do doctors use the availability heuristic, whereby they are more likely to consider diagnoses that come to mind easily? Several studies of medical diagnoses suggest that the answer is yes (Eraker & Politser, 1988; Schiffmann, Cohen, Nowik, & Selinger, 1978; Weber, Bockenholt, Hilton, & Wallace, 1993).

Consider Dr. Robert Marion's diagnosis of Nicole, a bright, sweet, 9-year-old girl who came to his office one day. Nicole was normal in every way except that once or twice a year she had strange neurological attacks, characterized by

Availability Heuristic
A mental rule of thumb whereby people base a judgment on the ease with which they can bring something to mind

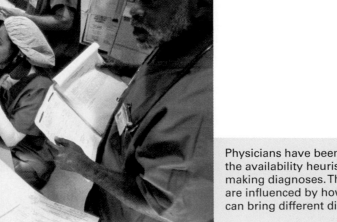

Physicians have been found to use the availability heuristic when making diagnoses. Their diagnoses are influenced by how easily they can bring different diseases to mind.

disorientation, insomnia, slurred words, and strange mewing sounds. Nicole had been hospitalized three times, had seen over a dozen specialists, and had undergone many diagnostic tests, including CT scans, brain-wave tests, and virtually every blood test there is. Still, the doctors were stumped. Within minutes of seeing her, however, Dr. Marion correctly diagnosed her problem as a rare inherited blood disorder called acute intermittent porphyria (AIP). The blood chemistry of people with this disorder often gets out of sync, causing a variety of neurological symptoms. It can be controlled with a careful diet and by avoiding certain medications.

How did Dr. Marion diagnose Nicole's disorder so quickly when so many other doctors failed to do so? He had just finished writing a book on the genetic diseases of historical figures, including a chapter on King George III of England, who—you guessed it—suffered from AIP. "I didn't make the diagnosis because I'm a brilliant diagnostician or because I'm a sensitive listener," Dr. Marion admitted. "I succeeded where others failed because [Nicole] and I happened to run into each other in exactly the right place, at exactly the right time" (Marion, 1995, p. 40).

In other words, Dr. Marion used the availability heuristic. AIP happened to come to mind quickly because in Dr. Marion had just read about it, making the diagnosis easy. Though this was a happy outcome of the use of the availability heuristic, it is easy to see how it can go wrong. As Dr. Marion says, "Doctors are just like everyone else. We go to the movies, watch TV, read newspapers and novels. If we happen to see a patient who has symptoms of a rare disease that was featured on the previous night's 'Movie of the Week,' we're more likely to consider that condition when making a diagnosis" (Marion, 1995, p. 40). That's fine if your disease happens to be the topic of last night's movie. It's not so good if your illness doesn't happen to be available in your doctor's memory, as was the case with the twelve doctors Nicole had seen previously.

Do people use the availability heuristic to make judgments about themselves? It might seem like we have well-developed ideas about our own personalities, such as how assertive we are, but often we lack firm schemas about our own traits (Markus, 1977). We thus might make judgments about ourselves based on how easily we can recall examples of our own behavior. To see if this is true, researchers performed a clever experiment in which they altered how easy it was for people to remember examples of their own past behaviors (Schwarz et al., 1991). In one condition, they asked people to think of six times they had acted assertively. Most people readily thought of times they turned down persistent salespeople and stood up for themselves. In another condition, the researchers asked people to think of twelve times they had acted assertively. This group had to try very hard to think of this many examples. All participants were then asked to rate how assertive they thought they really were.

The question was, did people use the availability heuristic (the ease with which they could bring examples to mind) to infer how assertive they were? As seen on the left-hand side of Figure 3.7, they did. People asked to think of six ex-

FIGURE 3.7

Availability and assertiveness.

People asked to think of six times they behaved assertively found it easy to do so and concluded that they were pretty assertive people. People asked to think of twelve times they behaved assertively found it difficult to think of so many examples and concluded they were not very assertive people (see the left-hand side of the graph). Similar results were found among people asked to think of six or twelve times they behaved unassertively (see the right-hand side of the graph). These results show that people often base their judgments on availability, or how easily they can bring information to mind.

(Adapted from Schwartz et al., 1991)

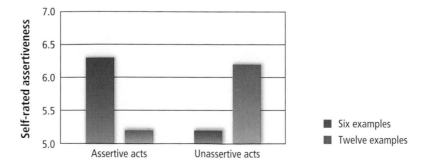

amples rated themselves as relatively assertive because it was easy to think of this many examples ("Hey, this is easy—I guess I'm a pretty assertive person"). People asked to think of twelve examples rated themselves as relatively unassertive because it was difficult to think of this many examples ("Hmm, this is hard—I must not be a very assertive person"). Other people were asked to think of six or twelve times they had acted unassertively, and similar results were found—those asked to think of six examples rated themselves as relatively unassertive (see the right-hand side of Figure 3.7). In short, people use the availability heuristic—the ease with which they can bring examples to mind—when making judgments about themselves and other people.

How Similar Is A to B? The Representativeness Heuristic   Suppose that you attend a state university in New York. At the student union one day, you meet a student named Brian. Brian has blond hair and a deep tan, seems to be very mellow, and likes to go to the beach. What state do you think Brian is from? Because Brian matches a common stereotype for Californians, you might guess that he was from there. If so, you would be using the **representativeness heuristic,** which is a mental shortcut we use to classify something according to how similar it is to a typical case, such as how similar Brian is to your conception of Californians (Gilovich & Savitsky, 2002; Kahneman & Tversky, 1973; Kahneman & Frederick, 2002; Tversky & Kahneman, 1974).

Categorizing things according to representativeness is often a perfectly reasonable thing to do. If we did not use the representativeness heuristic, how else would we decide where Brian comes from? Should we just randomly choose a state, without making any attempt to judge his similarity to our conception of students from New York State versus out-of-state students? Actually, there is another source of information we might use. If we knew nothing about Brian, it would be wise to guess that he was from New York State, because at state universities there are more in-state than out-of-state students. If we guessed New York State, we would be using what is called **base rate information,** information about the relative frequency of members of different categories in the population (e.g., the percentage of students at New York state universities who are from New York).

What do people do when they have both base rate information (e.g., knowing that there are more New Yorkers than Californians at a university) and contradictory information about the person in question (e.g., knowing that Brian is blond and mellow and likes to hang out at the beach)? Kahneman and Tversky (1973) found that people do not use base rate information sufficiently, paying most attention to how representative the information about the specific person is of the general category (e.g., Californians). Though this is not a bad strategy if the information about the person is very reliable, it can get us into trouble when the information is flimsy. Given that the base rate of Californians attending state universities in New York is low, you would need to have very good evidence that this person was a Californian before ignoring the base rate and guessing that he is one of the few exceptions. And given that it is not that unusual to find people from eastern states who have blond hair, are laid-back, and like to go to the beach, you would be wise to use the base rate in this instance.

We don't mean to imply that people totally ignore base rate information (Koehler, 1993, 1996). Baseball managers consider the overall likelihood of left-handed batters getting a hit off of left-handed pitchers when deciding who to send up as a pinch hitter, and birdwatchers consider the prevalence of different species of birds in their area when identifying individual birds ("That probably wasn't a bay-breasted warbler because they've never been seen in this area"). The point is that people often focus too much on individual characteristics of what they observe ("But it did seem to have a chestnut-colored throat; hmm, maybe it was a bay-breasted warbler") and too little on the base rates.

Is this woman from California or Michigan? People often make such judgments by using the representativeness heuristic, a mental shortcut whereby we classify something according to how similar it is to a typical case, such as how similar the woman is to your conception of Californians.

Representativeness Heuristic

A mental shortcut whereby people classify something according to how similar it is to a typical case

Base Rate Information

Information about the frequency of members of different categories in the population

Throughout history, for example, people have assumed that the cure for a disease must resemble—be representative of—the symptoms of the disease, even when this isn't the case. At one time, eating the lungs of a fox was thought to be a cure for asthma, because foxes have a strong respiratory system (Mill, 1843). Such a reliance on representativeness may even impede the discovery of the actual cause of a disease. Around the turn of the twentieth century, an editorial in a Washington newspaper denounced the foolhardy use of federal funds to research far-fetched ideas about the causes of yellow fever, such as the absurd contention of one Walter Reed that yellow fever was caused by, of all things, a mosquito (Nisbett & Ross, 1980).

Taking Things at Face Value: The Anchoring and Adjustment Heuristic Suppose you are a judge who is trying to decide what sentence to give a defendant who has been convicted of rape. There are all kinds of relevant facts you could bring to bear on this important decision, such as the severity of the crime, sentencing guidelines from state or federal law, and your sense of how likely the defendant is to commit rape again. Surprisingly, you might also be influenced by quite irrelevant numbers that happen to be on your mind, such as the sentence you gave to the previous defendant or the fact that you are attending someone's seventy-fifth birthday party that night. If you are thinking about the number 75, you might give a higher sentence than if the number 5 were on you mind.

If so, you would be using the **anchoring and adjustment heuristic** (Tversky & Kahneman, 1974), a mental shortcut in which people use a number or value as a starting point and then adjust insufficiently from this anchor. If the number 75 is on your mind, you might begin by saying, "Hmm, seventy-five—that sounds a little high; I'll give the guy sixty years." If the number 5 was on your mind, you might start with this and adjust a little upward, ending up with a substantially lower sentence than if you had started with 75.

Like all the other mental shortcuts we have considered, the anchoring and adjustment heuristic is a good strategy under many circumstances. If you have reason to believe that a starting value is valid and informative, then it can be a logical place to start. Suppose, for example, that an experienced prosecutor whom you respect recommends a prison sentence of seventy-five years. Using this as a starting point would be quite reasonable, because the prosecutor knows many more details about the case than you do and probably has a good reason for this recommendation. This is in fact what judges did in a recent study (Englich & Mussweiler, 2001). They gave a significantly longer prison sentence in a hypothetical rape case when the prosecutor recommended a high sentence versus a low one.

The problem with anchoring and adjustment is that people are sometimes influenced by completely arbitrary anchor values. The same study, for example, found that judges gave higher sentences when they read that a first-year computer science student recommended a long sentence than when the computer science student recommended a short sentence, even though virtually all of the judges said that the computer science student's recommendation had no bearing on their decision. Many other studies have found that completely arbitrary starting values influence people's judgments. Tversky and Kahneman (1974), for example, spun a wheel of fortune and asked people to consider whether the number that came up was higher or lower than the percentage of African nations in the United Nations. People gave a higher estimate when the wheel of fortune stopped on a high number than when it stopped on a low number. Similar anchoring effects have been found in many other studies (Chapman & Johnson, 2002; Epley & Gilovich, 2001; Mussweiler & Strack, 1999; Slovic & Lichtenstein, 1971; Wilson, Houston, Etling, & Brekke, 1996).

Anchor values can influence us in two ways. First, when we consider a starting point, we selectively retrieve from memory information that is consistent

Anchoring and Adjustment Heuristic

A mental shortcut whereby people use a number or value as a starting point and then adjust insufficiently from this anchor

with it. A judge who initially considers seventy-five years as a possible sentence, for example, is likely to bring to mind information consistent with that number: "Well, it was a heinous crime, and the person seems like he might be a serial rapist." Because information consistent with a long prison term is in mind, the judge is likely to stick to a high number when making the final decision ("Seventy-five years is a little high, but sixty years sounds about right"; Mussweiler & Strack, 1999). This effect of anchoring is related to the role of accessibility we discussed earlier. The starting point increases the accessibility of thoughts that are consistent with it (e.g., reasons why the criminal deserves a long sentence).

Sometimes, however, a starting point does not make us generate thoughts consistent with it because we know it is wrong. This is particularly true with values that people generate themselves as a starting point but that they know are incorrect. When asked what year George Washington was elected president of the United States, for example, most Americans start with the year that the United States declared independence from Britain, 1776. They know that this year is incorrect—Washington wasn't elected president until well after the Revolutionary War. Therefore, this year is unlikely to make people think of reasons it might be true (that is, people are unlikely to generate reasons why Washington was elected that year). Instead, they use 1776 as a starting point and adjust upward ("Well, I know it was a little after that; I'll say 1780"). The problem is that people do not adjust enough from their starting points, even when they know they are wrong (Epley & Gilovich, 2001). They stick too closely to the value they started with. How do heuristics influence your thinking? Take the quiz in the Try It! exercise on page 80 to find out.

The Pervasiveness of Automatic Thinking

At this point, you might be wondering why we have spent so much time on the automatic, nonconscious type of social cognition. Didn't we say earlier that there are two modes of thinking, automatic and controlled? Isn't it possible to think about the social world slowly, carefully, and deliberately, such as when we take time to sit down and really think a problem through? Indeed it is. We've spent so much time on automatic thinking, however, because it is so pervasive and dominates much of our mental lives. Just as modern jetliners fly mostly on automatic pilot, so do people rely on a great deal on automatic thinking to get through their days.

But how can this be when it seems like so much of our lives is governed by our conscious deliberations? Many decisions, such as where to go to college or whom to date, are accompanied by deliberative, conscious, thinking. Yet even big decisions like these can be influenced by automatic thinking, such as when we use judgmental heuristics when deciding where to apply to college. Obviously, conscious thinking is extremely important, though, especially when people try to correct or fix mistakes in their automatic thinking.

We cannot leave this topic, however, without pointing out that just because people think they are consciously controlling their actions does not necessarily mean they are. Daniel Wegner (2002) argues that the sense that people have of consciously willing an action can be an illusion, a feeling that we create when our actions were really controlled by either our automatic thinking or the external environment.

Have you ever seen children in a video arcade furiously working the controls, believing that they are playing the game, when in fact they never put money in the machine and are watching the demonstration program? Occasionally, when the children pushed the controls in one direction, the game did appear to respond to the commands, making it hard for the children to realize that in fact they had no control over what was happening (Wegner, 2002). Adults are not immune from such illusions of control. People who are able to

Answer each of the following questions.

1. Consider the letter *R* in the English language. Do you think that this letter occurs more often as the first letter of words (e.g., *rope*) or more often as the third letter of words (e.g., *park*)?
   a. more often as the first letter
   b. more often as the third letter
   c. about equally often as the first and as the third letter

2. Which of these do you think causes more fatalities in the United States?
   a. accidents
   b. strokes
   c. accidents and strokes in approximately equal numbers

3. Suppose you flipped a fair coin six times. Which sequence is more likely to occur, HTTHTH or HHHTTT? (H = heads, T = tails)
   a. HTTHTH is more likely
   b. HHHTTT is more likely
   c. both sequences are equally likely

4. After flipping a coin and observing the sequence TTTTT, what is the probability that the next flip will be heads?
   a. less than .5
   b. .5
   c. greater than .5

See page 91 for the answers.

choose their lottery numbers, for example, are more confident that they will win than people who are assigned numbers (Langer, 1975). And what sports fans haven't felt that they helped a favorite team by crossing their fingers at a key moment in the game?

Sometimes people believe they are exerting less control over their actions than they really are. A number of years ago, for example, a new technique called facilitated communication was developed to allow communication-impaired people, such as those suffering from autism and cerebral palsy, to express themselves. A trained facilitator held the fingers and arm of a communication-impaired client at a computer keyboard to make it easier for the client to type answers to questions. This technique caused great excitement. People who had been unable to communicate with the outside world suddenly seemed to become quite verbose, voicing all sorts of thoughts and feelings with the aide of the facilitator. Parents were thrilled by the sudden opportunity to communicate with their previously silent autistic children.

Facilitated communication was soon discredited, however, when it became clear that it was not the communication-impaired person who was doing the typing but, unwittingly, the facilitator. In one well-designed study, for example, researchers asked separate questions of the facilitator and the communication-impaired person over headphones. The facilitator might have heard "How do you feel about today's weather?" while the communication-impaired person heard "How did you like your lunch today?" The answers that were typed matched the questions the facilitator heard (e.g., "I wish it were sunnier"), not the ones posed to the communication-impaired client (Wegner, Fuller, & Sparrow, in press; Wheeler, Jacobson, Paglieri, & Schwartz, 1993). The facilitators were not deliberating faking it; they genuinely believed that it was the communication-impaired person who was choosing what to type and that they were simply helping them move their fingers on the keyboard.

These examples illustrate that there can be a disconnect between our conscious sense of how much we are causing our own actions and how much we really are causing them. Sometimes we overestimate the amount of control we have, as when we believe that crossing our fingers will help our favorite sports team. Sometimes we underestimate the amount of control we have, as with the facilitators who thought it was the client choosing what to type when they were unconsciously doing it themselves (Wegner, 2002).

We turn now to the kind of thinking we are most aware of: slow, deliberate, and conscious. The way in which controlled, conscious thinking interacts with automatic thinking is one of the most intriguing issues in social cognition, as we will now see.

CONTROLLED SOCIAL COGNITION: HIGH-EFFORT THINKING

Richard Wilkins, a Washington, D.C., lawyer, was returning from his grandfather's funeral in Maryland when a state trooper pulled him over and asked to search his car. Wilkins refused, but the trooper let loose a drug-sniffing dog anyway. While Wilkins and his family sat in the car helplessly, the dog sniffed the entire exterior, including the windshield and taillights. The dog found nothing. "We were completely humiliated," Wilkins said ("Driving while Black," 1999). Wilkins, an African American, may have been a victim of racial profiling, whereby the police target and stop pedestrians, airline passengers, and motorists on the basis of their race.

Racial profiling has received a great deal of attention since the events of September 11, 2001. Because the terrorists who flew the planes into the World Trade Center towers were of Middle Eastern descent, some people feel that anyone who looks like they might be of a similar background should receive special scrutiny when flying on commercial airlines. On the New Year's Eve after the attacks, for example, Michael Dasrath and Edgardo Cureg boarded a Continental Airlines flight from New Jersey to Tampa. Dasrath was a U.S. citizen who was born in South America, and Cureg was a U.S. resident from the Philippines. Both had successfully passed through extensive security checks. Dasrath, seated in first class, was removed from the plane when a woman with a dog complained that he made her uncomfortable. Dasrath was also removed from the flight, allegedly because he made other passengers nervous. Neither man posed a threat, but because they had brown skin, they were singled out and refused service. Both are suing the airlines for violating their civil rights ("Judge Rules," 2002).

These examples of racial profiling bear some similarities to the tragedy of Amadou Diallo, discussed at the beginning of the chapter. In both cases, innocent people were suspected of a crime because of the color of their skin. In other respects, however, the examples are quite different. In Diallo's case, the police had very little time to react—seconds or less—and could not think carefully about what Diallo was reaching for. More than likely, the police officers' automatic thinking took over. In Wilkins's case, the police officer had ample time to decide whether to pull him over. Presumably, the officer's decision was a more conscious and deliberative one. In fact, there is evidence that some police departments in the United States have encouraged their officers to stop black and Hispanic motorists in disproportionately high numbers, suggesting that racial

Racial profiling is official action toward people based on their race, ethnicity, or national origin instead of their behavior. Since the tragic events of September 11, 2001, some innocent people who looked like they might be of Middle Eastern descent have not been allowed on airplanes.

profiling is a conscious policy decision in these departments and not the result of automatic thinking (Drummond, 1999). Similarly, in the case of the men removed from the airplane, the airline officials presumably had ample time to think about and consider their actions.

Racial prejudice can thus be the result of automatic thinking or conscious, deliberative thinking—an issue we will take up in detail in Chapter 13. For now, we use this example to illustrate the more conscious, controlled type of social cognition. **Controlled thinking** is defined as thinking that is conscious, intentional, voluntary, and effortful. People can usually turn on or turn off this type of thinking at will and are fully aware of what they are thinking. Further, this kind of thinking is effortful in the sense that it requires mental energy. People have the capacity to think in a conscious, controlled way about only one thing at a time; they cannot be thinking about what they will eat for lunch today at the same time they are thinking through a complex math problem. Automatic thinking, in contrast, can occur in the background with no conscious effort at all.

One purpose of controlled thinking is to provide checks and balances for automatic thinking. Just as an airline captain can turn off the automatic pilot and take control of the plane when trouble occurs, controlled thinking takes over when unusual events occur. Unlike automatic thinking, however, controlled thinking requires motivation and effort. We have to want to do it, and we have to have the time and energy to devote to it. Thus when the stakes are low and we do not particularly care about the accuracy of a decision or judgment, we often let our automatic thinking do the job without bothering to check or correct it. If we are idly watching television after a long day, for example, we might be judging the people we see on the tube rather automatically. Similarly, we might react to the commercials in a mindless way, expending little mental effort to examine what is being said. The message that "nine out of ten doctors recommend this brand of pain reliever" might register automatically, without much critical thinking to evaluate the claim.

Sometimes, though, people have the motivation and mental capacity to analyze the commercial. Suppose that you have been looking around for a new car and have been considering all-wheel-drive station wagons. When a commercial for one of these cars comes on, you are likely to sit up and take notice, analyzing what is said in much more detail. As we will see in Chapter 7, there is considerable evidence that when people are motivated to analyze a message carefully and have the mental capacity to do so (that is, if they are not tired or distracted), they

Controlled Thinking

Thinking that is conscious, intentional, voluntary, and effortful go off automatic pilot and engage in more controlled thinking, paying closer attention to the merits of what is being said. When people are not very motivated ("ho-hum, another commercial for pain relievers") or are distracted (the kids are screaming in the background), they remain on automatic pilot and are influenced more by the surface characteristics of the message (Chaiken, 1987; Petty & Cacioppo, 1986; Petty, Priester, & Brinol, 2002; Petty & Wegener, 1999).

Similarly, when people care enough to analyze a problem thoughtfully, they can sometimes avoid the kinds of biases that result from automatic thinking. In some of the studies we reviewed earlier, the tasks were not all that important to people. Several studies show that when more consequential tasks are involved, people make more complex and more accurate inferences (e.g., Kruglanski & Webster, 1996; Martin, Seta, & Crelia, 1990; Strack & Hannover, 1996). In one study, for example, female participants read about another student named Tom Ferguson. They learned how interested Tom was in dating each of several women and learned several things about these women, such as how good their sense of humor was. They were asked to judge the relationship between the qualities of the women (e.g., their sense of humor) and Tom's willingness to date them. As with many other studies that have examined people's ability to judge such relationships, the participants used simple strategies that were not particularly accurate (Harkness, DeBono, & Borgida, 1985).

Unless, that is, they were highly motivated to make careful judgments. Some of the participants thought that they were taking part in a dating study and that they themselves would be dating Tom for several weeks. Now that the women cared more about what Tom liked and disliked in a dating partner, they put their high-effort thinking into gear and made judgments that were more accurate. When the stakes are high, people use more sophisticated, effortful strategies than when the stakes are low and hence make more accurate judgments (Dunn & Wilson, 1990; Kruglanski, 1989; Stangor & McMillan, 1992; Tetlock, 1992; Trope & Lieberman, 1996).

We do not mean to imply that with a little motivation, people become perfect reasoners. In later chapters we'll see examples of people making erroneous judgments about the social world despite their best efforts and intentions. Human judgment is not like a car engine, where it is easy to tell when it breaks down and what is wrong with it. It is often hard to know exactly how we formed a judgment, whether it is biased, and how much, if at all, we should correct it (Martin, 1986; Schwarz & Bless, 1992; Wegener & Petty, 1997; Wilson & Brekke, 1994). Nonetheless, it is often true that the more motivated we are to form unbiased judgments, the greater the likelihood is that we will do so.

Automatic Believing, Controlled Unbelieving

There are other interesting ways in which controlled thinking provides checks and balances on automatic thinking. As we saw earlier, when people use the anchoring and adjustment heuristic, they use starting points in their judgments and fail to adjust sufficiently from these points. One explanation for this process is that people automatically use whatever they encounter as a starting point without even fully realizing that they are doing so and then attempt to adjust from this starting point with controlled thinking. Three centuries ago, the philosopher Benedict Spinoza observed that when people initially see, hear, or learn something, they take it at face value and assume it is true. Only after accepting the veracity of a fact do they go to the effort of deciding whether it might be false. Although other philosophers (e.g., René Descartes) have disagreed, recent research has shown that Spinoza was right (Gilbert, 1991; 2002; Krull & Dill, 1996).

Daniel Gilbert argues that people are programmed to believe automatically everything they hear and see. This automatic "seeing is believing" process is built into human beings because pretty much everything people hear and see *is* true. If we had to stop and deliberate about the truthfulness of everything we encountered, life would be difficult indeed ("Let's see, it looks like a car careening toward me down the street, but maybe it's really an illusion . . . CRASH!"). Occasionally, however, what we see or hear is not true; thus we need a check-and-balance system to be able to "unaccept" what we have initially believed. When we hear a politician say, "If elected, I will lower your taxes, balance the budget, reduce crime, and wash your car every Sunday afternoon," we are in automatic thinking mode and initially believe what we hear. However, the "unacceptance" part of the process quickly kicks in, making us doubt the truth of what we've just heard. ("Now wait just a minute . . ."). The process is depicted in Figure 3.8.

The interesting thing about this process is that the initial acceptance part occurs automatically, which, as we have seen, means that it occurs unconsciously and without effort or intention. The assessment and unacceptance part of the process is the product of controlled thinking, however, which means that people have to have the energy and motivation to do it. When we are preoccupied, tired, or unmotivated, the acceptance part of the process will operate unchecked, and this can lead to the acceptance of falsehoods. If we are mindlessly watching television and not thinking very carefully about what is being said, for example, we might automatically accept the outlandish claims being made in the commercials (see Chapter 7).

Thought Suppression and Ironic Processing

Being preoccupied and unable to engage in controlled thinking has another interesting consequence: It reduces our ability to engage in **thought suppression**— the attempt to avoid thinking about something we would just as soon forget, such as a lost love, an unpleasant encounter with one's boss, or a delectable piece of cheesecake in the refrigerator. According to Daniel Wegner (1992, 1994; Wenzlaff & Wegner, 2000), successful thought suppression depends on the interaction of two processes, one relatively automatic and the other relatively controlled. The automatic part of the system, called the *monitoring process*, searches for evidence that the unwanted thought is about to intrude on consciousness. Once the unwanted thought is detected, the more controlled part of the system, called the *operating process*, comes into play. This is the effortful, conscious attempt to distract oneself by finding something else to think about. These two processes operate in tandem, like two parents conspiring to keep their kids away from junk food outlets at a mall. One parent's job, akin to the monitoring process, is to keep a watch out for the food joints and let the other one know when they are in the vicinity ("McDonald's alert!"). The other parent's job, akin to the operating process, is then to divert the kids' attention away from

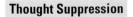

Thought Suppression

The attempt to avoid thinking about something we would prefer to forget

FIGURE 3.8

Gilbert's theory of automatic believing.

According to Daniel Gilbert (1991), people initially believe everything they hear and see. They then assess whether what they heard or saw is really true and "unaccept" it if necessary. The second and third parts of the process, in which people assess and unaccept information, take time and effort. If people are tired or preoccupied, these parts of the process are difficult to execute, increasing the likelihood that people will believe false information.

(Adapted from Gilbert, 1991)

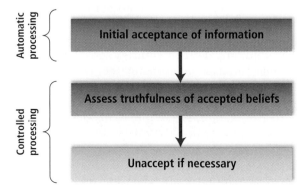

the food places ("Hey, kids, look at the giant picture of SpongeBob in that store window"). This system works pretty well as long as each process (parent) does its job, one ever alert for the topic we want to avoid and the other diverting our attention from this topic.

What happens, though, when the controlled operating process is unable to do its job because the person is tired or preoccupied? The monitoring process continues to find instances of the unwanted thought, which then intrude on consciousness unchecked by the controlled system. A state of hyperaccessibility results in which the unwanted thought occurs with high frequency. If the parent whose job it is to distract the children falls down on the job, for example, the kids will become even more aware that fast-food joints are in the vicinity because they will keep hearing the other parent point them out (Renaud & McConnell, 2002; Wenzlaff & Bates, 2000).

The irony is that when people are trying their hardest not to think about something (e.g., you are on guard not to think about jokes about short people because your 4-foot-8-inch boss is standing next to you), if people are tired or preoccupied—that is, under *cognitive load*—these thoughts are especially likely to spill out unchecked. Further, there can be an emotional and physical cost to thought suppression. In one study, medical school students wrote about a personal topic once a day for three days (Petrie, Booth, & Pennebaker, 1998). After each writing episode, some participants were asked to suppress all thoughts about what they had just written for five minutes. Compared to people who did not suppress their thoughts, people in the suppress condition showed a significant decrease in immune system functioning. In another study, women who had had an abortion were asked how much they had tried to suppress thoughts about the abortion (Major & Gramzow, 1999). The more the women reported that they tried not to think about the abortion, the greater their reported psychological distress. As you will see in the first Social Psychology in Action module, "Social Psychology and Health," it is generally better to open up about one's problems by writing about or discussing them than to try to suppress thoughts about the problems.

Mentally Undoing the Past: Counterfactual Reasoning

There is one final condition under which people are likely to go off automatic pilot and think about things more slowly and consciously: when they experience a negative event that was a "close call," such as failing a test by just a point or two. Under these conditions, we engage in **counterfactual thinking,** mentally changing some aspect of the past as a way of imagining what might have been (Gilovich & Medvec, 1995b; Kahneman & Miller, 1986; Roese, 1997; Tetlock, 2002). "If only I had answered that one question differently," you might think, "I would have passed the test."

Counterfactual thoughts can have a big influence on our emotional reactions to events. The easier it is to mentally undo an outcome, the stronger the emotional reaction to it (Landman, 1993; Miller & Taylor, 2002; Niedenthal, Tangney, & Gavanski, 1994). One group of researchers, for example, interviewed people who had suffered the loss of a spouse or child. As expected, the more people imagined ways in which the tragedy could have been averted, by mentally undoing the circumstances preceding it, the more distress they reported (Davis, Lehman, Wortman, Silver, & Thompson, 1995; see also Branscombe, Owen, Garstka, & Coleman, 1996).

Counterfactual reasoning can lead to some paradoxical effects on people's emotions. For example, who do you think would be happier, an Olympic athlete who won a silver medal (came in second) or an Olympic athlete who won a bronze medal (came in third)? Though it might seem like the athlete who performed better (the silver medal winner) would be happier, that is not what researchers predicted (Medvec, Madey, & Gilovich, 1995). They reasoned that the

Counterfactual Thinking

Mentally changing some aspect of the past as a way of imagining what might have been

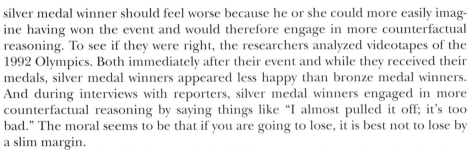

These Nigerian women look as if they'd taken first place, but actually, they came in third in the 100-meter relay at the Summer Olympics in Barcelona, Spain. Research suggests they are happier than if they'd run second. The reason is that it is harder for them to engage in counterfactual reasoning, imaging ways in which they could have won the event (Medvec, Madey, & Gilovich, 1995).

silver medal winner should feel worse because he or she could more easily imagine having won the event and would therefore engage in more counterfactual reasoning. To see if they were right, the researchers analyzed videotapes of the 1992 Olympics. Both immediately after their event and while they received their medals, silver medal winners appeared less happy than bronze medal winners. And during interviews with reporters, silver medal winners engaged in more counterfactual reasoning by saying things like "I almost pulled it off; it's too bad." The moral seems to be that if you are going to lose, it is best not to lose by a slim margin.

Earlier we described controlled thinking as conscious, intentional, voluntary, and effortful; but like automatic thinking, different kinds of controlled thought meet these requirements to different degrees. Counterfactual reasoning is clearly conscious and effortful; we know we are obsessing about the past, and this kind of thinking often takes up so much mental energy that we cannot think about anything else. It is not, however, always intentional or voluntary. Even when we want to stop dwelling on the past and move on to something else, it can be difficult to turn off the kind of "if only" thinking that characterizes counterfactual reasoning.

This is not so good if counterfactual thinking results in rumination, whereby people repetitively focus on negative things in their lives. Rumination has been found to be a contributor to depression (Lyubomirsky, Caldwell, & Nolen-Hoeksema, 1993). Thus it is not advisable to ruminate constantly about a bad test grade to the point where you can't think about anything else. Counterfactual thinking can be useful, however, if it focuses people's attention on ways that they can cope better in the future. Thinking such thoughts as "If only I had studied a little harder, I would have passed the test" can be beneficial, to the extent that it gives people a heightened sense of control over their fate and motivates them to study harder for the next test (Nasco & Marsh, 1999; Roese & Olson, 1997).

The greatest of all faults, I should say, is to become conscious of none.

—Thomas Carlyle

THE AMADOU DIALLO CASE REVISITED

By now we have seen two very different modes of social cognition, one that is effortless, involuntary, unintentional, and unconscious (automatic thinking) and another that is more effortful, voluntary, intentional, and conscious (controlled thinking). We have also seen that both kinds of thinking can lead to consequential errors. Amadou Diallo's death may have been the result of an automatic assumption made by the police officers who shot him, based on his race. Other kinds of racial prejudice may be the result of more controlled thinking, such as racial profiling. So how good a thinker is the typical human being anyway? How can we reconcile the fact that human beings have amazing cognitive abilities that have resulted in dazzling cultural and intellectual achievements but at the same time humans are prone to making consequential mental errors like the ones documented in this chapter?

One way of addressing this question is to ask which kind of thinking—automatic or controlled—is more important in human functioning. The answer to this question has engendered a lively debate among social psychologists. It is fair to say that there has been an increasing appreciation of the role of automatic thinking in human thought; more and more research has shown that people operate on automatic pilot when thinking about the social world. Some researchers have gone so far as to argue that the role of conscious, controlled thinking may be quite limited in human functioning (Bargh & Chartrand, 1999; Wegner, 2002; Wilson, 2002). Others have argued that although it can be difficult, it is possible to gain conscious control over unwanted automatic responses, such as prejudiced ones (Devine, 1989b; Devine & Monteith, 1999; Fiske, 1989a). Debate over these fundamental issues, such as the role of consciousness in human functioning, is likely to generate a good deal of research in the next several years.

What is clear is that despite the troubles they can cause, both kinds of thinking are extremely useful. It would be difficult to live without the ability to process information about the social world automatically and make quick assumptions about our environments; we would be a like a primitive, extremely slow computer, chugging away constantly as we tried to understand what was happening around us. And it is clearly to our advantage to be able to switch to controlled mode, where we can think about ourselves and the social world more slowly and carefully.

The following portrait of the social thinker has emerged: First, people are very sophisticated social thinkers who have amazing cognitive abilities. No one has been able to construct a computer that comes anywhere close to matching the power of the human brain. But there is plenty of room for improvement. The shortcomings of social thinking we have documented can be quite consequential, as demonstrated by the examples of racial prejudice in this chapter (Gilovich, 1991; Nisbett & Ross, 1980; Slusher & Anderson, 1989). Tim Wilson and colleagues have gone so far as to use the term *mental contamination* to describe the kinds of biases in our thinking that are pervasive in everyday life (Wilson & Brekke, 1994; Wilson, Centerbar, & Brekke, 2002). Perhaps the best metaphor of human thinking is that people are "flawed scientists"— brilliant thinkers who are attempting to discover the nature of the social world in a logical manner but do not do so perfectly. People are often blind to truths that don't fit their schemas and sometimes treat others in ways that make their schemas come true—something that good scientists would never do.

> Modest doubt is called the beacon of the wise. *—William Shakespeare*

Improving Human Thinking

Given that human reasoning is sometimes flawed and can have unpleasant and even tragic consequences, it is important to consider how these mistakes can be corrected. Is it possible to teach people to make better inferences, thereby avoiding some of the mistakes we have discussed in this chapter?

One approach is to make people a little more humble about their reasoning abilities. Often we have greater confidence in our judgments than we should

> The sign of a first-rate intelligence is the ability to hold two opposed ideas at the same time.
>
> —F. Scott Fitzgerald

(Blanton, Pelham, DeHart, & Carvallo, 2001; Buehler, Griffin, & Ross, 2002; Vallone, Griffin, Lin, & Ross, 1990). Teachers, for example, sometimes have greater confidence in their beliefs about the abilities of boys versus girls than is warranted. Anyone trying to improve human inference is thus up against an **overconfidence barrier** (Metcalfe, 1998). Many people seem to think that their reasoning processes are just fine the way they are and hence that there is no need for any remedial action. One approach, then, might be to address this overconfidence directly, getting people to consider the possibility that they might be wrong. This tack was taken by one team of researchers (Lord, Lepper, & Preston, 1984), who found that when asked to consider the opposite point of view to their own, people realized there were other ways to construe the world than their own way; consequently, they made fewer errors in judgment (Anderson, Lepper, & Ross, 1980; Hirt & Markman, 1995; Mussweiler, Strack, & Pfeiffer, 2000).

Another approach is to teach people directly some basic statistical and methodological principles about how to reason correctly, with the hope they will

Try it!

How Well Do You Reason?

1. The city of Middleopolis has had an unpopular police chief for a year and a half. He is a political appointee who is a crony of the mayor and he had little previous experience in police administration when he was appointed. The mayor has recently defended the chief in public, announcing that in the time since he took office, crime rates decreased by 12 percent. Which of the following pieces of evidence would most deflate the mayor's claim that his chief is competent?
   a. The crime rates of the two cities closest to Middleopolis in location and size have decreased by 18 percent in the same period.
   b. An independent survey of the citizens of Middleopolis shows that 40 percent more crime is reported by respondents in the survey than is reported in police records.
   c. Common sense indicates that there is little a police chief can do to lower crime rates. These are for the most part due to social and economic conditions beyond the control of officials.
   d. The police chief has been discovered to have business contacts with people who are known to be involved in organized crime.

2. After the first two weeks of the major league baseball season, newspapers begin to print the top ten batting averages. Typically, after two weeks, the leading batter has an average of about .450. Yet no batter in major league history has ever averaged .450 at the end of a season. Why do you think this is?
   a. A player's high average at the beginning of the season may be just a lucky fluke.
   b. A batter who has such a hot streak at the beginning of the season is under a lot of stress to maintain his performance record. Such stress adversely affects his playing.
   c. Pitchers tend to get better over the course of the season as they get more in shape. As pitchers improve, they are more likely to strike out batters, so batters' averages go down.
   d. When a batter is known to be hitting for a high average, pitchers bear down more when they pitch to him.
   e. When a batter is known to be hitting for a high average, he stops getting good pitches to hit. Instead, pitchers "play the corners" of the plate because they don't mind walking him.

See page 91 for the answers.

(Questions from Lehman, Lempert, & Nisbett, 1988, p. 442)

apply these principles in their everyday lives. Many of these principles are already taught in courses in statistics and research design, such as the idea that if you want to generalize from a sample of information (e.g., a group of welfare mothers) to a population (e.g., all welfare mothers), you must have a large, unbiased sample. Do people who take such courses apply these principles in their everyday lives? Are they less likely to make the kinds of mistakes we have discussed in this chapter? A number of recent studies have provided encouraging answers to these questions, showing that people's reasoning processes can be improved by college statistics courses, graduate training in research design, and even brief onetime lessons (Crandall & Greenfield, 1986; Malloy, 2001; Nisbett, Fong, Lehman, & Cheng, 1987; Schaller, Asp, Rosell, & Heim, 1996).

Richard Nisbett and his colleagues (1987), for example, examined how different kinds of graduate training influenced people's reasoning on everyday problems involving statistical and methodological reasoning—precisely the kind of reasoning we have considered in this chapter, such as people's understanding of how to generalize from small samples of information (see the Try It! exercise on page 88 for sample questions). The researchers predicted that students in psychology and medicine would do better on the statistical reasoning problems than students in law and chemistry would because graduate programs in psychology and medicine include more training in statistics than programs in the other two disciplines do.

As Figure 3.9 shows, after two years of graduate work, students in psychology and medicine improved on the statistical reasoning problems more than students in law and chemistry did. The improvement among the psychology graduate students was particularly impressive. Interestingly, the students in the different disciplines performed equally well on sample items from the Graduate Record Exam, suggesting that they did not differ in overall intelligence. Instead, the different kinds of training they had received appeared to influence how accurately and logically they reasoned on everyday problems (Nisbett et al., 1987). Thus there are grounds for being optimistic about people's ability to overcome the kinds of mistakes we have documented in this chapter. And you don't have to go to graduate school to do it. Sometimes it helps simply to consider the opposite, as participants in the Lord and colleagues (1984) study did. Beyond this, formal training in statistics helps, at both the graduate and undergraduate levels. So if you were dreading taking a college statistics course, take heart: It might not only satisfy a requirement for your major but improve your reasoning as well!

Overconfidence Barrier

The fact that people usually have too much confidence in the accuracy of their judgments

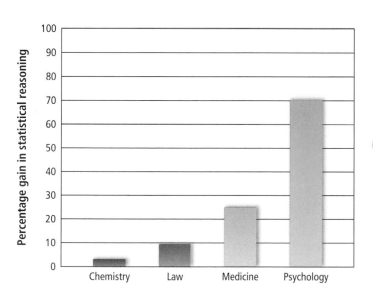

FIGURE 3.9

Performance on a test of statistical reasoning abilities by graduate students in different disciplines.

After two years of graduate study, students in psychology and medicine showed more improvement on statistical reasoning problems than students in law and chemistry did.

(Adapted from Nisbett, Fong, Lehman, & Cheng, 1987)

SUMMARY

On Automatic Pilot: Low-Effort Thinking

Social cognition is the study of how people select, interpret, and use information to make judgments and decisions. One kind of social cognition involves **automatic thinking,** thinking that is nonconscious, unintentional, involuntary, and effortless. For example, people automatically use **schemas,** cognitive structures that organize information around themes or subjects. Schemas have a powerful effect on what information we notice, think about, and remember. Although schemas are typically quite useful, they have a downside. Schemas about other people can lead to automatic stereotyping; for example, studies have found that some people automatically associate African Americans with weapons. One determinant of the schema people apply in a given situation is **accessibility,** the extent to which schemas and concepts are at the forefront of the mind and are therefore likely to be used when we are making judgments about the social world. Schemas can become accessible through **priming,** the process by which recent experiences increase the accessibility of a schema, trait, or concept. Relying on schemas is adaptive and functional up to a point, but people can be overzealous. For example, sometimes we persevere in our beliefs even when they're disproved, as shown in research on the **perseverance effect.** Finally, schemas also affect our behavior—we act on the basis of our schemas. The most fascinating example of this is the **self-fulfilling prophecy,** whereby our schemas come true by unconsciously treating others in such a way that makes them act consistently with our schemas.

In addition to schemas, people automatically use **judgmental heuristics** to help them deal with the large amount of social information they face. Heuristics are rules of thumb people follow in order to make judgments quickly and efficiently. The **availability heuristic,** the ease with which we can think of something, has a strong effect on how we view the world. The **representativeness heuristic** helps us decide how similar one thing is to another; we use it to classify people or situations on the basis of their similarity to a typical case. When using this heuristic, we have a tendency to ignore **base rate information**—the prior probability that something or someone belongs in that classification. People also rely on the **anchoring and adjustment heuristic,** in which an initial piece of information acts as an anchor, or starting point, for subsequent thoughts on the topic. One example of anchoring and adjustment is biased sampling, whereby people make generalizations from samples of information they know are biased or atypical. Although all three heuristics are useful, they can lead to incorrect conclusions. Automatic thinking has been found to be quite pervasive.

Controlled Social Cognition: High-Effort Thinking

A second kind of social cognition is **controlled thinking,** thinking that is conscious, intentional, voluntary, and effortful. People can usually turn on or turn off this type of thinking at will and are fully aware of what they are thinking. Further, this kind of thinking is effortful in the sense that it requires mental energy. People have the capacity to think in a conscious, controlled way about only one thing at a time. When people are unmotivated or preoccupied, however, controlled thinking is difficult to do. In such cases, people are more likely to accept false information and to have difficulty engaging in **thought suppression:** the attempt to avoid thinking about something they would prefer to forget. Another example of controlled thinking is **counterfactual thinking,** whereby people mentally change some aspect of the past as a way of imagining what might have been. This type of thinking influences people's emotional reactions to events.

The Amadou Diallo Case Revisited

Human beings have amazing cognitive abilities that have resulted in dazzling cultural and intellectual achievements, but at the same time humans are prone to making tragic errors, such as the shooting of Amadou Diallo. Perhaps the best metaphor of human thinking is that people are like flawed scientists—brilliant thinkers who often blind themselves to truths that don't fit their theories and who sometimes treat others in ways that make those theories come true. Though people often use strategies effectively, there is room for improvement in social thinking. For one thing, people are up against an **overconfidence barrier;** they are too confident in the accuracy of their judgments. Fortunately, recent research has indicated that some of the shortcomings of human reasoning can be improved, particularly by training in statistics.

CRITICAL THINKING QUESTIONS

1. Give examples of ways in which automatic thinking is beneficial to humans and ways in which it is harmful. If you could design the perfect human, would you change anything about the way in which automatic and controlled thinking operates?

2. Why might teachers develop an expectation about a child's academic performance that is not true? How might that expectation lead to a self-fulfilling prophecy?

3. Imagine high school students trying to decide where to apply to college. Give examples of how students might use the availability, representativeness, and an-choring and adjustment heuristics when forming impressions of different colleges and deciding where to apply.

4. Suppose you were asked to design a program to help college students think better, avoiding many of the problems discussed in this chapter. What would you do?

Answers, *Try it!* Page 80

1. The correct answer is (b), the third letter. Tversky and Kahneman (1974) found that most people thought that the answer was (a), the first letter. Why do people make this mistake? Because, say Tversky and Kahneman, they find it easier to think of examples of words that begin with *R*. By using the availability heuristic, they assumed that the ease with which they could bring examples to mind meant that such words were more common.

2. The correct answer is (b). Slovic, Fischhoff, and Lichtenstein (1976) found that most people think that (a) is correct (accidents). Why did people make this error? Again, it's the availability heuristic: Accidental deaths are more likely to be reported by the media, so people find it easier to bring to mind examples of such deaths than deaths from strokes.

3. The correct answer is (c). Both outcomes are equally likely, given that the outcomes of coin flips are random events. Tversky and Kahneman (1974) argue that due to the representativeness heuristic, people expect a sequence of random events to "look" random. That is, they expect events to be representative of their conception of randomness.

Many people therefore choose HTTHTH because this sequence is more representative of people's idea of randomness than HHHTTT. In fact, the chance that either sequence will occur is 1 out of 2^6 times, or 1 in 64. As another illustration of this point, if you were to buy a lottery ticket with four numbers, would you rather have the number 6957 or 1111? Many people prefer the former number because it seems more "random" and thus more likely to be picked. In fact, both numbers have a 1 in 1,000 chance of being picked.

4. The correct answer is (b). Many people choose (c) because they think that after five tails in a row, heads is more likely "to even things out." This is called the gambler's fallacy, which is the belief that prior random events (e.g., five tails in a row) have an influence on subsequent random events. Assuming that the coin is fair, prior tosses have no influence on future ones. Tversky and Kahneman (1974) suggest that the gambler's fallacy is due in part to the representativeness heuristic: Five tails and one head seems more representative of a chance outcome than six tails in a row.

Answers, *Try it!* Page 88

1. (a) This question assesses methodological reasoning, the recognition that there are several reasons why crime has gone down other than actions taken by the police chief and that a better test of the major's claim is to compare the crime rate in Middleopolis with other, similar cities.

2. (a) This question assesses statistical reasoning, the recognition that large samples of information are more likely to reflect true scores and abilities than small samples of information. For example, if you

flip a fair coin four times, it is not unusual to get all heads or all tails, but if you flip the coin a thousand times, it is extremely unlikely that you will get all heads or all tails. Applied to this example, this statistical principle says that when baseball players have a small number of at-bats, it is not unusual to see very high (or very low) averages just by chance. By the end of the season, however, when baseball players have hundreds of at-bats, it is highly unlikely that they will have a very high average just by luck.

Social Perception:

How We Come to Understand Other People

O ther people are not easy to figure out. Why are they the way they are? Why do they do what they do? The frequency and urgency with which we pose these questions is clear in this touching story, sent in by a reader to the *New York Times:*

> After ending an office romance, a female friend of mine threw a bag full of her former paramour's love letters, cards, and poems into an outside dumpster. The following day he called and wanted to know why she would throw out his letters. She was stunned. He explained that a homeless person going through the garbage read the correspondence and called the number found on a piece of stationery. The homeless man was curious as to why two people who seemed so in love could now be apart. "I would have called you sooner," he told the former boyfriend, "but this was the first quarter I was given today."
> (De Marco, 1994)

The homeless man was down on his luck—no home, no money, reduced to rifling through garbage cans—and yet that endless fascination with the human condition still asserted itself. He needed to know why the couple broke up. He even spent his only quarter to find out.

We all have a fundamental fascination with explaining other people's behavior. But the reasons people behave as they do are usually hidden from us. All we have to go on is observable behavior: what people do, what they say, their facial expressions, gestures, tone of voice. Unfortunately, we can't read other people's minds; we can't know, truly and completely, who they are and what they mean. Instead, we rely on our impressions and personal theories, putting them together as well as we can, hoping they will lead to reasonably accurate and useful conclusions.

Our desire to understand other people is so fundamental that it carries over into our hobbies and recreational lives. We go to movies, read novels, watch soap operas, and "people watch" at airports because thinking about the behavior even of strangers and fictional characters fascinates us (Weiner,

1985). This basic aspect of human cognition has been exploited brilliantly by "reality TV" programmers, who cast television shows with real people, not actors, and place them in unusual or even difficult situations. This new genre of television show has proved a powerhouse. Since the original version of *Survivor,* shot in 2000 on an island in the South China Sea, reality shows have crowded the top ten list of most watched shows every year (Carter, 2000, 2003). And they are multiplying—*Fear Factor, The Osbournes, American Idol, The Bachelorette, Joe Millionaire*— with new ones arriving every month. Why are these shows so popular with the American public? Because we enjoy figuring people out.

We do it all day long, as a necessary part of social survival, and then we go home, turn on the TV, and do it for fun and entertainment. For example, take two popular reality shows that are particularly interesting from a social psychological perspective: *Survivor* and *The Osbournes.* In both, the "cast members" are together for a long time (in *Survivor,* for over a month; in *The Osbournes,* for life, as they are a real family), are dependent on each other for many things, and have personal goals and desires that cause problems with the others. (This does sound like real life!)

In the *Survivor* shows, the contestants scheme, lie, and form alliances as one by one they vote their fellow contestants off the show in the hope of being the last survivor, collecting the reward of $1 million. A typical segment from one show featured one contestant confiding to another her plans and strategy for remaining on the island, then presenting a totally different story to another contestant, and finally, speaking directly into the camera to us, the TV audience, telling yet a third version that contradicted the other two (Gilbert, 2000; James, 2000). What was the truth? What would she really do? And what was she really like as a person—a deceitful, manipulative opportunist or just someone who knows how to play the game?

In *The Osbournes,* we watch a real family, consisting of heavy-metal recording star Ozzy Osbourne, his manager-wife, Sharon, and their two teenage children, Kelly and Jack. To say the family is unique is an understatement. TV cameras record nearly every moment of their home life, and the family members certainly don't seem to edit their behavior just because the cameras are present. As viewers watch the weekly episodes, they form opinions about the individual family members and their relationships with one another. As with all reality shows, *The Osbournes* poses fascinating questions about what people are going to do next, what motivates them to do what they do, and what they're really like.

Why do we care? Why do we spend so much time and energy trying to explain other people's behavior? Because doing so helps us understand and predict our social world (Heider, 1958; Kelley, 1967). In this chapter, we will discuss **social perception**—the study of how we form impressions of other people and how we make inferences about them. One important source of information that we use is people's nonverbal behavior, such as their facial expressions, body movements, and tone of voice.

NONVERBAL BEHAVIOR

What do we know about people when we first meet them? We know what we can see and hear, and even though we know we should not judge a book by its cover, this kind of easily observable information is crucial to our first impression. Physical characteristics such as attractiveness and facial type (e.g., a "baby face") influence the way we judge people (Hatfield & Sprecher, 1986; Zebrowitz, 1997; Zebrowitz & Montepare, 1992). We also pay a great deal of attention to what people say. After all, our most noteworthy accomplishment as a species is the development of verbal language.

But our words tell only part of the story. With no words at all, we can communicate volumes (Ambady & Rosenthal, 1992, 1993; De Paulo & Friedman, 1998; Gifford, 1991, 1994). **Nonverbal communication** refers to how people communicate, intentionally or unintentionally, without words. Facial expressions, tone of voice, gestures, body positions and movement, the use of touch, and eye gaze are the most frequently used and most revealing channels of nonverbal communication (Henley, 1977; Knapp & Hall, 1997). Even in a setting where you might think the verbal channel is paramount—a courtroom—various forms of nonverbal communication can prove so powerful and disruptive that a judge may be forced to prohibit them. For instance, during the famous O. J. Simpson trial, the judge reprimanded everyone in the courtroom for displaying emotions. Judge Lance Ito said, "Let me remind you that any reactions, gestures, . . . [or] facial expressions . . . made during these court sessions, especially when the jury is here, . . . are inappropriate and will result in your expulsion" (Pertman, 1995).

How does nonverbal communication work? Nonverbal cues serve many functions in communication. The primary uses of nonverbal behavior are (1) *expressing emotion* ("I'm angry"—your eyes narrow, your eyebrows lower, you stare intently, your mouth is set in a thin, straight line), (2) *conveying attitudes* ("I like you"—smiles, extended eye contact—or "I don't like you"—eyes averted, flat tone of voice, body turned away), (3) *communicating one's personality traits* ("I'm outgoing"—broad gestures, changes in inflection when speaking, an energetic tone of voice), and (4) *facilitating verbal communication* (you lower your voice and look away as you finish your sentence so that your conversational partner knows you are done and it is his or her turn to speak) (Argyle, 1975). You can explore how you use your voice to communicate in the Try It! exercise on page 96.

In addition, some nonverbal cues repeat or complement the spoken message, as when you smile while saying "I'm so happy for you!" Others actually contradict the spoken words. Communicating sarcasm is the classic example of verbal-nonverbal contradiction. Think about how you'd say "I'm so happy for you" sarcastically. (You could use your tone of voice, stressing the word *so* with an ironic twist, or you could roll your eyes as you speak, a sign of sarcasm in North American culture.) Nonverbal cues can also substitute for the verbal message. Hand gestures such as flashing the "OK" sign or drawing a finger across your throat convey clear messages without any words at all (Ekman, 1965).

> An eye can threaten like a loaded and leveled gun, or can insult like hissing or kicking; or, in its altered mood, by beams of kindness, it can make the heart dance with joy.
>
> —Ralph Waldo Emerson, The Conduct of Life

Social Perception
The study of how we form impressions of and make inferences about other people

Nonverbal Communication
The way in which people communicate, intentionally or unintentionally, without words; nonverbal cues include facial expressions, tone of voice, gestures, body position and movement, the use of touch, and gaze

Try it!

Using Your Voice as a Nonverbal Cue

Even though the words you say are full of information, the way you say them gives your listener even more of an idea of what you mean. You can take a perfectly straightforward sentence like "I don't know her" and give it many different meanings, depending on how you say it. Try saying that sentence out loud so that it communicates each of the emotions listed below. Experiment with the pitch of your voice (high or low), the speed with which you speak, the loudness or softness of your voice, and whether you stress some words and not others.

"I don't know her."

- You're angry.
- You're being sarcastic.
- You're scared.
- You're surprised.
- You're disgusted.
- You're very happy.

Now try this exercise with a friend. Turn your back to your friend as you say each sentence; you want your friend to have to rely on your voice as the only cue, without help from any facial expressions you might make. How well does he or she guess the emotions you are expressing? Have your friend try the exercise too—can you understand his or her nonverbal vocal cues? If you don't always correctly identify each other's voices, discuss what was missing or confusing about the voice. In this way, you'll be able to figure out, for example, what a "disgusted" voice sounds like as compared to an "angry" or "scared" voice.

Nonverbal forms of communication have typically been studied individually, in their separate "channels" (e.g., eye gaze or gestures), even though in everyday life nonverbal cues of many kinds occur all at the same time in a quite dazzling orchestration of information (Archer & Akert, 1980, 1984). Let's focus on a few of these channels and then turn to how we interpret the full symphony of nonverbal information as it naturally occurs.

Facial Expressions of Emotion

The crown jewel of nonverbal communication is the facial expressions channel. This aspect of communication has the longest history of research, beginning with Charles Darwin's book *The Expression of the Emotions in Man and Animals* (1872). Its primacy is due to the exquisite communicativeness of the human face (Kappas, 1997; McHugo & Smith, 1996; Wehrle, Kaiser, Schmidt, & Scherer, 2000). Look at the photographs on page 97. We bet you can figure out the meaning of these expressions with very little effort.

Evolution and Facial Expressions   Darwin's research on facial expressions has had a major impact on the field in many areas. We will focus on his belief that the primary emotions conveyed by the face are universal: All humans **encode** or express these emotions in the same way, and all humans can **decode** or interpret them with equal accuracy. Darwin's interest in evolution led him to believe that nonverbal forms of communication were "species-specific" and not "culture-specific." He stated that facial expressions were vestiges of once useful physio-

Encode

To express or emit nonverbal behavior, such as smiling or patting someone on the back

Decode

To interpret the meaning of the nonverbal behavior other people express, such as deciding that a pat on the back was an expression of condescension and not kindness

These photographs depict facial expressions of the six major emotions. Can you guess the emotion expressed on each face?

Answers: (beginning in the upper left): Anger, fear, disgust, happiness, surprise and sadness.

logical reactions. For example, if early hominids ate something that tasted terrible, they would have wrinkled their noses in displeasure and expelled the food from their mouths. Note that the photograph showing the disgusted expression demonstrates this sort of reaction. Darwin (1872) argued that such facial expressions then acquired evolutionary significance; being able to communicate such emotional states (e.g., the feeling of disgust, not for food but for another person or a situation) had survival value for the developing species (Hansen & Hansen, 1988; Izard, 1994; McArthur & Baron, 1983). Was Darwin right? Are facial expressions of emotion universal?

The answer is yes, for the six major emotional expressions: anger, happiness, surprise, fear, disgust, and sadness. For example, in a particularly well-designed study, Paul Ekman and Walter Friesen (1971) traveled to New Guinea, where they studied the decoding ability of the South Fore, a preliterate tribe that had had no contact with Western civilization. They told the Fore people brief stories with emotional content and then showed them photographs of American men and women expressing the six emotions; the Fore's job was to match the facial expressions of emotion to the stories. They were as accurate as Western subjects had been. The researchers then asked the Fore people to demonstrate, while being photographed, facial expressions that would match the stories they were told. These photographs, when later shown to American research participants, were also decoded accurately. Thus there is considerable evidence that the ability to interpret at least the six major emotions is cross-cultural—part of being human and not a product of people's cultural experience (Biehl et al., 1997; Ekman, 1993, 1994; Ekman et al., 1987; Elfenbein & Ambady, 2002; Haidt & Keltner, 1999; Izard, 1994).

> When the eyes say one thing, and the tongue another, a practiced man relies on the language of the first.
>
> —*Ralph Waldo Emerson,* The Conduct of Life

Darwin's idea of the evolutionary significance of facial expressions of emotion was supported by a simple but elegant experiment conducted by Christine Hansen and Ranald Hansen (1988). They reasoned that if the ability to pass emotional signals (e.g., via the face) from one individual to another had survival value in our species, then detecting angry faces should be particularly important, since another's anger can signal a direct threat to survival. The researchers took photographs of an encoder with three different expressions: angry, happy, and neutral (the face "at rest"). Next, they constructed photographs of "crowds," made up of many images of the person's face in one photo. Like the *Where's Waldo?* preschool book, they placed one angry face in a sea of happy or neutral faces; they also placed one happy or neutral face in a sea of the other facial expressions. The task of research participants was to find the discrepant face in the crowd as quickly as they could, and their reaction time was measured. Which face was found the fastest? The angry face, every time. For example, the angry face was found faster in the happy crowd than the happy face in the angry crowd. It appears that not only are humans good decoders of facial expressions in general, but they are particularly quick at decoding the expression that most signals potential danger: anger.

Besides the six major emotions, are there other emotional states that are communicated with distinctive and readily identifiable facial expressions? Researchers are exploring just this question for emotions such as anxiety, contempt, shame, pride, and embarrassment (Ekman, O'Sullivan, & Matsumoto, 1991, Harrigan & O'Connell, 1996; Keltner & Shiota, 2003; Matsumoto, 1992). For example, research by Dacher Keltner (1995) suggests that embarrassment has a distinctive nonverbal display as tested in his sample of Caucasian and African American undergraduates (Keltner & Buswell, 1996). Keltner's research participants were asked to perform difficult tasks that often made them feel lacking in ability or poise, all the while receiving explicit feedback from the experimenter on how they were doing. Needless to say, they often felt embarrassed (and experienced other emotions, such as amusement).

Keltner carefully coded photographs of the various expressions on their faces during the tasks, and he later asked other research participants to decode them. He concluded that a distinctive expression of embarrassment existed, composed of turning the head away, looking down, shifting the gaze to the side, evincing a controlled smile (e.g., with the lips pressed), and sometimes touching the face with one's hand—all lasting about four to five seconds in a typical instance (Keltner, 1995).

Finally, recent research suggests that there may be even more universal expressions of emotion than previously thought (Hejmadi, Davidson & Rozin, 2000). Participants viewed videotaped expressions of ten classic Hindu emotional expressions as described in the *Natyasastra,* which dates from the first to second century A.D. Translated from the Sanskrit, these emotions are anger, disgust, fear, heroism, humor-amusement, love, peace, sadness, shame-embarrassment, and wonder. The nonverbal depictions of these emotions are somewhat different from those we've discussed so far in that they combine facial expression with body movements, especially hand gestures. The researchers found that both Indian and American research participants could decode these nonverbal emotional displays with a good degree of accuracy.

Why Is Decoding Sometimes Inaccurate?   Decoding facial expressions accurately is more complicated than we have indicated, for three reasons. First, people frequently display **affect blends** (Ekman & Friesen, 1975): One part of their face registers one emotion while another part registers a different emotion. Take a look at the accompanying photographs and see if you can tell which two emotions are being expressed in each face. In the photograph on the left, we see a

Affect Blend

A facial expression in which one part of the face registers one emotion while another part of the face registers a different emotion

blend of anger (the eye and eyebrow region) and disgust (the nose and mouth region). (It may help to cover half of the photograph with your hand to see each emotional expression clearly.) This is the sort of expression you might display if a person told you something that was both horrible and inappropriate— you'd be disgusted with the content and angry that the person told you.

Second, at times people try to appear less emotional than they are so that no one will know how they really feel. For example, if someone says something mean to you, you may hide your hurt feelings, allowing nothing to show on your face. By suppressing your emotional response, you are not giving your tormentor the satisfaction of knowing he or she has upset you. Psychologists have studied what happens when people suppress their negative facial expressions; their results present an interesting cautionary tale (Gross 1998; Gross & Levenson, 1993, 1997). For example, research participants viewed several slides of people who had been physically injured (Richards & Gross, 1999). The injuries ranged from very mild to very severe (the latter being upsetting to look at). In addition, biographical information was presented about each injured person orally during the slide show. Half the research participants were told to watch the slides and listen to the background information; the other half were also told, "If you have any feelings as you watch the slides, please try your best not to let those feelings show" (p. 1036). The research participants were surreptitiously videotaped, and those who had been told to suppress their emotional expressions did a very good job of doing so. But at what cost?

The researchers found that suppressing negative emotions led participants to have significantly poorer memory for the biographical information and significantly higher blood pressure readings when compared to the participants who were allowed to express whatever emotion they felt. Thus emotional suppression impaired one aspect of cognitive functioning—memory for information encountered at the same time—and had a negative effect on one aspect of cardiovascular functioning—systolic and diastolic blood pressure.

Similar results have been found by other researchers. For example, research participants who were told to suppress their emotions during a conversation with a stranger on an upsetting topic experienced an increase in blood pressure, reported more negative emotions, and felt less rapport with their conversational partner than participants who did not engage in suppression (Butler, Egloff, Wilhelm, Smith, & Erickson, 2003). Research that focused on women with sexual-assault-related PTSD(posttraumatic stress disorder) found that the more the women suppressed their negative facial expressions while discussing the

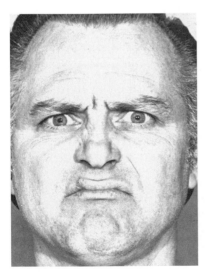

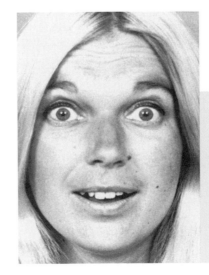

Often people express more than one emotion at the same time. Can you tell which emotions these people are expressing? The answers are printed below. (Adapted from Ekman & Friesen, 1975)

Answers: The man is expressing a blend of anger and disgust. The woman is expressing a blend of surprise and happiness.

sexual assault, the more negative emotions they reported feeling (Wagner, Roemer, Orsillo, & Litz, 2003). These data suggest that hiding your facial expressions of negative emotions such as disgust, anger, fear, or sadness may not only present difficulties for people who are trying to decode you accurately but also cause problems for you. A third reason that decoding facial expressions can be difficult has to do with culture.

Culture and the Channels of Nonverbal Communication

For decades, Paul Ekman and his colleagues have studied the influence of culture on the facial display of emotions (Ekman & Davidson, 1994; Ekman & Friesen, 1969; Matsumoto & Ekman, 1989; Matsumoto & Kudoh, 1993). They have concluded that **display rules** are particular to each culture and dictate what kinds of emotional expressions people are supposed to show.

For example, American cultural norms discourage emotional displays in men, such as grief or crying, but allow the facial display of such emotions in women. In Japan, traditional cultural rules dictate that women should not exhibit a wide, uninhibited smile (Ramsey, 1981). Japanese women will often hide a wide smile behind their hands, whereas Western women are allowed—indeed, encouraged—to smile broadly and often (Henley, 1977; La France, Hecht, & Paluck, 2003). In fact, the cultural display rules that govern Japanese nonverbal expression are surprisingly different from Western ones. Japanese norms lead people to cover up negative facial expressions with smiles and laughter and to display fewer facial expressions in general than is true in the West (Argyle, 1986; Aune & Aune, 1996; Gudykunst, Ting-Toomey, & Nishida, 1996; Richmond & McCroskey, 1995). This is undoubtedly what lies behind the Western stereotype that Asians are "inscrutable" and "hard to read."

There are, of course, other channels of nonverbal communication besides facial expressions. These nonverbal cues are shaped by culture as well. Eye contact and gaze are particularly powerful nonverbal cues. Members of American culture become suspicious when a person doesn't "look them in the eye" while speaking, and they find talking to someone who is wearing dark sunglasses quite disconcerting. However, as you can see in Figure 4.1, in other parts of the world, direct eye gaze is considered invasive or disrespectful. Another form of nonverbal communication is how people use personal space. Imagine you are talking to a person who stands too close to you (or too far away); these deviations from "normal" spacing will affect your impressions of that person. Cultures vary greatly in what is considered normative use of personal space (Hall, 1969). For example, most Americans like to have a bubble of open space, a few feet in radius, surrounding them; in comparison, in some other cultures, strangers think nothing of standing right next to each other, to the point of touching.

Gestures of the hands and arms are also a fascinating means of communication. Americans are very adept at understanding certain gestures, such as the "OK" sign, in which one forms a circle with the thumb and forefinger and the rest of the fingers curve above the circle, and "flipping the bird," in which one bends all the fingers down at the first knuckle except the longest, middle finger. Gestures like these, for which there are clear, well-understood definitions, are called **emblems** (Ekman & Friesen, 1975; Archer, 1997a). The important point about emblems is that they are not universal; each culture has devised its own emblems, and these need not be understandable to people from other cultures (see Figure 4.1). Thus "flipping the bird" will be a clear communicative sign in American society, whereas in some parts of Europe, you'd need to make a quick gesture with a cupped hand under your chin to convey the same message. President George H. W. Bush once used the "V for victory" sign (where two fingers form a V shape), but he did it backward—the palm of his hand was facing him instead of the audience. Unfortunately, he flashed this gesture to a large

Display Rules

Culturally determined rules about which nonverbal behaviors are appropriate to display

Emblems

Nonverbal gestures that have well-understood definitions within a given culture; they usually have direct verbal translations, such as the "OK" sign

Cultural Differences in Nonverbal Communication

Many forms of nonverbal behavior are specific to a given culture. Not only do some of the nonverbal behaviors of one culture mean nothing in another, but the same nonverbal behavior can exist in two cultures but have very different meanings in each. Such nonverbal differences can lead to misunderstanding when people from different societies interact. Some of these cultural differences are noted here.

Eye contact and gaze

In American culture, direct eye contact is valued; a person who won't "look you in the eye" is perceived as being evasive or even lying. However, in many parts of the world, direct eye contact is considered disrespectful, especially with superiors. For example, in Nigeria, Puerto Rico, and Thailand, children are taught not to make direct eye contact with their teachers and other adults. Cherokee, Navajo, and Hopi Native Americans use minimal eye contact as well. Japanese use far less direct eye contact than Americans. In contrast, Arabs use a great deal of eye contact, with a gaze that would be considered piercing by people from some other cultures.

Personal space and touching

Societies vary in whether they are high-contact cultures, where people stand close to each other and touch frequently, or low-contact cultures, where people maintain more interpersonal space and touch less often. High-contact cultures include Middle Eastern countries, South American countries, and southern European countries. Low-contact cultures include North American countries, northern European countries, Asian countries, Pakistan, and Native American peoples. Cultures also differ in how appropriate they consider same-sex touching among friends. For example, in Korea and Egypt, men and women hold hands, link arms, or walk hip to hip with their same-sex friends, and these nonverbal behaviors carry no sexual connotation. In the United States, such behavior is much less common, particularly between male friends.

Hand and head gestures

The "OK" sign: The OK sign is formed by making a circle with your thumb and index finger, with your three other fingers extended upward. In the United States, this means "OK." However, in Japan, this hand gesture means "money." In France, it means "zero"; in Mexico, it means "sex." In Ethiopia, it means "homosexuality." Finally, in some South American countries, like Brazil, it is an obscene gesture, carrying the same meaning as the American "flipping the bird" sign, where the middle finger is the only one extended.

The "thumb up" gesture: In the United States, raising one thumb upward with the rest of the fingers in the fist means "OK." Several European countries have a similar meaning for this gesture; for example, in France it means "excellent!" However, in Japan, the same gesture means "boyfriend," while in Iran and Sardinia, it is an obscene gesture.

The "hand-purse" gesture: This gesture is formed by straightening the fingers and thumb of one hand and bringing them together so the tips touch, pointing upwards. This gesture has no clear meaning in American culture. However, in Italy, it means "What are you trying to say?"; in Spain, it means "good"; in Tunisia, it means "slow down"; and in Malta, it means "you may seem good, but you are really bad."

Nodding the head: In the United States, nodding one's head up and down means "yes" and shaking it from side to side means "no." However, in some parts of Africa and India, the opposite is true: nodding up and down means "no," and shaking from side to side means "yes." To complicate this situation even more, in Korea, shaking one's head from side to side means "I don't know" (which in the United States is communicated by a shrug of the shoulders). Finally, Bulgarians indicate disagreement by throwing their heads back and then returning them to an upright position—which is frequently mistaken by Americans as meaning agreement.

FIGURE 4.1

Cultural differences in nonverbal communication.

These photographs depict French nonverbal emblems. These gestures are clearly understood in France but are difficult for an American to interpret. (The one on the left means, "How boring." The one on the right means, "You can't fool me!") (Adapted from Wylie, 1977.)

crowd in Australia—and in Australia, this emblem is the equivalent of "flipping the bird" (Archer, 1997a)!

Multichannel Nonverbal Communication

Except for certain specific situations, such as talking on the telephone, everyday life is made up of multichannel nonverbal social interaction (Archer & Akert, 1998; Rosenthal, Hall, Di Matteo, Rogers, & Archer, 1979). Typically, many nonverbal cues are available to us when we talk to or observe other people. How do we use this information? And how accurately do we use it?

To study multichannel nonverbal decoding, Dane Archer and Robin Akert have constructed a nonverbal communication decoding task that closely mirrors real-life interpretive situations. The Social Interpretations Task (SIT) videotape is composed of twenty scenes of naturally occurring nonverbal behavior (Archer & Akert, 1977a, 1977b, 1980, 1984). Real people, not actors, are seen and heard having real conversations, not scripted ones. The scenes last a minute or so, giving the viewer a slice of a real interaction. Following each scene, the viewer is asked a question about the people in the scene or their relationship to each other. For example, in one scene, two women are seen playing with a baby. The viewer is asked, "Which woman is the mother of the baby?" A clear criterion for accuracy exists for each of the scenes; one of the women really is the mother of the baby. However, neither of the women states this fact out loud; nor did the women realize this would be the interpretative question paired with their scene.

To get this and the other scenes right, the viewer must pay attention to and interpret the nonverbal behavior of the people in the scenes. Archer and Akert (1980) found that 64 percent of the more than fourteen hundred people tested were able to decode this scene accurately, far above the chance level of accuracy of 33 percent. People reported using several different channels of nonverbal communication to help them choose the right answer. For example, they compared the tone of voice of the real mother when talking to the baby to the other woman's tone of voice; they noted the body position and posture of the nonmother as she held the baby, as well as the way she held the baby; they relied on eye contact cues, especially the baby's eye contact with the mother versus the nonmother; and they focused on the way the mother touched the baby versus the nonmother's touch.

Further research with the SIT videotape has shown that the important, or diagnostic, nonverbal information is actually diffused throughout each scene (Archer & Akert, 1980). In other words, it is not typically the case that only one significant clue signals the right answer. Instead, useful nonverbal information is present via many channels in each scene. This makes the decoder's job easier: If you fail to notice the eye gaze behavior, you may notice the tone of voice or the unusual gesture and still arrive at an accurate judgment. Research has also shown that some people are particularly talented at decoding nonverbal cues accurately, while others are dismally poor at this task. For example, extraverts were more accurate decoders of nonverbal cues on a SIT-like task than introverts (Akert & Panter, 1986; Lieberman & Rosenthal, 2001).

Gender and Nonverbal Communication

Who is better at decoding nonverbal cues—men or women? And who is better at encoding nonverbal information? Many studies have found that women are better at both decoding and encoding (Hall, 1979, 1984; Rosenthal & De Paulo, 1979).

As with most rules, however, there is an exception: Although women are more accurate in interpreting nonverbal cues when a person is telling the truth, men are better at detecting lies (De Paulo, Epstein, & Wyer, 1993; Rosenthal & De Paulo, 1979). Given that women are generally superior decoders, why do they lose their advantage when faced with deceit? It may be because women are more polite than men. While women have the ability to decode nonverbal cues of lying, they tend to turn off this skill in the face of deception, in polite deference to the speaker (Rosenthal & De Paulo, 1979).

This interpretation fits nicely with a theory of sex differences offered by Alice Eagly (1987). According to Eagly's **social role theory,** most societies have a division of labor based on gender: Men work in jobs outside the home, and women work within the home. This division of labor has two important consequences. First, gender-role expectations arise: Members of the society *expect* men and women to have certain attributes that are consistent with their role. Thus women are expected to be more nurturing, friendly, expressive, and sensitive than men because of their primary role as caregivers to children and elderly family members (Eagly & Karau, 2002). Second, men and women develop different sets of skills and attitudes, based on their experiences in their gender roles (Barrett, Lane, Sechrest, & Schwartz, 2000). Finally, because women are less powerful in many societies and less likely to occupy roles of higher status, it is more important for women to learn to be accommodating and polite than it is for men (Deaux & Major, 1987; Henley, 1977). According to Eagly (1987), gender-role expectations and sex-typed skills combine to produce sex differences in social behavior, such as the differences in nonverbal behavior we just discussed.

One way to test this theory would be to examine sex differences in cultures that have different gender-role expectations and sex-typed skills. If women are more polite in reading nonverbal cues because of the social roles they occupy in society, then this tendency to be polite should be especially strong in cultures where women are most oppressed. This is exactly what Judith Hall (1979) found in her cross-cultural study of nonverbal behavior. First, she classified eleven countries as to the level of oppression of women, based on such statistics as the number of women who go to college and the prevalence of women's groups in each country. She then examined how likely women in each country were to show the "politeness pattern" when reading other people's nonverbal behaviors—that is, to focus on nonverbal cues that convey what people want others to see and to ignore nonverbal cues that "leak" people's true feelings. Sure enough, the tendency of women to be nonverbally polite in this manner was especially strong in those cultures where women are most oppressed.

To summarize, we can learn quite a lot about people from their nonverbal behavior, including their attitudes, emotions, and personality traits. Nonverbal behavior gives us many bits of information—"data" that we then use to construct our overall impressions or theories about people. But nonverbal cues are just the beginning of social perception. We turn now to the cognitive processes people use when forming impressions of others.

Social Role Theory

The theory that sex differences in social behavior are due to society's division of labor between the sexes; this division leads to differences in gender-role expectations and sex-typed skills, both of which are responsible for differences in men's and women's social behavior

IMPLICIT PERSONALITY THEORIES: FILLING IN THE BLANKS

As we saw in Chapter 3, when people are unsure about the nature of the social world, they use their schemas to fill in the gaps. A schema is a mental shortcut: When all we have is a small amount of information, our schemas provide additional information to fill in the gaps (Fiske & Taylor, 1991; Markus & Zajonc, 1985). Thus when we are trying to understand other people, we can use just a few observations of a person as a starting point and then, using our schemas, create a much fuller understanding (Dweck, Chiu, & Hong, 1995; Kim & Rosenberg, 1980). Schemas allow us to form impressions quickly, without having to spend weeks with people to figure out what they are like.

This kind of schema is called an **implicit personality theory**: It consists of our ideas about what kinds of personality traits go together (Asch, 1946; Schneider, 1973; Sedikides & Anderson, 1994; Werth & Foerster, 2002). We use a few known traits to determine what other characteristics a person has. If someone is kind, our implicit personality theory tells us he or she is probably generous as well; similarly, we assume that a stingy person is also irritable. But relying on schemas can also lead us astray. We might make the wrong assumptions about an individual; we might even resort to stereotypical thinking, where our schema, or stereotype, leads us to believe that the individual is like all the other members of his or her group. (We will discuss these issues in more depth in Chapter 13.)

Culture and Implicit Personality Theories

Implicit personality theories are developed over time and with experience. Though each of us may have a few idiosyncratic theories about which personality traits go together, we also share many similar theories with one another (Gervey, Chiu, Hong, & Dweck, 1999; Hamilton, 1970; Kuusinen, 1969; Pedersen, 1965). This occurs because implicit personality theories are strongly tied to culture. Like other beliefs, they are passed from generation to generation in a society, and one culture's implicit personality theory may be very different from another's (Anderson, 1995; Chiu, Morris, Hong, & Menon, 2000; Cousins, 1989; Vonk, 1995).

For example, when Americans perceive someone as "helpful," they also perceive them as "sincere"; a "practical" person is also "cautious" (Rosenberg, Nelson, & Vivekananthan, 1968). Another strong implicit personality theory in this culture involves physical attractiveness. We presume that "what is beautiful is good"—that people with physical beauty will also have a whole host of other wonderful qualities (Dion, Berscheid, & Walster, 1972; Eagly, Ashmore, Makhijani, & Longo, 1991; Jackson, Hunter, & Hodge, 1995). In China, an implicit personality theory describes a person who embodies traditional Chinese values: creating and maintaining interpersonal harmony, inner harmony, and *ren qin* (a focus on relationships) (Cheung et al., 1996).

Cultural variation in implicit personality theories was demonstrated in an intriguing study (Hoffman, Lau, and Johnsons 1986). The researchers noted that cultures have different ideas about personality types—the kinds of people for whom there are simple, agreed-on verbal labels. For example, in Western cultures, saying someone has an "artistic personality" implies that the person is creative, intense, and temperamental and has an unconventional lifestyle. The Chinese, however, do not have a schema or implicit personality theory for an artistic type. Granted, there are Chinese words to describe the individual characteristics of such people, such as *creative*, but there are no labels like "artistic" or "bohemian" that convey the whole constellation of traits implied by the English

> Others are to us like the "characters" in fiction, external and incorrigible; the surprises they give us turn out in the end to have been predictable—unexpected variations on the theme of being themselves.
>
> —Mary McCarthy

Implicit Personality Theory

A type of schema people use to group various kinds of personality traits together; for example, many people believe that someone who is kind is generous as well

Implicit personality theories differ from culture to culture. Westerners assume there is an artistic type of person—someone who is creative, intense, temperamental, and unconventional (for example, the artist Andy Warhol, on the left). The Chinese have no such implicit personality theory. The Chinese have a category of a *shi gú* person—someone who is worldly, devoted to his or her family, socially skillful, and somewhat reserved. Westerners do not have this implicit personality theory.

term. Conversely, in China, there are categories of personality that do not exist in Western cultures. For example, a *shi gú* person is someone who is worldly, devoted to his or her family, socially skillful, and somewhat reserved.

Hoffman and his colleagues (1986) hypothesized that these cultural implicit personality theories influence the way people form impressions of others. To test this hypothesis, they wrote stories in English and Chinese, describing someone behaving like an artistic type or a *shi gú* type, without using those labels. They gave the English versions to a group of native English speakers who spoke no other languages and to a group of Chinese-English bilinguals. Another group of Chinese-English bilinguals received the versions written in Chinese.

If people were using their cultural theories to understand the stories they read, what would you expect to happen? One measure of the use of theories (or schemas) is the tendency to fill in the blanks—to believe that information fitting the schema was observed when in fact it was not. The researchers asked the participants to write down their impressions of the characters in the stories; they then looked to see whether the participants listed traits that were not in the stories but did fit the artistic or *shi gú* personality type. For example, the term *unreliable* was not used in the "artistic personality type" story but is consistent with that implicit personality theory.

When the native English speakers read about the characters in English, they were much more likely to form an impression that was consistent with the artistic type than with the *shi gú* type (see Figure 4.2). Similarly, when the Chinese-English bilinguals read the descriptions of the characters in English, they too formed an impression that was consistent with the artistic type but not with the *shi gú* type, because English provides a convenient label for the artistic type. In comparison, Chinese-English bilinguals who read the descriptions in Chinese showed the opposite pattern of results. Their impression of the *shi gú* character was more consistent with that schema than their impression of the artist was, because the Chinese language provides a convenient label or implicit personality theory for this kind of person.

These results are consistent with a well-known argument by Benjamin Whorf (1956) that the language people speak influences the way they think about the world. Characters described identically were perceived differently by the bilingual research participants, depending on the language (and therefore the implicit personality theory) that was used. Thus one's culture and one's language produce widely shared implicit personality theories, and these theories can influence the kinds of inferences people form about one another.

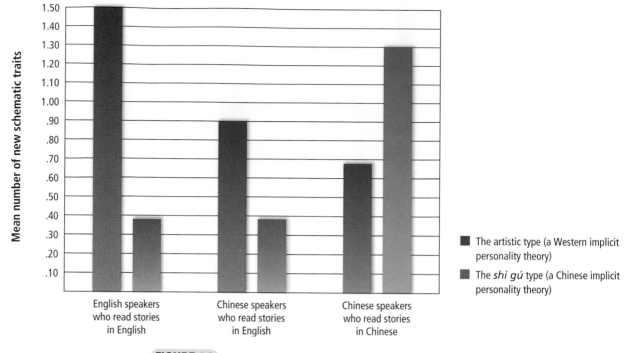

FIGURE 4.2

Implicit personality theories: How our culture and language shape our impressions of others.

People formed an impression of other people that was consistent with the implicit personality theory contained in their language. For example, when Chinese-English bilinguals read stories about people in English, they were likely to form impressions consistent with a Western implicit theory, the artistic personality. When Chinese-English bilinguals read the same stories in Chinese, they were likely to form impressions consistent with a Chinese implicit theory, the *shi gú* personality.

(Adapted from Hoffman, Lau, & Johnson, 1986)

Decoding nonverbal behaviors and relying on implicit personality theories tend to occur automatically—we are not always consciously aware of using this information. What about those times when we must work consciously to explain another's behavior?

CAUSAL ATTRIBUTION: ANSWERING THE "WHY" QUESTION

In the beginning was not the word, not the deed, not the silly serpent. In the beginning was why? Why did she pluck the apple? Was she bored? Was she inquisitive? Was she paid? Did Adam put her up to it? If not, who did?

—*John le Carré, The Russia House, 1989*

We have seen that when we observe other people, we have a rich source of information—their nonverbal behavior—on which to base our impressions. From their nonverbal behavior, we can also make guesses about people's personalities, such as how friendly or outgoing they are. And once we get this far, we use our implicit personality theories to fill in the blanks: If a person is friendly, we generally infer that he or she must be sincere as well.

However, nonverbal behavior and implicit personality theories are not fail-safe indicators of what a person is really thinking or feeling. If you meet an acquaintance and she says, "It's great to see you!" does she really mean it? Perhaps she is acting more thrilled than she really feels, out of politeness. Perhaps she is outright lying and really can't stand you. The point is that even though nonverbal communication is sometimes easy to decode and our implicit personality theories can streamline the way we form impressions, there is still substantial ambiguity as to what a person's behavior really means (De Paulo, 1992; De Paulo, Stone, & Lassiter, 1985; Schneider, Hastorf, & Ellsworth, 1979).

Why did that acquaintance behave as she did? To answer this "why" question, we will use our immediate observations to form more elegant and complex inferences about what people are really like and what motivates them to act as they do. How we go about answering these questions is the focus of **attribution theory,** the study of how we infer the causes of other people's behavior.

The Nature of the Attribution Process

Fritz Heider (1958) is frequently referred to as the father of attribution theory. His influential book defined the field of social perception, and his legacy is still very much evident in current research (Gilbert, 1998a; Ross, 1998). Heider discussed what he called "naive" or "commonsense" psychology. In his view, people were like amateur scientists, trying to understand other people's behavior by piecing together information until they arrived at a reasonable explanation or cause. Heider was intrigued by what seemed reasonable to people and by how they arrived at their conclusions.

One of Heider's most valuable contributions is a simple dichotomy: When trying to decide why people behave as they do—for example, why a father has just yelled at his young daughter—we can make one of two attributions. One option is to make an **internal attribution,** deciding that the cause of the father's behavior was something about him—his disposition, personality, attitudes, or character—an explanation that assigns the causes of his behavior internally. For example, we might decide that the father has poor parenting skills and disciplines his child in inappropriate ways. Alternatively, we might make an **external attribution,** deciding that something in the situation, not in the father's personality or attitudes, caused his behavior. If we conclude that he yelled because his daughter had just stepped into the street without looking, we would be making an external attribution for his behavior.

Notice that our impression of the father will be very different, depending on the type of attribution we make. If we make an internal attribution, we'll have a negative impression of him. If we make an external attribution, we won't learn much about him—after all, most parents would have done the same thing if they were in that situation and their child had just disobeyed them by stepping into the street. Quite a difference!

This internal/external attribution dichotomy plays an extraordinarily important role in even the most intimate parts of our lives. Indeed, spouses in happy, satisfied marriages make very different attributions about their partners than spouses in troubled, distressed marriages. Satisfied spouses tend to make internal attributions for their partners' positive behaviors (e.g., "She helped me because she's such a generous person") and external attributions for their partners' negative behaviors (e.g., "He said something mean because he's so stressed at work this week"). In contrast, spouses in distressed marriages tend to display the opposite pattern: Their partners' positive behaviors are chalked up to external causes (e.g., "She helped me because she wanted to impress our friends"), while negative behaviors are attributed to internal causes (e.g., "He said something mean because he's a totally self-centered jerk"). When an intimate relationship becomes troubled, this second pattern of attributions about one's partner only makes the situation worse and can have dire consequences for the health and future of the relationship (Bradbury & Fincham, 1991; Fincham, Bradbury, Arias, Byrne, & Karney, 1997; Karney & Bradbury, 2000).

Another of Heider's important contributions was his discussion of our preference for internal attributions over external ones. Although either type of attribution is always possible, Heider (1958) noted that we tend to see the causes of a person's behavior as residing in that person. We are perceptually focused on

Attribution Theory

A description of the way in which people explain the causes of their own and other people's behavior

Internal Attribution

The inference that a person is behaving in a certain way because of something about the person, such as attitude, character, or personality

External Attribution

The inference that a person is behaving a certain way because of something about the situation he or she is in; the assumption is that most people would respond the same way in that situation

According to Fritz Heider, we tend to see the causes of a person's behavior as internal. For example, when a person on the street asks for money, we are likely to assume that he is at fault for being poor—perhaps lazy or drug-addicted. If we knew the person's situation—perhaps he has lost his job due to a factory closing or has a spouse whose medical bills have bankrupted them—we might come up with a different, external attribution.

people—they are who we notice—and the situation (the external explanation), which is often hard to see and hard to describe, may be overlooked (Bargh, 1994; Fletcher, Reeder, & Bull, 1990; Gilbert, 1998b; Jones, 1979, 1990; Jones & Davis, 1965; Miller, 1998). You can observe people making attributions in their conversations using the Try It! exercise on page 109.

The Covariation Model: Internal versus External Attributions

The first, essential step in the process of social perception is determining how people decide whether to make an internal or an external attribution. Harold Kelley's major contribution to attribution theory was the idea that we notice and think about more than one piece of information when we form an impression of another person (1967, 1973). For example, let's say you ask your friend to lend you her car, and she says no. Naturally, you wonder why. What explains her behavior? Kelley's theory, called the **covariation model,** says that you will examine multiple instances of behavior, occurring at different times and in different situations, in order to answer this question. Has your friend refused to lend you her car in the past? Does she lend it to other people? Does she normally lend you other possessions?

Kelley, like Heider before him, assumes that when we are in the process of forming an attribution, we gather information, or data. The data we use, according to Kelley, are how a person's behavior "covaries" or changes across time, place, different actors, and different targets of the behavior. By discovering covariation in people's behavior (e.g., your friend refuses to lend you her car; she agrees to lend it to others), you are able to reach a judgment about what caused their behavior.

When we are forming an attribution, what kinds of information do we examine for covariation? Kelley (1967) identified three key types of information: *consensus*, *distinctiveness*, and *consistency*. Suppose that you are working at your part-time job at the Gap, and you observe your boss yelling at another employee, Hannah, telling her that she's an idiot. Automatically, you ask that attributional question: "Why is the boss yelling at Hannah and being so critical—is it something about the boss, something about Hannah, or something about the situation that surrounds and affects him?"

Covariation Model

A theory that states that to form an attribution about what caused a person's behavior, we systematically note the pattern between the presence or absence of possible causal factors and whether or not the behavior occurs

Try it!

Listen as People Make Attributions

Forming attributions is a major part of daily life—note the Ann Landers column on page 118! You can watch the attribution process in action too. All it takes is a group of friends and an interesting topic to discuss. Perhaps one of your friends is telling you about something that happened to her that day, or perhaps your group is discussing another person whom everybody knows. As they talk, pay very close attention to what they say. They will be trying to figure out why the person being discussed did what she did or said what he said. In other words, they will be making attributions. Your job is to try to keep track of their comments and label the attributional strategies they are using.

In particular, do they make internal attributions, about a person's character or personality, or do they make situational attributions, about all the other events and variables that make up a person's life? Do your friends seem to prefer one type of attribution over the other? If their interpretation is dispositional, what happens when you suggest another possible interpretation, one that is situational? Do they agree or disagree with you? What kinds of information do they offer as "proof" that their attribution is right? Observing people when they are making attributions in real conversations will show you just how common and powerful this type of thinking is when people are trying to understand each other.

How would Kelley's (1967, 1972, 1973) model of covariation assessment answer this question? **Consensus information** refers to how other people behave toward the same stimulus—in this case, Hannah. Do other people at work also yell at Hannah and criticize her? **Distinctiveness information** refers to how the actor (the person whose behavior we are trying to explain) responds to other stimuli. Does the boss yell at and demean other employees in the store? **Consistency information** refers to the frequency with which the observed behavior between the same actor and the same stimulus occurs across time and circumstances. Does the boss yell at and criticize Hannah regularly and frequently, whether the store is filled with customers or empty?

According to Kelley's theory, when these three sources of information combine into one of two distinct patterns, a clear attribution can be made. People are most likely to make an internal attribution (deciding that the behavior was due to something about the boss) when the consensus and distinctiveness of the act are low but its consistency is high (see Figure 4.3 on page 110). We would be pretty confident that the boss yelled at Hannah because he is a mean and vindictive person if we knew that no one else yells at Hannah, that the boss yells at other employees, and that the boss yells at Hannah every chance he gets. People are likely to make an external attribution (in this case, about Hannah) if consensus, distinctiveness, and consistency are all high (see Figure 4.3). Finally, when consistency is low, we cannot make a clear internal or external attribution and so resort to a special kind of external or situational attribution, one that assumes something unusual or peculiar is going on in these circumstances—for example, the boss just received very upsetting news and lost his temper with the first person he saw.

The covariation model assumes that people make causal attributions in a rational, logical way. People observe the clues, such as the distinctiveness of the act, and then draw a logical inference about why the person did what he or she did. Several studies have confirmed that people often do make attributions the way that Kelley's model says they should (Forsterling, 1989; Gilbert, 1998a; Hewstone & Jaspars, 1987; Hilton, Smith, & Kim, 1995; Orvis, Cunningham, & Kelley, 1975; White, 2002)—with two exceptions. First, studies have shown that people don't

Consensus Information

Information about the extent to which other people behave the same way toward the same stimulus as the actor does

Distinctiveness Information

Information about the extent to which one particular actor behaves in the same way to different stimuli

Consistency Information

Information about the extent to which the behavior between one actor and one stimulus is the same across time and circumstances

FIGURE 4.3

The covariation model.

Why did the boss yell at his employee Hannah? To decide whether a behavior was caused by internal (dispositional) factors or by external (situational) factors, people use consensus, distinctiveness, and consistency information.

Why did the boss yell at his employee, Hannah?			
People are likely to make an ***internal attribution***—it was something about the boss—if they see this behavior as	***low*** in consensus: the boss is the only person working in the store who yells at Hannah	***low*** in distinctiveness: the boss yells at all the employees	***high*** in consistency: the boss yells at Hannah almost every time he sees her
People are likely to make an ***external attribution***—it was something about Hannah—if they see this behavior as	***high*** in consensus: all of the employees yell at Hannah too	***high*** in distinctiveness: the boss doesn't yell at any of the other employees	***high*** in consistency: the boss yells at Hannah almost every time he sees her
People are likely to think it was something peculiar about the particular circumstances in which the boss yelled at Hannah if they see this behavior as	***low or high*** in consensus	***low or high*** in distinctiveness	***low*** in consistency: this is the first time that the boss has yelled at Hannah

use consensus information as much as Kelley's theory predicted; they rely more on consistency and distinctiveness information when forming attributions (McArthur, 1972; Wright, Luus, & Christie, 1990). Second, people don't always have the relevant information they need on all three of Kelley's dimensions. For example, you may not have consistency information because this is the first time you have ever asked your friend to borrow her car. In these situations, research has shown that people proceed with the attribution process using the information they do have and, if necessary, making inferences about the missing data (Fiedler, Walther, & Nickel, 1999; Kelley, 1973).

To summarize, the covariation model portrays people as master detectives, deducing the causes of behavior as systematically and logically as Sherlock Holmes would. However, as noted in Chapters 3 and 6, people aren't always logical or rational when forming judgments about others. Sometimes they distort information to satisfy their need for high self-esteem (see Chapter 6). At other times they use mental shortcuts that, though often helpful, can lead to inaccurate judgments (see Chapter 3). Unfortunately, the attributions we make are sometimes just plain wrong. In the next section, we will discuss some specific errors or biases that plague the attribution process. One shortcut is very common: the idea that people do what they do because of the kind of people they are, not because of the situation they are in. This has been termed the *fundamental attribution error.*

The Correspondence Bias: People as Personality Psychologists

Martha Stewart. The name conjures up images of domestic perfection that few mortals hope to attain. Over the past two decades, Stewart grew her small Connecticut catering business into a multimedia, billion-dollar company

(Sorkin, 2003). Books, magazines, newspaper columns, TV and radio shows, Internet commerce, and department store product lines communicate her vision of homemaking: meticulous, artistic, and time-consuming ways of doing everyday chores (Kahn, 2003).

Though millions of people have embraced Stewart's vision of home life (hence the billion-dollar company), others have found her ripe for parody and criticism. Her flagship magazine, *Martha Stewart Living*, spawned a parody titled *Is Martha Stewart Really Living?* The TV show *Saturday Night Live* has an ongoing skit making fun of her excruciatingly complex projects and "domestic diva" behavior. A biography, made into an NBC movie in 2003, presented a very unflattering picture of both her personality and way of interacting with people (Krasner, 2003). But the *coup de grâce* for Stewart and her company occurred on June 4, 2003, when she was indicted on nine counts of conspiracy, obstruction of justice, and securities fraud by the federal government.

An investigation by the Securities and Exchange Commission and the FBI alleges that Stewart engaged in insider trading, receiving illegal information that allowed her to sell a stock one day before its value plummeted. Stewart maintained that she had a standing order to sell the stock when it dropped to a certain price. The government believes she is lying (Aoki & Robertson, 2003; Hays, 2003).

CONNECTIONS

Martha Stewart: Control Queen or Unfair Target?

Following Martha Stewart's indictment, a flurry of explanations appeared in the press, made by both reporters and the general public they interviewed. Their attempts to understand Stewart's behavior offer an excellent real-life example of the prevalence of internal, or dispositional, attributions.

Martha Stewart's detractors offered strong internal attributions. Described in the press as the "queen of micromanagement" (Sorkin, 2003, p. C1), Stewart was "so detail oriented that, even with a net worth of hundreds of millions, she could not resist an illegal stock trade that netted her $45,000" ("Martha Stewart's troubled world," 2003, p. A34). These critics note that she worked as a stockbroker on Wall Street in the 1960s and thus cannot plead ignorance or naivete (Robertson, 2003). Some feel that this is "the classic story of an extremely successful yet irritating person getting her comeuppance" (Kahn, 2003, p. D6).

On the left, we see Martha Stewart in happier days, hosting her very successful television show. On the left, Ms. Stewart is exiting a federal courthouse after her criminal indictment. Attributionally, how do we make sense of this startling change in her life?

Stewart's attorney—and her supporters—counter with a situational attribution to explain her current troubles: Innocent of the crime, she is being singled out because she is a celebrity and a highly successful woman in the predominantly male businesss world (Robertson, 2003). Thus it is not anything about her personality or values that got her into this predicament (a dispositional attribution) but rather aspects of the situation, such as animosity toward her gender or occupation (a situational attribution), that have caused her to be unfairly targeted.

The resolution of this case will occur sometime in the future. But soon after her indictment, her company stock lost two-thirds of its value, and she resigned as chair and CEO (Sorkin, 2003).

The pervasive, fundamental theory or schema most of us have about human behavior is that people do what they do because of the kind of people they are, not because of the situation they are in. When thinking this way, we are more like personality psychologists, who see behavior as stemming from internal dispositions and traits, than like social psychologists, who focus on the impact of social situations on behavior. This tendency to infer that people's behavior corresponds to, or matches, their dispositions and personality has been called the **correspondence bias** (Fiske & Taylor, 1991; Gilbert, 1998b; Gilbert & Jones, 1986; Gilbert & Malone, 1995; Jones, 1979, 1990). The correspondence bias is so pervasive that many social psychologists call it the **fundamental attribution error** (Heider, 1958; Jones, 1990; Ross, 1977; Ross & Nisbett, 1991).

There have been many empirical demonstrations of the tendency to see people's behavior as a reflection of their dispositions and beliefs, rather than as influenced by the situation (Gawronski, 2003; Jones, 1979, 1990; Miller, Ashton, & Mishal, 1990; Miller, Jones, & Hinkle, 1981; Vonk, 1999). For example, in a classic study, Edward Jones and Victor Harris (1967) asked college students to read an essay written by a fellow student that either supported or opposed Fidel Castro's rule in Cuba and then to guess how the author of the essay really felt about Castro (see Figure 4.4). In one condition, the researchers told the students that the author freely chose which position to take in the essay, thereby making it easy to guess how he really felt. If he chose to write in favor of Castro, then clearly he must be sympathetic to Castro. In another condition, however, the students learned that the author had been assigned the position as a participant in a debate. One should not assume, then, that the writer believes what he or she wrote. Yet the participants in this study, and in dozens of others like it, assumed that the author really believed what he wrote, even when they knew he could not choose which position to take. As you can see in Figure 4.4, people

Correspondence Bias

The tendency to infer that people's behavior corresponds to (matches) their disposition (personality)

Fundamental Attribution Error

The tendency to overestimate the extent to which people's behavior is due to internal, dispositional factors and to underestimate the role of situational factors

FIGURE 4.4

The fundamental attribution error.

Even when people knew that the author's choice of an essay topic was externally caused (i.e., in the no-choice condition), they assumed that what he wrote reflected how he really felt about Castro. That is, they made an internal attribution from his behavior.

(Adapted from Jones & Harris, 1967)

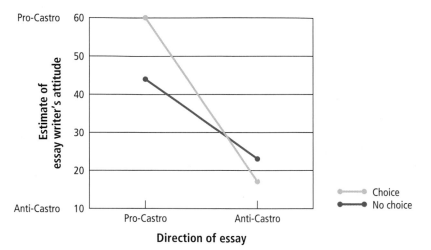

moderated their guesses a little bit—there was not as much difference in their estimates of the author's attitude in the pro-Castro and anti-Castro conditions—but they still assumed that the content of the essay reflected the author's true feelings.

Why is this correspondence bias, the tendency to explain behavior in terms of people's dispositions, often called the fundamental attribution error? It is not always wrong to make an internal attribution; clearly, people often do what they do because of the kind of people they are. However, considerable evidence indicates that social situations can strongly affect behavior; indeed, the major lesson of social psychology is that these influences can be extremely powerful. The point of the fundamental attribution error is that *people tend to underestimate external influences when explaining other people's behavior.* Even when the influence of the situation on behavior is obvious, as in the Jones and Harris (1967) experiment, people persist in making internal attributions (Lord, Scott, Pugh, & Desforges, 1997; Newman, 1996; Ross, 1977; Ross, Amabile, & Steinmetz, 1977; Ross & Nisbett, 1991).

The Role of Perceptual Salience in the Correspondence Bias   Why do people commit the fundamental attribution error? One reason is that when we try to explain someone's behavior, our focus of attention is usually on the person, not on the surrounding situation (Baron & Misovich, 1993; Heider, 1944, 1958; Jones & Nisbett, 1972). In fact, the situational causes of another person's behavior are practically invisible to us (Gilbert & Malone, 1995). If we don't know what happened to someone earlier in the day (e.g., she received an F on her midterm), we can't use that situational information to help us understand her current behavior. And even when we know her situation, we still don't know how she interprets it—for example, the F may not have upset her because she's planning to drop the course anyway. If we don't know the meaning of the situation for her, we can't accurately judge its effects on her behavior. Much of the time, in fact, information about the situational causes of behavior is unavailable or difficult to interpret accurately (Gilbert, 1998b; Gilbert & Malone, 1995).

What information does that leave us? Although the situation may be close to invisible, the individual is extremely "perceptually prominent"—people are what our eyes and ears notice. And what we notice seems to be the reasonable and logical cause of the observed behavior (Heider, 1958). We can't see the situation, so we ignore its importance. People, not the situation, have **perceptual salience** for us; we pay attention to them, and we tend to think that they alone cause their behavior.

Several studies have confirmed the importance of perceptual salience—especially an elegant one by Shelley Taylor and Susan Fiske (1975). In this study, two male students engaged in a "get acquainted" conversation. (They were actually both accomplices of the experimenters and were following a script during their conversation.) At each session, six actual research participants also took part. They sat in assigned seats, surrounding the two conversationalists (see Figure 4.5). Two of them sat on each side of the actors; they had a clear, profile view of both individuals. Two observers sat behind each actor; they could see the back of one actor's head but the face of the other. Thus who was visually salient—that is, the individual the participants could see the best—was cleverly manipulated in this study.

After the conversation, the research participants were asked questions about the two men—for example, who had taken the lead in the conversation and who had chosen the topics to be discussed? What happened? The person they could see the best was the person they thought had the most impact on the conversation (see Figure 4.6). Even though all the observers heard the same conversation, those who were facing student A thought he had taken the lead and chosen

> Be not swept off your feet by the vividness of the impression, but say, "Impression, wait for me a little. Let me see what you are and what you represent."
>
> —*Epictetus,*
> Discourses

Perceptual Salience

The seeming importance of information that is the focus of people's attention

FIGURE 4.5

Manipulating perceptual salience.

This is the seating arrangement for two actors and the six research participants in the Taylor and Fiske study. Participants rated each actor's impact on the conversation. Researchers found that people rated the actor they could see most clearly as having the largest role in the conversation.

(Adapted from Taylor & Fiske, 1975)

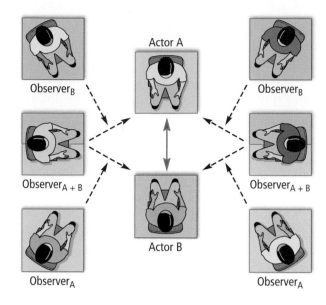

the topics, whereas those who were facing student B thought he had taken the lead and chosen the topics. In comparison, those who could see both students equally well thought both were equally influential.

Perceptual salience, or our visual point of view, helps explain why the fundamental attribution error is so widespread. We focus our attention more on people than on the surrounding situation because the situation is so hard to see or know; we underestimate or even forget about the influence of the situation when we are explaining human behavior. But this is only part of the story. Why should the simple fact that we are focused on a person make us exaggerate the extent to which that person determines his or her actions?

The culprit is one of the mental shortcuts we discussed in Chapter 3: the *anchoring and adjustment heuristic*. We saw several examples in which people began with a reference point when making a judgment and then did not adjust sufficiently away from that point. The fundamental attribution error is another byproduct of this shortcut. When making attributions, people use the focus of their attention as a starting point. For example, when we hear someone argue strongly in favor of Castro's regime in Cuba, our first inclination is to explain this in dispositional terms: "This person must hold radical political views." We realize that this explanation might not be the whole story, however. We might think, "On the other hand, I know he was assigned this position as part of a debate,"

FIGURE 4.6

The effects of perceptual salience.

These are the ratings of each actor's causal role in the conversation. People thought that the actor they could see the best had the most impact on the conversation.

(Adapted from Taylor & Fiske, 1975)

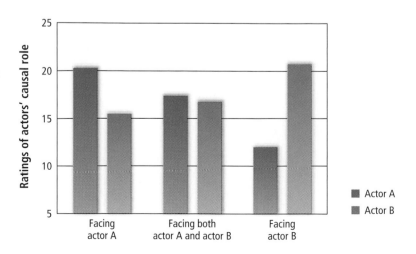

and adjust our attributions more toward a situational explanation. However, the problem is that people often don't adjust their judgments enough. In the Jones and Harris (1967) experiment, participants who knew that the essay writer did not have a choice of topics nevertheless thought he believed what he had written, at least to some extent. They adjusted insufficiently from their anchor, the position advocated in the essay (Quattrone, 1982).

The Two-Step Process of Making Attributions In sum, we go through a **two-step process** when we make attributions (Gilbert, 1989, 1991, 1993; Krull, 1993). First, we make an internal attribution; we assume that a person's behavior was due to something about that person. Then we attempt to adjust this attribution by considering the situation the person was in. But we often don't make enough of an adjustment in this second step. Indeed, when we are distracted or preoccupied, we often skip the second step, making an extreme internal attribution (Gilbert & Hixon, 1991; Gilbert & Osborne, 1989; Gilbert, Pelham, & Krull, 1988). Why? Because the first step (making the internal attribution) occurs quickly and spontaneously, whereas the second step (adjusting for the situation) requires more effort and conscious attention (see Figure 4.7).

We will engage in this second step of attributional processing if we consciously slow down and think carefully before reaching a judgment, if we are motivated to reach as accurate a judgment as possible, or if we are suspicious about the behavior of the target person, for example, believing that he or she is lying or has ulterior motives (Burger, 1991; Fein, 1996; Hilton, Fein, & Miller, 1993; Webster, 1993).

Two-Step Process of Attribution

Analyzing another person's behavior first by making an automatic internal attribution and only then thinking about possible situational reasons for the behavior, after which one may adjust the original internal attribution

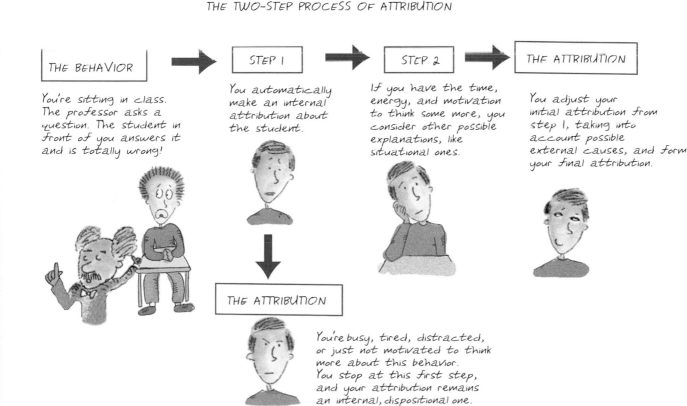

THE TWO-STEP PROCESS OF ATTRIBUTION

THE BEHAVIOR → STEP 1 → STEP 2 → THE ATTRIBUTION

You're sitting in class. The professor asks a question. The student in front of you answers it and is totally wrong!

You automatically make an internal attribution about the student.

If you have the time, energy, and motivation to think some more, you consider other possible explanations, like situational ones.

You adjust your initial attribution from step 1, taking into account possible external causes, and form your final attribution.

THE ATTRIBUTION

You're busy, tired, distracted, or just not motivated to think more about this behavior. You stop at this first step, and your attribution remains an internal, dispositional one.

FIGURE 4.7
The two-step process of attribution.

Our Intuitive Beliefs about the Correspondence Bias   We've seen that we prefer to make internal attributions about others and that we jump to dispositional conclusions easily. Now let's look at the fundamental attribution error from the other side. Do *we* realize that other people are busily making internal attributions about us? In other words, do we have an intuitive understanding that the fundamental attribution error is operating all the time and that like a lightning rod, we attract such internal, dispositional attributions?

Although you may never have thought about this before, recent research indicates that we do have an intuitive understanding that people prefer internal attributions, even when they're forming attributions about us (Van Boven, Kamada, & Gilovich, 1999). For example, let's say you raise your hand and ask a question in a large class. The professor answers you curtly, sounding and looking annoyed, and several of your classmates send you rather hostile looks. Later, you learn that your question was covered thoroughly in an earlier class, when you were out with the flu. At this point, you realize that your professor and classmates have probably made an internal (and negative) attribution about you—for example, that you aren't too bright or that you don't pay attention (Van Boven, Kamada, & Gilovich, 1999).

Thus we are aware that others are going to focus on us and not on the situation when forming attributions about us. However, in addition, we tend to believe that our actions and appearance are noticed and evaluated by others to a greater extent than is really the case, as if we are in a perpetual spotlight (Savitsky, Epley, & Gilovich, 2001). Indeed, one group of social psychologists dubbed these intuitive beliefs the **spotlight effect** (Gilovich, Medvec, & Savitsky, 2000). As a result of the spotlight effect, we are more embarrassed or concerned about our inadequacies than we need to be, whether these inadequacies involve our performance (e.g., saying something we think is stupid when answering a question in class), our social interactions (e.g., dropping a tray of food in front of everyone in the cafeteria), or our appearance (e.g., the unfortunate "bad hair day"). Why do we fall prey to the spotlight effect? Why do we think that other people notice the variability in our appearance and behavior more than they really do?

One team of researchers focused on the variability question (Gilovich, Kruger, & Medvec, 2002). Their research participants were members of real groups: students enrolled in seminar classes and students on the school volleyball team. In a series of studies, the researchers asked each participant to rate himself or herself, as well as all the other members of the group, on some attribute.

For the seminar classes, the attribute was physical appearance. Several times over the course of the semester, the students were asked to make the following ratings: how each person in the class looked that day compared to how they typically looked, and when rating themselves, how they thought the rest of the group would rate their appearance compared to how they typically looked. For the volleyball team, the attribute that was rated was their athletic performance. Again, several times during the semester, the volleyball team members rated one another on how they had played during that day's scrimmage compared to their typical level of play and how they thought the rest of their team members would rate their own athletic performance that day relative to their typical performance.

Comparing the two types of ratings, the researchers found that participants in both groups substantially overestimated how variable their appearance or their athletic performance was to the other members of the group. A given individual was sure that the others had noticed the bad hairdo or the ill-fitting outfit, the botched volleyball serve or the ball that hit the net. But in fact, the other members did not notice such variability in appearance and performance as much as the actor did.

The moral here is that we don't have to feel so anxious or embarrassed about every detail of our appearance or performance. Although we think the

Spotlight Effect
The tendency to overestimate the extent to which our actions and appearance are salient to others

"This week on 'Celebrity Fear Factor,' contestants are threatened with total anonymity."

spotlight is shining on us, other people may fail to notice many of these details and thus are not making attributions about us based on them. In fact, further research tells us one reason we fall prey to the spotlight effect (Epley, Savitsky, & Gilovich, 2002). Even when we commit an embarrassing blunder, others judge us less harshly than we think they have because they empathize with us. Through empathy, observers can imagine themselves committing the same embarrassing faux pas, leading them to take the situation into account and thus making fewer negative dispositional attributions about the poor blunderer. However, the spotlight effect occurs for the individual caught in the embarrassing mistake because he or she underestimates this empathic response in others and instead believes he or she will be judged harshly.

Thus although it's true that we, not situational factors, are salient to observers (and therefore the fundamental attribution error occurs), it is also the case that we are not as salient as we think (and worry) we are. So take comfort. You know you're having a "bad hair day," but most likely no one else does.

The Actor/Observer Difference

An interesting twist on the fundamental attribution error is that it applies unevenly: Whereas we are very likely to find internal causes for other people's behavior, we tend to look beyond ourselves, to the situation, to explain our own.

This creates an interesting attributional dilemma: The same behavior can trigger dispositional attributions in people observing the behavior and situational attributions in the person performing the behavior. For example, we observe a woman yelling at her child in the grocery store. We make the attribution that she's a mean, bad parent. However, when she thinks about her behavior, she attributes it to the anxiety and stress she's under since she lost her job. This difference in attributions is called the **actor/observer difference** (Jones & Nisbett, 1972; Hansen, Kimble, & Biers, 2001; Nisbett, Caputo, Legant, & Marecek, 1973; Robins, Spranka, & Mendelson, 1996; Watson, 1982).

The letter to Ann Landers (see page 118) demonstrates the actor/observer difference. The writer is focusing on the external forces that are affecting her life and shaping her behavior. She would rather focus outside of herself—on what she calls her mother's "obsession"—than on her own reaons for staying in a destructive relationship. Ann Landers, however, will have none of it. She responds with a strong, internal attribution—the woman herself, not her mother's disapproval (the situation), is the cause of her problems. As you might guess, the actor-observer difference can lead to some striking disagreements between peo-

Actor/Observer Difference

The tendency to see other people's behavior as dispositionally caused but focusing more on the role of situational factors when explaining one's own behavior

The letter and its response depict actor/observer differences in attribution. Schoeneman and Rubanowitz (1985) examined letters to the "Ann Landers" and "Dear Abby" advice columns and found strong evidence for actor/observer differences. The letter writers tended to attribute their problems to external factors (e.g., this letter writer says her biggest problem is her mother), whereas the advice columnists tended to make dispositional attributions to the letter writers (e.g., "Get into counseling at once").

Dear Ann Landers:

I'm writing you in desperation, hoping you can help me with a problem I'm having with my mother.

A little over a year ago, I moved in with my boyfriend despite my mother's protests. She has never liked "Kevin." I'll admit he's far from perfect and we've had our problems. He's an alcoholic, has a bad temper, is mentally abusive, is a compulsive liar and cannot hold a job. I am in debt over my head because of him but my biggest problem is that my mother is obsessed with my situation. I understand her concern, but I can take only so much. . . .
OVER-MOTHERED IN MICHIGAN

Dear Over-Mothered:
Your mother didn't write to me. You did. So you're the one who is going to get the advice. Get into counseling at once and find out why you insist on hanging on to an alcoholic, abusive, unemployed liar. . . .

ple. Why, at times, do the attributions made by actors and observers diverge so sharply?

> Resemblances are the shadows of differences. Different people see different similarities and similar differences.
>
> —Vladimir Nabokov, Pale Fire

Perceptual Salience Revisited One reason for such divergence is our old friend perceptual salience (Jones & Nisbett, 1972). As we said earlier, just as we notice other people's behavior more than their situation, we notice our own situation more than our own behavior. None of us is so egotistic or self-centered that we walk through life holding up a full-length mirror in order to observe ourselves constantly. We are looking outward; what is perceptually salient to us is other people, objects, and the events that unfold. We don't pay as much attention to ourselves. Consequently, when the actor and the observer think about what caused a given behavior, they are swayed by the information that is most salient and noticeable to them: the actor for the observer and the situation for the actor (Malle & Knobe, 1997; Nisbett & Ross, 1980; Ross & Nisbett, 1991; Storms, 1973).

The Role of Information Availability in the Actor/Observer Difference The actor/observer difference occurs for another reason as well. Actors have more information about themselves than observers do. Actors know how they've behaved over the years; they know what happened to them that morning. They are far more aware than observers are of both the similarities and the differences in their behavior over time and across situations (Greenwald & Banaji, 1989; Jones & Nisbett, 1972; Krueger, Ham, & Linford, 1996; Malle & Knobe, 1997). In Kelley's (1967) terms, actors have far more consistency and distinctiveness information about themselves than observers do.

For example, if you are quiet and sit alone at a party, an observer is likely to make a dispositional attribution about you—"That person is quite an introvert." In fact, you may know that this is not the way you usually behave at a party. Perhaps you are shy only at parties where you don't know anyone. Maybe you are just feeling tired or depressed by some recent bad news. It is not surprising, then, that actors' self-attributions often reflect situational factors, because they know

An interesting arena for studying self-serving attributions is sports. We can conjecture about what kinds of attributions were made by members of the 1999 World's Cup soccer teams after the U.S. team won the tournament.

more about how their behavior varies from one situation to the next than most observers do, who see them in limited contexts.

So far, our discussion of the mental shortcuts people use when making attributions has covered the role of perceptual salience and information availability. But what about a person's needs, desires, hopes, and fears—do these more emotional factors also create biases in our attributions? Are you motivated to see the world in certain ways because these views make you feel better, about both yourself and life in general? The answer is yes. The shortcuts we will discuss have a motivational basis; they are attributions that protect our self-esteem and our belief that the world is a safe and just place.

Self-Serving Attributions

Imagine that Alison goes to her chemistry class one day feeling anxious because she's getting her midterm grade that day. The professor returns her exam. Alison turns it over and sees that she has received an A. What will Alison think explains her grade? As you would guess, people tend to take personal credit for their successes but to blame their failures on external events beyond their control. Alison is likely to think that her success was due to the fact that she's good at chemistry and just plain smart.

How can we explain this departure from the typical actor-observer pattern of attributions? The answer is that when people's self-esteem is threatened, they often make **self-serving attributions.** Simply put, these attributions refer to our tendency to take credit for our successes (by making internal attributions) but to blame others or the situation (by making external attributions) for our failures (Carver, De Gregorio, & Gillis, 1980; McAllister, 1996; Miller & Ross, 1975; Pronin, Lin, & Ross, 2002; Robins & Beer, 2001).

A particularly interesting arena for studying self-serving attributions is professional sports. When explaining their victories, athletes and coaches both point overwhelmingly to aspects of their own teams or players. In fact, an analysis of professional athletes' and coaches' explanations for their team's wins and losses

Self-Serving Attributions

Explanations for one's successes that credit internal, dispositional factors and explanations for one's failures that blame external, situational factors

Try it!

Self-Serving Attributions in the Sports Pages

Do athletes and coaches tend to take credit for their wins but make excuses for their losses? Find out for yourself the next time you read the sports section of the newspaper or watch television interviews after a game. Analyze the sports figures' comments to see what kinds of attributions they make about their performance. Is the pattern a self-serving one?

For example, after a win, does the athlete make internal attributions like "We won because of excellent teamwork; our defensive line really held today" or "My serve was totally on"? After a loss, does the athlete make external attributions like "All the injuries we've had this season have really hurt us" or "That line judge made every call against me"? According to the research, these self-serving attributions should occur more often than the opposite pattern, for example, where a winner says, "We won because the other team played so badly it was like they were dead" (external) or where a loser says, "I played terribly today. I stank" (internal).

Next, see if you can find examples that fit Roesch & Amirkhan's (1997) research. Are self-serving attributions more common among solo-sport athletes than team-sport athletes? Do the athlete "stars" make more self-serving attributions than their less talented colleagues? Finally, think about the three reasons we identify for why people make self-serving attributions (maintaining self-esteem, presenting yourself positively to others, and personal knowledge about your past performances). When a sports figure makes a self-serving attribution, which one of these three motives do you think is at work? For example, if Michael Jordan attributed his team's loss to factors outside of himself, do you think he was protecting his self-esteem, trying to look good in front of others, or making the most logical attribution he could given his experience (i.e., he was so talented, most team losses weren't his fault)?

found that 80 percent of the attributions for wins were to such internal factors Lau & Russell (1980). For example, when explaining why the New York Yankees defeated the Los Angeles Dodgers in game 4 of the 1977 World Series, Yankees manager Billy Martin attributed it to a player on his team: "Pinella has done it all" (Lau & Russell, 1980, p. 32). Losses were more likely to be attributed to external causes, outside of the team's control. For example, the Dodgers attributed their loss not to their inferior ability or poor play but instead to bad luck or the superior play of the Yankees. Tommy Lasorda, the Dodgers' manager, said, "It took a great team to beat us, and the Yankees definitely are a great team" (p. 32).

Who is more likely to make self-serving attributions? Roesch and Amirkhan (1997) wondered if in the realm of sports, a player's skill, experience, and type of sport (team sports versus solo sports like tennis) affected the type of attribution the player made about a sports outcome. They found that less experienced athletes were more likely to make self-serving attributions than experienced ones. Experienced athletes realize that losses are sometimes their fault and that they can't always take credit for wins. Highly skilled athletes made more self-serving attributions than those with lower ability. The highly talented athlete believes that success is due to his or her prowess, while failure, an unusual and upsetting outcome, is due to teammates or other circumstances of the game. Finally, athletes in solo sports made more self-serving attributions than those in team sports. Solo athletes know that winning and losing rests on their shoulders. You can explore self-serving attributions by sports figures in the Try It! exercise above.

Why do we make self-serving attributions? Most people try to maintain their self-esteem whenever possible, even if that means distorting reality by changing a thought or belief. (We will discuss this concept at length in Chapter 6.) Here we see a specific attributional strategy that can be used to maintain or raise self-esteem: Just locate "causality"—the reason something happened—where it does you the most good (Greenberg, Pyszczynski, & Solomon, 1982; Snyder & Higgins, 1988; Wann & Schrader, 2000). We are particularly likely to engage in self-serving attributions when we fail at something and we feel we can't improve at it. The external attribution truly protects our self-esteem, as there is little hope we can do better in the future. But if we believe we can improve, we're more likely to attribute our current failure to internal causes and then work on improving (Duval & Silvia, 2002).

A second reason has to do with how we present ourselves to others, a topic we'll explore in the next chapter (Goffman, 1959). We want people to think well of us and to admire us. Telling others that our poor performance was due to some external cause puts a "good face" on failure; many people call this strategy "making excuses" (Greenberg et al., 1982; Tetlock, 1981; Weary & Arkin, 1981).

A third reason people make self-serving attributions has to do with our earlier discussion about the kind of information that is available to people. Let's imagine the attributional process of another student in the chemistry class, Ron, who did poorly on the midterm. Ron knows that he studied very hard for the midterm, that he typically does well on chemistry tests, and that in general he is a very good student. The D on the chemistry midterm comes as a surprise. The most logical attribution Ron can make is that the test was unfair—the D grade wasn't due to a lack of ability or effort. The professor, however, knows that some students did well on the test; given the information that is available to the professor, it is logical for him to conclude that Ron, and not the fact that it was a difficult test, was responsible for the poor grade (Miller & Ross, 1975; Nisbett & Ross, 1980).

People also alter their attributions to deal with other kinds of threats to their self-esteem. One of the hardest things to understand in life is the occurrence of tragic events, such as rapes, terminal diseases, and fatal accidents. Even when they happen to strangers we have never met, they can be upsetting. They remind us that if such tragedies can happen to someone else, they can happen to us. Of all the kinds of self-knowledge that we have, the knowledge that we are mortal and that bad things can happen to us is perhaps the hardest to accept (Greenberg, Pyszczynski, & Solomon, 1986; Greening & Chandler, 1997). So we take steps to deny this fact. One way we do this is by making **defensive attributions,** which are explanations for behavior that defend us from feelings of vulnerability and mortality.

One form of defensive attribution is **unrealistic optimism,** believing that good things are more likely to happen to oneself than to others and that bad things are less likely to happen to oneself than to others (Harris, 1996; Klein, 1996; McKenna & Albery, 2001; Regan, Snyder, & Kassin, 1995; Weinstein & Klein, 1996). To see how this works, estimate how likely it is that each of the following will happen to you, compared to how likely it is that they will happen to other students at your college or university: owning your own home, liking your postgraduate job, living past age 80, having a drinking problem, getting divorced, and being unable to have children. When college students were asked to answer these and similar questions, they were too optimistic (Weinstein, 1980). Virtually everyone thought that the good things were more likely to happen to them than to their peers and that the bad things were less likely to happen to them than to their peers. Further research has indicated that unrealistic optimism describes women's attitudes about getting breast cancer and men's attitudes about getting prostate cancer (Clarke, Lovegrove, Williams, &

Defensive Attributions

Explanations for behavior that avoid feelings of vulnerability and mortality

Unrealistic Optimism

A form of defensive attribution wherein people think that good things are more likely to happen to them than to their peers and that bad things are less likely to happen to them than to their peers

Macpherson, 2000), heroin users' attitudes about the risk of overdosing on the drug (McGregor, Darke, Ali, & Christie, 1998), gamblers' attitudes about winning the lottery (Rogers, 1998), and motorcycle riders' attitudes about having a serious bike accident (Rutter, Quine, & Albery, 1998).

Unrealistic optimism undoubtedly explains what lies behind the popularity of "extreme sports"—athletic activities that take place under very dangerous conditions where the chance of death is definitely present. Consider bungee jumping. To bungee jump, a person ties a high-strength elastic cord around one ankle and then leaps off a very high tower or bridge, free-falling and then bouncing at the end of the tether. Curious to know how people can take such risks, researchers interviewed British bungee jumpers right before they jumped (Middleton, Harris, & Surman, 1996). The researchers found strong support for unrealistic optimism among the jumpers: Each jumper perceived his or her own risk of injury to be less than that of the typical jumper. Being overly optimistic, then, is one way we try to protect ourselves from unpleasant feelings of mortality.

On a much sadder note, battered women have also been found to be unrealistically optimistic about the personal risks they run when they return to live with the man who abused them. They estimate their own risk as significantly lower than the risk of most battered women. In addition, their estimate of their personal risk is not related to the actual risk factors that describe their situation (Martin et al., 2000). Although unrealistic optimism may help us feel better in the short term, in the long term, it can be a potentially fatal attributional error.

Of course, just picking up a newspaper tells us that terrible things happen to people every day. How do we deal with these unsettling reminders? By believing that bad things happen only to bad people or at least to people who make stupid mistakes, poor choices, and so on. Therefore, bad things won't happen to us because we won't be that stupid or careless. Melvin Lerner (1980) has called this the **belief in a just world**—the assumption that people get what they deserve and deserve what they get. Because most of us view ourselves as decent, sensible, and capable human beings, surely bad things won't happen to us (Lambert, Burroughs, & Nguyen, 1999; Lipkus, Dalbert, & Siegler, 1996).

The just world belief has some sad and even tragic consequences. For example, suppose a female student on your campus was the victim of a date rape by a male fellow student. How do you think you and your friends would react? Would you wonder if she'd done something to trigger the rape? Was she acting suggestively earlier in the evening? Had she invited the man into her room?

Research by Elaine Walster (1966) and others has focused on such attributions, which these investigators call "blaming the victim" (e.g., Burger, 1981; Lerner & Miller, 1978; Stormo, Lang, & Stritzke, 1997). In several experiments, they have found that the victims of crimes or accidents are often seen as causing their fate. For example, not only do people tend to believe that rape victims are to blame for the rape (Abrams, Viki, Masser, & Bohner, 2003; Bell, Kuriloff, & Lottes, 1994), but battered wives are often seen as responsible for their abusive husbands' behavior (Summers & Feldman, 1984). By using this attributional bias, the perceiver does not have to acknowledge that there is a certain randomness in life, that an accident or criminal may be waiting just around the corner for an innocent person like oneself. The belief in a just world keeps anxiety-provoking thoughts about one's own safety at bay.

Belief in a Just World

A form of defensive attribution wherein people assume that bad things happen to bad people and that good things happen to good people

CULTURE AND ATTRIBUTIONS

For decades, the attributional biases we've discussed (the fundamental attribution error, the actor-observer difference, and defensive attributions) were thought to be universal: People everywhere, we thought, applied these cognitive shortcuts when forming attributions (Norenzayan, Choi, & Nisbett, 1999). But social psychologists are focusing more and more on the role of culture in many aspects of social behavior. Given that social psychology is the study of how the situation affects the individual, we can think of culture as an all-encompassing, higher-level situational variable. You are born into a culture; as you grow up, you learn the rules, norms, and ways of labeling reality that define your culture. In short, culture is one of the biggest "situations" affecting your daily life. In the past decade, social psychologists have explored attributional biases cross-culturally, with very interesting results. For example, do people everywhere make the fundamental attribution error? Or is culture, specifically Western culture, a cause of the correspondence bias and therefore of the fundamental attribution error? Let's look at the evidence.

Culture and the Correspondence Bias

North American and some other Western cultures stress individual autonomy. A person is perceived as independent and self-contained; his or her behavior reflects internal traits, motives, and values (Markus & Kitayama, 1991). The intellectual history of this cultural value can be traced from the Judeo-Christian belief in the individual soul and the English legal tradition of individual rights (Menon, Morris, Chiu, & Hong, 1999). In contrast, East Asian cultures such as those in China, Japan, and Korea stress group autonomy. The individual derives his or her sense of self from the social group to which he or she belongs. The intellectual history of this belief derives from the Confucian tradition, for example, the "community man" (*qunti de fenzi*) or "social being" (*shehui de renge*) (Menon et al., 1999, p. 703).

The question is, does Western culture, which emphasizes individual freedom and autonomy, socialize its members to prefer dispositional attributions over situational ones? Are Westerners brought up to look inward to explain their actions rather than looking at the situation? (Dix, 1993; Rholes, Newman, & Ruble, 1990). In comparison, do collectivist (often Eastern) cultures, which emphasize group membership, interdependence, and conformity to group norms, socialize their members to prefer situational dispositions over dispositional ones? In these cultures, are children raised to think that the situation, more than the individual, explains behavior? (Fletcher & Ward, 1988; Hong, Morris, Chiu, & Benet-Martinez, 2000; Markus & Kitayama, 1991; Triandis, 1990, 2001). As a result of this very different socialization, do people in collectivist cultures show less of a correspondence bias than people in individualistic cultures? Do they therefore make fewer fundamental attribution errors than Westerners do?

The answer is both simple and complex: People in individualist cultures do prefer dispositional attributions about others, relative to people in collectivist cultures, who prefer situational attributions. However, it is a mistake to think that members of collectivist cultures don't make dispositional attributions. They do—it's just that they are more aware of how the situation affects behavior and more likely to take situational effects into account (Choi, Dalal, Kim-Prieto, & Park, 2003; Choi & Nisbett, 1998; Choi, Nisbett, & Norenzayan, 1999; Krull et al., 1999; Miyamoto & Kitayama, 2002). Recent research suggests that a tendency to think dispositionally about others—the correspondence bias—appears in many cultures. The difference is that people in collectivist cultures go beyond individual explanations, including information about the situation as well.

Let's look at the evidence. Several researchers have conducted studies that are variations of the design used by Edward Jones and Victor Harris (1967), which we discussed earlier in this chapter. In this design, a target person is told to write an essay or give a speech after being assigned a specific position (e.g., pro or con) on the topic. Afterward, research participants are asked to rate the target person's real attitude on the topic. Remember, the position of the essay was assigned and not necessarily the target's true attitude. Nonetheless, as we saw earlier, American participants show a correspondence bias between the topic and the speaker and commit the fundamental attribution error: *They assume that the attitude expressed by the target person is the person's true attitude.* The same thing happens in Korea, Japan, and China: Participants believe the content of the target's speech or essay indicates what he or she is really like (Choi & Nisbett, 1998; Krull et al., 1999; Kashima, Siegel, Tanaka, & Kashima, 1992; Kitayama & Masuda, 1997; Masuda & Kitayama, 1996).

What if we made the situation more salient in an essay-writing type of study? Would participants from collectivistic cultures show less of a correspondence bias than partipants from individualistic cultures? Researchers made the situational information more salient in these studies by having the participants go through the same procedure as the target person they are judging. Like the target, the observers are also assigned to write an essay on a position they did not choose. Sometimes they are also given prepared statements to include in their essays. When later asked to judge the target's attitude, the observers should realize that the target was just as constrained by the situation as they were, so the content of the target's essay shouldn't reveal much about the target. What happens? American participants still make the fundamental attribution error when judging the target person; they still think the essay tells them something about what the target is really like. But in collectivist cultures, participants take this situational information into account and make far fewer dispositional attributions about the target (Choi & Nisbett, 1998; Kitayama & Masuda, 1997; Masuda & Kitayama, 1996).

To sum up, there is indeed something "fundamental" about the correspondence bias and the fundamental attribution error—people, regardless of their culture, like to think dispositionally about others and therefore demonstrate the correspondence bias. However, people in collectivist cultures like the East Asian ones, because of their values and experience, also seem able to override this dispositionalist tendency. They are more likely than people in Western, individualistic cultures to take situational information into account when forming attributions, especially if the situational information is particularly salient and noticeable.

CONNECTIONS

Attributions East and West

Does this cultural difference apply to attributions people make in their real lives as opposed to those they make in the lab? Evidence suggests that it does. For example, Joan Miller (1984) asked people of two cultures—Hindus living in India and Americans living in the United States—to think of various examples of behaviors performed by their friends and to explain why those behaviors occurred. The American participants preferred dispositional explanations for the behaviors. They were more likely to say that the causes of their friends' behaviors were the kind of people they were, rather than the situation or context in which the behaviors occurred. In contrast, Hindu participants preferred situational explanations for their friends' behaviors. Thinking about their friends was an interesting and important task, making situational information more salient to them than it was to Americans.

But, you might be thinking, perhaps the Americans and Hindus generated different kinds of examples. Perhaps the Hindus thought of behaviors that really were more situationally caused, whereas the Americans thought of behaviors that really were more dispositionally caused. To test this alternative hypothesis, Miller (1984) took some of the behaviors generated by the Hindu participants and gave them to Americans to explain. The difference in internal and external attributions appeared again: Americans still found internal, dispositional causes for the behaviors that the Hindus had thought were caused by the situation.

Another study that found cultural differences in the prevalence of the correspondence bias compared newspaper articles in Chinese- and English-language newspapers. The researchers targeted two mass murders, one committed by a Chinese graduate student in Iowa and one committed by a Caucasian postal worker in Michigan (Morris & Peng, 1994). They coded all the news articles about the two crimes that appeared in the *New York Times* and the *World Journal,* a Chinese-language U.S. newspaper. The results showed that journalists writing in English made significantly more dispositional attributions about both mass murderers than journalists writing in Chinese did. For example, American reporters described one murderer as a "darkly disturbed man" with a "sinister edge" to his personality. Chinese reporters, when describing the same murderer, emphasized more situational causes, such as "not getting along with his adviser" and his "isolation from the Chinese community."

Thus people in Western cultures appear to be more like personality psychologists, viewing behavior in dispositional terms. In contrast, people in Eastern cultures seem to be more like social psychologists, considering the situational causes of behavior.

In conclusion, how can we summarize cultural differences in the attribution process that underlies the fundamental attribution error? Recall the two-step process we discussed earlier (see Figure 4.7). What are people in collectivist cultures doing differently from people in individualist cultures? At what stage in this process do the two cultures diverge? People everywhere start off at the same point, showing the correspondence bias: They automatically make dispositional attributions about other people. What happens next is that people in collectivistic cultures look to the situation. They revise and correct their first impressions, taking the situation into account. Westerners tend to avoid this second step. Their first impression, the dispositional attribution, sticks (Choi et al., 2003; Knowles, Morris, Chiu, & Hong, 2001).

Culture and Other Attributional Biases

Continuing to explore the link between culture and attributional biases, social psychologists have examined the actor/observer difference in Korea and the United States (Choi & Nisbett, 1998). They found that Korean and American research participants did not differ in the attributions they made to themselves—the "actors." They both made situational attributions about their behavior. They differed only in the attributions they formed about others, and in a familiar way. Americans were more likely to think another person's behavior was due to his or her disposition (the fundamental attribution error), while the Koreans were more likely to think the other person's behavior was due to the situation.

Similarly, a few researchers have examined the self-serving bias and found a strong cultural component to it as well. For example, traditional Chinese culture values modesty and harmony with others. Thus Chinese students are expected to attribute their success to other people, such as their teachers or parents, or to other aspects of the situation, such as the high quality of their school (Bond, 1996; Leung, 1996). Their cultural tradition does not encourage them to attribute their success to themselves (such as to their talent or intelligence), as it does in the United States and other Western countries. As you might expect, Chinese research participants took less credit for their successes than U.S. participants did (Anderson, 1999; Lee & Seligman, 1997). Instead,

Research has shown that people vary in their *belief in the just world* due to their culture. For example, whites in South Africa subscribe to this belief strongly, believing that the poor and the rich each have what they deserve.

Things are seldom as they seem, Skim milk masquerades as cream.

—W. S. Gilbert, H.M.S. Pinafore

Chinese students attributed their success to aspects of their situation, reflecting the values of their culture. Interestingly, Chinese Americans, despite living in the United States, did not demonstrate the self-serving bias of non-Asian Americans (Lee & Seligman, 1997). Their attributional pattern was identical to that of mainland Chinese students. What about failure? Recall that in individualistic cultures like the United States, people tend toward the self-serving bias, looking outside of themselves—to the situation—to explain failure. In collectivist cultures like China, the reverse is true: People attribute failure to internal causes, not to external ones (Anderson, 1999; Fry & Ghosh, 1980; Oishi, Wyer, & Colcombe, 2000).

Recall that the belief in a just world is a defensive attribution that helps people maintain their vision of life as safe, orderly, and predictable. Is there a cultural component to it as well? Adrian Furnham (1993) argues that in a society where most people tend to believe the world is a just place, economic and social inequities are considered "fair." In such societies, people believe that the poor and disadvantaged have less because they deserve less. Thus the just world attribution can be used to explain and justify injustice. Preliminary research suggests that this is the case: In cultures with extremes of wealth and poverty, just world attributions are more common than in cultures where wealth is more evenly distributed (Dalbert & Yamauchi, 1994; Furnham, 1993; Furnham & Procter, 1989). For example, research participants in India and South Africa received higher scores on the just world belief scale than participants in the United States, Australia, Hong Kong, and Zimbabwe, who had scores in the middle of the scale. The lowest-scoring groups in the sample—those who believed the least in a just world—were the British and the Israelis (Furnham, 1993).

Finally, does the spotlight effect shine as brightly around the world as it does in the United States? Given all that we've discussed so far, you'd predict that the collectivist culture of Japan should make its members more sensitive to situational explanations for other people's behavior. Therefore, the Japanese should not magnify or overestimate the correspondence bias in people who are judging them. This is exactly what researchers found. Japanese intuitive beliefs about the fundamental attribution error are indeed weaker than American intuitive beliefs (Van Boven et al., 1999).

HOW ACCURATE ARE OUR ATTRIBUTIONS AND IMPRESSIONS?

When we make attributions, we are trying to understand other people and predict their behavior. But how accurate are we? Sometimes, not as accurate as we think we are. First impressions—the quick, attributional snapshots we form when we first meet someone—are often wrong (De Paulo, Kenny, Hoover, Webb, & Oliver, 1987; Funder & Colvin, 1988), but our ability to form accurate impressions of others improves as we get to know them (Wegener & Petty, 1995).

Our impressions are sometimes wrong because of the mental shortcuts we use when forming social judgments. The first culprit is our familiar friend, the fundamental attribution error. People are too ready to attribute others' actions to their personalities rather than to the situation.

That doesn't mean that people are always wrong when making dispositional attributions. Even if people underestimate the power of social situations, their impressions can still be correct. After all, our personalities lead us to seek certain situations and to avoid others (Gilbert & Malone, 1995; Snyder & Ickes, 1985). For example, suppose you are forming an attribution about a new acquaintance, Andrea, whom you met at a party. Let's say that Andrea is an outgoing person who chooses to go to lots of parties. In this case, it is not so much the situation that is affecting her behavior as it is her disposition that is choosing her situations. It really doesn't matter whether you decide that Andrea is outgoing because of the situation (the party) or her disposition, because *both* are true—her outgoing nature draws her to situations that encourage her to act in an outgoing way. Nevertheless, situations can be very powerful and sometimes override personality, so to the extent that we fail to take the situation into account, our impressions will be inaccurate.

Another reason our impressions can be wrong concerns our use of schemas. We've seen that people use implicit personality theories to fill in the gaps in their knowledge about others. Our impressions are therefore only as accurate as our theories. While many of our theories are likely to be correct, they can lead us astray, often dramatically, as in the case of stereotypes.

To improve the accuracy of your attributions and impressions, remember that the correspondence bias, the fundamental attribution error, the actor/observer difference, and defensive attributions exist, and try to counteract these biases. Even with such biases operating, we are quite accurate perceivers of other people. We do very well most of the time (Funder, 1995; Kenny, Albright, Malloy, & Kashy, 1994). We are adept at reading and interpreting nonverbal forms of communication; in fact, most of us are actually better at this than we realize (Ambady, Bernieri, & Richeson, 2000; Archer & Akert, 1980; Costanzo & Archer, 1989). We become more accurate at perceiving others as we get to know them better, and since most of our truly important social interactions involve people we know well, this is good news. In short, we are capable of making both stunningly accurate assessments of people and horrific attributional mistakes.

SUMMARY

Nonverbal Behavior

Social perception is the study of how people form impressions and make inferences about other people. People constantly form such impressions because doing so helps them understand and predict their social worlds.

One source of information people use is the nonverbal behavior of others. **Nonverbal communication** is used to **encode** or express emotion, convey attitudes, communicate personality traits, and facilitate and regulate verbal speech. Many studies show that people can accurately **decode** subtle nonverbal cues. For example, the six major facial expressions of emotion are perceived accurately around the world. Sometimes facial expressions are **affect blends,** where one part of the face registers one emotion and another part of the face registers another. Facial expressions can vary according to culturally determined **display rules.** These rules dictate which expressions are appropriate to display. **Emblems**—nonverbal gestures that have specific meanings—are also culturally determined. In general, women are better at understanding and conveying emotion nonverbally. One exception, though, is that women are less accurate at detecting deception when observing nonverbal behavior. According to the **social role theory** of sex differences, this may be because in many societies women have learned different skills, one of which is to be polite in social interactions, overlooking the fact that someone may be lying.

Implicit Personality Theories: Filling In the Blanks

Often it is difficult to tell how someone feels or what kind of person he or she is solely from the person's nonverbal behavior. As a result, we go beyond the information given in people's behavior, making inferences about their feelings, traits, and motives. One way we do this is to rely on an **implicit personality theory** to fill in the blanks. Such a theory is composed of our general notions about which personality traits go together in one person. Culture plays a role in the formation of our implicit personality theories.

Causal Attribution: Answering the "Why" Question

According to **attribution theory,** we try to determine why people do what they do in order to uncover the feelings and traits that are behind their actions. The **covariation model** focuses on observations of behavior across time, place, actors, and targets of the behavior and examines how the perceiver chooses either an **internal** or an **external attribution.** We make such choices by using **consensus, distinctiveness,** and **consistency information.**

People also use various mental shortcuts when making attributions, including the use of schemas and theories. One common shortcut is the **correspondence bias,** the tendency to believe that behavior corresponds to dispositions. This bias can lead to the **fundamental attribution error,** which is the tendency to overestimate the extent to which people do what they do because of internal, dispositional factors. A reason for this error is that a person's behavior usually has greater **perceptual salience** than the surrounding situation does. The **two-step process of attribution** indicates that the initial, automatic attribution about another person's behavior tends to be dispositional, but it can be corrected at the second step with conscious and effortful thinking, bringing to mind possible situational explanations. The **actor-observer difference** is a qualification of the fundamental attribution error: We are more likely to commit this error when explaining other people's behavior than when explaining our own behavior. The actor-observer effect occurs because perceptual salience and information availability differ for the actor and the observer.

Culture and Attributions

Finally, culture plays an important role in the formation of attributions. People from collectivist and individualist cultures demonstrate a correspondent bias. However, members of collectivist cultures are more aware of situational explanations of behavior and thus less likely to make the fundamental attribution error than members of individualist cultures, as long as situational variables are salient. People in Western countries understand intuitively that the fundamental attribution error occurs and therefore fall prey to the **spotlight effect,** overestimating how salient they are to other people.

Self-Serving Attributions

People's attributions are also influenced by their personal needs. **Self-serving attributions** occur when people make internal attributions for their successes and external attributions for their failures. This may be an attributional style found only in individualist cultures. **Defensive attributions** help people avoid feelings of mortality. One type of defensive attribution is **unrealistic optimism** about the future, whereby we think that good things are more likely to happen to us than to other people and bad things are less likely to happen to us than to others. Another type of defensive attribution is the **belief in a just world,** whereby we believe that bad things happen to bad people and good things happen to good people.

How Accurate Are Our Attributions and Impressions?

Not surprisingly, the more we get to know someone, the more accurate we are at describing their traits and motives. Even when judging people we know well, however, the shortcuts we use sometimes lead to mistaken impressions. For example, we tend to make more dispositional attributions about other people than are warranted.

CRITICAL THINKING QUESTIONS

1. Consider the "dark side" of implicit personality theories. Sometimes when we meet people, an aspect of their identity triggers stereotypes in our minds. Do these stereotypes have an implicit personality component? That is, do we believe that certain personality characteristics describe a person just because he or she is a member of a certain group? Why does this matter?

2. Think about your first impressions of a person—for example, when you met your college roommate or when you went out on a first date (especially a blind date). To what extent did you rely on dispositional attributions to get an initial understanding of that person? Were you accurate, or was the correspondence bias operating?

3. When we feel threatened, we sometimes resort to the defensive attribution of belief in a just world (bad things happen to other people because they made mistakes that we wouldn't make). Can this defensive attribution be applied to the tragic loss of thousands of lives on September 11, 2001? How does this affect people's anxiety about future terrorist attacks and the probability that they might themselves be harmed?

CHAPTER

5

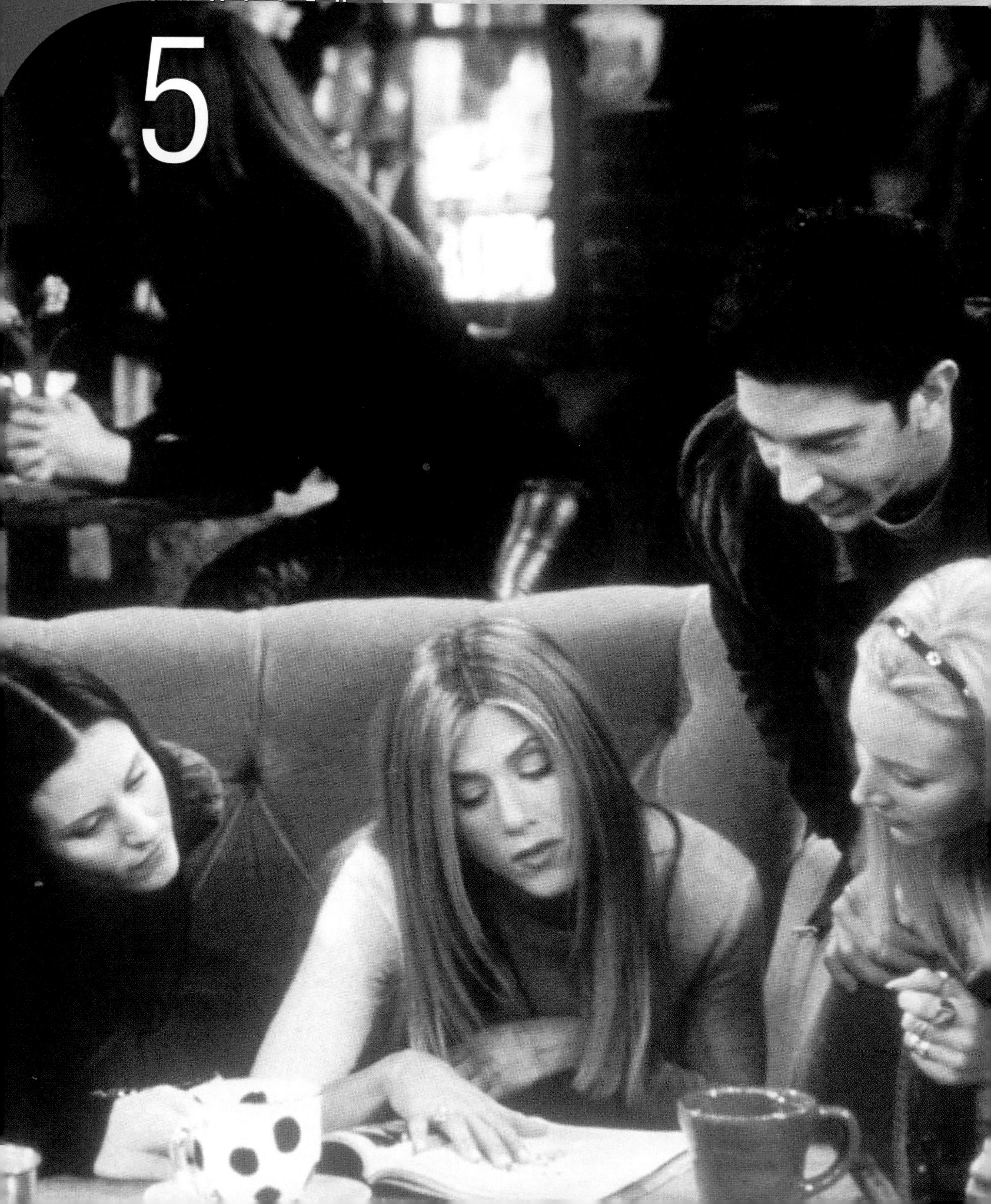

Self-Knowledge:

How We Come to Understand Ourselves

In an episode of the television show *Friends,* Ross faces a dilemma. Rachel, whom he has pursued for years, has finally showed a romantic interest in him, and they shared their first kiss. The problem is that Ross is currently dating Julie, whom he also likes a great deal. What to do? Urged on by his friends Chandler and Joey, Ross makes a list of the things he likes and dislikes about each woman, to try to clarify his thoughts.

Ross was in good company in taking the "pluses and minuses" approach. Over two centuries ago, Benjamin Franklin gave this advice about how to make difficult choices:

> My way is to divide half a sheet of paper by a line into two columns, writing over the one Pro, and over the other Con. Then . . . I put down . . . short hints of the different motives. . . . When each is thus considered, separately and comparatively, and the whole lies before me, I think I can judge better, and am less likely to make a rash step. (quoted in Goodman, 1945, p. 746)

Not everyone, however, believes in listing pros and cons. Consider the Peruvian writer Mario Vargas Llosa's reaction to judging films at the Berlin film festival:

> I went to every screening with a fresh pack of notecards that I would dutifully cover with my impressions of each and every film. The result, of course, was that the movies ceased to be fun and turned into problems, a struggle against time, darkness and my own esthetic emotions, which these autopsies confused. I was so worried about evaluating every aspect of every film that my entire system of values went into shock, and I quickly realized that I could no longer easily tell what I liked or didn't or why. (Vargas Llosa, 1986, p. 23)

What is the best way to decipher one's feelings when facing a difficult choice? Is it best to make careful lists of pros and cons, as Franklin recommended, or to go with one's gut feelings, as Varga Llosa implied? More generally,

Researchers have examined whether other species have a self-concept, by seeing whether they recognize that an image in a mirror is themselves and not another member of their species. The same procedure has been used with humans, revealing that people develop a self-concept around the age of two.

what is the nature of the self, and how do people discover it? These are the questions to which we turn.

THE NATURE OF THE SELF

Who are you? How did you come to be this person you call "myself"? The founder of American psychology, William James (1842–1910), described the basic duality of our perception of self. First, the self is composed of our thoughts and beliefs about ourselves, or what James (1890) called the "known," or, more simply, the "me." Second, the self is also the active processor of information, the "knower," or "I." In modern terms, we refer to the known aspect of the self as the **self-concept,** which is the content of the self (our knowledge about who we are), and to the knower aspect as **self-awareness,** which is the act of thinking about ourselves. These two aspects of the self combine to create a coherent sense of identity: Your self is both a book (full of fascinating content collected over time) and the reader of that book (who at any moment can access a specific chapter or add a new one). In this chapter, we will consider both aspects of the self—the nature of the self-concept and how we come to know ourselves through self-awareness.

A good place to begin is with the question of whether we are the only species with a sense of self. Some fascinating studies suggest that we are not alone in this regard (Gallup, 1977, 1997; Gallup & Suarez, 1986). Researchers placed a mirror in an animal's cage until the mirror became a familiar object. The animal was then briefly anesthetized and an odorless red dye was painted on its brow or ear. What happened when the animal woke up and looked in the mirror? Chimpanzees and orangutans immediately touched the area of their heads marked with the red spot. Dolphins have also shown signs of recognizing themselves in mirrors. When a spot was drawn on their bodies (with a nontoxic marker), the dolphins swam directly to mirrors and twisted their bodies to see the spot (Reiss & Marino, 2001).

These studies suggest that chimps and orangutans, and possibly dolphins, have a rudimentary self-concept. They realize that the image in the mirror is themselves and not another animal, and they recognize that they look different from how they looked before (de Veer, Gallup, Theall, van den Bos, & Povinelli, 2003; Gallup, 1997; Povinelli, 1994; Mitchell, 2003).

Wondering when a sense of self develops in humans, researchers used a variation of the red-dye test with toddlers and found that self-recognition develops at around age 2 (Asendorf, Warkentin, & Baudonniere, 1996; Lewis, 1997; Povinelli, Landau, & Perilloux, 1996). As we grow older, this rudimentary self-concept becomes more complex. One way psychologists have studied how people's self-concept changes from childhood to adulthood is to ask people of different ages to answer the simple question "Who am I?" Typically, a child's self-concept is concrete, with references to clear-cut, easily observable characteristics like age, sex, neighborhood, and hobbies. A 9-year-old answered the question this way: "I have brown eyes. I have brown hair. I have brown eyebrows. . . . I'm a boy. I have an uncle that is almost 7 feet tall" (Montemayor & Eisen, 1977, p. 317).

As we mature, we place less emphasis on physical characteristics and more on psychological states (our thoughts and feelings) and on considerations of how other people judge us (Hart & Damon, 1986; Livesley & Bromley, 1973; Montemayor & Eisen, 1977). Consider this twelfth-grade high school student's answer to the "Who am I?" question:

Self-Concept

The content of the self; that is, our knowledge about who we are

Self-Awareness

The act of thinking about ourselves

I am a human being. . . . I am a moody person. I am an indecisive person. I am an ambitious person. I am a very curious person. I am not an individual. I am a loner. I am an American (God help me). I am a Democrat. I am a liberal person. I am a radical. I am a conservative. I am a pseudoliberal. I am an atheist. I am not a classifiable person (i.e., I don't want to be). (Montemayor & Eisen, 1977, p. 318)

Clearly, this teenager has moved well beyond descriptions of her hobbies and appearance (Harter, 2003).

Functions of the Self

Why do human adults have such a multifaceted, complex definition of self? Researchers have found that the self serves both an organizational function and an executive function (Baumeister, 1998; Graziano, Jensen-Campbell, & Finch, 1997; Leary & Tangney, 2003).

Organizational Function of the Self As we saw in Chapter 3, schemas help us organize what we know about the social world; schemas also influence the information we notice, think about, and remember. Similarly, we use **self-schemas,** mental structures that help us to organize our knowledge about ourselves (Dunning & Hayes, 1996; Kihlstrom & Klein, 1994; Markus, 1977; Pincus & Morley, 2001; von Hippel, Hawkins, & Schooler, 2001).

Suppose that over the course of a day, Sarah and Caitlin play volleyball together and watch an old movie on television. How will they organize, remember, and think about these experiences? It depends on their self-schemas. Say that Sarah plays a lot of sports and that athleticism is an important self-schema for her. She is likely to think about and remember the volleyball game more than the movie. Caitlin, on the other hand, has performed in several plays and loves to act. Because acting is more likely to be one of Caitlin's self-schemas, she will think about and remember the movie more than the volleyball game. Self-schemas also act as lenses through which people view others. Suppose that Sarah and Caitlin meet Sam, a talented athlete and actor. Sarah is more likely notice and remember his athletic skills, whereas Caitlin is more likely to notice and remember his acting talents (Showers & Zeigler-Hill, 2003).

Here's a consequence of having a rich set of self-schemas that you can try out on your friends. Read them a list of twenty adjectives, such as *warm, colorful, quiet,* and *soft.* Ask one group of friends to think about how much each adjective describes themselves, and ask another group to think about the meaning of each adjective or how much it describes someone else. Then ask both groups to write down as many of the words as they can remember. More than likely you will find a **self-reference effect,** which is the tendency for people to remember information better if they relate it to themselves (Markus, 1977; Kihlstrom, Beer, & Klein, 2003; Symons & Johnson, 1997). Integrating information with our self-schemas helps us organize it better and connect it to other information about ourselves, which makes us more likely to remember it later.

Self-Schemas

Mental structures that people use to organize their knowledge about themselves and that influence what they notice, think about, and remember about themselves

Self-Reference Effect

The tendency for people to remember information better if they relate it to themselves

Self-Regulation: The Executive Function The self also serves an executive function, regulating people's behavior, choices, and plans for the future, much like the chief executive officer of a corporation (Baumeister & Vohs, 2003; Carver & Scheier, 1998; Higgins, 1989). We appear to be the only species, for example, that can imagine events that have not yet occurred and engage in long-term planning, and it is the self that does this planning and exerts control over our actions. Regulating our behavior and choices in optimal ways, of course, can be easier said than done, as anyone who has been on a diet or tried to quit smoking knows. An interesting question, then, is how the self engages in

When Harvard-educated Masako Owada abandoned her promising career to marry Crown Prince Naruhito of Japan and assumed the traditional roles required of her, many Western women questioned her decision. At issue for many were cultural differences relating to interdependence versus emphasis on independence of the self.

self-regulation. When we face a difficult choice ("Should I go to the party or study for my midterm?"), what determines how successful we will be at exerting self-control?

We discuss these questions in relation to health-related behaviors (e.g., trying to quit smoking) in the first Social Psychology in Action module, "Social Psychology and Health." For now, consider an intriguing approach to self-control called the *self-regulatory resource model.* According to this model, self-control is a limited resource, kind of like a muscle that gets tired with frequent use but then rebounds in strength (Baumeister & Hetherington, 1996; Baumeister, Muraven, & Tice, 2000; Vohs & Hetherington, 2000). The idea is that people have a limited amount of energy to devote to self-control and that spending it on one task limits the amount that can be spent on another task, just as going for a 5-mile run makes it difficult to immediately play a game of basketball.

To test this idea, researchers ask participants to exert self-control on one task, to see if this reduces their ability to exert control on a subsequent and completely unrelated task. In one study, for example, people who were instructed to suppress a thought (don't think about a white bear) were worse at trying to regulate their emotions on a second task (try not to laugh while watching a comedy film), compared to people who did not first have to suppress their thoughts (Muraven, Tice, & Baumeister, 1998). Although the tasks were quite different, the researchers suggest that the first one depleted the resource people use to control their behaviors and feelings, making it difficult to engage in a subsequent act of self-control.

These findings help explain why we often fail at self-control when we are under stress. Former smokers, for example, are more likely to take up smoking again when experiencing life's slings and arrows. Dealing with stress depletes the "self resource," such that there is less to spend in other areas. Similarly, efforts at self-control are more likely to fail at night, when the self resource has been depleted by a day of making choices and resisting temptations; dieters are more likely to break their diets at night, and bulimics are more likely to engage in binge eating at night (Baumeister et al., 2000). People are best at self-control when they are well-rested, such as in the morning after a good night's sleep.

Cultural Differences in Defining the Self

In June 1993, Masako Owada, a 29-year-old Japanese woman, married Crown Prince Naruhito of Japan. Masako was a very bright career diplomat in the foreign ministry, educated at Harvard and Oxford. She spoke five languages and was on the fast track to a prestigious diplomatic career. Her decision to marry the prince surprised many observers, because it meant she would have to give up her career. Indeed, she gave up any semblance of an independent life, becoming subservient to the prince and the rest of the royal family and spending much of her time participating in rigid royal ceremonies. Although some people hoped that she would modernize the monarchy, "so far the princess has not changed the imperial family as much as it has changed her" ("Girl Born to Japan's Princess," 2001).

How do you feel about Masako's decision to marry the prince? Your answer may say something about the nature of your self-concept and the culture in which you grew up. In many Western cultures, people have an **independent view of the self,** which is a way of defining oneself in terms of one's own internal thoughts, feelings, and actions and not in terms of the thoughts, feelings, and actions of others (Cross & Gore, 2003; Markus & Kitayama, 1991, 2001; Nisbett, 2003; Triandis, 1995). Westerners learn to define themselves as quite separate from other people and to value independence and uniqueness. Consequently, many Western observers were mystified by Masako's decision to marry the crown

Independent View of the Self

A way of defining oneself in terms of one's own internal thoughts, feelings, and actions and not in terms of the thoughts, feelings, and actions of other people

prince. They assumed that she was coerced into the marriage by a backward, sexist society that did not properly value her worth as an individual with an independent life of her own.

In contrast, many Asian and other non-Western cultures have an **interdependent view of the self,** which is a way of defining oneself in terms of one's relationships to other people and recognizing that one's behavior is often determined by the thoughts, feelings, and actions of others. Connectedness and interdependence between people is valued, whereas independence and uniqueness are frowned on. For example, when asked to complete sentences beginning with "I am . . . ," people from Asian cultures are more likely to refer to social groups, such as their family or religious group, than people from Western cultures are (Bochner, 1994; Triandis, 1989). To many Japanese and other Asians, Masako's decision to give up her career was not at all surprising and was a positive, natural consequence of her view of herself as connected and obligated to others, such as her parents and the royal family. What is viewed as positive and normal behavior by one culture may be viewed very differently by another.

Ted Singelis (1994) developed a questionnaire that measures the extent to which people view themselves as interdependent or independent. Sample items from this scale are given in the Try It! exercise on page 136. Singelis administered the questionnaire to students at the University of Hawaii at Manoa and found that Asian Americans agreed more with the interdependence than the independence items, whereas Caucasian Americans agreed more with the independence than the interdependence items.

We do not mean to imply that every member of a Western culture has an independent view of the self and that every member of an Asian culture has an interdependent view of the self. Within cultures, there are differences in the self-concept, and these differences are likely to increase as contact between cultures increases. It is interesting to note, for example, that Masako's decision to marry the prince was unpopular among at least some young Japanese women, who felt that her choice was not a positive sign of interdependence but a betrayal of the feminist cause in Japan (Sanger, 1993).

Nonetheless, the differences between the Western and Eastern sense of self is real and has interesting consequences for communication between the cultures. Indeed, the differences in the sense of self are so fundamental that it is very difficult for people with independent selves to appreciate what it is like to have an interdependent self, and vice versa. Western readers might find it difficult to appreciate the Asian sense of interdependence; similarly, many Japanese find it difficult to comprehend that Americans could possibly know who they are separate from the social groups to which they belong. After giving a lecture on the Western view of the self to a group of Japanese students, one psychologist reported that the students "sighed deeply and said at the end, 'Could this really be true?'" (Kitayama & Markus, 1994, p. 18). To paraphrase William Shakespeare, in Western society the self is the measure of all things. But however natural we consider this conception of the self to be, it is important to remember that it is socially constructed and therefore may differ from culture to culture.

The squeaky wheel gets the grease.

—American proverb

The nail that stands out gets pounded down.

—Japanese proverb

Gender Differences in Defining the Self

Is there any truth to the stereotype that when women get together, they talk about interpersonal problems and relationships, whereas men talk about anything but their feelings (usually sports)? Although this stereotype of "clueless men" is clearly an exaggeration, it does have a grain of truth and reflects a difference in women's and men's self-concept (Baumeister & Sommer, 1997; Cross, Bacon, & Morris, 2000; Cross & Madson, 1997; Gabriel & Gardner, 1999).

Interdependent View of the Self
A way of defining oneself in terms of one's relationships to other people; recognizing that one's behavior is often determined by the thoughts, feelings, and actions of others

Try it!

A Measure of Independence and Interdependence

Instructions: Indicate the extent to which you agree or disagree with each of these statements.

	Strongly Disagree						Strongly Agree
1. My happiness depends on the happiness of those around me.	1	2	3	4	5	6	7
2. I will sacrifice my self-interest for the benefit of the group I am in.	1	2	3	4	5	6	7
3. It is important to me to respect decisions made by the group.	1	2	3	4	5	6	7
4. If my brother or sister fails, I feel responsible.	1	2	3	4	5	6	7
5. Even when I strongly disagree with group members, I avoid an argument.	1	2	3	4	5	6	7
6. I am comfortable with being singled out for praise or rewards.	1	2	3	4	5	6	7
7. Being able to take care of myself is a primary concern for me.	1	2	3	4	5	6	7
8. I prefer to be direct and forthright when dealing with people I've just met.	1	2	3	4	5	6	7
9. I enjoy being unique and different from others in many respects.	1	2	3	4	5	6	7
10. My personal identity, independent of others, is very important to me.	1	2	3	4	5	6	7

Note: These questions are taken from a scale developed by Singelis (1994) to measure the strength of people's interdependence and independent views of themselves. The actual scale consists of twelve items that measure interdependence and twelve items that measure independence. We have reproduced five of each type of item here: The first five are designed to measure interdependence, and the last five are designed to measure independence.

For scoring instructions, turn to page 163.

(Adapted from Singelis, 1994)

Women have more *relational interdependence,* meaning that they focus more on their close relationships, such as how they feel about their spouse or their child. Men have more *collective interdependence,* meaning that they focus on their memberships in larger groups, such as the fact that they are Americans or that they belong to a fraternity (Brewer & Gardner, 1996; Gabriel & Gardner, 1999). Starting in early childhood, American girls are more likely to develop intimate friendships, cooperate with others, and focus their attention on social relationships, whereas boys are more likely to focus on their group memberships (Cross & Madson, 1997). These differences persist into adulthood, such that women focus more on intimacy and cooperation with a small number of close others and are in fact more likely to discuss personal topics and disclose their emotions than men are (Caldwell & Peplau, 1982; Davidson & Duberman, 1982).

Men focus more on their social groups like sports teams. For example, when women and men were asked to describe either a positive or negative emotional event in their lives, women tended to mention personal relationships, such as becoming engaged or the death of a family member (Gabriel & Gardner, 1999). Men talked about events involving larger groups, such as the time they joined a fraternity or their sports team lost an important game (see Figure 5.1). To see how much your self-concept is based on a sense of relational interdependence, answer the questions in the Try It! exercise on page 138.

When considering gender differences such as these, we need to be cautious: The psychological differences between men and women are far fewer than the ways in which they are the same (Deaux & LaFrance, 1998). Nevertheless, there

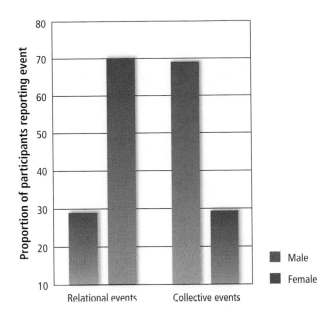

FIGURE 5.1

Gender differences in types of interdependence.

Male and female college students were asked to describe an important emotional event in their lives. Women reported more relational events, ones that had to do with close personal relationships. Men reported more collective events, ones that had to do with their membership in larger groups.

(From Gabriel & Gardner, 1999, p. 648)

do appear to be differences in the way women and men define themselves in the United States, with women having a greater sense of relational interdependence than men.

To summarize, the self-concept serves basic adaptive functions common to all cultures, but cultural and gender also shape the content of our self-concept. But how do we learn who we are in the first place? How did you discover the things that make you uniquely you? It turns out that there are some basic motives that govern how people view themselves, as we discussed in Chapter 1 (Baumeister, 1998; Dweck, Higgins, & Grant-Pillow, 2003; Fiske, 2003; Sedikides & Strube, 1997). People want accurate self-knowledge (selfassessment), confirmations of what they already believe (self-verification), and positive feedback (self-enhancement). The emphasis on these motives differs from culture to culture and, within cultures, at different points of the life cycle (Graziano et al., 1997; Heine, Lehman, Markus, & Kitayama, 1999; Tesser, 2003). Nonetheless, most psychologists agree that the motives are fundamental and common to all people. In the remainder of this chapter, we will discuss self-assessment, or the ways in which people attempt to gain accurate knowledge about themselves. We will discuss the other self-motives in Chapter 6.

KNOWING OURSELVES THROUGH INTROSPECTION

When we told you we were going to describe the sources of information you use to construct a self-concept, you may have thought, "Good grief! I don't need a social psychology textbook to tell me that! It's not exactly a surprise; I just think about myself. No big deal." In other words, you rely on **introspection,** looking inward to examine the "inside information" that you, and you alone, have about your thoughts, feelings, and motives. And indeed, you do find some answers when you introspect. But there are two interesting things about introspection: (1) People do not rely on this source of information as often as you might think—actually, people spend very little time thinking about themselves—and (2) even when people do introspect, the reasons for their feelings and behavior can be hidden from conscious awareness (Wilson, 2002). In short, self-scrutiny

Introspection

The process whereby people look inward and examine their own thoughts, feelings, and motives

A Measure of Relational Interdependence

Instructions: Indicate the extent to which you agree or disagree with each of these statements.

	Strongly Disagree						Strongly Agree
1. My close relationships are an important reflection of who I am.	1	2	3	4	5	6	7
2. When I feel close to someone, it often feels to me like that person is an important part of who I am.	1	2	3	4	5	6	7
3. I usually feel a strong sense of pride when someone close to me has an important accomplishment.	1	2	3	4	5	6	7
4. I think one of the most important parts of who I am can be captured by looking at my close friends and understanding who they are.	1	2	3	4	5	6	7
5. When I think of myself, I often think of my close friends or family also.	1	2	3	4	5	6	7
6. If a person hurts someone close to me, I feel personally hurt as well.	1	2	3	4	5	6	7
7. In general, my close relationships are an important part of my self-image.	1	2	3	4	5	6	7
8. Overall, my close relationships have very little to do with how I feel about myself.	1	2	3	4	5	6	7
9. My close relationships are unimportant to my sense of what kind of person I am.	1	2	3	4	5	6	7
10. My sense of pride comes from knowing who I have as close friends.	1	2	3	4	5	6	7
11. When I establish a close friendship with someone, I usually develop a strong sense of identification with that person.	1	2	3	4	5	6	7

For scoring instructions, turn to page 163.

(Adapted from Cross, Bacon, & Morris, 2000)

> Introspection is difficult and fallible. . . . The difficulty is simply that of all observation of whatever kind.
>
> —William James, 1890

isn't all it's cracked up to be, and if this were our only source of knowledge about ourselves, we would be in trouble.

Focusing on the Self: Self-Awareness Theory

How often do people think about themselves? To find out, researchers asked 107 employees, who ranged in age from 19 to 63 and worked at five different companies, to wear beepers for one week. The beepers went off at random intervals between 7:30 A.M. and 10:30 P.M., a total of seven to nine times a day (Csikszentmihalyi & Figurski, 1982). At the sound of the beeper, the participants answered a series of questions about their activities, thoughts, and moods at that time. The responses were content-analyzed into categories, including thoughts about oneself (e.g., "How lazy I've been all day," "It hurts," "Why did I get this fat?"). As you can see in Figure 5.2, people thought about themselves surprisingly little. Only 8 percent of the total thoughts recorded were about the self; more often, the participants thought about work, chores, and time. In fact, the response of "no thoughts" was more frequent than that of thoughts about the self. So although we do engage in introspection at times, it is not a frequent cognitive activity. Mundane thoughts about everyday life, and indeed thoughts about other people and our conversations with them, account for the vast majority of our daily thoughts (see Figure 5.2).

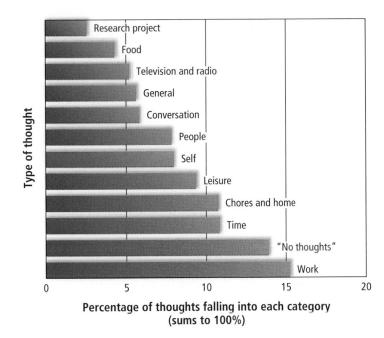

FIGURE 5.2

"What are you thinking about?"

For a week, people wore beepers that went off at random intervals several times a day. Each time the beepers went off, people described what they had just been thinking about. Thoughts about the self were surprisingly infrequent.

(Adapted from Csikszentmihalyi & Figurski, 1982)

When we are thinking about ourselves, what happens? What are the consequences of turning the spotlight of consciousness on ourselves, instead of focusing our attention on the world around us? As we just saw, we do not focus on ourselves very often. Sometimes, however, we encounter something in the environment that triggers self-awareness, such as knowing that people are watching us, hearing our tape-recorded voice, seeing ourselves on videotape, or staring at ourselves in a mirror. For example, if you are watching a home video taken by a friend with her new camcorder and you are the featured attraction, you will be in a state of self-awareness, you become the focus of your attention.

According to **self-awareness theory,** when we focus our attention on ourselves, we evaluate and compare our current behavior to our internal standards and values (Carver, 2003; Duval & Silvia, 2002; Duval & Wicklund, 1972). In short, we become self-conscious, in the sense that we become objective, judgmental observers of ourselves. Let's say that you believe it is important for you to be honest with your friends. One day, while chatting with a friend, you tell a lie. In the midst of this conversation, you catch sight of your friend staring at you. How do you think you will feel?

Seeing yourself through the eyes of your friend will make you aware of the disparity between your behavior and your moral standards. If you can change your behavior to match your internal guidelines (e.g., say something particularly nice to your friend or admit you lied and ask for forgiveness), you will do so. If you feel you can't change your behavior, then being in a state of self-awareness will be very uncomfortable, for you will be confronted with disagreeable feedback about yourself (Duval & Silvia, 2002; Fejfar & Hoyle, 2000; Mor & Winquist, 2002). In this situation, you will stop being self-aware as quickly as possible (e.g., by avoiding your friend's stare or leaving the room). Or when you get home, you might find yourself glued to the television; watching television is a good way for people to distract themselves and avoid thinking about their shortcomings (Moskalenko & Heine, 2002). Figure 5.3 (page 140) illustrates how self-awareness makes us conscious of our internal standards and directs our subsequent behavior.

Sometimes people go even further in their attempt to escape the self. Such diverse activities as alcohol abuse, binge eating, and sexual masochism have one thing in common: All are effective ways of turning off the internal spotlight on

But as
I looked into the mirror,
I screamed, and
my heart shuddered:
for I saw not myself but
the mocking,
leering, face
of a devil.

—Friedrich Nietzsche, Thus Spake Zarathustra

Self-Awareness Theory

The idea that when people focus their attention on themselves, they evaluate and compare their behavior to their internal standards and values

FIGURE 5.3

Self-awareness theory: The consequences of self-focused attention.

When people focus on themselves, they compare their behavior to their internal standards.

(Adapted from Carver & Scheier, 1981)

oneself (Baumeister, 1991). Getting drunk, for example, is one way of avoiding negative thoughts about oneself (at least temporarily). The fact that people regularly engage in such dangerous behaviors, despite their risks, is an indication of how aversive self-focus can be (Hull, 1981; Hull & Young, 1983; Hull, Young, & Jouriles, 1986).

Not all means of escaping the self, however, are so damaging. Many forms of religious expression and spirituality are also effective means of avoiding self-focus (Baumeister, 1991). Further, self-focus is not always aversive. If you have just achieved a life goal or experienced a major success, focusing on yourself can be pleasant indeed, because it highlights your positive accomplishments (Greenberg & Musham, 1981; Silvia & Abele, 2002). Further, self-focus can also be a way of keeping you out of trouble, by reminding you of your sense of right and wrong. For example, several studies have found that when people are self-aware (e.g., in front of a mirror), they are more likely to follow their moral standards, such as avoiding the temptation to cheat on a test (Beaman, Klentz, Diener, & Svanum, 1979; Diener & Wallbom, 1976; Gibbons, 1978).

To summarize, self-awareness is particularly aversive when it reminds people of their shortcomings, and under these circumstances (e.g., right after doing poorly on a test), people try to avoid it. At other times, however—such as when that little devil is on your shoulder pushing you into temptation—a dose of self-

> I swear to you . . . that to be overly conscious is a sickness, a real, thorough sickness.
>
> *—Fyodor Dostoevsky, Notes from Underground, 1864*

"Steer clear of that group. They're all terribly self-aware."

awareness is not such a bad thing because it makes you more aware of your morals and ideals. How self-aware do you tend to be? Complete the Try It! exercise on page 142 to find out.

Judging Why We Feel the Way We Do: Telling More than We Can Know

Even when we are self-aware and introspect to our heart's content, it can be difficult to know *why* we feel the way we do. Imagine trying to decide why you love someone. Being in love typically makes you feel giddy, euphoric, and preoccupied; in fact, the ancient Greeks thought love was a sickness. But why do you feel this way? Exactly what is it about your sweetheart that made you fall in love? We know it is something about our loved one's looks, personality, values, and background. But precisely what? How can we possibly describe the special chemistry that exists between two people? A friend once claimed he was in love with a woman because she played the saxophone. Was this really the reason? The heart works in such mysterious ways that it is difficult to tell.

Unfortunately, it's not just love that is difficult to explain. As we saw in Chapter 3, many of our basic mental processes occur outside of awareness (Kihlstrom, 1987; Wilson, 2002). This is not to say that we are thinkers without a clue—we are usually aware of the final result of our thought processes (e.g., that we are in love) but often unaware of the cognitive processing that led to the result. It's as if the magician pulled a rabbit out of a hat: You see the rabbit, but you don't know how it got there. How do we deal with this rabbit problem? Even though we often don't know why we feel a certain way, it seems we are always able to come up with an explanation. We are the proud owners of the most powerful brain to evolve on this planet, and we certainly put it to use. Unfortunately, it didn't come with an owner's manual. Introspection may not lead us to the true causes of our feelings and behavior, but we'll manage to convince ourselves that it did. Richard Nisbett and Tim Wilson referred to this phenomenon as "telling more than we can know" because people's explanations of their feelings and behavior often go beyond what they can reasonably know (Nisbett & Ross, 1980; Nisbett & Wilson, 1977; Wilson, 2002).

I have often wished I had time to cultivate modesty. . . . But I am too busy thinking about myself.

—Dame Edith Sitwell

Try it!

Measure Your Private Self-Consciousness

How much do you focus on yourself when you are alone? The following questions are taken from a scale developed by Fenigstein, Scheier, and Buss (1975) to measure private self-consciousness—the consistent tendency to be self-aware.

Instructions: Answer the following questions as honestly as possible on a scale from 1 to 5, where

      1 = extremely uncharacteristic (not at all like me)
      2 = somewhat uncharacteristic
      3 = neither characteristic nor uncharacteristic
      4 = somewhat characteristic
      5 = extremely characteristic (very much like me)

1. I'm always trying to figure myself out. _____
2. Generally, I'm not very aware of myself. _____
3. I reflect about myself a lot. _____
4. I'm often the subject of my own fantasies. _____
5. I never scrutinize myself. _____
6. I'm generally attentive to my inner feelings. _____
7. I'm constantly examining my motives. _____
8. I sometimes have the feeling that I'm off somewhere watching myself. _____
9. I'm alert to changes in my mood. _____
10. I'm aware of the way my mind works when I work through a problem. _____

For scoring instructions, turn to page 163.

(Adapted from Fenigstein, Scheier, & Buss, 1975)

Causal Theories

Theories about the causes of one's own feelings and behaviors; often we learn such theories from our culture (e.g., "absence makes the heart grow fonder")

In one study, for example, college students recorded their daily moods every day for five weeks (Wilson, Laser, & Stone, 1982). The students also kept track of things that might predict their daily moods, such as the weather, their workload, and how much sleep they had gotten the night before. At the end of the five weeks, the students estimated how much their mood was related to these other variables. An analysis of the actual data showed that in many cases, people were wrong about what predicted their mood. For example, most people believed that the amount of sleep they got predicted how good a mood they were in the next day when in fact this wasn't true: Amount of sleep was unrelated to people's moods. The participants had introspected and found or generated some logical-sounding theories that in fact weren't always right (Niedenthal & Kitayama, 1994; Wegner, 2002, Wilson, 2002).

What these participants had relied on, at least in part, were their **causal theories.** People have many theories about what influences their feelings and behavior (e.g., "My mood should be affected by how much sleep I got last night") and often use these theories to help them explain why they feel the way they do (e.g., "I'm in a bad mood; I'll bet the fact that I got only six hours of sleep last night has a lot to do with it"). We learn many of these theories from the culture in which we grow up—ideas such as absence makes the heart grow fonder, people are in bad moods on Mondays, or people who have been divorced are a poor choice for a successful second marriage. The only problem is that, as discussed in Chapter 3, our schemas and theories are not always correct and thus can lead to incorrect judgments about the causes of our actions.

Consider this example of causal theories in action from researchers who have studied them. One night, Dick Nisbett and Tim Wilson were meeting in an office at the University of Michigan. They were trying to think of ways to test the hypothesis that introspection often can't tell us why people feel the way they do and that they rely on causal theories when trying to uncover the reasons for their feelings, judgments, and actions. Brilliant insights were not bubbling forth, and the researchers were frustrated by their lack of progress. Then they realized that a source of their frustration (or so they thought) was the annoying whine of a vacuum cleaner that a custodial worker was operating right outside the office. Because it took them a while to realize that the noise of the vacuum was disrupting their meeting, they experienced what seemed like an inspiration. Maybe distracting background noises were an example of the very kind of occurrence they were looking for—one that would influence people's judgments but, because their causal theories did not adequately cover this possibility, would be overlooked when people explained their behavior.

Nisbett and Wilson (1977) designed a study to test this possibility (after shutting the door). They showed people a documentary in the presence of an annoying noise. About a minute into the film, a construction worker (played by Dick Nisbett) turned on a power saw right outside the door to the room in which the film was shown and ran the machine intermittently for several seconds until Tim Wilson, the experimenter, went to the door and asked him to please stop sawing until the film was over. At the end of the film, the participants rated how much they had enjoyed it; then the experimenter asked them to indicate whether the noise had influenced their evaluations. To see if the noise really did have an effect, there was a control condition in which other participants viewed the film without any distracting noise. The hypothesis was that the noise would lower people's evaluation of the film but that people would not realize the noise was responsible for their negative evaluation.

Does this seem like a reasonable hypothesis? It did to the researchers, but as it turned out, they were completely wrong. The participants who watched the film with the annoying background noise did not like it any less than those who saw the film without the distracting noise (in fact, they liked the film slightly more). When the participants were asked how much the noise had influenced their ratings, however, their hypothesis agreed with Nisbett and Wilson's. Even though the noise had no detectable effect on people's feelings about the film, it influenced their explanations for their feelings: Most reported that the noise had lowered their ratings of the film. In this case, both the participants and the researchers had the same causal theory, but the theory wasn't true—at least not when it came to watching a documentary while hearing construction noise.

In further studies, other factors that seem like they should not influence people's judgments—factors that are not part of people's causal theories—actually did have an effect. For example, in one study, people evaluated the quality of items of clothing, such as pantyhose, in a shopping mall (Nisbett & Wilson, 1977). Much to the surprise of the researchers, the position of the items on the display table had a large effect on people's preferences. The farther to the right an item was, the more people liked it. The researchers knew that it was the position and not something distinctive about the different pairs of pantyhose that influenced people's judgments, because in fact all the pairs were identical. However, the participants were completely in the dark about this effect of position on their judgments. Such an odd reason for their choice of pantyhose was not evident when they introspected about the reasons for their choice.

> We can never, even by the strictest examination, get completely behind the secret springs of action.
>
> —*Immanuel Kant*

We do not mean to imply that people rely solely on their causal theories when introspecting about the reasons for their feelings and behaviors. In addition to culturally learned causal theories, people have a great deal of information about themselves, such as how they have responded in the past and what they happen to have been thinking about before making a choice (Gavanski & Hoffman, 1987; Wilson, 2002). The fact remains, however, that introspecting about our past actions and current thoughts does not always yield the right answer about why we feel the way we do.

The Consequences of Introspecting about Reasons

At the beginning of this chapter, we posed the question of whether people should be very analytical about their feelings, making lists of pros and cons. Was Benjamin Franklin right that this is a fine strategy when facing an important decision? Or was Mario Vargas Llosa correct when he said that making lists can be confusing or even paralyzing?

Tim Wilson and his colleagues have found that analyzing the reasons for our feelings is not always the best strategy and in fact can make matters worse (Wilson, 2002; Wilson, Dunn, Kraft, & Lisle, 1989; Wilson, Hodges, & LaFleur, 1995). As we have just seen, it is often difficult to know exactly why we feel the way we do about something, so we bring to mind reasons that sound plausible. The reasons that sound plausible, however, may not be the correct reasons. Even worse, we might convince ourselves that these reasons are correct, thereby changing our minds about how we feel in order to match our reasons.

Suppose that we asked you to take out a piece of paper and write down exactly why you feel the way you do about a romantic partner. When people list reasons in this manner, they often change their attitudes toward their partners, at least temporarily (Wilson, Dunn, Bybee, Hyman, & Rotondo, 1984; Wilson & Kraft, 1993). Why? It is difficult to dissect the exact causes of our romantic feelings, so we latch on to reasons that sound good and that happen to be on our minds (remember our friend who claimed he was in love with a woman because she played the saxophone?). In Wilson's studies, people report such reasons as how well they communicate with their dating partner and how similar they are in their interests and backgrounds. Though these reasons may often be correct, people probably overlook other reasons that are not so easy to verbalize, such as the special chemistry that can exist between two people.

The trouble is that reasons that sound plausible to people and are easy to verbalize sometimes imply a different attitude from the one they had before. Suppose that things are going well between you and your dating partner but you have trouble verbalizing exactly why this is so. What comes to mind is the fact that you have rather different backgrounds and interests. "We really don't have much in common," you might think. "I guess this relationship doesn't have much of a future." Consequently, you are likely to change your mind about how you feel, resulting in **reasons-generated attitude change,** which is attitude change resulting from thinking about the reasons for your attitudes; you assume that your attitudes match the reasons that are plausible and easy to generate (Levine, Halberstadt, & Goldstone, 1996; Wilson & Kraft, 1993).

Remember the *Friends* episode we mentioned in which Ross makes a list of reasons for his feelings toward Rachel and Julie? As in the research studies, Ross found it easiest to verbalize reasons that did not match his feelings. Although he loved Rachel, he seemed unable to explain why, and so he put on his list things like "She's just a waitress" and "She's a little ditzy." If the script of the show had followed real life, Ross would have assumed that he did not love Rachel as much as he thought, because all he could think of were negative reasons. Fiction does not always reflect real life, however; when Ross started to list the reasons for his feelings toward Julie, all he could think of was "She's not Rachel," and he real-

Reasons-Generated Attitude Change
Attitude change resulting from thinking about the reasons for one's attitudes; people assume their attitudes match the reasons that are plausible and easy to verbalize

ized it was Rachel that he loved, waitress or not. That is, unlike participants in the research studies, he did not show reasons-generated attitude change.

A key question in real life is which attitude is the "right" one—the attitude people have before analyzing reasons or the reasons-generated attitude they have afterward. Wilson and his colleagues have found that the attitudes people express immediately after analyzing reasons should not be trusted too much. The real reasons people feel the way they do (e.g., the special chemistry between you and your romantic partner) do not go away when people analyze reasons; they just get obscured temporarily by focusing on reasons that are easier to put into words (Wilson, Lindsey, & Schooler, 2000). Consequently, if people base an important decision on their reasons-generated attitude ("Hmm, maybe my partner and I don't have much of a future"), they might regret it later, when their original feelings return (Wilson et al., 1993). Several studies, for example, have found that the attitudes people express after analyzing their reasons do not predict their future attitudes and behavior very well (Halberstadt & Levine, 1997; Reifman, Larrick, Crandall, & Fein, 1996; Wilson & LaFleur, 1995).

In sum, it is often difficult for people to know exactly why they feel the way they do, and it can be dangerous to think too much about one's reasons. If introspection has its limits, how else might we find out what sort of person we are and what our attitudes are? We turn now to another source of self-knowledge—observations of our own behavior.

KNOWING OURSELVES BY OBSERVING OUR OWN BEHAVIOR

Suppose that a friend of yours asks you how much you like classical music. You hesitate, because you never listened to classical music much when you were growing up, but lately you have found yourself listening to symphonies on the radio every now and again. "Well, I don't know," you reply. "I guess I like some kinds of classical music. Just yesterday, I heard Beethoven's Fifth while I was driving to work." If so, you used an important source of self-knowledge: observations of one's own behavior (in this case, what you chose to listen to on the radio).

Self-perception theory argues that when our attitudes and feelings are uncertain or ambiguous, we infer these states by observing our behavior and the situation in which it occurs (Bem, 1972). Let's consider each part of this theory. First, we infer our inner feelings from our behavior only when we are not sure how we feel. If you've always known that you love classical music, you do not need to observe your behavior to figure this out (Andersen, 1984; Andersen & Ross, 1984). Maybe, though, your feelings are murky; you've never really thought about how much you like it. If so, you are especially likely to use your behavior as a guide to how you feel (Chaiken & Baldwin, 1981; Kunda, Fong, Sanitioso, & Reber, 1993; Wood, 1982).

Second, people judge whether their behavior really reflects how they feel or whether it was the situation that made them act that way. If you freely choose to listen to the classical music station—no one makes you do it—you are especially likely to conclude that you listen to that station because you like classical music. If it is your spouse and not you who turned to the station playing Beethoven, you are unlikely to conclude that you listen to classical music in your car because you like it.

Sound familiar? In Chapter 4, we discussed attribution theory—the way in which people infer someone else's attitudes and feelings by observing that person's behavior. According to self-perception theory, people use the same

> I've alway written poems. . . . I never know what I think until I read it in one of my poems.
> —Virginia Hamilton Adair

Self-Perception Theory

The theory that when our attitudes and feelings are uncertain or ambiguous, we infer these states by observing our behavior and the situation in which it occurs

attributional principles to infer their own attitudes and feelings. For example, if you were trying to decide whether a friend likes classical music, you would observe her behavior and explain why she behaved that way. You might notice, for example, that she is always listening to classical music in the absence of any situational pressures or constraints—no one makes her play those Mozart CDs. You would make an internal attribution for her behavior and conclude that she likes Mozart. Self-perception theory says we infer our own feelings in the same way: We observe our behavior and explain it to ourselves; that is, we make an attribution about why we behaved that way (Albarracin & Wyer, 2000; Dolinsky, 2000; Fazio, 1987; Wilson, 1990). A large number of studies have supported self-perception theory, as we will now see.

Intrinsic versus Extrinsic Motivation

Imagine that you are an elementary school teacher who wants your students to develop a love of reading. Not only do you want your student to read more, but you also want them to look in the mirror and see someone who loves books, perhaps engendering a lifetime love of reading. How might you go about accomplishing this? It is not going to be easy, because so many other things compete for your students' attention, such as television, video games, and the Internet.

If you are like many educators, you might decide that a good approach would be to reward the children for reading. Maybe that will get them to put down those joysticks and pick up a book—and develop a love of reading in the process. Teachers have always rewarded kids with a smile or a pat on the head or a gold star on an assignment, of course, but recently they have turned to more powerful incentives. A chain of pizza restaurants offers elementary school students in some school districts a certificate for a free pizza when they have read a certain number of books (see "Book It!" at http://www.bookitprogram.com). In others, teachers offer candy, brownies, and toys for academic achievement (Perlstein, 1999).

A few years ago, Mel Steely, a professor at West Georgia College, decided to offer underprivileged children an even more lucrative reward. He started a program called Earning by Learning in which low-income children were offered $2 for every book they read (financed in part by a friend of Steely's, former Speaker

Many programs try to get children to read more by rewarding them. Do such rewards influence a child's self-concept? Do they increase or decrease a child's love of reading?

of the House Newt Gingrich). The program has since been expanded to schools in several states, including Florida, North Carolina, Texas, and Washington (Kimel, 2001). In Dallas, for example, more than ten thousand students have earned $140,000 by reading seventy thousand books (see "Earning by Learning of Dallas" at http://www.eblofdallas.org).

There is no doubt that rewards are powerful motivators and that pizzas and money will get kids to read more. One of the oldest and most fundamental psychological principles is that giving a reward each time a behavior occurs will increase the frequency of that behavior. Whether it be a rat pressing a bar in order to obtain a food pellet or a child reading to get a free pizza, rewards can change behavior.

But people are not rats, and we have to consider the effects of rewards on what's inside—people's thoughts about themselves, their self-concept, and their motivation to read in the future. Does getting money for reading, for example, change people's ideas about *why* they are reading? The danger of reward programs such as Earning by Learning is that kids will begin to think they are reading to earn money, not because they find reading to be an enjoyable activity in its own right. When the reward programs end and dollars or pizzas are no longer forthcoming, children may actually read less than they did before.

This is especially likely to happen to children who already liked to read. Such children have high **intrinsic motivation**—the desire to engage in an activity because they enjoy it or find it interesting, not because of external rewards or pressures (Harackiewicz & Elliot, 1993, 1998; Hirt, Melton, McDonald, & Harackiewicz, 1996; Ryan & Deci, 2000; Senko & Harackiewicz, 2002). Your reasons for engaging in the activity have to do with you—the enjoyment and pleasure you feel when reading a book. In other words, reading is play, not work.

The Overjustification Effect What happens when the children start getting rewards for reading? Their reading, originally stemming from intrinsic motivation, is now also spurred by **extrinsic motivation,** the desire to engage in an activity because of external rewards or pressures, not because you enjoy the task or find it interesting. According to self-perception theory, rewards can hurt intrinsic motivation. Whereas before many children read because they enjoyed it, now they are reading so that they will get the reward. The unfortunate outcome is that replacing intrinsic motivation with extrinsic motivation makes people lose interest in the activity they initially enjoyed. This result is called the **overjustification effect,** which results when people view their behavior as caused by compelling extrinsic reasons (e.g., a reward), making them underestimate the extent to which their behavior was caused by intrinsic reasons (Deci, Koestner, & Ryan, 1999a, 1999b; Harackiewicz, 1979; Lepper, 1995; Lepper, Henderlong, & Gingras, 1999).

Again, no one doubts that rewards are powerful motivators and can change what people do. It's the changes that occur inside people's heads that are often overlooked. Once reward programs such as Earning by Learing end, children might actually be less likely to read than they were before the programs began. Why? They might think, "I was reading to get money. Now that there is nothing in it for me, why should I read? I think I'll play a video game."

In one study, for example, fourth- and fifth-grade teachers introduced four new math games to their students, and during a thirteen-day baseline period, they noted how long each child played each math game. As seen in the leftmost graph of Figure 5.4, the children had some intrinsic interest in the math games initially, in that they played them for several minutes during this baseline period. For the next several days, a reward program was introduced. Now, the children could earn credits toward certificates and trophies by playing the math games. The more time they spent playing the games, the more credits they earned. As the middle graph of Figure 5.4 shows, the reward program was effective in

Intrinsic Motivation

The desire to engage in an activity because we enjoy it or find it interesting, not because of external rewards or pressures

Extrinsic Motivation

The desire to engage in an activity because of external rewards or pressures, not because we enjoy the task or find it interesting

Overjustification Effect

The tendency of people to view their behavior as caused by compelling extrinsic reasons, making them underestimate the extent to which it was caused by intrinsic reasons

FIGURE 5.4

The overjustification effect.

During the initial baseline phase, researchers measured how much time elementary school children played math games. During the reward program, they rewarded the children with prizes for playing the games. When the rewards were taken away (during the follow-up), the children played the games even less than they had during the baseline phase, indicating that the rewards had lowered their intrinsic interest in the games.

(Adapted from Greene, Sternberg, & Lepper, 1976)

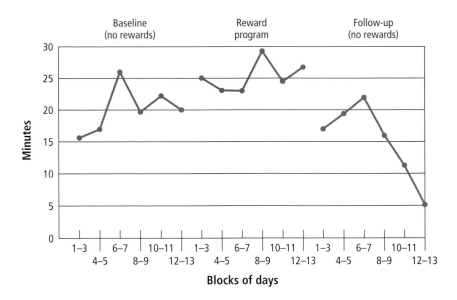

> I remember that the game [of basketball] lost some of its magical qualities for me once I thought seriously about playing for a living.
>
> —Bill Russell, 1979

increasing the amount of time the kids spent on the math games, showing that the rewards were an effective motivator.

The key question is what happened after the program ended and the kids could no longer earn rewards for playing the games. As predicted by the overjustification hypothesis, the children spent significantly less time on the math games than they had initially, before the rewards were introduced (see the rightmost graph in Figure 5.4). The researchers determined, by comparing these results to those of a control condition, that it was the rewards that made people like the games less and not the fact that everyone became bored with the games as time went by. In short, the rewards destroyed the children's intrinsic interest in the games; by the end of the study, they were hardly playing the games at all (Greene, Sternberg, & Lepper, 1976).

Preserving Intrinsic Interest   What can we do to protect intrinsic motivation from the dangers of society's reward system? Fortunately, there are conditions under which overjustification effects can be avoided. First, rewards will undermine interest only if interest was high initially (Calder & Staw, 1975; Tang & Hall, 1995). If a child has no interest in reading, then getting him or her to read by offering free pizzas is not a bad idea, because there is no initial interest to undermine.

Second, the type of reward makes a difference. So far, we have discussed **task-contingent rewards,** meaning that people get them only for doing a task, regardless of how well they do it. Sometimes **performance-contingent rewards** are used, whereby the reward depends on how well people perform the task. For example, grades are performance-contingent, because you get a high reward (an A) only if you do well. This type of reward is less likely to decrease interest in a task—and may even increase interest—because it conveys the message that you are good at the task (Deci & Ryan, 1985; Sansone & Harackiewicz, 1997). Thus rather than giving kids a reward for playing math games regardless of how well they do (i.e., a task-contingent reward), it is better to reward them for doing well in math. Even performance-contingent rewards must be used with care, because they too can backfire. Though people like the positive feedback these rewards convey, they do not like the apprehension caused by being evaluated (Harackiewicz, 1989; Harackiewicz, Manderlink, & Sansone, 1984). The trick is to convey positive feedback without making people feel nervous and apprehensive about being evaluated.

Task-Contingent Rewards

Rewards that are given for performing a task, regardless of how well the task is done

Performance-Contingent Rewards

Rewards that are based on how well we perform a task

CONNECTIONS

How Should Parents Praise Their Children?

If you were to visit a home where parents are helping their kids with their homework, you would find the parents doling out a lot of praise, at least in Western cultures. "Nice job on your geography project, Johnny. Your map of South America looks great!" "You got every math problem right, Susie—keep up the good work." Many adults assume that it is beneficial to praise children because it makes them feel good about themselves and enhances their intrinsic motivation. As we have just seen, however, sometimes rewards can actually undermine intrinsic motivation. What should parents do?

The key is the message that the praise conveys to children (Henderlong & Lepper, 2002). Praise has positive effects if it makes children feel like competent people whose effort has paid off. It is also helpful if it makes them feel that they chose the activity on their own and not because of external rewards and if it conveys reasonable expectations about how they should do in the future. As we have seen, praise has negative effects if it convinces children that they performed the activity just to get the praise (the overjustification effect). It also has negative effects if it makes kids compare themselves too much to their peers, conveys expectations that are too high for them to meet, or focuses children's attention too much on their ability (because if they have difficulties in the future, they will assume they have low ability).

Here are some specific recommendations about how to dole out praise: It is a good idea to praise children for their effort on a hard task ("Wow, you really worked hard on that science fair project") to convey the lesson that hard work pays off when the going gets tough (Dweck, 1999). You shouldn't go overboard and praise children too much for their effort, however, because they might infer that this means they are low on ability, like the player on a basketball team who gets the Best Effort award instead of the Most Valuable Player award. Along with praise for effort, it is a good idea to make children feel that they have some competence in the area (e.g., "You worked hard on your science project and really learned a lot; you've become quite an expert on plant pesticides"). Note that this praise avoids conveying the message that there is a fixed amount of ability in this area that people have or don't have; if children hold that view and run into difficulties in the future, they are likely to give up, assuming that they don't really have what it takes (Dweck, 1999). Instead, the praise should convey the message that they gained competence through hard work.

Praise is also helpful if it makes kids feel that they chose to do the task on their own initiative, with no outside pressure or inducement (e.g., "It was so smart of you to work on you project in your free time well before it was due"); this helps avoid an overjustification effect (the inference that they were doing it because of outside pressure or rewards). It is also advisable to avoid praise that compares children to their peers (e.g., "You got an even

What kinds of praise from parents helps children develop an intrinsic interest in an activity, and what kinds of praise can be harmful?

higher grade than Jimmie!") because they might give up if they encounter people in the future who do better than they do.

You may have noticed our comment that parents dole out a lot of praise "in Western cultures." There is some evidence that the situation is different in Eastern cultures, where people have a more interdependent sense of self. First, praise is much less frequent in China and Japan because it is viewed as potentially harmful to children's character (Salili, 1996). Second, children in these countries appear to be more intrinsically motivated to begin with and more concerned with the desire to improve their performance (Heine et al., 1999; Lewis, 1995). Consequently, praise from adults may not be as necessary to motivate children in these cultures to engage in academic pursuits.

Understanding Our Emotions: The Two-Factor Theory of Emotion

Consider how happy, angry, or afraid you feel at any given time. How do you know which emotion you are experiencing? This question probably sounds kind of silly; don't we know how we feel without having to think about it? The way in which we experience emotions, however, has a lot in common with the kinds of self-perception processes we have been discussing.

Stanley Schachter (1964) proposed a theory of emotion that says we infer what our emotions are in the same way that we infer what kind of person we are or how interested we are in math games: In each case, we observe our behavior and then explain why we are behaving that way. The only difference is in the kind of behavior we observe. Schachter says we observe our internal behaviors—how physiologically aroused we feel. If we feel aroused, we then try to figure out what is causing this arousal. For example, suppose you go for a 3-mile run one day and are walking back to your apartment. You go around a corner and nearly walk right into an extremely attractive person from your psychology class that you are just getting to know. Your heart is pounding and you feel a little sweaty. Is it because love is blossoming between you and your new friend or simply because you just went for a run?

Schachter's theory is called the **two-factor theory of emotion** because understanding our emotional states requires two steps: First, we must experience physiological arousal, and second, we must seek an appropriate explanation or label for it. Because our physical states are difficult to label on their own, we use infor-

Two-Factor Theory of Emotion

The idea that emotional experience is the result of a two-step self-perception process in which people first experience physiological arousal and then seek an appropriate explanation for it

mation in the situation to help us make an attribution about why we feel aroused (see Figure 5.5).

Imagine that you were a participant in a classic study by Stanley Schachter and Jerome Singer (1962) that tested this theory. When you arrive, the experimenter tells you he is studying the effects of a vitamin compound called Suproxin on people's vision. After a physician injects you with a small amount of Suproxin, the experimenter asks you to wait while the drug takes effect. He introduces you to another participant, who, he says, has also been given some Suproxin. The experimenter gives each of you a questionnaire to fill out, saying he will return in a little while to give you the vision tests.

You look at the questionnaire and notice that it contains some highly personal and insulting questions. For example, one question asks, "With how many men (other than your father) has your mother had extramarital relationships?" (Schachter & Singer, 1962, p. 385). The other participant reacts angrily to these offensive questions, becoming more and more furious, until he finally tears up his questionnaire, throws it on the floor, and stomps out of the room. How do you think you would feel? Would you feel angry as well?

As you've probably guessed, the real purpose of this experiment was not to test people's vision. The researchers set up a situation in which the two crucial

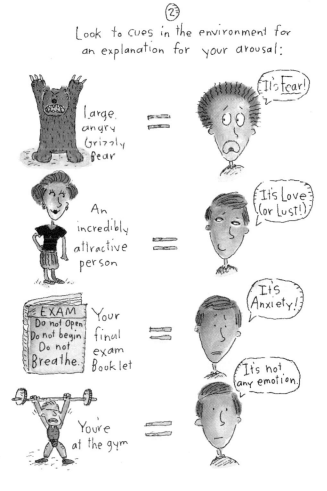

FIGURE 5.5

The two-factor theory of emotion.

People first experience physiological arousal and then attach an explanation to it.

variables—arousal and an emotional explanation for that arousal—would be present or absent and then observed which, if any, emotions people experienced. The participants did not really receive an injection of a vitamin compound. Instead, some participants received epinephrine, a hormone produced naturally by the human body that causes arousal (body temperature and heart and breathing rates increase), and the other half received a placebo that had no physiological effects.

Imagine how you would have felt had you received the epinephrine: As you read the insulting questionnaire, you begin to feel aroused. (Remember, the experimenter didn't tell you the shot contained epinephrine, so you don't realize that the injection is making you feel this way.) The other participant—who was actually an accomplice of the experimenter—reacts with rage. You are likely to infer that you are feeling flushed and aroused because you too are angry. You have met the conditions Schachter (1964) argues are necessary to experience an emotion—you are aroused, you have sought out and found a reasonable explanation for your arousal in the situation that surrounds you, and so you become furious. This is indeed what happened—participants who had been given epinephrine reacted much more angrily than participants who had been given the placebo.

A fascinating implication of Schachter's theory is that people's emotions are somewhat arbitrary, depending on what the most plausible explanation for their arousal happens to be. Schachter and Singer (1962) demonstrated this idea in two ways. First, they showed that they could prevent people from becoming angry by providing a nonemotional explanation for why they felt aroused. They did this by informing some of the people who received epinephrine that the injection would increase their heart rate, make their face feel warm and flushed, and cause their hands to shake slightly. When people actually began to feel this way, they inferred that it was not because they were angry but because the injection was taking effect. As a result, these participants did not react angrily to the questionnaire.

Even more impressively, Schachter and Singer showed that they could make participants experience a very different emotion by changing the most plausible explanation for their arousal. In another condition, participants did not receive the insulting questionnaire and the accomplice did not respond angrily. Instead, the accomplice acted in a euphoric, devil-may-care fashion, playing basketball with rolled-up pieces of paper, making paper airplanes, and playing with a Hula-Hoop he found in the corner. How did the real participants respond? If they had received epinephrine but had not been told of its effects, they inferred that they must be feeling happy and euphoric and often joined the accomplice's antics.

> I could feel all the excitement of losing the big fish going through the transformer and coming out as anger at my brother-in-law.
>
> —Norman Maclean, A River Runs Through It, 1976

The Schachter and Singer experiment has become one of the most famous studies in social psychology because it shows that emotions can be the result of a self-perception process: People look for the most plausible explanation for their arousal. Sometimes the most plausible explanation is not the right one, and so people end up experiencing a mistaken emotion. The people who became angry or euphoric in the Schachter and Singer (1962) study did so because they felt aroused and thought this arousal was due to the obnoxious questionnaire or to the infectious, happy-go-lucky behavior of the accomplice. The real cause of their arousal, the epinephrine, was hidden from them; so they relied on situational cues to explain their behavior.

Finding the Wrong Cause: Misattribution of Arousal

To what extent do the results found by Schachter and Singer (1962) generalize to everyday life? (Recall from Chapter 2 that a test of a study's external validity is whether the results hold up outside the lab.) Do people form mistaken emotions in the same way as participants in that study did? In everyday life, one might argue, people usually know why they are aroused. If a mugger points a gun at us and says, "Give me your wallet!" we feel aroused and correctly identify this arousal as fear. If our heart is thumping while we walk on a deserted moonlit beach with the man or woman of our dreams, we correctly label this arousal love or sexual attraction.

Many everyday situations, however, present more than one plausible cause for our arousal, and it is difficult to identify how much of the arousal is due to one source or another. Imagine that you go to see a scary movie with an extremely attractive date. As you are sitting there, you notice that your heart is thumping and you are a little short of breath. Is this because you are wildly attracted to your date or because the movie is terrifying you? It is unlikely that you could say, "Fifty-seven percent of my arousal is due to the fact that my date is gorgeous, 32 percent is due to the scary movie, and 11 percent is due to indigestion from all the popcorn I ate." Because of this difficulty in pinpointing the precise causes of our arousal, we sometimes misidentify our emotions. You might think that most of your arousal is a sign of attraction to your date when in fact a lot of it is due to the movie (or maybe even indigestion).

If so, you have demonstrated **misattribution of arousal,** whereby people make mistaken inferences about what is causing them to feel the way they do (Ross & Olson, 1981; Savitsky, Medvec, Charlton, & Gilovich, 1998; Sinclair, Hoffman, Mark, Martin, & Pickering, 1994; Zillmann, 1978). Consider how this worked in a field experiment by Donald Dutton and Arthur Aron (1974). An attractive young woman asked men visiting a park in British Columbia if they would fill out a questionnaire for her as part of a psychology project on the effects of scenic attractions on people's creativity. When they had finished, she said that she would be happy to explain her study in more detail when she had more time. She tore off a corner of the questionnaire, wrote down her name and phone number, and told the participant to give her a call if he wanted to talk with her some more. How attracted do you think you the men were to this woman? Would they telephone her and ask for a date?

This is a hard question to answer. Undoubtedly, it depends on whether the men were dating someone else, how busy they were, and so on. It might also depend, however, on how they interpreted any bodily symptoms they are experiencing. If they were aroused for some extraneous reason, they might mistakenly think some of the arousal is the result of attraction to the young woman. To test this idea, Dutton and Aron (1974) had the woman approach males in the park under two very different circumstances.

In one condition, the men were walking across a 450-foot-long suspension bridge that spanned a deep canyon. The bridge was made of wooden planks attached to wire cables, and as they walked across, they had to stoop to hold on to the low handrail. A little way out over the canyon, the wind tended to catch the bridge and make it wobble from side to side. This is a scary experience, and most people who cross the bridge become more than a little aroused—their heart pounds against their chest, they breathe rapidly, and they begin to perspire. It was at this point that the attractive woman approached a man on the bridge and asked him to fill out her questionnaire. How attracted do you think he felt toward her?

In another condition, the woman waited until a man had crossed the bridge and rested for a while on a bench in the park before approaching them. They had a chance to calm down—their heart was no longer pounding, and their breathing rate had

Misattribution of Arousal

The process whereby people make mistaken inferences about what is causing them to feel the way they do

Misattribution. When people are aroused for one reason, such as occurs when they cross a scary bridge, they often attribute this arousal to the wrong source—such as attraction to the person they are with.

returned to normal. They were peaceably admiring the scenery when the woman asked them to fill out her questionnaire. How attracted were these men to the woman? The prediction from Schachter's two-factor theory is clear: The men approached on the bridge would be considerably more aroused and might mistakenly think some of this arousal is the result of attraction to the beautiful woman. That is exactly what happened. A large proportion of the men approached on the bridge telephoned the woman later to ask her for a date, whereas relatively few of the men approached on the bench telephoned the woman (see Figure 5.6). This type of misattribution of arousal has been found in numerous subsequent studies, in both men and women (e.g., Sinclair et al., 1994; Zillmann, 1978). The moral is this: If you encounter an attractive man or woman and your heart is going thump-thump, think carefully about why you are aroused—you might fall in love for the wrong reasons!

Interpreting the Social World: Cognitive Appraisal Theories of Emotion

Though many studies have confirmed that people can misattribute the cause of their arousal, sometimes we experience an emotion in a situation in which we don't feel aroused at all. Many events can be viewed in different ways; our emotional reactions depend on how we interpret those events. Suppose that your best friend tells you she was just admitted to one of the top medical schools in the country. What emotion will you feel? A central idea of **cognitive appraisal theories of emotion** is that it depends on the way in which you interpret or explain this event, in the absence of any physiological arousal (Ellsworth, 1994; Frijda, 1986; Lazarus, 1995; Ortony, Clore, & Collins, 1988; Roseman & Smith, 2001; Russell & Barrett, 1999; Scherer & Schorr, 2001). Two kinds of appraisals are especially important: (1) Do you think the event has good or bad implications for you? and (2) How do explain what caused the event?

If you have been dreaming all your life about becoming a doctor and you are worried about being admitted to any medical school rather than feeling good about your friend's spectacular acceptance, you might feel envious and resentful: You have interpreted her success as a threat to your own. On the other hand, if you have no desire to go to medical school, you will probably feel happy about her success and may even bask in her reflected glory (Tesser, 1988). The emotion you will feel also depends on how you explain the cause of the event. If you think you contributed to your friend's success (she wouldn't have made it through that tough physics course without your help), you will probably feel pride. (Of course, if you were rejected by that same medical school, you might

Cognitive Appraisal Theories of Emotion

Theories holding that emotions result from people's interpretations and explanations of events, even in the absence of physiological arousal

FIGURE 5.6

Misattribution of arousal.

When a woman approached men on a scary bridge and asked them to fill out a questionnaire, a high percentage of them were attracted to her and called her for a date. When the same woman approached men after they had crossed the bridge and had rested, relatively few called her for a date.

(Adapted from Dutton & Aron, 1974)

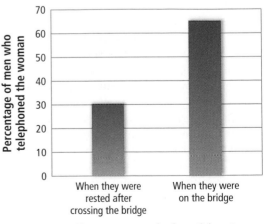

Woman approached participants

not feel so happy for the friend who benefited from your help.) If you think she did it entirely on her own, you will probably feel admiration, assuming that you do not feel threatened by her success.

Cognitive appraisals are similar to one of the two factors in Schachter's two-factor theory—the part whereby people try to explain the causes of an event and their reactions to it (see Figure 5.5). The main difference between Schachter's theory and cognitive appraisal theories concerns the role of arousal. According to cognitive appraisal theories, arousal does not always come first; the cognitive appraisals alone are a sufficient cause of emotional reactions. The two theories are not incompatible, however. When people are aroused and not certain where this arousal comes from, how they explain the arousal determines their emotional reaction (Schachter's two-factor theory). When people are not aroused, how they interpret and explain what happens to them determines their emotional reaction (cognitive appraisal theories). The theories agree that one way people learn about themselves is by observing events—including their own behavior—and then trying to explain those events.

USING OTHER PEOPLE TO KNOW OURSELVES

The self-concept does not develop in a solitary context but is shaped by the people around us. If we never interacted with other people, our own image would be a blur, because we would not see ourselves as having selves distinct from other people. Remember the mirror and red-dye test we discussed earlier, used to determine if animals have a self-concept? Variations of this test have been used to show that social contact is indeed crucial to the development of a self-concept. Gordon Gallup (1977) compared the behavior of chimpanzees raised in normal family groupings with that of chimps who were raised alone, in complete social isolation. The socially experienced chimps "passed" the mirror test; after red dye was put on their foreheads and they looked at themselves in a mirror, they immediately used their mirrored image to explore the red areas of their heads. However, the socially isolated chimps did not react to their reflections at all—they did not recognize themselves in the mirror, suggesting that they had not developed a sense of self.

Knowing Ourselves by Comparing Ourselves to Others

How do we use others to define ourselves? One way is to measure our own abilities and attitudes by seeing how we stack up against other people. Suppose you work in an office that subscribes to a charity fund: You can donate whatever you want from your monthly paycheck to worthy organizations. You decide to donate $50 a month. How generous is this? Should you be feeling particularly proud of your philanthropic nature? One way to answer this question is to compare yourself to others. If you find out that your friend Sue donated only $10 per month, you are likely to feel that you are a very generous person who cares a lot about helping others. If you find out, however, that your friend Sue donated $100 per month, you probably will not view yourself as quite so generous.

This example illustrates **social comparison theory,** which holds that people learn about their own abilities and attitudes by comparing themselves to others (Festinger, 1954; Suls & Wheeler, 2000; Wood, 1996). The theory revolves around two important questions: (1) When do you engage in social comparison? and (2) With whom do you choose to compare yourself? The answer to the first question is that people socially compare when there is no objective standard to measure themselves against and when they experience some uncertainty about themselves in a particular area (Suls & Fletcher, 1983; Suls & Miller, 1977). If the

Social Comparison Theory

The idea that we learn about our own abilities and attitudes by comparing ourselves to other people

office donation program is new and you are not sure what amount would be generous, you are especially likely to compare yourself to others.

As to the second question—With whom do people compare themselves?—research reveals a surprising answer (Gilbert, Giesler, & Morris, 1995). People's initial impulse is to compare themselves with anyone who is around, and this initial comparison occurs quickly and automatically (see our discussion of automatic judgment in Chapter 3). After a quick assessment of how our performance compares to others', however, we then decide how appropriate that comparison is, realizing that not all comparisons are equally informative.

Suppose that it is the first day of a college Spanish class and you are wondering about your abilities and how well you will do in the class. With whom should you compare yourself: a student who mentions that she lived in Spain for two years, a student who says she took the course on a lark and has never studied Spanish before, or a student who has a similar background to yours? Not surprisingly, people find it most informative to compare themselves to others who have a similar background in the area in question (Goethals & Darley, 1977; Miller, 1982; Suls, Martin, & Wheeler, 2000). Comparing yourself to a student with a very similar background in Spanish—the one who, like you, took Spanish in high school but has never traveled to a Spanish-speaking country—will be most informative. If that student is doing well in the class, you probably will too.

If we want to know what excellence is—the top level to which we can aspire—we engage in **upward social comparison:** We compare ourselves to people who are better than we are on a particular ability (Blanton, Buunk, Gibbons, & Kuyper, 1999). If we want to know the "best of the best" so that we can dream of getting there some day, then clearly we should compare ourselves to the student who lived in Spain and see how well she is doing in the class. In terms of self-knowledge, however, it is often more useful to compare ourselves to someone who is similar to us (Thornton & Arrowood, 1966; Wheeler, Koestner, & Driver, 1982; Zanna, Goethals, & Hill, 1975).

But forming an accurate image of ourselves is only one reason we engage in social comparison—we also use social comparison to boost our egos (Helgeson & Mickelson, 1995). Is it very important to you to believe that you are a fabulous Spanish speaker? Then compare your performance in the class to the student who is taking Spanish for the first time, because you will surely have her beat.

Upward Social Comparison
Comparing ourselves to people who are better than we are on a particular trait or ability

"Of course you're going to be depressed if you keep comparing yourself with successful people."

This use of **downward social comparison**—comparing yourself to people who are worse than you on a particular trait or ability—is a self-protective, self-enhancing strategy (Aspinwall & Taylor, 1993; Buunk, Oldersma, & de Dreu, 2001; Gibbons et al., 2002; Lockwood, 2002). If you compare yourself to people who are not as well off as you are, you'll feel better about yourself. For example, when interviewed by researchers, the vast majority of cancer patients spontaneously compared themselves to other patients who were more ill than they were, presumably as a way of making them feel more optimistic about the course of their own disease (Wood, Taylor & Lichtman, 1985).

Another way we can feel better about ourselves is to compare our current performance with our own past performance. In a sense, people use downward social comparison here as well, though the point of comparison is a "past self," not someone else. In one study, people made themselves feel better by comparing their current self with a past self who was worse off. One student, for example, said that her "college self" was more outgoing and sociable than her "high school self," who had been shy and reserved (Ross & Wilson, 2002; Wilson & Ross, 2000).

In short, the nature of our goals affects the comparisons we make. When we want an accurate assessment of our abilities and opinions, we compare ourselves to people who are similar to us. When we want information about what we can strive toward, we make upward social comparisons. Finally, when our goal is self-enhancement, we compare ourselves to those who are less fortunate (including our past selves); such downward comparisons make us look better by comparison.

> There is little satisfaction in the contemplation of heaven for oneself if one cannot simultaneously contemplate the horrors of hell for others.
>
> —*P. D. James*, The Children of Men, *1992*

Seeing Ourselves through the Eyes of Others

Have you ever been with a couple at a restaurant and heard one say to the other, "Honey, what do I feel like eating?" Or has a close friend ever disagreed with you about what you want or what you are like? "Come on, I know you will enjoy the party tonight if you just give it a chance," a friend might say, and she might be right, even though you feel like staying home and reading a book. Similarly, a close friend might notice before we are even aware of it that we are tired of dating a boyfriend or girlfriend or are interested in the person we sit next to in our psychology class.

Sometimes other people view our personalities and feelings differently than we do. Who is right? Often we are; after all, we know ourselves better than anyone else. Sometimes, though, our friends might be right. Some studies have compared a person's predictions about what he or she will actually do in the future with friends' or acquaintances' predictions about what he or she will do. Surprisingly, the friends and acquaintances often make more accurate predictions than the person him- or herself (Kenny, 1994a; Spain, Eaton, & Funder, 2000). In one study, for example, college students were not very accurate at predicting whether they would purchase a flower as part of a charity drive, but they were very accurate at predicting whether other people would (Epley & Dunning, 2000). In other words, if you wanted to predict whether individual students would buy a flower, you would be more accurate asking their classmates than asking the students themselves.

People are obviously not clueless about what they are like and how they will behave. They can make mistakes, however, for at least two reasons. First, they might not want to acknowledge a negative trait in themselves; it is easier to admit that other people will fail to help a needy charity than to admit that we will. Second, as seen in this chapter and in Chapter 3, much of our thinking about the world occurs automatically and unconsciously, and sometimes other people can better deduce what we are thinking and feeling than can we ourselves. Jenny's friends might notice that she is flirting with the guy in her psychology

Downward Social Comparison

Comparing ourselves to people who are worse than we on a particular trait or ability class before she notices it herself. To increase our self-knowledge, then, sometimes it is wise to view ourselves through the eyes of other people and at least entertain the possibility that their view is accurate (Wilson, 2002).

> The truth is,
> we never know
> for sure about ourselves. . . .
> Only after we've done a thing
> do we know what we'll do. . . .
> [That] is why we have spouses
> and children and parents
> and colleagues and friends,
> because someone has to
> know us better than
> we know ourselves.
>
> —Richard Russo, Straight Man, 1997

IMPRESSION MANAGEMENT: ALL THE WORLD'S A STAGE

In 1991, David Duke decided to run for governor of Louisiana as a mainstream conservative Republican. He had some obstacles to overcome in convincing people to vote for him, however, because for most of his adult life he had been a white supremacist and anti-Semite who in 1989 had sold Nazi literature from his office ("Duke," 1991). To improve his appeal, he claimed that he no longer supported Nazi ideology or the Ku Klux Klan, of which he had been a leader (or Grand Wizard) in the 1970s. He also tried to improve his appearance by undergoing facial cosmetic surgery. Duke's campaign rhetoric didn't fool too many Louisiana voters. They perceived the same racist message disguised in new clothes, and he was defeated by the Democratic candidate, Edwin Edwards. In 2003, he was sentenced to fifteen months in federal prison for allegedly using funds raised from supporters for personal investments and gambling (Murr & Smalley, 2003).

Though few politicians attempt as extreme a remake as David Duke did, managing public opinion is hardly a new concept in politics. President John F. Kennedy presented himself as a healthy, vigorous man ready to face any challenge that came his way when in fact he suffered from degenerative bone disease and chronic back pain and was under heavy medication for much of his presidency (Dallek, 2002).

These are extreme examples of **impression management,** which is the attempt by people to get others to see them the way they want to be seen (Goffman, 1959; Knowles & Sibicky, 1990; Leary, 1995; Schlenker, 1980; Spencer, Fein, Zanna, & Olson, 2003). Just as politicians try to put the best possible spin

Impression Management

The attempt by people to get others to see them as they want to be seen

Impression management in action: In the 1970s, David Duke was a leader in the Ku Klux Klan; in 1991, he ran for governor of Louisiana as a mainstream conservative Republican. A remarkable change occurred in Duke's presentation of self during this time. Besides undergoing facial cosmetic surgery to improve his appearance, he claimed during his campaign that he no longer supported Nazi ideology or the Ku Klux Klan.

Virtually all politicians try to manage the impressions they convey to the public, sometimes distorting reality. President John F. Kennedy presented himself as a healthy, vigorous man ready to face any challenge that came his way, when in fact he suffered from degenerative bone disease and chronic back pain, and was under heavy medication for much of his presidency.

on their actions and manage the impressions others have of them, so do we in our everyday lives. As Erving Goffman (1959) pointed out, we are all like stage actors who are trying our best to convince the "audience" (the people around us) that we are a certain way, even if we really are not.

People have many different impression management strategies (Jones & Pittman, 1982). One is **ingratiation**—using flattery or praise to make yourself likable to another, often higher-status person (Gordon, 1996; Jones & Wortman, 1973; Vonk, 2002). We can ingratiate through compliments, by agreeing with another's ideas, by commiserating and offering sympathy, and so on. If your boss drones on at a staff meeting, nearly putting the entire office to sleep, and you say, "Great job today, Sue. Loved your presentation," you are probably ingratiating. Ingratiation is a powerful technique, since we all enjoy having someone be nice to us—which is what the ingratiator is good at. However, such a ploy can backfire if the recipient of your ingratiation senses that you're being insincere (Jones, 1964; Kauffman & Steiner, 1968).

Another strategy, and the one that has attracted the most research attention, is **self-handicapping.** In this case, people create obstacles and excuses for themselves so that if they do poorly on a task, they can avoid blaming themselves. Doing poorly or failing at a task is damaging to your self-esteem. In fact, just doing less well than you expected or than you have in the past can be upsetting, even if it is a good performance. How can you prevent this disappointment? Self-handicapping is a rather surprising solution: You can set up excuses, before the fact, just in case you do poorly (Arkin & Oleson, 1998; Jones & Berglas, 1978).

Let's say it's the night before the final exam in one of your courses. It's a difficult course, required for your major, and one in which you'd like to do well. A sensible strategy would be to eat a good dinner, study for a while, and then go to bed early and get a good night's sleep. The self-handicapping strategy would be to pull an all-nighter, do some heavy partying, and then wander into the exam

> Keep up appearances whatever you do.
> —Charles Dickens, 1843

> To succeed in the world, we do everything we can to appear successful.
> —François de La Rochefoucauld, 1678

Ingratiation

The process whereby people flatter, praise, and generally try to make themselves likable to another person, often of higher status

Self-Handicapping

The strategy whereby people create obstacles and excuses for themselves so that if they do poorly on a task, they can avoid blaming themselves

the next morning bleary-eyed and muddle-headed. If you don't do well on the exam, you have an external attribution to offer to others to explain your performance, one that deflects the potential negative, internal attribution they might otherwise make (that you're not smart). If you ace the exam, well, so much the better—you did it under adverse conditions (no sleep), which suggests that you are especially bright and talented.

There are two major ways in which people self-handicap. In its most extreme form, people create obstacles that reduce the likelihood they will succeed on a task so that if they do fail, they can blame it on these obstacles rather than on their lack of ability. The obstacles people have been found to use include drugs, alcohol, reduced effort on the task, and failure to prepare for an important event (Deppe & Harackiewicz, 1996; Silvera, 2000; Spalding & Hardin, 1999; Thill & Curry, 2000).

The second type of self-handicapping is less extreme. Rather than creating obstacles to success, people devise ready-made excuses in case they fail (Baumgardner, Lake, & Arkin, 1985; Greenberg, Pyszczynski, & Paisley, 1984; Hirt, Deppe, & Gordon, 1991). We might not go so far as to pull an all-nighter the night before an important exam, but we might complain that we are not feeling well. People can arm themselves with all kinds of excuses: They blame their shyness, test anxiety, bad moods, physical symptoms, and adverse events from their past.

A problem with preparing ourselves with excuses in advance, however, is that we may come to believe these excuses and hence exert less effort on the task. Why work hard at something if you are going to do poorly anyway? Self-handicapping may prevent unflattering attributions for our failures, but it often has the adverse effect of causing the poor performance we feared to begin with. Further, even if self-handicappers avoid unflattering attributions about their performance (e.g., people thinking they aren't smart), they risk being disliked by their peers. People do not like others whom they perceive as engaging in self-handicapping strategies (Hirt, McCrea, & Boris, 2003; Rhodewalt, Sanbonmatsu, Tschanz, Feick, & Waller, 1995). In general, people are better off studying hard and trying their best, rather than worrying too much about what other people will think if they fail.

Culture, Impression Management, and Self-Enhancement

People in all cultures are concerned with the impression they make on others, but the nature of this concern and the impression management strategies people use differ considerably from culture to culture. We have seen, for example, that people in Asian cultures tend to have a more interdependent view of themselves than people in Western cultures do. One consequence of this identity is that "saving face," or avoiding public embarrassment, is extremely important in Asian cultures. In Japan, people are very concerned that they have the "right" guests at their weddings and the appropriate number of mourners at the funerals of their loved ones—so concerned, in fact, that if guests or mourners are unavailable, they can go to a local "convenience agency" and rent some. These agencies (benriya) have employees who are willing to pretend—for a fee—that they are your closest friends. A woman named Hiroko, for example, worried that too few guests would attend her second wedding. No problem—she rented six, including a man to pose as her boss, at a cost of $1,500. Her "boss" even delivered a flattering speech about her at the wedding (Jordan & Sullivan, 1995).

Although such impression management attempts might seem extreme to Western readers, the desire to manage public impressions is as strong in the West—it just takes different forms (as in David Duke's attempts to change the way the public viewed him). Exactly how do attempts to manage impressions differ across cultures? Debate on this issue is lively. Some argue that people in the

West are much more likely to engage in self-enhancement strategies, whereby they put themselves in as positive a light as possible—not only in how they present themselves to others but also in how they view themselves. People in East Asian cultures, according to this argument, are less likely to engage in self-enhancement and are more willing to criticize themselves (Heine et al., 1999). Indeed, college students in the United States view themselves more positively than their friends do, whereas college students in Japan view themselves more negatively than their friends do. And when told they had done poorly on a test of their creativity, college students in Canada dismissed the negative feedback and maintained a positive view of themselves, whereas college students in Japan embraced the negative feedback and viewed it as an opportunity for self-improvement (Heine, Kitayama, & Lehman, 2002; Heine & Renshaw, 2002).

Others argue, however, that the desire to view oneself in a positive light is universal—it's just the form that self-enhancement takes that differs from culture to culture. According to this view, people in Western cultures are most likely to self-enhance in areas that are important in their culture, particularly individualistic behaviors (e.g., tests of their individual abilities), whereas people in East Asian cultures are more likely to self-enhance in areas that are important in their culture, particularly collectivistic behaviors (e.g., behaviors that promote their group). In one study, American and Japanese college students rated how likely they were to engage in several behaviors, relative to their peers in their own culture. American students showed self-enhancement on individualistic actions, saying that they were more likely than their peers to do things like stand up for their own rights when they disagreed with their group. Japanese students showed self-enhancement on collectivistic actions, saying they were more likely than their peers to do things like blending in with the group and following the rules (Sedikes, Gaertner, & Toguchi, 2003). In other words, both groups were immodest in some of their predictions, but the Americans said they would excel at individualistic behaviors, whereas the Japanese said they would excel at collectivistic behaviors.

It will take more research to answer the question of the ways in which impression management strategies differ across cultures. For now, we can say that the desire to manage the image we present to others is strong in all cultures, though the kinds of images we want to present depend on the culture in which we live.

SUMMARY

The Nature of the Self

In this chapter we explored the nature of the self, the function of the self, and how people come to know themselves. The **self-concept** is the content of the self, namely our knowledge about who we are. **Self-awareness** refers to the act of thinking about ourselves. Whereas primates have a rudimentary self-concept, the human sense of self is uniquely complex and multifaceted. The self-concept serves two important functions. The first is the organizational function, whereby people store information in **self schemas,** mental structures that people use to organize their knowledge about themselves and that influence what they notice, think, and remember. People remember information better if they relate it to themselves, for example; this is called the **self-reference effect.** The self

also serves an executive function, regulating people's behavior, choices, and plans for the future. Recent evidence suggests that the executive function is served by a depletable resource that is like a muscle, and that success at self-control depends on how tired it is or how much it has been strengthened through exercise.

There are interesting cross-cultural and gender differences in the self-concept. In many Western cultures, people have an **independent view of the self,** whereby they define themselves mainly in terms of their own thoughts, feelings, and actions. In many Asian cultures, people have an **interdependent view of the self,** whereby they define themselves primarily in terms of their relationships with other people. Recent evidence suggests that in the United States, women have more relational interdependence, focusing more on their close relationships, whereas men have more collective interdependence, focusing more on their memberships in larger groups.

Knowing Ourselves Through Introspection

How do people come to know themselves? One way is through **introspection,** the process whereby people look inward and examine their own thoughts, feelings, and motives. Research on **self-awareness theory** has found that introspecting about ourselves can be unpleasant, because it focuses our attention on how we fall short of our internal standards. Thinking about why we feel the way we do can also be problematic. Many studies show that people's introspections about the reasons for their feelings and actions are often incorrect, in part because people rely on **causal theories** when explaining their behavior. Further, the act of thinking about reasons can cause **reasons-generated attitude change,** convincing us that our feelings match the reasons that happen to come to mind.

Knowing Ourselves by Observing Our Own Behavior

Self-perception theory holds that we come to know ourselves through observations of our own behavior, just as an outsider would. This occurs in particular when our internal states are unclear and there appears to be no external reason for our behavior. One interesting application of self-perception theory is the **overjustification effect,** which is the **discounting** of our **intrinsic motivation** for a task, as a result of inferring that we are engaging in the task because of **extrinsic motivation.** That is, rewards and other kinds of external influences can undermine our intrinsic interest; an activity we once liked seems like work instead of play. The overjustification effect is especially likely to occur when **task-contingent rewards** are used. These rewards are given for completing a task, regardless of people's level of performance. **Performance-contingent rewards** are based on how well people perform a task. These rewards are less likely to decrease interest in a task and may even increase interest, if they convey the message that people are competent without making them feel nervous and apprehensive about being evaluated. Another example of self-perception is the **two-factor theory of emotion,** whereby we determine our emotions by observing how aroused we are and making inferences about the causes of that arousal. **Misattribution of arousal** can occur, whereby people attribute their arousal to the wrong source. Attributions about arousal are not the only source of emotions; **cognitive appraisal theories of emotion** argue that emotions can also result from our interpretations and explanations of events in the absence of any physiological arousal.

Using Other People to Know Ourselves

People also come to know themselves through by comparing themselves to other people. **Social comparison theory** states that we will compare ourselves to others when we are unsure of our standing on some attribute and there is no objective criterion we can use. Typically, we choose to compare ourselves to similar others, for this is most diagnostic. **Upward social comparison,** comparing ourselves to those who are superior on the relevant attribute, can help define what the standard of excellence is. **Downward social comparison,** comparing ourselves to those who are inferior on the relevant attribute, can make us feel better about our current plight.

Impression Management: All the World's a Stage

Once we know ourselves, we often attempt to manage the self we present to others through the processes of **self-presentation** and **impression management.** Social life is much like the theater, where we present selves (or roles) to others. Two self-presentational strategies are **ingratiation** and **self-handicapping.** Self-handicapping involves lining up a behavior, trait, or situational event before a performance so that we can later use it as an excuse if we don't do well. One problem with preparing ourselves with excuses in advance, however, is that we may come to believe these excuses and thus exert less effort on the task. Whereas self-handicapping may prevent unflattering attributions for our failures, it often has the adverse effect of causing the poor performance that is so feared.

CRITICAL THINKING QUESTIONS

1. Why is the study of the self an important topic in social psychology? How is the self-concept shaped by other people? How is it shaped by the culture in which we live?

2. How accurate do you think self-knowledge is? What are some ways in which people can make mistaken inferences about themselves?

3. What advice would you give to parents about how to use rewards and praise with their children? What are the dangers of using too much praise, or the wrong kind of praise?

4. What advice would you give employees about how to make a good impression on their boss? What kinds of impression management strategies are likely to be effective, and which are likely to backfire?

Scoring the *Try it!* Exercises

Page 136

To estimate your degree of interdependence, take the average of your answers to questions 1–5. To estimate your degree of independence, take the average of your answers to questions 6–10. On which measure did you come out higher? Singelis (1994) found that Asian Americans agreed more with the interdependence than the independence items, whereas Caucasian Americans agreed more with the independence than the interdependence items.

Page 138

To compute your score, first reverse the rating you gave to questions 8 and 9. That is, if you circled a 1, change it to a 7; if you circled a 2, change it to a 6; if you circled a 7, change it to a 1; and so on.

Then add up your answers to the eleven questions. High scores reflect more of a tendency to define yourself in terms of relational interdependence. Cross, Bacon, & Morris (2000) found that women tend to score higher than men; in eight samples of college students, women averaged 57.2 and men averaged 53.4.

Page 142

First, reverse your answers to questions 2 and 5. If you answered 1 to these questions, change it to a 5; if you answered 2, change it to a 4; and so on. Then add your ratings for all ten questions. The higher your score, the more likely you are to focus your attention on yourself. Fenigstein, Scheier, and Buss (1975) found that the average score was 26 in a sample of college students.

The Need to Justify Our Actions

On March 26, 1997, thirty-nine people were found dead at a luxury estate in Rancho Santa Fe, California—participants in a mass suicide. They were all members of an obscure cult called Heaven's Gate, founded by Marshall Herff Applewhite, a former college professor. Each body was laid out neatly, feet clad in brand-new black Nikes, face covered with a purple shroud. The cult members died willingly and peacefully—and didn't really consider it suicide. They left behind detailed videotapes describing their beliefs and intentions: They believed that the Hale-Bopp Comet, at the time clearly visible in the western sky, was their ticket to a new life in paradise. They were convinced that Hale-Bopp's wake was a gigantic spaceship whose mission was to carry them off to a new incarnation. To be picked up by the spaceship, they first needed to rid themselves of their current "containers." That is, they needed to leave their own bodies by ending their lives. Alas, no spaceship ever came.

Several weeks before the mass suicide, when Hale-Bopp was still too distant to be seen with the naked eye, some members of the cult walked into a specialty store and purchased a very expensive high-powered telescope. They wanted to get a clearer view of the comet and the spaceship that they believed was traveling behind it. A few days later, they made their way back to the store, returned the telescope, and politely asked for their money back. When the store manager asked them if they had problems with the scope, they replied, "Well, gosh, we found the comet, but we can't find anything following it" (Ferris, 1997). Although the store manager tried to convince them that there was nothing wrong with the telescope and that there was nothing following the comet, they remained unconvinced. Their attitude was clear, and given their premise, their logic was impeccable: (1) We know an alien spaceship is following behind the Hale-Bopp Comet, and (2) if an expensive telescope failed to reveal that spaceship, then (3) there must be something wrong with the telescope.

Their thinking might strike you as strange, irrational, or stupid, but generally speaking, the members of the Heaven's Gate cult were not stupid or

> When the heart speaks, the mind finds it indecent to object.
>
> —*Milan Kundera*

irrational or crazy. Neighbors who knew them considered them pleasant, smart, reasonable people. Moreover, they were expert at using computers and the Internet and earned their living by setting up highly innovative Web pages. Clients who worked closely with them were impressed, describing them as unusually bright, talented, and creative. What is the process by which intelligent, sane people can succumb to such fantastic thinking and self-destructive behavior? We will attempt to explain their actions near the end of this chapter. For now, we will simply state that their behavior is not unfathomable—it is simply an extreme example of a normal human tendency: the need to justify our actions.

MAINTAINING A STABLE, POSITIVE SELF-IMAGE

During the past half-century, social psychologists have discovered that one of the most powerful determinants of human behavior stems from our need to preserve a stable, positive self-image. In other words, we humans strive to maintain a relatively favorable view of ourselves, particularly when we encounter evidence that contradicts our typically rosy self-image (Aronson, 1969, 1992a, 1998; Wicklund & Brehm, 1998). Most of us want to believe that we are reasonable, decent folks who make wise decisions, do not behave immorally, and have integrity. In short, we want to believe that we do not do stupid, cruel, or absurd things. But maintaining this belief is not always easy. As we go through life, we encounter a great many challenges to it. The topic of this chapter is how human beings deal with those challenges.

The Theory of Cognitive Dissonance

Most of us have a need to see ourselves as reasonable, moral, and smart. When we are confronted with information implying that we may have behaved in ways that are irrational, immoral, or stupid, we experience a good deal of discomfort. This feeling of discomfort caused by performing an action that runs counter to one's customary (typically positive) conception of oneself is referred to as **cognitive dissonance.** A half-century of research has demonstrated that cognitive dissonance is a major motivator of human thought and behavior. Leon Festinger (1957) was the first to investigate the precise workings of this powerful phenomenon and elaborated his findings into what is arguably social psychology's most important and most provocative theory, the theory of cognitive dissonance. At first, social psychologists believed that cognitive dissonance could be caused by *any* two conflicting cognitions (thoughts or opinions) (Brehm & Cohen, 1962; Festinger, 1957; Festinger & Aronson, 1960). But later research made it clear that not all cognitive inconsistencies are equally upsetting. Rather, it was discovered that dissonance is most powerful and most upsetting when people behave in ways that threaten their self-image. This is upsetting precisely because it forces us to confront the discrepancy between who we *think* we are and how we have in fact behaved (Aronson, 1968, 1969, 1992a, 1998; Greenwald & Ronis, 1978).

Cognitive dissonance always produces discomfort, and in response, we try to reduce it. The process is very similar to the effects of hunger and thirst: Discomfort motivates us to eat or drink. But unlike satisfying hunger or thirst by

Cognitive Dissonance

A drive or feeling of discomfort, originally defined as being caused by holding two or more inconsistent cognitions and subsequently defined as being caused by performing an action that is discrepant from one's customary, typically positive self-conception

eating or drinking, the path to reducing dissonance is not always simple or obvious. In fact, it can lead to fascinating changes in the way we think about the world and the way we behave. How can we reduce dissonance? There are three basic ways (see Figure 6.1 on page 168):

- By changing our behavior to bring it in line with the dissonant cognition
- By attempting to justify our behavior through changing one of the dissonant cognitions
- By attempting to justify our behavior by adding new cognitions

To illustrate, let's look at a behavior that millions of people engage in several times a day—smoking cigarettes. If you are a smoker, you are likely to experience dissonance because you know that this behavior can lead to a painful, early death. How can you reduce this dissonance? The most direct way is to change your behavior—to give up smoking. Your behavior would then be consistent with your knowledge of the link between smoking and cancer. Though many people have succeeded in doing just that, it's not easy—many have tried to quit and failed. What do these people do? It would be wrong to assume that they simply swallow hard and prepare to die. They don't. Researchers studied the behavior and attitudes of heavy smokers who attended a smoking cessation clinic and succeeded in quitting smoking for a while but then relapsed into heavy smoking again. What do you suppose the researchers discovered? Heavy smokers who tried to quit and failed actually succeeded in lowering their perception of the dangers of smoking. In this way, they could continue to smoke without feeling terrible about it (Gibbons, Eggleston, & Benthin, 1997).

Smokers can come up with some pretty creative ways to justify their smoking. Some succeed in convincing themselves that the data linking cigarette smoking to cancer are inconclusive. Others try to add new cognitions—for example, the erroneous belief that filters trap most of the harmful chemicals and thus reduce

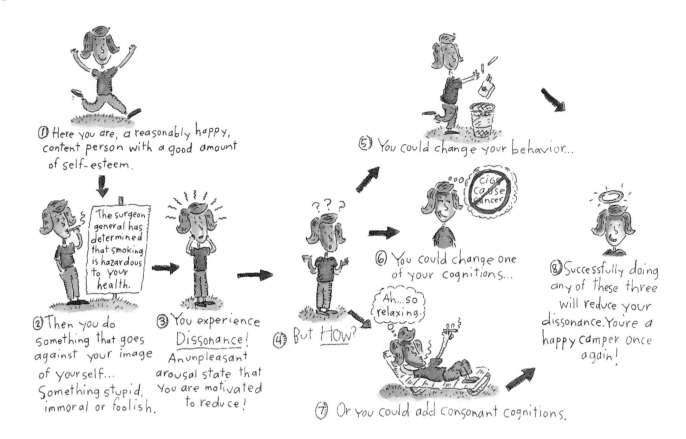

FIGURE 6.1

How we reduce cognitive dissonance.

the threat of cancer. Some add a cognition that allows them to focus on the vivid exception: "Look at my grandfather. He's 87 years, and he's been smoking a pack a day since he was 12. That proves it's not always bad for you." Still others add the cognition that smoking is an extremely enjoyable activity, one for which it is worth risking cancer. Others even succeed in convincing themselves that all things considered, smoking is worthwhile because it relaxes them, reduces nervous tension, and so on.

These justifications may sound silly to the nonsmoker. That is precisely our point. As the smokers' rationales show, people experiencing dissonance will often deny or distort reality to reduce it. People who try and fail to lose weight, who refuse to practice safer sex, or who receive bad news about their general health can be equally "creative" in denying risk and reducing their discomfort (Aronson, 1997b; Croyle & Jemmott, 1990; Goleman, 1982; Kassarjian & Cohen, 1965; Leishman, 1988). Occasionally, these illusions can be helpful; for example, Shelley Taylor and her colleagues have demonstrated that individuals who harbor unrealistically positive illusions about surviving a terminal illness like AIDS live longer than those who are more "realistic" (Taylor, 1989; Taylor & Armor, 1996; Taylor & Brown, 1988; Taylor & Gollwitzer, 1995). Far more often (as in the case of smoking), such illusions are destructive.

Rational Behavior versus Rationalizing Behavior

Most people think of themselves as rational beings, and generally, they are right: We are certainly capable of rational thought. But as we've seen, the need to maintain our self-esteem leads to thinking that is not always rational; rather, it is *rationalizing*. People who are in the midst of reducing dissonance are so involved

This youngster may be thinking: "There's nothing wrong with putting on a little extra weight. After all, some professional football players weigh more than 300 pounds and earn millions of dollars a year. Pass the fries."

with convincing themselves that they are right that they frequently end up behaving irrationally and maladaptively.

During the late 1950s, when segregation was still widespread, Edward Jones and Rika Kohler (1959) performed a simple experiment in a southern town. First, they selected people who were deeply committed to a position on the issue of racial segregation—some strongly supported segregation; others opposed it just as strongly. Next, the researchers presented these individuals with a series of arguments on both sides of the issue. Some of the arguments on each side were plausible, and others on each side were rather silly. The question was, which of the arguments would people remember best?

If the participants were behaving in a purely rational way, we would expect them to remember the plausible arguments best and the implausible arguments least, regardless of how they felt about segregration. After all, why would anyone want to remember implausible arguments? What does dissonance theory predict? A silly argument that supports your own position arouses some dissonance because it raises doubts about the wisdom of that position or the intelligence of people who agree with it. Likewise, a sensible argument on the other side of the issue also arouses some dissonance because it raises the possibility that the other side might be closer to the truth than you had thought. Because these arguments arouse dissonance, we try not to think about them.

This is exactly what Jones and Kohler found. The participants remembered the plausible arguments agreeing with their own position *and* the *implausible* arguments agreeing with the *opposing* position (see Figure 6.2). Subsequent research has yielded similar results on many issues, from whether or not the death penalty deters people from committing murder to the risks of contracting AIDS through heterosexual contact (e.g., Biek, Wood, & Chaiken, 1996; Edwards & Smith, 1996).

All of this research indicates that we humans do not always process information in an unbiased way. Rather, we distort it in a way that fits our preconceived notions. This probably explains why on issues such as politics and religion, people who are deeply committed to a view different from our own will almost never come to see things our way (the proper way!), no matter how powerful and balanced our arguments might be.

Decisions, Decisions, Decisions

Every time we make a decision, we experience dissonance. How come? Let's take a close look at the process. Suppose you are about to buy a car, but you are torn between a van and a subcompact. You know that each has advantages and

FIGURE 6.2

The effects of plausibility on the learning of controversial statements.

People tend to remember plausible arguments that support their position and implausible arguments that support the opposing position. To remember either implausible arguments that support your position or plausible arguments that support the opposing position would arouse dissonance.

(Adapted from Jones & Kohler, 1959)

Well, perhaps the price of gasoline will drop!

disadvantages: The van would be convenient; you can haul things in it, you can sleep in it during long trips, and it has plenty of power, but it gets poor mileage and it's hard to park. The subcompact is a lot less roomy, and you wonder about its safety. But it is less expensive to buy and operate, it's a lot zippier to drive, and it has a pretty good repair record. Before you decide, you will probably get as much information as you can. Chances are you will read *Consumer Reports* to find out what this expert, unbiased source has to say. You'll talk with friends who own a van or a subcompact. (You may even talk to your parents.) You'll probably visit automobile dealers to test-drive the vehicles to see how each one feels. All of this predecision behavior is perfectly rational. Let's assume you decide to buy the subcompact.

What happens next? We predict that your behavior will change in a specific way: You will begin to think more and more about the number of miles to the gallon as though it were the most important thing in the world. Simultaneously, you will almost certainly downplay the fact that you can't sleep in your subcompact. Similarly, you will barely remember that your new car can put you at considerable risk of harm in a collision. How does this shift in thinking happen?

Distorting Our Likes and Dislikes In any decision, whether it is between two cars, two colleges, or two potential lovers, the chosen alternative is seldom entirely positive, and the rejected alternative is seldom entirely negative. So while making the decision, you have your doubts. After the decision, your cognition that you are a smart person is dissonant with all of the negative things about the car, college, or lover you chose; that cognition is also dissonant with all of the *positive* aspects of the car, college, or lover you *rejected*. We call this **postdecision dissonance.** Cognitive dissonance theory predicts that to help yourself feel better about the decision, you will do some mental work to try to reduce the dissonance.

What kind of work? An early experiment by Jack Brehm (1956) will clarify. Brehm posed as a representative of a consumer testing service and asked women to rate the attractiveness and desirability of several kinds of appliances, such as toasters and electric coffeemakers. Each woman was told that as a reward for having participated in the survey, she could have one of the appliances as a gift. She was given a choice between two of the products she had rated as being equally

Postdecision Dissonance

Dissonance aroused after making a decision, typically reduced by enhancing the attractiveness of the chosen alternative and devaluating the rejected alternatives

attractive. After she made her decision, her appliance was wrapped up and given to her. Twenty minutes later, each woman was asked to rerate all the products. Brehm found that after receiving the appliance of their choice, the women rated its attractiveness somewhat higher than they had the first time. Not only that, but they drastically lowered their rating of the appliance they might have chosen but decided to reject.

In other words, following a decision, to reduce dissonance we change the way we feel about the chosen and unchosen alternatives, cognitively spreading them apart in our own minds in order to make ourselves feel better about the choice we made. (See the Try It! exercise below.)

The Permanence of the Decision   It stands to reason that the more important the decision, the greater the dissonance. Deciding which car to buy is clearly more important than deciding between a toaster and a coffeemaker; deciding which person to marry is clearly more important than deciding which car to buy. Decisions also vary in terms of how permanent they are—that is, how difficult they are to revoke. It is a lot easier to trade in your new car for another one than it is to get out of an unhappy marriage. The more permanent and less revocable the decision, the greater the need to reduce dissonance.

An excellent place to investigate the significance of irrevocability is the racetrack. Experienced bettors typically spend a lot of time poring over the "dope sheets," trying to decide which horse to put their money on. When they make a decision, they head for the betting windows. While they are standing in line, they have already made their decision, but we would hypothesize that because it is still revocable, they have no urge to reduce dissonance. However, once they get to the window and place their bet—even if it's for only $2—it is absolutely irrevocable. Therefore, if irrevocability is an important factor, we would expect bettors to be engaged in much more dissonance reduction a few minutes after placing the bet than a few minutes before placing the bet.

In a simple but clever experiment, social psychologists intercepted people who were on their way to place $2 bets and asked them how certain they were that their horses would win (Knox & Inkster, 1968). The investigators also approached other bettors just as they were leaving the $2 window, after having placed their bets, and asked them the same question. Almost invariably, people who had already placed their bets gave their horses a much better chance of winning than those who had not yet placed their bets did. Since only a few minutes separated one group from another, nothing real had occurred to increase the probability of winning; the only thing that had changed was the finality of the decision—and hence the dissonance it produced.

Try it!

Justifying Decisions

The distinguished news show *Meet the Press* usually focuses on a current, controversial political issue. The typical format of the show is that articulate people, representing both sides of the issue, present their views in a forceful and articulate manner. Read the TV listings to see what issue is going to be debated on the next show.

In advance, poll two or three of your friends or family members to ascertain their feelings about the issue. Try to get them to watch the show that week. Discuss their feelings about the issue and their feelings about the debaters after watching the show.

Lowballing

An unscrupulous strategy whereby a salesperson induces a customer to agree to purchase a product at a very low cost, subsequently claims it was an error, and then raises the price; frequently, the customer will agree to make the purchase at the inflated price

Lowballing: The Illusion of Irrevocability The irrevocability of a decision always increases dissonance and the motivation to reduce it. Because of this, unscrupulous salespeople have developed techniques for creating the illusion that irrevocability exists. One such technique is called **lowballing** (Cialdini, Cacioppo, Basset, & Miller, 1978; Weyant, 1996). Robert Cialdini, a distinguished social psychologist, temporarily joined the sales force of an automobile dealership to observe this technique closely. Here's how it works: You enter an automobile showroom intent on buying a particular car. Having already priced it at several dealerships, you know you can purchase it for about $18,000. You are approached by a personable, middle-aged man who tells you he can sell you one for $17,679. Excited by the bargain, you agree to write out a check for the down payment so that the salesman can take it to the manager as proof you are a serious customer. Meanwhile, you imagine yourself driving home in your shiny new bargain. But alas, ten minutes later the salesperson returns, looking forlorn. He tells you that in his zeal to give you a good deal, he miscalculated, and the sales manager caught it. The price of the car actually comes to $18,178. You are disappointed. Moreover, you are pretty sure you can get it a bit cheaper elsewhere. The decision to buy is not irrevocable. And yet in this situation, research by Cialdini and his colleagues (1978) suggests that far more people will go ahead with the deal than if the original asking price had been $18,178, even though the reason for buying the car from this particular dealer—the bargain price—no longer exists. How come?

There are at least three reasons why lowballing works. First, while the customer's decision to buy is certainly reversible, a commitment of sorts does exist. Signing a check for a down payment creates the illusion of irrevocability, even though, if the car buyer really thought about it, he or she would quickly realize it is a nonbinding contract. However, in the world of high-pressure sales, even temporary illusion can have powerful consequences. Second, the feeling of commitment triggered the anticipation of an exciting event: driving out with a new car. To have had the anticipated event thwarted (by not going ahead with the deal) would have produced dissonance and disappointment. Third, although the final price is substantially higher than the customer thought it would be, it is probably only slightly higher than the price at another dealership. Under these circumstances, the customer in effect says, "Oh, what the heck. I'm here, I've already filled out the forms, I've written out the check—why wait?" Thus by using dissonance reduction and the illusion of irrevocability, high-pressure salespeople increase the probability that you will decide to buy their product at their price.

The Decision to Behave Immorally Of course, decisions about cars, appliances, racehorses, and even presidential candidates are the easy ones. Often our choices involve moral and ethical issues. When is it OK to lie to a friend, and when is it not? When is an act stealing, and when is it borrowing? Resolving moral dilemmas is a particularly interesting area in which to study dissonance because of the powerful implications for one's self-esteem. Even more interesting is the fact that dissonance reduction following a difficult moral decision can cause people to behave either more *or less* ethically in the future.

Take the issue of cheating on an exam. Suppose you are a college sophomore taking the final exam in a physics course. Ever since you can remember, you have wanted to be a surgeon, and you think that your admission to medical school will depend heavily on how well you do in this physics course. The key question on the exam involves some material you know fairly well, but because so much is riding on this exam, you experience acute anxiety and draw a blank. The minutes tick away. You become increasingly anxious. You simply cannot think. You look up and notice that you happen to be sitting next to the smartest person in the class. You glance at her paper and discover that she is just completing her answer to the crucial question. You know you could easily read her

After she cheats, she will try to convince herself that everybody would cheat if they had the chance.

answer if you chose to. Time is running out. What do you do? Your conscience tells you it's wrong to cheat—and yet if you don't cheat, you are certain to get a poor grade. And if you get a poor grade, you are convinced that there goes medical school. You wrestle with your conscience.

Regardless of whether you decide to cheat or not, the threat to your self-esteem arouses dissonance. If you cheat, your belief or cognition "I am a decent, moral person" is dissonant with your cognition "I have just committed an immoral act." If you decide to resist temptation, your cognition "I want to become a surgeon" is dissonant with your cognition "I could have nailed a good grade and admission to medical school, but I chose not to. Wow, was I stupid!"

In this situation, some students would decide to cheat; others would decide not to cheat. What happens to the students' attitudes about cheating after their decision? Suppose that after a difficult struggle, you decide to cheat. How do you reduce the dissonance? According to dissonance theory, it is likely that you would try to justify the action by finding a way to minimize the negative aspects of the action you chose. In this case, an efficient path to reducing dissonance would involve changing your attitude about cheating. You would adopt a more lenient attitude toward cheating, convincing yourself that it is a victimless crime that doesn't hurt anybody, that everybody does it, and so it's not really that bad.

Suppose, by contrast, that after a difficult struggle, you decide not to cheat. How would you reduce your dissonance? Once again, you could change your attitude about the morality of the act—but this time in the opposite direction. That is, to justify giving up a good grade, you must convince yourself that cheating is a heinous sin, that it's one of the lowest things a person can do, and that cheaters should be rooted out and severely punished.

How Dissonance Affects Personal Values What has happened is not merely a rationalization of your own behavior but an actual change in your system of values. People facing this kind of choice will undergo either a softening or a hardening of their attitudes toward cheating on exams, depending on whether or not they decided to cheat. The interesting and important thing to remember is that two people acting in two different ways could have started out with almost identical attitudes toward cheating. One came within an inch of cheating but decided to resist, while the other came within an inch of resisting but decided to cheat. Once they had made their decisions, however, their attitudes toward cheating would diverge sharply as a consequence of their actions.

These speculations were tested by Judson Mills (1958) in an experiment he performed in an elementary school. Mills first measured the attitudes of sixth graders toward cheating. He then had them participate in a competitive exam, with prizes awarded to the winners. The situation was arranged so that it was almost impossible to win without cheating. Mills made it easy for the children to cheat and created the illusion that they could not be detected. Under these conditions, as one might expect, some of the students cheated and others did not. The next day, the sixth graders were again asked to indicate how they felt about cheating. Sure enough, the children who had cheated became more lenient toward cheating, and those who had resisted the temptation to cheat adopted a harsher attitude.

Classic experiments conducted in the laboratory often inspire contemporary research in the real world. A case in point: While conducting research among mid-level business executives in India, two social psychologists came up with some interesting data pertinent to Mills's results (Viswesvaran & Deshpande, 1996). They reasoned that executives who were in the process of making a decision about whether to behave ethically or not were in a vulnerable state: On the one hand, they wanted to behave ethically; on the other hand, they were undoubtedly concerned that they might need to behave unethically in order to succeed. The investigators found that executives who had substantial reason to

The harsh training required to become a marine will increase the recruits' feelings of cohesiveness and their pride in the corps.

believe that managerial success could be achieved only through unethical behavior experienced far greater dissonance (in the form of job dissatisfaction) than those who were given no reason to believe this. Our guess is that if the investigators had returned a year or two later, they would have found a reduction in dissonance in this group; that is, as with Mills's subjects, most of those who behaved unethically would have found a way to justify that behavior after the fact.

Justifying Your Effort

Most people are willing to work hard to get something they really want. For example, if you are really interested in pursuing a particular career, you are likely to go the extra mile to get it. You'll probably study hard to meet graduate school entrance requirements, study some more for graduate school admissions exams, and submit to a series of stressful interviews.

Let's turn that proposition inside out. Suppose you expend a great deal of effort to get into a particular club and it turns out to be a totally worthless organization, consisting of boring, pompous people engaged in trivial activities. You would feel pretty foolish, wouldn't you? A sensible person doesn't work hard to gain something worthless. Such a circumstance would produce a significant amount of dissonance; your cognition that you are a sensible, adept human being is dissonant with your cognition that you worked hard to get into a dismal club. How would you reduce this dissonance? How would you justify your behavior?

You might start by finding a way to convince yourself that the club and the people in it are nicer, more interesting, and more worthwhile than they appeared to be at first glance. How can one turn boring people into interesting people and a trivial club into a worthwhile one? Easy. Even the most boring people and trivial clubs have some redeeming qualities. Activities and behaviors are open to a variety of interpretations; if we are motivated to see the best in people and things, we will tend to interpret these ambiguities in a positive way. We call this the **justification of effort**—the tendency for individuals to increase their liking for something they have worked hard to attain.

In a classic experiment, Elliot Aronson and Judson Mills (1959) explored the link between effort and dissonance reduction. In their experiment, college students volunteered to join a group that would be meeting regularly to discuss various aspects of the psychology of sex. To be admitted to the group, they volunteered to go through a screening procedure. For one-third of the participants, the procedure was extremely demanding and unpleasant; for one-third, it was only mildly unpleasant; and one-third were admitted to the group without any screening at all.

Each participant was then allowed to listen in on a discussion being conducted by the members of the group they would be joining. Although they were led to believe that the discussion was live, they actually heard a prerecorded tape. The taped discussion was arranged so that it was as dull and bombastic as possible. After the discussion was over, each participant was asked to rate it in terms of how much he or she liked it, how interesting it was, how intelligent the participants were, and so forth. The major findings are shown in Figure 6.3.

The results supported the predictions: Participants who underwent little or no effort to get into the group did not enjoy the discussion very much. They were able to see it for what it was—a dull and boring waste of time. They regret-

Justification of Effort

The tendency for individuals to increase their liking for something they have worked hard to attain

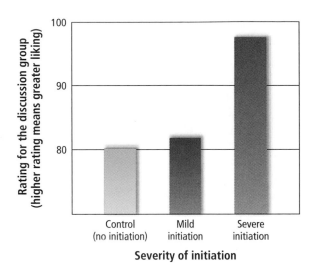

FIGURE 6.3

The tougher the initiation, the more we like the group.

The more effort we put into gaining group membership, the more we like the group we have just joined.

(Adapted from Aronson & Mills, 1959)

ted that they had agreed to participate. Participants who went through a severe initiation, however, convinced themselves that the same discussion, though not as scintillating as they had hoped, was dotted with interesting and provocative tidbits and was therefore, in the main, a worthwhile experience. In short, they justified the effort they had expended by interpreting all the ambiguous aspects of the group discussion in the most positive way possible. Similar results have been obtained by other researchers in comparable circumstances (e.g., Cooper, 1980; Gerard & Mathewson, 1966).

It should be clear that we are not suggesting that most people enjoy difficult, unpleasant experiences—they do not. Nor are we suggesting that people enjoy things that are merely associated with unpleasant experiences—they do not. What we are asserting is that if a person agrees to go through a demanding or an unpleasant experience in order to attain some goal or object, that goal or object becomes more attractive. Thus if you were walking to the discussion group and a passing car splashed mud all over you, you would not like that group any better. However, if you volunteered to jump into a mud puddle in order to be admitted to a group that turned out to be trivial and boring, you *would* like the group better. (See the Try It! exercise below.)

Try it!

Justifying Actions

Think about something that you have gone after in the past that necessitated your going through a lot of trouble or effort. Perhaps you waited for several hours in a long line to get tickets to a concert; perhaps you sat in your car through an incredible traffic jam because it was the only way you could visit a close friend.

1. Specifically, list the things you had to go through in order to attain your goal.
2. Do you think you might have tried to justify all that effort? Did you find yourself exaggerating the good things about the goal and minimizing any negative aspects of the goal? List some of the ways you might have exaggerated the value of the goal.
3. The next time you find yourself in that kind of situation, you might want to monitor your actions and cognitions carefully to see if there is any self-justification involved.

Sara Krulwich/The New York Times

"Don't you just LOVE my new dress?"

The Psychology of Insufficient Justification

When we were little, we were taught never to tell a lie. Indeed, our elementary school history courses were full of mythical stories (disguised as truths) like that of George Washington and the cherry tree, apparently aimed at convincing us that we had better be truthful if we aspired to the presidency. Alas, there may be some people who have never told a lie, but most of us have yet to meet one. At times, most of us feel that for good reason, we need to be less than perfectly truthful. One such reason involves something else that we were taught—to be kind to one another. Occasionally, in order to be kind to someone, we find it necessary to tell a lie.

Suppose your friend Jen shows you her expensive new dress and asks your opinion. You think it is atrocious and are about to say so when she tells you that she has already had it altered, which means that she cannot return it. What do you say? Chances are you go through something like the following thought process: "Jen seems so happy and excited about her new dress. She spent a lot of money for it, and she can't take it back. If I if say what I really think, I'll upset her."

So you tell Jen that you like her dress very much. Do you experience much dissonance? We doubt it. There are a great many thoughts that are consonant with having told this lie, as outlined in your reasoning in the preceding paragraph. In effect, your cognition that it is important not to cause pain to people you like provides ample **external justification** for having told a harmless lie.

Counterattitudinal Advocacy   What happens if you say something you don't really believe, but there isn't a good external justification for being insincere? That is, what if your friend Jen was fabulously wealthy and could easily afford to absorb the cost of her ugly new dress? What if she sincerely wanted to know what you thought? What if in the past you'd told her that she had bought something awful and your friendship survived? Now the external justifications—the reasons for lying to Jen about the dress are minimal. If you still withhold your true opinion (saying instead, "Gee, Jen, it's, uh, interesting"), you will experience dissonance. When you can't find external justification for your behavior, you will attempt to find **internal justification**—you will try to reduce dissonance by changing something about yourself (e.g., your attitude or behavior).

How can you do this? You might begin looking harder for positive things about the dress that you hadn't noticed before. If you look hard enough, you will probably find something. Within a short time, your attitude toward the dress will have moved in the direction of the statement you made—and that is how saying becomes believing. This phenomenon is generally referred to as **counterattitudinal advocacy.** It occurs when we claim to have an opinion or attitude that differs from our true beliefs. When we do this with little external justification, that is, without being motivated by something outside of ourselves, what we believe begins to look more and more like the lie we told.

This proposition was first tested in a groundbreaking experiment by Leon Festinger and J. Merrill Carlsmith (1959). College students were induced to spend an hour performing a series of excruciatingly boring and repetitive tasks. The experimenter then told them that the purpose of the study was to determine whether or not people would perform better if they had been informed in advance that the tasks were interesting. They were each informed that they had been randomly assigned to the control condition—that is, they had not been told anything in advance. However, he explained, the next participant, a young woman who was just arriving in the anteroom, was going to be in the experimental condition. The researcher said that he needed to convince her that the task was going to be interesting and enjoyable. Since it was much more convincing if a fellow student rather than the experimenter delivered this message, would the participant do so? Thus with his request the experimenter induced the participants to lie about the task to another student.

External Justification

A reason or an explanation for dissonant personal behavior that resides outside the individual (e.g., in order to receive a large reward or avoid a severe punishment)

Internal Justification

The reduction of dissonance by changing something about oneself (e.g., one's attitude or behavior)

Counterattitudinal Advocacy

Stating an opinion or attitude that runs counter to one's private belief or attitude

Half of the students were offered $20 for telling the lie (a large external justification), while the others were offered only $1 for telling the lie (a small external justification). After the experiment was over, an interviewer asked the lie-tellers how much they had enjoyed the tasks they had performed earlier in the experiment. The results validated the hypothesis: The students who had been paid $20 for lying—that is, for saying that the tasks had been enjoyable—rated the activities as the dull and boring experiences they were. But those who were paid only $1 for saying the task was enjoyable rated the task as significantly more enjoyable. In other words, people who had received an abundance of external justification for lying told the lie but didn't believe it, whereas those who told the lie without a great deal of external justification succeeded in convincing themselves that what they said was closer to the truth.

Does the same thing happen when important attitudes are involved? Can you induce a person to change an attitude about things that matter? Subsequent research has shown that the Festinger-Carlsmith paradigm has wide ramifications in areas of great significance. Consider an experiment by Arthur R. Cohen (1962), for example. Cohen was a social psychologist at Yale University during a turbulent political period when the city police were often called to the campus to control the behavior of students who were demonstrating against the war in Southeast Asia. Occasionally, the police reacted with excessive force. After one such incident, Cohen visited a dormitory, pretending that he worked for a well-known research institute. He told the students that there were two sides to every issue and that the institute was interested in looking at both sides of the police-student issue. He then asked the students to write forceful essays supporting the behavior of the police. Moreover, he told them he was able to offer them an incentive for writing the essay. Depending on the condition to which the students were assigned, he offered them 50 cents, $1, $5, or $10. (In 1962, $10 bought about thirty beers.) None of the students knew what the others were offered. After the students wrote their essays, Cohen assessed their real attitude toward the actions of the city police.

The results were clear: The smaller the incentive, the more favorable people became toward the city police. In other words, when the students were given a great deal of external justification for writing the essay, they did not need to convince themselves that they really believed what they had written. However, when they faced the fact that they had written positive things about the police for 50 cents or $1, they needed to convince themselves that there may have been some truth in what they had written.

In a similar experiment, researchers approached college students who initially believed that marijuana was harmful and induced them to compose and recite a videotaped speech favoring its use and legalization (Nel, Helmreich, & Aronson, 1969). Some were offered large incentives; others were offered small incentives. Again, the findings were clear: The smaller the incentive, the greater the softening of the attitude toward the use and legalization of marijuana.

In many of these experiments, people behaved without integrity (told a lie) in a manner that also might have harmed another person. For example, if you believe that marijuana is dangerous and you tell someone that it is not, in your own mind, you might be doing that person a great deal of harm. Accordingly, it is reasonable to ask the following question: Is lying enough? Is harming another person a necessary condition for dissonance, or is dissonance produced simply by behaving without integrity, even if no harm results? An experiment by Eddie Harmon-Jones and his colleagues (1996) made it clear that behaving without integrity, in and of itself, produces dissonance. In their experiment, people who drank an awful-tasting beverage and then volunteered to say that it tasted good actually came to believe that it tasted good (compared to the rating of a control group). The way they "said" it tasted good was to write their false opinion down on a small slip of paper, which they then immediately crumpled up and threw away. Thus even though their lie could not possibly harm anyone, the act of lying produced changes in belief aimed at softening the dissonance and restoring a sense of integrity.

Counterattitudinal Advocacy, Race Relations, and Preventing AIDS

What happens outside the laboratory? Can the experiments on counterattitudinal advocacy be used to tackle social problems? Let's look at race relations and racial prejudice, surely one of our nation's most important and enduring problems. Would it be possible to get people to endorse a policy favoring a minority group and then see if their attitudes become more favorable toward that group? Absolutely.

In an important set of experiments, Mike Leippe and Donna Eisenstadt (1994, 1998) induced white college students to write a counterattitudinal essay publicly endorsing a controversial proposal at their university to double the amount of funds available for academic scholarships for African American students. Because the total amount of funds was limited, this meant cutting by half the amount of scholarship funds available to white students. As you might imagine, this was a highly dissonant situation. How might the students reduce dissonance? The best way would be to convince themselves that they really believed deeply in that policy. Moreover, it is reasonable to suggest that dissonance reduction might generalize beyond the specific policy—that is, the theory would predict that their general attitude toward African Americans would become more favorable and more supportive. And that is exactly what Leippe and Eisenstadt found.

In the past decade, this aspect of dissonance theory has also been applied to another important social issue—preventing the spread of AIDS. Since the early 1980s, when the first few cases were diagnosed, the virus (known as HIV) that causes AIDS has killed approximately 15 million people across the globe, and in Asia and Africa, the number of infected people keeps rising. The greatest tragedy, perhaps, is that AIDS is largely preventable. By practicing "safe sex," including the use of condoms, people can significantly reduce their risk of contracting the HIV virus. To get this message across, the U.S. government has spent millions of dollars on AIDS information and prevention campaigns. But it turned out that information alone is not enough to prevent people from engaging in risky sexual behavor. As with many things, there is a wide gap between knowing what you should do and actually doing it. For example, although college students know that AIDS is a serious problem, only a small percentage use condoms every time they have sex. The reason seems to be that condoms are inconvenient and unromantic, and they remind people of disease—the last thing they want to be thinking about when preparing to make love. Rather, as researchers have consistently discovered, sexual behavior is often accompanied by denial. In this case, we tend to believe that although AIDS is a problem for most people, we ourselves are not at risk. How can this dangerous belief be overcome?

During the 1990s, Elliot Aronson and his students found that the counterattitudinal advocacy paradigm could help solve this problem (Aronson, Fried, & Stone, 1991; Stone, Aronson, Crain, Winslow, & Fried, 1994). The researchers asked two groups of college students to compose a speech describing the dangers of AIDS and advocating the use of condoms every time a person has sex. In one group, the students merely composed the arguments. In the second group, after composing their arguments, they were to recite them in front of a video camera and were told that an audience of high school students would watch the resulting tape. In addition, half the students in each group were made mindful of their own failure to use condoms by making a list of the circumstances in which they had found it particularly difficult, awkward, or impossible to use them.

Essentially, then, the participants in one group—those who made a video for high school students after the experimenter got them to think about their own failure to use condoms—experienced high dissonance. Why? They were made aware of their own hypocrisy: They had to deal with the fact that that they were preaching behavior that they themselves were not practicing. To remove the hypocrisy and maintain their self-esteem, they would need to start practicing what they were preaching. And that is exactly what the researchers found: They gave each student the chance to buy condoms very cheaply. The results demonstrated that the students in the hypocrisy condition were far more likely to buy condoms than students in any of the other conditions (see Figure 6.4). To find out if the results were long-lasting, the researchers phoned the students several months after the experiment and found that the effects held up. People in the hypocrisy condition—the students who would have felt the most cognitive dissonance—reported far greater use of condoms than those in the control conditions.

Insufficient Punishment   All societies run, in part, on punishment or the threat of punishment. For example, while cruising down the highway at 75 miles an hour, we know that if a cop spots us, we will pay a substantial fine, and if we get caught often, we will lose our license. So we learn to obey the speed limit when patrol cars are in the vicinity. By the same token, youngsters in school know that if they cheat on an exam and get caught, they could be humiliated by the teacher and severely punished. So they learn not to cheat while the teacher is in the room watching them. But does harsh punishment teach adults to want to obey the speed limit? Does it teach youngsters to value honest behavior? We don't think so. Rather, we believe that all it teaches is to try to avoid getting caught.

Let's look at bullying behavior. It is extremely difficult to persuade children that it's not right or enjoyable to beat up smaller children (Olweus, 2002). But theoretically, it is conceivable that under certain conditions they will persuade themselves that such behavior is unenjoyable. Imagine that you are the parent of a 6-year-old boy who often beats up his 4-year-old brother. You've tried to reason with your older son, to no avail. In an attempt to make him a nicer person (and to preserve the health and welfare of his little brother), you begin to punish him for his aggressiveness. As a parent, you can use a range of punishments, from the extremely mild (a stern look) to the extremely severe (a hard spanking, forcing the child to stand in the corner for two hours, depriving him of TV privileges for a month). The more severe the threat, the greater the likelihood the youngster

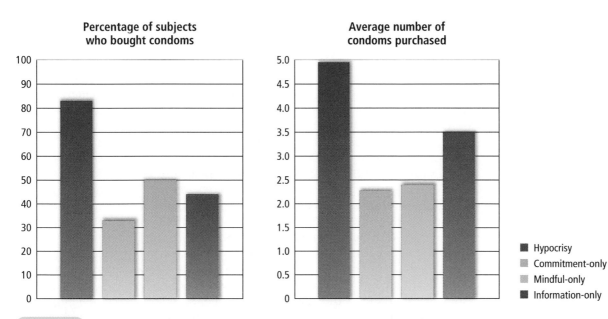

FIGURE 6.4

People who are made mindful of their hypocrisy begin to practice what they preach.

(Adapted from Stone, Aronson, Crain, Winslow, & Fried, 1994)

A parent can intervene to stop bullying after it takes place, but what might she do to make it less likely to happen in the future?

will cease and desist—while you are watching him. But he may very well hit his brother again as soon as you are out of sight. In short, just as most drivers learn to watch for the highway patrol while speeding, your 6-year-old still enjoys bullying his little brother; he has merely learned not to do it while you are around to punish him. Suppose that you threaten him with a mild punishment. In either case—under threat of severe punishment or of mild punishment—the child experiences dissonance. He is aware that he is not beating up his little brother, and he is also aware that he would like to beat him up. When he has the urge to hit his brother and doesn't, he implicitly asks himself, "How come I'm not beating up my little brother?" Under severe threat, he has a convincing answer in the form of a sufficient external justification: "I'm not beating him up because if I do, my parents are going to really punish me." This serves to reduce the dissonance.

The child in the mild threat situation experiences dissonance too. But when he asks himself, "How come I'm not beating up my little brother?" he doesn't have a very convincing answer because the threat is so mild that it does not provide a superabundance of justification. In short, this is **insufficient punishment.** The child is refraining from doing something he wants to do, and while he does have some justification for not doing it, he lacks complete justification. In this situation, he continues to experience dissonance. Therefore, the child must find another way to justify the fact that he is not aggressing against his kid brother.

The less severe you make the threat, the less external justification there is; the less external justification, the greater the need for internal justification. The child can reduce his dissonance by convincing himself that he doesn't really want to beat up his brother. In time, he can go further in his quest for internal justification and decide that beating up little kids is not fun. We would predict, then, that allowing children the leeway to construct their own internal justification enables them to develop a permanent set of values.

So far, we have been speculating that threats of mild punishment for any behavior will make that behavior less likely than severe threats will. To find out if this is in fact what happens, Elliot Aronson and J. Merrill Carlsmith (1963) devised an experiment with preschoolers. Because very young children were involved, the researchers thought it would be unethical to try to influence important values, like those concerning aggressive behavior. Instead, they attempted to change something that was unimportant to society but very important to the children—their desire for different kinds of toys. The experimenter first asked each child to rate the attractiveness of several toys. He then pointed to a toy that the child considered among the most attractive and told the child that he or she was not allowed to play with it. Half the children were threatened with mild punishment if they disobeyed; the other half were threatened with severe punishment. The experimenter left the room for a few minutes, giving the children the time and opportunity to play with the other toys and to resist the temptation to play with the forbidden toy. None of the children played with the forbidden toy.

Next, the experimenter returned and asked each child to rate how much he or she liked each of the toys. Initially, everyone had wanted to play with the forbidden toy, but during the temptation period, when they had the chance, not one child played with the toy. Clearly, the children were experiencing dissonance. How did they respond to this uncomfortable feeling? The children who had received a severe threat had ample justification for their restraint. They knew why they hadn't played with the toy, and therefore, they had no reason to change their attitude about it. These children continued to rate the forbidden

Insufficient Punishment

The dissonance aroused when individuals lack sufficient external justification for having resisted a desired activity or object, usually resulting in individuals' devaluing the forbidden activity or object

toy as highly desirable; indeed, some even found it more desirable than they had before the threat.

But what about the others? Without much external justification for avoiding the toy—they had little to fear if they played with it—the children in the mild threat condition needed an *internal* justification to reduce their dissonance. They succeeded in convincing themselves that the reason they hadn't played with the toy was that they didn't really like it. They rated the forbidden toy as less attractive than they had when the experiment began. What we have here is a clear example of self-justification leading to self-persuasion in the behavior of very young children. The implications for child rearing are fascinating. Parents who use punishment to encourage their children to adopt desirable values should keep the punishment mild—barely enough to produce a change in behavior—and the values will follow.

Does Self-Persuasion Last? Let's say you've attended a lecture on the evils of cheating. It might have a temporary effect on your attitudes toward cheating. But if a week or two later you found yourself in a highly tempting situation, would your new attitude keep you from cheating? Probably not. Social psychologists know that mere lectures do not usually result in permanent or long-lasting attitude change. But suppose that your experience was similar to the children's in Judson Mills's (1958) experiment on cheating, discussed earlier in this chapter. Here we would expect that your new attitude would endure. The children who were tempted to cheat but resisted came to believe that cheating is bad, not because someone told them so but through **self-persuasion:** They persuaded themselves of this belief to justify the fact that by not cheating, they had given up something they really wanted. Self-persuasion is more permanent than direct attempts at persuasion precisely because, with self-persuasion, the persuasion takes place internally and not because of external coaxing or pressure.

To test the long-lasting effects of attitudes that result from self-justification, Jonathan Freedman (1965) replicated Aronson and Carlsmith's (1963) forbidden toy experiment. Several weeks later, a young woman came to the school, telling the children she was there to administer some paper-and-pencil tests. In fact, she was working for Freedman. Coincidentally, she was administering her tests in the same room Freedman had used for his experiment—the room where the same toys were casually scattered about. After administering the test, she asked the children to wait for her while she scored it in another room. She then casually suggested that the scoring might take a while and that—how lucky!—someone had left some toys around and the children could play with anything they liked.

The results were striking: The overwhelming majority of the children whom Freedman had mildly threatened several weeks earlier decided, on their own, not to play with the forbidden toy. By contrast, the great majority of the children who had been severely threatened played with the forbidden toy. A single mild threat was still very effective several weeks later; the severe threat was not.

Again, the power of this phenomenon rests on the fact that the reason the children didn't play with the toy was not that some adult told them the toy was undesirable: That kind of information would not have had much effect after the adult left. The reason the mild threat persisted for at least several weeks was that *the children were motivated to convince themselves the toy was undesirable*. The results of Freedman's experiment are presented in Figure 6.5 on the next page.

Not Just Tangible Rewards or Punishments As we have seen, a sizable reward or a severe punishment provides strong external justification for an action. So if you want a person to do something or not to do something only once, the best strategy would be to promise a large reward or threaten a severe punishment. But if you want a person to become committed to an attitude or to a behavior, the *smaller* the reward or punishment that will lead to momentary compliance, the *greater* will be the eventual change in attitude and therefore the more permanent the effect.

How can we induce this child to give up playing with an attractive toy?

Self-Persuasion

A long-lasting form of attitude change that results from attempts at self-justification

Several weeks afterward, children who had received a threat of mild punishment were far less likely to play with the forbidden toy than children who had received a threat of severe punishment. Those given a mild threat had to provide their own justification by devaluing the attractiveness of the toy.

(Adapted from Freedman, 1965)

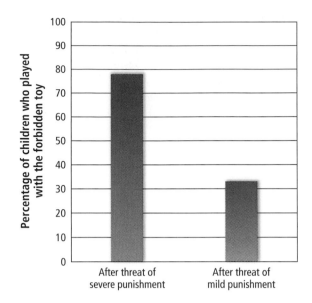

Large rewards and severe punishments, because they are strong external justifications, encourage compliance but prevent real attitude change (see Figure 6.6.)

This phenomenon is not limited to tangible rewards and punishments; justifications can also come in more subtle packages. Take friendship, for example. We like our friends; we trust our friends; we do favors for our friends. Suppose you are at a formal dinner party at the home of a close friend. Your friend is passing around a strange-looking appetizer. "What is it?" you ask. "Oh, it's a fried grasshopper; I'd really like you to try it." She's a good friend and you don't want to embarrass her in front of the other guests, so you pick one up and eat it. How much do you think you will like this new snack food?

Keep that in mind for a moment. Now suppose you are a dinner guest at the home of a person you don't like very much, and he hands you, as an appetizer, a fried grasshopper and tells you that he'd really like you to try it. You comply. Now the crucial question: In which of these two situations will you like the taste of the grasshopper better? Common sense might suggest that the grasshopper would taste better when recommended by a friend. But think about it for a moment; which condition involves less external justification? Common sense notwithstanding, dissonance theory makes the opposite prediction. In the first case, when you ask yourself, "How come I ate that disgusting insect?" you have ample justification: You ate it because your good friend asked you to. In the second case, you don't have this kind of outside justification, so you must create it. Namely, you must convince yourself that you actually *liked* the grasshopper. While this may seem a rather bizarre example of dissonance-reducing behavior, it's not as far-fetched as you might think. Indeed, Philip Zimbardo and his colleagues conducted an experiment directly analogous to our example (Zimbardo, Weisenberg, Firestone, & Levy, 1965). In this experiment, army

FIGURE 6.6

The Power of Insufficient Justification

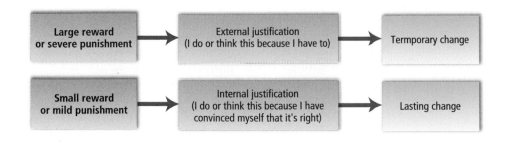

reservists were asked to eat fried grasshoppers as part of a research project on survival foods. Reservists who ate grasshoppers at the request of a stern, unpleasant officer increased their liking for grasshoppers far more than those who ate grasshoppers at the request of a well-liked, pleasant officer. Those who complied with the unfriendly officer's request had little external justification for their actions. As a result, they adopted more positive attitudes toward eating grasshoppers in order to justify their otherwise strange and dissonance-arousing behavior.

Good and Bad Deeds

Whenever we act either kindly or cruelly toward a person, we never quite feel the same way about that person again. (See the Try It! exercise below.)

The Ben Franklin Effect When we like people, we show it by treating them well. The reverse is also true. We might even go out of our way to snub someone we dislike. But what happens when we do a person a favor? In particular, what happens when we are subtly induced to do a favor for a person we do not like—will we like the person more? Or less? Dissonance theory predicts that we will like the person more after doing the favor. Can you see why? Jot down your answer in the margin.

> We do not love people so much for the good they have done us as for the good we have done them.
>
> —Leo Tolstoy, 1869

This phenomenon has been a part of folk wisdom in several cultures for a very long time. The great Russian novelist Leo Tolstoy wrote about it in 1869, and more than a century before that, Benjamin Franklin confessed to having used this bit of folk wisdom as a political strategy. While serving in the Pennsylvania state legislature, Franklin was disturbed by the political opposition and animosity of a fellow legislator. So he set out to win him over.

> *I did not . . . aim at gaining his favour by paying any servile respect to him but, after some time, took this other method. Having heard that he had in his library a certain very scarce and curious book I wrote a note to him expressing my desire of perusing that book and requesting he would do me the favour of lending it to me for a few days. He sent it immediately and I returned it in about a week with another note expressing strongly my sense of the favour. When we next met in the House he spoke to me (which he had never done before), and with great civility; and he ever after manifested a readiness to serve me on all occasions, so that we became great friends and our friendship continued to his death. This is another instance of the truth of an old maxim I had learned, which says, "He that has once done you a kindness will be more ready to do you another than he whom you yourself have obliged." (Franklin, 1868/1900, pp. 216–217)*

Try it!

Good Deeds

When you walk down a city street and view people sitting on the sidewalk, panhandling, or pushing their possessions around in a shopping cart, how do you feel about them? Think about it for a few moments, and write down a list of your feelings. If you are like most college students, your list will reflect some mixed feelings. That is, you probably feel some compassion but also think these people are a nuisance, that if they really tried, they could get their lives together. Consider doing volunteer work at a shelter for the homeless—serving food, for example. After a few sessions, pay close attention to your feelings. Do you notice any changes?

Without realizing it, Ben Franklin may have been the first dissonance theorist.

Benjamin Franklin was clearly pleased with the success of his blatantly manipulative strategy. But as rigorous scientists, we should not be convinced by his anecdote. We have no way to know whether Franklin's success was due to this particular gambit or simply to his general, all-around charm. To be certain, it is important to design and conduct an experiment that controls for such things as charm. Such a study was conducted by Jon Jecker and David Landy (1969), more than 240 years after Franklin's more casual experiment. In the Jecker and Landy experiment, students participated in an intellectual contest that enabled them to win a substantial sum of money. After the experiment was over, one-third of the participants were approached by the experimenter, who explained that he was using his own funds for the experiment and was running short, which meant he might be forced to close down the experiment prematurely. He asked, "As a special favor to me, would you mind returning the money you won?" The same request was made to a different group of subjects, except this time not by the experimenter but by the departmental secretary, who asked them if they would return the money as a special favor to the (impersonal) psychology department's research fund, which was running low. The remaining participants were not asked to return their winnings at all. Finally, all of the participants were asked to fill out a questionnaire that included an opportunity to rate the experimenter. Participants who had been cajoled into doing a special favor for the experimenter found him the most attractive; that is, after they did him a favor, they convinced themselves he was a wonderful, deserving fellow. The others thought he was a pretty nice guy but not anywhere near as wonderful as the people who had been asked to do him a favor (see Figure 6.7).

Recall the experiment by Mike Leippe and Donna Eisenstadt in which white students developed more favorable attitudes toward African Americans after having said publicly that they favored preferential treatment for African American students. Can you see how the "Ben Franklin effect" might apply here—how this act of helping might have contributed to their change in attitudes?

Suppose you find yourself in a situation where you have an opportunity to lend a helping hand to an acquaintance but because you are in a hurry or because it is inconvenient, you decline to help that person. How do you think this act of omission might affect your feelings for this person? This is precisely the kind of situation investigated by Gail Williamson and her colleagues (Williamson, Clark, Pegalis, & Behan, 1996). As you might expect, this refusal led to a decline in the attractiveness of the acquaintance. This was an act of omission. But suppose you actually did harm to another person. What do you suppose might happen then? We will discuss that in the following section.

FIGURE 6.7

If we have done someone a favor, we are more likely to feel more positively toward that person.

(Adapted from Jecker & Landy, 1969)

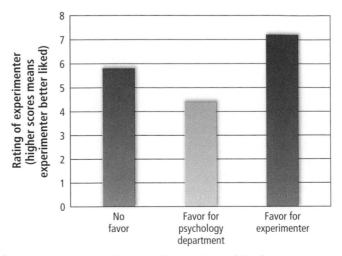

Who was the recipient of the favor?

Hating Our Victims   During the height of the war in Vietnam, Elliot Aronson hired a young man to help paint his house.

The painter was a gentle and sweet-natured person who had graduated from high school, joined the army, and fought in Vietnam. After leaving the army, he took up housepainting and was a good and reliable craftsman and an honest businessman. I enjoyed working with him. One day while we were taking a coffee break, we began to discuss the war and the intense opposition to it, especially at the local university. It soon became apparent that he and I were in sharp disagreement on this issue. He felt that the American intervention was reasonable and just and would "make the world safe for democracy." I argued that it was a terribly dirty war, that we were killing, maiming, and napalming thousands of innocent people—old people, women, children—people who had no interest in war or politics. He looked at me for a long time; then he smiled sweetly and said, "Hell, Doc, those aren't people; those are Vietnamese! They're gooks." He said it matter-of-factly, without obvious rancor or vehemence. I was astonished and chilled by his response. I wondered how it could be that this apparently good-natured, sane, and gentle young man could develop that kind of attitude. How could he dismiss an entire national group from the human race?

Over the next several days, as we continued our dialogue, I got to know more about him. It turned out that during the war he had participated in actions in which Vietnamese civilians had been killed. What gradually emerged was that initially he had been racked by guilt—and it dawned on me that he might have developed this attitude toward the Vietnamese people as a way of assuaging his guilt. That is, if he could convince himself that the Vietnamese were not fully human, it would make him feel less awful about having hurt them, and it would reduce the dissonance between his actions and his self-concept as a decent person.

Clearly, these speculations about the causes of the housepainter's attitude are far from conclusive. While he may have derogated the Vietnamese people as a way of reducing dissonance, the situation is complex; for example, he might always have had a negative and prejudiced attitude toward the Vietnamese, and this might have made it easier for him to behave brutally toward them. To be certain that the justification of cruelty can occur in such situations, it is essential for the social psychologist to temporarily step back from the helter-skelter of the real world and test the proposition in the more controlled setting of the experimental laboratory.

Ideally, if we want to measure attitude change as a result of dissonant cognitions, we should know what the attitudes were before the dissonance-arousing behavior occurred. Such a situation was produced in an experiment performed by Keith Davis and Edward Jones (1960). Each student's participation consisted of watching a young man being interviewed and then, on the basis of this observation, providing him with an analysis of his shortcomings as a human being. Specifically, the participants were told to tell the young man (a confederate of the researchers) that they thought he was a shallow, untrustworthy, boring person. The participants succeeded in convincing themselves that they didn't like the victim of their cruelty—after the fact. In short, after saying things they knew were certain to hurt him, they convinced themselves that he deserved to be hurt. They found him less attractive than they had prior to saying the hurtful things to him.

Let's go back to our housepainter example. Suppose for a moment that all the people he killed and injured in Vietnam had been fully armed enemy soldiers rather than noncombatants. Do you think he would have experienced as much dissonance? We think it is unlikely. When engaged in combat with an enemy soldier, it is a "you or me" situation; if the housepainter had not killed the enemy soldier, the enemy soldier might have killed him. So even though hurting or killing another person is probably never taken lightly, it is not nearly so heavy

During wartime, especially when defenseless civilians such as old people, women, and children are targets of military violence, the soldiers committing such acts of violence will become inclined to derogate or dehumanize their victims, after the fact, in order to reduce their own dissonance.

> There's nothing people can't contrive to praise or condemn and find justification for doing so.
>
> —*Molière, The Misanthrope*

a burden as it would be if the victim were an unarmed civilian—a child, a woman, an old person.

These speculations are supported by the results of an experiment by Ellen Berscheid and her colleagues (Berscheid, Boye, & Walster, 1968). College students volunteered for an experiment in which each of them administered a (supposedly) painful electric shock to a fellow student. As one might expect, these students derogated their victim as a result of having administered the shock. However, half of the students were told there would be a turnabout: The other student would be given the opportunity to retaliate against them at a later time. Those who were led to believe that their victim would be able to retaliate later did not derogate the victim. In short, because the victim was going to be able to even the score, there was very little dissonance, and therefore the harm-doers had no need to belittle their victim in order to convince themselves that he or she deserved it.

The results of these laboratory experiments lend credence to our speculations about the behavior of the housepainter; the results suggest that during a war, military personnel have a greater need to derogate civilian victims (because these individuals can't retaliate) than military victims. Moreover, several years after Aronson's encounter with the housepainter, a similar set of events emerged during the court-martial of Lieutenant William Calley for his role in the slaughter of innocent civilians at My Lai in Vietnam. In long and detailed testimony, Calley's psychiatrist made it clear that the lieutenant had come to regard the Vietnamese people as less than human.

As we have seen, systematic research in this area demonstrates that people do not perform acts of cruelty and come out unscathed. We can never be completely certain of how the housepainter, Lieutenant Calley, and thousands of other American military personnel came to regard the Vietnamese as subhuman, but it seems reasonable to assume that when people are engaged in a war where a great number of innocent people are being killed, they might try to derogate the victims in order to justify their complicity. They might poke fun at them, refer to them as "gooks," and dehumanize them. Ironically, success at dehumanizing the victim virtually guarantees a continuation or even an escalation of the cruelty. It becomes easier to hurt and kill subhumans than to hurt and kill fellow human beings. Reducing dissonance in this way therefore has sobering future consequences: It increases the likelihood that the atrocities people are willing to commit will become greater and greater through an endless chain of violence followed by self-justification (in the form of dehumanizing the victim), followed by greater violence and still more intense dehumanization. In this manner, unbelievable acts of human cruelty—such as the Nazi "Final Solution" that led to the murder of 6 million European Jews—can occur. Unfortunately, atrocities are not a thing of the past but are as recent as today's newspaper.

CONNECTIONS

Was Osama bin Laden Capitalizing on Dissonance?

Following the catastrophic destruction of the World Trade Center by suicide bombers on September 11, 2001, political analysts struggled to understand how hatred can be so strong that people would destroy themselves in order to kill thousands of innocent people—when they must have known that their action could not possibly produce any direct political advantage. Most analysts have explained the behavior of the suicide bombers in terms of religious fanaticism. But this explanation does not add much to our understanding. Thomas Friedman, a Pulitzer Prize–winning journalist and one of our nation's most astute observers of the Middle East, has taken a different approach. He has offered a partial answer to this most difficult question based on the theory of cognitive dissonance. Friedman (2002) suggests that there are thousands of young Muslim men all over the Middle East and Europe who are suffering from a loss of dignity. According to Friedman (pp. 334–335), these young men were

> *taught from youth in the mosque that theirs is the most complete and advanced form of the three monotheistic faiths—superior to both Christianity and Judaism—yet who become aware that the Islamic world has fallen behind both the Christian West and the Jewish state in education, science, democracy, and development. This produces a cognitive dissonance in these young men—a cognitive dissonance that is the original spark for all their rage. . . . They reconcile this by concluding that the Islamic world has fallen behind the rest of the world either because the Europeans, Americans, and Israelis stole something from the Muslims, or because the Europeans, Americans, and Israelis are deliberately retarding the progress of Muslims, or because those who are leading the Muslim world have drifted away from the true faith and are behaving in un-Islamic ways, but are being kept in power by America. . . . They see America as the most powerful lethal weapon destroying their religious universe, or at least the universe they would like to build. And that is why they transform America into the ultimate evil, even more than Western Europe, an evil that needs to be weakened and, if possible, destroyed. Even by suicide? Why not? If America is destroying the source of meaning in their lives, then it needs to be destroyed back.*

Culture and Dissonance

We can find the effects of dissonance in almost every part of the world (e.g., Beauvois & Joule, 1996, 1998; Sakai, 1999), but it does not always take the same form. Harry Triandis (1995) has argued that in societies where the needs of the group matter more than the needs of the individual, dissonance-reducing behavior might be less prevalent—at least on the surface. In such cultures, we'd be more likely to find behavior aimed at maintaining group harmony and less likely to see self-justification, which is an individual drive. Others have argued that dissonance-reducing behavior may be less extreme in Japan than it is in the West because Japanese culture considers an individual's acceptance of inconsistency to be a sign of maturity and broad-mindedness (Hong, 1992).

It may also be that self-justification does occur in less individualistic societies but is triggered in more communal ways. In a striking set of experiments,

Japanese social psychologist Haruki Sakai (1999) investigated dissonance-reducing behavior in Japan by combining his interest in dissonance with his expert knowledge of Japanese community orientation. In a nutshell, what Sakai found was that in Japan, not only does a person reduce dissonance after saying that a boring task is interesting and enjoyable (as in the classic Festinger and Carlsmith experiment), but in addition, if a person merely observes someone he knows and likes saying that a boring task is interesting and enjoyable, that will cause the observer to experience dissonance. Consequently, in that situation, the observers' attitudes change. In short, the observers bring their evaluation more in line with the lie their friend has told!

VARIATIONS ON THE THEME OF SELF-JUSTIFICATION

Throughout this chapter, we've seen that people generally need to see themselves as intelligent, sensible, and decent folks who behave with integrity. Indeed, what triggers the behavior change and cognitive distortion that occurs when we try to reduce feelings of dissonance is precisely our need to maintain this picture of themselves. At first glance, much of the behavior described in this chapter may seem startling—people coming to dislike others more after doing them harm; people liking others more after doing them a favor; people believing a lie they've told only if there is little or no reward for telling it. These behaviors would be difficult for us to understand if it weren't for the insights provided by the theory of cognitive dissonance.

Social psychologists have continued to explore this basic premise in greater depth and in new contexts. What are they finding?

Self-Discrepancy Theory

Most of the classic dissonance experiments we've looked at have involved behavior that in some way doesn't measure up to most people's standards of competence or morality, such as working hard for something of questionable value or lying for no good reason. Tory Higgins and his colleagues (Higgins, 1987, 1989, 1996b, 1999; Higgins, Klein, & Strauman, 1987) were curious about the emotional distress we feel when we fall short of our ideals and standards. According to their **self-discrepancy theory**, we become distressed when our sense of who we truly are—our actual self—differs from our personal standards or from our desired self-concept.

For Higgins and his colleagues, these standards are reflected most clearly in the various beliefs we hold about the type of person we aspire to be—our *ideal self*—and the type of person we believe we should be—our *ought self*. Comparing our actual self with our ideal and ought selves provides us with an important means of self-evaluation. We make judgments about our abilities, our personal attributes, our behavior, and the extent to which we are adhering to our goals.

What happens when we become aware that we have failed to measure up to our standards? Like dissonance theory, self-discrepancy theory predicts that this blow to our self-esteem will generate psychological distress, along with the motivation to reduce the inconsistency associated with the self-discrepancy. Engaging in various forms of self-justification allows us to narrow the gap that sometimes exists between who we are, as implied by our self-discrepant actions, and who we aspire to be.

To illustrate, consider the predicament of Ana, a first-year college student who has always had very high academic standards. In terms of self-discrepancy theory, academic competence is a central component of her ideal self. Moreover, she's become accustomed to living up to these high standards over

Self-Discrepancy Theory

The idea that people become distressed when their sense of their actual self differs from their ideal self

the years: With only a modest level of effort, it was pretty much a breeze in high school to earn A's in most subjects and B's in the others. In her first semester at a competitive, prestigious college, however, Ana has discovered those A's much harder to come by. It seems that the courses she has enrolled in are far more rigorous and demanding than she had anticipated. As a matter of fact, in her introductory chemistry course—a prerequisite for her major—she barely managed to earn a C. Given this scenario, how is Ana likely to experience this discrepancy between her ideal and actual selves?

To begin with, we might imagine that the threat to her self-concept as a high achiever would almost certainly generate fairly strong levels of emotional discomfort—for example, disappointment in herself and perhaps an unaccustomed sense of uncertainty regarding her abilities. Self-discrepancy research supports this view. In a series of studies, Higgins and his colleagues (Higgins, 1989; Higgins, Bond, Klein, & Strauman, 1988) have found that when people are made aware of a discrepancy between their actual and ideal selves, they tend to experience a pattern of feelings involving dejection, sadness, dissatisfaction, and other depression-related emotions.

What happens when there is a discrepancy between Ana's ideal self-concept (as an excellent student) and her actual performance?

Now consider what would happen if Ana had encountered a self-discrepancy involving her ought self—not the ideal self she aspired to but the "should" self she felt obligated to uphold. Imagine that Ana didn't need to be a top-notch student to satisfy her own ideal self-aspirations. Instead, suppose that her parents had always held this standard as highly important and that Ana, out of respect for them, was very responsive to their expectations regarding academic excellence. How, then, would Ana experience this discrepancy between her actual and ought selves in the face of a mediocre performance in her first semester at college? Higgins and his colleagues have found that a different pattern of emotions would tend to occur than in the case of actual-ideal self-discrepancy. Specifically, their research indicates that Ana would be likely to experience fear, worry, tension, and other anxiety-related emotions.

How might Ana attempt to cope with the dissonance arousal and negative feelings generated by either of these two forms of self-discrepancy? According to the theory, self-discrepancies not only produce emotional discomfort but also provoke strivings to minimize the gap between the actual and the ideal or ought selves. As we've seen throughout this chapter, self-justifying thoughts and behaviors can restore a positive self-concept when it has been threatened by a self-discrepant experience. For example, recall the predicament of subjects in Festinger and Carlsmith's (1959) classic study who, for a paltry $1, told a "fellow student" that a tedious experimental task was actually quite fascinating. Let's assume that the ideal or ought selves of these subjects included the notion of behaving with honesty and integrity. Lying, then, would have signaled a discrepancy between their actual selves and their standards. How did they reduce the dissonance associated with this self-discrepancy? By minimizing the extent of their dishonesty— that is, by expressing greater liking for the boring task.

In Ana's case, reducing dissonance might involve interpreting her poor grades in a way that protects her belief in herself as an excellent student. In fact, in several experiments, undergraduate students who received a failing grade on an exam reacted in precisely this way: Failing students blamed their poor performance on the alleged unfairness of the test, rather than attributing it to personal factors such as poor ability or insufficient effort. In other words, when faced with a discrepancy between their actual and desired selves, they reduced the discrepancy by rejecting personal responsibility for their failure (Arkin & Maruyama, 1979; Davis & Stephan, 1980). Similarly, Ana might convince herself that the grading was unfair, that her chemistry instructor was totally inept, or that something else caused her mediocre performance. Of course, self-justification, though a self-protective strategy in the short run, might not be the most adaptive approach for Ana to use in coming to terms with dissonance arousal. She would benefit far more from reassessing her situation—concluding, perhaps, that maintaining her high academic standards might require more effort than it did in high school.

Maintaining Our Self-Image

Most dissonance research concerns how our self-image is threatened by our own behavior, such as acting contrary to our attitudes or making a difficult decision. Abraham Tesser and his colleagues have explored how other people's behavior can threaten our self-image in ways that have important implications for our interpersonal relationships (Beach, Tesser, Mendolia, & Anderson, 1996; Tesser, 1988).

Suppose you consider yourself a good tennis player—in fact, you typically beat all of your friends. Then you move to another town and discover that your favorite new friend plays like a pro. How does that make you feel? Probably, you are more than a little uneasy about the fact that your friend outdoes you in your area of expertise.

Now suppose that your new best friend is not a tennis star but a very talented artist. Will you feel uncomfortable? Undoubtedly not; in fact, you will probably bask in the reflected glory of your friend's success. You might even brag to your other friends, "I have a new friend who has sold some of her paintings in a really hot New York gallery." The difference between these two scenarios is that in the first one, your friend excels at something that is important to you and may even be a central part of how you define yourself. We all have abilities and traits that we treasure—we are especially proud of being talented cooks, artists, musicians, or baseball players. Whatever our most treasured ability, if we meet someone who is better at it than we are, there is likely to be trouble—trouble of the dissonance variety. How can we be proud of our ability to cook if our closest friend is a far better chef than we are?

This is the basic premise of Tesser's (1988) **self-evaluation maintenance theory:** One's self-concept can be threatened by another individual's behavior; the level of the threat is determined by both the closeness of the other individual and the personal relevance of the behavior.

So there is no problem if a close friend outperforms us on a task that is not particularly relevant to us. In fact, we feel even better about ourselves for having such a talented friend. Dissonance occurs when a close friend outperforms us on a task that is important to the way we define ourselves.

Reducing Dissonance We can try to change any one of the three components that produced this dissonance. First, we can distance ourselves from the person who outperforms us, deciding that he or she is not such a close friend after all. Researchers tested this possibility by having college students compete against another student, who was actually an accomplice of the experimenter, on general knowledge questions (Pleban & Tesser, 1981). They rigged it so that in some conditions, the questions were on topics that were highly relevant to people's self-definitions and the accomplice got many more of the questions correct. Just as predicted, this was the condition in which people distanced themselves the most from the accomplice, saying they would not want to work with him again. It is too dissonance-producing to be close to someone who is better than we in our treasured areas of expertise (Wegner, 1986).

A second way to reduce such threats to our self-esteem is to change how relevant the task is to our self-definition. If our new friend is a far better tennis player than we are, we might lose interest in tennis and decide that running is really our thing. In a test of this prediction, people received feedback about how well they and another student had done on a test of a newly discovered ability. Those who learned that the other student was similar to them and had done better on the test were especially likely to say that this ability was not very important to them—just as the theory predicts (Tesser & Paulus, 1983).

Self-Evaluation Maintenance Theory
The idea that one's self-concept can be threatened by another individual's behavior and that the level of threat is determined by both the closeness of the other individual and the personal relevance of the behavior

Finally, people can deal with self-esteem threats by changing the third component in the equation—their performance relative to the other person's. Suppose that being a good cook is important to us and our new best friend is a superb cook. We can reduce the dissonance by trying to make ourselves even better in the kitchen. But no matter how hard we try, she still outdoes us. We might then resort to a more diabolical route: We try to undermine our friend's performance so that it is not as good as ours. If our friend asks for a recipe, we might leave out a crucial ingredient so that the resulting *saumon en brioche* is not nearly as good as ours.

Why Might We Help a Stranger More than a Friend?   Are people really so mean-spirited that they try to sabotage their friends' performances? Surely not always, but if our self-esteem is on the line, we are not as helpful as we would like to think (Tesser & Smith, 1980). Students in a study were asked to play a word game: One person gives clues to help another guess a word. Students were paired with both friends and strangers, and they could choose to give clues that would make it easy for the other player to guess the word or hard. The researchers set it up so that people first performed poorly themselves, then had the opportunity to help the other players by giving them easy or difficult clues. Whom would they help more, the strangers or their friends?

You can probably see what self-evaluation maintenance theory predicts. If the task is not self-relevant to people, they should want their friends to do especially well so that they can bask in the reflected glory. If the task is self-relevant, however, it would be threatening to people's self-esteem to have their friends outperform them. So they might make it difficult for their friends by giving them especially hard clues. This is exactly what Tesser and Smith (1980) found. They made the task self-relevant for some participants by telling them that performance on the game was highly correlated with their intelligence and leadership skills. Under these conditions, people gave more difficult clues to their friends than to the strangers because they did not want their friends to shine on a task that was highly important to them. When the task was not self-relevant, people gave more difficult clues to the strangers than to their friends.

In sum, research on self-evaluation maintenance theory has shown that threats to our self-concept have fascinating implications for our interpersonal relationships. Though much of the research has been with college students in laboratory settings, the theory has been confirmed in field and archival studies as well. For example, Tesser (1980) examined biographies of male scientists, noting how close these scientists were to their fathers. As the theory predicts, when the scientists' field of expertise was the same as their fathers', they had a more distant and strained relationship with their fathers. Similarly, the greatest amount of friction between siblings was found to occur when the siblings were close in age and one sibling was significantly better on key dimensions, such as popularity or intelligence. When performance and relevance are high, it can be difficult to avoid conflicts with family members (Tesser, 1980). Consider how the novelist Norman Maclean (1983) describes his relationship with his brother in *A River Runs through It*: "One of the earliest things brothers try to find out is how they differ from each other. . . . Undoubtedly, our differences would not have seemed so great if we had not been such a close family" (p. 83).

Self-Affirmation Theory

Sometimes threats to our self-concept can be so strong and difficult to avoid that the usual means of reducing dissonance are difficult to apply. For example, millions of people have discovered that quitting smoking is very hard. It is also difficult for most smokers to ignore or distort all the evidence indicating that smoking can harm our health and might even kill us. So what can people do in this situation? Are smokers doomed to wallow in a constant state of dissonance? **Self-affirmation theory** suggests that people will reduce the impact of a

If being a good cook is an important aspect of her self-concept, and her best friend is a superb cook, she will try harder. Where *are* those capers?

Self-Affirmation Theory

The idea that people will reduce the impact of a dissonance-arousing threat to their self-concept by focusing on and affirming their competence on some dimension unrelated to the threat

dissonance-arousing threat to their self-concept by focusing on and affirming their competence on some dimension unrelated to the threat.

Research has revealed how self-affirmation comes about (Aronson, Cohen, & Nail, 1999; Steele, 1988). "Yes, it's true that I smoke," you might say, "but I am a great cook" (a terrific tennis player, a wonderful friend, a promising scientist). Self-affirmation occurs when our self-esteem is threatened; if all else fails, we will attempt to reduce the dissonance by reminding ourselves of some other aspect of our self-concept that we cherish as a way of feeling good about ourselves in spite of some stupid or immoral action we have just committed.

In a series of clever experiments, Claude Steele and his colleagues demonstrated that if you give people an opportunity for self-affirmation before the onset of dissonance, they will often grab it. For example, the researchers replicated Jack Brehm's (1956) classic experiment on postdecision dissonance reduction (Steele, Hoppe, & Gonzales, 1986). They asked students to rank ten record albums, ostensibly as part of a marketing survey. As a reward, the students were then told that they could keep either their fifth- or sixth-ranked album. Ten minutes after making their choice, they were asked to rate the albums again. You will recall that in Brehm's experiment, after selecting a kitchen appliance, the participants rated the one they had chosen much higher than the one they had rejected. In this manner, they convinced themselves that they had made a smart decision. And that is what the students did in this experiment as well.

But Steele and his colleagues built an additional set of conditions into their experiment. Half of the students were science majors, and half were business majors. Half of the science majors and half of the business majors were asked to put on a white lab coat while participating in the experiment. Why the lab coat? A lab coat is associated with science. Steele and his colleagues suspected that the lab coat would serve a "self-affirmation function" for the science majors but not for the business majors. The results supported their predictions. Whether or not they were wearing a lab coat, business majors reduced dissonance just as the people in Brehm's experiment did: After their choice, they increased their evaluation of the chosen album and decreased their evaluation of the one they had rejected. Similarly, in the absence of a lab coat, science majors reduced their dissonance in the same way. However, science majors who were wearing the lab coat resisted the temptation to distort their perceptions. The lab coat reminded these students that they were promising scientists and thereby short-circuited the need to reduce dissonance by changing their attitudes toward the albums. In effect, they said, "I may have made a dumb choice in record albums, but I can live with that because I have other things going for me; at least I'm a promising scientist!"

WHY WOULD ANYONE WANT TO MAINTAIN A POOR SELF-IMAGE?

We've said repeatedly that people experience dissonance when their self-concepts are threatened. But what about people who have a poor opinion of themselves? What threatens a poor self-image? Think back to our example of smokers who continue to smoke, knowing that smoking jeopardizes their health. Smokers are likely to experience high levels of dissonance: How can you feel good about yourself if you knowingly risk your health? But this conclusion rests on an important premise: It assumes that the smoker in question has a favorable self-image, one that would be inconsistent with foolish behavior. But what if we're dealing with smokers who have negative self-concepts? Such people would already think of themselves as fairly incompetent and thus capable of engaging in a self-destructive habit. In this case, they wouldn't need to reduce dissonance to reestablish a positive sense of self, because a positive sense of self isn't there to begin with. Although such individuals would almost certainly experience some discomfort, smoking wouldn't threaten the stability of their self-concepts in the way that it would for smokers who think highly of themselves.

It turns out that the vast majority of dissonance experiments have been conducted among college student populations, who for the most part have moderate to high levels of self-esteem. For such people, acting foolishly or immorally threatens both their self-esteem and the stability of their self-conceptions. As a result, self-justification works to maintain our sense of self: By reducing dissonance, people with favorable self-images can restore a positive sense of self as well as a consistent and stable one.

As you might expect from this reasoning, research that has taken self-esteem into account reveals that people with negative self-concepts do not usually engage in the kinds of self-justifying behaviors that are typical of people with relatively high self-esteem. Consider this study, for example. Participants were induced to deliver what they believed to be painful electric shocks to an innocent "fellow student," who was actually a confederate of the experimenter. Before doing so, however, they were given bogus feedback on a personality test, designed to temporarily lower or raise their self-esteem. In one condition, the test results enhanced esteem by depicting participants as compassionate, mature, and otherwise virtuous individuals. For others, however, the feedback described them as fairly self-centered, insensitive to others' feelings, and so forth. The researcher found that after "shocking" the confederate, the two groups of people did not react in the same way to this potentially dissonance-arousing situation. Specifically, participants in the high-self-esteem condition reduced dissonance by justifying their immoral behavior. They rated the "fellow student," whom they believed they had injured, as less attractive, less likable, and so forth. In contrast, the people whose self-esteem had been temporarily lowered did not show this tendency to derogate the "victim." Why was this the case? For low-self-esteem participants, acting immorally was apparently consistent with their self-concepts. As a result, they had no need to derogate the "fellow student." Instead, they maintained their unfavorable self-concepts (Glass, 1964).

Confirming Our Self-Concept or Enhancing It?

William Swann and his colleagues have explored this tendency we have to preserve our customary self-beliefs, even when those beliefs are unfavorable (Swann, 1990, 1996; Swann & Pelham, 1988). Swann calls this **self-verification theory**, suggesting that people need to seek confirmation of their self-concept whether the self-concept is positive or negative. In some circumstances, this tendency can conflict with the desire to uphold a favorable view of oneself. For example, consider Patrick, who has always thought of himself as a lousy writer with poor verbal skills. When a friend who writes well reads his term paper and says it is skillfully crafted, beautifully written, and superbly articulate, how will Patrick feel? You might predict that he'd feel pleased and gratified because the friend's praise boosts Patrick's self-esteem. In fact, he might not. Why?

The praise he receives challenges Patrick's long-standing view of himself as a poor writer, and he might be motivated to maintain this negative view. Why? For two reasons. First, like dissonance theory, self-verification theory rests on the basic premise that it is unsettling and confusing to have our views of ourselves disconfirmed. If we changed our self-concept every time we met someone with a different opinion of us, maintaining a coherent, consistent self-concept would be impossible. Second, self-verification theory holds that interacting with people who view us differently from the way we view ourselves can be embarrassing. People who don't know us might have unrealistic expectations, and we might be

> The mind is a strange machine which can combine the materials offered to it in the most astonishing ways.
> —Bertrand Russell

Self-Verification Theory

The idea that people have a need to seek confirmation of their self-concept, be it positive or negative, which in some circumstances can conflict with the desire to uphold a favorable view of oneself

embarrassed when they find out that we are not as smart or as artistic or as athletic as they think we are. Better to let them know our weaknesses at the outset.

In short, when people with negative opinions of themselves receive positive feedback, opposing needs go head to head—the desire to feel good about themselves by believing the positive feedback (self-enhancement needs) versus the desire to maintain a consistent, coherent picture of themselves and avoid the embarrassment of being found out (self-verification needs). Which needs win out?

Throughout this chapter, we have been telling you that human beings have a powerful need to feel good about themselves—in short, that the need for **self-justification** is a major determinant of our attitudes and behaviors. We now have to qualify this statement. Several studies suggest that when the two motives conflict, our need to maintain a stable self-concept frequently overpowers our desire to view ourselves in a positive light. This is especially true when people feel that they might be able to change a negative part of themselves with a little effort. Under these conditions, they prefer accurate feedback, because this information can help them figure out what they need to do to improve (Aronson & Carlsmith, 1962; Steele, Spencer, & Josephs, 1992). However, if they believe that there is nothing they can do to improve their ability in a particular area, they generally prefer positive feedback to accurate feedback (Aronson, 1992a). After all, why remind ourselves that we don't measure up in some way if there is nothing we can do to change it?

SOME FINAL THOUGHTS ON DISSONANCE: LEARNING FROM OUR MISTAKES

Self-Justification

The tendency to justify one's actions in order to maintain one's self-esteem

Rationalization Trap

The potential for dissonance reduction to produce a succession of self-justifications that ultimately result in a chain of stupid or immoral actions

Throughout this chapter, we've seen that dissonance-reducing behavior can be useful because it restores our sense of stability and allows us to maintain our self-esteem. But if we human beings were to spend all of our time and energy defending our egos, we would never learn from our mistakes. Instead, we would try to ignore them or, worse still, attempt to turn them into virtues. If we did not learn from our mistakes, we would get stuck within the confines of our narrow minds and never grow or change.

At times, the process of dissonance-reducing behavior can lead us into the **rationalization trap**, a series of self-justifications that can result in a chain of

Some members of this team, those with high self-esteem, will develop a self-justifying "story" about their loss that helps them believe that they can win the next one. Those with low self-esteem will be less likely to use the face-saving, dissonance-reducing strategies discussed in this chapter and more likely to blame themselves.

stupid or irrational actions, sometimes with tragic consequences. The irony, of course, is that to avoid thinking of ourselves as stupid or immoral, we set the stage for increasing our acts of stupidity or immorality. For example, people who hurt others can derogate their victims to the point where the perpetrators' actions seem not only justified but even heroic in their own eyes. (We will elaborate on this phenomenon in Chapters 12 and 13.) Similarly, we have seen how people who say something they don't really believe will come to believe the statement—and some of those beliefs might be tragically erroneous. The memoirs of some of our most beleaguered former presidents are full of the kinds of self-serving, self-justifying statements that can best be summarized as "If I had it all to do over again, I would not change anything important" (Johnson, 1971; Nixon, 1990; Reagan, 1990).

An interesting and more complex example of this phenomenon can be found in the memoirs of Robert McNamara (1995), who was secretary of defense and one of President Lyndon Johnson's principal military advisers during the Vietnam War. In a painful revelation, McNamara admits he came to the realization that the war was unwinnable in 1967—several years before our eventual withdrawal. But he chose to remain silent on this issue after leaving office while the war raged on, wasting several thousand additional American lives as well as countless Vietnamese lives. Most knowledgeable analysts believe that to have been a tragic and catastrophic error, arguing that if he had spoken out publicly, it could have shortened the war and saved thousands of people. In his book, McNamara makes a spirited but unconvincing attempt to justify his public silence out of some sort of personal and professional loyalty to Lyndon Johnson.

To learn from our mistakes, we need to tolerate dissonance long enough to examine the situation critically and dispassionately. We then stand a chance of breaking out of the cycle of action followed by self-justification followed by more intense action. For example, suppose that Mary has acted unkindly toward a fellow student. To learn from that experience, she must be able to resist the need to derogate her victim. Ideally, it would be effective if she were able to stay with the dissonance long enough to say, "OK, I blew it; I did a cruel thing. But that doesn't necessarily make me a cruel person. Let me think about why I did what I did." This is easier said than done. But a clue as to how such behavior might come about is contained in some of the research on self-affirmation we discussed previously (Steele, 1988).

Suppose that immediately after Mary acted cruelly but before she had an opportunity to derogate her victim, she was reminded of the fact that she had recently donated several pints of blood to the Red Cross to be used by earthquake victims or that she had recently gotten a high score on her physics exam. This self-affirmation would be likely to provide her with the ability to resist engaging in typical dissonance-reducing behavior. In effect, Mary might be able to say, "It's true—I just did a cruel and stupid thing. But I am also capable of some really decent, intelligent, and generous behavior. I can do better." Indeed, self-affirmation can serve as a cognitive buffer, protecting a person from caving in to temptation and committing a cruel or immoral act.

> Both salvation and punishment for man lie in the fact that, if he lives wrongly, he can befog himself so as not to see the misery of his position.
> *—Leo Tolstoy*

HEAVEN'S GATE REVISITED

At the beginning of this chapter, we raised a vital question regarding the followers of Marshall Herff Applewhite of Heaven's Gate. Similar questions were raised in Chapter 1 about the followers of the Reverend Jim Jones and those of David Koresh in Waco, Texas. How could intelligent people allow themselves to be led into what to the overwhelming majority of us is obviously senseless and tragic behavior, resulting in mass suicide? Needless to say, the situation is complex; there were many factors operating, including the charismatic, persuasive power of each of these leaders, the existence of a great deal of social support for the views of the group (from other members of the group), and the relative isolation of each group from dissenting views, producing a closed system—a little like living in a roomful of mirrors.

In addition to these factors, we are convinced that one of the single most powerful forces common to all of these groups was the existence of a high degree of cognitive dissonance within the minds of the participants. After reading this chapter, you now realize that when individuals make an important decision and invest heavily in that decision (in terms of time, effort, sacrifice, and commitment), this results in a strong need to justify those actions and that investment. The more they give up and the harder they work, the greater will be the need to convince themselves that their views are correct; indeed, they may even begin to feel sorry for others who do not share their beliefs. The members of the Heaven's Gate cult sacrificed a great deal for their beliefs: They abandoned their friends and families, turned their backs on their professions, relinquished their money and possessions, moved to another part of the world, and worked hard and long for the particular cause they believed in—all increasing their commitment to the belief. Those of us who have studied the theory of cognitive dissonance were not surprised to learn that the Heaven's Gate people, having bought a telescope that failed to reveal a spaceship that wasn't there, concluded that the telescope was faulty. To have believed otherwise would have created too much dissonance to bear. That they went on to abandon their "containers," believing that they were moving on to a higher incarnation, although tragic and bizarre, is not unfathomable. It is simply an extreme manifestation of a process that we have seen in operation over and over again throughout this chapter.

SUMMARY

Maintaining a Stable, Positive Self-Image

One of the most powerful determinants of human behavior stems from our need to justify our actions. How does this come about? According to **cognitive dissonance theory,** people experience discomfort (dissonance) whenever they are confronted with cognitions about some aspect of their behavior that is inconsistent with their self-concept. We are motivated to reduce this dissonance by either changing our behavior or by finding ways to justify our past behavior, bringing it into line with a generally positive view of ourselves. The resulting change in attitude stems from a process we call **self-persuasion.** Beliefs and attitudes resulting from self-persuasion are deeper and more permanent than if their source is outside the person—such as information conveyed by the media.

Dissonance inevitably occurs after a person makes an important decision. The thought "I chose alternative X" is inconsistent with the thought "I might have been a lot better off with alternative Y." This is called **postdecision dissonance.** People reduce this form of dissonance by increasing their liking for the chosen alternative and decreasing their liking for the other alternatives.

Unscrupulous salespeople have been known to take advantage of this human tendency through the use of a strategy called **lowballing,** which increases the probability that the customer will feel that he or she has already made a commitment to purchase the product when in fact no such commitment exists.

Another major source of dissonance takes place when people exert effort to attain something that turns out not to be worth the effort. This typically results in a **justification of effort** leading people to minimize the negative aspects of the thing they attained. For example, people who go through a lot of effort to join a group will like that group better than people who joined the group without exerting effort.

A third important source of dissonance occurs when people commit foolish, immoral, or absurd acts for little reward or refrain from performing a desirable act for no good reason. Thus when people advocate a position contrary to their own attitude (**counterattitudinal advocacy**) with little or no **external justification,** they find **internal justification** for their behavior by convincing themselves that there is some truth in what they said. Similarly, if people avoid doing something desirable in the face of

insufficient punishment, they will come to believe that the activity wasn't really all that desirable. Similarly, if people find themselves doing someone a favor for insufficient justification, they assume that they did so because the person is likable. The flip side of this kind of dissonance reduction has sinister effects: If people find themselves acting cruelly toward someone for insufficient justification, they typically will derogate the victim, convincing themselves that he or she is a terrible person and therefore must have deserved such treatment.

Variations on the Theme of Self-Justification

In recent years, social psychologists have expanded dissonance theory in new directions. One of the spin-offs from dissonance theory is **self-discrepancy theory,** which suggests that people will behave in a way that reflects a need to maintain a sense of consistency among their various beliefs and perceptions about themselves.

Most dissonance research concerns how our self-image is threatened by our own behavior, such as acting contrary to our attitudes. **Self-evaluation maintenance theory** suggests that dissonance is produced in interpersonal relationships whenever someone close to us outperforms us on a task that is highly relevant to our self-definition. People can reduce this dissonance in a number of ways: by distancing themselves from the person, by improving their performance, by lowering the other person's performance, or by reducing the relevance of the task.

Another spin-off, **self-affirmation theory,** argues that people are flexible at dealing with threats to their self-esteem. When dissonance cannot be reduced by directly eliminating a specific threat to their self-esteem, people can feel better about themselves by affirming their strengths or abilities in some other area.

Why Would Anyone Want to Maintain a Poor Self-Image?

Research on **self-verification theory** suggests that the need to bolster our self-esteem sometimes conflicts with the need to verify our self-views. Because people with negative self-views fear that other people might discover that they are not who they appear to be, they will frequently prefer feedback that confirms their low opinion of themselves to feedback that is self-enhancing.

Some Final Thoughts on Dissonance: Learning from Our Mistakes

The problem with reducing dissonance in ways that make us feel better about ourselves (**self-justification**) is that it can result in a **rationalization trap,** whereby we set the stage for acts of increasing stupidity or immorality. As suggested by self-affirmation theory, we can avoid this trap by reminding ourselves that we are generally good and decent people so that we do not have to justify and rationalize every stupid or immoral act we perform.

Heaven's Gate Revisited

When individuals make an important decision and invest their time, effort, sacrifice, and commitment in that decision, they have a strong need to justify those actions and that investment. The members of the Heaven's Gate cult sacrificed a great deal for their beliefs, abandoning friends and families, leaving their jobs, relinquishing their money and possessions—all increasing their commitment to the belief. So even when the spaceship didn't appear, they needed to believe that abandoning their "containers" would take them to a higher incarnation. At that point, to have believed otherwise would have created too much dissonance to bear.

CRITICAL THINKING QUESTIONS

1. Why is self-persuasion more powerful and more permanent than persuasion induced by another person, such as Michael Jordan, the president of the United States, your best friend, or even your psychology professor?

2. Suppose that you are the principal of a junior high school where bullying is a serious problem. How would you use "hypocrisy induction" to reduce bullying?

3. What do the dissonance theorists mean by "insufficient justification"? In what way is the justification insufficient? Why is that an important concept?

"Reach for a Lucky - instead of a sweet"

LUCKY STRIKE
"IT'S TOASTED"
CIGARETTES

TWENTY

"A flavor that completely satisfies"

Billie Burke

Billie Burke
Popular American Actress

"It's toasted"

No Throat Irritation-No Cough.

© 1929, The American Tobacco Co., Manufacturers

Attitudes and Attitude Change:

Influencing Thoughts and Feelings

It is hard to go anywhere these days without encountering an advertisement. Ads have always been on television and radio, of course, and in newspapers and magazines. Now they appear on the Internet, on the floors of grocery stores, on the inside door of stalls in public restrooms, and on video screens at cash machines and gasoline pumps (Cropper, 1998). There are even companies that pay people to wrap their cars in advertisements. A college administrator agreed to cover her car with ads for an Internet service company and earned enough to pay off her car loan. "My car was cute as the dickens before," she said, "and the advertising just makes it cuter" (Wollenberg, 2000).

It is easy to shrug off advertisements as minor annoyances that have become part of the fabric of modern life. Not all advertising is so benign, however. Consider the history of cigarette ads. In the nineteenth century, most consumer goods, including tobacco products, were made and sold locally. But with the Industrial Revolution came the mass production of many consumer products, and manufacturers sought broader markets. Advertising was the natural result. In the 1880s, for example, cigarettes were being mass-produced for the first time, and moguls such as James Buchanan Duke began to market their brands aggressively. Duke placed ads for his brands in newspapers, rented space on thousands of billboards, hired famous actresses to endorse his brands, and gave gifts to retailers who stocked his products. Other cigarette manufacturers soon followed suit (Kluger, 1996).

Although these efforts were phenomenally successful—sales of cigarettes skyrocketed in the United States—there was still a vast untapped market, namely women. Until the early twentieth century, men bought 99 percent of cigarettes sold. It was socially unacceptable for women to smoke; those who did were considered to have questionable morals. This began to change with the burgeoning women's rights movement and the fight to achieve the right to vote; ironically, smoking cigarettes became a symbol of women's emancipation (Kruger, 1996). Cigarette manufacturers were happy to cultivate and encourage this view. They began to target women in their advertisements. It remained unacceptable for women to smoke in public for many years, so early cigarette ads never showed a woman actually smoking. Instead, they tried to associate smoking with sophistication and glamour or convey that cigarettes helped control weight ("Reach for a Lucky instead of a sweet"). By the 1960s, cigarette advertisements were making a direct link between women's liberation and smoking, and a new brand was started (Virginia Slims) specifically for this purpose ("You've come a long way, baby"). The percentage of cigarettes purchased by women steadily increased. In 1955, there were twice as many male as female smokers in the United States; by 2000, the gap had narrowed considerably (26 percent of adult men smoked in 2000, compared to 21 percent of adult women).

As the dangers of smoking became more widely known, however, sales of cigarettes began to drop in the United States. Undeterred, tobacco companies aggressively marketed cigarettes in other countries to increase sales. For example, they spend billions of dollars on advertising and the sponsorship of concerts and sporting events around the globe. The World Health Organization estimates that fifty thousand teenagers a day begin smoking in Asia alone and that smoking may eventually kill *one-quarter* of the young people currently living in Asia (Teves, 2002).

Is advertising responsible? To what extent can advertising shape people's attitudes and behavior? Exactly what is an attitude, anyway, and how is it changed? These questions, which are some of the oldest in social psychology, are the subject of this chapter.

THE NATURE AND ORIGIN OF ATTITUDES

It would be odd to hear someone say, "My feelings toward anchovies, snakes, chocolate cake, and my roommate are completely neutral." People are not neutral observers of the world; they have attitudes toward most of what they encounter. Simply put, **attitudes** are evaluations of people, objects, or ideas (Eagly & Chaiken, 1998; Fazio, 2000; Olson & Zanna, 1993; Petty & Wegener, 1998). Attitudes are made up of three parts that together form our evaluation of the "attitude object"—another person, a social issue, or an object such as a food item or consumer product (Crites, Fabrigar, & Petty, 1994; McGuire, 1985; Zanna & Rempel, 1988):

1. An *affective* component, consisting of your emotional reactions toward the attitude object
2. A *cognitive* component, consisting of your thoughts and beliefs about the attitude object
3. A *behavioral* component, consisting of your actions or observable behavior toward the attitude object

Attitudes

Evaluations of people, objects, and ideas

For example, consider your attitude toward a particular model of car, such as a sports utility vehicle (SUV). What is your affective reaction when you see the car? Perhaps you have feelings of excitement and power. If you are a U.S. autoworker examining a new foreign-made model, maybe you feel anger and resentment. Second, what is your cognitive reaction? What beliefs do you hold about the car's attributes? Perhaps you think that SUVs get poor gas mileage and are at greater risk of rollover than some other cars. Third, what is your behavioral reaction? Do you go to a dealership and test-drive the car and actually buy one? Each of these components combine to form your overall attitude toward the SUV.

Where Do Attitudes Come From?

One provocative answer to the question of where attitudes come from is that some attitudes, at least, are linked to our genes (Tesser, 1993). Evidence for this conclusion comes from the fact that identical twins share more attitudes than fraternal twins, even when the identical twins were raised in different homes and never knew each other. One study, for example, found that identical twins had more similar attitudes toward such things as the death penalty and jazz than fraternal twins did (Martin et al., 1986). Now, we should be careful how to interpret this evidence. No one is arguing that there are specific genes that determine our attitudes; it is highly unlikely, for example, that there is a "jazz-loving" gene that determines your music preferences. It appears, though, that some attitudes are an indirect function of our genetic makeup. They are related to things like our temperament and personality, which are directly related to our genes. People may have inherited a temperament and personality from their parents that made them predisposed to like jazz more than rock-and-roll.

Even if there is a genetic component, our social experiences clearly play a large role in shaping our attitudes. Social psychologists have focused primarily on the way in which attitudes are created by people's cognitive, affective, and behavioral experiences. One important finding is that not all attitudes are created equally. Though all attitudes have affective, cognitive, and behavioral components, any given attitude can be based more on one type of experience than another (Zanna & Rempel, 1988).

Cognitively Based Attitudes   Sometimes our attitudes are based primarily on the relevant facts, such as the objective merits of an automobile. How many miles to the gallon does it get? Does it have side-impact air bags? To the extent that people's evaluation is based primarily on people's beliefs about the properties of an attitude object, we say it is a **cognitively based attitude**. The purpose of this kind of attitude is to classify the pluses and minuses of an object so that we can quickly tell whether we want to have anything to do with it. Consider your attitude toward a utilitarian object like a vacuum cleaner. Your attitude is likely to be based on your beliefs about the objective merits of particular brands, such as how well they vacuum up dirt and how much they cost—not on how sexy they make you feel.

Affectively Based Attitudes   An attitude based more on emotions and values than on an objective appraisal of pluses and minuses is called an **affectively based attitude** (Breckler & Wiggins, 1989; Zanna & Rempel, 1988). Sometimes we simply like a car, regardless of how many miles to the gallon it gets. Occasionally we even feel great about something—such as another person—in spite of having negative beliefs (see the quote on the next page from Smokey Robinson's song, "You've Really Got a Hold on Me").

As a guide to which attitudes are likely to be affectively based, consider the topics that etiquette manuals suggest should not be discussed at a dinner party:

We never desire passionately what we desire through reason alone.

—François de La Rochefoucauld, Maxims, 1665

Cognitively Based Attitude
An attitude based primarily on people's beliefs about the properties of an attitude object

Affectively Based Attitude
An attitude based more on people's feelings and values than on their beliefs about the nature of an attitude object

I don't like you, but I love you. Seems that I'm always thinking of you. You treat me badly, I love you madly. You've really got a hold on me.

—Smokey Robinson, "You've Really Got a Hold on Me," 1962

That is the way we are made; we don't reason; where we feel, we just feel.

—Mark Twain, A Connecticut Yankee in King Arthur's Court, 1885

politics, sex, and religion. People seem to vote more with their hearts than their minds, for example, caring more about how they feel about a candidate than their beliefs about his or her specific policies (Abelson, Kinder, Peters, & Fiske, 1982; Granberg & Brown, 1989). In fact, it has been estimated that one-third of the electorate knows virtually nothing about specific politicians but nonetheless has strong feelings about them (Redlawsk, 2002; Wattenberg, 1987).

If affectively based attitudes do not come from examining the facts, where do they come from? They have a variety of sources. First, they can stem from people's values, such as their basic religious and moral beliefs. People's feelings about such issues as abortion, the death penalty, and premarital sex are often based more on their values than on a cold examination of the facts. The function of such attitudes is not so much to paint an accurate picture of the world as to express and validate one's basic value system (Maio & Olson, 1995; Schwartz, 1992; Smith, Bruner, & White, 1956; Snyder & DeBono, 1989). Other affectively based attitudes can result from a sensory reaction, such as liking the taste of chocolate (despite its number of calories), or an aesthetic reaction, such as admiring a painting or the lines and color of a car. Still others can be the result of conditioning (Walther, 2002).

Classical conditioning works this way: A stimulus that elicits an emotional response is accompanied by a neutral stimulus that does not until eventually the neutral stimulus elicits the emotional response by itself (Olson & Fazio, 2001). For example, suppose that when you were a child, you experienced feelings of warmth and love when you visited your grandmother. Suppose also that her house always smelled faintly of mothballs. Eventually, the smell of mothballs alone will trigger the emotions you experienced during your visits, through the process of classical conditioning (Cacioppo, Marshall-Goodell, Tassinary, & Petty, 1992; De Houwer, Baeyens, & Eelen, 1994).

In **operant conditioning,** behaviors that we freely choose to perform become more or less frequent, depending on whether they are followed by a reward (positive reinforcement) or punishment. How does this apply to attitudes? Imagine that a 4-year-old white girl goes to the playground with her father and begins to play with an African American girl. Her father expresses strong disapproval, telling her, "We don't play with that kind of child." It won't take long before the child associates interacting with African Americans with disapproval, thereby adopting her father's racist attitudes. Attitudes can take on a positive or negative affect through either classical or operant conditioning, as shown in Figure 7.1 (Cacioppo et al., 1992; Kuykendall & Keating, 1990).

Although affectively based attitudes come from many sources, we can group them into one family because they (1) do not result from a rational examination of the issues, (2) are not governed by logic (e.g., persuasive arguments about the issues seldom change an affectively based attitude), and (3) are often linked to people's values, so that trying to change them challenges those values (Katz, 1960; Smith et al., 1956). How can we tell if an attitude is more affectively or cognitively based? See the Try It! exercise on page 204 for one way to measure the bases of people's attitudes.

Behaviorally Based Attitudes   A **behaviorally based attitude** stems from people's observations of how they behave toward an object. This may seem a little odd—how do we know how to behave if we don't already know how we feel? According to Daryl Bem's (1972) *self-perception theory*, under certain circumstances, people don't know how they feel until they see how they behave. For example, suppose you asked a friend how much she likes to exercise. If she replies, "Well, I guess I like it, because I always seem to be going for a run or heading over to the gym to work out," we would say she has a behaviorally based attitude. Her at-

Classical Conditioning

The phenomenon whereby a stimulus that elicits an emotional response is repeatedly paired with a neutral stimulus that does not until the neutral stimulus takes on the emotional properties of the first stimulus

Operant Conditioning

The phenomenon whereby behaviors that people freely choose to perform increase or decrease in frequency, depending on whether they are followed by positive reinforcement or punishment

Behaviorally Based Attitude

An attitude based on observations of how one behaves toward an attitude object

Some attitudes are based more on emotions and values than on facts and figures. Attitudes towards abortion may be such a case.

titude is based more on an observation of her behavior than on her cognitions or affect.

As noted in Chapter 5, people infer their attitudes from their behavior only under certain conditions. First, their initial attitude has to be weak or ambiguous. If your friend already has a strong attitude toward exercising, she does not have to observe her behavior to infer how she feels about it. Second, people infer their attitudes from their behavior only when there are no other plausible explanations for their behavior. If your friend believes she exercises to lose weight or because her doctor has or-

> How can I know what I think till I see what I say?
> —Graham Wallas, The Art of Thought, 1926

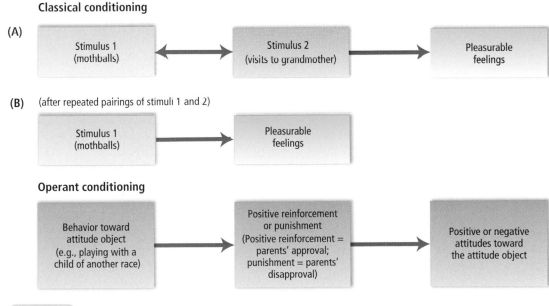

Classical conditioning

(A)

| Stimulus 1 (mothballs) | ⬌ | Stimulus 2 (visits to grandmother) | ➡ | Pleasurable feelings |

(B) (after repeated pairings of stimuli 1 and 2)

| Stimulus 1 (mothballs) | ➡ | Pleasurable feelings |

Operant conditioning

| Behavior toward attitude object (e.g., playing with a child of another race) | ➡ | Positive reinforcement or punishment (Positive reinforcement = parents' approval; punishment = parents' disapproval) | ➡ | Positive or negative attitudes toward the attitude object |

FIGURE 7.1

Classical and operant conditioning of attitudes.

Affectively based attitudes can result from either classical or instrumental conditioning.

Affective and Cognitive Bases of Attitudes

Fill out this questionnaire to see how psychologists measure the affective and cognitive components of attitudes.

1. Circle the number on each scale that best describes your feelings toward snakes:

hateful	−3	−2	−1	0	1	2	3	love
sad	−3	−2	−1	0	1	2	3	delighted
annoyed	−3	−2	−1	0	1	2	3	happy
tense	−3	−2	−1	0	1	2	3	calm
bored	−3	−2	−1	0	1	2	3	excited
angry	−3	−2	−1	0	1	2	3	relaxed
disgusted	−3	−2	−1	0	1	2	3	acceptance
sorrowful	−3	−2	−1	0	1	2	3	joy

2. Circle the number on each scale that best describes the traits or characteristics of snakes:

useless	−3	−2	−1	0	1	2	3	useful
foolish	−3	−2	−1	0	1	2	3	wise
unsafe	−3	−2	−1	0	1	2	3	safe
harmful	−3	−2	−1	0	1	2	3	beneficial
worthless	−3	−2	−1	0	1	2	3	valuable
imperfect	−3	−2	−1	0	1	2	3	perfect
unhealthy	−3	−2	−1	0	1	2	3	wholesome

Add up your responses to question 1 and, separately, your responses to question 2.

Question 1 measures the affective component of your attitude toward snakes, whereas question 2 measures the cognitive component of attitudes. Most people's attitudes toward snakes are more affectively than cognitively based. If this was true of you, your total score for question 1 should depart more from zero (in a negative direction, for most people) than your total score for question 2.

Now go back and fill out the scales again, substituting "vacuum cleaners" for "snakes." Most people's attitudes toward a utilitarian object such as a vacuum cleaner are more cognitively than affectively based. If this were true of you, your total score for question 2 should depart more from zero than your total score for question 1.

dered her to, she is unlikely to assume that she runs and works out because she enjoys it. (See Chapter 5 for a more detailed description of self-perception theory.)

Explicit versus Implicit Attitudes

Once an attitude develops, it can exist at two levels. **Explicit attitudes** are ones we consciously endorse and can easily report; they are what we think of as our evaluations when someone asks us a question like "What is you opinion about affirmative action?" People can also have **implicit attitudes,** which are involuntary, uncontrollable, and at times unconscious evaluations (Fazio & Olson, 2003; Greenwald & Banaji, 1995; Wilson, Lindsey, & Schooler, 2000).

Consider Sam, a white, middle-class college student who genuinely believes that all races are equal and abhors any kind of racial bias. This is Sam's explicit attitude, in the sense that it is his conscious evaluation of members of other races that governs how he chooses to act; for instance, consistent with his explicit atti-

Explicit Attitudes

Attitudes that we consciously endorse and can easily report

Implicit Attitudes

Attitudes that are involuntary, uncontrollable, and at times unconscious

tude, Sam recently signed a petition in favor of affirmative action policies at his university. Sam has grown
up in a culture in which there are many negative
stereotypes about minority groups, however, and it is
possible that some of these negative ideas have seeped
into him in ways of which he is not fully aware
(Devine, 1989a). When he is around African
Americans, for example, perhaps some negative feelings are triggered automatically and unintentionally.
If so, he has a negative implicit attitude toward
African Americans, which is likely to influence behaviors he is not monitoring or controlling, such as how
nervous he acts around African Americans (Dovidio,
Kawakami, & Gaertner, 2002).

We will discuss such automatic prejudice in
Chapter 13 (see also our discussion of automatic
thinking in Chapter 3). For now, we point out that
people can have explicit and implicit attitudes toward
virtually anything, not just other races. For example,
students can believe explicitly that they hate math but have a more positive attitude at an implicit level (Nosek, Banaji, & Greenwald, 2002).

How do we know? A variety of techniques have been developed to measure
people's implicit attitudes, some of which we discussed in Chapter 3. One of the
most popular is the Implicit Association Test or IAT (Greenwald, McGhee, &
Schwartz, 1998; Greenwald & Nosek, 2001), in which people categorize words
or pictures on a computer. Rather than going into detail about how this test
works, we encourage you to visit a Web site where you can take the test yourself
and read more about how it is constructed (http://implicit.harvard.edu/
implicit).

Research on implicit attitudes is in its infancy, and psychologists are actively
investigating their origins, how to measure them, and their relation to explicit attitudes. The focus in the remainder of this chapter will be on how explicit attitudes change and their relation to behavior. We will return to a discussion of
implicit attitudes in Chapter 13 as they apply to stereotyping and prejudice.

People can have explicit and
implicit attitudes toward the same
topic. Explicit attitudes are those
we consciously endorse and can
easily report, implicit attitudes
are involuntary, uncontrollable,
and at least at times, unconscious.
Social psychologists have been
especially interested in people's
explicit and implicit attitudes
toward members of other races.

HOW DO ATTITUDES CHANGE?

Attitudes do sometimes change. In America, for example, the popularity of the
president often seems to rise and fall with surprising speed. In the weeks before
the tragic events of September 11, 2001, for example, only about 50 percent of
Americans said that they approved of the job that George W. Bush was doing as
president. In the days right after 9/11, his approval rating jumped to 82 percent.
By March of 2003, right before the U.S. invasion of Iraq, the figure had dropped
back down to 53 percent; a month later, it had risen to 71 percent
(PollingReport.com, 2003).

When attitudes change, they often do so in response to social influence. Our
attitudes toward everything from a presidential candidate to a brand of laundry
detergent can be influenced by what other people do or say. This is why attitudes
are of such interest to social psychologists—even something as personal and internal as an attitude is a highly social phenomenon, influenced by the imagined
or actual behavior of other people. The entire premise of advertising, for example, is that your attitudes toward consumer products (e.g., cigarettes) can be influenced by seeing the kinds of ad shown at the beginning of this chapter. Let's
take a look at the conditions under which attitudes are most likely to change.

Sometimes attitudes change dramatically over short periods of time. In America, for example, the popularity of the president often seems to rise and dip with surprising speed. In the weeks before the tragic events of September 11, 2001, for example, only about 50% of Americans said that they approved of the job that George W. Bush was doing as president. In the days right after 9-11, his approval ratings soared to 82%. In this photo, taken in May, 2003 President Bush, wearing a flight suit, speaks to sailors and pilots on the USS Abraham Lincoln after landing in a small jet to declare that major combat in Iraq was over. By September of 2003, after months of continuing American casualties in Iraq, his ratings had dropped back down to 52%.

Changing Attitudes by Changing Behavior: Cognitive Dissonance Theory Revisited

We have already discussed one way that attitudes change—when people behave inconsistently with their attitudes and cannot find external justification for their behavior. We refer, of course, to cognitive dissonance theory. As we noted in Chapter 6, people experience dissonance when they do something that threatens their image of themselves as decent, kind, and honest, particularly if there is no way they can explain away this behavior as due to external circumstances.

> By persuading others, we convince ourselves.
>
> —Junius

Suppose that you are meeting your future in-laws for the first time and the conversation turns to politics. You are the vice-president of the Young Republicans, and you've recently interviewed for a job with Microsoft. Your fiancé's parents turn out to be survivors of some sort of 1960s hippie commune and start talking about the horrors of the "fascist right wing" and "oppression caused by the corporate state." "So," your future father-in-law says, "don't you agree that both political parties are in the pockets of corporate America?"

You pause, your mind racing. You could be honest; your future in-laws are bound to find out sooner or later that their child is going to marry a (gasp) Republican. But why bring it up at your first meeting and risk an ugly scene? You want to make a good first impression, and what if they tried to cancel the wedding? Besides, your fiancé is shooting mental darts at you from across the table. "Well," you say, "I know what you mean. Companies like Microsoft do have too much power." You probably wouldn't experience much dissonance under these circumstances. There are a great many thoughts that are consonant with having told this fib. For example, your belief that it is important not to ruffle people's feathers unnecessarily or to risk an argument with your fiancé provides *external justification* for having bent the truth a little.

But what happens if you say something you don't really believe without much external justification? What if your future in-laws were not so extreme in their views and your fiancé couldn't care less if you contradicted them? Or if earlier in the evening you mentioned your job interview with Microsoft to your fiancé's uncle, who didn't have any problems with it, even though he was wearing beads? If you still refrain from giving your true opinion and agree with your in-laws about the dangers of the corporate state, you will experience dissonance.

When you can't find external justification for your behavior, you will attempt to find *internal justification*—by bringing the two cognitions (your attitude and your behavior) closer together. How do you do this? You begin to believe what you said, at least to some extent. "Microsoft does have an awful lot of power," you think. "Maybe I should look for a job with a nonprofit group instead." When people do not have a strong external justification for their behavior, "saying is believing." This phenomenon is generally referred to as *counterattitudinal advocacy*, a process by which people are induced to state publicly an opinion or attitude that runs counter to their own private attitudes. When this is accomplished with a minimum of external justification, it results in a change in people's private attitude in the direction of the public statement.

As we saw in Chapter 6, counterattitudinal advocacy is a powerful way to change someone's attitudes. If you wanted to change a friend's attitude toward smoking, you might succeed by getting him or her to give an antismoking speech, under conditions of low external justification. But what if your goal was to change attitudes on a mass scale? Suppose you were hired by the American Cancer Society to come up with an antismoking campaign that could be used nationwide, to counteract the kind of tobacco advertisement we saw at the beginning of this chapter. Though dissonance techniques are powerful, they are very difficult to carry out on a mass scale (e.g., it would be hard to have all American smokers make antismoking speeches under just the right conditions of low external justification). In order to change as many people's attitudes as possible, you would have to resort to other techniques of attitude change. You would probably construct some sort of **persuasive communication,** which is a communication such as a speech or television advertisement that advocates a particular side of an issue. How should you construct your message so that it would really change people's attitudes?

Persuasive Communications and Attitude Change

Suppose the American Cancer Society has given you a six-figure budget to develop your advertising campaign. You have a lot of decisions ahead of you. Should you pack your public service announcement with facts and figures? Or should you take a more emotional approach, including frightening visual images of diseased lungs in your message? Should you hire a movie star to deliver your message or a Nobel Prize–winning medical researcher? Should you take a friendly tone and acknowledge that it is hard to quit smoking, or should you take a hard line and tell smokers to (as the Nike ads put it) "just do it"? You can see the point—constructing a truly persuasive communication is complicated.

Luckily, social psychologists have conducted many studies over the years on what makes a persuasive communication effective, beginning with Carl Hovland and his colleagues (Hovland, Janis, & Kelley, 1953). Drawing on their experiences during World War II, when they worked for the United States armed forces to increase the morale of U.S. soldiers (Stouffer, Suchman, De Vinney, Star, & Williams, 1949), Hovland and his colleagues conducted many experiments on the conditions under which people are most likely to be influenced by persuasive communications. In essence, they studied "who says what to whom," looking at the source of the communication (e.g., how expert or attractive the speaker is), the communication itself (e.g., the quality of the arguments; whether the speaker presents both sides of the issue), and the nature of the audience (e.g., which kinds of appeals work with hostile or friendly audiences). Because these researchers were at Yale University, this approach to the study of persuasive communications is known as the **Yale Attitude Change approach.**

Persuasive Communication

Communication (e.g., a speech or television ad) advocating a particular side of an issue

Yale Attitude Change Approach

The study of the conditions under which people are most likely to change their attitudes in response to persuasive messages, focusing on "who said what to whom"—the source of the communication, the nature of the communication, and the nature of the audience

> Of the modes of persuasion furnished by the spoken word there are three kinds. The first kind depends on the personal character of the speaker; the second on putting the audience into a certain frame of mind; the third on the proof, or apparent proof, provided by the words of the speech itself.
>
> —*Aristotle,*
> *Rhetoric*

This approach yielded a great deal of useful information on how people change their attitudes in response to persuasive communications; some of this information is summarized in Figure 7.2. As the research mounted, however, a problem became apparent: Many aspects of persuasive communications turned out to be important, but it was not clear which were more important than others—that is, it was unclear when one factor should be emphasized over another.

For example, let's return to that job you have with the American Cancer Society. The marketing manager wants to see your ad next month! If you were to read the many Yale Attitude Change studies, you might find lots of useful information about who should say what to whom in order to construct a persuasive communication. However, you might also find yourself saying, "There's a lot of information here, and I'm not sure where I should place the most emphasis. Should I focus on who delivers the ads? Or should I worry more about the content of the message?"

The Central and Peripheral Routes to Persuasion Some well-known attitude researchers have asked the same questions: When is it best to stress factors central to the communication—such as the strength of the argu-

FIGURE 7.2
The Yale Attitude Change approach.

The Yale Attitude Change Approach

The effectiveness of persuasive communications depends on who says what to whom.

Who: The Source of the Communication

- Credible speakers (e.g., those with obvious expertise) persuade people more than speakers lacking in credibility (Hovland & Weiss, 1951; Jain & Posavac, 2000).
- Attractive speakers (whether due to physical or personality attributes) persuade people more than unattractive speakers do (Eagly & Chaiken, 1975; Petty, Wegener, & Fabrigar, 1997).

What: The Nature of the Communication

- People are more persuaded by messages that do not seem to be designed to influence them (Petty & Cacioppo, 1986; Walster & Festinger, 1962).
- Is it best to present a one-sided communication (one that presents only arguments favoring your position) or a two-sided communication (one that presents arguments for and against your position)? In general, two-sided messages work better, if you are sure to refute the arguments on the other side (Allen, 1991; Crowley & Hoyer, 1994; Lumsdaine & Janis, 1953).
- Is it best to give your speech before or after someone arguing for the other side?

If the speeches are to be given back to back and there will be a delay before people have to make up their minds, it is best to go first. Under these conditions, there is likely to be a *primacy effect,* wherein people are more influenced by what they hear first. If there is a delay between the speeches and people will make up their minds right after hearing the second one, it is best to go last. Under these conditions, there is likely to be a *recency effect,* wherein people remember the second speech better than the first one (Haugtvedt & Wegener, 1994; Miller & Campbell, 1959).

To Whom: The Nature of the Audience

- An audience that is distracted during the persuasive communication will often be persuaded more than one that is not (Festinger & Maccoby, 1964; Albarracin & Wyer, 2001).
- People low in intelligence tend to be more influenceable than people high in intelligence, and people with moderate self-esteem tend to be more influenceable than people with low or high self-esteem (Rhodes & Wood, 1992).
- People are particularly susceptible to attitude change during the impressionable ages of 18 to 25. Beyond those ages, people's attitudes are more stable and resistant to change (Krosnick & Alwin, 1989; Sears, 1981).

ments—and when is it best to stress factors peripheral to the logic of the arguments, such as the credibility or attractiveness of the person delivering the speech? This question has been answered by two influential theories of persuasive communication: the *heuristic-systematic model* of persuasion (Chaiken, 1987; Chaiken, Wood, & Eagly, 1996) and the *elaboration likelihood model* (Petty & Cacioppo, 1986; Petty, Priester, & Brinol, 2002).

These theories specify when people will be influenced by what the speech says (i.e., the logic of the arguments) and when they will be influenced by more superficial characteristics (e.g., who gives the speech or how long it is). The theories have much in common; to avoid confusion, we will discuss here the ideas and the terminology of the **elaboration likelihood model** and will return later to some of the specifics of the heuristic-systematic model.

Both theories state that under certain conditions, people are motivated to pay attention to the facts in a communication, and so they will be most persuaded when these facts are logically compelling. That is, sometimes people elaborate on what they hear, carefully thinking about and processing the content of the communication. Petty and Cacioppo (1986) call this the **central route to persuasion.** Under other conditions, people are not motivated to pay attention to the facts; instead, they notice only the surface characteristics of the message, such as how long it is and who is delivering it. Here people will not be swayed by the logic of the arguments because they are not paying close attention to what the communicator says. Instead, they are persuaded if the surface characteristics of the message—such as the fact that it is long or is delivered by an expert or attractive communicator—make it seem like a reasonable one. Petty and Cacioppo call this the **peripheral route to persuasion** because people are swayed by things peripheral to the message itself.

What are the conditions under which people take the central versus the peripheral route to persuasion? The key is whether people have the motivation and the ability to pay attention to the facts. To the extent that people are truly interested in the topic and thus motivated to pay close attention to the arguments, they are more likely to take the central route. Similarly, if people have the ability to pay attention—for example, if nothing is distracting them—they are more likely to take the central route (see Figure 7.3 on page 210).

Elaboration Likelihood Model

An explanation of the two ways in which persuasive communications can cause attitude change: *centrally*, when people are motivated and have the ability to pay attention to the arguments in the communication, and *peripherally*, when people do not pay attention to the arguments but are instead swayed by surface characteristics (e.g., who gave the speech)

Central Route to Persuasion

The case whereby people elaborate on a persuasive communication, listening carefully to and thinking about the arguments, as occurs when people have both the ability and the motivation to listen carefully to a communication

Peripheral Route to Persuasion

The case whereby people do not elaborate on the arguments in a persuasive communication but are instead swayed by peripheral cues

Sometimes attitude change occurs via a peripheral route, whereby people are persuaded by things other than arguments about the facts. For example, sometimes we are swayed more by who delivers a persuasive communication than by the strength of the message. An endorsement by Oprah Winfrey, for example, can turn a book into an instant best seller.

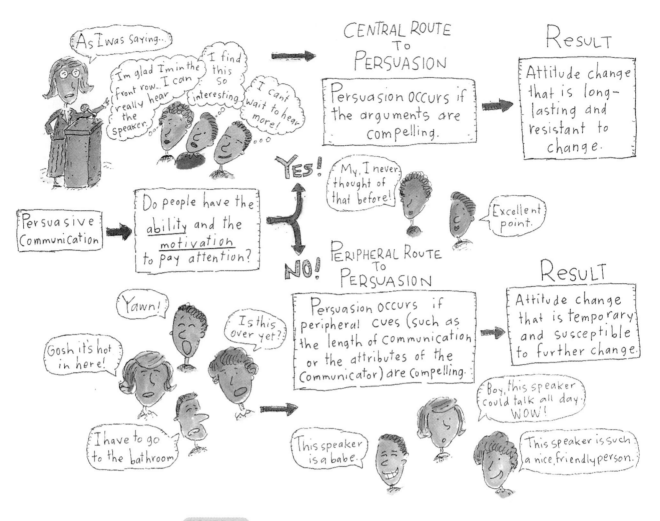

FIGURE 7.3

The elaboration likelihood model.

The elaboration likelihood model describes how people change their attitudes when they hear persuasive communications.

The Motivation to Pay Attention to the Arguments   One thing that determines whether people are motivated to pay attention to a communication is the personal relevance of the topic: How important is the topic to a person's well-being? For example, consider the issue of whether Social Security benefits should be reduced. How personally relevant is this to you? If you are a 72-year-old whose sole income is from Social Security, the issue is extremely relevant; if you are a 20-year-old from a well-to-do family, the issue has little personal relevance.

The more personally relevant an issue is, the more willing people are to pay attention to the arguments in a speech, and therefore the more likely people are to take the central route to persuasion. In one study, for example, college students were asked to listen to a speech arguing that all college seniors should be required to pass a comprehensive exam in their major before they graduate (Petty, Cacioppo, & Goldman, 1981). Half of the participants were told that their university was seriously considering requiring comprehensive exams. For these participants, the issue was personally relevant. For the other half, the issue was of the "ho-hum" variety—the students were told that their university might require such exams but would not implement them for ten years.

The researchers then introduced two variables that might influence whether people would agree with the speech. The first was the strength of the arguments presented. Half of the participants heard arguments that were strong and persuasive (e.g., "The quality of undergraduate teaching has improved at schools with the exams"), whereas the others heard arguments that were weak and unpersuasive (e.g., "The risk of failing the exam is a challenge most students would welcome"). The second was a peripheral cue—the prestige of the speaker. Half of the participants were told that the author of the speech was an eminent professor at Princeton University, whereas the others were told that the author was a high school student.

When deciding how much to agree with the speaker's position, the participants could use one or both of these different kinds of information. They could listen carefully to the arguments and think about how convincing they were, or they could simply go by who said them (i.e., how prestigious the source was). As predicted by the elaboration likelihood model, the way in which people were persuaded depended on the personal relevance of the issue. The left-hand panel of Figure 7.4 shows what happened when the issue was highly relevant to the listeners. These students were greatly influenced by the quality of the arguments (i.e., persuasion occurred via the central route). Those who heard strong arguments agreed much more with the speech than those who heard weak arguments. It didn't matter who presented the arguments, the Princeton professor or the high school student. A good argument was a good argument, even if it was written by someone who lacked prestige.

What happens when a topic is of low relevance? As seen in the right-hand panel of Figure 7.4, what mattered was not the strength of the arguments but who the speaker was. Those who heard the strong arguments agreed with the

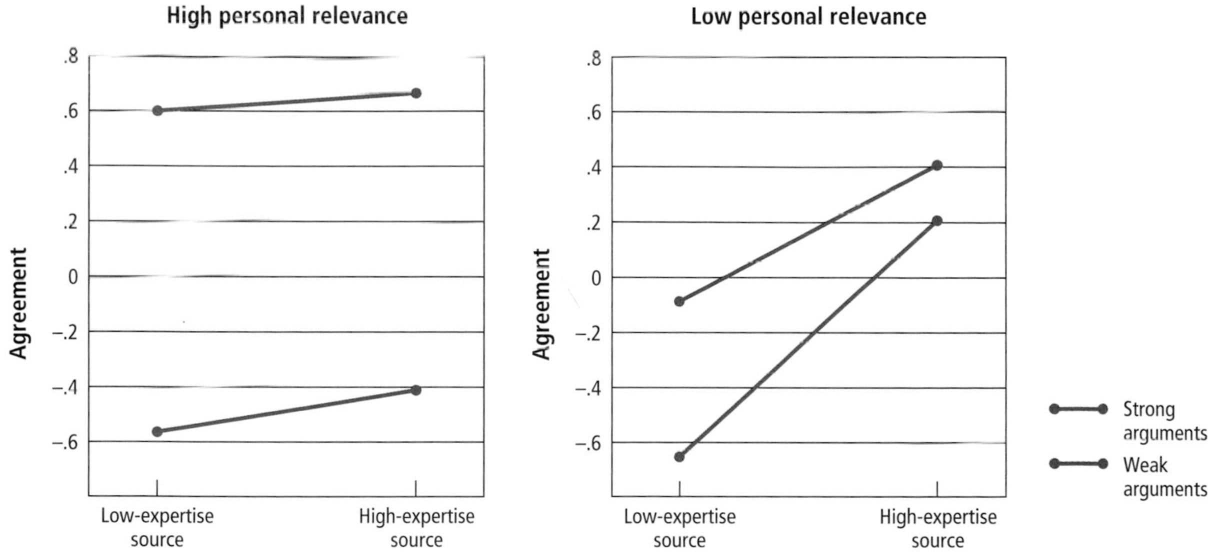

> The ability to kill or capture a man is a relatively simple task compared with changing his mind.
>
> —Richard Cohen, 1991

FIGURE 7.4

Effects of personal relevance on type of attitude change.

The higher the number, the more people agreed with the persuasive communication—namely, that their university should adopt comprehensive exams. *Left panel:* When the issue was highly relevant, people were swayed by the quality of the arguments more than the expertise of the speaker. This is the central route to persuasion. *Right panel:* When the issue was low in relevance, people were swayed by the expertise of the speaker more than the quality of the arguments. This is the peripheral route to persuasion.

(Adapted from Petty & Cacioppo, 1986, based on Petty, Cacioppo, & Goldman, 1981)

> I'm not convinced by proofs but signs.
>
> —Coventry Patmore

speech only slightly more than those who heard the weak arguments, whereas those who heard the Princeton professor were much more swayed than those who heard the high school student.

This finding illustrates a general rule: When an issue is personally relevant, people pay attention to the arguments in a speech and will be persuaded to the extent that the arguments are sound—the "proof" of the speech, in Aristotle's words. When an issue is not personally relevant, people pay less attention to the arguments. Instead, they will take a mental shortcut, following such peripheral rules as "Prestigious speakers can be trusted" (Chen & Chaiken, 1999; Fabrigar, Priester, Petty, & Wegener, 1998).

In addition to the personal relevance of a topic, people's motivation to pay attention to a speech depends on their personality. Some people enjoy thinking things through more than others do; they are said to be high in the **need for cognition** (Cacioppo, Petty, Feinstein, & Jarvis, 1996). This is a personality variable that reflects the extent to which people engage in and enjoy effortful cognitive activities. People high in the need for cognition are more likely to form their attitudes by paying close attention to relevant arguments (i.e., via the central route), whereas people low in the need for cognition are more likely to rely on peripheral cues, such as how attractive or credible a speaker is. The Try It! exercise on page 213 can show you how high you are in the need for cognition.

The Ability to Pay Attention to the Arguments   Sometimes it is difficult to pay attention to a speech, even if we want to. Maybe we're tired; maybe we're distracted by construction noise outside the window; maybe the issue is too complex and hard to evaluate. When people are unable to pay close attention to the arguments, they are swayed more by peripheral cues (Petty & Brock, 1981; Petty, Wells, & Brock, 1976). For example, a few years ago, an exchange of letters appeared in the Ann Landers advice column about whether drugs such as cocaine and marijuana should be legalized. Readers wrote in with all sorts of compelling arguments on both sides of the issue, and it was difficult to figure out which arguments had the most merit. One reader resolved this dilemma by relying less on the content of the arguments than on the prestige and expertise of the source of the arguments. The reader noted that several eminent people have supported the legalization of drugs, including a Princeton professor who wrote in the prestigious publication *Science,* the eminent economist Milton Friedman; Kurt Schmoke, the former mayor of Baltimore; columnist William F. Buckley; and former Secretary of State George Schultz. She decided to support legalization as well, not because of the strength of pro-legalization arguments he or she had read, but because that's the way several people she trusted felt—a clear case of the peripheral route to persuasion.

So if you are worried that your message is rather weak, you might consider distracting your audience—perhaps by arranging for some loud music just outside the room in which you are speaking. If your arguments are strong and convincing, however, make sure you have your audience's full attention, so that they can listen to (and be swayed by) your arguments.

How to Achieve Long-Lasting Attitude Change   Now that you know a persuasive communication can change people's attitudes in either of two ways—via the central or the peripheral route—you may be wondering what difference it makes. Does it really matter whether it was the logic of the arguments or the expertise of the source that changed students' minds about comprehensive exams in the Petty and colleagues (1981) study? Given the bottom line—they changed their attitudes—why should any of us care how they got to that point?

If we are interested in creating long-lasting attitude change, we should care a lot. People who base their attitudes on a careful analysis of the arguments will be

Need for Cognition

A personality variable reflecting the extent to which people engage in and enjoy effortful cognitive activities

Try it!

The Need for Cognition

Indicate to what extent each statement is characteristic of you, using the following scale:

1 = extremely uncharacteristic of you (not at all like you)
2 = somewhat uncharacteristic
3 = uncertain
4 = somewhat characteristic
5 = extremely characteristic of you (very much like you)

1. I would prefer complex to simple problems. _____
2. I like to have the responsibility of handling a situation that requires a lot of thinking. _____
3. Thinking is not my idea of fun. _____
4. I would rather do something that requires little thought than something that is sure to challenge my thinking abilities. _____
5. I try to anticipate and avoid situations where there is a likely chance I will have to think in depth about something. _____
6. I find satisfaction in deliberating hard and for long hours. _____
7. I only think as hard as I have to. _____
8. I prefer to think about small, daily projects to long-term ones. _____
9. I like tasks that require little thought once I've learned them. _____
10. The idea of relying on thought to make my way to the top appeals to me. _____
11. I really enjoy a task that involves coming up with new solutions to problems. _____
12. Learning new ways to think doesn't excite me very much. _____
13. I prefer my life to be filled with puzzles that I must solve. _____
14. The notion of thinking abstractly is appealing to me. _____
15. I would prefer a task that is intellectual, difficult, and important to one that is somewhat important but does not require much thought. _____
16. I feel relief rather than satisfaction after completing a task that required a lot of mental effort. _____
17. It's enough for me that something gets the job done; I don't care how or why it works. _____
18. I usually end up deliberating about issues even when they do not affect me personally. _____

This scale measures the *need for cognition*, which is a personality variable reflecting the extent to which people engage in and enjoy effortful cognitive activities (Cacioppo, Petty, Feinstein, & Jarvis, 1996). People high in the need for cognition are more likely to form their attitudes by paying close attention to relevant arguments (i.e., via the central route), whereas people low in the need for cognition are more likely to rely on peripheral cues, such as how attractive or credible a speaker is.

Note: Turn to p. 235 for instructions on how to add up your score on this measure.

IT HAD EVERY SAFETY FEATURE
IN THE WORLD.
EXCEPT A DESIGNATED DRIVER.

SOMETIMES DRINKING RESPONSIBLY MEANS NOT DRINKING AT ALL. DESIGNATE A DRIVER

JOSEPH E. SEAGRAM & SONS, INC.
Those who appreciate quality enjoy it responsibly.

This ad is clearly trying to scare people into changing their attitudes and behavior. Based on research on fear-arousing communications, do you think this ad would work?

Fear-Arousing Communications

Persuasive messages that attempt to change people's attitudes by arousing their fears

more likely to maintain this attitude over time, more likely to behave consistently with this attitude, and more resistant to counterpersuasion than people who base their attitudes on peripheral cues (Chaiken, 1980; Mackie, 1987; Petty, Haugtvedt, & Smith, 1995; Petty & Wegener, 1998). In one study, for example, people changed their attitudes either by analyzing the logic of the arguments or by using peripheral cues. When the participants were telephoned ten days later, those who had analyzed the logic of the arguments were more likely to have maintained their new attitude—that is, attitudes that changed via the central route to persuasion lasted longer (Chaiken, 1980).

Emotion and Attitude Change

Now you know exactly how to construct your ad for the American Cancer Society, right? Well, not quite. Before people will consider your carefully constructed arguments, you have to get their attention. If you are going to show your antismoking ad on television, for example, how can you be sure people will watch the ad when it comes on, instead of changing the channel or heading for the refrigerator? One way is to grab people's attention by playing to their emotions.

Fear-Arousing Communications One way to get people's attention is to scare them—for example, by showing pictures of diseased lungs and presenting alarming data about the link between smoking and lung cancer. This kind of persuasive message—attempting to change people's attitudes by stirring up their fears—is called a **fear-arousing communication.** Public service ads often take this approach by trying to scare people into practicing safer sex, wearing seat belts, and staying away from drugs. For example, as of January, 2001, cigarette packs sold in Canada are required to display graphic pictures of diseased gums and other body parts that cover at least 50% of the outside label. (Canada's Scare Tactics: Graphic Labels on Cigarette Packs, http://www.geocities.com/rmcra2/cigpack.html)

Do fear-arousing communications work? It depends on whether the fear influences people's ability to pay attention to and process the arguments in a message. If a moderate amount of fear is created and people believe that listening to the message will teach them how to reduce this fear, they will be motivated to analyze the message carefully and will likely change their attitudes via the central route (Petty, 1995; Rogers, 1983).

Consider a study in which a group of smokers watched a graphic film depicting lung cancer and then read pamphlets with specific instructions about how to quit smoking (Leventhal, Watts, & Pagano, 1967). As shown in the bottom line in Figure 7.5, people in this condition reduced their smoking significantly more than people who were shown only the film or only the pamphlet. Why? Watching the film scared people, and giving them the pamphlet reassured them that there was a way to reduce this fear—by following the instructions on how to quit. Seeing only the pamphlet didn't work very well because there was little fear motivating people to read it carefully. Seeing only the film didn't work very well either because people are likely to tune out a message that raises fear but does not give information about how to reduce it. This may explain why some attempts to frighten people into changing their attitudes and behaviors fail: They succeed in scaring people but do not provide specific recommendations to help them reduce their fear (Ruiter, Abraham, & Kok, 2001; Soames, 1988).

Fear-arousing appeals will also fail if they are so strong that they threaten people. If people are scared to death, they will become defensive, deny the importance of the threat, and be unable to think rationally about the issue (Janis & Feshbach, 1953; Liberman & Chaiken, 1992). So if you have decided to arouse people's fear in your ad for the American Cancer Society, keep these points in

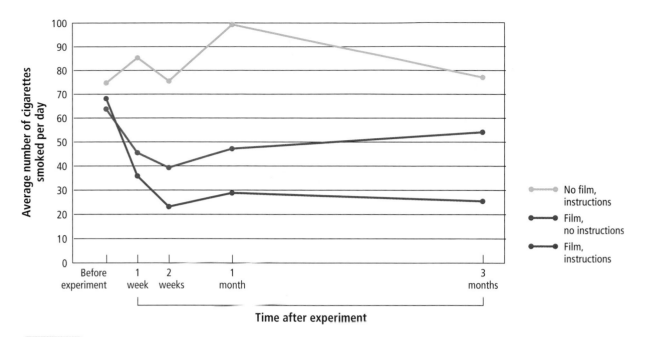

FIGURE 7.5

Effects of fear appeals on attitude change.

People were shown a scary film about effects of smoking, instructions about how to stop smoking, or both. Those who were shown both reduced the number of cigarettes they smoked the most.

(Adapted from Leventhal, Watts, & Pagano, 1967)

mind: First, try to create enough fear to motivate people to pay attention to your arguments but not so much fear that people will tune out or distort what you say. Second, include some specific recommendations about how to stop smoking so that people will be reassured that paying close attention to your arguments will help them reduce their fear.

Emotions as a Heuristic   Another way in which emotions can cause attitude change is by acting as a signal for how we feel about an issue. According to the **heuristic–systematic model of persuasion** (Chaiken, 1987), when people take the peripheral route to persuasion, they often use heuristics. Recall from Chapter 3 that heuristics are mental shortcuts people use to make judgments quickly and efficiently. In the present context, a heuristic is a simple rule people use to decide what their attitude is without having to spend a lot of time analyzing every little detail about the matter. Examples of such heuristics are "Experts are always right" and "Length equals strength" (i.e., long messages are more persuasive than short ones).

Interestingly, our emotions and moods can themselves act as heuristics to determine our attitudes. When trying to decide what our attitude is about something, we often rely on the "How do I feel about it?" heuristic (Clore et al., 2001; Forgas, 1995; Schwarz & Clore, 1988). If we feel good, we must have a positive attitude; if we feel bad, it's thumbs down. Now this probably sounds like a pretty good rule to follow, and like most heuristics, it is—most of the time. Suppose you need a new couch and go to a furniture store to look around. You see one in your price range and are trying to decide whether to buy it. If you use the "How do I feel about it?" heuristic, you do a quick check of your feelings and emotions. If you feel great while you're sitting in the couch in the store, you will probably buy it.

The only problem is that sometimes it is difficult to tell where our feelings come from. Is it really the couch that made you feel great, or is it something

Heuristic–Systematic Model of Persuasion

An explanation of the two ways in which persuasive communications can cause attitude change: either systematically processing the merits of the arguments or using mental shortcuts (heuristics), such as "Experts are always right"

completely unrelated? Maybe you were in a good mood to begin with, or maybe on the way to the store you heard your favorite song on the radio. Or perhaps a salesperson greeted you with a big smile and an ice-cold drink when you walked in the door, and that brightened your mood. The problem with the "How do I feel about it?" heuristic is that we can make mistakes about what is causing our mood, misattributing feelings created by one source (the cold drink) to another (the couch; see Chapter 5 on misattribution). If so, people might make a bad decision. Once you get the new couch home, you might discover that it no longer makes you feel all that great. It makes sense, then, that advertisers and retailers want to create good feelings while they present their product (e.g., by playing appealing music or showing pleasant images), hoping that people will attribute at least some of those feelings to the product they are trying to sell.

> It is useless to attempt to reason a man out of a thing he was never reasoned into.
>
> —Jonathan Swift

Emotion and Different Types of Attitudes   The success of various attitude change techniques depends on the type of attitude we are trying to change. As we saw earlier, not all attitudes are created equally; some are based more on beliefs about the attitude object (cognitively based attitudes), whereas others are based more on emotions and values (affectively based attitudes). Several studies have shown that it is best to fight fire with fire: If an attitude is cognitively based, try to change it with rational arguments; if it is affectively based, try to change it with emotional appeals (Fabrigar & Petty, 1999; Shavitt, 1989; Snyder & DeBono, 1989).

Consider a study of the effectiveness of different kinds of advertisements (Shavitt, 1990). Some ads stress the objective merits of a product, such as an ad for an air conditioner or a vacuum cleaner that discusses its price, efficiency, and reliability. Other ads stress emotions and values, such as ones for perfume or designer jeans that try to associate their brands with sex, beauty, and youthfulness, rather than saying anything about the objective qualities of the product. Which kind of ad is most effective?

To find out, participants looked at different kinds of advertisements. Some were for "utilitarian products," such as air conditioners and coffee. People's attitudes toward such products tend to be formed after an appraisal of the utilitarian aspects of the products (e.g., how energy-efficient an air conditioner is) and thus are cognitively based. The other items were "social identity products," such as perfume and greeting cards. People's attitudes toward these types of products tend to reflect a concern with how they appear to others and are more affectively based.

As shown in Figure 7.6, people reacted most favorably to the ads that matched the type of attitude they had. If people's attitudes were cognitively based (e.g., toward air conditioners or coffee), the ads that focused on the utilitarian aspects of these products, such as the features of the air conditioner, were most successful. If people's attitudes were more affectively based (e.g., toward perfume or greeting cards), the ads that focused on values and social identity concerns were most successful. The graph displayed in Figure 7.6 shows the number of favorable thoughts people had in response to the different kinds of ads. Similar results were found on a measure of how much people intended to buy the products. Thus if you ever get a job in advertising, the moral is to know what type of attitude most people have toward your product and then tailor your advertising accordingly.

Culture and Different Types of Attitudes   Are there differences across cultures in the kinds of attitudes people have toward the same products, re-

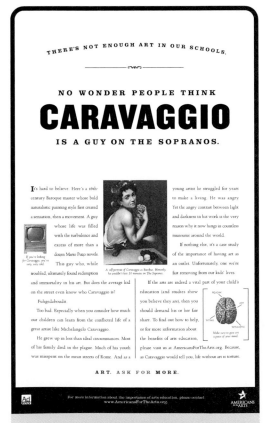

Many advertisements attempt to use emotions to persuade people. This ad uses a combination of humor (comparing Michelangelo to a character on the TV show, "The Sopranos") and fear (depriving kids of art is bad for their development).

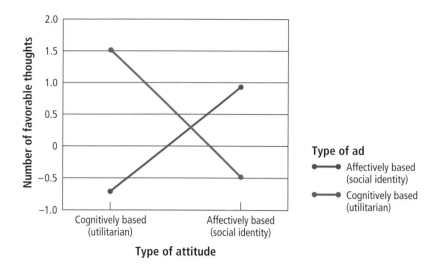

FIGURE 7.6

Effects of affective and cognitive information on affectively and cognitively based attitudes.

When people had cognitively based attitudes (e.g., toward air conditioners and coffee), cognitively based advertisements that stressed the utilitarian aspects of the products worked best. When people had more affectively based attitudes (e.g., toward perfume and greeting cards), affectively based advertisements that stressed values and social identity worked best. (The higher the number, the more favorable thoughts people listed about the products after reading the advertisements.)

(Adapted from Shavitt, 1990)

flecting the differences in self-concept we discussed in Chapter 5? As we saw, Western cultures tend to stress independence and individualism, whereas many Asian cultures stress interdependence and collectivism. Maybe these differences influence the kinds of attitudes people have and hence how those attitudes change.

Perhaps people in Western cultures base their attitudes more on concerns about individuality and self-improvement, whereas people in Asian cultures base their attitudes more on concerns about their standing in their social group, such as their families. If so, advertisements that stress individuality and self-improvement might work better in Western cultures, and advertisements that stress one's social group might work better in Asian cultures. To test this hypothesis, researchers created different ads for the same product that stressed independence (e.g., an ad for shoes said, "It's easy when you have the right shoes") or interdependence (e.g., "The shoes for your family") and showed them to both Americans and Koreans (Han & Shavitt, 1994). The Americans were persuaded most by the ads stressing independence, and the Koreans were persuaded by the ads stressing interdependence. The researchers also analyzed actual magazine advertisements in the United States and Korea and found that these ads were in fact different: American ads tended to emphasize individuality, self-improvement, and benefits of the product for the individual consumer, whereas

Do you think this Mercedes ad will work better with people who have affectively-based or cognitively-based attitudes toward cars? In general, ads work best if they are tailored to the kind of attitude they are trying to change. Given that this ad seems to be targeting people's emotions (indeed, it doesn't present any information about the car, such as its safety record, gas mileage, or reliability), it will probably work best on people whose attitudes are affectively-based.

Korean ads tended to emphasize the family, concerns about others, and benefits for one's social group. In general, then, advertisements work best if they are tailored to the kind of attitude they are trying to change.

RESISTING PERSUASIVE MESSAGES

By now you are no doubt getting nervous (and not just because the chapter hasn't ended yet): With all these clever methods to change your attitudes, are you ever safe from persuasive communications? Indeed you are, or at least you can be, if you use some strategies of your own. Here's how to make sure all of those persuasive messages that bombard you don't turn you into a quivering mass of constantly changing opinion.

Attitude Inoculation

One thing you can do is consider the arguments against your attitude before someone attacks it. The more people have thought about pro and con arguments beforehand using the technique known as **attitude inoculation** (Bernard, Maio, & Olson, 2003; McGuire, 1964), the better they can ward off attempts to change their minds using logical arguments. By considering "small doses" of arguments against their position, people become immune to later, full-blown attempts to change their attitudes. Having considered the arguments beforehand, people are relatively immune to the effects of the later communication, just as exposing people to a small amount of a virus can inoculate them against exposure to the full-blown viral disease. In contrast, if people have not thought much about the issue—that is, if they formed their attitude via the peripheral route—they are particularly susceptible to an attack on that attitude using logical appeals.

> The chief effect of talk on any subject is to strengthen one's own opinions and, in fact, one never knows exactly what he does believe until he is warmed into conviction by the heat of the attack and defense.
>
> —*Charles Dudley Warner, Backlog Studies, 1873*

In one study, for example, William McGuire (1964) "inoculated" people by giving them brief arguments against *cultural truisms,* beliefs that most members of a society accept uncritically, such as the idea that we should brush our teeth after every meal. Two days later, people came back and read a much stronger attack on the truism, one that contained a series of logical arguments about why brushing your teeth too frequently is a bad idea. The people who had been inoculated against these arguments were much less likely to change their attitudes than a control group who had not been inoculated. Why? The individuals who were inoculated with weak arguments had time to think about why these arguments were false, making them more able to contradict the stronger attack they heard two days later. The control group, never having thought about how often people should brush their teeth, was particularly susceptible to the strong communication arguing against frequent brushing.

Being Alert to Product Placement

When an advertisement comes on during a TV show, people often decide to press the mute button on the remote control or to get up and get a snack. To counteract this tendency to tune out, advertisers look for ways of displaying their wares during the show itself. With this technique, called *product placement,* companies pay the makers of a TV show or movie to incorporate their product into the script. In the movie *E.T. the Extra-Terrestrial,* for example, Elliot left a trail of Reese's Pieces to draw out E.T., after which sales of the candy boomed. In a 1996 James Bond movie, Agent 007 abandoned his usual Aston Martin and drove a BMW Z3 roadster, reportedly in return for a $3 million fee from the BMW com-

Attitude Inoculation

Making people immune to attempts to change their attitudes by initially exposing them to small doses of the arguments against their position

pany. Moviegoers responded with $240 million in advance sales for the car (York, 2001). More recently, companies have paid to have their products appear in television shows like *Survivor* and in MTV videos (Leeds, 2003). And there is increasing evidence that people are influenced by what they see on television and in the movies. One study, for example, found that the more children in grades 5–8 had seen movies in which adults smoked cigarettes, the more positive were their attitudes toward smoking (Sargent et al., 2002).

One reason product placement may be so successful is that people do not realize that someone is trying to influence their attitudes and behavior. People's defenses are down; when we see E.T. eating Reese's Pieces or James Bond driving a BMW, we don't think about the fact that someone is trying to influence our attitudes and start generating counterarguments (e.g., "Is the BMW really better than the Aston Martin that 007 used to drive?"). This leads to the question of whether forewarning people that someone is about to try to change their attitudes is an effective tool against advertising, product placement, or persuasion more generally.

It turns out that it is. Several studies have found that warning people about an upcoming attempt to change their attitudes makes them less susceptible to that attempt. When people are forewarned, they analyze what they see and hear more carefully and as a result are likely to avoid attitude change. Without such warnings, people pay little attention to the persuasive attempts and tend to accept them at face value (Sagarin, Cialdini, Rice, & Serna, 2002; Wood & Quinn, 2003). So before letting kids watch TV or sending them off to the movies, it is good to remind them that they are likely to encounter several attempts to change their attitudes.

Resisting Peer Pressure

We've seen that many attacks on our attitudes consist of appeals to our emotions. Can we ward off this kind of opinion change technique, just as we can ward off the effects of logical appeals? This is an important question, because many critical changes in attitudes and behaviors occur not in response to logic but via more emotional appeals. Consider the way in which many adolescents begin to smoke, drink, or take drugs. Often they do so in response to pressure from their peers, at an age when they are particularly susceptible to such pressure. Indeed, one study found that the best predictor of whether an adolescent smokes marijuana is whether he or she has a friend who does so (Yamaguchi & Kandel, 1984).

Think about how this occurs. It is not as if peers present a set of logical arguments ("Hey, Jake, did you know that recent studies show that moderate drinking may have health benefits?"). Instead, peer pressure is linked more to people's values and emotions, playing on their fear of rejection and their desire for freedom and autonomy. In adolescence, peers become an important source of social approval—perhaps the most important—and can dispense powerful rewards for holding certain attitudes or behaving in certain ways, such as using drugs or engaging in unprotected sex. What is needed is a technique that will make young people more resistant to attitude change attempts via peer pressure so that they will be less likely to engage in dangerous behaviors.

One possibility is to extend the logic of McGuire's inoculation approach to more affectively based persuasion techniques, such as peer pressure. In addition to inoculating people with doses of logical arguments that they might hear, we could also inoculate them with samples of the kinds of emotional appeals they might encounter.

Consider Jake, a 13-year-old who is hanging out with some classmates, many of whom are smoking cigarettes. The classmates begin to tease Jake about not smoking, calling him a wimp. One of them even lights a cigarette and holds it in

> A companion's words of persuasion are effective.
>
> —Homer

front of Jake, daring him to take a puff. Many 13-year-olds, facing such pressure, would cave in. But suppose that we immunized Jake to such social pressures by exposing him to mild versions of them and showing him ways to combat these pressures. We might have him role-play a situation where a friend calls him a chicken for not smoking a cigarette and teach him to respond by saying, "I'd be more of a chicken if I smoked it just to impress you." Would this help him resist the more powerful pressures exerted by his classmates?

Several programs designed to prevent smoking in adolescents suggest that it would. In one, psychologists used a role-playing technique with seventh graders, very much like the one we described (McAlister, Perry, Killen, Slinkard, & Maccoby, 1980). The researchers found that these students were significantly less likely to smoke three years after the study, compared to a control group that had not participated in the program. This result is encouraging and has been replicated in similar programs designed to reduce smoking (Chassin, Presson, & Sherman, 1990; Falck & Craig, 1988; Killen, 1985).

When Persuasion Attempts Boomerang: Reactance Theory

It is important not to use too heavy a hand when trying to immunize people against assaults on their attitudes. Suppose you want to make sure that your child never smokes. "Might as well err on the side of giving too strong a message," you might think, absolutely forbidding your child to even look at a pack of cigarettes. "What's the harm?" you figure. "At least this way, my child will get the point about how serious a matter this is."

Actually, there is harm to administering strong prohibitions—the stronger they are, the more likely they will boomerang, causing an increase in interest in the prohibited activity. According to **reactance theory** (Brehm, 1966), people do not like to feel that their freedom to do or think whatever they want is being threatened. When they feel that their freedom is threatened, an unpleasant state of reactance is aroused, and people can reduce this reactance by performing the threatened behavior (e.g., smoking).

In one study, for example, researchers placed one of two signs in the bathrooms on a college campus, in an attempt to get people to stop writing graffiti on the restroom walls (Pennebaker & Sanders, 1976). One sign read, "Do not write on these walls under any circumstances." The other gave a milder prohibition: "Please don't write on these walls." The researchers returned two weeks later and observed how much graffiti had been written since they posted the signs. As they predicted, significantly more people wrote graffiti in the bathrooms with the "Do not write . . ." sign than with the "Please don't write . . ." sign. Similarly, people who receive strong admonitions against smoking, taking drugs, or getting their nose pierced become more likely to perform these behaviors in order to restore their sense of personal freedom and choice (Bushman & Stack, 1996; Dowd et al., 1988).

SMOKE-FREE

IT'S THE NEW EVOLUTION

Boyz II Men

A number of programs designed to prevent smoking in adolescents have had some success. Many celebrities have lent their names and pictures to the effort, as in this ad featuring Boyz II Men.

Reactance Theory

The idea that when people feel their freedom to perform a certain behavior is threatened, an unpleasant state of reactance is aroused, which they can reduce by performing the threatened behavior

WHEN WILL ATTITUDES PREDICT BEHAVIOR?

If you change people's attitudes, does that mean they will do what you want them to do? What is the relationship between attitudes and people's actual behavior? Companies spend billions of dollars on advertising because they believe that changing attitudes will boost sales. And political campaigners assume that if they can get enough people to feel positively toward their candidate, those feelings will translate into votes.

Actually, the relationship between attitudes and behavior is not so straightforward, as shown in a classic study (LaPiere, 1934). In the early 1930s, Richard LaPiere embarked on a cross-country sightseeing trip with a young Chinese couple. Prejudice against Asians was common in the United States at this time, so at each hotel, campground, and restaurant they entered, LaPiere worried that his friends would be refused service. To his surprise, of the 251 establishments he and his friends visited, only one refused to serve them.

Struck by this apparent lack of prejudice, LaPiere decided to explore people's attitudes toward Asians in a different way. After his trip, he wrote a letter to each establishment he and his friends had visited, asking if it would serve a Chinese visitor. Of the many replies, only *one* said it would. More than 90 percent said they definitely would not; the rest were undecided. Why were the attitudes people expressed in writing the reverse of their actual behavior?

LaPiere's study was not, of course, a controlled experiment. As he acknowledged, there are several reasons why his results may not show an inconsistency between people's attitudes and behavior. He had no way of knowing whether the proprietors who answered his letter were the same people who had served him and his friends, and even if they were, people's attitudes could have changed in the months between the time they served the Chinese couple and the time they received the letter. Nonetheless, the lack of correspondence between people's attitudes and what they actually did was so striking that we might question our earlier assumption that behavior routinely follows from attitudes. This is especially the case in light of research performed after LaPiere's study, which also found that people's attitudes were poor predictors of their behavior (Wicker, 1969).

How can this be? Does a person's attitude toward Asians or political candidates really tell us nothing about how he or she will behave? How can we reconcile LaPiere's findings—and other studies like it—with the fact that many times behavior and attitudes *are* consistent? It turns out that attitudes do predict behavior, but only under certain specifiable conditions (DeBono & Snyder, 1995; Zanna & Fazio, 1982). One key factor is knowing whether the behavior we are trying to predict is spontaneous or is deliberative and planned (Fazio, 1990).

> We give advice but we do not influence people's conduct.
>
> —François de La Rouchefoucauld, *Maxims, 1665*

Predicting Spontaneous Behaviors

Sometimes we act spontaneously, thinking little about what we are about to do. When LaPiere and his Chinese friends entered a restaurant, the manager did not have a lot of time to reflect on whether to serve them; he or she had to make a snap decision. Similarly, when someone stops us on the street and asks us to sign a petition in favor of a change in the local zoning laws, we usually don't stop to deliberate; we decide whether to sign the petition on the spot.

Attitudes will predict spontaneous behaviors only when they are highly accessible to people (Fazio, 1990, 2000; Kallgren & Wood, 1986). **Attitude accessibility** refers to the strength of the association between an object and an evaluation of it, which is typically measured by the speed with which people can report how they feel about an issue or object (Fazio, 2000). When accessibility is high, your attitude comes to mind whenever you see or think about the attitude object. When accessibility is low, your attitude comes to mind more slowly. It follows that highly accessible attitudes will be more likely to predict spontaneous behaviors because people are more likely to be thinking about their attitude when they are called on to act.

One study demonstrated the role of accessibility by looking at people's attitudes and behaviors toward consumer items (Fazio, Powell, & Williams, 1989). People first rated their attitudes toward several products, such as different brands of gum and candy. The accessibility of these attitudes was assessed by

Attitude Accessibility

The strength of the association between an attitude object and a person's evaluation of that object, measured by the speed with which people can report how they feel about the object

measuring how long it took the people to respond to the attitude questions. Then the researchers placed ten of the products on a table (in two rows of five) and told people they could choose five of them to take home as a reward for being in the study. To what extent did people's attitude toward the products determine which ones they chose?

As predicted, it depended on the accessibility of their attitudes. Attitude-behavior consistency was high among people with accessible attitudes and relatively low among people with inaccessible attitudes. That is, people acted in accordance with their attitudes only if their attitudes came quickly to mind when they were making their choice. What about people with inaccessible attitudes—what determined which products they chose? They were more influenced by an arbitrary aspect of the situation—which products happened to be in the first row on the table in front of them. The closer an item was, the more likely they were to choose it. When attitudes are inaccessible, people are more influenced by situational variables—in this case, how noticeable and within reach the products were. Now you know why companies compete to have their products placed at eye level on supermarket shelves.

Predicting Deliberative Behaviors

In many circumstances, behavior is not spontaneous but deliberative and planned. Most of us think seriously about where to go to college, whether to accept a new job, or where to spend our vacation. Under these conditions, the accessibility of our attitude is not important. Given enough time to think about an issue, even people with inaccessible attitudes can bring to mind how they feel. It is only when we have to decide how to act on the spot, without time to think it over, that accessibility matters (Eagly & Chaiken, 1993; Fazio, 1990).

The best-known theory of how attitudes predict deliberative behaviors is the **theory of planned behavior** (Ajzen & Fishbein, 1980; Ajzen & Sexton, 1999; Fishbein & Ajzen, 1975). According to this theory, when people have time to contemplate how they are going to behave, the best predictor of their behavior is their intention, which is determined by three things: their attitudes toward the specific behavior, their subjective norms, and their perceived behavioral control (see Figure 7.7). Let's consider each of these in turn.

Theory of Planned Behavior
The idea that the best predictors of a person's planned, deliberate behaviors are the person's attitudes toward specific behaviors, subjective norms, and perceived behavioral control

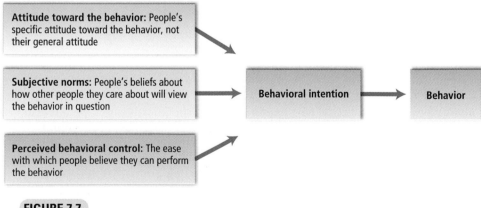

FIGURE 7.7

The theory of planned behavior.

According to this theory, the best predictors of people's planned, deliberative behaviors are their behavioral intentions. The best predictors of their intentions are their attitudes toward the specific behavior, their subjective norms, and their perceived behavioral control of the behavior.

(Adapted from Ajzen, 1985)

TABLE 7.1

Specific Attitudes Are Better Predictors of Behavior

Different groups of women were asked about their attitudes toward birth control. The more specific the question, the better it predicted their actual use of birth control. *Note:* If a correlation is close to 0, it means that there is no relationship between the two variables. The closer the correlation is to 1, the stronger the relationship between attitudes and behavior.

ATTITUDE MEASURE	ATTITUDE-BEHAVIOR CORRELATION
Attitude toward birth control	.08
Attitude toward birth control pills	.32
Attitude toward using birth control pills	.53
Attitude toward using birth control pills during the next two years	.57

(Adapted from Davidson & Jaccard, 1979)

Specific Attitudes   The theory of planned behavior holds that only specific attitudes toward the behavior in question can be expected to predict that behavior. In one study, researchers asked a sample of married women for their attitudes toward birth control pills, ranging from the general (their attitude toward birth control) to the specific (their attitude toward using birth control pills during the next two years; see Table 7.1). Two years later, they asked the women whether they had used birth control pills at any time since the last interview. As Table 7.1 shows, the women's general attitude toward birth control did not predict their use of birth control at all. This general attitude did not take into account other factors that could have influenced their decision, such as concern about the long-term effects of the pill and their attitude toward other forms of birth control. The more specific the question was about the act of using birth control pills, the better this attitude predicted their actual behavior (Davidson & Jaccard, 1979).

This study helps explain why LaPiere (1934) found such inconsistency between people's attitudes and behaviors. His question to the proprietors—whether they would serve "members of the Chinese race"—was very general. Had he asked a much more specific question—such as whether they would serve an educated, well-dressed, well-to-do Chinese couple accompanied by a white American college professor—the proprietors might have given an answer that was more in line with their behavior.

> If actions are to yield all the results they are capable of, there must be a certain consistency between them and one's intentions.
>
> —*François de La Rochefoucauld, Maxims, 1665*

Subjective Norms   In addition to measuring attitudes toward the behavior, we also need to measure people's subjective norms—their beliefs about how people they care about will view the behavior in question (see Figure 7.7). To predict someone's intentions, knowing these beliefs can be as important as knowing the person's attitudes. For example, suppose we want to predict whether Kristen intends to go to a hip-hop concert, and we know that she doesn't like hip-hop music. We would probably say she won't go. But suppose we also know that Kristen's best friend, Tony, really wants her to go. Knowing this subjective norm—her belief about how a close friend views her behavior—we might make a different prediction.

Perceived Behavioral Control   Finally, as seen in Figure 7.7, people's intentions are influenced by the ease with which they believe they can perform the behavior, or *perceived behavioral control*. If people think it is difficult to perform the behavior, such as remembering to use condoms when having sex, they will not form a strong intention to do so. If people think it is easy to perform the behavior, such as remembering to buy milk on the way home from work, they are more likely to form a strong intention to do so.

Considerable research supports the idea that asking people about these determinants of their intentions—attitudes toward specific behaviors, subjective norms, and perceived behavioral control—increases the ability to predict their planned, deliberative behaviors, such deciding what job to accept, whether to wear a seat belt, whether to check oneself for disease, and whether to use condoms when having sex (Albarracin, Johnson, Fishbein, & Muellerleile, 2001; Armitage & Conner, 2001; Sheeran & Taylor, 1999; Trafimow & Finlay, 1996).

THE POWER OF ADVERTISING

A curious thing about advertising is that most people think it works on everyone but themselves (Wilson & Brekke, 1994). People typically comment, "There is no harm in watching commercials. Some of them are fun, and they don't have much influence on me." Are they right? This is an important question for social psychology, because most of the research on attitudes and behavior we have discussed so far was conducted in the laboratory with college students. As we saw at the beginning of the chapter, each of us is confronted with hundreds of attempts to change our attitudes every day in the form of advertisements. Do these ads really work, or are companies wasting the billions of dollars a year they are spending on advertising?

> You can tell the ideals of a nation by its advertisements.
>
> ---George Norman Douglas, South Wind, 1917

It turns out that people are influenced by advertisements more than they think (Abraham & Lodish, 1990; Liebert & Sprafkin, 1988; Ryan, 1991; Wells, 1997; Wilson, Houston, & Meyers, 1998). The best evidence that advertising works comes from studies using what are called *split cable market tests*. Advertisers work in conjunction with cable television companies and grocery stores, showing a target commercial to a randomly selected group of people. They keep track of what people buy by giving potential consumers special ID cards that are scanned at checkout counters; thus they can tell whether people who saw the commercial for ScrubaDub laundry detergent actually buy more ScrubaDub—the best measure of advertising effectiveness.

The results of over three hundred split cable market tests indicate that advertising does work, particularly for new products (Lodish et al., 1995). About 60 percent of the advertisements for new products led to an increase in sales, compared to 46 percent of the advertisements for established brands. When an ad was effective, how much did it increase sales? The difference in sales between people who saw an effective ad for a new product and those who did not averaged 21 percent. Although this figure might seem modest, it translates into millions of dollars when applied to a national advertising campaign. Further, these effective ads worked quickly, increasing sales substantially within the first six months they were shown.

CONNECTIONS

Do Media Campaigns to Reduce Drug Use Work?

At the 2002 MTV Video Music Awards, the pop star Pink interrupted her acceptance speech to declare that she was "too drunk for this." Later in the evening, when accepting her award, Michelle Branch declared that she was "drunker than Pink." Smoking and drinking are common in movies, and sometimes public figures admired by many youth glamorize the use of drugs and alcohol. Advertising, product placement, and the behavior of admired figures can have powerful effects on people's behavior, including tobacco and alcohol use (Pechmann & Knight, 2002; Saffer, 2002). This raises an important question: Do public service ads designed to reduce people's use of drugs such as alcohol, tobacco, and marijuana work?

By now you know that changing people's attitudes and behavior can be difficult, particularly if people are not very motivated to pay attention to a persuasive message or are distracted while trying to pay attention. If persuasive messages are well crafted, they can have an effect, however, and we have seen many successful attempts to change people's attitudes in this chapter. What happens when researchers take these techniques out of the laboratory and try to change real-life attitudes and behavior, such as people's attraction to and use of illegal drugs?

A recent meta-analysis of studies that tested the effects of a media message (conveyed via television, radio, electronic, and print media) on substance abuse (including illegal drugs, alcohol, and tobacco) in youths was encouraging (Derzon & Lipsey, 2002). After a media campaign that targeted a specific substance, such as tobacco, kids became more negative toward the use of that substance. The effects on actual use of the substance were reliable but of lesser magnitude. Television and radio messages had bigger effects than messages in the print media.

In a particularly impressive study, researchers developed 30-second television spots in which teen actors conveyed the risks of smoking marijuana, such as its effects on people's relationships, level of motivation, and judgment (Palmgreen, Donohew, Lorch, Holye, & Stephenson, 2001). The ads were shown for four-month intervals at different times in two similar communities, Fayette County, Kentucky, and Knox County, Tennessee. The researchers interviewed randomly chosen teenagers in both communities and assessed their attitudes and use of marijuana during the previous thirty days.

The ads had no detectable effect among teenagers who were low in sensation seeking, which is a personality trait having to do with how much people are attracted to novel, emotionally exciting activities. These people did not use marijuana much to begin with, so we would not expect the public service ads to change their behavior. Among the teenagers who were high in sensation seeking, however, the ads had an impact. When the ads were shown in Fayette County but not Knox County, the percentage of Fayette teenagers who reported using marijuana in the preceding thirty days dropped from about 38 percent to 28 percent. The percentage of Knox County teenagers who said they used marijuana increased during this same time period. When the ads were shown in Knox County, reported marijuana use also dropped by about 10 percent. These drops were not huge; it is not as if every teenager who saw the ads decided against smoking marijuana. Undoubtedly, some teenagers never saw the ads, and many who did were unaffected. From a public health perspective, however, a 10 percent drop is impressive, providing some hope for the success of media campaigns to lead to healthier behavior.

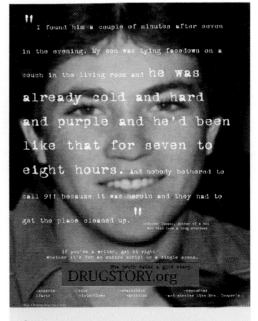

A recent meta analysis showed that public campaigns to reduce drug use can work. Do you think this ad is effective, based on the research on fear-arousing communications we discussed earlier in the chapter?

How Advertising Works

How does advertising work, and what types of ads work best? The answers follow from our earlier discussion of attitude change. Advertisers should consider the kind of attitude they are trying to change. If they are trying to change an

"How about one of those sunny old grandpas who make things look honest?"

affectively based attitude, then as we have seen, it is best to fight emotions with emotions. Many advertisements take the emotional approach—for example, ads for different brands of soft drinks. Given that different brands of colas are not all that different, many people do not base their purchasing decisions on the objective qualities of the different brands. Consequently, soda advertisements do not stress facts and figures. As one advertising executive noted, "The thing about soda commercials is that they actually have nothing to say" ("Battle for Your Brain," 1991). Instead of presenting facts, soft drink ads play to people's emotions, trying to associate feelings of excitement, youth, energy, and sexual attractiveness with the brand.

If people's attitudes are more cognitively based, we need to ask an additional question: How personally relevant is the issue? Does it have important consequences for people's everyday lives, or is it a remote issue that does not directly affect them? Consider, for example, the problem of heartburn. This is not a

Advertisements for sodas tend to be emotion-based, trying to associate feelings of excitement, youth, and sexiness with a particular brand, as in this ad featuring Brittany Spears. Rarely do ads for sodas say anything about the product, such as how its taste compares to its competitors.

topic that evokes strong emotions and values in most people—it is more cognitively based. To people who suffer from frequent heartburn, however, the topic clearly has direct personal relevance. In this case, the best way to change people's attitudes is to use logical, fact-based arguments—convince people that your product will reduce heartburn the best or the fastest, and people will buy it (Chaiken, 1987; Petty & Cacioppo, 1986).

What if you are dealing with a cognitively based attitude that is not of direct personal relevance to people? For example, what if you are trying to sell a heartburn medicine to people who experience heartburn only every now and then and do not consider it a big deal? Here you have a problem, because people are unlikely to pay close attention to your advertisement. You might succeed in changing their attitudes via the peripheral route, such as having attractive movie stars endorse your product. The problem here, as we have seen, is that attitude change triggered by simple peripheral cues is not long-lasting (Chaiken, 1987; Petty & Cacioppo, 1986). So if you have a product that does not trigger people's emotions and is not directly relevant to their everyday lives, you are in trouble.

But don't give up. The trick is to *make* your product personally relevant. Let's take a look at some actual ad campaigns to see how this is done. Consider the case of Gerald Lambert, who early in the twentieth century inherited a company that made a surgical antiseptic used to treat throat infections—Listerine. Seeking a wider market for his product, Lambert decided to promote it as a mouthwash. The only problem was that no one at the time used a mouthwash or even knew what one was. So having invented the cure, Lambert invented the disease. Look at the ad for Listerine, which appeared in countless magazines over the years.

Even though today we would find this ad incredibly sexist, at the time most Americans did not find it offensive. Instead, the ad successfully played on people's fears about social rejection and failure. The phrase "Often a bridesmaid, never a bride" became one of the most famous in the history of advertising. In a few cleverly chosen words, it succeeded in making a problem—*halitosis*—personally relevant to millions of people. Listerine became a best-selling product. And *halitosis* was an obscure medical term until Gerald Lambert and his advertising team made it a household word, presenting it as a dreadful disease that we must avoid at all costs—and could be by going to the nearest drugstore and stocking up on mouthwash.

Lambert's success at playing to people's fears and sense of shame was not lost on other advertisers. Similar ads have been designed to create new markets for many new products, most having to do with personal hygiene or health: underarm deodorants, deodorant soaps, vitamin supplements, oat bran, fish oil, and more. These campaigns work by convincing people that they have problems of great personal relevance that only the advertised product can solve.

Many advertisements also try to make people's attitudes more affectively based by associating the product with important emotions and values (recall our earlier discussion of classical conditioning). Consider, for example, advertisements for long-distance telephone service. This topic does not, for most of us, evoke deep-rooted emotional feelings—until we see an ad in which a man calls his estranged brother to tell him he loves him or a man calls his mother to tell her he has just bought her a plane ticket so that she can come for a visit. There is nothing logically compelling about these ads. After all, there is no reason to believe that using AT&T will magically make you closer to your family than using

This ad is one of the most famous in the history of advertising. Although today it is easy to see how sexist and offensive it is, when it appeared in the 1930s it succeeded in making a problem (bad breath) personally relevant by playing on people's fears and insecurities about personal relationships. Can you think of contemporary ads that try to raise similar fears?

Verizon or Sprint. However, by associating positive emotions with a product, an advertiser can turn a bland product into one that evokes feelings of nostalgia, love, warmth, and general goodwill.

Subliminal Advertising: A Form of Mind Control?

In September 2000, during the heat of the United States presidential campaign, a man in Seattle was watching a political advertisement on television. At first, the ad looked like a run-of-the-mill political spot, in which an announcer praised the benefits of George W. Bush's prescription drug plan and criticized Al Gore's plan. But the viewer thought that he noticed something odd, so he videotaped the ad the next time it ran and played it back at a slow speed. Sure enough, he *had* noticed something unusual: As the announcer said, "The Gore prescription plan: Bureaucrats decide," the word RATS flashed on the screen very quickly— for one-thirtieth of a second at normal viewing speed. The alert viewer notified officials in the Gore campaign, who quickly contacted the press. Soon the country was abuzz about a possible attempt by the Bush campaign to use subliminal messages to create a negative impression of Al Gore. The Bush campaign denied that anyone had deliberately inserted the word RATS, claiming that it was "purely accidental" (Berke, 2000).

The RATS incident was hardly the first such controversy over the use of **subliminal messages,** defined as words or pictures that are not consciously perceived but may influence people's judgments, attitudes, and behaviors. In the late 1950s, James Vicary supposedly flashed the messages "Drink Coca-Cola" and "Eat popcorn" during a commercial movie and claimed that sales at the concession counter skyrocketed. According to some reports, Vicary made up these claims (Weir, 1984), but his was not the last attempt at subliminal persuasion. Wilson Bryan Key (1973, 1989) has written several best-selling books on hidden persuasion techniques, which claim that advertisers routinely implant sexual messages in print advertisements, such as the word *sex* in the ice cubes of an ad for gin, and male and female genitalia in everything from pats of butter to the icing in an ad for cake mix. Key (1973) argues that these images are not consciously perceived but put people in a good mood and make them pay more attention to the advertisement.

Subliminal messages are not just visual; they can be auditory as well. There is a large market for audiotapes that contain subliminal messages to help people lose weight, stop smoking, improve their study habits, raise their self-esteem, and even shave a few strokes off their golf scores. In 1990, sales of subliminal self-help tapes were estimated to be $50 million. But are subliminal messages effective? Do they really make us more likely to buy consumer products or help us lose weight and stop smoking? Most members of the public believe that subliminal

Subliminal Messages

Words or pictures that are not consciously perceived but may nevertheless influence people's judgments, attitudes, and behaviors

messages can shape their attitudes and behaviors, even though they are not aware that the messages have entered their minds (Zanot, Pincus, & Lamp, 1983). Are they right?

Debunking the Claims about Subliminal Advertising   Few of the proponents of subliminal advertising have conducted controlled studies to back up their claims. Fortunately, many controlled studies of subliminal perception have been conducted, allowing us to evaluate the sometimes outlandish claims that are made. Simply stated, there is no evidence that the types of subliminal messages encountered in everyday life have any influence on people's behavior. Hidden commands do not cause us to line up and buy popcorn any more than we normally do, and the subliminal commands on self-help tapes do not (unfortunately!) help us quit smoking or lose weight (Brannon & Brock, 1994; Merikle, 1988; Moore, 1992; Pratkanis, 1992; Theus, 1994; Trappey, 1996).

Consider one study that evaluated subliminal self-help tapes (Greenwald, Spangenberg, Pratkanis, & Eskenazi, 1991). Half the participants listened to tapes that, according to the manufacturer, contained subliminal messages designed to improve memory (e.g., "My ability to remember and recall is increasing daily"); the others listened to tapes that had subliminal messages designed to raise self-esteem (e.g., "I have high self-worth and high self-esteem"). Neither of the tapes had any effect on people's memory or self-esteem. It would be nice if we could all improve ourselves simply by listening to music with subliminal messages, but this study and others like it show that subliminal tapes are no better at solving our problems than patent medicines or visits to an astrologist.

Interestingly, the research participants thought the subliminal tapes were working, even though they were not. The researchers were a little devious, in that they correctly informed half the participants about which tape they listened to but misinformed the others (i.e., half the people who got the memory tape were told it was designed to improve their memory, and the other half were told it was designed to improve their self-esteem). Those who thought they had listened to the memory tape believed their memory had improved, even if they had really heard the self-esteem tape. And people who thought they had listened to the self-esteem tape believed their self-esteem had improved, even if they had heard the memory tape. This finding explains why subliminal tapes are big business: Even though the tapes don't work, people think they do.

Laboratory Evidence for Subliminal Influence   We've seen that subliminal messages are ineffective when used in advertising. Actually, there is evidence for subliminal effects in carefully controlled laboratory studies. In one study, for example, people saw a series of Chinese ideographs (characters used in the Chinese written language) and rated how much they liked the appearance of each one (Murphy & Zajonc, 1993). Unbeknown to the participants, the Chinese characters were preceded by another picture—a human face expressing happiness, a human face expressing anger, or a polygon conveying no emotion. These pictures were flashed for only four milliseconds, which is too fast for people to perceive consciously. Nonetheless these subliminal flashes influenced people's evaluations of the Chinese ideographs (see Figure 7.8). The same ideograph was liked the most when it was preceded by a happy face, second most when it was preceded by an unemotional polygon, and least when it was preceded by an angry face—even though people didn't know that these images had been flashed. Several other researchers have found similar effects of pictures or words flashed at subliminal levels (e.g., Bargh & Pietromonaco, 1982; Bornstein,

PEOPLE HAVE BEEN TRYING TO FIND THE BREASTS IN THESE ICE CUBES SINCE 1957.

The advertising industry is sometimes charged with sneaking seductive little pictures into ads.

Supposedly, these pictures can get you to buy a product without your even seeing them.

Consider the photograph above. According to some people, there's a pair of female breasts

hidden in the patterns of light refracted by the ice cubes.

Well, if you really searched you probably *could* see the breasts. For that matter, you could also see Millard Fillmore, a stuffed pork chop and a 1946 Dodge.

The point is that so-called "subliminal advertising" simply

doesn't exist. Overactive imaginations, however, most certainly do.

So if anyone claims to see breasts in that drink up there, they aren't in the ice cubes.

They're in the eye of the beholder.

ADVERTISING
ANOTHER WORD FOR FREEDOM OF CHOICE.
American Association of Advertising Agencies

There is no scientific evidence that implanting sexual images in advertising boosts sales of the product. The public is very aware of this subliminal technique, however—so much so that some advertisers have begun to poke fun at subliminal messages in their ads.

FIGURE 7.8

Effects of subliminal exposure to faces on the liking of Chinese ideographs.

There is evidence from carefully controlled laboratory studies that subliminal exposures to words and faces can influence people's judgments and attitudes. In this study, people were shown pictures of Chinese ideographs (characters used in the Chinese written language) for two seconds and asked how much they liked the appearance of each one. Unbeknown to the participants, the ideographs were preceded by quick flashes of happy faces (top panel), unemotional polygons (middle panel), or angry faces (bottom panel). These flashed images influenced how much people liked the ideographs, even though the images could not be perceived consciously. The only successful demonstrations of subliminal messages, however, have been done under carefully controlled laboratory conditions that would be difficult to duplicate in everyday life. Further, there is no evidence that subliminal messages can get people to do things they prefer not to do.

(Adapted from Murphy & Zajonc, 1993)

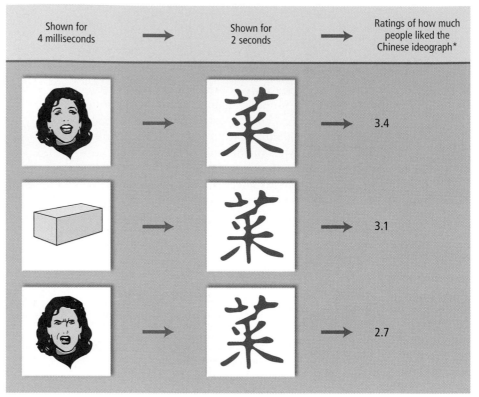

Shown for 4 milliseconds		Shown for 2 seconds		Ratings of how much people liked the Chinese ideograph*
😀	→	菜	→	3.4
▱	→	菜	→	3.1
😠	→	菜	→	2.7

*On a scale from 1 ("did not like at all") to 5 ("liked quite a bit")

Leone, & Galley, 1987; Dijksterhuis & Aarts, 2002; Strahan, Spencer, & Zanna, 2002).

Although it might be frightening to think that our attitudes can be influenced by information we do not even know we have seen, we should mention some qualifications. All of the successful demonstrations of subliminal stimuli have been conducted under carefully controlled laboratory conditions that are probably difficult to reproduce in everyday life. To get subliminal effects, researchers have to make sure that the illumination of the room is just right, that people are seated just the right distance from a viewing screen, and that nothing else is occurring to distract them as the subliminal stimuli are flashed. Further, even in the laboratory, there is no evidence that subliminal messages can get people to act counter to their wishes, values, or personalities (Neuberg, 1988). These messages might have subtle influences on people's liking for an ambiguous stimulus (e.g., a Chinese ideograph), but they cannot override their wishes and desires, making them march off to the supermarket to buy products they don't want or vote for candidates they despise. Thus it is highly unlikely that the word RATS in the Bush campaign ad converted people from Gore supporters to Bush supporters.

Advertising, Cultural Stereotypes, and Social Behavior

Ironically, the hoopla surrounding subliminal messages has obscured the fact that ads are more powerful when people consciously perceive them. We have seen plenty of evidence that the ads people perceive consciously every day can substantially influence their behavior, even though the ads do not contain subliminal messages. It is interesting that people fear subliminal advertising more than regular advertising when it is regular advertising that is more powerful (Wilson, Gilbert, & Wheatley, 1998). The Try It! exercise on page 231 will help you see whether this is true of people you know.

Try it!

Advertising and Mind Control

Here is an exercise on people's beliefs about the power of advertising that you can try on your friends. Ask about ten friends the following questions—preferably friends who have not had a course in social psychology! See how accurate their beliefs are about the effects of different kinds of advertising.

1. Do you think that you are influenced by subliminal messages in advertising? (Define *subliminal messages* for your friends as words or pictures that are not consciously perceived but nevertheless supposedly influence people's judgments, attitudes, and behaviors.)

2. Do you think that you are influenced by everyday advertisements that you perceive consciously, such as television ads for laundry detergent and painkillers?

3. Suppose you had a choice to listen to one of two speeches that argued against a position you believe in, such as whether marijuana should be legalized. In speech A, a person presents several arguments against your position. In speech B, all of the arguments are presented subliminally—you will not perceive anything consciously. Which speech would you rather listen to, A or B?

Tally the results here:

Question 1	Question 2	Question 3
Yes:	Yes:	Yes:
No:	No:	No:

Turn to page 235 to see if your results match those of actual studies. Show off your knowledge to your friends. Ask them why they are more wary of subliminal messages than everyday advertising when it is everyday ads and not subliminal messages that change people's minds. Why do *you* think that people are most afraid of the kinds of ads that are least effective? What does this say about people's awareness of their own thought processes?

Further, advertising influences more than just our consumer attitudes. Advertisements transmit cultural stereotypes in their words and images, subtly linking products with desired images (e.g., Marlboro ads linking cigarettes with the rugged, macho Marlboro Man; beer ads linking beer consumption with sex). Advertisements can also reinforce and perpetuate stereotypical ways of thinking about social groups. Until recently, ads almost always showed groups of whites (token individuals of color are now mixed into the group), couples who are heterosexual, families that are traditional (with a mom, dad, son, and daughter), and so on. You would think that divorced families, the middle-aged and the elderly, people of color, lesbians and gay men, the physically disabled, and others just didn't exist.

Gender stereotypes are particularly pervasive in advertising imagery. Men are doers; women are observers. Several studies have examined television commercials throughout the world and coded how men and women are portrayed. As seen in Figure 7.9 on the next page, one review found that women were more likely to be portrayed in dependent roles (that is, not in a position of power but dependent on someone else) than men in every country that was examined (Furnham & Mak, 1999).

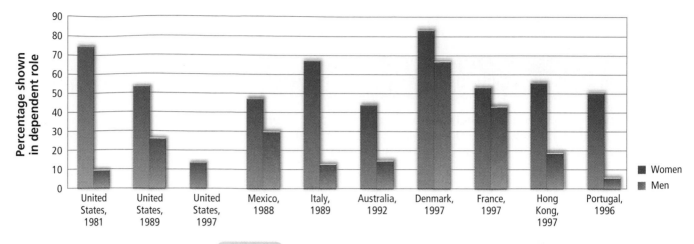

FIGURE 7.9

Portrayals of women and men in television advertising.

The ways in which women and men are portrayed in television commercials have been examined throughout the world. In every country, women were more likely to be portrayed in powerless, dependent roles than men were.

(Adapted from Furnham & Mak, 1999)

Well, you might think, television commercials reflect the stereotypes of a society but play little role in shaping those stereotypes or influencing people's behavior. Actually, the stereotypes conveyed in advertisements are far from harmless, as shown in a recent study of stereotype threat. **Stereotype threat** is the apprehension experienced by members of a group that their behavior might confirm a cultural stereotype. As we will see in Chapter 13, when people are thinking about the negative stereotypes toward their group, the apprehension they feel can hinder their performance. For example, women do worse on math tests when they think the test is the kind on which women might do worse than men, and white men do worse on math tests when they think they are competing with Asians. In each case, anxiety about confirming the stereotype—that women are worse at math than men and that whites are worse at math than Asians—lowered the performance of the target of the stereotype.

Where do commercials fit in? A recent study found that advertisements that portray women in stereotypical ways can trigger stereotype threat (Davies, Spencer, Quinn, & Gerhardstein, 2002). College women and men who were good at math watched television ads that showed women in stereotypical ways (e.g., an ad for an acne product in which a young woman bounced up and down on a bed) or counterstereotypical ways (e.g., an ad in which a woman impressed a man with her knowledge about cars). The students then took a difficult math test. As you can see in Figure 7.10, women and men performed at similar levels when they saw the counterstereotypical ads (there was no significant difference between men and women in this condition). Women performed significantly worse than men when they saw the stereotypical commercials.

The stereotypical commercials triggered thoughts about gender stereotypes in both men and women but impaired performance only for women. Subsequent studies by the same authors showed that women who watched the stereotypical commercials expressed less interest in careers that involved math (e.g., engineering and computer science) than women who watched neutral commercials that did not convey any stereotypes. If watching a couple of commercials in the laboratory can have such dramatic effects, we can only wonder about the effects of seeing hundreds of commercials in everyday life that portray people in stereotypical ways.

Stereotype Threat

The apprehension experienced by members of a group that their behavior might confirm a cultural stereotype

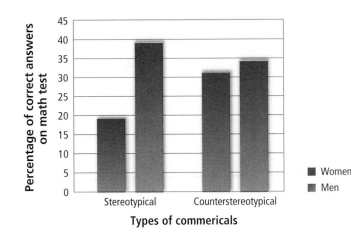

FIGURE 7.10

Effect of television commercials on math performance.

Male and female college students took a difficult math test after watching commercials that portrayed women in stereotypical or counterstereotypical ways. Women who saw the stereotypical ads did worse on the test. The commercials triggered stereotype threat in the women, which is apprehension experienced by members of a group when they believe that their behavior might confirm a cultural stereotype.

(Adapted from Davies, Spencer, Quinn, & Gerhardstein, 2002)

SUMMARY

The Nature and Origin of Attitudes

An **attitude** is a person's enduring evaluation of people, objects, and ideas. Attitudes can be based on affective, cognitive, or behavioral components. A **cognitively based attitude** is based mostly on people's beliefs about the properties of the attitude object. An **affectively based attitude** is based more on people's emotions and values; it can be created through **classical conditioning** or **operant conditioning**. A **behaviorally based attitude** is based on people's actions toward the attitude object. Once an attitude develops, it can exist at two levels. **Explicit attitudes** are ones that people consciously endorse and can easily report, whereas **implicit attitudes** are involuntary, uncontrollable, and at times unconscious.

How Do Attitudes Change?

As shown by research on cognitive dissonance theory, attitudes change when people engage in counterattitudinal advocacy for low external justification. When this occurs, people find internal justification for their behavior, bringing their attitudes in line with their behavior. Chapter 6 provides a detailed discussion of these topics. Attitudes can also change in response to a **persuasive communication**. According to the **Yale Attitude Change approach**, the effectiveness of a persuasive communication depends on aspects of the communicator, or source of the message; aspects of the message itself (e.g., its content); and aspects of the audience. The **elaboration likelihood model** specifies when people are persuaded more by the strength of the arguments in the communication and when they are persuaded more by surface characteristics, such as the attractiveness of the speaker. People will take the **central route to persuasion** when they have both the motivation and the ability to pay close attention to the arguments. This is likely to occur when the topic of the communication is high in personal relevance or when people are high in the **need for cognition.** People will take the **peripheral route to persuasion** when they either do not want to pay close attention to the arguments or cannot do so. Under these conditions, they are persuaded by such peripheral cues as the attractiveness of the speaker or the length of the speech. Attitude change is longer-lasting and more resistant to attack when it occurs via the central route.

Emotions influence attitude change in a number of ways. **Fear-arousing communications** can cause lasting attitude change if a moderate amount of fear is aroused and people believe they will be reassured by the content of the message. Consistent with the **heuristic-systematic model of persuasion,** emotions can also be used as heuristics to gauge one's attitude; if people feel good in the presence of an object, they often infer that they like it, even if those good feelings were caused by something else. Finally, the effectiveness of persuasive communications also depends on the type of attitude people have. Appeals to emotion and social identity work best if the attitude is based on emotion and social identity.

Resisting Persuasive Messages

Attitude inoculation is the technique whereby people are exposed to small doses of arguments against their position, making it easier for them to refute these arguments when they hear the arguments later. This approach may also inoculate people against attacks that play on their emotions and values, if people are first given small doses of these kinds of attacks. Another way to make people resistant is to warn them in advance that someone will be trying to change their attitudes. When people were forewarned, they analyze what they see and hear more carefully and as a result are likely to avoid attitude change. Attempts to manage people's attitudes, however, should not be used with too heavy a hand. Strongly prohibiting people from engaging in certain behaviors can actually cause an increase in liking for those activities. According to **reactance theory,** people experience an unpleasant state called reactance when their freedom of choice is threatened. One way people can reduce reactance is to perform the behavior that was threatened.

When Will Attitudes Predict Behavior?

To understand when attitudes will predict behavior, we need to distinguish between behaviors that are spontaneous and those that are more planned and deliberative. Attitudes predict spontaneous behaviors only when they are relatively accessible. **Attitude accessibility** refers to the strength of the association between an object and an evaluation of it, which is typically measured by the speed with which people can report how they feel about an issue or object. When attitudes are inaccessible, behavior is more likely to be influenced by situational and social factors. The **theory of planned behavior** specifies how we can predict people's planned and deliberative behaviors. Here it is necessary to know people's attitudes toward the specific act in question, their subjective norms (people's beliefs about how others view the behavior in question), and how much people believe they can control the behavior.

The Power of Advertising

Advertising has been found to be quite effective at changing people's attitudes, as indicated by split cable market tests. It is most effective when the ad is tailored to the kind of attitude people have and when the product is made to appear to be personally relevant to people. One kind of advertising that has caused public concern is the use of words or pictures that are supposedly perceived unconsciously—**subliminal messages.** Despite people's fears, this type of advertising has not been shown to influence consumer behavior. Under controlled laboratory conditions, subliminal messages can have subtle effects on people's preferences, but there is no evidence that subliminal messages have been used successfully in real-world marketing campaigns. The use of such messages in self-help tapes is also ineffective.

Regular advertisements transmit cultural stereotypes in their words and images, as well as influence consumer attitudes. Advertisements that portray women in stereotypical ways, for example, can trigger **stereotype threat,** which is the apprehension experienced by members of a group that their behavior might confirm a cultural stereotype. In one study, women who saw an ad that portrayed women in stereotypical ways performed more poorly on a math test than women who saw an ad that portrayed women in counterstereotypical ways.

CRITICAL THINKING QUESTIONS

1. Suppose you were hired by the marketing department of a fast-food company to increase sales. You will be responsible for designing a new line of advertisements to create positive attitudes toward the company's restaurants. What would you do and why, based on the research discussed in this chapter?

2. Now suppose you were hired by the health department to get people to resist ads for fast-food restaurants and eat healthier diets. How would you make people resistant to the advertisements you designed in question 1?

3. Why is it that people seem to change some of their attitudes frequently (e.g., approval ratings of U.S. presidents often fluctuate widely over short periods of time), whereas other attitudes are very hard to change?

4. Think about some recent advertisements you have seen on television or in magazines. Can you think of examples of ads that targeted different kinds of attitudes? How did they do so? Do you think the ad campaigns will be successful, given the kinds of attitudes they are trying to change? Why or why not?

Answers, *Try it!* Page 213

Scoring: First, reverse your responses to items 3, 4, 5, 7, 8, 9, 12, 16, and 17. Do so as follows: If you gave a 1 to these questions, change it to a 5; if you gave a 2, change it to a 4; if you gave a 3, leave it the same; if you gave a 4, change it to a 2; if you gave a 5, change it to a 1. Then add up your answers to all eighteen questions.

People who are high in the need for cognition score slightly higher in verbal intelligence but no higher in abstract reasoning. And there are no gender differences in the need for cognition.

Answers, *Try it!* Page 231

Question 1: Wilson, Gilbert, and Wheatley (1998) found that 80 percent of college students preferred not to receive a subliminal message because it might influence them in an undesirable way

Question 2: Wilson, Gilbert, and Wheatley (1998) found that only 28 percent of college students preferred not to receive a regular everyday TV ad because it might influence them in an undesirable way

Question 3: When Wilson, Houston, & Meyers (1998) asked college students to choose to listen to the type of speech they thought would influence them the least, 69 percent chose the regular speech and 31 percent chose the subliminal speech. Ironically, it was the regular speech that changed people's minds the most.

Conformity:

Influencing Behavior

Consider the recent case of Shannon Faulkner, who found that no matter how hard she tried to obey and conform to a group's rules, she was rejected. Shannon was an entering cadet at the Citadel, a military college in Charleston, South Carolina. For 153 years, the Citadel had been an all-male institution, but a federal court ruled that as a public institution supported by South Carolina taxpayers, the Citadel could not exclude a state resident just because she was female. Shannon Faulkner was admitted.

The students and faculty of the Citadel were not pleased. Faulkner followed all the rules of the Citadel during her first week, but her gender made her deviant from the group norm, and she was punished. On her first day, the beginning of what the school calls "Hell Week," signs saying "Shannon go home" greeted her. "You should have heard the way they were talking to me, calling me names," Faulkner said. "I never looked in their direction. I did what the other guys were doing. I got in line and did what I was supposed to do" (Rogers, Dampier, & Sieder, 1995, p. 78).

The stress of being different, of having no support, soon made Shannon sick, and after a few days in the school infirmary, Faulkner withdrew from the Citadel. As a male junior cadet said, "You just don't make it here on your own. You have to rely on each other, [but] she had no one. No one spoke to her, and that wasn't going to change" (p. 80). When news spread that Faulkner had left the campus, the cadets rejoiced boisterously and enthusiastically. (Since the Faulkner case, other women have entered the freshman class at the Citadel. Norms for appropriate conduct have changed at the institution, and the women have successfully completed their education.)

More problems with conformity and obedience struck the military academies in 2003. The United States Air Force Academy was rocked by allegations that female cadets had been raped by male cadets. When the women reported the sexual assaults, they stated that they were ignored by the male commanding officers or punished for infractions; their attackers were not punished. Other women acknowledged that they had not reported rape or sexual har-

237

rassment because they were afraid of what would happen to them if they did. These allegations prompted Pentagon and congressional investigations, criminal proceedings against the accused rapists, the replacement of the top four commanding officers of the academy, and a demotion in military rank for the general who was the superintendent (Sarche, 2003; Schemo, 2003).

What had gone so horribly wrong? In a setting where conformity and obedience are highly valued norms, manipulation can occur. For example, first-year cadets have to obey the orders of older students, who outrank them. This cadet command structure can be abused; some of the women reported that they were ordered by a male student to meet him at a certain time and place, where they were raped. In addition, the strong honor code of the academies promotes conformity and makes it difficult for a given individual to violate the norms. A professor who studies the military put it this way: "Part of the strong honor code system is the idea that you owe your loyalty to the Academy, to the service, and to your superiors. You don't want to rat out your peers. Individuals are worried about being labeled as someone who is not part of the team" (Bender, 2003, p. A10).

Issues surrounding conformity are not limited to special settings like the military academies. Every social setting that you encounter has "rules." Some of the rules are explicit. They may even be laws, such as those in the criminal code or those that govern driving a car. Other rules are implicit and therefore subtle. They include expectations that people have for appropriate behavior: for example, behaving respectfully in conversations with one's professors or joining the end of a line instead of cutting in at the front.

Both conformity and obedience are our responses to the social influence tactics of others. We usually do what others want because they have explicitly ordered us to do so (obedience) or because they have more subtly indicated to us what is appropriate and it seems in our best interest to go along (conformity). In this chapter, we will focus on the potentially positive and negative effects of these social influence processes.

CONFORMITY: WHEN AND WHY

Which one of the two quotations on page 239 do you find more appealing? Which one describes your immediate reaction to the word *conformity*? We wouldn't be surprised if you preferred the second quotation. American culture stresses the importance of not conforming (Hofstede, 1986; Markus, Kitayama, & Heiman, 1996). We think of ourselves as a nation of rugged individualists, people who think for themselves, who stand up for the underdog, who go against the tide for what they think is right. This cultural self-image has been shaped by the manner in which our nation was founded, by our system of government, and by our society's historical experience with western expansion—the "taming" of the Wild West (Turner, 1932).

American mythology has celebrated the rugged individualist in many ways. For example, one of the longest-running and most successful advertising campaigns in American history features the "Marlboro Man." Since 1955, the photograph of a cowboy alone on the range has been an archetypal image. It has also sold a lot of cigarettes. People who have never seen a horse, let alone the American West, have responded for nearly half a century to this simple, evocative image. Clearly, it tells us something about ourselves that we want and like to hear: that we make up our own minds; that we're not spineless, weak conformists; that we're not puppets but players (Buehler & Griffin, 1994).

But are we, in fact, nonconforming creatures? Are the decisions we make always based on what we think, or do we sometimes use other people's behavior to help us decide what to do? As we saw in Chapter 6, the mass suicide of the Heaven's Gate cult members suggests that people sometimes conform in extreme and surprising ways—even when making such a fundamental decision as whether or not to take their own lives. But, you might argue, this is an unusual and extreme case. Perhaps the followers of Marshall Applewhite were disturbed people who were somehow predisposed to do what a charismatic leader told them to do. There is, however, another, more chilling possibility: Maybe most of us would have acted the same way, had we been exposed to the same long-standing, powerful conformity pressures as the members of Heaven's Gate. According to this view, almost anyone would have conformed in these same extreme circumstances.

If this statement is true, we should be able to find other situations in which people, put under strong social pressures, conform to a surprising degree. For example, in 1961, activists in the American civil rights movement incorporated Mohandas Gandhi's principles of nonviolent protest into their demonstrations to end segregation. They trained their "Freedom Riders" in the passive acceptance of violent treatment. Thousands of southern African Americans, joined by a smaller number of northern whites, many from college campuses, demonstrated against the segregationist laws of the South. In one confrontation after another, the civil rights activists reacted nonviolently as they were beaten, clubbed, hosed, whipped, raped, and even killed by southern sheriffs and police (Powledge, 1991). Their powerful show of conformity to the ideal of nonviolent protest helped usher in a new era in America's fight for equality—passage of the Civil Rights Act of 1964.

Now consider the case of the My Lai massacre in Vietnam. On the morning of March 16, 1968, at the height of the Vietnam War, a company of American soldiers boarded helicopters that would take them to the village of My Lai. The soldiers were very apprehensive because they had never been in combat before and the village was rumored to be occupied by the Forty-Eighth Vietcong Battalion, one of the most feared units of the enemy. One of the helicopter pilots radioed that he saw Vietcong soldiers below, and so the American soldiers jumped off the helicopters, rifles blazing. They soon realized that the pilot was wrong—there were no enemy soldiers. Instead, the Americans found several villagers, all women, children, and elderly men, cooking breakfast over small fires. Inexplicably, the leader of the platoon, Lieutenant William Calley, ordered one of the soldiers to kill the villagers. Other soldiers began firing too, and the carnage spread. The Americans rounded up and systematically murdered all the villagers of My Lai. They shoved women and children into a ravine and shot them; they threw hand grenades into huts filled with cowering villagers. Though no one knows the exact number of deaths, the estimates range from 450 to 500 Vietnamese civilians (Hersh, 1970).

> Do as most do, and [people] will speak well of thee.
> —Thomas Fuller

> It were not best that we should all think alike; it is difference of opinion that makes horse races.
> —Mark Twain

Under strong social pressure, individuals will conform to the group, even when this means doing something immoral. During the Vietnam War, American soldiers massacred several hundred Vietnamese civilians—old men, women, and children—in the village of My Lai. This award-winning photograph of some of the victims chilled the nation. Why did the soldiers commit this atrocity? As you read this chapter, you will see how the social influence pressures of conformity and obedience can cause decent people to commit indecent acts.

In all of these examples, people found themselves caught in a web of social influence. In response, they changed their behavior and conformed to the expectations of others. For social psychologists, this is the essence of **conformity:** changing one's behavior due to the real or imagined influence of others (Kiesler & Kiesler, 1969). As these examples show, the consequences of conformity can span a wide range, from usefulness and nobility to hysteria and tragedy. But why did these people conform? Some probably conformed because they did not know what to do in a confusing or unusual situation. The behavior of the people around them served as a cue as to how to respond, and they decided to act in a similar manner. Other people probably conformed because they did not wish to be ridiculed or punished for being different from everybody else. They chose to act the way the group expected them to act so that they wouldn't be rejected or thought less of by group members. Let's see how each of these reasons for conforming operates.

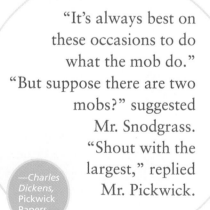

"It's always best on these occasions to do what the mob do." "But suppose there are two mobs?" suggested Mr. Snodgrass. "Shout with the largest," replied Mr. Pickwick.

—*Charles Dickens,* Pickwick Papers

INFORMATIONAL SOCIAL INFLUENCE: THE NEED TO KNOW WHAT'S "RIGHT"

How should you address your psychology professor—as "Dr. Berman," "Professor Berman," "Ms. Berman," or "Patricia"? How should you vote in the upcoming referendum that would raise your tuition to cover expanded student services? Do you cut a piece of sushi or eat it whole? Did the scream you just heard in the hallway come from a person joking with friends or from the victim of a mugging?

In these and many other situations, we feel uncertain about what to think or how to act. We simply don't know enough to make a good or accurate choice. Luckily, we have a powerful and useful source of knowledge available to us—the behavior of other people. Asking others what they think or watching what they do helps us reach a definition of the situation (Kelley, 1955; Thomas, 1928). When we subsequently act like everyone else, we are conforming, but not because we are weak, spineless individuals with no self-reliance. Instead, the influence of other people leads us to conform because we see them as a source of information to guide our behavior. We conform because we believe that others' interpretation of an ambiguous situation is more accurate than

Conformity

A change in one's behavior due to the real or imagined influence of other people ours and will help us choose an appropriate course of action. This is called **informational social influence** (Cialdini, 2000; Cialdini, Kallgren, & Reno, 1991; Deutsch & Gerard, 1955; MacNeil & Sherif, 1976).

As an illustration of how other people can be a source of information, imagine that you are a participant in the following experiment by Muzafer Sherif (1936). In the first phase of the study, you are seated alone in a dark room and asked to focus your attention on a dot of light 15 feet away. The experimenter asks you to estimate in inches how far the light moves. You stare earnestly at the light, and yes, it moves a little. You say, "About two inches," though it is not easy to tell exactly. The light disappears and then comes back; you are asked to judge again. The light seems to move a little more, and you say, "Four inches." After several of these trials, the light seems to move about the same amount each time—about 2 to 4 inches.

The interesting thing about this task is that the light was not actually moving at all. It looked like it was moving because of a visual illusion called the autokinetic effect. If you stare at a bright light in a uniformly dark environment (e.g., a star on a dark night), the light will appear to waver back and forth. This occurs because you have no stable reference point to anchor the position of the light. The distance that the light appears to move varies from person to person but becomes consistent for each person over time. In Sherif's experiment, the subjects all arrived at their own stable estimate during the first phase of the study, but these estimates differed from person to person. Some people thought the light was moving only an inch or so; others thought it was moving as much as 10 inches.

Sherif chose to use the autokinetic effect because he wanted a situation that would be ambiguous—where the correct definition of the situation would be unclear to his participants. In the second phase of the experiment, a few days later, the participants were paired with two other people, each of whom had had the same prior experience alone with the light. Now the situation became a truly social one, as all three made their judgments out loud. Remember, the autokinetic effect is experienced differently by different people; some see a lot of movement and some see not much at all. After hearing their partners give judgments that were different from their own, what did people do?

Over the course of several trials, people reached a common estimate, and each member of the group conformed to that estimate. These results indicate that people were using each other as a source of information, coming to believe that the group estimate was the correct one (see Figure 8.1). An important feature of informational social influence is that it can lead to **private acceptance,** when people conform to the behavior of others because they genuinely believe that these other people are right.

Informational Social Influence

The influence of other people that leads us to conform because we see them as a source of information to guide our behavior; we conform because we believe that others' interpretation of an ambiguous situation is more correct than ours and will help us choose an appropriate course of action

Private Acceptance

Conforming to other people's behavior out of a genuine belief that what they are doing or saying is right

FIGURE 8.1

One group's judgments in Sherif's (1936) autokinetic studies.

People estimated how far a point of light appeared to move in a dark room. When they saw the light by themselves, their estimates varied widely. When they were brought together in groups and heard other people announce their estimates, people conformed to the group's estimate of how much the light moved.

(Adapted from Sherif, 1936)

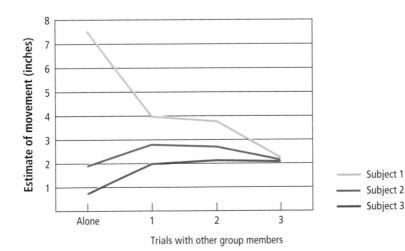

critical trials. In the high-importance condition, participants conformed to the confederates' judgments on 51 percent of the critical trials.

As we've noted, when a situation is ambiguous and choosing the right answer is difficult, we look to others to give us the additional information we need. Baron and his colleagues found that in such situations, the more important the decision is to us, the more we will rely on other people for information and guidance.

Other researchers have explored decision making in groups where the task was a very difficult one involving recognition memory (Levine, Higgins, & Choi, 2000). The three-person groups consisted of research participants (there were no confederates in the group). They were shown brief glimpses of nonsense words (sequences of letters that do not spell a real word) and then a big list of more nonsense words, some of which they'd just seen and some of which were new. Their job was to say, out loud, whether each test word on the big list was new or one they'd seen before. The researchers explored the role of importance in a new way—they manipulated what kind of answer was important. Half the research participants were told that their group would start with $3, to be divided equally among them. However, they would receive an additional $3 if the answers of all three of them were at least 80 percent correct. We'll call this the "risky strategy" condition.

The other half were told that their group would start with $6, to be divided equally. However, they would lose $3 if the answers of all three of them were more than 20 percent incorrect. We'll call this the "cautious strategy" condition. Note that these two sets of instructions are actually identical. The most money both types of groups could get was $6 and the least $3, and they both had to give the right answers at least 80 percent of the time. But the way the instructions were worded gives a very different feeling—in one case, it sounds like a good idea to "go for it," take risks, and get that extra money. In the other case, it sounds like a good idea to be cautious so as not to lose the initial money. In the study, the groups then responded to the memory recognition task, which is a very difficult, ambiguous task. How did the members of the group respond?

The experimenters found that the group members' answers converged, just as they had in Sherif's study on the autokinetic effect. Over the trials, the participants in each group increasingly gave the same answers. What's interesting is that they converged in one direction or the other, depending on their initial instructions. The "risky strategy" group made increasingly risky judgments (defined on a recognition memory task as giving more "Yes, seen that word before" responses), while the "cautious strategy" group made increasingly cautious judgments (giving more "No, didn't see it before" responses). This occurred without the participants' discussing strategy or anything else. They simply paid attention to each other's responses. They used these responses to help them make sense of an ambiguous situation, which in turn enabled them to make their own judgments (Levine, Higgins, & Choi, 2000).

In real life, informational conformity can lead a group to adopt a "risky strategy"—with tragic results. On February 1, 2003, the space shuttle *Challenger* exploded during reentry over the United States, killing all the astronauts aboard. A piece of insulating foam had broken off the shuttle and hit its wing during the launch. The resulting gash in the wing allowed superheated gases to enter the shuttle, with catastrophic results (Schwartz, 2003). NASA was aware that foam pieces had broken off during prior launches of the shuttle, but it was not perceived as a problem within the agency. An independent investigating panel formed by the government stated in its report that the accident was the result of "a flawed institutional culture" that play(ed) down "problems . . . (and) risky anomalies" and consider(ed) them "to be . . . part of the realm of the acceptable" (Schwartz & Wald, 2003, pp. A1, A12).

Thus when you aren't sure what to think or do and it is important that you figure out an answer, you are more likely to engage in informational conformity.

In an ambiguous situation, this is a good strategy, but it does come with risks: What if the other people are wrong?

When Informational Conformity Backfires

A dramatic form of informational social influence occurs during crises, when an individual is confronted with a frightening, potentially dangerous situation to which he or she is ill-equipped to respond (Killian, 1964). The person may have no idea of what is really happening or what he or she should do. When one's personal safety is involved, the need for information is acute—and the behavior of others is very informative.

Consider what happened on Halloween Night in 1938. Orson Welles, the gifted actor and film director, and the Mercury Theater broadcast a radio play based loosely on H. G. Wells's science fiction fantasy *War of the Worlds*. Remember, this was the era before television; radio was a primary source of entertainment, with music, comedy, and drama programs, and the only source for fast-breaking news. That night, the drama that Welles and his fellow actors broadcast—portraying the invasion of Earth by hostile Martians—was so realistic that at least a million listeners became frightened and alerted the police; several thousand were so panic-stricken that they tried to flee the "invasion" in their cars (Cantril, 1940).

Why were so many Americans convinced that what they heard was a real news report of an actual invasion by aliens? Hadley Cantril (1940), who studied this real-life "crisis," suggested two reasons. One was that the play parodied existing radio news shows very well, and many listeners missed the beginning of the broadcast (when it was clearly identified as a play) because they had been listening to the nation's top-rated show, *Charlie McCarthy*, on another station. The other culprit, however, was informational social influence. Many people were listening with friends and family and naturally turned to each other, out of uncertainty, to see whether they should believe what they heard. Seeing looks of concern and worry on their loved ones' faces added to the panic people were beginning to feel. "We all kissed one another and felt we would all die," reported one listener (Cantril, 1940, p. 95).

In addition, many frightened listeners misinterpreted actual events so that they fit the news on the radio program: "We looked out the window and Wyoming Avenue was black with cars. People were rushing away, I figured," or "No cars came down my street. Traffic is jammed on account of the roads being destroyed, I thought" (Cantril, 1940, p. 93). When a situation is highly ambiguous and people begin to believe they know what is happening, they will even reinterpret potentially disconfirming evidence so that it fits their definition of the situation.

> Ninety-nine percent of the people in the world are fools, and the rest of us are in great danger of contagion.
>
> —*Thornton Wilder, The Matchmaker*

The New York Times headlined the War of the Worlds incident. Partly because of informational social influences, many listeners believed that Orson Welles' radio broadcast about an invasion by Martians was true.

The *Southern Standard* headlined a frightening and mysterious event at a local Tennessee high school. In fact, an investigation proved that the "poisonings" were a case of mass psychogenic illness.

A late-nineteenth-century social scientist, Gustav Le Bon (1895), was the first researcher to document how emotions and behavior can spread rapidly through a crowd—an effect he called **contagion** (Gump & Kulik, 1997; Hatfield, Cacioppo, & Rapson, 1993; Levy & Nail, 1993). As we have learned, in a truly ambiguous situation, people will most likely rely on the interpretation of others. Unfortunately, in a truly ambiguous and confusing situation, other people may be no more knowledgeable or accurate than we are. If other people are misinformed, we will adopt their mistakes and misinterpretations. Depending on others to help us define the situation can therefore sometimes lead us into serious inaccuracies.

An example of extreme and misdirected informational social influence is **mass psychogenic illness** (Bartholomew & Wessely, 2002; Colligan, Pennebaker, & Murphy, 1982), the occurrence of similar physical symptoms, with no known physical cause, in a group of people. For example, in 1998, a teacher at a high school in Tennessee reported the smell of gasoline in her classroom; soon she experienced headache, nausea, shortness of breath, and dizziness. As her class was being evacuated, others in the school reported similar symptoms. The decision was made to evacuate the entire school. Everyone watched as the teacher and some students were placed in ambulances. Local experts investigated and could find nothing wrong with the school. Classes resumed—and more people reported feeling sick. Again, the school was evacuated and closed. Experts from numerous government agencies were called in to conduct an environmental and epidemiological investigation. Again, nothing was found to be wrong with the school. When it reopened this time, the epidemic of mysterious illness was over (Altman, 2000).

Timothy Jones, of the Tennessee Department of Health, led a study of this unusual case. In all, more than 170 students, teachers, and staff had gone to the hospital with symptoms for which no organic cause was ever found. Jones and his colleagues (2000) determined that mass psychogenic illness was the cause. This form of contagion usually begins with just one person or a few people reporting physical symptoms; typically, these people are experiencing some kind of stress in their lives. Other people around them construct what seems to be a reasonable explanation for their illness. This explanation, a new definition of the situation, spreads, and more people begin to think that they, too, have symptoms. As the number of afflicted people grows, both the physical symptoms and their supposed explanation become more credible and thus more widespread (Colligan et al., 1982; Kerckhoff & Back, 1968; Singer, Baum, Baum, & Thew, 1982). In the Tennessee high school case, the students who became sick were more likely than students who did not get sick to report having directly observed an ill person during the outbreak or to have known a classmate who was ill. Clearly, the "information" that defined vague symptoms (or even no symptoms) as a frightening, building-caused illness had spread through direct contact. In addition, dramatic and extensive media coverage of the event increased people's anxiety and spread more "information" about what was supposedly happening.

Donald Johnson conducted a now classic study on mass psychogenic illness, that of the "phantom anesthetist" of Mattoon, Illinois. It began when a woman told police that someone had gassed her through her bedroom window. Soon, many residents claimed they too had been gassed; the state police were eventually called in to handle the investigation. In fact, there was no psychopathic "gasser" on the loose. It was 1944 and people were feeling stress due to World War II. How did this contagion spread? How did some people come to believe that their physical ailments were symptoms of a bizarre attack? Johnson (1945)

Contagion

The rapid spread of emotions or behaviors through a crowd

Mass Psychogenic Illness

The occurrence, in a group of people, of similar physical symptoms with no known physical cause

determined that informational social influence had occurred primarily via newspaper articles. Few of the victims knew each other, and so they had not spread the information interpersonally. Instead, blaring headlines and sensationalistic articles in the town newspapers were the means by which a new definition of the situation was communicated.

What is particularly interesting about modern cases of mass psychogenic illness (as well as other peculiar forms of conformity) is the powerful role that the mass media play in their dissemination. Through television, radio, newspapers, magazines, the Internet, and e-mail, information is spread quickly and efficiently to all segments of the population. Whereas in the Middle Ages it took two hundred years for the "dancing manias" (a kind of psychogenic illness) to crisscross Europe (Sirois, 1982), today it takes only minutes for most of the inhabitants of the planet to learn about an unusual event. Luckily, the mass media also have the power to quickly squelch these uprisings of contagion by introducing more logical explanations for ambiguous events.

When Will People Conform to Informational Social Influence?

Let's review the situations that are the most likely to produce conformity because of informational social influence.

When the Situation Is Ambiguous   Ambiguity is the most crucial variable for determining how much people use each other as a source of information. When you are unsure of the correct response, the appropriate behavior, or the right idea, you will be most open to influence from others. The more uncertain you are, the more you will rely on others (Allen, 1965; Baron et al., 1996; Tesser, Campbell, & Mickler, 1983). Situations such as My Lai were ambiguous ones for the people involved, ideal circumstances for informational social influence to take hold. The soldiers were young (typically 18 or 19) and very inexperienced. For most of them, this was their first combat situation. When they saw a few other soldiers begin shooting at the villagers, most of them thought this is what they were supposed to do too, and they joined in.

When the Situation Is a Crisis   Crisis, another variable that promotes the use of others as a source of information, often occurs simultaneously with ambiguity. In a crisis situation, we usually do not have time to stop and think about exactly which course of action we should take. We need to act—immediately. If we feel scared and panicky and are uncertain what to do, it is only natural for us to see how other people are responding and to do likewise. Unfortunately, the people we imitate may also feel scared and panicky and not be behaving rationally.

The soldiers at My Lai, for example, expected to experience combat with the Vietcong when they arrived at the village of My Lai. They were undoubtedly scared and on edge. Further, it was not easy to tell who the enemy was. In the Vietnam War, Vietnamese civilians who were sympathizers of the Vietcong were known to have laid mines in the path of U.S. soldiers, fired guns from hidden locations, and thrown or planted grenades. In a guerrilla war like Vietnam, it was often difficult to tell if people were civilians or combatants, allies or enemies. So when one or two soldiers began firing on the villagers in My Lai, it is perhaps not surprising that others followed suit, believing this to be the proper course of action. Had the soldiers not been in a crisis situation and instead had more time to think about their actions, perhaps the tragedy would have been avoided.

When Other People Are Experts   Typically, the more expertise or knowledge a person has, the more valuable he or she will be as a guide in an ambiguous situation (Allison, 1992; Bickman, 1974; Cialdini & Trost, 1998). For example, a

Try it!

One of the most interesting examples of informational social influence in action is the behavior of bystanders in emergencies. An emergency is by definition a crisis situation. In many respects, it is an ambiguous situation as well; sometimes there are "experts" present, but sometimes there aren't. In an emergency, the bystander is thinking: What's happening? Is help needed? What should I do? What's everybody else doing?

As you'll recall from the story told by Robin Akert on page xxxv, trying to decide if an emergency is really happening and if your help is really needed can be very difficult. Bystanders often rely on informational social influence to help them figure out what to do, but as we saw in the story in the Preface, if other people are acting like nothing is wrong, you could be misled by their behavior and interpret the situation as a nonemergency too. In that case, informational social influence has backfired.

To explore informational social influence, gather some stories about people's reactions to emergencies when they were bystanders (not victims). Think about your own experiences, and ask your friends to tell you about emergencies they have been in. As you recollect your own experience or talk to your friends about their experiences, note how informational social influence played a role:

1. How did you (and your friends) decide that an emergency was really occurring? Did you glance at other passersby and watch their response? Did you talk to other people to help you figure out what was going on?

2. Once you decided that it was an emergency, how did you decide what to do? Did you do what other people were doing? Did you show or tell them what to do?

3. Were there any experts present, people who knew more about the situation or how to offer assistance? Did you do what the experts told you to do? If you were in the role of expert (or were at least knowledgeable) at the scene of the emergency, did people follow your lead?

The issues raised by these questions are all examples of informational social influence in action.

passenger who sees smoke coming out of an airplane engine will probably check the flight attendants' reaction rather than their seatmates'. However, experts are not always reliable sources of information. Imagine the fear felt by the young man listening to the *War of the Worlds* broadcast who called his local police department for an explanation, only to learn that the police, too, thought the events described on the radio were actually happening (Cantril, 1940)! (In the Try It! exercise above, you can explore how the informational social influence variables of ambiguity, crisis, and expertise have operated in your life and your friend's lives.)

Resisting Informational Social Influence

Relying on others to help us define what is happening can be an excellent idea, or it can be a tragedy in the making. How can we tell when other people are a good source of information and when we should resist their definition of a situation?

First, remember that it is possible to resist illegitimate or inaccurate informational social influence. In all of our examples, some people resisted conforming to what they perceived to be incorrect information. At My Lai, not all the soldiers took part in the atrocity. One sergeant said he'd been ordered to "destroy the village," but he simply refused to follow the order. Another soldier, watching as the others fired on civilians, intentionally shot himself in the foot so that he would have an excuse to be evacuated from the killing scene. One helicopter pilot, looking down on the grisly sight, landed and scooped up fifteen Vietnamese children and ferried them off to safety deep in the forest. Thus some soldiers rejected the behavior of others as a correct definition of what they should do. Instead, they relied on what they knew was right and moral and refused to take part in the massacre of innocent people.

Similarly, during the *War of the Worlds* broadcast, not all listeners panicked (Cantril, 1940). Some engaged in rational problem solving; they checked other stations on the radio dial and discovered that no other station was broadcasting the same news. Instead of relying on others and being caught up in the contagion and mass panic, they searched for and found information on their own.

One reason that the decision about whether to conform is so important is that it influences how people define reality. If you decide to accept other people's definition of the situation, you will come to see the world as they do. This basic fact was demonstrated in an interesting study (Buehler & Griffin, 1994). Researchers asked students to read newspaper reports of a real and highly controversial incident in which an African American teenager driving a stolen car was shot and killed by white police officers. Many of the details of the situation were ambiguous, such as how much the youth had threatened the officers and how much the officers feared for their lives.

Participants were asked first how they interpreted the situation: How fast was the victim's car going? Was the victim trying to ram the police car? Did he realize that his pursuers were the police? What were the police officers thinking and feeling? Each participant was then told that other participants had agreed with the statement that the police were 75 percent responsible and the victim 25 percent responsible. After indicating whether they agreed with this assessment, the participants were asked how they interpreted the situation. The question was, did people's interpretation of the situation change, depending on whether they agreed with other people's assessments?

First, not everyone conformed to other people's views. In fact, only 32 percent of the participants agreed that the police were 75 percent responsible for the incident. Clearly, we can resist informational influence. Did people's decision about whether to conform influence their definition of the situation? The answer is yes: Participants who agreed with others that the police were responsible changed their interpretations to be consistent with the group; they now believed that the victim had not threatened the police and that police were not in fear of their lives. What about the people who did not conform? Interestingly, they also changed their interpretations, but in the opposite direction—they now believed that the victim's car was about to ram the police and that the police feared for their lives. In short, people changed their interpretations of reality to bolster their decision about whether to agree with the majority opinion.

Your decision as to whether to conform to informational influence, then, will affect not only your behavior but also your interpretation of reality (Bless, Strack, & Walther, 2001; Hoffman, Granhag, See, & Loftus, 2001). Evaluating whether other people's reaction to a situation is any more legitimate than your own, then, is extremely important. Ask yourself:

- Do other people know any more about what is going on than I do? Is there an expert handy, someone who should know more?
- Do the actions of other people or experts seem sensible? If I behave the way they do, will it go against my common sense or against my internal moral compass, my sense of right and wrong?

> Yes, we must, indeed, all hang together or, most assuredly, we shall all hang separately.
>
> —*Benjamin Franklin at the signing of the Declaration of Independence, 1776*

The desire to be accepted and liked by others can lead to dangerous behavior. Here, Brazilian teenagers "surf" on top of trains because it has become the popular thing to do in their peer group.

By knowing how informational social influence works in daily life, you are in a better position to know when it is useful and when it is not.

NORMATIVE SOCIAL INFLUENCE: THE NEED TO BE ACCEPTED

In the 1990s in Rio de Janeiro, Brazil, teenage boys and girls engaged in a dangerous and reckless game: "surfing" on the tops of trains, standing with arms outstretched as the trains sped along. Despite the fact that an average of 150 teenagers died each year from this activity and 400 more were injured by falling off the trains or hitting the 3,000-volt electric cable, the surfing continued (Arnett, 1995). In the United States, one teenager died and two more were critically injured when they responded to a dare to reenact a scene from the movie *The Program.* Like the movie's protagonist, they lay down in the middle of a highway at night. Unlike the movie's protagonist, they were run over (Hinds, 1993).

Why do some adolescents engage in such risky behavior? Why does anyone follow the group's lead when the resulting behavior is less than sensible and may even be dangerous? We doubt that the Brazilian or American teenagers risked their lives due to informational conformity—it is difficult to argue that a boy or girl staring at a train would say, "Gee, I don't know what to do. I guess standing on top of a train going 60 miles an hour makes a lot of sense; everybody else is doing it." This example tells us that something else explains why we conform besides the need for information: We also conform so that we will be liked and accepted by other people. We conform to the group's **social norms,** which are implicit (and sometimes explicit) rules for acceptable behaviors, values, and beliefs (Deutsch & Gerard, 1955; Kelley, 1955; Miller & Prentice, 1996). Groups have certain expectations about how the group members should behave, and members in good standing conform to these rules. Members who do not are perceived as different, difficult, and eventually deviant.

Social Norms

The implicit or explicit rules a group has for the acceptable behaviors, values, and beliefs of its members

Deviant members can be ridiculed, punished, or even rejected by other group members (Kruglanski & Webster, 1991; Levine, 1989; Miller & Anderson, 1979; Schachter, 1951), sometimes with tragic consequences. In Japan, a whole class (even the entire school) will turn against one student perceived as different. The students will alternate between harassing and shunning the individual. In a highly cohesive, group-oriented culture like Japan, this kind of treatment has had profound and tragic results: Twelve teenage victims of bullying killed themselves in one year (Jordan, 1996). (In Chapter 12, we'll consider the circumstances of two outsiders at Columbine High School in Colorado who killed a dozen classmates, a teacher, and themselves.)

We human beings are by nature a social species. Few of us could live happily as hermits, never seeing or talking to another person. Through interactions with others, we receive emotional support, affection, and love, and we partake of enjoyable experiences. Other people are extraordinarily important to our sense of well-being. Research on individuals who have been isolated for long periods of time indicates that being deprived of human contact is stressful and traumatic (Baumeister & Leary, 1995; Curtiss, 1977; Schachter, 1959; Zubek, 1969).

Given this fundamental human need for social companionship, it is not surprising that we often conform in order to be accepted by others. Conformity for normative reasons occurs in situations where we do what other people are doing not because we are using them as a source of information but because we won't attract attention, be made fun of, get into trouble, or be rejected. Thus **normative social influence** occurs when the influence of other people leads us to conform in order to be liked and accepted by them. This type of conformity results in public compliance with the group's beliefs and behaviors but not necessarily in private acceptance (Cialdini et al., 1991; Deutsch & Gerard, 1955; Levine, 1999; Nail, McDonald, & Levy, 2000).

You probably don't find it too surprising that people sometimes conform in order to be liked and accepted by others. You might be thinking, where's the harm? If the group is important to us and wearing the right clothes or using hip words will gain us acceptance, why not go along? But when it comes to more important kinds of behaviors, such as hurting another person, surely we will resist such conformity pressures. And surely we won't conform when we are certain of what the correct way of behaving is and the pressures are coming from a group that we don't care all that much about. Or will we?

Conformity and Social Approval: The Asch Line Judgment Studies

To find out, Solomon Asch (1951, 1956) conducted a series of now classic studies exploring the power of normative social influence. Asch devised the studies assuming that there are limits to how much people will conform. Naturally, people conformed in the Sherif studies (see page 241), he reasoned, because the situation was highly ambiguous—trying to guess how much a light was moving. But when a situation was completely unambiguous, Asch expected that people would act like rational, objective problem solvers. When the group said or did something that contradicted an obvious truth, surely people would resist social pressures and decide for themselves what was going on.

To test his hypothesis, Asch conducted the following study. Had you been a participant, you would have been told that this was an experiment on perceptual judgment and that you would be taking part with seven other students. Here's the scenario: The experimenter shows everyone two cards, one with a single line on it, the other with three lines labeled 1, 2, and 3. He asks each of you to judge

Normative Social Influence

The influence of other people that leads us to conform in order to be liked and accepted by them; this type of conformity results in public compliance with the group's beliefs and behaviors but not necessarily private acceptance of those beliefs and behaviors

FIGURE 8.2

The judgment task in Asch's line studies.

In a study of normative social influence, participants judged which of the three comparison lines on the right was closest in length to the standard line on the left. The correct answer was obvious (as it is here). However, members of the group (actually confederates) gave the wrong answer out loud. Now the participant was in a dilemma: Should he give the right answer and go against the whole group, or should he conform to their behavior and give the obviously wrong answer?

(Adapted from Asch, 1956)

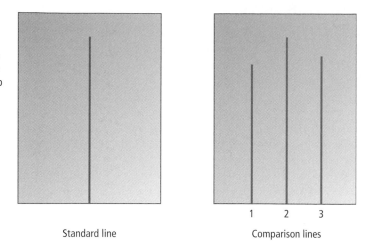

Standard line

Comparison lines

and then announce out loud which of the three lines on the second card is closest in length to the line on the first card (see Figure 8.2).

It is crystal-clear that the correct answer is the second line. Not surprisingly, each participant says, "Line 2." Your turn comes next to last, and of course you say, "Line 2" as well. The last participant concurs. The experimenter then presents a new set of cards and asks the participants again to make their judgments and announce them out loud. Again, the answer is obvious, and everyone gives the correct answer. At this point, you are probably thinking to yourself, "What a waste of time. I've got a paper due tomorrow. I need to get out of here."

As your mind starts to wander, something surprising happens. The experimenter presents a third set of lines, and again the answer is obvious—line 3 is clearly the closest in length to the target line. But the first participant announces that the correct answer is line 1! "This guy must be so bored that he fell asleep," you think. Then the second person announces that line 1 is the correct answer. The third, fourth, fifth, and sixth participants agree; then it's your turn to judge. By now startled, you are probably looking at the lines very closely to see if you missed something. But no, line 3 is clearly the right answer. What will you do? Will you bravely blurt out, "Line 3," or will you go along with the group and give the obviously wrong answer, "Line 1"?

As you can see, Asch set up a situation to discover if people would conform even when the right answer was absolutely obvious. In each group, all of the participants but one had been told earlier to give the wrong answer on twelve of the eighteen trials. What happened? Contrary to what Asch expected, a considerable

Participants in an Asch line study. The real participant is seated in the middle. He is surrounded by the experimenter's accomplices, who have just given the wrong answer on the line task.

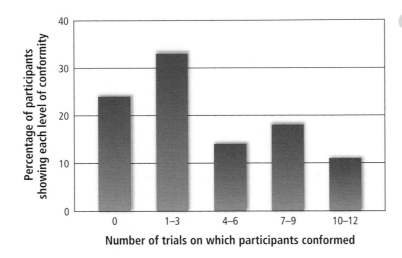

FIGURE 8.3

Results of the Asch line judgment study.

Participants in the Asch line study showed a surprisingly high level of conformity, given how obvious it was that the group was wrong in its judgments. Seventy-six percent of the participants conformed on at least one trial; only 24 percent of participants never conformed at all (see bar labeled zero). Most participants conformed on one to three of the twelve trials in which the group gave the wrong answer. However, a sizable number of participants conformed to the group's response nearly every time it gave the wrong answer (see the two bars on the right).

(Adapted from Asch, 1957)

amount of conformity occurred: Seventy-six percent of the participants conformed on at least one trial. On average, people conformed on about a third of the twelve trials on which the accomplices gave the incorrect answer (see Figure 8.3).

Why did people conform so much of the time? Participants couldn't have needed information from others to help them decide, as in the Sherif study, because the situation was not ambiguous. The right answers were so obvious that when people in a control group made the judgments by themselves, they were accurate more than 98 percent of the time. Instead, normative pressures came into play. Even though the other participants were strangers, the fear of being the lone dissenter was so strong that people conformed, at least occasionally. One participant explained: "Here was a group; they had a definite idea; my idea disagreed; this might arouse anger. . . . I was standing out [like] a sore thumb. . . . I didn't want particularly to make a fool of myself. . . . I felt I was definitely right . . . [but] they might think I was peculiar" (Asch, 1956, Whole No. 416).

These are classic normative reasons for conforming: People know that what they are doing is wrong but go along anyway so as not to feel peculiar or look like a fool. These reasons illustrate an important fact about normative pressures: In contrast to informational social influence, normative pressures usually result in *public compliance without private acceptance*—people go along with the group even if they do not believe in what they are doing or think it is wrong.

What is especially surprising about Asch's results is that people were concerned about looking foolish in front of complete strangers. It is not as if the participants were in danger of being ostracized by a group that was important to them. Nor was there any risk of open punishment or disapproval for failing to conform or of losing the esteem of people they really cared about, such as friends and family members. Yet decades of research indicate that conformity for normative reasons can occur simply because we do not want to risk social disapproval, even from complete strangers we will never see again (Crutchfield, 1955; Tanford & Penrod, 1984).

In a variation of his study, Asch (1957) demonstrated the power of social disapproval in shaping a person's behavior. The confederates gave the wrong answer twelve out of eighteen times, as before, but this time the participants wrote their answers on a piece of paper instead of saying them out loud. Now people did not have to worry about what the group thought of them because the group would never find out what their answers were. Conformity dropped dramatically, occurring on an average of only 1.5 of the twelve trials (Insko, Smith, Alicke, Wade, & Taylor, 1985; Nail, 1986). As Serge Moscovici (1985) observed, the Asch studies are "one of the most dramatic illustrations of conformity, of blindly going

> It isn't difficult to keep alive, friends—just don't make trouble—or if you must make trouble, make the sort of trouble that's expected.
>
> —Robert Bolt, A Man for All Seasons

along with the group, even when the individual realizes that by doing so he turns his back on reality and truth" (p. 349).

The Importance of Being Accurate, Revisited

Now, you may be thinking, "OK, so we conform to normative social influence, but hey, only when it's something little. Who cares whether you give the right answer on the line judgment task? It doesn't matter, nothing is at stake, and so it's easier to go along with the group. I wouldn't conform to the group's wrong answer if something important was involved!" And this would be a very good criticism. Recall our discussion of importance in connection with informational social influence; we found that the more important the decision or choice a person has to make is, the more the person conforms for informational reasons in ambiguous situations. What about in nonambiguous situations? Maybe the more important the decision or choice is, the less the person would conform for normative reasons. When it's important to you to be right, are you strong enough to withstand group pressure and disagree with the group?

In the study of eyewitness identification of perpetrators that we discussed earlier, Baron and his colleagues (1996) included experimental conditions that triggered normative social influence. Recall that their research participants viewed pairs of slides, one of the perpetrator alone and one of the perpetrator in a lineup. Participants watched the slides in groups with two confederates. When studying informational conformity, the researchers made the task fiendishly difficult and therefore ambiguous—the slides were projected for only half a second. In order to study normative social influence, the researchers made the same task ridiculously easy: The participants viewed each slide for a full five seconds, and to make it even easier, they were shown each pair of slides twice. Now the task is analogous to Asch's line-judging task; basically, if you're awake, you'll get the right answer. Baron and colleagues proved that the task was easy by having a control group view the slides alone. The controls answered correctly on 97 percent of the trials, very close to Asch's control group's performance of 98 percent on the line-judging task.

Baron and colleagues again manipulated the importance of the participants' being accurate, in ways we discussed earlier. Half thought it was very important that they give the right answers, and half thought it really didn't matter to the experimenters how they did. Now how will participants respond when the confederates give the obviously wrong answer? Will they, like the participants in the Asch study did, conform to the group on at least some of the trials? Or will the participants who are motivated to do well stand up to the group, ignore their wrong answers and the normative pressure to agree with them, and give the right answers every time?

> Customs do not concern themselves with right or wrong or reason. But they have to be obeyed; one reasons all around them until [one] is tired, but [one] must not transgress them, it is sternly forbidden.
>
> —Mark Twain

The researchers found that participants in the low-importance condition conformed to the group on 33 percent of the critical trials. (These findings are very close to Asch's on the line-judgment task.) What happens when it is important to the participants to be accurate? They conform less to the obviously wrong answers of the group; on only 16 percent of the critical trials did they echo the group's blatantly wrong answer. Note, however, that they still conformed sometimes! Instead of standing up to the group, they caved in on at least some trials. These findings underscore the power of normative social influence: Even when the group is wrong, the right answer is obvious, and there are strong incentives to be accurate, people will find it difficult to risk social disapproval, even from strangers (Baron et al., 1996).

Normative social influence most closely reflects the negative stereotype of conformity we referred to earlier. At times, conforming for normative reasons can be spineless and weak; it can have negative consequences. Even in a dangerous situation, like that faced by the Brazilian teenagers who surf on top of trains, you might go ahead and conform because normative social pressures can be difficult to resist. The desire to be accepted is part of human nature, but it can have tragic consequences.

The Importance of Accountability

We've seen how the importance of being accurate affects conformity: It tends to increase people's informational conformity and decrease their normative conformity. But what if people have to explain and justify their decisions? For example, what if you had to explain to members of the group why you did or did not agree with them? In this situation, you are being held accountable for your decision. How will it affect your tendency to conform?

Some research has found that accountability tends to increase conformity. By agreeing, you gain the group's approval, and your normative conformity needs are met (Lerner & Tetlock, 1999; Pennington & Schlenker, 1999). However, other researchers have argued that accountability, because it involves social interaction, is a powerful variable that can make salient whatever goal a person in the group has (Quinn & Schlenker, 2002; Schlenker & Weigold, 1989). Thus if you are motivated to get along with the group, the presence of accountability will increase your conformity. But if you are motivated to reach an accurate solution to a problem, accountability should make you less likely to conform to the group's less than accurate recommendations.

To test this hypothesis, research participants were presented first with a series of vignettes that stressed the importance of working cooperatively with others and getting along with them (the "cooperative" condition) or with vignettes that stressed the importance of working objectively toward an accurate solution no matter what (the "accurate" condition) (Quinn & Schlenker, 2002). With one of these two approaches primed in their minds, the participants proceeded to the main task.

They were given a business school type of case study about a small American brewing company that had recently introduced two new beers, one in the United States and one in Europe. Over the prior two years, the company had spent 80 percent of its advertising budget on the European beer. However, the European sales had been disappointing, while sales of the American beer had exceeded expectations. Participants were asked to decide how the company should allocate this year's advertising budget—how much should be spent in each of these two markets?

Participants were seated in a room alone during this study, but half of them were told that they would be discussing their decision with another student. This was the "accountable" condition. They learned what this other person had decided before they had to make their own decision. Their future partner had decided that the company should continue to devote most of the advertising budget to the European market (the less than optimal choice). The other half of the participants were in the "not accountable" condition. They too would learn what the other person's decision was, but they would not meet with the person, nor would their own decision be revealed. Recall that half of the participants were already primed, by the prior task, to focus on accuracy, while half were primed to work cooperatively with others.

What happened? Participants who had been motivated to be accurate and who thought they would be accountable for their decision did not conform normatively to the other person's recommendation. They decided that more of the advertising budget should be devoted to the American beer. In comparison, the participants who were motivated to cooperate and who also believed they would be held accountable allocated significantly more of the budget to the European beer—indicating normative conformity to the other person's position. In the "not accountable" condition, participants tended to conform to the other person regardless of whether they were focusing on accuracy or cooperation. This suggests that some informational conformity was at work here too. The issues surrounding the advertising budget were not completely clear-cut; with some ambiguity present and no motivation to be accurate, participants tended to trust the other person's judgment and agree to some extent. Thus only the combination of accountablity and the desire to be accurate led participants to ignore conformity pressures in this situation and to make their own independent decisions.

The Consequences of Resisting Normative Social Influence

One way to observe the power of normative social pressures is to see what happens when people manage to resist them. If a person refuses to do as the group asks and thereby violates its norms, what happens? Think about the norms that operate in your group of friends. Some friends have an egalitarian norm for making group decisions. For example, when choosing a movie, everyone gets to state a preference; the choice is then discussed until agreement is reached on one movie. What would happen if, in a group with this kind of norm, you stated at the outset that you only wanted to see *Rebel Without a Cause*? Your friends would be surprised by your behavior; they would also be annoyed with you or even angry. If you continued to disregard the friendship norms of the group by failing to conform to them, two things would most likely happen. First, the group would try to bring you "back into the fold," chiefly through increased communication with you. Teasing comments and long discussions would ensue as your friends tried to figure out why you were acting so strangely and would try to get you to conform to their expectations (Garfinkle, 1967). If these discussions didn't work, your friends would most likely start to withdraw from you (Festinger & Thibaut, 1951; Gerard, 1953). Now, in effect, you've been rejected (Kruglanski & Webster, 1991; Levine, 1989; Milgram & Sabini, 1978).

Stanley Schachter (1951) demonstrated how the group responds to an individual who ignores the group's normative influence. He asked groups of college students to read and discuss a case history of "Johnny Rocco," a juvenile delin-

Male cadets at The Citadel, a military academy, celebrate after learning that Shannon Faulkner, the first female cadet at the school, has dropped out.

Try it!

Unveiling Normative Social Influence by Breaking the Rules

Every day, you talk to a lot of people—friends, professors, co-workers, and strangers. When you have a conversation (whether long or short), you follow certain interaction "rules" that operate in American culture. These rules for conversation include nonverbal forms of behavior that Americans consider "normal" as well as "polite." You can find out how powerful these norms are by breaking them and noting how people respond to you; their response is normative social influence in action.

For example, in conversation, we stand a certain distance from each other—not too far and not too close. About 2 to 3 feet is typical in this culture. In addition, we maintain a good amount of eye contact when we are listening to the other person; in comparison, when we're talking, we look away from the person more often.

What happens if you break these normative rules? For example, have a conversation with a friend and stand either too close or too far away (e.g., 1 foot or 7 feet). Have a typical, normal conversation with your friend; only the spacing from what you normally use with this person should be different. Note how your friend responds. If you're too close, your friend will probably back away; if you continue to keep the distance small, he or she may act uncomfortable and even terminate your conversation sooner than usual. If you're too far away, your friend will probably come closer; if you back up, he or she may think you are in a strange mood. In either case, your friend's response will probably include looking at you a lot, having a puzzled look on his or her face, acting uncomfortable or confused, and talking less than normal or ending the conversation.

You have acted in a nonnormative way, and your conversational partner is first, trying to figure out what is going on, and second, responding in a way to get you to stop acting oddly. From this one brief exercise, you will get the idea of what would happen if you behaved oddly all the time—people would try to get you to change, and then they would probably start avoiding or ignoring you.

When you're done, please "debrief" your friend, explaining the exercise, so that your behavior is understood.

quent. Most of the students took a middle-of-the-road position about the case, believing that Rocco should receive a judicious mixture of love and discipline. Unbeknown to the participants, however, Schachter had planted an accomplice in the group who was instructed to disagree with the group's recommendations. He consistently argued that Rocco should receive the harshest amount of punishment, regardless of what the other group members argued.

How was the deviant treated? He received the most comments and questions from the real participants throughout the discussion until near the end, when communication with him dropped sharply. The other group members had tried to convince the deviant to agree with them; when it appeared that that wouldn't work, they ignored him. In addition, they punished the deviant. After the discussion, they were asked to fill out questionnaires that supposedly pertained to future discussion meetings of their group. The participants were asked to nominate one group member who should be eliminated from further discussions if the size had to be reduced. They nominated the deviant. They were also asked to assign group members to various tasks in future discussions. They assigned the unimportant or boring jobs, such as taking notes, to the deviant. Social groups are well versed in how to bring a nonconformist into line. No wonder we respond as often as we do to normative pressures! You can find out what it's like to resist normative social influence in the Try It! exercise above.

> Success or failure lies in conformity to the times.
>
> *—Niccolò Machiavelli, The Prince*

In 1969, hippie fashions in clothing and hairstyles were all the rage.

Normative Social Influence in Everyday Life

Normative social influence operates on many levels in our daily lives. For example, although few of us are slaves to fashion, we tend to wear what is considered appropriate and stylish at a given time. The wide ties popular in the 1970s gave way to narrow ties in the 1980s; and hemlines dropped from mini to maxi and rose again in the 1990s. Normative social influence is at work whenever you notice a look shared by people in a certain group, and no matter what it is, it will look outdated just a few years later until the fashion industry declares it stylish again.

Fads are another fairly frivolous example of normative social influence. Certain activities or objects can suddenly become popular and sweep the country. In the late 1950s, every child had to have a Hula-Hoop or risk social ostracism. College students swallowed live goldfish in the 1930s, crammed as many people as possible into telephone booths in the 1950s, and "streaked" (ran naked) at official gatherings in the 1970s.

Social Influence and Women's Body Image   A more sinister form of normative social influence involves women's attempts to conform to cultural definitions of an attractive body. While many, if not most, world societies consider plumpness in females attractive, Western culture and particularly American culture currently value extreme thinness in the female form (Anderson, Crawford, Nadeau, & Lindberg, 1992; Fouts & Burggraf, 1999; Jackson, 1992; Thompson & Heinberg, 1999).

Why should preference for female body type vary by culture? To explore this question, Judith Anderson and her colleagues (1992) analyzed what people in fifty-four cultures considered the ideal female body: a heavy body, a body of moderate weight, or a slender body. The researchers also analyzed how reliable the food supply was in each culture. They hypothesized that in societies where food was frequently scarce, a heavy body would be considered the most beautiful: These would be women who had enough to eat and therefore were healthy and fertile. As you can see in Figure 8.4, their hypothesis was supported. Heavy women were preferred over slender or moderate ones in cultures with unreliable or somewhat unreliable food supplies. As the reliability of the food supply increases, the preference for heavy-to-moderate bodies decreases. Most dramatic is the increase in preference for the slender body across cultures. Only in cultures with very reliable food supplies (like the United States) was the slender body type highly valued.

"No woman can be too slim or too rich."

—Wallis Simpson, Duchess of Windsor

FIGURE 8.4

What is the "ideal" female body across cultures?

Researchers divided fifty-four cultures into groups, depending on the reliability of their food supply. They then determined what was considered the "ideal" female body in each culture. Heavy female bodies were considered the most beautiful in cultures with unreliable or somewhat unreliable food supplies. As the reliability of the food supply increases, the preference for a moderate to heavy body type decreased. Only in cultures where food was very readily available was the slender body valued.

(Adapted from Anderson, Crawford, Nadeau, & Lindberg, 1992)

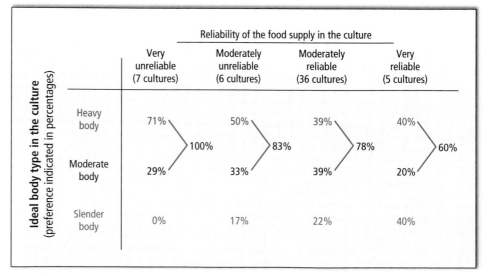

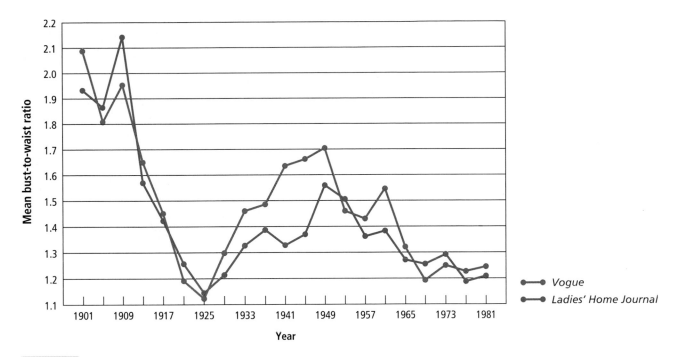

The mean bust-to-waist ratios of models in *Vogue* and *Ladies' Home Journal,* 1901–1981.

What has been considered an attractive female body changed dramatically during the twentieth century, from heavy women at the beginning of the 1900s to rail-thin women during the 1920s to somewhat heavier and more curvaceous women during the 1940s and 1950s, to a return to very thin women in the 1960s and thereafter.

(Adapted from Silverstein, Perdue, Peterson, & Kelly, 1986)

What is the American standard for the female body? Has it changed over time? In the 1980s, Brett Silverstein and her colleagues (Silverstein, Perdue, Peterson, & Kelly, 1986) analyzed photographs of women appearing in *Ladies' Home Journal* and *Vogue* magazines from 1901 to 1981. The researchers measured the women's busts and waists in centimeters, creating a bust-to-waist ratio. A high score indicates a heavier, more voluptuous body, while a lower score indicates a thin, lean body type. Their results show a startling series of changes in the cultural definition of female bodily attractiveness during the twentieth century (see Figure 8.5).

At the turn of the twentieth century, an attractive woman was voluptuous and heavy; by the "flapper" period of the 1920s, the correct look for women was rail-thin and flat-chested. The normative body changed again in the 1940s, when World War II "pinup girls" like Betty Grable exemplified a heavier standard. The curvaceous female body remained popular during the 1950s; witness, for example, Marilyn Monroe. However, the "swinging 1960s" fashion look, exemplified by the reed-thin British model Twiggy, introduced a very thin silhouette again. The average bust-to-waist ratio has been very low since 1963, marking the longest period of time in the past century that American women have been exposed to an extremely thin standard of feminine physical attractiveness (Barber, 1998; Garner, Garfinkel, Schwartz, & Thompson, 1980; Wiseman, Gray, Mosimann, & Ahrens, 1992).

Interestingly, the standards for physical attractiveness for Japanese women have also undergone changes in recent decades. Since World War II, the preferred look has taken on a "Westernized" element—long-legged, thin bodies or what is called the "*hattou shin* beauty" (Mukai, Kambara, & Sasaki, 1998). And this cultural shift has had an effect—Japanese women experience strong norma-

Cultural standards for women's bodies are changeable. Whereas today's female models and movie stars tend to be lean and muscle-toned, the female icons of the 1940s and 1950s, like Marilyn Monroe, were curvaceous, heavier, and less muscular.

tive pressures to be thin (Mukai, 1996). In fact, researchers who studied Japanese and American college-aged women found that the Japanese women were even more likely than the American women to perceive themselves as being overweight. They also reported greater dissatisfaction with their bodies than the American women did. All this occurred despite the fact that the Japanese women were significantly thinner than the American women. In addition, these researchers found that participants' "need for social approval" as measured on a questionnaire was a significant predictor of eating disorders for the Japanese women but not for the American women. Japanese culture places a greater emphasis on conformity than American culture, and hence the normative pressure to be thin operates with even more serious consequences for Japanese women (Mukai et al., 1998).

Informational social influence is the mechanism by which women learn what kind of body is considered attractive at a given time in their culture. Women learn what an attractive body is (and how they compare) from family and friends and from the media. All forms of media have been implicated in sending a message that the ideal female body is thin. For example, researchers have coded the articles and advertisements in magazines aimed at teenage girls and adult women, as well as female characters on television shows (Cusumano & Thompson, 1997; Levine & Smolak, 1996; Nemeroff, Stein, Diehl & Smilack Stein, Diehl, & Smilack, 1995). Women tend to perceive themselves as overweight and as heavier than they actually are (Cohn & Adler, 1992), and this effect is heightened if they've just been exposed to media portrayals of thin women (Fredrickson, Roberts, Noll, Quinn, & Twenge, 1998; Heinberg & Thompson, 1995; Lavine, Sweeney, & Wagner, 1999).

Normative social influence explains women's attempts to create the ideal body through dieting and, more disturbingly, through eating disorders like anorexia nervosa and bulimia (Gimlin, 1994; Stice & Shaw, 1994). As early as the 1960s, researchers found that 70 percent of the high school girls surveyed were unhappy with their bodies and wanted to lose weight (Heunemann, Shapiro, Hampton, & Mitchell, 1966; Sands & Wardle, 2003). The sociocultural pressure for thinness that is currently operating on women is a potentially fatal form of normative social influence. The last time that a very thin standard of bodily attractiveness for women existed, in the mid-1920s, an epidemic of eating disorders appeared (Killen et al., 1994; Silverstein, Peterson, & Perdue, 1986). And it is happening again, but with even younger girls: The American Anorexia Bulimia Association recently released statistics indicating that one-third of 12- to 13-year-old girls are actively trying to lose weight by dieting, vomiting, using laxatives, or taking diet pills (Ellin, 2000). Research has given us some insights about conformity pressures and eating disorders.

CONNECTIONS

Bulimia as a Normative Social Influence

Curious about the effects of pressures to conform and eating disorders, Christian Crandall (1988) focused on bulimia, an eating pattern characterized by periodic episodes of uncontrolled binge eating, followed by periods of purging through fasting, vomiting, or using laxatives.

Crandall's research participants belonged to two college sororities. He found, first, that each sorority had its own social norm for binge eating. In one sorority, the group norm was that the more one binged, the more popular one was in the group. In the other sorority, popularity was associated with bingeing the right amount—the most popular women binged not too often and not too infrequently, compared to the others.

Did binge eating operate as a form of normative social influence? Yes, it did. Crandall tested the women throughout the school year and found that new members had conformed to the eating patterns of their friends. Probably, the initial conforming behavior was informational, as a new pledge learned from the group how to manage her weight. However, normative conformity processes would then take over as the woman matched her bingeing behavior to the sorority's standard and that of her friends. Not to engage in the behavior or to do it differently from the others could easily have resulted in a loss of popularity and even ostracism.

Social Influence and Men's Body Image   What about cultural definitions of an attractive *male* body? Have these changed over time as well? Do men engage in normative conformity too, trying to achieve the perfect-looking body? Surprisingly, there is very little research on these questions, but the initial studies suggest that yes, cultural norms have changed in that men are beginning to come under the same pressure to achieve an ideal body that women have experienced for decades (Morry & Staska, 2001; Petrie et al., 1996).

Specifically, some evidence suggests that if sociocultural expectations of attractiveness for males have changed over recent decades, it is that the ideal is now much more muscular. For example, Harrison Pope and his colleagues (Pope, Olivardia, Gruber, & Borowiecki, 1999) analyzed boys' toys such as GI Joe dolls by measuring their waists, chests, and biceps. The changes in the GI Joe from 1964 to 1998 are startling, as you can see in the photographs from Pope's research.

They also coded advertisements in two women's magazines, *Glamour* and *Cosmopolitan*, since 1950, for how often male and female models were pictured in some state of undress. For women, the percentage remained at about 20 percent over the decades, but for men a change was clear. In 1950, less than 5 percent of ads showed men in some state of undress; by 1995, that figure had risen to as much as 35 percent (Pope, Phillips, & Olivardia, 2000).

In other research, Pope and colleagues (Pope, Gruber et al., 2000) asked men in the United States, France, and Austria to alter a computer image of a male body in terms of fat and muscle until it reflected first, their own bodies; second, the body they'd like to have; and finally, the body they thought women would find most attractive. The men were quite accurate in their depiction of their own bodies. However, men in all three countries chose an ideal body that had on average 28 more pounds of muscle than their own. This ideal standard was also the body they chose for what they thought women would find attractive. (In fact, when women participants did the task, they chose a very normal, typical-looking male body as their ideal.) All of these data suggest that informational

> You cannot make a man by standing a sheep on its hind-legs. But by standing a flock of sheep in that position you can make a crowd of men.
>
> *—Sir Max Beerbohm, Zuleika Dobson*

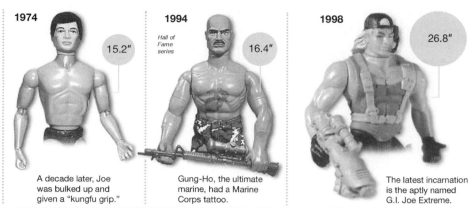

1964 12.2"
The original G.I. Joe from 1964 had relatively normal proportions.

1974 15.2"
A decade later, Joe was bulked up and given a "kungfu grip."

1994 16.4"
Hall of Fame series
Gung-Ho, the ultimate marine, had a Marine Corps tattoo.

1998 26.8"
The latest incarnation is the aptly named G.I. Joe Extreme.

Has the American cultural ideal of the male body changed over time? Harrison Pope and his colleagues (1999) measured the waist, chest, and biceps of the most popular action figure toys of the last three decades, including G.I. Joe dolls, pictured here. The researchers found that the toy figures had grown much more muscular over time, far exceeding the muscularity of even the largest human bodybuilders. The researchers suggest that such images of the male body may contribute to body image disorders in boys.

and normative social influence may now be operating on men, affecting their perceptions of their bodies' attractiveness.

CONNECTIONS

The Power of Propaganda

One example of extraordinary social influence is propaganda, especially as perfected by the Nazi regime in the 1930s. Propaganda is defined as "the deliberate, systematic attempt to shape perceptions, manipulate cognitions, and direct behavior to achieve a response that furthers the desired intent of the propagandist" (Jowett & O'Donnell, 1999, p. 6).

Adolf Hitler was well aware of the power of propaganda as a tool of the state. In *Mein Kampf* (1925), written before he came to power, Hitler stated, "Its task is not to make an objective study of the truth . . . and then set it out before the masses with academic fairness; its task is to serve our right, always and unflinchingly" (pp. 182–183). In 1933, Hitler appointed Joseph Goebbels as head of the newly created Nazi Ministry of Popular Enlightenment and Propaganda. It was a highly efficient agency that permeated every aspect of Germans' lives. Nazis controlled all forms of the media, such as newspapers, films, and radio. They also disseminated Nazi ideology through the extensive use of posters and "spectacles"—lavish public rallies that aroused powerful emotions of loyalty and patriotism in the massive crowds (Jowett & O'Donnell, 1999; Zeman, 1995). Nazi propaganda was taught in schools and further promoted in Hitler Youth groups. The propaganda always presented a consistent, dogmatic message: The German people must take action to protect their racial purity and to increase their *Lebensraum* (living space) through conquest (Staub, 1989).

The concerns with *Lebensraum* led to World War II; the concerns with racial purity led to the Holocaust. How could the German people have

To swallow and follow, whether old doctrine or new propaganda, is a weakness still dominating the human mind.

—Charlotte Perkins Gilman

acquiesed to the destruction of European Jewry? A major factor was prejudice (which we will discuss further in Chapter 13). Anti-Semitism was not a new or a Nazi idea. It had existed in Germany and in many other parts of the Continent for hundreds of years. Propaganda is most successful when it taps into an audience's preexisting beliefs. Thus the German people's anti-Semitism could be quite easily strengthened and expanded by Goebbels' ministry. Jews were described in the Nazi propaganda as destroyers of Arayan racial purity and thus a threat to German survival. They were "pests, parasites, bloodsuckers" (Staub, 1989, p. 103) and were compared to "a plague of rats that needed to be exterminated" (Jowett & O'Donnell, 1999, p. 242). However, anti-Semitism is not a sufficient cause in and of itself. Germany was initially no more prejudiced against Jews than its neighboring countries (and the United States) in the 1930s. None of these other countries came up with the concept of a "final solution" as Germany did (Tindale, Munier, Wasserman, & Smith, 2002).

Although prejudice was an important precursor, more is needed to explain the Holocaust. Clearly, the propaganda operated as persuasive messages leading to attitude change, as we discussed in Chapter 7. But the propaganda also initiated social influence processes. In a totalitarian, fascist regime, the state is the "expert," always present, always right, and always to be obeyed. Propaganda would persuade many Germans through informational conformity. They learned new "facts" (which were really lies) about the Jews and learned new solutions to what the Nazis had defined as the "Jewish problem." The propaganda did an excellent job of convincing Germans that the Jews were a threat. As we saw earlier, people experiencing a crisis are more likely to conform to information delivered by an expert.

Nazi propaganda permeated every facet of German life in the 1930s and 1940s. Here, huge crowds attend the 1934 Nuremberg rally. Such large public gatherings were a technique frequently used by Goebbels and Hitler to promote loyalty and conformity to the Nazi party.

But surely, you are thinking, there must have been Germans who did not agree with the Nazi propaganda. Yes, but think about the position they were in. The Nazi ideology so permeated daily life that children and teenagers in Hitler Youth groups were encouraged to spy on their own parents and report them to the Gestapo if they were not "good" Nazis (Staub, 1989). Neighbors, co-workers, salespeople in shops—they could all turn you in if you said or did something that indicated you were not loyal. This situation is ripe for normative conformity, where public compliance occurs without, necessarily, private acceptance. Rejection, ostracism, even torture or death by the Gestapo would all be strong motivators for normative conformity.

Whether people conformed to Nazi propaganda for informational or normative reasons, their conformity allowed the Holocaust to occur. In the early years of the Third Reich, Hitler was very concerned about public resistance to his ideas (Staub, 1989). Unfortunately, because of social influence processes, prejudice, and the totalitarian system, public resistance never arose.

When Will People Conform to Normative Social Influence?

People don't always cave in to peer pressure. Although conformity is commonplace, we are not lemmings who always do what everyone else is doing. And we certainly do not agree on all issues, like abortion, affirmative action, or same-sex marriages. Exactly when are people most likely to conform to normative pressures?

The answer to this question is provided by Bibb Latané's (1981) **social impact theory.** According to this theory, the likelihood that you will respond to social influence from other people depends on three variables:

1. *Strength:* How important to you is the group?
2. *Immediacy:* How close is the group to you in space and time during the attempt to influence you?
3. *Number:* How many people are in the group?

Social impact theory predicts that conformity will increase as strength and immediacy increase. Clearly, the more important a group is to us and the more we are in its presence, the more likely we will be to conform to its normative pressures. For example, the sorority sisters that Crandall (1988) studied experienced a high level of strength and immediacy in their groups, with serious consequences. You can explore a more benign version of normative social influence in the Try It! exercise on p. 266.

Number operates differently. As the size of the group increases, each additional person has less of an influencing effect—going from three people to four makes more of a difference than going from fifty-three people to fifty-four. If we feel pressure from a group to conform, adding another person to the majority makes much more of a difference if the group consists of three rather than fifteen people. Latané constructed a mathematical model that captures these hypothesized effects of strength, immediacy, and number and has applied this formula to the results of many conformity studies. It has effectively predicted the actual amount of conformity that occurred (Latané, 1981; Latane & Bourgeois, 2001; Latané & L'Herrou, 1996).

For example, gay men who lived in communities that were highly involved in AIDS awareness activities (where strength, immediacy, and number would all be high) reported feeling more social pressure to avoid risky sexual behavior and stronger intentions to do so than gay men who lived in less involved communities (Fishbein et al., 1993). Similarly, a sample of heterosexual college students reported that what governed the likelihood of their engaging in risky sexual behavior was the norms for sexual behavior that operated in their group of friends (Winslow, Franzini, & Hwang, 1992).

Let's see in more detail what social impact theory says about the conditions under which people will conform to normative social pressures.

When the Group Size Is Three or More   At what point does group size stop influencing conformity? Asch (1955) and later researchers found that conformity increased as the number of people in the group increased, but once the group reached four or five other people, conformity does not increase much (Campbell & Fairey, 1989; Gerard, Wilhelmy, & Conolley, 1968; McGuire, 1968; Rosenberg, 1961)—just as social impact theory suggests (see Figure 8.6). In short, it does not take an extremely large group to create normative social influence. As Mark Twain wrote in *The Adventures of Huckleberry Finn,* "Hain't we got all the fools in town on our side? And ain't that a big enough majority in any town?"

When the Group Is Important   Another tenet of social impact theory is that the strength of the group—defined as how important the group is to us—makes a difference. Normative pressures are much stronger when they come from people whose friendship, love, and respect we cherish, because there is a large cost to losing this love and respect. Thus groups to which we are highly attracted and with which we strongly identify will exert more normative influence on us than groups for which we have little or no attachment (Abrams, Wetherell, Cochrane, Hogg, & Turner, 1990; Clark & Maass, 1988; Guimond, 1999; Hogg, 1992; Lott

Social Impact Theory

The idea that conforming to social influence depends on the strength of the group's importance, its immediacy, and the number of people in the group

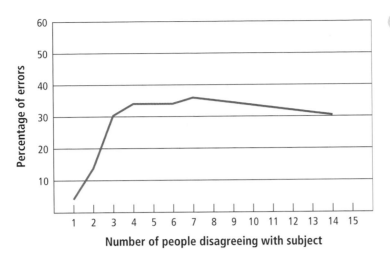

FIGURE 8.6

Effects of group size on conformity.

Asch varied the size of the unanimous major-ity and found that once the majority num-bered four people, adding more people had little influence on conformity.

(Adapted from Asch, 1955)

& Lott, 1961; Nowak, Szamrej, & Latané, 1990; Sakurai, 1975; Wolf, 1985). One consequence is that it can be dangerous to have policy decisions made by highly cohesive groups, because they care more about pleasing each other and avoid-ing conflict than arriving at the soundest, most logical decision. We will see sev-eral examples of this phenomenon in Chapter 9.

When One Has No Allies in the Group   Normative social influence is most power-fully felt when everyone in the group says or believes the same thing—for exam-ple, when your group of friends all believe that *101 Dalmatians* was the greatest movie ever made. Resisting such unanimous social influence is difficult or even impossible—unless you have an ally. If another person disagrees with the group—say, by nominating *Citizen Kane* as the best movie ever—this behavior will help you buck the tide as well.

To test the importance of having an ally, Asch (1955) conducted another version of his conformity experiment. He had six of the seven confederates give the wrong answer and one confederate give the right answer on every trial. Now the subject was not alone. Though still disagreeing with the majority of the group, having one ally helped the subject resist normative pressures. People con-formed on an average of only 6 percent of the trials in this study, compared to 32 percent in the version where all of the confederates gave the wrong answer. Several other studies have found that observing another person resist normative social influence emboldens the individual to do the same (Allen & Levine, 1969; Morris & Miller, 1975; Nemeth & Chiles, 1988).

The effect of having allies produces some interesting anomalies in everyday life—people who hold unpopular beliefs can maintain them in the face of group pressure if they can convince at least a few others to agree with them. For exam-ple, the members of the Heaven's Gate cult persevered in their belief that they would be transported by aliens to outer space. Clearly, the fact that the other cult members continued to believe helped each individual in the group engage in the ultimate behavior required by their cult: suicide.

When the Group's Culture Is Collectivistic   "In America, the squeaky wheel gets the grease. In Japan, the nail that stands out gets pounded down" (Markus & Kitayama, 1991, p. 224). Is it true that the society in which one is raised affects the frequency of normative social influence? Perhaps not surprisingly, the an-swer is yes. Stanley Milgram (1961, 1977) replicated the Asch studies in Norway and France and found that the Norwegian participants conformed to a greater degree than the French participants did. Milgram (1961, p. 51) describes Nor-

Try it!

Fashion: Normative Social Influence in Action

You can observe social impact theory in action by focusing on fashion—specifically, the clothes and accessories that you and your group of friends wear, as well as the look of other groups on campus. You can also observe what happens when you break those normative rules for fashion, for example, by dressing in a way that deviates from your group.

When you are with a group of friends and acquaintances, note carefully how everyone is dressed. Pretend that you are from another culture and not acquainted with the norms of this group; this will help you notice details that you might otherwise overlook. For example, what kinds of pants, shoes, shirts, jewelry, and other items are worn by this group? Are there similarities in their haircuts? Can you discover their fashion "rules"?

Next, spend some time on campus "people-watching," specifically observing what other groups of people are wearing. Can you discern different subgroups on your campus, defined by their style of dress? If so, there are different types of normative conformity operating on your campus; groups of friends are dressing according to the rules of their subgroup and not according to the rules of the campus as a whole.

Finally, if you are brave, break the fashion rules of your normative group. You can do this subtly or you can be very obvious. (But do be sensible; don't get yourself arrested!) For example, if you're male, you could wear a skirt around campus. That would definitely attract attention; you will be not conforming to normative influence in a very major way! If you're female, you'll have to get more creative to break the normative rules, since women's fashion includes male-type clothing. You could wear a garbage bag (with holes cut out for your head and arms) over your clothing. In either case, just walk around campus as usual, seeming unaware that you are wearing anything strange at all. How do people react to you? What will your friends say? Will strangers stare at you?

Your group of friends (as well as the students at your school in general) may well have the qualities that social impact theory discusses: The group is important to you, the group has more than three members, and the group is unanimous (which is the case if your group of friends or your college has definite fashion norms). If you stop conforming to this normative social influence, the other group members will exert some kind of pressure on you, trying to get you to return to conformity.

wegian society as "highly cohesive" with "a deep feeling of group identification," while French society, in comparison, shows "far less consensus in both social and political life." In another cross-cultural study of normative social influence, people in Lebanon, Hong Kong, and Brazil conformed to a similar extent (both to each other and to the American sample), whereas participants from the Bantu tribe of Zimbabwe conformed to a much greater degree (Whittaker & Meade, 1967). As the researchers point out, conformity has a very high social value in Bantu culture.

Although Japanese culture is more highly conforming than our own in many areas, two Asch-type studies found that when the group unanimously gave the incorrect answer, Japanese students were less conformist in general than North Americans (Frager, 1970; Williams & Sogon, 1984). In Japan, cooperation and loyalty are directed to the groups to which one belongs and with which one identifies; there is little expectation that one should conform to the behavior of complete strangers, especially in such an artificial setting as a psychology experiment. Similarly, conformity was much higher in a British sample when the participants thought the other group members were psychology majors like themselves rather than art history majors (Abrams et al., 1990). Similarly, German research participants have shown less conformity in the Asch experiment than North Americans (Timaeus, 1968); in Germany, conformity to strangers is less valued than conformity to a few well-defined groups (Moghaddam, Taylor, & Wright, 1993).

In a meta-analysis of 133 Asch line-judgment studies conducted in seventeen countries, researchers found that cultural values affected normative social influence (Bond & Smith, 1996). (The countries were the United States, Canada, Britain, France, the Netherlands, Belgium, Germany, Portugal, Japan, Hong Kong, Fiji, Zimbabwe, Congo (Zaïre), Ghana, Brazil, Kuwait, and Lebanon.) Participants in collectivistic cultures showed higher rates of conformity on the line task than participants in individualistic cultures. In collectivistic cultures, conformity is a valued trait, not a negative one as in the United States. Agreeing with others may not be so much an act of conformity in collectivist cultures as an act of tact or sensitivity (Smith & Bond, 1999). Because the emphasis is on the group and not the individual, people in collectivistic cultures value normative social influence because it promotes harmony and supportive relationships in the group (Guisinger & Blatt, 1994; Kim, Triandis, Kagitcibasi, Choi, & Yoon, 1994; Markus et al., 1996).

J. W. Berry (1967; Kim & Berry, 1993) explored the issue of conformity as a cultural value by comparing two cultures that had very different strategies for accumulating food. He hypothesized that societies that relied on hunting or fishing would value independence, assertiveness, and adventurousness in their members—traits that were needed to find and bring home food—whereas societies that were primarily agricultural would value cooperativeness, conformity, and acquiescence—traits that made close living and interdependent farming more successful. Berry compared the Inuit people of Baffin Island in Canada, a hunting and fishing society, to the Temne of Sierra Leone in Africa, a farming society, on an Asch-type conformity task. The Temne showed a significant tendency to accept the suggestions of the group, while the Inuit almost completely disregarded them. As one Temne put it, "When the Temne people choose a thing, we must all agree with the decision—this is what we call cooperation"; in contrast, the few times the Inuit did conform to the group's wrong answer, they did so with "a quiet, knowing smile" (Berry, 1967, p. 417).

Finally, there is intriguing evidence that the level of conformity is changing in the United States. For example, replications of the Asch study conducted twenty-five to forty years after the original, in Western countries like the United States and Britain, have found that conformity percentages are decreasing (Bond & Smith, 1996; Lalancette & Standing, 1990; Larsen, 1990; Nicholson, Cole, & Rocklin, 1985; Perrin & Spencer, 1981).

We turn now from conditions within the group that influence normative conformity to aspects of the individual. Is a certain sort of person more likely to conform to normative pressures than another? Research in this area has focused on personality and gender.

The Effect of Low Self-Esteem   It seems reasonable to propose that some people are just conforming types, while others' personalities make them highly resistant to normative pressures. Solomon Asch (1956) suggested that people with low self-esteem may be particularly likely to conform because they fear rejection or punishment by the group. In the first study examining personality traits and conformity, Richard Crutchfield (1955) found evidence for this relationship between self-esteem and normative conformity. Later studies found that people who perceived themselves as having a strong need for approval were more likely to demonstrate normative conformity (Snyder & Ickes, 1985), but the relationship between personality traits and conforming behavior is not always so clearcut. In some studies, the relationship appeared weak or nonexistent (Marlowe & Gergen, 1970). The reason is that people are often inconsistent in how they respond in different social situations (McGuire, 1968; Mischel, 1968). In other

The extent to which conformity is valued varies across cultures. Hunting cultures that prize independence and assertiveness, like the Inuit, show low levels of conformity.

words, they don't always conform, at different times and in different situations, the way they would if their personalities alone were affecting their behavior. Instead, the situation affects their behavior as well, so that in some situations they conform and in other situations they don't, regardless of what type of person they are. You may recall from Chapter 1 that this is a fundamental principle of social psychology: Often the social situation is more important than personality in accounting for a person's behavior.

Gender Differences in Conformity   The second personal variable that has been studied is gender. Do women and men differ in how readily they conform to social pressures? For many years, the prevailing wisdom has been to answer this question in the affirmative: Women are more conforming than men (Crutchfield, 1955). For decades, this was presented as a fact. Reviews of the literature, however, have shown that matters are not so simple. Researchers have taken an objective look at this question by conducting meta-analyses. (Recall from Chapter 2 that a meta-analysis is a statistical technique that allows you to combine results across a large number of studies and come up with a meaningful statistical summary.) Alice Eagly and Linda Carli (1981), for example, performed a meta-analysis of 145 studies of influenceability that included more than 21,000 participants. As previous reviews of this literature showed, they found that on average, men are less prone to being influenced than women. But the size of the difference was very small. It shows up when one averages across thousands of participants, but that does not mean that every man you meet will be less influenceable than every woman. In fact, Eagly and Carli found that only slightly more than half of men are less influenceable than the average woman. (This means, of course, that just under one-half of men are *more* influenceable than the average woman.)

Not only are sex differences in influenceability small, but they depend on the type of conformity pressures impinging on people. Gender differences are especially likely to be found in group pressure situations, where an audience can directly observe how much you conform (e.g., the Asch study, where everyone can tell whether you give the same answer as the other participants). When facing this kind of social pressure, women are more likely to conform than men are. In other situations, when we are the only ones who know whether we conform, such as when we listen to someone give a speech against our views and then decide, privately, how much we agree with the speech, sex differences in influence-ability virtually disappear (Becker, 1986; Eagly, 1987). Eagly (1987) suggests that this pattern of results stems from the social roles men and women are taught in our society. Women are taught to be more agreeable and supportive, whereas men are taught to be more independent in the face of direct social pressures. Eagly further suggests that both women and men are more likely to exhibit such gender-consistent behaviors in public situations, where everyone can see how they respond (e.g., the Asch-type conformity study). But remember, the size of these differences is small.

One other finding in this area is surprising and controversial. The gender of the person conducting conformity studies makes a difference too. Eagly and Carli (1981) found that male researchers were more likely than female researchers to find that men were less influenceable. They suggest that researchers may be more likely to use experimental materials and situations that are familiar to their own gender. Male researchers, for example, may be more likely than female researchers to study how people conform to persuasive messages about sports. We've seen that people are more likely to conform when confronted with an unfamiliar, ambiguous situation; thus women may be more likely to conform in the unfamiliar situations designed by male experimenters.

> People create social conditions, and people can change them.
>
> —Tess Onwueme

Resisting Normative Social Influence

Normative social influence is often useful and appropriate, but there are times when it is not. What can we do to resist inappropriate normative social influence? First, simply be aware that it is operating. Is the presence of others causing you to change your behavior from what you think is right? The second step of resistance is to take action. Why do we fail to take action? Because of the possible ridicule, embarrassment, or rejection we may experience. However, we know that having an ally helps us resist normative pressures. So if you are in a situation where you don't want to go along with the crowd but you fear the repercussions if you don't, try to find another person or group who thinks the way you do.

In addition, the very act of conforming to normative influence most of the time earns you the right to deviate occasionally without serious consequences. This interesting observation was made by Edwin Hollander (1958, 1960), who stated that conforming to a group over time earns you **idiosyncrasy credits,** much like putting money in the bank. It's as if your past conformity allows you, at some point in the future, to deviate from the group (to act idiosyncratically) without getting into too much trouble. If you refuse to lend your car, for example, your friends may not become upset with you if you have followed their friendship norms in other areas in the past, for you've earned the right to deviate from their normative rules in this area. Thus resisting normative influence may not be as difficult (or as scary) as you might think, if you have earned idiosyncrasy credits with the group.

Minority Influence: When the Few Influence the Many

We shouldn't leave our discussion of normative social influence with the impression that the individual never has an effect on the group. As Serge Moscovici (1985, 1994; Moscovici, Mucchi-Faina, & Maass, 1994) says, if groups really did succeed in silencing nonconformists, rejecting deviants, and persuading everyone to go along with the majority point of view, how could change ever be introduced into the system? We would all be like little robots, marching along with everyone else in monotonous synchrony, never able to adapt to changing reality.

Instead, Moscovici (1985, 1994) argues, the individual, or the minority of group members, can influence the behavior or beliefs of the majority. This is called **minority influence.** The key is consistency: People with minority views must express the same view over time, and different members of the minority must agree with one another. If a person in the minority wavers between two different viewpoints or if two individuals express different minority views, the majority will dismiss them as people who have peculiar and groundless opinions. If, however, the minority expresses a consistent, unwavering view, the majority is likely to take notice and may even adopt the minority view (Moscovici & Nemeth, 1974). For example, a minority of scientists began to raise concerns about global warming two decades ago. Today the majority is paying attention; political leaders from the industrialized nations have met to discuss possible worldwide solutions. In a meta-analysis of nearly one hundred studies, Wendy Wood and her colleagues describe how minority influence operates (Wood, Lundgren, Ouellette, Busceme, & Blackstone, 1994).

People in the majority can cause other group members to conform through normative influence. As in the Asch experiments, the conformity that occurs may be a case of public compliance without private acceptance. People in the minority can rarely influence others through normative means—the majority has little concern for how the minority views them. In fact, majority group members may be loath to agree publicly with the minority; they don't want anyone to think

> Never let anyone keep you contained, and never let anyone keep your voice silent.
>
> —*Adam Clayton Powell*

Idiosyncrasy Credits

The tolerance a person earns, over time, by conforming to group norms; if enough idiosyncrasy credits are earned, the person can, on occasion, behave deviantly without retribution from the group

Minority Influence

The case where a minority of group members influence the behavior or beliefs of the majority

Here we see the aftermath of a large festival in Australia. By invoking conformity to social norms, we can encourage people to behave in socially desirable ways, such as refraining from littering.

that they agree with those unusual, strange views of the minority. Minorities therefore exert their influence on the group via the other principal method, informational social influence. The minority introduces new and unexpected information to the group and causes the group to examine the issues more carefully. Such careful examination may cause the majority to realize that the minority view has merit, leading the group to adopt all or part of the minority's view. In short, majorities often obtain public compliance because of normative social influence, whereas minorities often achieve private acceptance because of informational social influence (Levine & Moreland, 1998; Levine & Russo, 1987; Maass & Clark, 1984; Peterson & Nemeth, 1996; Smith, Tindale, & Dugoni, 1996; Wood, Leck, & Purvis, 1996).

USING SOCIAL INFLUENCE TO PROMOTE BENEFICIAL BEHAVIOR

We have seen how informational and normative conformity occurs. Even in a highly individualistic culture such as the United States, conformity of both types is common. Is there a way that we can use this tendency to conform to affect people's behavior for the common good? Robert Cialdini, Raymond Reno, and Carl Kallgren have developed a model of normative conduct in which social norms (the rules that a society has for acceptable behaviors, values, and beliefs) can be used to subtly induce people to conform to correct, socially approved behavior (Cialdini, Kallgren, & Reno, 1991; Kallgren, Reno, & Cialdini, 2000).

For example, we all know that littering is wrong. When we've finished our Big Mac, do we toss the wrapper on the ground or out the car window? Or do we carry it with us until we come to a trash receptacle? Let's say we wanted to decrease littering or increase voter registration or encourage people to donate blood. How would we go about doing it?

Cialdini and his colleagues (1991) suggest that first we need to focus on what kind of norm is operating in the situation. Only then can we invoke a form of social influence that will encourage people to conform in socially beneficial ways. A culture's social norms are of two types. **Injunctive norms** have to do with what we think other people approve or disapprove of. Injunctive norms motivate behavior by promising rewards (or punishments) for normative (or nonnorma-

Injunctive Norms

People's perceptions of what behaviors are approved or disapproved of by others

Descriptive Norms

People's perceptions of how people actually behave in given situations, regardless of whether the behavior is approved or disapproved of by others

tive) behavior. For example, an injunctive norm in our culture is that littering is wrong. **Descriptive norms** concern our perceptions of the way people actually behave in a given situation, regardless of whether the behavior is approved or disapproved of by others. Descriptive norms motivate behavior by informing people about what is effective or adaptive behavior. For example, while we all know that littering is wrong (an injunctive norm), we also all know that there are times and situations when people are likely to do it (a descriptive norm)—for example, dropping peanut shells on the ground at a baseball game or leaving your trash behind at your seat in a movie theater. Thus an injunctive norm is what most people in a culture approve or disapprove; a descriptive norm is what people actually do (Kallgren et al., 2000).

Now let's examine how we can use social influence processes to promote beneficial social behavior.

The Role of Injunctive and Descriptive Norms

In a series of studies, Cialdini, Kallgren, and Reno have explored how injunctive and descriptive norms affect people's likelihood to litter. For example, in one field experiment, patrons of a city library were returning to their cars in the parking lot when a confederate approached them (Reno, Cialdini, & Kallgren, 1993). In one condition, the control group, the confederate just walked by, saying and doing nothing. In the *descriptive norm condition,* the confederate was carrying an empty bag from a fast-food restaurant and dropped the bag on the ground before passing the participant. By littering, the confederate was subtly communicating "what people do in this situation." In the *injunctive norm condition,* the confederate was not carrying anything but instead picked up a littered fast-food bag from the ground before passing the participant. By picking up someone else's litter, the confederate was subtly communicating that "littering is wrong." These three conditions occurred in one of two environments—either the parking lot was heavily littered (by the experimenters, using paper cups, candy wrappers, and so on), or the area was clean and unlittered (cleaned up by the experimenters).

At this point, research participants have been exposed to one of two types of norms about littering or to no norm (the control group), and they've done this in a littered or a clean environment. What about their chance to litter? When they got to their cars, they found a large handbill slipped under the driver's side of the windshield. The handbill appeared on all the other cars too (not surprising, since the experimenters put them there). The participant had two choices at this point: throw the handbill on the ground, littering, or take the handbill in the car and dispose of it later. What will they do? Who refrains from littering?

The control group tells us what percentage of people will litter in this situation. As you can see in Figure 8.7 on page 272, the researchers found that slightly more than one-third of people threw the handbill on the ground; it didn't matter if the area was already littered or if it was clean. In the descriptive norm condition, the confederate's littering communicated two different messages, depending on the condition of the parking lot. In the littered parking lot, the confederate's behavior communicated. "Littering is what most people do here." In the clean parking lot, the confederate's behavior communicated "Littering is not what people do here." Hence we would expect the descriptive norm to reduce littering more in the clean environment than in the littered one, and this is what the researchers found (see Figure 8.7). Finally, what about the injunctive norm condition? This kind of norm supplies the most powerful social influence information: Seeing the confederate picking up someone else's litter invokes the injunctive norm ("Littering is wrong") in both the clean and the littered environments and leads to the lowest amount of littering in the study (see Figure 8.7). (Reno et al., 1993.)

FIGURE 8.7

The effect of injunctive and descriptive norms on littering.

The data for the control group (left) indicate that 37 to 38 percent of people litter a handbill found on their car windshield whether the environment (a parking lot) is littered or clean. When a descriptive norm is made salient to them, littering decreases significantly only in the clean environment (middle). When an injunctive norm is made salient, littering decreases significantly in both types of environment, indicating that injunctive norms are more effective at changing behavior.

(Adapted from Reno, Cialdini, & Kallgren, 1993)

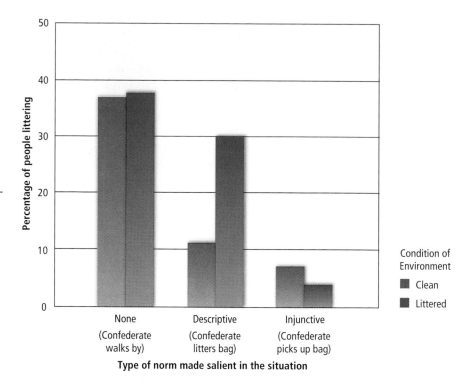

Following this and other studies, the researchers concluded that injunctive norms are more powerful than descriptive norms in producing desirable behavior (Kallgren et al., 2000). This should not surprise you, since injunctive norms tap into normative conformity—we conform (for example, refrain from littering) because someone's behavior has reminded us that our society disapproves of littering. We will look like selfish slobs if we litter, and we will feel embarrassed or worse if other people see us litter. It's true that norms are always present—we know that littering is bad—but they are not always *salient* to us (Kallgren et al., 2000). In order to promote socially beneficial behavior, something in the situation needs to draw our attention to the relevant norm so that we think about it. Thus information that communicates *injunctive norms*—what society approves and disapproves of—is the type that needs to be present to create positive behavioral change.

OBEDIENCE TO AUTHORITY

Obedience is a social norm that is valued in every culture. You simply can't have people doing whatever they want all the time—it would result in chaos. Consequently, we are socialized, beginning as children, to obey authority figures whom we perceive as legitimate (Blass, 2000; Staub, 1989). We internalize the social norm of obedience such that we usually obey rules and laws even when the authority figure isn't present—you stop at red lights even if the cops aren't parked at the corner. However, obedience can have extremely serious and even tragic consequences. People will obey the orders of an authority figure to hurt or even kill other human beings.

Why did the My Lai massacre occur? In this instance, the reasons that people conform combined to produce an atrocity. The behavior of the other soldiers made the killing seem like the right thing to do (*informational influence*), and the soldiers wanted to avoid rejection by their peers and superior officers (*normative influence*). In addition, some of the soldiers later testified at the congressional investigation of the atrocity that they had received direct orders from their officer, Lieutenant Calley, to shoot the civilians. Thus the My Lai tragedy occurred in part because some of the soldiers followed the social norm of obedience to authority too readily, without questioning or taking personal responsibility for what they were doing. It was the power of these conformity pressures that led to the tragedy, not personality defects in the soldiers. This makes the incident all the more frightening, because it implies that similar incidents can occur with any group if similar pressures of social influence are present.

The twentieth century was marked by repeated atrocities and genocides—in Germany and the rest of Europe, Armenia, the Ukraine, Rwanda, Cambodia, Bosnia, and elsewhere. One of the most important questions facing the world's inhabitants therefore becomes, where does obedience end and personal responsibility begin? The philosopher Hannah Arendt (1965) was particularly interested in understanding the causes of the Holocaust. How could Hitler's Nazi regime in Germany accomplish the murder of 6 million European Jews? Arendt argued

Victims of the Holocaust, Nordhausen, Germany, April 1945. According to social psychologists, most of the German guards and citizens who participated in the Holocaust were not madmen but ordinary people exposed to extraordinary social influences.

that most participants in the Holocaust were not sadists or psychopaths who enjoyed the mass murder of innocent people but ordinary citizens subjected to complex and powerful social pressures. She covered the trial of Adolf Eichmann, the Nazi official responsible for the transportation of Jews to the death camps, and concluded that he was not the monster that many people made him out to be but a commonplace bureaucrat like any other bureaucrat who did what he was told without questioning his orders (Miller, 1995).

Our point is not that Eichmann—or the soldiers at My Lai or the Khmer Rouge in Cambodia or the Serbs in Bosnia—should be excused for the crimes they committed. The point is that it is too easy to explain their behavior as the acts of madmen. It is more fruitful—and more frightening—to view their behavior as the acts of ordinary people exposed to extraordinary social influence. But how can we be sure that the Holocaust, My Lai, and other mass atrocities were not caused solely by evil, psychopathic people but by powerful social forces operating on people of all types? The way to find out is to study social pressure in the laboratory under controlled conditions. We could take a sample of ordinary citizens, subject them to various kinds of social influence, and see to what extent they will conform and obey. Can an experimenter influence ordinary people to commit immoral acts, such as inflicting severe pain on an innocent bystander? Stanley Milgram (1963, 1974, 1976) decided to find out, in what has become the most famous series of studies in social psychology.

Imagine that you were a participant in one of Milgram's studies. You answer an ad in the newspaper asking for participants in a study on memory and learning. When you arrive at the laboratory, you meet another participant, a 47-year-old, somewhat overweight, pleasant-looking fellow. The experimenter, wearing a white lab coat, explains that one of you will play the role of a teacher and the other a learner. You draw a slip of paper out of a hat and discover that you will be the teacher. It turns out that your job is to teach the other participant a list of word pairs (e.g., *blue–box, nice–day*) and then test him on the list. The experimenter instructs you to deliver an electric shock to the learner whenever he makes a mistake because the purpose of the study is to examine the effects of punishment on learning.

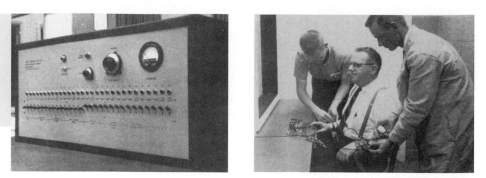

Left: The shock generator used in the Milgram experiments. *Right:* The learner (an accomplice of the experimenter) is strapped into the chair, and electrodes are attached to his arm. (Adapted from Milgram, 1974)

You watch as the other participant—the learner—is strapped into a chair in an adjacent room and electrodes are attached to his arm. You are seated in front of a shock generator whose thirty switches deliver varying levels of shock in 15-volt increments, from 15 to 450 volts. There are labels accompanying these switches, from "Slight Shock" to "Danger: Severe Shock" to an ominous "XXX" next to the highest levels (see the photos on this page). The experimenter tells you that the first time the learner makes a mistake, you should give him a shock of 15 volts—the smallest amount—and then increase the amount by 15 volts for each subsequent mistake he makes. So that you will know what the shocks are like, the experimenter gives you a sample shock of 45 volts, which is rather painful.

You read the list of word pairs to the learner and then begin the testing phase. After announcing the first word of a pair, you give four possible answers; the learner responds by pressing one of four switches, which illuminates a light on the answer box in front of you. Everything begins smoothly as the learner gets the first few right. Then he gets some wrong, and as instructed, you deliver the shocks. At this point, you are probably getting concerned about the number and severity of the shocks you will have to give. When you get to the 75-volt level, the learner, whom you can hear over an intercom, emits a painful "Ugh!" Perhaps you pause and ask the experimenter what you should do. "Please continue," he responds. As the learner continues to make mistakes, you deliver a few more shocks. The learner protests, shouting, "Ugh! Experimenter! That's all! Get me out of here!" You look at the experimenter with grave concern. He tells you, "It is absolutely essential that you continue." (See Figure 8.8.)

What would you do? How many people do you think would continue to obey the experimenter and increase the levels of shock until they had delivered the maximum amount, 450 volts?

When this question was posed to psychology majors at Yale University, they estimated that only about 1 percent of the population would go to this extreme. A sample of middle-class adults and a panel of psychiatrists made similar predictions. However, from our discussion of conformity thus far, you are probably not so optimistic. Whereas no one would have believed that such travesties as the Holocaust could have occurred, they did. Most of Milgram's participants succumbed to the pressure of an authority figure. The average maximum shock delivered was 360 volts, and 62.5 percent of the participants went all the way, delivering the 450-volt shock. A full 80 percent of the participants continued giving the shocks even after the learner, who earlier had mentioned that he had a heart condition, screamed, "Let me out of here! Let me out of here! My heart's bothering me. Let me out of here! . . . Get me out of here! I've had enough. I won't be in the experiment any more" (Milgram, 1974, p. 56).

It is important to note that the learner was actually an accomplice of the experimenter who play-acted his role; he did not receive any actual shocks. It is equally important to note that the study was very convincingly done so that peo-

Learner's Protests

75 volts: Ugh!

90 volts: Ugh!

105 volts: Ugh! (louder)

120 volts: Ugh! Hey this really hurts.

135 volts: Ugh!!

150 volts: Ugh!!! Experimenter! That's all. Get me out of here. I told you I had heart trouble. My heart's starting to bother me now. Get me out of here, please. My heart's starting to bother me. I refuse to go on. Let me out.

165 volts: Ugh! Let me out! (shouting)

180 volts: Ugh! I can't stand the pain. Let me out of here! (shouting)

195 volts: Ugh! Let me out of here. Let me out of here. My heart's bothering me. Let me out of here! You have no right to keep me here! Let me out! Let me out of here! Let me out! Let me out of here! My heart's bothering me. Let me out! Let me out!

210 volts: Ugh! Experimenter! Get me out of here. I've had enough. I won't be in the experiment any more.

225 volts: Ugh!

240 volts: Ugh!

255 volts: Ugh! Get me out of here.

270 volts: Ugh! (Agonized scream) Let me out of here. Let me out of here. Let me out of here. Let me out. Do you hear? Let me out of here.

285 volts: Ugh! (Agonized scream)

300 volts: Ugh! (Agonized scream) I absolutely refuse to answer any more. Get me out of here. You can't hold me here. Get me out. Get me out of here.

315 volts: Ugh! (Intensely agonized scream) I told you I refuse to answer. I'm no longer part of this experiment.

330 volts: Ugh! (Intense and prolonged agonized scream) Let me out of here. Let me out of here. My heart's bothering me. Let me out, I tell you. (Hysterically) Let me out of here. Let me out of here. You have no right to hold me here. Let me out! Let me out! Let me out of here! Let me out!

Instructions used by the Experimenter to Achieve Obedience

Prod 1: Please continue *or* Please go on.

Prod 2: The experiment requires that you continue.

Prod 3: It is absolutely essential that you continue.

Prod 4: You have no other choice; you must go on.

The prods were always made in sequence: Only if prod 1 had been unsuccessful could prod 2 be used. If the subject refused to obey the experimenter after prod 4, the experiment was terminated. The experimenter's tone of voice was at all times firm but not impolite. The sequence was begun anew on each occasion that the subject balked or showed reluctance to follow orders.

Special prods. If the subject asked whether the learner was likely to suffer permanent physical injury, the experimenter said:

Although the shocks may be painful, there is no permanent tissue damage, so please go on. [Followed by prods 2, 3, and 4 if necessary.]

If the subject said that the learner did not want to go on, the experimenter replied: Whether the learner likes it or not, you must go on until he has learned all the word pairs correctly. So please go on. [Followed by prods 2, 3, and 4 if necessary.]

FIGURE 8.8

Transcript of the learner's protests in Milgram's obedience study and of the prods used by the experimenter to get people to continue giving shocks.

(Adapted from Milgram, 1963, 1974)

ple believed they really were shocking the learner. Here is Milgram's description of one participant's response to the teacher role:

> *I observed a mature and initially poised businessman enter the laboratory smiling and confident. Within 20 minutes he was reduced to a twitching, stuttering wreck, who was rapidly approaching a point of nervous collapse. He constantly pulled on his earlobe, and twisted his hands. At one point he pushed his fist into his forehead and muttered, "Oh God, let's stop it." And yet he continued to respond to every word of the experimenter, and obeyed to the end. (Milgram, 1963, p. 377)*

Why did so many research participants (who ranged in age from the twenties to the fifties and included blue-collar, white-collar, and professional workers) conform to the wishes of the experimenter, to the point where they (at least in their own minds) were inflicting great pain on another human being? Why were the college students, middle-class adults, and psychiatrists so wrong in their predictions about what people would do? Each of the reasons that explain why people conform combined in a dangerous way, causing Milgram's participants to obey—just as the soldiers did at My Lai. Let's take a close look at how this worked in the Milgram experiments.

The Role of Normative Social Influence

First, it is clear that normative pressures made it difficult for people to refuse to continue. As we have seen, if someone really wants us to do something, it can be difficult to say no. This is particularly true when the person is in a position of authority over us. Milgram's participants probably believed that if they refused to continue, the experimenter would be disappointed, hurt, or maybe even angry—all of which put pressure on them to continue. It is important to note that this study, unlike the Asch study, was set up so that the experimenter actively attempted to get people to conform, giving stern commands such as "It is absolutely essential that you continue." When an authority figure is so insistent that we obey, it is difficult to say no (Blass, 1991, 2000, 2003; Hamilton, Sanders, & McKearney, 1995; Meeus & Raaijmakers, 1995; Miller, 1986).

The fact that normative pressures were present in the Milgram experiments is clear from a variation of the study that he conducted. This time, there were three teachers, two of whom were confederates of the experimenter. One confederate was instructed to read the list of word pairs; the other, to tell the learner whether his response was correct. The (real) participant's job was to deliver the shocks, increasing their severity with each error, as in the original experiment. At 150 volts, when the learner gave his first vehement protest, the first confederate refused to continue, despite the experimenter's command that he do so. At 210 volts, the second confederate refused to continue. The result? Seeing their peers disobey made it much easier for the actual participant to disobey too. Only 10 percent of the participants gave the maximum level of shock in this experiment (see Figure 8.9). This result is similar to Asch's finding that people did not conform nearly so much when one accomplice bucked the majority and consistently gave the correct answer.

FIGURE 8.9

Results of different versions of the Milgram experiment.

Obedience is highest in the standard version, where the participant is ordered to deliver increasing levels of shock to another person (left panel). Obedience drops when other participants model disobedience or when the authority figure is not present (two middle panels). Finally, when no orders are given to increase the shocks, almost no participants do so (right panel). The contrast in behavior between the far-left and far-right panels indicates just how powerful the social norm of obedience is.

(Adapted from Milgram, 1974)

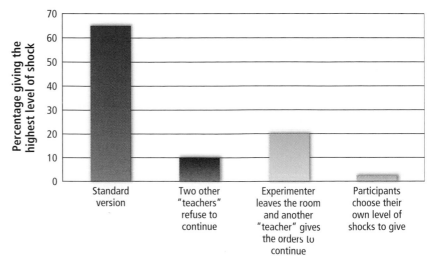

The Role of Informational Social Influence

Despite the power of the normative pressures in Milgram's original study, they are not the sole reason people complied. The experimenter was authoritative and insistent, but he was not pointing a gun at participants and telling them to "conform or else." The participants were free to get up and leave anytime they wanted to. Why didn't they, especially when the experimenter was a stranger they had never met before and probably would never see again?

As we saw earlier, when people are in a confusing situation and unsure of what they should do, they use other people to help define the situation. Informational social influence is especially powerful when the situation is ambiguous, when it is a crisis, and when the other people in the situation have some expertise. The situation Milgram's participants faced was clearly confusing, unfamiliar, and upsetting. It all seemed straightforward enough when the experimenter explained it to them, but then it turned into something else altogether. The learner cried out in pain, but the experimenter told the participant that although the shocks were painful, they did not cause any permanent damage. The participant didn't want to hurt anyone, but he or she had agreed to be in the study and to follow the directions. When in such a state of conflict, it was only natural for the participants to use an expert—the experimenter—to help them decide what was the right thing to do (Hamilton et al., 1995; Krakow & Blass, 1995; Miller, 1986; Miller, Collins, & Brief, 1995).

Another version of the experiment that Milgram performed supports the idea that informational influence was operative. This version was identical to the original one except for three critical changes: First, the experimenter never said which shock levels were to be given, leaving this decision up to the teacher (the real participant). Second, before the study began, the experimenter received a telephone call and had to leave the room. He told the participant to continue without him. Third, there was a confederate playing the role of an additional teacher, whose job was to record how long it took the learner to respond. When the experimenter left, this other teacher said that he had just thought of a good system: How about if they increased the level of shock each time the learner made a mistake? He insisted that the real participant follow this procedure.

Note that in this situation, the expertise of the person giving the commands has been removed: He was just a regular person, no more knowledgeable than the participants themselves. Because he lacked expertise, people were much less likely to use him as a source of information about how they should respond. As seen in Figure 8.9, in this version, compliance dropped from 62.5 percent giving the maximum shock to only 20 percent. (The fact that 20 percent still complied suggests that some people were so uncertain about what to do that they used even a nonexpert as a guide.)

An additional variation conducted by Milgram underscores the importance of authority figures as experts in eliciting such conformity and obedience. In this variation, two experimenters gave the real participants their orders. At 150 volts, when the learner first cried out that he wanted to stop, the two experimenters began to disagree about whether they should continue the study. At this point, 100 percent of the participant-teachers stopped responding. Note that nothing the victim ever did caused all the participants to stop obeying; however, when the authorities' definition of the situation became unclear, the participants broke out of their conforming role.

Other Reasons Why We Obey

Both normative and informational social influences were very strong in Milgram's experiments. However, these reasons for complying still fall short of fully explaining why people acted so inhumanely. They seem to account for why

> When you think of the long and gloomy history of man, you will find more hideous crimes have been committed in the name of obedience than in the name of rebellion.
>
> —C. P. Snow, *Either-Or*

people initially complied, but after it became increasingly obvious to people what they were doing to the learner, why didn't they realize that what they were doing was terribly wrong and stop? Just as the soldiers at My Lai persisted in killing the villagers long after it was obvious that they were unarmed and defenseless civilians, many of Milgram's participants pulled the shock levers time after time after time, despite the cries of anguish from a fellow human being.

Conforming to the Wrong Norm   To understand this continued compliance, we need to consider additional aspects of the situation. We don't mean to imply that Milgram's participants were completely mindless or unaware of what they were doing. All were terribly concerned about the plight of the victim. The problem was that they were caught in a web of conflicting norms, and it was difficult to determine which one to follow. At the beginning of the experiment, it was perfectly reasonable to heed the norm that says, "Obey expert, legitimate authority figures." The experimenter was confident and knowledgeable, and the study seemed like it was a reasonable test of an interesting hypothesis. So why not cooperate and do as you are told?

But gradually the rules of the game changed, and this "obey authority" norm was no longer appropriate. The experimenter, who seemed so reasonable before, was now asking people to inflict great pain on their fellow participant. But once people are following one norm, it can be difficult to switch midstream, realizing that this norm is no longer appropriate and that another norm, "Do not inflict needless harm on a fellow human being," should be followed. For example, suppose the experimenter had explained, at the outset, that he would like people to deliver possibly fatal shocks to the other participant. How many people would have agreed? Very few, we suspect, because it would have been clear that this violated an important social and personal norm about inflicting harm on others. Instead, the experimenter pulled a kind of "bait and switch" routine whereby he first made it look like an "obey authority" norm was appropriate and then gradually violated this norm (Collins & Brief, 1995).

It was particularly difficult for people to abandon the "obey authority" norm in the Milgram experiments because of two key aspects of the situation. First, the experiment was fast-paced, preventing the participants from reflecting on what they were doing. They were busy recording the learner's responses, keeping track of which word pairs to test him on next, and determining whether his responses were right or wrong. Given that they had to attend carefully to these details and move along at a fast pace, it was difficult for them to realize that the norm that was guiding their behavior—cooperating with the authority figure—was, after a while, no longer appropriate. We suspect that if halfway through the experiment, Milgram's participants had been told to take a break and go sit in a room by themselves, many more would have successfully redefined the situation and refused to continue.

Self-Justification   Second, it is important to remember that the experimenter asked people to increase the shocks in very small increments. The participants did not go from giving a small shock to giving a potentially lethal one. Instead, at any given point, they faced the decision about whether to increase the amount of shock they had just given by 15 volts. As we saw in Chapter 6, every time a person makes an important or difficult decision, dissonance is produced, with resultant pressures to reduce it. An effective way of reducing dissonance produced by a difficult decision is to decide that the decision was fully justified. But because reducing dissonance provides a justification for the preceding action, in some situations it makes a person vulnerable to pressures leading to an escalation of the chosen activity.

Thus in the Milgram study, the participants' initial agreement to administer the first shock created internal pressure on them to continue to obey. As the participants administered each successive level of shock, they had to justify it in their own minds. Once they had justified a particular shock level, it became very difficult for them to decide on a place where they should draw the line and stop. How could they say, in effect, "OK, I gave him 200 volts, but not 215—never 215!"? Each succeeding shock and its justification laid the groundwork for the next shock and would have been dissonant with quitting; 215 volts is not that different from 200, and 230 is not that different from 215. Those who did break off the series did so against enormous internal pressure to continue (Darley, 1992; Gilbert, 1981; Miller et al., 1995; Modigliani & Rochat, 1995).

Mika Haritos-Fatouros (1988; see also Staub, 1989) reports that this incremental approach was used by the Greek military dictatorship of the late 1960s to train torturers. In interviews with former torturers, Haritos-Fatouros learned that their first contact with political prisoners was to bring them food and "occasionally" give them some blows. Next, they were put on guard while others conducted torture sessions. Next, they would take part in a few group floggings or beatings. The last step, being in charge of a torture session, "was announced suddenly to the [man] by the commander-in-chief without leaving him any time for reflection" (1988, p. 1117).

It's Not about Aggression   Before leaving our discussion of the Milgram studies, we should mention one other possible interpretation of his results: Did the participants act so inhumanely because there is an evil side to human nature, lurking just below the surface, ready to be expressed with the flimsiest excuse? After all, it was socially acceptable to inflict harm on another person in the Milgram experiment; in fact, subjects were ordered to do so. Perhaps this factor allowed the expression of a universal aggressive urge. To test this hypothesis, Milgram conducted another version of his study. Everything was the same except that the experimenter told the participants that they could choose any level of shock they wished to give the learner when he made a mistake. Milgram gave people permission to use the highest levels, telling them that there was a lot to be learned from all levels of shock. This instruction should have allowed any aggressive urges to be expressed unchecked. Instead, the participants chose to give very mild shocks (see Figure 8.8). Only 2.5 percent of the participants gave the maximum shock. Thus the Milgram studies do not show that people have an evil streak that shines through when the surface is scratched. Instead, these studies demonstrate that social pressures can combine in insidious ways to make humane people act in an inhumane manner. Let us conclude this chapter with the words of Stanley Milgram (1976, pp. 183–184):

> *Even Eichmann was sickened when he toured the concentration camps, but in order to participate in mass murder he had only to sit at a desk and shuffle papers. At the same time the man in the camp who actually dropped [the poison] into the gas chambers is able to justify his behavior on the grounds that he is only following orders from above. Thus there is fragmentation of the total human act; no one man decides to carry out the evil act and is confronted with its consequences. The person who assumes full responsibility for the act has evaporated. Perhaps this is the most common characteristic of socially organized evil in modern society.*

SUMMARY

Conformity: When and Why

In this chapter, we focused on **conformity,** or how people change their behavior due to the real (or imagined) influence of others. We found that there are two main reasons people conform: because of informational and normative social influences.

Informational Social Influence: The Need to Know What's "Right"

Informational social influence occurs when people do not know what is the correct (or best) thing to do or say. This reaction typically occurs in new, confusing, or crisis situations, where the definition of the situation is unclear. People look to the behavior of others as an important source of information and use it to choose appropriate courses of action for themselves. Informational social influence usually results in **private acceptance,** wherein people genuinely believe in what other people are doing or saying.

People are most likely to use others as a source of information when the situation (and thus what they should do) is ambiguous; here a person is open to the influence of others. Experts are powerful sources of influence, since they typically have the most information about appropriate responses. A special type of ambiguous situation is a crisis; fear, confusion, and panic increase our reliance on others to help us decide what to do.

Using others as a source of information can backfire, however, as when people panic because others are doing so. **Contagion** occurs when emotions and behaviors spread rapidly throughout a group; one example is research on **mass psychogenic illness.** You can best resist the inappropriate use of others as a source of information by checking the information you are getting against your common sense and internal moral compass.

Normative Social Influence: The Need to Be Accepted

Normative social influence occurs for a different reason: We change our behavior to match that of others not because they seem to know better what is going on but because we want to remain a member of the group, continue to gain the advantages of group membership, and avoid the pain of ridicule and rejection. We conform to the group's **social norms,** implicit or explicit rules for acceptable behaviors, values, and attitudes. Normative social influence can occur even in unambiguous situations; people will conform to others for normative reasons even if they know that what they are doing is wrong. Normative social influence usually results in **public compliance** but not private acceptance of other people's ideas and behaviors.

Social impact theory specifies when normative social influence is most likely to occur by referring to the strength, immediacy, and size of the group. We are more likely to conform when the group is one we care about, when the group members are unanimous in their thoughts or behaviors, and when the group has three or more members. Failure to respond to normative social influence can be painful.

Normative social influence operates on many levels in social life: It influences our eating habits, hobbies, fashion, body image, and so on, and it promotes correct (polite) behavior in society.

We can resist inappropriate normative pressures by gathering **idiosyncrasy credits** over time, from a group whose membership we value. Furthermore, **minority influence,** whereby a minority of group members influence the beliefs and behavior of the majority, can occur under certain conditions.

Using Social Influence to Promote Beneficial Behavior

Social influence techniques can be used to promote socially beneficial behavior in others. Communicating **injunctive norms** is a more powerful way to create change than communicating **descriptive norms.**

Obedience to Authority

In the most famous series of studies in social psychology, Stanley Milgram examined the limits of obedience to authority figures. Informational and normative pressures combined to cause chilling levels of obedience, to the point where a majority of participants administered what they thought were near-lethal shocks to a fellow human being. In addition, the participants were caught in a web of conflicting social norms and were asked to increase the level of shocks in small increments. After justifying to themselves that they had delivered one level of shock, it was very difficult for people to decide that a slightly higher level of shock was wrong.

Unfortunately, the conditions that produced such extreme antisocial behavior in Milgram's laboratory have been present in real-life tragedies, such as the Holocaust and the mass murders at My Lai in Vietnam.

CRITICAL THINKING QUESTIONS

1. Groups of friends have their own social norms—expectations for how they expect group members to think and behave. Can you identify some of the social norms in your friendship group? What happens when one of your friends breaks a group norm? How does the group respond to the deviant?

2. To what extent do you think informational and normative conformity affects your body image? Do you think you are immune from such pressures, or do you think they have affected how you feel about your appearance, now or when you were younger?

3. Think about the people at your school, and identify some aspect of their behavior that you would like to change. How would you go about doing it, first, using a descriptive norm approach, and second, using an injunctive norm approach?

CHAPTER 9

LIFE

**RAW UNTOLD TRUTH
BY MEN WHO FOUGHT**

Bay of Pigs

**Heartbreaking Price
They Paid for
U.S. Miscalculations**

**NEW
YORK
EDITION**

Group Processes:
Influence in Social Groups

On a cold January day in 1961, John F. Kennedy was inaugurated as the thirty-fifth president of the United States. The author of a romance novel could not have written a better script: Kennedy was young, bright, and handsome; he came from a wealthy, well-connected family; he was a war hero. He had an intelligent, beautiful wife and two adorable children. In his election victory over Richard Nixon, Kennedy proved to be a master political strategist whose dashing good looks, wit, and charm were perfect for the new medium of television. He surrounded himself with advisers and cabinet members who were so talented that one writer dubbed them "the best and the brightest" (Halberstam, 1972).

As Kennedy took the helm in these heady times, he was immediately confronted with a major foreign policy decision. Should he go ahead with a plan, initiated by the Eisenhower administration, to invade Cuba? It might seem odd, from our twenty-first-century perspective, that a tropical island 90 miles off the coast of Florida was considered a major threat to U.S. security. But this was the middle of the Cold War, and Fidel Castro, who had recently led a Communist revolution in Cuba (with the support of the Soviet Union), was seen as an enormous threat. The Eisenhower plan was to land a small force of CIA-trained Cuban exiles on the Cuban coast, who would then instigate and lead a mass uprising against Castro.

Kennedy assembled his advisers to examine the pros and cons of such a plan. The group became a tightly knit, cohesive unit that brought a great deal of expertise to the topic. After lengthy deliberation, they decided to go ahead, and on April 17, 1961, a force of fourteen hundred exiles invaded an area of Cuba known as the Bay of Pigs. Disaster followed. Castro's forces captured or killed nearly all the invaders. Friendly Latin American countries were outraged that the United States had invaded one of their neighbors, and Cuba became even more closely allied with the Soviet Union. Later, President Kennedy would ask, "How could we have been so stupid?" (Sorenson, 1966).

Good question. How could such a remarkably talented group of people, who met at great length to analyze the options, come up with such a disastrous plan? Most of us assume that groups make better decisions than individuals. However, in this case, a committee of experts made an astonishing number of errors. Would President Kennedy have been better off making the decision by himself, without consulting his advisers?

Though you might think so, consider Kennedy's next foreign policy crisis, which also involved Cuba. The following October, the CIA discovered that the Soviet Union had placed nuclear missiles in Cuba. The missiles were aimed toward U.S. cities, and the resulting crisis brought us the closest we have ever come to World War III (Rhodes, 1995). Kennedy and his advisers deftly avoided war with a brilliant strategy of threats, naval blockades, and conciliatory gestures that succeeded in getting Nikita Khrushchev, the leader of the Soviet Union, to back down and remove the missiles. What did Kennedy and his advisers do differently this time? Did they simply stumble onto a good strategy, or had they learned from their earlier mistakes at the Bay of Pigs? In this chapter, we will focus on questions such as these about the nature of groups and how they influence people's behavior, which are some of the oldest topics in social psychology (Cartwright & Zander, 1968; Forsyth, 2000; Levine, 1999; Levine & Moreland, 1990, 1998).

WHAT IS A GROUP?

Six students sitting around a table in the library are not a group. But if they meet to study for their psychology final together, they are. A **group** consists of two or more people who interact and are interdependent in the sense that their needs and goals cause them to influence each other (Cartwright & Zander, 1968; Lewin, 1948). Like Kennedy's advisers working together to reach a foreign policy decision, citizens meeting to solve a community problem, or people who have gathered to blow off steam at a party, groups are people who have assembled for some common purpose.

Think for a moment of the number of groups to which you belong. Don't forget to include your family, campus groups (such as fraternities, sororities, or political organizations), community groups (such as churches or synagogues), sports teams, and more temporary groups (such as your classmates in a small seminar). All of these count as groups, because you interact with the other members and you are interdependent: You influence them, and they influence you.

Why Do People Join Groups?

Forming relationships with other people fulfills a number of basic human needs—so basic, in fact, that there may be an innate need to belong to groups. Some researchers argue that in our evolutionary past, there was a substantial survival advantage to establishing bonds with other people (Baumeister & Leary, 1995). People who bonded together were better able to hunt for and grow food, find mates, and care for children. Consequently, they argue, the need to belong has become innate and is present in all societies. Consistent with this view, people in all cultures are motivated to form relationships with other people and to

Group

Two or more people who interact and are interdependent in the sense that their needs and goals cause them to influence each other

resist the dissolution of these relationships (Gardner, Pickett, & Brewer, 2000; Manstead, 1997).

Groups have a number of other benefits. As we saw in Chapter 8, other people can be an important source of information, helping us resolve ambiguity about the nature of the social world. Groups become an important part of our identity, helping us define who we are—witness the number of times people wear shirts with the name of one of their groups (e.g., a fraternity or sorority) emblazoned on it. Groups also help establish social norms, the explicit or implicit rules defining what is acceptable behavior.

The Composition and Functions of Groups

The groups to which you belong probably vary in size from two or three members to several dozen members. Most groups, however, have two to six members (Desportes & Lemaine, 1988; Levine & Moreland, 1998; McPherson, 1983). This is due in part to our definition of groups as involving interaction between members. If groups become too large, you cannot interact with all the members; for example, the college or university that you attend is not a group because you are unlikely to meet and interact with every other student.

Another important feature of groups is that the members tend to be alike in age, sex, beliefs, and opinions (George, 1990; Levine & Moreland, 1998; Magaro & Ashbrook, 1985). There are two reasons for the homogeneity of groups. First, many groups tend to attract people who are already similar before they join (Feld, 1982). As we'll see in Chapter 10, people are attracted to others who share their attitudes and thus are likely to recruit fellow group members who are similar to them. Second, groups tend to operate in ways that encourage similarity in the members (Moreland, 1987). This can happen in a number of important ways, some of which we discussed in Chapter 8.

Social Norms As we saw in Chapter 8, *social norms* are a powerful determinant of our behavior. All societies have norms about which behaviors are acceptable, some of which all members are expected to obey (e.g., we should be quiet in libraries) and some of which vary from group to group (e.g., rules about what to wear to weddings and funerals). If you belong to a fraternity or sorority, you can probably think of social norms that govern behavior in your group, such as whether alcoholic beverages are consumed and how you are supposed to feel about rival fraternities or sororities. It is unlikely that other groups to which you belong share these norms. The power of norms to shape behavior becomes clear when we violate them too often: We are shunned by other group members and, in extreme cases, pressured to leave the group (Marques, Abrams, & Serodio, 2001; Schachter, 1951; see also Chapter 8).

Social Roles Most groups have a number of well-defined **social roles,** which are shared expectations in a group about how particular people are supposed to behave. Whereas norms specify how all group members should act, roles specify how people who occupy certain positions in the group should behave. A boss and an employee in a business occupy different roles and are expected to act in different ways in that setting. Like social norms, roles can be very helpful, because people know what to expect from each other. When members of a group follow a set of clearly defined roles, they tend to be satisfied and perform well (Barley & Bechky, 1994; Bettencourt & Sheldon, 2001).

There are, however, two potential costs to social roles. First, people can get so far into a role that their personal identities and personalities get lost. Suppose that you agreed to take part in a two-week psychology experiment in which you were randomly assigned to play the role of a prison guard or a prisoner in a simulated prison. You might think that the role you were assigned to play would not

Social Roles

Shared expectations in a group about how particular people are supposed to behave

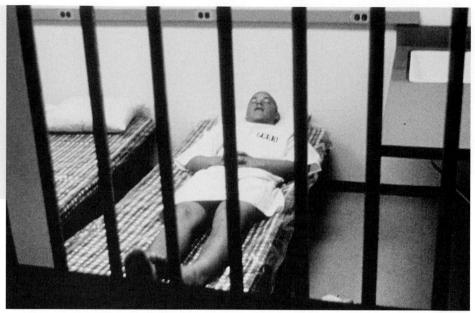

Philip Zimbardo and his colleagues randomly assigned students to play the role of prisoner or guard in a mock prison. The students assumed these roles all too well. Those playing the role of guard became quite aggressive, and those playing the role of prisoner became passive, helpless, and withdrawn. People got into their roles so much that their personal identities and sense of decency somehow got lost.

be very important; after all, everyone knows that it is only an experiment and that people are just pretending to be guards or prisoners. Philip Zimbardo and his colleagues, however, had a different hypothesis. They believed that social roles can be so powerful that they "take over" our personal identities to the point that we become the role we are playing.

To see if this is true, Zimbardo and colleagues conducted an unusual study. They built a mock prison in the basement of the psychology department at Stanford University and paid students to play the role of guard or prisoner (Haney, Banks, & Zimbardo, 1973). The role students played was determined by the flip of a coin. The guards were outfitted with a uniform of khaki shirts and pants, a whistle, a police nightstick, and reflecting sunglasses, and the prisoners were outfitted with a loose-fitting smock with an identification number stamped on it, rubber sandals, a cap made from a nylon stocking, and a locked chain attached to one ankle.

The researchers planned to observe the students for two weeks, to see whether they began to act like real prison guards and prisoners. As it turned out, the students quickly assumed these roles—to such an extent that the researchers ended the experiment after only six days. Many of the guards became quite abusive, thinking of creative ways of verbally harassing and humiliating the prisoners. The prisoners became passive, helpless, and withdrawn. Some prisoners, in fact, became so anxious and depressed that they had to be released from the study earlier than the others. Remember, everyone knew that they were in a psychology experiment and that the prison was only make-believe. The roles of guard and prisoner were so compelling and powerful, however, that this simple truth was often overlooked. People got so far into their roles that their personal identities and sense of decency somehow got lost.

If social roles are so powerful in make-believe prisons, imagine how powerful they are in real prisons and in other institutions with well-defined roles. The roles we assume can shape our behavior in powerful and unexpected ways. Parents of young children, for example, can often be heard exclaiming, "I swore I would never yell at my child in the way my parents yelled at me, and yet I just did!"

The second drawback of social roles is that there is a cost to acting inconsistently with the expectations associated with them. The next time you report to your job, try telling your boss that you're going to decide what she should do that day. Role expectations are especially problematic when they are arbitrary or unfair. All societies, for example, have expectations about how people who occupy the roles of women and men should behave. As we discuss in Chapter 13, these role expectations can constrain the way in which people behave and result in negative attitudes toward people who decide to act inconsistently with how they are expected to behave. The Try It! exercise on this page describes a way you can experience this for yourself.

Gender Roles   In many cultures, women are expected to assume the role of wife and mother and have limited opportunities to pursue other careers. In the United States and other countries, these expectations are changing, and women have more opportunities than ever before. Conflict can result, however, when expectations change for some roles but not for others assumed by the same person. In India, for instance, women were traditionally permitted to take only the roles of wife, mother, agricultural laborer, and domestic worker. As their rights have improved, women are increasingly working at other professions. At home, though, many husbands still expect their wives to assume the traditional role of child rearer and household manager, even if their wives have other careers. Conflict results, because many women are expected to "do it all"—maintain a career, raise the children, clean the house, and attend to their husband's needs (Brislin, 1993). Such conflicts are not limited to India; many American readers will find this kind of role conflict all too familiar (Rudman, 1998).

Changing roles do more than cause us conflict; they can actually affect our personalities. In a historical study, researchers tracked women's social status in the United States between 1931 and 1993 and compared those results to women's ratings of their own assertiveness (Twenge, 2001). Women's status improved between the years of 1931 and 1945. During this time, women increasingly earned college degrees and worked outside the home; by 1945, for example, over half of all college degrees were earned by women. If World War II increased opportunities for women while men were away fighting, when the men came home, so did the women. During the years 1946–1967, the stay-at-home mom became the norm; women increasingly dropped out of the workforce, and fewer women went to college. In 1950, for example, about 25 percent of college degrees were earned by women. Between 1968 and 1993, women's status

Try it!

What Happens When You Violate a Role?

Pick a behavior that is part of the role for your gender in your culture, and deliberately violate it. For example, if you are male in the United States, you might decide to put on makeup or carry a purse to your next class. If you are female, you might wear a jacket and tie to a party. Keep a journal describing how others react to you. More than likely, you will encounter a good deal of social disapproval, such as people staring at you or questioning your behavior. For this reason, you want to avoid role violations that are too extreme.

The social pressure that is brought to bear on people who do not conform to their roles explains why it can be so difficult to break out of the roles to which we are assigned, even when they are arbitrary. Of course, there is safety in numbers; when enough people violate role expectations, others do not act nearly so negatively, and the roles begin to change. For example, it is now much more acceptable for men to wear earrings than it was twenty years ago. To illustrate this safety in numbers, enlist the help of several same-sex friends and violate the same role expectation together. Again, note carefully how people react to you. Did you encounter more or less social disapproval in the group than you did as an individual?

FIGURE 9.1

Women's assertiveness scores over time.

A study examining women's social status in the United States between 1931 and 1993 found that women's status improved between 1931 and 1945, decreased between 1946 and 1967, and increased again between 1963 and 1993. As seen in the figure, women's ratings of their own assertiveness mirrored these societal trends. The roles that people assume in groups, and in society at large, appear to be powerful determinants of how they view themseleves.

(Adapted from Twenge, 2001)

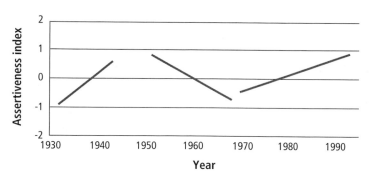

improved as the feminist movement took hold in the United States. By the early 1990s, women were again earning more college degrees than men.

As seen in Figure 9.1, women's ratings of assertiveness mirrored these societal trends. As women's role in the United States changed from independent to dependent, their ratings of assertiveness dropped. Then, as they became more independent, their ratings of assertiveness increased. The roles that people assume in groups, and in society at large, are powerful determinants of their feelings, behavior, and personality (Eagly & Steffen, 2000; Wood, Christensen, Hebl, & Rothgerber, 1997).

Group Cohesiveness   Another important aspect of group composition is how cohesive the group is. The qualities of a group that bind members together and promote mutual liking are known as **group cohesiveness** (Dion, 2000; Hogg, 1993; Prentice, Miller, & Lightdale, 1994). If a group has formed primarily for social reasons, such as a group of friends who like to go to the movies together on weekends, then the more cohesive the group is, the better. This is pretty obvious; would you rather spend your free time with a bunch of people who don't care much for each other or a tight-knit bunch of people who feel committed to you and the other members of the group? As might be expected, the more cohesive a group is, the more its members are likely to stay in the group, take part in group activities, and try to recruit new like-minded members (Levine & Moreland, 1998; Pickett, Silver, & Brewer, 2002; Sprink & Carron, 1994).

If the function of the group is to work together and solve problems, however, as it is for a sales team at a company or a military unit, then the story is not quite so simple. Doing well on a task causes a group to become more cohesive (Mullen & Cooper, 1994), but is the reverse true? Does cohesiveness cause a group to perform well? It does if the task requires close cooperation between the group members, such as a football team executing a difficult play or a military unit carrying out a complicated maneuver (Gully, Devine, & Whitney, 1995). Sometimes, however, cohesiveness can get in the way of optimal performance, if maintaining good relations among group members becomes more important than finding good solutions to a problem. Is it possible, for example, that the cohesiveness felt by Kennedy and his advisers got in the way of clear thinking about the Bay of Pigs invasion? We will return to this question later in the chapter, when we discuss group decision making.

GROUPS AND INDIVIDUALS' BEHAVIOR

Group Cohesiveness

Qualities of a group that bind members together and promote liking between members

Do you act differently when other people are around? Simply being in the presence of other people can have a variety of interesting effects on our behavior. We will begin by looking at how a group affects your performance on something with which you are very familiar—taking a test in a class.

Social Facilitation:
When the Presence of Others Energizes Us

It is time for the final exam in your psychology class. You have spent countless hours studying the material, and you feel ready. When you arrive, you see that the exam is scheduled in a tiny room already packed with students. You squeeze into an empty desk, elbow to elbow with your classmates. The professor arrives and says that if any students are bothered by the close quarters, they can take the test by themselves in one of several smaller rooms down the hall. What should you do?

The question is whether being with other people will affect your performance (Geen, 1989; Guerin, 1993; Kent, 1994; Sanna, 1992). The presence of others can mean one of two things: (1) performing a task with co-workers who are doing the same thing you are or (2) performing a task in front of an audience that is not doing anything but observing you. Note that the question is a basic one about the mere presence of other people, even if they are not part of a group that is interacting. Does the simple fact that other people are around make a difference, even if you never speak or interact with them in any way?

To answer this question, we need to talk about insects—cockroaches, in fact. Believe it or not, a classic study using cockroaches as research participants suggests an answer to the question of how you should take your psychology test. Robert Zajonc and his colleagues (Zajonc, Heingartner, & Herman, 1969) built a contraption to see how a cockroach's behavior was influenced by the presence of its peers. The researchers placed a bright light (which cockroaches dislike) at the end of a runway and timed how long it took a roach to escape the light by running to the other end, where it could scurry into a darkened box (see the left-hand side of Figure 9.2). The question was, did roaches perform this simple feat faster when they were by themselves or when they were in the presence of other cockroaches?

You might be wondering how the researchers managed to persuade other cockroaches to be spectators. They simply placed other roaches in clear plastic boxes next to the runway. These roaches were in the bleachers, so to speak, observing the solitary cockroach do its thing (see Figure 9.2). The results? The individual cockroaches performed the task faster when other roaches were there than when they were by themselves.

> Mere social contact begets . . . a stimulation of the animal spirit that heightens the efficiency of each individual workman.
>
> —*Karl Marx,*
> *Das Kapital,*
> *1867*

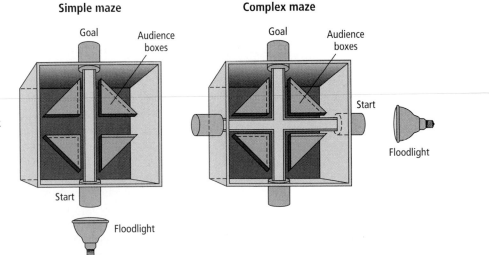

FIGURE 9.2

Cockroaches and social facilitation.

In the maze on the left, cockroaches had a simple task: to go from the starting point down the runway to the darkened box. They performed this feat faster when other roaches were watching than when they were alone. In the maze on the right, the cockroaches had a more difficult task. It took them longer to solve this maze when other roaches were watching than when they were alone.

(Adapted from Zajonc, Heingartner, & Herman, 1969)

Simple maze — Goal, Audience boxes, Start, Floodlight

Complex maze — Goal, Audience boxes, Start, Floodlight

Now, we would not give advice on how you should take your psychology test based on one study that used cockroaches. But the story does not end here. Dozens of studies have been done on the effects of the mere presence of other people, involving human beings as well as other species, such as ants and birds (e.g., Aiello & Douthitt, 2001; Rajecki, Kidd, & Ivins, 1976; Thomas, Skitka, Christen, & Jurgena, 2002). The findings of these studies are remarkably consistent: As long as the task is a relatively simple, well-learned one—as escaping a light is for cockroaches—the mere presence of others improves performance. For example, in one of the first social psychology experiments ever done, Norman Triplett (1898) asked children to wind up fishing line on a reel, either by themselves or in the presence of other children. They did so faster when in the presence of other children than when by themselves.

Simple versus Difficult Tasks Before concluding that you should stay in the crowded classroom to take your exam, we need to consider a different set of findings. Remember that we said the presence of others enhances performance on simple, well-learned tasks. Escaping a light is old hat for a cockroach, and winding fishing line on a reel is not difficult, even for a child. What happens when we give people a more difficult task to do and place them in the presence of others? To find out, Zajonc and his colleagues (1969) included another condition in the cockroach experiment. This time, the cockroaches had to solve a maze that had several runways, only one of which led to the darkened box (see the right-hand side of Figure 9.2). When working on this more difficult task, the opposite pattern of results occurred: The roaches took *longer* to solve it when other roaches were present than when they were alone. Many other studies have also found that people and animals do worse in the presence of others when the task is difficult (e.g., Bond & Titus, 1983; Geen, 1989).

Arousal and the Dominant Response In an influential article published in 1965, Robert Zajonc offered an elegant theoretical explanation for why the presence of others facilitates a well-learned response but inhibits a less practiced or new response. His argument has two steps: First, the presence of others increases physiological arousal (i.e., our bodies become more energized), and second, when such arousal exists, it is easier to do something that is simple but harder to do something complex or learn something new. Consider, for example, a behavior that is second nature to you, such as riding a bicycle or writing your name. Arousal, caused by the presence of other people watching you, should make it even easier to perform these well-learned tasks. But let's say you have to do something more complex, such as learning a new sport or working on a difficult math problem. Now arousal will lead you to feel flustered and do less well than if you were alone (Schmitt, Gilovich, Goore, & Joseph, 1986). This phenomenon became known as **social facilitation,** which is the tendency for people to do better on simple tasks and worse on complex tasks when they are in the presence of others and their individual performance can be evaluated.

Why the Presence of Others Causes Arousal Why does the presence of others lead to arousal? Researchers have developed three theories to explain the role of arousal in social facilitation: Other people cause us to become particularly alert and vigilant, they make us apprehensive about how we're being evaluated, and they distract us from the task at hand.

The first explanation suggests that the presence of other people makes us more alert. When we are by ourselves reading a book, we don't have to pay attention to anything but the book; we don't have to worry that the lamp will ask us a question. When someone else is in the room, however, we have to be alert to the possibility that he or she will do something that requires us to respond. Because other people are less predictable than lamps, we are in a state of greater

Social Facilitation

The tendency for people to do better on simple tasks and worse on complex tasks when they are in the presence of others and their individual performance can be evaluated

Research on social facilitation finds that people do better on a well-learned task when in the presence of others than when they are alone. Actors, like these cast members of London's Globe Theatre, who know their lines well, should perform better when the theater is full than when it is empty.

alertness in their presence. This alertness, or vigilance, causes mild arousal. The beauty of this explanation (the one preferred by Zajonc, 1980) is that it explains both the animal and the human studies. A solitary cockroach need not worry about what the cockroach in the next room is doing. However, it needs to be alert when in the presence of another member of its species—and the same goes for human beings.

The second explanation focuses on the fact that people are not cockroaches and are often concerned about how other people are evaluating them. When other people can see how you are doing, the stakes are raised: You feel like the other people are evaluating you and will feel embarrassed if you do poorly and pleased if you do well. This concern about being judged, called *evaluation apprehension,* can cause mild arousal. According to this view, then, it is not the mere presence of others but the presence of others who are evaluating us that causes arousal and subsequent social facilitation (Blascovich, Mendes, Hunter, & Salomon, 1999; Bond, Atoum, & Van Leeuwen, 1996; Seta & Seta, 1995).

The third explanation centers on how distracting other people can be (Baron, 1986; Huguet, Galvaing, Monteil, & Dumas, 1999; Sanders, 1983). It is similar to Robert Zajonc's (1980) notion that we need to be alert when in the presence of others, except that it focuses on the idea that any source of distraction—be it the presence of other people or noise from the party going on in the apartment upstairs—will put us in a state of conflict because it is difficult to pay attention to two things at the same time. This divided attention produces arousal, as any parent knows who has ever tried to read the newspaper while his or her 2-year-old clamors for attention. Consistent with this interpretation, nonsocial sources of distraction, such as a flashing light, cause the same kinds of social facilitation effects as the presence of other people (Baron, 1986).

We have summarized research on social facilitation in the top half of Figure 9.3 (we will discuss the bottom half in a moment). This figure illustrates that there is more than one reason that the presence of other people is arousing. The consequences of this arousal, however, are the same: When people are around other people, they do better on tasks that are simple and well learned, but they do worse on tasks that are complex and require them to learn something new.

Where, then, should you take your psychology exam? We recommend that you stay with your classmates, assuming you know the material well, so that it is

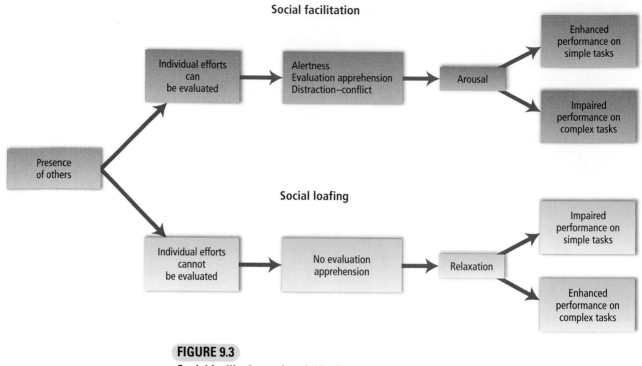

Social facilitation

Social loafing

FIGURE 9.3

Social facilitation and social loafing.

The presence of others can lead to social facilitation or social loafing. The important variables that distinguish the two are evaluation, arousal, and the complexity of the tasks.

(Adapted from Cottrell, Wack, Sekerak, & Ritter, 1968)

relatively simple for you to recall it. The arousal produced by being elbow to elbow with your classmates should improve your performance. But when you study for an exam—that is, when you learn new material—you should do so by yourself, away from other people. In this situation, the arousal caused by others will make it more difficult to concentrate.

Social Loafing: When the Presence of Others Relaxes Us

When you take your psychology exam, your individual efforts will be evaluated (you will be graded on the test). This is typical of the research on social facilitation we have reviewed: People are working on something (either alone or in the presence of others), and their individual efforts are easily observed and evaluated. When people are in the presence of others, however, their individual efforts often cannot be distinguished from those of the people around them. Such is the case when you clap after a concert (no one can tell how loudly you are clapping) or when you play an instrument in a marching band (your instrument blends in with all the others).

These situations are just the opposite of the kinds of social facilitation settings we have just considered. In social facilitation, the presence of others puts the spotlight on you, making you aroused. But if being with other people means we can merge into a group, becoming less noticeable than when we are alone, then we should become relaxed. Because no one can tell how well we are doing, we should feel less evaluation apprehension and thus be less willing to try our hardest. What happens then? Will this relaxation produced by becoming lost in the crowd lead to better or worse performance? Once again, the answer depends on whether we are working on a simple or a complex task.

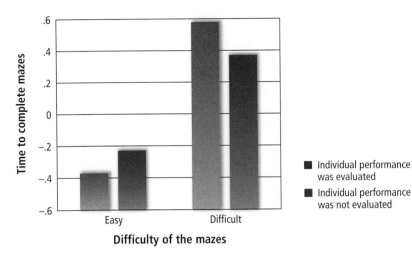

FIGURE 9.4
Social loafing.

When students worked on easy mazes, those who thought their individual performance would not be evaluated did worse (they took more time to complete them, as seen on the left-hand side of the graph). When students worked on difficult mazes, those who thought their individual performance would not be evaluated did better (they took less time to complete them, as seen on the right-hand side of the graph).

(Adapted from Jackson & Williams, 1985)

Let's first consider simple tasks, such as trying to pull as hard as you can on a rope. The question of how working with others would influence performance on such a task was first studied in the 1880s by a French agricultural engineer, Max Ringelmann (1913). He found that when a group of men pulled on a rope, each individual exerted less effort than when he did it alone. A century later, social psychologists Bibb Latané, Kipling Williams, and Stephen Harkins (1979) called this **social loafing,** which is the tendency for people to do worse on simple tasks but better on complex tasks when they are in the presence of others and their individual performance cannot be evaluated. Social loafing in groups has since been found on a variety of simple tasks, such as clapping your hands, cheering loudly, and thinking of as many uses for an object as you can (Karau & Williams, 2001; Shepperd & Taylor, 1999).

What about complex tasks? Recall that when performance in a group cannot be identified, people become more relaxed. Recall also our earlier discussion of the effects of arousal on performance: Arousal enhances performance on simple tasks but impairs performance on complex tasks. By the same reasoning, becoming relaxed should impair performance on simple tasks—as we have just seen—but improve performance on complex tasks. The idea is that when people are not worried about being evaluated, they are more relaxed and should thus be less likely to "clam up" on a difficult task and do it better as a result.

In one study, participants worked on either simple or complex mazes that appeared on a computer screen (Jackson & Williams, 1985). Another participant worked on identical mazes on another computer in the same room. The researchers either said that they would evaluate each person's individual performance (causing evaluation apprehension) or stated that a computer would average the two participants' scores and no one would ever know how well any one person performed (reducing evaluation apprehension). The results were just as predicted. When people thought their score was being averaged with another person's, they were more relaxed, and this relaxation led to better performance (i.e., less time) on the difficult mazes (see the right-hand side of Figure 9.4) but worse performance (i.e., more time) on the easy mazes (see the left-hand side of Figure 9.4).

Gender and Cultural Differences in Social Loafing: Who Slacks Off the Most?

Jane and John are working with several classmates on a class project, and no one can assess their individual contributions. Who is more likely to slack off and let the others do most of the work, John or Jane? If you said John, you are probably

> Which of us . . . is to do the hard and dirty work for the rest—and for what pay?
>
> *—John Ruskin*

Social Loafing

The tendency for people to do worse on simple tasks but better on complex tasks when they are in the presence of others and their individual performance cannot be evaluated right. In a review of more than 150 studies of social loafing, the tendency to loaf was found to be stronger in men than in women (Karau & Williams, 1993). As discussed in Chapter 5, women tend to be higher than men in *relational interdependence,* which is the tendency to focus on and care about personal relationships with other individuals. Perhaps it is this focus that makes women less likely to engage in social loafing when in groups (Eagly, 1987; Wood, 1987).

It was also found that the tendency to loaf is stronger in Western cultures than Asian cultures, which may be due to the different self-definitions prevalent in these cultures (Karau & Williams, 1993). Asians are more likely to have an *interdependent view of the self,* which is a way of defining oneself in terms of relationships to other people (see Chapter 5). This self-definition may reduce the tendency toward social loafing when in groups. We should not, however, exaggerate these gender and cultural differences. Women and members of Asian cultures do engage in social loafing when in groups; they are just less likely to do so than men or members of Western cultures (Chang & Chen, 1995).

To summarize, you need to know two things to predict whether the presence of others will help or hinder your performance: whether your individual efforts can be evaluated and whether the task is simple or complex. If your performance can be evaluated, the presence of others will make you alert and aroused. This will lead to social facilitation effects, where people do better on simple tasks but worse on complex tasks (see the top of Figure 9.3). If your efforts cannot be evaluated (i.e., you are one cog in a machine), you are likely to become more relaxed. This leads to social loafing effects, where people do worse on simple tasks but better on complex ones (see the bottom of Figure 9.3).

These findings have numerous implications for the way in which groups should be organized. On the one hand, if you are a manager who wants your employees to work on a relatively simple problem, a little evaluation apprehension is not such a bad thing—it should improve performance. You shouldn't place your employees in groups where their individual performance cannot be observed, because social loafing (lowered performance on simple tasks) is likely to result. On the other hand, if you want your employees to work on a difficult, complex task, then lowering their evaluation apprehension—by placing them in groups in which their individual performance cannot be observed—is likely to result in better performance.

Deindividuation: Getting Lost in the Crowd

If you are going to make people more anonymous, you should be aware of other consequences of being a face in the crowd. So far, we have discussed the ways in which a group affects how hard people work and how successfully they learn new things. Being in a group can also cause **deindividuation,** which is the loosening of normal constraints on behavior when people are in a crowd, leading to an increase in impulsive and deviant acts (Lea, Spears, & de Groot, 2001). In other words, getting lost in a crowd can lead to an unleashing of behaviors that we would never dream of doing by ourselves. Throughout history, there have been many examples of groups of people committing horrendous acts that no individual would do on his or her own. The massacre at My Lai during the Vietnam War, when a group of American soldiers systematically murdered hundreds of defenseless women, children, and elderly men (see Chapter 8), was one such instance. In Europe, mobs of soccer fans sometimes attack and bludgeon each other. In the United States, hysterical fans at rock concerts have trampled each other to death. And the United States has a shameful history of whites—often cloaked in the anonymity of white robes—lynching African Americans.

Brian Mullen (1986) content-analyzed newspaper accounts of sixty lynchings committed in the United States between 1899 and 1946 and discovered an interesting fact: The more people there were in the mob, the greater the savagery and

Deindividuation

The loosening of normal constraints on behavior when people are in a crowd, leading to an increase in impulsive and deviant acts

viciousness with which they killed their victims. Similarly, Robert Watson (1973) studied twenty-four cultures and found that warriors who hid their identities before going into battle—for example, by using face and body paint—were significantly more likely to kill, torture, or mutilate captive prisoners than warriors who did not hide their identities.

Fortunately, lynch mobs and wars are relatively uncommon. It is not so uncommon, however, to be asked to wear uniforms that make us look like everyone else in the vicinity, an arrangement that might also make us feel less accountable for our actions and hence more aggressive. Does wearing a uniform, as when on a sports team, increase aggressiveness? A German study indicated that it does (Rehm, Steinleitner, & Lilli, 1987). The researchers randomly assigned fifth graders in German schools to teams of five people and then watched the teams play handball against each other. In every game, all the members of one team wore orange shirts and all the members of the other team wore their normal street clothes. The children who wore the orange shirts (and were thus harder to tell apart) played the game significantly more aggressively than the children who wore their everyday clothing (and were thus easier to identify).

The robes and hoods of the Ku Klux Klan cloak its members in anonymity; their violent behavior is consistent with research on deindividuation.

Deindividuation Makes People Feel Less Accountable Exactly what is it about deindividuation that leads to impulsive (and often violent) acts? There are two factors. First, deindividuation makes people feel less accountable for their actions because it reduces the likelihood that any individual will be singled out and blamed (Diener, 1980; Postmes & Spears, 1998; Zimbardo, 1970). In Harper Lee's novel *To Kill a Mockingbird*, for example, a mob of white southerners has assembled to lynch Tom Robinson, a black man falsely accused of rape. Only Atticus Finch, the defendant's lawyer, stands between the mob and the jail. But then Scout, Atticus's 8-year-old daughter, walks into the middle of the crowd. Here is what the mob looked like through her eyes:

> I looked around the crowd. It was a summer's night, but the men were dressed, most of them, in overalls and denim shirts buttoned up to the collars. I thought they must be cold natured, as their sleeves were unrolled and buttoned at the cuffs. Some wore hats pulled firmly down over their ears. They were sullen-looking, sleepy-eyed men who seemed unused to later hours. (Lee, 1960, p. 153)

In other words, the men were highly deindividuated. It was night, they were dressed alike, and it was difficult to tell one from another. It was a mob with one purpose, not a collection of individuals. At that moment, however, Scout recognized one of the men, a farmer named Mr. Cunningham, and greeted him by name:

> "Don't you remember me, Mr. Cunningham? I'm Jean Louise Finch. You brought us some hickory nuts one time, remember?" I began to sense the futility one feels when unacknowledged by a chance acquaintance.
> "I go to school with Walter," I began again. "He's your boy, ain't he? Ain't he, sir?"
> Mr. Cunningham was moved to a faint nod. He did know me, after all.
> "He's in my grade," I said, "and he does right well. He's a good boy," I

If you can keep your head when all about you are losing theirs . . .
—Rudyard Kipling, "If", 1909

In the movie *To Kill a Mockingbird,* Scout succeeded in turning a faceless, deindividuated lynch mob into a collection of individual citizens by singling out Mr. Cunningham and asking him about his son. The mob soon dispersed without harming anyone.

added, "a real nice boy. We brought him home for dinner one time. Maybe he told you about me, I beat him up one time but he was real nice about it. Tell him hey for me, will you?" (pp. 153–154)

At first, the crowd did not respond, so Scout continued her banter.

I was slowly drying up, wondering what idiocy I had committed. I looked around and up at Mr. Cunningham, whose face was equally impassive. Then he did a peculiar thing. He squatted down and took me by both shoulders.
   "I'll tell him you said hey, little lady," he said.
   Then he straightened up and waved a big paw. "Let's clear out," he called. "Let's get going, boys." (p. 154)

Scout succeeded in turning a faceless mob into a collection of individual citizens, who had children who went to school together and to dinner at each other's houses. She had unwittingly performed a brilliant social psychological intervention by increasing the extent to which the mob felt like individuals who were accountable for their actions.

Deindividuation Increases Obedience to Group Norms   Let's consider another explanation of deindividuation. In a meta-analysis of more than sixty studies, researchers found that becoming deindividuated also increases the extent to which people obey the group's norms (Postmes & Spears 1998). Sometimes the norms of a specific group of which we are a member conflict with the norms of other groups or of society at large. When group members are together and deindividuated, they are more likely to act according to the group norms than the other norms. In *To Kill a Mockingbird,* for example, the norms of the lynch mob were to take the law into their own hands, but clearly these norms conflicted with other rules and laws (e.g., "Thou shalt not kill"). Because of the conditions promoting deindividuation, they were about to act on the group's norms and ignore the others until Scout stepped in and reminded them that they were individuals. Thus it is not just that deindividuation reduces the likelihood that one person will stand out and be blamed but also that it increases adherence to the specific group's norms.

   Consequently, deindividuation does not always lead to aggressive or antisocial behavior—it depends on what the norm of the group is. Imagine that you are at a raucous college party at which everyone is dancing wildly to very loud music. To the extent that you feel deindividuated—it is dark, and you are dressed similarly to other people—you are more likely to join the group and let loose on the dance floor. Thus it is the specific norm of the group that determines whether deindividuation will lead to positive or negative behaviors (Gergen, Gergen, & Barton, 1973; Johnson & Downing, 1979). If the group is angry and the norm is to act violently, then deindividuation will make people in the group act aggressively. If we are at a party and the norm is to eat a lot, then being deindividuated will increase the likelihood that we will eat the entire bowl of guacamole.

GROUP DECISIONS: ARE TWO (OR MORE) HEADS BETTER THAN ONE?

We have just seen that the presence of other people influences individual behavior in a number of interesting ways. We turn now to one of the major functions of groups: to make decisions. Most important decisions in the world today are made by groups because it is assumed that groups make better decisions than individuals. In the American judicial system, many verdicts are determined by groups of individuals (juries), not single individuals (for a discussion of jury decision making, see the third Social Psychology in Action module, "Social Psychology and the Law"). The United States Supreme Court is made up of nine justices, not just one member of the judiciary. Similarly, governmental and corporate decisions are often made by groups of people who meet to discuss the issues, and U.S. presidents have a cabinet and the National Security Council to advise them.

Is it true that two (or more) heads are better than one? Most of us assume the answer is yes. A lone individual may be subject to all sorts of whims and biases, whereas several people together can exchange ideas, catch each other's errors, and reach better decisions. We have all taken part in group decisions in which we listened to someone else and thought to ourselves, "Hmm, that's a really good point—I never would have thought of that." In general, groups will do better than individuals if they rely on the person with the most expertise (Davis & Harless, 1996) and are stimulated by each other's comments.

Sometimes, though, two or more heads are not better than one, or at least no better than two heads working alone (Kerr, MacCoun, & Kramer, 1996; McGrath, 1984; Tindale, 1993). At the beginning of this chapter, for example, we saw that President Kennedy and his advisers, after deliberating at length, made a foolhardy decision to invade Cuba. Several factors, as we will see, can cause groups to make worse decisions than individuals.

> Nor is the people's judgement always true: The most may err as grossly as the few.
> —*John Dryden, Absalom and Achitophel, 1682*

Process Loss: When Group Interactions Inhibit Good Problem Solving

One problem is that a group will do well only if the most talented member can convince the others that he or she is right—which is not always easy, given that many of us bear a strong resemblance to mules when it comes to admitting we are wrong (Henry, 1995; Laughlin, 1980; Maier & Solem, 1952). You undoubtedly know what it's like to try to convince a group to follow your idea, be faced with opposition and disbelief, and then have to sit there and watch the group make the wrong decision. This is called **process loss,** which is any aspect of group interaction that inhibits good problem solving (Steiner, 1972). Process loss can occur for a number of reasons. Groups might not try hard enough to

Process Loss

Any aspect of group interaction that inhibits good problem solving find out who the most competent member is and instead rely on someone who really doesn't know what he or she is talking about. The most competent member might find it difficult to disagree with everyone else in the group (recall our discussion of normative social pressures in Chapter 8). Other causes of process loss involve communication problems within the group—in some groups, people don't listen to each other; in others, one person is allowed to dominate the discussion while the others tune out (Sorkin, Hays, & West, 2001; Watson, Johnson, Kumar, & Critelli, 1998).

Failure to Share Unique Information Another interesting example of process loss is the tendency for groups to focus on what its members already know in common, failing to discuss information that only some members have (Geitemeyer & Schulz-Hardt, 2003; Stasser & Titus, 1985). In any group, members share some common knowledge but also know unique things not shared by other members. Consider a medical team trying to decide on the course of treatment of a person with abdominal pain. All members share some knowledge, such as the fact that the patient is a male in his fifties with a history of digestive problems. Some members of the team, however, know things the other members do not. The doctor who first examined the patient in the emergency room may be the only one who knows that the patient had mussels for dinner that night, whereas one of the attending physicians may be the only one to have seen the results of a blood test showing that the patient has an abnormally high white blood cell count. Obviously, to make the most informed decision, the group needs to pool all of the information and use it to decide on the best course of treatment.

As obvious as this is, there is a funny thing about groups: They tend to focus on the information they share and ignore facts known to only some members of the group. In one study, for example, participants met in groups of four to discuss which candidate for student body president was the most qualified (Stasser & Titus, 1985). In the shared information condition, each participant was given the same packet of information to read, data indicating that candidate A was the best choice for office. As seen at the top of Figure 9.5, all participants in this condition knew that candidate A had eight positive qualities and four negative qualities, making him superior to the other candidates. Not surprisingly, when this group met to discuss the candidates, almost all of the members chose candidate A.

In the unshared information condition, each participant received a different packet of information. As seen at the bottom of Figure 9.5, each person knew that candidate A had two positive qualities and four negative qualities. However, the two positive qualities cited in each person's packet were unique—different from those listed in other participants' packets. Everyone learned that candidate A had the same four negative qualities; thus if the participants shared with each other the information that was in their packets, they would learn that candidate A had a total of eight positive qualities and four negative qualities—just as people in the shared information condition knew. Most of the groups in the unshared information condition never realized that candidate A had more good than bad qualities, however, because they focused on the information they shared rather than on the information they did not. As a result, few of these groups chose candidate A.

Subsequent research has focused on ways to get groups to focus more on unshared information (Kelly & Karau, 1999; Postmes, Spears, & Cihangir, 2001). Unshared information is also more likely to be brought up later over time, suggesting that group discussions should last long enough to get beyond what everyone already knows (Larson, Christensen, Franz, & Abbott, 1998; Larson, Foster-Fishman, & Franz, 1998). Another approach is to assign different group members to specific areas of expertise so that they know that they alone are

SHARED INFORMATION CONDITION

UNSHARED INFORMATION CONDITION

FIGURE 9.5

When people are in groups, do they share information that only they know?

Participants in a study met to discuss candidates for an election. In the shared information condition (top half of figure), each person was given the same positive and negative facts about the candidates. Candidate A was clearly the superior candidate, and most groups preferred him. In the unshared information condition (bottom half of figure), each person was given the same four negative facts about candidate A as well as two unique positive facts. In discussion, these people focused on the information they all shared and failed to mention their unique information; these groups were less likely to see candidate A as superior.

(Adapted from Stasser & Titus, 1985)

responsible for certain types of information. If only one doctor's job is to monitor the blood tests, he or she is more likely to bring up this information and other members are more likely to pay attention to it (Stasser, Stewart, & Wittenbaum, 1995; Stewart & Stasser, 1995).

This last lesson has been learned by many couples, who know to rely on each other's memories for different kinds of information. One member of a couple might be responsible for remembering the times of social engagements, whereas the other might be responsible for remembering when to pay the bills (Wegner, Erber, & Raymond, 1991). The combined memory of two people that is more efficient than the memory of either individual is called **transactive memory** (Hollingshead, 2001; Wegner, 1995). By learning to specialize their memories and knowing what their partner is responsible for, couples often do quite well in remembering important information. The same can be true of groups of strangers, if they develop a system whereby different people are responsible for remembering different parts of a task (Liang, Moreland, & Argote, 1995; Moreland, 1999; Moreland, Argote, & Krishnan, 1996). In sum, the tendency for groups to fail to share important information known to only some of the members can be overcome if people learn who is responsible for what kinds of information and take the time to discuss these unshared data (Stasser, 2000).

Groupthink: Many Heads, One Mind Earlier we mentioned that group cohesiveness can get in the way of clear thinking and good decision making. Perhaps that was the problem with Kennedy and his advisers when they decided to invade Cuba; they were more concerned with maintaining morale than with rocking the boat.

Using real-world events, Irving Janis (1972, 1982) developed an influential theory of group decision making that he called **groupthink,** a kind of thinking in which maintaining group cohesiveness and solidarity is more important than considering the facts in a realistic manner. According to Janis's theory, groupthink is most likely to occur when certain preconditions are met, such as when the group is highly cohesive, isolated from contrary opinions, and ruled by a

> The only sin which we never forgive in each other is difference of opinion.
>
> —Ralph Waldo Emerson, *Society and Solitude, 1870*

Transactive Memory

The combined memory of two people that is more efficient than the memory of either individual

Groupthink

A kind of thinking in which maintaining group cohesiveness and solidarity is more important than considering the facts in a realistic manner

directive leader who makes his or her wishes known. Kennedy and his advisers were riding high on their close victory in the 1960 election and were a tight-knit, homogeneous group. Since they had not yet made any major policy decisions, they lacked well-developed methods for discussing the issues. Moreover, Kennedy made it clear that he favored the invasion, and he asked the group to consider only details of how it should be executed instead of questioning whether it should proceed at all.

When these preconditions of groupthink are met, several symptoms appear (see Figure 9.6). The group begins to feel that it is invulnerable and can do no wrong. People do not voice contrary views (they exercise self-censorship) because they are afraid of ruining the group's high morale or because they fear being criticized by the others. For example, Arthur Schlesinger, one of Kennedy's advisers, reported that he had severe doubts about the Bay of Pigs invasion but did not express these concerns during the discussions out of a fear that "others would regard it as presumptuous of him, a college professor, to take issue with august heads of major government institutions" (Janis, 1982, p. 32). If anyone does voice a contrary viewpoint, the rest of the group is quick to criticize, pressuring the person to conform to the majority view. Schlesinger did share some of his doubts with Dean Rusk, the secretary of state. When Robert Kennedy, the attorney general and the president's brother, got wind of this, he took Schlesinger aside at a party and told him that the president had made up his mind to go ahead with the invasion and that his friends should support him. This kind of behavior creates an illusion of unanimity, where it looks as if everyone agrees. On the day the group voted on whether to invade, President Kennedy asked all those present for their opinion—except Arthur Schlesinger.

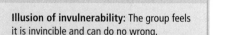

Antecedents of groupthink	Symptoms of groupthink	Defective decision making
The group is highly cohesive: The group is valued and attractive, and people very much want to be members.	**Illusion of invulnerability:** The group feels it is invincible and can do no wrong.	**Incomplete survey of alternatives**
Group isolation: The group is isolated, protected from hearing alternative viewpoints.	**Belief in the moral correctness of the group:** "God is on our side."	**Failure to examine risks of the favored alternative**
A directive leader: The leader controls the discussion and makes his or her wishes known.	**Stereotyped views of out-group:** Opposing sides are viewed in a simplistic, stereotyped manner.	**Poor information search** **Failure to develop contingency plans**
High stress: The members perceive threats to the group.	**Self-censorship:** People decide themselves not to voice contrary opinions so as not to "rock the boat."	
Poor decision-making procedures: No standard methods to consider alternative viewpoints.	**Direct pressure on dissenters to conform:** If people do voice contrary opinions, they are pressured by others to conform to the majority.	
	Illusion of unanimity: An illusion is created that everyone agrees for example, by not calling on people known to disagree.	
	Mindguards: Group members protect the leader from contrary viewpoints.	

FIGURE 9.6

Groupthink: Antecedents, symptoms, and consequences.

Under some conditions, maintaining group cohesiveness and solidarity is more important to a group than considering the facts in a realistic manner (see "Antecedents"). When this happens, certain symptoms of groupthink occur, such as the illusion of invulnerability (see "Symptoms"). These symptoms lead to defective decision making.

(Adapted from Janis, 1982)

The perilous state of groupthink causes people to implement an inferior decision-making process. As seen at the far right in Figure 9.6, for example, the group does not consider the full range of alternatives, does not develop contingency plans, and does not adequately consider the risks of its preferred choice. Can you think of other governmental decisions that were plagued by groupthink? Janis (1972, 1982) discusses several, such as the failure of the U.S. military commanders in Pearl Harbor to anticipate the Japanese attack in 1941; President Truman's decision to invade North Korea in 1950, despite explicit warnings from the Chinese that they would attack with massive force; President Johnson's decision to escalate the Vietnam War in the mid-1960s; and the Watergate coverup by President Nixon and his advisers. A nonpolitical example was the decision in 1986 by NASA to go ahead with the launch of the space shuttle *Challenger* despite the objections of engineers who said that the freezing temperatures presented a severe danger to the rubber O-ring seals. The seals failed during the launch, causing the rocket to explode, killing all aboard. All these decisions were plagued by many of the symptoms and consequences of groupthink, outlined in Figure 9.6 (Esser & Lindoerfer, 1989). As we write, the explosion of the space shuttle *Columbia* in 2003 is still being investigated; it remains to be seen whether any of the decisions in this tragedy were characterized by groupthink.

Since the theory of groupthink was first proposed, it has been put to the test by numerous researchers, with mixed results (Paulus, 1998). For example, group cohesiveness does not seem to be as related to groupthink as Janis had assumed (Aldag & Fuller, 1993; Mohamed & Wiebe, 1996; Tetlock, Peterson, McGuire, Chang, & Field, 1992). Janis's theory, however, suggests that group cohesiveness will increase groupthink only if other conditions are met, such as the presence of a directive leader and high stress (see Figure 9.6). And indeed, the experimental evidence is consistent with this idea: Group cohesiveness does not increase groupthink by itself but does so when it is accompanied by other risk factors (Ahlfinger & Esser, 2001; Mullen, Anthony, Salas, & Driskell, 1994; Turner, Pratkanis, Probasco, & Leve, 1992). Thus support for the groupthink model has been found both in systematic analyses of historical events and in well-controlled laboratory experiments (Esser, 1998; Hogg & Hains, 1998; Schafer & Crichlow, 1996).

The decision to launch the space shuttle *Challenger,* which tragically exploded due to defective O-ring seals, appears to have been the result of groupthink on the part of NASA officials, who disregarded engineers' concerns about the quality of the seals.

Avoiding the Groupthink Trap   A wise leader can take several steps to ensure that his or her group is immune to the groupthink style of decision making (Flowers, 1977; McCauley, 1989; Zimbardo & Andersen, 1993).

- *Remain impartial.* The leader should not take a directive role but should remain impartial.

- *Seek outside opinions.* The leader should invite outside opinions from people who are not members of the group and who are thus less concerned with maintaining group cohesiveness.

- *Create subgroups.* The leader should divide the group into subgroups that first meet separately and then meet together to discuss their different recommendations.

- *Seek anonymous opinions.* The leader might also take a secret ballot or ask group members to write down their opinions anonymously; doing so would ensure that people give their true opinions, uncensored by a fear of recrimination from the group.

Fortunately, President Kennedy learned from his mistakes with the Bay of Pigs decision, and when he encountered his next major foreign policy decision, the Cuban missile crisis, he took many of these steps to avoid groupthink. When his advisers met to decide what to do about the discovery of Soviet missiles in

Cuba, Kennedy often absented himself from the group so as not to inhibit discussion. He also brought in outside experts (e.g., Adlai Stevenson) who were not members of the in-group. That Kennedy successfully negotiated the removal of the Soviet missiles was almost certainly due to the improved methods of group decision making he adopted.

Group Polarization: Going to Extremes

Maybe you are willing to grant that groups sometimes make poor decisions. Surely, though, groups will usually make less risky decisions than a lone individual will—one individual might be willing to bet the ranch on a risky proposition, but if others help make the decision, they will interject reason and moderation. Or will they? The question of whether groups or individuals make more risky decisions has been examined in numerous studies. Participants are typically given the Choice Dilemmas Questionnaire (CDQ), a series of stories that present a dilemma for the main character and ask the reader to choose how much probability of success there would have to be before the reader would recommend the risky alternative (Kogan & Wallach, 1964). An example of a CDQ item about a chess player appears in the Try It! exercise below. People choose their answers

Try it!

Choice Dilemmas Questionnaire

You'll need four or five friends for this exercise. First, copy the questionnaire below and give it to each of your friends to complete individually, without talking to anyone else. Then bring them all together and ask them to discuss the dilemma and arrive at a unanimous decision. They should try to reach a consensus such that every member of the group agrees at least partly with the final decision. Finally, compare people's initial decisions (made alone) with the group decision. Who made the riskier decisions on average, people deciding by themselves or the group?

The Choice Dilemmas Questionnaire

A low-ranked participant in a national chess tournament, playing an early match against a highly favored opponent, has the choice of attempting or not attempting a deceptive but risky maneuver that might lead to quick victory if it is successful or almost certain defeat if it fails. Indicate the lowest probability of success that you would accept before recommending that the chess player play the risky move.

_____ 1 chance in 10 of succeeding

_____ 3 chances in 10 of succeeding

_____ 5 chances in 10 of succeeding

_____ 7 chances in 10 of succeeding

_____ 9 chances in 10 of succeeding

_____ I would not recommend taking the chance.

Remember, groups tend to make riskier decisions than individuals on problems such as these. Did you find the same thing? Why or why not? If the group did make a riskier decision, was it due more to the persuasive arguments interpretation discussed in the text, the social comparison interpretation, or both?

(Adapted from Wallach, Kogan, & Bem, 1962)

alone and then meet in a group to discuss the options, arriving at a unanimous group decision for each dilemma.

Many of the initial studies found, surprisingly, that groups make riskier decisions than individuals do. For example, when deciding alone, people said that the chess player should make the risky gambit only if there was at least a 30 percent chance of success. But after discussing the problem with others in a group, people said that the chess player should go for it even if there were only a 10 percent chance of success (Wallach, Kogan, & Bem, 1962). Findings such as these became known as the *risky shift*. But further research has made clear that such shifts are not the full story. It turns out that groups tend to make decisions that are more extreme in the same direction as the individual's initial predispositions, which happened to be risky in the case of the chess problem. What would happen if people were initially inclined to be conservative? In cases such as these, groups tend to make even more conservative decisions than individuals do.

Consider this problem: Roger, a young married man with two children, has a secure but low-paying job and no savings. Someone gives him a tip about a stock that will triple in value if the company's new product is successful but will plummet if the new product fails. Should Roger sell his life insurance policy and invest in the company? Most people recommend a safe course of action here: Roger should buy the stock only if the new product is very certain to succeed. When they talk it over in a group, they become even more conservative, deciding that the new product would have to have a nearly 100 percent chance of success before they would recommend that Roger buy stock in the company.

The tendency for groups to make decisions that are more extreme than the initial inclination of its members—toward greater risk if people's initial tendency is to be risky and toward greater caution if people's initial tendency is to be cautious—is known as **group polarization** (Brown, 1965; Ohtsubo, Masuchi, & Nakanishi, 2002; Rodrigo & Ato, 2002; Teger & Pruitt, 1967). Group polarization occurs for two main reasons. According to the persuasive arguments interpretation, all individuals bring to the group a set of arguments, some of which other individuals have not considered, supporting their initial recommendation. For example, one person might stress that cashing in the life insurance policy is an unfair risk to Roger's children, should he die prematurely. Another person might not have considered this possibility; thus he or she becomes more conservative as well. A series of studies supports this interpretation of group polarization, whereby each member presents arguments that other members had not considered (Burnstein & Sentis, 1981; Burnstein & Vinokur, 1977).

According to the social comparison interpretation, when people discuss an issue in a group, they first check out how everyone else feels. What does the group value—being risky or being cautious? In order to be liked, many people then take a position that is similar to everyone else's but a little more extreme. In this way, the individual supports the group's values and also presents himself or herself in a positive light—a person in the vanguard, an impressive thinker. Both the persuasive arguments and the social comparison interpretations of group polarization have received research support (Blaskovich, Ginsburg, & Veach, 1975; Brown, 1986; Isenberg, 1986; Zuber, Crott, & Werner, 1992).

The Culture-Value Theory Though group polarization can go either way, Roger Brown (1965) has proposed that relatively speaking, Americans value risk more than caution. In his culture-value theory, Brown discusses how American culture, based on the economic system of capitalism, requires a willingness to take risks and try new approaches. In comparison, other cultures operate under a dominant cultural value of caution—a relatively high level of wariness and conservatism. Hence the hypothesis derived from culture-value theory is that some cultures should be more likely to evince risky shifts while others should be more likely to evince cautious shifts.

Group Polarization

The tendency for groups to make decisions that are more extreme than the initial inclinations of its members

In support of Brown's theory, research has indicated that Americans perceive people who take risks more positively than those who make cautious decisions (Madaras & Bem, 1968), find the riskier alternatives more admirable than the cautious ones (Lamm, Schaude, & Trommsdorff, 1971), and believe high risk takers are more competent than people who choose cautious alternatives (Jellison & Riskind, 1970). Thus it appears that risk does have value in the United States. In comparison, two cross-cultural studies have found evidence for a general cultural value of caution in African countries. In both Uganda and Liberia, groups made choices on the CDQ that were typically more cautious than those made by the individual members alone and that were more cautious than those made by Western research participants (Carlson & Davis, 1971; Gologor, 1977). Thus when group discussion occurs, it reinforces whichever cultural value predominates in that society—for example, group polarization toward caution occurs when individuals learn that they are not as cautious as others in the group and caution is valued in their culture.

Leadership in Groups

A critical question we have not yet considered is the role of the leader in group decision making. The question of what makes a great leader has intrigued psychologists, historians, and political scientists for some time (Bass, 1990; Chemers, 2000; Fiedler, 1967; Hogg, 2001; Hollander, 1985; Klenke, 1996; Simonton, 1987). One of the best-known answers to this question is the **great person theory,** which maintains that certain key personality traits make a person a good leader, regardless of the nature of the situation the leader faces.

There is properly no history, only biography.

—Ralph Waldo Emerson, Essays, History, 1841

If the great person theory is true, we ought to be able to isolate the key aspects of personality that make someone a great leader. Is it a combination of intelligence, charisma, and courage? Is it better to be introverted or extraverted? Should we add a dollop of ruthlessness to the mix as well, as Niccoló Machiavelli suggested in 1513, in his famous treatise on leadership, *The Prince*? Or do highly moral people make the best leaders?

Leadership and Personality Numerous studies have found weak relationships between personality and leadership abilities. Compared to nonleaders, for example, leaders tend to be slightly more intelligent, extraverted, driven by the desire for power, charismatic, socially skilled, open to new experiences, confident in their leadership abilities, and less neurotic (Albright & Forziati, 1995; Chemers, Watson, & May, 2000; Hogan, Curphy, & Hogan, 1994; Judge, Bono, Ilies, & Gerhardt, 2002). What is most telling, however, is the absence of strong relationships. Surprisingly few personality characteristics correlate strongly with leadership effectiveness, and the relationships that have been found tend to be modest. For example, Dean Simonton (1987, 2001) gathered information about one hundred personal attributes of all U.S. presidents, such as their family backgrounds, educational experiences, occupations, and personalities. Only three of these variables—height, family size, and the number of books a president published before taking office—correlated with how effective the presidents were in office. Tall presidents, those from small families, and those who have published books are most likely to become effective leaders, as rated by historians. The other ninety-seven characteristics, including personality traits, were not related to leadership effectiveness at all.

Great Person Theory

The idea that certain key personality traits make a person a good leader, regardless of the situation

The Right Person in the Right Situation As you know by now, one of the most important tenets of social psychology is that to understand social behavior, it is not enough to consider personality traits alone—we must take the social situation into account as well. The inadequacy of the great person theory does not mean that personal characteristics are irrelevant to good leadership. Instead, being good social psychologists, we should consider both the nature of the leader and the situation in which the leading takes place. This view of leadership argues that it is not enough to be a great person; you have to be the right person at the right time in the right situation.

A business leader, for example, can be highly successful in some situations but not in others. Consider Steve Jobs, who, at age 21, founded the Apple Computer company with Stephen Wozniak. Jobs was anything but an M.B.A. type of corporate leader. A product of the 1960s counterculture, he turned to computers only after experimenting with LSD, traveling to India, and living on a communal fruit farm. In the days when there were no personal computers, Jobs's offbeat style was well suited to starting a new industry. Within five years, he was the leader of a billion-dollar company. But Jobs's unorthodox style was ill-suited to managing a large corporation in a competitive market. Apple's earnings began to suffer, and in 1985, Jobs was forced out (Patton, 1989). Interestingly, a decade later, the Apple company faced some of the same technological challenges it did at its inception, having to revamp the operating system for its Macintosh computers and regain market share. Whom did Apple hire to lead this new challenge? Steve Jobs, of course (Markoff, 1996).

Several theories of leadership focus on characteristics of the leader, the followers, and the situation (e.g., Hollander, 1958; House, 1971; Sternberg & Vroom, 2002). The best-known theory of this type is the **contingency theory of leadership,** which argues that leadership effectiveness depends both on how task-oriented or relationship-oriented the leader is and on the amount of control and influence the leader has over the group (Fiedler, 1967, 1978). The first assumption of the theory is that there are two kinds of leaders, those who are task-oriented and those who are relationship-oriented. The **task-oriented leader** is concerned more with getting the job done than with workers' feelings and relationships. For the **relationship-oriented leader,** workers' feelings and relationships are the primary concern.

The crux of contingency theory is that neither type of leader is always more effective than the other; it depends on the situation—specifically, on the amount of control and influence a leader has over the group. In so-called high-control work situations, the leader has excellent interpersonal relationships with subordinates, his or her position in the company is clearly perceived as powerful, and the work needing to be done by the group is structured and well defined. In low-control work situations, the opposite holds—the leader has poor relationships with subordinates, and the work needing to be done is not clearly defined. As seen in Figure 9.7, on the next page, task-oriented leaders are most effective in situations that are either very high or very low in control. When situational control is very high, people are happy, everything is running smoothly, and there is no need to worry about people's feelings and relationships. The leader who pays attention only to the task will get the most accomplished. When situational control is very low, the task-oriented leader is best at taking charge, imposing some order on a confusing, ill-defined work environment. Relationship-oriented leaders, however, are most effective in situations that are moderate in control. Under these conditions, the wheels are turning fairly smoothly, but some attention to the squeakiness caused by poor relationships and hurt feelings is needed. The leader who can soothe such feelings will be most successful.

The contingency theory of leadership has been tested with numerous groups of leaders, including business managers, college administrators, military commanders, and postmasters. These studies have generally been supportive, conforming well to the pattern shown in Figure 9.7 (Chemers, 2000; Peters, Hartke, & Pohlmann, 1985; Schriesheim, Tepper, & Tetrault, 1994; Van Vugt & DeCremer, 1999).

What determines whether someone is a great leader, such as Martin Luther King, Jr.? Is it a certain constellation of personality traits, or is it necessary to have the right person in the right situation at the right time?

Leadership cannot really be taught. It can only be learned.

—*Harold Geneen, 1984*

Contingency Theory of Leadership

The idea that leadership effectiveness depends both on how task-oriented or relationship-oriented the leader is and on the amount of control and influence the leader has over the group

Task-Oriented Leader

A leader who is concerned more with getting the job done than with workers' feelings and relationships

Relationship-Oriented Leader

A leader who is concerned primarily with workers' feelings and relationships

FIGURE 9.7

Fiedler's contingency theory of leadership.

According to Fiedler, task-oriented leaders perform best when situational control is high or low, whereas relationship-oriented leaders perform best when situational control is moderate.

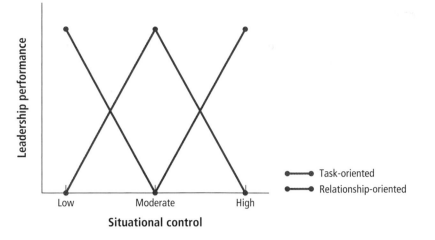

Research shows that women seeking leadership roles can find themselves in a double-bind. If they conform to society's expectations about how they ought to behave, by being warm and communal, they are often perceived to have low leadership potential. If, like Senator Hillary Rodham Clinton, they become leaders and act in ways that leaders are expected to act, namely in agentic, forceful ways, they are often perceived negatively for not "acting like a woman should."

Gender and Leadership An old adage says that because of sex discrimination, a woman has to be "twice as good as a man" in order to advance. Unfortunately, there do seem to be differences in the ways female and male leaders are evaluated (Biernat, Crandall, Young, Kobrynowicz, & Halpin, 1998). If a woman's style of leadership is stereotypically "masculine," in that she is autocratic, "bossy," and task-oriented, she is evaluated more negatively than men who have the same style are (Eagly, Makhijani, & Klonsky, 1992). This is especially true if men are doing the evaluating.

In one study, researchers instructed male and female accomplices to assume leadership roles in groups of students attempting to solve a business problem (Butler & Geis, 1990). Both the male and the female leaders were assertive but cordial, taking charge of the group discussion. How did the other members of the group react to these assertive leaders? The results were discouraging. When a man took charge of the group and acted assertively, the group members reacted favorably. When a woman acted in the same fashion, the group members reacted much more negatively—especially the males. It appears that many men are uncomfortable with women who use the leadership techniques that men typically use.

As more and more women enter the workforce, perhaps people are becoming less biased. But stereotypes change slowly, and it is still the case that women are expected to be more *communal* (concerned with the welfare of others, warm, helpful, kind, affectionate) and men are expected to be more *agentic* (assertive, controlling, dominant, independent, self-confident). Do these gender roles influence how women are perceived in leadership roles? To find out, Alice Eagly and her colleagues have written several reviews of the literature on gender and leadership (Carli & Eagly, 1999; Eagly & Karau, 2002; Eagly, Karau, & Makhijani, 1995). The bad news is that there are two forms of prejudice against women. First, if women behave in the way they are "supposed" to according to societal norms (namely, in a communal fashion), they are often perceived as having less leadership potential. This is because people typically expect successful leaders to be more agentic than communal, especially in high-powered positions such as the head of a large corporation or a military leader.

Second, once women become leaders, they are evaluated more negatively than men when they exhibit agentic leadership behavior, again because these behaviors are contrary to how women are "supposed" to behave. Thus there is a double bind for women: If they conform to societal expectations about how they ought to behave, by being warm and communal, they are often perceived to have low leadership potential. If they succeed in attaining a leadership position and act in ways that leaders are expected to act—namely, in agentic, forceful ways—they are often perceived negatively for not "acting like a woman should." These two kinds of prejudice might help explain why there is a shortage of women in leadership roles in the United States. Women make up 46 percent of the workforce, and 51 percent of all people who hold college degrees are women, yet less than 1 percent of the CEOs of Fortune 500 companies are women, and only 4 percent of the top managers of these companies are women (Eagly & Karau, 2002).

The better news is that prejudice toward women leaders appears to be lessening over time. In a Gallup poll conducted in 1953, for example, 75 percent of men and 57 percent of women said that they preferred a man as a boss, whereas in a similar poll conducted in 2000, 45 percent of men and 50 percent of women said that they preferred a man as a boss (Eagly & Karau, 2002). Further, there is some evidence that people are becoming more accepting of women who act in stereotypical "male" ways (Twenge, 1997) and that there is a growing recognition that effective leaders must often be able to act in stereotypical female (communal) ways as well as stereotypical male (agentic) ways (Eagly & Karau, 2002).

> I wonder men dare trust themselves with men.
>
> *—William Shakespeare, The Life of Timon of Athens*

CONFLICT AND COOPERATION

We have just examined how people work together to make decisions; in these situations, group members have a common goal. Often, however, people have incompatible goals, placing them in conflict with each other. This can be true of two individuals, such as romantic partners who disagree about who should clean the kitchen, or two groups, such as a labor union and company management who disagree over wages and working conditions. It can also be true of nations, such as the long-standing conflict between Israel and its Arab neighbors or between the Serbs, Croats, and Muslims in the former Yugoslavia. The opportunity for interpersonal conflict exists whenever two or more people interact. Sigmund Freud (1930) went so far as to argue that conflict is an inevitable byproduct of civilization because the goals and needs of individuals often clash with the goals and needs of their fellow human beings. The nature of conflict, and how it can be resolved, has been the topic of a great deal of social psychological research (Deutsch, 1973; Levine & Thompson, 1996; Pruitt, 1998; Thibaut & Kelley, 1959).

Many conflicts are resolved peacefully, with little rancor. Couples can find a way to resolve their differences in a mutually acceptable manner, and labor disputes are sometimes settled with a handshake. All too often, however, conflict erupts into open hostilities. The divorce rate in the United States is distressingly high. People sometimes resort to violence to resolve their differences, as shown by the high rate of murders in the United States, which has been called "the murder capital of the civilized world." Warfare between nations remains an all-too-common solution to international disputes. In fact, when wars over the past five centuries are examined, the twentieth century ranks first in the severity of wars (defined as the number of deaths per war) and second in their frequency (Levy & Morgan, 1984). It is therefore of great importance to find ways of resolving conflicts peacefully.

Sometimes negotiations fail and armed conflict results, as in the United States invasion of Iraq. Other times conflicts can be resolved peacefully. Social psychologists have performed experiments to test ways in which conflict resolution is most likely to occur.

Social Dilemmas

What is best for an individual is not always best for the group as a whole. Consider a recent publishing venture by the novelist Stephen King. He wrote two installments of a novel called *The Plant* and posted them on the Internet, asking readers to pay $1 per installment. The deal he offered was simple: If at least 75 percent of the people who downloaded the installments paid the fee, he would keep writing and posting new installments. If fewer than 75 percent of the people paid, he would stop writing, and people would never get the rest of the novel.

King had devised a classic **social dilemma,** a conflict in which the most beneficial action for an individual will, if chosen by most people, be harmful to everyone. It was to any individual's financial advantage to download King's novel free of charge and let other people pay. However, if too many people took this approach, everyone would lose, because King said he would stop writing the novel.

At first, people acted for the good of all; more than 75 percent paid for the first installment. As with many social dilemmas, however, people eventually acted in their own self-interest, to the detriment of all. The number of people who paid for their later installments dropped below 75 percent, and King stopped posting new ones, saying on his Web site that the novel is "on hiatus."

There are many perspectives on how people respond to social dilemmas, including sociological studies of social movements and historical, economic, and political analyses of international relations. The social psychological approach is unique in its attempt to study these conflicts experimentally, testing both their causes and resolutions in the laboratory.

One of the most common ways of studying social dilemmas in the laboratory is with a game called the *prisoner's dilemma.* In this game, two people have to choose one of two options without knowing what the other person will choose. The number of points they win depends on the options chosen by both people. Suppose that you were playing the game with a friend. As shown in the Try It! exercise on page 309, you have to choose option X or option Y, without knowing which option your friend will choose. Your payoff—the amount of money you win or lose—depends on the choices of both you and your friend. For instance, if both you and your friend choose option X, you both win $3. If, however, you choose option Y and your friend chooses option X, you win $6 and your friend loses $6. Which option would you choose?

Many people begin by choosing option Y. At worst, you will lose $1, and at best, you will win the highest possible amount, $6. Choosing option X raises the possibility that both sides will win some money, but this is also a risky choice. If your partner chooses Y while you choose X, you stand to lose a great deal. Because people often do not know how much they can trust their partners, option Y frequently seems like the safest choice (Rapoport & Chammah, 1965). The rub is that both players will probably think this way, ensuring that both sides lose (see the lower right-hand corner of the figure in the exercise).

People's actions in these games seem to mirror many conflicts in everyday life. To find a solution desirable to both parties, people must trust each other. Often they do not, and this lack of trust leads to an escalating series of competitive moves so that in the end no one wins (Batson & Ahmad, 2001; Insko & Schopler, 1998; Kelley & Thibaut, 1978; Pruitt, 1998). Two countries locked in an arms race may feel that they cannot afford to disarm out of fear that the other side will take advantage of their weakened position. The result is that both sides add furiously to their stockpile of weapons, neither gaining superiority over the other and both spending money they could use to solve domestic problems (Deutsch, 1973). Such an escalation of conflict is also seen all too often among couples who are divorcing. Sometimes the goal seems more to hurt the other person than to further one's own needs (or the children's). In the end, both suffer, because metaphorically speaking, they both choose option Y too often.

Increasing Cooperation in the Prisoner's Dilemma Such escalating conflict, though common, is not inevitable. Many studies have found that when people play a prisoner's dilemma game, they will, under certain conditions, adopt the more cooperative response (option X), ensuring that both sides end up with a positive outcome. Not surprisingly, if people are playing the game with a friend or if they expect to interact with their partner in the future, they are more likely to adopt a cooperative strategy that maximizes both their profits and their partner's (Pruitt & Kimmel, 1977). In addition, growing up in some societies, such

Social Dilemma

A conflict in which the most beneficial action for an individual will, if chosen by most people, have harmful effects on everyone

Try it!

The Prisoner's Dilemma

Your Friend's Options	Your Options	
	Option X	**Option Y**
Option X	You win $3 / Your friend wins $3	You win $6 / Your friend loses $6
Option Y	You lose $6 / Your friend wins $6	You lose $1 / Your friend loses $1

Play this version of the prisoner's dilemma game with a friend. First, show the table above to the friend, and explain how the game works: On each trial of the game, you and your friend can choose option X or option Y, without knowing what the other will choose. You should each write your choice on folded pieces of paper that are opened at the same time. The numbers in the table represent imaginary money that you and your friend win or lose on each trial. For example, if you choose option X on the first trial and your friend chooses option Y, you lose an imaginary $6 and your friend wins an imaginary $6. If both of you choose option Y, you both lose an imaginary $1. Play the game for ten trials, and keep track of how much each of you wins or loses. Did you and your friend choose the cooperative option (option X) or the competitive option (option Y) more often? Why? Did a pattern of trust or mistrust develop over the course of the game?

as Asian cultures, seems to foster a more cooperative orientation than growing up in the West does (Bonta, 1997; Markus & Kitayama, 1991).

To increase cooperation, you can also try the **tit-for-tat strategy,** which is a way of encouraging cooperation by at first acting cooperatively but then always responding the way your opponent did (cooperatively or competitively) on the previous trial. This strategy communicates a willingness to cooperate and an unwillingness to sit back and be exploited if the partner does not cooperate. The tit-for-tat strategy is usually successful in getting the other person to respond with the cooperative, trusting response (Axelrod, 1984; Messick & Liebrand, 1995; Parks & Rumble, 2001; Sheldon, 1999; Van Lange, Ouwerkerk, & Tazelaar, 2002). The analogy to the arms race would be to match not only any military buildup made by an unfriendly nation but also any conciliatory gesture, such as a ban on nuclear testing.

Another proven strategy is to allow individuals to resolve a conflict rather than opposing groups, because two individuals who play the prisoner's dilemma are more likely to cooperate than two groups who play the same game (Schopler & Insko, 1999). The reason for this is that people are more likely to assume that another individual is cooperative at heart and can be trusted but that most groups of individuals will, given the opportunity, stab us in the back. Does this mean that world leaders would be more cooperative when negotiating one-on-one than when groups of advisers from the two nations meet? Possibly. In 1985,

Tit-for-Tat Strategy

A means of encouraging cooperation by at first acting cooperatively but then always responding the way your opponent did (cooperatively or competitively) on the previous trial

Ronald Reagan and Mikhail Gorbachev, the leaders of the United States and the Soviet Union, met in Switzerland for the first time to discuss arms reduction. After formal meetings between the leaders and their aides stalled, Reagan and Gorbachev took a walk to a boathouse accompanied only by translators. According to some reports, the two men came close to agreeing to dismantle all of their nuclear missiles—until their aides got wind of this "preposterous" idea and squelched it (Korda, 1997).

Other Kinds of Social Dilemmas   A number of other kinds of social dilemmas have been studied as well. A **public goods dilemma** occurs when individuals must contribute to a common pool in order to maintain the public good, such as paying taxes for public schools. It is to each individual's advantage to pay as little as possible, but if everyone adopts this strategy, everyone suffers.

The **commons dilemma** is a situation in which everyone takes from a common pool of goods that will replenish itself if used in moderation but will disappear if overused. This dilemma got its name from an example in which there is a common grassy area in the middle of a town on which all residents are permitted to let their sheep graze. This is a classic social dilemma because it is to each individual farmer's benefit to let his or her sheep graze as much as possible, but if all farmers do this, the commons will be overgrazed and the grass will disappear (Hardin, 1968). Modern examples include the use of limited resources such as water and energy. Individuals benefit by using as much as they need, but if everyone does so, shortages often result. We discuss commons dilemmas in the second Social Psychology in Action module, "Social Psychology and the Environment," in the context of how to get people to avoid environmentally damaging behaviors.

Using Threats to Resolve Conflict

When involved in a conflict, many of us are tempted to use threats to get the other party to cave in to our wishes, believing that we should, in the words of Teddy Roosevelt, "speak softly and carry a big stick." Parents commonly use threats to get their children to behave, and teachers often threaten their students with demerits or a visit to the principal. More alarming is the increasing number of youths in the United States who carry weapons and use them to resolve conflicts that used to be settled with a playground scuffle. Threats are commonly used on an international scale as well, to further the interests of one nation over another (Turner & Horvitz, 2001).

A classic series of studies by Morton Deutsch and Robert Krauss (1960, 1962) indicates that threats are not an effective means of reducing conflict. These researchers developed a game in which two participants imagined they were in charge of trucking companies named Acme and Bolt. The goal of each company was to transport merchandise as quickly as possible to a destination. The participants were paid 60 cents for each "trip" but had 1 cent subtracted for every second it took them to make the trip. The most direct route for each company was over a one-lane road on which only one truck could travel at a time. This placed the two companies in direct conflict, as seen in Figure 9.8. If Acme and Bolt both tried to take the one-lane road, neither truck could pass, and both would lose money. Each company could take an alternate route, but this was much longer, guaranteeing they would lose at least 10 cents on each trial. The game lasted until each side had made twenty trips.

How did the participants respond to this dilemma? After a while, most of them worked out a solution that allowed both trucks to make a modest amount of money. They took turns waiting until the other party crossed the one-lane road; then they would take that route as well. In another version of the study, the researchers gave Acme a gate that could be lowered over the one-lane road, thereby blocking Bolt from using that route. You might think that using force—

Public Goods Dilemma

A social dilemma in which individuals must contribute to a common pool in order to maintain the public good

Commons Dilemma

A social dilemma in which everyone takes from a common pool of goods that will replenish itself if used in moderation but will disappear if overused

The Deutsch and Krauss trucking game

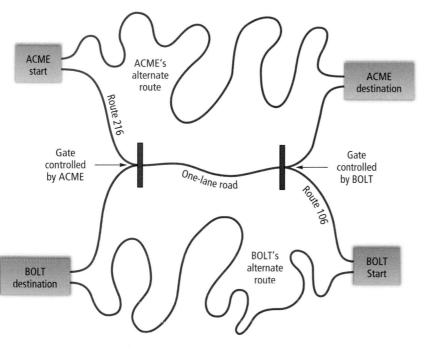

FIGURE 9.8

The trucking game.

Participants play the role of the head of either Acme or Bolt Trucking Company. In order to earn money, they have to drive their truck from the starting point to their destination as quickly as possible. The quickest route is the one-lane road, but both trucks cannot travel on this road at the same time. In some versions of the studies, participants were given gates they used to block the other's progress on the one-lane road.

(Adapted from Deutsch & Krauss, 1962)

the gate—would increase Acme's profits, because all Acme had to do was to threaten Bolt to "stay off the one-lane road or else." In fact, quite the opposite happened. When one side had the gate, both participants lost more than when neither side had the gate—as seen in the left-hand panel of Figure 9.9 on page 312. This figure shows the total amount earned or lost by both sides. (Acme won slightly more than Bolt when it had the gate but won substantially more when neither side had a gate.) Bolt did not like to be threatened and often retaliated by parking its truck on the one-lane road, blocking the other truck's progress. Meanwhile, the seconds ticked away, and both sides lost money.

What would happen if the situation were more equitable, with both sides having gates? Surely they would learn to cooperate very quickly, recognizing the stalemate that would ensue if both of them used their gates—right? To the contrary (as you can see in the left-hand panel of Figure 9.9), both sides lost more money in the bilateral threat condition than in any of the others. The owners of the trucking companies both threatened to use their gates and did so with great frequency. Once Acme used the gate to block Bolt, Bolt retaliated and blocked Acme the next time its truck came down the road, producing a stalemate that was in neither party's interest. Sound familiar? For many decades, the United States and the former Soviet Union were locked in an escalating nuclear arms race, each threatening the other with destruction.

> My own belief is that Russian and Chinese behavior is as much influenced by suspicion of our intentions as ours is by suspicion of theirs. This would mean that we have great influence over their behavior—that, by treating them as hostile, we assure their hostility.
>
> —J. William Fulbright

Effects of Communication

There is a way in which the Deutsch and Krauss trucking game does not approximate real life: The two sides were not allowed to communicate with each other. Would the two adversaries work out their differences if they could talk them over? To find out, Deutsch and Krauss ran a version of their study in which the participants could communicate over an intercom. In one condition, the

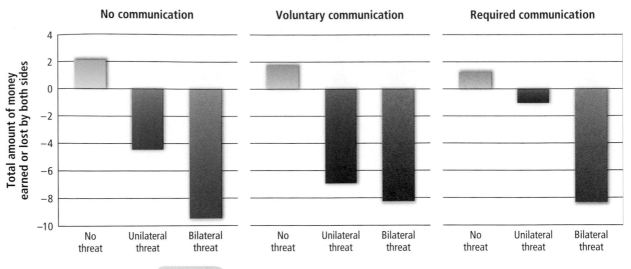

FIGURE 9.9

Results of the trucking game studies.

The left-hand panel shows the amount of money the participants made (summed over Acme and Bolt) when they could not communicate. When threats were introduced by giving one or both sides a gate, both sides lost more money. The middle panel shows the amount of money the participants made when they could communicate as little or as much as they wanted. Once again, giving them gates reduced the amount of money they won. The right-hand panel shows the amount of money the participants made when they were required to communicate on every trial. Once again, giving them gates reduced their winnings.

(Adapted from Deutsch & Krauss, 1962)

participants were allowed to speak as often or as little as they liked, but this had very little effect (compare the middle panel of Figure 9.9 with the left-hand panel). Interestingly, people chose not to say much to each other in this condition, communicating on only about five of the twenty trials.

In another condition, the researchers required the participants to communicate on every trial. Surely if people were forced to talk to each other, they would cooperate more. But again, no dramatic increase in profits occurred (see the right-hand panel of Figure 9.9). Making people communicate reduced losses somewhat when Acme alone had the gate (the unilateral threat condition) but failed to increase cooperation in either of the two other conditions (no threat; bilateral threat). Overall, requiring people to communicate did not raise profits dramatically. Why not?

The problem with the communication in the trucking studies is that it did not foster trust. In fact, people used the intercom to threaten each other. Other studies have found that communication is helpful if people learn to use it to establish trust (Kerr & Kaufman-Gilliland, 1994). Krauss and Deutsch demonstrated this fact in a later version of their trucking study in which they specifically instructed people in how to communicate, telling them to work out a solution that was fair to both parties—that they would be willing to accept if they were in the other person's shoes. Under these conditions, verbal communication increased the amount of money both sides won because it fostered trust instead of adding fuel to the competitive fires (Deutsch, 1973, 1990; Krauss & Deutsch, 1966; Pruitt, 1998).

Negotiation and Bargaining

In the laboratory games we have discussed so far, people's options are limited. They have to choose option X or Y in the prisoner's dilemma, and they have only a couple of ways of getting their truck to its destination in the trucking game. In everyday life, we often have a wide array of options. Consider two people haggling over the price of a car. Both the buyer and the seller can give in to all of the other's demands, to some of them, or to none of them. Either party can walk away from the deal at any time. Given that there is considerable latitude in how people can resolve the conflict, communication between the parties is all the more important. By talking, bargaining, and negotiating, people can arrive at a satisfactory settlement. **Negotiation** is a form of communication between opposing sides in a conflict in which offers and counteroffers are made and a solution occurs only when both parties agree (Bazerman & Neale, 1992; DeDreu, Weingart, & Kwon, 2000; Galinsky, Mussweiler, & Medvec, 2002). How successful are people at negotiating mutually beneficial solutions?

One limit to successful negotiation is that people often assume they are locked in a conflict in which only one party can come out ahead. They don't realize that as in the conflicts we have reviewed, solutions favorable to both parties are available. Consider a labor union and a company that are negotiating a new contract. The company has proposed a 2 percent salary increase and no additional days of annual vacation, and the union has proposed a 6 percent salary increase and six additional days of annual vacation. After protracted negotiations, the two sides decide to compromise on both issues, agreeing to a 4 percent salary increase and three additional days of annual vacation. Sounds fair, doesn't it? The problem with such compromises is that they assume that both issues (in this case, the salary increase and additional vacation days) are equally important to both parties, and often that is not true.

Suppose that the labor union cared much more about increasing salaries than getting additional vacation days, whereas the company cared much more about minimizing vacation days than keeping salaries in check. In this case, a better solution for both sides would be to trade off issues such that the union got the 6 percent salary increase (which it cared about the most) in return for no increase in vacation days (which the company cared about the most). This type of compromise, called an **integrative solution,** is a solution to a conflict whereby the parties make trade-offs on issues according to their different interests; each side concedes the most on issues that are unimportant to it but important to the other side.

It might seem that such integrative solutions would be relatively easy to achieve. After all, the two parties simply have to sit down and figure out which issues are the most important to each. However, people often find it difficult to identify integrative solutions (Hoffman et al., 1999; Thompson, 1997). For instance, the more people have at stake in a negotiation, the more biased their perceptions of their opponent. They will tend to distrust proposals made by the other side and to overlook interests they have in common (O'Connor & Carnevale, 1997; Ross & Ward, 1995, 1996).

In one study, for example, students were asked to take sides in a hypothetical conflict between an employee and an employer (Thompson, 1995). As in our example, the employee had interests somewhat different from the employer's; for example, obtaining a high salary was more important to the employee than the employer, whereas keeping medical benefits down was more important to the employer than the employee. Neither party knew the importance of the issues to the opponent; the point was to see how well each side figured this out as they negotiated a solution.

It turned out that people were not very good at discovering their opponents' true interests. And those who were directly involved in the negotiations were even worse at this task than those who were not. Other students watched videotapes of the negotiations and were simply asked to estimate how important each issue was to each side. These uninvolved observers of the negotiations made more accurate judgments than the people actually involved in the negotiations. When negotiators are in the heat of the battle and care deeply about the

Negotiation

A form of communication between opposing sides in a conflict in which offers and counteroffers are made and a solution occurs only when both parties agree

Integrative Solution

A solution to a conflict whereby the parties make trade-offs on issues according to their different interests; each side concedes the most on issues that are unimportant to it but important to the other side

Resolving international conflicts, such as promoting peace in the Middle East, is not easy. Social psychologists have studied negotiation strategies that can increase the chances that conflicts will be reduced. Here, President George W. Bush encourages talks between the Israeli and Palestinian Prime Ministers.

> Yet there remains another wall. This wall constitutes a psychological barrier between us, . . . [a] barrier of distorted and eroded interpretation of every event and statement. . . . I ask, why don't we stretch our hands with faith and sincerity so that together we might destroy this barrier?
>
> *—Former Egyptian president Anwar al-Sadat, speaking before the Israeli Knesset, 1977*

outcome, they tend to distrust the other side, making it more difficult to realize that there is common ground beneficial to both parties. This is one reason people often use neutral mediators to solve labor disputes, legal battles, and divorce proceedings: Mediators are often in a better position to recognize that there are mutually agreeable solutions to a conflict (Carnevale, 1986; Kressel & Pruitt, 1989; Ross & LaCroix, 1996).

The bottom line? When you are negotiating with someone, it is important to keep in mind that integrative solutions are often available. Try to gain the other side's trust, and communicate your own interests in an open manner. Remember that the way you construe the situation is not necessarily the same as the way the other party construes the situation. You may well discover that the other side communicates its interests more freely as a result, increasing the likelihood that you will find a solution beneficial to both parties.

SUMMARY

What Is a Group?

A **group** consists of two or more people who interact with each other and are interdependent, in the sense that their needs and goals cause them to influence each other. Groups have a number of benefits; in fact, there may be an innate need to belong that drives us to establish bonds with other people. Groups tend to consist of homogeneous members, in part because groups have *social norms* that people are expected to obey. Groups also have well-defined **social roles,** shared expectations about how people are supposed to behave. The roles that people assume in groups, and the expectations that come with those roles, are powerful determinants of people's feelings and behavior in groups. **Group cohesiveness,** qualities of a group that bind members together and promote liking between members, is another important property of groups that influences the group's performance.

Groups and Individuals' Behavior

When people's individual efforts on a task can be evaluated, the mere presence of others leads to **social facilitation:** Their performance is enhanced on simple tasks but impaired on complex tasks. When their individual efforts cannot be evaluated, the mere presence of others leads to **social loafing:** Performance is impaired on simple tasks but enhanced on complex tasks. Finally, the mere presence of others can lead to **deindividuation,** which is the loosening of normal constraints on behavior when people are in crowds, leading to an increase in impulsive and deviant acts.

Group Decisions: Are Two (or More) Heads Better than One?

One of the major functions of groups is to make decisions. Groups make better decisions than individuals if they are good at pooling ideas and listening to the expert members of the group. Often, however, **process loss** occurs, whereby the most expert individual is unable to sway the rest of the group. Further, groups often focus on the information they have in common and fail to share unique information. This latter problem can be avoided if the group knows that individual members have been assigned to specific areas of expertise. Many couples know that one member is responsible for remembering things the other is not. Consequently, they have an effective **transactive memory,** which is the combined memory of two people that is more efficient than the memory of either individual.

Tightly knit, cohesive groups are also prone to **groupthink,** which occurs when maintaining group cohesiveness and solidarity becomes more important than considering the facts in a realistic manner. **Group polarization** causes groups to make more extreme decisions in the direction toward which its members were initially leaning; these group decisions can be more risky or more cautious, depending on which attitude is valued in the group.

Leaders usually play crucial roles in group decisions. There is little support for the **great person theory,** which argues that good leadership is a matter of having the right personality traits. Leadership effectiveness is a function of both the kind of person a leader is and the nature of the work situation. Research on Fiedler's **contingency theory of leadership** has found that leadership performance depends both on whether a group has a **task-oriented leader** or a **relationship-oriented leader** and on whether the work environment is high or low in situational control. There is a double bind for women leaders: If they conform to societal expectations about how they ought to behave, by being warm and communal, they are often perceived as having low leadership potential. If they succeed in attaining a leadership position and act in ways that leaders are expected to act—namely, in agentic, forceful ways—they are often perceived negatively for not "acting like a woman should."

Conflict and Cooperation

Often people have incompatible goals, placing them in conflict with each other. A particularly interesting kind of conflict is a **social dilemma,** in which the most beneficial action for an individual will, if chosen by most people, have harmful effects on everyone. A commonly studied social dilemma is the prisoner's dilemma, in which two people must decide whether to look out for only their own interests or for their partner's interests as well. The **tit-for-tat strategy** is a useful way of dealing with conflict, allowing one to respond cooperatively or competitively, mirroring the other person's response. Creating trust is crucial in solving this kind of conflict. Other kinds of social dilemmas are the **public goods dilemma,** in which individuals must contribute to a common pool in order to maintain the public good, and the **commons dilemma,** in which everyone takes from a public pool of goods that will replenish itself if used in moderation but will disappear if overused. Finally, we examined the conditions under which hostilities are likely to increase or decrease, including how the use of threats and the inability to communicate can exacerbate a conflict. In **negotiation,** it is important to look for an **integrative solution,** whereby each side concedes the most on issues that are unimportant to it but very important to its adversary.

CRITICAL THINKING QUESTIONS

1. Think of several groups you belong to. Do these groups meet the definition of a group presented in the text? What kinds of benefits do you get by being a member of these groups?

2. Give some examples of social roles you are expected to assume. Are you comfortable performing these roles? Why or why not? What would be the consequences if you decided not to act according to these social roles anymore?

3. Think of times that you experienced deindividuation when in a group. How did this influence you?

4. Suppose that you are the leader of a country that is in conflict with a neighboring country over where the border should be and who should have access to valuable natural resources near the border. Based on the research discussed in this chapter, discuss several ways in which you might try to resolve this conflict peacefully.

Interpersonal Attraction:
From First Impressions to Close Relationships

In the village of Junigau, Nepal, 100 miles southwest of Kathmandu, young men and women have the same hopes and goals as their peers around the world—to find someone to love and share their life with. But the path they follow to matrimony is strikingly different from that of people in Western countries like the United States. In Nepalese villages, dating is forbidden, and even casual meetings between young men and women are considered inappropriate. Traditionally, one's future spouse is chosen by one's parents, who focus on the potential suitor's social standing: family, caste, and economic resources. In these arranged marriages, the bride and groom often speak to each other for the first time on their wedding day. It is not unusual for the bride to cry during the ceremony and for the groom to look stunned and resigned (Goode, 1999). Despite what might seem an inauspicious beginning, many of these unions turn out to be very successful. (The high divorce rate in the United States suggests that the Western process of choosing one's own mate is not necessarily the most successful way!)

After the ceremony, the bride moves in with her husband's family, where she is considered of low status. She has to perform the hardest work and is expected to wash her husband's feet every morning and then drink the washwater (a tradition that some women have abandoned in recent years) (Goode, 1999).

It is not just the process of finding a romantic partner that varies around the world, but even how "love" is defined and experienced. As we have discussed throughout this book, Western and Eastern cultures vary in their definitions of the needs of individuals and of the group or the society. Western societies are individualistic, emphasizing that the individual is autonomous, self-sufficient, and defined by his or her personal qualities. Eastern cultures are collectivistic, emphasizing loyalty to the group and defining the individual through membership in the group (Hofstede, 1984; Hui & Triandis, 1986; Markus, Kitayama, & Heiman, 1996; Triandis, 1995).

Social psychologists have noted that romantic love is an important, even crucial basis for marriage in individualistic societies but has less value in collectivistic ones. In individualistic societies, romantic love is a heady, highly personal experience. One immerses oneself in the new partner, virtually ignoring friends and family for a while. The decision regarding whom to become involved with or marry is for the most part a personal one. In comparison, in collectivistic societies, the individual in love must consider the wishes of family and other group members, which sometimes includes agreeing to an arranged marriage (K. L. Dion & K. K. Dion, 1988, 1993; Fiske, Kitayama, Markus, & Nisbett, 1998; Levine, Sato, Hashimoto, & Verma, 1995).

Nevertheless, Western ways of finding a partner have permeated collectivistic cultures through the media, and these media portrayals have had an effect (Hatfield & Rapson, 2002). In Nepal, for example, prospective suitors now write letters to each other, getting to know each other a bit before the wedding. In their letters, the couple do not communicate romantic love as Westerners idealize it. Instead, they discuss serious economic issues that suggest what their future life together will be like, as well as reassure each other they they are trustworthy and honest (Goode, 1999). Even further from tradition is the outcome of these letters: The couple may choose to "elope," marrying at the groom's home (if they have his family's blessing). The couple still must get the bride's family's acceptance of the marriage after the fact; otherwise, the bride can be disinherited.

Similarly, South Asians in London have taken the finding of mates into their own hands to a certain extent. Traditionally, Indians and Pakistanis in Britain, as in their homelands, have viewed marriage as a union between families, not individuals. As one young Indian woman put it, marriage "is not based on love, which can fizzle out," but on similarities in education, income, family standing, religion, and character (Alvarez, 2003, p. 3). Nevertheless, modern Western-style courtship techniques, including "speed dating," are changing traditional ways of meeting. (See the photograph on page 316.)

Speed dating involves meeting many potential mates in a public setting for a few minutes of conversation with each; Hindus are seated at one table and Muslims at another. Someone who strikes a speed dater's fancy is quickly taken home to "meet the parents." Although this ritual occurs in individualistic cultures too, it has far deeper ramifications in collectivistic cultures. In this new version of an arranged marriage, the South Asian suitors play an important role in the beginning, but the families of both still make the ulitimate decision (Alvarez, 2003).

Thus even something as basic to the human condition as falling in love and choosing a life partner shows the effects of social psychology: the influence of the situation—in this case, one's culture. In this chapter, we will explore what makes us feel attracted to other people, whether as friends or lovers, and how relationships develop and progress.

WHAT CAUSES ATTRACTION?

When social psychologist Ellen Berscheid asked people of various ages what made them happy, at or near the top of their lists were making and maintaining friendships and having positive, warm relationships (Berscheid, 1985; Berscheid & Peplau, 1983; Berscheid & Reis, 1998). The absence of meaningful relationships with other people makes people feel lonely, worthless, hopeless, helpless, powerless, and alienated (Baumeister & Leary, 1995; Hartup & Stevens, 1997; Peplau & Perlman, 1982; Stroebe & Stroebe, 1996). In this chapter, we will discuss the antecedents of attraction, from the initial liking of two people meeting for the first time to the love that develops in close relationships.

The Person Next Door: The Propinquity Effect

One of the simplest determinants of interpersonal attraction is proximity (sometimes called *propinquity*). The people who, by chance, are the ones you see and interact with the most often are the most likely to become your friends and lovers (Berscheid & Reis, 1998).

Now, this might seem obvious. But the striking thing about proximity and attraction, or the **propinquity effect,** as social psychologists call it, is that it works in a very narrow sense. For example, consider a classic study conducted in a housing complex for married students at MIT. Leon Festinger, Stanley Schachter, and Kurt Back (1950) tracked friendship formation among the couples in the various apartment buildings. For example, one section of the complex, Westgate West, was composed of seventeen two-story buildings, each having ten apartments. The residents had been assigned to their apartments at random, as a vacancy opened up, and nearly all of them were strangers when they moved in. The researchers asked the residents to name their three closest friends in the entire housing project. Just as the propinquity effect would predict, 65 percent of the friends mentioned lived in the same building, even though the other buildings were not far away.

Even more striking was the pattern of friendships within a building. Each Westgate West building was designed like the drawing in Figure 10.1: Most of the

Propinquity Effect

The finding that the more we see and interact with people, the more likely they are to become our friends

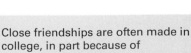

Close friendships are often made in college, in part because of prolonged propinquity.

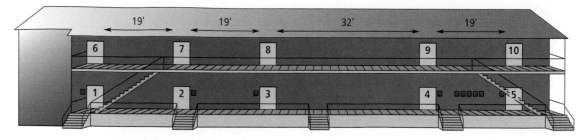

FIGURE 10.1

The floor plan of a Westgate West building.

All the buildings in the housing complex had the same floor plan.

(Adapted from Festinger, Schachter, & Back, 1950)

> Contrary to popular belief, I do not believe that friends are necessarily the people you like best; they are merely the people who got there first.
>
> —Sir Peter Ustinov, Dear Me, 1977

front doors were only 19 feet apart, and the greatest distance between apartment doors was only 89 feet. The researchers found that 41 percent of the next-door neighbors indicated they were close friends, 22 percent of those who lived two doors apart said so, and only 10 percent of those who lived on opposite ends of the hall indicated they were close friends.

Festinger and his colleagues (1950) demonstrated that attraction and propinquity rely not only on actual physical distance but also on "functional distance." Functional distance refers to certain aspects of architectural design that make it more likely that some people will come into contact with each other more often than with others. For example, consider the friendship choices of the residents of apartments 1 and 5 in Figure 10.1. Living at the foot of the stairs and in one case near the mailboxes meant that these couples saw a great deal of upstairs residents. Sure enough, apartment dwellers in apartments 1 and 5 throughout the complex had more friends upstairs than dwellers in the other first-floor apartments did. (You can map out propinquity effects in your life with the Try It! exercise on page 321.)

The propinquity effect works because of familiarity, or the **mere exposure effect:** The more exposure we have to a stimulus, the more apt we are to like it. We see certain people a lot, and the more familiar they become, the more friendship blooms. Of course, if the person in question is an obnoxious jerk, then, not surprisingly, the more exposure you have, the greater your dislike (Swap, 1977). But in the absence of such negative qualities, familiarity breeds attraction and liking (Bornstein, 1989; Griffin & Sparks, 1990; Moreland & Zajonc, 1982; Zajonc, 1968).

A good example of the propinquity and mere exposure effects is your college classroom. All semester long, you see the same people. Does this increase your liking for them? Researchers tested this hypothesis by planting female research confederates in a large college classroom (Moreland & Beach, 1992). The women did not interact with the professor or the other students; they just walked in and sat quietly in the first row, where everyone could see them. The confederates differed in how many classes they attended, from fifteen down to the control condition of none. At the end of the semester, the students in the class were shown slides of the women, whom they rated on several measures of liking and attractiveness. As you can see in Figure 10.2, mere exposure had a definite effect on liking. Even though they had never interacted, the students liked the women more the more often they had seen them in class.

Mere Exposure Effect

The finding that the more exposure we have to a stimulus, the more apt we are to like it

Computers: Long-Distance Propinquity Computer-mediated communication offers a new twist on the propinquity effect; the fact that someone is thousands of miles away no longer means that the two of you can't meet in a chat room or

Try it!

Mapping the Effect of Propinquity in Your Life

In this exercise, you will be examining the relationship between who your friends and acquaintances are and the places where you spend time regularly. Does propinquity explain who your friends are?

First, pick a physical space to focus on. You could choose your dormitory, your apartment building, or the building where you work. (We'll use a dormitory as an example.) Draw a rough floor plan of your dormitory floor. Include the location of all the dorm room doors, the stairs or elevator, the restroom, living room, and so on. Mark your room with a large X. (You can decide whether you need to draw just your floor or more of the building.)

Second, think about who your close friends on the floor are. Mark their dorm rooms with the number 1. Next, think about who your friends are; mark their rooms with a 2. Finally, think about your acquaintances—people you say hello to or chat with briefly now and then. Mark their rooms with a 3.

Now examine the pattern of friendships on your map. Are your friends clustered near your room in physical space? Are the dorm rooms with the numbers 1 and 2 among the closest to your room in physical space? Are they physically closer to your room than the ones with number 3? And what about the dorm rooms that didn't get a number (meaning that you don't really know these people or interact with them)—are these rooms the farthest from yours?

Finally, examine your propinquity map for the presence of functional distance as well. Do aspects of the architectural design of your dorm make you more likely to cross paths with some dorm members more than others? For example, the location of the restroom, kitchen, living room, stairs or elevator, and mailboxes can play an important role in propinquity and friendship formation. These are all places that you go to frequently; when walking to and from them, you pass some people's rooms and not others'. Are the people who live along your path the ones you know the best? If so, propinquity has played an important role in determining the people with whom you have formed relationships!

through e-mail. Propinquity and functional distance, in a sense, are defined by your computer screen. How are computer-based relationships different from the ones formed in everyday life? Do computer relationships survive when they move from the computer screen to face-to-face interactions? Researchers are beginning to explore these questions (Fehr, 1996; Lea & Spears, 1995; Walther, Anderson, & Park, 1994).

We do know that meeting people online poses inherent problems due to the medium itself. First, people may exaggerate or even lie about themselves in an e-mail, and the recipient has no way to detect dishonesty. Second, the flurry of e-

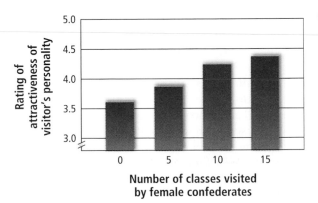

FIGURE 10.2

The effects that mere exposure in the classroom has on attraction.

The more often students saw a female confederate in their classroom, the more positively they rated her personality, even though they had never interacted with her.

(Adapted from Moreland & Beach, 1992)

mails between two people tends to create a high level of emotional intimacy—sometimes too quickly. With no real information about the person (such as you'd get from a face-to-face interaction), you may create an idealized image of the person that quickly dies upon meeting him or her. Third, words alone do not predict attraction. As we saw in Chapter 4, nonverbal cues are an important source of information that we use to form attributions about others. Without real behavior, including nonverbal cues, we don't really know if we're compatible with another person.

So how successful are online dating services? Match.com reports that over a six-year period, it had 5 million members and 1,100 confirmed marriages. Although marriage is only one measure of a successful match, these data indicate that only .045 percent of members who met through Match.com married (Cohen, 2001).

Similarity

Although propinquity does affect friendship choices, we don't become good friends with everyone who is near us in physical space. Researchers describe two types of situations in which relationships begin: *closed-field situations,* in which people are forced to interact with each other, and *open-field situations,* in which people are free to interact or not as they choose (Berscheid & Reis, 1998; Murstein, 1970; Thibaut & Kelley, 1959). Life is made up of many closed-field situations, such as those that exist with your dorm or apartment roommate, your biology lab partner, or your colleagues at work. As we saw, propinquity increases familiarity, which leads to liking, but something more is needed to fuel a growing friendship or a romantic relationship. (Otherwise, every pair of roommates would be best friends!) That "fuel" is *similarity*—a match between our interests, attitudes, values, background, or personality and those of another person. Folk wisdom captures this idea in the expression "Birds of a feather flock together" (the concept of *similarity*). But folk wisdom also has another saying, "Opposites attract" (the concept of *complementarity,* or that we are attracted to people who are our opposites). Luckily, we don't have to remain forever confused by contradictory advice from old sayings; research evidence proves that it is similarity and not complementarity that draws people together (Berscheid & Reis, 1998; Byrne, 1997; McPherson, Smith-Lovin, & Cook, 2001).

Opinions and Personality   In dozens of tightly controlled experiments, if all you know about a person (whom you've never met) are his or her opinions on several issues, the more similar those opinions are to yours, the more you will like the person (e.g., Byrne & Nelson, 1965). And what happens when you do meet? In a classic study, Theodore Newcomb (1961) randomly assigned male college students at the University of Michigan to be roommates in a particular dormitory at the start of the school year. Would similarity predict friendship formation? The answer was yes: Men became friends with those who were demographically similar (e.g., shared a rural background), as well as with those who were similar in attitudes and values (e.g., were also engineering majors or also held liberal political views). It's not just attitudes or demographics that are important. Similar personality characteristics also promote liking and attraction. For example, in a study of gay men's relationships, men sought men with similar personalities. Those who scored high on a test of stereotypical male traits desired a partner who was most of all logical—a stereotypical masculine trait. Gay men who scored high on a test of stereotypical female traits desired a partner who was most of all expressive—a stereotypical feminine trait (Boyden, Carroll, & Maier, 1984). Similar personality characteristics are important for heterosexual couples and for friends as well (Aube & Koestner, 1995; Caspi & Harbener, 1990; Martin & Anderson, 1995).

An administrator in the Housing Office of Barnard College sorts through roommate applications, placing them in piles according to their similar answers to questions about living habits and interests.

Interpersonal Style We are also attracted to people whose interpersonal style and communication skills are similar to ours. In one study, people were attracted to peers who were similar to them in how they thought about people and how they liked to talk about interpersonal interactions (Burleson & Samter, 1996). High-skill people saw social interactions as complicated and complex; they focused on the psychological aspects of the interaction and valued communication with others that included this psychological component. Low-skill people saw social interactions in a more straightforward, less complicated way; they focused on the instrumental aspects of the interaction (e.g., what can be accomplished and what actually happened) and were less interested in the personalities or motivation of the participants. Pairs of friends had similar levels of communication skill—low with low, high with high. In fact, researchers have found that relationships with people who do not share your interpersonal communication style are frustrating and less likely to flourish (Burleson, 1994; Duck & Pittman, 1994). This is probably a great predictor of satisfaction in relationships and marriage—and of breakups and divorce!

S. GROSS

"I don't care if she is a tape dispenser. I love her."

Interests and Experiences Finally, similarity operates in another, more subtle way. The situations that you choose to be in are, by definition, populated by people who have chosen them for similar reasons. You're sitting in a social psychology class, surrounded by people who also chose to take social psychology this semester. You sign up for salsa dance lessons; the others in your class are there because they too want to learn Latin dancing. Thus we choose to enter into certain types of social situations where we then find similar others. For example, in a study of the patterns of students' friendships that focused on the effects of "tracking" (grouping students by academic ability), researchers found that students were significantly more likely to choose friends from their track than from outside it (Kubitschek & Hallinan, 1998). Clearly, propinquity and initial similarity play a role in the formation of these friendships. However, the researchers add that similarity plays yet another role: Over time, students in the same academic track share many of the same experiences, which are different from the experiences of those in other tracks. Thus new similarities are created and discovered between them, fueling the friendships.

Why is similarity so important in attraction? There are at least three possibilities. First, we tend to think that people who are similar to us will also like us, so we are likely to initiate a relationship (Aronson & Worchel, 1966; Berscheid, 1985; Condon & Crano, 1988). Second, people who are similar validate our own characteristics and beliefs—that is, they provide us with the feeling that we are right (Byrne & Clore, 1970). Third, we make negative inferences about someone who disagrees with us on important issues. We suspect that the individual's opinion is indicative of the kind of person whom we have found to be unpleasant, immoral, weak, or thoughtless. In short, disagreement on important attitudes leads to repulsion (Rosenbaum, 1986). Thus the desire to be liked, the need to be validated, and the conclusions we draw about character all play a role in boosting the attractiveness of a like-minded person and diminishing the attractiveness of someone who is dissimilar (Byrne, Clore, & Smeaton, 1986; Condon & Crano, 1988; Houts, Robins, & Huston, 1996; Tan & Singh, 1995).

Reciprocal Liking

> Life is to be fortified by many friendships. To love, and to be loved, is the greatest happiness of existence.
>
> —Sydney Smith, 1855

We all like to be liked. In fact, just knowing that someone likes us fuels our attraction to the person. Liking is so powerful that it can even make up for the absence of similarity. For example, in one experiment, when a young woman expressed interest in male research participants simply by maintaining eye contact, leaning toward them, and listening attentively, the men expressed great liking for her despite the fact that they knew she disagreed with them on important issues (Gold, Ryckman, & Mosley, 1984). Whether the clues are nonverbal or verbal, perhaps the most crucial determinant of whether we will like person A is the extent to which we believe person A likes us (Berscheid & Walster, 1978; Kenny, 1994b; Kenny & La Voie, 1982; Kubitschek & Hallinan, 1998).

Reciprocal liking sometimes happens because of a self-fulfilling prophecy (see Chapter 3). Researchers demonstrated this process by conducting the following experiment (Curtis & Miller, 1986). College students participated in the study in pairs; they had not known each other before meeting at the study. One member of each pair was randomly chosen to receive special information. The researchers led some to believe that the other student liked them and led others to believe that the other student disliked them. The pairs of students were then allowed to meet and talk to each other again. Just as predicted, those who thought they were liked behaved in more likable ways with their partner; they disclosed more about themselves, disagreed less about the topic under discussion, and generally behaved in a warmer, more pleasant manner than the individuals who thought they were disliked. Moreover, those who believed they were liked came to be liked by the other student to a far greater extent than those who believed they were disliked. In short, the partner tended to mirror the behaviors of the person with whom he or she was paired.

Most of the time, being liked by a person is a powerful determinant of our liking for them. But the amount of self-esteem a person has affects this process (Swann, 1992). People with a positive or moderate self-concept respond to other's liking with reciprocal liking, as we've discussed. But people with a negative self-concept respond quite differently—in an experimental setting, such people indicate that they'd prefer to meet and talk to a person they know has criticized them earlier than meet and talk to a person they know has praised them earlier (Swann, Stein-Seroussi, & McNulty, 1992). Thus if people think of themselves as not being worth very much or even as unlikable, another person's friendly behavior toward them will seem unwarranted, and they may not respond, setting in motion a self-fulfilling prophecy (Murray, Holmes, McDonald, & Ellsworth, 1998).

> Love to faults is always blind, Always is to joy inclin'd.
>
> —William Blake, "Love to Faults"

Physical Attractiveness and Liking

Propinquity, similarity, and reciprocal liking are not the only determinants of who we will come to like. How important is physical appearance to our first impressions of people? In field experiments investigating people's actual behavior (rather than what they say they will do), people overwhelmingly go for physical attractiveness. For example, in a classic study, Elaine Walster Hatfield and her colleagues (Walster, Aronson, Abrahams, & Rottman, 1966) randomly matched 752 incoming students at the University of Minnesota for a blind date at a dance during freshman orientation week. Although the students had previously taken a battery of personality and aptitude tests, the researchers paired them up at random. On the night of the dance, the couples spent a few hours together dancing and chatting. They then evaluated their date and indicated the strength of their desire to date that person again. Of the many possible characteristics that could have determined whether they liked each other—such as their partner's intelligence, independence, sensitivity, or sincerity—the overriding determinant was physical attractiveness.

What's more, there was no great difference between men and women on this score. This is an interesting point, for while several studies have found that men and women pay equal attention to the physical attractiveness of others (Duck, 1994a, 1994b; Lynn & Shurgot, 1984; Speed & Gangestad, 1997; Woll, 1986), other studies have reported that men value attractiveness more than women do (Buss, 1989; Buss & Barnes, 1986; Howard, Blumstein, & Schwartz, 1987). A meta-analysis of many studies found that while both sexes value attractiveness, men value it somewhat more (Feingold, 1990). However, this gender difference was greater when men's and women's attitudes were being measured than when their actual behavior was being measured. Thus it may be that men are more likely than women to *say* that physical attractiveness is important to them in a potential friend, date, or mate, but when it comes to actual behavior, the sexes are more similar in their response to the physical attractiveness of others.

> It is only shallow people who do not judge by appearances.
>
> —Oscar Wilde, The Picture of Dorian Gray, 1891

Recent research continues to find that men and women rank physical attractiveness as equally important. Two researchers focused on an important distinction: They asked male and female participants to rate the desirability of twenty-three traits (including physical attractiveness) in a potential sexual partner (i.e., in a short-term, uncommitted relationship) and in a potential marriage partner (i.e., in a committed, long-term relationship) (Regan & Berscheid, 1997). Both sexes ranked physical attractiveness as the most highly desirable characteristic in a potential sexual partner. (Only when it came to rating a marriage partner did men rate physical attractiveness higher than women did,

Research has found that we share some standards of beauty. In females, large eyes, prominent cheekbones and narrow cheeks, high eyebrows, and a small chin were associated with beauty; in males, large eyes, prominent cheekbones, and a large chin were rated as most beautiful. Today's popular models and film stars, such as Brad Pitt, Michelle Pfeiffer, Denzel Washington, Naomi Campbell, Benjamin Bratt, and Lucy Liu, fit these criteria.

though it was not one of the top characteristics desired by men.) In other studies, both genders rated physical attractiveness as the single most important characteristic that triggers sexual desire (Graziano, Jensen-Cambell, Shebilske, & Lundgren, 1993; Regan & Berscheid, 1995).

Finally, the powerful role that physical appearance plays in attraction is not limited to heterosexual relationships. When gay men participated in a "blind date" study like the one described earlier, they responded just as the heterosexual men and women had in the earlier study: The physical attractiveness of their dates was the strongest predictor of their liking for them (Sergios & Cody, 1985).

What Is Attractive? Is physical attractiveness "in the eye of the beholder," or do we all share some of the same notions of what is beautiful and handsome? From early childhood on, the media tell us what is beautiful, and they tell us that this definition of beauty is associated with goodness. For example, illustrators of most traditional children's books, as well as the people who draw the characters in Disney movies, have taught us that the heroines—as well as the princes who woo and win them—all look alike. For example, the heroines all have regular features; small, pert noses; big eyes;

Oh, what vileness human beauty is, corroding, corrupting everything it touches.

—Orestes, 408 B.C.

shapely lips; blemish-free complexions; and slim, athletic bodies—pretty much like Barbie dolls.

Bombarded as we are with media depictions of attractiveness, it is not surprising to learn that we share a set of criteria for defining beauty (Fink & Penton-Voak, 2002; Tseëlon, 1995). Look at the photographs on page 326 of models and actors who are considered very attractive in Western culture. Can you describe the facial characteristics that have earned them this label? Michael Cunningham (1986) designed a creative study to determine these standards of beauty. He asked college men to rate the attractiveness of fifty photographs of women, taken from a college yearbook and from an international beauty pageant program. Cunningham then carefully measured the relative size of the facial features in each photograph. He found that high attractiveness ratings were associated with faces with large eyes, a small nose, a small chin, prominent cheekbones and narrow cheeks, high eyebrows, large pupils, and a big smile. Researchers then examined women's ratings of male beauty in the same way (Cunningham, Barbee, & Pike, 1990). They found that men's faces with large eyes, prominent cheekbones, a large chin, and a big smile received higher attractiveness ratings.

There is some overlap in the men's and women's ratings. Both sexes admire large eyes in the opposite sex; these are considered a "babyface" feature, for newborn mammals have very large eyes for the size of their faces. Babyface features are thought to be attractive because they elicit feelings of warmth and nurturance in perceivers—think of our typical response to babies, kittens, and puppies (e.g., Berry, 1995; McArthur & Berry, 1987; Zebrowitz, 1997; Zebrowitz & Montepare, 1992). Both sexes also admire prominent cheekbones in the opposite sex, an adult feature that is found only in the faces of those who are sexually mature. Note that the female face that is considered beautiful has more babyface features (small nose, small chin) than the handsome male face, suggesting that beauty in the female is associated more with childlike qualities than male beauty is.

Cultural Standards of Beauty   Are people's perceptions of what is beautiful or handsome similar across cultures? The answer is a surprising yes (Cunningham, Roberts, Barbee, Druen, & Wu, 1995; Jones & Hill, 1993; McArthur & Berry, 1987; Rhodes et al., 2001). Even though racial and ethnic groups do vary in specific facial features, people from a wide range of cultures agree on what is physically attractive in the human face. Researchers asked participants from various countries, ethnicities, and racial groups to rate the physical attractiveness of photographed faces of people who also represented various countries, ethnicities, and racial groups. The participants' ratings agreed to a remarkable extent. For example, one review of this literature found that the correlations between participants' ratings ranged from .66 to .93 (Langlois & Roggman, 1990), which are very strong correlations (see Chapter 2). A meta-analysis of many studies by Judith Langlois and her colleagues (2000) also found evidence for cross-cultural agreement in what constitutes a beautiful or handsome face. Although people's judgments vary, across large groups a consensus emerges: Perceivers think some faces are just better-looking than others, regardless of cultural background (Berscheid & Reis, 1998).

How can we explain these results? Langlois and Roggman have suggested that humans came to find certain dimensions of faces attractive during the course of our evolution (Langlois & Roggman, 1990; Langlois, Roggman, & Musselman, 1994). Several studies led the researchers toward this hypothesis. We know, for example, that infants prefer photographs of attractive faces to unattractive ones, and infants prefer the same photographs adults prefer (Langlois, Ritter, Roggman, & Vaughn, 1991; Langlois, Roggman, & Rieser-Danner, 1990;

> Beauty is a greater recommendation than any letter of introduction.
>
> —*Aristotle, fourth century B.C.*

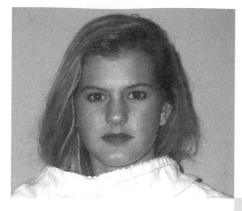
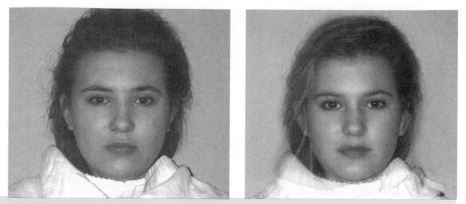

Physical attractiveness of composite faces. Langlois & Roggman (1990) created composites of faces using a computer. Pictured here is the first step in the process: The two women's photos on the left are merged to create the "composite person" on the right. This composite person has facial features that are the mathematical average of the facial features of the two original women. The final step of the process occurs when thirty-two individuals' faces have been merged to create one face, the average of all of the prior thirty-two faces. Perceivers rated the thirty-two-photograph composite face as more physically attractive than any of the individual faces that had created it. (From Langlois, Roggman, & Musselman, 1994)

Langlois et al., 1987). They further hypothesized that attractive faces for both sexes are those whose features are the arithmetic mean—or average—for the species and not the extremes.

To test these hypotheses, Langlois and her colleagues (Langlois & Roggman, 1990; Langlois et al., 1994) designed an elegant and original study. They took photographs of many college students (mostly Caucasians, with some Hispanics and Asians) and digitized each photograph by scanning it into a computer. They then took two people's photographs (men or women) and, using the computer, merged the two photographs into one. The resulting composite was the exact mathematical average of the facial features of the two original people's photographs. The photographs on this page show the result of this operation: The composite photograph, or average, is a blend of the two original women.

Langlois and Roggman (1990) continued adding new photographs until they created a single photograph composite based on sixteen different faces and another based on thirty-two faces. (The composite was created by averaging in the facial features of each added photograph.) Next, they asked research participants to rate the physical attractiveness of the composite photograph and the individual photographs that made up the composite. Would the composite photograph—the arithmetic average of all the faces—be judged more attractive than all the separate faces that helped create that composite? The answer was yes, for both male and female photographs and across many different sets of photographs. The sixteen- and thirty-two-face composites produced what the researchers called a typical or "familiar" face. Individual variation in facial features melted away in the composite; what was left was a good-looking human being whose face had a familiar and highly pleasing aspect.

Do these results mean that "average" faces are the most attractive? Clearly not, for we respond to the physical appearance of movie stars and models because their looks are atypical or "above average" compared to most humans. What Langlois and her colleagues found was that the "average" composite face was perceived as more attractive than all the faces that made it up. But that does not mean these composite "average" faces had all the physical qualities that people cross-culturally agree are highly attractive.

Other research makes this distinction clear (Perrett, May, & Yoshikawa, 1994). These researchers also created composite faces of two types: One composite was composed of sixty individual photographs and was called the "average attractive" composite. The other composite was a new kind, composed of fifteen photos from the original sixty that had received the highest ratings of attractiveness in a pretest. This composite was called the "highly attractive" composite.

The researchers made separate composites of these two types using photographs of Caucasian women, Caucasian men, Japanese women, and Japanese men. They then asked research participants in Great Britain and Japan to rate all the composite faces for attractiveness. They found, first, that the "highly attractive" composites were rated significantly more attractive than the "average attractive" composites. Second, the Japanese and British participants showed the same pattern when judging the faces, reinforcing the idea that similar perceptions of facial attractiveness exist cross-culturally and exist for ethnic groups that are the same or different from one's own. Finally, what did those "highly attractive" composites look like? Their facial shapes, whether Japanese or Caucasian, matched the descriptions for men and women that Michael Cunningham and his colleagues (Cunningham, 1986; Cunningham, Barbee, & Pike, 1990) found in their research. For example, the Japanese and Caucasian "highly attractive" female composites had higher cheekbones, a thinner jaw, and larger eyes relative to the size of the face than the "average attractive" composites did (Perrett et al., 1994). Thus the "average" composite face is attractive to us because it has lost some of the atypical or unfamiliar variation that makes up individual faces. However, the most attractive composite face is one that started out above average and only became more so as variation was smoothed over.

The Power of Familiarity   The crucial variable that explains interpersonal attraction may actually be familiarity (Berscheid & Reis, 1998). We've seen that "averaging" many faces together produces one face that looks typical, familiar, and physically attractive (see also Halberstadt & Rhodes, 2000). Recent research has found evidence for an even more startling effect for familiarity: When research participants rated the attractiveness of faces, they preferred the faces that most resembled their own! The researchers then computer-morphed a picture of each participant's face (without the participant's knowledge) into that of a person of the opposite sex. When they presented this photo to participants, they gave the photo of their opposite-sex "clone" even higher ratings of attractiveness (Little & Perrett, 2002).

Familiarity also underlies the other concepts we've been discussing: propinquity (people we see frequently become familiar through mere exposure), similarity (people who are similar to us will also seem familiar to us), and reciprocal liking (people who like each other get to know and become familiar with each other). All of these attraction variables may be expressions of our "underlying preference for the familiar and safe over the unfamiliar and potentially dangerous" (Berscheid & Reis, 1998, p. 210).

Assumptions about Attractive People   In many studies, participants attributed positive qualities to beautiful people that had nothing to do with their looks. Some researchers (Dion, Berscheid, & Walster, 1972) have called this tendency the "what is beautiful is good" stereotype (Ashmore & Longo, 1995; Calvert, 1988; Moore, Graziano, & Millar, 1987).

The stereotype is relatively narrow, affecting people's judgments about an individual only in specific areas. Meta-analyses have revealed that physical attractiveness has the largest effect on both men's and women's attributions when they are judging social competence: The beautiful are thought to be more sociable, extraverted, and popular than the less attractive (Eagly, Ashmore, Makhijani, & Longo, 1991; Feingold, 1992b). They are also seen as more sexual, happier, and more assertive.

In Western cultures, where independence is valued, the "beautiful" stereotype includes traits of personal strength. In more collectivistic Asian cultures, beautiful people are assumed to have traits such as integrity and concern for others.

Do these stereotypes about beautiful people operate across cultures? The answer appears to be yes (Albright et al., 1997; Chen, Shaffer, & Wu, 1997). For example, college students in Seoul, South Korea, were asked to rate a number of yearbook photographs that varied in physical attractiveness (Wheeler & Kim, 1997). Both male and female participants thought the more physically attractive people would also be more socially skilled, friendly, and well adjusted—the same group of traits that North American participants thought went with physical attractiveness (see Table 10.1). But Korean and North American students differed in some of the other traits they assigned to the beautiful, highlighting what is important and valuable in each culture (Markus et al., 1996; Triandis, 1995). For the American and Canadian students, who live in individualistic cultures that value independence, individuality, and self-reliance, the "beautiful" stereotype included traits of personal strength. These traits were not part of the Korean "beautiful" stereotype. Instead, for the Korean students, who live in a collectivistic culture that values harmonious group relations, the "beautiful" stereotype included integrity and concern for others, traits that were not part of the North American stereotype (see Table 10.1).

Interestingly, the stereotype that the beautiful are particularly gifted in the area of social competence has some research support; highly attractive people do develop good social interaction skills and report having more satisfying interactions with others than the less attractive do (Feingold, 1992b; Langlois et al., 2000; Reis, Nezlek, & Wheeler, 1980; Reis et al., 1982). Undoubtedly, this "kernel of truth" in the stereotype occurs because the beautiful, from a young age, receive a great deal of social attention that in turn helps them develop good social skills. You probably recognize the self-fulfilling prophecy at work here (see Chapter 3): The way we treat people affects how they behave and ultimately how they perceive themselves.

TABLE 10.1

How Culture Affects the "What Is Beautiful Is Good" Stereotype

The "what is beautiful is good" stereotype has been explored in both an individualistic culture (North America) and a collectivistic culture (Asia). Male and female research participants in the United States and Canada and in South Korea rated photographs of people with varying degrees of physical attractiveness. Their responses indicated that some of the traits that make up the stereotype are the same across cultures, while other traits that are associated with the stereotype are different in the two cultures. In both cultures, the physically attractive are seen as having more of the characteristics that are valued in that culture than the less physically attractive have.

Traits Shared in the Korean, American, and Canadian Stereotype

sociable	extraverted	likable
happy	popular	well-adjusted
friendly	mature	poised
sexually warm and responsive		

Additional Traits Present in the American and Canadian Stereotype

strong	assertive	dominant

Additional Traits Present in the Korean Stereotype

sensitive	empathic	generous
honest	trustworthy	

Sources: Eagly, Ashmore, Makhijani, & Longo (1991); Feingold (1992b); Wheeler & Kim (1997).

Can a "regular" person be made to act like a "beautiful" one through the self-fulfilling prophecy? To find out, researchers gave college men a packet of information about another research participant, including her photograph (Snyder, Tanke, & Berscheid, 1977). The photograph was rigged; it was either of an attractive woman or of an unattractive woman. The men were told that they would have a telephone conversation with this woman (in this experimental condition, only verbal communication—no gestures or facial expressions—was used). The experimental purpose of the photograph was to invoke the men's stereotype that "what is beautiful is good"—that the woman would be more warm, likable, poised, and fun to talk to if she was physically attractive than if she was unattractive. In fact, the photograph the men were given was not a photo of the woman with whom they spoke. Did the men's beliefs create reality?

Yes—the men who thought they were talking to an attractive woman responded to her in a warmer, more sociable manner than the men who thought they were talking to an unattractive woman. Not only that, but the men's behavior influenced how the women themselves responded. When independent observers listened to a tape recording of only the woman's half of the conversation (without looking at the photograph), they rated the women whose male partners thought they were physically attractive as more attractive, confident, animated, and warm than the women whose male partners thought they were unattractive. In short, because the male partner thought he was talking to an attractive woman, he spoke to her in a way that brought out her best and most sparkling qualities.

This study was later replicated with the roles switched: Women participants looked at a photograph of an attractive or an unattractive man and then spoke with him on the phone (Andersen & Bem, 1981). The men were unaware of the women's belief about them, and just as in the original study, the women acted on their "prophecy" and the unknowing men responded accordingly. These data remind us that it is a myth that physical attractiveness affects women's lives more than men's. Three meta-analyses that have examined the effect of attractiveness on behavior and perceptions across hundreds of studies have found no gender differences: Physical attractiveness is as important a factor in men's lives as women's (Eagly et al., 1991; Feingold, 1992b; Langlois et al., 2000).

Recollections of Initial Attraction

We've now discussed several predictors of initial attraction and liking: propinquity, similarity, reciprocal liking, and physical attractiveness. At the beginning of the chapter, we asked you to think about why you were first attracted to your friends and romantic partners. In a research study, college students and older adults were asked to give accounts of how they fell in love or formed a friendship with specific people in their lives (Aron, Dutton, Aron, & Iverson, 1989). The researchers then coded these accounts for the presence of the classic social psychological variables we have discussed. Do people spontaneously report such factors as the cause for their initial feelings of attraction?

Yes, they do. First, for the falling-in-love accounts, reciprocal liking and attractiveness (involving both physical and personality qualities) were mentioned spontaneously with very high frequency (Aron et al., 1989; Duck, 1994a). The power of these two variables together led the researchers to conclude that "People are just waiting for an attractive person to do something they can interpret as liking them" (Aron et al., 1989, p. 251). Mentioned with moderate frequency were variables such as being ready for or looking for a romantic relationship and being unhappy in a current relationship. Finally, similarity and propinquity were mentioned with low to moderate frequency. The researchers suggest that these two variables may be underreported because people do not remember or notice experiencing them or because they are seen as too mundane

Research indicates that reciprocal liking and attractiveness are powerful predictors of falling in love among many people, including Anglo, Mexican and Chinese Americans, as well as Russians and Japanese.

Don't threaten me with love, baby. Let's go walking in the rain.

—Billie Holiday

to explain something so exciting as falling in love. It is also possible that that similarity and propinquity may play an important role before one falls in love, by narrowing the field to only those people who are "eligible" (Aron et al., 1989). This basic pattern of results for falling in love appears cross-culturally as well, for Chinese American and Mexican American students in the United States (Aron & Rodriguez, 1992) and for students in Japan and Russia (Sprecher, Aron et al., 1994).

Second, for the forming-friendship accounts, the researchers again found that reciprocal liking and attractiveness were the most frequently mentioned reasons, though they were mentioned less often than in the falling-in-love accounts. For friendship attraction, similarity and propinquity were mentioned very frequently, and more so than in the falling-in-love accounts (Aron et al., 1989). Other research has found an interesting gender difference in the pattern of attraction for friendships. For women, a strong predictor of friendship attraction was the quality of the conversation. When experiencing friendship attraction, women appear respond positively to quality conversation to a greater extent than men do (Duck, 1994a; Fehr, 1996; Johnson & Aries, 1983; Reisman, 1990). Thus the variables of attractiveness, reciprocal liking, similarity, and propinquity not only predict people's behavior in laboratory experiments but appear as well when people are asked to spontaneously recall their real-life experiences with attraction (Aron & Aron, 1996).

Theories of Interpersonal Attraction: Social Exchange and Equity

So far, we've examined the determinants of attraction that concern aspects of the situation (propinquity, repeated exposure), the individual's attributes (physical attractiveness, similarity, self-esteem), and the individual's behavior (conveying liking). We turn now to theories of interpersonal attraction that link these phenomena together.

Social Exchange Theory Many of the variables we have discussed can be thought of as examples of social rewards. It is pleasing to have our attitudes validated; thus the more similar a person's attitudes are to ours, the more rewarded we feel. Likewise, it is rewarding to be around someone who likes us and is physically attractive. One way of summarizing much of our discussion so far is to say that the more social rewards a person provides us with (and the fewer costs), the more we will like the person. The flip side of this equation is that if a relationship costs (e.g., in terms of emotional turmoil) far more than it gives (e.g., in terms of validation or praise), chances are that it will not last.

This simple notion that relationships operate on an economic model of costs and benefits, much like the marketplace, has been expanded by psychologists and sociologists into complex theories of social exchange (Blau, 1964; Homans, 1961; Kelley & Thibaut, 1978; Secord & Backman, 1964; Thibaut & Kelley, 1959). **Social exchange theory** holds that how people feel (positively or negatively) about their relationships will depend on (1) their perception of the rewards they receive from the relationship, (2) their perception of the costs they incur, and (3) their perception of what kind of relationship they deserve and the probability that they could have a better relationship with someone else. In other words, we buy the best relationship we can get, one that gives us the most value for our emotional dollar. The basic concepts of social exchange theory are reward, cost, outcome, and comparison level.

Rewards are the positive, gratifying aspects of the relationship that make it worthwhile and reinforcing. They include the kinds of personal characteristics and behaviors of our relationship partner that we have already discussed and our ability to acquire external resources by virtue of knowing this person (e.g., gaining access to money, status, activities, or other interesting people; Lott & Lott, 1974). For example, in Brazil, friendship is openly used as an exchange value. Brazilians will readily admit that they need a *pistolão* (literally, a big, powerful handgun), meaning they need a person who will use his or her personal connections to help them get what they want (Rector & Neiva, 1996). Costs are, obviously, the other side of the coin, and all friendships and romantic relationships have some costs attached to them (such as putting up with those annoying habits and characteristics of the other person). The outcome of the relationship is a direct comparison of its rewards and costs; you can think of it as a mathematical formula where outcome equals rewards minus costs. (If you come up with a negative number, your relationship is not in good shape.)

How satisfied you are with your relationship depends on another variable—your **comparison level,** or what you expect the outcome of your relationship to be in terms of costs and rewards (Kelley & Thibaut, 1978; Thibaut & Kelley, 1959). Over time, you have amassed a long history of relationships with other people, and this history has led you to have certain expectations as to what your current and future relationships should be like. Some people have a high comparison level, expecting lots of rewards and few costs in their relationships. If a given relationship doesn't match this expected comparison level, they will be unhappy and unsatisfied. In contrast, people who have a low comparison level would be happy in the same relationship because they expect relationships to be difficult and costly.

Finally, your satisfaction with a relationship also depends on your perception of the likelihood that you could replace it with a better one—or your **comparison level for alternatives.** There are a lot of people out there; could a relationship with a different person give you a better outcome or greater rewards for fewer costs than your current one? People who have a high comparison level for alternatives, either because they believe the world is full of fabulous people dying to meet them or because they know of a fabulous person dying to meet them, are more likely to get into circulation and make a new friend or find a new lover. People with a low comparison level for alternatives will be more likely to stay in a costly relationship because to them, what they have is not great but is better than their expectation of what they could find elsewhere (Simpson, 1987).

Love is often nothing but a favorable exchange between two people who get the most of what they can expect, considering their value on the personality market.

—*Erich Fromm*, The Sane Society, 1955

Social Exchange Theory

The idea that people's feelings about a relationship depend on their perceptions of the rewards and costs of the relationship, the kind of relationship they deserve, and their chances for having a better relationship with someone else

Comparison Level

People's expectations about the level of rewards and punishments they are likely to receive in a particular relationship

Comparison Level for Alternatives

People's expectations about the level of rewards and punishments they would receive in an alternative relationship

"This is goodbye, gentlemen. I have met another board of directors, and we have fallen in love."

Social exchange theory has received a great deal of empirical support; friends and romantic couples do pay attention to the costs and rewards in their relationships, and these affect how positively people feel about the status of the relationship (Bui, Peplau, & Hill, 1996; Le & Agnew, 2003; Rusbult, 1983; Rusbult, Martz, & Agnew, 1998; South & Lloyd, 1995).

Equity Theory Some researchers have criticized social exchange theory for ignoring an essential variable in relationships—the notion of fairness, or equity. Proponents of **equity theory** argue that people are not just out to get the most rewards for the least cost; they are also concerned about equity in their relationships, wherein the rewards and costs they experience and the contributions they make to the relationship are roughly equal to those of the other person (Homans, 1961; Walster, Walster, & Berscheid, 1978). These theorists describe equitable relationships as the happiest and most stable. In comparison, inequitable relationships result in one person feeling overbenefited (getting a lot of rewards, incurring few costs, having to devote little time or energy to the relationship) or underbenefited (getting few rewards, incurring a lot of costs, having to devote a lot of time and energy to the relationship).

According to equity theory, both underbenefited and overbenefited partners should feel uneasy about this state of affairs, and both should be motivated to restore equity to the relationship. This makes sense for the underbenefited person (who wants to continue feeling miserable?), but why should the overbenefited individual want to give up what social exchange theory indicates is a cushy deal—lots of rewards for little cost and little work? Some theorists argue that equity is a powerful social norm—people will eventually feel uncomfortable or even guilty if they get more than they deserve in a relationship. However, being overbenefited just doesn't seem as bad as being underbenefited, and research has borne out that inequity is perceived as more of a problem by the underbenefited individual (Buunk & Van Yperen, 1991; Hatfield, Greenberger, Traupmann, & Lambert, 1982; Sprecher & Schwartz, 1994; Van Yperen & Buunk, 1990).

> Friendship is a scheme for the mutual exchange of personal advantages and favors.
>
> *—François de La Rochefoucauld, Maxims, 1665*

Equity Theory
The idea that people are happiest with relationships in which the rewards and costs experienced and the contributions made by both parties are roughly equal

CLOSE RELATIONSHIPS

After getting to this point in the chapter, you should be in a pretty good position to make a favorable first impression the next time you meet someone. Suppose you want Claudia to like you. You should hang around her so that you become familiar, act in ways that are rewarding to her, emphasize your similarity to her, and let her know you enjoy her company. But what if you want to do more than make a good impression? What if you want to have a close friendship or a romantic relationship?

Until recently, social psychologists had little to say in answer to this question; research on interpersonal attraction focused almost exclusively on first impressions. Why? Primarily because close, long-term relationships are much more difficult to study scientifically than first impressions. As we saw in Chapter 2, random assignment to different conditions is the hallmark of an experiment. When studying first impressions, a researcher can randomly assign you to a get-acquainted session with someone who is similar or dissimilar to you. But a researcher can't randomly assign you to the similar or dissimilar "lover" condition and make you have a relationship! In addition, the feelings and intimacy associated with close relationships can be difficult to measure. Psychologists face a daunting task when trying to measure such complex feelings as love and passion.

> Love is something so divine, Description would but make it less; 'Tis what I feel, but can't define, 'Tis what I know, but can't express.
>
> *—Beilby Porteus*

Defining Love

Despite the difficulties in studying close relationships, social psychologists have made some interesting discoveries about the nature of love, how it develops, and how it flourishes. Let's begin with perhaps the most difficult question: What, exactly, is love? Early attempts to define love distinguished between liking and loving, showing that as you might expect, love is something different from "lots of liking," and it isn't just sexual desire either (Rubin, 1970).

> Try to reason about love, and you will lose your reason.
>
> *—French proverb*

Companionate versus Passionate Love For Shakespeare's Romeo and Juliet, love was passionate, turbulent, and full of longing. Your grandparents, if they've remained married for a long time, probably exemplify a calmer, more tranquil

Gwyneth Paltrow and Joseph Fiennes exemplify the early stages of passionate love in this scene from "Shakespeare in Love."

TABLE 10.2

Cross-Cultural Evidence for Passionate Love Based on Anthropological Research in 166 Societies

CULTURAL AREA	PASSIONATE LOVE PRESENT	PASSIONATE LOVE ABSENT
Mediterranean	22 (95.7%)	1 (4.3%)
Sub-Saharan Africa	20 (76.9%)	6 (23.1%)
Eurasia	32 (97.0%)	1 (3.0%)
Insular Pacific	27 (93.1%)	2 (6.9%)
North America	24 (82.8%)	5 (17.2%)
South and Central America	22 (84.6%)	4 (15.4%)

Source: Data from Jankowiak & Fischer (1992).

kind of love. We use the word *love* to describe both of these relationships, though each seems to be of a different kind (Berscheid & Meyers, 1996, 1997; Fehr, 1994; Fehr & Russell, 1991).

Social psychologists have recognized that a good definition of love must include the passionate, giddy feelings of romantic love as well as the deep, long-term devotion of a long-married couple, lifelong friends, or siblings. In defining love, then, we generally distinguish between *companionate love* and *passionate love* (Hatfield, 1988; Hatfield & Rapson, 1993; Hatfield & Walster, 1978). **Companionate love** consists of feelings of intimacy and affection we have for someone that are not accompanied by passion or physiological arousal. People can experience companionate love in nonsexual relationships, such as close friendships, or in sexual relationships, where they experience great feelings of intimacy (companionate love) but not a great deal of the heat and passion they may once have felt.

Passionate love involves an intense longing for another person, characterized by the experience of physiological arousal, the feeling of shortness of breath and a thumping heart in our loved one's presence (Regan, 1998; Regan & Berscheid, 1999). When things are going well—the other person loves us too—we feel great fulfillment and ecstasy. When things are not going well—our love is unrequited—we feel great sadness and despair. Cross-cultural research comparing an individualistic culture (the United States) and a collectivistic culture (China) indicates that American couples tend to value passionate love more than Chinese couples do, and Chinese couples tend to value companionate love more than American couples do (Gao, 1993; Jankowiak, 1995; Ting-Toomey & Chung, 1996). In comparison, the Taita of Kenya, in East Africa, value both equally; they conceptualize romantic love as a combination of companionate love and passionate love. The Taita consider this the best kind of love, and achieving it is a primary goal in the society (Bell, 1995). Reviewing the anthropological research on 166 societies, William Jankowiak and Edward Fischer (1992) found evidence for passionate love in 147 of them, as you can see in Table 10.2.

Elaine Hatfield and Susan Sprecher (1986a) developed a questionnaire to measure passionate love. As measured by this scale, passionate love consists of strong, uncontrollable thoughts; intense feelings; and overt acts toward the target of one's affection. Find out if you are experiencing (or have experienced) passionate love by filling out the questionnaire in the Try It! exercise on page 337.

Triangular Theory of Love Robert Sternberg (1986, 1988, 1997; Sternberg & Beall, 1991) has developed the **triangular theory of love.** According to this

Companionate Love

The intimacy and affection we feel when we care deeply for a person but do not experience passion or arousal in the person's presence

Passionate Love

An intense longing we feel for a person, accompanied by physiological arousal; when our love is reciprocated, we feel great fulfillment and ecstasy, but when it is not, we feel sadness and despair

Triangular Theory of Love

The idea that different kinds of love consist of varying degrees of three components: intimacy, passion, and commitment

Try it!

The Passionate Love Scale

These items ask you to describe how you feel when you are passionately in love. Think of the person whom you love most passionately right now. If you are not in love right now, think of the last person you loved passionately. If you have never been in love, think of the person you came closest to caring for in that way. Choose your answers remembering how you felt when your feelings were the most intense.

For each of the fifteen items, choose the number between 1 and 9 that most accurately describes your feelings. The answer scale ranges from 1, not at all true, to 9, definitely true. Write the number you choose next to each item.

```
1     2     3     4     5     6     7     8     9
↑                       ↑                       ↑
Not at all true     Moderately true     Definitely true
```

1. I would feel deep despair if _____ left me.
2. Sometimes I feel I can't control my thoughts; they are obsessively on _____.
3. I feel happy when I am doing something to make _____ happy.
4. I would rather be with _____ than anyone else.
5. I'd get jealous if I thought _____ were falling in love with someone else.
6. I yearn to know all about _____.
7. I want _____—physically, emotionally, mentally.
8. I have an endless appetite for affection from _____.
9. For me, _____ is the perfect romantic partner.
10. I sense my body responding when _____ touches me.
11. _____ always seems to be on my mind.
12. I want _____ to know me—my thoughts, my fears, and my hopes.
13. I eagerly look for signs indicating _____'s desire for me.
14. I possess a powerful attraction for _____.
15. I get extremely depressed when things don't go right in my relationship with _____.

Scoring: Add up your scores for the fifteen items. The total score can range from a minimum of 15 to a maximum of 135. The higher your score, the more your feelings for the person reflect passionate love; the items to which you gave a particularly high score reflect those components of passionate love that you experience most strongly.

(Adapted from Hatfield & Sprecher, 1986)

theory, love consists of three basic ingredients: intimacy, passion, and commitment. Intimacy refers to feelings of being close to and bonded with a partner. Passion refers to the "hot" parts of a relationship—the arousal you experience toward your partner, including sexual attraction. Commitment consists of two decisions: the short-term one that you love your partner and the long-term one to maintain that love and stay with your partner. Sternberg (1988) developed a scale to measure the three components of love, including such questions as "I have a relationship of mutual understanding with _____" (intimacy), "I find myself thinking about _____ frequently during the day" (passion), and "I expect my love for _____ to last for the rest of my life" (commitment).

FIGURE 10.3

The triangle of love.

According to the triangle theory of love, there are seven different forms of love, each made up of varying degrees of intimacy, passion, and commitment.

(Adapted from Sternberg, 1988)

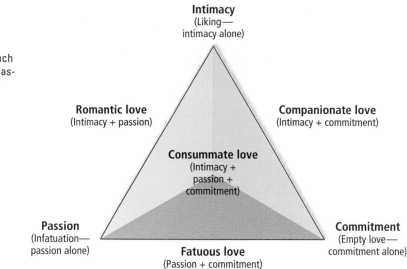

> Love is or it ain't. Thin love ain't love at all.
>
> —Toni Morrison

These three ingredients—intimacy, passion, and commitment—can be combined in varying degrees to form any of the different kinds of love (see Figure 10.3). Love can consist of one component alone or of any combination of these three parts. For example, a person may feel a great deal of passion or physical attraction for another (infatuation love) but not know the person well enough to experience intimacy and not be ready to make any kind of commitment. As the relationship develops, it might blossom into romantic love, characterized by passion and intimacy, and maybe even consummate love—the blending of all three components. Companionate love is characterized by intimacy and commitment but not passion (Aron & Westbay, 1996; Hassebrauck & Buhl, 1996; Lemieux & Hale, 1999).

Culture and Love

Although love is is a universal emotion, how we experience it (and what we expect from close relationships) is linked to culture. For example, the Japanese describe *amae* as an extremely positive emotional state in which one is a totally passive love object, indulged and taken care of by one's romantic partner, much like a mother-infant relationship. *Amae* has no equivalent word in English or in any other Western language; the closest is the word *dependency,* an emotional state that Western cultures consider unhealthy in adult relationships (K. K. Dion & K. L. Dion, 1993; Doi, 1988).

Similarly, the Chinese concept of *gan qing* differs from the Western view of romantic love. *Gan qing* is achieved by helping and working for another person; for example, a "romantic" act would be fixing someone's bicycle or helping someone learn new material (Gao, 1996). In Korea, a special kind of relationship is expressed by the concept of *jung.* Much more than "love," *jung* is what ties two people together. Couples in new relationships may feel strong love for each other, but they have not yet developed strong *jung*—that takes time and many mutual experiences. Interestingly, *jung* can develop in negative relationships too—for example, between business rivals who dislike each other. *Jung* may unknowingly grow between them over time, with the result that they will feel that a strange connection exists between them (Lim & Choi, 1996).

Phillip Shaver and his colleagues (Shaver, Wu, & Schwartz, 1992) wondered if romantic or passionate love was associated with the same emotions in different cultures. They asked research participants in the United States, Italy, and China to sort more than a hundred emotional words into categories; their analysis indicated that love has similar and different meanings cross-culturally. The most striking difference was the presence of a "sad love" cluster in the Chinese sample. The Chinese had many love-related concepts that were sad, such as words for "sorrow-love," "tenderness-pity," and "sorrow-pity." Although this "sad love" cluster made a small appearance in the U.S. and Italian samples, it was not perceived as a major aspect of love in these Western societies.

Other researchers wondered what the lyrics of popular American and Chinese (Mainland China and Hong Kong) love songs would reveal about the experience of love in each culture (Rothbaum & Tsang, 1998). Finding that the Chinese love songs had significantly more references to suffering and to negative outcomes than the American love songs, the researchers looked to the Chinese concept of *yuan*. This is the belief that interpersonal relations are predestined. According to the traditional Buddhist belief in *karma*, fate determines what happens in a relationship. The romantic partners have little control over this process (Goodwin, 1999). If a relationship is not working, it cannot be saved; one must accept fate and the suffering that accompanies it (Rothbaum & Tsang, 1998). Though Chinese songs were sadder than American ones, there was no difference in the intensity with which love was described in the two countries. The researchers found that love in Chinese songs was as "passionate and erotic" as love expressed in American songs.

How romantic love is defined and experienced can vary across individualistic and collectivistic cultures, as we discussed earlier. Researchers have found that Canadian college students have different attitudes about love, depending on their ethnocultural background: Asian (Chinese, Korean, Vietnamese, Indian, Pakistani), Anglo-Celtic (English, Irish, Scottish), or European (Scandinavian, Spanish, German, Polish). In comparison to their peers, the Asian respondents were significantly more likely to identify with a companionable, friendship-based romantic love, a "style of love that would not disrupt a complex network of existing family relationships" (K. L. Dion & K. K. Dion, 1993, p. 465). In a similar study, researchers surveyed college students in eleven countries around the world, asking them, "If a man (woman) had all the qualities you desired, would you marry this person if you were not in love with him (her)?" These researchers found that marrying for love was most important to participants in Western and Westernized countries (e.g., the United States, Brazil, England, and Australia) and of least importance to participants in less developed Eastern countries (i.e., India, Pakistan, and Thailand; Levine et al., 1995).

The results of these studies indicate that the concept of romantic love is to some extent culturally specific (Dion & Dion, 1996; Gao & Gudykunst, 1995; Hatfield & Rapson, 1996, 2002; Hatfield & Sprecher, 1995; Sprecher, Aron et al., 1994). Love can vary in definition and behavior in different societies. We all love, but we do not necessarily all love in the same way—or at least we don't describe it in the same way. As noted earlier, anthropologists found evidence of romantic (passionate) love in 147 of the 166 cultures sampled (Jankowiak, 1995; Jankowiak & Fischer, 1992); it was present even in societies "that do not accept" romantic love "or embrace it as a positive ideal" (Jankowiak, 1995, p. 4). Thus it may be that romantic love is nearly universal in the human species, but cultural rules alter how that emotional state is experienced, expressed, and remembered (Levinger, 1994). As Robert Moore (1998) noted in summarizing his research in the People's Republic of China, "Young Chinese do fall deeply in love and experience the same joys and sorrows of romance as young Westerners do. But they do so according to standards that require . . . the individual [to] sacrifice personal interests for the sake of the family. . . . This means avoiding fleeting infatuations, casual sexual encounters, and a dating context [where] family concerns are forgotten" (p. 280).

Although people all over the world experience love, how love is defined varies across cultures.

LOVE AND RELATIONSHIPS

Are the causes of love similar to the causes of initial attraction? How do the factors we discussed earlier as determinants of first impressions play out in intimate relationships? And do other variables come into play when we are developing and maintaining a close relationship?

Evolution and Love: Choosing a Mate

The poet Robert Browning asked, "How do I love thee? Let me count the ways." For psychologists, the question is "Why do I love thee?" For many, the answer lies in an **evolutionary approach to love.** The basic tenet of evolutionary biology is that an animal's "fitness" is measured by its reproductive success—that is, its ability to pass on its genes to the next generation. Reproductive success is not just part of the game; it *is* the game. This biological concept has been applied to social behavior by psychologists, who define **evolutionary psychology** as the attempt to explain social behavior in terms of genetic factors that evolved over time according to the principles of natural selection. Has human behavior evolved in specific ways to maximize reproductive success? Evolutionary psychologists say yes; they argue that men and women have very different agendas due to their differing roles in producing offspring.

For women, reproduction is costly in terms of time, energy, and effort: They must endure the discomforts of pregnancy and birth and then care for their infants until maturity. Reproducing, then, is a serious business, so women, the theory goes, must consider carefully when and with whom to reproduce. In comparison, reproduction has few costs for men. The evolutionary approach to love concludes that reproductive success for the two sexes translates into two very different behavior patterns: Throughout the animal world, males' reproductive success is measured by the quantity of their offspring. They pursue frequent pairings with many females in order to maximize the number of their surviving progeny. In contrast, females' reproductive success lies in successfully raising each of their offspring to maturity. They pair infrequently and only with a carefully chosen male because the cost of raising and ensuring the survival of each offspring is so high (Berkow, 1989; Symons, 1979).

Now, what does this have to do with falling in love? David Buss and his colleagues state that this evolutionary approach explains the different strategies of

Evolutionary Approach to Love

A theory derived from evolutionary biology that holds that men and women are attracted to different characteristics in each other (men are attracted by women's appearance; women are attracted by men's resources) because this maximizes their chances of reproductive success

Evolutionary Psychology

The attempt to explain social behavior in terms of genetic factors that evolved over time according to the principles of natural selection

men and women in romantic relationships (Buss, 1985, 1988a, 1996a, 1996b; Buss & Schmitt, 1993). Buss (1988b) explains that finding (and keeping) a mate requires one to display one's resources—the aspects of oneself that will appear attractive to potential mates. This approach argues that across millennia, human beings have been selected through evolution to respond to certain external cues in the opoposite sex. Women, facing high reproductive costs, will look for a man who can supply the resources and support she needs to bear a child. Men will look for a woman who appears capable of reproducing successfully. More specifically, men will respond to the physical appearance of women, since age and health denote reproductive fitness, and women will respond to the economic and career achievements of men, since these variables represent resources they and their offspring will need (Buss, 1988b).

Several studies have found support for these predictions. For example, Buss and his colleagues (Buss, 1989; Buss et al., 1990) asked more than nine thousand adults in thirty-seven countries how important and desirable various characteristics were in choosing a marriage partner. In general, the women participants valued ambition, industriousness, and good earning capacity in a potential mate more than the men did. The men valued physical attractiveness in a mate more than the women did, a finding echoed in other research. (However, it should be noted that the top characteristics on both men's and women's lists were the same, involving such characteristics as honesty, trustworthiness, and a pleasant personality [Buss & Barnes, 1986; Hatfield & Sprecher, 1995; Regan & Berscheid, 1997; Sprecher, Sullivan, & Hatfield, 1994].) As we discussed earlier, men are more likely than women to say that physical attractiveness is important to them in a potential date (Feingold, 1990). Other survey studies have indicated that men prefer spouses who are younger than they are (youth indicating greater reproductive fitness), while women prefer spouses around their own age (Buss, 1989; Kenrick & Keefe, 1992). When college students were asked to imagine that their romantic partner had been sexually unfaithful or emotionally unfaithful, the men were more upset by the sexual infidelity scenario than the women were, while the women were relatively more upset by the emotional infidelity story (Buss, Larsen, Westen, & Semmelroth, 1992).

An elaboration of the evolutionary approach to love and mate selection has been offered by Steven Gangestad and David Buss (1993). If physical attractiveness in women is preferred by men because it signals reproductive fitness, then female physical attractiveness should be particularly valued in regions of the world where disease is very common—the idea being that the physically attractive are both healthy and possibly resistant to local diseases. Gangestad and Buss found that in areas of the world where disease-transmitting parasites are prevalent, people did indicate a stronger preference for physically attractive mates than in areas with a low prevalence of parasites. However, this preference for the physically attractive mate was just as strong among women as it was among men. Thus this study offers support for the fundamental points of the evolutionary approach but calls into question the proposed gender difference between men and women regarding attractiveness in mate selection.

The evolutionary approach to love has attracted its share of criticism. Some social psychologists argue that the theory is untestable: We can't do an experiment to prove that evolutionary forces are the primary cause of current human behavior (Sternberg & Beall, 1991). Others suggest that it is an oversimplification of extremely complex human behavior (Travis & Yeager, 1991). It has been argued that men may value physical attractiveness in a partner simply because they have been taught to value it; they have been conditioned by decades of advertising and media images to value beauty in women and to have a recreational approach to sex (Hatfield & Rapson, 1993).

Men seek to propagate widely, whereas women seek to propagate wisely.

—Robert Hinde

She's beautiful and therefore to be woo'd.

—William Shakespeare

Attachment theory predicts that the attachment style we learn as infants and young children stays with us throughout life and generalizes to all of our relationships with other people.

Other studies have found that women value physical attractiveness as much as men when they are considering a potential sexual partner as opposed to a potential marriage partner (Regan & Berscheid, 1997; Simpson & Gangestad, 1992). Research results are also mixed as to whether women are attracted to potential mates because of the men's ability to provide economic resources (Buss et al., 1990; Cochran & Peplau, 1985; Feingold, 1992a; Hatfield & Sprecher, 1995; Jensen-Campbell, Graziano, & West, 1995; Regan & Berscheid, 1995, 1997; Speed & Gangestad, 1997).

Finally, some researchers note that the preference for different qualities in a mate can be explained without resorting to evolutionary principles: Around the world, women have less power, status, wealth, and other resources than men do. If women need to rely on men to achieve economic security, they must consider this characteristic when choosing a husband (Rosenblatt, 1974). Thus in the framework of equity theory, female youth and beauty are considered a fair exchange for male career and economic success.

Steven Gangestad (1993) tested this hypothesis by correlating the extent to which women in several countries had access to financial resources and the extent to which women reported male physical attractiveness as an important variable in a mate. (In this study, parasite prevalence was controlled, so it was not a factor in the results.) He found an association between the two: The more economic power women had in a given culture, the more women were interested in a physically attractive man. In the United States, women have access to economic resources (e.g., education, well-paid jobs, high-status occupations) to a greater extent than most other women in the world. How does this affect American mate preferences? A recent survey of nearly one thousand young adults in the northeast found that similarity in physical attractiveness and wealth was a stronger predictor of mate choice than the "beauty for money" exchange. People from wealthy families wanted a partner who was also wealthy, whether they were male or female. Similarly, men and women who were physically attractive wanted to find their match: a beautiful or handsome mate (Buston & Emlen, 2003). As you can see, when discussing human mate preference, it is difficult to disentangle "nature" (inborn preferences) from "nurture" (cultural norms and gender roles). The evolutionary approach is an interesting, exciting, and somewhat controversial theory; further theorizing and research will reveal more about the role that biology plays in love.

Attachment Styles in Intimate Relationships

Most of the influences on love and intimacy we have discussed so far have been in the here-and-now of a relationship: the attractiveness and similarity of the partners, how they treat each other, and so on. The evolutionary approach takes the long view—that how people act today is based on behavior patterns that evolved from our species' hominid past. Another recent theory of love takes the middle ground, stating that our behavior in adult relationships is based on our experiences in the early years of life with our parents or caregivers. This approach focuses on attachment styles and draws on the groundbreaking work of John Bowlby (1969, 1973, 1980) and Mary Ainsworth (Ainsworth, Blehar, Waters, & Wall, 1978) on how infants form bonds with their primary caregivers (e.g., their mothers or fathers). According to the theory of **attachment styles,** the kinds of bonds we form early in life influence the kinds of relationships we form as adults.

Ainsworth and her colleagues (1978) identified three types of relationships between infants and their mothers. Infants with a **secure attachment style** typically have caregivers who are responsive to their needs and who show positive emotions when interacting with them. These infants trust their caregivers, are not worried about being abandoned, and come to view themselves as worthy and

Attachment Styles

The expectations people develop about relationships with others, based on the relationship they had with their primary caregiver when they were infants

Secure Attachment Style

An attachment style characterized by trust, a lack of concern with being abandoned, and the view that one is worthy and well liked

well liked. Infants with an **avoidant attachment style** typically have caregivers who are aloof and distant, rebuffing the infants' attempts to establish intimacy. These infants desire to be close to their caregiver but learn to suppress this need, as if they know that attempts to be intimate will be rejected. People with this style find it difficult to develop intimate relationships. Infants with an **anxious/ambivalent attachment style** typically have caregivers who are inconsistent and overbearing in their affection. These infants are unusually anxious because they can never predict when and how their caregivers will respond to their needs.

The key assumption of attachment theory is that the particular attachment style we learn as infants and young children becomes our working model or schema (as we discussed in Chapter 3) for what relationships are like. This early childhood relationship schema typically stays with us throughout life and generalizes to all of our relationships with other people (Collins & Sroufe, 1999; Fury, Carlson, & Sroufe, 1997; Hartup & Laursen, 1999). Thus people who had a secure relationship with their parents or care-givers are able to develop mature, lasting relationships as adults; people who had avoidant relationships with their parents are less able to trust others and find it difficult to develop close, intimate relationships; and people who had anxious/ambivalent relationships with their parents want to become close to their adult partners but worry that their partners will not return their affections (Reis & Patrick, 1996; Shaver, Collins, & Clark, 1996). This has been borne out in numerous studies that measure adults' attachment styles with questionnaires or interviews and then correlate these styles with the quality of their romantic relationships.

For example, researchers asked adults to choose one of the three statements shown in Table 10.3 according to how they typically felt in romantic relationships (Hazan & Shaver, 1987). Each of these statements was designed to capture the three kinds of attachment styles we have described. The researchers also asked people questions about their current relationships. The results of this study—and several others like it—were consistent with an attachment theory perspec-tive. Securely attached adults report that they easily become close to other

> In my very own self, I am part of my family.
>
> —D. H. Lawrence

TABLE 10.3

Measuring Attachment Styles

As part of a survey of attitudes toward love published in a newspaper, people were asked to choose the statement that best described their romantic relationships. The attachment style each statement was designed to measure and the percentage of people who chose each alternative are indicated.

Secure style	56%	"I find it relatively easy to get close to others and am comfortable depending on them and having them depend on me. I don't often worry about being abandoned or about someone getting too close."
Avoidant style	25%	"I am somewhat uncomfortable being close to others; I find it difficult to trust them completely, difficult to allow myself to depend on them. I am nervous when anyone gets close, and often love partners want me to be more intimate than I feel comfortable being."
Anxious style	19%	"I find that others are reluctant to get as close as I would like. I often worry that my partner doesn't really love me or won't stay with me. I want to merge completely with another person, and this desire sometimes scares people away."

Source: Adapted from Hazan & Shaver (1987).

Avoidant Attachment Style

An attachment style characterized by a suppression of attachment needs, because attempts to be intimate have been rebuffed; people with this style find it difficult to develop intimate relationships

Anxious/Ambivalent Attachment Style

An attachment style characterized by a concern that others will not reciprocate one's desire for intimacy, resulting in higher-than-average levels of anxiety

people, readily trust others, and have satisfying romantic relationships. People with an avoidant style report that they are uncomfortable becoming close to others, find it hard to trust others, and have less satisfying romantic relationships. And people with an anxious/ambivalent style tend to have less satisfying relationships but of a different type: They are likely to be obsessive and preoccupied with their relationships, fearing that their partners do not want to be as intimate or as close as they desire them to be (Feeney, Noller, & Roberts, 2000; Hazan & Shaver, 1994a, 1994b; Shaver, Hazan, & Bradshaw, 1988; Simpson & Rholes, 1994).

Many researchers have reported similar findings: Securely attached individuals have the most enduring, long-term romantic relationships of the three attachment types. They experience the highest level of commitment to the relationship as well as the highest level of satisfaction with their relationships. The anxious/ambivalently attached individuals have the most short-lived romantic relationships of the three. They enter into romantic relationships the most quickly, often before they know their partners well. (For example, a study conducted at a marriage license bureau found that anxious men acquired marriage licenses after a shorter courtship than either secure or avoidant men; Senchak & Leonard, 1992.) They are also the most upset and angriest of the three types when their love is not reciprocated. Finally, avoidant individuals are the least likely to enter into a romantic relationship and the most likely to report never having been in love. They maintain their distance in relationships and have the lowest level of commitment to their relationships of the three types (Feeney & Noller, 1990; Keelan, Dion, & Dion, 1994; Morgan & Shaver, 1999).

Finally, attachment styles have also been found to affect men's and women's behavior in an experimental setting. Researchers brought heterosexual dating couples into the lab and measured their attachment styles using a questionnaire (Simpson, Rholes, & Nelligan, 1992). They then told the woman of each pair that in the next part of the study, she would experience an experimental procedure that aroused considerable anxiety and distress in most people. The researchers added that they couldn't tell her any more about it at that time. Each woman was then asked to wait a few minutes, with her boyfriend, before the procedure began. Their interactions were recorded by the experimenters and later analyzed. Securely attached women turned to their boyfriends for support and comfort during the anxious waiting period, while avoidant women did not; they withdrew from their boyfriends. And what about the men? When the girlfriends of securely attached men began to signal their distress, the men responded with more comfort and reassurance. In contrast, when the girlfriends of avoidant men began indicating that they were upset, the men responded with less comfort and support.

Attribution and Attachment Style You can see how attachment style can affect communication in a relationship as well as the attributions that partners make about each other (Feeney et al., 2000). For example, what would happen if an anxious person became involved with an avoidant one? Research has found that anxious and avoidant people become couples because they both match each other's relationship schema: Anxious people expect to be more invested in their relationships than their partners, and avoidant people expect to be less committed than their partners (Kirkpatrick & Davis, 1994). *Voilà!* Expectations met! But are these relationships happy ones? Not really; anxious-avoidant pairs report little satisfaction with their relationships and negative, problematic communication patterns (Morgan & Shaver, 1999). You would probably expect that romantic relationships made up of these pairs would also be short-lived, but there's an interesting twist here. One type of anxious-avoidant pair had very stable relationships: anxious women involved with avoidant men (Kirkpatrick & Davis, 1994). Their relationships were as stable over a four-year period as those of the secure woman–secure man couples in the sample. The researchers suggest that gender stereotypes play an important role in maintaining anxious woman–avoidant man relationships. Anxious women display stereotypically feminine traits in their relationships: They invest a lot of energy in the relationship, they demonstrate concern about how the relationship is doing, and they engage in "caretaking" behavior toward their partners. Avoidant men display stereotypically masculine traits in their relationships: They invest little energy in the relationship, they show and share little emotion in the relationship, and they avoid discussions about the relationship. Thus while these couples have far less positive relationships than secure–secure couples, they believe that the problems are due to their partner's gender—"He's just being a guy" or "Women are like that." Thus they tolerate their partner's behavior because it fits their stereotype or schema for the opposite sex. And what of romantic couples where the man is anxious and the woman is avoidant? Researchers have found that these relationships don't last long. Each partner views the other's behavior as especially troubling and negative because it deviates so far from the stereotypical pattern of gender behavior (Morgan & Shaver, 1999).

Attachment theory does not mean that if people had unhappy relationships with their parents, they are doomed to repeat this same kind of unhappy relationship with everyone they ever meet (Simms, 2002). For example, some researchers have recontacted their research participants months or years after the original studies and asked them to take the attachment style scale again. They have found that 25 to 30 percent of their participants had changed from one attachment style to another (Feeney & Noller, 1996; Kirkpatrick & Hazan, 1994). People can and do change, their experiences in relationships can help them learn new and more healthy ways of relating to others than what they experienced as children. In fact, it may be that people can develop more than one attachment style over time, as a result of their various experiences in close relationships (Baldwin & Fehr, 1995). At any given time, the attachment style that they display is the one that is called into play by their partner's behavior and the type of relationship that they've created as a couple. Thus people may respond to situational variables in their relationships, displaying a more secure attachment style in one relationship and a more anxious one in another (Baldwin, Keelan, Fehr, Enns, & Koh-Rangarajoo, 1996; Hammond & Fletcher, 1991).

As interesting as the results are on attachment theory and adult relationships, you should remember that they are often correlational rather than experimental. As we saw in Chapter 2, it is risky to infer causation from correlational data. Moreover, these studies rely in part on adults' memories of their childhood and how their parents behaved toward them—and these early childhood memories can be inaccurate.

Taken as a whole, however, these studies are highly suggestive and do lend support to the contention that the kind of relationship we had with our parents is likely to influence our relationships with others in adulthood. When you find yourself having problems in your close relationships, think about these research findings in attachment theory and see if they help you understand your behavior and your partner's.

Social Exchange in Long-Term Relationships

According to the rule of social exchange, if we want other people to like us, we must dole out social rewards to them (Blau, 1964; Homans, 1961). Research has shown ample support for social exchange theory in intimate relationships in cultures as different as Taiwan and the Netherlands (Lin & Rusbult, 1995; Rusbult & Van Lange, 1996; Van Lange et al., 1997). For example, college-age dating couples focused much more on rewards during the first three months of their relationships (Rusbult, 1983). If the relationships were perceived as offering a lot of

What, after all, is our life but a great dance in which we are all trying to fix the best going rate of exchange?

—Malcolm Bradbury, 1992

rewards, the people reported feeling happy and satisfied. The perception of rewards continued to be important over time. At seven months, couples who were still together believed their rewards had increased over time. The perception and importance of costs came into play a few months into the relationships; this is when the glow created by all those rewards begins to be dimmed by the realization that costs are involved too. Not surprisingly, satisfaction with the relationship decreased markedly over time for those who reported that costs were increasing in their relationships. Thus rewards are always important to the outcome; costs become increasingly important over time.

Of course, we know that many people do not leave their partners, even when they are dissatisfied and their other alternatives look bright. Research indicates that we need to consider at least one additional factor to understand close relationships—a person's level of investment in the relationship (Impett, Beals, & Peplau, 2001–2002; Kelley, 1983; Rusbult et al., 1998). In her **investment model** of close relationships, Caryl Rusbult (1983) defines investments as anything people have put into a relationship that will be lost if they leave it. Examples include tangible things, such as financial resources and possessions (e.g., a house), as well as intangible things, such as the emotional welfare of one's children, the time and emotional energy spent building the relationship, and the sense of personal integrity that will be lost if one gets divorced. As seen in Figure 10.4, the greater the investment individuals have in a relationship, the less likely they are to leave, even if satisfaction is low and other alternatives look promising. In short, to predict whether people will stay in an intimate relationship, we need to know (1) how satisfied they are with the relationship, (2) what they think of the alternatives, and (3) how great their investment in the relationship is.

Investment Model

The theory that people's commitment to a relationship depends not only on their satisfaction with the relationship in terms of rewards, costs, and comparison level and their comparison level for alternatives but also on how much they have invested in the relationship that would be lost by leaving it

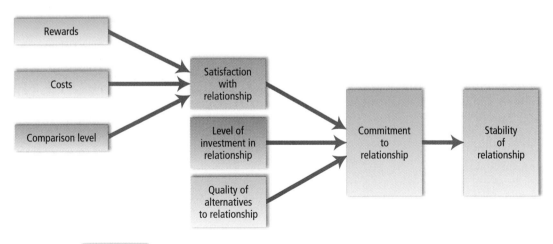

FIGURE 10.4

The investment model of commitment.

People's commitment to a relationship depends on several variables. First, their *satisfaction* with the relationship is based on their comparing their *rewards* to their *costs* and determining if the outcome exceeds their general expectation of what they should get in a relationship (or *comparison level*). Next, their *commitment* to the relationship depends on three variables: how *satisfied* they are, how much they feel they have *invested* in the relationship, and whether they have good *alternatives* to this relationship. These commitment variables in turn predict how *stable* the relationship will be. For example, a woman who feels her relationship has more costs and fewer rewards than she considers acceptable would have a low satisfaction. If she also felt she had little invested in the relationship and a very attractive person had just asked her for a date, she would have a low level of commitment. The end result is low stability; most likely, she will break up with her current partner.

(Adapted from Rusbult, 1983)

To test this model, Rusbult (1983) asked college students involved in heterosexual dating relationships to fill out questionnaires for seven months. Every three weeks or so, people answered questions about each of the components of the model shown in Figure 10.4. Rusbult also kept track of whether the students stayed in the relationships or broke up. As you can see in Figure 10.5, people's satisfaction, alternatives, and investments all predicted how committed they were to the relationship and whether it lasted. (The higher the number on the scale, the more each factor predicted the commitment to and length of the relationship.) Subsequent studies have found results similar to those shown in Figure 10.5 for married couples of diverse ages, for lesbian and gay couples, for close (nonsexual) friendships, and for residents of both the United States and Taiwan (Kurdek, 1992; Lin & Rusbult, 1995; Rusbult, 1991; Rusbult & Buunk, 1993). A further test of the model focused on couples' willingness to make personal sacrifices for their partner or for the sake of the relationship (Van Lange et al., 1997). The researchers found that couples willing to make sacrifices for each other were strongly committed to their relationship, a commitment stemming from a a high degree of satisfaction and investment in the relationship and the low quality of alternatives to the relationship.

Does the same model hold for destructive relationships? To find out, Rusbult and a colleague interviewed women who had sought refuge at a shelter for battered women, asking them about their abusive romantic relationships and marriages (Rusbult & Martz, 1995). Why had these women stayed in these relationships, even to the point that some of them returned to the abusive male partner when they left the shelter? As the theory would predict, feelings of commitment to the abusive relationship were greater among women who had poorer economic alternatives to the relationship, were more heavily invested in the relationship (e.g., were married, had children), and were less dissatisfied with the relationship (i.e., reported receiving less severe forms of abuse). In long-term relationships, then, commitment is based on more than just the amount of rewards and punishments people dole out; it also depends on people's perceptions of their investments in, satisfaction with, and alternatives to the relationship.

> The friendships which last are those wherein each friend respects the other's dignity to the point of not really wanting anything from him.
>
> —Cyril Connolly

Equity in Long-Term Relationships

Does equity theory operate in long-term relationships the same way it does in new or less intimate relationships? Not exactly: The more we get to know someone, the more reluctant we are to believe that we are simply exchanging favors

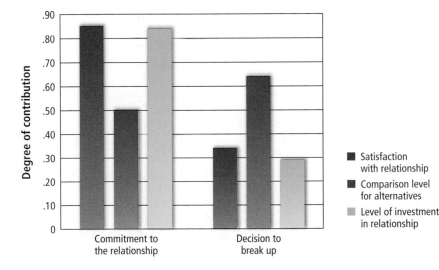

FIGURE 10.5

A test of the investment model.

This study examined the extent to which college students' satisfaction with a relationship, their comparison level for alternatives, and their investment in the relationship predicted their commitment to the relationship and their decision about whether to break up with their partner. The higher the number, the more each variable predicted commitment and breakup, independent of the two other variables. All three variables were good predictors of how committed people were and whether or not they broke up.

(Adapted from Rusbult, 1983)

Close relationships can have either exchange or communal properties. Family relationships are typically communal; friendships are typically based on exchange, although they can become communal over time.

and the less inclined we are to expect immediate compensation for a favor done. In casual relationships, we trade "in kind"—you lend someone your class notes, he buys you a beer. But in intimate relationships, we trade very different resources, so determining if equity has been achieved can be difficult. Does "dinner at an expensive restaurant on Monday balance out three nights of neglect due to a heavy workload" (Hatfield & Rapson, 1993, p. 130)? In other words, long-term, intimate relationships seem to be governed by a looser give-and-take notion of equity rather than a rigid tit-for-tat strategy (Kollack, Blumstein, & Schwartz, 1994; Laursen & Hartup, 2002).

According to Margaret Clark and Judson Mills, interactions between new acquaintances are governed by equity concerns and are called **exchange relationships.** In exchange relationships, people keep track of who is contributing what and feel taken advantage of when they feel they are putting more into the relationship than they are getting out of it.

In comparison, interactions between close friends, family members, and romantic partners are governed less by an equity norm and more by a desire to help each other in times of need (Clark, 1984, 1986; Clark & Mills, 1993; Mills & Clark, 1982, 1994, 2001). In these **communal relationships,** people give in response to the other's needs, regardless of whether they are paid back.

In a series of experiments, Clark and her colleagues varied whether people desired an exchange or a communal relationship with another person and then observed the extent to which they were concerned with equity in the relationship. In such experiments, participants interacted with an interesting person and were told either that this person was new to the area and wanted to make new friends (thereby increasing their interest in establishing a communal relationship with the person) or that the other person was married and visiting the area for only a brief time (thereby making them more inclined to favor an exchange relationship with the person). As predicted, people in the exchange condition operated according to the equity norm, as summarized in Figure 10.6. People in the communal condition, thinking there was a chance for a long-term relationship, were relatively unconcerned with a tit-for-tat accounting of who was contributing what (Clark, 1984; Clark & Mills, 1979; Clark & Waddell, 1985; Williamson & Clark, 1989, 1992). These results are not limited to exchange and

Exchange Relationships

Relationships governed by the need for equity (i.e., for an equal ratio of rewards and costs)

Communal Relationships

Relationships in which people's primary concern is being responsive to the other person's needs

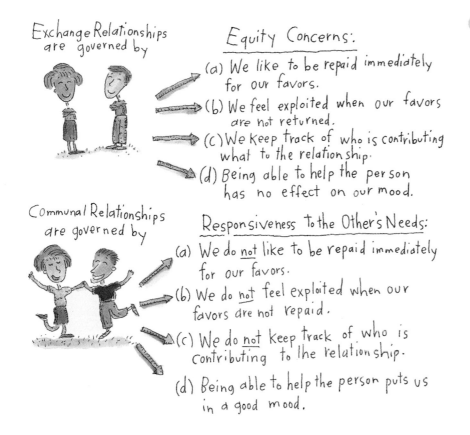

FIGURE 10.6
Exchange versus communal relationships.

Exchange Relationships are governed by

Equity Concerns:

(a) We like to be repaid immediately for our favors.

(b) We feel exploited when our favors are not returned.

(c) We keep track of who is contributing what to the relationship.

(d) Being able to help the person has no effect on our mood.

Communal Relationships are governed by

Responsiveness to the Other's Needs:

(a) We do <u>not</u> like to be repaid immediately for our favors.

(b) We do <u>not</u> feel exploited when our favors are not repaid.

(c) We do <u>not</u> keep track of who is contributing to the relationship.

(d) Being able to help the person puts us in a good mood.

communal relationships created in the laboratory. Other studies show, unsurprisingly, that ongoing friendships are more communal than relationships between strangers (Clark, Mills, & Corcoran, 1989).

Are people in communal relationships completely unconcerned with equity? No; as we saw earlier, people do feel distressed if they believe their intimate relationships are inequitable (Canary & Stafford, 2001; Walster et al., 1978). However, equity takes on a somewhat different form in communal relationships than it does in less intimate ones. In communal relationships, the partners are more relaxed about what constitutes equity at any given time; they believe that things will eventually balance out and a rough kind of equity will be achieved over time. If this is not the case—if they come to feel there is an imbalance—the relationship may end.

ENDING INTIMATE RELATIONSHIPS

The current American divorce rate is nearly 50 percent of the current marriage rate and has been for the past two decades (Thernstrom, 2003); some demographers estimate that two-thirds of all current first marriages will eventually end in separation or divorce (Spanier, 1992). And of course, countless romantic relationships between unmarried individuals end every day. After several years of studying what love is and how it blooms, social psychologists are now beginning to explore the end of the story—how it dies.

The Process of Breaking Up

Ending a romantic relationship is one of life's more painful experiences. In recent years, researchers have begun to examine what makes people end their relationships and the disengagement strategies they use (Baxter, 1986; Femlee,

"Somehow I remember this one differently."

Sprecher, & Bassin, 1990; Frazier & Cook, 1993; Helgeson, 1994; Rusbult & Zembrodt, 1983; Simpson, 1987). For example, Steve Duck (1982) reminds us that relationship dissolution is not a single event but a process with many steps (see Figure 10.7). Duck theorizes that four stages of dissolution exist, ranging from the intrapersonal (the individual thinks a lot about his or her dissatisfaction with the relationship) to the dyadic (the individual discusses the breakup with the partner) to the social (the breakup is announced to other people) and

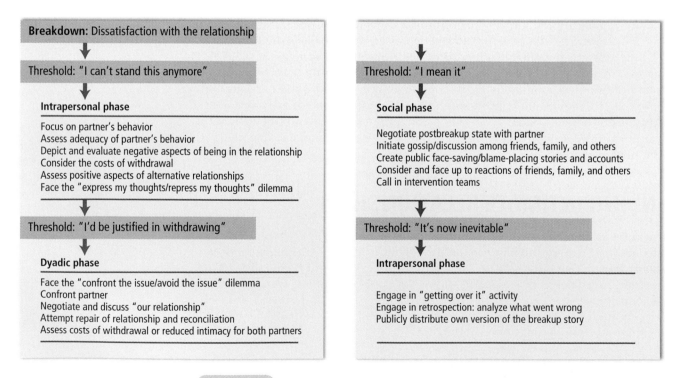

FIGURE 10.7

Steps in dissolving close relationships.

(Adapted from Duck, 1982)

back to the intrapersonal (the individual recovers from the breakup and forms an account, or version, of how and why it happened). In terms of the last stage in the process, John Harvey and his colleagues (Harvey, 1995; Harvey, Flanary, & Morgan, 1986; Harvey, Orbuch, & Weber, 1992) have found that the version of "why the relationship ended" that we present to close friends can be very different from the official (i.e., cleaned-up) version that we present to co-workers or neighbors. Take a moment to examine the stages outlined in Figure 10.7; see if they mirror your experience.

Why relationships end has been studied from several angles. One approach has used the investment model, which we discussed earlier (Bui et al., 1996; Drigotas & Rusbult, 1992). Caryl Rusbult's work on social exchange theory has led her to identify four types of behavior that occur in troubled relationships (Rusbult, 1987; Rusbult & Zembrodt, 1983). The first two types are destructive behaviors: actively harming the relationship (e.g., abusing the partner, threatening to break up, actually leaving) and passively allowing the relationship to deteriorate (e.g., refusing to deal with problems, ignoring the partner or spending less time together, putting no energy into the relationship). The other two responses are positive, constructive behaviors: actively trying to improve the relationship (e.g., discussing problems, trying to change, going to a therapist) and passively remaining loyal to the relationship (e.g., waiting and hoping that the situation will improve, being supportive rather than fighting, remaining optimistic).

Rusbult and her colleagues have found that destructive behaviors harm a relationship a lot more than constructive behaviors help it. Furthermore, when one partner acts destructively, the other partner tends to accommodate this behavior by responding constructively in order to save the relationship. When both partners act destructively, the relationship typically ends (Rusbult, Johnson, & Morrow, 1986; Rusbult, Yovetich, & Verette, 1996).

Another approach to studying why relationships end focuses on what attracts people to someone in the first place. In this research, college men and women were asked to focus on a romantic relationship that had ended and to list the qualities that first attracted them to the person and the characteristics they ended up disliking the most about the person (Femlee, 1995). Thirty percent of these breakups were examples of "fatal attractions." The very qualities that were initially so attractive (e.g., "He's so unusual and different," "She's so exciting and unpredictable") became the very reasons why the relationship ended ("He and I have nothing in common," "I can never count on her").

In further research, Femlee (1998a, 1998b) explored exactly what qualities turn out to be fatal attractions in close relationships. First, fatal attractions can occur when the person is different from you in a specific way. For example, you find someone attractive because he is a lot older than you and seems so mature. Later, the quality you dislike about him is . . . that he's so much older and has little in common with you. This finding reminds us again of the overriding importance of similarity between partners, and not complementarity, as a characteristic of successful relationships. Second, the person is different because he or she has a quality that is unique in a general sense. For example, you find someone attractive because she is so different and strange; perhaps she has an "offbeat personality" or she's "mysterious." Later, the quality that you dislike about her is that very strangeness—now she's "weird" or even "unbalanced." Third, the person is different because he or she has a quality that is extreme in a general sense. For example, you find someone attractive because he demonstrates such a deep and intense interest in you. Later, you perceive him as "jealous and possessive." Femlee (1998a) notes that while people in relationships will always differ from each other to some extent, these differences are not always the

> Love is like war; easy to begin but very hard to stop.
>
> —H. L. Mencken

Relationships can end for many reasons. For example, in "fatal attractions," the very qualities that once attracted you ("He's so mature and wise") can become the very reason you break up ("He's too old").

reason they were attracted to each other initially. When they are the reason, the attraction could turn out to be "fatal."

If a romantic relationship is in bad shape, can we predict who will end it? Much has been made about the tendency in heterosexual relationships for women to end relationships more often than men (Rubin, Peplau, & Hill, 1981). Recent research has found, however, that neither sex ends romantic relationships more frequently than the other (Akert, 1998; Hagestad & Smyer, 1982; Rusbult et al., 1986).

The Experience of Breaking Up

Can we predict the different ways people will feel when their relationship ends? One key is the role people play in the decision to end the relationship (Akert, 1998; Helgeson, 1994; Lloyd & Cate, 1985). For example, Robin Akert asked 344 college-age men and women to focus on their most important romantic relationship that had ended and to respond to a questionnaire focusing on their experiences during the breakup. One question asked to what extent they or their partner had been responsible for the decision to break up. Participants who indicated a high level of responsibility for the decision were labeled breakers; those who reported a low level of responsibility, breakees; and those who shared the decision making with their partners about equally, mutuals.

Akert found that the role people played in the decision to end the relationship was the single most powerful predictor of their breakup experiences. Not surprisingly, breakees were miserable—they reported high levels of loneliness, depression, unhappiness, and anger, and virtually all reported experiencing physical disorders in the weeks after the breakup as well. Breakers found the end of the relationship the least upsetting, the least painful, and the least stressful of the three. Although breakers did report feeling guilty and unhappy, they had the fewest negative physical symptoms (39 percent), such as headaches and stomachaches and eating and sleeping irregularities.

The mutual role, which carries with it a component of shared decision making, helped individuals evade some of the negative emotional and physical reactions to breaking up. Mutuals were not as upset or hurt as breakees, but they were not as unaffected as breakers. Some 60 percent of the mutuals reported

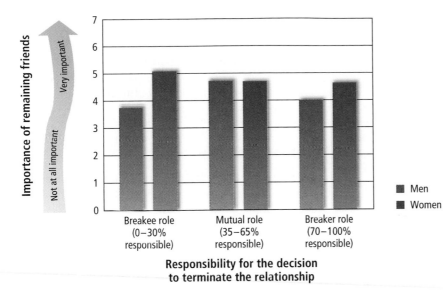

FIGURE 10.8

Importance of remaining friends after the breakup.

After ending a romantic relationship, do people want to remain friends with their ex-partner? It depends on both the role they played in the decision to break up and on their gender. Women are more interested than men in staying friends when they are in the breakee or breaker role; men and women are equally interested in staying friends when the relationship ends by mutual decision.

(Akert, 1998)

physical symptoms, indicating that a mutual conclusion to a romantic relationship is a more stressful experience than simply deciding to end it on one's own. Finally, gender played a role in the emotional and physical responses of the respondents, with women reporting somewhat more negative reactions to breaking up than men.

Do people want to stay friends when they break up? It depends on the role one plays in the breakup, as well as one's gender. Akert (1998) found that men are not very interested in remaining friends with their ex-girlfriends when they are in either the breaker or the breakee role, while women are more interested in remaining friends, especially when they are the breakees (see Figure 10.8). Interestingly, the mutual role is the one where men's and women's interest in future friendship matches the most. These data suggest that when men experience either great control (breaker) or little control (breakee) over the ending of the relationship, they tend to want to "cut their losses" and move on, severing ties with their ex-partner. In comparison, women tend to want to continue feeling connected to their ex-partner, hoping to reshape the intimate relationship into a platonic friendship. The mutual breakup is the one in which each partner effectively plays the breaker and breakee roles simultaneously. This equality in roles appears to be important in producing an equivalent interest in future friendship for men and women (see Figure 10.8).

The breakup moral? If you find yourself in a romantic relationship and your partner seems inclined to break it off, try to end it mutually. Your experience will be less traumatic because you will share some control over the process (even if you don't want it to happen). Unfortunately for your partner, if you are about to be in the role of breaker, you will experience less pain and suffering if you continue to play that role; however, changing your role from breaker to mutual would be an act of kindness toward your soon-to-be ex–loved one.

SUMMARY

What Causes Attraction?

In the first part of this chapter, we discussed the variables that cause initial attraction between two people. One such variable is physical proximity, or the **propinquity effect:** People who, by chance, you come into contact with the most are the most likely to become your friends and lovers. This occurs because of the **mere exposure effect;** in general, exposure to any stimulus produces liking for it. Similarity between people, whether in attitudes, values, personality traits, or demographic characteristics, is also a powerful cause of attraction and liking. Similarity is a more powerful predictor of attraction than complementarity—the idea that opposites attract. How people behave toward us is also of obvious importance. Reciprocal liking holds that in general, we like others who behave as if they like us. Though most people are reluctant to admit it, physical attractiveness also plays an important role in liking. Physical attractiveness of the face has a cross-cultural component: People from different cultures rate photographs quite similarly. The "what is beautiful is good" stereotype indicates that people assume that physical attractiveness is associated with other desirable traits. Exactly which desirable traits are linked to attractiveness depends on what is valued in one's culture.

Many of these determinants of attractiveness can be explained by **social exchange theory,** which argues that how people feel about their relationships depends on their perception of the rewards they receive from the relationship and the costs they incur. In addition, in order to determine whether people will stay in a relationship, we also need to know their **comparison level**—their expectations about the outcomes of their relationship—and their **comparison level for alternatives**—their expectations about how happy they would be in other relationships.

There are, however, exceptions to the rule of social exchange. Under some conditions, people do not prefer the person who is most rewarding. For example, some theorists argue that the most important determinant of satisfaction is the amount of equity in the relationship. **Equity theory** states that we are happiest when the ratio of rewards and costs we experience is roughly equal to the ratio of rewards and costs the other person experiences.

Close Relationships

Next, we examined attraction and love in long-term, intimate relationships. Social psychologists have offered several definitions of love. One important distinction is between **companionate love**—feelings of intimacy that are not accompanied by intense longing and arousal—and **passionate love**—feelings of intimacy that are accompanied by intense longing and arousal. The

triangular theory of love distinguishes among three components of love: intimacy, passion, and commitment. Although love is universal, cultural variations in the definition of love do occur.

Love and Relationships

Evolutionary psychology attempts to explain social behavior in terms of genetic factors that evolved over time according to the principles of natural selection. As applied here, the **evolutionary approach to love** states that men and women are attracted to different characteristics in each other because this maximizes their reproductive success. This view maintains that when choosing a marriage partner, women care more about men's resources and men care more about women's appearance.

The theory of **attachment styles** points to people's past relationships with their parents as a significant determinant of the quality of their close relationships as adults. Infants can be classified as having one of three types of attachment relationships with their primary caregiver: **secure, avoidant,** and **anxious/ambivalent.** There is evidence that people who were securely attached as infants have the most intimate and satisfying romantic relationships of the three types.

Social exchange theories of close relationships, such as the **investment model,** say that to predict whether a couple will stay together, we need to know each person's level of investment in and satisfaction with the relationship, as well as each person's comparison level and comparison level for alternatives. The notion of equity of rewards and costs is different in long-term versus short-term relationships. Short-term ones are usually **exchange relationships,** in which people are concerned about a fair distribution of rewards and costs. Long-term, intimate relationships are usually **communal relationships,** in which people are less concerned with an immediate accounting of who is contributing what and are more concerned with helping their partner when he or she is in need.

Ending Intimate Relationships

Unfortunately, intimate relationships can end; the breaking-up process is composed of stages; it is not a single event. Strategies for responding to problems in a romantic relationship include both constructive and destructive behaviors. Problems can occur because of fatal attractions when the qualities in a person that once were attractive become the very qualities that repel. Although the experience of breaking up is never pleasant, a powerful variable that predicts how a person will weather the breakup is the role he or she plays in the decision to terminate the relationship.

CRITICAL THINKING QUESTIONS

Think about a friendship or romantic relationship you had that has ended. Go through the following list of questions. Does thinking about these issues gives you a greater understanding of your relationship and breakup?

1. First, think about how your relationship started. To what extent did propinquity, similarity, reciprocal liking, and physical attractiveness bring the two of you together?

2. Think about which attachment styles best describe yourself and your friend or partner. Did you have matching or dissimilar styles? Do you think a difference in your attachment styles played a role in the ending of your relationship?

3. According to the investment model, satisfaction, investment, and alternatives predict whether people will stay together or break up. How would you describe yourself and your friend or partner in terms of these three variables? Was one of you more invested than the other? What about your respective comparison levels of alternatives?

4. Did your breakup follow the steps described in Figure 10.8? If you skipped some steps, do you think this made the breakup more or less painful?

5. Was your relationship a "fatal attraction" for either or both of you?

Prosocial Behavior:

Why Do People Help?

September 11, 2001, was truly a day of infamy in American history, with terrible loss of life at the World Trade Center, the Pentagon, and the field in Pennsylania where United Air Lines flight 93 crashed. It was also a day of incredible courage and sacrifice by people who did not hesitate to help their fellow human beings. Many people lost their lives while helping others, including 403 New York firefighters and police officers who died trying to rescue people from the World Trade Center.

Many of the heroes of September 11 were ordinary citizens who found themselves in extraordinary circumstances. Imagine that you were working in the World Trade Center towers when they were hit by the planes and how strong the desire must have been to flee and seek personal safety. This is exactly what William Wik's wife urged him to do when he called her from the ninety-second floor of the South Tower shortly after the attacks. "No, I can't do that; there are still people here," he replied (Lee, 2001, p. 28). Wik's body was found in the rubble of the South Tower after it collapsed, wearing work gloves and holding a flashlight.

Abe Zelmanowitz worked on the twenty-seventh floor of the North Tower and could easily have walked down the stairs to safety when the plane struck the floors above. Instead he stayed behind with his friend Ed Beyea, a quadriplegic, waiting for help to carry him down the stairs. Both died when the tower collapsed.

Rick Rescorla was head of security for the Morgan Stanley brokerage firm. After the first plane hit the North Tower, Rescorla and the other employees in the South Tower were instructed to remain at their desks. Rescorla, who had spent years studying the security of the towers, had drilled his employees repeatedly in what to do in an emergency like this—find a partner, avoid the elevators, and evacuate the building. He invoked this plan immediately, and when the plane hit the South Tower, he was on the forty-fourth floor supervising the evacuation, yelling instructions through a bullhorn. After most of the Morgan Stanley employees made it out of the building, Rescorla decided to do a final sweep of the offices to make sure no one was left behind, and perished when the South Tower collapsed. Rescorla is credited with saving the lives of the thirty-seven hundred employees he guided to safety (Stewart, 2002).

And then there were the passengers on United flight 93. Based on phone calls made from the plane in the fateful minutes after it was hijacked, it appears that several passengers, including Todd Beamer, Jeremy Glick, and Thomas Burnett, all fathers of young children, stormed the cockpit and struggled with the terrorists. They could not prevent the plane from crashing, killing everyone on board, but they did prevent an even worse tragedy. The plane was headed for Washington, D.C., with the White House or the U.S. Capitol its likely target.

BASIC MOTIVES UNDERLYING PROSOCIAL BEHAVIOR: WHY DO PEOPLE HELP?

How can we explain acts of great self-sacrifice and heroism when people are also capable of acting in uncaring, heartless ways? In this chapter, we will consider the major causes of **prosocial behavior**—any act performed with the goal of benefiting another person. We are particularly concerned with prosocial behavior that is motivated by **altruism,** which is the desire to help another person even if it involves a cost to the helper. Someone might act in a prosocial way out of self-interest, hoping to get something in return. Altruism is helping purely out of the desire to benefit someone else, with no benefit (and often a cost) to oneself. Many of the heroes of September 11, for example, gave their lives in order to help strangers.

We begin by considering the basic origins of prosocial behavior and altruism: Is the willingness to help a basic impulse with genetic roots? Must it be taught and nurtured in childhood? Is there a pure motive for helping? Or do people typically help only when there is something in it for them? Let's see how psychologists have addressed these centuries-old questions.

Evolutionary Psychology: Instincts and Genes

According to Charles Darwin's (1859) theory of evolution, natural selection favors genes that promote the survival of the individual (see Chapter 10). Any gene that furthers our survival and increases the probability that we will produce offspring is likely to be passed on from generation to generation. Genes that lower our chances of survival, such as those causing life-threatening diseases, reduce the chances that we will produce offspring and thus are less likely to be passed on. Evolutionary biologists like E. O. Wilson (1975) and Richard Dawkins (1976) have used these principles of evolutionary theory to explain such social behaviors as aggression and altruism. Several psychologists have pursued these ideas, spawning the field of *evolutionary psychology,* which is the attempt to explain social behavior in terms of genetic factors that evolved over time according to the principles of natural selection (Barkow, Cosmides, & Tooby, 1992; Buss, 1999; Pinker, 2002). In Chapter 10, we discussed how evolutionary psychology attempts to explain love and attraction; here we discuss how it attempts to explain prosocial behavior (McAndrew, 2002).

Darwin realized early on that there was a problem with evolutionary theory: How can it explain altruism? If people's overriding goal is to ensure their own

Prosocial Behavior

Any act performed with the goal of benefiting another person

Altruism

The desire to help another person even if it involves a cost to the helper

survival, why would they ever help others at a cost to themselves? It would seem that over the course of human evolution, altruistic behavior would disappear, because people who acted that way would, by putting themselves at risk, produce fewer offspring than people who acted selfishly. Genes promoting selfish behavior should be more likely to be passed on—or should they?

Kin Selection   One way that evolutionary psychologists attempt to resolve this dilemma is with the notion of **kin selection,** the idea that behaviors that help a genetic relative are favored by natural selection (Hamilton, 1964; Meyer, 1999). People can increase the chances that their genes will be passed along not only by having their own children but also by ensuring that their genetic relatives have children. Because a person's blood relatives share some of his or her genes, the more that person ensures their survival, the greater the chance that his or her genes will flourish in future generations. Thus natural selection should favor altruistic acts directed toward genetic relatives.

In one study, for example, people reported that they would be more likely to help genetic relatives than nonrelatives in life-and-death situations, such as a house fire. People did not report that they would be more likely to help genetic relatives when the situation was non-life-threatening, which supports the idea that people are most likely to help in ways that ensure the survival of their own genes. Interestingly, both males and females, and both American and Japanese participants, followed this rule of kin selection in life-threatening situations (Burnstein, Crandall, & Kitayama, 1994).

Of course, in this study, people reported what they thought they would do; this doesn't prove that in a real fire they would indeed be more likely to save their sibling than their cousin. Anecdotal evidence from real emergencies, however, is consistent with these results. Survivors of a fire at a vacation complex reported that when they became aware there was a fire, they were much more likely to search for family members before exiting the building than they were to search for friends (Sime, 1983).

Evolutionary psychologists are not suggesting that people consciously weigh the biological importance of their behavior before deciding whether to help: We don't compute the likelihood that our genes will be passed on before deciding whether to help someone push his or her car out of a ditch. According to evolutionary theory, however, the genes of people who follow this "biological importance" rule are more likely to survive than the genes of people who do not. Over the millennia, kin selection may have become ingrained in human behavior.

The Reciprocity Norm   To explain altruism, evolutionary psychologists also point to the **norm of reciprocity,** which is the expectation that helping others will increase the likelihood that they will help us in the future. The idea is that as human beings were evolving, a group of completely selfish individuals, each living in his or her own cave, would have found it more difficult to survive than a group who had learned to cooperate. Of course, if people cooperated too readily, they might have been exploited by an adversary who never helped in return. Those who were most likely to survive, the argument goes, were people who developed an understanding with their neighbors about reciprocity: "I will help you now, with the agreement that when I need help, you will return the favor." Because of its survival value, such a norm of reciprocity may have become genetically based (Cosmides & Tooby, 1992; de Waal, 1996; Shackelford & Buss, 1996; Trivers, 1971). The Try It! exercise on page 360 describes a way you can use the reciprocity norm to collect money for charity.

Learning Social Norms   Nobel laureate Herbert Simon (1990) offered one more link between evolution and altruism. He argued that it is highly adaptive for

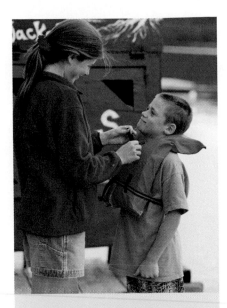

According to evolutionary psychology, prosocial behavior occurs in part because of kin selection, such as this young woman helping her little brother.

Altruism based on kin selection is the enemy of civilization. If human beings are to a large extent guided to favor their own relatives and tribe, only a limited amount of global harmony is possible.

—E. O. Wilson, 1978

Kin Selection

The idea that behaviors that help a genetic relative are favored by natural selection

Norm of Reciprocity

The expectation that helping others will increase the likelihood that they will help us in the future

Try it!

Does the Reciprocity Norm Work?

If you help people in some way, they will probably feel obligated to help you in the future. This exercise takes advantage of the reciprocity norm to help you collect money for a good cause. See if it works for you.

1. Choose a charity or cause for which you would like to collect money.
2. Make a list of ten to fifteen friends and acquaintances whom you are willing to ask to give money to this charity.
3. Go down the list, and flip a coin for each name. If the coin comes up tails, assign the person to the "favor" condition. If it comes up heads, assign the person to the "no favor" condition.
4. Find a way to do a small favor for each person in the "favor" condition. For example, if you're going to the soda machine, offer to buy a soda for your friend. If you have a car, provide a ride somewhere. The exact favor doesn't matter and doesn't have to be the same for each person in your "favor" condition. The key is that it be a little out of the ordinary so that your friend feels obligated to you.
5. A day later, ask everyone on your list to make a donation to your charity. Keep track of how much each person gives. Chances are, people in your "favor" condition will give more, on average, than people in your "no favor" condition.

Warning: This technique can backfire if your friends perceive your favor as an attempt to manipulate them. That is why it is important to allow a day or so to pass between the time you help them and the time you ask them for a donation; if you ask them right after the favor, they are likely to feel that you helped only to get them to give money—and to resent this intrusion. Also, when you ask them for a donation, do not say anything about your earlier favor. After you are done with this exercise, you may want to discuss it with your friends and explain why you did what you did.

individuals to learn social norms from other members of a society. People who are the best learners of the norms and customs of a society have a survival advantage, because over the centuries, a culture learns such things as which foods are poisonous and how best to cooperate, and the person who learns these rules is more likely to survive than the person who does not. Consequently, through natural selection, the ability to learn social norms has become part of our genetic makeup. One norm that people learn is the value of helping others—considered a valuable norm in virtually all societies. In short, people are genetically programmed to learn social norms, and one of these norms is altruism (Hoffman, 1981; Kameda, Takezawa, & Hastie, 2003).

In sum, evolutionary psychologists believe that people help others because of three factors that have become ingrained in our genes: kin selection, the norm of reciprocity, and the ability to learn and follow social norms. As we saw in Chapter 10, evolutionary psychology is a challenging and creative approach to understanding prosocial behavior, though it does have its critics (Batson, 1998; Caporael & Brewer, 2000; Gould, 1997; Wood & Eagly, 2002). How, for example, can evolutionary theory explain why complete strangers sometimes help each other, even when there is no reason for them to assume that they share some of the same genes or that their favor will ever be returned? It seems absurd to say that the heroes of September 11, who lost their lives while saving others, somehow calculated how genetically similar they were to the others before deciding to help. Further, just because people are more likely to save family members than strangers from a fire does not necessarily mean that they are genetically programmed to help genetic relatives. It may simply be that they cannot bear the thought of losing a loved one and so go to greater lengths to save the ones they love over people they have never met. We turn now to other possible motives behind prosocial behavior that do not necessarily originate in people's genes.

Social Exchange: The Costs and Rewards of Helping

Although some social psychologists disagree with evolutionary approaches to prosocial behavior, they share the view that altruistic behavior can be based on self-interest. In fact, *social exchange theory* (see Chapter 10) argues that much of what we do stems from the desire to maximize our rewards and minimize our costs (Homans, 1961; Lawler & Thye, 1999; Thibaut & Kelley, 1959). The difference from evolutionary approaches is that social exchange theory doesn't trace this desire back to our evolutionary roots; nor does it assume that the desire is genetically based. Social exchange theorists assume that just as people in an economic marketplace try to maximize the ratio of their monetary profits to their monetary losses, people in their relationships with others try to maximize the ratio of social rewards to social costs.

This does not mean that we keep a little notebook handy, entering a plus every time our friends are nice to us and a minus every time they treat us badly. Social exchange theory does argue, however, that we keep track, at a more implicit level, of the rewards and costs in social relationships. Helping can be rewarding in a number of ways. As we saw with the norm of reciprocity, it can increase the likelihood that someone will help us in return. Helping someone is an investment in the future, the social exchange being that someday, someone will help us when we need it. Helping can also relieve the personal distress of a bystander. Considerable evidence indicates that people are aroused and disturbed when they see another person suffer and that they help at least in part to relieve their own distress (Dovidio, 1984; Dovidio, Piliavin, Gaertner, Schroeder, & Clark, 1991; Eisenberg & Fabes, 1991). By helping others, we can also gain such rewards as social approval from others and increased feelings of self-worth.

The other side of the coin, of course, is that helping can be costly. Helping decreases when the costs are high, as when it would put us in physical danger, result in pain or embarrassment, or simply take too much time (Dovidio et al., 1991; Piliavin, Dovidio, Gaertner, & Clark, 1981; Piliavin, Piliavin, & Rodin, 1975). The basic assumption of social exchange theory is that people help only when the benefits outweigh the costs. Perhaps Abe Zelmanowitz, who stayed behind with his friend Ed Beyea in the World Trade Center, simply found the prospect of walking away and letting his friend die too distressing. Basically,

> Let him who neglects to raise the fallen, fear lest, when he falls, no one will stretch out his hand to lift him up.
>
> —Saadi, The Orchard, 1257

> I once saw a man out of courtesy help a lame dog over a stile, and [the dog] for requital bit his fingers.
>
> —William Chillingworth

Calvin and Hobbes   by Bill Watterson

RRIINGG RRINGG

HELLO? NO, MY DAD'S NOT HERE RIGHT NOW.

WILL I TAKE A MESSAGE? I DON'T KNOW - WHAT'S IN IT FOR *ME*?

PEOPLE ALWAYS ASSUME YOU'RE SOME KIND OF ALTRUIST.

> What seems to be generosity is often no more than disguised ambition.
>
> —François de la Rochefoucauld, Maxims, 1665

social exchange theory argues that true altruism, in which people help even when doing so is costly to themselves, does not exist. People help when the benefits outweigh the costs.

If you are like many of our students, you may think this is an overly cynical view of human nature. Is true altruism, motivated only by the desire to help someone else, really such a mythical act? Must we trace all prosocial behavior, such as large charitable gifts made by wealthy individuals, to the self-interest of the helper? Well, a social exchange theorist might reply, there are many ways in which people can obtain gratification, and we should be thankful that one way is by helping others. After all, wealthy people could decide to get their pleasure only from lavish vacations, expensive cars, and meals at fancy restaurants. We should applaud their decision to give money to the disadvantaged, even if, ultimately, it is just a way for them to feel good about themselves. Prosocial acts are doubly rewarding in that they help both the giver and the recipient of the aid. Thus it is to everyone's advantage to promote and praise such acts.

Still, many people are dissatisfied with the argument that all helping stems from self-interest. How can it explain why people give up their lives for others, as many of the heroes of September 11th did? According to some social psychologists, people do have hearts of gold and sometimes help only for the sake of helping.

Empathy and Altruism: The Pure Motive for Helping

C. Daniel Batson (1991) is the strongest proponent of the idea that people often help purely out of the goodness of their hearts. Batson acknowledges that people sometimes help others for selfish reasons, such as to relieve their own distress at seeing another person suffer. But he also argues that people's motives are sometimes purely altruistic, in that their only goal is to help the other person, even if doing so involves some cost to themselves. Pure altruism is likely to come into play, he maintains, when we feel **empathy** for the person in need of help, putting ourselves in the shoes of another person and experiencing events and emotions the way that person experiences them.

Suppose that while you are food shopping, you see a man holding a baby and a bag full of diapers, toys, and rattles. As he reaches for a box of Wheat Chex, the man drops the bag, and everything spills onto the floor. Will you help him pick up his things? According to Batson, it depends first on whether you feel empathy for him. If you do, you will help, regardless of what you have to gain. Your goal will be to relieve the other person's distress, not to gain something for yourself. This is the crux of Batson's **empathy-altruism hypothesis:** When we feel empathy for another person, we will attempt to help the person for purely altruistic reasons, regardless of what we have to gain.

If you do not feel empathy, then, Batson says, social exchange concerns come into play. What's in it for you? If there is something to be gained, such as obtaining approval from the man or from onlookers, you will help the man pick up his things. If you will not profit from helping, you will go on your way without stopping. Batson's empathy-altruism hypothesis is summarized in Figure 11.1.

Batson and his colleagues would be the first to acknowledge that it can be very difficult to isolate the exact motives behind complex social behaviors. If you saw someone help the man pick up his possessions, how could you tell whether the person was acting out of empathic concern or to gain some sort of social reward? Consider a famous story about Abraham Lincoln. One day, while riding in a coach, Lincoln and a fellow passenger were debating the very question we are considering: Is helping ever truly altruistic? Lincoln argued that helping always stems from self-interest, whereas the other passenger took the view that true al-

Empathy

The ability to put oneself in the shoes of another person and to experience events and emotions (e.g., joy and sadness) the way that person experiences them

Empathy-Altruism Hypothesis

The idea that when we feel empathy for a person, we will attempt to help that person purely for altruistic reasons, regardless of what we have to gain

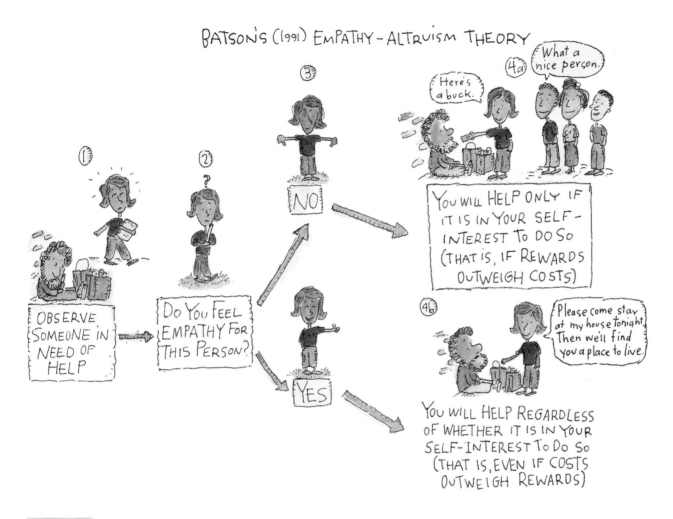

FIGURE 11.1

Batson's (1991) empathy-altruism theory.

truism exists. Suddenly the men were interrupted by the screeching of a pig who was trying to save her piglets from drowning in a creek. Lincoln ordered the coach to stop, jumped out, ran down to the creek, and lifted the piglets to the safety of the bank. When he returned, his companion said, "Now, Abe, where does selfishness come in on this little episode?" "Why, bless your soul, Ed," Lincoln replied. "That was the very essence of selfishness. I should have had no peace of mind all day had I gone on and left that suffering old sow worrying over those pigs. I did it to get peace of mind, don't you see?" (Sharp, 1928, p. 75).

As this example shows, an act that seems truly altruistic is sometimes motivated by self-interest. How, then, can we tell which is which? Batson and his colleagues have devised a series of clever experiments to unravel people's motives (Batson, 2002; Batson & Powell, 2003). Imagine that you were one of the introductory psychology students in one of these studies (Toi & Batson, 1982). You are asked to evaluate some tapes of new programs for the university radio station, one of which is called *News from the Personal Side*. There are lots of different pilot tapes for this program, and you are told that only one person will be listening to each tape. The one you hear is an interview with a student named Carol Marcy. She describes a bad automobile accident in which both of her legs were broken and talks about how hard it has been to keep up with her classwork as a result of the accident,

> It is one of the beautiful compensations of this life that no one can sincerely try to help another without helping himself.
>
> *—Charles Dudley Warner, 1873*

especially because she is still in a wheelchair. Carol says she is especially concerned about how far she has fallen behind in her introductory psychology class and mentions that she will have to drop the class unless she can find another student to tell her what she has missed.

After you listen to the tape, the experimenter hands you an envelope marked "To the student listening to the Carol Marcy pilot tape." The experimenter says she doesn't know what's in the envelope but was asked by the professor supervising the research to hand it out. You open the envelope and find a note from the professor, saying that he was wondering if the student who listened to Carol's tape would be willing to help her out with her psychology class. Carol was reluctant to ask for help, he says, but because she is so far behind in the class, she agreed to write a note to the person listening to her tape. The note asks if you could meet with her and share your introductory psychology lecture notes.

As you have guessed, the point of the study was to look at the conditions under which people agreed to help Carol. The researchers pitted two motives against each other—self-interest and empathy. First, they varied how much empathy people felt toward Carol by telling different participants to adopt different perspectives when listening to the tape. In the high-empathy condition, people were told to try to imagine how Carol felt about what happened to her and how it changed her life. In the low-empathy condition, people were told to try to be objective and not be concerned with how Carol felt. As expected, people in the high-empathy condition reported feeling more sympathy for Carol than people in the low-empathy condition did.

Second, the researchers varied how costly it would be *not* to help Carol. In one condition, participants learned that she would start coming back to class the following week and happened to be in the same psychology section as they were; thus they would see her every time they went to class and would be reminded that she needed help. This was the high-cost condition, because it would be unpleasant to refuse to help Carol and then run into her every week in class. In the low-cost condition, people learned that Carol would be studying at home and would not be coming to class; thus they would never have to face her in her wheelchair and feel guilty about not helping her.

When deciding whether to help Carol, did people take into account the costs involved? According to the empathy-altruism hypothesis, people should have been motivated purely by altruistic concerns and helped regardless of the costs—if empathy was high (see Figure 11.1). As you can see in the right-hand side of Figure 11.2, this prediction was confirmed: In the high-empathy condition, about as many people agreed to help when they thought they would see Carol in class as when they thought they would not see her in class. This suggests that people had Carol's interests in mind and not their own. In the low-empathy condition, however, many more people agreed to help when they thought they

FIGURE 11.2

Altruism versus self-interest.

Under what conditions did people agree to help Carol with the work she missed in her introductory psychology class? When empathy was high, people helped regardless of the costs and rewards (i.e., regardless of whether they would encounter her in their psychology class). When empathy was low, people were more concerned with the rewards and costs for them—they helped only if they would encounter Carol in their psychology class and thus feel guilty about not helping.

(Adapted from Toi & Batson, 1982)

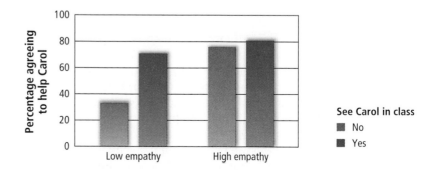

would see Carol in class than when they thought they would not see her in class (see the left-hand side of Figure 11.2). This suggests that when empathy was low, social exchange concerns came into play, in that people based their decision to help on the costs and benefits to themselves. They helped when it was in their interests to do so (i.e., when they would see Carol in her wheelchair and feel guilty for not helping) but not otherwise (i.e., when they thought they would never see her again).

These results suggest that true altruism exists when people experience empathy toward the suffering of another. But as we learned from Abraham Lincoln and the pigs, unraveling people's exact motives for helping someone is a formidable task, and the empathy-altruism hypothesis has sparked a lively debate. Some researchers have questioned whether people who experience empathy help purely out of concern for the person in need or, like Abe Lincoln, offer help to relieve their own distress at seeing someone suffer (e.g., Cialdini, Brown, Lewis, Luce, & Neuberg, 1997; Maner et al., 2002; Preston & De Waal, 2002).

To sum up, we've identified three basic motives underlying prosocial behavior:

1. Helping is an instinctive reaction to promote the welfare of those genetically similar to us (evolutionary psychology).

2. The rewards of helping often outweigh the costs, so helping is in our self-interest (social exchange theory).

3. Under some conditions, powerful feelings of empathy and compassion for the victim prompt selfless giving (the empathy-altruism hypothesis).

Each of these approaches has its supporters and critics.

PERSONAL QUALITIES AND PROSOCIAL BEHAVIOR: WHY DO SOME PEOPLE HELP MORE THAN OTHERS?

If basic human motives were all there was to it, then why are some people so much more helpful than others? Clearly, we need to consider the personal qualities that distinguish the helpful person from the selfish one.

Individual Differences: The Altruistic Personality

When you read the descriptions of the September 11 heroes at the beginning of this chapter, did you think about the personalities of the people we described? It is natural to assume that William Wik, Abe Zelmanowitz, Rick Rescorla, and the passengers of United flight 93 were cut from a different cloth—selfless, caring people who would never dream of ignoring someone's pleas for help. Remember Kitty Genovese, the woman was murdered within earshot of thirty-eight of her neighbors, none of whom called the police or helped her in any way (see Chapter 2)? If the heroes of September 11 had heard her cries, surely they would have helped in some way.

Study: Cavemen helped disabled

United Press International
NEW YORK—The skeleton of a dwarf who died about 12,000 years ago indicates that cave people cared for physically disabled members of their communities, a researcher said yesterday.

The skeleton of the 3-foot-high youth was initially discovered in 1963 in a cave in southern Italy but was lost to anthropologists until American researcher David W. Frayer reexamined the remains and reported his findings in the British journal Nature.

Frayer, a professor of anthropology at the University of Kansas at Lawrence, said in a telephone interview that the youth "couldn't have taken part in normal hunting of food or gathering activities so he was obviously cared for by others."

Archaeologists have found the remains of other handicapped individuals who lived during the same time period, but their disabilities occurred when they were adults, Frayer said.

"This is the first time we've found someone who was disabled since birth . . . .", Frayer said. He said there was no indication that the dwarf, who was about 17 at the time of his death, had suffered from malnutrition or neglect.

He was one of six individuals buried in the floor of a cave and was found in a dual grave in the arms of a woman, about 40 years old.

This touching story of early hominid prosocial behavior is intriguing to think about in terms of different theories of prosocial behavior. Evolutionary psychologists might argue that the caregivers helped the dwarf because he was a relative and that people are programmed to help those who share their genes (kin selection). Social exchange theory would maintain that the dwarf's caregivers received sufficient rewards from their actions to outweigh the costs of caring for him. The empathy-altruism hypothesis would hold that the caregivers helped out of strong feelings of empathy and compassion for him—an interpretation supported by the article's final paragraph.

Helping behavior is common in virtually all species of animals, and sometimes it even crosses species lines. In August 1996, a 3-year-old boy fell into a pit containing seven gorillas at the Brookfield, Illinois, zoo. Binti, a 7-year-old gorilla, immediately picked up the boy. After cradling him in her arms, she placed the boy near a door where zookeepers could get to him. Why did she help? Evolutionary psychologists would argue that prosocial behavior is selected for and thus becomes part of the genetic makeup of the members of many species. Social exchange theorists would argue that Binti had been rewarded for helping in the past. In fact, because she had been rejected by her mother, she had received training in parenting skills from zookeepers, in which she was rewarded for caring for a doll (Bils & Singer, 1996).

> On reflecting at dinner that he had done nothing to help anybody all day, he uttered these memorable and praise-worthy words: "Friends, I have lost a day."
>
> —*Suetonius,* Lives of the Twelve Caesars, *first century* A.D.

Altruistic Personality

The qualities that cause an individual to help others in a wide variety of situations

Or so it seems, to the extent that helping is determined by personality qualities that set some people apart from others. Psychologists have been interested in the nature of the **altruistic personality,** the qualities that cause an individual to help others in a wide variety of situations (Eisenberg et al., 2002; Penner, Fritzsche, Craiger, & Freifeld, 1995; Penner & Finkelstein, 1998). To what extent are some people more helpful than others?

As we have seen throughout this book, personality alone does not determine behavior. Social psychologists argue that to understand human behavior, we need to consider the pressures of the situation as well as an individual's personality. Predicting how helpful people will be is no exception. Consider a classic study by Hugh Hartshorne and Mark May (1929). They observed how helpful ten thousand elementary and high school students were in a variety of situations, including the students' willingness to find stories and pictures to give to hospitalized children, donate money to charity, and give small gifts to needy children. The researchers assumed that they were measuring the extent to which each students had an altruistic personality.

Surprisingly, though, the extent to which the students were prosocial in one situation (e.g., finding many stories and pictures for the hospitalized children) was not highly related to how prosocial the same children were in another. The average correlation between helping in one situation and helping in another was only .23. This means that if you knew how helpful a child was in one situation, you could not predict with much confidence how helpful he or she would be in another. Moreover, studies of both children and adults indicate that people with high scores on personality tests of altruism are not much more likely to help than those with lower scores (Batson, 1998; Magoo & Khanna, 1991; Piliavin & Charng, 1990).

Does this mean that any two people—be they like Mother Teresa or Osama bin Laden—are equally likely to help in an emergency or assist a neighbor who is seriously ill? Of course not. It's just that individual differences in personality are not the only predictors of how helpful someone will be. We need to consider several other critical factors as well, such as the situational pressures that are affecting people, their gender, the culture in which they grew up, and even their current mood.

Gender Differences in Prosocial Behavior

Consider two scenarios. In one, someone performs a dramatic, heroic act, like storming the cockpit of United flight 93 to fight the terrorists. In the other, someone is involved in a long-term helping relationship, such as assisting a disabled neighbor with chores around the house. Are men or women more likely to help in each situation?

The answer is males in the first situation and females in the second (Eagly, 1987; Eagly & Crowley, 1986). In virtually all cultures, norms prescribe different traits and behaviors for males and females, learned as boys and girls are growing up. In Western cultures, the male sex role includes being chivalrous and heroic; females are expected to be nurturant and caring and to value close, long-term relationships.

Indeed, of the seven thousand people who received medals from the Carnegie Hero Fund Commission for risking their lives to save a stranger, 91 percent have been men. Researchers have focused less on helping that involves more nurturance and commitment, but a few studies have found that women do help more in long-term, nurturant relationships than men do (George, Carroll, Kersnick, & Calderon, 1998; McGuire, 1994; Otten, Penner, & Waugh, 1988; Smith, Wheeler, & Diener, 1975). Cross-cultural evidence suggests the same pattern. In a survey of adolescents in seven countries, more girls than boys reported doing volunteer work in their communities (Flanagan, Bowes, Jonsson, Csapo, & Sheblanova, 1998).

> If an accident happens on the highway, everyone hastens to help the sufferer. If some great and sudden calamity befalls a family, the purses of a thousand strangers are at once willingly opened and small but numerous donations pour in to relieve their distress.
>
> *—Alexis de Tocqueville, Democracy in America, 1835*

> Both men and women belie their nature when they are not kind.
>
> *—Gamaliel Bailey*

MotherTeresa. Clearly, some people have more of an altruistic personality than others, causing them to engage in more prosocial behavior. Personality, however, is not the whole story; the nature of the social situation also determines whether people help.

Whereas men are more likely to perform chivalrous and heroic acts, women are more likely to be helpful in long-term relationships that involve greater commitment.

Cultural Differences in Prosocial Behavior

Let's look again at Western and non-Western cultures (see Chapter 5). Does an independent view of the self versus a more interdependent, group-oriented outlook affect people's willingness to help others? Because people with an interdependent view of the self are more likely to define themselves in terms of their social relationships and have more of a sense of "connectedness" to others, we might predict that they'd be more likely to help a person in need.

However, people in all cultures are more likely to help someone they define as a member of their **in-group,** the group with which an individual identifies. People everywhere are less likely to help someone they perceive to be a member of an **out-group,** a group with which they do not identify (Brewer & Brown, 1998; see also Chapter 13). Cultural factors come into play in determining how strongly people draw the line between in-groups and out-groups. In many interdependent cultures, the needs of in-group members are considered more important than those of out-groups, and consequently, people in these cultures are more likely to help in-group members than members of individualistic cultures are (Leung & Bond, 1984; Miller, Bersoff, & Harwood, 1990; Moghaddam, Taylor, & Wright, 1993). However, because the line between "us" and "them" is more firmly drawn in interdependent cultures, people in these cultures are *less* likely to help members of out-groups than people in individualistic cultures are (L'Armand & Pepitone, 1975; Leung & Bond, 1984; Triandis, 1994). Thus to be helped by other people, it is important that they view you as a member of their in-group—as "one of them"—and this is especially true in interdependent cultures (Ting & Piliavin, 2000).

A particular cultural value that strongly relates to prosocial behavior is *simpatía.* Prominent in Spanish-speaking countries, *simpatía* refers to a range of social and emotional traits, including being friendly, polite, good-natured, pleasant, and helpful toward others (interestingly, it has no direct English translation). A recent study tested the hypothesis that helping would be higher in cultures that value *simpatía* (Levine, Norenzayan, & Philbrick, 2001). The researchers staged helping incidents in large cities in twenty-three countries and observed what people did. In one scenario, a researcher posing as a blind person stopped at a busy intersection and observed whether pedestrians offered help in crossing or informed the researcher when the light turned green.

In-Group

The group with which an individual identifies as a member

Out-Group

Any group with which an individual does not identify

If you look at Table 11.1, you'll see that the percentage of people who helped (averaged across the three incidents) varied. On average, people in countries that value *simpatía* helped more than in countries that did not, 83 to 66 percent. The researchers noted that these results are only suggestive, because the five Latin American and Spanish countries differed from the others in ways other than the value they placed on *sympatía*. And some countries not known for their *sympatía* had high rates of helping. Nevertheless, if a culture strongly values friendliness and prosocial behavior, people may be more likely to help strangers on city streets (Janoff-Bulman & Leggatt, 2002).

The Effects of Mood on Prosocial Behavior

Imagine that you are at your local shopping mall. As you walk from one store to another, a fellow in front of you drops a manila folder and papers go fluttering in all directions. He looks around in dismay, then bends down and starts picking up the papers. Would you stop and help him? What do you think the average shopper would do? By now you know that thinking about how many altruistic people there are in the world won't predict the answer. Other factors, including

TABLE 11.1

Helping in Twenty-Three Cultures

In twenty-three cities around the world, researchers observed how many people helped in three situations: helping a person with a leg brace who dropped a pile of magazines, helping someone who did not notice that he or she had dropped a pen, and helping a blind person across a busy intersection. The percentages in the table are averaged across the three situations. The cities in boldface are in countries that have the cultural value of *simpatía*, which prizes friendliness, politeness, and helping others.

CITY	PERCENT HELPING
Rio de Janeiro, Brazil	**93**
San José, Costa Rica	**91**
Lilongwe, Malawi	86
Calcutta, India	83
Vienna, Austria	81
Madrid, Spain	**79**
Copenhagen, Denmark	78
Shanghai, China	77
Mexico City, Mexico	**76**
San Salvador, El Salvador	**75**
Prague, Czech Republic	75
Stockholm, Sweden	72
Budapest, Hungary	71
Bucharest, Romania	69
Tel Aviv, Israel	68
Rome, Italy	63
Bangkok, Thailand	61
Taipei, Taiwan	59
Sofia, Bulgaria	57
Amsterdam, Netherlands	54
Singapore	48
New York, United States	45
Kuala Lumpur, Malaysia	40

(Adapted from Levine, Norenzayan, & Philbrick, 2001)

the mood people happen to be in at the time, can strongly affect behavior—in this case, whether or not they will offer help.

Effects of Positive Moods: Feel Good, Do Good To explore the effect of good moods on prosocial behavior, researchers set up an experiment in shopping malls in San Francisco and Philadelphia (Isen & Levin, 1972). First, they boosted the mood of shoppers by leaving dimes in the coin-return slot of a pay telephone at the mall, and then waited for someone to find the coins. (Note the year this study was done; it would be like finding 35 cents today.) As the lucky shoppers left the phone with their newly found dime, a research assistant played the role of the man with the manila folder. He intentionally dropped the folder a few feet in front of the shopper to see whether he or she would stop and help him pick up his papers. It turned out that finding the dime had a dramatic effect on helping. Only 4 percent of the people who did not find a dime helped the man pick up his papers, whereas 84 percent of the people who found a dime stopped to help.

Researchers have found this "feel good, do good" effect in diverse situations and have shown that it is not limited to the little boost we get when we find some money. People are more likely to help others when they are in a good mood for a number of reasons, including doing well on a test, receiving a gift, thinking happy thoughts, and listening to pleasant music. And when people are in a good mood, they are more helpful in many ways, including contributing money to charity, helping someone find a lost contact lens, tutoring another student, donating blood, and helping co-workers on the job (Carlson, Charlin, & Miller, 1988; Isen, 1999; Salovey, Mayer, & Rosenhan, 1991). See the Try It! exercise below for a way of doing your own test of the "feel good, do good" hypothesis.

Try it!

Feel Good, Do Good?

Think back to the last time you smelled the delicious aroma of fresh-baked chocolate chip cookies. Did it put you in a good mood? A recent field study assumed that people's moods are improved by pleasant fragances and that this improved mood would make them more helpful (R. A. Baron, 1997). Consistent with his prediction, shoppers were more likely to help a stranger (by giving change for a dollar) when they were approached in locations with pleasant smells than when they were approached in locations with neutral smells.

See if you can replicate this effect. Pick locations in a local mall that have either pleasant aromas or neutral aromas. In the actual study, the researcher used locations near a cookie store, a bakery, and a gourmet coffeeshop for the pleasant aromas. The areas with neutral smells should be as identical as possible in all other respects; for example, the researcher picked locations that were similar in the volume of pedestrians, lighting, and proximity to mall exits, such as areas outside of clothing stores.

At each location, approach someone who is alone. Take out a $1 bill and ask the passerby for change for a dollar. If the person stops and gives you change, count it as helping. If the person ignores you or says he or she does not have any change, count it as not helping. In the actual study, 57 percent of people helped in the locations with pleasant aromas, whereas only 19 percent of people helped in the locations with neutral aromas. Did you replicate these results?

Note: Before conducting this study, you should seek permission from the of the manager of the mall. The manager of the mall in which the actual study was conducted requested that the researchers only approach persons of the same gender as themselves because of a concern that cross-gender requests for change would be perceived as "pickup" attempts.

Being in a good mood can increase helping for three reasons. First, good moods make us look on the bright side of life. If you saw the man drop his manila folder full of papers, you might think, "What a klutz. Let him clean up his own mess." Or you might have some sympathy for him, thinking, "Oh, the poor guy, he probably feels really frustrated." When we're in a good mood, we tend to see the good side of other people, giving them the benefit of the doubt. A victim who might normally seem clumsy or annoying will, when we are feeling cheerful, seem like a decent, needy person who is worthy of our help (Carlson et al., 1988; Forgas & Bower, 1987).

Second, helping other people is an excellent way of prolonging our good mood. If we see someone who needs help, then being a Good Samaritan spawns even more good feelings, and we can walk away feeling terrific. In comparison, not helping when we know we should is a surefire "downer," deflating our good mood (Clark & Isen, 1982; Isen, 1987; Williamson & Clark, 1989).

Finally, good moods increase self-attention. As we noted in Chapters 5 and 9, at any given time, people vary in how much attention they pay to their feelings and values versus the world around them. Sometimes we are particularly attuned to our internal worlds, and sometimes we are not. Good moods increase the amount of attention we pay to ourselves, and this factor in turn makes us more likely to behave according to our values and ideals. Because most of us value altruism and because good moods increase our attention to this value, good moods increase helping behavior (Berkowitz, 1987; Carlson et al., 1988; Salovey & Rodin, 1985).

Negative-State Relief: Feel Bad, Do Good   What about when we are in a bad mood? Suppose that when you saw the fellow in the mall drop his folder, you were feeling down. Would this influence the likelihood that you would help the man pick up his papers? One kind of bad mood clearly leads to an increase in helping—feeling guilty (Baumeister, Stillwell, & Heatherton, 1994; Estrada-Hollenbeck & Heatherton, 1998). People often act on the idea that good deeds cancel out bad deeds. When they have done something that has made them feel guilty, helping another person balances things out, reducing their guilty feelings. For example, one study found that churchgoers were more likely to donate money to charities before attending confession than afterward, presumably because confessing to a priest reduced their guilt (Harris, Benson, & Hall, 1975). Thus if you just realized you had forgotten your best friend's birthday and you felt guilty about it, you would be more likely to help the fellow in the mall, to repair your guilty feelings.

But suppose you just had a fight with a friend or just found out you did poorly on a test and you were feeling sad. Given that feeling happy leads to greater helping, it might seem that feeling sad would decrease helping. Surprisingly, however, sadness can also lead to an increase in helping, at least under certain conditions (Carlson & Miller, 1987; Salovey et al., 1991). When people are sad, they are motivated to engage in activities that make them feel better (Wegener & Petty, 1994). To the extent that helping is rewarding, it can lift us out of the doldrums.

The idea that people help in order to alleviate their own sadness and distress is called the **negative-state relief hypothesis** (Cialdini, Darby, & Vincent, 1973; Cialdini & Fultz, 1990; Cialdini et al., 1987). It is an example of the social exchange theory approach to helping that we discussed earlier. People help someone else with the goal of helping themselves—namely, to relieve their own sadness and distress. This is pretty obvious if we help in a way that deals with the cause of our sadness. If our best friend is depressed, we might feel a little depressed as well, so if we do something to cheer up our friend, we've reduced the cause of our own sadness. However, when we feel blue, we are also more likely to

> If you want others to be happy, practice compassion. If you want to be happy, practice compassion.
>
> —The Dalai Lama

Negative-State Relief Hypothesis
The idea that people help in order to alleviate their own sadness and distress

help in some totally unrelated way. If we are feeling down because our best friend is unhappy, we are more likely to donate money to a charity. The warm glow of helping the charity reduces our gloom, even though the charity and our friend's unhappiness are unrelated (Cialdini et al., 1973).

SITUATIONAL DETERMINANTS OF PROSOCIAL BEHAVIOR: WHEN WILL PEOPLE HELP?

Personality, gender, culture, and mood all contribute a piece to the puzzle of why people help others, but they do not complete the picture. To understand more fully why people help, we need to consider the social situation in which people find themselves.

> Do not wait for extraordinary circumstances to do good actions; try to use ordinary situations.
>
> —John Paul Richter, 1763

Environment: Rural versus Urban

Suppose you are riding your bike, and as you zoom around a corner, your front wheel slams into a pothole, sending you flying over the handlebars. You're stunned for a moment; then you feel a sharp pain in your shoulder. You've broken a bone, and there is no way you can get up and get help by yourself. Now consider this question: Where would you rather have this accident—on Main Street in a small rural town or on a busy street in a large city? In which place would passersby be more likely to help you?

If you picked the small town, you are right. Consider this evidence: You are walking down a street when you notice a man limping. Suddenly, he falls and cries with pain. He rolls up his pants leg, and you see that his bandaged shin is bleeding heavily. What would you do? When researchers staged this scene in a small town, about half the pedestrians who witnessed it stopped and offered to help. In large cities, only 15 percent of pedestrians helped the injured man (Amato, 1983). Besides helping strangers who have had an accident, people in small towns also assist more when asked to help a lost child, give directions, and return a lost letter. The same relationship between size of town and helping has

People are less helpful in big cities than in small towns, not because of a difference in values but because the stress of urban life causes them to keep to themselves.

been found in several countries, including the United States, Canada, Israel, Australia, Turkey, Great Britain, and the Sudan (Hedge & Yousif, 1992; Steblay, 1987).

Is there something about growing up in a small town that enhances the altruistic personality, while growing up in a big city diminishes it? If that were the case, you'd be more likely to be helped by someone who grew up in a small town, even if that person were visiting a big city. The key is the values the small-town resident has internalized, not the immediate surroundings. Alternatively, it might be that people's immediate surroundings are the key and not their internalized values. Stanley Milgram (1970), for example, suggested that people living in cities are constantly being bombarded with stimulation and that they keep to themselves in order to avoid being overwhelmed by it. According to this **urban overload hypothesis,** if you put urban dwellers in a calmer, less stimulating environment, they would be as likely as anyone else to reach out to others.

Research has supported the urban overload hypothesis more than the idea that living in cities makes people less altruistic by nature. A review of dozens of studies found that when an opportunity for helping arises, it matters more whether the incident occurs in a rural or urban area than where the witnesses happened to grow up (Steblay, 1987). And in field studies conducted in thirty-six cities in the United States, population density (the number of people per square mile) was more related to helping than population size was (Levine, Martinez, Brase, & Sorenson, 1994). The greater the density of people, the less likely people were to help. This makes sense, according to the urban overload hypothesis: There should be more stimulation in a small area packed with a lot of people than in a large area where the same number of people are spread out. In short, it would be better to have a city slicker witness your bicycle accident in a small town than to have a small-town person witness it in a big city packed with people. The hustle and bustle in cities can be so overwhelming that even caring, altruistic people turn inward, responding less to the people around them.

The Number of Bystanders: The Bystander Effect

Remember Kitty Genovese? We have just seen one reason why her neighbors turned a deaf ear to her cries for help: The murder took place in New York City, one of the most densely populated areas in the world. Perhaps her neighbors were so overloaded with urban stimulation that they dismissed Genovese's cries as one small addition to the surrounding din. Though it is true that people help less in urban environments, that isn't the only reason Genovese's neighbors failed to help. Her desperate cries surely must have risen above the everyday noises of garbage trucks and car horns. And there have been cases where people ignored the pleas of their neighbors even in small towns. In Fredericksburg, Virginia, a convenience store clerk was beaten in front of customers who did nothing to help, even after the assailant had fled and the clerk lay bleeding on the floor (Hsu, 1995). Fredericksburg has only twenty thousand residents.

Bibb Latané and John Darley (1970) are two social psychologists who taught at universities in New York at the time of the Genovese murder. As we discussed in Chapter 2, they too were unconvinced that the only reason her neighbors failed to help was the stresses and stimulation of urban life. They focused on the fact that so many people heard her cries. Paradoxically, they thought, it might be that the greater the number of bystanders who observe an emergency, the less likely any one of them is to help. As Latané (1987) put it, "We came up with the insight that perhaps what made the Genovese case so fascinating was itself what made it happen—namely, that not just one or two, but thirty-eight people had watched and done nothing" (p. 78).

In a series of now classic experiments, Latané and Darley (1970) found that in terms of receiving help, there is no safety in numbers. Think back to the

Urban Overload Hypothesis
The theory that people living in cities are constantly being bombarded with stimulation and that they keep to themselves to avoid being overwhelmed by it

Kitty Genovese and the alley in which she was murdered. Ironically, she would probably not have died if fewer people had heard her desperate cries for help.

seizure experiment we discussed in Chapter 2. In that study, people sat in individual cubicles, participating in a group discussion of college life (over an intercom system) with students in other cubicles. One of the other students suddenly had a seizure, crying out for help, choking, and finally falling silent. There was actually only one real participant in the study. The other "participants," including the one who had the seizure, were prerecorded voices. The point of the study was to see whether the real participant would attempt to help the seizure victim by trying to find him or by summoning the experimenter or whether, like Kitty Genovese's neighbors, the person would simply sit there and do nothing.

As Latané and Darley anticipated, the answer depended on how many people the participant thought witnessed the emergency. When people believed they were the only ones listening to the student having the seizure, most of them (85 percent) helped within sixty seconds. By two and a half minutes, 100 percent of the people who thought they were the only bystander had offered assistance (see Figure 11.3). In comparison, when the research participants believed there was one other student listening, fewer helped—only 62 percent within sixty seconds. As you can see in Figure 11.3, helping occurred more slowly when there were two bystanders and never reached 100 percent, even after six minutes, when the experiment was ended. Finally, when the participants believed there were four other students listening in addition to themselves, the percentage of people who helped dropped even more dramatically. Only 31 percent helped in the first sixty seconds, and after six minutes, only 62 percent had offered help. Dozens of other studies, conducted in the laboratory and in the field, have found the same thing: The greater the number of bystanders who witness an emergency, the less likely any one of them is to help the victim—a phenomenon called the **bystander effect.**

Why is it that people are less likely to help when others are present? Latané and Darley (1970) developed a step-by-step description of how people decide whether to intervene in an emergency (see Figure 11.4 on page 376). Part of this description is an explanation of how the number of bystanders can make a difference. But let's begin with the first step—whether people notice that someone needs help.

Noticing an Event If you are hurrying down a crowded street, you might not notice that someone has collapsed in a doorway. Obviously, if people don't notice

Bystander Effect

The finding that the greater the number of bystanders who witness an emergency, the less likely any one of them is to help

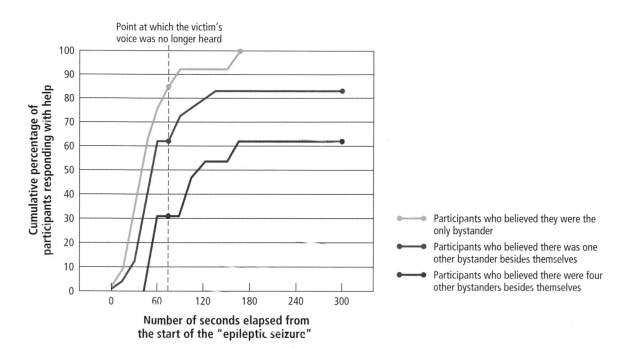

FIGURE 11.3

Bystander intervention: The presence of bystanders reduces helping.

When people believed they were the only one witnessing a student having a seizure—when they were the lone bystander—most of them helped him immediately, and all did within a few minutes. When they believed that someone else was listening as well—that there were two bystanders—they were less likely to help and did so more slowly. And when they believed that four others were listening— that there were five bystanders—they were even less likely to help.

(Adapted from Darley & Latané, 1968)

that an emergency situation exists, they will not intervene and offer to help. What determines whether people notice an emergency? John Darley and Daniel Batson (1973) demonstrated that something as seemingly trivial as how much of a hurry people are in can make more of a difference than what kind of person they are. These researchers conducted a study that mirrored the parable of the Good Samaritan, wherein many passersby failed to stop to help a man lying unconscious at the side of the road. The research participants were people we might think would be extremely altruistic—seminary students preparing to devote their lives to the ministry. The students were asked to walk to another building, where the researchers would record them making a brief speech. Some were told that they were late and should hurry to keep their appointment. Others were told that there was no rush because the assistant in the other building was running a few minutes behind schedule. As they walked to the other building, each of the students passed a man who was slumped in a doorway. The man (an accomplice of the experimenters) coughed and groaned as each student walked by. Did the seminary students stop and offer to help him? If they were not in a hurry, most of them (63 percent) did. If they were hurrying to keep their appointment, however, only 10 percent stopped to help. Many of the students who were in a hurry did not even notice the man.

Surely if people were deeply religious, they would be less influenced by such a small matter as how hurried they were. Surprisingly, though, Darley and Batson (1973) found that the seminary students who were the most religious were no more likely to help than those who were the least religious. What about if they were thinking about helping people in need? The researchers also varied the topic of the speech they asked the students to give: Some were asked to discuss

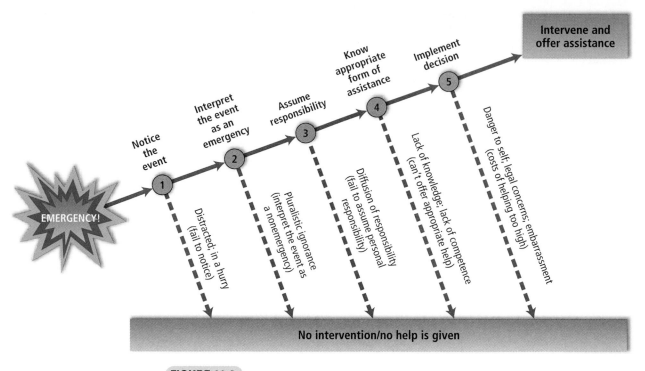

FIGURE 11.4

Bystander intervention decision tree: Five steps to helping in an emergency.

Latané and Darley (1970) showed that people go through five decision-making steps before they help someone in an emergency. If bystanders fail to take any one of the five steps, they will not help. Each step, as well as the possible reasons for why people decide not to intervene, is outlined here.

(Adapted from Latané & Darley, 1970)

the kinds of jobs seminary students preferred; others were asked to discuss the parable of the Good Samaritan. You might think that seminary students who were thinking about the parable of the Good Samaritan would be especially likely to stop and help a man slumped in a doorway, given the similarity of this incident to the parable, but the topic of the speech made little difference in whether they helped. Students in a hurry were unlikely to help, even if they were very religious and about to give a speech about the Good Samaritan.

Interpreting the Event as an Emergency Even if people do notice someone slumped in a doorway, they might not stop and help. The next determinant of helping is whether the bystander interprets the event as an emergency—as a situation where help is needed (see Figure 11.4). Is the person in the doorway drunk or seriously ill? If we see white smoke coming out of a vent, is it something innocuous, such as mist from an air conditioner, or a sign that the building is on fire? Did that scream we just heard come from someone having a good time at a party, or is someone being attacked? If people assume that nothing is wrong when an emergency is taking place, they will not help.

When other bystanders are present, people are more likely to assume that an emergency is something innocuous. To understand why, think back to our discussion of informational social influence in Chapter 8. This type of social influence occurs when we use other people to help us define reality. When we are uncertain about what's going on, such as whether the smoke we see is a sign of a fire, one of the first things we do is look around to see how other people are responding. If other people look up, shrug, and go about their business, we are likely to assume there is nothing to worry about. If other people look panic-stricken and yell, "Fire!" we immediately assume the building is indeed on fire. As we saw in Chapter 8, it's often a good strategy to use other people as a source of information when we are uncertain about what's going on. The danger is that sometimes no one is sure what is happening. Since an emergency is often a sudden and confusing event, bystanders tend to freeze, watching and listening with blank expressions as they try to figure out what's going on. When they glance at each other, they see an apparent lack of concern on the part of everyone else. This results in a state of **pluralistic ignorance.** Bystanders assume that nothing is wrong in an emergency because no one else looks concerned.

Emergency situations can be confusing. Does this man need help? Have the bystanders failed to notice him, or has the behavior of the others led each of them to interpret the situation as a nonemergency—an example of pluralistic ignorance?

Consider another classic experiment by Latané and Darley (1970). You are participating in a study of people's attitudes toward the problems of urban life, and you arrive at the appointed time. A sign tells you to fill out a questionnaire while you're waiting for the study to begin, so you take a seat and get started. Then you notice something odd: White smoke is trickling into the room through a small vent in the wall. Before long, the room is so filled with smoke that you can barely see the questionnaire. What will you do?

In fact, there was no real danger—the experimenters were pumping smoke into the room to see how people would respond to this potential emergency. Not surprisingly, when people were alone, most of them took action. Within two minutes, 50 percent of the participants left the room and found the experimenter down the hall, reporting that there may have been a fire in the building; by six minutes, 75 percent of the participants had left the room to alert the experimenter.

But what would happen if people were not alone? Given that 75 percent of the participants who were by themselves reported the smoke, it would seem that the larger the group, the greater the likelihood that someone would report the smoke. In fact, this can be figured mathematically: If there is a 75 percent chance that any one person will report the smoke, then there is a 98 percent chance that at least one person in a three-person group will do so.

To find out if there really is safety in numbers, Latané and Darley (1970) included a condition in which three participants took part at the same time. Everything was identical except that three people sat in the room as the smoke began to seep in. Surprisingly, in only 12 percent of the three-person groups did someone report the smoke within two minutes, and in only 38 percent of the groups did someone report the smoke within six minutes. In the remaining groups, the participants sat there filling out questionnaires even when they had to wave away the smoke with their hands to see what they were writing. What went wrong?

Unsure whether the smoke signaled an emergency, participants used each other as a source of information. If the people next to you glance at the smoke and then continue filling out their questionnaires, you will feel reassured that nothing is wrong; otherwise, why would they be acting so unconcerned? The problem is that they are probably looking at you as well, and if you seem untroubled, they too are reassured that everything is OK. In short, each group member is reassured because they assume that everyone else knows more about what's going on than they do. And when the event is ambiguous—as when smoke is coming from a vent—people in groups will convince each other that nothing is wrong (Clark & Word, 1972; Solomon, Solomon, & Stone, 1978).

Pluralistic Ignorance

Bystanders' assuming that nothing is wrong in an emergency because no one else looks concerned

Assuming Responsibility Sometimes it is obvious that an emergency is occurring, as when Kitty Genovese cried out, "Oh my God, he stabbed me! Please help me! Please help me!" (Rosenthal, 1964, p. 33). Genovese's neighbors must have believed that something terrible was happening and that she desperately needed help. That they did nothing indicates that even if we interpret an event as an emergency, we have to decide that it is *our* responsibility—not someone else's—to do something about it. Here again the number of bystanders is a crucial variable.

Think back to the Latané and Darley (1968) seizure experiment in which participants believed they were the only one listening to the student while he had a seizure. The responsibility was totally on their shoulders. If they didn't help, no one would, and the student might die. As a result, in this condition most people helped almost immediately, and all helped within a few minutes.

But what happens when there are many witnesses? A **diffusion of responsibility** occurs: Each bystander's sense of responsibility to help decreases as the number of witnesses increases. Because other people are present, no single bystander feels a strong personal responsibility to act. Recall from our earlier discussion that helping often entails costs—we might be putting ourselves in danger or end up looking foolish by overreacting or doing the wrong thing. Why should we risk these costs when many other people who can help are present? The problem is that everyone is likely to feel the same way, making all the bystanders less likely to help. This is particularly true if people cannot tell whether someone else has already intervened. When participants in the seizure experiment believed that other students were witnesses as well, they couldn't tell whether another student had already helped, because the intercom system allowed only the voice of the student having the seizure to be transmitted. Each student probably assumed that he or she did not have to help because surely someone else had already done so. Similarly, Kitty Genovese's neighbors had no way of knowing whether someone else had called the police. Most likely, they assumed there was no need to do so because someone else had already made the call. Tragically, everyone assumed it was somebody else's responsibility to act, and Genovese was left to fight her assailant alone. The sad irony of Genovese's murder is that she probably would be alive today if fewer people had heard her cries for help.

Knowing How to Help Even if people have made it this far in the helping sequence, another condition must still be met (step 4 in Figure 11.4): They must decide what kind of help is appropriate. Suppose that on a hot summer day, you see a woman collapse in the street. No one else seems to be helping, and so you decide it is up to you. But what should you do? Has the woman had a heart attack? Is she suffering from heatstroke? Should you call an ambulance, administer CPR, or try to get her out of the sun? If people don't know what form of assistance to give, obviously they will be unable to help.

Deciding to Implement the Help Finally, even if you know exactly what kind of help is appropriate, there are still reasons why you might decide not to intervene. For one thing, you might not be qualified to deliver the right kind of help. Even if the woman is complaining of chest pains, indicating a heart attack, you may not know how to give her CPR. Or you might be afraid of making a fool of yourself, of doing the wrong thing and making matters worse, or even of placing yourself in danger by trying to help. Consider the fate of three television network technicians who in 1982 saw a man beating a woman in a New York parking lot, tried to intervene, and were shot and killed by the assailant. Even when we know what kind of intervention is needed, we have to weigh the costs of trying to help.

Diffusion of Responsibility

The phenomenon whereby each bystander's sense of responsibility to help decreases as the number of witnesses increases

What about helping situations that are not emergencies? The Latané and Darley model applies here as well. Consider an Internet chat room, for example, in which someone needs help figuring out how to use the software. Are people less likely to help each other as the number of people in the chat room increases? Researchers in one study entered chat groups on Yahoo! Chat, in which two to nineteen people were discussing a wide variety of topics (Markey, 2000). The researchers posed as either a male or female participant and typed this request for help: "Can anyone tell me how to look at someone's profile?" (p. 185). (A profile is a brief biographical description that each person in the chat group provides.) The message was addressed either to the group as a whole or to one randomly selected person in the chat room. Then the researchers timed how long it took someone in the group to respond to the request for help.

When the request was addressed to the group as a whole, Latané and Darley's results were replicated closely: The more people were in the chat room, the longer it took for anyone to respond to the request for help. But when the request was directed to a specific person, that person responded quickly, regardless of the size of the group. These results suggest that the diffusion of responsibility was operating. When a general request for help is made, a large group makes people feel that they do not have much responsibility to respond. When addressed by name, though, people are more likely to feel a responsibility to help, even when many others are present. The implication is clear: If you do have that bicycle accident and there are lots of people present, do not yell out, "Will someone please help me?" If you single out one person—"Hey, you in the blue shirt and sunglasses—could you please call 911?"—you will probably receive help more quickly.

Even if people are by themselves, however, they can still experience a diffusion of responsibility. In a recent study, people who were asked to think about going out to dinner with ten friends were less likely to donate money to charity or volunteer to help with another experiment than people who were asked to think about going out to dinner with one friend (Garcia, Weaver, Moskowitz, & Darley, 2002). Simply imagining ourselves in a group is enough to make us feel less responsible for helping others.

The Nature of the Relationship: Communal versus Exchange Relationships

A great deal of research on prosocial behavior has looked at helping between strangers, such as Latané and Darley's research on bystander intervention. Although this research is very important, most helping in everyday life occurs between people who know each other well, such as family members and close friends. What determines whether people help in these kinds of relationships?

Earlier we noted the view that people will help only if there are immediate short-term benefits for doing so (the negative-state relief hypothesis.) When people know each other well, however, they are often more concerned with the long-term benefits of helping than with the immediate effects (Salovey et al., 1991). Consider the mother of a 4-year-old. One Saturday morning, she sits down with a cup of coffee to read the newspaper. She wants nothing more than a moment's peace while she catches up on the news. Her daughter, however, has other ideas: She asks her mother to read her *The Berenstain Bears Visit the Dentist* for the fiftieth time. Reading to the child has few short-term benefits in this situation. The coffee gets cold, the newspaper goes unread, and the moment's peace disappears. Even when there are no short-term benefits, however, helping can reap large long-term rewards. Parents who sit around sipping coffee and reading the newspaper while ignoring their children are less likely to obtain the long-term satisfaction of having a good relationship with their kids and seeing their kids flourish. Thus parents might read to their children with this long-term goal in

In communal relationships, such as those between parents and their children, people are concerned less with who gets what and more with how much help the other person needs.

mind, enduring the short-term annoyance of being interrupted and having to recite the story of Brother and Sister Bear's cavities yet again.

Even more fundamentally, in some types of relationships people may not be concerned at all with the rewards they receive. In Chapter 10, we distinguished between communal and exchange relationships. *Communal relationships* are those in which people's primary concern is with the welfare of the other person (e.g., a child), whereas *exchange relationships* are governed by concerns about equity—that what you put into the relationship equals what you get out of it. How does helping occur in communal relationships, such as our example of the parent whose child is clamoring for attention?

One possibility is that the rewards for helping are as important in communal as exchange relationships, but the rewards differ (Batson, 1993). In exchange relationships, we expect our favors to be repaid pretty quickly. If we invite our new friend Sam to a party, we expect that he will invite us to his next party. If we help a co-worker learn how to access the Internet on Monday, we expect that the co-worker will help us learn how to use the new fax machine next week. Maybe people in communal relationships also expect an equal exchange of benefits, but the benefits are different from those in exchange relationships. When parents are deciding whether to help their children, for example, they seldom think, "Well, what have they done for me lately?" Nonetheless, they might help with the expectation that they will eventually be rewarded for their help. In our example of the mother and her 4-year-old, perhaps the mother was motivated by the rewards of seeing her daughter become a healthy, well-adjusted adult. Maybe this relationship involves an exchange of long-term instead of short-term benefits.

Margaret Clark and Judson Mills (1993; Mills & Clark, 2001), however, argue that communal relationships are fundamentally different from exchange relationships: It's not just that different kinds of rewards govern the relationship; people in communal relationships are concerned less with the benefits they will receive by helping and more with simply satisfying the needs of the other person. In support of this argument, Clark and her colleagues have found that people in communal relationships pay less attention to who is getting what than people in exchange relationships do (Clark, 1984; Clark & Grote, 1998; Clark, Mills, & Corcoran, 1989).

Does this mean that people are more helpful toward friends than strangers? Yes—at least under most circumstances. We are more likely to have communal relationships with friends and are therefore more likely to help even when there is nothing in it for us. In fact, we like to help a partner in a communal relationship more than a partner in an exchange relationship (Williamson, Clark, Pegalis, & Behan, 1996). There is, however, an interesting exception to this rule. Research by Abraham Tesser (1988) on self-esteem maintenance (see Chapter 6) has shown that when a task is not important to us, we do indeed help friends more than strangers. But suppose that the most important thing in the world for you is to be a doctor, that you are struggling to pass a difficult premed physics course, and that two other people in the class—your best friend and a complete stranger—ask you to lend them your notes from a class they missed. According to Tesser's research, you will be more inclined to help the stranger than your friend (Tesser, 1991; Tesser & Smith, 1980). Why? Because it hurts to see a close friend do better than we do in an area of great importance to our self-esteem. Consequently, we are less likely to help a friend in these important areas than in areas we don't care as much about.

HOW CAN HELPING BE INCREASED?

Most religions stress some version of the Golden Rule, urging us to do unto others as we would have others do unto us. There are many saintly people in the world who succeed in following this rule, devoting their lives to the welfare of others. We would all be better off, however, if prosocial behavior were more common than it is. How can we get people, when faced with an emergency, to act more like Abe Zelmanowitz and less like Kitty Genovese's neighbors?

Before addressing this question, we should point out that people do not always want to be helped. Imagine that you are sitting at a computer terminal at the library and are struggling to learn a new e-mail system. You can't figure out how to send and receive mail and are becoming increasingly frustrated as the computer responds with messages like "Invalid Command." A confident-looking guy whom you know only slightly walks over to you and looks over your shoulder for a few minutes. "You have a lot to learn," he says. "Let me show you how this baby works." How would you react? You might feel some gratitude, but you will probably also feel some resentment. His offer of help comes with a message: "You are too stupid to figure this out for yourself." Because receiving help can make people feel inadequate and dependent, they do not always react positively when someone offers them aid. People do not want to appear incompetent, and so they often decide to suffer in silence, even if doing so lowers their chances of successfully completing a task (Nadler, 1991; Nadler & Fisher, 1986; Schneider, Major, Luhtanen, & Crocker, 1996).

Nevertheless, the world would be a better place if more people helped those in need. How can we increase everyday acts of kindness, such as looking out for an elderly neighbor or volunteering to read to kids at the local school? The answer to this question lies in our discussion of the causes of prosocial behavior. For example, we saw that several personal characteristics of potential helpers are important, and promoting those factors can increase the likelihood that these people will help (Clary, Snyder, Ridge, Miene, & Haugen, 1994; Snyder, 1993). But even kind, altruistic people will fail to help if certain situational constraints are present, such as being in an urban environment or witnessing an emergency in the presence of numerous bystanders.

> When death, the great reconciler, has come, it is never our tenderness that we repent of, but our severity.
>
> —*George Eliot (Marian Evans)*, Adam Bede, *1859*

Increasing the Likelihood that Bystanders Will Intervene

There is evidence that simply being aware of the barriers to helping in an emergency can increase people's chances of overcoming those barriers. A few years ago at Cornell University, several students intervened to prevent another student

Learning about the barriers preventing people from helping in emergencies has been found to increase the likelihood that people will help if they subsequently encounter an emergency.

from committing suicide. As is often the case with emergencies, the situation was very confusing, and at first, the bystanders were not sure what was happening or what they should do. The student who led the intervention said that she was reminded of a lecture she had heard on bystander intervention in her introductory psychology class a few days before and realized that if she didn't act, no one would (Savitsky, 1998). Or consider a recent incident at Vassar College, where some students looked outside their dormitory and saw a student being attacked by a mugger. Like Kitty Genovese's neighbors, most of them did nothing, probably because they assumed that someone had already called the police. One of the students, however, immediately called the campus police because she was struck by how similar the situation was to the studies on bystander intervention she had read about in her social psychology course—even though she had taken the class more than a year earlier (Coats, 1998).

Were these helpful people really spurred on by what they had learned in their psychology classes? This question has been addressed experimentally (Beaman, Barnes, Klentz, & McQuirk, 1978). The reseachers randomly assigned students to listen to a lecture on Latané and Darley's (1970) bystander intervention research or a lecture on an unrelated topic. Two weeks later, all the students participated in what they thought was a completely unrelated sociology study, during which they encountered a student lying on the floor. Was he in need of help? Had he fallen and injured himself, or was he simply a student who had fallen asleep after pulling an all-nighter? As we have seen, when in an ambiguous situation such as this, people look to see how other people are reacting. Because an accomplice of the experimenter (posing as another participant) intentionally acted unconcerned, the natural thing to do was to assume that nothing was wrong. This is exactly what most participants did if they had not heard the lecture about bystander intervention research; in this condition, only 25 percent of them stopped to help the student. However, if the participants had heard the lecture about bystander intervention, 43 percent stopped to help the student. Thus knowing how we can be unwittingly influenced by others can by itself help overcome this type of social influence. We can only hope that knowing about other barriers to prosocial behavior will make them easier to overcome as well.

An increasing number of schools and businesses are requiring people to perform community service. These programs can actually lower interest in volunteering if people feel they are doing so because of an external requirement. Encouraging people to volunteer while preserving the sense that they freely choose to do so is likely to increase people's intentions to volunteer again in the future.

CONNECTIONS:

Increasing Volunteerism

There are many important kinds of prosocial behavior besides intervening in emergencies, including volunteerism and community service. Social psychologists have studied this kind of helping as well, whereby people commit to helping strangers on a more long-term basis (Omoto & Snyder, 2002; Penner, 2002).

Surveys of Western European and North American countries have found that many people engage in volunteer work, with the highest rate in the United States (47 percent; Ting & Piliavin, 2000). Of course, that means that even in the United States, more than half of the population is not volunteering, raising the question of how to increase people's willingness to spend time helping others. Some institutions have responded by requiring their members to perform community service. Some high schools, colleges, and businesses, for example, require their students or employees to engage in volunteer work.

These programs have the benefit of increasing the pool of volunteers available to help community organizations such as homeless shelters, medical clinics, and day-care centers. The question arises, however, as to the effect of such "mandatory volunteerism" on the motivation of the people who do the helping. Many of these organizations assume that they are increasing the likelihood that their members will volunteer in the future, even after they leave the organizations. That is, making people volunteer is assumed to foster volunteerism by enlightening people about its benefits.

As we discussed in Chapter 5, however, giving people strong external reasons for performing an activity can actually undermine their intrinsic interest in that activity. This is called the *overjustification effect:* People see their behavior as caused by compelling extrinsic reasons (e.g., being required to do volunteer work), making them underestimate the extent to which their behavior was caused by intrinsic reasons (e.g., that they like to do volunteer

Try it!

The Lost Letter Technique

Leave some stamped letters lying on the ground and see whether people pick them up and mail them. This procedure, called the "lost letter technique," was invented by Stanley Milgram (1969). He found that people were more likely to mail letters addressed to organizations they supported; for example, 72 percent of letters addressed to "Medical Research Associates" were mailed, whereas only 25 percent of letters addressed to "Friends of the Nazi Party" were mailed (all were addressed to the same post office box so that Milgram could count how many were returned).

Use the lost letter technique to test some of the hypotheses about helping behavior we have discussed in this chapter or hypotheses that you come up with on your own. Put your address on the letters so that you can count how many are returned, but vary where you put the letters or to whom they are addressed. For example, drop some letters in a small town and in an urban area to see whether people in small towns are more likely to mail them (be sure to mark the envelopes in some way that will let you know where they were dropped; e.g., put a little pencil mark on the back of the ones dropped in small towns). Did you replicate the finding of previous studies that people living in small towns are more likely to mail the letters (Bridges & Coady, 1996; Hansson & Slade, 1977)? Or you might vary the ethnicity of the name of the person on the address to see if people are more likely to help members of some ethnic groups more than others. Be creative!

After deciding what you want to vary (e.g., the ethnicity or gender of the addressee), be careful to place envelopes of both types (e.g., those addressed to males and females) in similar locations. It is best to use a fairly large number of letters (e.g., a minimum of fifteen to twenty in each condition) to get reliable results. Obviously, you should not leave more than one letter in the same location. You might want to team up with some classmates on this project so that you can split the cost of the stamps.

work). Consistent with this research, the more that people feel they are volunteering because of external requirements, the less likely they are to volunteer freely in the future (Batson, Coke, Jasnoski, & Hanson, 1978; Kunda & Schwartz, 1983; Stukas, Snyder, & Clary, 1999). The moral is that organizations should be careful about how heavy-handedly they impose requirements to volunteer. If people feel that they are complying only because they have to, they may actually become less likely to volunteer in the future. Encouraging people to volunteer while preserving the sense that they freely choose to do so has been shown to increase people's intentions to volunteer again in the future (Stukas et al., 1999). If you would like to learn more about the conditions under which people help others in an experiment of your own design, see the Try It! exercise above.

Positive Psychology and Prosocial Behavior

In recent years, a new field known as *positive psychology* has emerged (Seligman, 2002; Snyder & Lopez, 2002). Martin Seligman, an influential clinical psychologist, observed that much of psychology—particularly clinical psychology—had focused on mental disorders, largely ignoring how to define and nurture psychological health. Psychology should not just be the study of "disease, weakness, and damage," he argued, but the study of "strength and virtue" (2002, p. 4). Largely through Seligman's efforts, many psychologists are now focusing on such topics as the nature of healthy human functioning, how to define and categorize human strengths, and how to improve people's lives.

The positive psychology movement is a useful and necessary corrective to the emphasis on mental illness in clinical psychology and has led to many fascinating research programs. As we have seen in this book, though, social psychology has not concentrated solely on negative behaviors. For many years, there have been active social psychological research programs on such topics as how people develop intrinsic interest in an activity (Chapter 5), how people maintain high self-esteem (Chapter 6), and how people form impressions of and lasting relationships with others (Chapter 10). To be sure, social psychology has documented many negative behaviors that can result from powerful social influences, such as obedience to authority and other kinds of conformity (Chapter 8). By studying the basic ways in which humans process information about themselves and their social worlds, however, it has been possible to understand both the dark and bright side of human behavior, such as when people will help others and when they will not.

An excellent example of the social psychological approach is the topic of this chapter, the study of the conditions under which people fail to help their fellow humans. Is this the study of positive psychology or a focus on the dark side? Both, because social psychologists study the condition under which people are likely to help (e.g., when people feel empathy toward another) and the conditions under which they are likely to fail to help (e.g., when they experience a diffusion of responsibility).

As noted earlier, Daniel Batson and his colleagues have been the strongest proponents of the idea that many people have a pure, unselfish motive for helping others and will do so when they feel empathy (Batson, Ahmad, Lishner, & Tsang, 2002). In the experiment we reviewed earlier, for example, when people felt empathy toward a classmate who had been in an automobile accident, they were willing to help her regardless of whether there was a cost to themselves of doing so (see Figure 11.2).

Batson and his colleagues also wondered whether feeling empathy toward a member of a stigmatized group improves feelings toward the group in general (Batson et al., 1997). That is, in addition to helping the person in need, do people who experience empathy also develop more positive feelings toward the group to which the person belongs? To find out, they performed studies much like the earlier one, in which college students were asked to evaluate tapes for the university radio station. They listened to interviews with either a young woman who had contracted the AIDS virus or a homeless man. As in the earlier study, half of the participants were asked to adopt an empathic perspective while listening to the tape, imagining how the person felt. The others were asked to adopt an objective perspective in which they remained detached and did not get caught up in the person's feelings. Unlike the earlier study, the dependent measure was not whether they helped the person in the interview but whether they changed their attitudes toward the group as a whole—AIDS patients or homeless people. As it turns out, they did—*if* they adopted the empathy perspective. People in the empathy condition developed more positive attitudes toward people with AIDS if they had heard the interview with the AIDS patient and more positive attitudes toward homeless people if they had heard the interview with the homeless person.

As we will see in Chapter 13, deep-seated prejudices can be difficult to change, and feeling empathy toward one member of a stigmatized group is unlikely to erase a lifetime of negative attitudes. It can make a difference to feel empathy toward someone who is suffering harm, however; doing so makes people more likely to help that person and to feel more positively toward the group of which the person is a member. Research on empathy and prosocial behavior is an excellent example of the way in which social psychologists have been interested in positive psychology, the study of people's strengths and virtues.

SUMMARY

Basic Motives Underlying Prosocial Behavior: Why Do People Help?

For centuries, people have debated the determinants of **prosocial behavior**—acts performed with the goal of benefiting another person. People have been particularly intrigued with the causes of **altruism,** which is the desire to help another person even if it involves a cost to the helper. One approach is *evolutionary psychology,* which attempts to explain social behavior in terms of genetic factors that evolved over time according to the principles of natural selection. According to this approach, prosocial behavior has genetic roots because it has been selected for in three ways: People further the survival of their genes by helping genetic relatives (**kin selection**); there is a survival advantage to following the **norm of reciprocity,** whereby people help strangers in the hope that they will receive help when they need it; and there is a survival advantage to the ability to learn and follow social norms of all kinds, including altruism. Social exchange theory views helping behavior as a weighing of rewards and costs; helping occurs due to self-interest—that is, in situations where the rewards for helping are greater than the costs. Rewards include recognition, praise, and the relief of personal distress. Neither of these theories sees helping behavior as a form of altruism; self-gain is always involved. In comparison, the **empathy-altruism hypothesis** sees prosocial behavior as motivated only by empathy and compassion for those in need.

Personal Qualities and Prosocial Behavior: Why Do Some People Help More than Others?

Prosocial behavior is multidetermined, and both personal and situational factors can override or facilitate basic motives to help. Personal determinants of helping include the **altruistic personality,** the idea that some people are more helpful than others. Although important, personality is not the sole determinant of prosocial behavior. Gender is another personal factor that comes into play. Though one sex is not more altruistic than the other, the ways in which men and women help often differs, with men more likely to help in heroic, chivalrous ways and women more likely to help in ways that involve a long-term commitment. People's cultural background also matters. Compared to members of individualistic cultures, members of interdependent cultures are more likely to help people they view as members of their **in-group** and less likely to help people they view as members of an **out-group.**

Mood also affects helping. Interestingly, being in either a good or a bad mood—compared to being in a neutral mood—can increase helping. Good moods increase helping for several reasons, including the fact that they make us see the good side of other people, making us more willing to help them. Bad moods increase helping because of the **negative-state relief hypothesis,** which maintains that helping someone makes us feel good, lifting us out of the doldrums.

Situational Determinants of Prosocial Behavior: When Will People Help?

Social determinants of prosocial behavior include rural versus urban environments, with helping behavior more likely to occur in rural settings. One reason for this is the **urban overload hypothesis,** which says that cities bombard people with so much stimulation that they keep to themselves to avoid being overwhelmed. The **bystander effect** points out the impact of the number of bystanders on whether help is given—the fewer the bystanders, the more inclined a person is to help. The bystander decision tree indicates that a potential helper must make five decisions before providing help: notice the event, interpret the event as an emergency (**pluralistic ignorance** can occur if everyone assumes that nothing is wrong because no one else looks concerned—an example of informational social influence), assume personal responsibility (a **diffusion of responsibility** created by the presence of several bystanders may lead us to think it's not our responsibility to act), know how to help, and implement the help. In addition, the nature of the relationship between the helper and the person in need is important. In exchange relationships, people are concerned with equity and keep track of who is contributing what to the relationship. In communal relationships, people are concerned less with who gets what and more concerned with how much help the other person needs.

How Can Helping Be Increased?

Teaching people about the determinants of prosocial behavior makes them more aware of why they sometimes don't help, with the happy result that they help more in the future. Programs that require community service can actually lower interest in volunteering if people feel they are doing so because of external requirements. Encouraging people to volunteer while preserving the sense that they freely choose to do so is likely to increase people's intentions to volunteer again in the future.

The new subfield of *positive psychology* focuses on people's strengths and virtues (e.g., what makes people helpful) rather than the negative side of human behavior (e.g., why people fail to help). Recent research has shown, for example, that when people feel empathy toward another person, they become more helpful toward that individual and more sympathetic to the group to which the person belongs (e.g., homeless people).

CRITICAL THINKING QUESTIONS

1. Why do people help others at a cost to themselves? Compare and contrast the major theories that explain altruistic behavior.

2. What factors will influence whether someone will intervene in an emergency, such as helping a person who slips and breaks an ankle on a patch of ice? What factors will determine whether someone will help on a more long-term basis, such as volunteering at a homeless shelter?

3. Some psychologists have begun studying positive psychology, arguing that clinical psychology has focused too much on mental problems and other negative aspects of human behavior. Does social psychology focus too much on negative parts of behavior? Using research on prosocial behavior as an example, does social psychology focus on the negative, the positive, or both?

CHAPTER 12

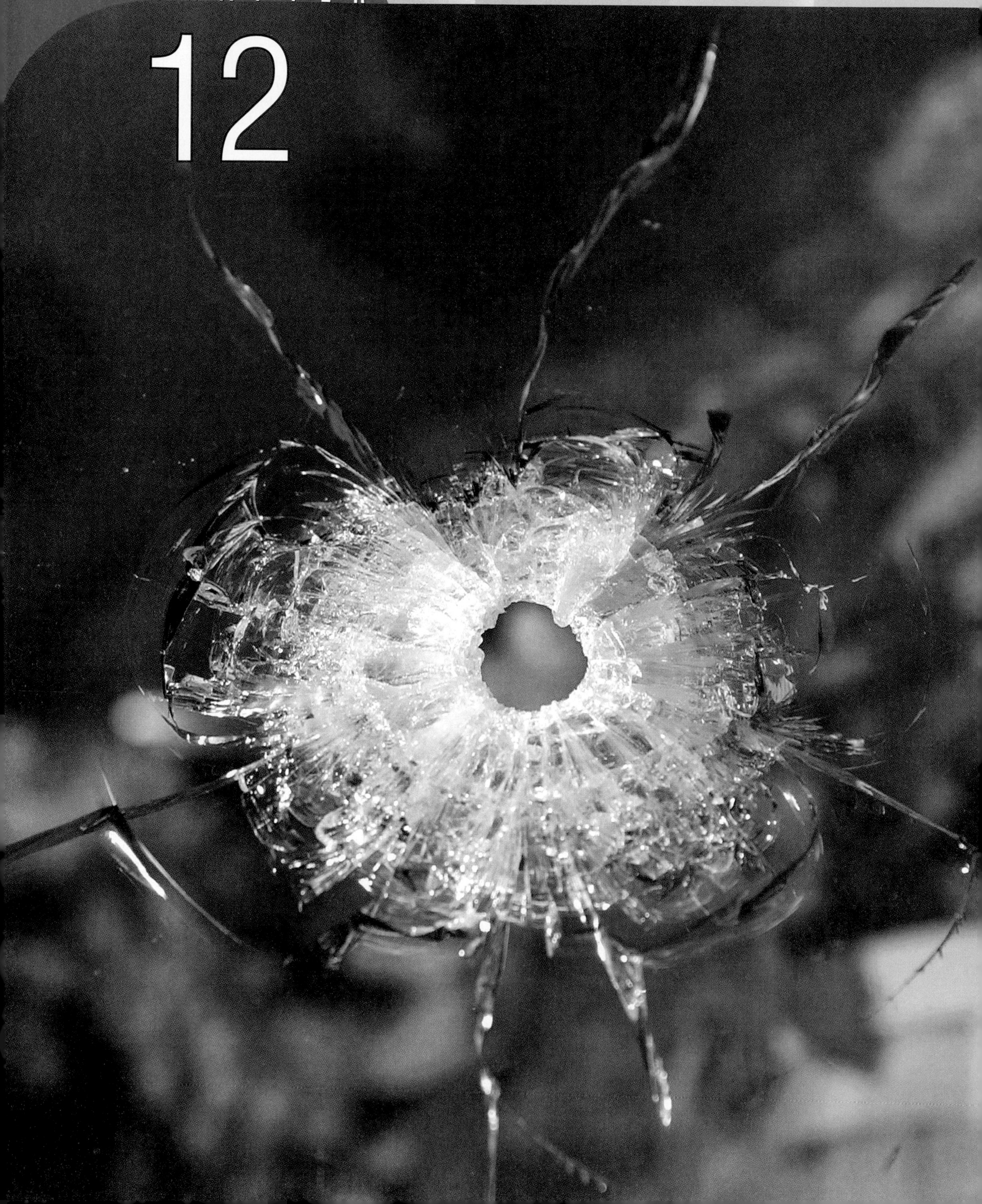

Aggression:
Why Do We Hurt Other People?
Can We Prevent It?

On April 20, 1999, the corridors and classrooms of Columbine High School in Littleton, Colorado, reverberated with the sound of gunshots. Two students, Eric Harris and Dylan Klebold, armed with assault weapons and explosives, had gone on a rampage, killing a teacher and several of their fellow students. They then turned their guns on themselves. After the smoke had cleared, fifteen people lay dead (including the shooters) and twenty-three others were hospitalized, some with severe wounds. It was the worst school massacre in American history. As horrendous as it was, we now know that the toll could have been much higher. The two shooters made some videotapes a few weeks before the massacre, and from these we have learned that they actually prepared ninety-five explosive devices that failed to go off. Of these, one set was placed a few miles from the school, intended to explode first and distract police by keeping them busy away from the school.

A second set was intended to explode in the cafeteria, killing a large number of students and causing hundreds to evacuate the building, in terror, with Harris and Klebold waiting to gun them down. They planted a third set of explosives in their own cars in the school parking lot, timed to explode after the police and paramedics had arrived on the scene as a way of further increasing the number of casualties and creating even more chaos. The videotape shows the perpetrators gleefully predicting that before the day was over, they would have killed 250 people.

The Columbine massacre was the deadliest of nine multivictim school shootings that took place in the United States during a period of 2½ years. In the sad aftermath of a school shooting—especially one as terrible as Columbine—the country needed someone or something to blame. Almost everyone wondered, were these youngsters crazy? If they were crazy, why didn't their parents and teachers notice their pathology before it erupted into violence? How could reasonably observant parents not know that their sons kept guns in their bedrooms and were manufacturing bombs in their garage?

And where were the school authorities? Didn't these students' teachers notice behaviors that would have predicted such violence? Some people even wondered if schools should give students personality tests to identify the ones most likely to commit acts of this kind.

Certain observers quickly concluded that the major cause of such violence is the easy availability of guns, claiming that if we could only control the use and sale of guns, we could eliminate the problem. Others were quick to blame the Supreme Court for outlawing prayer in the schools—wouldn't prayer prevent this sort of outrage? Still others pointed to the prevalence of violence in films, on TV, and in video games. If we could ban violent entertainment, wouldn't that make our schools safe again? And some people felt that these outrageous acts grew out of a general lack of respect among teenagers in our culture. One state legislature responded to the massacre by actually passing a law requiring students to call their teachers "sir" or "ma'am" as a way of showing respect—as if respect can be mandated (Aronson, 2000).

The Columbine tragedy is a stark reminder that humans are capable of acts of extreme aggression. It also underscores the importance of our trying to understand the causes of aggression so that the awful losses suffered at Columbine are not repeated elsewhere.

In this chapter, we will focus on aggression and try to understand what causes it. Are human beings instinctively aggressive? Can normal people be inspired to commit violence by the example of violent characters on TV or in films or by the easy availability of weapons of destruction? Can a society, a school, or a parent do anything to reduce aggression? If so, specifically, what? These are social psychological questions of the utmost importance. Needless to say, we don't have all the answers. But we do have some of them. By the time you get to the end of this chapter, we hope you will have gained some insight into those issues.

WHAT IS AGGRESSION?

For social psychologists, aggressive action is intentional behavior aimed at causing either physical or psychological pain. It should not be confused with assertiveness—even though most people loosely refer to others as "aggressive" if they stand up for their rights, write letters to the editor complaining about real or imagined injustices, or are real "go-getters." Similarly, in a sexist society, a woman who simply speaks her mind or takes the initiative and invites a man to dinner might be called aggressive by some. Our definition is far more specific: **Aggression** is intentional action aimed at doing harm or causing pain. The action might be physical or verbal; it might succeed in its goal or not. It is still aggression. So if someone throws a beer bottle at your head and you duck so that the bottle misses your head, it was still an aggressive act. The important thing is

Aggression

Intentional behavior aimed at doing harm or causing pain to another person

the intention. By the same token, if a drunk driver unintentionally runs you down while you're attempting to cross the street, that is not an act of aggression, even though the damage would be far greater than that caused by the beer bottle that missed.

It is also useful to distinguish between hostile aggression and instrumental aggression (Berkowitz, 1993). **Hostile aggression** is an act of aggression stemming from feelings of anger and aimed at inflicting pain or injury. In **instrumental aggression,** there is an intention to hurt the other person, but the hurting takes place as a means to some goal other than causing pain. For example, in a professional football game, a defensive lineman will usually do whatever it takes to thwart his opponent (the blocker) and tackle the ball carrier. This typically includes intentionally inflicting pain on his opponent if doing so is useful in helping him get the blocker out of the way so that he can get to the ball carrier. This is instrumental aggression. By contrast, if he believes his opponent has been playing dirty, he might become angry and go out of his way to hurt his opponent, even if doing so does not increase his opportunity to tackle the ball carrier. This is hostile aggression.

Is Aggression Inborn or Learned?

For centuries, scientists, philosophers, and other serious thinkers have been arguing about the human capacity for aggression. Some are convinced that aggression is an inborn, instinctive human trait. Others are just as certain that aggressive behavior must be learned (Baron & Richardson, 1994; Berkowitz, 1993; Geen, 1998). The political philosopher Thomas Hobbes, in his classic work *Leviathan*, first published in 1651, argued that human beings, in our natural state, are brutes and that only by enforcing the law and order of society could we curb the natural instinct toward aggression. A century later, Jean-Jacques Rousseau argued just the opposite. Humans, he wrote in 1762, are "noble savages"—naturally gentle creatures born into a restrictive society that forces them to become hostile and aggressive.

Hobbes's more pessimistic view was elaborated in the twentieth century by Sigmund Freud (1930), who theorized that humans are born with an instinct toward life, which he called **Eros,** and an equally powerful instinct toward death, which he called **Thanatos.** About the death instinct, Freud wrote: "It is at work in every living being and is striving to bring it to ruin and to reduce life to its original condition of inanimate matter" (p. 67). Freud believed that aggressive energy must come out somehow, lest it continue to build up and produce illness. Freud's notion can best be characterized as a "hydraulic theory"—the analogy is to water pressure building up in a container: Unless energy is released, it will produce some sort of explosion.

According to Freud, society performs an essential function in regulating these instincts and in helping people *sublimate* them, that is, turn the energy into acceptable or useful behavior. For example, Freud believed that the energy behind artistic creation or the innovations that created railroads were sublimations of aggressive (or sexual) energy.

Is Aggression Instinctual? Situational? Optional?

As elegant as it is, Freud's theory has never been proved scientifically, in part because it is difficult or unethical to experiment on these factors using humans. Accordingly, much of the evidence on aggression in human beings is based on observation and experimentation involving other species. The idea behind this research is that if we can demonstrate that certain so-called instinctive aggressive behaviors in the lower animals are not rigidly preprogrammed, then surely aggression is not rigidly preprogrammed in humans. For example, consider the

Hostile Aggression

Aggression stemming from feelings of anger and aimed at inflicting pain

Instrumental Aggression

Aggression as a means to some goal other than causing pain

Eros

The instinct toward life, posited by Freud

Thanatos

According to Freud, an instinctual drive toward death, leading to aggressive actions

common belief about cats and rats. Most people assume that cats will instinctively stalk and kill rats. Biologist Zing Yang Kuo (1961) attempted to demonstrate that this was a myth. He performed a simple little experiment: He raised a kitten in the same cage with a rat. What did he find? Not only did the cat refrain from attacking the rat, but the two became close companions. Moreover, when given the opportunity, the cat refused either to chase or to kill other rats; thus the benign behavior was not confined to this one buddy but generalized to rats the cat had never met.

Although this experiment is charming, it fails to prove that aggressive behavior is not instinctive; it merely demonstrates that the aggressive instinct can be inhibited by early experience. What if an organism grows up without any experience with other organisms? Will it or won't it show normal aggressive tendencies? Another scientist showed that rats raised in isolation (i.e., without any experience in fighting other rats) will attack a fellow rat when one is introduced into the cage; moreover, the isolated rat uses the same pattern of threat and attack that experienced rats use (Eibl-Eibesfeldt, 1963). So even though aggressive behavior can be modified by experience (as shown by Kuo's experiment), aggression apparently does not need to be learned.

But this evidence alone does not mean that aggression is necessarily instinctive. To draw this conclusion, we'd need to see evidence of a spontaneous stimulation for fighting that arises from within the body alone (Scott, 1958). The stimulus in the second experiment, in which the rat had been raised in isolation, came from the outside—the sight of a new rat stimulated the isolated rat to fight. Scott concluded from his analysis of the evidence that there is no inborn need for fighting: If an organism can arrange its life so that there is no outside stimulation to fight, it will experience no physiological or mental damage as a result of not expressing aggression.

The argument continues to go back and forth. Scott's conclusion was called into question by the Nobel Prize-winning ethologist Konrad Lorenz (1966), who observed the behavior of cichlids—highly aggressive tropical fish. Male cichlids will attack other males of the same species to establish and defend their territory. In its natural environment, the male cichlid does not attack female cichlids; nor does it attack males of a different species—it attacks only males of its own species. What happens if all other male cichlids are removed from an aquarium, leaving only one male alone with no appropriate target? The cichlid will attack

Is this kind of aggression "only natural"?

males of other species—males it previously ignored. Moreover, if all other males are removed, the male cichlid will eventually attack and kill females.

The universality of aggression among vertebrates strongly suggests that aggressiveness has evolved and has been maintained because it has survival value (Lore & Schultz, 1993). At the same time, these researchers underscore the point that nearly all organisms also seem to have evolved strong inhibitory mechanisms that enable them to suppress aggression when it is in their best interests to do so. Even in the most violence-prone species, then, aggression is an optional strategy—whether it is expressed or not. It is determined by the animal's previous social experiences as well as by the specific social context in which the animal finds itself.

Aggression and Culture

Most social psychologists agree that aggression is an optional strategy. Moreover, where humans are concerned, because of the complexity and importance of our social interactions, the social situation becomes even more important than it is among the lower organisms (Bandura, 1973; Berkowitz, 1968, 1993; Lysak, Rule, & Dobbs, 1989). We humans seem to have an inborn tendency to respond to certain provocative stimuli by striking out against the perpetrator (Berkowitz, 1993). Whether or not the aggressive action is actually expressed depends on a complex interplay between these innate tendencies, a variety of learned inhibitory responses, and the precise nature of the social situation. For example, although it is true that many animals, from insects to apes, will usually attack another animal that invades their territory, we *cannot* conclude, as some popular writers have, that human beings are likewise programmed to protect their territory and behave aggressively in response to specific stimuli. Instead, much evidence supports the view of most social psychologists that for humankind, innate patterns of behavior are infinitely modifiable and flexible. Cross-cultural studies have found, in fact, that human cultures vary widely in their degree of aggressiveness. European history, when condensed, consists of one major war after another; in contrast, certain "primitive" tribes, such as the Lepchas of Sikkim, the Pygmies of Central Africa, and the Arapesh of New Guinea, live in apparent peace and harmony, with acts of aggression being extremely rare (Baron & Richardson, 1994).

Human cultures vary widely in their degree of aggressiveness. European history is marked by frequent wars, but in other cultures, such as the Efe shown here, acts of aggression are extremely rare.

Aggression among the Iroquois Within a given culture, changing social conditions frequently lead to striking changes in aggressive behavior. For example, for hundreds of years, the Iroquois of North America lived peacefully, as a hunting nation, without engaging in aggressive behavior against other tribes. But in the seventeenth century, barter with the newly arrived Europeans brought the Iroquois into direct competition with the neighboring Hurons over furs, which dramatically increased in value, because they could now be traded for manufactured goods. A series of skirmishes with the Hurons ensued, and within a short time, the Iroquois developed into ferocious warriors. It would be hard to argue that they were spectacular warriors because of uncontrollable aggressive instincts; rather, their aggressiveness almost certainly came about because a social change produced increases in competition (Hunt, 1940).

Aggression and a Culture of Honor In our own society, there are some striking regional differences in aggressive behavior and in the kinds of events that trigger violence. For example, Richard Nisbett (1993) has shown that homicide rates for white southern males are substantially higher than those for white northern males, especially in rural areas. But this is true only for "argument-related" homicides. Nisbett's research shows that southerners do not endorse violence more than northerners when survey questions are expressed in general terms. However, southerners are more inclined to endorse violence for protection and in response to insults. This pattern suggests that the "culture of honor" may be characteristic of particular economic and occupational circumstances, including the herding society of the early South, where protection of the herd was vital.

In a follow-up study, Nisbett and his colleagues (Cohen, Nisbett, Bowdle, & Schwarz, 1996) conducted a series of experiments in which they demonstrated that these norms characteristic of a "culture of honor" manifest themselves in the cognitions, emotions, behaviors, and physiological reactions of contemporary southern white males enrolled at the University of Michigan. In these experiments, each participant was "accidentally" bumped into by the experimenter's confederate, who then insulted him by calling him a denigrating name. Compared with northern white males (who tended to simply shrug off the insult), southerners were more likely to think their masculine reputation was threatened, became more upset (as shown by a rise in cortisol levels in their bloodstream), were more physiologically primed for aggression (as shown by a rise in testosterone levels in their bloodstream), became more cognitively primed for aggression, and were ultimately more likely to engage in aggressive and dominant behavior following the incident.

We would conclude, then, that although an instinctual component of aggression is almost certainly present in human beings, aggression is not brought forth entirely by instinct. And although situational and social events can produce aggressive behavior, such behavior can also be modified by situational and social factors. In short, aggressive behavior can be changed.

NEURAL AND CHEMICAL INFLUENCES ON AGGRESSION

Aggressive behaviors in human beings, as well as in the lower animals, are associated with an area in the core of the brain called the **amygdala.** When the amygdala is stimulated, docile organisms become violent; similarly, when neural activity in that area is blocked, violent organisms become docile (Moyer, 1976). But there is flexibility here also: The impact of neural mechanisms can be modified by social factors, even in nonhumans. For example, if a male monkey is in the presence of other less dominant monkeys, he will attack the other monkeys

Amygdala

An area in the core of the brain that is associated with aggressive behaviors when the amygdala is stimulated. But if the amygdala is stimulated while the monkey is in the presence of more dominant monkeys, he will not attack but will run away instead.

Certain chemicals have been shown to influence aggression. For example, **serotonin,** a chemical substance that occurs naturally in the midbrain, seems to have an *inhibiting* effect on impulsive aggression. In animals, when the flow of serotonin is disrupted, increases in aggressive behavior frequently follow; among humans, researchers have found that violent criminals have particularly low levels of naturally produced serotonin (Davidson, Putnam, & Larson, 2000). Moreover, in laboratory experiments on normal people, when the natural production of serotonin is interrupted, aggressive behavior increases (Bjork, Dougherty, Moeller, Cherek, & Swann, 1999).

Too little serotonin can lead to increases in aggression, but so can too much **testosterone,** a male sex hormone. Laboratory animals injected with testosterone became more aggressive (Moyer, 1983), and there is a parallel finding in humans: Naturally occurring testosterone levels are significantly higher among prisoners convicted of violent crimes than among those convicted of nonviolent crimes. Also, once incarcerated, prisoners with higher testosterone levels violated more prison rules, especially those involving overt confrontation (Dabbs, Carr, Frady, & Riad, 1995; Dabbs, Ruback, Frady, Hopper, & Sgoutas, 1988). Similarly, juvenile delinquents have higher testosterone levels than college students (Banks & Dabbs, 1996). Comparing fraternities at a given college, those generally considered most rambunctious, less socially responsible, and "cruder" were found to have the highest average testosterone levels (Dabbs, 2000; Dabbs, Hargrove, & Heusel, 1996).

Gender and Aggression

If testosterone level affects aggressiveness, does that mean that men are more aggressive than women? Apparently so; in a classic survey of research on children, Eleanor Maccoby and Carol Jacklin (1974) demonstrated that boys appear to be more aggressive than girls. For example, in one study, the investigators closely observed children at play in a variety of cultures, including the United States, Switzerland, and Ethiopia. Among boys, there was far more "nonplayful" pushing, shoving, and hitting than among girls (Deaux & La France, 1998).

But the research on gender differences is a bit more complicated than it might seem on the surface. For example, although research shows that young boys tend to be more overtly aggressive than young girls (in the sense that they lash out directly at the target person), girls tend to express their aggressive feelings more covertly—by gossiping, engaging in more backbiting, and spreading false rumors about the target person (Coie et al., 1999; Dodge & Schwartz, 1997; McFadyen-Ketchum, Bates, Dodge, & Pettit, 1996). Moreover, a meta-analysis of sixty-four separate experiments found that although it is true that men are far more aggressive than women under ordinary circumstances, the gender difference becomes much smaller when men and women are actually provoked (Bettencourt & Miller, 1996).

In other words, in everyday life situations, when nothing special is going on, men behave far more aggressively than women; but when people are subjected to frustration or insult, women will react almost as aggressively as men. It seems as though men are more likely to interpret ambiguous situations as provocative than women are—and are therefore more likely to react aggressively in what we would consider everyday situations. A good example is road rage: Many men seem to regard being cut off in traffic as a personal insult and respond aggressively. Women are more likely to take such occurrences in stride.

This might help explain why the great majority of persons arrested for aggressive offenses are men. Women are arrested typically for property crimes

Serotonin

A chemical in the brain that may inhibit aggressive impulses

Testosterone

A hormone associated with aggression

(forgery, fraud, larceny) rather than violent crimes (murder, aggravated assault). How can we explain these differences? Are males naturally predisposed to be more physically aggressive than females, or have they learned to behave that way? In short, does biology or social learning have the greater influence? We cannot be sure, but there is some evidence of a biological difference. Specifically, in the United States, the enormous social changes affecting women during the past forty years have not produced increases in the incidence of violent crimes committed by women relative to those committed by men. In fact, the data indicate that women have shown a far greater increase in *nonviolent* crimes relative to that shown by men (Wilson & Herrnstein, 1985).

Again, this does not necessarily mean that aggressiveness among women is rare, but women are much less likely to behave aggressively in nonprovocative circumstances than men are. Furthermore, when women do commit acts of overt aggression, they tend to feel more guilt or anxiety about such acts than men do (Eagly & Steffen, 1986).

Does Culture Make a Difference?   Sex differences in aggressive behaviors tend to hold up across cultures. In one study, teenagers from eleven different countries, mostly in Europe and Asia, read stories involving conflict among people and were asked to write their own endings (Archer & McDaniel, 1995). In every one of the eleven countries, young men showed a greater tendency toward violent solutions to conflict than young women did.

From these data, we can conclude that there are biochemical differences between men and women; but biochemical differences were not the only cause of these findings. Although within a given culture, men showed consistently higher levels of aggression than women, culture also played a major role. For example, women from Australia and New Zealand showed greater evidence of aggressiveness than men from Sweden and Korea did.

Violence Among Intimate Partners   Finally, we must address the enormous gender difference in violence committed against intimate partners. Of all the violent crimes against women in 2000, some 22 percent were committed by their intimate male partners; for men, the figure is 3 percent (U.S. Department of Justice, 2000). Husbands are far more likely to murder their wives than vice versa. For example, in 1998, of the 3,419 women killed in the United States, 32 percent died at the hands of a husband, boyfriend, former husband, or former boyfriend. The comparable figure for men being killed by an intimate partner or former partner is 4 percent. The shocking frequency of women being murdered by intimate partners prompted one senior health official to remark: "Women worry when they go out; perhaps they should worry when they stay in" (Goode, 2000, p. F1).

Again, these data do not prove that testosterone is the sole cause of this gender difference. When dealing with such a complex phenomenon, there is probably more than one simple cause. The gender difference in intimate homicide could be due, at least in part, to testosterone. In addition, it could be at least partly social—the reflection of a sexist society in which some men may come to feel entitled to exercise power and control over women (Eisenstat & Bancroft, 1999). Nevertheless, even if the cause is partly biological, it does not excuse violent behavior, nor does it mean that such behavior cannot be altered by a social intervention—as we shall see.

Alcohol and Aggression

As most socially active college students know, alcohol is a social lubricant that lowers our inhibitions against committing behaviors frowned on by society, including acts of aggression (Desmond, 1987; Taylor & Leonard, 1983). The link

Why are women more likely to be the victims of spousal aggression?

between alcohol and aggressive behavior is well known among researchers, and it appears even among people who have not been provoked and who do not usually behave aggressively when sober (Bailey & Taylor, 1991; Bushman & Cooper, 1990; White, 1997; Yudko, Blanchard, Henne, & Blanchard, 1997). This might explain why fistfights frequently break out in bars and nightclubs and why family violence is often associated with alcohol abuse.

Why can alcohol increase aggressive behavior? Alcohol often serves as a disinhibitor—it reduces our social inhibitions, making us less cautious than we usually are (MacDonald, Zanna, & Fong, 1996). But it is more than that. Alcohol appears to disrupt the way we usually process information (Bushman, 1993, 1997; Bushman & Cooper, 1990). This means that intoxicated people often respond to the earliest and most obvious aspects of a social situation and tend to miss the subtleties. For example, in practical terms, if you are sober and someone steps on your toe, you would notice that the person didn't do it on purpose. But if you were drunk, you might miss the subtlety of the situation and respond as if he had purposely stomped on your foot. Accordingly (especially if you are a male), you might slug him. This is typical of the kinds of ambiguous situations that males might interpret as provocative—especially under the influence of alcohol. In fact, crime statistics reveal that most people arrested for murder, assault, and other violent crimes were legally drunk at the time of their arrest (Henneberg, 2001). In addition, controlled laboratory experiments demonstrate that when individuals ingest enough alcohol to make them legally drunk, they tend to respond more violently to provocations than those who have ingested little or no alcohol (Bushman, 1993; Lipsey, Wilson, Cohen, & Derzon, 1997; Taylor & Leonard, 1983).

"Oh, that wasn't me talking. It was the alcohol talking."

Pain, Discomfort, and Aggression

If an animal experiences pain and cannot flee the scene, it will almost invariably attack; this is true of rats, mice, hamsters, foxes, monkeys, crayfish, snakes, raccoons, alligators, and a host of other creatures (Azrin, 1967; Hutchinson, 1983). In those circumstances, animals will attack members of their own species, members of different species, or anything else in sight, including stuffed dolls and tennis balls. Do you think this is true of human beings as well? A moment's reflection might help you guess that it may very well be. Most of us have experienced becoming irritable when subjected to a sharp, unexpected pain (e.g., when we stub our toe) and hence being prone to lash out at the nearest available target. In a series of experiments, students who underwent the pain of having their hand immersed in very cold water were far more likely to act aggressively against other students (Berkowitz, 1983).

By the same token, many theorists have speculated that other forms of bodily discomfort, such as heat, humidity, air pollution, and offensive odors, lower the threshold for aggressive behavior (Stoff & Cairns, 1997). During the late 1960s and early 1970s, when tensions in the United States ran high over the war in Vietnam and racial injustice, national leaders worried about "the long, hot summer." The phrase was a code for the fear that the summer's heat would cause simmering tensions to explode. Their fears were justified. An analysis of disturbances in seventy-nine cities between 1967 and 1971 found that riots were far more likely to occur on hot days than on cold ones (Carlsmith & Anderson, (1979) (see Figure 12.1). Similarly, in major American cities, from Houston, Texas, to Des Moines, Iowa, the hotter it is on a given day, the greater the likelihood that violent crimes will occur (Anderson & Anderson, 1984; Harries & Stadler, 1988).

As you know by now, one must be cautious about interpreting events that take place in natural settings, outside the laboratory. For example, the scientist in you might be tempted to ask whether increases in aggression are due to the

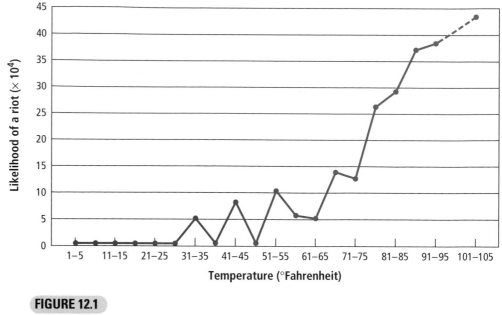

FIGURE 12.1

The long, hot summer.

Warm temperatures increase the likelihood that violent riots and other aggressive acts will occur.

(Adapted from Carlsmith & Anderson, 1979)

temperature itself or merely to the fact that more people are apt to be outside (getting in one another's way) on hot days than on cold or rainy days. So how might we determine that it's the heat that caused the aggression and not merely the greater opportunity for contact? We can bring the phenomenon into the laboratory; in fact, it is remarkably easy to do so. In one such experiment, students took the same test under different conditions: Some worked in a room at normal room temperature while others worked in a room where the temperature reached 90 degrees (Griffitt & Veitch, 1971). The students in the hot room not only reported feeling more aggressive but also expressed more hostility toward a stranger whom they were asked to describe and rate. Similar results have been reported by a number of investigators (Anderson, Anderson, & Deuser, 1996; Rule, Taylor, & Dobbs, 1987).

Additional evidence from the natural world helps bolster our belief in the relationship between heat and aggression. Not only are violent crimes more frequent during hotter years than cooler ones (Anderson, Bushman, & Groom 1997), but even on the baseball field, heat and hostility seem to go together. In major league baseball games, significantly more batters are hit by pitched balls when the temperature rises above 90 degrees (Reifman, Larrick, & Fein, 1988). And in the desert city of Phoenix, Arizona, drivers in non-air-conditioned cars are more likely to honk their horns in traffic jams than drivers in air-conditioned cars (Kenrick & MacFarlane, 1986). See the Try It! exercise on page 399.

SOCIAL SITUATIONS AND AGGRESSION

We've seen the effects of body chemistry, alcohol, and unpleasant physical experiences like pain and heat on aggression. Aggression can also be caused by unpleasant social situations. Imagine that your friend Sam is driving you to the airport so that you can fly home for the Christmas holidays. Sam has picked you up a bit later than you feel comfortable with; he accuses you of being overly

Try it!

The next time you find yourself caught in a traffic jam, try doing a simple, naturalistic replication of the Kenrick and MacFarlane (1986) experiment. Consider the following hypothesis: The greater the heat and humidity, the greater the aggression.

• Take notes on how much aggression you notice (in the form of horn-honking).

• Note down the heat and humidity that day.
• The next two or three times you get caught in a traffic jam, do the same thing.

Can you discern a relationship between heat and humidity and horn-honking?

---

anxious and assures you that he knows the route well and that you will arrive there with thirty minutes to spare. Halfway to the airport, you are standing still in bumper-to-bumper traffic. Sam assures you that there is plenty of time—but this time he sounds less confident. After a few minutes, your palms are sweating. You open the car door and survey the road ahead: Not a car is moving, as far ahead as you can see. You get back in the car, slam the door, and glare at Sam. He smiles lamely and says, "How was I supposed to know there would be so much traffic?" Should he be prepared to duck?

Frustration and Aggression

As this all-too-familiar story suggests, the unpleasant experience of frustration is a major cause of aggression. Frustration occurs when a person is thwarted on the way to an expected goal or gratification. All of us have experienced some degree of frustration from time to time; indeed, it's unlikely we can get through a week without experiencing it. Research has shown that the experience of frustration can increase the probability of an aggressive response. This tendency is referred to as **frustration-aggression theory,** which holds that people's perception that they are being prevented from attaining a goal will increase the probability of their responding aggressively. This does not mean that frustration always leads to aggression—but it frequently does, especially when the frustration is a decidedly unpleasant experience.

In a classic experiment by Roger Barker, Tamara Dembo, and Kurt Lewin (1941), young children were led to a roomful of attractive toys that were kept out of their reach by a wire screen. After a long wait, the children were finally allowed to play with the toys. In a control condition, a different group of children were allowed to play with the toys immediately, without first being frustrated. These children played joyfully with the toys, but the frustrated group, when finally given access to the toys, were extremely destructive: Many smashed the toys, threw them against the wall, stepped on them, and so forth.

Several things can increase frustration and, accordingly, will increase the probability that some form of aggression will occur. One such factor involves your closeness to the goal or the object of your desire. The closer the goal, the greater the expectation of pleasure that is thwarted; the greater the expectation, the more likely the aggression. This was demonstrated in a field experiment (Harris, 1974). A confederate cut in line in front of people who were waiting in a variety of places—for movie tickets, outside crowded restaurants, or at the

Frustration-Aggression Theory

The idea that frustration—the perception that you are being prevented from attaining a goal—increases the probability of an aggressive response

Road rage is often caused by frustration among motorists.

checkout counter of a supermarket. On some occasions, the confederate cut in front of the second person in line; at other times, the confederate cut in front of the twelfth person. The results were clear: The people standing behind the intruder were much more aggressive when the confederate cut into the second place in line.

Aggression also increases when the frustration is unexpected (Kulik & Brown, 1979). Experimenters hired students to telephone strangers and ask for donations to a charity. The students worked on a commission basis—they received a small fraction of each dollar pledged. Some of the students were led to expect a high rate of contributions; others, to expect far less success. The experiment was rigged so that none of the potential donors agreed to make a contribution. What happened? The callers with high expectations were more verbally aggressive toward the nondonors, speaking more harshly and slamming down the phone with more force than the callers with low expectations.

As we've said, frustration does not always produce aggression. Rather, it seems to produce anger or annoyance and a readiness to aggress if other things about the situation are conducive to aggressive behavior (Berkowitz, 1978, 1988, 1989, 1993; Gustafson, 1989). What are those other things? Well, one obvious other thing would be the size and strength of the person responsible for your frustration, as well as that person's ability to retaliate. It is undoubtedly easier to slam the phone down on a reluctant donor who is miles away and has no idea who you are than to take out your anger against your frustrator if he turned out to be the middle linebacker of the Green Bay Packers and was staring you right in the face. Similarly, if the frustration is understandable, legitimate, and unintentional, the tendency to aggress will be reduced. For example, in one experiment, when a confederate "unwittingly" sabotaged the problem solving of his groupmates because his hearing aid stopped working, the resulting frustration did not lead to a measurable degree of aggression (Burnstein & Worchel, 1962).

It should be clear that frustration is not the same as deprivation. For example, children who simply don't have toys do not aggress more than children who do. In the toy experiment, frustration and aggression occurred because the children had every reason to expect to play with the toys, and their reasonable expectation was thwarted; this thwarting was what caused the children to behave destructively.

Accordingly, Rev. Jesse Jackson (1981), with great insight, pointed out that the race riots of 1967 and 1968 occurred in the middle of rising expectations and increased, though inadequate, social spending. In short, Jackson was suggesting that thwarted expectations were largely responsible for the frustration and aggression of the rioters. This is consistent with the observations of psychiatrist Jerome Frank (1978), who noted that the most serious riots in that era occurred not in the geographic areas of greatest poverty but in Los Angeles and Detroit, where things were not nearly so bad for African Americans as they were in most other large urban centers. The point is that things were bad relative to the rioters' perception of how white people were doing and relative to the positive changes many African Americans had a right to expect. Thus what causes aggression is not deprivation but *relative deprivation:* the perception that you (or your group) have less than you deserve, less than what you have been led to expect, or less than what people similar to you have.

A similar phenomenon occurred in eastern Europe in 1991, when serious rebellion against the Soviet Union took place only after the chains had been loosened somewhat. In the same vein, Primo Levi (1986), a survivor of Auschwitz, contended that even in concentration camps, the few instances of rebellion were performed not by the inmates at the very bottom of the camp totem pole—the suffering victims of unrelenting horror—but "by prisoners who were privileged in some way" (p. 203).

Being Provoked and Reciprocating

Another unpleasant experience involves direct provocation. Suppose you are working at your part-time job behind the counter, flipping hamburgers in a crowded fast-food restaurant. Today, you are working harder than usual because the other short-order cook went home sick, and the customers are lining up at the counter, clamoring for their burgers. In your eagerness to speed up the process, you spin around too fast and knock over a large jar of pickles, which smashes on the floor just as the boss enters the workplace. "Boy, are you clumsy!" he screams. "I'm gonna dock your pay $10 for that one; grab a broom and clean up, you moron! I'll take over here!" You glare at him. You'd love to tell him what he can do with this lousy job!

Aggression frequently stems from the need to reciprocate after being provoked by aggressive behavior from another person. While the Christian plea to "turn the other cheek" is wonderful advice, most people don't take it, as has been illustrated in countless experiments in and out of the laboratory. Typical of this line of research is an experiment by Robert Baron (1988) in which subjects prepared an advertisement for a new product; their ad was then evaluated and criticized by an accomplice of the experimenter. In one condition, the criticism, though strong, was done in a gentle and considerate manner ("I think there's a lot of room for improvement"); in the other condition, the criticism was given in an insulting manner ("I don't think you could be original if you tried"). When provided with an opportunity to retaliate, subjects who were treated harshly were far more likely to do so than those in the "gentle" condition.

> Nothing is more costly, nothing is more sterile, than revenge.
>
> —Winston Churchill

But even when provoked, people do not always reciprocate. We ask ourselves, was the provocation intentional or not? When convinced it was unintentional, most of us will not reciprocate (Kremer & Stephens, 1983). Similarly, if there are mitigating circumstances, counteraggression will not occur. But to curtail an aggressive response, these mitigating circumstances must be known at the time of the provocation (Johnson & Rule, 1986). In one study, students were insulted by the experimenters' assistant. Half of them were first told that the assistant was upset after receiving an unfair low grade on a chemistry exam; the other students received this information only after the insult was delivered. All subjects later had an opportunity to retaliate by choosing the level of unpleasant noise with which to zap the assistant. Those students who knew about the mitigating

Insults and Aggression

Think about the last time you were insulted.

- Who insulted you?
- What were the circumstances?
- Did you take it personally or not?

- How did you respond?

  How does your behavior relate to the material you have just finished reading?

circumstances before being insulted delivered less intense bursts of noise. Why the difference? At the time of the insult, the informed students simply did not take it personally and therefore had no strong need to retaliate. This interpretation is bolstered by evidence of their physiological arousal: At the time of the insult, the heartbeat of the insulted students did not increase as rapidly if they knew about the assistant's unhappy state of mind beforehand. See the Try It! exercise above.

Aggressive Objects as Cues

Certain stimuli seem to impel us to action. Is it conceivable that the mere presence of an **aggressive stimulus**—an object that is associated with aggressive responses—might increase the probability of aggression?

In a classic experiment by Leonard Berkowitz and Anthony Le Page (1967), college students were made angry. Some of them were made angry in a room in which a gun was left lying around (ostensibly from a previous experiment), and others were made angry in a room in which a neutral object (a badminton racket) was substituted for the gun. Subjects were then given the opportunity to administer what they believed were electric shocks to a fellow college student. Those individuals who had been made angry in the presence of the gun administered more intense electric shocks than those made angry in the presence of the racket (see Figure 12.2). The basic findings have been replicated a great many times in the United States and Europe (Frodi, 1975; Turner & Leyens, 1992; Turner, Simons, Berkowitz, & Frodi, 1977). These findings are provocative

Aggressive Stimulus

An object that is associated with aggressive responses (e.g., a gun) and whose mere presence can increase the probability of aggression

FIGURE 12.2

The trigger can pull the finger.

Aggressive cues, such as weapons, tend to increase levels of aggression.

(Adapted from Berkowitz & Le Page, 1967)

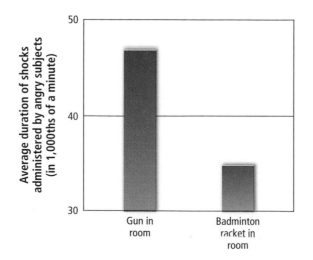

Guns to the left of me, guns to the right of me . . . Does the easy availability of guns in the United States contribute to the frequency and intensity of violence?

and point to a conclusion opposite to a familiar slogan often used by opponents of gun control that "guns don't kill; people do." Guns do kill. As Leonard Berkowitz (1981, p. 12) put it, "An angry person can pull the trigger of his gun if he wants to commit violence; but the trigger can also pull the finger or otherwise elicit aggressive reactions from him, if he is ready to aggress and does not have strong inhibitions against such behavior."

Consider Seattle, Washington, and Vancouver, British Columbia. They are twin cities in a lot of ways; they have very similar climates, populations, economies, general crime rates, and rates of physical assault. They differ in two respects: (1) Vancouver severely restricts handgun ownership, while Seattle does not, and (2) the murder rate in Seattle is more than twice as high as that in Vancouver (Sloan et al., 1988). Is one thing the cause of the other? We cannot be sure. But the laboratory experiments just described strongly suggest that the ubiquitous presence of aggressive stimuli such as guns in the United States might be a factor.

This speculation receives additional support from a cross-national study that found that the homicide rate in countries around the world is highly correlated with the availability of handguns (Archer & Gartner, 1984). Britain, for example, where handguns are banned, has one-fourth the population of the United States and one-sixteenth as many homicides.

In a large-scale follow-up study, Archer and his colleagues (Archer, 1994; Archer & McDaniel, 1995) asked teenagers from the United States and ten other countries to read stories involving conflict among people and to predict the outcome of the conflict. The results? American teenagers were more likely to anticipate a violent conclusion to the conflict than teenagers from other countries. Moreover, the violent conclusions drawn by American teenagers were far more likely to be "lethal, gun-laden and merciless" (Archer, 1994, p. 19). The conclusions are undeniable: Lethal violence, especially involving guns, is simply a major part of American society—and therefore plays a major role in the expectations and fantasies of American youngsters.

Children have never been very good at listening to their elders, but they have never failed to imitate them.

—James Baldwin, Nobody Knows My Name

Imitation and Aggression

One of the major cues to aggressive action is the presence of other people behaving aggressively. This is especially true for children. Children frequently learn to solve conflicts aggressively by imitating adults and their peers, especially when

It is clear from the studies of Bandura, Ross, and Ross (1961, 1963) that children learn aggressive behavior through imitation and modeling.

they see that the aggression is rewarded. For example, in most high-contact sports (e.g., football and hockey), the more aggressive players often achieve the greatest fame (and the highest salaries), and the more aggressive teams win more games. In these sports, it usually doesn't pay to be a gentle soul—as famed baseball manager Leo Duroscher once pointed out, "Nice guys finish last!" The data bear him out. In professional hockey, for example, with few exceptions, those players most frequently sent to the penalty box for overly aggressive play also scored the most goals and earned the highest salaries (McCarthy & Kelly, 1978). To the extent that athletes serve as role models for children and adolescents, what is being modeled might be that fame and fortune go hand in hand with excessive aggressiveness.

The people children imitate the most, of course, are their parents. And if the parents were abused as children, this can set a chain of abuse in motion. Indeed, a large percentage of physically abusive parents were themselves abused by their own parents when they were kids (Silver, Dublin, & Lourie, 1969; Strauss & Gelles, 1980). Many experts speculate that when children are physically abused by their parents, they learn that violence is an acceptable way to socialize their own kids. But of course, that is not the only conclusion one might draw from these family data.

We've seen that aggression has a strong inborn component, so might aggressive parents simply breed aggressive children? How can one determine whether or not imitation might be operating here? As you might guess, a laboratory study could provide useful evidence. In a classic series of experiments, Albert Bandura and his associates (Bandura, Ross, & Ross, 1961, 1963) demonstrated the power of social learning.

Social learning theory holds that we learn social behavior (e.g., aggression) by observing others and imitating them. The basic procedure in the Bandura experiments was to have an adult knock around a plastic, air-filled "Bobo" doll (the kind that bounces back after it's been knocked down). The adult would smack the doll around with the palm of a hand, strike it with a mallet, kick it, and yell aggressive things at it. The kids were then allowed to play with the doll. In these experiments, the children imitated the aggressive models and treated the doll in an abusive way. Children in a control condition, who did not see the aggressive adult in action, almost never unleashed any aggression against the hapless doll. Moreover, the children who watched the aggressive adult used identical actions and identical aggressive words as the adult. And many went beyond mere imitation—they also engaged in novel forms of aggressive behavior. This research

Social Learning Theory

The idea that we learn social behavior (e.g., aggression) by observing others and imitating them offers strong support for our belief that aggressive behavior is often learned by the simple process of watching and imitating the behavior of others.

Violence in the Media: TV, Movies, and Video Games

If just watching people behave aggressively causes children to mistreat dolls, what does watching violence on television do to them—to all of us? And what about violent video games in which children participate in the destruction of cities and the lopping off of heads and limbs of characters on their computer screens?

> Television has brought murder back into the home—where it belongs.
> *—Alfred Hitchcock, 1965*

Effects on Children   The average American child watches two to four hours of TV every day, (Huston & Wright, 1996). Concerned about the amount and intensity of violence children were seeing during those hours, social psychologist Leonard Eron told a Senate committee that by the time the average American child finishes elementary school, he or she would have seen 8,000 murders and more than 100,000 other acts of violence (reported in Eron, 2001). Since then, Eron's figures have been amply documented. Dozens of studies (e.g., Seppa, 1997) have demonstrated that 58 percent of all TV programs contain violence—and of those, 78 percent contain not a shred of remorse, criticism, or penalty for that violence. Indeed, some 40 percent of the violent incidents seen on TV during a particular year were initiated by characters portrayed as heroes or other attractive role models for children (Cantor et al., 2001).

Exactly what do children learn from watching violence on TV? A number of long-term studies have indicated that the more violence individuals watch on TV as children, the more violence they exhibit later as teenagers and young adults (Eron, 1982, 1987; Eron, Huesmann, Lefkowitz, & Walder, 1996). In a typical study of this kind, teenagers are asked to recall which shows they watched on TV when they were kids and how frequently they watched them. Next, the shows are independently rated by judges as to how violent they are. Finally, the general aggressiveness of the teenagers is independently rated by their teachers and classmates. Not only is there a high correlation between the amount of violent TV watched and the viewer's subsequent aggressiveness, but the impact also accumulates over time—that is, the strength of the correlation increases with age.

Although these are fairly powerful data, they do not definitively prove that watching a lot of violence on TV causes children to become violent teenagers. After all, it is at least conceivable that the aggressive kids were born with a tendency to enjoy violence and that this enjoyment manifests itself in both their aggressive behavior and their liking for watching violence on TV. Once again, we see the value of the controlled experiment in helping us sort out what causes what. To demonstrate conclusively that watching violence on TV actually causes violent behavior, the relationship must be shown experimentally.

Because this is an issue of great importance to society, it has been well researched. Though not all of the research is consistent, the overwhelming thrust of the experimental evidence demonstrates that watching violence does indeed increase the frequency of aggressive behavior in children (for reviews of the literature, see Cantor et al, 2001; Geen, 1994, 1998; Huesmann & Miller, 1994). For example, in an early experiment on this issue, Robert Liebert and Robert Baron (1972) exposed a group of children to an extremely violent TV episode of a police drama. In a control condition, a similar group of children were exposed to an exciting but nonviolent TV sporting event for the same length of time. Each child was then allowed to play in another room with a group of other children. Those who had watched the violent police drama showed far more aggression against their playmates than those who had watched the sporting event (see Figure 12.3 on the next page).

FIGURE 12.3

TV violence and aggression.

Being exposed to violence on TV increases aggressive behavior in children.

(Adapted from Liebert & Baron, 1972)

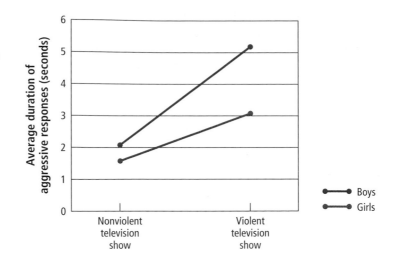

A subsequent experiment by Wendy Josephson (1987) showed, as one might expect, that watching TV violence has the greatest impact on youngsters who are somewhat prone to violence to begin with. In this experiment, youngsters were exposed to either a film depicting a great deal of police violence or an exciting, nonviolent film about bike racing. The youngsters then played a game of floor hockey. Watching the violent film had the effect of increasing the number of aggressive acts committed during the hockey game—primarily by the youngsters who had previously been rated as highly aggressive by their teachers. These kids hit others with their sticks, threw elbows, and yelled aggressive things at their opponents to a much greater extent than either the kids rated as nonaggressive who had also watched the violent film or the kids rated as aggressive who had watched the nonviolent film. Thus it may be that watching media violence in effect serves to give aggressive kids permission to express their aggression. Josephson's experiment suggests that youngsters who do not have aggressive tendencies to begin with do not necessarily act aggressively—at least not on the basis of seeing only one violent film.

That last phrase is an important one because it may be that even children who are not inclined toward aggression will become more aggressive if exposed to a steady diet of violent films over a long period. That is exactly what was found in field experiments performed in Belgium by J. Philippe Leyens and his

"At last, a movie without all those filthy sex scenes!"

colleagues (Leyens, Camino, Parke, & Berkowitz, 1975; Parke, Berkowitz, Leyens, West, & Sebastian, 1977). In these experiments, groups of children were exposed to differing amounts of media violence over a longer period than is typical of "one-shot" laboratory experiments. In these field experiments, the great majority of the kids (even those without strong aggressive tendencies) who were exposed to a high degree of media violence over a long period were more aggressive than those who watched more benign programs.

As noted earlier, the average 12-year-old has seen an estimated 100,000 acts of televised violence (Signorielli, Gerbner, & Morgan, 1995). We mention this because we believe that one of the crucial factors involved in the findings on the behavior of children exposed to violence, in addition to social learning and imitation, is the simple phenomenon of *priming*. That is, just as exposing children to rifles and other weapons left lying around the house or the laboratory has a tendency to increase the probability of an aggressive response when children subsequently experience pain or frustration, exposing children to an endless stream of violence in films and on TV might have a similar tendency to prime an aggressive response.

Playing violent video games seems to have the same kind of impact on children that watching TV violence does. In one study, violent video game playing was positively correlated with aggressive behavior and delinquency in children, and the relationship was stronger for children who had been more prone to violence beforehand (Anderson & Dill, 2000). In a second study, the researchers showed that the relationship was more than correlational. Exposing a random sample of children to a graphically violent video game had a direct and immediate impact on their aggressive thoughts and behavior (Anderson & Dill, 2000).

What about Adults?   So far, we've focused on children—and for good reason. Youngsters are by definition much more malleable than adults—their attitudes and behaviors are almost certainly deeply influenced by the things they view. Moreover, children are not as adept as adults at distinguishing between reality and fantasy. But the effects of media violence on violent behavior are not limited to children.

Media violence has a major impact on the aggressive behavior of adolescents and young adults as well. In a recent longitudinal study, researchers monitored the behavior of more than seven hundred families over a period of seventeen

Does playing violent games lead to violence in everyday life?

years. Their findings are striking: They found a significant association between the amount of time spent watching television during adolescence and early adulthood and the likelihood of subsequent violent acts against others. This association was significant *regardless of parental education, family income, and neighborhood violence.* Moreover, unlike most laboratory experiments on aggression, which, understandably must use rather pallid measures of aggression (like administering fake electric shocks or loud noises to the victim), this study, because it took place in the real world over a long period of time, was able to examine severe aggressive behavior like assault and armed robbery (Johnson, 2002).

On numerous occasions, adult violence seems to be a case of life imitating art. For example, a few years ago, a man drove his truck through the window of a crowded cafeteria in Killeen, Texas, emerged from the cab, and began shooting people at random. By the time the police arrived, he had killed twenty-two people, making this the most destructive shooting spree in American history. He then turned the gun on himself. In his pocket, police found a ticket stub to *The Fisher King,* a film depicting a deranged man firing a shotgun into a crowded bar, killing several people.

> Death has been tidied up, cleansed of harmful ingredients, and repackaged in prime-time segments that pander to baser appetites but leave no unpleasant aftertaste. The Caesars of network television permit no mess on the living room floor.
>
> —Donald Goddard, 1977

Did seeing the film cause the violent act? We cannot be sure. But we do know that violence in the media can and does have a profound impact on the behavior of adults. Several years ago, David Phillips (1983, 1986) scrutinized the daily homicide rates in the United States and found that they almost always increased during the week following a heavyweight boxing match. Moreover, the more publicity surrounding the fight, the greater the subsequent increase in homicides. Still more striking, the race of prizefight losers was related to the race of victims of murders after the fights: After white boxers lost fights, there was a corresponding increase in murders of white men but not of black men. After black boxers lost fights, there was a corresponding increase in murders of black men but not of white men. Phillips's results are far too consistent to be dismissed as a fluke. Moreover, his findings have received strong confirmation from a meta-analysis by showing that across a wide range of ages, there is a reliable relationship between viewing violence on TV and the antisocial behavior of the viewer (Paik & Comstock, 1994). Again, these data should not be construed as indicating that all people or even a sizable percentage of people are motivated to commit violence through watching media violence. But the fact that some people are influenced—and that the results can be tragic—cannot be denied.

The Numbing Effect of TV Violence Repeated exposure to difficult or unpleasant events tends to have a numbing effect on our sensitivity to those events. In one experiment, researchers measured the physiological responses of several young men while they were watching a rather brutal and bloody boxing match (Cline, Croft, & Courier, 1973). Those who watched a lot of TV in their daily lives seemed relatively indifferent to the mayhem in the ring—that is, they showed little physiological evidence of excitement, anxiety, or other arousal. They were unmoved by the violence. But those who typically watched relatively little TV experienced major physiological arousal—the violence really agitated them.

Studies have also found that viewing television violence can subsequently numb people's reactions when they face real-life aggression (Thomas, Horton, Lippincott, & Drabman, 1977). The researchers had their subjects watch either a violent police drama or an exciting but nonviolent volleyball game. After a short break, they were allowed to observe a verbally and physically aggressive interaction between two preschoolers. Those who had watched the police show responded less emotionally than those who had watched the volleyball game. It seems that viewing the initial violence served to desensitize them to further acts of violence—they were not upset by an incident that by all rights should have upset them. While such a reaction may psychologically protect us from upset, it may also have the unintended effect of increasing our indifference to victims of violence and perhaps render us more accepting of violence as an aspect of life in the modern world. In a follow-up experiment, Margaret Thomas (1982) took this reasoning a step further. She demonstrated that college students exposed to a great deal of TV violence not only showed physiological evidence of greater acceptance of violence but in addition, when subsequently given the opportunity to administer electric shocks to a fellow student, administered more powerful electric shocks than those in the control condition.

How Does Media Violence Affect Our View of the World?   If I am watching all this murder and mayhem on the TV screen, wouldn't it be logical for me to conclude that it simply isn't safe to leave the house—especially after dark? That is precisely what many heavy TV viewers do conclude (Gerbner, Gross, Morgan, Signorielli, & Shanahan, 2002). Adolescents and adults who are heavy TV viewers (who watch more than four hours per day) are more likely than light TV viewers (who watch less than two hours per day) to have an exaggerated view of the degree of violence taking place outside their own home. Moreover, heavy TV viewers have a much greater fear of being personally assaulted.

Why Does Media Violence Affect Viewers' Aggression?   As suggested throughout this discussion, there are at least five distinct reactions that explain why exposure to violence via the media might increase aggression:

1. *"If they can do it, so can I."* When people see characters on TV behaving violently, it may simply weaken their previously learned inhibitions against violent behavior.
2. *"Oh, so that's how you do it!"* When people see characters on TV behaving violently, it might trigger imitation, providing them with ideas as to how they might go about it.

Media violence may serve to give kids already prone to aggression permission to be aggressive. It also may make children not prone to aggression more aggressive.

3. *"I think it must be aggressive feelings that I'm experiencing."* Watching violence may put people more in touch with their feelings of anger and make an aggressive response more likely simply through priming, as discussed in Chapter 4. Having recently viewed violence on TV, someone might interpret his or her own feelings of mild irritation as intense anger and then be more likely to lash out.

4. *"Ho-hum, another brutal beating; what's on the other channel?"* Watching a lot of mayhem seems to reduce both our sense of horror about violence and our sympathy for the victims, making it easier for us to live with violence and perhaps easier for us to act aggressively.

5. *"I had better get him before he gets me!"* If watching a lot of TV makes me think the world is a dangerous place, I might be more apt to be hostile to a stranger who approaches me on the street.

Does Violence Sell?

Everyone knows that violence on TV is popular. People might complain about all that mayhem, but most people also seem to enjoy watching it. What message does that send to advertisers? Does violence sell? After all, the goal of advertising is not simply to get a lot of people to tune in to the ad; the ultimate goal of advertising is to present the product in such a way that the public will end up purchasing it over a long period of time. What if it turns out that certain kinds of shows produce so much mental turmoil that the sponsor's product is soon forgotten? If people cannot remember the name of the product, seeing the show will not lead them to buy it.

In a striking experiment, Brad Bushman & Angelica Bonacci (2002) got people to watch TV shows that were either violent, sexually explicit, or neutral. Each of the shows contained the same nine ads. Immediately after seeing the show, the researchers asked the viewers to recall the brands and to pick them out from photos of supermarket shelves. Twenty-four hours later, they telephoned the viewers and asked them to recall the brands they had seen during the viewing. The people who saw the ads during the viewing of a neutral (nonviolent, nonsexually explicit) show were able to recall the advertised brands better than the people who saw the violent show or the sexually explicit show. This was true both immediately after viewing and twenty-four hours after viewing and was true for both men and women of all ages. It seems that violence and sex impair the memory of viewers. In terms of sales, advertisers might be well advised to sponsor nonviolent shows.

Violent Pornography and Violence against Women

A particularly troubling aspect of aggression in the United States involves violence expressed by some men against women in the form of rape. According to national surveys, during the past three decades, almost half of all rapes or attempted rapes do not involve assaults by a stranger but are instances of "date rape," in which the victim is acquainted with or even dating the assailant. Many date rapes occur because the male refuses to take no for an answer. Why does this happen?

Part of the answer lies in the "sexual scripts" adolescents learn as they grow toward sexual maturity. **Scripts** are ways of behaving socially that we learn implicitly from the culture. The sexual scripts adolescents are exposed to suggest that the traditional female role is to resist the male's sexual advances and the male's role is to be persistent (Check & Malamuth, 1983; White, Donat, & Humphrey,

Scripts

Ways of behaving socially that we learn implicitly from our culture

1995). This may explain why, in one survey of high school students, although 95 percent of the males and 97 percent of the females agreed that the man should stop his sexual advances as soon as the woman says no, nearly half of those same students also believed that when a woman says no, she doesn't always mean it (Monson, Langhinrichsen-Rohling, & Binderup, 2002). During the 1990s, this confusion prompted several colleges to suggest that dating couples negotiate an explicit contract about their sexual conduct and limitations at the very beginning of the date. Given the problems associated with sexual scripts and the emotionally destructive consequences of miscommunication, it is understandable that college administrators would have resorted to these extreme precautions. But social critics (e.g., Roiphe, 1994) lambasted these measures on the grounds that they encouraged fear and paranoia, destroyed the spontaneity of romance, and reduced the excitement of dating to something resembling a field trip to a lawyer's office. They were eventually dropped.

Coincidental with the increase in date rape has been an increase in the availability of magazines, films, and videocassettes depicting vivid, explicit sexual behavior. For better or worse, in recent years our society has become increasingly freer and more tolerant of pornography. If viewing aggression in films and on television contributes to aggressiveness, doesn't it follow that viewing pornographic material could increase the incidence of rape? Although this possibility has been presented as a fact by certain self-appointed guardians of morality, scientific research suggests that it is still an open question. Because pornography is a hot button issue, research findings often get distorted or ignored in the heat of rhetoric. In 1970, after studying the existing evidence, the Presidential Commission on Obscenity and Pornography concluded that explicit sexual material, in and of itself, does not contribute to sexual crimes, violence against women, or other antisocial acts. But as you will recall, in Chapter 2 we discussed the fact that in 1985, the attorney general's commission disagreed with the findings of the earlier report and concluded that pornography has a major impact on violent crimes against women. Which commission was right?

As is often the case in such politically motivated disputes, the truth is more complex than either of these conclusions. Careful scientific research suggests an important distinction between simple pornography and violent pornography. By "violent pornography," we mean exactly what you might think: pornographic material that contains an element of violence against women.

During the past two decades, a team of researchers has conducted careful studies, in both naturalistic and laboratory settings, to determine the effects of violent pornography. Taken as a whole, these studies indicate that exposure to violent pornography promotes greater acceptance of sexual violence toward women and is almost certainly a factor associated with actual aggressive behavior toward women (Dean & Malamuth, 1997; Donnerstein & Linz, 1994; Malamuth, Linz, Heavey, Barnes, & Acker, 1995). In one experiment (Donnerstein & Berkowitz, 1981), male subjects were angered by a female accomplice. They were then shown one of three films—an aggressive-erotic one involving rape, a purely erotic one without violence, or a film depicting noneurotic violence against women. After viewing one of these films, the men took part in a supposedly unrelated experiment that involved teaching the female accomplice by means of administering electric shocks to her whenever she gave incorrect answers. They were also allowed to choose whatever level of shock they wished to use. (As with other experiments using this procedure, no shocks were actually received.) Only the men who had earlier seen the violent pornographic film subsequently administered intense shocks to the female accomplice. There is also evidence showing that under these conditions, subjects who view violent pornographic films will administer more intense shocks to a female confederate than to a male confederate (Donnerstein, 1980). This indicates that viewing pornographic violence against women does tend to focus aggressive feelings on women as a target.

In a similar experiment, male college students watched one of two erotic films (Malamuth, 1981). One version showed two mutually consenting adults making love; in the other version, the male raped the woman. After watching the film, the men were asked to engage in sexual fantasy. What would you predict? Men who had watched the rape version of the film created more violent sexual fantasies than those who had watched the mutual-consent version. Further, just as we saw with violence, prolonged exposure to depictions of sexual violence against women makes viewers more accepting of this kind of violence and less sympathetic toward the victim (Linz, Donnerstein, & Penrod, 1984, 1988). Interestingly, this applies to female viewers as well as male viewers.

All of this does not mean that viewing nonviolent pornographic films has zero impact on aggressive feelings directed toward women. Here the data are mixed: Some researchers have found no relationship, and some have found small effects.

Trying to make sense out of the mixed results, a team of psychologists analyzed data from thirty studies (a meta-analysis; see Chapter 2). They found that exposure to violent pornographic material produced a high degree of aggression against women (Allen, D'Alessio, & Brezgel, 1995). They also found that nonviolent pornographic material had a small but measurable effect on aggressive behavior against women. Making this issue even more complex, they found, too, that men who were exposed to images of nude women not engaged in sexual activity were actually less prone to commit violence against women than men in control conditions. Given the complexity of the data, the only firm conclusion we are able to draw at this time is that only violent pornography presents a clear and unambiguous problem for our society.

HOW TO REDUCE AGGRESSION

"Stop hitting your brother!" "Turn off the TV and go to your room!" Trying to curb the aggressive behavior of their children, most parents use some form of punishment. Some deny privileges; others use force, believing in the old saying, "Spare the rod and spoil the child." How well does punishment work?

> All punishment is mischief; all punishment itself is evil.
>
> —Jeremy Bentham, Principles of Morals and Legislation, 1789

Does Punishing Aggression Reduce Aggressive Behavior?

Punishment is a complex event, especially as it relates to aggression. On the one hand, you might think that punishing any behavior, including aggression, would reduce its frequency. On the other hand, if the punishment takes the form of an aggressive act, the punishers are actually modeling aggressive behavior for the person whose aggressive behavior they are trying to stamp out and might induce that person to imitate their action. This seems to be true—for children. As we have seen, children who grow up with punitive, aggressive parents tend to be prone toward violence when they grow up (Vissing, Straus, Gelles, & Harrop, 1991).

Moreover, as we saw in Chapter 6, several experiments with preschoolers demonstrated that the threat of relatively severe punishment for committing a transgression does not make the transgression less appealing to the child. On the other hand, the threat of mild punishment—of a degree just powerful enough to get the child to stop the undesired activity temporarily—leads the child to try to justify his or her restraint and, as a result, can make the behavior less appealing (Aronson & Carlsmith, 1963; Freedman, 1965).

CONNECTIONS:

Curbing Schoolyard Bullying

These findings were confirmed by psychologist
Dan Olweus (1991, 1995a, 1995b, 1996, 1997) in a
pioneering intervention aimed at curbing bullying
in Norway in which he used a combination of education and mild punishment. This remarkable effort blanketed the entire country, prompted by the
Norwegian government's concern over the suicides of three young victims of bullying. Take the
example of Henry, a Norwegian sixth grader who
did not succeed in killing himself:

Schoolyard bullying, derision,
and taunting makes life
miserable for a sizeable
proportion of children in most
countries.

> On a daily basis, Henry's classmates called him
> "Worm," broke his pencils, spilled his books
> on the floor, and mocked him whenever he
> answered a teacher's questions. Finally, a few
> boys took him to the bathroom and made him lic, face down, in the
> urinal drain. After school that day he tried to kill himself. His par-
> ents found him unconscious, and only then learned about his tor-
> ment. (Olweus, 1991, p. 413)

At the request of the government, Olweus surveyed all of Norway's ninety
thousand schoolchildren. He concluded that bullying was serious and widespread, that teachers and parents were only dimly aware of bullying incidents, and that even when adults were aware of these incidents, they rarely
intervened. The government sponsored a campaign in every school to
change the social dynamic that breeds bullies and victims. First, community-
wide meetings were held to explain the problem. Parents were given
brochures detailing symptoms of victimization. Teachers received training on
handling bullying. Students watched videotapes to evoke sympathy for victims of bullying.

Second, classes discussed ways to prevent bullying and befriend lonely
children. Teachers organized cooperative learning groups and moved quickly
to stop name-calling and other aggression that escalates into bullying.
Principals ensured that lunchrooms, bathrooms, and playgrounds were adequately supervised.

A third set of measures came into play if bullying occurred despite these
preventive steps. Counselors intervened using a combination of mild punishment and intensive therapy with the bully and counseling with the parents
and sometimes assigned the bully to a different class or school.

Twenty months after the campaign began, Olweus found that bullying
overall had decreased by half, with improvements at every grade level. He
concluded, "It is no longer possible to avoid taking action about bullying
problems at school using lack of awareness as an excuse—it all boils down to
a matter of will and involvement on the part of adults" (1991, p. 415).

Using Punishment on Violent Adults The criminal justice system of most cultures
administers harsh punishments both as retribution and as a means of deterring
violent crimes like murder, manslaughter, and rape. Does the threat of harsh
punishments for violent crimes make such crimes less likely? Do people who are
about to commit violent crimes say to themselves, "I'd better not do this because
if I get caught, I'm going to jail for a long time; I might even be executed." The

scientific evidence is mixed. Laboratory experiments indicate that punishment can indeed act as a deterrent (Bower & Hilgard, 1981), but only if two "ideal conditions" are met: punishment must be both prompt and certain. It must follow quickly after the violence occurred, and it must be unavoidable. In the real world, these ideal conditions are almost never met, especially in a complex society with a high crime rate and a slow criminal justice system like our own. In most American cities, the probability that a person who commits a violent crime will be apprehended, charged, tried, and convicted is not high. Moreover, given the volume of cases in our courts, as well as the necessary cautions with which the criminal justice system must operate, promptness is almost impossible. Typically, punishment is delayed by months or even years. Consequently, in the complex world of criminal justice, severe punishment is unlikely to have the kind of deterrent effect that it does in the controlled conditions of the laboratory.

Given these realities, severe punishment does not seem to deter violent crimes. Countries that invoke the death penalty for murder do not have fewer murders per capita than those without it. Similarly, U.S. states that have abolished the death penalty have not experienced the increase in capital crimes that some experts predicted (Archer & Gartner, 1984; Nathanson, 1987). Ruth Peterson and William Bailey (1988) examined a period in the United States just after a national hiatus on the death penalty, resulting from a Supreme Court ruling that it constituted cruel and unusual punishment. When the Court reversed itself in 1976, there was no indication that the return to capital punishment produced a decrease in homicides. During the past thirty years, the homicide rate in the United States has fluctuated between 6 and 10 murders per year for every 100,000 people in the population (see Figure 12.4). This statistic is striking when one compares it to other industrialized countries like Germany, England, and France, where the homicide rate has remained stable at less than 1 per 100,000. Similarly, a study by the National Academy of Sciences (see Berkowitz, 1993) demonstrated that consistency and certainty of punishment were far more effective deterrents of violent behavior than severe punishment.

Catharsis and Aggression

Conventional wisdom suggests that one way to reduce feelings of aggression is to do something aggressive. "Get it out of your system" has been a common piece of advice for a great many years. So if you are feeling angry (the belief goes), yell, scream, curse, throw a dish at the wall. Express the anger, the wisdom goes, and it won't build up into something truly uncontrollable. This common belief is

FIGURE 12.4

U.S. homicide rate, 1900–2000.

(National Center for Vital Statistics, 2002)

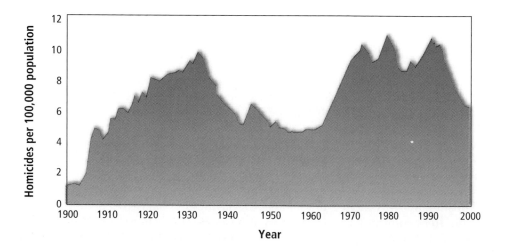

based on an oversimplification of the psychoanalytic notion of **catharsis** (see Dollard, Doob, Miller, Mowrer, & Sears, 1939; Freud, 1933) that has filtered down to the popular culture. As we noted earlier, Freud held a "hydraulic" idea of aggressive impulses; he believed that unless people were allowed to express their aggression in relatively harmless ways, the aggressive energy would be dammed up, pressure would build, and the energy would seek an outlet, either exploding into acts of extreme violence or manifesting itself as symptoms of mental illness.

Some evidence suggests that stifled feelings can produce illness (Pennebaker, 1990; Pennebaker & Francis, 1996), but this does not necessarily mean that venting those feelings indiscriminately is either healthy or useful. Freud was a brilliant and complex thinker whose conclusions and advice were never simplistic. Unfortunately, his theory of catharsis has been boiled down to the dictum that youngsters should be taught to vent their anger. The idea is that blowing off steam will not only make angry people feel better but also serve to make them less likely to engage in subsequent acts of destructive violence. Does this square with the data?

> Something of vengeance I had tasted for the first time; an aromatic wine it seemed, on swallowing, warm and racy; its after-flavour, metallic and corroding, gave me a sensation as if I had been poisoned.
>
> *—Charlotte Brontë, Jane Eyre, 1847*

The Effects of Aggressive Acts on Subsequent Aggression   When frustrated or angry, many of us do feel less tense after blowing off steam by yelling, cursing, or perhaps even hitting someone. But does aggression reduce the need for further aggression? Does playing competitve games, for example, serve as a harmless outlet for our instinctive aggressive drive (Menninger, 1948)? Generally, the answer is no, and in fact, the reverse seems to be true (Patterson, 1974).

Arthur Patterson (1974) measured the hostility of high school football players, rating them both one week before and one week after the football season. If it were true that the intense competitiveness and aggressive behavior that are part of playing football serve to reduce the tension caused by pent-up aggression, the players would be expected to exhibit a decline in hostility over the course of the season. Instead, the results showed that feelings of hostility *increased* significantly.

What about watching aggressive games? Will that reduce aggressive behavior? A Canadian sports psychologist tested this proposition by measuring the hostility of spectators at an especially violent hockey game (Russell, 1983). As the game progressed, the spectators became increasingly belligerent; toward the end of the final period, their level of hostility was extremely high and did not return to the pregame level until several hours after the game was over. Similar results have been found among spectators at football games and wrestling matches (Arms, Russell, & Sandilands, 1979; Branscombe & Wann, 1992; Goldstein & Arms, 1971). As with participating in an aggressive sport, watching one also increases aggressive behavior. Finally, does direct aggression against the source of your anger reduce further aggression? The answer is no (Geen, 1998; Geen & Quanty, 1977). In fact, by far the most common finding resembles the research on watching violence: When people commit acts of aggression, such acts increase the tendency toward future aggression. For example, in an experiment by Russell Geen and his associates (Geen, Stonner, & Shope, 1975), college students were paired with another student who was actually a confederate of the experimenters. First, the student was angered by the confederate; during this phase, which involved the exchanging of opinions on various issues, the student was given phony electric shocks when his partner disagreed with his opinion. Next, during a bogus study of "the effects of punishment on learning," the student acted as a teacher while the confederate served as learner. On the first learning task, some of the students were required to deliver electric shocks to the confederate each time he made a mistake; others merely recorded his errors. On

Catharsis

The notion that "blowing off steam"—by performing an aggressive act, watching others engage in aggressive behaviors, or engaging in a fantasy of aggression—relieves built-up aggressive energies and hence reduces the likelihood of further aggressive behavior

Fans watching aggressive sports do not become less aggressive; in fact, they may become more aggressive than if they hadn't watched at all.

In war, the state is sanctioning murder. Even when the war is over, this moral corruption is bound to linger for many years.

—Erasmus, 1514

the next task, all the students were given the opportunity to deliver shocks. If a cathartic effect were operating, we would expect the students who had previously given shocks to the confederate to administer fewer and less intense shocks the second time. This didn't happen; in fact, those students who had previously delivered shocks to the confederate expressed even greater aggression when given the subsequent opportunity to attack him.

Outside the lab, in the real world, we see the same phenomenon: Verbal acts of aggression are followed by further attacks (Ebbesen, Duncan, & Konecni, 1975). All in all, the weight of the evidence does not support the catharsis hypothesis.

Blaming the Victim of Our Aggression   When somebody angers us, venting our hostility against that person does seem to relieve tension and make us feel better. But "feeling better" should not be confused with a reduction in hostility. With human beings, aggression is dependent not merely on tensions—what a person feels—but also on what a person thinks.

Imagine yourself in the experiments just described. After you've administered what you think are shocks to another person or expressed hostility against your ex-boss, it becomes easier to do so a second time. Aggressing the first time can reduce your inhibitions against committing other such actions; in a sense, the aggression is legitimized, making it easier to carry out such assaults. Further, and more important, the main thrust of the research on this issue indicates that committing an overt act of aggression against a person changes your feelings about that person, increasing your negative feelings toward the target and making future aggression against that person more likely.

Does this material begin to sound familiar? It should. As we saw in Chapter 6, harming someone sets in motion cognitive processes aimed at justifying the act of cruelty. Specifically, when you hurt another person, you experience cognitive dissonance. The cognition "I have hurt Charlie" is dissonant with the cognition "I am a decent, reasonable person." A good way for you to reduce dissonance is somehow to convince yourself that hurting Charlie was not a bad thing to do. You can accomplish this by ignoring Charlie's virtues and emphasizing his faults, by convincing yourself that Charlie is a bad person who deserved to be hurt. This would especially hold if the target was an innocent victim of your aggression. Thus, as in experiments described in Chapter 6 (Davis & Jones, 1960; Glass, 1964), participants inflicted either psychological or physical harm on an innocent person who had done them no prior harm. Participants then derogated their victims, convincing themselves they were not nice people and therefore deserved what they got. This reduces dissonance, all right—and it also sets the stage for further aggression, for once a person has succeeded in derogating someone, it makes it easier to do further harm to the victim in the future.

What happens if the victim isn't totally innocent? For example, what if the victim has done something that hurt or disturbed you and therefore deserves your retaliation? Here the situation becomes more complex and more interesting. One of several experiments to test this idea was performed several years (Kahn, 1966). A young man posing as a medical technician, taking some physiological measurements from college students, made derogatory remarks about the students. In one experimental condition, the participants were allowed to vent their hostility by expressing their feelings about the technician to his

During World War II, we derogated the Japanese by depicting them as less than human. This helped justify our own violence against them, as in the bombing of Nagasaki.

employer—an action that looked as though it would get the technician into serious trouble, perhaps even cost him his job. In another condition, participants did not have the opportunity to express any aggression against the person who had aroused their anger. Those who were allowed to express their aggression subsequently felt greater dislike and hostility for the technician than those who were inhibited from expressing their aggression did. In other words, expressing aggression did not inhibit the tendency to aggress; rather, it tended to *increase* it—even when the target was not simply an innocent victim.

These results suggest that when people are angered, they frequently engage in overkill. In this case, costing the technician his job is much more devastating than the minor insult delivered by the technician. The overkill produces dissonance in much the same way that hurting an innocent person produces dissonance: If there is a major discrepancy between what the person did to you and the force of your retaliation, you must justify that discrepancy by derogating the object of your wrath.

If our reasoning is correct, it might help explain why it is that when two nations are at war, few members of the victorious nation feel much sympathy for the innocent victims of the nation's actions. For example, near the end of World War II, American planes dropped atomic bombs on Hiroshima and Nagasaki. More than one hundred thousand civilians—including a great many children— were killed, and countless thousands suffered severe injuries. Shortly thereafter, a poll taken of the American people indicated that less than 5 percent felt we should not have used those weapons, whereas 23 percent felt we should have used many more of them before giving Japan the opportunity to surrender. Why would so many Americans favor the death and disfigurement of innocent victims? Our guess is that in the course of the war, a sizable proportion of Americans gradually adopted increasingly negative attitudes toward the Japanese that made it increasingly easy to accept the fact that we were causing them a great deal of misery. The more misery we inflicted on them, the more these Americans derogated them—leading to an endless spiral of aggression and the justification of aggression, even to the point of favoring a delay in the ending of the war so that still more destruction might be inflicted.

How could this be? Are Americans such callous, unsympathetic people? We don't believe so. You now have the tools to begin to understand the mechanics of how that phenomenon comes about.

> To jaw-jaw is better than to war-war.
>
> —Winston Churchill, 1954

This spiral of self-justification was bolstered by the way the Japanese people were depicted in American newspapers and magazines as well as in Hollywood films: as sneaky, treacherous, diabolical, and evil (see Chapter 7). After all, they did attack Pearl Harbor without provocation. It is important to note that in our government's information and propaganda campaigns, these traits were specifically attributed to the Japanese people as a whole, not simply their leaders or their military.

Of course, the nature of the propaganda and the details of the justification spiral will vary according to the specific events and the political objectives of the war. With this in mind, it is interesting to compare the war against Japan with the Iraq war of 2003. In World War II, our aim was to defeat Japan as quickly and as totally as possible. The Allies were fighting for our lives. The thinking of our leaders was that if this meant breaking the will of the Japanese people by indiscriminately bombing heavily populated cities, so be it. Indeed, during World War II, the intentional bombing of densely populated cities was a strategy employed by both sides. London, Berlin, Tokyo, Rotterdam, and Dresden were heavily bombed, resulting in a huge loss of civilian life (Aron, 2002).

In contrast, in 2003 the stated American objective was not to conquer Iraq or to break the will of its people but merely to get rid of Saddam Hussein and his weapons of mass destruction. Accordingly, our leaders deemed it important to win the hearts and minds of the people of Iraq so that they would welcome us as liberators and cooperate with us as we endeavored to put a more democratic regime in place. This necessitated a serious attempt to limit "collateral damage" (a chilling military euphemism for the unintentional killing and maiming of noncombatants) and to inform the American people that Iraqi civilians were not the enemy but rather were innocent victims of their ruthless dictator. Because our military killed relatively few civilians, Americans felt no inclination to dislike or derogate the Iraqi people.

The Effect of War on General Aggression

We all know that war is hell, but the consequences of war extend far beyond the battlefield. When a nation is at war, the circumstance has a major impact on the aggressive feelings of its ciitzens. Specifically, when a nation is at war, its people are more likely to commit aggressive acts against one another (Archer & Gartner, 1976, 1984). Crime rates for 110 countries from 1900 on show that compared with similar nations that remained at peace, after a country had fought a war, its homicide rates rose substantially (see Figure 12.5). This is consistent with

FIGURE 12.5

The effects of war on combatants versus noncombatants.

Immediately after a war, combatant countries are more likely to show an increase in violent crimes than countries not involved in a war. How would you explain this?

(Adapted from Archer & Gartner, 1976)

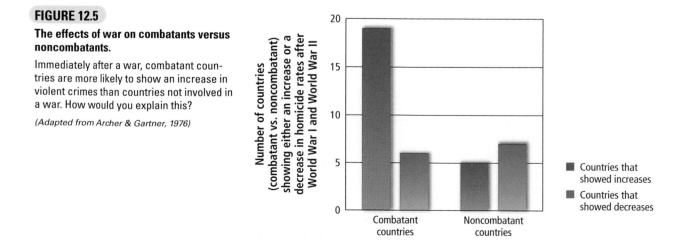

everything we have been saying about the social causes of aggression. In a sense, when a nation is at war, it's like one big, violent TV drama. Just as with overexposure to TV violence, the fact that a nation is at war (1) weakens the population's inhibitions against aggression, (2) leads to imitation of aggression, (3) makes aggressive responses more acceptable, and (4) numbs our senses to the horror of cruelty and destruction, making us less sympathetic toward the victims. In addition, being at war serves to legitimize violence as a way to address difficult problems. This phenomenon is likely to be more powerful now than ever before because thanks to the magic of satellite transmission, we and our children can watch the war unfold in our own living rooms as it happens, twenty-four hours a day.

What Are We Supposed to Do with Our Anger?

If violence leads to self-justification, which in turn breeds more violence, what are we to do with our angry feelings toward someone? Surely, Freud was not totally wrong when he indicated that stifled anger might be harmful to the individual. Indeed, as mentioned earlier, stifling powerful emotions can lead to physical illness (Pennebaker, 1990). But if keeping our feelings bottled up and expressing them are both harmful, what are we supposed to do? The answer is simpler than it might seem.

First, it is possible to control our anger by actively enabling it to dissipate. "Actively enabling" means using such simple devices as counting to ten before speaking (as Thomas Jefferson is said to have recommended). Taking deep breaths or engaging in a distracting activity (working a crossword puzzle, listening to soothing music, taking a bike ride, or even doing a good deed) are good ways of actively enabling the anger to dissipate.

Venting versus Self-Awareness Dissipating anger is not always best for yourself or for a relationship. If your close friend or spouse does something that makes you angry, you may want to express that anger in a way that helps you gain insight into yourself and the dynamics of the relationship. But for that to happen, the anger must be expressed in a nonviolent and nondemeaning way. You can do this (after counting to ten!) by making a clear, calm, and simple statement indicating that you are feeling angry and describing, nonjudgmentally, precisely what your friend or spouse did to bring about those feelings. Such a statement in itself will probably relieve tension and make the angered person feel better. At the same time, because you haven't actually harmed the target of your anger, such a response does not set in motion the cognitive processes that would lead you to justify your behavior by ridiculing or derogating your friend. Moreover, when such feelings are expressed among friends or acquaintances in a clear, open, nonpunitive manner, greater mutual understanding and a strengthening of the friendship can result. It almost seems too simple. Yet we have found such behavior to be a reasonable option that will have more beneficial effects than shouting, name-calling, and throwing dishes, on the one hand, or suffering in silence as you grin and bear it, on the other (Aronson, 1999).

> I was angry with my friend;
> I told my wrath, my wrath did end.
> —William Blake

Although it is probably best to reveal your anger to the friend who provoked it, it can also help to talk about your anger with someone else. In general, when we are experiencing emotional stress, it helps to reveal that emotion to another person (Pennebaker, 1990). In experiments with people undergoing a wide range of traumatic events, those who were induced to reveal the details of the event, as well as their feelings at the time they were experiencing the event, felt healthier and suffered fewer physical illnesses six months later than either people who were allowed to suffer in silence or those who were induced to talk about the details of the events but not the underlying feelings. The benefits of "opening up" are due not simply to the venting of feeling but primarily to the insights and self-awareness that usually accompany such self-disclosure (Pennebaker, 1990).

Some independent corroboration of this suggestion comes from a rather different experiment by Leonard Berkowitz and Bartholomeu Troccoli (1990). In this experiment, young women listened to another woman talk about herself as part of a job interview. Half of the listeners did so while extending their nondominant arm, unsupported (causing discomfort and mild pain), while the others listened with their arms resting comfortably on the table. In each condition, half of the subjects were asked to rate their feelings while they were listening to the job interview; according to the researchers, this procedure provided those subjects with a vehicle for understanding their discomfort and a way to gain insight into it. The results were striking: The subjects who experienced pain and discomfort during the interview but were not given the opportunity to process it experienced the most negative feelings toward the interviewee—and the more unpleasant the experience was for them, the more negative they felt toward the interviewee. By contrast, the subjects who were given the opportunity to process their pain were able to avoid being unfairly harsh to the interviewee.

Defusing Anger through Apology   Earlier, we noted that when people had been frustrated by someone and then learned that the person simply couldn't do any better, that frustration was less likely to bubble over into anger or aggression. This suggests that one way to reduce aggression is for the individual who caused the frustration to take responsibility for the action, apologize for it, and indicate that it is unlikely to happen again. Suppose you are taking a friend to a concert that starts at 8:00 P.M. She's been looking forward to it, and you've arranged to be at her house at 7:30. You leave your house with barely enough time to get there and discover that you have a flat tire. By the time you change the tire and get to her house, you are already twenty minutes late for the concert. Imagine her response if you (a) casually walk in, smile, and say, "Hey, it probably wouldn't have been such a good concert anyway. Lighten up; it's not a big deal" or (b) run in looking upset, show her your dirty hands, explain what happened, tell her you left your house in time to make it but got a flat, apologize sincerely, and vow to make it up to her.

We would predict that your friend would be prone toward aggression in the first case but not in the second, and a host of experiments support our prediction (Baron, 1988, 1990; Ohbuchi & Sato, 1994; Weiner, Amirkhan, Folkes, & Verette, 1987). Typically, any apology sincerely given and in which the perpetrator took full responsibility was effective at reducing aggression.

With this in mind, Elliot Aronson has speculated about the great advantages that might be gained by equipping automobiles with "apology" signals. Picture the scene: You stop at a stop sign and then proceed, but too late you realize that the right of way wasn't really yours. What happens? In most urban centers, the offended driver will honk angrily at you or open the window and give you that ancient near-universal symbol of anger and contempt that consists of the middle finger pointed skyward (Wagner & Armstrong, 2003). Because nobody likes to be the recipient of such abuse, you might be tempted to honk back—and the escalating anger and aggression produces classic "road rage." Such escalation might be avoided, though, if in addition to the horn (which throughout the world is most often used as an instrument of aggression), every car were equipped with an apology signal—perhaps at the push of a button, a little flag could pop up, saying, "Oops! Sorry!" In the foregoing scenario, had you pushed such a button as soon as you became aware of your transgression, you might have defused the cycle of anger and retaliation.

The Modeling of Nonaggressive Behavior We've seen that children will be more aggressive (toward dolls as well as other children) if they've seen people behaving aggressively in similar situations. What if we reverse the situation and expose children to nonaggressive models—to people who, when provoked, expressed themselves in a restrained, rational, pleasant manner? This has been tested in several experiments (Baron, 1972; Donnerstein & Donnerstein, 1976; Vidyasagar & Mishra, 1993) and found to work. In those experiments, children first watched youngsters behaving nonaggressively when provoked. Later, when the children were put in a situation in which they themselves were provoked, they were much less likely to respond aggressively than children who had not seen the nonaggressive models.

Training in Communication and Problem-Solving Skills It is impossible to go through life—or sometimes to get through the day—without experiencing frustration, annoyance, anger, or conflict. Feeling anger is part of being human, but what causes the problem is the *expression* of anger in violent ways. Yet we are not born knowing how to express anger or annoyance in constructive, nonviolent, nondisruptive ways. Indeed, it seems almost natural to lash out when we are angry. In most societies, it is precisely the people who lack proper social skills who are most prone to violent solutions to interpersonal problems (Toch, 1980). One way to reduce violence, then, is to teach people such techniques as how to communicate anger or criticism in constructive ways, how to negotiate and compromise when conflicts arise, and how to be more sensitive to the needs and desires of others.

There is some evidence that such formal training can be an effective means of reducing aggression (Studer, 1996). For example, in a classic experiment by Joel Davitz (1952), children were allowed to play in groups of four. Some of these groups were taught constructive ways to relate to one another and were rewarded for such behavior; others were rewarded for aggressive or competitive behavior. Next, the children were deliberately frustrated. They were told that

> Man must evolve for all human conflict a method which rejects revenge, aggression, and retaliation.
>
> —*Martin Luther King Jr., Nobel Prize acceptance speech, 1964*

Martin Luther King Jr. was effective in reducing and preventing violence by using and modeling nonviolence. Being nonviolent in the face of violence is difficult but effective.

they would see some entertaining movies and would be allowed to have fun. The experimenter began to show a movie and to hand out candy bars, but then he abruptly stopped the movie at the point of highest interest and took the candy bars away. Now the children were allowed to play freely as the researchers watched for aggressive or constructive behavior. The results? Children who had been trained for constructive behavior showed far more constructive activity and far less aggressive behavior than those in the other group.

Many elementary and secondary schools now train students to employ nonaggressive strategies for resolving conflict (Eargle, Guerra, & Tolan, 1994; Educators for Social Responsibility, 2001).

Building Empathy Let's look at horn-blowing again. Picture the following scene: A long line of cars is stopped at a traffic light at a busy intersection; the light turns green; the lead car hesitates for ten seconds. What happens? Almost inevitably, there will be an eruption of horn-honking. In a controlled experiment, Robert Baron (1976) found that when the lead car failed to move after the light turned green, almost 90 percent of the drivers of the second car honked their horn in a relentless, aggressive manner. As part of the same experiment, a pedestrian crossed the street between the first and the second car while the light was still red and was out of the intersection by the time the light turned green.

As you might imagine, this did not have an effect on the behavior of the drivers of the next car in line—almost 90 percent honked their horn when the light turned green. But in another condition, the pedestrian was on crutches. He hobbled across the street before the light turned green. Interestingly, however, in this condition, only 57 percent of the drivers honked their horn. How come? Apparently, seeing a person on crutches evoked feelings of empathy, which you will recall from Chapter 11 is the ability to put oneself in the shoes of another person and vicariously experience some of the same feelings that person is experiencing. In this instance, once evoked, the feeling of empathy infused the consciousness of the potential horn-honkers and decreased their urge to be aggressive.

Most people find it difficult to inflict pain on a stranger unless they can find a way to dehumanize their victim (Feshbach & Feshbach, 1969; N.D. Feshbach, 1978; S. Feshbach, 1971). Thus when the United States was fighting wars against Asians (Japanese in the 1940s, Koreans in the 1950s, Vietnamese in the 1960s), military personnel frequently referred to them as "gooks." We see this as a dehumanizing rationalization for acts of cruelty; it's easier to commit violent acts against someone you think is subhuman than against a fellow human being. This kind of rationalization guarantees that we will continue to aggress against that person. Once we accept that our enemy is not really human, it lowers our inhibitions for committing all kinds of atrocities.

Understanding the process of dehumanization is the first step toward reversing it. Specifically, if it is true that most individuals must dehumanize their victims in order to commit an extreme act of aggression, then by building empathy among people, aggressive acts should be more difficult to commit. The research data lend strong support to this contention. In one study, students who had been trained to empathize—that is, to take the perspective of the other person—behaved far less aggressively toward that person than students who had not received the training (Richardson, Hammock, Smith, & Gardner, 1994). In a similar study, Japanese students were told to shock another student as part of a learning experiment (Ohbuchi & Baba, 1988; Ohbuchi, Ohno, & Mukai, 1993). In one condition, the "victims" first revealed something personal about themselves; in the other condition, they were not given this opportunity. Participants gave less severe shocks to the "victim" who had revealed personal information.

CONNECTIONS

Teaching Empathy in School

"What would the world look like to you if you were as small as a cat?" "What birthday present would make each member of your family happiest?" These questions form the basis of some of the exercises for elementary school children in Los Angeles who participated in a thirty-hour program designed by Norma Feshbach, who has pioneered the teaching of empathy in elementary schools. Thinking hard about the answers to such questions expands children's ability to put themselves in another's situation. In addition, the children listened to stories and then retold them from the point of view of each of the different characters in each story. The children played the role of each of the characters. The performances were videotaped. The children then viewed the tapes and analyzed how people look and sound when they express different feelings.

At the end of the program, the children not only had learned to be more empathic but also showed higher self-esteem, greater generosity, more positive attitudes, and less aggressiveness than students who had not participated in the program.

At first glance, such a program may seem unrelated to academics. Yet role playing and close analysis of stories is just what students do when putting on a play or analyzing a piece of literature. Interestingly, in reminiscing about his childhood, the Nobel Prize-winning physicist Richard Feynman reported that his father challenged his intellect by asking him to pretend he was a tiny creature living in their living room carpet. To deal with that challenge, Feynman needed, in effect, to crawl into the skin and persona of that tiny creature and get a feel for what his life would be like in those circumstances. Such questions also encourage the kind of cognitive flexibility taught in corporate creativity programs. Accordingly, it should not surprise us when Norma Feshbach reports that students who have learned to develop greater empathic ability also tend to have higher academic achievement (Feshbach, 1989, 1997).

One study has shown that children who were taught to put themselves in others' shoes, to be empathic, exhibited higher self-esteem, greater generosity, and less aggressiveness.

COULD THE COLUMBINE MASSACRE HAVE BEEN PREVENTED?

At the beginning of this chapter, we described the massacre at Columbine High School as well as other recent school shootings and discussed some of the speculations about what might have caused those horrifying events. The key question is, could those events have been prevented? Before we can hope to prevent such events, we must have some idea as to their cause. After reading this chapter, perhaps you can see that several factors might have been involved—factors such as the easy availability of guns and the prevalence of violence in the media and in video games. But these factors are almost certainly not the root cause of these shootings. It is also possible that the shooters were crazy. In his analysis of the Columbine massacre, Elliot Aronson (2000), while acknowledging that these violent acts were pathological, suggested that it would be a serious mistake to dismiss them as "simply" the result of individual pathology and let it go at that. Such an explanation leads nowhere, because Harris and Klebold (as well as the other recent school shooters) were functioning quite effectively. They were getting good grades, attended class regularly, and did not present serious behavior problems to their parents or to the school authorities. True, they were loners and they did dress in a strange manner. But this was typical of hundreds of other students at Columbine High School. In short, their pathological behavior was not readily predictable from their day-to-day interactions with parents, teachers, or friends. It was not even detected by Eric Harris's psychiatrist (whose care he was under for a mild depression). This was not due to negligence on the part of these adults; it was due to the fact that Harris and Klebold's observable behavior was not far from the norm.

But more important, to dismiss this horrifying deed as "merely" the result of mental illness would lead us to miss something of vital importance, something that might help us prevent similar tragedies in the future: the power of the social situation. Specifically, Aronson (2000) argued that the spate of school shootings may be the pathological tip of a very large iceberg.

Harris and Klebold were almost certainly reacting in an extremely pathological manner to a general school atmosphere that creates an environment of exclusion, mockery, and taunting, making life difficult for a sizable number of students. Most high schools are cliquish places where students are shunned if they are the "wrong" race or the "wrong" ethnic group, if they come from the wrong side of the tracks, wear the wrong clothes, are too short, too fat, too tall, or too thin.

After the shootings, Columbine students recalled that Harris and Klebold suffered greatly by being taunted and bullied by the in-group. Indeed, one student, a member of the in-group, justified this behavior by saying:

> "Most kids didn't want them there. They were into witchcraft. They were into voodoo. Sure we teased them. But what do you expect with kids who come to school with weird hairdos and horns on their hats? If you want to get rid of someone, usually you tease 'em. So the whole school would call them homos. . . ." (Gibbs & Roche, 1999, p. 154)

The image that many young people can identify with is that of a lone student, standing in the cafeteria with a tray full of food, searching the crowded room in vain for a friendly face who might welcome the student to join a group at a table. Describing the alienating nature of the underlying social atmosphere is not intended to excuse the behavior of Harris and Klebold, merely to try to understand it so that we might try to prevent further occurrences of this kind.

This specific analysis of what might have been going on in the young men's minds is supported by the videocassette they left behind, which depicts them angrily talking about the insults and bullying they experienced at Columbine. According to psychiatrist James Gilligan (1996), the director of mental health for the Massachusetts prison system, the motivation behind the vast majority of rampage killings is an attempt to transform feelings of shame and humiliation into feelings of pride. "Perhaps now we will get the respect we deserve," said Klebold on the videotape, brandishing a sawed-off shotgun.

Aronson's analysis received more general support from the dozens of messages submitted to Internet chat groups in the immediate aftermath of the Columbine massacre. The overwhelming majority expressed anguish and unhappiness, describing how awful it feels to be rejected and taunted by more popular classmates. Several months before the Harris-Klebold videotapes were released, many of the writers were convinced that Harris and Klebold must have had similar experiences of rejection and exclusion. We hasten to note that none of these teenagers condoned the shootings; yet their Internet postings revealed a surprisingly high degree of understanding and empathy for the suffering the two adolescents must have endured. Most students suffer in silence—but they do suffer. Some contemplate suicide; according to recent research, 20 percent of all high school students have seriously contemplated suicide (Aronson, 2000). Thus far, blessedly few go so far over the edge that they blast away at their fellow students.

A typical Internet posting was written by a 16-year-old girl, who said: "I know how they feel. Parents need to realize that a kid is not overreacting all the time they say that no one accepts them. Also, all of the popular conformists need to learn to accept everyone else. Why do they shun everyone who is different?" If Aronson's analysis of the Columbine massacre is correct, then it should be possible to make our schools safer by bringing about a change in the negative, exclusionary social atmosphere. If one could achieve this, not only would it make the schools safer, but it would make them more pleasant, more exciting, and more humane as well. A clue as to how this might come about comes from two lines of research discussed in this chapter: the success of Dan Olweus's program to reduce bullying in the schools of Norway and Norma and Seymour Feshbach's successful attempt to build empathy among schoolchildren in the United States. These and other successful programs will be discussed in greater detail in the following chapter.

We end here with a letter from a Columbine parent.

June 18, 2002

Dear Dr. Aronson,

As a parent of a Columbine High School student whose life was spared but forever changed by the events of April 20, 1999, I am compelled to write to thank you for your powerful book. In just a few short pages, you have summarized all that I have been feeling about the complexity of the events that preceded that horrific day. In addition, you have provided insight into how we can create healthy school environments so that such tragedies can become a thing of the past.

I must tell you that I . . . have intentionally avoided all books and articles about Columbine because so many people have attempted to gather up the loose ends and tattered pieces of April 20th and then tie them up in ribbons of simplistic self-righteousness. However, . . . your book Nobody Left to Hate *offers deep insight into the situation and actually suggests solutions that renounce the typical "pump-handle" responses. I believe that your simple strategies for classroom organization and interaction can truly make a difference.*

Again, I thank you.
Carolyn L. Mears
Littleton, Colorado

SUMMARY

What Is Aggression?

Aggression is intentional behavior aimed at doing harm or causing pain to another person. **Hostile aggression** involves having the goal of inflicting pain; **instrumental aggression** involves inflicting pain on the way to some other goal. Aggression has become an increasingly serious concern to Americans because of the rapid increase in violent crimes, especially in major urban centers.

Over the centuries, scholars have disagreed over whether aggressiveness is primarily instinctive or learned. Sigmund Freud theorized that human beings are born with an instinct toward life, called **Eros,** and a death instinct, **Thanatos.** The death instinct, when turned inward, manifests itself as suicide and, when turned outward, as hostility, destructiveness, and murder. Freud's hydraulic theory states that aggressive energy must be released to avoid a buildup resulting in an explosion.

Because aggressiveness has had survival value, most contemporary social psychologists accept the proposition that it is part of our evolutionary heritage. At the same time, we know that human beings have developed exquisite mechanisms for controlling their aggressive impulses and that human behavior is flexible and adaptable to changes in the environment. Whether or not aggression is actually expressed therefore depends on a complex interplay between our biological propensities, our innate and learned inhibitory responses, and the precise nature of the social situation.

Neural and Chemical Influences on Aggression

There are many factors that arouse aggression, from the neurological and chemical to the social. The area in the core of the brain called the **amygdala** is thought to control aggression. Recent evidence suggests that the chemical **serotonin** serves to inhibit aggressive behavior. When the body's natural production of serotonin is disrupted, aggression increases. It is also reasonably clear that the hormone **testosterone** is positively correlated with aggressive behavior; prisoners convicted of violent crimes tend to have higher levels of testosterone than those convicted of nonviolent crimes. This is consistent with the more general finding that men are more aggressive than women. At least one other chemical, alcohol, is associated with increases in aggression, due to the fact that alcohol acts as a general disinhibitor, lowering a person's inhibitions against violent behavior as well as a variety of other behaviors frowned on by society. It has also been shown that pain and other physical discomforts will increase aggressive behavior.

Social Situations Leading to Aggression

Many causes of aggression are social. Among these, frustration is prominent. The **frustration-aggression theory** states that the experience of frustration can increase the probability of an aggressive response. However, frustration alone does not automatically lead to aggression; it is more likely to produce aggression if one is thwarted on the way to a goal in a manner that is either illegitimate or unexpected. In addition, frustration is the result not simply of deprivation but of relative deprivation—the feeling that you have less than what you deserve, less than what you have been led to expect, or less than what people similar to you have.

Aggression can also be produced by social provocation or the mere presence of an **aggressive stimulus,** or an object associated with aggressive responses, such as a gun. **Social learning theory** states that aggression can also be produced through the imitation of aggressive models, either in face-to-face situations or by viewing violence in films or on TV. The possible effects of viewing violence in the media are of particular interest to social psychologists in our country because of the pervasiveness of violent programming. Violence in the media has been shown not only to lead to greater aggressiveness in the viewer but also to create a numbing effect, making us more accepting of violence in society. The viewing of pornographic material appears to be relatively harmless; however, if the pornographic material depicts hostile acts directed against women, it promotes greater acceptance of sexual violence toward women and is almost certainly a factor associated with actual aggressive behavior toward women.

How to Reduce Aggression

Aggression can be reduced in a number of ways. These include distracting ourselves from the anger, discussing the reasons for anger and hostility, modeling nonaggressive behavior, training people in the use of nonviolent solutions to conflict and in communication and negotiation skills, and building people's empathy toward others. Building empathy is particularly useful as a means of thwarting the human tendency to dehumanize one's victim.

Punishing aggressive behavior in order to reduce it is tricky; punishment can be effective if it is not too severe and if it follows closely on the heels of the aggressive act. But severe or delayed punishment is not an effective way to reduce aggression. Similarly, there is no evidence to support the notion of **catharsis**—the idea that committing an aggressive action or watching others behave aggressively is a good way to get the impulse toward aggression out of one's system. On the contrary, careful research has shown that committing an act of aggression can trigger the tendency to justify that action and might thus eventually produce an increase in aggressive behavior.

Could the Columbine Massacre Have Been Prevented?

A humiliating social atmosphere prevalent in high schools may have been one of the root causes of the Columbine massacre. Changing that atmosphere might be an effective way of reducing the frequency of such occurrences.

CRITICAL THINKING QUESTIONS

1. Is it important to know whether aggressiveness in humans is inborn? Why or why not?

2. Does exposure to violence in the media make people more violent?

3. Everyone who has gone to public school knows that schoolyard bullying is a pervasive problem. How might bullying be reduced?

Prejudice:

Causes and Cures

I n the 1930s, when Thurgood Marshall was a young lawyer working for the National Association for the Advancement of Colored People (NAACP), he was sent to a small town in the South to defend a black man who was accused of a serious crime. When he arrived, he was shocked and dismayed to learn that the defendant was already dead—lynched by an angry white mob. With a heavy heart, Marshall returned to the railroad station to wait for a train back to New York. While waiting, he realized he was hungry and noticed a small food stand on the platform. Walking toward the stand, he debated whether to go right up to the front and order a sandwich (as was his legal right) or to go around to the back of the stand (as was the common practice for African Americans in the South at that time). But before he reached the stand, he was approached by a large, heavyset white man who looked at him suspiciously. Marshall took him to be a lawman of some sort because he walked with an air of authority and had a bulge in his pants pocket that could only have been made by a handgun.

"Hey, boy," the man shouted at Marshall. "What are you doing here?"

"I'm just waiting for a train," Marshall replied. The man scowled, took a few steps closer, glared at him menacingly, and said, "I didn't hear you. What did you say, boy?"

Marshall realized that his initial reply had not been sufficiently obsequious. "I beg your pardon, sir, but I'm waiting for a train." There was a long silence, during which the man slowly looked Marshall up and down, and then said, "And you'd better catch that train, boy—and soon, because in this town, the sun has never set on a live nigger."

As Marshall later recalled, at that point his debate about how to get the sandwich proved academic. He decided not to get a sandwich at all but to catch the very next train out—no matter where it was headed. Besides, somehow he didn't feel hungry anymore (Williams, 1998).

Thurgood Marshall's distinguished career spanned an incredible period of increased justice for minorities in this country. Needless to say, Marshall was a major contributor to that progress.

Thurgood Marshall went on to become chief counsel for the NAACP; in 1954, he argued the case of *Brown* v. *Board of Education* before the U.S. Supreme Court. His victory there put an end to legalized racial segregation in public schools. Subsequently, Marshall was appointed to the Supreme Court, where he served with distinction until his retirement in 1991. We are not sure what became of the man with the bulge in his pocket.

Of all the social behaviors we discuss in this book, prejudice is among the most common and the most dangerous. Prejudice touches nearly everyone's life. We are all victims or potential victims of stereotyping and discrimination, for no other reason than our membership in an identifiable group, whether on the basis of ethnicity, religion, gender, national origin, sexual orientation, body size, or disability—to name a few.

More than seventy years have passed since the incident involving the future Justice Marshall. No one can deny that the civil rights movement made enormous progress during his lifetime. But even though manifestations of prejudice today tend to be both less frequent and less flagrant than they used to be, prejudice continues to exact a heavy toll on its victims. There are still hate crimes, church burnings, and countless miscellaneous acts of prejudice-induced violence, as well as "lesser" outrages like the futility of trying to get a cab to stop for you late at night in an American metropolis if you happen to be a black man (Fountain, 1997).

Moreover, on a wide variety of important social issues, a huge racial divide exists in this country in terms of attitude and experience. While sophisticated observers have long been aware of this divide, it was brought home with stunning force in the mid-1990s during the trial of O. J. Simpson for the murders of his ex-wife, Nicole Brown Simpson, and her friend, Ronald Goldman. The trial captured the rapt attention of millions of Americans, but from the outset, it seemed as if white Americans and black Americans were watching two different trials. Overwhelmingly, whites believed Simpson was guilty; and overwhelmingly, blacks found the evidence unconvincing at best.

Social critics will be pondering this particular example of the "racial divide" for many years to come. Among other things, they will try to decide whether this huge difference was due to differences among the racial groups in their respective experiences with the criminal justice system or differences in the degree to which they found the defendant to be attractive and sympathetic (Bugliosi, 1997; Cochran & Rutten, 1998; Dershowitz, 1997; Gates, 1995; Petroselli & Knobler, 1998; Toobin, 1995). In order to understand this phenomenon and others like it, we must take a long look at prejudice as a social psychological phenomenon.

PREJUDICE:
THE UBIQUITOUS SOCIAL PHENOMENON

It would be wrong to conclude that only minority groups are the targets of prejudice at the hands of the dominant majority. Of course, this aspect of prejudice is both powerful and poignant. But the truth is that prejudice is ubiquitous; in one form or another, it affects us all. For one thing, prejudice is a two-way street; it often flows from the minority group to the majority group as well as in the other direction. And any group can be a target of prejudice.

Let us take one of the most superordinate groups to which you belong—your nationality. As you well know, Americans are not universally loved, respected, and admired; at one time or another, we Americans have been the target of prejudice in just about every corner of the world. In the 1960s and 1970s, North Vietnamese Communists referred to Americans as the "running dogs of capitalist imperialism." In the twenty-first century, the majority of people living in the Middle East think of America as a ruthless, power-hungry, amoral nation, referring to us as "the great Satan." In our own hemisphere, many of our neighbors to the south consider us overfed economic and military bullies.

On a more subtle level, even our political allies do not always see us clearly. For example, in research on stereotyping, it turns out that British citizens tend to label Americans as intrusive, forward, pushy, and excessively patriotic (Campbell, 1967). This is not a recent development: Historian Simon Schama (2003) points out that the British and other Europeans have held such stereotypes of Americans for at least two hundred years. But stereotyping cuts both ways: Americans tend to label the British as cold, unemotional, and detached. Similarly, during the U.N. debates prior to the invasion of Iraq in 2002, the French viewed Americans as brash and bellicose, while Americans viewed the French as cowardly appeasers.

Your nationality is only one of a number of aspects of your identity that can cause you to be labeled and discriminated against. Racial and ethnic identity is a major focal point for prejudiced attitudes. All Americans of mixed heritage and nationality (e.g., African Americans, Asian Americans, Hispanic Americans, or Native Americans) are targets of prejudice. So are some groups of Anglo or white Americans: Note the long-standing popularity of Polish jokes or the negative stereotypes used over the past century to describe Italian Americans and Irish Americans. Other aspects of your identity also leave you vulnerable to prejudice—for example, your gender, your sexual orientation, and your religion. Your appearance or physical state can arouse prejudice as well; obesity, disabilities, and diseases like AIDS, for instance, cause people to be treated unfairly by others.

Or consider the old stereotype that blondes are ditzy bimbos. Finally, even your profession or hobbies can lead to your being stereotyped. We all know the "dumb jock" and the "computer nerd" stereotypes. Some people have negative attitudes about blue-collar workers; others, about Fortune 500 CEOs. The point is that none of us emerges completely unscathed by prejudice; it is a problem common to all humankind.

In addition to being widespread, prejudice is dangerous. Simple dislike of a group can be relentless and can escalate to extreme hatred, to thinking of its members as less than human, and to torture, murder, and even genocide. But even when murder or genocide is not the culmination of prejudiced beliefs, the targets of prejudice will suffer in less dramatic ways. One nearly inevitable consequence of being the target of relentless prejudice is a diminution of one's self-esteem. As we discussed in Chapter 6, self-esteem is a vital aspect of a person's life. Who we think we are is a key determinant of how we behave and who we become. A person with low self-esteem will, by definition, conclude that he or she is

> A little black girl yearns for the blue eyes of a little white girl, and the horror at the heart of her yearning is exceeded only by the evil of fulfillment.
> —Toni Morrison, The Bluest Eye

unworthy of a good education, a decent job, an exciting romantic partner, and so on. Thus a person with low self-esteem is more likely to be unhappy and unsuccessful than a person with well-grounded high self-esteem. In a democracy, such a person is also less likely to take advantage of available opportunities.

Prejudice and Self-Esteem

For the targets of relentless prejudice, the seeds of low selfesteem are usually sown early in life. In a classic experiment conducted in the late 1940s, social psychologists Kenneth Clark and Mamie Clark (1947) demonstrated that African American children—some of them only 3 years old—were already convinced that it was not particularly desirable to be black. In this experiment, the children were offered a choice between playing with a white doll and playing with a black doll. The great majority of them rejected the black doll, feeling that the white doll was prettier and generally superior.

In his argument before the Supreme Court in 1954, Thurgood Marshall cited this experiment as evidence that psychologically, segregation did irreparable harm to the selfesteem of African American children. Taking this evidence into consideration, the Court ruled that separating black children from white children on the basis of race alone "generates a feeling of inferiority as to their status in the community that may affect their hearts and minds in a way unlikely ever to be undone. . . . Separate educational facilities are therefore inherently unequal" (Justice Earl Warren, speaking for the majority in the case of *Brown* v. *Board of Education of Topeka*, 1954).

Lowered self-esteem has affected other oppressed groups as well. For example, Philip Goldberg (1968) demonstrated that like African Americans, women in this culture had learned to consider themselves intellectually inferior to men. In his experiment, Goldberg asked female college students to read scholarly articles and to evaluate them in terms of their competence and writing style. For some students, specific articles were signed by male authors (e.g., "John T. McKay"), while for others, the same articles were signed by female authors (e.g., "Joan T. McKay"). The female students rated the articles much higher if they were attributed to a male author than if the same articles were attributed to a female author. In other words, these women had learned their place; they regarded the output of other women as inferior to that of men, just as the African American youngsters learned to regard black dolls as inferior to white dolls. This is the legacy of a prejudiced society.

A Progress Report

Clark and Clark's experiment was conducted more than fifty years ago; Goldberg's, more than thirty. Significant changes have taken place in American society since then. For example, the number of blatant acts of overt prejudice and discrimination has decreased sharply, legislation on affirmative action has opened the door to greater opportunities for women and minorities, and the media have increased our exposure to women and minorities doing important work in positions of power and influence. As one might expect, these changes are reflected in the gradual increase in self-esteem of people in these groups, an increase underscored by the fact that most recent research has failed to replicate the results of those earlier experiments. African American children have gradually become more content with black dolls than they were in 1947 (Gopaul-McNicol, 1987; Porter, 1971; Porter & Washington, 1979, 1989), and people no longer discriminate against a piece of writing simply because it is attributed to a woman (Swim, 1994; Swim, Borgida, Maruyama, & Myers, 1989). Similarly, recent research suggests that there might not be any major differences in global self-esteem between blacks and whites or between men and women (Aronson,

If an African American girl believes that white dolls are more desirable than black dolls, should we be concerned about her self-esteem?

Quinn, & Spencer, 1998; Crocker & Major, 1989; Steele, 1992, 1997). While this progress is real, it would be a mistake to conclude that prejudice has ceased to be a serious problem in the United States. As mentioned earlier, prejudice exists in countless subtle and not-so-subtle ways. For the most part, in America, prejudice has gone underground and become less overt (Pettigrew, 1985, 1989). During the past half-century, social psychologists have contributed greatly to our understanding of the psychological processes underlying prejudice and have begun to identify and demonstrate some possible solutions. What is prejudice? How does it come about? How can it be reduced?

PREJUDICE, STEREOTYPING, AND DISCRIMINATION

Prejudice is an attitude. As we discussed in Chapter 7, attitudes are made up of three components: an affective or emotional component, representing both the type of emotion linked with the attitude (e.g., anger, warmth) and the extremity of the attitude (e.g., mild uneasiness, outright hostility); a cognitive component, involving the beliefs or thoughts (cognitions) that make up the attitude; and a behavioral component, relating to one's actions—people don't simply hold attitudes; they usually act on them as well.

As these headlines show, anyone can be the target of prejudice.

Prejudice: The Affective Component

Prejudice refers to the general attitude structure and its affective (emotional) component. Technically, there are positive and negative prejudices. For example, you could be prejudiced against Texans or prejudiced in favor of Texans. In one case, your emotional reaction is negative; when a person is introduced to you as "This is Bob from Texas," you will expect him to act in particular ways that you associate with "those obnoxious Texans." Conversely, if your emotional reaction is positive, you will be delighted to meet another one of "those wonderful, uninhibited Texans," and you'll expect Bob to demonstrate many positive qualities, such as warmth and friendliness. While prejudice can involve either positive or negative affect, social psychologists (and people in general) use the word *prejudice* primarily when referring to negative attitudes about others. In this context, **prejudice** is a hostile or negative attitude toward people in a distinguishable group, based *solely* on their membership in that group. For example, when we say that someone is prejudiced against blacks, we mean that he or she is primed to behave coolly or with hostility toward blacks and that he or she feels that all blacks are pretty much the same. Thus the characteristics this individual assigns to blacks are negative and applied to the group as a whole. The individual traits or behaviors of the individual target of prejudice will either go unnoticed or be dismissed.

Stereotypes: The Cognitive Component

Close your eyes for a moment and imagine the looks and characteristics of the following people: a high school cheerleader, a New York cab driver, a Jewish doctor, a black musician. Our guess is that this task was not difficult. We all walk around with images of various "types" of people in our heads. The distinguished

Prejudice

A hostile or negative attitude toward a distinguishable group of people, based solely on their membership in that group

Is this roughly the stereotypical image that comes to mind when you are asked to imagine a New York cab driver?

journalist Walter Lippmann (1922), who was the first to introduce the term *stereotype*, described the distinction between the world out there and stereotypes—"the little pictures we carry around inside our heads." Within a given culture, these pictures tend to be remarkably similar. For example, we would be surprised if your image of the high school cheerleader was anything but bouncy, peppy, pretty, nonintellectual, and (of course!) female. We would also be surprised if the Jewish doctor or the New York cab driver in your head was female—or if the black musician was playing classical music.

It goes without saying that there are male cheerleaders, women doctors who are Jewish, and black classical musicians. Deep down, we know that New York cab drivers come in every size, shape, race, and gender. But we tend to categorize according to what we regard as normative. And within a given culture, what people regard as normative is very similar, in part because these images are perpetuated and broadcast widely by the media of that culture. Stereotyping, however, goes a step beyond simple categorization. A **stereotype** is a generalization about a group of people in which identical characteristics are assigned to virtually all members of the group, regardless of actual variation among the members. Once formed, stereotypes are resistant to change on the basis of new information.

But be aware that stereotyping is not necessarily emotional and does not necessarily lead to intentional acts of abuse. Often stereotyping is merely a technique we use to simplify how we look at the world—and we all do it to some extent. For example, Gordon Allport (1954) described stereotyping as "the law of least effort." According to Allport, the world is just too complicated for us to have a highly differentiated attitude about everything. Instead, we maximize our cognitive time and energy by developing elegant, accurate attitudes about some topics while relying on simple, sketchy beliefs for others. (Recall the many facets of social cognition that we discussed in Chapter 3.) Given our limited capacity for processing information, it is reasonable for human beings to behave like "cognitive misers"—to take shortcuts and adopt certain rules of thumb in our attempt to understand other people (Fiske, 1989b; Fiske & Depret, 1996; Jones, 1990; Taylor, 1981). To the extent that the resulting stereotype is based on experience and is at all accurate, it can be an adaptive shorthand way of dealing with complex events. However, if the stereotype blinds us to individual differences within a class of people, it is maladaptive, unfair, and potentially abusive. (See the Try It! exercise on page 435.)

Sports, Race, and Attribution The potential abuse of stereotyping's mental shortcuts can be blatant and obvious—as when one ethnic group is considered lazy or another ethnic group is considered greedy. But the potential abuse can be more subtle—and it might even involve a stereotype about a positive attribute. For example, in 1992, Twentieth Century Fox produced an amusing film about two-on-two street basketball (starring Wesley Snipes, Woody Harrelson, and Rosie Perez) called *White Men Can't Jump*. The implication is that African American men are better at basketball than white men. Well, it turns out that during the past twenty-five years, some 75 to 80 percent of the players in the National Basketball Association have been African American (Gladwell, 1997; Hoose, 1989). This figure is far greater than one would expect from comparative population statistics (approximately 13 percent of the U.S. population is African American).

So what here is abusive to the minority? What's wrong with the implication that black men can jump? The abuse enters when we ignore the overlap in the distributions—that is, when we ignore the fact that a great many African American kids are not adept at basketball and a great many white kids are. Thus if we meet a young African American man and are astonished at his ineptitude on the basketball court, we are, in a very real sense, denying him his individuality. And there is ample evidence that this kind of potentially abusive stereotyping

Stereotype

A generalization about a group of people in which identical characteristics are assigned to virtually all members of the group, regardless of actual variation among the members

Try it!

Stereotype and Aggression

Close your eyes. Imagine a very aggressive construction worker. How is this person dressed, where is this person located, and what, specifically, is this person doing to express aggression? Write it all down, being specific about the person's actions.

Now imagine a very aggressive lawyer. How is this person dressed, where is this person located, and what, specifically, is this person doing to express aggression? Write it all down, being specific about the person's actions.

If you are like the experimental subjects in a research study, your stereotype of the construction worker and of the lawyer would have influenced the way you construed the term *aggression:* Most of the study subjects imagined the construction worker using physical aggression and the lawyer using verbal aggression (Kunda, Sinclair, & Griffin, 1997).

occurs (Brinson & Robinson, 1991; Edwards, 1973). In a clever experiment, college students listened to a twenty-minute audiotape recording of a college basketball game. They were asked to focus on one of the players, Mark Flick, and were allowed to look at a folder containing information about him, including a photograph—allegedly of Flick. Half of the participants saw a photo of an African American male; the others saw a photo of a white male. After listening to the game, the students rated Flick's performance. Their ratings reflected the prevailing stereotypes: Students who believed Flick was African American rated him as having more athletic ability and as having played a better game than those who thought he was white. Those who thought he was white rated him as having greater hustle and greater basketball sense (Stone, Perry, & Darley, 1997).

Stereotypes, Attribution, and Gender   A particularly interesting manifestation of stereotyping takes place in the perception of gender differences. Almost universally, women are thought to be more nurturant and less assertive than men (Deaux & Lewis, 1984). It is possible that this perception may be entirely role-related—that is, women have traditionally been assigned the role of homemaker and thus may be seen as more nurturant (see Deaux & La France, 1998). At the other end of the continuum, evolutionary social psychologists (Buss, 1995, 1996b; Buss & Kenrick, 1998) suggest that female behavior and male behavior differ in precisely those domains in which the sexes have faced different adaptive problems. From a Darwinian perspective, there are powerful biological reasons why women might have evolved as more nurturant than men. Specifically, among our ancient ancestors, for anatomical reasons, women were always the early caregivers of infants; women who were not nurturant did not have many babies who survived. Therefore, their nonnurturing genes were less likely to be passed on.

Although there is no clear way of determining whether or not caregiving is more likely to be part of a woman's genetic nature than a man's, it does turn out that the cultural stereotype is not far from reality. Research has shown that compared to men, women do tend to manifest behaviors that can best be described as more socially sensitive, friendlier, and more concerned with the welfare of others, while men tend to behave in ways that are more dominant, controlling,

Gary Hallgren.

and independent (Eagly, 1994; Eagly & Wood, 1991; Swim, 1994). Indeed, if anything, some of the data indicate that the stereotype tends to underestimate the actual gender differences (Swim, 1994). Again, as with our basketball example, considerable overlap exists between men and women on these characteristics. Nonetheless, as Eagly (1995, 1996) has argued, the differences are too consistent to be dismissed as unimportant.

Needless to say, the phenomenon of gender stereotyping often does not reflect reality and can cut deeply. In one experiment, for example, when confronted with a highly successful female physician, male undergraduates perceived her as being less competent and having had an easier path toward success than a successful male physician (Feldman-Summers & Kiesler, 1974). Female undergraduates saw things differently: Although they saw the male physician and the female physician as being equally competent, they saw the male as having had an easier time of it. Both males and females attributed higher motivation to the female physician. It should be noted that attributing a high degree of motivation to a woman can be one way of implying that she has less skill than her male counterpart (i.e., "She's not very smart, but she tries hard").

This possibility comes into clear focus when we examine a similar study (Deaux & Emsweiler, 1974). Male and female students were shown a highly successful performance on a complex task by a fellow student and were asked how it came about. When a man succeeded, both male and female students attributed his achievement almost entirely to his ability; when it was a woman who succeeded, students of *both* genders thought the achievement was largely a matter of luck. Apparently, if the sexual stereotype is strong enough, even members of the stereotyped group tend to buy it.

But this research was done three decades ago. American society has undergone a great many changes since then. Have these changes affected the stereotypes held of women? Not so you'd notice. In a careful analysis of some fifty-eight more recent experiments Janet Swim and Lawrence Sanna (1996) found that the results were remarkably consistent with the earlier research. Specifically, they found that if a man was successful on a given task, observers of both sexes attributed his success to ability; if a woman was successful at that same task, observers attributed her success to hard work. If a man failed on a given task, observers attributed his failure either to bad luck or to lower effort; if a woman failed, observers felt the task was simply too hard for her ability level.

Even as children, girls have a tendency to downplay their own ability. In one experiment, while fourth-grade boys attributed their own successful outcomes on a difficult intellectual task to their ability, girls tended to derogate their own successful performance. Moreover, this experiment also showed that while boys had learned to protect their egos by attributing their own failures to bad luck, girls took more of the blame for failures on themselves (Nichols, 1975). In a subsequent study, the tendency girls have to downplay their own ability appeared most prevalent in traditionally male domains like math (Stipek & Gralinski, 1991). Specifically, junior high school girls attributed their success on a math exam to luck, while boys attributed their success to ability. Girls also showed less feelings of pride than boys following success on a math exam.

These self-defeating beliefs do not develop in a vacuum. They can be influenced by the attitudes of our society in general and, most powerfully, by the most important people in the young girl's life—her parents. In this regard, Janis Jacobs and Jacquelynne Eccles (1992) explored the influence of mothers' gender-stereotypical beliefs on the way these same mothers perceived the abili-

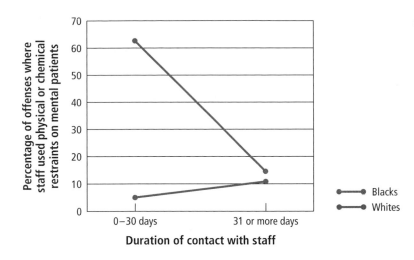

FIGURE 13.1

Use of extreme measures against black mental patients.

During the first thirty days of confinement, there appeared to be an assumption that blacks would be more violent than whites.

(Adapted from Bond, DiCandia, & McKennon, 1988)

ties of their 11- and 12-year-old sons and daughters. The researchers then tested to see what impact this might have on the children's perceptions of their own abilities. As you might predict, mothers who held the strongest gender-stereotypical beliefs also believed that their own daughters had relatively low math ability and that their sons had relatively high math ability. Mothers who did not hold stereotypical beliefs did not see their daughters as less able in math than their sons. How did the mothers' beliefs affect the beliefs of their children? The daughters of women with strong gender stereotypes believed that they had poor math ability; the opposite was true as well: Mothers who did not hold strong gender stereotypes had daughters without this self-defeating mind-set. This is an interesting variation on the self-fulfilling prophecy discussed in Chapters 3 and 4: Here, if your mother doesn't expect you to do well, chances are you will not do as well as you otherwise might.

Discrimination: The Behavioral Component

This brings us to the final component of prejudice—the action component. Stereotypical beliefs often result in unfair treatment. We call this **discrimination:** an unjustified negative or harmful action toward the members of a group simply because of their membership in that group.

If you are a fourth-grade math teacher and you have the stereotypical belief that little girls are hopeless at math, you might be less likely to spend as much time in the classroom coaching a girl than coaching a boy. If you are a police officer and you have the stereotypical belief that African Americans are more violent than whites, this might affect your behavior toward a specific black man you are trying to arrest.

In one study, researchers compared the treatment of patients in a psychiatric hospital run by an all-white professional staff (Bond, Di Candia, & McKinnon, 1988). The results of the study are illustrated in Figure 13.1. The researchers examined the two most common methods used by staff members to handle patients' violent behavior: secluding the individual in a timeout room and restraining the individual in a straitjacket and administering tranquilizing drugs. An examination of hospital records over eighty-five days revealed that the harsher method—physical and chemical restraint—was used with black patients nearly four times as often as with white patients. This was the case despite the virtual lack of differences in the number of violent incidents committed by the black and the white patients. Moreover, this discriminatory treatment occurred even though the black patients, on being admitted to the hospital, had been diagnosed as slightly less violent than the white patients.

> Prejudices are the props of civilization.
>
> —André Gide, 1939

Discrimination

Unjustified negative or harmful action toward a member of a group simply because of his or her membership in that group

This study did uncover an important positive finding: After several weeks, reality managed to overcome the effects of the existing stereotype. The staff eventually noticed that the black and the white patients did not differ in their degree of violent behavior, and they began to treat black and white patients equally. While this is encouraging, the overall meaning of the study is both clear and disconcerting: The existing stereotype resulted in undeserved, harsher initial treatment of black patients by trained professionals. At the same time, the fact that reality overcame the stereotype is a tribute to the professionalism of the staff, because, as we shall see, in most cases, deeply rooted prejudice, stereotypes, and discrimination are not easy to change.

Discrimination against Homosexuals   In the summer of 2003, the Supreme Court struck down state laws against sodomy, echoing the softening attitudes towards homosexuality in American society. Nevertheless, several studies during the past two decades have shown that homosexuals face a good deal of discrimination and antipathy in their day-to-day lives (Fernald, 1995; Franklin, 2000; Herek, 1991).

Unlike women, ethnic minorities, and people with disabilities, homosexuals are not protected by national laws banning discrimination in the workplace, and only eleven states have such laws. So it would seem that homosexuals would be vulnerable to job discrimination. If you were applying for a job, how would you be treated by your potential employers if they had prior information that you were a homosexual? Would they refuse to hire you? Would they treat you with less warmth than they treat heterosexuals?

In a field experiment, Michelle Hebl and her colleagues (Hebl, Foster, Mannix, & Dovidio, 2002) tried to find out. Sixteen college students (eight males and eight females), who were actually confederates of the experimenters, applied for jobs at local stores. In some of their interviews, they were portrayed as being homosexual; in others, they were not. In order to standardize the interactions, the applicants were all dressed similarly in jeans and pullover jackets.

The researchers looked at two kinds of discrimination: formal discrimination and interpersonal discrimination. To gauge formal discrimination, they sought to determine if there were differences in what the employer said about the availability of jobs, differences in whether the employer allowed them to fill out a job application, differences in whether or not they received a call-back, and differences in the employer's response to a request to use the bathroom. On these issues, the investigators found no significant differences. That is, in terms of formal discrimination, there was no evidence of discrimination against those portrayed as homosexuals. The employers could not be accused of treating "homosexual" applicants unjustly.

On the other hand, there were strong indications of interpersonal discrimination against those portrayed as homosexuals. Compared to the way they interacted with "nonhomosexuals," employers were less verbally positive, spent less time interviewing them, used fewer words while chatting with them, and made less eye contact with them. In other words, it was clear from their behavior that the potential employers were either uncomfortable or more distant with people they believed to be homosexual.

WHAT CAUSES PREJUDICE?

What makes people prejudiced? Is it "natural" or "unnatural"? Evolutionary psychologists have suggested that animals have a strong tendency to feel more favorably toward genetically similar others and to express fear and loathing toward genetically dissimilar organisms, even if the latter have never done them any harm (Buss & Kenrick, 1998; Rushton, 1989; Trivers, 1985). Thus prejudice might be built in—an essential part of our biological survival mechanism inducing us to favor our own family, tribe, or race and to express hostility toward outsiders. Conversely, it is also conceivable that humans are different from the lower animals; perhaps our natural inclination is to be friendly, open, and cooperative. If this were the case, prejudice would not come naturally. Rather, the culture (parents, the community, the media) might, intentionally or unintentionally, instruct us to assign negative qualities and attributes to people who are different from us.

The bottom line is that although we human beings might have inherited biological tendencies that predispose us toward prejudicial behavior, no one knows for sure whether or not prejudice is a vital and necessary part of our biological makeup. In any case, most social psychologists would agree that the specifics of prejudice must be learned. But even when young children pick up their parents' prejudices, they do not necessarily retain those prejudices in adulthood. Indeed, when researchers examined the similarity of attitudes and values of parents and their adult children, they discovered an interesting pattern (Rohan & Zanna, 1996). They found that when parents held egalitarian attitudes and values, their adult children did as well. And when parents held prejudice-related attitudes and values, their adult children were less likely to hold the same views. Why would this be true? It is likely that the discrepancy occurs because the culture as a whole is more egalitarian than the bigoted parents. So when children of bigoted parents leave home (e.g., to go off to college), they are more likely to be exposed to competing views.

At the same time, it is reasonably clear that children can be taught prejudice. Jane Elliot (1977), a third-grade teacher in Riccville, Iowa, was concerned that her young students were leading too sheltered a life. The children all lived in rural Iowa, they were all white, and they were all Christian. Elliot felt it was important for their development to give them some direct experience about what stereotyping and discrimination felt like from both sides. To achieve this end, she divided her class by eye color. She told her students that blue-eyed people were superior to brown-eyed people—smarter, nicer, more trustworthy, and so on. The brown-eyed youngsters were required to wear special cloth collars

Children may pick up prejudices espoused by their parents, but they do not necessarily retain those prejudices when they leave home and are exposed to competing views.

around their necks so that they would be instantly recognizable as a member of the inferior group. She gave special privileges to the blue-eyed youngsters: They got to play longer at recess, could have second helpings at the cafeteria, were praised in the classroom, and so on. How did the children respond?

In just hours, Elliot created a microcosm of a prejudiced society in her classroom. The children had been a cooperative, cohesive group, but once the seeds of divisiveness were planted, there was trouble. The "superior" blue-eyed kids made fun of the brown-eyed kids, refused to play with them, tattled on them to the teacher, thought up new restrictions and punishments for them, and even started a fistfight in the schoolyard. The "inferior" brown-eyed kids became self-conscious, depressed, and demoralized. They performed poorly on classroom tests that day.

The next day, Elliot switched the stereotypes about eye color. She said she'd made a dreadful mistake—that brown-eyed people were really the superior ones. She told the brown-eyed kids to put their collars on the blue-eyed kids. They gleefully did so. The tables had turned—and the brown-eyed kids exacted their revenge.

On the morning of the third day, Elliot explained to her students that they had been learning about prejudice and discrimination and how it feels to be a person of color in this society. The children discussed the two-day experience and clearly understood its message. In a follow-up, Elliot met with these students at a class reunion, when they were in their mid-twenties. Their memories of the exercise were startlingly clear—they reported that the experience had had a powerful and lasting impact on their lives. They felt that they were less prejudiced and more aware of discrimination against others because of this childhood experience.

The world is full of pots jeering at kettles.

—François de la Rochefoucauld, Maxims, 1665

The Way We Think: Social Cognition

Our first explanation for what causes prejudice is that it is the inevitable byproduct of the way we process and organize information—in other words, it is the dark side of human social cognition (see Chapter 3). Our tendency to categorize and group information, to form schemas and use them to interpret new or unusual information, to rely on potentially inaccurate heuristics (shortcuts in mental reasoning), and to depend on what are often faulty memory processes—all of these aspects of social cognition can lead us to form negative stereotypes and to apply them in a discriminatory way. Let's examine this dark side of social cognition more closely.

Social Categorization: Us versus Them   The first step in prejudice is the creation of groups—putting some people into one group based on certain characteristics and others into another group based on their different characteristics. This kind of categorization is the underlying theme of human social cognition (Brewer & Brown, 1998; Rosch & Lloyd, 1978; Taylor, 1981; Wilder, 1986). For example, we make sense out of the physical world by grouping animals and plants into taxonomies based on their physical characteristics; similarly, we make sense out of our social world by grouping people according to other characteristics, including gender, nationality, ethnicity, and so on. When we encounter people with these characteristics, we rely on our perceptions of what people with similar characteristics have been like in the past to help us determine how to react to someone else with the same characteristics (Andersen & Klatzky, 1987). Thus social categorization is both useful and necessary; however, this simple cognitive process has profound implications.

For example, in Jane Elliot's third-grade classroom, children grouped according to eye color began to act differently based on that social categorization. Blue-eyed children, the superior group, stuck together and actively promoted and used their higher status and power in the classroom. They formed an in-group, defined as the group with which an individual identifies. The blue-eyed kids saw the brown-eyed ones as outsiders—different and inferior. To the blue-eyed children, the brown-eyed kids were the out-group, the group with which the individual does not identify.

In-Group Bias Kurt Vonnegut captures the in-group versus out-group concept beautifully in his novel *Cat's Cradle* (1963). A woman discovers that a person she has just met, casually, on a plane, is from Indiana. Even though they have almost nothing else in common, a bond immediately forms between them:

> *"My God," she said, "are you a Hoosier?"*
> *I admitted I was.*
> *"I'm a Hoosier too," she crowed. "Nobody has to be ashamed of being a Hoosier."*
> *"I'm not," I said. "I never knew anybody who was." (pp. 42–43)*

What is the mechanism that produces this in-group bias—positive feelings and special treatment for people we have defined as being part of our in-group and negative feelings and unfair treatment for others simply because we have defined them as being in the out-group? The British social psychologist Henri Tajfel (1982a) discovered that the major underlying motive is self-esteem: Individuals seek to enhance their self-esteem by identifying with specific social groups. Yet self-esteem will be enhanced only if the individual sees these groups as superior to other groups. Thus for members of the Ku Klux Klan, it is not enough to believe that the races should be kept separate; they must convince themselves of the supremacy of the white race in order to feel good about themselves.

To get at the pure, unvarnished mechanisms behind this phenomenon, Tajfel and his colleagues have created entities that they refer to as *minimal groups* (Tajfel, 1982a; Tajfel & Billig, 1974; Tajfel & Turner, 1979). In these experiments, complete strangers are formed into groups using the most trivial criteria imaginable. For example, in one experiment, participants watched a coin toss that randomly assigned them to either group X or group W. In another experiment,

Wearing our school colors is a way of demonstrating that we are a member of the in-group.

participants were first asked to express their opinions about artists they had never heard of and were then randomly assigned to a group that appreciated either the "Klee style" or the "Kandinsky style," ostensibly due to their picture preferences. The striking thing about this research is that despite the fact that the participants were strangers before the experiment and didn't interact with one another during it, they behaved as if those who shared the same meaningless label were their dear friends or close kin. They liked the members of their own group better; they rated the members of their in-group as more likely to have pleasant personalities and to have done better work than out-group members. Most striking, the participants allocated more money and other rewards to those who shared their label and did so in a rather hostile, cutthroat manner—for example, when given a clear choice, they preferred to give themselves only $2, if it meant giving the out-group person $1, over giving themselves $3, if that meant the out-group member received $4 (Brewer, 1979; Hogg & Abrams, 1988; Mullen, Brown, & Smith, 1992; Wilder, 1981).

In short, even when the reasons for differentiation are minimal, being in the in-group makes you want to win against members of the out-group and leads you to treat the latter unfairly, because such tactics build your self-esteem. And when your group does win, it strengthens your feelings of pride and identification with that group. For example, our casual observation suggests that there was much more flag-waving among the public and patriotic speechmaking by politicians following the recent victorious war in Iraq than there was following the less than victorious war in Vietnam. In a more systematic observation, Robert Cialdini and his colleagues (1976; Cialdini, 1993) simply counted the number of college insignia T-shirts and sweatshirts worn to classes on the Monday following a football game at seven different universities. The results? You guessed it: Students were more likely to wear their university's insignia after victory than after defeat.

Out-Group Homogeneity Besides the in-group bias, another consequence of social categorization is the perception of **out-group homogeneity,** the belief that "they" are all alike (Linville, Fischer, & Salovey, 1989; Quattrone, 1986). In-group members tend to perceive those in the out-group as more similar to each other (homogeneous) than they really are, as well as more homogeneous than the in-group members are. Does your college have a traditional rival, whether in athletics or academics? If so, as an in-group member, you probably value your institution more highly than this rival (thereby raising and protecting your self-esteem), and you probably perceive students at this rival school to be more similar to each other (e.g., as a given type) than you perceive students at your own college to be.

Consider a study of students in two rival universities: Princeton and Rutgers (Quattrone & Jones, 1980). The rivalry between these colleges is based on athletics, academics, and even class-consciousness (Princeton is private and Rutgers is public). Male research participants at the two schools watched videotaped scenes in which three different young men were asked to make a decision—for example, in one videotape, an experimenter asked a man whether he wanted to listen to rock music or classical music while he participated in an experiment on auditory perception. The participants were told that the man was either a Princeton or a Rutgers student, so for some of them the student in the videotape was an in-group member and for others an out-group member. Participants had to predict what the man in the videotape would choose. After they saw the man make his choice (e.g., rock or classical music), they were asked to predict what percentage of male students at that institution would make the same choice. Did the predictions vary due to the in- or out-group status of the target men? As you can see in Figure 13.2, the results support the out-group homogeneity hypothesis: When the target person was an out-group member, the participants believed his choice was more predictive of what his peers would choose than when he was an

Out-Group Homogeneity

The perception that individuals in the out-group are more similar to each other (homogeneous) than they really are, as well as more similar than the members of the in-group are

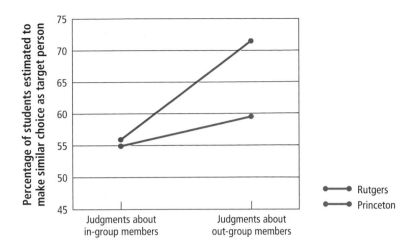

FIGURE 13.2

Judgments about in-group and out-group members.

After watching the target person make a choice between two alternatives, participants were asked to estimate what percentage of students at their school (in-group) and their rival school (out-group) would make the same choice. An out-group homogeneity bias was found: Students' estimates for out-group members were higher (greater similarity) than for in-group members.

(Adapted from Quattrone & Jones, 1980)

in-group member (a student at their own school). In other words, if you know something about one out-group member, you are more likely to feel you know something about all of them. Similar results have been found in a wide variety of experiments in the United States, Europe, and Australia (Duck, Hogg, & Terry, 1995; Hartstone & Augoustinos, 1995; Judd & Park, 1988; Ostrom & Sedikides, 1992; Park & Rothbart, 1982).

The Failure of Logic   If you've ever argued with people holding deep-seated prejudices, you know how hard it is to get them to change their minds. Even people who are usually sensible and reasonable about most topics become relatively immune to rational, logical arguments when it comes to the topic of their prejudice. Why is this so? There are two reasons, involving the affective and cognitive aspects of an attitude. First, it is primarily the emotional aspect of attitudes that makes a prejudiced person so hard to argue with; logical arguments are not effective in countering emotions. The difficulty of using reason to change prejudiced attitudes is beautifully illustrated by Gordon Allport in his landmark book *The Nature of Prejudice* (1954). Allport reports a dialogue between Mr. X and Mr. Y:

> *Mr. X:* The trouble with the Jews is that they only take care of their own group.
>
> *Mr. Y:* But the record of the Community Chest campaign shows that they gave more generously, in proportion to their numbers, to the general charities of the community than did non-Jews.
>
> *Mr. X:* That shows they are always trying to buy favor and intrude into Christian affairs. They think of nothing but money; that is why there are so many Jewish bankers.
>
> *Mr. Y:* But a recent study shows that the percentage of Jews in the banking business is negligible, far smaller than the percentage of non-Jews.
>
> *Mr. X:* That's just it; they don't go in for respectable business; they are only in the movie business or run night clubs. (pp. 13–14)

Because Mr. X is emotionally caught up in his beliefs about Jews, his responses are not logical. In effect, the prejudiced Mr. X is saying, "Don't trouble me with facts; my mind is made up." Rather than refuting the powerful data presented by Mr. Y, he distorts the facts so that they support his hatred of Jews, or he

> Our minds thus grow in spots; and like grease spots, the spots spread. But we let them spread as little as possible; we keep unaltered as much of our old knowledge, as many of our old prejudices and beliefs, as we can.
>
> *—William James, 1907*

> The mind of a bigot is like the pupil of the eye; the more light you pour upon it, the more it will contract.
>
> *—Oliver Wendell Holmes Jr., 1901*

"It's a cat calendar, so it may not be all that accurate."

simply ignores them and initiates a new line of attack. The prejudiced attitude remains intact, despite the fact that the specific arguments Mr. X began with are now lying in tatters at his feet.

Second, as we discussed in earlier chapters, an attitude tends to organize the way we process relevant information about the targets of that attitude. This presents difficulties for the person trying to reduce a friend's prejudice. None of us is a 100 percent reliable accountant when it comes to processing social information we care about. The human mind simply does not tally events objectively. Accordingly, individuals who hold specific opinions (or schemas) about certain groups will process information about those groups differently from the way they process information about other groups. Specifically, information consistent with their notions about these target groups will be given more attention, will be rehearsed (or recalled) more often, and will therefore be remembered better than information that contradicts these notions (Bodenhausen, 1988; Dovidio, Evans, & Tyler, 1986; O'Sullivan & Durso, 1984; Wyer, 1988). These are the familiar effects of *schematic processing* that we discussed in Chapter 4. Applying these effects to the topic of prejudice, we can see that whenever a member of a group behaves as we expect, the behavior confirms and even strengthens our stereotype. Thus stereotypes become relatively impervious to change; after all, proof that they are accurate is always out there—when our beliefs guide us to see it.

The Activation of Stereotypes   Stereotypes reflect cultural beliefs—within a given society, they are easily recognized descriptions of members of a particular group. For example, we all know the stereotype of the woman driver or the overemotional female. Even if we don't believe these stereotypes, we can easily recognize them as common beliefs held by others. For instance, in a series of studies conducted at Princeton University over a span of thirty-six years (1933–1969), students were asked to assign traits to members of various ethnic and national groups (Gilbert, 1951; Karlins, Coffman, & Walters, 1969; Katz & Braly, 1933). The participants could do so easily, and to a large extent they agreed with each other. They knew the stereotypes, even for groups about whom they had little real knowledge, such as Turks. Table 13.1 shows some of the results of these studies. Note how negative the early stereotypes were in 1933 and how they became somewhat less negative over time. What is particularly interesting about these studies is that participants in 1951 began to voice discomfort with the task (discomfort that didn't exist in 1933). By 1969, many participants not only felt discomfort but seemed reluctant to admit that these stereotypes even existed because they did not believe the stereotypes themselves (Karlins et al., 1969). A quarter of a century later, Patricia Devine and Andrew Elliot (1995) showed that the stereotypes were not really fading at all; virtually all the participants were fully aware of the negative stereotypes of African Americans, whether they believed them personally or not.

Why Do Unwanted Stereotypes Persist?   This brings us to an intriguing social cognition puzzle: If you know a stereotype, will it affect your cognitive processing about a target person, even if you neither believe the stereotype nor consider yourself prejudiced against this group? Imagine this scenario: You are a member of a group, judging another person's performance. Someone in your group makes an ugly, stereotypical comment about the individual. Will the comment affect your judgment of his or her performance? "No," you are probably

TABLE 13.1

Some Common Stereotypes Held by Princeton Students over the Years

Note the general stability as well as changes in these stereotypes.

GROUP	1933	1951	1969
Americans	industrious intelligent materialistic ambitious progressive	materialistic intelligent industrious pleasure-loving individualistic	materialistic ambitious pleasure-loving industrious conventional
Japanese	intelligent industrious progressive shrewd sly	imitative sly extremely nationalistic treacherous	industrious ambitious efficient intelligent progressive
Jews	shrewd mercenary industrious grasping intelligent	shrewd intelligent industrious mercenary ambitious	ambitious materialistic intelligent industrious shrewd
Negroes (African Americans)	superstitious lazy happy-go-lucky ignorant musical	superstitious musical lazy ignorant pleasure-loving	musical happy-go-lucky lazy pleasure-loving ostentatious

Adapted from Gilbert (1951); Karlins, Coffman, & Walters (1969); Katz & Braly (1933)

thinking; "I'd disregard it completely." But would you be able to do so? Is it possible that the comment would trigger in your mind all the other negative stereotypes and beliefs about people in that group and affect your judgment about this particular person?

Attempting to find out, researchers had two confederates, one African American and one white, stage a debate about nuclear energy for groups of participants (Greenberg & Pyszczynski, 1985). For half the groups, the African American debater presented far better arguments and clearly won the debate; for the other half, the white debater performed far better and won the debate. The participants were asked to rate both debaters' skill. However, just before subjects were to do this, the critical experimental manipulation occurred. A confederate planted in the group did one of three things: (1) He made a highly racist remark about the African American debater—"There's no way that nigger won the debate"; (2) he made a nonracist remark about the African American debater—"There's no way the pro [or con] debater won the debate"; or (3) he made no comment at all.

The researchers reasoned that if those participants who heard the racist comment were able to disregard it completely, they would not rate the African American debater any differently from the way participants in the other conditions, who had not heard such a comment, rated him. Was that the case? Figure 13.3 (on the next page) clearly shows that the answer is no. The data compared the ratings of skill given to the African American and white debaters when they were each in the losing role. As you can see, the participants rated the African American and white debaters as equally skillful when no comment was made;

Activation of a stereotypical belief.

When a derogatory comment was made about the black debater, it activated the latent stereotype held by the observers, causing them to lower their rating of his performance.

(Adapted from Greenberg & Pyszczynski, 1985)

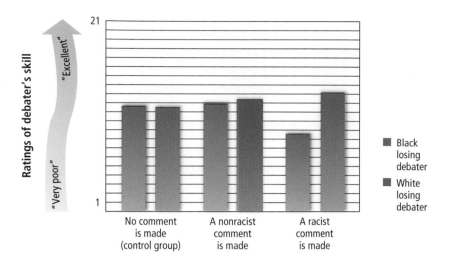

similarly, when a nonracist, nonstereotypical comment was made about the African American debater, he was rated as being just as skillful as the white debater. However, after the racist comment evoked racial stereotypes, participants rated the African American debater *significantly lower* than participants in the other groups did. Why? The derogatory comment activated other negative stereotypes about African Americans so that those who heard it rated the same performance by the debater as less skilled than those who had not heard the racist remark.

In a similar study, all it took was one negative action by one African American (actually a confederate of the experimenters) to activate the negative stereotypes against blacks and to discourage the participants from wanting to interact with a different African American (Henderson-King & Nisbett, 1996). These findings suggest that in most of us, stereotypes lurk just beneath the surface. It doesn't take much to activate the stereotype, and once activated, it can have dire consequences for how a particular member of that out-group is perceived and treated.

Automatic and Controlled Processing of Stereotypes   How does this activation process work? Patricia Devine and her colleagues (Devine, 1989a; Zuwerink, Montieth, Devine, & Cook, 1996) have done some fascinating research on how stereotypical and prejudiced beliefs affect cognitive processing. Devine differentiates between automatic processing of information and controlled processing of information. An automatic process is one over which we have no control. For example, even if you score very low on a prejudice scale, you are certainly familiar with certain stereotypes that exist in the culture, such as "African Americans are hostile," "Jews are materialistic," or "Homosexual men are effeminate." These stereotypes are automatically triggered under certain conditions—they just pop into one's mind. Since the process is automatic, you can't control it or stop it from occurring. You know the stereotypes, and they simply come to mind—say, when you are meeting someone or rating a person's performance. However, for people who are not deeply prejudiced, their control processes can suppress or override these stereotypes. For example, such a person can think, "Hey, that stereotype isn't fair and it isn't right—African Americans are no more hostile than whites. Ignore the stereotype about this person's ethnicity."

What Devine's theory suggests, therefore, is a two-step model of cognitive processing: The automatic processing brings up information—in this case, stereotypes—but the controlled (or conscious) processing can refute or ignore it. But what happens if you are busy, overwhelmed, distracted, or not paying much attention? You may not initiate that controlled level of processing, meaning that the information supplied by the automatic process—the stereotype—is still in your mind and unrefuted. Devine (1989a) set out to study exactly this process: that a stereotype is automatically activated when a member of an outgroup is encountered, and the stereotype can be ignored through conscious processing—for example, by people who are not prejudiced (see Figure 13.4).

First, Devine administered a test of prejudice to a large number of students and, according to their scores, divided them into high-prejudice and low-prejudice groups. Next, she demonstrated that regardless of prejudice, both groups possessed equal knowledge of racial stereotypes. Next came the test of automatic and conscious processing: She flashed stereotyped words (e.g., *black, hostile, lazy, welfare*) and neutral words (e.g., *however, what, said*) on a screen so quickly that the words were just below the participants' perceptual (conscious) awareness. They saw something, but they weren't sure what—that is, their conscious processing couldn't identify the words. However, their automatic processing could recognize the words. How could Devine be sure?

After flashing the words, she asked the participants to read a story about "Donald" (his ethnicity was not mentioned) and to rate their impressions of him. Donald was described somewhat ambiguously; he did some things in the story that could be interpreted either positively or negatively. The participants who had seen the words reflecting the stereotype of black Americans interpreted Donald significantly more negatively than those who had seen the neutral words

FIGURE 13.4

A two-step model of the cognitive processing of stereotypes.

did. Thus for one group the negative stereotype had been primed (activated unconsciously through automatic processing); without their awareness, the participants were affected by these hostile and negative words, as indicated in their ratings of the Donald character. Because these stereotypes were operating outside their conscious cognitive control, white students who were low in prejudice were just as influenced by the cultural stereotype (e.g., that blacks are hostile) as the prejudiced students.

In her final experiment, Devine gave the students a task that involved their conscious processing: She asked them to list all the words they could think of that are used to describe black Americans. The high-prejudice students listed significantly more negative words than the low-prejudice students did. In other words, the less prejudiced participants used their conscious processing to edit out the negative stereotype and therefore were able to respond in a manner that was free of its influence.

While Devine's work is of great interest, recent research has suggested some important correctives—primarily, that the phenomenon is not as universal as she believed. Let us explain: According to Devine, pretty much everyone in American society has learned the negative stereotype of African Americans; this negative stereotype is therefore activated automatically in everyone. Accordingly, to be nonprejudiced, we must learn to suppress or overcome this automatic response. But Russell Fazio and his colleagues (Fazio, Jackson, Dunton, & Williams, 1995) have shown that considerable variability exists in people's automatic processing of negative stereotypes.

Fazio and colleagues developed a clever way of measuring people's automatic processing of stereotypes. They presented people with words on a computer screen and asked them to judge whether the meaning of each word was good or bad. For example, when people saw the word *attractive*, they pressed a key to indicate that this word has a good meaning, and when they saw the word *disgusting*, they pressed a key to indicate that this word has a bad meaning.

On some trials, the words were preceded by a quick flash of a picture of a human face. People were told to look at the faces but to respond only to the meaning of the word that subsequently appeared on the screen. Thus if you were a participant, you would have seen a quick flash of a face, then a word such as *attractive*, and pressed a key to indicate that this was a "good" word. Now here's the interesting part: Some of the faces were of African Americans and some were of whites. Remember, these faces were flashed very quickly (for about a third of a second). This was long enough for people to see the faces and have an automatic emotional reaction to them but too brief for people to control or suppress this reaction. As soon as they had a positive or negative reaction to the face, the word appeared on the screen and they had to decide whether the word was good or bad.

The point of the study was to see whether or not the presentation of the faces influenced how long it took people to respond to positive and negative words. Think about how this would work: If a participant is prejudiced against African Americans and this prejudice is ingrained and automatic, then negative feelings will be triggered automatically when the person sees a picture of an African American. This negative reaction should make it easier to respond "bad" to a negative word such as *disgusting*, because negative feelings are already present when the word appears. A negative reac-

According to Patricia Devine's theory, we exhibit both automatic and controlled processing of information. So even though your automatic response to this man might reflect prejudice, you could override the stereotypes behind that response by more controlled processing.

tion should make it harder to respond "good" to a positive word such as *attractive* because this feeling is opposite to the meaning of the word.

The researchers constructed an index of automatic prejudice by computing the extent to which faces of African Americans slowed down responses to positive words and sped up responses to negative words. Fazio and his colleagues found considerable variability in people's level of automatic prejudice. Some people appeared to have automatic negative reactions to African Americans, whereas others did not. Further, this amount of automatic prejudice was found to predict people's behavior. At the end of the study, all participants were debriefed by an experimenter who "happened" to be an African American woman. This experimenter rated how friendly the participants treated her. Those who had shown the highest level of automatic prejudice on the word judgment task tended to be cold and distant toward the experimenter, whereas those who had shown the lowest amount of prejudice were far more likely to be warm and friendly.

Fazio and his colleagues suggest that regarding attitudes toward African Americans, there are three kinds of people: (1) those who do not have an automatic negative reaction to African Americans, (2) those who do have an automatic negative reaction and have no qualms about expressing these feelings (i.e., are willing to be prejudiced), and (3) those who have an automatic negative reaction but want to suppress this reaction.

John Bargh has taken the idea of automatic prejudice a step further, showing that it can be triggered when certain ideas about the target group come to mind. Bargh and his colleagues examined negative reactions of men toward women (Bargh, Raymond, Pryor, & Strack, 1995). Some men are particularly inclined to employ sexual violence against women. Bargh and his colleagues investigated the possibility that for such men, there may be an automatic link between power and aggressive sex. Would thinking about power automatically trigger aggressive sexual attraction without the men even recognizing this link?

To test this idea, Bargh and his colleagues gave men a questionnaire that measured how prone they were toward sexual aggression (e.g., how much of a "turn-on" they found rape fantasies to be). The men also participated in a laboratory study in which the concept of power was primed in some men but not in others. (Recall that priming is a technique designed to activate a concept and make it salient.)

In the experiment, the men participated in the company of a young woman who they believed was another participant but who was really a confederate of the experimenter. After the priming procedure, the men were asked to rate how attractive they thought this woman was. Did priming the concept of power increase their attraction to the woman? The answer was yes for men who scored high on the sexual aggression questionnaire but no for the men who scored low on that questionnaire. In other words, for some men but not for others, there is an automatic link in their minds between power and sexual attractiveness; priming or activating the concept of power increases the extent to which they find women attractive. The disturbing implication of this research is that these men are not aware of the link between power and sex in their minds and thus may not know that their attraction to women is influenced by feelings of power (Bargh & Raymond, 1995; Bargh & Barndollar, 1996; Chartand & Bargh, 1996).

The Illusory Correlation   Another way that our cognitive processing perpetuates stereotypical thinking is through the phenomenon of **illusory correlation** (Fiedler, 2000; Garcia-Marques & Hamilton, 1996; Shavitt, Sanbonmatsu, Smittipatana, & Posavac, 1999). When we expect two things to be related, we fool ourselves into believing that they are—even when they are actually unrelated. Many illusory correlations exist in our society. For example, there is a common belief that couples who haven't been able to have children will conceive a child after

Illusory Correlation

The tendency to see relationships, or correlations, between events that are actually unrelated

Distinctiveness can lead to an illusory correlation. For example, you may be tempted to believe that Whoopi Goldberg's personal style is more common among African American women than it in fact is.

they adopt a child—apparently because after the adoption, they feel less anxious and stressed. Guess what: This correlation is entirely illusory. Occasionally, an apparently infertile couple does conceive after adopting a child, but this occurs with no greater frequency than for apparently infertile couples who do not adopt. The former event, because it is so charmingly vivid, simply makes more of an impression on us when it happens, creating the illusory correlation (Gilovich, 1991).

What does all this have to do with prejudice and stereotypes? Illusory correlations are most likely to occur when the events or people are distinctive or conspicuous—that is, when they are different from the run-of-the-mill, typical social scene we are accustomed to (Hamilton, 1981; Hamilton, Stroessner, & Mackie, 1993). Minority group members—for example, as defined by race—are, by definition, distinctive, since fewer of them are present in the society. Other groups who are not distinctive in terms of numbers—such as women, who make up 50 percent of the species—may nonetheless become distinctive or conspicuous because of a nonstereotypical profession or talent—for example, a woman member of the U.S. Senate. David Hamilton and Robert Gifford (1976) have shown that such distinctiveness leads to the creation of and belief in an illusory correlation—a relationship between the distinctive target person and the behavior he or she displays. This illusory correlation is then applied to all members of the target group.

How does this work in everyday life? Let's say you don't know many Jews, so for you, interacting with a Jew is a distinctive event and for you, Jews in general are distinctive people. Let's say you meet a Jewish individual who is an investment banker. Let's say you meet a second Jew who is an economist. An illusory correlation between Jews and money is created. If you also are aware of the stereotype that Jews are materialistic, the correlation you perceived based on your personal experiences seems all the more sound. The result is that in the future, you will be more likely to notice situations in which Jews are behaving materialistically, you will be less likely to notice situations in which Jews are not behaving materialistically, and you will be less likely to notice situations in which non-Jews are behaving materialistically. You will have processed new information guided by your illusory correlation, seeing what you expect to see. You will also have strengthened your illusory correlation, confirming in your mind that your stereotype is right (Hamilton & Sherman, 1989; Mullen & Johnson, 1988).

We should note that illusory correlations are created in a far more passive fashion too. It is not necessary to have personal experience with people in a distinctive group—television, newspapers, and other media create illusory correlations when they portray women, minorities, and other groups in stereotypical roles (Busby, 1975; Deaux & La France, 1998; Friedman, 1977; McArthur & Resko, 1975).

Can We Change Stereotypical Beliefs?   How do you get people to change their negative stereotypical beliefs? Would simply providing them with accurate information refute their stereotypes? Unfortunately, it's not that simple. Let's say your next-door neighbor believes that African Americans and Asian Americans lack leadership ability and are unpatriotic. What if you reminded him that General Colin Powell, former chairman of the Joint Chiefs of Staff and the U.S. secretary of state, is African American? What if you also informed him that the most highly decorated combat unit in World War II was composed solely of Asian Americans? Would this information affect your neighbor's stereotypes?

Not necessarily. Researchers have found that when people are presented with an example or two that seems to refute their existing stereotype, most of them do not change their general belief. Indeed, in one experiment, some people presented with this kind of disconfirming evidence actually *strengthened* their stereotypical belief because the disconfirming evidence challenged them to come up with additional reasons for holding on to that belief (Kunda & Oleson, 1997).

It *is* possible to change a stereotype; a great deal depends on how the disconfirming information is presented. Research has shown that when you present people with only two or three powerful disconfirming pieces of evidence (as the Colin Powell example), it is not effective because participants simply dismiss the disconfirming examples as "the exceptions that prove the rule." But when the participants are bombarded with many examples that are inconsistent with the stereotype, they gradually modify their beliefs (Webber & Crocker, 1983).

To sum up this discussion, two points need to be emphasized: (1) We all stereotype others to some extent—it is part of being a cognitive miser—and (2) emotional attitudes are harder to change than nonemotional ones. Thus a strongly prejudiced person engages in stereotyping in a deeper, more thorough

> A fanatic is one who can't change his mind and won't change the subject.
>
> *—Winston Churchill, 1944*

General Colin Powell, a popular hero and secretary of state, was one of the first African Americans to have been given serious consideration for the presidency. Might a bigoted person vote for him? Perhaps—if the bigot characterized Powell as "the exception that proves the rule."

manner than the rest of us. Through this process, prejudiced attitudes become like a fortress—a closed circuit of cognitions, if you will—and this fortress drastically reduces the effectiveness of logical argument or scattered pieces of disconfirming information.

How We Assign Meaning: Attributional Biases

As we discussed in Chapter 4, people and situations don't come with neon signs telling us everything we need to know about them. Instead, we must rely on one aspect of social cognition—attributional processes—to try to understand why people behave as they do. Just as we form attributions to make sense out of one person's behavior, we also make attributions about whole groups of people. As you shall see, the attributional biases we discussed in Chapter 4 come back to haunt us now in a far more damaging and dangerous form: prejudice and discrimination.

Dispositional versus Situational Explanations One reason stereotypes are so insidious and persistent is the human tendency to make dispositional attributions—that is, to leap to the conclusion that a person's behavior is due to some aspect of his or her personality rather than to some aspect of the situation. This is the familiar fundamental attribution error we discussed in Chapter 4. Although attributing people's behavior to their dispositions is often accurate, human behavior is also shaped by situational forces. Relying too heavily on dispositional attributions, therefore, often leads us to make attributional mistakes. Given that this process operates on an individual level, you can only imagine the problems and complications that arise when we overzealously act out the fundamental attribution error for a whole group of people—an out-group.

Stereotypes are dispositional attributions—negative ones. Thomas Pettigrew (1979) has called our tendency to make dispositional attributions about an entire group of people the **ultimate attribution error.** For example, some of the stereotypes that characterize anti-Semitism are the result of Christians committing the fundamental attribution error when interpreting the behavior of Jews. These stereotypes have a long history, extending over several centuries. When the Jews were first forced to flee their homeland during the third Diaspora, some 2,500 years ago, they were not allowed to own land or become artisans in the new regions in which they settled. Needing a livelihood, some took to lending money—one of the few professions to which they were allowed easy access. Although this choice of occupation was an accidental byproduct of restrictive laws, it led to a dispositional attribution about Jews: that they were interested only in dealing with money and not in honest labor, like farming. As this attribution became an ultimate attribution error, Jews were labeled conniving, vicious parasites of the kind dramatized and immortalized by Shakespeare in the character of Shylock in *The Merchant of Venice* or of Fagin in Dickens's *Oliver Twist*. This dispositional stereotype contributed greatly to the barbarous consequences of anti-Semitism in Europe during the 1930s and 1940s, when Hitler's Nazi regime murdered 6 million European Jews, and has persisted even in the face of clear, disconfirming evidence such as that produced by the birth of the state of Israel, where Jews tilled the soil and made the desert bloom.

Similarly, many Americans have a stereotype about African American and Hispanic men that involves aggression and the potential for violence—a very powerful dispositional attribution. In one study, college students, playing the role of jurors in a mock trial, were more likely to find a defendant guilty of a given crime simply if his name was Carlos Ramirez rather than Robert Johnson (Bodenhausen, 1988). Thus any situational information or extenuating circumstances that might have explained the defendant's actions were ignored when

The cause is hidden, but the result is known.
—Ovid, first century A.D.

Ultimate Attribution Error
The tendency to make dispositional attributions about an entire group of people

the powerful dispositional attribution was stereotypically triggered—in this case, by the Hispanic name.

In another study, researchers set up another dispositional versus situational possibility. College students read fictionalized files on prisoners who were being considered for parole and used that information to make a parole decision (Bodenhausen & Wyer, 1985). Sometimes the crime matched the common stereotype of the offender—for example, when a Hispanic male, Carlos Ramirez, committed assault and battery, or when an upper-class Anglo-American, Ashley Chamberlaine, committed embezzlement. In other instances, the crimes were inconsistent with the stereotypes. When the prisoners' crimes were consistent with participants' stereotypes, the students' recommendations for parole were harsher. Most of the students also ignored additional information that was relevant to a parole decision but was inconsistent with the stereotype, such as evidence of good behavior in prison.

These results indicate that when people conform to our stereotype, we tend to blind ourselves to clues about why they might have behaved as they did. Instead, we assume that something about their character or disposition, and not their situation or life circumstances, caused their behavior. In other words, when the fundamental attribution error rears its ugly head, we make dispositional attributions (based on our stereotypical beliefs about an ethnic or racial group) and not situational ones.

***The Bell Curve* Revisited**   Over the past decade, we have witnessed the reemergence of a heated debate that has raged in our society for almost two centuries. The most recent flare-up occurred when a scholarly book, *The Bell Curve* (Herrnstein & Murray, 1994), suggested that the statistically significant difference in academic performance between African Americans and Anglo-Americans might have a genetic component.

What are the facts? There is a statistical difference in academic test performance among various cultural groups in this country. In general, although there is considerable overlap, Asian Americans as a group perform slightly better than Anglo Americans, who in turn perform better than African Americans. This difference is undeniably real. The key question is, why does it occur? Is the reason for the difference dispositional or situational? In a striking series of experiments, Claude Steele, Joshua Aronson, and their colleagues have demonstrated that at least one major contributing factor is clearly situational and is based on a phenomenon they call **stereotype threat** (Aronson et al., 1998, 1999; Steele, 1997; Steele & Aronson, 1995a, 1995b). Specifically, when African American students find themselves in highly evaluative educational situations, most tend to experience apprehension about confirming the existing negative cultural stereotype of "intellectual inferiority." In effect, they are saying, "If I perform poorly on this test, it will reflect poorly on me and on my race." This extra burden of apprehension in turn interferes with their ability to perform well in these situations. For example, in one of their experiments, Steele and Aronson administered a difficult verbal test, the GRE, individually to African American and white students at Stanford University. Half the students of each race were led to believe that the investigator was interested in measuring their intellectual ability; the other half were led to believe that the investigator was merely trying to develop the test itself—and because the test was not yet valid or reliable (recall the discussion in Chapter 2), they were assured that their performance would mean nothing in terms of their actual ability.

The results confirmed the researchers' speculations. White students performed equally well regardless of whether or not they believed the test was being used as a diagnostic tool. The African American students who believed their abilities were not being measured performed as well as the white students. But the

> I will look at any additional evidence to confirm the opinion to which I have already come.
>
> *—Lord Molson, British politician*

Stereotype Threat

The apprehension experienced by members of a minority group that their behavior might confirm a cultural stereotype

Stereotype threat occurs when people feel they are being evaluated against an existing negative cultural stereotype. In studies, African American students show poorer performance on standardized tests if they feel they are being evaluated; if they are led to believe the test doesn't count, they perform as well as white students. The same sorts of results have been found with women and men and white males placed in competition on a math exam with Asian males.

> We all decry prejudice, yet all are prejudiced.
>
> —*Herbert Spencer, 1873*

African American students who thought the test *was* measuring their abilities did not perform as well as the white students or as well as the African Americans in the other group. In subsequent experiments in the same series, Steele and Aronson also found that if race is made more salient, the decrease in performance among African Americans is even more pronounced.

Stereotype threat applies to gender as well. A similar pattern of results was found for women (compared to men) when taking math tests (Spencer, Steele, & Quinn, 1999). The common stereotype has it that men are better at math than women are. In this experiment, when women were led to believe that a particular test was designed to show differences in math abilities between men and women, they did not perform as well as men. In another condition, when women were told that the same test had nothing to do with male-female differences, they performed as well as men. The phenomenon even shows itself among white males if you put them in a similarly threatening situation. For example, in a series of experiments, Joshua Aronson and his colleagues (1999) demonstrated that white males perform less well on a math exam when competing with Asian males—a group that they considered to have superior math ability.

Expectations and Distortions   When a member of an out-group behaves as we expect, it confirms and even strengthens our stereotype. But what happens when an out-group member behaves in an unexpected, nonstereotypical fashion? Attribution theory provides the answer: We can simply engage in some attributional fancy footwork and emerge with our dispositional stereotype intact. Principally, we can make situational attributions about the exception—for example, that the person really is as we believe, but it just isn't apparent in this situation.

This phenomenon was beautifully captured in the laboratory (Ickes, Patterson, Rajecki, & Tanford, 1982). College men were scheduled, in pairs, to participate in the experiment. In one condition, the experimenter casually informed one participant that his partner was extremely unfriendly; in the other condition, the experimenter told one participant that his partner was extremely friendly. In both conditions, the participants went out of their way to be nice to their partner, and their partner returned their friendliness—that is, he behaved warmly and smiled a lot, as college men tend to do when they are treated nicely.

The difference was that the participants who expected their partner to be unfriendly interpreted his friendly behavior as phony—as a temporary, fake response to their own nice behavior. They were convinced that underneath it all, he really was an unfriendly person. Accordingly, when the observed behavior—friendliness—was unexpected and contrary to their dispositional attribution, participants attributed it to the situation: "He's just pretending to be friendly." The dispositional attribution emerged unscathed.

The cartoon on this page demonstrates this ability to explain away disconfirming situational evidence and maintain a dispositional stereotype. This cartoon, from 1951, capitalizes on the stereotype of Mexicans as lazy. While ten Mexicans are seen in the background working hard, the cartoon focuses on the stereotypical image in the foreground. The cartoon's message is that the lazy individual is the true exemplar of his ethnic group. No matter how many others refute the stereotype, the cartoon is implying, it is still true. (Note that half a century ago, not only was this message considered acceptable, but this cartoon was chosen as one of the best of the year.)

Blaming the Victim   Try as they might, it is hard for people who have rarely been discriminated against to fully understand what it's like to be a target of prejudice. Well-intentioned members of the dominant majority will sympathize with the plight of African Americans, Hispanic Americans, Asian Americans, Jews, women, homosexuals, and other groups who are targets of discrimination, but true empathy is difficult for those who have routinely been judged on the basis of their own merit and not their racial, ethnic, religious, or other group membership. And when empathy is absent, it is sometimes hard to avoid falling into the trap of **blaming the victim** for his or her plight. This may take the form of the "well-deserved reputation." It goes something like this: "If the Jews have been victimized throughout their history, they must have been doing something to deserve it." Such suggestions constitute a demand that members of the outgroup conform to more stringent standards of behavior than those set for the majority.

Ironically, as we discussed in Chapter 4, this tendency to blame victims for their victimization—attributing their predicaments to deficits in their abilities and character—is typically motivated by an understandable desire to see the world as a fair and just place, one where people get what they deserve and deserve what they get. Most people, when confronted with evidence of an unfair outcome that is otherwise difficult to explain, find a way to blame the victim (Lerner, 1980, 1991; Lerner & Grant, 1990). For example, in one experiment, two people worked equally hard on the same task and, by the flip of a coin, one received a sizable reward and the other received nothing. After the fact, observers tended to reconstruct what happened and convince themselves that the unlucky person must have worked less hard. Similarly, negative attitudes toward the poor and the homeless—including blaming them for their own plight—are more prevalent among individuals who display a strong belief in a just world (Furnham & Gunter, 1984).

How does the belief in a just world lead to derogation of a victim and the perpetuation of prejudice? When something bad happens to another person (as when someone is mugged or raped), we will undoubtedly feel sorry for the person but at the same time will also feel relieved that this horrible thing didn't happen to us. We will also feel scared that such a thing might happen to us in the future. How can we cope with these fears and worries? We can protect ourselves from the fear we feel by convincing ourselves that the person must have done something to cause the tragedy. We feel safe, then, because we would have behaved more cautiously (Jones & Aronson, 1973).

Most of us are very good at reconstructing situations after the fact in order to support our belief in a just world. It simply requires making a dispositional

Blaming the Victim

The tendency to blame individuals (make dispositional attributions) for their victimization, typically motivated by a desire to see the world as a fair place

attribution—to the victim—and not a situational one—to the scary, random events that can happen to anyone at any time. In a fascinating experiment, college students who were provided with a description of a young woman's friendly behavior toward a man judged that behavior as completely appropriate (Janoff-Bulman, Timko, & Carli, 1985). Another group of students was given the same description, plus the information that the encounter ended with the young woman being raped by the man. This group rated the young woman's behavior as inappropriate; she was judged as having brought the rape on herself.

Such findings are not limited to American college students reading hypothetical cases. In a survey conducted in England, a striking 33 percent of the respondents believed that victims of rape are almost always to blame for it (Wagstaff, 1982).

How can we account for such harsh attributions? Most of us find it frightening to think that we live in a world where people, through no fault of their own, can be raped, discriminated against, deprived of equal pay for equal work, or denied the basic necessities of life. By the same token, if 6 million Jews are exterminated for no apparent reason, it is, in some strange way, comforting to believe that they must have done something to bring those events on themselves. The irony is overwhelming: Such thinking makes the world seem safer to us.

Self-Fulfilling Prophecies   All other things being equal, if you believe that Amy is stupid and treat her accordingly, chances are that she will not say a lot of clever things in your presence. This is the well-known **self-fulfilling prophecy,** discussed in Chapter 3. How does this come about? If you believe that Amy is stupid, you probably will not ask her interesting questions, and you will not listen intently while she is talking; indeed, you might even look out the window or yawn. You behave this way because of a simple expectation: Why waste energy paying attention to Amy if she is unlikely to say anything smart or interesting? This is bound to have an important impact on Amy's behavior, for if the people she is talking to aren't paying much attention, she will feel uneasy and will probably clam up and not come out with all the poetry and wisdom within her. This serves to confirm the belief you had about her in the first place. The circle is closed; the self-fulfilling prophecy is complete.

Researchers demonstrated the relevance of this phenomenon to stereotyping and discrimination in an elegant experiment (Word, Zanna, & Cooper, 1974). White college undergraduates were asked to interview several job applicants; some of the applicants were white, and others were African American. Unwittingly, the college students displayed discomfort and lack of interest when interviewing African American applicants. They sat farther away, tended to stammer, and ended the interview far sooner than when they were interviewing white applicants. Can you guess how this behavior might have affected the African American applicants? To find out, the researchers conducted a second experiment in which they systematically varied the behavior of the interviewers (actually confederates) so that it coincided with the way the real interviewers had treated the African American or white interviewees in the first experiment. But in the second experiment, all of the interviewees were white. The researchers videotaped the proceedings and had the applicants rated by independent judges. They found that those applicants who were interviewed the way African Americans had been interviewed in the first experiment were judged to be far more nervous and far less effective than those who were interviewed the way whites had been interviewed in the first experiment. In sum, these experiments demonstrate clearly that when African Americans are interviewed by whites, they are unintentionally placed at a disadvantage and are likely to perform less well than their white counterparts (see Figure 13.5).

On a societal level, the insidiousness of the self-fulfilling prophecy goes even further. Suppose that there is a general belief that a particular group is

Self-Fulfilling Prophecy

The case whereby people (1) have an expectation about what another person is like, which (2) influences how they act toward that person, which (3) causes that person to behave in a way consistent with people's original expectations

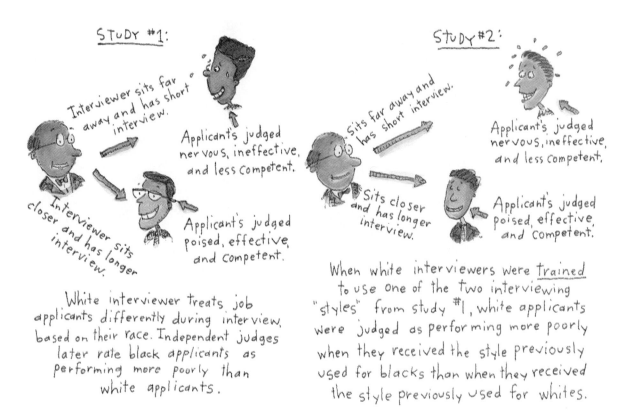

FIGURE 13.5
An experiment demonstrating self-fulfilling prophecies.

irredeemably stupid, uneducable, and fit only for menial jobs. Why waste educational resources on them? Hence they are given inadequate schooling. Thirty years later, what do you find? An entire group that with few exceptions is fit only for menial jobs. "See? I was right all the while," says the bigot. "How fortunate that we didn't waste our precious educational resources on such people!" The self-fulfilling prophecy strikes again.

Prejudice and Economic Competition: Realistic Conflict Theory

One of the most obvious sources of conflict and prejudice is competition—for scarce resources, for political power, and for social status. Indeed, whatever problems result from the simple in-group versus out-group phenomenon, they will be magnified by real economic, political, or status competition. **Realistic conflict theory** holds that limited resources lead to conflict among groups and result in prejudice and discrimination (J. W. Jackson, 1993; Sherif, 1966; White, 1977). Thus prejudiced attitudes tend to increase when times are tense and conflict exists over mutually exclusive goals. For example, prejudice has existed between Anglos and Mexican American migrant workers over a limited number of jobs, between Arabs and Israelis over disputed territory, and between northerners and southerners over the abolition of slavery.

Economic and Political Competition   In his classic study of prejudice in a small industrial town, John Dollard (1938) was among the first to document the relationship between discrimination and economic competition. At first, there was

Realistic Conflict Theory

The idea that limited resources lead to conflict between groups and result in increased prejudice and discrimination

Economic competition drives a good deal of prejudice. As long as white Americans have work, they are happy to let Mexican American migrant workers pick crops; but when unemployment is high, they may see these same workers as a threat to their well-being.

no discernible hostility toward the new German immigrants; prejudice flourished, however, as jobs grew scarce:

> *Local whites largely drawn from the surrounding farms manifested considerable direct aggression toward the newcomers. Scornful and derogatory opinions were expressed about these Germans, and the native whites had a satisfying sense of superiority toward them. . . . The chief element in the permission to be aggressive against the Germans was rivalry for jobs and status in the local woodenware plants. The native whites felt definitely crowded for their jobs by the entering German groups and in case of bad times had a chance to blame the Germans, who by their presence provided more competitors for the scarcer jobs. There seemed to be no traditional pattern of prejudice against Germans unless the skeletal suspicion against all out-groupers (always present) can be invoked in its place.*

Similarly, the prejudice, violence, and negative stereotyping directed against Chinese immigrants in the United States fluctuated wildly throughout the nineteenth century as a result of changes in economic competition. Chinese who joined the California gold rush, competing directly with white miners, were described as "depraved and vicious," "gross gluttons," and "bloodthirsty and inhuman" (Jacobs & Landau, 1971, p. 71). However, only a few years later, when they were willing to accept backbreaking work as laborers on the transcontinental railroad—work few white Americans were willing to do—they were regarded as sober, industrious, and law-abiding. They were so highly regarded, in fact, that Charles Crocker, one of the great tycoons financing the railroad, wrote, "They are equal to the best white men. . . . They are very trusty, very intelligent, and they live up to their contracts" (p. 81). With the end of the Civil War came an influx of former soldiers into an already tight job market. This was immediately followed by a dramatic increase in negative attitudes toward the Chinese: The stereotype changed to criminal, conniving, crafty, and stupid (Jacobs & Landau, 1971).

These changes suggest that when times are tough and resources are scarce, in-group members will feel more threatened by the out-group, and incidents of prejudice, discrimination, and violence toward out-group members will increase. How might the hypothesis be tested? We might look for increases in violent acts directed at minority group members during times of economic hardship. Carl Hovland and Robert Sears (1940) did just that by correlating two sets of very different data: the price of cotton in the southern states from 1882 to 1930 and the number of lynchings of southern African Americans during that same period. During this period, cotton was by far the most important crop in the South; as cotton went, so went the economy. Hovland and Sears found that a significant correlation existed between the two variables: As the price of cotton dropped, the number of lynchings increased. In short, as members of the in-group experienced the hardships of an economic depression, they became more hostile toward out-group members, whom they almost certainly perceived as a threat to their livelihood. Note, however, that this research is correlational. As we discussed in Chapter 2, experimental research designs allow us to make cause-and-effect statements with far more confidence than we can on the basis of correlational research. How might we study the relationship between competition and prejudice experimentally?

In a classic experiment, Muzafer Sherif and his colleagues (1961) tested group conflict theory using the natural environment of a Boy Scout camp. The participants in the camp were normal, well-adjusted 12-year-old boys who were randomly assigned to one of two groups, the Eagles or the Rattlers. Each group stayed in its own cabin; the cabins were located quite a distance apart to reduce contact between the two groups. The youngsters were placed in situations designed to increase the cohesiveness of their own group. This was done by arranging enjoyable activities such as hiking and swimming and by having the campers work with their group on various building projects, preparing group meals, and so on.

After feelings of cohesiveness developed within each group, the researchers set up a series of competitive activities in which the two groups were pitted against each other—for example, in games like football, baseball, and tug-of-war, where prizes were awarded to the winning team. These competitive games aroused feelings of conflict and tension between the two groups. In addition, the investigators created other situations to further intensify the conflict. For example, a camp party was arranged, but each group was told it started at a different time, thereby ensuring that the Eagles would arrive well before the Rattlers. The refreshments at the party consisted of two different kinds of food: Half the food was fresh, appealing, and appetizing, while the other half was squashed, ugly, and unappetizing. As you'd expect, the early-arriving Eagles ate well, and the latecoming Rattlers were not happy with what they found. They began to curse at the exploitive group. Because the Eagles believed they deserved what they got (first come, first served), they resented the name-calling and responded in kind. Name-calling escalated into food-throwing, and within a short time, punches were thrown and a full-scale riot ensued.

Following this incident, the investigators tried to reverse the hostility they had promoted. Competitive games were eliminated, and a great deal of nonconflictual social contact was initiated. Once hostility had been aroused, however, simply eliminating the competition did not eliminate the hostility. Indeed, hostility continued to escalate, even when the two groups were engaged in such benign activities as watching movies together. Eventually, the investigators did manage to reduce the hostility between the two groups; exactly how will be discussed at the end of this chapter.

The Role of the Scapegoat A special case of the conflict-competition theory is the *scapegoat theory* (Allport, 1954; Gemmill, 1989; Miller & Bugelski, 1948). As indicated earlier, if times are tough and things are going poorly, individuals have a tendency to lash out at members of an out-group with whom they compete directly for scarce resources. But there are situations in which a logical competitor does not exist. For example, in Germany following World War I, inflation was out of control, and people were extremely poor, demoralized, and

FIGURE 13.6

Scapegoating.

When insulted, people are more prone to aggress against minorities.

(Adapted from Rogers & Prentice-Dunn, 1981)

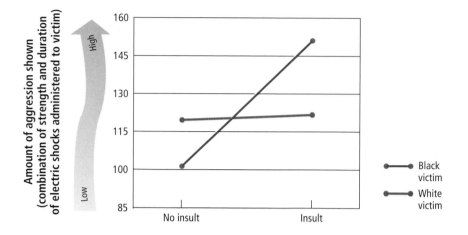

FIGURE 13.6

Scapegoating.

When insulted, people are more prone to aggress against minorities.

(Adapted from Rogers & Prentice-Dunn, 1981)

frustrated. When the Nazis gained power in the 1930s, they managed to focus the frustration of the German population on the Jews, an easily identifiable, powerless out-group. The Jews were not the reason the German economy was in such bad shape, but who was? It's hard to fight back against world events or one's government—particularly when one's government is evading responsibility by blaming someone else. Thus the Nazis created the illusion that if the Jews could be punished, deprived of their civil rights, and ultimately eliminated, all of the problems then plaguing Germany would disappear. The Jews served as a convenient scapegoat because they were easily identifiable and were not in a position to defend themselves or strike back (Berkowitz, 1962). Does scapegoating occur whenever people are feeling frustrated and angry, even in the absence of direct competition or conflict? In an experiment at the University of Alabama, white students were told to administer a series of electric shocks to another student as part of a learning experiment (Rogers & Prentice-Dunn, 1981). The students were free to adjust the level of intensity of the shocks. In actuality, the learner was a confederate who was not really connected to the shock apparatus. There was no conflict or competition involved in this study; however, for some participants, feelings of frustration and anger were aroused. The confederate was trained to be either friendly or insulting to the participant. In addition, the confederate was either black or white. Would angry white students respond more aggressively toward a black peer than a white one? The answer is yes. When the confederate insulted them, the students administered far more intense shocks to the black student than to the white student; when the confederate was friendly, the students administered slightly less intense shocks to the black student. The results of this experiment are shown in Figure 13.6.

The research on **scapegoating** shows that individuals, when frustrated or unhappy, tend to displace aggression onto groups that are disliked, are visible, and are relatively powerless. Moreover, the form the aggression takes depends on what is allowed or approved by the in-group in question. Since the 1940s and 1950s, lynchings of African Americans and pogroms against Jews have diminished dramatically because these are now deemed illegal by the dominant culture. But not all progress is linear. In the past decade, we have seen many eastern European countries emerge from the shadow of the former Soviet Union. But the new freedoms in the region have been accompanied by increased feelings of nationalism ("us versus them") that have in turn intensified feelings of rancor and prejudice against out-groups. In the Baltic States and the Balkans, the rise in nationalistic feelings has led to the outbreak of hostility and even war among Serbs, Muslims, and Croats, Azerbaijanis and Armenians, and other groups.

Scapegoating

The tendency for individuals, when frustrated or unhappy, to displace aggression onto groups that are disliked, visible, and relatively powerless

And there is evidence of increases in hostility toward the world's favorite scapegoat, with anti-Semitism on the rise throughout eastern Europe (Poppe, 2001; Singer, 1990).

The Way We Conform: Normative Rules

We've seen that prejudice is created and maintained by many forces in the social world. Some operate within the individual, such as the ways we process information and assign meaning to observed events; some operate on whole groups of people, such as the effects of competition, conflict, and frustration. Our final explanation for what causes prejudice also occurs on the group level—conformity to normative standards or rules in the society. As we discussed in Chapter 8, conformity is a frequent part of social life, whether we conform to gain information (informational conformity) or to fit in and be accepted (normative conformity). Again, a relatively innocuous social behavior—in this case, conformity—becomes particularly dangerous and debilitating when the conforming involves prejudiced beliefs and behaviors.

When Prejudice Is Institutionalized   Norms are beliefs held by a society as to what is correct, acceptable, and permissible. Obviously, norms vary widely across cultures. Important regional differences in norms also occur within the same country. For example, until not long ago, racial segregation in hotels, eating places, motion picture theaters, drinking fountains, and toilet facilities was normative in the American South but not in the North. Indeed, it can be said that prior to 1954, segregation controlled most aspects of social life in the South. These norms do not have to be taught directly. Simply by living in a society where stereotypical information abounds and where discriminatory behavior is the norm, the vast majority of us will unwittingly develop prejudiced attitudes and discriminatory behavior to some extent. We call this institutional discrimination or, more specifically, as **institutionalized racism** and **institutionalized sexism.** For example, if you grow up in a society where few minority group members and women have professional careers and where most people in these groups hold menial jobs, then simply living in that society will increase your likelihood of developing certain (negative) attitudes about the inherent abilities of minorities and women. This state of affairs can come about without anyone actively teaching you that minorities and women are inferior and without any law or decree banning minorities and women from college faculties, boardrooms, or medical schools. Instead, social barriers have created a lack of opportunity for these groups that makes their success extremely unlikely.

How does normative prejudice work? In Chapter 8, we discussed the strong tendency to go along with the group in order to fulfill the group's expectations and gain acceptance, a phenomenon known as **normative conformity.** Being a nonconformist can be painful. As Thomas Pettigrew (1958, 1985, 1991) has noted, many people consequently adopt prejudiced attitudes and engage in discriminatory behaviors in order to conform to, or fit in with, the prevailing majority view of their culture. It's as if people say, "Hey, everybody else thinks Xs are inferior; if I behave cordially toward Xs, people will think I'm weird. They won't like me. They'll say bad things about me. I don't need the hassle. I'll just go along with everybody else." Pettigrew argues convincingly that while economic competition, frustration, and social cognition processes do account for some prejudice, by far the greatest determinant of prejudice is slavish conformity to social norms.

For example, Ernest Campbell and Thomas Pettigrew (1959) studied the ministers of Little Rock, Arkansas, after the 1954 Supreme Court decision struck

Institutionalized Racism

Racist attitudes that are held by the vast majority of people living in a society where stereotypes and discrimination are the norm

Institutionalized Sexism

Sexist attitudes that are held by the vast majority of people living in a society where stereotypes and discrimination are the norm

Normative Conformity

The tendency to go along with the group in order to fulfill the group's expectations and gain acceptance

down school segregation. Most ministers favored integration and equality for all American citizens, but they kept these views to themselves. They were afraid to support desegregation from their pulpits because they knew that their white congregations were violently opposed to it. Going against the prevailing norm would have meant losing church members and contributions, and under such normative pressure, even ministers found it difficult to do the right thing.

Another way to determine the role of normative conformity is to track changes in prejudice and discrimination over time. As social norms change, so should the strength of prejudiced attitudes and the amount of discriminatory behavior. For example, what happens when people move from one part of the country to another? If conformity is a factor in prejudice, we would expect individuals to show dramatic increases in their prejudice when they move to an area in which the norm is more prejudicial and to show dramatic decreases when they move to an area in which the norm is less prejudicial. And that is just what happens.

Researchers have found that people who had recently moved to New York City and had come into direct contact with an anti-Semitic norm became more anti-Semitic themselves. Similarly, when southerners entered the army and came into contact with a less prejudiced set of social norms, their prejudice against African Americans gradually decreased (Pettigrew, 1958; Watson, 1950). Researchers in a small mining town in West Virginia found even more dramatic evidence of shifting norms: Over the years, African American miners and white miners developed a pattern of living that consisted of total integration while they were under the ground and total segregation while they were above the ground (Minard, 1952; Reitzes, 1952).

Moreover, surveys conducted over the past six decades make it clear that what is going on inside the minds of Americans has changed a great deal. For example, in 1942, the overwhelming majority of white Americans believed that it was a good idea to have separate sections for African American and white people on buses. Two out of every three white Americans surveyed believed that schools should be segregated. In the South, the numbers were even more striking: In 1942, fully 98 percent of the white population was opposed to desegregating schools (Hyman & Sheatsley, 1956). In contrast, by 1988, only 3 percent of white Americans said they wouldn't want their child to attend school with black children. That is a dramatic change indeed!

Shifting cultural norms are well illustrated by the two photographs on page 463, each depicting Governor George Wallace of Alabama. In one, the governor, along with his state militia, is attempting to block the doors of the University of Alabama as the first African American students seek to register for college. Only the presence of federal troops and telephone intervention by President John Kennedy caused Governor Wallace to back down. And yet just a decade later, the normative climate of Alabama had changed to the extent that Governor Wallace could be seen—as in the second photograph—congratulating the young African American woman whom the University of Alabama student body had chosen to be homecoming queen (Knopke, Norrell, & Rogers, 1991).

"Modern" Prejudice As the norm swings toward tolerance for out-groups, many people simply become more careful—outwardly acting unprejudiced yet inwardly maintaining their stereotyped views. This phenomenon is known as **modern racism.** People have learned to hide prejudice in order to avoid being labeled as racist, but when the situation becomes "safe," their prejudice will be revealed (Dovidio & Gaertner, 1996; McConahay, 1986).

Modern Racism

Outwardly acting unprejudiced while inwardly maintaining prejudiced attitudes

For example, while it is true that few Americans say they are generally opposed to school desegregation, it is interesting that most white parents oppose busing their own children to achieve racial balance. When questioned, these parents insist that their opposition has nothing to do with prejudice; they simply

What a difference a decade makes! On the left, in 1963, Governor George Wallace defies a federal order by physically blocking the entrance of the first black student to the University of Alabama. On the right, ten years later, Governor Wallace happily congratulates the University of Alabama homecoming queen.

don't want their kids to waste a lot of time on a bus. But as John McConahay (1981) has shown, most white parents are quite tranquil about busing when their kids are simply being bused from one white school to another; most show vigorous opposition only when the busing is interracial.

Given the properties of modern prejudice, it can best be studied with subtle or unobtrusive measures (Crosby, Bromley, & Saxe, 1980). One team of researchers created an ingenious contraption to get at the real attitudes—not simply the socially desirable ones—of their research participants (Jones & Sigall, 1971). They showed research participants an impressive-looking machine, described as a kind of lie detector. In fact, this "bogus pipeline" was just a pile of electronic hardware whose dials the experimenter could secretly manipulate. Here's how researchers use the pipeline: Participants are randomly assigned to one of two conditions, in which they indicate their attitudes either on a paper-and-pencil questionnaire (where it is easy to give socially correct responses) or by using the bogus pipeline (where they believe the machine will reveal their true attitudes if they lie). The researchers found that students' responses showed more racial prejudice when the bogus pipeline was used (Sigall & Page, 1971). Similarly, college men and women expressed almost identical positive attitudes about women's rights and women's roles in society on a paper-and-pencil measure. However, when the bogus pipeline was used, most of the men displayed far less sympathy to women's issues than the women did (Tourangeau, Smith, & Rasinski, 1997).

Subtle and Blatant Prejudice in Western Europe   We've been discussing prejudice and stereotyping in the United States, but Americans have no franchise on prejudice. Examples of blatant prejudice abound in daily newspaper headlines: ethnic cleansing in Bosnia, violent conflict between Arabs and Jews in the Middle East, mass murder between warring tribes in Rwanda. This prejudice exists in "modern" forms as well (Pettigrew, 1998; Pettigrew et al., 1998). A transnational study, for example, found both blatant and more "modern," subtle racism in France, the Netherlands, and Great Britain (Meertens & Pettigrew, 1997; Pettigrew & Meertens, 1995).

The researchers showed that the difference between blatant and subtle racism is important and has interesting consequences. One of their major findings is that although the targets of prejudice differ in the three countries, the behavior of the native population toward recent immigrants can be predicted from their scores on both blatant and subtle measures of prejudice. For example, in all three countries, people who score high on the blatant prejudice scale want to send immigrants back to their home country and wish to restrict their meager rights even further. Those who score low on both scales want to improve the rights of immigrants, are prepared to take action to help them remain in the country, and are willing to act forcefully to improve relations between immigrants and natives. Those who score high on the subtle racism scale but low on the blatant scale tend to reject immigrants in ways that are more covert and socially acceptable. Specifically, while they will not act to send immigrants back to their home country, they will also not do anything to help improve their relations with the immigrant population, nor will they join any attempt to increase that population's civil rights (Pettigrew, 1998).

Subtle Sexism

Subtle forms of prejudice can also be directed toward women. As we have seen, not all prejudice consists of feelings of antipathy toward the target group. Because we live in a patriarchal society, many men have feelings of ambivalence toward women. Peter Glick and Susan Fiske (2001) have shown that this ambivalence can take one of two forms: *hostile sexism* or *benevolent sexism*. Hostile sexists hold stereotypical views of women that suggest that women are inferior to men (e.g., that they are less intelligent, less competent, and so on). Benevolent sexists hold stereotypically positive views of women. Indeed, their views are actually chivalrous in nature. As we suggested earlier, harboring stereotypically positive feelings about a group (as is true of benevolent sexists) can be damaging to the target because it is limiting. But benevolent sexism goes a bit further. According to Glick and Fiske, underneath it all, benevolent sexists (like hostile sexists) assume that women are the weaker sex. Benevolent sexists tend to idealize women romantically, may admire them as wonderful cooks and mothers, and want to protect them when they do not need protection. Thus in the final analysis, both hostile sexism and benevolent sexism—for different reasons—serve to justify relegating women to traditional stereotyped roles in society.

> It is never too late to give up our prejudices.
>
> —Henry David Thoreau, 1854

HOW CAN PREJUDICE BE REDUCED?

Sometimes subtle, sometimes brutally overt, prejudice is indeed ubiquitous. Does this mean that prejudice is an essential aspect of human social interaction and will therefore always be with us? We social psychologists do not take such a pessimistic view. We tend to agree with Thoreau that "it is never too late to give up our prejudices." People can change. But how? What can we do to eliminate or at least reduce this noxious aspect of human social behavior?

Because stereotypes and prejudice are based on false information, for many years social observers believed that education was the answer: All we needed to do was expose people to the truth and their prejudices would disappear. But this has proved a naive hope (Lazarsfeld, 1940). After reading this chapter to this point, you can see why this might be the case. Because of the underlying emotional aspects of prejudice, as well as some of the cognitive ruts we get into (e.g., attributional biases, biased expectations, and illusory correlations), stereotypes based on misinformation are difficult to modify simply by providing people with the facts. But there is hope. As you may have experienced, repeated contact with members of an out-group can modify stereotypes and prejudice. But mere contact is not enough; it must be a special kind of contact. What exactly does this mean?

The Contact Hypothesis

In 1954, when the U.S. Supreme Court outlawed segregated schools, social psychologists were excited and optimistic. Because segregation lowered the self-esteem of minority children, most social psychologists believed that desegregating the schools would lead to increases in these youngsters' self-esteem. It was hoped, too, that school desegregation would be the beginning of the end of prejudice. The idea was that contact between children of different races and ethnicities would eventually erode prejudice.

"I wish we could have met under different circumstances..."

There was good reason for this optimism, for not only did it make sense theoretically, but empirical evidence supported the power of contact among races. As early as 1951, Morton Deutsch and Mary Ellen Collins examined the attitudes of white Americans toward African Americans in two public housing projects that differed in their degree of racial integration. In one, black and white families had been randomly assigned to separate buildings in the same project. In the other project, black and white families lived in the same building. After several months, white residents in the integrated project reported a greater positive change in their attitudes toward blacks than residents of the segregated project did, even though the former had not chosen to live in an integrated building initially.

Although contact among the races is generally a good thing (Pettigrew & Tropp, 2003), the desegregation of schools did not work as smoothly as most knowledgeable people had expected. Indeed, far from producing the hoped-for harmony, school desegregation frequently led to tension and turmoil in the classroom. In his careful analysis of the research examining the impact of desegregation, Walter Stephan (1978, 1985) was unable to find a single study demonstrating a significant increase in self-esteem among African American children, and 25 percent of the studies showed a significant decrease in their self-esteem following desegregation. In addition, prejudice was not reduced. Stephan (1978) found that in 53 percent of the studies, prejudice actually increased; in 34 percent of the studies, no change in prejudice occurred. And if one had taken an aerial photograph of the schoolyards of most desegregated schools, one would have found that there was very little true integration: White kids tended to cluster with white kids, black kids tended to cluster with black kids, Hispanic kids tended to cluster with Hispanic kids, and so on (Aronson, 1978; Aronson & Gonzalez, 1988; Aronson & Thibodeau, 1992; Schofield, 1986). Clearly, in this instance, mere contact did not work as we had hoped.

What went wrong? Why did desegregated housing work better than desegregated schools? Let's take a closer look at the contact hypothesis. Clearly, not all kinds of contact will reduce prejudice and raise self-esteem. For example, in the South, blacks and whites have had a great deal of contact, dating back to the time when Africans first arrived on American shores; however, prejudice flourished nonetheless. Obviously, the kind of contact they were having—as master and slave—was not the kind that would reduce prejudice. In his strikingly prescient masterwork *The Nature of Prejudice*, Gordon Allport (1954) stated the contact hypothesis this way:

> *Prejudice may be reduced by equal-status contact between majority and minority groups in the pursuit of common goals. The effect is greatly enhanced if this contact is sanctioned by institutional supports (i.e., by law, custom or local*

Intergroup relations.

Intergroup tensions were eased only after members engaged in cooperative activities.

(Adapted from Sherif, Harvey, White, Hood, & Sherif, 1961)

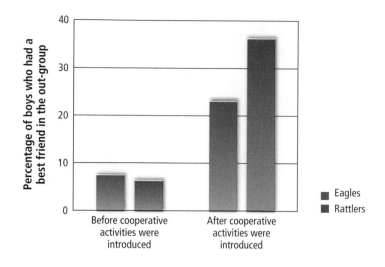

atmosphere), and provided it is of a sort that leads to the perception of common interests and common humanity between members of the two groups. (p. 281)

In short, prejudice will decrease when two conditions are met: Both groups are of equal status and both share a common goal. Note that implicit in the Deutsch and Collins (1951) housing study was the fact that the two groups were of equal status in the project and that no obvious issues of conflict existed between them. Decades of research have substantiated Allport's early claim that these conditions must be met before contact will lead to a decrease in prejudice between groups (Cook, 1985). Let's now turn to a discussion of these conditions.

When Contact Reduces Prejudice: Six Conditions

Remember Sherif and colleagues' (1961) study at the boys' camp, involving the Eagles and the Rattlers? When conflict and competition were instigated, stereotyping and prejudice resulted. As part of the study, Sherif and his colleagues also staged several events at the camp to reduce the prejudice they had created. Their findings tell us a great deal about what contact can and cannot do.

First, the researchers found that once hostility and distrust were established, simply removing the conflict and the competition did not restore harmony. In fact, bringing the two groups together in neutral situations actually *increased* their hostility and distrust. The children in these groups had trouble with each other even when they were simply watching a movie together.

How did Sherif succeed in reducing their hostility? He placed the two groups of boys in situations where they experienced **mutual interdependence,** the need to depend on each other to accomplish a goal that is important to each group. For example, the investigators set up an emergency situation by damaging the water supply system. The only way the system could be repaired was if all the Rattlers and Eagles cooperated immediately. On another occasion, the camp truck broke down while the boys were on a camping trip. To get the truck going again, it was necessary to pull it up a rather steep hill. This could be accomplished only if all the youngsters pulled together, regardless of whether they were Eagles or Rattlers. Eventually, these sorts of situations brought about a diminution of hostile feelings and negative stereotyping among the campers. In fact, after these cooperative situations were introduced, the number of boys who said their closest friend was in the other group increased dramatically (see Figure 13.7). Thus two of the key factors in the success of contact are *mutual interdependence* and a *common goal* (Amir, 1969, 1976).

> We must recognize that beneath the superficial classification of sex and race the same potentialities exist, recurring generation after generation only to perish because society has no place for them.
>
> —*Margaret Mead, Male and Female, 1943*

Mutual Interdependence

The situation that exists when two or more groups need each other and must depend on each other to accomplish a goal that is important to each of them

It is crucial that individuals believe that out-group members he or she comes to know are typical of their group. If this man perceives his partner as an exception, his prejudice against women on the force won't be affected by his personal acceptance of her value as a fellow officer.

The third condition is *equal status*. At the boys' camp (Sherif et al., 1961) and in the public housing project (Deutsch & Collins, 1951), the group members were very much the same in terms of status and power. No one was the boss, and no one was the less powerful employee. When status is unequal, interactions can easily follow stereotypical patterns. The whole point of contact is to allow people to learn that their stereotypes are inaccurate; contact and interaction should lead to disconfirmation of negative, stereotyped beliefs. If status is unequal between the groups, their interactions will be shaped by that status difference—the bosses will act like stereotypical bosses, the employees like stereotypical subordinates—and no one will learn new, disconfirming information about the other group (Pettigrew, 1969; Wilder, 1984).

Fourth, contact must occur in a *friendly, informal setting* where in-group members can interact with out-group members on a one-to-one basis (Brewer & Miller, 1984; Cook, 1984; Wilder, 1986). Simply placing two groups in contact in a room where they can remain segregated will do little to promote their understanding or knowledge of each other.

Fifth, through friendly, informal interactions with *multiple members* of the out-group, an individual will learn that his or her beliefs about the out-group are wrong. It is crucial for the individual to believe that the out-group members he or she comes to know are typical of their group; otherwise, the stereotype can be maintained by labeling one out-group member as the exception (Wilder, 1984). For example, a study of male police officers assigned female partners in Washington, D.C., found that although the men were satisfied with their female partner's performance, they still opposed hiring women police officers. Their stereotypes about women's ability to do police work hadn't changed; in fact, they matched those of male officers with male partners (Milton, 1971). Why? They perceived their partner as an exception.

Sixth and last, contact is most likely to lead to reduced prejudice when *social norms that promote and support equality among groups* are operating in the situation (Amir, 1969; Wilder, 1984). Social norms are powerful; here they can be harnessed to motivate people to reach out to members of the out-group. For example, if the boss or the professor creates and reinforces a norm of acceptance and tolerance at work or in the classroom, group members will change their behavior to fit the norm.

To sum up, suspicious or even hostile groups will reduce their stereotyping, prejudice, and discriminatory behavior when these six conditions of contact are met (Aronson & Bridgeman, 1979; Cook, 1984; Riordan, 1978):

1. Mutual interdependence
2. A common goal
3. Equal status
4. Informal, interpersonal contact
5. Multiple contacts
6. Social norms of equality

Why Early Desegregation Failed

Knowing now what conditions must exist for contact to work, we can better understand the problems that occurred when schools were first desegregated. Imagine a typical scenario. Carlos, a Mexican American sixth grader, has been attending schools in an underprivileged neighborhood his entire life. Because the schools in his neighborhood were not well equipped or well staffed, his first five years of education were somewhat deficient. Suddenly, without much warning or preparation, he is bused to a school in a predominantly white, middle-class neighborhood.

As you know from experience, the traditional classroom is a highly competitive environment. The typical scene involves the teacher asking a question; immediately, several hands go into the air as the children strive to show the teacher that they know the answer. When a teacher calls on one child, several others groan because they've missed an opportunity to show the teacher how smart they are. If the child who is called on hesitates or comes up with the wrong answer, there is a renewed and intensified flurry of hands in the air, perhaps even accompanied by whispered, derisive comments directed at the student who failed. Carlos finds he must compete against white, middle-class students who have had better preparation than he and who have been reared to hold white, middle-class values, which include working hard in pursuit of good grades, raising one's hand enthusiastically whenever the teacher asks a question, and so on. In effect, Carlos has been thrust into a highly competitive situation for which he is unprepared and in which payoffs are made for abilities he has not yet developed. He is virtually guaranteed to lose. After a few failures, Carlos, feeling defeated, humiliated, and dispirited, stops raising his hand and can hardly wait for the bell to ring to signal the end of the school day.

In the typical desegregated classroom, to use Allport's (1954) terminology, the students were not of equal status and were not pursuing common goals. Indeed, one might say that they were in a tug-of-war on an uneven playing field. When one examines the situation closely, it is easy to see why Stephan (1978) found a general decrease in the self-esteem of minority children following desegregation. Moreover, given the competitive atmosphere of the classroom, it is likely that the situation would have exacerbated whatever stereotypes existed before desegregation. Specifically, given that the minority kids were not prepared for the competitiveness of the classroom, it is not surprising that some of the white kids quickly concluded that the minority kids were stupid, unmotivated, and sullen—just as they had suspected (Wilder & Shapiro, 1989). Moreover, it is likely that the minority kids might conclude that the white kids were arrogant showoffs. This is an example of the self-fulfilling prophecy we discussed earlier.

How could we change the atmosphere of the classroom so that it comes closer to Gordon Allport's prescription for the effectiveness of contact?

Specifically, how could we get white students and minority students to be of equal status, mutually dependent, and in pursuit of common goals? The following is a firsthand account.

CONNECTIONS

Cooperation and Interdependence: The Jigsaw Classroom

In 1971, Austin, Texas, desegrated its schools. Within just a few weeks, African American, white, and Mexican American children were in open conflict; fistfights broke out in the corridors and schoolyards. Austin's school superintendent called on Elliot Aronson, then a professor at the University of Texas, to find a way to create a more harmonious environment. After spending a few days observing the dynamics of several classrooms, Aronson and his graduate students were strongly reminded of the situation that existed in the Sherif and colleagues (1961) camp experiment. With the findings of that study in mind, they developed a technique that created an interdependent classroom atmosphere, designed to place the students of various racial and ethnic groups in pursuit of common goals. They called it the **jigsaw classroom** because it resembled the assembling of a jigsaw puzzle (Aronson, 1978; Aronson & Gonzalez, 1988; Aronson & Patnoe, 1997; Walker & Crogan, 1998; Wolfe & Spencer, 1996).

Here is how the jigsaw classroom works: Students are placed in diverse six-person learning groups. The day's lesson is divided into six segments, and each student is assigned one segment of the written material. For example, if the students are to learn the life of Eleanor Roosevelt, her biography is broken into six parts and distributed to the six students, each of whom has possession of a unique and vital part of the information, which, like the pieces of a jigsaw puzzle, must be put together before anyone can view the whole picture. Each student must learn his or her own section and teach it to the other members of the group, who do not have any other access to that material. Therefore, if Debbie wants to do well on the exam about the life of Eleanor Roosevelt, she must pay close attention to Carlos (who is reciting on Roosevelt's girlhood years), to Shamika (who is reciting on Roosevelt's years in the White House), and so on.

Unlike the traditional classroom, where students are competing against each other, the jigsaw classroom has students depending on each other. In the traditional classroom, if Carlos, because of anxiety and discomfort, is having difficulty reciting, the other students can easily ignore him (or even put him down) in their zeal to show the teacher how smart they are. But in the jigsaw classroom, if Carlos is having difficulty reciting, it is now in the best interests of the other students to be patient, make encouraging comments, and even ask friendly, probing questions to make it easier for Carlos to bring forth the knowledge within him.

Through the jigsaw process, the children begin to pay more attention to each other and to show respect for each other. As you might expect, a child like Carlos would respond to this treatment by simultaneously becoming more relaxed and more engaged; this would inevitably produce an improvement in his ability to communicate. In fact, after a couple of weeks, the other students were struck by their realization that Carlos was a lot smarter than

> Two are better than one because they have a good reward for their toil. For if they fail, one will lift up his fellow, but woe to him who is alone when he falls and has not another to lift him up. Again, if two lie together, they are warm; but how can one be warm alone?
>
> —*Ecclesiastes 4: 9–12*

Jigsaw Classroom

A classroom setting designed to reduce prejudice and raise the self-esteem of children by placing them in small desegregated groups and making each child dependent on the other children in the group to learn the course material and do well in the class

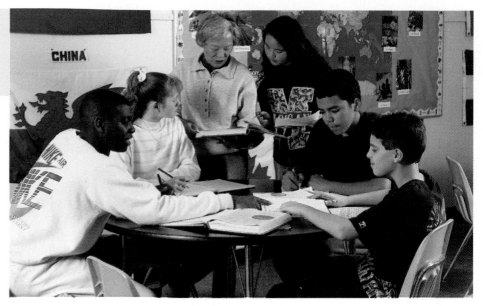

When the classroom is structured so that students of various ethnic groups work together cooperatively, prejudice decreases and self-esteem increases.

they had thought he was. They began to like him. Carlos began to enjoy school more and began to see the Anglo students in his group not as tormentors but as helpful and responsible teammates. Moreover, as he began to feel increasingly comfortable in class and started to gain more confidence in himself, Carlos's academic performance began to improve. As his academic performance improved, so did his self-esteem. The vicious circle had been broken; the elements that had been causing a downward spiral were changed, and the spiral moved dramatically upward.

The formal data gathered from the jigsaw experiments were clear and striking: Compared to students in traditional classrooms, students in jigsaw groups showed a decrease in prejudice and stereotyping and an increase in their liking for their groupmates, both within and across ethnic boundaries. In addition, children in the jigsaw classrooms performed better on objective exams and showed a significantly greater increase in self-esteem than children in traditional classrooms. Children in the jigsaw classrooms also showed far greater liking for school than those in traditional classrooms. Moreover, children in schools where the jigsaw technique was practiced showed substantial evidence of true integration—in the schoolyard, there was far more intermingling among the various races and ethnic groups than on the grounds of schools using more traditional classroom techniques.

Why Does Jigsaw Work?

One reason for the success of this technique is that the process of participating in a cooperative group breaks down in-group versus out-group perceptions and allows the individual to develop the cognitive category of "oneness" wherein no one is excluded from group membership (Gaertner, Mann, Dovidio, & Murrell, 1990). In addition, the cooperative strategy places people in a "favor-doing" situation. Recall that in Chapter 6, we discussed an experiment by Mike Leippe and Donna Eisenstadt (1994, 1998) demonstrating that people who acted in a way that benefited others subsequently came to feel more favorably toward the people they helped, a finding also echoed in Chapter 11.

There is at least one additional reason why jigsaw learning produces such positive interpersonal outcomes: The process of working cooperatively encourages the development of empathy. Here's why: In the competitive classroom, the goal is simply to show the teacher how smart you are. You don't have to pay much attention to the other students in your classroom. But to participate effectively in the jigsaw classroom, each student needs to pay close attention to whichever member of the group is reciting. In doing so, the participants begin to learn that great results can accrue if each of their classmates is approached in a way that is tailored to fit his or her special needs. For example, Alicia may learn that Carlos is a bit shy and needs to be prodded gently, while Trang is so talkative that she might need to be reined in occasionally. Peter can be joked with, but Darnell responds only to serious suggestions.

If our analysis is sound, it should follow that working in jigsaw groups would lead to the sharpening of a youngster's general empathic ability—a change that will reduce the tendency to rely on stereotypes. To test this notion, Diane Bridgeman conducted a clever experiment with 10-year-old children. Just prior to her experiment, half of the children had spent two months participating in jigsaw classes and half in traditional classrooms. In her experiment, Bridgeman (1981) showed the children a series of cartoons aimed at testing children's ability to empathize—to put themselves in the shoes of the cartoon characters. For example, in one cartoon, the first panel shows a little boy looking sad as he waves good-bye to his father at the airport. In the next panel, a letter carrier delivers a package to the boy. In the third panel, the boy opens the package, finds a toy airplane inside, and bursts into tears. Bridgeman asked the children why they thought the little boy burst into tears at the sight of the airplane. Nearly all of the children could answer correctly—because the toy airplane reminded him of how much he missed his father. Then Bridgeman asked the crucial question: "What did the letter carrier think when he saw the boy open the package and start to cry?"

Most children of this age make a consistent error; they assume that everyone knows what they know. Thus the youngsters in the control group thought that the letter carrier would know the boy was sad because the gift reminded him of his father leaving. But the children who had participated in the jigsaw classroom responded differently. Because of their experience with jigsaw, they had developed the ability to take the perspective of the letter carrier—to put themselves in his shoes—and they realized that he would be confused at seeing the boy cry over receiving a nice present because the letter carrier hadn't witnessed the farewell scene at the airport. (See the Try It! exercise on page 472.)

Offhand, this might not seem very important. After all, who cares whether kids have the ability to figure out what is in the mind of a cartoon character? In point of fact, we should all care—a great deal. Recall our discussion of the Columbine tragedy in Chapter 12. In that chapter, we suggested how important empathy is in curbing aggression. The extent to which children can develop the ability to see the world from the perspective of another human being has profound implications for interpersonal relations in general. When we develop the ability to understand what another person is going through, it increases the probability that our heart will open to that person. Once our heart opens to another person, it becomes virtually impossible to feel prejudice against that person, to bully that person, to taunt that person, to humiliate that person. Our guess is that if the jigsaw strategy had been used in Columbine High School and in the elementary and middle schools feeding into Columbine, the tragedy would have been averted.

The Gradual Spread of Cooperative Learning The jigsaw approach was first tested in 1971; since then, educational researchers have developed a variety of similar cooperative techniques (Cook, 1985; Johnson & Johnson, 1987; Slavin & Cooper, 1999). The striking results Aronson and his colleagues obtained have now been successfully replicated in hundreds of classrooms in all regions of the country and abroad (Jurgen-Lohmann, Borsch, & Giesen, 2001; Sharan, 1980).

Jigsaw-Type Group Study

The next time a quiz is coming up in one of your courses, try to organize a handful of your classmates into a jigsaw-type group for purposes of studying for the quiz.

Assign each person a segment of the reading. That person is responsible for becoming the world's greatest expert on that material. That person will organize the material into a report that will be given to the rest of the group. The rest of the group will feel free to ask questions to make sure they fully understand the material. At the end of the session, ask the group members the following questions:

1. Compared to studying alone, was this more or less enjoyable?
2. Compared to studying alone, was this more or less efficient?
3. How are you feeling about each of the people in the group, compared to how you felt about them prior to the session?
4. Would you like to do this again?

You should realize that this situation is probably a lot less powerful than the jigsaw groups described in this book. Why?

Cooperative learning is now generally accepted by educational researchers as one of the most effective ways of improving race relations, building empathy, and improving instruction in our schools (Deutsch, 1997; McConahay, 1981; Slavin, 1996). What began as a simple experiment in one school system is slowly becoming an important force in the field of public education. Unfortunately, the operative word in the preceding sentence is *slowly*. The educational system, like all bureaucracies, tends to resist change. As the Columbine massacre illustrates, this slowness can have tragic consequences (Aronson, 2000).

SUMMARY

Prejudice: The Ubiquitous Social Phenomenon

Prejudice is a widespread phenomenon, present in all societies of the world. Social psychologists define **prejudice** as a hostile or negative attitude toward a distinguishable group of people based solely on their group membership. A **stereotype** is the cognitive component of the prejudiced attitude; it is defined as a generalization about a group whereby identical characteristics are assigned to virtually all members, regardless of actual variation among the members. **Discrimination,** the behavioral component of the prejudiced attitude, is an unjustified negative or harmful action toward members of a group based on their membership in that group.

What Causes Prejudice?

As a broad-based and powerful attitude, prejudice has many causes. We discussed four aspects of social life that bring about prejudice: the way we think, the way we assign meaning or make attributions, the way we allocate resources, and the way we conform to social rules.

The processes of social cognition are important in the creation and maintenance of stereotypes and prejudice. Categorization of people into groups leads to the perception of in-groups and out-groups. In-group bias means that we will treat members of our own group more positively than members of the out-group. Another consequence of categorization is the perception of **out-group homogeneity:** In-group members perceive out-group members as being more similar to each other than the in-group members are.

Stereotypes are widely known in a culture; even if you do not believe in them, they can affect your cognitive processing of information about an out-group member. For example, research has shown that stereotypes are activated by automatic processing; they must be ignored or suppressed by conscious, controlled processing. The **illusory correlation** is another way that cognitive processing perpetuates stereotypical thinking; we tend to see correlations where they don't exist, particularly if the events or people are distinctive.

The fundamental attribution error applies to prejudice—we tend to overestimate the role of dispositional forces when making sense out of others' behavior. Stereotypes can be described as the **ultimate attribution error**—making negative dispositional attributions about an entire out-group. When out-group members act nonstereotypically, we tend to make situational attributions about them, thereby maintaining our stereotypes. For their part, members of an out-group experience **stereotype threat**—a fear they might behave in a manner that confirms an existing stereotype about their group. Our belief in a just world leads us to derogate victims as well as members of out-groups—we see them as causing their fate and circumstances, a phenomenon known as **blaming the victim.** Finally, **self-fulfilling prophecies** are an attributional process by which we find confirmation and proof for our stereotypes by unknowingly causing stereotypical behavior in out-group members through our treatment of them.

Realistic conflict theory states that prejudice is the inevitable byproduct of real conflict between groups for limited resources—whether involving economics, power, or status. Competition for resources leads to derogation of and discrimination against the competing out-group. **Scapegoating** is a process whereby frustrated and angry people tend to displace their aggression from its real source to a convenient target—an out-group that is disliked, visible, and relatively powerless. Social learning theory states that we learn the appropriate norms of our culture—including stereotypes and prejudiced attitudes—from adults, peers, the media, and other aspects of the culture.

Institutionalized racism and **institutionalized sexism** are norms operating throughout the society's structure. **Normative conformity,** or the desire to be accepted and "fit in," leads us to go along with stereotyped beliefs and not challenge them. **Modern racism** is an example of a shift in normative rules about prejudice: Nowadays, people have learned to hide their prejudice in situations where it would lead them to be labeled as racist. Given the more hidden nature of prejudice today, techniques like the bogus pipeline are used to study people's real attitudes about out-groups.

How Can Prejudice Be Reduced?

The most important way to reduce prejudice is through contact—bringing in-group and out-group members together. However, mere contact, as occurred when public schools were first desegregated, is not enough and can even exacerbate existing negative attitudes. Instead, contact situations must include the following six conditions: **mutual interdependence;** a common goal; equal status; informal, interpersonal contact; multiple contacts; and social norms of equality. The **jigsaw classroom,** a learning atmosphere in which children must depend on each other and work together to learn and to reach a common goal, has been found to be a powerful way to reduce stereotyping and prejudice among children of different ethnicities.

CRITICAL THINKING QUESTIONS

1. What are some of the factors that might cause differences in test performance between African American students and white students?

2. How does the belief in a just world perpetuate prejudice?

3. What are the underlying mechanisms that make the jigsaw classroom an effective means of reducing prejudice?

1 SOCIAL PSYCHOLOGY *IN ACTION*

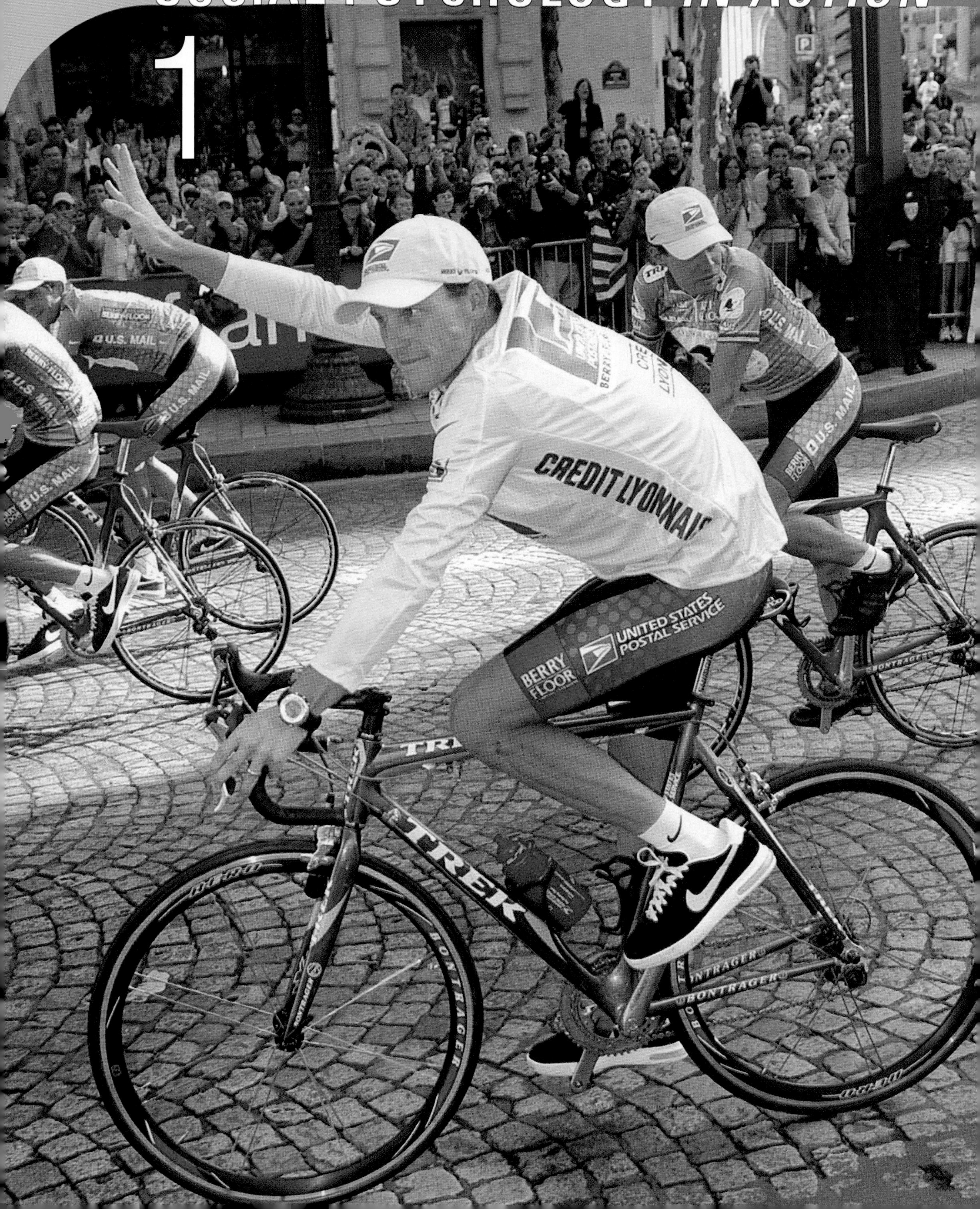

Social Psychology and Health

When Lance Armstrong was 22 years old, he received some devastating news: He had testicular cancer, so advanced that it had spread to his abdomen, lungs, and brain. One of the experts he visited estimated (to himself) that Armstrong had no better than a 3 percent chance of survival. But Armstrong, one of the top cyclists in the world, was not about to admit defeat. He underwent surgery to remove the brain tumors and began an aggressive course of chemotherapy to deal with the cancer in the rest of his body. He learned everything he could about the disease, rallied his friends and family, and approached his treatment as a challenge:

> The more I thought about it, the more cancer began to seem like a race to me. Only the destination had changed. They shared grueling physical aspects, as well as a dependence on time, and progress reports every interval, with checkpoints and a slavish reliance on numbers and blood tests. The only difference was that I had to focus better and harder than I ever did on a bike. (Armstrong, 2000, p. 89)

Remarkably, Armstrong began to recover from the cancer. The surgery to remove the tumors from his brain was successful. The chemotherapy took a tremendous toll on his body, causing skin burns, muscle loss, and near-constant nausea. But it worked: After several months, he was free of cancer. He was so physically weak that no one believed he would ever be the cyclist he once was, but Armstrong got back on his bike and resumed training.

Fast-forward to 1999, three years after Armstrong was diagnosed with cancer. He entered the Tour de France, the most grueling race in the world. Indeed, it may be the most punishing athletic event of any kind: a 23-day race that covers over 2,000 miles, much of it up and down steep mountains in rain and sleet. Almost no one believed Armstrong could win the race, which routinely defeats the top athletes in the world (many of whom drop out before the end). Not only did Armstrong compete, he won the race by more than seven minutes over his nearest competitor. Armstrong went on to win the race the next four years as well, an astonishing feat for any athlete.

Why was Armstrong able to beat the odds and overcome his cancer? Is it a coincidence that he is the kind of person who meets a challenge head on, an optimist who took control of his treatment like a CEO running a major company? Did it have to do with the fact that he was a professional athlete who was in excellent physical shape? Or was he just extremely lucky? It is impossible to answer these questions definitively. Armstrong himself is unsure; in his autobiography, he says he will never know how much to credit himself, medical science, or a miracle. Fortunately, however, some questions about the connection between people's mental outlook and their health can be addressed in carefully controlled studies. Does having a sense of control over one's life aid in recovery from serious diseases? Are optimists likely to be healthier than pessimists? Questions such as these about the relation between the mind and the body have intrigued human beings for centuries, and recent research suggests some fascinating answers.

This chapter is concerned with the application of psychology to physical and mental health, which is a flourishing area of research. We will focus primarily on topics that connect social psychology and health: how people cope with stress in their lives, the relationship between their coping styles and their physical and mental health, and how we can get people to behave in healthier ways.

STRESS AND HUMAN HEALTH

There is more to our physical health than germs and disease—we also need to consider the amount of stress in our lives and how we deal with that stress (Inglehart, 1991). Early research in this area documented some extreme cases in which people's health is influenced by stress. Consider these examples, reported by psychologist W. B. Cannon (1942):

- A New Zealand woman eats a piece of fruit and then learns that it came from a forbidden supply reserved for the chief. Horrified, her health deteriorates, and the next day she dies—even though it was a perfectly fine piece of fruit.

- A man in Africa has breakfast with a friend, eats heartily, and goes on his way. A year later, he learns that his friend had made the breakfast from a wild hen, a food strictly forbidden in his culture. The man immediately begins to tremble and is dead within twenty-four hours.

- An Australian man's health deteriorates after a witch doctor casts a spell on him. He recovers only when the witch doctor removes the spell.

These examples probably sound bizarre, like something you would read in "Ripley's Believe It or Not." But let's shift to the present in the United States, where many similar cases of sudden death occur following a psychological trauma. When people undergo a major upheaval in their lives, such as losing a spouse, declaring bankruptcy, or being forced to resettle in a new culture, their chance of dying increases (Morse, Martin, & Moshonov, 1991). Soon after a major earthquake in the Los Angeles area on January 17, 1994, there was an increase in the number of people who died suddenly of heart attacks (Leor, Poole, & Kloner, 1996). And many people experienced psychological and physical problems after the terrorist attacks on September 11, 2001 (Schlenger et al., 2002; Silver, Holman, McIntosh, Poulin, & Gil-Rivas, 2002). One study measured the heart rates of a sample of adults in New Haven, Connecticut, the week after the attacks. Compared to a control group of people studied before the attacks, the post–September 11 sample showed lower heart rate variability, which is a risk factor for sudden death (Lampert, Baron, McPhearson, & Lee, 2002). To understand findings such as these, we need to understand exactly how to define stress and how it is related to people's health.

Effects of Negative Life Events

Among the pioneers in research on stress was Hans Selye (1956, 1976), who defined *stress* as the body's physiological response to threatening events. Selye focused on how the human body adapts to threats from the environment, regardless of the source, be it a psychological or physiological trauma. Later researchers have examined what it is about a life event that makes it threatening. Holmes and Rahe (1967), for example, suggested that stress is the degree to which people have to change and readjust their lives in response to an external event. The more change that is required, the greater the stress we experience. For example, if a spouse or partner dies, just about every aspect of a person's life is disrupted, leading to a great deal of stress. This definition of stress applies to happy events as well, if the event causes big changes in one's daily routine. Graduating from college is a happy occasion, but it can be stressful because it is often accompanied by a separation from friends and adapting to a new situation, such as looking for a job, working full time, or going to graduate school.

To assess the amount of change in people's lives, Holmes and Rahe (1967) developed a measure called the Social Readjustment Rating Scale (see Table SPA1.1 on page 478). Some events, such as the death of a spouse or partner, have many "life change units" because they involve the most change in people's daily routines. Other events, such as getting a traffic ticket, have relatively few life change units. Here's how the scale works: Participants check all the events they have experienced in the past year and add up their score for the total number of life change units associated with those events. The scores are then correlated with the frequency with which the participants become sick or have physical complaints. Several studies have found that the higher the score people report, the worse their mental and physical health (Seta, Seta, & Wang, 1990; Tesser & Beach, 1998).

These findings probably don't come as much of a surprise; it seems pretty obvious that people who are experiencing a lot of change and upheaval in their lives are more likely to feel anxious and get sick. But these findings aren't all that straightforward. One problem, as you may have recognized, is that most studies in this area use correlational designs, not experimental designs. Just because life changes are correlated with health problems does not mean that the life changes *caused* the health problems (see Chapter 2 on correlation and causality). Some researchers have argued persuasively for the role of "third variables," whereby certain kinds of people are more likely to be experiencing difficult life changes and to report that they are ill (Schroeder & Costa, 1984; Watson & Pennebaker, 1989). According to these researchers, it is not life changes that cause health problems. Instead, people with certain personality traits, such as the tendency to experience negative moods, are more likely to experience life difficulties and to have health problems.

Another problem with inventories such as Holmes and Rahe's is that they focus on stressors experienced by the middle class and underrepresent stressors

TABLE SPA1.1

The Social Readjustment Scale

According to Holmes and Rahe (1967), the greater the number of "life change units" you are experiencing right now, the greater the likelihood that you will become physically ill.

RANK	LIFE EVENT	LIFE CHANGE UNITS
1	Death of spouse	100
2	Divorce	73
3	Marital separation	65
4	Jail term	63
5	Death of a close family member	63
6	Personal injury or illness	53
7	Marriage	50
8	Fired at work	47
9	Marital reconciliation	45
10	Retirement	45
11	Change in health of a family member	44
12	Pregnancy	40
13	Sex difficulties	39
14	Gain of new family member	39
15	Business readjustment	39
16	Change in financial state	38
17	Death of close friend	37
18	Change to different line of work	36
19	Change in number of arguments with spouse	35
20	Mortgage over $10,000	31
21	Foreclosure of mortgage or loan	30
22	Change in responsibilities at work	29
23	Son or daughter leaving home	29
24	Trouble with in-laws	29
25	Outstanding personal achievement	28
26	Spouse begins or stops work	26
27	Begin or end school	26
28	Change in living conditions	25
29	Revision of personal habits	24
30	Trouble with boss	23
31	Change in work hours or conditions	20
32	Change in residence	20
33	Change in schools	20
34	Change in recreation	19
35	Change in church activities	19
36	Change in social activities	18
37	Mortgage or loan less than $10,000	17
38	Change in sleeping habits	16
39	Change in number of family get-togethers	15
40	Change in eating habits	15
41	Vacation	13
42	Christmas	12
43	Minor violations of the law	11

Adapted from Holmes & Rahe, 1967

experienced by the poor and members of minority groups. Variables such as poverty and racism are potent causes of stress (Clark, Anderson, Clark, & Williams, 1999; Jackson & Inglehart, 1995; Jackson et al., 1996). Moreover, the way in which these variables influence health is not always obvious. It might not surprise you to learn that the more racism minority groups experience, the

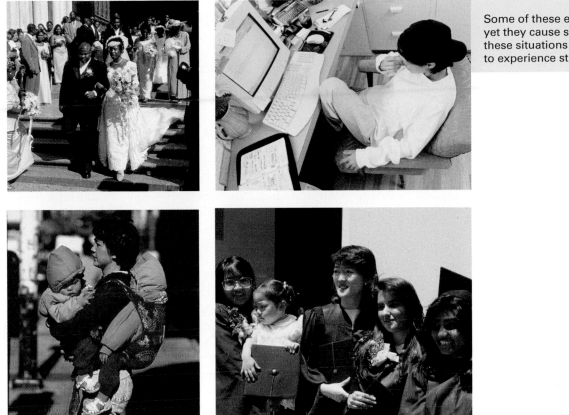

Some of these events are happy, yet they cause stress. Which of these situations might cause you to experience stress?

worse their health. It might come as more of a surprise to learn that majority groups who express the most racist attitudes also experience diminished health (Jackson & Inglehart, 1995). Racism is often associated with hostility and aggression, and as we will see later in this chapter, there is evidence that hostility is related to health problems such as coronary heart disease. Clearly, to understand the relationship between stress and health, we need to understand better such community and cultural variables as poverty and racism.

Perceived Stress and Health

Simply totting up the number of negative life events that people experience—such as losing one's job or divorcing—violates a basic principle of social psychology: Subjective situations have more of an impact on people than objective situations (Griffin & Ross, 1991). Of course, some situational variables are hazardous to our health regardless of how we interpret them (Jackson & Inglehart, 1995; Taylor, Repetti, & Seeman, 1997). Children growing up in smog-infested areas such as Los Angeles, for example, have been found to have 10 to 15 percent less efficiency in their lungs than children who grow up in less polluted areas (see the second Social Psychology in Action module, "Social Psychology and the Environment" on page 504). Nonetheless, some environmental events are open to interpretation and seem to have negative effects only on people who construe these events in certain ways. Some people view getting a traffic ticket as a major hassle, whereas others view it as a minor inconvenience. Some people view a major life change such as getting divorced as a liberating escape from an abusive relationship, whereas others view it as a devastating personal failure. As recognized by Richard Lazarus (1966, 1993, 2000) in his pioneering work on stress, it is subjective, not objective, stress that causes problems. An event is stressful for people only if they interpret it as stressful; thus we can define **stress** as the negative feelings and beliefs that occur whenever people feel unable to cope with demands from their environment (Lazarus & Folkman, 1984).

Consider Lance Armstrong's life during his treatment for cancer. If he had filled out the Social Readjustment Rating Scale, he would have scored a very high number of life change units: "personal injury or illness," "change in financial state," "change to a different line of work" (he could no longer race), and so on. According to the theory, he should have been experiencing a great deal of stress, so much so that he was at great risk for further physical problems. To be sure, it was a tremendously stressful time; Armstrong's life was disrupted in nearly every way. But Armstrong approached these life changes like a fighter, taking an active role in his treatment, finding out everything he could about the disease, and maintaining his optimism. Whereas many people would have found the life changes he experienced to be devastating, Armstrong treated them more as challenges than stressors. Thus a totally objective approach to stress, assuming that everyone reacts in the same way, fails to take into account how different people interpret disruptions and challenges in their lives.

In a classic series of studies, Lazarus (1966) showed that it is people's interpretation of an event that influences how stressful they find it, not the event itself. In one study, for example, he asked people to watch a film of gory industrial accidents, such as a scene in which a worker operating a power saw accidentally cuts off his finger. How upsetting was this film? It depended on how people interpreted it. Lazarus instructed some participants to adopt an intellectual stance while watching the film, concentrating less on the accident and more on the relationships between the workers. Compared to people who were given no special instructions, this group was relatively unaffected by the film. Just as an emergency room nurse reacts to blood and gore differently from how most other people do, these participants succeeded in adopting a detached, clinical view of the accidents, turning a stressful experience into a relatively neutral one.

Studies using this subjective definition of stress confirm the idea that negative life experiences are bad for our health. In fact, stress caused by negative interpretations of events can directly affect our immune systems, making us more susceptible to disease. Consider the common cold. When people are exposed to the virus that causes a cold, only 20 to 60 percent of them become sick. Is it possible that stress is one determinant of who these 20 to 60 percent will be? To find out, researchers asked volunteers to spend a week at a research institute in southern England (Cohen, Tyrrell, & Smith, 1991, 1993). As a measure of stress, the participants listed recent events that had had a negative impact on their lives. (Consistent with our definition of stress, the participants listed only events they perceived as negative.)

The researchers then gave participants nasal drops that contained either the virus that causes the common cold or saline (salt water). The participants were subsequently quarantined for several days so that they had no contact with other people. The results? The people who were experiencing a great deal of stress in their lives were more likely to catch a cold from the virus (see Figure SPA1.1). Among people who reported the least amount of stress, about 27 percent came down with a cold. This rate increased steadily the more stress people reported, topping out at a rate of nearly 50 percent in the group that was experiencing the most stress. This effect of stress was found even when several other factors that influence catching a cold were taken into account, such as the time of year people participated and the participants' age, weight, and gender. This study, along with others like it, shows that the more stress people experience, the lower their immunity to disease (S. Cohen, 2001; O'Leary, 1990; Stone et al., 1993).

You may have noticed that the Cohen and colleagues study used a correlational design; this must make us cautious about its interpretation. The amount of stress people were experiencing was measured and correlated with the likeli-

Stress

The negative feelings and beliefs that arise whenever people feel unable to cope with demands from their environment

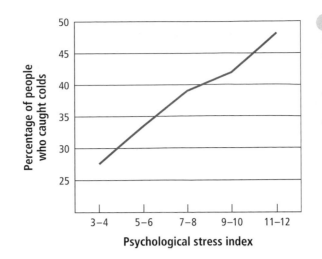

FIGURE SPA1.1

Stress and the likelihood of catching a cold.

People were first exposed to the virus that causes the common cold and then isolated. The greater the amount of stress they were experiencing, the greater the likelihood that they caught a cold from this virus.

(Adapted from Cohen, Tyrrell, & Smith, 1991)

hood that people caught a cold. It is possible that stress itself did not lower people's immunity but rather that some variable correlated with stress did. It would have been ethically impermissible, of course, to conduct an experimental study in which people were randomly assigned to a condition in which they experienced a great deal of prolonged stress. There are studies, however, in which people's immune responses are measured before and after undergoing mildly stressful tasks in the laboratory, such as solving mental arithmetic problems continuously for six minutes or giving speeches on short notice. Even relatively mild stressors such as these can lead to a suppression of the immune system (Cacioppo, 1998; Cacioppo et al., 1998).

The finding that stress negatively affects health raises an important question: What exactly is it that makes people perceive a situation as stressful? One important determinant is the amount of control they believe they have over the event.

Feeling in Charge: The Importance of Perceived Control

Lance Armstrong did not believe in the standard doctor-patient relationship, in which the patient is a passive recipient of medical treatment.

> *Previously, I thought of medicine as something practiced by individual doctors on individual patients. The doctor was all-knowing and all-powerful, the patient was helpless. But it was beginning to dawn on me that there was nothing wrong with seeking a cure from a combination of people and sources, and that the patient was as important as the doctor. . . . No one person could take sole responsibility for the state of my health, and most important, I began to share the responsibility with them. (Armstrong, 2000, p. 93)*

Is it possible that Armstrong's recovery was related to the sense of control that he felt over his disease? We can't tell in any single case, but research with the chronically ill suggests that there is a relationship between perceived control and health. Shelley Taylor and her colleagues (Taylor, Lichtman, & Wood, 1984), for example, interviewed women with breast cancer and found that many of them believed they could control whether their cancer returned. Here is how one man described his wife: "She got books, she got pamphlets, she studied, she talked to cancer patients. She found out everything that was happening to her and she fought it. She went to war with it. She calls it 'taking in her covered wagons and surrounding it'" (quoted in Taylor, 1989, p. 178). The researchers found that women who believed their cancer was controllable were better adjusted psychologically (Folkman & Moskowitz, 2000). Subsequent studies have found that a high sense of **perceived control,** defined as the belief that we can influence our environment in ways that determine whether we experience positive or negative outcomes, is associated with good physical and mental health (Averill, 1973; Burger, 1992; Skinner, 1995, 1996; Thompson, 1999). For example, among people who had undergone a coronary angioplasty because of diseased arteries, those who had a high sense of control over their futures were less likely to experience subsequent heart problems than people with a low sense of control (Helgeson, 2003; Helgeson & Fritz, 1999).

Again, we need to remember that studies of perceived control in the chronically ill use correlational rather than experimental designs. Researchers measure the amount of control people are experiencing and correlate this with their psychological and physical adjustment to the disease. These studies cannot prove that feelings of control *cause* one's health to improve; for example, it is possible that improving health causes one to feel more in control (or that breast cancer patients who feel most in control also have the least serious forms of the disease). To address the question of whether feelings of control have beneficial causal effects, we need to conduct experimental studies in which people are randomly assigned to conditions of "high" versus "low" perceived control. A number of such experimental studies have been conducted (Heckhausen & Schulz, 1995; Rodin, 1986).

Increasing Perceived Control in Nursing Homes   Some of the most dramatic effects of perceived control have been found in studies of older people in nursing homes. Many people who end up in nursing homes and hospitals feel they have lost control of their lives (Raps, Peterson, Jonas, & Seligman, 1982). People are often placed in long-term care facilities against their wishes and, once there, have little say in what they do, whom they see, or what they eat. Two psychologists believed that boosting their feelings of control would help such people (Langer & Rodin, 1976). They asked the director of a nursing home in Connecticut to convey to the residents that contrary to what they might think, they had a lot of responsibility for their own lives. Here is an excerpt of his speech:

> *Take a minute to think of the decisions you can and should be making. For example, you have the responsibility of caring for yourselves, of deciding whether or not you want to make this a home you can be proud of and happy in. You should be deciding how you want your rooms to be arranged—whether you want it to be as it is or whether you want the staff to help you rearrange the furniture. You should be deciding how you want to spend your time. . . . If you are unsatisfied with anything here, you have the influence to change it. . . . These are just a few of the things you could and should be deciding and thinking about now and from time to time every day. (Langer & Rodin, 1976, pp. 194–195)*

The director went on to say that a movie would be shown on two nights the next week and that the residents should decide which night they wanted to attend. Finally, he gave each resident a gift of a house plant, emphasizing that it was up to the resident to take care of it. The director also gave a speech to residents assigned to a comparison group. This speech was different in one crucial way—all references to making decisions and being responsible for oneself were deleted. He emphasized that he wanted the residents to be happy, but he did not say anything about the control they had over their lives. He said that a movie would be shown on two nights the next week but that the residents would be assigned to see it on one night or the other. He gave plants to these residents as well but said that the nurses would take care of the plants.

The director's speech might not seem like a major change in the lives of the residents. The people in the induced control group heard one speech about the responsibility they had for their lives and were given one plant to water. That

Perceived Control

The belief that we can influence our environment in ways that determine whether we experience positive or negative outcomes

Giving senior citizens a sense of control over their lives has been found to have positive benefits, both physically and psychologically.

doesn't seem like very strong stuff, does it? But to an institutionalized person who feels helpless and constrained, even a small boost in control can have a dramatic effect. Indeed, the residents in the induced control group became happier and more active than residents in the comparison group (Langer & Rodin, 1976). Most dramatically of all, the intervention improved the residents' health and reduced the likelihood that they would die in the next year and a half (Rodin & Langer, 1977). Eighteen months after the director's speech, 15 percent of the residents in the induced control group had died, compared to 30 percent in the comparison condition (see the left side of Figure SPA1.2).

Another researcher increased feelings of control in residents of nursing homes in a different way (Schulz, 1976). Undergraduates visited the residents of a North Carolina nursing home once a week for two months. In the induced control condition, the residents decided when the visits would occur and how long they would last. In a randomly assigned comparison condition, it was the students, not the residents, who decided when the visits would occur and how long they would last. Thus the residents received visits in both conditions, but in

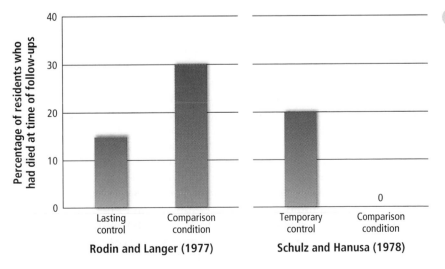

Rodin and Langer (1977) **Schulz and Hanusa (1978)**

FIGURE SPA1.2

Perceived control and mortalilty.

In two studies, elderly residents in nursing homes were made to feel more in control of their lives. In one (Rodin & Langer, 1977), the intervention endured over time, so that people continued to feel in control. As seen on the left side of the figure, this intervention had positive effects on mortality rates. Those who received it were more likely to be alive eighteen months later than those who did not. In the other study (Schulz & Hanusa, 1978), the intervention was temporary. Being given control and then having it taken away had negative effects on mortality rates, as seen on the right side of the figure.

(Adapted from Rodin & Langer, 1977; Schulz & Hanusa, 1978)

only one could they control the visits' frequency and duration. This may seem like a minor difference, but again, giving the residents some semblance of control over their lives had dramatic effects. After two months, those in the induced control condition were happier, healthier, more active, and taking fewer medications than those in the comparison group.

Schulz returned to the nursing home several months later to assess the long-term effects of his intervention, including its effect on mortality rates. Based on the results of the Langer and Rodin (1976) study, we might expect that the residents who could control the students' visits would be healthier and more likely still to be alive than the residents who could not. But there is a crucial difference between the two studies: The residents in the Langer and Rodin study were given an enduring sense of control, whereas the residents in the Schulz study experienced control and then lost it. Langer and Rodin's participants could continue to choose which days to participate in different activities, continue to take care of their plant, and continue to feel they could make a difference in what happened to them, even after the study ended. By contrast, when Schulz's study was over, the student visits ended. The residents who could control the visits suddenly had that control removed.

Unfortunately, Schulz's intervention had an unintended effect: Once the program ended, the people in the induced control group did worse (Schulz & Hanusa, 1978). Compared to people in the comparison group, they were more likely to have experienced deteriorating health and zest for life, and they were more likely to have died (see the right side of Figure SPA1.2). This study has sobering implications for the many college-based volunteer programs in which students visit residents of nursing homes, prisons, and mental hospitals. These programs might be beneficial in the short run but do more harm than good after they end.

Disease, Control, and Well-Being We end this discussion with some words of caution. First, the relationship between perceived control and distress is more important to members of Western cultures than members of Asian cultures. One study found that Asians reported that perceived control was less important to them than Westerners did and that there was less of a relationship between perceived control and psychological distress in Asians than in Westerners (Sastry & Ross, 1998). The researchers argue that in Western cultures, where individualism and personal achievement are prized, people are more likely to be distressed if they feel that they cannot personally control their destinies. A lowered sense of control is less of an issue in Asian cultures, they argue, because Asians place greater value on collectivism and putting the social group ahead of individual goals.

Second, even in Western societies, there is a danger in exaggerating the relationship between perceived control and health. The social critic Susan Sontag (1978, 1988) has perceptively observed that when a society is plagued by a deadly but poorly understood disease, such as tuberculosis in the nineteenth century and AIDS today, the illness is often blamed on some kind of human frailty, such as a lack of faith, a moral weakness, or a broken heart. As a result, people sometimes blame themselves for their illnesses, even to the point where they do not seek effective treatment. Even though it helps people to feel that they are in control of their illnesses, the downside of this strategy is that if they do not get better, they may blame themselves for failing to recover. Tragically, diseases such as cancer can be fatal no matter how much control a person feels. As one of Lance Armstrong's doctors put it, "I've seen wonderful, positive people not make it in the end . . . and some of the most miserable, ornery people survive to resume their ornery lives" (Armstrong, 2000, p. 127). It only adds to the tragedy if people with serious diseases feel a sense of moral failure, blaming themselves for a disease that is unpredictable and incurable.

For people living with serious illnesses, keeping some form of control even when their health is failing has benefits. Researchers have found that even when people who are seriously ill with cancer or AIDS feel no control over the disease, many of them believe they could control the *consequences* of the disease, such as their emotional reactions and some of the physical symptoms of the disease, such as how tired they felt. And the more people felt they could control the consequences of their disease, the better adjusted they were, even if they knew they could not control the eventual course of their illness. In short, it is important to feel in control of something, even if it is not the disease itself. Maintaining such a sense of control is likely to improve one's psychological well-being, even if one's health fails (Heckhausen & Schulz, 1995; Thompson, 2002; Thompson, Nanni, & Levine, 1994).

Knowing You Can Do It: Self-Efficacy

Believing that we have control over our lives is one thing; believing that we can actually execute the specific behaviors that will get us what we want is another. Sam might have a general sense that he is in control of his life, but will this mean that he will find it easy to stop smoking? According to Albert Bandura, we have to examine his **self-efficacy** in this domain—the belief in one's ability to carry out specific actions that produce desired outcomes (Bandura, 1997; Bandura & Locke, 2003). If Sam believes that he is can perform the behaviors that will enable him to quit smoking—throwing away his cigarettes, avoiding situations in which he is most tempted to smoke, distracting himself when he craves a cigarette—then chances are he will succeed. If he has low self-efficacy in this domain, believing that he can't perform the behaviors necessary to quit, then he is likely to fail (Carey & Carey, 1993; Holden, 1991).

People's level of self-efficacy has been found to predict a number of important health behaviors, such as the likelihood that they will quit smoking, lose weight, lower their cholesterol, and exercise regularly (Bandura, 1997; Maddux, 1995; Salovey, Rothman, Detweiler, & Steward, 2000). Again, it is not a general sense of control that predicts these behaviors but the confidence that one can perform the specific behaviors in question. A person might have high self-efficacy in one domain, such as high confidence that she can lose weight, but low self-efficacy in another domain, such as low confidence that she can quit smoking.

Self-efficacy helps in two ways. First, it influences our persistence and effort at a task. People with low self-efficacy tend to give up easily, whereas those with high self-efficacy set higher goals, try harder, and persist more in the face of failure—thereby increasing the likelihood that they will succeed (Cervone & Peake, 1986; Litt, 1988). Second, self-efficacy influences the way our bodies react while we are working toward our goals. For example, people with high self-efficacy experience less anxiety while working on a difficult task, and their immune systems function more optimally (Bandura, Cioffi, Taylor, & Brouillard, 1988; Wiedenfeld et al., 1990). In short, self-efficacy operates as a kind of self-fulfilling prophecy. The more you believe that you can accomplish something, such as quitting smoking, the greater the likelihood that you will.

Other people can help us gain self-efficacy. In one study, for example, participants took part in a fourteen-week program to help them quit smoking (Blittner, Goldberg, & Merbaum, 1978). The program was especially successful if the researchers first instilled self-efficacy, by telling people that they had been chosen for the study because they had "strong willpower and great potential to control and conquer their desires and behavior" (p. 555). The people in this condition did not really have stronger willpower than anyone else, because they were randomly assigned to receive the self-efficacy feedback. The *belief* that they were likely to succeed, however, led to greater success. More people in the

Self-Efficacy

The belief in one's ability to carry out specific actions that produce desired outcomes

FIGURE SPA1.3

The role of self-efficacy in smoking cessation.

Adult smokers were randomly assigned to one of three conditions. In the self-efficacy condition, people were told that they were selected for the study because they had great potential to quit. They then underwent a fourteen-week smoking cessation program. People in the treatment-alone condition participated in the same program but were told that they had been randomly selected for it. People in the no-treatment control did not take part in the program. At the end of the fourteen-week period, substantially more people in the self-efficacy condition had quit smoking. Believing that one has the ability to carry out beneficial behaviors—having high self-efficacy—is an important determinant of whether people succeed.

(Adapted from Blittner, Goldberg, & Merbaum, 1978)

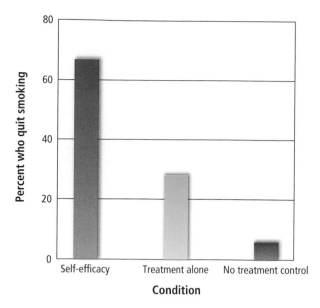

Learned Helplessness

The state of pessimism that results from attributing a negative event to stable, internal, and global factors

Stable Attribution

The belief that an event is caused by factors that will not change over time (e.g., your intelligence), as opposed to factors that will change over time (e.g., the amount of effort you put into a task)

Internal Attribution

The belief that an event is caused by things about you (e.g., your own ability or effort), as opposed to factors that are external to you (e.g., the difficulty of a test)

Global Attribution

The belief that an event is caused by factors that apply in a large number of situations (e.g., your intelligence, which will influence your performance in many areas) rather than factors that are specific and apply in only a limited number of situations (e.g., your musical ability, which will affect your performance in music courses but not in other courses)

self-efficacy condition quit smoking than in a condition that underwent the same treatment but without the self-efficacy instructions or a control condition that did not receive any treatment (see Figure SPA1.3). Believing that we can do something has a powerful influence on whether we succeed.

Explaining Negative Events: Learned Helplessness

What happens when we experience a setback? Despite believing in ourselves, perhaps we failed to quit smoking or did poorly on a midterm. Another important determinant of our physical and mental health is how we explain to ourselves why a negative event occurred. Consider two college students who both got poor grades on their first calculus test. Student A says to herself, "I'll bet the professor deliberately made the test difficult, to motivate us to do better. I'll just have to study harder. If I really buckle down for the next test, I'll do better." Student B says to himself, "Wow, I guess I can't really cut it here at State U. I was worried that I wasn't smart enough to make it in college, and boy, was I ever right." Which student do you think will do better on the next test? Clearly the first one, because she has explained her poor performance in a way that is more flattering to herself and makes her feel more in control. In contrast, the second student is expressing **learned helplessness,** pessimism that results from attributing a negative event to stable, internal, and global factors (Abramson, Seligman, & Teasdale, 1978; Overmier, 2002; Seligman, 1975).

If we think a negative event had a stable cause, we've made a **stable attribution**—we believe that the event was caused by things that will not change over time (e.g., our intelligence), as opposed to factors that can change over time (e.g., the amount of effort we put into a task). Explaining a negative event as due to an internal cause—that is, making an **internal attribution**—means we believe that something about us caused the event (e.g., our own ability or effort), as opposed to factors that are external to us (e.g., the difficulty of a test). Finally, explaining an event as due to a global cause—that is, making a **global attribution**—is the belief that the event is caused by factors that apply in a large number of situations (e.g., our general intelligence, which will influence our performance in many areas) rather than factors that are specific and apply in only a limited number of situations (e.g., how good we are at math, which will affect our performance in math courses but not in other courses). According to learned helplessness theory, making stable, internal, and global attributions for negative events leads to hopelessness, depression, reduced effort, and difficulty in learning (see Figure SPA1.4).

Student B, for example, believes that the cause of his poor grade is stable (being unintelligent will last forever), internal (something about him is to blame), and global (being unintelligent will affect him in many situations other than calculus classes). This kind of explanation will lead to learned helplessness, thereby producing depression, reduced effort, and the inability to learn new things. Student A, by contrast, believes that the cause of her poor grade is unstable (the professor will make the tests easier, and she can study harder next time), external (the professor intentionally made the test hard), and specific (the things that caused her poor calculus grade are unlikely to affect anything else, such as her grade in English). People who explain bad events in this more optimistic way are less likely to be depressed and more likely to do better on a broad range of tasks (Joiner & Wagner, 1995; Peterson & Seligman, 1984; Sweeney, Anderson, & Bailey, 1986).

Consider Lance Armstrong's comeback after he had recovered from cancer. In his first races, he did fairly well, finishing fourteenth in a five-day race through Spain and nineteenth in an eight-day race from Nice to Paris. He was used to winning, however, and initially explained his failure to do so like this: "Well, I've just been through too much. I've been through three surgeries, three months of chemo, and a year of hell, and that's the reason I'm not riding well. My body is

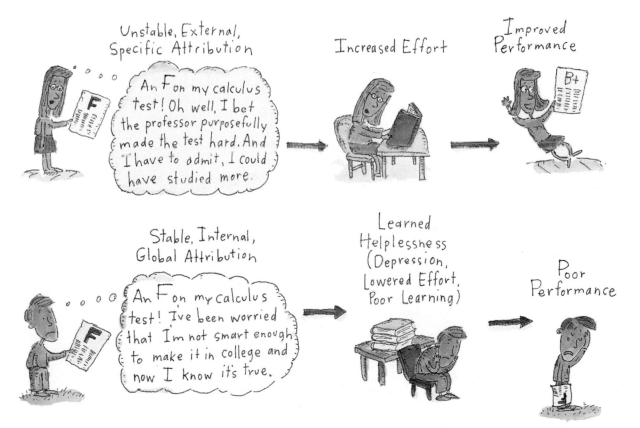

THE THEORY OF LEARNED HELPLESSNESS

Unstable, External, Specific Attribution

An F on my calculus test! Oh well, I bet the professor purposefully made the test hard. And I have to admit, I could have studied more.

Increased Effort

Improved Performance

B+

Stable, Internal, Global Attribution

An F on my calculus test! I've been worried that I'm not smart enough to make it in college and now I know it's true.

Learned Helplessness (Depression, Lowered Effort, Poor Learning)

Poor Performance

FIGURE SPA1.4

The theory of learned helplessness.

Explaining a negative event in a pessimistic manner leads to learned helplessness (depression, lowered effort, poor learning).

just never going to be the same" (Armstrong, 2000, p. 188). Note that he attributed his poor performance to a cause that was internal (his lowered physical abilities), stable (a condition that would not change), and global (a condition that would influence many aspects of his life, not just one race). Had he persisted in explaining his performance in this way, surely he never would have gone on to win the Tour de France. Instead, he had the insight to recognize that every cyclist has ups and downs and no one wins every race. "What I really should have been saying," Armstrong realized, "was, 'Hey, it's just a bad day'"—an attribution to a cause that was external (the particular circumstances, not something about him), unstable (something likely to change), and specific (something limited to that one situation).

Learned helplessness theory is intimately related to attribution theory (see Chapter 4). Attribution theorists assume that your attitudes and behaviors depend on how you interpret the causes of events, an assumption that learned helplessness shares. Note that we do not know the real reason our hypothetical students did poorly on their calculus test. Instead, learned helplessness theory states that it is more important to consider people's perceptions of these causes. The real causes, of course, are not irrelevant. Students who truly lack ability in calculus are likely to do poorly on future calculus tests. Often in life, however, what actually causes our behavior is not so clear-cut or fixed. In such situations, people's attributions about the causes of their problems can be very important.

To explore this link between learned helplessness and academic performance, Tim Wilson and Patricia Linville (1982, 1985) conducted a study with first-year college students. They assumed that many first-year students experience academic difficulties because of a damaging pattern of attributions. Due to the difficulty of adjusting to a new academic and social environment, the first year of college has its rough spots for nearly everyone. The problem is, many first-year students do not realize how common such adjustment problems are and assume that their problems are due to personal predicaments that are unlikely to change—just the kind of attribution that leads to learned helplessness.

Wilson and Linville tried to combat this pessimism by convincing students that the causes of poor performance are often temporary. At Duke University, first-year students who were concerned about their academic performance took part in what they thought was a survey of college experiences. In the treatment condition, the students watched videotaped interviews of four upper-class stu-

Students who realize that poor academic performance in the first year of college is common and likely to improve will probably do better than students who believe that poor performance is due to personal shortcomings that are unlikely to change.

dents, each of whom, during the interviews, mentioned that his or her grades were poor or mediocre during the first year but had improved significantly since then. The students were also given statistics indicating that academic performance is often poor in the first year of college but improves thereafter. The researchers hypothesized that this simple message would help prevent learned helplessness, increasing the students' motivation to try harder and removing needless worries about their abilities. Judging by the students' future performance, this is just what happened. Compared to students in a control group who participated in the study but did not watch the videotaped interviews or see the statistics, students in the treatment condition improved their grades more in the following year and were less likely to drop out of college. Similar results have been found in studies in other countries, such as Canada and Belgium (Menec et al., 1994; Van Overwalle & DeMetsenaere, 1990; Wilson, Damiani, & Shelton, 2002).

Because people's attributions were not measured in the Wilson and Linville (1982) study, we can only infer that the students improved their academic performance because of a beneficial change in their attributions. Other studies have directly measured people's attributions and found that those who explain bad events in optimistic ways are less depressed, are in better health, and do better in school and in their careers (Dweck, 1999; Nolen-Hoeksema, Girgus, & Seligman, 1986; Snyder, Irving, & Anderson, 1991).

Stereotype Threat, Achievement, and Health

Suppose an African American and a white college student are taking the same test and are having difficulty solving one of the problems. Both students are likely to be worried about their performance, but the African American has a worry the white student does not—the fear of confirming the cultural stereotype that African Americans are unintelligent. If the white student does poorly, it reflects badly only on that student. If the African American does poorly, it not only reflects badly on the student but also reinforces the negative stereotype about African Americans.

Claude Steele and his colleagues have called this worry *stereotype threat*, the fear of confirming a negative stereotype of one's group (Steele, Spencer, & Aronson, 2002). As we saw in Chapter 13, stereotype threat can hinder academic performance, whereas removing it can improve performance. African Americans college students who believed that a difficult verbal test was measuring their academic ability did worse than white college students, whereas African American students who believed the test was not a measure of their ability as well as the white students (Steele & Aronson, 1995a). Similarly, female college students who believed that women tended to do worse on a difficult math test did, in fact, do more poorly than male college students. However, female college students were told that men and women score equally on the test performed as well as men (Spencer, Steele, & Quinn, 1999).

Stereotype threat has been found to have negative effects on many types of performance among many different populations. In one study, for example, white athletes did worse than black athletes in a miniature golf game when they were told that the game measures "natural athletic ability." Because part of the stereotype of whites is that they possess less athletic ability than blacks, the whites experienced stereotype threat in this condition. However, when the athletes were told that the game measures "sport strategic intelligence," blacks did worse than whites, because they were at risk of confirming the stereotype that blacks are less intelligent than whites (Stone, Lynch, Sjomeling, & Darley, 1999).

It is bad enough that stereotype threat can hinder people's performance in domains that are important to them, but recent research suggests that it also take a toll on people's health (Blascovich, Spencer, Quinn, & Steele, 2001). It is well known that African Americans have a higher incidence of hypertension (high blood pressure) than European Americans in the United States, and many reasons for this difference have been offered, including genetic differences and higher levels of stress in African Americans (Anderson, 1989). Is it possible that stereotype threat is one of the culprits? In their daily lives, African Americans often encounter situations in which they might be stereotyped and are often concerned about whether they will act in ways that confirm those stereotypes. Do such encounters increase hypertension?

To find out, the researchers asked African American and European Americans to take a standardized test of verbal abilities. Half of the participants were told that they were taking the test to see if it was culturally biased (high stereotype threat condition), whereas the other half were told that the test was culturally unbiased (low stereotype threat condition). As in previous research, African Americans performed worse when under high stereotype threat. When under low stereotype threat, they performed as well as the European Americans (who did equally under both conditions).

The researchers also measured participants' blood pressure during the study and found sobering results. The African Americans in the high stereotype threat conditions showed an increase in blood pressure when they took the verbal test, and their blood pressure remained relatively high for the rest of the experiment. The participants in the other three conditions—African Americans in the low stereotype condition and European Americans in both the high and low threat conditions—did not show an increase in blood pressure over the course of the experiment. The results of the Blascovich et al. (2001) study suggest that stereotype threat might be an important cause of hypertension among African Americans.

In summary, our feelings of control and self-efficacy, the kinds of attributions we make for our performance, and stereotype threat are important determinants of our psychological and physical health. The power of our minds over our bodies is, of course, limited. But research shows that people's psychological reactions to life events, such as the amount of control they feel they have over negative events and how they explain them, can have a big influence on their mental and physical health.

COPING WITH STRESS

No one always feels in control, of course, and sometimes it is difficult to avoid being pessimistic after something bad happens. The death of a loved one, an acrimonious divorce, and the loss of a job are extremely stressful events. Considerable research indicates that people exhibit various reactions, or **coping styles,** in the face of threatening events (Aspinwall & Taylor, 1997; Lazarus & Folkman, 1984; Lehman, Davis, De Longis, & Wortman, 1993; Salovey et al.,

Coping Styles
The ways in which people react to threatening events

2000; Somerfield & McCrae, 2000; Taylor & Aspinwall, 1993). We examine a few coping styles here, beginning with research on gender differences in the ways people respond to stress.

Gender Differences in Coping with Stress

Tim Wilson often takes the family dog, Jackson, to a park with a fenced-in area where dogs are allowed to run free. Most of the time, the neighborhood dogs get along quite well, romping together with abandon. Occasionally, the romping gets out of hand, and one of the more aggressive dogs goes on the attack. The other dogs react in one of two ways: Sometimes they respond in kind, and a dog-fight occurs (soon broken up by the owners). At other times the picked-on dogs seem not to like their chances and take off as fast as they can, tails between their legs. (Fortunately, Jackson is quite fast and can often be seen running just ahead of a dog with bared teeth.)

Walter Cannon (1932) termed this the **fight-or-flight response,** defined as responding to stress by either attacking the source of the stress or fleeing from it. For years, the fight-or-flight response has been viewed as the way in which all mammals respond to stress. When under threat, mammals are energized by the release of hormones such as norepinephrine and epinephrine, and like the dogs in the park, they either go on the attack or retreat as quickly as they can. That, at least, has been the accepted story for many years. Recently, Shelley Taylor and her colleagues (2000) pointed out a little-known fact about research on the fight-or-flight syndrome: Most of it has been done on males (particularly male rats). Is it possible that females respond differently to stressful events?

Taylor and her colleagues argue that the fight-or-flight response does not work well for females because they typically play a greater role in caring for children. Fighting is not always a good option for a pregnant female or one tending offspring. Similarly, fleeing is difficult when an adult is responsible for the care of young children or in the later months of pregnancy.

Consequently, Taylor and her colleagues argue, a different way of responding to stress has evolved in females, the **tend-and-befriend response.** Instead of fighting or fleeing, women respond to stress with nurturant activities designed to protect oneself and one's offspring (tending) and creating social networks that provide protection from threats (befriending). Tending has a number of benefits for both the mother and the child (e.g., a quiet child is less likely to be noticed by predators, and nurturing behavior leads to lower stress and improved immune functioning in mammals). Befriending involves the creation of close ties with other members of the species, which also confers a number of advantages. A close-knit group can exchange resources, watch out for predators, and share child care. As we saw in Chapter 5, human females are more likely than males to develop intimate friendships, cooperate with others, and focus their attention on social relationships. This is especially so when people are under stress; under these circumstances, women are more likely to seek out others, particularly other women (Tamres, Janicki, & Helgeson, 2002).

It is possible that the tend-and-befriend response has a biological basis, just as the fight-and-flight response does in males. Specifically, females are more likely to show increased levels of the hormone oxytocin when under stress, and there is evidence that oxytocin has calming properties and promotes affiliation with others (Ennis, Kelly, & Lambert, 2001; Taylor et al., 2000). However, the tendency for women to seek social support could also be due to the way women and men are socialized. There is evidence, for example, that women are more rewarded than men for turning to others during stress and discussing their problems (Collins & Miller, 1994).

It is easy to oversimplify gender differences such as these. Although gender differences in coping do exist, the magnitude of these differences is not very

Fight-or-Flight Response

Responding to stress by either attacking the source of the stress or fleeing from it

Tend-and-Befriend Response

Responding to stress with nurturant activities designed to protect oneself and one's offspring (tending) and creating social networks that provide protection from threats (befriending)

Females are somewhat more likely than males to develop intimate friendships, cooperate with others, and focus their attention on social relationships, particularly when under stress. Shelley Taylor and her colleagues (2000) have referred to this as a tend-and-befriend strategy, responding to stress with nurturant activities designed to protect oneself and one's offspring (tending) and creating social networks that provide protection from threats (befriending).

large (Tamres et al., 2002). Further, seeking social support can benefit both women and men.

Social Support: Getting Help from Others

One of the striking things about Lance Armstrong's recovery from cancer was the amount of support he received from his family and friends. His mother, to whom he was very close, took an active role in his treatment and recovery. She stayed by his side as much as possible and organized his schedule, prescription medicines, and diet. A close circle of friends stayed with him as well, many traveling great distances to visit him at the hospital and nurse him through the treatments. Twenty-four hours after his brain surgery, for example, a group of friends took him to dinner at a restaurant across the street from the hospital. Armstrong developed close friendships with many of the doctors and nurses who treated him.

Social support, perceiving that others are responsive and receptive to one's needs, is very helpful for dealing with stress (Cohen & Wills, 1985; Helgeson & Cohen, 1996; Hobfoll & Vaux, 1993; Ryff & Singer, 2001; Stroebe & Stroebe, 1996). For example, after devastating hurricanes killed dozens of people and destroyed the homes and property of thousands of others in South Carolina and Florida, researchers found that the people who coped the best were those who felt that they had the most social support, such as having others to talk to and to help solve problems (Norris & Kaniasty, 1996). In general, people who have someone to lean on deal better with life's problems and show improved health (Uchino, Cacioppo, & Keicolt-Glaser, 1996).

What about in cases of life-threatening illnesses, such as Lance Armstrong's battle with cancer? Controlled studies suggest that social support may play a role in the course of such diseases. In one of the most dramatic studies, women with advanced breast cancer were randomly assigned to a social support condition or a control condition (Spiegel, Bloom, Kraemer, & Gottheil, 1989). People in the social support condition met weekly with other patients and doctors to discuss their problems and fears, whereas people in the control group did not have access to this support system. Not only did the social support improve women's moods and reduce their fears, but it also lengthened their lives by an average of

Social Support

The perception that others are responsive and receptive to one's needs

eighteen months (Cunningham, Phillips, Lockwood, Hedley, & Edmonds, 2000; Helgeson, Cohen, & Fritz, 1998; Walker, Heys, & Eremin, 1999).

Research in different cultures also provides evidence for the importance of social support. People who live in cultures that stress interdependence and collectivism suffer less from stress-related diseases than people who live in cultures that stress individualism, possibly because it is easier for people in collectivist cultures to obtain social support (Bond, 1991; Brislin, 1993; Cross & Vick, 2001). Individualistic cultures' emphasis on "going it alone" can take its toll on our health. In a study of a large sample of American men and women in the years 1967–1969, men with a low level of social support were two to three times more likely to die over the next dozen years than men with a high level of social support (House, Robbins, & Metzner, 1982). Women with a low level of social support were 1.5 to 2 times more likely to die than women with a high level of social support (Berkman & Syme, 1979; Schwarzer & Leppin, 1991; Stroebe & Stroebe, 1996).

Does this mean that you should always seek out comfort and advice from others? Not necessarily. According to the **buffering hypothesis,** we need social support only when we are under stress (Cohen & Wills, 1985; Koopman, Hermanson, Diamond, Angell, & Spiegel, 1998; Peirce, Frone, Russell, & Cooper, 1996). When times are tough—we've just broken up with our girlfriend or boyfriend, or our parents have gone off the deep end again—social support helps in two ways. First, it can help us interpret an event as less stressful than we otherwise would. Suppose you've just found out that you have midterms in your psychology and calculus classes on the same day. If you have several friends in these classes who can commiserate with you and help you study, you are likely to find the tests less of a big deal than if you had to cope with them on your own. Second, even if we do interpret an event as stressful, social support can help us cope. Say you've just done poorly on a midterm and feel badly about it. It's best to have close friends nearby to help you deal with this and figure out how to do better on the next test (Stroebe & Stroebe, 1996). To get an idea of the amount of social support you feel is available in your life, complete the Try It! exercise on page 494.

Personality and Coping Styles

Some people, of course, are more likely to seek help from others or, more generally, to react in an adaptive way when under stress. Others seem to react badly when the going gets tough. As seen earlier in our discussion of learned helpless-

Buffering Hypothesis

The theory that we need social support only when we are under stress because it protects us against the detrimental effects of this stress

Social Support

This list contains statements that may or may not be true about you. For each statement that is probably true about you, circle T; for each that is probably not true about you, circle F.

You may find that many of the statements are neither clearly true nor clearly false. In these cases, try to decide quickly whether probably true (T) or probably false (F) is more descriptive of you. Although some questions will be difficult to answer, it is important that you pick one alternative or the other. Circle only one of the alternatives for each statement.

Read each item quickly but carefully before responding. This is not a test, and there are no right or wrong answers.

1. There is at least one person I know whose advice I really trust.   T   F

2. There is really no one I can trust to give me good financial advice.   T   F

3. There is really no one who can give me objective feedback about how I'm handling my problems.   T   F

4. When I need suggestions for how to deal with a personal problem, I know there is someone I can turn to.   T   F

5. There is someone who I feel comfortable going to for advice about sexual problems.   T   F

6. There is someone I can turn to for advice about handling hassles over household responsibilities.   T   F

7. I feel that there is no one with whom I can share my most private worries and fears.   T   F

8. If a family crisis arose, few of my friends would be able to give me good advice about how to handle it.   T   F

9. There are very few people I trust to help solve my problems.   T   F

10. There is someone I could turn to for advice about changing my job or finding a new one.   T   F

Scoring instructions appear on page 503.

(Adapted from Cohen, Mermelstein, Kamarack, & Hoberman, 1985)

ness, part of this is due to the way people explain the causes of a particular setback; explaining the setback in an optimistic way leads to better coping than explaining events in a pessimistic way. Other researchers have looked at this from the vantage point of individual differences, the aspects of people's personalities that make them different from other people. Some people are by nature optimistic, generally expecting the best out of life, whereas others always see the dark underside. And there is evidence that optimistic people react better to stress and are generally healthier than pessimists (Armor & Taylor, 1998; Carver & Scheier, 2003; Salovey et al., 2000). To get an idea of how optimistic you tend to be, complete the Try It! exercise on page 495.

The good news is that most people have been found to have an optimistic outlook on life. In fact, most people seem to be unrealistically optimistic about their lives (Armor & Taylor, 1998; Taylor & Brown, 1988, 1994). In one study, college students estimated how likely a variety of events were to happen to them, compared to how likely these events were to happen to their peers (Weinstein, 1980). The events included both positive things, such as liking a postgraduation job and living past 80, and negative things, such as getting divorced and contracting lung cancer. People were overly optimistic: Nearly everyone thought

Try it!

The Life Orientation Test

Please indicate the extent of your agreement with each of the following ten statements, using the following scale:

0 = strongly disagree
1 = disagree
2 = neither agree nor disagree
3 = agree
4 = agree strongly

Be as accurate and honest as you can on all items, and try not to let your answer to one question influence your answer to other questions. There are no right or wrong answers.

1. In uncertain times, I usually expect the best.   _____
2. It's easy for me to relax.   _____
3. If something can go wrong for me, it will   _____
4. I'm always optimistic about my future.   _____
5. I enjoy my friends a lot.   _____
6. It's important for me to keep busy   _____
7. I hardly ever expect things to go my way.   _____
8. I don't get upset too easily.   _____
9. I rarely count on good things happening to me.   _____
10. Overall, I expect more good things to happen to me than bad.   _____

Scoring instructions are on page 503.

(Adapted from Scheier, Carver, & Bridges, 1994)

that the good events were more likely to happen to them than their peers and that the negative events were less likely to happen to them than their peers (we know that people were wrong, on average, because it is not possible that everyone could be more likely than others to experience the good things and avoid the bad things).

This kind of unrealistic optimism would be a problem if it caused people to make serious mistakes about their prospects in life. Obviously, it would not be a good idea to convince ourselves that we will never get lung cancer and therefore we're free to smoke as much as we want. Most people seem to have a healthy balance of optimism and reality monitoring. We manage to put a positive spin on many aspects of our lives, which leads to increased feelings of control and self-efficacy. At the same time, most people are able to keep their optimistic biases in check when they face a real threat and to take steps to deal with that threat (Armor & Taylor, 1998). Consider Lance Armstrong's battle with cancer. In one sense, he was quite realistic, finding out all he could about the disease and the latest treatments and seeking the advice of many experts. He even learned to read X-rays as well as the doctors. Despite the severity of his disease, however, and the very real possibility that it might kill him, he was able to maintain a sense of

People with a Type A personality—those who are impatient, competitive, and hostile—are more likely to develop coronary disease than people with a Type B personality—those who are relaxed, patient, and nonhostile. Recent research suggests that it is hostility in particular that is most related to coronary disease.

Twixt the optimist and
the pessimist
the difference is droll:
The optimist sees
the doughnut
But the pessimist
sees the hole.

*—McLandburgh
Wilson, 1915*

Type A Personality

The type of person who is typically competitive, impatient, hostile, and control-oriented, when confronting a challenge

Type B Personality

The type of person who is typically patient, relaxed, and noncompetitive when confronting a challenge

optimism: "What is stronger, fear or hope? . . . Initially, I was very fearful and without much hope, but as I sat there and absorbed the full extent of my illness, I refused to let the fear completely blot out my optimism" (Armstrong, 2000, p. 99).

Another personality variable that has received a great deal of attention is the **Type A** versus **Type B personality,** which has to do with how people typically confront challenges in their lives (Rosenman, 1993). The Type A person is typically competitive, impatient, hostile, aggressive, and control-oriented. Type Bs are typically patient, relaxed, and noncompetitive. We are all familiar with the Type A pattern; this is the person who honks and yells at other drivers when they don't drive to his or her satisfaction. People with this personality trait appear to deal with stress efficiently and aggressively. Their hard-driving, competitive approach to life pays off in some respects; Type A individuals tend to get good grades in college and to be successful in their careers (Kleiwer, Lepore, & Evans, 1990; Ovcharchyn, Johnson, & Petzel, 1981). However, this success comes with some costs. Type A individuals spend relatively little time on nonwork activities and have more trouble in balancing their work and family lives (Burke & Greenglass, 1990; Greenglass, 1991). Further, numerous studies show that Type A individuals are more prone than Type B people to developing coronary heart disease, (Matthews, 1988).

Subsequent studies have tried to narrow down what it is about the Type A personality that is most related to heart disease. The most likely culprit is hostility (Farber & Burge-Callaway, 1998; Krantz & McCeney 2002; Salovey et al., 2000; Williams, 2002). Competitiveness and a fast-paced life might not be so bad by themselves, but for a person who is chronically hostile, they increase the risk for coronary disease.

A number of factors affect whether you are Type A or Type B. You are more likely to be Type A if you are male, your parents are Type A, and you live in an urban rather than a rural area (Rosenman, 1993). The culture in which you grow up may also play a role. There is a higher rate of coronary disease in many Western cultures than in many Asian cultures, such as Japan. Again, each culture's emphasis on independence and indvidualism versus interdependence and collectivism may play a role (Triandis, 1995). These emphases might be related to heart disease in two ways: In Western cultures, where individualism and competitiveness are prized, personality types more like Type A might be encouraged. Second, people who live in cultures that stress collectivism might have more support from other people when they experience stress, and as we have seen, such social support is a valuable way of making stress more manageable (Triandis, 1995).

Questions like "What is it that makes one person more resistant to health problems than another person?" are typically explored by personality psychologists. Social psychologists takes a different tack, asking instead: Can we identify ways of coping with stress that everyone can use?

Opening Up: Confiding in Others

When something traumatic happens to you, is it best to try to bury it as deep as you can and never talk about it or to open up and discuss your problems with others? Although folk wisdom has long held that it is best to open up, only recently has this assumption been put to the test. James Pennebaker and his colleagues (Pennebaker, 1990, 1997; Niederhoffer & Pennebaker, 2002; Smyth, 1998) have conducted a number of interesting experiments on the value of confiding in others. Pennebaker and Beale (1986), for example, asked college students to write, for fifteen minutes on each of four consecutive nights, about a traumatic event that had happened to them. Students in a control condition wrote for the same amount of time about a trivial event. The traumas that people chose to write included tragedies such as rape and the death of a sibling. Writing about these events was certainly upsetting in the short run: Students who wrote about traumas reported more negative moods and showed greater increases in blood pressure. But there were also dramatic long-term benefits: The same students were less likely to visit the student health center during the next six months, and they reported having fewer illnesses. Similarly, first-year college students who wrote about the problems of entering college and survivors of the Holocaust who disclosed the most about their World War II experiences improved their health over the next several months (Pennebaker, Barger, & Tiebout, 1989; Pennebaker, Colder, & Sharp, 1990).

What is it about opening up that leads to better health? Pennebaker (1997) argues that people who write about negative events construct a more meaningful narrative or story that explains the events. Pennebaker has analyzed the

Research by James Pennebaker (1990) on opening up to others shows that there are long-term health benefits to writing or talking about one's personal traumas.

hundreds of pages of writing his participants provided and found that the people who improved the most were those who began with rather incoherent, disorganized descriptions of their problem and ended with coherent, organized stories that explained the event and gave it meaning. Once an event is explained, people do not have to think about it as much. Further, people might be less inclined to try to suppress thoughts about the event. Trying to suppress negative thoughts can lead to a preoccupation with those very thoughts, because the act of trying not to think about them can actually make us think about them more (Wegner, 1994). Writing about or confiding in others about a traumatic event may help people gain a better understanding of the event and thus move forward with life.

PREVENTION: IMPROVING HEALTH HABITS

Beyond helping people reduce stress, social psychology can offer some insights into how to get people to change their health habits more directly—to stop smoking, lose weight, eat a healthier diet, stop abusing alcohol or other drugs, and practice safer sex.

Americans are doing a pretty good job of improving some of these health habits. Smoking among high school students has become less frequent in recent years, after showing an alarming increase in the 1990s ("Trends in Cigarette Smoking," 2002). And a recent survey found an increase in seat belt usage, an increase in mammography exams for women 40 and over, and an increase in flu shots for people over 65 (Nelson et al., 2002). But there is still room for improvement. Binge drinking occurs at alarming rates on college campuses; one study found that 49 percent of college men and 41 percent of college women engage in binge drinking (Wechsler et al., 2002). Although most binge drinkers believe that it will be easy to stop after leaving college, many find it very hard to do so and develop serious drinking problems. Americans are among the heaviest people in the world, and obesity is increasing in virtually all countries (Visscher & Seidell, 2001). And people who are at risk for getting AIDS are not taking as many precautions as they should. In one poll, only 58 percent of single, sexually active Americans reported that they use condoms (Clement & Hales, 1997).

Suppose you were hired to design public service ads encouraging people to act in healthier ways. What would you do? What kinds of techniques would you use? If you are like many people, the first approach that might occur to you is to scare people into changing their behavior.

Fear-Arousing Communications

Public service ads often use fear as a tactic to get people to act in healthier ways, such as the ad designed by the New York State Department of Health depicting a corpse in a morgue with a tag on its toe that says "AIDS." As we saw in Chapter 7, fear-arousing communications can work under some circumstances. It is best to arouse a moderate amount of fear that motivates people to pay careful attention to the ad and to include information about how people can reduce their fear (e.g., by using condoms). Fear-arousing ads will not work if they trigger so much fear that people "shut down" and are unable to think rationally about the issue or if they fail to provide people with recommendations about how to act in healthier ways (Devos-Comby & Salovey, 2002). In one study, for example, a scary ad about AIDS actually led to riskier sexual behavior in a sample of gay men, possibly because it produced so much fear that it made the men feel helpless and as if contracting AIDS were inevitable (Rosser, 1991). Fear-arousing ads therefore need to be designed very carefully and tested on sample audiences before being put into widespread circulation.

Message Framing: Stressing Gains versus Losses

It is also important to think carefully about how to word a public service ad. The same message can be framed in terms of the benefits of following the recommendations (e.g., "If you use condoms, you can stay healthy and avoid sexually transmitted diseases") or the costs of not following the recommendations (e.g., "If you don't use condoms, you could get AIDS"). It might seem as if these different messages would have the same effect; after all, they convey the same information—that it's a good idea to use condoms. It turns out, though, that framing messages in terms of gains versus losses can make a big difference (Jones, Sinclair, & Courneya, 2003; Rothman & Salovey, 1997).

When trying to get people to *detect* the presence of a disease, it is best to use a "loss frame," emphasizing what they have to lose by avoiding this behavior (e.g., the costs of not using condoms or not examining one's skin for cancer; Meyerowitz & Chaiken, 1987; Rothman, 2000). When trying to get people to behave in positive ways that will *prevent* disease, it is best to use a "gain frame," emphasizing what they have to gain by engaging in these behaviors (e.g., the benefits of using condoms or sunscreen; Higgins, 1998; Rothman, Salovey, Antone, Keough, & Martin, 1993). In one study, for example, framing a message in terms of losses increased college women's intentions to examine their skin for cancer (a detection behavior), whereas framing a message in terms of gains increased college women's intentions to use sunscreen (a prevention behavior; Rothman et al., 1993; see Figure SPA1.5).

Why does the way in which a message is framed make a difference? It may change the way we think about our health (Rothman & Salovey, 1997). A loss frame focuses our attention on the possibility that we might have a problem that can be dealt with by performing detection behaviors (e.g., examining our skin for cancer). A gain frame focuses our attention on the fact that we are in a good state of health and that to stay that way, we should perform preventive behaviors (e.g., using sunscreen when exposed to the sun and condoms when having sex). So before designing your public health ad, decide which kind of behavior you want to encourage—a prevention or detection behavior—and design your ad accordingly.

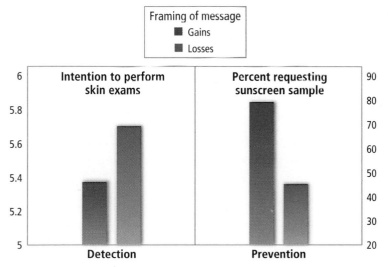

FIGURE SPA1.5

Framing health messages in terms of gains or losses.

Researchers presented women with information trying to get them to avoid skin cancer. Some participants received a message framed in terms of gains that focused on the positive benefits of being concerned about skin cancer (e.g., "If detected early, most of these cancers are curable"). Other participants received a message framed in terms of losses that focused on the negative consequences of not being concerned about skin cancer (e.g., "Unless detected and treated early, most of these cancers are not curable"). As seen on the left side of the figure, the loss frame message worked best on detection behaviors (people's intention to perform exams of their skin). As seen on the right side of the figure, the gain frame message worked best with a prevention behavior (requesting a sample of sunscreen).

(Adapted from Rothman, Salovey, Antone, Keough, & Martin, 1993)

Changing Health-Relevant Behaviors Using Dissonance Theory

Unfortunately, when it comes to changing some ingrained health habits, public service ads may not help very much. The problem is that with many health problems, there are overwhelming barriers to change. Consider the use of condoms. Most people are aware that AIDS is a serious problem and that using condoms provides substantial protection against AIDS. Still, a surprisingly small percentage of people use condoms. One reason is that many people find condoms inconvenient and unromantic, as well as a reminder of disease—something they don't want to think about when they are having sex. Where sexual behavior is involved, there is a strong tendency to go into denial—in this case, to decide that even though AIDS is a real problem, we are not at risk. What can be done to change this potentially fatal attitude?

One of the most important messages of social psychology is that an effective way of changing people's behavior is to challenge their self-esteem in such a way that it becomes to their advantage, psychologically, to act differently. By doing so, they feel good about themselves, maintaining their self-esteem. Sound familiar? This is a basic tenet of dissonance theory. As we discussed in Chapter 6, Elliot Aronson and his colleagues applied the principles of dissonance theory to get people to behave in healthier ways, including using condoms more often. To review briefly, college students were asked to compose a speech describing the dangers of AIDS and advocating the use of condoms "every single time you have sex." The students gave their speech in front of a video camera, after being informed that the resulting videotape would be played to an audience of high school students (Aronson, Fried, & Stone 1991; Stone, Aronson, Crain, Winslow, & Fried, 1994). Was giving this speech sufficient to change their own behavior, making the students more likely to use condoms themselves?

Americans are making progress in improving some areas of health; for example, more and more people are quitting smoking. But Americans are not doing very well in other areas. Many people find it difficult to lose weight and maintain a regular exercise program. How can social psychology help people act in healthier ways?

The answer is yes—but only when the students were also made mindful of their own failures to use condoms by making a list of the circumstances in their own lives when they found it particularly difficult, awkward, or "impossible" to use condoms. These students were most aware of their own hypocrisy—that they were preaching behavior to high school students that they themselves were not practicing. Because no one likes to feel like a hypocrite, these participants needed to take steps to fix their damaged self-esteem. A clear way of doing this would be to start practicing what they were preaching. This is exactly what Aronson and his colleagues found: Students in the hypocrisy condition showed the greatest willingness to use condoms in the future and, when given the opportunity, purchased significantly more condoms for their own use than students in the nonhypocrisy conditions did.

Try it!

Changing Your Health Habits

Pick a health habit of yours and try to improve it, using the principles we have discussed in this chapter. For example, you might try to lose a few pounds, exercise more, or cut down on your smoking. This is not easy, of course—if it were, we would all be svelte, physically fit nonsmokers! We suggest that you start small with a limited goal; try to increase your exercise by one or two hours a week, or aim to lose 5 pounds, or smoke fewer cigarettes each day. Here are some specific suggestions as to how to change your behavior:

- Increase your feelings of control over your behavior, particularly your self-efficacy in this domain. One way to do this is to start small. If you are trying to lose weight, for example, begin slowly with some easy-to-control behaviors. You might start by eliminating one food or beverage from your diet that you do not like all that much but is pretty fattening. Suppose you drink a 200-calorie fruit juice five times a week. Replacing the juice with water will save 52,000 calories a year, which is equivalent to 13 pounds! The idea is to gain mastery over your behavior slowly, improving your feelings of self-efficacy. When you've mastered one behavior, try another. You can do it!

- If you experience a setback, such as eating two pieces of cake at a birthday party when you really didn't mean to or not going to the gym when you planned to, avoid a damaging pattern of attributions. Do not assume that the setback was due to internal, stable, global causes—this will cause learned helplessness. Remember, almost everyone fails the first time they try to diet or quit smoking. It often takes people several attempts; therefore, a setback or two are not due to something unchangeable about you. Keep trying.

- Try your own little dissonance experiment, such as the one we discussed by Aronson, Fried, & Stone (1991) on safer sex. There are two steps: First, make a speech to others urging them to adopt the behaviors you are trying to change. For example, tell all your friends about the dangers of obesity (e.g., the World Health Organization estimates that each year, 300,000 Americans die prematurely because they are overweight; Fumento, 1997). The more involved and detailed you make your speech and the wider your audience, the better. Second, make a detailed list of times when you did not practice what you preached (e.g., when you gained weight). You might find it easier to lose weight once you have put yourself through this "hypocrisy" procedure.

- It can be stressful to change a firmly ingrained habit, and it is at times of stress that social support is most important. Talk with your friends and family about your attempts to change your behavior. Seek their advice and support. Even better, convince several friends to try these techniques with you. Make it a group project in which you and your friends support each other's efforts to alter your behavior.

The condom study is yet another illustration of a familiar point: Sometimes the best way to change people's behavior is to change their interpretation of themselves and the social situation. No attempt was made to modify the research participants' behavior (their use of condoms) directly. They were not rewarded for using condoms, nor were they given any information about what would happen if they didn't. Instead, the researchers altered the way in which the participants interpreted their failure to use condoms. In the hypocrisy condition, the failure to use condoms took on a new meaning. Before the study, the students probably viewed failing to use a condom as no big deal; after all, surely they would never contract AIDS. After delivering a speech for high school students and thinking about their own behavior, not using a condom took on a very different meaning: It became an unprincipled, hypocritical act, and—presto!—the students now wanted to use condoms more. We cannot overemphasize this important social psychological message: One of the best ways to get people to change their behavior is to change their interpretation of the situation. Now that you have read about several of the factors that influence health behaviors, see if you can improve your habits by completing the Try It! exercise on page 501.

SUMMARY

Stress and Human Health

Stress, defined as the negative feelings that occur when people feel they cannot cope with the environment, has been found to have a number of negative effects, such as an impairment of the immune system. One key determinant of stress is how much **perceived control** people have over their environment. The less control people believe they have, the more likely it is that the event will cause them physical and psychological problems. For example, the loss of control experienced by many older people in nursing homes can have negative effects on their health. It is also important for people to have high **self-efficacy** in a particular domain, which is the belief in one's ability to carry out specific actions that produce desired outcomes. In addition, the way in which people explain the causes of negative events is critical to how stressful those events will be. When bad things happen, **learned helplessness** results if people make **stable, internal,** and **global attributions** for those events. Learned helplessness leads to depression, reduced effort, and difficulty in learning new material. Stereotype threat, the fear of confirming a negative stereotype of one's group, is another source of stress. It can also lead to health problems such as high blood pressure. Removing stereotype threat—for example, by telling African Americans or women that there are no race or gender differences on a particular test—has been found to improve performance.

Coping with Stress

Coping styles refer to the ways in which people react to stressful events. Recent research suggests that men are more likely to react to stress with a **fight-or-flight reaction,** responding to stress by either attacking the source of the stress or fleeing from it. Women are more likely to react to stress with a **tend-and-befriend reaction,** responding to stress with nurturant activities designed to protect oneself and one's offspring (tending) and creating social networks that provide protection from threats (befriending). **Social support**—the perception that other people are responsive to one's needs—is beneficial for men and women. According to the **buffering hypothesis,** social support is especially helpful in times of stress by making people less likely to interpret an event as stressful and helping them cope with stressful events.

Research on personality traits, such as optimism and the **Type A** versus **Type B personality,** focuses on how people typically deal with stress and how these styles are related to their physical health. Optimistic people tend to react better to stress and to be healthier. Type A individuals—particularly those with high levels of hostility—are more at risk for coronary disease. Other researchers focus on ways of coping with stress that everyone can adopt. Several studies show that opening up, by writing or talking about one's problems, has long-term health benefits.

Prevention: Improving Health Habits

It is also important to explore how to get people to act in healthier ways. One approach is to present people with persuasive communications that arouse fear. To be successful, the message should arouse a moderate amount of fear that motivates people to pay careful attention to the ad and includes information about how people can reduce their fear (e.g., by using condoms). It is also important to tailor these messages to the kinds of behaviors you want people to adopt. To get people to perform detection behaviors, such as examining their skin for cancer, it is best to use messages framed in terms of losses (the negative consequences of failing to act). To get people to perform preventive behaviors, such as using sunscreen, it is best to use messages framed in terms of gains (the positive consequences of performing the behaviors). Even more powerful are techniques that arouse dissonance that can be reduced by changing one's health habits, such as making people feel hypocritical about their failure to use condoms.

CRITICAL THINKING QUESTIONS

1. Think of a personal example of an event that some people found to be stressful and others did not. Why was it stressful for some people but not others? Were some of the factors mentioned in this chapter involved, such as perceived control, self-efficacy, learned helplessness, or stereotype threat?

2. Design a program to help first-year college students adjust to the academic demands of their institution, using the principles discussed in this chapter.

3. Design a public health campaign to get college students to engage in less binge drinking, using the principles discussed in this chapter.

Scoring the *Try it!* Questions, Page 494

You get 1 point each time you answered true (T) to questions 1, 4, 5, 6, and 10 and 1 point for each time you answered false (F) to questions 2, 3, 7, 8, and 9.

This scale was developed to measure what the researchers call appraisal social support, or "the perceived availability of someone to talk to about one's problems" (Cohen, Mermelstein, Kamarack, & Hoberman, 1985, pp. 75–76). One of their findings was that when people were not under stress, those low in social support had no more physical symptoms than people high in social support did.

However, when people were under stress, those low in social support had more physical symptoms than people high in social support did. This reinforces the buffering hypothesis talked about in the text: We need social support the most when times are tough. Another finding was that women scored reliably higher on the social support scale than men did. If you scored lower than you would like, you might want to consider reaching out to others more when you are under stress.

Scoring the *Try it!* Questions, Page 495

First, reverse your answers to questions 3, 7, and 9. That is, for these questions, change 0 to 4, 1 to 3, 3 to 1, and 4 to 0. Then add these reversed scores to the scores you gave to questions 1, 4, and 10. (Ignore questions 2, 5, 6, and 8; they were filler items.)

This measure of dispositional optimism was created by Scheier, Carver, and Bridges (1994).

According to these researchers, the higher your score, the more optimistic your approach to life. The average score for college students in their study was 14.3, with no significant differences between women and men. Several studies have found that optimistic people cope better with stress and are generally healthier than their pessimistic counterparts.

Social Psychology and the Environment

As an enduring symbol of current environmental problems, there is no more poignant image than the barge full of trash that nobody wanted. In 1987, a load of trash from New York City was rejected by a landfill in Islip, New York, because the landfill was already overflowing. The company hauling the trash hired some entrepreneurs to take it somewhere else. These unlucky transporters filled a barge called the *Mobro 4000* with the trash and departed for a dump in Morehead City, North Carolina. Their idea was to dump it at a gas conversion project there, profiting from the methane gas that would be released as the trash decayed. This plan was quickly rejected by North Carolina authorities, who would not even allow the barge to dock. You see, in the modern world, trash is not simply trash. Many of the things we throw away contain toxic chemicals and dangerous metals, and the North Carolinians did not want their state poisoned with the decay from New York's toxic waste.

Thus began the lonely, meandering, 6,000-mile voyage of the *Mobro 4000*. For six months, the barge owners searched for someone to take the trash, making ports of call in Florida, Alabama, Mississippi, Louisiana, Mexico, Belize, and the Bahamas. But there were no takers. Finally, the barge returned home. After considerable wrangling by local and state officials, the trash was incinerated and buried in—you guessed it—the landfill in Islip, New York.

Where we deposit our trash is no laughing matter and in fact may be quite consequential to our health. A recent study found that people who lived within 3 kilometers (1.9 miles) of toxic landfill sites in Europe were 40 percent more likely to have children with birth defects (Vrijheid et al., 2002).

As the human population grows, our physical world is becoming an increasingly important source of stress. Many areas are running out of places to deposit their trash. The presence of other people can be quite aggravating as overcrowding occurs in more and more urban areas. It is getting more difficult to escape the noise caused by such things as jetliners and heavy traffic. How do people deal with stress from their physical environment?

Just as our environment exerts stress on us, we exert stress on our environment. Few problems are as pressing as the damage we are doing to the environment, including toxic waste, overflowing landfills, pollution, global warming, and the destruction of rain forests. In this chapter, we will consider two general issues: the environment as a source of stress and how we can get people to behave in more environmentally friendly ways.

THE ENVIRONMENT AS A SOURCE OF STRESS

Looking back over the centuries, it is impressive to what extent we have learned to master the harsh environmental hazards that plagued our ancestors (although, tragically, in many areas of the world, starvation and preventable diseases are still major causes of premature death). The irony is that at the same time as we have found ways to master the environment, we have created new environmental stressors that our ancestors did not have to face. Chief among these hazards is our phenomenal reproductive success.

Crowding as a Source of Stress

More than 6 billion human beings inhabit the earth—more than the total number of persons who have ever lived before. The world's population is increasing at the rate of 250,000 people every day. At our current rate of growth, the world population will double by the year 2025 and double again at increasingly shorter intervals. Two hundred years ago, the English clergyman Thomas Malthus warned that the human population was expanding so rapidly that soon there would not be enough food to feed everyone. He was wrong about when such a calamity would occur, largely because of technological advances in agriculture that have vastly improved grain yields. The food supply is dwindling, however, and the number of malnourished people in the world is increasing (Sadik, 1991). Malthus's timing may have been a little off, but many scientists fear that his predictions are becoming truer every day.

Even when there is enough food, overcrowding can be a source of considerable stress to both animals and human beings. When animals are crowded together, in either their natural environment or the laboratory, they reproduce more slowly, take inadequate care of their young, and become more susceptible to disease (Calhoun, 1973; Christian, 1963). Studies of crowding in human beings show similar negative effects. As crowding increases in prisons, for example, disciplinary problems, suicides, and overall death rates also increase (Paulus & Dzindolet, 1992; Paulus, McCain, & Cox, 1981). Studies at universities find that students living in crowded dorms (e.g., ones that have long corridors with common bathroom and lounge facilities) are more withdrawn socially and more likely to show signs of learned helplessness than students living in less crowded dorms (e.g., ones with smaller suites that have their own bathrooms; Baum & Valins, 1977; Evans, Lepore, & Schroeder, 1996; Kaya & Erkip, 2001).

What is it about crowding that is so aversive? To answer this question, we must first recognize that the presence of other people is not always unpleasant. Many people love living in large cities. When Saturday night arrives, many of us are ready to join our friends for an evening of fun, feeling that the more people we round up, the merrier. This fact has led researchers to distinguish between two terms: **Density** is a neutral term that refers to the number of people who occupy a given space. A classroom with twenty students in it has a lower density of people than the same classroom with fifty students in it. **Crowding** is the subjec-

Density
The number of people occupying a given space

Crowding
The subjective feeling of unpleasantness due to the presence of other people

As the human population explodes, our planet is becoming more and more crowded. Under what conditions will crowding be experienced as stressful?

tive feeling of unpleasantness due to the presence of other people; it is the stress we feel when density becomes unpleasant. Under certain circumstances, the class with twenty students might feel more crowded than the class with fifty students.

Crowding and Perceived Control   When does density turn into crowding? One factor pertains to how people interpret the presence of others, including how much control they feel they have over the crowded conditions (Baron & Rodin, 1978; Schmidt & Keating, 1979; Sherrod & Cohen, 1979). If the presence of others reduces our sense of control—for example, if it makes us feel that it is harder to move around as freely as we would like or harder to avoid running into people we would just as soon avoid—we are likely to experience a crowd as stressful. If we feel we have control over the situation—for example, if we know we can leave the crowd at any point and find solace in a quiet spot—we are unlikely to experience it as stressful.

One study tested this hypothesis by asking high school students to work on some problems in a room that was jam-packed with other people (Sherrod, 1974). In one condition, the researcher told the students that they were free to leave at any point. "In the past, some people who have been in the experiment have chosen to leave," he said. "Others have not. We would prefer that you do not, but that's entirely up to you" (p. 176). Students in a second condition worked under identical crowded conditions but were not given the choice to leave. Finally, students in a third condition worked in uncrowded conditions. After working on the initial set of problems, the participants were moved to uncrowded quarters, where they worked on a series of difficult puzzles.

At first, the students who were crowded—regardless of whether or not they had a sense of control—solved as many problems as students who were not crowded. Initially, they were able to concentrate, ignoring the fact that they were shoulder to shoulder with other people. However, in the crowded condition in which the students thought they could not escape, the lack of control eventually took its toll. As seen in Figure SPA2.1 (on page 508), the students who had no control over the crowded conditions in the first session tried to solve significantly fewer puzzles in the second session, compared to students in the other conditions. The students who had a sense of perceived control over the crowded conditions worked on almost as many difficult puzzles as the students who had not been crowded at all.

The thing which in the subway is called congestion is highly esteemed in the night spots as intimacy.
—Simeon Strunsky, 1954

FIGURE SPA2.1

Crowding and perceived control.

People who believed they had control over the crowded conditions tried almost as hard on a subsequent task as people who were not crowded at all.

(Adapted from Sherrod, 1974)

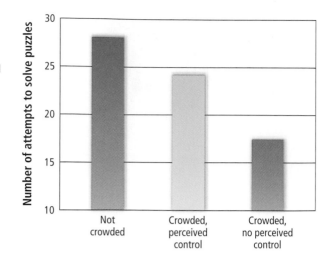

The moral? It is not crowding itself that causes stress but the feeling that one cannot control or escape crowded conditions. It might seem that this sense of control is much easier to achieve in some parts of the world than in others. If you live in a high-rise in New York City, for example, it would seem to be more difficult to avoid crowded conditions than if you live on a farm in Iowa. Similarly, homes and apartments are much smaller in Japan than in the United States, and to Americans, at least, it might seem that it is more difficult to escape crowded conditions in Japan than in the United States. Yet even in areas where the density of people is quite high, norms develop to protect people's privacy and to allow an escape from feeling overcrowded. Richard Brislin (1993) notes, for instance, that in both Japan and the inner cities of Mexico, both of which have a very high density of people, norms about visiting people in their homes are different from those in the United States. In Mexico, people's homes are respected as sacrosanct places where people can be by themselves and escape the stress of crowded conditions; it is virtually unheard of for someone to "drop in" at someone else's house (Pandey, 1990). Similarly, the Japanese entertain in their homes much less than Americans do; they are more likely to invite guests for a meal in a restaurant. The way in which people in different cultures gain control over crowding differs, then, but the need for control appears to be universal (Fuller, Edwards, Vorakitphokatorn, & Sermsri, 1996).

Crowding and Attribution In addition to perceived control, other factors determine how aversive people will find crowded conditions. It is well known, for example, that the presence of others makes people physiologically aroused (Zajonc, 1965). As we saw in Chapter 5, arousal can have intriguing consequences. It can lead to quite different emotions, depending on the attributions people make about the source of their arousal (Schachter & Singer, 1962). Thus as we might expect, an important determinant of how aversive crowding will be is the nature of the attributions people make for the arousal caused by crowding. If people attribute their arousal to the presence of the other people, they will interpret it as a sign that the setting is too crowded and will feel uncomfortable, cramped, and irritated. If they attribute the arousal to another source, they will not feel crowded (Aiello, Thompson, & Brodzinsky, 1983; Schmidt & Keating, 1979). For example, if a student in a class of three hundred people attributes her arousal to the stimulating and fascinating lecture she is hearing, she will feel less crowded than if she attributes her arousal to the fact that she feels like a sardine in a can.

Sensory Overload

Receiving more stimulation from the environment than we can pay attention to or process at a given time

Crowding and Sensory Overload Finally, crowding will be aversive if it leads to **sensory overload** (Cohen, 1978; Milgram, 1970), which occurs when we receive more stimulation from the environment than we can pay attention to or process. Since other people are a key source of stimulation, one instance in which sensory overload can occur is when so many people are around that we cannot pay attention to everyone. For example, if you were being interviewed for a job by a committee of ten persons, you'd feel that you had to pay close attention to everything each interviewer said and did. The result: a severe demand placed on your attentional system—and most likely negative consequences for you. To examine density and crowding in your life, see the Try It! exercise below.

Noise as a Source of Stress

In many urban areas, the police carry an extra piece of equipment, along with their nightsticks, revolvers, and radios: a noise meter. As the human population grows and urban areas become denser, complaints about the noise humans generate have skyrocketed. When night falls in Rehoboth Beach, an ocean resort town in Delaware, for example, the bands in the bars crank up, and complaints from nearby residential areas soon follow. The police come by and take readings with their noise meters and can issue $100 tickets to businesses that exceed spec-

Try it!

When Do People Feel Crowded?

Over a period of a few days, observe people in a variety of situations in which crowding might occur, such as a party, busy bus stop, line to enter a movie theater or dining hall, or concert. In each situation, make the following ratings:

1. What is the density of people in this setting? That is, how many people are there per square yard? Obviously, this will be hard to measure exactly, but come up with a rough estimate.

2. How much control do people have in this situation? Specifically, how easily could they leave and find a less crowded setting, if they so desired? Make your rating based on this scale:

In this situation, people seem to feel

       1   2   3   4   5   6   7   8   9
    very little control   *complete control*

3. How crowded do people seem to feel? Specifically, how negative an experience is it to be in this setting? Make your ratings based on this scale:

People seem to find this setting

       1   2   3   4   5   6   7   8   9
    very unpleasant   *very pleasant*

After sampling several situations, see which predicts your answers to item 3 the best: the density of people (item 1) or how much control people feel (item 2). If you have had a course in statistics, you can compute the correlation coefficient between your answers to items 1 and 3 and between your answers to items 2 and 3, to see which one is bigger. If you haven't, no big deal—just examine the pattern of answers and see whether your answers to item 3 seem to follow your answers to item 1 or item 2 more. Based on the research discussed in the text, it is likely that your answers to item 3 depended more on the amount of control people felt (item 2) than the objective density of people in the situation (item 1).

As the human population increases, the physical world is becoming an increasingly important source of stress. Noise from airplanes and traffic, for example, is an increasingly common feature of urban life.

ified limits (Pressley, 2003). The *San Francisco Chronicle* recently issued noise meters to its restaurant critics and includes ratings of noise levels in its restaurant reviews (Weiss, 2003).

People can choose whether to frequent a noisy restaurant or bar. Others are not so fortunate, because they live in areas where noise is difficult to escape. Christopher Marzec and his wife, for example, moved to an apartment in Englewood, New Jersey, to escape their noisy neighborhood in Hoboken. They enjoyed the peace and quiet of Englewood for a couple of years until the Federal Aviation Administration revised the landing patterns at Newark Airport, routing hundreds of planes directly over the Marzecs' apartment. One day, Marzec came home and found his wife in tears. "We've pretty much arranged now to be gone during the bulk of the hours when the jets are passing over," Marzec said. "Psychologically, we don't live here anymore. It's not like living under a bridge, but there's a sense of homelessness" ("Jet Noise," 1991, p. 32).

Compare the Marzecs' experiences with people known as the Mabaan who live in the Sudan in northeastern Africa, near the equator. When studied in the early 1960s by Samuel Rosen and his colleagues (Rosen, Bergman, Plester, El-Mofty, & Satti, 1962), this culture was relatively untouched by modern civilization. The Mabaan lived in bamboo huts, wore little clothing, and thrived on a diet of grains, fish, and small game. Their environment was quiet and uncrowded, free of many of the stressors associated with modern urban life. There were no sleep-jarring noises from sirens and trucks, no traffic jams to endure at the end of the day, and little fear of crime. Rosen and his colleagues found that compared to adults in the United States, the Mabaan had less hypertension (high blood pressure), less obesity, and superior hearing.

We cannot be sure, of course, that the absence of modern environmental stressors, such as those of urban life, was responsible for the excellent health of the Mabaan. Even if it was, we might not want to conclude that living in a modern, urban area is always stressful, inevitably causing health problems. Some people thrive in the hustle and bustle of a large city. Further, the identical event—such as loud music—can be enjoyable on some occasions but highly stressful on others. Nonetheless, urban noise can be stressful. One town in New Jersey went so far as to ban music from ice-cream trucks because people complained that it was loud and bothersome (Herszenhorn, 1998).

To understand why noise is bothersome at some times but not at others, we need to revisit a basic assumption of social psychology: It is not objective but sub-

The earth we abuse and the living things we kill, in the end, take their revenge; for in exploiting their presences we are diminishing our future.

—Marya Mannes, 1958

jective situations that influence people. The same stimulus, such as loud music, is interpreted as a source of pleasure on some occasions and as an annoying interruption on others. To understand when our environment will be stressful, then, we need to understand how and why people construe that environment as a threat to their well-being. Just as with crowding, noise is especially stressful when people feel they cannot control it.

Noise and Perceived Control   David Glass and Jerome Singer (1972) performed a series of studies to test the conditions under which noise is experienced as stressful. In a typical experiment, participants were given several problems to solve, such as complex addition problems and a proofreading task. While they worked on these problems, they heard very loud bursts of noise. The noise was of such things as a mimeograph machine, a typewriter, and two people speaking in Spanish, played at 108 decibels—about what you would hear if you were operating a riveting machine or were standing near the runway when a large commercial jet took off.

In one condition, the bursts of noise occurred in unpredictable lengths and at unpredictable intervals over the course of the twenty-five-minute session. In a second condition, people heard the same sequence of noises but were given a sense of control over them. The experimenter told participants that they could stop the noise at any point by pressing a button. "Whether or not you press the button is up to you," explained the experimenter. "We'd prefer that you do not, but that's entirely up to you" (Glass & Singer, 1972, p. 64). A key fact to remember is that no one actually pressed the button. Thus people in this condition heard the same amount of noise as people in the uncontrollable noise condition; the only difference was that they believed they could stop the noise whenever they wanted. Finally, a third condition was included wherein people worked on the problems in peace and quiet. After the twenty-five-minute session was over, people in all conditions worked on new problems without any noise being played.

The noise had little effect on people during the initial twenty-five-minute session. As long as a task was not too complex, people could bear down and ignore unpleasant noises, doing just as well on the problems as people who worked on them in quiet surroundings. A different picture emerged, however, when people worked on problems in the next session, in which everyone could work in peace and quiet. As you can see in Figure SPA2.2, those who had endured the uncontrollable noises made significantly more errors during this session than the people who had not heard noises during the first session. In contrast, the people who heard the noises but believed they could control them did almost as well on the subsequent problems as the people who heard no noise

> Noise, *n.* A stench in the ear. . . . The chief product and authenticating sign of civilization.
>
> —*Ambrose Bierce,* Devil's Dictionary, 1906

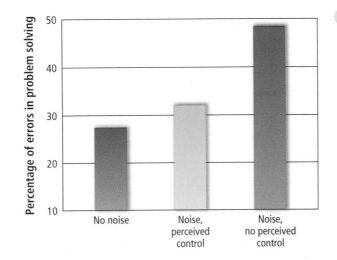

FIGURE SPA2.2

Noise and perceived control.

People who believed they could control the noxious noise did about as well on a subsequent task as people who heard no noise at all.

(Adapted from Glass & Singer, 1972)

at all. When people knew they could turn off the noise at any point, the noise was much easier to tolerate and did not impair later performance—even though people never actually turned it off.

Why did it take some time for the noise to hurt people's performance, and why did this occur only in the condition where the noise couldn't be controlled? When people are initially exposed to uncontrollable, negative events, they often attempt to overcome them as best they can. But if negative, uncontrollable events continue despite our best efforts to overcome them, learned helplessness sets in (Abramson, Seligman, & Teasdale, 1978; Wortman & Brehm, 1975). As discussed in the first Social Psychology in Action module, learned helplessness occurs when people explain a negative event in a pessimistic way—by, for example, assuming that the event is caused by things that can't be changed. One consequence of learned helplessness is reduced effort, which makes it more difficult to learn new material. Thus the participants who could not control the noise were able to deal with it and do well on the problems initially, but the lack of control they experienced eventually took its toll, causing them to do poorly on the second task. In contrast, the participants who believed they could control the noise never experienced learned helplessness and thus were able to do well on the second set of problems.

Noise and Urban Life Unfortunately, in modern urban life, loud noises are often not controllable, and they last a lot longer than the twenty-five-minute sessions in the Glass and Singer study. Several studies have shown that people who are exposed to real-life noises respond like the participants in the uncontrollable noise condition of Glass and Singer's study. For example, children who live near busy highways and airports have higher blood pressure, are more easily distracted, and do more poorly on reading tests than children who live in quieter areas (Cohen, Evans, Krantz, Stokols, & Kelly, 1981; Cohen, Glass, & Singer, 1973). These deficits are classic signs of learned helplessness.

Obviously, the researchers in these studies could not randomly assign children to live near or far from an airport. Whereas the researchers did their best to match the children on such variables as race, social class, and economic background, there is always the possibility that the children differed in some way other than their exposure to uncontrollable noise. The opening of a new airport in Munich, Germany, and the closing of the old airport provided a unique opportunity to study the effects of noise over time in the same neighborhoods. Researchers gave reading tests to children who lived near the old airport, both before and after it closed, and to children who lived near the new airport, both

Frequent, unpredictable noises are an unavoidable fact of urban life. Studies have shown that children who are exposed to constant noises have higher blood pressure, are more easily distracted, and are more likely to give up when working on difficult puzzles than other children.

before and after it opened (Hygge, Evans, & Bullinger, 2002). Confirming previous studies, the children who were exposed to aircraft noise did significantly worse on the reading tests than the children who were not. That is, the children who lived near the old airport before it closed did poorly on the reading test, as did the children who lived near the new airport after it opened.

This study also examined a new question: whether the effects of the aircraft noise are reversed when the noise ends. By a year after the old airport closed, the children who lived nearby were doing as well on the reading tests as children who lived farther away. This finding is encouraging, suggesting that attempts to reduce urban noise will pay off relatively quickly. Due in part to studies such as these, attempts have recently been made to reduce the amount of noise to which people are subjected—for example, by adding soundproofing materials to schools and devices to jet engines that make them less noisy (Bronzaft, 2002).

In sum, as humans have evolved, we have learned to master many environmental hazards but in the process have produced new ones, such as noise and crowding. We turn now to another consequence of having become a crowded and technologically advanced society: People are harming the physical environment in multiple ways. Changes in attitudes and behaviors are urgently needed in order to avoid environmental catastrophe. Social psychologists have studied a number of techniques involving social influence and social interaction that encourage people to behave in more environmentally sound ways (Sundstrom, Bell, Busby, & Asmus, 1996; Vining & Ebreo, 2002).

USING SOCIAL PSYCHOLOGY TO CHANGE ENVIRONMENTALLY DAMAGING BEHAVIORS

We humans have been treating the planet as a huge garbage can, rapidly filling up the ground, water, and atmosphere with all sorts of pollutants. When people lived in small groups of hunters and gatherers, they could get away with discarding their trash wherever they pleased; now that there are more than 6 billion of us, and we have developed toxic wastes that will remain poisonous for centuries, we have to change our ways (Gilbert, 1990). We have also taken for granted that the resources we need to sustain life will always be plentiful, but in fact, water is becoming a scarce resource in many communities. Recently, in the area in which one of us lives in Virginia, there was such a severe drought that mandatory water restrictions were imposed. The water was turned off in the sinks in public restrooms at airports and colleges. Restaurants were ordered to use disposable plates and glasses to save water from washing dishes (which only, of course, added to the landfill problem). Fortunately, these restrictions ended when there was finally sufficient rainfall, but as the population continues to expand in the United States, many people believe that such shortages will become commonplace.

Clearly, it is important to learn more about such environmental problems and to find ways of solving them. This will involve convincing people to treat the environment better. Naturally, you will recognize this as a classic social psychological question, in that it concerns how we can change people's attitudes and behaviors. Let's see what solutions social psychologists have come up with for the planet's pressing environmental problems (Geller, 2002; Oskamp, 1995).

Resolving Social Dilemmas

The first step is to realize that we are dealing with a classic social dilemma. As we discussed in Chapter 9, a social dilemma is a conflict in which the most beneficial action for an individual will, if chosen by most people, have harmful effects

"Help!"

on everyone. Of particular relevance to the environment is a variant called the *commons dilemma,* a situation in which everyone takes from a common pool of goods that will replenish itself if used in moderation but will disappear if overused. Examples include the use of limited resources such as water and energy. Individuals benefit by using as much as they need, but if everyone does so, shortages often result (Dawes, 1980; Hardin, 1968; Kortenkamp & Moore, 2001; Levine & Moreland, 1998; Pruitt, 1998). How can we resolve social dilemmas, convincing people to act for the greater good of everyone, rather than purely out of self-interest?

Social psychologists have devised some fascinating laboratory games to try to answer this question. For example, imagine you arrive for a study and discover that there are six other participants you have never met before. The experimenter gives you and the other participants $6 and says each of you can keep the money. There is, however, another option. Each person can donate his or her money to the rest of the group, to be divided equally among the six other members. If anyone does so, the experimenter will double the contribution. For example, if you donate your money, it will be doubled to $12 and divided evenly among the six other participants. If other group members donate their money to the pot, it will be doubled and you will get a share.

Think about the dilemma you face. If everyone (including you) cooperates by donating his or her money to the group, once it is doubled and divided up, your share will be $12—double what you started with. Donating your money is risky, however; if you are the only one who does so, you will end up with nothing while having increased everyone else's winnings (see Table SPA2.1). Clearly, the most selfish (and safest) course of action is to keep your money, hoping that everyone else donates theirs. That way, you would make up to $18—your $6, plus your share of the money everyone else threw into the pot. Of course, if everyone thinks this way, you'll make only $6, because no one will donate any money to the group. If you were like most of the participants in the actual study, you would keep your six bucks (Orbell, van de Kragt, & Dawes, 1988). After all, as you can see in Table SPA2.1, you will always earn more money by keeping your $6 than by giving it away (i.e., the winnings in the top row of Table SPA2.1 are always higher than the winnings in the bottom row). The only problem with this strategy is that because most people adopted it, everyone suffered. That is, the total pool of money to be divided remained low because few people allowed the experi-

TABLE SPA2.1

Amount of Money You Stand to Win in the Orbell, van de Kragt, and Dawes Experiment

You can either keep your $6 or donate it to the six other group members. If you donate it, the money will be doubled, so that each group member will receive $2. Most people who play this game want to keep their money, to maximize their own gains. The more people who keep their money, however, the more everyone loses.

OTHER PEOPLE'S DECISIONS:	6 KEEP, 0 GIVE	5 KEEP, 1 GIVES	4 KEEP, 2 GIVE	3 KEEP, 3 GIVE	2 KEEP, 4 GIVE	1 KEEPS, 5 GIVE	0 KEEP 6 GIVE
Your Decision							
Keep your $6	$6	$8	$10	$12	$14	$16	$18
Give your $6	$0	$2	$4	$6	$8	$10	$12

Adapted from Orbell, van de Kragt, & Dawes (1988)

menter to double the money by donating it to the group. As with many social dilemmas, most people looked out for themselves, and as a result, everyone lost.

How can people be convinced to trust their fellow group members, cooperating in such a way that everyone benefits? It is notoriously difficult to resolve social dilemmas, as indicated by the difficulty of getting people to conserve water when there are droughts, recycle their waste goods, and clean up a common area in a dormitory or apartment. In another condition of their experiment, however, the researchers found an intriguing result: Simply allowing the group to talk with each other for ten minutes dramatically increased the number of people who donated money to the group, from 38 to 79 percent. The increase in the number of donators led to a larger pool of money to be divided, rising from an average of $32 to $66 (Orbell et al., 1988). Communication works because it allows each person to find out whether the others are planning to act cooperatively or competitively, as well as to persuade others to act for the common good (e.g., "I'll donate my money if you donate yours") (Bouas & Komorita, 1996; De Cremer, 2002).

This finding is encouraging, but it may be limited to small groups that are able to communicate face to face. What happens when an entire community is caught in a social dilemma? It would be impossible for all the farmers in Nebraska to gather together and talk about land management practices. When large groups are involved, alternative approaches are needed. One approach is to make it easier for individuals to monitor their own behavior. A problem with some environmental social dilemmas is that it is not easy for people to keep track of how much of a resource they are using, such as water or electricity. During a drought, for example, people may be asked to conserve water, but it is not easy for them to monitor how many gallons a month they are using. One pair of researchers reasoned that making it easy for people to keep track of their water use would make it easier for them to act on their concern for the greater good (Van Vugt & Samuelson, 1999). They compared two communities in the Hampshire region of England during a severe drought in the summer of 1995. The houses in one community had been equipped with water meters that allowed residents to monitor how much water they were consuming. The houses in the other community did not have meters. As expected, when people felt that the water shortage was severe, those in the metered houses consumed less water than those in the unmetered houses. Further, there was evidence that they did so not purely out of self-interest (using less water would save money) but also out of concern for the collective good. Thus one simple way to resolve an environmental social dilemma is to make it easier for people to monitor their consumption, which makes it easier for them to act on their good intentions (Van Vugt, 2001).

Another approach is to make people's behavior as public as possible. If people can take the selfish route privately, undiscovered by their peers, they will often do so. But if their actions are public, the kinds of normative pressures we discussed in Chapter 8 come into play, making people's behavior more consistent with group norms. For example, some farmers might be tempted to allow runoff of fertilizers from their land if no one will find out about it, but if they believe they will become the object of derision and scorn from their neighbors, they will most likely refrain from doing so.

Another proven technique is to change the way in which people perceive themselves and their social behavior. In the first Social Psychology in Action module, we saw that Aronson, Fried, and Stone (1991) succeeded in getting people to behave in healthier and more socially responsible ways—purchasing (and presumably using) more condoms—by making them see their own past actions as hypocritical. Could similar techniques be used to convince people to behave in more environmentally sound ways, such as conserving water?

Conserving Water

Several years ago, when California was experiencing severe water shortages, the administrators at one campus of the University of California realized that an enormous amount of water was being wasted by students using the university athletic facilities. The administrators posted signs in the shower rooms of the gymnasiums, exhorting students to conserve water by taking briefer, more efficient showers. The signs appealed to the students' conscience by urging them to take brief showers and to turn off the water while soaping up. The administrators were confident the signs would be effective because the vast majority of students at this campus were ecology-minded and believed in preserving natural resources. However, systematic observation revealed that fewer than 15 percent of the students complied with the conservation message on the posted signs.

> In an age where man has forgotten his origins and is blind even to his most essential needs for survival, water along with other resources has become the victim of his indifference.
>
> *—Rachel Carson, The Silent Spring, 1962*

The administrators were puzzled—perhaps the majority of the students hadn't paid attention to the sign? After all, a sign on the wall is easy to ignore. So administrators made each sign more obtrusive, putting it on a tripod at the entrance to the showers so that the students needed to walk around the sign in order to get into the shower room. While this increased compliance slightly (19 percent turned off the shower while soaping up), it apparently made a great many students angry—the sign was continually being knocked over and kicked around, and a large percentage of students took inordinately long showers, apparently as a reaction against being told what to do. The sign was doing more harm than good, puzzling the administrators even more. Time to call in the social psychologists.

Elliot Aronson and his students (Dickerson, Thibodeau, Aronson, & Miller, 1992) decided to apply the hypocrisy technique they had used in the condom study to this new situation. The procedure involved intercepting female students who were on their way from the swimming pool to the women's shower room, introducing the experimental manipulations, and then having a research assistant casually follow them into the shower room, where she unobtrusively timed their showers. Research participants in one condition were asked to respond to a brief questionnaire about their water use, a task designed to make them mindful of how they sometimes wasted water while showering. In another condition, research participants made a public commitment, exhorting others to take steps to conserve water. Specifically, these participants were asked to sign their names to a public poster that read, "Take Shorter Showers. Turn Shower Off While Soaping Up. If I Can Do It, So Can YOU!" In the crucial condition—the "hypocrisy" condition—the participants did both; that is, they were made mindful of their own wasteful behavior, and they indicated publicly (on the poster) that they were practicing water conservation. In short, they were made aware that they were preaching behavior they themselves were not practicing. Just as in the condom study described in Chapter 6, those participants who were made to feel like hypocrites changed their behavior so that they could feel good about themselves. In this case, they took very brief showers. Indeed, the procedure was so effective that the average time students in this condition spent showering was reduced to 3.5 minutes. The hypocrisy procedure has been found to increase other environmentally sound practices as well, such as recycling (Fried & Aronson, 1995).

Conserving Energy

It may be possible to draw on other social psychological techniques to increase environmentally sound behaviors. Consider the case of energy conservation. As a nation, the United States consumes far more energy, per capita, than any other nation on earth. Historically, we have felt perfectly content using as much energy as we needed, assuming that the planet had an infinite supply of oil, natural gas, and electric power. But this is not true. We have already depleted many of our national oil reserves, and we must import much of our oil from other countries, including many Middle Eastern countries.

Let's take private homes as an example. By taking such simple measures as increasing ceiling, wall, and floor insulation, plugging air leaks, using more efficient light bulbs, and maintaining furnaces properly, the typical American energy consumer could reduce the amount of energy used to heat, light, and cool his or her home from 30 to 75 percent (Williams & Ross, 1980, U.S. Environmental Protection Agency, 2001.). The technology needed to increase energy efficiency currently exists and is well within the financial means of most homeowners. Not only would this technology save energy, but it would also save the individual homeowner a great deal of money. Yet despite the fact that the social and financial advantages of conservation have been well publicized, the vast majority of homeowners have not taken action. How come? Why have Americans been slow to act in a manner that is in their economic self-interest? This lack of compliance has puzzled economists and policymakers because they have failed to see that the issue is partly a social psychological one.

Making Energy Loss Vivid   In Chapter 5, we noted that people's attention is typically directed to the aspects of their environment that are conspicuous and

College students who were made aware that they were advocating water conservation behaviors they themselves were not practicing changed their behavior by taking shorter showers.

vivid. Elliot Aronson and his colleagues (Aronson, 1990; Aronson & Yates, 1985; Coltrane, Archer, & Aronson, 1986; Stern & Aronson, 1984) reasoned that energy conservation in the home is not a particularly vivid problem, and so people do not spend much time thinking about it. The bill for natural gas and electricity comes only once a month and is spread out over dozens of appliances; thus the homeowner has no clear idea which of the many appliances is using the most energy. It is as if you were buying food in a supermarket where the prices of individual items were unmarked and you were billed a lump sum at the end of the month. How would you know what to do to save money on your purchases? Perhaps if the sources of home energy consumption were made more vivid, people would take action.

To test this hypothesis, Aronson and his colleagues (Aronson & Gonzales, 1990; Gonzales, Aronson, & Costanzo, 1988) worked with several energy auditors in California. As in many states, California utility companies offer a free service wherein an auditor will come to people's homes and give them a customized assessment of what needs to be done to make their homes more energy-efficient. What a deal! The problem was that fewer than 20 percent of the individuals requesting audits were actually following the auditors' recommendations.

To increase compliance, the Aronson research team trained the auditors to present their findings in a more vivid manner. For example, let's consider weatherstripping. For most people, a small crack under the door didn't seem like a huge drain of energy, so when an auditor told them they should put in some weatherstripping, they thought, "Yeah, big deal." Aronson and his colleagues told the auditors to make this statement more vivid:

> *If you were to add up all the cracks around and under the doors of your home, you'd have the equivalent of a hole the size of a football in your living room wall. Think for a moment about all the heat that would escape from a hole that size. That's precisely why I'm recommending that you install weather stripping. (Gonzales et al., 1988, p. 1052)*

Similar attempts were made to make other problems more vivid—for example, referring to an attic that lacks insulation as a "naked attic" that is like "facing winter not just without an overcoat but without any clothing at all" (p. 1052).

The results were striking. The percentage of homeowners who followed the vivid recommendations jumped to 61 percent. This study demonstrates that people will act in a manner that is sensible in terms of national goals and their own economic self-interest, but if old habits are involved, the communication must be vivid enough to break through those established habits.

Making Conservation Competitive   Other researchers have demonstrated a simple but powerful way to get people to conserve energy in the workplace (Siero, Bakker, Dekker, & Van Den Burg, 1996). At one unit of a factory in the Netherlands, the employees were urged to engage in energy-saving behaviors. For example, announcements were placed in the company magazine asking people to close windows during cold weather and to turn off lights when leaving a room. In addition, the employees got weekly feedback on their behavior; graphs were posted that showed how much they had improved their energy-saving behaviors, such as how often they had turned off the lights. This intervention resulted in modest improvement. By the end of the program, for example, the number of times people left the lights on decreased by 27 percent.

Another unit of the factory took part in an identical program, with one difference. In addition to receiving weekly feedback on their own energy-saving actions, they received feedback about how the other unit was doing. The researchers hypothesized that this social comparison information would motivate people to do better than their colleagues in the other unit. As seen in Figure

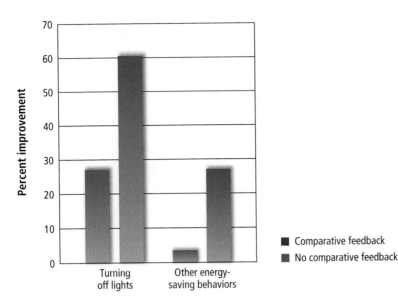

FIGURE SPA2.3

Effects of comparative feedback on energy-saving behaviors.

Two units of a factory were urged to conserve energy and received feedback about how their unit was doing. Only one of the units, however, received comparative feedback about how it was doing relative to the other unit. As seen in the graph, this second unit improved its behavior the most, especially by turning off lights more.

(Adapted from Siero, Bakker, Dekker, & Van Den Burgh, 1996)

SPA2.3, they were right. By the end of the program, the number of times people left lights on had decreased by 61 percent. Engaging people's competitive spirit can have a large impact on their behavior.

Reducing Litter

Compared to other environmental problems, littering may not seem to be all that serious a matter. Although billboards implore us to "Keep America Beautiful," most people seem to think it isn't a big deal to leave their paper cup at the side of the road instead of in a trash barrel. Unfortunately, those paper cups add up. In California, for example, littering has increased steadily to the point that $100 million of tax money is spent cleaning it up every year (Cialdini, Kallgren, & Reno, 1991). The stuff we discard is polluting our water systems, endangering wildlife, and costing us millions of dollars.

Littering is another classic social dilemma. Sometimes it's a pain to find a trash can, and from an individual's point of view, big deal—what's one more paper cup added to the side of the road? As with all social dilemmas, the problem is that if everyone thinks this way, everyone suffers (Sibley & Lui, 2003). How can we get people to act less selfishly when they have that empty paper cup in hand?

As we saw in Chapter 8, one answer is to remind people of the social norms against littering. Robert Cialdini, Raymond Reno, and Carl Kallgren have pointed out that there are two important kinds of social norms that can influence whether people litter (Cialdini et al., 1991; Kallgren, Reno, & Cialdini, 2000; Reno, Cialdini, & Kallgren, 1993). First, there are **injunctive norms,** which are socially sanctioned behaviors—people's perceptions of what behaviors are approved or disapproved by others. For example, we may be in an environment where many people are littering but know there is an injunctive norm against littering—most people disapprove of it. Second, there are **descriptive norms,** which are people's perceptions of how people are actually behaving in a given situation, regardless of whether the behavior is approved or disapproved by others.

In Chapter 8, we discussed a field experiment by Reno and his colleagues (1993) in which an experimental accomplice conveyed an injunctive norm against littering by picking up a fast-food bag that had been discarded on the ground and putting it in the trash. The researchers hypothesized that seeing the accomplice pick up the fast-food bag would be a vivid reminder of the injunctive norm—littering is bad, and other people disapprove of it—and hence would

Injunctive Norms

People's perceptions of what behaviors are approved or disapproved of by others

Descriptive Norms

People's perceptions of how people actually behave in a given situation, regardless of whether the behavior is approved or disapproved of by others

lower people's inclination to litter. To find out, they placed a large handbill under the windshield wiper of people's cars and observed whether people threw the handbill on the ground or took it with them (presumably to throw away when they got home). As predicted, only 7 percent of the people who had seen the accomplice pick up the fast-food bag tossed the handbill on the ground, compared to 37 percent in a control condition in which there was no fast-food bag on the ground and the accomplice simply walked by. If you would like to try to replicate this effect in an experiment of your own, see the Try It! exercise below.

What is the best way to communicate descriptive norms against littering? The most straightforward way, it would seem, would be to clean up all the litter in an environment, to illustrate that "no one litters here." In general, this is true: The less litter there is in an environment, the less likely people are to litter (Huffman, Grossnickle, Cope, & Huffman, 1995; Krauss, Freedman, & Whitcup, 1978; Reiter & Samuel, 1980). There is, however, an interesting exception to this finding. Cialdini, Reno, and Kallgren (1990) figured that seeing one conspicuous piece of litter on the ground, spoiling an otherwise clean environment, would be a better reminder of descriptive norms than seeing a completely clean environment. The single piece of trash sticks out like a sore thumb, reminding people that no one has littered here except one thoughtless person. In contrast, if there is no litter on the ground, people might be less likely to think about what the descriptive norm is. Ironically, then, littering may be more likely to occur in a totally clean environment than in one containing a single piece of litter.

> We live in an environment whose principal product is garbage.
>
> —Russell Baker, 1968

To test this hypothesis, the researchers stuffed students' mailboxes with handbills and then observed, from a hidden vantage point, how many of the students dropped the handbills on the floor (Cialdini et al., 1990). In the first condition, the researchers cleaned up the mailroom so that there were no other

Try it!

Reducing Littering with Injunctive Norms

See if you can get people to pick up litter by invoking injunctive norms, using the techniques discovered by Raymond Reno and his colleagues (Reno, Cialdini, & Kallgren, 1993). This exercise is easiest to do in pairs with a friend.

First, find an environment in which people are likely to litter. For example, at many universities, the student newspaper often comes with an advertising insert. When people pick up a copy of the newspaper, they often discard the insert on the floor. This exercise is best done with a friend who can observe people unobtrusively to see if they litter.

Next, plant a conspicuous piece of litter in this environment. Reno et al. (1993) used a fast-food bag stuffed with trash. Place it in a location that people are sure to see, such as near a doorway.

In one condition, wait until an individual enters the environment and is in full view of the piece of trash you planted. Then pick up the trash, throw it away, and go on your way. It is crucial that the person realize that it wasn't your bag but that you decided to pick it up and throw it away anyway. In a second condition, walk by the trash, glance at it, and continue on your way without picking it up. Make sure to randomly assign passersby to one of these two conditions.

The observer should watch to see whether people litter; for example, whether they throw the advertising insert on the floor or put it in a trash can. As discussed in the text, Reno et al. (1993) found that when people saw someone pick up another person's litter, they were much less likely to litter themselves. Did you replicate this effect? Why or why not, do you think?

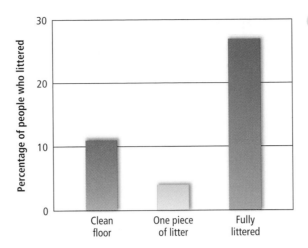

FIGURE SPA2.4

Descriptive norms and littering.

Who littered the least—people who saw that no one else had littered, people who saw one piece of litter on the floor, or people who saw several pieces of litter? As shown in the figure, it was people who saw one piece of litter. Seeing the single piece of litter was most likely to draw people's attention to the fact that most people had not littered, making people less likely themselves to litter.

(Adapted from Cialdini, Reno, & Kallgren, 1990)

pieces of litter to be seen. In the second condition, they placed one very noticeable piece of litter on the floor—a hollowed-out piece of watermelon. In the third condition, they not only put the watermelon rind on the floor but also spread out dozens of discarded handbills. As predicted, the lowest rate of littering occurred in the condition where there was a single piece of trash on the floor (see Figure SPA2.4). The single violation of a descriptive norm highlighted the fact that no one had littered but the one doofus who had dropped the watermelon rind on the floor. Now that people's attention was focused on the descriptive norm against littering, virtually none of the students littered. The highest percentage of littering occurred when the floor was littered with lots of handbills; here it was clear that there was a descriptive norm in favor of littering, and many of the students followed suit.

Clearly, drawing people's attention to both injunctive and descriptive norms can reduce littering. Of the two kinds of norms, these researchers suggest that injunctive norms work better. Descriptive norms work only if everyone cooperates—for example, by keeping an environment relatively free of litter. This method is not perfect, however; if trash starts accumulating, the descriptive norm becomes "Lots of people litter here!" and littering will increase. In contrast, reminding people of the injunctive norm works in a wide variety of situations (Kallgren et al., 2000; Reno et al., 1993). Once we are reminded that "people disapprove of littering," we are less likely to litter in virtually all circumstances.

Besides being unsightly, litter can cost millions of dollars to clean up. Social psychologists have found that emphasizing different kinds of social norms against littering is an effective way to prevent it.

Getting People to Recycle

Suppose we succeeded in getting people to stop littering. That would be wonderful, because roadsides would look pretty and we wouldn't have to spend millions of dollars in tax money to clean up people's litter. But the problem of what to do with our trash, once it is collected and thrown away, would remain, as seen by the fruitless journey of the trash barge discussed at the beginning of this chapter.

To reduce the amount of trash that ends up in landfills, many cities are encouraging their residents to recycle materials such as glass, paper, and aluminum. But as you know, it can be inconvenient to do so; in some areas, you have to load your car with boxes of cans and bottles and drop them off at a recycling center, which might be several miles from your house. Other cities have curbside recycling, whereby a truck picks up recycling materials that you set out at the curb on a designated day. Even here, though, you have to remember to separate your cans and bottles from the rest of the trash and find a place to store them until the pickup day. We thus have another social dilemma—a behavior (recycling) that, while good for us all, is effortful and unpleasant for individuals. As you might imagine, several social psychologists have turned their attention to ways of getting people to recycle more.

There have been two general approaches to this problem. First, some psychologists have focused on ways of changing people's attitudes and values in a pro-environment direction, with the assumption that their behavior will follow suit. This assumption is consistent with social psychological research on attitudes, which has found that under many conditions, people's attitudes are good predictors of their behavior (see Chapter 7). Several studies have found that people's attitudes toward recycling are in fact good predictors of their recycling behaviors, suggesting that a mass media campaign that targets people's attitudes is a good way to go (Cheung, Chan, & Wong, 1999; Ewing, 2001; Oskamp, Burkhardt, Schultz, Hurin, & Zelezny, 1998).

Sometimes, though, we might fail to act consistently with our attitudes, despite our best intentions. Perhaps the recycling center is too far away or we just can't find the time to sort our trash, even though we know we should. Kurt Lewin (1947), one of the founders of social psychology, made the observation that big social changes can sometimes occur by removing small barriers from people's

More and more communities are encouraging people to recycle materials such as bottles, cans, and newspapers. Social psychologists have identified several ways of increasing the likelihood that people will recycle.

environments (Ross & Nisbett, 1991). In the context of recycling, it might be better simply to remove some of the hassles involved, such as instituting curbside recycling, than to try to change people's attitudes toward the environment. A number of studies have found this to be true. Increasing the number of recycling bins in a community, instituting curbside recycling, and allowing residents to mix materials, instead of having to sort them, have all been found to increase people's recycling behaviors (Domina & Koch, 2002; Ludwig, Gray, & Rowell, 1998; Schultz, Oskamp, & Mainieri, 1995).

Consider a natural experiment that was conducted in Fairfax County, Virginia (Guagnano, Stern, & Dietz, 1995). Curbside recyling had recently begun in the county, and only about a quarter of the residents had received plastic bins in which to put their recyclable materials. Others had to find their own containers in which to put their bottles and cans. Now, it might seem like this would not be much of an impediment to recycling; if people really cared about the environment, they should be able to find their own box. As Lewin argued, however, sometimes little barriers have big effects, and indeed, the people who had the bins were much more likely to recycle. The researchers also measured people's attitudes toward recycling to see if those with positive attitudes were more likely to recycle than those who were not. Interestingly, people's attitudes predicted behavior only when they did not possess a recycling bin. When there was a barrier preventing easy compliance—people had to search through the

Try it!

Changing Environmentally Damaging Behaviors

Use the techniques discussed in this chapter to change people's behavior in ways that help the environment. Here's how to proceed:

1. Choose the behavior you want to change. You might try to increase the amount that you and your roommates recycle, reduce the amount of energy wasted in your dorm, or increase water conservation.

2. Choose the technique you will use to change the behavior. For example, you might use the comparative feedback technique used by Frans Siero and colleagues (1996) to increase energy conservation. Encourage two areas of your dormitory to reduce energy usage or to recycle, and give each feedback about how it is doing relative to the other area. (To do this, you will have to have an easy, objective way of measuring people's behavior, such as the number of times lights are left on at night or the number of cans that are recycled.) Or you might try the hypocrisy technique used by Elliot Aronson and colleagues (Dickerson et al., 1992) to increase water conservation, whereby you ask people to sign a public poster that encourages recycling and have them fill out a questionnaire that makes them mindful of times they have failed to recycle. Be creative, and feel free to use more than one technique.

3. Measure the success of your intervention. Find an easy way to measure people's behavior, such as the amount that they recycle. Assess their behavior before and after your intervention. Best of all, include a control group of people who do not receive your intervention (randomly assigned, of course). In the absence of such a control group, it will be difficult to gauge the success of your intervention; for example, if people's behavior changes over time, you won't be able to tell if it is because of your intervention or some other factor (e.g., an article on recycling that happened to appear in the newspaper). By comparing the changes in behavior in your target group to the control group, you will have a better estimate of the success of your intervention.

garage to find a suitable box—only those with positive attitudes exerted the energy to circumvent the barrier. When there was no barrier—people had a convenient container provided by the county—attitudes did not matter as much. People were likely to conform even if they did not have strong pro-environmental attitudes.

The moral? There are two ways to get people to act in more environmentally sound ways. First, you can try to change people's attitudes in a pro-environmental direction; this will motivate them to act in environmentally friendly ways, even if there are barriers that make it hard to do so (such as having to find a box for your bottles and cans and taking it to a recycling center). It is often easier, however, simply to remove the barriers (as by instituting curbside recycling and giving people containers). When it is easy to comply, many people will do so, even if they do not have strong pro-environmental attitudes.

Now that you have read about several approaches for changing people's behavior in ways that help the environment, you are in a position to try them out yourself. See the Try It! exercise on page 523 for suggestions on how to do this.

SUMMARY

The Environment as a Source of Stress

As we human beings continue to populate the earth at an alarming rate, our physical world is becoming a crowded and noisy place to live. Social psychologists have focused on how people interpret and explain crowded conditions and noise. One key interpretation is how much perceived control people have over the event. The less control people believe they have, the more likely it is that the event will cause them physical and psychological problems. For example, if people in settings in which **density** is high feel they have a low level of control (i.e., they believe it is difficult to escape to a less dense setting), they will experience **crowding,** the subjective feeling of unpleasantness due to the presence of other people. Crowding can also be aversive if it leads to **sensory overload,** which occurs when other people place a severe demand on our attentional system. In addition, the way in which people explain the causes of negative events is critical to how an event is interpreted and thus to how stressful it will be.

Using Social Psychology to Change Environmentally Damaging Behaviors

We also discussed the effects people are having on the environment and the ways in which social influence techniques can be used to get people to behave in more envi-ronmentally sound ways. This is not easy because many environmental problems are classic social dilemmas, wherein actions that are beneficial for individuals are, if performed by most people, harmful to everyone. Using proven techniques to change people's attitudes and behaviors, however, social psychologists have had some success in getting people to act in more environmentally sound ways. One technique is to arouse dissonance in people by making them feel that they are not practicing what they are preaching—for example, that even though they believe in water conservation, they are taking long showers. Another is to remind people of both **injunctive** and **descriptive norms** against environmentally damaging acts, such as littering. Focusing people's attention on injunctive norms against littering—the idea that throwing trash on the ground is not a socially accepted behavior—was found to be especially effective. Finally, removing barriers that make pro-environmental behaviors difficult, such as instituting curbside recycling and providing people with recycling bins, has been shown to be effective.

CRITICAL THINKING QUESTIONS

1. Suppose you were asked to help design a new dormitory at a university. Based on what you have learned about the stressful effects of crowding and noise, what design approach would you take?

2. Based on research on social dilemmas, how might you try to get the residents of a dormitory to recycle more and consume less energy?

3. Suppose you are hired as the city manager of a mid-sized town in the United States. You are running out of landfill space to deposit the city's trash, and it is expensive to ship your trash elsewhere. Based on what you have learned in this chapter, what might you do to get the residents of the town to produce less trash and recycle more?

SOCIAL PSYCHOLOGY *IN ACTION*

3

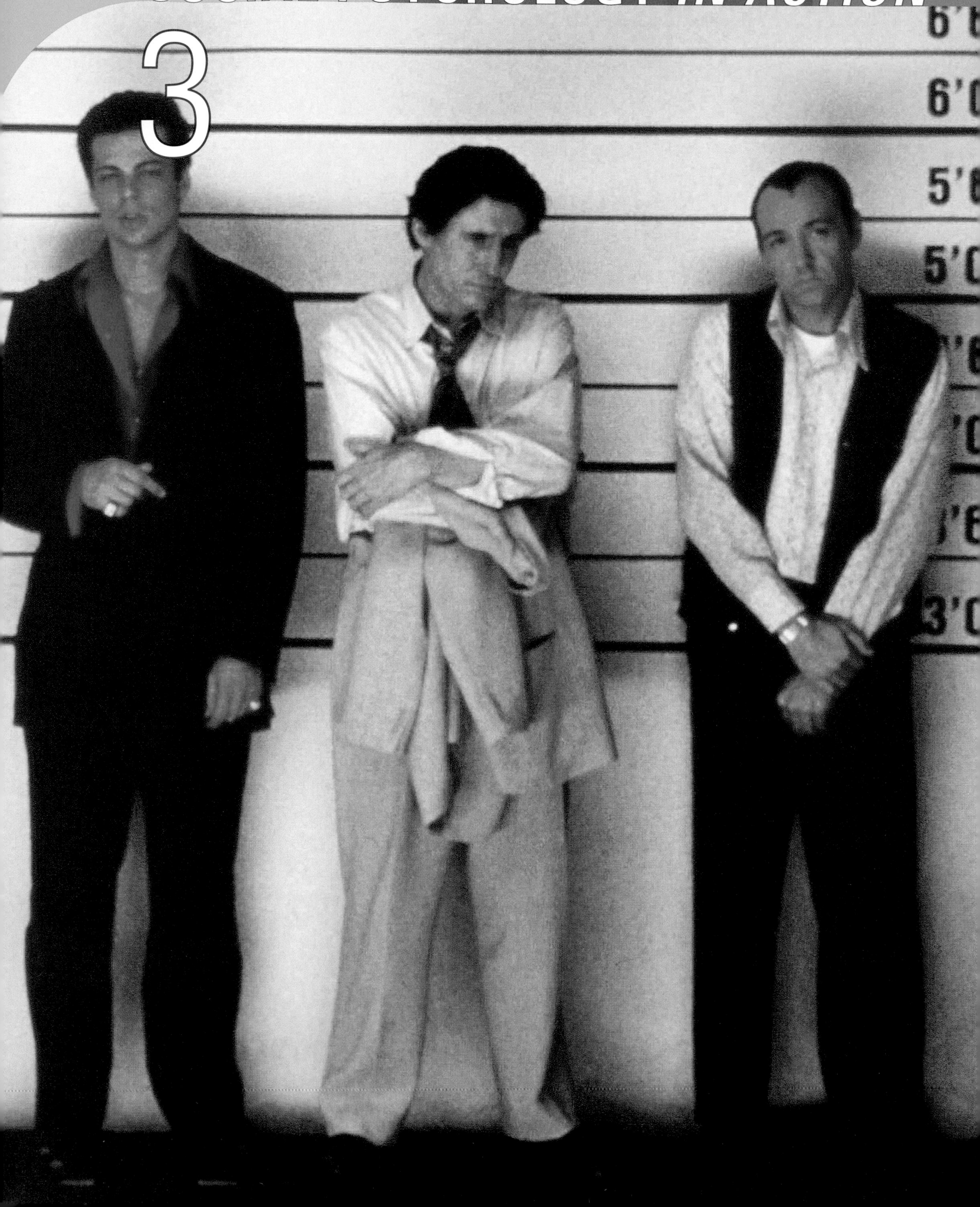

Social Psychology and the Law

You be the jury and decide how you would vote, after hearing the following testimony from an actual case in Texas.

On a cold, dark night in November 1976, police officer Robert Wood and his partner spotted a car driving with its headlights off. Wood signaled the car to pull over, got out, and walked up to the driver's side. He intended only to tell the driver to turn on his lights, but he never got the chance. Before Wood could even speak, the driver pointed a handgun at Wood and shot him, killing him instantly. Wood's partner emptied her revolver at the car as it sped away, but the killer escaped.

A month later, the police picked up a suspect, 16-year-old David Harris. Harris admitted that he had stolen a neighbor's car and revolver the day before the murder, that this was the car Officer Wood had pulled over that night, and that he was in the car when the murder occurred. Harris denied, however, that he was the one who shot Wood. He said he had picked up a hitchhiker by the name of Randall Adams and had let Adams drive. It was Adams, he claimed, who reached under the seat, grabbed the revolver, and shot the officer.

When the police questioned Randall Adams, he admitted he had gotten a ride from David Harris but said Harris had dropped him off at his motel three hours before the murder occurred. It was Harris, he claimed, who was the murderer. Who was telling the truth? It was Harris's word against Adams's— until the police found three eyewitnesses who corroborated Harris's story. Emily and Robert Miller testified that they drove by just before Officer Wood was shot. Though it was very dark, they said they got a good look at the driver of the car, and both identified him as Randall Adams. "When he rolled down the window, that's what made his face stand out," said Robert Miller. "He had a beard, mustache, kind of dishwater blond hair" (Morris, 1988). David Harris was clean-shaven, and at the time of the murder, Randall Adams did indeed fit Miller's description (see the photo on the next page). Michael Randell, a salesman, also happened to be driving by right before the murder and claimed to have seen two people in the car. He too said the driver had long hair and a mustache.

Randall Adams (left) and David Harris (right). The fact that eyewitnesses said the murderer had long hair and a mustache was the main reason Adams was convicted of murdering Officer Wood.

Who do you think committed the murder? The real jury believed the eyewitnesses and convicted Adams, sentencing him to death. However, as Adams languished in jail, waiting for the courts to hear his appeals, several experts began to doubt that he was guilty. New evidence came to light (largely because of a film made about the case, *The Thin Blue Line*), and it is now almost certain that David Harris was the murderer. Harris was later convicted of another murder and while on death row strongly implied that he, not Randall Adams, had shot Officer Wood. An appeals court finally overturned Adams's conviction. He was a free man—after spending twelve years in prison for a crime he did not commit.

If Adams was innocent, why did the eyewitnesses say that the driver of the car had long hair and a mustache? And why did the jury believe them? How common are such miscarriages of justice? In this chapter, we will discuss the answers to these questions, focusing on the role social psychological processes play in the legal system.

Let's begin with a brief review of the American justice system. When someone commits a crime and the police arrest a suspect, a judge or a grand jury decides whether there is enough evidence to press formal charges. If there is, lawyers for the defense and the prosecution gather evidence and negotiate with each other. As a result of these negotiations, the defendant often pleads guilty to a lesser charge. About a quarter of the cases go to trial, in which a jury or a judge decides the defendant's fate. There are also civil trials, where one party (the plaintiff) brings a complaint against another (the defendant) for violating the former's rights in some way.

All of these steps in the legal process are related to central social psychological questions. For example, first impressions of the accused and of the witnesses have a powerful effect on police investigators and the jury; attributions about what caused the criminal behavior are made by police, lawyers, jurors, and the judge; prejudiced beliefs and stereotypical ways of thinking affect those attributions; attitude change and persuasion techniques abound in the courtroom as lawyers for each side argue their case and jurors later debate with one another; and the processes of social cognition affect the jurors' decision making when deciding guilt or innocence. Social psychologists have studied the legal system a great deal in recent years, both because it offers an excellent applied setting in which to study basic psychological processes and because of its immense importance in daily life. If you, through no fault of your own, become the accused in a court trial, what do you need to know to convince the system of your innocence?

We will begin our discussion with eyewitness testimony, the most troubling aspect of the Randall Adams case. We saw in Chapter 4 that although people do form accurate impressions of others, systematic biases can come into play, leading to serious misunderstandings. A closely related question is, how accurate are people at identifying someone who has committed a crime?

EYEWITNESS TESTIMONY

The American legal system assigns a great deal of significance to eyewitness testimony. If an eyewitness fingers you as the culprit, you are quite likely to be convicted, even if considerable circumstantial evidence indicates that you are innocent. Randall Adams was convicted largely because of the eyewitnesses who identified him, even though in other ways the case against him was weak: He had no criminal record, he had just found steady employment, and he had no reason to be concerned about being pulled over by the police—he was only a hitchhiker (if, indeed, he really was in the car at the time of the shooting). In comparison, David Harris had many reasons to fear the police: He had stolen the car and was in possession of a stolen, loaded handgun. Given these facts, why would Randall Adams murder a police officer? Doesn't David Harris seem the more logical suspect? Despite the implausibility of the Adams-as-murderer scenario and despite the lack of physical evidence linking Adams to the scene of the crime, the eyewitness testimony that Adams was driving the car was enough to convict him.

Systematic experiments have confirmed that jurors and law enforcement professionals rely heavily on eyewitness testimony when they are deciding whether someone is guilty. Unfortunately, jurors also tend to overestimate the accuracy of eyewitnesses (Ellsworth & Mauro, 1998; Loftus, 1979; Wells & Olson, 2003). Rod Lindsay and his colleagues (Lindsay, Wells, & Rumpel, 1981) conducted a clever experiment that illustrates both of these points. The researchers first staged the theft of a calculator in front of unsuspecting students and then saw how accurately the students could pick out the "thief" from a set of six photographs. In one condition, identifying the thief was difficult because he had worn a knit cap pulled over his ears and was in the room for only twelve seconds. In the second condition, the thief had worn the knit cap higher on his head, revealing some of his hair, so that it was easier to identify him. In the third condition, the thief had worn no hat and stayed in the room for twenty seconds, making it easiest to identify him.

FIGURE SPA3.1

The accuracy of eyewitness identification.

The accuracy of eyewitness identification depends on the viewing conditions at the time the crime was committed. As in this study, however, most jurors believe that witnesses can correctly identify the criminal even when viewing conditions are poor.

(Adapted from Lindsay, Wells, & Rumpel, 1981)

The first set of results is as we'd expect: The more visual information available about the thief, the higher the percentage of students who correctly identified him in the photo lineup (see the bottom line in Figure SPA3.1). In the next stage of the experiment, a researcher playing the role of lawyer questioned the students about their eyewitness identifications, just as a real lawyer would cross-examine witnesses in a trial. These question-and-answer sessions were videotaped. A new group of participants, playing the role of jurors, watched the videotapes of these cross-examinations and rated the extent to which they believed the witnesses had correctly identified the thief. As shown by the top line in Figure SPA3.1, the jurors overestimated the accuracy of the witnesses, especially in the condition where the thief was difficult to identify.

How accurate are eyewitnesses to real crimes? Although it is impossible to say exactly what percentage of the time eyewitnesses are accurate, there is reason to believe that they often make mistakes. Researchers have documented many cases of wrongful arrests, and in a remarkably high proportion of these cases, the wrong person was convicted because an eyewitness mistakenly identified him or her as the criminal. For example, Gary Wells and his colleagues (1998) examined forty cases in which DNA evidence, obtained after the conviction of a suspect, indicated that the suspect was innocent. In thirty-six of these cases, an eyewitness had falsely identified the suspect as the criminal. Five of these falsely accused people were on death row when they were exonerated. The most common cause of an innocent person's being convicted of a crime is an erroneous eyewitness (Brandon & Davies, 1973; Sporer, Koehnken, & Malpass, 1996; Wells, Wright, & Bradfield, 1999).

Why Are Eyewitnesses Often Wrong?

The problem is that our minds are not like video cameras, which can record an event, store it over time, and play it back later with perfect accuracy. Think back to our discussion of social perception in Chapter 4, the study of how we form impressions of and make inferences about other people. We saw that a number of distortions can occur. Because eyewitness identification is a form of social perception, it is subject to similar problems, particularly those involving memory. To be an accurate eyewitness, a person must successfully complete three stages of memory processing: acquisition, storage, and retrieval of the events witnessed. **Acquisition** refers to the process whereby people notice and pay attention to information in the environment. Because people cannot perceive everything that is happening around them, they acquire only a subset of the information available in the environment. **Storage** refers to the process by which people store in

Acquisition

The process by which people notice and pay attention to information in the environment; because people cannot perceive everything that is happening around them, they acquire only a subset of the information available in the environment

Storage

The process by which people store in memory information they have acquired from the environment

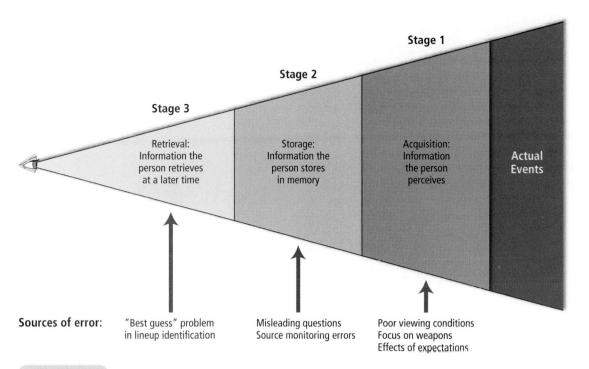

FIGURE SPA3.2

Acquisition, storage, and retrieval.

To be an accurate eyewitness, people must complete three stages of memory processing. Error may creep in at each of the three stages.

memory information they have acquired from the environment. **Retrieval** refers to the process by which people recall information stored in their memories (see Figure SPA3.2). Eyewitnesses can be inaccurate because of problems at any of these three stages.

Acquisition   How accurate is our ability to observe the unexpected? Not very. Consider the following incident, described nearly a century ago by the psychologist Hugo Münsterberg (1908). During a scientific meeting attended by psychologists, lawyers, and physicians, a clown burst into the room, followed closely by a man with a revolver. The two men shouted wildly, grabbed each other, and then fell to the ground in a fierce struggle. One of them fired a shot; then both men ran out of the room.

All the witnesses were asked to write down an exact account of what they had just seen (which was actually an event staged by two actors). Even though the eyewitnesses were educated people with (presumably) good memories, their accounts were far from accurate. Most of them omitted or wrote mistaken accounts of about half the actions that had occurred, and most made errors about the duration of the incident. Though the two men were in the room for about twenty seconds, the witnesses' estimates ranged from a few seconds to several minutes.

Many years later, a team of psychologists found similar eyewitness errors in a study of actual criminal cases (Tollestrup, Turtle & Yuille, 1994) . They examined police records of robbery and fraud cases in which a suspect was caught and confessed to the crime. They then assessed the accuracy of both victims' and bystanders' descriptions of the criminal by comparing the witness's initial descriptions of the criminal to the criminal's actual physical characteristics (for example, were witnesses correct that the criminal had blond hair and a mustache?). Eyewitnesses weren't too bad at remembering some details; 100 percent of bystanders correctly remembered whether or not the criminal had facial hair

Retrieval

The process by which people recall information stored in their memories

Imagine that you are on this street corner and suddenly witness a holdup across the street. A thief robs a man of his wallet and is gone in a matter of seconds. How accurate do you think your description of the thief will be?

(although crime victims correctly remembered this only 60 percent of the time). Only 48 percent of the bystanders and 38 percent of the victims correctly remembered the suspect's hair color, however. Most important, neither bystanders nor victims did a very good job of picking the criminal out of a lineup; overall, they correctly identified the criminal only 48 percent of the time.

A number of factors limit the amount of information about a crime that people take in, such as how much time they have to watch an event and the nature of the viewing conditions. As obvious as this may sound, people sometimes forget how these factors limit eyewitness reports of crimes. Crimes usually occur under the very conditions that make acquisition difficult: quickly, unexpectedly, and under poor viewing conditions, such as at night. These conditions certainly describe the scene of the murder of Officer Wood. Eyewitnesses were driving down a dimly lit road, past a pulled-over car, when the unexpected happened—shots were fired and a policeman crumpled to the ground. How well could they see? How much information could they take in, in the few seconds it took to drive by?

We should also remember that eyewitnesses who are the victims of a crime will be terribly afraid, and this alone can make it difficult to take in everything that is happening. As we saw, robbery victims tend to make more mistakes than bystanders (Tollestrup et al., 1994). Another reason why victims of crimes have a poor memory for a suspect is that they focus their attention mostly on any weapon they see and less on the suspect's features (Christianson, 1992; Loftus, Loftus, & Messo, 1987; Pickel, 1998; Shaw & Skolnick, 1999). If someone points a gun at you and demands your money, your attention is likely to be more on the gun than on whether the robber has blue or brown eyes.

The information people notice and pay attention to is also influenced by what they expect to see. Consider our friend Alan, a social psychologist who is an expert on social perception. One Sunday, Alan was worried because his neighbor, a frail woman in her eighties, did not appear for church. After knocking on her door repeatedly and receiving no response, Alan jimmied open a window and searched her house. Soon his worst fears were realized: The woman was lying dead on the floor of her bedroom.

Shaken, Alan went back to his house and telephoned the police. After spending a great deal of time in the woman's house, a detective came over and asked Alan increasingly detailed questions, such as whether he had noticed any suspicious activity in the past day or two. Alan was confused by this line of questioning and finally burst out, "Why are you asking me these questions? Isn't it obvious that my neighbor died of old age? Shouldn't we be notifying her family?" Now it was the detective's turn to look puzzled. "Aren't you the one who discovered the body?" he asked. Alan said he was. "Well," said the detective, "didn't you notice that her bedroom had been ransacked, that there was broken glass everywhere, and that there was a belt tied around her neck?"

It turned out that Alan's neighbor had been strangled by a man who had come to spray her house for insects. There had been a fierce struggle, and the fact that the woman was murdered could not have been more obvious. But Alan saw none of the signs. He was worried that his elderly neighbor had

> When an actual perceptual fact is in conflict with expectation, expectation may prove a stronger determinant of perception and memory than the situation itself.
>
> —Gordon Allport and Leo Postman, 1947

passed away. When he discovered that she had in fact died, he was quite upset, and the farthest thing from his mind was that she had been murdered. As a result, he saw what he expected and failed to see what he did not expect. When the police later showed him photographs of the crime scene, he felt as though he had never been there. He recognized almost nothing. Alan's experiences are consistent with our discussion in Chapter 3 of how people use theories and schemas. We have many theories about the world and the people in it, and these theories influence what we notice and remember.

Similarly, the information we take in is influenced by how familiar we are with it. Unfamiliar things are more difficult to remember than familiar things. For example, people are better at recognizing faces that are of the same race as they are, a phenomenon known as **own-race bias.** Whites are better at recognizing white faces than black or Asian faces, blacks are better at recognizing black than white faces, and Asians are better at recognizing Asian than white faces (Levin, 2000; Meissner & Brigham, 2001b; Ng & Lindsay, 1994; Shapiro & Penrod, 1986).

Own-race bias is due to the fact that people have more contact with members of their own race, allowing them to learn better how to distinguish one individual from another (Meissner & Brigham, 2001b). For example, there is evidence that when people examine same-race faces, they pay close attention to individuating features that distinguish that face from others, such as the height of the cheekbones or the contour of the forehead. When people examine different-race faces, however, they are drawn more to features that distinguish that face from their own race, rather than individuating features (Levin, 2000). Daniel Levin, a researcher who has investigated this hypothesis, puts it like this: "When a white person looks at another white person's nose, they're likely to think to themselves, 'That's John's nose.' When they look at a black person's nose, they're likely to think, 'That's a black nose'" (quoted in Carpenter, 2000, p. 44). Because people usually have less experience with features that characterize individuals of other races, they find it more difficult to tell members of that race apart. One study found a similar effect with age: College students were better at recognizing faces of people their own age than faces of middled-aged people, whereas middle-aged people were better at recognizing faces of people their own age than faces of college students (Wright & Stroud, 2002).

Storage   We have just seen that several variables limit what people perceive and thus what they are able to store in their memories. Once a piece of information is in memory, it might seem like it stays there, unaltered, until we recall it at a later time. Many people think memory is like a photograph album. We record a picture of an event, such as the face of a robber, and place it in the memory "album." In reality, few of us have photographic memories. Memories, like real photographs, fade with age. Further, it is tempting to believe that a picture, once stored, cannot be altered or retouched, and that details cannot be added to or subtracted from the image. If the robber we saw was clean-shaven, surely we will not pencil in a mustache at some later time. Hence the fact that the witnesses who testified at the Randall Adams trial remembered that the driver of the car had long hair and a mustache seems like pretty incriminating evidence against Randall Adams.

Unfortunately, memories are far from indelible. People can get mixed up about where they heard or saw something; memories in one "album" can get confused with memories in another. As a result, people can have quite inaccurate recall about what they saw. This is the conclusion reached after years of research on **reconstructive memory,** the distortion of memories of an event by information encountered after the event occurred (Hirt, McDonald, & Erikson, 1995; Loftus, 1979; Loftus & Hoffman, 1989; McDonald & Hirt, 1997; Schacter,

Own-Race Bias

The fact that people are better at recognizing faces of their own race than those of other races

Reconstructive Memory

The process whereby memories of an event become distorted by information encountered after the event occurred

1996). According to this research, information we obtain after witnessing an event can change our memories of the event.

In one study, Elizabeth Loftus showed students thirty slides depicting different stages of an automobile accident. The content of one slide varied; some students saw a car stopped at a stop sign, and others saw the same car stopped at a yield sign. After the slide show, the students were asked several questions about the car accident they had "witnessed." The key question varied how the traffic sign was described. In one version, the question asked, "Did another car pass the red Datsun while it was stopped at the stop sign?" In the other version, the question asked, "Did another car pass the red Datsun while it was stopped at the yield sign?" Thus for half the participants, the question described the traffic sign as they had in fact seen it. But for the other half, the wording of the question subtly introduced new information—for example, if they had seen a stop sign, the question described it as a yield sign. Would this small change (akin to what might occur when witnesses are being questioned by police investigators or attorneys) have an effect on people's memories of the actual event?

All the students were shown the two pictures reproduced here and asked which one they had originally seen. Most people (75 percent) who were asked about the sign they had actually seen chose the correct picture; that is, if they had seen a stop sign and were asked about a stop sign, most of them correctly identified the stop sign photograph (note that 25 percent made a crucial mistake on what would seem to be an easy question). However, of those who had received the misleading question, only 41 percent chose the correct photograph (Loftus, Miller, & Burns, 1978).

In subsequent experiments, Loftus and her colleagues have found that misleading questions can change people's minds about how fast a car was going,

Students saw one of these pictures and then tried to remember whether they had seen a stop sign or a yield sign. Many of those who heard leading questions about the street sign made mistaken reports about which sign they had seen. (From Loftus, Miller, & Burns, 1978)

whether broken glass was at the scene of an accident, whether a traffic light was green or red, and—of relevance to the Randall Adams trial—whether a robber had a mustache (Loftus, 1979). Her studies show that the way in which the police and lawyers question witnesses can change the witnesses' reports about what they saw. (There is some suspicion that in the Randall Adams case, the police may have led the witnesses by asking questions that implicated Adams and not Harris. At the time of the murder, Harris was a juvenile and could not receive the death penalty for killing a police officer; Adams was in his thirties and was eligible for the death penalty. According to this reasoning, Adams was a "better" suspect in the eyes of the police). But, we might ask, do misleading questions alter what is stored in eyewitnesses' memories, or do the questions change only what these people are willing to report, without retouching their memories?

Though some controversy exists over the answer to this question (Koriat, Goldsmith, & Pansky, 2000; Loftus & Hoffman, 1989; McCloskey & Zaragoza, 1985; Smith & Ellsworth, 1987), most researchers endorse the following position: Misleading questions cause a problem with **source monitoring,** the process people use to try to identify the source of their memories (Johnson, Hashtroudi, & Lindsay, 1993; Mitchell, Johnson, & Mather, 2003). People who saw a stop sign but received the misleading question about a yield sign now have two pieces of information in memory, the stop sign and the yield sign. This is all well and good as long as they remember where these memories came from: the stop sign from the accident they saw earlier and the yield sign from the question they were asked later. The problem is that people often get mixed up about where they heard or saw something, mistakenly believing that the yield sign looks familiar because they saw it during the slide show. This process is similar to the misattribution effects we discussed in Chapter 5, when people are unsure about what has caused their arousal. It's easy to get confused about the source of our memories as well. When information gets stored in memory, it is not always well "tagged" as to where it came from.

> Give us a dozen healthy memories, well-formed, and . . . we'll guarantee to take any one at random and train it to become any type of memory we might select—hammer, screwdriver, wrench, stop sign, yield sign, Indian chief—regardless of its origin or the brain that holds it.
>
> —*Elizabeth Loftus and Hunter Hoffman, 1989*

The implications for legal testimony are sobering. Eyewitnesses who are asked misleading questions often report seeing things that were not really there. In addition, eyewitnesses might be confused as to why a suspect looks familiar. It is likely, for example, that the eyewitnesses in the Randall Adams trial saw pictures of Adams in the newspaper before they testified about what they saw the night of the murder. When asked to remember what they saw that night, they might have become confused because of a source monitoring error. They remembered seeing a man with long hair and a mustache, but they may have gotten mixed up about where they had seen his face before.

Another source monitoring error may have occurred in the Oklahoma City bombing incident. On April 19, 1995, a bomb went off in the Alfred P. Murrah Federal Building in Oklahoma City, killing 168 people. Timothy McVeigh was later convicted of the crime and received the death penalty. But did he act alone? Tom Kessinger, a mechanic in a truck rental office, said that he saw McVeigh and another man rent a Ryder truck the day before the blast. Kessinger described the second suspect, who became known as "John Doe No. 2," as a large, muscular man wearing a black T-shirt and a baseball hat. A worldwide search for this suspect ensued, but the police were never able to find him, triggering suspicion that one of the bombers was still at large. It later came to light, though, that Kessinger had made a source monitoring error. Feeling pressure to identify McVeigh's companion, Kessinger mixed him up with a man who had

Source Monitoring

The process whereby people try to identify the source of their memories

Police distributed this sketch of "John Doe No. 2," a suspect in the Oklahoma City bombing in April 1995. The sketch was based on a description given by a mechanic in a truck rental office, who said that he saw Timothy McVeigh and the man in the sketch rent a truck. The employee later acknowledged, however, that he was confused and had actually described a man who had been in the office the day before McVeigh and who had nothing to do with the bombing. This appears to be a classic source monitoring error. The employee had an actual memory of the person he described but was mistaken about where he had seen the person.

been in the office the day before McVeigh, Private Todd Bunting from Fort Riley, Kansas, who had nothing to do with the bombing (Thomas, 1997).

Retrieval   Suppose that the police have arrested a suspect and want to see if you, the eyewitness, can identify the person. Typically, the police arrange a lineup at the police station, where you will be asked whether one of several people is the perpetrator. Sometimes you will be asked to look through a one-way mirror at an actual lineup of the suspect and some foils (people known not to have committed the crime). Other times you will be asked to examine videotapes of a lineup or photographs of the suspect and the foils. In each case, if a witness identifies a suspect as the culprit, the suspect is likely to be charged and convicted of the crime. After all, the argument goes, if an eyewitness saw the suspect commit the crime and then picked the suspect out of a lineup later, that's pretty good evidence the suspect is the guilty party.

Just as there are problems with acquisition and storage of information, so too can there be problems with how people retrieve information from their memories (Ellsworth & Mauro, 1998; Koehnken, Malpass, & Wogalter, 1996). In fact, identification errors from lineups are the most common cause of wrongful convictions in the United States (Wells et al., 1998). A number of things other than the image of a person that is stored in memory can influence whether eyewitnesses will pick someone out of a lineup. Witnesses often choose the person in a lineup who most resembles the criminal, even if the resemblance is not very strong.

Suppose that a 19-year-old woman committed a robbery and the police mistakenly arrest you, a 19-year-old woman, for the crime. They put you in a lineup and ask witnesses to pick out the criminal. Which do you think would be more fair: if the other people in the lineup were a 20-year-old man, a 3-year-old child, and an 80-year-old woman, or if the other people were all 19-year-old women? In the former case, the witnesses might pick you only because you are the one who most resembles the actual criminal (Buckhout, 1974). In the latter case, it is much less likely that the witnesses will mistake you for the criminal, because everyone in the lineup is the same age and sex as the culprit (Wells, 1993; Wells & Luus, 1990).

To avoid this "best guess" problem, where witnesses pick the person who looks most like the suspect, as well as other problems with lineup identifications, social psychologists recommend that police follow these steps:

- *Make sure everyone in the lineup resembles the witness's description of the suspect.* Doing so will minimize the possibility that the witness will simply choose the person who looks most like the culprit (Wells et al., 1998).

- *Tell the witnesses that the person suspected of the crime may or may not be in the lineup.* If witnesses believe the culprit is present, they are much more likely to choose the person who looks most like the culprit, rather than saying that they aren't sure or that the culprit is not present. As a result, false identifications are more likely to occur when people believe the culprit is in the lineup (Gonzalez, Ellsworth, & Pembroke, 1993; Malpass & Devine, 1981; Steblay, 1997; Wells et al., 1998, 2000).

- *Do not always include the suspect in an initial lineup.* If a witness picks out someone as the culprit from a lineup that includes only foils, you will know the witness is not reliable (Wells, 1984).

- *Make sure that the person conducting the lineup does not know which person in the lineup is the suspect.* This avoids the possibility that the person will unintentionally communicate to the witness who the suspect is (Wells et al., 1998).

- *Ask witnesses how confident they are that they can identify the suspect before they receive any feedback about their lineup performance.* People often increase their confidence after receiving feedback on their performance, and this confidence influences jurors. If a witness's confidence is much higher at a trial than at the time of the identification, there is reason not to trust this confidence (Wells et al., 1998).

- *Present pictures of people sequentially instead of simultaneously.* Doing so makes it more difficult for witnesses to compare all the pictures, choosing the one that most resembles the criminal, even when the criminal is not actually in the lineup (Lindsay & Wells, 1985; Steblay, Dysart, Fulero, & Lindsay, 2001).

- *Present witnesses with both photographs of people and sound recordings of their voices.* Witnesses who both see and hear members of a lineup are much more likely to identify the person they saw commit a crime than people who only see the pictures or only hear the voice recordings (Melara, De Witt–Rickards, & O'Brien, 1989).

"Take your time, Mrs. Scradler, and tell us which of these men you saw looking in your second-story window."

Judging Whether Eyewitnesses Are Mistaken

Suppose you are a police detective or a member of a jury who is listening to a witness describe a suspect. How can you tell whether the witness's memory is accurate or whether the witness is making one of the many mistakes in memory we have just documented? It might seem that the answer to this question is pretty straightforward: Pay careful attention to how confident the witness is. Consider the case of Jennifer Thompson, who was raped when she was a 22-year-old college student. During the rape, Thompson reports, she "studied every single detail on the rapist's face" to help her identify him. She was determined that if she survived, she was going to make sure he was caught and went to prison. After the ordeal, she went to the police station and looked through hundreds of police photos. When she saw Ronald Cotton's picture, she was certain that he was the rapist. "I knew this was the man. I was completely confident. I was sure."

The police brought Cotton in and put him in a lineup, and Thompson picked him out without hesitation. Certain that Cotton was the man who had raped her, she testified against him in court. "I was sure. I knew it. I had picked the right guy." On the basis of her convincing testimony, Cotton was sentenced to life in prison.

A few years later, the police asked Thompson to go to court and look at another man, Bobby Poole, who had been bragging in prison that he had committed the rape. When asked if she recognized him, Thompson replied, "I have never seen him in my life. I have no idea who he is."

As the years passed, and Cotton remained in jail for the rape, DNA testing became more widely available. The police decided to see if evidence from the case matched Cotton or Poole's DNA. In 1995, eleven years after the crime, the police informed Thompson of the results: "I was standing in my kitchen when the detective and the district attorney visited. They were good and decent people who were trying to do their jobs—as I had done mine, as anyone would try to do the right thing. They told me: 'Ronald Cotton didn't rape you. It was Bobby Poole.'" (Thompson, 2000, p. 15). Cotton was released from prison after serving eleven years for a crime he did not commit.

Does Certainty Mean Accuracy? One reason Cotton was convicted in the first place was that Thompson was so certain that he was the man who had raped her. It is only natural for jurors and law enforcement officers to go by how confident a witness is; surely witnesses who are confident are more likely to be correct. The U.S. Supreme Court concurred with this reasoning, ruling that the amount of confidence witnesses express is a good indicator of their accuracy (*Neil* v. *Biggers,* 1972).

> No subjective feeling of certainty can be an objective criterion for the desired truth.
>
> —*Hugo Münsterberg, On the Witness Stand, 1908*

Nevertheless, numerous studies have shown that a witness's confidence is only weakly related to his or her accuracy (Lindsay, Read, & Sharma, 1998; Olsson, 2000; Smith, Kassin, & Ellsworth, 1989; Wells, Olson, & Charman, 2002). When law enforcement officials and jurors assume that a witness who is very confident is also correct, they can make serious mistakes. For example, in the Lindsay and colleagues (1981) experiment we discussed earlier, witnesses who saw the crime under poor viewing conditions (in which the thief wore the cap over his ears) had as much confidence in their identifications as witnesses who saw the crime under moderate or good viewing conditions, even though they were considerably less accurate (see Figure SPA3.1 on page 530).

Why isn't confidence always a sign of accuracy? One reason is that the things that influence people's confidence are not necessarily the same things that influence their accuracy. After identifying a suspect, for example, a person's confidence increases if he or she finds out that other witnesses identified the same suspect and decreases if he or she finds out that other witnesses identified a different suspect (Penrod & Cutler, 1995; Wells & Bradfield, 1998). This change in confidence cannot influence the accuracy of the identification the person made earlier. Therefore, just because a witness is confident does not mean that he or she is accurate, as the cases of Randall Adams and Ronald Cotton illustrate so tragically.

Signs of Accurate Testimony How, then, can we tell whether a witness's testimony is correct? It is by no means easy, but research by David Dunning and Lisa Beth Stern (1994; Stern & Dunning, 1994) suggests some answers. They showed participants a film in which a man stole some money from a woman's wallet, asked participants to pick the man out of a photo lineup, and then asked the participants to describe how they had made up their minds. Accurate witnesses tended to say that they didn't really know how they recognized the man, that his face just "popped out" at them. Inaccurate witnesses tended to say that they used a process of elimination, deliberately comparing one face to another. Ironically, taking more time and thinking more carefully about the pictures were associated with making more mistakes. We should thus be more willing to believe a witness who says, "I knew it was the defendant as soon as I saw him in the lineup," than one who says, "I compared everyone in the lineup to each other, thought about it, and decided it was the defendant."

The research by Dunning and Stern, while intriguing, leaves unanswered an important question: Did taking more time on the identification task make people less accurate, or did people who were less accurate to begin with simply take more time? Maybe some people did not pay close attention to the film of the robbery and thus had difficulty recognizing the robber in the lineup. Consequently, they had to spend more time thinking about it and comparing the faces, such that inaccuracy caused a longer decision time. Alternatively, there might have been something about making identifications thoughtfully and deliberatively that impaired accuracy.

The Problem with Verbalization Some fascinating studies by Jonathan Schooler and Tonya Engstler-Schooler (1990) support this second possibility and suggest that trying to put an image of a face into words can cause problems. They showed students a film of a bank robbery and asked some of the students to write detailed descriptions of the robber's face (the verbalization condition). The others spent the same amount of time completing an unrelated task (the no-verbalization condition). All students then tried to identify the robber from a photo lineup of eight faces. It might seem that writing a description of the robber would be a good memory aid and make people more accurate. In fact, the reverse was true: Only 38 percent of the people in the verbalization condition correctly identified the robber, compared to 64 percent of the people in the no-verbalization condition.

Schooler and Engstler-Schooler (1990; see also Meissner & Brigham, 2001a; Schooler, Fiore, & Brandimonte, 1997) suggest that trying to put a face into words is difficult and impairs memory for that face. Using the word *squinty* to describe a robber's eyes, for example, might be a general description of what his eyes looked like but probably does not capture the subtle contours of his eyes, eyelids, eyelashes, eyebrows, and upper cheeks. When you see the photo lineup, you look for eyes that are squinty, and doing so interferes with your attention to the finer details of the faces. If you ever witness a crime, then, you should not try to put into words what the criminal looked like. And if you hear a witness say that he or she wrote down a description of the criminal and then took a while deciding whether the person was present at a lineup, you might doubt the accuracy of the witness's identification.

To sum up, several factors make eyewitness testimony inaccurate, leading to all too many false identifications. Perhaps the legal system in the United States should rely less on eyewitness testimony than it now does. In the legal systems of some countries, a suspect cannot be convicted on the basis of a sole eyewitness; at least two independent witnesses are needed. Adopting this more stringent standard in the United States might mean that some guilty people go free, but it would avoid many false convictions. To see how accurate you and your friends are at eyewitness testimony and to illustrate some of the pitfalls, do the Try It! exercise on page 540.

Judging Whether Witnesses Are Lying

There is yet another reason eyewitness testimony can be inaccurate: Even if witnesses have very accurate memories for what they saw, they might deliberately lie when on the witness stand. After Randall Adams was tried and convicted, new evidence suggested that some of the eyewitnesses who testified against him had lied. One witness may have struck a deal with the police, agreeing to say what they wanted her to say in return for lenient treatment of her daughter, who had been arrested for armed robbery. If this witness was lying, why couldn't the jurors tell?

Several studies have tested people's ability to detect deception (Bond & Atoum, 2000; DePaulo & Friedman, 1998; Ekman, 2002; Gordon & Miller, 2000). When people watch videotapes of actors who are either lying or telling the truth, their ability to tell who is lying is only slightly better than chance guessing (DePaulo, Stone, & Lassiter, 1985). But surely some people must be very good at detecting deception; after all, some jobs require exactly that skill. To find out, researchers tested various groups of people, some of whom might be expected to be better at detecting lies than others (Ekman, O'Sullivan & Frank, 1999). For example, one group consisted of federal officers attending a workshop on deception, most of whom worked for the Central Intelligence Agency in the United States. Others were clinical psychologists, some of whom had experience working with criminal defendants and some of whom did not. All participants viewed videotapes of men who were either lying or telling the truth about controversial social issues about which they felt very strongly. The percentage of times the participants correctly guessed whether the men were lying or telling the truth was recorded.

> If falsehood, like truth, had only one face, we would be in better shape. For we would take as certain the opposite of what the liar said. But the reverse of truth has a hundred thousand shapes.
>
> —*Montaigne, Essays, 1595*

Try this demonstration with a group of friends who you know will be gathered in one place, such as a dorm room or an apartment. The idea is to stage an incident in which someone comes into the room suddenly, acts in a strange manner, and then leaves. Your friends will then be asked to recall as much as they can about this person to see if they are good eyewitnesses. Here are some specific instructions about how you might do this.

1. Take one friend, whom we will call the actor, into your confidence before you do this exercise. Ideally, the actor should be a stranger to the people who will be the eyewitnesses. The actor should suddenly rush into the room where you and your other friends are gathered and act in a strange (but nonthreatening) manner. For example, the actor could hand someone a flower and say, "The flower man cometh!" Or he or she could go up to each person and say something unexpected, like "Meet me in Moscow at the mosque." Ask the actor to hold something in his or her hand during this episode, such as a pencil, shoelace, or banana.

2. Important note: The actor should not act in a violent or threatening way or make the eyewitnesses uncomfortable. The goal is to act in unexpected and surprising ways, not to frighten people.

3. After a few minutes, the actor should leave the room. Inform your friends that you staged this event as a demonstration of eyewitness testimony and that if they are willing, they should try to remember, in as much detail as possible, what occurred. Ask them to write down answers to these questions:
   a. What did the actor look like? Write down a detailed description.
   b. What did the actor say? Write down his or her words as best as you can remember.
   c. How much time did the actor spend in the room?
   d. Did the actor touch anyone? If yes, who?
   e. What was the actor holding in his or her hand?

4. After all participants have answered these questions, ask them to read their answers aloud. How much did they agree? How accurate were people's answers? Discuss with your friends why they were correct or incorrect in their descriptions.

Note: This demonstration will work best if you have access to a video camera and can record the actor's actions. That way, you can play the tape to assess the accuracy of the eyewitnesses' descriptions. If you cannot videotape it, keep track of how much time elapsed so that you can judge the accuracy of people's time estimates.

As seen in Figure SPA3.3, the groups who had the most experience with detecting deception did better than the other groups. The federal officers (mostly CIA employees) did the best, correctly identifying 73 percent of the statements as lies or truths. Clinical psychologists who had experience with defendants also did well (68 percent), as did a group of sheriffs who had been identified as outstanding interrogators (67 percent). A group of law enforcement officers who were not identified as outstanding interrogators did the worst (51 percent, statistically the same as chance accuracy). Thus people with a good deal of experience are fairly good at telling when someone is lying, but even the best group in this study was wrong 27 percent of the time, which is not very reassuring if you are being interrogated by a law enforcement officer.

Are Polygraph Machines Accurate?   Guy and Venita DiCastro had an important decision to make. Should Anthony, Shane, or Camron be the one to spend a

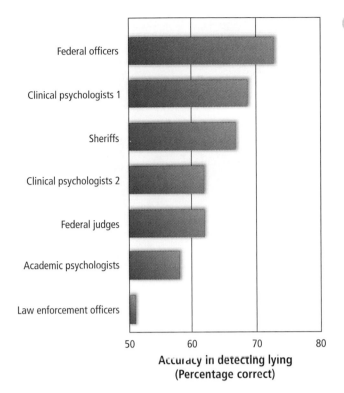

Accuracy in detecting lying
(Percentage correct)

FIGURE SPA3.3

Does experience in law enforcement improve the ability to detect deception?

Different groups of participants viewed videotapes of men who were either lying or telling the truth about controversial social issues, to see how accurate the observers were at telling if someone was lying. Experienced law enforcement officers did better than inexperienced law enforcement officers or academic psychologists. The federal officers were mostly from the Central Intelligence Agency. The "clinical psychologists 1" were psychologists who had experience working with criminal defendants. The sheriffs had been chosen because they were excellent interrogators. The "clinical psychologists 2" did not have experience working with criminal defendants. The law enforcement officers had not been selected because they were excellent interrogators. People could get 50 percent correct simply by guessing.

(Adapted from Ekman, O'Sullivan, & Frank, 1999)

week in Hawaii with their daughter Jessica? That was the choice they were given on the initial episodes of the NBC reality show, *Meet My Folks*. Guy and Venita spent a weekend observing each bachelor and asking him revealing questions about his past and his darkest secrets. But how could they be sure that the men were telling the truth and not just putting their best foot forward, telling Guy and Venita what they wanted to hear? Not to worry—the producers of the show installed a polygraph in the basement of the DiCastros' home, with an expert operator ready to strap in each man. The **polygraph**, or "lie detector," is a machine that measures people's physiological responses, such as heart rate and breathing rate. As Guy DiCastro asked each bachelor difficult questions, the expert looked at the scribbling polygraph pen that indicated the man's heart rate and breathing rate and then gave the verdict: thumbs up if the man was telling the truth and thumbs down if he was lying.

Whereas this procedure made for some amusing television (Guy and Venita are crestfallen when the polygraph operator gives an emphatic thumbs down after Anthony says that he likes Venita's cooking), the polygraph is not infallible. There are two types of polygraph tests used in real life, as in law enforcement. In one, called the *control question test*, the operator asks people both relevant questions about a crime (e.g., "Did you steal money from the cash register of the restaurant?") and control questions that are known to produce truthful responses (e.g., "Have you ever stolen anything in your whole life?"). The assumption is that when people lie, they become anxious, and this anxiety can be detected by increases in heart rate, breathing rate, and so on. Thus the operator can see whether you have a greater physiological response to the relevant question than the control question.

The other approach is called the *guilty knowledge test*. Here people answer multiple-choice questions about specific aspects of a crime, the answers to which are known only by the police and the culprit. For example, you might be asked, "Was the amount stolen from the cash register: $10, $23, $34, $54, or $110?" The idea is that only the criminal would know the correct answer and thus will be anxious when that answer is read. For example, the thief who knows that he stole

Polygraph

A machine that measures people's physiological responses (e.g., their heart rate); polygraph operators attempt to tell if someone is lying by observing that person's physiological responses while answering questions

Although polygraphs can detect whether someone is lying at levels better than chance, they are far from infallible.

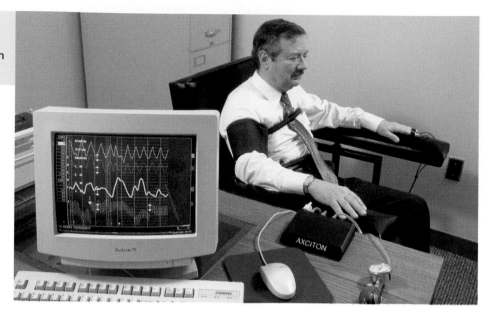

$23 will probably have more of a reaction when this amount is read than an innocent person who does not know how much money was stolen.

Polygraphs have both strong supporters (e.g., Raskin, Honts, & Kircher, 1997) and steadfast critics (e.g., Lykken, 1998). How well do these tests work? First, polygraph results are only as good as the person operating and interpreting the test. With several responses being measured, it is not always easy to tell whether a person has had more of a physiological response to one question versus another. One disturbing finding is that operators often disagree with one another, suggesting that the test is by no means infallible (Ellsworth & Mauro, 1998).

When administered under optimal conditions by an experienced examiner, the test does reveal whether someone is lying or telling the truth at levels better than chance. But even then it is not perfect (Ben-Shakhar & Elaad, 2003; Ellsworth & Mauro, 1998; Iacono & Patrick, 1999). The error rates vary somewhat, depending on the technique used to administer the test. Some studies have found that false negatives, in which liars are found to be telling the truth, are the most common kind of error (Honts, 1994). Others have found very high rates of false positives, in which innocent people are found to be lying (Patrick & Iacono, 1989). One review concluded that averaging across all the different techniques, the polygraph typically misidentifies between 10 and 15 percent of liars as truth-tellers (false negatives) and between 10 and 15 percent of truth-tellers as liars (false positives; Ekman, 2002).

Psychologists continue to look for the perfect lie detection machine. One approach tried a camera that records blood flow in the face using high-definition thermal imaging technology (Pavlidis, Eberhardt, & Levine, 2002). The researchers hypothesized that when people are lying, they might show a specific "thermal signature" around their eyes, reflecting the fact that there was increased blood flow, possibly due to nervousness. An initial study showed that the thermal imaging technique did distinguish liars from nonliars at a better than chance rate, but the technique was by no means perfect: 15 percent of the people were mislabeled as liars or truth-tellers, about the same error rate as is found with the polygraph.

A concern with all physiological measures of deception is whether guilty people can learn to beat the tests. There is some evidence that people can deliberately act in ways that reduce the validity of the results of polygraph tests, such as biting their tongue and doing mental arithmetic. The search continues, but there is still no perfect lie detection machine that can always differentiate lies from the truth (Iacono, 2000; Kleiner, 2002).

To see how well you and your friends can tell whether someone is lying, do the Try It! exercise below. How did you do? It would be nice if there were a fool-proof method of telling whether or not someone is lying. Randall Adams would never have had to endure twelve long years in prison for a crime he did not commit. Many psychologists doubt, though, that such a test will ever be developed; the nuances of human behavior are too rich and complex to allow foolproof tests of honesty.

Can Eyewitness Testimony Be Improved?

We have seen a number of ways in which eyewitness testimony can go wrong. Given the importance of such testimony in criminal trials, are there ways to improve it? Two general approaches have been tried, but neither has proved very successful.

The first involves hypnosis. You may have seen movies in which a witness to a terrible crime has no memory of what occurred—until he or she is put under hypnosis. Then, while in a trancelike state, the person is able to describe the murderer in great detail. Unfortunately, this is one area where the movies do not reflect real life. There is no hard evidence that people's memory improves when

Try it!

Lie Detection

The purpose of this exercise, which should be done with a group of friends, is to see how well people can tell if someone is lying. Ask for a volunteer to be the speaker and the others to be the audience. The speaker's job will be to lie about how much he or she likes five high school acquaintances and to tell the truth about how much he or she likes five other high school acquaintances. The audience's job is to try to guess when the speaker is telling the truth and when he or she is lying. Here are some specific instructions:

Instructions for the speaker: Make a list of ten people you knew in high school, and think about how much you like each person. Randomly choose five people and put a T next to their names. These are the people about whom you will be truthful. Put an L next to the other names. These are the people about whom you will lie. Take a few minutes to think about what you will say. When you are ready, describe your feelings toward each person (truthfully or not) to the audience. Give a few sentences about each person.

Instructions for the audience: The speaker will be describing her or his feelings toward ten high school acquaintances. He or she will be telling the truth about half the people and lying about the other half. Listen carefully and try to guess when the speaker is telling the truth and when he or she is lying. You may use any cues you want to make your decision. Write down the numbers 1 to 10, and put "truth" or "lie" next to the number corresponding to each person the speaker describes.

Variation: Have half the audience members sit with their backs to the speaker so that they can hear but not see him or her. The other half should face the speaker. Which group was better at detecting when the speaker was lying? Bella DePaulo, Dan Lassiter, and Julie Stone (1983) found that people who were instructed to pay special attention to a speaker's tone of voice did better at lie detection than people instructed to pay attention to how the speaker looked. When people can see a speaker, they tend to focus on facial cues that they think are good indications of lying but in fact are not. The group of people who cannot see the speaker might rely more on his or her tone of voice and thus may be more accurate.

Note: Turn to page 557 for instructions on scoring.

they are hypnotized (Ellsworth & Mauro, 1998; Erdelyi, 1984; Kebbell & Wagstaff, 1998). There is some evidence that when people are under hypnosis, they are more susceptible to suggestion, coming to believe that they saw things that they did not (Lynn, Lock, Loftus, Krackow, & Lilienfeld, 2003; Scoboria, Mazzoni, Kirsch, & Milling, 2002). Even worse, people tend to become more confident in their memories after they have been hypnotized, even if they are no more accurate (Spiegel & Spiegel, 1987). This is dangerous, because as we saw earlier, juries often use confidence as a gauge of a witness's accuracy, even though confidence is not strongly related to accuracy.

The second way people have tried to increase eyewitness accuracy is with the use of the **cognitive interview** (Geiselman & Fischer, 1989). With this technique, a trained interviewer tries to improve eyewitnesses' memories by focusing their attention on the details and context of the event. This is done chiefly by asking the person to recall the event several times from different starting points (e.g., from the beginning of the event and from the middle of the event) and by asking the person to create a mental image of the scene. Some research using this technique looked promising (Holliday, 2003). Other research, however, has been more sobering, finding that the cognitive interview may increase errors and confabulations of memory, especially when used with children (Fisher, Brennan, & McCauley, 2001). One reason for this is that repeatedly imagining an event has been found to increase source monitoring errors, whereby people become confused about whether they actually witnessed an event or simply imagined it later (Johnson, Raye, Wang, & Taylor, 1979).

So far, then, researchers have not found a tried-and-true way to improve the accuracy of eyewitnesses' memories, other than trying to avoid the pitfalls we have discussed.

The Recovered Memory Debate

Another form of eyewitness memory has received a great deal of attention: the case in which a person recalls having been the victim of a crime, typically sexual abuse, after many years of being consciously unaware of that fact. Not surprisingly, the accuracy of such **recovered memories** has been hotly debated (McNally, 2003; Pezdek & Banks, 1996; Schooler & Eich, 2000).

One well-known case occurred in 1988 in Olympia, Washington, when Paul Ingram's daughters accused him of sexual abuse, satanic rituals, and murder, events they claimed to have recalled suddenly years after they occurred. The police could find no evidence for the crimes, and Ingram initially denied that they had ever occurred. Eventually, though, he became convinced that he, too, must have repressed his past behavior and that he must have committed the crimes, even though he could not remember having done so. According to experts who have studied this case, Ingram's daughters genuinely believed that the abuse and killing had occurred—but they were wrong. What they thought they remembered were actually false memories (Wright, 1994).

The question of the accuracy of recovered memories is controversial. On one side are writers such as Ellen Bass and Laura Davis (1994), who claim that it is not uncommon for women who were sexually abused to repress these traumas so that they have absolutely no memory of them. The abuse and its subsequent repression, according to this view, are responsible for many psychological problems, such as depression and eating disorders. Later in life, often with the help of a psychotherapist, these events can be "recovered" and brought back into memory. On the other side of the controversy are academic psychologists and others who argue that the accuracy of recovered memories cannot be accepted on faith (e.g., Loftus, 2003; Ofshe & Watters, 1994; Schacter, 1996; Schooler, 1999; Wegner, Quillian, & Houston, 1996). These writers acknowledge that sexual abuse and other childhood traumas are a terrible problem and are more

Cognitive Interview

A technique whereby a trained interviewer tries to improve eyewitnesses' memories by focusing their attention on the details and context of the event

Recovered Memories

Recollections of a past event, such as sexual abuse, that had been forgotten or repressed

In Olympia, Washington, in 1988, Paul Ingram was accused by his daughters of sexual abuse, satanic rituals, and murder. His daughters claimed to have suddenly recalled these events years after they occurred. According to experts who studied the case, Ingram's daughters genuinely believed the abuse and killing occurred, but in fact they were wrong: What they thought they remembered were actually false memories. Ingram eventually became convinced that he too must have repressed his past behavior and that he must have committed the crimes. Due to his "confession," he is currently serving a prison sentence.

common than we would like to think. They further agree that claims of sexual abuse should be investigated fully and that when sufficient evidence of guilt exists, the person responsible for the abuse should be prosecuted.

But here's the problem: What is "sufficient evidence"? Is it enough that someone remembers, years later, that she or he has been abused, in the absence of any other evidence of abuse? According to many researchers, the answer is no, because of a **false memory syndrome:** People can recall a past traumatic experience that is objectively false but that they believe is true (Kihlstrom, 1996). There is evidence that people can acquire vivid memories of events that never occurred, especially if another person—such as a psychotherapist—suggests that the events occurred (Johnson & Raye, 1981; Loftus, 1993; Schooler & Eich, 2000). In addition to numerous laboratory demonstrations of false memories, evidence from everyday life also indicates that memories of abuse can be false. Often these memories are contradicted by objective evidence (e.g., no evidence of satanic murders can be found); sometimes people who suddenly acquire such memories decide later that the events never occurred; and sometimes the memories are so bizarre (e.g., that people were abducted by aliens) as to strain credulity. Unfortunately, some psychotherapists do not sufficiently consider that by suggesting past abuse, they may be planting false memories rather than helping clients remember real events.

This is not to say, however, that all recovered memories are inaccurate. Although scientific evidence for repression and recovery—the idea that something can be forgotten for years and then recalled with great accuracy—is sparse, there may be instances in which people do suddenly remember traumatic events that really did occur (Schooler, 1999). Thus any claim of abuse should be taken with the utmost seriousness. Unfortunately, it is very difficult to distinguish the accurate memories from the false ones in the absence of any corroborating evidence. For this reason, claims of abuse cannot be taken on faith, especially if they are the result of suggestions from other people.

JURIES: GROUP PROCESSES IN ACTION

Ultimately, it is not a polygraph that decides whether witnesses are telling the truth but a judge or jury. Juries are of particular interest to social psychologists because the way they reach verdicts is directly relevant to social psychological

False Memory Syndrome

Remembering a past traumatic experience that is objectively false but nevertheless accepted as true

research on group processes and social interaction. The right to be tried by a jury of one's peers has a long tradition in English and American law. Trial by jury was an established institution in England at the beginning of the seventeenth century, and the people who founded the first permanent English settlement in North America, at Jamestown, Virginia, carried this tradition with them (though this right was not granted to Native Americans or other nonwhites or to a few rebellious English settlers who were summarily hanged). In the United States today, everyone has the right, under most circumstances, to be tried by a jury.

Despite this tradition, the jury system has often come under attack. Millions of television viewers placed themselves in the role of juror during the O. J. Simpson criminal trial and formed strong opinions about whether he was guilty of murder—sometimes disagreeing with the verdict of the actual jurors (not guilty). In the Randall Adams trial, it is now clear that the jury reached the wrong decision. One study found that judges who presided over criminal jury trials disagreed with the verdict rendered by the jury a full 25 percent of the time (Kalven & Zeisel, 1966). More recent observers have also criticized the jury system, questioning the ability of jurors to understand complex evidence and reach a dispassionate verdict (Arkes & Mellers, 2002; Devine, Clayton, Dunford, Seying, & Pryce, 2001).

As noted by a former dean of the Harvard Law School, "Why should anyone think that 12 persons brought in from the street, selected in various ways for their lack of general ability, should have any special capacity for deciding controversies between persons?" (Kalven & Zeisel, 1966, p. 5).

The jury system has its staunch supporters, of course, and few people argue that it should be abolished. The point is that it is not a perfect system and that based on research in social psychology, there are ways we might expect it to go wrong. Problems can arise at each of three phases of a jury trial: the way in which jurors use information they obtain before the trial begins, the way in which they process information during the trial, and the way in which they deliberate in the jury room, after all the evidence has been presented.

> 'Tis with our judgments as our watches, None go just alike, yet each believes his own.
>
> —*Alexander Pope*, *Essay on Criticism*, *1711*

Effects of Pretrial Publicity

Because the murder of Officer Wood in Texas received considerable attention in the media, it is possible that the jury members were biased by what they had read in the newspapers before the trial began. The press reported that a key eyewitness had picked Randall Adams out of a police lineup, but this information was false and was never presented to the jury during the trial. Nonetheless, two jurors mentioned during the deliberations that they believed the eyewitness had picked Adams out of the lineup (*Dallas Morning News*, May 4, 1987). Similarly, the jurors in the O. J. Simpson and Timothy McVeigh murder trials had probably heard a lot about these cases before the trial, given the amount of media attention they received. What are the effects of such pretrial publicity?

Even when the information reported by the media is accurate, it is often stacked against a suspect for a simple reason—the press gets much of its information from the police and the district attorney, who are interested in presenting as strong a case as they can against the suspect (Imrich, Mullin, & Linz, 1995). It is therefore not surprising that the more people hear about a case in the media, the more they believe the suspect is guilty (Fulero, 2002; Kerr, 1995; Steblay, Besirevic, Fulero, & Jimenez-Lorente, 1999).

Estate of Mischa Richter and Harald Bakken

"Since you have already been convicted by the media, I imagine we can wrap this up pretty quickly."

Especially biasing is the kind of emotional publicity that arouses public passions, such as lurid details about a murder. In one study, researchers contacted people who had just finished serving on juries in Michigan and asked them to watch a videotaped trial of a man accused of robbing a supermarket. Before the jurors viewed the trial, the researchers exposed them to emotional publicity (reports that a car matching the one used in the robbery struck and killed a 7-year-old girl after the robbery), factual publicity (a report that the suspect had an extensive prior criminal record), or no publicity. After watching the trial and deliberating in twelve-member mock juries, the participants rated whether they would vote to convict the suspect. The emotional publicity biased jurors the most, significantly increasing the percentage of jurors who gave guilty verdicts—even though the jurors knew they were not supposed to be influenced by any information they learned before viewing the trial (Kramer, Kerr, & Carroll, 1990).

Judges and lawyers have a variety of options to try to remedy this problem. First, lawyers are allowed to question prospective jurors before the trial (a process called *voir dire*). The lawyers ask people whether they have heard anything about the case, and if so, whether they feel they can render an unbiased verdict. One problem with this approach, however, is that people are often unaware they have been biased by pretrial publicity (Ogloff & Vidmar, 1994). In the study we just reviewed, for example, the researchers put the jurors through a *voir dire* process, removing from the study any jurors who said that because of the pretrial publicity they could not form an unbiased opinion (Kramer et al., 1990). Nonetheless, the emotional publicity still influenced the verdicts given by the remaining jurors.

Second, judges can instruct jurors to disregard what they have heard in the media. But these instructions do little to erase the effects of pretrial publicity and may even increase the likelihood that jurors use it (Fein, McCloskey, & Tomlinson, 1997; Kramer et al., 1990; Shaw & Skolnick, 1995). One reason this can happen is that it is very difficult to erase something from our minds once we have heard it. In fact, as we noted in Chapter 3, the more we try not to think about something, the more that very thing keeps popping into consciousness (Wegner, 1989, 1992, 1994).

Another problem with pretrial publicity is that linking a person's name with incriminating events can cause negative impressions of the person, even if the media explicitly deny any such connection. In one study, when participants read a headline denying any wrongdoing on someone's part—such as "Bob Talbert Not Linked with Mafia"—they had a more negative impression of the person than participants who read an innocuous headline—such as "Bob Talbert Arrives in City" (Wegner, Wenzlaff, Kerker, & Beattie, 1981) The mere mention of Bob Talbert and the Mafia in the same headline was enough to plant seeds of doubt in readers' minds, despite the headline's explicit denial of a connection. Thus media reports can have unintended negative effects, and once there, those effects are hard to erase. The best solution is to include in a trial only jurors who have heard nothing about the case. Sometimes a trial is moved to a new location where there has been less publicity. In highly publicized cases such as the sniper shootings in the Washington, D.C. area in 2002, finding such jurors can be very difficult.

> "A court is no better than each . . . of you sitting before me on this jury. A court is only as sound as its jury, and a jury is only as sound as the [people] who make it up."
>
> —Harper Lee, To Kill a Mockingbird, 1960

How Jurors Process Information during the Trial

How do individual jurors think about the evidence they hear during a trial? As we saw in Chapter 3, people often construct theories and schemas to interpret the world around them, and the same is true of jurors (Hart, 1995; Kuhn, Weinstock, & Flaton, 1994; Smith, 1991). Some psychologists suggest that jurors

"Your Honor, we're going to go with the prosecution's spin."

decide on one story that best explains all the evidence; they then try to fit this story to the possible verdicts they are allowed to render, and if one of those verdicts fits well with their preferred story, they are likely to vote to convict on that charge (Hastie & Pennington, 2000; Pennington & Hastie, 1992). This possibility has important implications for how lawyers present their cases. Lawyers typically present the evidence in one of two ways. In the first, called *story order,* they present the evidence in the sequence in which the events occurred, corresponding as closely as possible to the story they want the jurors to believe. In the second, called *witness order,* they present witnesses in the sequence they think will have the greatest impact, even if this means that events are described out of order. For example, a lawyer might save his or her best witness for last so that the trial ends on a dramatic, memorable note, even if this witness describes events that occurred early in the alleged crime.

If you were a lawyer, in which order would you present the evidence? You can probably guess which order researchers in this area hypothesized would be the most successful. If jurors are ultimately swayed by the story or schema they think best explains the sequence of events, then the best strategy should be to present the evidence in story order and not witness order. To test their hypothesis, researchers asked mock jurors to listen to a simulated murder trial and varied the order in which the defense attorney and the prosecuting attorney presented their cases (Pennington & Hastie, 1988). In one condition, both used story order whereas in another condition, both used witness order. In other conditions, one attorney used story order and the other used witness order.

The results provided clear and dramatic support for the story order strategy. As seen in Table SPA3.1, when the prosecutor used story order and the defense used witness order, the jurors were most likely to believe the prosecutor—78 percent voted to convict the defendant. When the prosecutor used witness order and the defense used story order, the tables were turned—only 31 percent voted to convict. One reason the conviction rate in felony trials in America is so high—approximately 80 percent—may be that in real trials, prosecutors usually present evidence in story order, whereas defense attorneys usually use witness order. If you are a budding lawyer, remember this when you are preparing for your first trial!

TABLE SPA3.1

How Should Lawyers Present Their Cases?

Lawyers can present their cases in a variety of ways. This study found that story order, in which lawyers present the evidence in the order that corresponds most closely to the story they want the jurors to believe, works best.

PERCENTAGE OF PEOPLE VOTING TO CONVICT THE DEFENDANT

PROSECUTION EVIDENCE	DEFENSE EVIDENCE	
	STORY ORDER	WITNESS ORDER
Story order	59	78
Witness order	31	63

Adapted from Pennington & Hastie (1988)

Deliberations in the Jury Room

As any lawyer can tell you, a crucial part of the jury process occurs out of sight, when jurors deliberate before deciding on the verdict. Even if most jurors are inclined to vote to convict, there might be a persuasive minority who change their fellow jurors' minds. Sometimes this can be a minority of one, as in the classic movie *Twelve Angry Men*. When the film begins, a jury has just finished listening to the evidence in a murder case, and all the jurors except one vote to convict the defendant. But over the course of the next ninety minutes, the lone holdout, played by Henry Fonda, persuades his peers that there is reason to doubt that the young Hispanic defendant is guilty. At first, the other jurors pressure Fonda to change his mind (using techniques of normative and informational conformity, as discussed in Chapter 8), but in the end, reason triumphs, and the other jurors come to see that Fonda is right.

As entertaining as this movie is, research indicates that it does not reflect the reality of most jury deliberations (Devine et al., 2001; Ellsworth & Mauro, 1998; Kalven & Zeisel, 1966; MacCoun, 1989). In the Randall Adams trial, for example, a majority of the twelve-person jury (seven men and five women) initially voted to convict Adams. After eight hours of deliberations, the majority prevailed: The holdouts changed their minds, and the jury voted unanimously to convict. In the O. J. Simpson trial, one juror initially voted guilty but quickly changed her mind. In a study of more than two hundred juries in actual criminal trials, researchers found that in 97 percent of the cases, the jury's final decision was the same as the one favored by a majority of the jurors on the initial vote (Kalven & Zeisel, 1966). Thus just as we saw in Chapter 8 on conformity, majority opinion usually carries the day, bringing dissenting jurors into line. If jury deliberation is stacked toward the initial majority opinion, why not just abandon the deliberation process, letting the jury's initial vote determine a defendant's guilt or innocence? For two reasons, this would not be a good idea. First, forcing juries to reach a unanimous verdict makes them consider the evidence more carefully, rather than simply assuming that their initial impressions of the case were correct (Hastie, Penrod, & Pennington, 1983). Second, even if minorities seldom succeed in persuading the majority to change their minds about guilt or innocence, minorities often do change people's minds about how guilty a person is. In criminal trials, juries

In the classic movie *Twelve Angry Men,* Henry Fonda convinces all of his fellow jurors to change their minds about a defendant's guilt. In real life, however, such cases of a minority in a jury convincing the majority to change its mind are rare.

usually have some discretion about the type of guilty verdict they can reach. In a murder trial, for example, they can often decide whether to convict the defendant of first-degree murder, second-degree murder, or manslaughter. One study found that people on a jury who have a minority point of view often convince the majority to change their minds about the specific verdict to render (Pennington & Hastie, 1990). Thus while a minority of jurors are unlikely to convince a majority of jurors to change their verdict from first-degree murder to not guilty, they might well convince the majority to change the verdict to second-degree murder.

Jury Size: Are Twelve Heads Better than Six?

Imagine that your worst nightmare has come true: You are falsely accused of murder and have to stand trial. Would you rather be judged by a jury of twelve people or a jury of six? Although juries have traditionally been composed of twelve people, the U.S. Supreme Court decided in 1970 that there was nothing sacrosanct about this number and allowed smaller juries in some cases. This decision was criticized by a number of social psychologists, and several experiments have since been performed to see how the size of a jury influences its decisions (Davis, Kerr, Atkin, Holt, & Meek, 1975; Horowitz & Bordens, 2002; Saks & Marti, 1997).

One problem with small juries is that they reduce the probability that minority members will be represented. Suppose that 10 percent of the members of a particular community are Hispanic. There is a 72 percent chance that at least one Hispanic will be a member of a twelve-person jury but only a 47 percent chance at least one Hispanic will be a member of a six-person jury. What about the decision processes of the group? Suppose that there is a small minority of the community that is likely to be sympathetic to your case and that on a six-person jury, there is one such person, whereas on a twelve-person jury, there are two such people. The Supreme Court reasoned that because the proportion of people with the minority viewpoint would be identical on both juries (1/6 versus 2/12), the overall size of the jury was unimportant. Ring any bells? Being a good social psychologist, you know that this is not true. Recall our discussion of the Asch conformity experiments in Chapter 8, where we saw that it is much more difficult to withstand pressure from a majority if you are a lone dissenter than if you have one other person who agrees with you. A minority of one on a six-person jury is much more likely to conform than two people on a twelve-person jury are.

In 1978, the Supreme Court rejected the use of five-person juries in Georgia, based in part on the results of social psychological research. However, the court still allowed six-person juries in some cases (e.g., civil trials). As noted by Phoebe Ellsworth and Robert Mauro (1998), this decision was ironic, because most of the arguments the court used to criticize five-person juries apply to six-person juries as well. Most social psychologists who have conducted research in this area believe that all juries should consist of twelve people.

WHY DO PEOPLE OBEY THE LAW?

Ultimately, the success of the legal system depends on keeping people out of it. We should, of course, find ways to improve the accuracy of eyewitness testimony and help juries make better decisions. Even more important, though, is finding ways of preventing people from committing crimes in the first place. We thus close with a discussion of how to get people to obey the law.

Do Severe Penalties Deter Crime?

By many indications, the crime rate is decreasing in the United States. According to FBI statistics, for example, violent crime dropped by 1.4 percent in 2002, compared to 2001 (Federal Bureau of Investigation, 2003). A striking illustration of this trend was seen in the power blackout in the northeastern United States and Canada in August, 2003. During previous blackouts, such as the one in New York City in 1977, crime rates skyrocketed when people broke into and looted many businesses. In the blackout of 2003, the crime rate was actually lower in New York, Detroit, and Cleveland than on typical summer days ("During Blackout, Fewer Crimes," 2003).

Why has the crime rate gone down? Some experts have attributed these promising trends to, among other things, stiffer penalties for crimes. It makes perfect sense that the harsher the penalty for a crime, the less likely people are to commit it. As we have seen many times in this book, however, common sense is not always correct, and in the case of crime and prison sentences, the story is not as straightforward as it might seem. Some analysts have suggested that the drop in violent crime is due not to stiffer penalties but to the fact that the population of adolescents and young adults, who are most responsible for violent crimes, has been declining in the past few years.

How can we tell which of these interpretations is correct? Unfortunately, it is not easy. Unlike many of the other questions we have posed in this book, this one cannot be answered by randomly assigning people to different experimental conditions. It would be not be feasible, for example, to take a group of people convicted of drunk driving and randomly assign half of them to get ten year prison sentences and the other half to get one-year sentences. The next best thing to an experiment, though, is to compare groups of people that have been naturally assigned to one "condition" or the other, such as residents of a state that has a severe penalty for drunk driving and residents of a state that has a milder penalty for drunk driving. Such data are imperfect, of course, because the residents of the two states might differ in other important ways. Nonetheless, such studies can be informative about the relationship between the severity of penalties and crime rates.

The rates of many kinds of crime have been dropping in the United States. For example, during the blackout in New York City in 1977, many people broke into and looted businesses. During the blackout in the United States and Canada in August, 2003, however, shown here, few crimes were committed; in fact, the crime rate was lower than on a typical summer day.

Let's begin with a theory that argues that stiff penalties do prevent crimes. **Deterrence theory** argues that people refrain from criminal activity because of the threat of legal punishment, as long as the punishment is perceived as severe, certain, and swift (Carlsmith, Darley, & Robinson, 2002; Gibbs, 1985; Williams & Hawkins, 1986). Undoubtedly, this theory is correct under some circumstances. Imagine, for example, that you are driving to an important appointment one day and get snarled in a traffic jam on the interstate. At last the traffic clears, but unless you hurry, you will be late. "Maybe I'll speed up just a little," you think, as the speedometer creeps up to 75. Your decision to exceed the speed limit was probably based on a consideration of the facts that (1) you are unlikely to get caught and that (2) if you do, the penalty won't be all that severe. But suppose you knew that the interstate is always patrolled by the state police and that the penalty for speeding is a five-year prison sentence. Chances are you would not dare to let your foot press too hard on the accelerator.

In this example, we have made a couple of important assumptions. First, we assumed that you know what the penalties for speeding are. Second, we assumed that you have good control over your behavior and that whether you speed is a rational decision that you make after reflecting about the consequences. For many crimes, these assumptions do not hold. Surveys have found that many people are ignorant of the penalties for different crimes; if they do not know what they are, obviously, the penalties cannot act as a deterrent. (To see how well you know the penalties for various federal crimes, complete the Try It! exercise on page 553.) Further, other types of crimes are not based on a rational decision process. Many murders, for example, are impulsive crimes of passion committed by people in highly emotional states, not by people who carefully weigh the pros and cons. In general, severe penalties will work only when people know what they are, believe they are relatively certain to be caught, and are able to weigh the consequences dispassionately before deciding whether to commit a crime.

To illustrate these points, let's consider two very different kinds of crimes: drunk driving and murder. The decision about whether to drink and drive is one that most of us can control; when we go to a party or a bar and know that we will be driving home afterward, we can decide how much we will drink. Given that this decision is a fairly rational one under most circumstances, we would expect that severe and certain penalties would act as a deterrent. To test this hypothesis, investigators have compared the number of alcohol-related motor vehicle accidents in states with severe versus mild drunk-driving laws or in communities that

Deterrence Theory

The hypothesis that the threat of legal punishment causes people to refrain from criminal activity as long as the punishment is perceived as relatively severe, certain, and swift

Increasing the certainty of being caught for drunk driving, by checking the blood alcohol level of all motorists stopped at sobriety checkpoints, is associated with fewer alcohol-related accidents.

Try it!

Are You Aware of the Penalties for Federal Crimes?

Deterrence theory holds that legal penalties will prevent crimes if people perceive them to be severe, certain, and swift. If people are unaware that a crime has a severe penalty, those penalties cannot act as a deterrent. Are you aware, for example, of which federal crimes are punishable by death? Take the following quiz to find out.

Which of the Following Federal Crimes Are Punishable by Death?

Crime	Punishable by Death?	
1. Drug trafficking in large quantities where no death results	No	Yes
2. Attempted killing of a public officer by a drug kingpin	No	Yes
3. Attempting to kill a juror or witness in a case involving a continuing criminal enterprise	No	Yes
4. Carjacking that results in death	No	Yes
5. Kidnapping that results in death	No	Yes
6. Train sabotage that results in death	No	Yes
7. Smuggling aliens where death results	No	Yes
8. Aircraft hijacking that results in death	No	Yes
9. Assassination of a member of Congress	No	Yes
10. Assassination of a major-party vice-presidential candidate	No	Yes
11. Assassination of a cabinet officer	No	Yes
12. Assassination of a Supreme Court justice	No	Yes
13. Assassination of the president	No	Yes
14. Espionage	No	Yes
15. Treason	No	Yes

For the answers, turn to page 557.

have instituted tough drunk-driving policies with communities in the same state that have not. These studies find that increasing the severity of penalties for drunk driving is not related, by itself, to fewer alcohol-related accidents. However, consistent with deterrence theory, increasing the certainty of being caught for drunk driving, by checking the blood alcohol level of all motorists stopped at sobriety checkpoints, is associated with fewer alcohol-related accidents (Evans, Neville, & Graham, 1991; Stuster & Blowers, 1995; Voas, Holder, & Gruenewald, 1999). These results suggest that severity itself does not act as a deterrent but that an increase in the certainty of being caught does.

Now consider a very different crime and a very different penalty—murder and capital punishment. A majority of Americans support the death penalty for murder, in part because they believe that it acts as a deterrent. There is no more severe penalty than death, of course, and if the death penalty prevents even a few murders, it might be worthwhile—or so the argument goes. To see if this argument is correct, a number of studies have compared the murder rates in American states that have the death penalty with those that do not, compared the murder rates in American states before and after they adopted the death penalty, and compared the murder rates in other countries before and after they adopted the death penalty. The results are unambiguous: There is no evidence that the death penalty prevents murders (Archer & Gartner, 1984; Bedau, 1997; Ellsworth & Mauro, 1998; Sorensen, Wrinkle, Brewer, & Marquart, 1999).

Opponents of the death penalty point out that, as we mentioned, most murders are crimes of passion that are not preceded by a rational consideration of the consequences. Because people are not considering the consequences of their actions, the death penalty does not act as a deterrent. Further, an astonishing number of mistakes have been made whereby innocent people have been sentenced to death. Since the death penalty was reinstated in the United States in 1976, one person has been freed from death row (often due to DNA evidence that was unavailable at the trial) for every seven people who have been executed. In January 2003, Illinois Governor George Ryan, an advocate of capital punishment, commuted the sentences of all death row prisoners in Illinois to life in prison because he was so concerned about the fairness of the process and the possibility that innocent people had been sentenced to death. No one knows how many innocent people have been executed in the United States. Given our earlier discussion of eyewitness testimony, however, it is sobering to realize that some defendants have been convicted and executed on the basis of the testimony of one eyewitness. For example, Gary Graham was put to death in Texas due largely to the testimony of a single witness who got only a brief look at him from her car more than 30 feet away. Two other witnesses who got a much better look claimed that Graham was not the killer, but they were not interviewed by Graham's court-appointed attorney. And as we saw at the beginning of this chapter, Randall Adams was almost executed for a crime he didn't commit, based on the faulty reports of eyewitnesses.

Proponents of the death penalty argue that these flaws in the system can be corrected, now that tests of DNA evidence are more widely available. Further, as argued by deterrence theory, severe penalties must be applied with certainty and speed. The last of these conditions is almost never met in the case of capital punishment. The time between a conviction for murder and the execution of the murderer is often many years because of the slowness of the judicial system and the many avenues of appeal open to prisoners on death row. Were the process speeded up, this argument goes, the death penalty would act as a deterrent.

Although this is an empirical question, there is reason to doubt that the death penalty would act as a deterrent, even if it were applied swiftly. We refer to a few studies that have found that executions are followed not by a decrease but an increase in murders (Archer & Gartner, 1984; Bailey & Peterson, 1997). This might seem like a bizarre finding; why would the execution of a convicted murderer increase the likelihood that someone else would commit murder? If you recall our discussion in Chapter 12, though, on aggression, the finding makes sense. As we saw, observing someone else commit a violent act weakens people's inhibitions against aggression, leads to imitation of aggression, and numbs their sense of horror over violence. Could it be that observing the government put someone to death lowers other people's inhibitions, making them more likely to commit murders? Though the data are not conclusive, this argument makes social psychological sense—and there is some evidence to support it (Bailey & Peterson, 1997).

Procedural Justice: People's Sense of Fairness

We have just seen that one reason people obey the law is that they fear being caught and punished. An even more important reason, however, is because of their moral values about what constitutes good behavior. People will obey a law if they think it is just, even if it is unlikely that they will be caught for breaking it. For example, many people are honest on their tax returns because they think cheating is wrong, not because they fear being caught for cheating.

American legislators suffer from a monumental illusion in their belief that long prison sentences will reduce the crime rate.

—Jack Gibbs, 1985

If you were a lawmaker, you could therefore try to prevent crime in two ways. You could increase the penalties for breaking the law and the probability that people will be caught, or you could try to convince people that the law is just and fair. As we have seen, the former approach is difficult and sometimes ineffective. If we wanted to prevent people from driving through red lights, we could increase the penalties for doing so and make sure that we stationed a police officer at every intersection. But it would be far simpler to convince people that it is wrong to run red lights so that they comply with the law even when no police officers are around.

What determines whether people think a law is just? One important factor is their perception of the fairness of legal proceedings. **Procedural justice** refers to people's judgments about the fairness of the procedures used to determine outcomes, such as whether they are innocent or guilty of a crime (Blader & Tyler, 2003; Kelley & Thibaut, 1978; Wenzel, 2000). People who feel that they have been treated fairly are more likely to comply with the law than people who feel that they have been treated unfairly (Tyler, 1990). Consider, for example, what happens when the police are called because of a domestic assault. What determines whether the person accused of assault will repeat this crime in the future? Surprisingly, it is not whether suspects are arrested or threatened with punishment; it is whether they feel that they were treated fairly by the police ("Misconceptions," 1997).

As another example, imagine that you receive a traffic ticket one day for failing to stop at a stop sign. You believe the ticket is unfair because your view of the stop sign was obstructed by branches from a large tree that should have been trimmed by the city. You decide to go to court to protest the ticket. You take photographs of the tree, make careful diagrams of the intersection, and spend hours practicing your testimony before your friends. Finally, you get your day in court. Now, imagine that one of two things occurs: In the first scenario, your ticket is dismissed without a hearing because the officer who gave you the ticket could not appear in court that day. In the second scenario, the judge listens carefully, asks you a number of questions, and compliments you on your photographs and diagrams. After carefully considering all the facts, however, she rules against you, arguing that the stop sign, though obstructed, was still visible. Which outcome would you prefer—the first or the second one?

Surely the first one, you might think, because here you receive a positive outcome—no fine, no points on your driving record, no increase in your insurance rates. Research by Tom Tyler (1990), however, suggests that most people prefer the second scenario. Even though the outcome is negative, people have a greater sense of procedural justice in this case—they have had their day in court and were treated with fairness and respect. It is often more important to people to maintain a sense of procedural justice than to receive a positive outcome.

In sum, social psychological research indicates that the American legal system can go wrong in a number of ways: Juries rely heavily on eyewitness testimony when in fact such testimony is often in error; determining when witnesses are telling the truth is difficult, even with the use of polygraphs; and because juries are groups of people who try to reach consensus by discussing, arguing, and bargaining, the kinds of conformity pressures and group processes we discussed in Chapters 8 and 9 can lead to faulty decisions. By illuminating these problems in their research, however, social psychologists can help initiate change in the legal system—change that will lead to greater fairness and equity and to a greater sense of procedural justice. Most important of all, heeding psychological research on these questions might reduce the number of cases in which people like Randall Adams and Ronald Cotton languish in prison for crimes they did not commit.

Procedural Justice

People's judgments about the fairness of the procedures used to determine outcomes, such as whether they are innocent or guilty of a crime

SUMMARY

Eyewitness Testimony

Many social psychological principles predict how people will respond in the legal arena. Because of the limitations of people's memory, eyewitness testimony is often inaccurate. A number of factors bias the **acquisition, storage,** and **retrieval** of what people observe, sometimes leading to the false identification of criminals. For example, research on **own-race bias** shows that people find it more difficult to recognize members of other races than members of their own race. Research on **reconstructive memory** indicates that errors in **source monitoring** can occur when people become confused about where they saw or heard something. Jurors often place a great deal of faith in eyewitness testimony, even though jurors are not very good at telling when someone is lying. The **polygraph** is also an imperfect measure of lie detection, which means that false testimony by eyewitnesses and others sometimes goes undetected. Because of these problems with eyewitness testimony, researchers have tried to develop ways of improving it. Although techniques such as hypnosis and the **cognitive interview** have been tried, neither is very successful at improving the accuracy of eyewitness testimony.

There is a great deal of controversy over another form of eyewitness memory, namely, the accuracy of people's memories about their own past traumatic experiences. How valid are **recovered memories,** the sudden recollection of events, such as sexual abuse, that had been forgotten or repressed? Though recovered memories may be true in some instances, they can also be the result of **false memory syndrome,** whereby people come to believe the memory is true when it actually is not. False memories are especially likely to occur when another person suggests to us that an event really occurred.

Juries: Group Processes in Action

Juries are of particular interest to social psychologists because the way they reach verdicts is directly relevant to social psychological research on group processes and social interaction. Jurors are susceptible to the same kinds of biases and social pressures we documented in earlier chapters. They are sometimes biased by pretrial publicity, even when trying to put it out of their minds. During a trial, jurors attempt to make sense out of the testimony and often decide on one story that explains all of the evidence. Juries are thus most swayed by lawyers who present the evidence in a way that tells a consistent story. During deliberations, jurors with minority views are often pressured into conforming to the view of the majority; thus verdicts usually correspond to the initial feelings of the majority of jurors. What about the size of juries—are six jurors as good as twelve, as suggested by the Supreme Court? Social psychological research suggests that twelve jurors are better than six. On larger juries, minorities are more likely to be represented, and people with minority viewpoints are less likely to be pressured to conform.

Why Do People Obey the Law?

It is also important to examine people's perception of the legal system, because these perceptions have a lot to do with how likely people are to obey the law. For example, **deterrence theory** holds that people refrain from criminal activity if they view penalties as severe, certain, and swift. Deterrence theory may be correct about crimes that are the result of rational thought but is unlikely to apply to crimes of passion that are not rational, such as many murders. There is no evidence, for example, that the death penalty deters murders, and there is even some evidence that it increases the murder rate. Finally, people are more likely to obey the law if their sense of **procedural justice** is high; that is, if they believe that the procedures used to determine their guilt or innocence are fair.

CRITICAL THINKING QUESTIONS

1. List several ways in which people can be falsely convicted of a crime, according to psychological research. What can be done to prevent such false convictions?

2. Take three key concepts from this chapter, and discuss how they are related to theories and research from previous chapters in the text. In what ways does basic research in social psychology speak to legal issues?

3. If you could design your own society, what would you do to keep the crime rate low? What are the pros and cons of different approaches, according to psychological research?

Scoring the *Try it!* Questions, Page 543

When the speaker is done, he or she should reveal when he or she was telling the truth versus lying. The audience members should tally how often they were right. People would be correct half the time just by guessing; scores that are substantially above 50 percent may indicate that you are good at detecting deception. Compare notes about what kinds of cues you paid attention to in the speaker. What did the person do that made you think he or she was telling a lie?

Answers, *Try it!* Questions, Page 553

All of the crimes listed are punishable by death (Bedau, 1997).

GLOSSARY

Accessibility   The extent to which schemas and concepts are at the forefront of people's minds and are therefore likely to be used when we are making judgments about the social world

Acquisition   The process by which people notice and pay attention to information in the environment; because people cannot perceive everything that is happening around them, they acquire only a subset of the information available in the environment

Actor/Observer Difference   The tendency to see other people's behavior as dispositionally caused but focusing more on the role of situational factors when explaining one's own behavior

Affect Blend   A facial expression in which one part of the face registers one emotion while another part of the face registers a different emotion

Affectively Based Attitude   An attitude based more on people's feelings and values than on their beliefs about the nature of an attitude object

Aggression   Intentional behavior aimed at doing harm or causing pain to another person

Aggressive Stimulus   An object that is associated with aggressive responses (e.g., a gun) and whose mere presence can increase the probability of aggression

Altruism   The desire to help another person even if it involves a cost to the helper

Altruistic Personality   The qualities that cause an individual to help others in a wide variety of situations

Amygdala   An area in the core of the brain that is associated with aggressive behaviors

Anchoring and Adjustment Heuristic   A mental shortcut whereby people use a number or value as a starting point and then adjust insufficiently from this anchor

Anxious/Ambivalent Attachment Style   An attachment style characterized by a concern that others will not reciprocate one's desire for intimacy, resulting in higher-than-average levels of anxiety

Applied Research   Studies designed to solve a particular social problem

Archival Analysis   A form of the observational method in which the researcher examines the accumulated documents, or archives, of a culture (e.g., diaries, novels, magazines, and newspapers)

Attachment Styles   The expectations people develop about relationships with others, based on the relationship they had with their primary caregiver when they were infants

Attitude Accessibility   The strength of the association between an attitude object and a person's evaluation of that object, measured by the speed with which people can report how they feel about the object

Attitude Inoculation   Making people immune to attempts to change their attitudes by initially exposing them to small doses of the arguments against their position

Attitudes   Evaluations of people, objects, and ideas

Attribution Theory   A description of the way in which people explain the causes of their own and other people's behavior

Automatic Thinking   Thinking that is nonconscious, unintentional, involuntary, and effortless

Availability Heuristic   A mental rule of thumb whereby people base a judgment on the ease with which they can bring something to mind

Avoidant Attachment Style   An attachment style characterized by a suppression of attachment needs, because attempts to be intimate have been rebuffed; people with this style find it difficult to develop intimate relationships

Base Rate Information   Information about the frequency of members of different categories in the population

Basic Research   Studies that are designed to find the best answer to the question of why people behave as they do and that are conducted purely for reasons of intellectual curiosity

Behaviorally Based Attitude   An attitude based on observations of how one behaves toward an attitude object

Behaviorism   A school of psychology maintaining that to understand human behavior, one need only consider the reinforcing properties of the environment—that is, how positive and negative events in the environment are associated with specific behaviors

Belief in a Just World   A form of defensive attribution wherein people assume that bad things happen to bad people and that good things happen to good people

Blaming the Victim   The tendency to blame individuals (make dispositional attributions) for their victimization, typically motivated by a desire to see the world as a fair place

Buffering Hypothesis   The theory that we need social support only when we are under stress because it protects us against the detrimental effects of this stress

Bystander Effect   The finding that the greater the number of bystanders who witness an emergency, the less likely any one of them is to help

Catharsis The notion that "blowing off steam"—by performing an aggressive act, watching others engage in aggressive behaviors, or engaging in a fantasy of aggression—relieves built-up aggressive energies and hence reduces the likelihood of further aggressive behavior

Causal Theories Theories about the causes of one's own feelings and behaviors; often we learn such theories from our culture (e.g., "absence makes the heart grow fonder")

Central Route to Persuasion The case whereby people elaborate on a persuasive communication, listening carefully to and thinking about the arguments, as occurs when people have both the ability and the motivation to listen carefully to a communication

Classical Conditioning The phenomenon whereby a stimulus that elicits an emotional response is repeatedly paired with a neutral stimulus that does not until the neutral stimulus takes on the emotional properties of the first stimulus

Cognitive Appraisal Theories of Emotion Theories holding that emotions result from people's interpretations and explanations of events, even in the absence of physiological arousal

Cognitive Dissonance A drive or feeling of discomfort, originally defined as being caused by holding two or more inconsistent cognitions and subsequently defined as being caused by performing an action that is discrepant from one's customary, typically positive

Cognitive Interview A technique whereby a trained interviewer tries to improve eyewitnesses' memories by focusing their attention on the details and context of the event

Cognitively Based Attitude An attitude based primarily on people's beliefs about the properties of an attitude object

Commons Dilemma A social dilemma in which everyone takes from a common pool of goods that will replenish itself if used in moderation but will disappear if overused

Communal Relationships Relationships in which people's primary concern is being responsive to the other person's needs

Companionate Love The intimacy and affection we feel when we care deeply for a person but do not experience passion or arousal in the person's presence

Comparison Level for Alternatives People's expectations about the level of rewards and punishments they would receive in an alternative relationship

Comparison Level People's expectations about the level of rewards and punishments they are likely to receive in a particular relationship

Conformity A change in one's behavior due to the real or imagined influence of other people

Consensus Information Information about the extent to which other people behave the same way toward the same stimulus as the actor does

Consistency Information Information about the extent to which the behavior between one actor and one stimulus is the same across time and circumstances

Construal The way in which people perceive, comprehend, and interpret the social world

Contagion The rapid spread of emotions or behaviors through a crowd

Contingency Theory of Leadership The idea that leadership effectiveness depends both on how task-oriented or relationship-oriented the leader is and on the amount of control and influence the leader has over the group

Controlled Thinking Thinking that is conscious, intentional, voluntary, and effortful

Coping Styles The ways in which people react to threatening events

Correlation Coefficient A statistical technique that assesses how well you can predict one variable from another—for example, how well you can predict people's weight from their height

Correlational Method The technique whereby two or more variables are systematically measured and the relationship between them (i.e., how much one can be predicted from the other) is assessed

Correspondence Bias The tendency to infer that people's behavior corresponds to (matches) their disposition (personality)

Counterattitudinal Advocacy Stating an opinion or attitude that runs counter to one's private belief or attitude

Counterfactual Thinking Mentally changing some aspect of the past as a way of imagining what might have been

Covariation Model A theory that states that to form an attribution about what caused a person's behavior, we systematically note the pattern between the presence or absence of possible causal factors and whether or not the behavior occurs

Cover Story A description of the purpose of a study, given to participants, that is different from its true purpose, used to maintain psychological realism

Cross-Cultural Research Research conducted with members of different cultures, to see whether the psychological processes of interest are present in both cultures or whether they are specific to the culture in which people were raised

Crowding The subjective feeling of unpleasantness due to the presence of other people

Debriefing Explaining to participants, at the end of an experiment, the true purpose of the study and exactly what transpired

Deception Misleading participants about the true purpose of a study or the events that will actually transpire

Decode To interpret the meaning of the nonverbal behavior other people express, such as deciding that a pat on the back was an expression of condescension and not kindness

Defensive Attributions Explanations for behavior that avoid feelings of vulnerability and mortality

Deindividuation The loosening of normal constraints on behavior when people are in a crowd, leading to an increase in impulsive and deviant acts

Density The number of people occupying a given space

Dependent Variable The variable a researcher measures to see if it is influenced by the independent variable; the researcher hypothesizes that the dependent variable will depend on the level of the independent variable

Descriptive Norms   People's perceptions of how people actually behave in given situations, regardless of whether the behavior is approved or disapproved of by others

Deterrence Theory   The hypothesis that the threat of legal punishment causes people to refrain from criminal activity as long as the punishment is perceived as relatively severe, certain, and swift

Diffusion of Responsibility   The phenomenon whereby each bystander's sense of responsibility to help decreases as the number of witnesses increases

Discrimination   Unjustified negative or harmful action toward a member of a group simply because of his or her membership in that group

Display Rules   Culturally determined rules about which nonverbal behaviors are appropriate to display

Distinctiveness Information   Information about the extent to which one particular actor behaves in the same way to different stimuli

Downward Social Comparison   Comparing ourselves to people who are worse than we on a particular trait or ability

Elaboration Likelihood Model   An explanation of the two ways in which persuasive communications can cause attitude change: centrally, when people are motivated and have the ability to pay attention to the arguments in the communication, and peripherally, when people do not pay attention to the arguments but are instead swayed by surface characteristics (e.g., who gave the speech)

Emblems   Nonverbal gestures that have well-understood definitions within a given culture; they usually have direct verbal translations, such as the "OK" sign

Empathy   The ability to put oneself in the shoes of another person and to experience events and emotions (e.g., joy and sadness) the way that person experiences them

Empathy-Altruism Hypothesis   The idea that when we feel empathy for a person, we will attempt to help that person purely for altruistic reasons, regardless of what we have to gain

Encode   To express or emit nonverbal behavior, such as smiling or patting someone on the back

Equity Theory   The idea that people are happiest with relationships in which the rewards and costs experienced and the contributions made by both parties are roughly equal

Eros   The instinct toward life, posited by Freud

Ethnography   The method by which researchers attempt to understand a group or culture by observing it from the inside, without imposing any preconceived notions they might have

Evolutionary Approach to Love   A theory derived from evolutionary biology that holds that men and women are attracted to different characteristics in each other (men are attracted by women's appearance; women are attracted by men's resources) because this maximizes their chances of reproductive success

Evolutionary Psychology   The attempt to explain social behavior in terms of genetic factors that evolved over time according to the principles of natural selection

Exchange Relationships   Relationships governed by the need for equity (i.e., for an equal ratio of rewards and costs)

Experimental Method   The method in which the researcher randomly assigns participants to different conditions and ensures that these conditions are identical except for the independent variable (the one thought to have a causal effect on people's responses)

Explicit Attitudes   Attitudes that we consciously endorse and can easily report

External Attribution   The inference that a person is behaving a certain way because of something about the situation he or she is in; the assumption is that most people would respond the same way in that situation

External Justification   A reason or an explanation for dissonant personal behavior that resides outside the individual (e.g., in order to receive a large reward or avoid a severe punishment)

External Validity   The extent to which the results of a study can be generalized to other situations and to other people

Extrinsic Motivation   The desire to engage in an activity because of external rewards or pressures, not because we enjoy the task or find it interesting

False Memory Syndrome   Remembering a past traumatic experience that is objectively false but nevertheless accepted as true

Fear-Arousing Communications   Persuasive messages that attempt to change people's attitudes by arousing their fears

Field Experiments   Experiments conducted in natural settings rather than in the laboratory

Fight-or-Flight Response   Responding to stress by either attacking the source of the stress or fleeing from it

Frustration-Aggression Theory   The idea that frustration—the perception that you are being prevented from attaining a goal—increases the probability of an aggressive response

Fundamental Attribution Error   The tendency to overestimate the extent to which people's behavior is due to internal, dispositional factors and to underestimate the role of situational factors

Gestalt Psychology   A school of psychology stressing the importance of studying the subjective way in which an object appears in people's minds, rather than the objective, physical attributes of the object

Global Attribution   The belief that an event is caused by factors that apply in a large number of situations (e.g., your intelligence, which will influence your performance in many areas) rather than factors that are specific and apply in only a limited number

Great Person Theory   The idea that certain key personality traits make a person a good leader, regardless of the situation

Group Cohesiveness   Qualities of a group that bind members together and promote liking between members

Group Polarization   The tendency for groups to make decisions that are more extreme than the initial inclinations of its members

Group   Two or more people who interact and are interdependent in the sense that their needs and goals cause them to influence each other

Groupthink A kind of thinking in which maintaining group cohesiveness and solidarity is more important than considering the facts in a realistic manner

Heuristic–Systematic Model of Persuasion An explanation of the two ways in which persuasive communications can cause attitude change: either systematically processing the merits of the arguments or using mental shortcuts (heuristics), such as "Experts are always right"

Hindsight Bias The tendency for people to exaggerate how much they could have predicted an outcome after knowing that it occurred

Hostile Aggression Aggression stemming from feelings of anger and aimed at inflicting pain

Idiosyncrasy Credits The tolerance a person earns, over time, by conforming to group norms; if enough idiosyncrasy credits are earned, the person can, on occasion, behave deviantly without retribution from the group

Illusory Correlation The tendency to see relationships, or correlations, between events that are actually unrelated

Implicit Attitudes Attitudes that are involuntary, uncontrollable, and at times unconscious

Implicit Personality Theory A type of schema people use to group various kinds of personality traits together; for example, many people believe that someone who is kind is generous as well

Impression Management The attempt by people to get others to see them as they want to be seen

Independent Variable The variable a researcher changes or varies to see if it has an effect on some other variable

Independent View of the Self A way of defining oneself in terms of one's own internal thoughts, feelings, and actions and not in terms of the thoughts, feelings, and actions of other people

Individual Differences The aspects of people's personalities that make them different from other people

Informational Social Influence The influence of other people that leads us to conform because we see them as a source of information to guide our behavior; we conform because we believe that others' interpretation of an ambiguous situation is more correct than ours and will help us choose an appropriate course of action

Informed Consent Agreement to participate in an experiment, granted in full awareness of the nature of the experiment, which has been explained in advance

Ingratiation The process whereby people flatter, praise, and generally try to make themselves likable to another person, often of higher status

In-Group The group with which an individual identifies as a member

Injunctive Norms People's perceptions of what behaviors are approved or disapproved of by others

Institutionalized Racism Racist attitudes that are held by the vast majority of people living in a society where stereotypes and discrimination are the norm

Institutionalized Sexism Sexist attitudes that are held by the vast majority of people living in a society where stereotypes and discrimination are the norm

Instrumental Aggression Aggression as a means to some goal other than causing pain

Insufficient Punishment The dissonance aroused when individuals lack sufficient external justification for having resisted a desired activity or object, usually resulting in individuals' devaluing the forbidden activity or object

Integrative Solution A solution to a conflict whereby the parties make trade-offs on issues according to their different interests; each side concedes the most on issues that are unimportant to it but important to the other side

Interdependent View of the Self A way of defining oneself in terms of one's relationships to other people; recognizing that one's behavior is often determined by the thoughts, feelings, and actions of others

Interjudge Reliability The level of agreement between two or more people who independently observe and code a set of data; by showing that two or more judges independently come up with the same observations, researchers ensure that the observations are not the sub

Internal Attribution (Chapter 4) The inference that a person is behaving in a certain way because of something about the person, such as attitude, character, or personality; (SPA1) the belief that an event is caused by things about you (e.g., your own ability or effort), as opposed to factors that are external to you (e.g., the difficulty of a test)

Internal Justification The reduction of dissonance by changing something about oneself (e.g., one's attitude or behavior)

Internal Validity Making sure that nothing besides the independent variable can affect the dependent variable; this is accomplished by controlling all extraneous variables and by randomly assigning people to different experimental conditions

Intrinsic Motivation The desire to engage in an activity because we enjoy it or find it interesting, not because of external rewards or pressures

Introspection The process whereby people look inward and examine their own thoughts, feelings, and motives

Investment Model The theory that people's commitment to a relationship depends not only on their satisfaction with the relationship in terms of rewards, costs, and comparison level and their comparison level for alternatives but also on how much they have in the relationship that would be lost by leaving it

Jigsaw Classroom A classroom setting designed to reduce prejudice and raise the self-esteem of children by placing them in small desegregated groups and making each child dependent on the other children in the group to learn the course material and do well in the class

Judgmental Heuristics Mental shortcuts people use to make judgments quickly and efficiently

Justification of Effort The tendency for individuals to increase their liking for something they have worked hard to attain

Kin Selection The idea that behaviors that help a genetic relative are favored by natural selection

Learned Helplessness The state of pessimism that results from attributing a negative event to stable, internal, and global factors

Lowballing   An unscrupulous strategy whereby a salesperson induces a customer to agree to purchase a product at a very low cost, subsequently claims it was an error, and then raises the price; frequently, the customer will agree to make the purchase at the inflated price

Mass Psychogenic Illness   The occurrence, in a group of people, of similar physical symptoms with no known physical cause

Mere Exposure Effect   The finding that the more exposure we have to a stimulus, the more apt we are to like it

Meta-Analysis   A statistical technique that averages the results of two or more studies to see if the effect of an independent variable is reliable

Minority Influence   The case where a minority of group members influence the behavior or beliefs of the majority

Misattribution of Arousal   The process whereby people make mistaken inferences about what is causing them to feel the way they do

Modern Racism   Outwardly acting unprejudiced while inwardly maintaining prejudiced attitudes

Mundane Realism   The extent to which an experiment is similar to real-life situations

Mutual Interdependence   The situation that exists when two or more groups need each other and must depend on each other to accomplish a goal that is important to each of them

Need for Cognition   A personality variable reflecting the extent to which people engage in and enjoy effortful cognitive activities

Negative-State Relief Hypothesis   The idea that people help in order to alleviate their own sadness and distress

Negotiation   A form of communication between opposing sides in a conflict in which offers and counteroffers are made and a solution occurs only when both parties agree

Nonverbal Communication   The way in which people communicate, intentionally or unintentionally, without words; nonverbal cues include facial expressions, tone of voice, gestures, body position and movement, the use of touch, and gaze

Norm of Reciprocity   The expectation that helping others will increase the likelihood that they will help us in the future

Normative Conformity   The tendency to go along with the group in order to fulfill the group's expectations and gain acceptance

Normative Social Influence   The influence of other people that leads us to conform in order to be liked and accepted by them; this type of conformity results in public compliance with the group's beliefs and behaviors but not necessarily private acceptance of those beliefs and behaviors

Observational Method   The technique whereby a researcher observes people and systematically records measurements or impressions of their behavior

Operant Conditioning   The phenomenon whereby behaviors that people freely choose to perform increase or decrease in frequency, depending on whether they are followed by positive reinforcement or punishment

Out-Group Homogeneity   The perception that individuals in the out-group are more similar to each other (homogeneous)

than they really are, as well as more similar than the members of the in-group are

Out-Group   Any group with which an individual does not identify

Overconfidence Barrier   The fact that people usually have too much confidence in the accuracy of their judgments

Overjustification Effect   The tendency of people to view their behavior as caused by compelling extrinsic reasons, making them underestimate the extent to which it was caused by intrinsic reasons

Own-Race Bias   The fact that people are better at recognizing faces of their own race than those of other races

Participant Observation   A form of the observational method in which the observer interacts with the people being observed but tries not to alter the situation in any way

Passionate Love   An intense longing, we feel for a person, accompanied by physiological arousal; when our love is reciprocated, we feel great fulfillment and ecstasy, but when it is not, we feel sadness and despair

Perceived Control   The belief that we can influence our environment in ways that determine whether we experience positive or negative outcomes

Perceptual Salience   The seeming importance of information that is the focus of people's attention

Performance-Contingent Rewards   Rewards that are based on how well we perform a task

Peripheral Route to Persuasion   The case whereby people do not elaborate on the arguments in a persuasive communication but are instead swayed by peripheral cues

Perseverance Effect   The finding that people's beliefs about themselves and the social world persist even after the evidence supporting these beliefs is discredited

Persuasive Communication   Communication (e.g., a speech or television ad) advocating a particular side of an issue

Pluralistic Ignorance   Bystanders' assuming that nothing is wrong in an emergency because no one else looks concerned

Polygraph   A machine that measures people's physiological responses (e.g., their heart rate); polygraph operators attempt to tell if someone is lying by observing that person's physiological responses while answering questions

Postdecision Dissonance   Dissonance aroused after making a decision, typically reduced by enhancing the attractiveness of the chosen alternative and devaluating the rejected alternatives

Prejudice   A hostile or negative attitude toward a distinguishable group of people, based solely on their membership in that group

Priming   The process by which recent experiences increase the accessibility of a schema, trait, or concept

Private Acceptance   Conforming to other people's behavior out of a genuine belief that what they are doing or saying is right

Probability Level (p-value)   A number calculated with statistical techniques that tells researchers how likely it is that the results of their experiment occurred by chance and not because of the independent variable or variables; the convention in science, including social psychology, is to consider results significant (trustworthy) if the probability level is less than 5 in 100 that the results might be due to chance factors and not the independent variables studied

Procedural Justice   People's judgments about the fairness of the procedures used to determine outcomes, such as whether they are innocent or guilty of a crime

Process Loss   Any aspect of group interaction that inhibits good problem solving

Propinquity Effect   The finding that the more we see and interact with people, the more likely they are to become our friends

Prosocial Behavior   Any act performed with the goal of benefiting another person

Psychological Realism   The extent to which the psychological processes triggered in an experiment are similar to psychological processes that occur in everyday life; psychological realism can be high in an experiment even if mundane realism is low

Public Compliance   Conforming to other people's behavior publicly without necessarily believing in what we are doing or saying

Public Goods Dilemma   A social dilemma in which individuals must contribute to a common pool in order to maintain the public good

Random Assignment to Condition   A process ensuring that all participants have an equal chance of taking part in any condition of an experiment; through random assignment, researchers can be relatively certain that differences in the participants' personalities or background

Random Selection   A way of ensuring that a sample of people is representative of a population by giving everyone in the population an equal chance of being selected for the sample

Rationalization Trap   The potential for dissonance reduction to produce a succession of self-justifications that ultimately result in a chain of stupid or immoral actions

Reactance Theory   The idea that when people feel their freedom to perform a certain behavior is threatened, an unpleasant state of reactance is aroused, which they can reduce by performing the threatened behavior

Realistic Conflict Theory   The idea that limited resources lead to conflict between groups and result in increased prejudice and discrimination

Reasons-Generated Attitude Change   Attitude change resulting from thinking about the reasons for one's attitudes; people assume their attitudes match the reasons that are plausible and easy to verbalize

Reconstructive Memory   The process whereby memories of an event become distorted by information encountered after the event occurred

Recovered Memories   Recollections of a past event, such as sexual abuse, that had been forgotten or repressed

Relationship-Oriented Leader   A leader who is concerned primarily with workers' feelings and relationships

Replication   Repeating a study, often with different subject populations or in different settings

Representativeness Heuristic   A mental shortcut whereby people classify something according to how similar it is to a typical case

Retrieval   The process by which people recall information stored in their memories

Scapegoating   The tendency for individuals, when frustrated or unhappy, to displace aggression onto groups that are disliked, visible, and relatively powerless

Schemas   Mental structures people use to organize their knowledge about the social world around themes or subjects and that influence the information people notice, think about, and remember

Scripts   Ways of behaving socially that we learn implicitly from our culture

Secure Attachment Style   An attachment style characterized by trust, a lack of concern with being abandoned, and the view that one is worthy and well liked

Self-Affirmation Theory   The idea that people will reduce the impact of a dissonance-arousing threat to their self-concept by focusing on and affirming their competence on some dimension unrelated to the threat

Self-Awareness Theory   The idea that when people focus their attention on themselves, they evaluate and compare their behavior to their internal standards and values

Self-Awareness   The act of thinking about ourselves

Self-Concept   The content of the self; that is, our knowledge about who we are

Self-Discrepancy Theory   The idea that people become distressed when their sense of their actual self differs from their ideal self

Self-Efficacy   The belief in one's ability to carry out specific actions that produce desired outcomes

Self-Esteem   People's evaluations of their own self-worth—that is, the extent to which they view themselves as good, competent, and decent

Self-Evaluation Maintenance Theory   The idea that one's self-concept can be threatened by another individual's behavior and that the level of threat is determined by both the closeness of the other individual and the personal relevance of the behavior

Self-Fulfilling Prophecy   The case whereby people (1) have an expectation about what another person is like, which (2) influences how they act toward that person, which (3) causes that person to behave consistently with people's original expectations, making the expectations come true

Self-Handicapping   The strategy whereby people create obstacles and excuses for themselves so that if they do poorly on a task, they can avoid blaming themselves

Self-Justification   The tendency to justify one's actions in order to maintain one's self-esteem

Self-Perception Theory   The theory that when our attitudes and feelings are uncertain or ambiguous, we infer these states by observing our behavior and the situation in which it occurs

Self-Persuasion   A long-lasting form of attitude change that results from attempts at self-justification

Self-Reference Effect   The tendency for people to remember information better if they relate it to themselves

Self-Schemas   Mental structures that people use to organize their knowledge about themselves and that influence what they notice, think about, and remember about themselves

Self-Serving Attributions   Explanations for one's successes that credit internal, dispositional factors and explanations for one's failures that blame external, situational factors

Self-Verification Theory   The idea that people have a need to seek confirmation of their self-concept, be it positive or negative, which in some circumstances can conflict with the desire to uphold a favorable view of oneself

Sensory Overload   Receiving more stimulation from the environment than we can pay attention to or process at a given time

Serotonin   A chemical in the brain that may inhibit aggressive impulses

Social Cognition   How people think about themselves and the social world, or more specifically, how people select, interpret, remember, and use social information to make judgments and decisions

Social Comparison Theory   The idea that we learn about our own abilities and attitudes by comparing ourselves to other people

Social Dilemma   A conflict in which the most beneficial action for an individual will, if chosen by most people, have harmful effects on everyone

Social Exchange Theory   The idea people's feelings about a relationship depend on their perceptions of the rewards and costs of the relationship, the kind of relationship they deserve, and their chances for having a better relationship with someone else

Social Facilitation   The tendency for people to do better on simple tasks and worse on complex tasks when they are in the presence of others and their individual performance can be evaluated

Social Impact Theory   The idea that conforming to social influence depends on the strength of the group's importance, its immediacy, and the number of people in the group

Social Influence   The effect that the words, actions, or mere presence of other people have on our thoughts, feelings, attitudes, or behavior

Social Learning Theory   The idea that we learn social behavior (e.g., aggression) by observing others and imitating them

Social Loafing   The tendency for people to do worse on simple tasks but better on complex tasks when they are in the presence of others and their individual performance cannot be evaluated

Social Norms   The implicit or explicit rules a group has for the acceptable behaviors, values, and beliefs of its members

Social Perception   The study of how we form impressions of and make inferences about other people

Social Psychology   The scientific study of the way in which people's thoughts, feelings, and behaviors are influenced by the real or imagined presence of other people

Social Role Theory   The theory that sex differences in social behavior are due to society's division of labor between the sexes; this division leads to differences in gender-role expectations and

sex-typed skills, both of which are responsible for differences in men's and women's social behavior

Social Roles   Shared expectations in a group about how particular people are supposed to behave

Social Support   The perception that others are responsive and receptive to one's needs

Source Monitoring   The process whereby people try to identify the source of their memories

Spotlight Effect   The tendency to overestimate the extent to which our actions and appearance are salient to others

Stable Attribution   The belief that an event is caused by factors that will not change over time (e.g., your intelligence), as opposed to factors that will change over time (e.g., the amount of effort you put into a task)

Stereotype Threat   The apprehension experienced by members of a group that their behavior might confirm a cultural stereotype

Stereotype   A generalization about a group of people in which identical characteristics are assigned to virtually all members of the group, regardless of actual variation among the members

Storage   The process by which people store in memory information they have acquired from the environment

Stress   The negative feelings and beliefs that arise whenever people feel unable to cope with demands from their environment

Subliminal Messages   Words or pictures that are not consciously perceived but may nevertheless influence people's judgments, attitudes, and behaviors

Surveys   Research in which a representative sample of people are asked (often anonymously) questions about their attitudes or behavior

Task-Contingent Rewards   Rewards that are given for performing a task, regardless of how well the task is done

Task-Oriented Leader   A leader who is concerned more with getting the job done than with workers' feelings and relationships

Tend-and-Befriend Response   Responding to stress with nurturant activities designed to protect oneself and one's offspring (tending) and creating social networks that provide protection from threats (befriending)

Testosterone   A hormone associated with aggression

Thanatos   According to Freud, an instinctual drive toward death, leading to aggressive actions

Theory of Planned Behavior   The idea that the best predictors of a person's planned, deliberate behaviors are the person's attitudes toward specific behaviors, subjective norms, and perceived behavioral control

Thought Suppression   The attempt to avoid thinking about something we would prefer to forget

Tit-for-Tat Strategy   A means of encouraging cooperation by at first acting cooperatively but then always responding the way your opponent did (cooperatively or competitively) on the previous trial

Transactive Memory The combined memory of two people that is more efficient than the memory of either individual

Triangular Theory of Love The idea that different kinds of love consist of varying degrees of three components: intimacy, passion, and commitment

Two-Factor Theory of Emotion The idea that emotional experience is the result of a two-step self-perception process in which people first experience physiological arousal and then seek an appropriate explanation for it

Two-Step Process of Attribution Analyzing another person's behavior first by making an automatic internal attribution and only then thinking about possible situational reasons for the behavior, after which one may adjust the original internal attribution

Type A Personality The type of person who is typically competitive, impatient, hostile, and control-oriented, when confronting a challenge

Type B Personality The type of person who is typically patient, relaxed, and noncompetitive when confronting a challenge

Ultimate Attribution Error The tendency to make dispositional attributions about an entire group of people

Unrealistic Optimism A form of defensive attribution wherein people think that good things are more likely to happen to them than to their peers and that bad things are less likely to happen to them than to their peers

Upward Social Comparison Comparing ourselves to people who are better than we are on a particular trait or ability

Urban Overload Hypothesis The theory that people living in cities are constantly being bombarded with stimulation and that they keep to themselves to avoid being overwhelmed by it

Yale Attitude Change Approach The study of the conditions under which people are most likely to change their attitudes in response to persuasive messages, focusing on "who said what to whom"—the source of the communication, the nature of the communication, and the nature of the audience

REFERENCES

Aarts, H., & Dijksterhuis, A. (2003) The silence of the library: Environment, situational norm, and social behavior. *Journal of Personality and Social Psychology, 84,* 18–28.

Abelson, R. P., Kinder, D. R., Peters, M. D., & Fiske, S. T. (1982). Affective and semantic components in political person perception. *Journal of Personality and Social Psychology, 42,* 619–630.

Abraham, M. M., & Lodish, L. M. (1990). Getting the most out of advertising and promotion. *Harvard Business Review, 68,* 50–60.

Abrams, D., Wetherell, M., Cochrane, S., Hogg, M. A., & Turner, J. C. (1990). Knowing what to think by knowing who you are: Self-categorization and the nature of norm formation, conformity and group polarization. *British Journal of Social Psychology, 29,* 97–119.

Abrams, D., Viki, G. T., Masser, B., & Bohner, G. (2003). Perceptions of stranger and acquaintance rape: The role of benevolent and hostile sexism in victim blame and rape proclivity. *Journal of Personality and Social Psychology, 84,* 111–125.

Abramson, L. Y., Seligman, M. E. P., & Teasdale, J. D. (1978). Learned helplessness in humans: Critique and reformulation. *Journal of Abnormal Psychology, 87,* 49–74.

Adler, J. (1997). It's a wise father who knows . . . *Newsweek,* p. 73.

Ahlfinger, N. R., & Esser, J. K. (2001). Testing the groupthink model: Effects of promotional leadership and conformity predisposition. *Social Behavior and Personality, 29,* 31–41.

Aiello, J. R., & Douthitt, E. A. (2001). Social facilitation from Triplett to electronic performance monitoring. *Group Dynamics: Theory, Research, and Practice, 5,* 163–180.

Aiello, J. R., Thompson, D. E., & Brodzinsky, D. M. (1983). How funny is crowding anyway? Effects of room size, group size, and the introduction of humor. *Basic and Applied Social Psychology, 4,* 193–207.

Ainsworth, M. D. S., Blehar, M. C., Waters, E., & Wall, S. (1978). *Patterns of attachment: A psychological study of the strange situation.* Hillsdale, NJ: Erlbaum.

Ajzen, I. (1985). From intentions to actions: A theory of planned behavior. In J. Kuhl & J. Beckmann (Eds.), *Action control: From cognition to behavior* (pp. 11–39). Heidelberg, Germany: Springer-Verlag.

Ajzen, I., & Fishbein, M. (1980). *Understanding attitudes and predicting social behavior.* Englewood Cliffs, NJ: Prentice Hall.

Ajzen, I., & Sexton, J. (1999). Depth of processing, belief congruence, and attitude-behavior correspondence. In S. Chaiken & Y. Trope (Eds.), *Dual-process theories in social psychology* (pp. 117–138). New York: Guilford Press.

Akert, R. M. (1998). *Terminating romantic relationships: The role of personal responsibility and gender.* Unpublished manuscript, Wellesley College.

Akert, R. M., Chen, J., & Panter, A. T. (1991). *Facial prominence and stereotypes: The incidence and meaning of face-ism in print and television media.* Unpublished manuscript. Wellesley College.

Akert, R. M., & Panter, A. T. (1986). Extraversion and the ability to decode nonverbal communication. *Personality and Individual Differences, 9,* 965–972.

Albarracin, D., & Wyer, R. S., Jr. (2000). The cognitive impact of past behavior: Influences on beliefs, attitudes, and future behavioral decisions. *Journal of Personality and Social Psychology, 79,* 5–22.

Albarracin, D., & Wyer, R. S., Jr. (2001). Elaborative and nonelaborative processing of a behavior-related communication. *Personality and Social Psychology Bulletin, 27,* 691–705.

Albarracin, D., Johnson, B. T., Fishbein, M., & Muellerleile, P. A. (2001). Theories of reasoned action and planned behavior as models of condom use: A meta-analysis. *Psychological Bulletin, 127,* 142–161

Albright, L., & Forziati, C. (1995). Cross-situational consistency and perceptual accuracy in leadership. *Personality and Social Psychology Bulletin, 21,* 1269–1276.

Albright, L., Malloy, T. E., Dong, Q., Kenny, D. A., Fang, X., Winquist, L., & Yu, D. (1997). Cross-cultural consensus in personality judgments. *Journal of Personality and Social Psychology, 72,* 558–569.

Aldag, R. J., & Fuller, S. R. (1993). Beyond fiasco: A reappraisal of the groupthink phenomenon and a new model of group decision processes. *Psychological Bulletin, 113,* 533–552.

Allen, M. (1991). Meta-analysis comparing the persuasiveness of one-sided and two-sided messages. *Western Journal of Speech Communication, 55,* 390–404.

Allen, M., D'Alessio, D., & Brezgel, K. (1995). *A meta-analysis summarizing the effects of pornography: Vol. 2. Aggression after exposure.* Thousand Oaks, CA: Sage.

Allen, V. L. (1965). Situational factors in conformity. In L. Berkowitz (Ed.), *Advances in experimental social psychology* (Vol. 2, pp. 133–175). New York: Academic Press.

Allen, V. L., & Levine, J. M. (1969). Consensus and conformity. *Journal of Personality and Social Psychology, 5,* 389–399.

Allison, P. D. (1992). The cultural evolution of beneficent norms. *Social Forces, 71,* 279–301.

Allport, G. W. (1954). *The nature of prejudice.* Reading, MA: Addison-Wesley.

Allport, G. W. (1985). The historical background of social psychology. In G. Lindzey & E. Aronson (Eds.), *The handbook of social psychology* (3rd ed., Vol. 1, pp. 1–46). New York: McGraw-Hill.

Altman, L. K. (2000, January 18). Mysterious illnesses often turn out to be mass hysteria. *New York Times,* pp. D7, D12.

Alvarez, L. (2003, June 22). Arranged marriages get a little rearranging. *New York Times,* p. 3.

Amato, P. R. (1983). Helping behavior in urban and rural environments: Field studies based on a taxonomic organization of helping episodes. *Journal of Personality and Social Psychology, 45,* 571–586.

Ambady, N., Bernieri, F. J., & Richeson, J. A. (2000). Toward a histology of social behavior: Judgmental accuracy from thin slices of the behavioral stream. In M. P. Zanna (Ed.), *Advances in experimental social psychology* (Vol. 32, pp. 201–271). San Diego, CA: Academic Press.

Ambady, N., & Rosenthal, R. (1992). Thin slices of expressive behavior as predictors of interpersonal consequences: A meta-analysis. *Psychological Bulletin, 111,* 256–274.

Ambady, N., & Rosenthal, R. (1993). Half a minute: Predicting teacher evaluations from thin slices of nonverbal behavior and physical attractiveness. *Journal of Personality and Social Psychology, 64,* 431–441.

American Psychological Association. (1992). Ethical principles of psychologists and code of conduct. *American Psychologist, 47,* 1597–1611.

American Psychological Association. (2002). *Ethical principles of psychologists and code of conduct.* Retrieved from http://www.apa.org/ethics

Amir, I. (1969). Contact hypothesis in ethnic relations. *Psychological Bulletin, 71,* 319–342.

Amir, I. (1976). The role of intergroup contact in change of prejudice and ethnic relations. In P. A. Katz (Ed.), *Towards the elimination of racism* (pp. 245–308). New York: Pergamon Press.

Andersen, S. M. (1984). Self-knowledge and social inference: II. The diagnosticity of cognitive/affective and behavioral data. *Journal of Personality and Social Psychology, 46,* 294–307.

Andersen, S. M., & Bem, S. L. (1981). Sex typing and androgyny in dyadic interaction: Individual differences in responsiveness to physical attractiveness. *Journal of Personality and Social Psychology, 41,* 74–86.

Andersen, S. M., & Klatzky, R. L. (1987). Traits and social stereotypes: Levels of categorization in person perception. *Journal of Personality and Social Psychology, 53,* 235–246.

Andersen, S. M., & Ross, L. D. (1984). Self-knowledge and social inference: I. The impact of cognitive/affective and behavioral data. *Journal of Personality and Social Psychology, 46,* 280–293.

Anderson, C. A. (1995). Implicit personality theories and empirical data: Biased assimilation, belief perseverance and change, and covariation detection sensitivity. *Social Cognition, 13,* 25–48.

Anderson, C. A. (1999). Attributional style, depression, and loneliness: A cross-cultural comparison of American and Chinese students. *Personality and Social Psychology Bulletin, 25,* 482–499.

Anderson, C. A., Anderson, B., & Deuser, W. (1996). Examining an affective aggression framework: Weapon and temperature effects on aggressive thoughts, affect, and attitudes. *Personality and Social Psychology Bulletin, 22,* 366–376.

Anderson, C. A., & Anderson, D. C. (1984). Ambient temperature and violent crime: Tests of the linear and curvilinear hypotheses. *Journal of Personality and Social Psychology, 46,* 91–97.

Anderson, C. A., & Bushman, B. J. (1997). External validity of "trivial" experiments: The case of laboratory aggression. *Review of General Psychology, 1,* 19–41.

Anderson, C. A., Bushman, B. J., & Groom, R. W. (1997). Hot years and serious and deadly assault: Empirical tests of the heat hypothesis. *Journal of Personality and Social Psychology, 73,* 1213–1223.

Anderson, C. A., & Dill, K. E. (2000). Video games and aggressive thoughts, feelings, and behavior in the laboratory and in life. *Journal of Personality and Social Psychology, 78,* 772–790.

Anderson, C. A., Lepper, M. R., & Ross, L. (1980). The perseverance of social theories: The role of explanation in the persistence of discredited information. *Journal of Personality and Social Psychology, 39,* 1037–1049.

Anderson, C. A., & Lindsay, J. J. (1998). The development, perseverance, and change of naive theories. *Social Cognition, 16,* 8–30.

Anderson, C. A., Lindsay, J. J., & Bushman, B. J. (1999). Research in the psychological laboratory: Truth or triviality? *Current Directions in Psychological Science, 8,* 3–9.

Anderson, J. L., Crawford, C. B., Nadeau, J., & Lindberg, T. (1992). Was the Duchess of Windsor right? A cross-cultural review of the socioecology of ideals of female body shape. *Ethology and Sociobiology, 13,* 197–227.

Anderson, N. B. (1989). Racial differences in stress-induced cardiovascular reactivity and hypertension: Current status and substantive issues. *Psychological Bulletin, 105,* 89–105.

Aoki, N. & Robertson, T. (2003, June 5). Stewart is indicted, steps down. *Boston Globe,* p. A1: E4.

Archer, D. (1991). *A world of gestures: Culture and nonverbal communication* [Videotape and manual]. Berkeley: University of California Extension Center for Media and Independent Learning.

Archer, D. (1994). American violence: How high and why? *Law Studies, 19,* 12–20.

Archer, D. (1997a). Unspoken diversity: Cultural differences in gestures. *Qualitative Sociology, 20,* 79–105.

Archer, D. (1997b). *A world of differences: Understanding cross-cultural communication* [Videotape and manual]. Berkeley: University of California Extension Center for Media and Independent Learning.

Archer, D., & Akert, R. M. (1977a, October). How well do you read body language? *Psychology Today,* pp. 68–69, 72, 119–120.

Archer, D., & Akert, R. M. (1977b). Words and everything else: Verbal and nonverbal cues in social interaction. *Journal of Personality and Social Psychology, 35,* 443–449.

Archer, D., & Akert, R. M. (1980). The encoding of meaning: A test of three theories of social interaction. *Sociological Inquiry, 50,* 393–419.

Archer, D., & Akert, R. M. (1984). Problems of context and criterion in nonverbal communication: A new look at the accuracy issue. In M. Cook (Ed.), *Issues in person perception* (pp. 114–144). New York: Methuen.

Archer, D., & Akert, R. M. (1998). *The interpretation of behavior: Verbal and nonverbal factors in person perception.* New York: Cambridge University Press.

Archer, D., & Gartner, R. (1976). Violent acts and violent times: A comparative approach to postwar homicide rates. *American Sociological Review, 41,* 937–963.

Archer, D., & Gartner, R. (1984). *Violence and crime in cross-national perspective.* New Haven, CT: Yale University Press.

Archer, D., Iritani, B., Kimes, D. D., & Barrios, M. (1983). Face-ism: Five studies of sex differences in facial prominence. *Journal of Personality and Social Psychology, 45,* 725–735.

Archer, D., & McDaniel, P. (1995). Violence and gender: Differences and similarities across societies. In R. B. Ruback & N. A. Weiner (Eds.), *Interpersonal violent behaviors: Social and cultural aspects* (pp. 63–88). New York: Springer-Verlag.

Arendt, H. (1965). *Eichmann in Jerusalem: A report on the banality of evil.* New York: Viking.

Argyle, M. (1975). *Bodily communication.* New York: International Universities Press.

Arkes, H. R., & Mellers, B. A. (2002). Do juries meet our expectations? *Law and Human Behavior, 26,* 625–639.

Arkin, R. M., & Maruyama, G. M. (1979). Attribution, affect, and college exam performance. *Journal of Educational Psychology, 71,* 85–93.

Arkin, R. M., & Oleson, K. C. (1998). Self-handicapping. In J. M. Darley & J. Cooper (Eds.), *Attribution and social interaction: The legacy of Edward E. Jones* (pp. 313–341). Washington, DC: American Psychological Association.

Armitage, C. J., & Conner, M. (2001). Social cognitive determinants of blood donation. *Journal of Applied Social Psychology, 31,* 1431–1457.

Armor, D. A., & Taylor, S. E. (1998). Situated optimism: Specific outcome expectancies and self-regulation. In M. P. Zanna (Ed.), *Advances in experimental social psychology* (Vol. 30, pp. 309–379). San Diego, CA: Academic Press.

Arms, R. L., Russell, G. W., & Sandilands, M. L. (1979). Effects on the hostility of spectators of viewing aggressive sports. *Social Psychology Quarterly, 42,* 275–279.

Armstrong, L. (2000). *It's not about the bike: My journey back to life.* New York: Putnam.

Arnett, J. (1995). The young and the reckless: Adolescent reckless behavior. *Current Directions in Psychological Science, 4,* 67–71.

Aron, A., & Aron, E. N. (1996). Self and self-expansion in relationships. In G. J. O. Fletcher & J. Fitness (Eds.), *Knowledge structures in close relationships: A social psychological approach* (pp. 325–344). Mahwah, NJ: Erlbaum.

Aron, A., Dutton, D. G., Aron, E. N., & Iverson, A. (1989). Experiences of falling in love. *Journal of Social and Personal Relationships, 6,* 243–257.

Aron, A., & Rodriguez, G. (1992). Scenarios of falling in love among Mexican, Chinese, and Anglo-Americans. In A. Aron (Chair), *Ethnic and cultural differences in love.* Symposium conducted at the Sixth International Conference on Personal Relationships, Orono, ME.

Aron, A., & Westbay, L. (1996). Dimensions of the prototype of love. *Journal of Personality and Social Psychology, 70,* 535–551.

Aron, R. (2002). *The dawn of universal history.* New York: Perseus Books

Aronson, E. (1968). Dissonance theory: Progress and problems. In R. P. Abelson, E. Aronson, W. J. McGuire, T. M. Newcomb, M. J. Rosenberg, & P. H. Tannenbaum (Eds.), *Theories of cognitive consistency: A sourcebook* (pp. 5–27). Chicago: Rand McNally.

Aronson, E. (1969). The theory of cognitive dissonance: A current perspective. In L. Berkowitz (Ed.), *Advances in experimental social psychology* (Vol. 4, pp. 1–34). New York: Academic Press.

Aronson, E. (1990). Applying social psychology to prejudice reduction and energy conservation. *Personality and Social Psychology Bulletin, 16,* 118–132.

Aronson, E. (1992). The return of the repressed: Dissonance theory makes a comeback. *Psychological Inquiry, 3,* 303–311.

Aronson, E. (1997). The theory of cognitive dissonance: The evolution and vicissitudes of an idea. In C. McGarty & S. A. Haslam (Eds.), *The message of social psychology: Perspectives on mind in society* (pp. 20–35). Oxford, England: Blackwell.

Aronson, E. (1998). Dissonance, hypocrisy, and the self-concept. In E. Harmon-Jones & J. S. Mills (Eds.), *Cognitive dissonance theory: Revival with revisions and controversies* (pp. 21–36). Washington, DC: American Psychological Association.

Aronson, E. (1999). *The social animal* (8th ed.). New York: Worth/Freeman.

Aronson, E. (2000). *Nobody left to hate: Teaching compassion after Columbine.* New York: Worth/Freeman.

Aronson, E. (2002) Drifting my own way: Following my nose and my heart. In R. Sternberg (Ed.), *Psychologists defying the crowd: Stories of those who battled the establishment and won* (pp. 132–148). Washington, DC: American Psychological Association.

Aronson, E., & Bridgeman, D. (1979). Jigsaw groups and the desegregated classroom: In pursuit of common goals. *Personality and Social Psychology Bulletin, 5,* 438–446.

Aronson, E., & Carlsmith, J. M. (1962). Performance expectancy as a determinant of actual performance. *Journal of Abnormal and Social Psychology, 65,* 178–182.

Aronson, E., & Carlsmith, J. M. (1963). Effect of severity of threat in the devaluation of forbidden behavior. *Journal of Abnormal and Social Psychology, 66,* 584–588.

Aronson, E., & Carlsmith, J. M. (1968). Experimentation in social psychology. In G. Lindzey & E. Aronson (Eds.), *The handbook of social psychology* (Vol. 2, pp. 1–79). Reading, MA: Addison-Wesley.

Aronson, E., Ellsworth, P. C., Carlsmith, J. M., & Gonzalez, M. H. (1990). *Methods of research in social psychology* (2nd ed.). New York: McGraw-Hill.

Aronson, E., Fried, C., & Stone, J. (1991). Overcoming denial and increasing the intention to use condoms through the induction of hypocrisy. *American Journal of Public Health, 81,* 1636–1638.

Aronson, E., & Gonzalez, A. (1988). Desegregation, jigsaw, and the Mexican-American experience. In P. A. Katz & D. Taylor (Eds.), *Towards the elimination of racism: Profiles in controversy* (pp. 310–330). New York: Plenum.

Aronson, E., & Gonzales, M. H. (1990). The social psychology of energy conservation. In J. Edwards (Ed.), *Social influence processes and prevention* (pp. 48–59). New York: Plenum.

Aronson, E., & Mills, J. S. (1959). The effect of severity of initiation on liking for a group. *Journal of Abnormal and Social Psychology, 59,* 177–181.

Aronson, E., & Patnoe, S. (1997). *Cooperation in the classroom: The jigsaw method.* New York: Longman.

Aronson, E., Stephan, C., Sikes, J., Blaney, N., & Snapp, M. (1978). *The jigsaw classroom.* Beverly Hills, CA: Sage.

Aronson, E., & Thibodeau, R. (1992). The jigsaw classroom: A cooperative strategy for reducing prejudice. In J. Lynch, C. Modgil, & S. Modgil (Eds.), *Cultural diversity in the schools* (pp. 110–118). London: Falmer Press.

Aronson, E., Wilson, T. D., & Brewer, M. B. (1998). Experimental methods. In D. T. Gilbert, S. T. Fiske, & G. Lindzey (Eds.), *The handbook of social psychology* (4th ed., Vol. 1, pp. 99–142). New York: McGraw-Hill.

Aronson, E., & Worchel, P. (1966). Similarity versus liking as determinants of interpersonal attractiveness. *Psychonomic Science, 5,* 157–158.

Aronson, E., & Yates, S. (1985). Social psychological aspects of energy conservation. In D. Hafemeister, H. Kelly, & B. Levi (Eds.), *Energy sources: Conservation and renewables* (pp. 81–91). New York: American Institute of Physics Press.

Aronson, J. M., Cohen, G., & Nail, P. R. (1999). Self-affirmation theory: An update and appraisal. In E. Harmon-Jones & J. S. Mills (Eds.), *Cognitive dissonance: Progress on a pivotal theory in social psychology* (pp. 127–147). Washington, DC: American Psychological Association.

Aronson, J. M., Lustina, M. J., Good, C., Keough, K., Steele, C. M., & Brown, J. (1999). When white men can't do math: Necessary and sufficient factors in stereotype threat. *Journal of Experimental Social Psychology, 35,* 29–46.

Aronson, J. M., Quinn, D., & Spencer, S. (1998). Stereotype threat and the academic underperformance of women and minorities. In J. K. Swim & C. Stangor (Eds.), *Stigma: The target's perspective* (pp. 83–103). San Diego, CA: Academic Press.

Asch, S. E. (1946). Forming impressions of personality. *Journal of Abnormal and Social Psychology, 41,* 258–290.

Asch, S. E. (1951). Effects of group pressure upon the modification and distortion of judgment. In H. Guetzkow (Ed.), *Groups, leadership, and men* (pp. 76–92). Pittsburgh, PA: Carnegie Press.

Asch, S. E. (1955). Opinions and social pressure. *Scientific American, 193,* 31–35.

Asch, S. E. (1956). Studies of independence and conformity: A minority of one against a unanimous majority. *Psychological Monographs, 70*(9, Whole No. 416).

Asch, S. E. (1957). An experimental investigation of group influence. In Walter Reed Army Institute of Research, *Symposium on preventive and social psychiatry* (pp. 15–17). Washington, DC: U.S. Government Printing Office.

Asendorf, J. B., Warkentin, V., & Baudonniere, P. (1996). Self-awareness and other-awareness: II. Mirror self-recognition, social contingency awareness, and synchronic imitation. *Developmental Psychology, 32,* 313–321.

Ashmore, R. D., & Longo, L. C. (1995). Accuracy of stereotypes: What research on physical attractiveness can teach us. In Y.-T. Lee, L. J. Jussim, & C. R. McCauley (Eds.), *Stereotype accuracy: Toward appreciating group difference* (pp. 63–86). Washington, DC: American Psychological Association.

Aspinwall, L. G., & Taylor, S. E. (1993). Effects of social comparison direction, threat, and self-esteem on affect, evaluation, and expected success. *Journal of Personality and Social Psychology, 64,* 708–722.

Aspinwall, L. G., & Taylor, S. E. (1997). A stitch in time: Self-regulation and proactive coping. *Psychological Bulletin, 121,* 417–436.

Aube, J., & Koestner, R. (1995). Gender characteristics and relationship adjustment: Another look at similarity-complementarity hypotheses. *Journal of Personality, 63,* 879–904.

Aune, K. S. & Aune, R. K. (1996). Cultural differences in the self-reported experience and expression of emotions in relationships. *Journal of Cross-Cultural Psychology, 27,* 67–81.

Averill, J. R. (1973). Personal control over aversive stimuli and its relationship to stress. *Psychological Bulletin, 80,* 286–303.

Axelrod, R. (1984). *The evolution of cooperation.* New York: Basic Books.

Azrin, N. H. (1967, May). Pain and aggression. *Psychology Today,* pp. 27–33.

Babad, E. (1993). Pygmalion—25 years after interpersonal expectations in the classroom. In P. D. Blank (Ed.), *Interpersonal expectations: Theory, research, and applications* (pp. 125–153). New York: Cambridge University Press.

Bailey, W. C., & Peterson, R. D. (1997). Murder, capital punishment, and deterrence: A review of the literature. In H. A. Bedau (Ed.), *The death penalty in America: Current controversies* (pp. 135–161). New York: Oxford University Press.

Baldwin, M. W., & Fehr, B. (1995). On the instability of attachment style ratings. *Personal Relationships, 2,* 247–261.

Baldwin, M. W., Keelan, J. P. R., Fehr, B., Enns, V., & Koh-Rangarajoo, E. (1996). Social-cognitive conceptualizations of attachment working models: Availability and accessibility effects. *Journal of Personality and Social Psychology, 71,* 94–109.

Bandura, A. (1973). *Aggression: A social learning analysis.* Englewood Cliffs, NJ: Prentice Hall.

Bandura, A. (1997). *Self-efficacy: The exercise of control.* New York: Freeman.

Bandura, A., Cioffi, D., Taylor, C. B., & Brouillard, M. E. (1988). Perceived self-efficacy in coping with cognitive stressors and opioid activation. *Journal of Personality and Social Psychology, 55,* 479–488.

Bandura, A., & Locke, E. A. (2003). Negative self-efficacy and goal effects revisited. *Journal of Applied Psychology, 88,* 87–99.

Bandura, A., Ross, D., & Ross, S. (1961). Transmission of aggression through imitation of aggressive models. *Journal of Abnormal and Social Psychology, 63,* 575–582.

Bandura, A., Ross, D., & Ross, S. (1963). Imitation of film-mediated aggressive models. *Journal of Abnormal and Social Psychology, 66,* 3–11.

Banks, T., & Dabbs, J. M., Jr. (1996). Salivary testosterone and cortisol in delinquent and violent urban subculture. *Journal of Social Psychology, 136,* 49–56.

Barber, N. (1998). Secular changes in standards of bodily attractiveness in American women: Different masculine and feminine ideals. *Journal of Psychology, 132,* 87–94.

Bargh, J. A. (1994). The four horsemen of automaticity: Awareness, intention, efficiency, and control in social cognition. In R. S. Wyer Jr. & T. K. Srull (Eds.), *Handbook of social cognition* (Vol. 1, pp. 1–40). Hillsdale, NJ: Erlbaum.

Bargh, J. A. (1996). Automaticity in social psychology. In E. T. Higgins & A. W. Kruglanski (Eds.), *Social psychology: Handbook of basic principles* (pp. 169–183). New York: Guilford Press.

Bargh, J. A., & Barndollar, K. (1996). Automaticity in action: The unconscious as repository of chronic goals and motives. In P. M. Gollwitzer & J. A. Bargh (Eds.), *The psychology of action: Linking cognition and motivation to behavior* (pp. 457–481). New York: Guilford Press.

Bargh, J. A., & Chartrand, T. L. (1999). The unbearable automaticity of being. *American Psychologist, 54,* 462–479.

Bargh, J. A., & Ferguson, M. J. (2000). Beyond behaviorism: On the automaticity of higher mental processes. *Psychological Bulletin, 126,* 925–945.

Bargh, J. A., & Pietromonaco, P. (1982). Automatic information processing and social perception: The influence of trait information presented outside of conscious awareness on impression formation. *Journal of Personality and Social Psychology, 43,* 437–449.

Bargh, J. A., & Raymond, P. (1995). The naive misuse of power: Nonconscious sources of sexual harassment. *Journal of Social Issues, 51,* 85–96.

Bargh, J. A., Raymond, P., Pryor, J. B., & Strack, F. (1995). Attractiveness of the underling: An automatic power-sex association and its consequences for sexual harassment and aggression. *Journal of Personality and Social Psychology, 68,* 768–781.

Barker, R., Dembo, T., & Lewin, K. (1941). Frustration and aggression: An experiment with young children. *University of Iowa Studies in Child Welfare, 18,* 1–314.

Barkow, L., Cosmides, L., & Tooby, J. (1992). *The adapted mind: Evolutionary psychology and the generation of culture.* New York: Oxford University Press.

Barley, S. R., & Bechky, B. A. (1994). In the backrooms of science: The work of technicians in science labs. *Work and Occupations, 21,* 85–126.

Baron, L., & Straus, M. A. (1984). Sexual stratification, pornography, and rape. In N. M. Malamuth & E. Donnerstein (Eds.), *Pornography and sexual aggression* (pp. 186–209). New York: Academic Press.

Baron, R. A. (1972). Reducing the influence of an aggressive model: The restraining effects of peer censure. *Journal of Experimental Social Psychology, 8,* 266–275.

Baron, R. A. (1976). The reduction of human aggression: A field study on the influence of incompatible responses. *Journal of Applied Social Psychology, 6,* 95–104.

Baron, R. A. (1988). Negative effects of destructive criticism: Impact on conflict, self-efficacy, and task performance. *Journal of Applied Psychology, 73,* 199–207.

Baron, R. A. (1990). Countering the effects of destructive criticism: The relative efficacy of four interventions. *Journal of Applied Psychology, 75,* 235–245.

Baron, R. A. (1997). The sweet smell of . . . helping: Effects of pleasant ambient fragrance on prosocial behavior in shopping malls. *Personality and Social Psychology Bulletin, 23,* 498–503.

Baron, R. A., & Richardson, D. R. (1994). *Human aggression* (2nd ed.). New York: Plenum.

Baron, R. M., & Misovich, S. J. (1993). Dispositional knowing from an ecological perspective. *Personality and Social Psychology Bulletin, 19,* 541–552.

Baron, R. M., & Rodin, J. (1978). Personal control as a mediator of crowding. In A. Baum, J. S. Singer, & S. Valins (Eds.), *Advances in environmental psychology* (Vol. 1, pp. 145–190). Hillsdale, NJ: Erlbaum.

Baron, R. S. (1986). Distraction/conflict theory: Progress and problems. In L. Berkowitz (Ed.), *Advances in experimental social psychology* (Vol. 19, pp. 1–40). Orlando, FL: Academic Press.

Baron, R. S., Vandello, J. A., & Brunsman, B. (1996). The forgotten variable in conformity research: Impact of task importance on social influence. *Journal of Personality and Social Psychology, 71,* 915–927.

Barrett, L. F., Lane, R. D., Sechrest, L., & Schwartz, G. E. (2000). Sex differences in emotional awareness. *Personality and Social Psychology Bulletin, 26,* 1027–1035.

Bartholomew, R. E., & Wessely, S. (2002). Protean nature of mass sociogenic illness: From possessed nuns to chemical and biological terrorism. *British Journal of Psychiatry, 180,* 300–306.

Bartlett, F. C. (1932). *Remembering.* Cambridge, England: Cambridge University Press.

Bass, B. M. (1990). *Bass and Stogdill's handbook of leadership: Theory, research, and managerial applications* (3rd ed.). New York: Free Press.

Bass, E., & Davis, L. (1994). *The courage to heal: A guide for women survivors of childhood sexual abuse* (3rd ed.). New York: HarperCollins.

Batson, C. D. (1991). *The altruism question: Toward a social-psychological answer.* Hillsdale, NJ: Erlbaum.

Batson, C. D. (1993). Communal and exchange relationships. What's the difference? *Personality and Social Psychology Bulletin, 19,* 677–683.

Batson, C. D. (1998). Altruism and prosocial behavior. In D. T. Gilbert, S. T. Fiske, & G. Lindzey (Eds.), *The handbook of social psychology* (4th ed., Vol. 2, pp. 282–316). New York: McGraw-Hill.

Batson, C. D. (2002). Addressing the altruism question experimentally. In S. G. Post & L. G. Underwood (Eds.), *Altruism and altruistic love: Science, philosophy, and religion in dialogue* (pp. 89–105). Oxford, England: Oxford University Press.

Batson, C. D., & Ahmad, N. (2001). Empathy-induced altruism in a prisoner's dilemma II: What if the target of empathy has defected? *European Journal of Social Psychology, 31,* 25–36.

Batson, C. D., Ahmad, N., Lishner, D. A., & Tsang, J. (2002). Empathy and altruism. In C. R. Snyder & S. J. Lopez (Eds.), *Handbook of positive psychology* (pp. 485–498). New York: Oxford University Press.

Batson, C. D., Coke, J. S., Jasnoski, M. L., & Hanson, M. (1978). Buying kindness: Effect of an extrinsic incentive for helping on perceived altruism. *Personality and Social Psychology Bulletin, 4,* 86–91.

Batson, C. D., Polycarpou, M. P., Harmon-Jones, E., Imhoff, H. J., Mitchener, E. C., Bednar, L. L., Klein, T. R., & Highberger, L. (1997). Empathy and attitudes: Can feeling for a member of a stigmatized group improve feelings toward the group? *Journal of Personality and Social Psychology, 72,* 105–118.

Batson, C. D., & Powell, A. A. (2003). Altruism and prosocial behavior. In T. Millon & M. J. Lerner (Eds.), *Handbook of psychology: Personality and social psychology* (Vol. 5, pp. 463–484). New York: Wiley.

Batson, C. D., Sager, K., Garst, E., Kang, M., Rubchinsky, K., & Dawson, K. (1997). Is empathy-induced helping due to self-other merging? *Journal of Personality and Social Psychology, 73,* 495–509.

Battle for your brain. (1991, August). *Consumer Reports,* pp. 520–521.

Baum, A., Revenson, T. A., & Singer, J. E. (Eds.). (2001). *Handbook of health psychology.* Boulder, CO: NetLibrary.

Baum, A., & Valins, S. (1977). *Architecture and social behavior: Psychological studies of social density.* Hillsdale, NJ: Erlbaum.

Baumeister, R. F. (1991). *Escaping the self: Alcoholism, spirituality, masochism, and other flights from the burden of selfhood.* New York: Basic Books.

Baumeister, R. F. (1998). The self. In D. T. Gilbert, S. T. Fiske, & G. Lindzey (Eds.), *The handbook of social psychology* (4th ed., Vol. 1, pp. 680–740). New York: McGraw-Hill.

Baumeister, R. F., & Hetherington, T. F. (1996). Self-regulation failure: An overview. *Psychological Inquiry, 7,* 1–15.

Baumeister, R. F., & Leary, M. R. (1995). The need to belong: Desire for interpersonal attachment as a fundamental human motivation. *Psychological Bulletin, 117,* 497–529.

Baumeister, R. F., Muraven, M., & Tice, D. M. (2000). Ego depletion: A resource model of volition, self-regulation, and controlled processing. *Social Cognition, 18,* 130–150.

Baumeister, R. F., & Sommer, K.L. (1997). What do men want? Gender differences and two spheres of belongingness: Comment on Cross and Madson (1997). *Psychological Bulletin, 122,* 38–44.

Baumeister, R. F., Stillwell, A. M., & Heatherton, T. F. (1994). Guilt: An interpersonal approach. *Psychological Bulletin, 115,* 243–267.

Baumeister, R. F., & Vohs, K. D. (2003). Self-regulation and the executive function of the self. In M. R. Leary & J. P. Tangney (Eds.), *Handbook of self and identity* (pp. 197–217). New York: Guilford Press.

Baumgardner, A. H., Lake, E. A., & Arkin, R. M. (1985). Claiming mood as a self-handicap. *Personality and Social Psychology Bulletin, 11,* 349–357.

Baxter, L. A. (1986). Gender differences in the heterosexual relationship rules embedded in break-up accounts. *Journal of Social and Personal Relationships, 3,* 289–306.

Bazerman, M., & Neale, M. (1992). *Negotiating rationally.* New York: Free Press.

Beach, S. R. H., Tesser, A., Mendolia, M., & Anderson, P. (1996). Self-evaluation maintenance in marriage: Toward a performance ecology of the marital relationship. *Journal of Family Psychology, 10,* 379–396.

Beaman, A. L., Barnes, P. J., Klentz, B., & McQuirk, B. (1978). Increasing helping rates through informational dissemination: Teaching pays. *Personality and Social Psychology Bulletin, 4,* 406–411.

Beaman, A. L., Klentz, B., Diener, E., & Svanum, S. (1979). Objective self-awareness and transgression in children: A field study. *Journal of Personality and Social Psychology, 37,* 1835–1846.

Beauvois, J., & Joule, R. (1996). *A radical dissonance theory.* London: Taylor & Francis.

Becker, B. J. (1986). Influence again: Another look at studies of gender differences in social influence. In J. S. Hyde & M. C. Linn (Eds.), *The psychology of gender: Advances through meta-analysis* (pp. 178–209). Baltimore: Johns Hopkins University Press.

Bedau, H. A. (Ed.). (1997). *The death penalty in America: Current controversies.* New York: Oxford University Press.

Bell, J. (1995). Notions of love and romance among the Taita of Kenya. In W. Jankowiak (Ed.), *Romantic passion: A universal experience?* (pp. 152–165). New York: Columbia University Press.

Bell, S. T., Kuriloff, P. J., & Lottes, I. (1994). Understanding attributions of blame in stranger-rape and date-rape situations: An examination of gender, race, identification, and students' social perceptions of rape victims. *Journal of Applied Social Psychology, 24,* 1719–1734.

Bem, D. J. (1972). Self-perception theory. In L. Berkowitz (Ed.), *Advances in experimental social psychology* (Vol. 6, pp. 1–62). New York: Academic Press.

Bender, B. (2003, June 15). Scandals rock military academies. *Boston Globe,* p. A10.

Ben-Shakhar, G., & Elaad, E. (2003). The validity of psychophysiological detection of information with the guilty knowledge test: A meta-analytic review. *Journal of Applied Psychology, 88,* 131–151.

Berke, R. L. (2000, September 12). Democrats see, and smell, "rats" in GOP ad. *New York Times on the Web,* http://www.nytimes.com

Berkman, L. F., & Syme, S. L. (1979). Social networks, host resistance, and mortality: A nine-year follow-up study of Alameda County residents. *American Journal of Epidemiology, 109,* 186–204.

Berkow, J. H. (1989). *Darwin, sex, and status: Biological approaches to mind and culture.* Toronto, Ontario, Canada: University of Toronto Press.

Berkowitz, L. (1962). *Aggression: A social psychological analysis.* New York: McGraw-Hill.

Berkowitz, L. (1968, September). Impulse, aggression, and the gun. *Psychology Today,* pp. 18–22.

Berkowitz, L. (1978). Whatever happened to the frustration-aggression hypothesis? *American Behavioral Scientist, 21,* 691–708.

Berkowitz, L. (1981, June). How guns control us. *Psychology Today,* pp. 11–12.

Berkowitz, L. (1983). Aversively simulated aggression. *American Psychologist, 38,* 1135–1144.

Berkowitz, L. (1987). Mood, self-awareness, and willingness to help. *Journal of Personality and Social Psychology, 52,* 721–729.

Berkowitz, L. (1988). Frustrations, appraisals, and aversively stimulated aggression. *Aggressive Behavior, 14,* 3–11.

Berkowitz, L. (1989). Frustration-aggression hypothesis: Examination and reformulation. *Psychological Bulletin, 106,* 59–73.

Berkowitz, L. (1993). *Aggression: Its causes, consequences, and control.* New York: McGraw-Hill.

Berkowitz, L., & Le Page, A. (1967). Weapons as aggression-eliciting stimuli. *Journal of Personality and Social Psychology, 7,* 202–207.

Berkowitz, L., & Troccoli, B., (1990). Feelings, direction of attention, and expressed evaluations of others. *Cognition and Emotion, 4,* 305–325.

Bernard, M. M., Maio, G. R., & Olson, J. M. (2003). The vulnerability of values to attack: Inoculation of values and value-relevant attitudes. *Personality and Social Psychology Bulletin, 29,* 63–75.

Berry, D. S. (1995). Beyond beauty and after affect: An event perception approach to perceiving faces. In R. A. Eder (Ed.), *Craniofacial anomalies: Psychological perspectives* (pp. 14–29). New York: Springer-Verlag.

Berry, J. W. (1967). Independence and conformity in subsistence-level societies. *Journal of Personality and Social Psychology, 7,* 415–418.

Berscheid, E. (1985). Interpersonal attraction. In G. Lindzey & E. Aronson (Eds.), *The handbook of social psychology* (3rd ed., Vol. 3, pp. 413–484). New York: McGraw-Hill.

Berscheid, E., Boye, D., & Walster, E. (1968). Retaliation as a means of restoring equity. *Journal of Personality and Social Psychology, 10,* 370–376.

Berscheid, E., & Meyers, S. A. (1996). A social categorical approach to a question about love. *Personal Relationships, 3,* 19–43.

Berscheid, E., & Meyers, S. A. (1997). The language of love: The difference a preposition makes. *Personality and Social Psychology Bulletin, 23,* 347–362.

Berscheid, E., & Peplau, L. A. (1983). The emerging science of relationships. In H. H. Kelley, E. Berscheid, A. Christensen, J. H. Harvey, T. L. Huston, G. Levinger, E. McClintock, L. A. Peplau, & D. R. Peterson (Eds.), *Close relationships* (pp. 1–19). New York: Freeman.

Berscheid, E., & Reis, H. T. (1998). Attraction and close relationships. In D. T. Gilbert, S. T. Fiske, & G. Lindzey (Eds.), *The handbook of social psychology* (4th ed., Vol. 2, pp. 193–281). New York: McGraw-Hill.

Berscheid, E., & Walster, E. (1978). *Interpersonal attraction.* Reading, MA: Addison-Wesley.

Bettencourt, B. A., & Miller, N. (1996). Gender differences in aggression as a function of provocation: A meta-analysis. *Psychological Bulletin, 119,* 422–447.

Bettencourt, B. A., & Sheldon, K. (2001). Social roles as mechanism for psychological need satisfaction within social groups. *Journal of Personality and Social Psychology, 81,* 1131–1143.

Bickman, L. (1974). The social power of a uniform. *Journal of Applied Social Psychology, 4,* 47–61.

Biehl, M., Matsumoto, D., Ekman, P., Hearn, V., Heider, K., Kudoh, T., & Ton, V. (1997). Matsumoto and Ekman's Japanese and Caucasian facial expressions of emotion (JACFEE): Reliability and cross-national differences. *Journal of Nonverbal Behavior, 21,* 3–21.

Biek, M., Wood, W., & Chaiken, S. (1996). Working knowledge, cognitive processing, and attitudes: On the determinants of bias. *Personality and Social Psychology Bulletin, 22,* 547–556.

Biernat, M., Crandall, C. S., Young, L. V., Kobrynowicz, D., & Halpin, S. M. (1998). All that you can be: Stereotyping of self and others in a military context. *Journal of Personality and Social Psychology, 75,* 301–317.

Biesanz, J. C., Neuberg, S. L., Smith, D. M., Asher, T., & Judice, T. N. (2001). When accuracy-motivated perceivers fail: Limited attentional resources and the reemerging self-fulfilling prophecy. *Personality and Social Psychology Bulletin, 27,* 621–629.

Bjork, J. M., Dougherty, D. M., Moeller, F. G., Cherek, D. R., & Swann, A. C. (1999). The effects of tryptophan depletion and loading on laboratory aggression in men: Time course and a food-restricted control. *Psychopharmacology, 142,* 24–30.

Blader, S. L., & Tyler, T. R. (2003). A four-component model of procedural justice: Defining the meaning of a "fair" process. *Personality and Social Psychology Bulletin, 6,* 747–758.

Blank, P. D. (1993). Interpersonal expectations in the courtroom: Studying judges' and juries' behavior. In P. D. Blank (Ed.), *Interpersonal expectations: Theory, research, and applications* (pp. 64–87). New York: Cambridge University Press.

Blanton, H., Buunk, B. P., Gibbons, F. X., & Kuyper, H. (1999). When better-than-others compare upward: Choice of comparison and comparative evaluation as independent predictors of academic performance. *Journal of Personality and Social Psychology, 76,* 420–430.

Blanton, H., Pelham, B. W., De Hart, T., & Carvallo, M. (2001). Overconfidence as dissonance reduction. *Journal of Experimental Social Psychology, 37,* 373–385.

Blascovich, J., Ginsburg, G. P., & Veach, T. L. (1975). A pluralistic explanation of choice shifts on the risk dimension. *Journal of Personality and Social Psychology, 31,* 422–429.

Blascovich, J., Mendes, W. B., Hunter, S. B., & Salomon, K. (1999). Social "facilitation" as challenge and threat. *Journal of Personality and Social Psychology, 77,* 68–77.

Blascovich, J., Spencer, S. J., Quinn, D., & Steele, C. (2001). African Americans and high blood pressure: The role of stereotype threat. *Psychological Science, 12,* 225–229.

Blass, T. (1991). Understanding behavior in the Milgram obedience experiment. *Journal of Personality and Social Psychology, 60,* 398–413.

Blass, T. (2000). *Obedience to authority: Current perspectives on the Milgram paradigm.* Mahwah, NJ: Erlbaum.

Blass, T. (2003). The Milgram paradigm after 35 years: Some things we now know about obedience to authority. *Journal of Applied Social Psychology,* (in press).

Blau, P. M. (1964). *Exchange and power in social life.* New York: Wiley.

Bless, H., Strack, F., & Walther, E. (2001). Memory as a target of social influence? Memory distortions as a function of social influence and metacognitive knowledge. In J. P. Forgas & W. D. Kipling (Eds.), *Social influence: Direct and indirect processes* (pp. 167–183). Philadelphia: Psychology Press.

Blittner, M., Goldberg, J., & Merbaum, M. (1978). Cognitive self-control factors in the reduction of smoking behavior. *Behavior Therapy, 9,* 553–561.

Bochner, S. (1994). Cross-cultural differences in the self-concept: A test of Hofstede's individualism/collectivism distinction. *Journal of Cross-Cultural Psychology, 25,* 273–283.

Bodenhausen, G. V. (1988). Stereotypic biases in social decision making and memory: Testing process models of stereotype use. *Journal of Personality and Social Psychology, 55,* 726–737.

Bodenhausen, G. V., & Wyer, R. S., Jr. (1985). Effects of stereotypes on decision making and information processing strategies. *Journal of Personality and Social Psychology, 18,* 267–282.

Bond, C., Di Candia, C., & McKinnon, J. R. (1988). Response to violence in a psychiatric setting. *Personality and Social Psychology Bulletin, 14,* 448–458.

Bond, C. F., Jr., & Atoum, A. O. (2000). International deception. *Personality and Social Psychology Bulletin, 26,* 385–395.

Bond, C. F., Jr., Atoum, A. O., & Van Leeuwen, M. D. (1996). Social impairment of complex learning in the wake of public embarrassment. *Basic and Applied Social Psychology, 18,* 31–44.

Bond, C. F., Jr., & Titus, L. J. (1983). Social facilitation: A meta-analysis of 241 studies. *Psychological Bulletin, 94,* 264–292.

Bond, M. H. (Ed.). (1988). *The cross-cultural challenge to social psychology.* Newbury Park, CA: Sage.

Bond, M. H. (1991). Chinese values and health: A culture-level examination. *Psychology and Health, 5,* 137–152.

Bond, M. H. (1996). Chinese values. In M. H. Bond (Ed.), *The handbook of Chinese psychology* (pp. 208–226). Hong Kong: Oxford University Press.

Bond, R., & Smith, P. B. (1996). Culture and conformity: A meta-analysis of studies using Asch's (1952b, 1956) line judgment task. *Psychological Bulletin, 119,* 111–137.

Bonta, B. D. (1997). Cooperation and competition in peaceful societies. *Psychological Bulletin, 121,* 299–320.

Bornstein, R. F. (1989). Exposure and affect: Overview and meta-analysis of research, 1968–1987. *Psychological Bulletin, 106,* 265–289.

Bornstein, R. F., Leone, D. R., & Galley, D. J. (1987). The generalizability of subliminal mere exposure effects: Influence of stimuli perceived without awareness on social behavior. *Journal of Personality and Social Psychology, 53,* 1070–1079.

Bouas, K. S., & Komorita, S. S. (1996). Group discussion and cooperation in social dilemmas. *Personality and Social Psychology Bulletin, 22,* 1144–1150.

Bower, G. H., & Hilgard, E. R. (1981). *Theories of learning* (15th ed.). Englewood Cliffs, NJ: Prentice Hall.

Bowlby, J. (1969). *Attachment and loss: Vol. 1. Attachment.* New York: Basic Books.

Bowlby, J. (1973). *Attachment and loss: Vol. 2. Separation: Anxiety and anger.* New York: Basic Books.

Bowlby, J. (1980). *Attachment and loss: Vol. 3. Loss.* New York: Basic Books.

Boyden, T., Carroll, J. S., & Maier, R. A. (1984). Similarity and attraction in homosexual males: The effects of age and masculinity-femininity. *Sex Roles, 10,* 939–948.

Bradbury, T. N., & Fincham, F. D. (1991). A contextual model for advancing the study of marital relationships. In G. J. O. Fletcher & F. D. Fincham (Eds.), *Cognition in close relationships* (pp. 127–147). Hillsdale, NJ: Erlbaum.

Brandon, R., & Davies, C. (1973). *Wrongful imprisonment: Mistaken convictions and their consequences.* London: Allen & Unwin.

Brannon, L. A., & Brock, T. C. (1994). The subliminal persuasion controversy. In S. Shavitt & T. C. Brock (Eds.), *Persuasion: Psychological insights and perspectives* (pp. 279–293). Needham Heights, MA: Allyn & Bacon.

Branscombe, N. R., Owen, S., Garstka, T. A., & Coleman, J. (1996). Rape and accident counterfactuals: Who might have done otherwise, and would it have changed the outcome? *Journal of Applied Social Psychology, 26,* 1042–1067.

Branscombe, N. R., & Wann, D. L. (1992). Physiological arousal and reactions to outgroup members during competitions that implicate an important social identity. *Aggressive Behavior, 18,* 85–93.

Breckler, S. J., & Wiggins, E. C. (1989). On defining attitude and attitude theory: Once more with feeling. In A. R. Pratkanis, S. J. Breckler, & A. G. Greenwald (Eds.), *Attitude structure and function* (pp. 407–427). Hillsdale, NJ: Erlbaum.

Brehm, J. W. (1956). Postdecision changes in the desirability of alternatives. *Journal of Abnormal and Social Psychology, 52,* 384–389.

Brehm, J. W. (1966). *A theory of psychological reactance.* New York: Academic Press.

Brehm, J. W., & Cohen, A. R. (1962). *Explorations in cognitive dissonance.* New York: Wiley.

Brewer, M. B. (1979). In-group bias in the minimal intergroup situation: A cognitive-motivational analysis. *Psychological Bulletin, 86,* 307–324.

Brewer, M. B., & Brown, R. J. (1998). Intergroup relations. In D. T. Gilbert, S. T. Fiske, & G. Lindzey (Eds.), *The handbook of social psychology* (4th ed., Vol. 2, pp. 554–594). New York: McGraw-Hill.

Brewer, M. B., & Gardner, W. L. (1996). Who is this "we"? Levels of collective identity and self-representations. *Journal of Personality and Social Psychology, 71,* 83–93.

Brewer, M. B., & Miller, N. (1984). Beyond the contact hypothesis: Theoretical perspectives on desegregation. In N. Miller & M. B. Brewer (Eds.), *Groups in contact: The psychology of desegregation* (pp. 281–302). New York: Academic Press.

Bridgeman, D. L. (1981). Enhanced role taking through cooperative interdependence: A field study. *Child Development, 52,* 1231–1238.

Bridges, F. S., & Coady, N. P. (1996). Affiliation, urban size, urgency, and cost of responses to lost letters. *Psychological Reports, 79,* 775–780.

Brinson, L., & Robinson, E. (1991). The African-American athlete: A psychological perspective. In L. Diamant (Ed.), *Psychology of sports, exercise, and fitness* (pp. 249–259). New York: Hemisphere.

Brislin, R. (1993). *Understanding culture's influence on behavior.* Fort Worth, TX: Harcourt Brace.

Bronzaft, A. L. (2002). Noise pollution: A hazard to physical and mental well-being. In R. B. Bechtel & A. Churchman (Eds.), *Handbook of environmental psychology* (pp. 499–510). New York: Wiley.

Brooke, J. (2000, January 20). Canada proposes scaring smokers with pictures on the packs. *New York Times on the Web,* http://www.nytimes.com

Brophy, J. E. (1983). Research on the self-fulfilling prophecy and teacher expectations. *Journal of Educational Psychology, 75,* 631–661.

Brown, R. (1965). *Social psychology.* New York: Free Press.

Brown, R. (1986). *Social psychology* (2nd ed.). New York: Free Press.

Buckhout, R. (1974). Eyewitness testimony. *Scientific American, 231,* 23–31.

Buehler, R., & Griffin, D. W. (1994). Change-of-meaning effects in conformity and dissent: Observing construal processes over time. *Journal of Personality and Social Psychology, 67,* 984–996.

Buehler, R., Griffin, D. W., & Ross, M. (2002). Inside the planning fallacy: The causes and consequences of optimistic time preferences. In T. Gilovich, D. W. Griffin, & D. Kahneman (Eds.), *Heuristics and biases: The psychology of intuitive judgment* (pp. 250–270). New York: Cambridge University Press.

Bugliosi, V. T. (1997). *Outrage: The five reasons why O. J. Simpson got away with murder.* New York: Dell.

Bui, K.-V. T., Peplau, L. A., & Hill, C. T. (1996). Testing the Rusbult model of relationship commitment and stability in a 15-year study of heterosexual couples. *Personality and Social Psychology Bulletin, 22,* 1244–1257.

Burger, J. M. (1981). Motivational biases in the attribution of responsibility for an accident: A meta-analysis of the defensive-attribution hypothesis. *Psychological Bulletin, 90,* 496–512.

Burger, J. M. (1991). Changes in attributions over time: The ephemeral fundamental attribution error. *Social Cognition, 9,* 182–193.

Burger, J. M. (1992). *Desire for control: Personality, social, and clinical perspectives.* New York: Plenum.

Burke, R. J., & Greenglass, E. R. (1990). Type A behavior and non-work activities. *Personality and Individual Differences, 11,* 945–952.

Burleson, B. R. (1994). Friendship and similarities in social-cognitive and communicative abilities: Social skill bases of interpersonal attraction in childhood. *Personal Relationships, 1,* 371–389.

Burleson, B. R., & Samter, W. (1996). Similarity in the communication skills of young adults: Foundations of attraction, friendship, and relationship satisfaction. *Communication Reports, 9,* 127–139.

Burnstein, E., Crandall, C. S., & Kitayama, S. (1994). Some neo-Darwinian decision rules for altruism: Weighing cues for inclusive fitness as a function of the biological importance of the decision. *Journal of Personality and Social Psychology, 67,* 773–789.

Burnstein, E., & Sentis, K. (1981). Attitude polarization in groups. In R. E. Petty, T. M. Ostrom, & T. C. Brock (Eds.), *Cognitive responses in persuasion* (pp. 197–216). Hillsdale, NJ: Erlbaum.

Burnstein, E., & Vinokur, A. (1977). Persuasive argumentation and social comparison as determinants of attitude polarization. *Journal of Experimental Social Psychology, 13,* 315–332.

Burnstein, E., & Worchel, P. (1962). Arbitrariness of frustration and its consequences for aggression in a social situation. *Journal of Personality, 30,* 528–540.

Busby, L. J. (1975). Defining the sex-role standard in commercial network television programming directed at children. *Journalism Quarterly, 51,* 690–696.

Bushman, B. J. (1993). Human aggression while under the influence of alcohol and other drugs: An integrative research review. *Current Directions in Psychological Science, 2,* 148–152.

Bushman, B. J. (1997). Effects of alcohol on human aggression: Validity of proposed explanations. In M. Galanter (Ed.), *Recent developments in alcoholism: Vol. 13. Alcohol and violence: Epidemiology, neurobiology, psychology, family issues* (pp. 227–243). New York: Plenum.

Bushman, B. J. (2002). Does venting anger feed or extinguish the flame? Catharsis, rumination, distraction, anger, and aggressive responding. *Personality and Social Psychology Bulletin, 28,* 724–731.

Bushman, B. J., & Bonacci, A. M. (2002). Violence and sex impair memory for television ads. *Journal of Applied Psychology, 87,* 557–564.

Bushman, B. J., & Cooper, H. M. (1990). Alcohol and human aggression: An integrative research review. *Psychological Bulletin, 107,* 341–354.

Bushman, B. J., & Stack, A. D. (1996). Forbidden fruit versus tainted fruit: Effects of warning labels on attraction to television violence. *Journal of Experimental Psychology: Applied, 2,* 207–226.

Buss, D. M. (1985). Human mate selection. *American Scientist, 73,* 47–51.

Buss, D. M. (1988a). The evolution of human intrasexual competition. *Journal of Personality and Social Psychology, 54,* 616–628.

Buss, D. M. (1988b). Love acts: The evolutionary biology of love. In R. J. Sternberg & M. L. Barnes (Eds.), *The psychology of love* (pp. 110–118). New Haven, CT: Yale University Press.

Buss, D. M. (1989). Sex differences in human mate preferences: Evolutionary hypotheses tested in 37 cultures. *Behavioral and Brain Sciences, 12,* 1–49.

Buss, D. M. (1995). Evolutionary psychology: A new paradigm for psychological science. *Psychological Inquiry, 6,* 1–30.

Buss, D. M. (1996a). The evolutionary psychology of human social strategies. In E. T. Higgins & A. W. Kruglanski (Eds.), *Social psychology: Handbook of basic principles* (pp. 3–38). New York: Guilford Press.

Buss, D. M. (1996b). Sexual conflict: Evolutionary insights into feminism and the "battle of the sexes." In D. M. Buss & N. M. Malamuth (Eds.), *Sex, power, conflict: Evolutionary and feminist perspectives* (pp. 296–318). New York: Oxford University Press.

Buss, D. M. (1999). *Evolutionary psychology: The new science of the mind.* Needham Heights, MA: Allyn & Bacon.

Buss, D. M., Abbott, M., Angleitner, A., Biaggio, A., Blanco-Villasenor, A., Bruchon-Schweitzer, M., et al. (1990). International preferences in selecting mates: A study of 37 cultures. *Journal of Cross-Cultural Psychology, 21,* 5–47.

Buss, D. M., & Barnes, M. L. (1986). Preferences in human mate selection. *Journal of Personality and Social Psychology, 50,* 559–570.

Buss, D. M., & Kenrick, D. T. (1998). Evolutionary social psychology. In D. T. Gilbert, S. T. Fiske, & G. Lindzey (Eds.), *The handbook of social psychology* (4th ed., Vol. 2, pp. 982–1026). New York: McGraw-Hill.

Buss, D. M., Larsen, R. J., Westen, D., & Semmelroth, J. (1992). Sex differences in jealousy: Evolution, physiology, and psychology. *Psychological Science, 3,* 251–255.

Buss, D. M., & Schmitt, D. P. (1993). Sexual strategies theory: An evolutionary perspective on human mating. *Psychological Bulletin, 100,* 204–232.

Buston, P. M., & Emlem, S. T. (2003). Cognitive processes underlying human mate choice: The relationship between self-perception and mate preference in Western society. *Proceedings of the National Academy of Sciences, 100,* 8805–8810.

Butler, D., & Geis, F. L. (1990). Nonverbal affect responses to male and female leaders: Implications for leadership evaluations. *Journal of Personality and Social Psychology, 58,* 48–59.

Butler, E. A., Egloff, B., Wilhelm, F. H., Smith, N. C., & Erickson, E. A. (2003). The social consequences of expressive suppression. *Emotion, 3,* 48–67.

Buunk, B. P., Oldersma, F. L., & de Dreu, C. K. W. (2001). Enhancing satisfaction through downward comparison: The role of relational discontent and individual differences in social comparison orientation. *Journal of Experimental Social Psychology, 37,* 452–467.

Buunk, B. P., & Van Yperen, N. W. (1991). Referential comparisons, relational comparisons, and exchange orientation: Their relation to marital satisfaction. *Personality and Social Psychology Bulletin, 17,* 709–717.

Byrne, D. (1997). An overview (and underview) of research and theory within the attraction paradigm. *Journal of Social and Personal Relationships, 14,* 417–431.

Byrne, D., & Clore, G. L. (1970). A reinforcement model of evaluative processes. *Personality, 1,* 103–128.

Byrne, D., Clore, G. L., & Smeaton, G. (1986). The attraction hypothesis: Do similar attitudes affect anything? *Journal of Personality and Social Psychology, 51,* 1167–1170.

Byrne, D., & Nelson, D. (1965). Attraction as a linear function of positive reinforcement. *Journal of Personality and Social Psychology, 1,* 659–663.

Cacioppo, J. T. (1998). Somatic responses to psychological stress: The reactivity hypothesis. In M. Sabourin & F. Craik (Eds.), *Advances in psychological science: Biological and cognitive aspects* (Vol. 2, pp. 87–112). Hove, England: Psychology Press.

Cacioppo, J. T., Berntson, G. G., Malarkey, W. B., Kiecolt-Glaser, J. K., Sheridan, J. F., Poehlmann, K. M., Burleson, M. H., Ernst, J. M., Hawkley, L. C., & Glaser, R. (1998). Autonomic, neuroendocrine, and immune responses to psychological stress: The reactivity hypothesis. In S. M. McCann & J. M. Lipton (Eds.), *Annals of the New York Academy of Sciences* (Vol. 840, pp. 664–673). New York: New York Academy of Sciences.

Cacioppo, J. T., Marshall-Goodell, B. S., Tassinary, L. G., & Petty, R. E. (1992). Rudimentary determinants of attitudes: Classical conditioning is more effective when prior knowledge about the attitude stimulus is low than high. *Journal of Experimental Social Psychology, 28,* 207–233.

Cacioppo, J. T., Petty, R. E., Feinstein, J., & Jarvis, B. (1996). Dispositional differences in cognitive motivation: The life and times of individuals low versus high in need for cognition. *Psychological Bulletin, 119,* 197–253.

Calder, B. J., & Staw, B. M. (1975). Self perception of intrinsic and extrinsic motivation. *Journal of Personality and Social Psychology, 31,* 599–605.

Caldwell, M., & Peplau, L. A. (1982). Sex differences in same-sex friendship. *Sex Roles, 8,* 721–732.

Calhoun, J. B. (1973). Death squared: The explosive growth and demise of a mouse population. *Proceedings of the Royal Society of Medicine, 66,* 80–88.

Calvert, J. D. (1988). Physical attractiveness: A review and reevaluation of its role in social skill research. *Behavioral Assessment, 10,* 29–42.

Campbell, D. T. (1967). Stereotypes and the perception of group differences. *American Psychologist, 22,* 817–829.

Campbell, D. T., & Stanley, J. C. (1967). *Experimental and quasi experimental designs for research.* Chicago: Rand McNally.

Campbell, E. Q., & Pettigrew, T. F. (1959). Racial and moral crisis: The role of Little Rock ministers. *American Journal of Sociology, 64,* 509–516.

Campbell, J. D., & Fairey, P. J. (1989). Informational and normative routes to conformity: The effect of faction size as a function of norm extremity and attention to the stimulus. *Journal of Personality and Social Psychology, 57,* 457–468.

Canary, D. J., & Stafford, L. (2001). Equity in the preservation of personal relationships. In J. Harvey & A. Wenzel (Eds.), *Close romantic relationships: Maintenance and enhancement* (pp. 133–151). Mahwah, NJ: Erlbaum.

Cannon, W. B. (1932). *The wisdom of the body.* New York: Norton.

Cannon, W. B. (1942). "Voodoo" death. *American Anthropologist, 44,* 169–181.

Cantor, J., Bushman, B. J., Huesmann, L. R., Groebel, J., Malamuth, N. M., Impett, E. A., Donnerstein, E., & Smith, S. (2001). Some hazards of television viewing: Fears, aggression, and sexual attitudes. In D. G. Singer & J. L. Singer (Eds.), *Handbook of children and the media* (pp. 207–307). Thousand Oaks, CA: Sage.

Cantril, H. (1940). *The invasion from Mars: A study in the psychology of panic.* New York: Harper & Row.

Caporael, L. R., & Brewer, M. B. (2000). Metatheories, evolution, and psychology: Once more with feeling. *Psychological Inquiry, 11,* 23–26.

Carey, K. B., & Carey, M. P. (1993). Changes in self-efficacy resulting from unaided attempts to quit smoking. *Psychology of Addictive Behaviors, 7,* 219–224.

Carli, L. L. (1999). Cognitive reconstruction, hindsight, and reactions to victims and perpetrators. *Personality and Social Psychology Bulletin, 25,* 966–979.

Carli, L. L., & Eagly, A. H. (1999). Gender effects on social influence and emergent leadership. In G. N. Powell (Ed.), *Handbook of gender and work* (pp. 203–222). Thousand Oaks, CA: Sage.

Carlsmith, J. M., & Anderson, C. A. (1979). Ambient temperature and the occurrence of collective violence: A new analysis. *Journal of Personality and Social Psychology, 37,* 337–344.

Carlsmith, K. M., Darley, J. M., & Robinson, P. H. (2002). Why do we punish? Deterrence and just deserts as motives for punishment. *Journal of Personality and Social Psychology, 83,* 284–299.

Carlson, J., & Davis, D. M. (1971). Cultural values and the risky shift: A cross-cultural test in Uganda and the United States. *Journal of Personality and Social Psychology, 20,* 392–399.

Carlson, M., Charlin, V., & Miller, N. (1988). Positive mood and helping behavior: A test of six hypotheses. *Journal of Personality and Social Psychology, 55,* 211–229.

Carlson, M., & Miller, N. (1987). Explanation of the relationship between negative mood and helping. *Psychological Bulletin, 102,* 91–108.

Carnevale, P. J. (1986). Strategic choice in mediation. *Negotiation Journal, 2,* 41–56.

Carpenter, S. (2000, December). Why do "they all look alike"? *Monitor on Psychology,* pp. 44–45.

Carter, B. (2000, August 24). "CBS is surprise winner in ratings contest." *New York Times,* p. A22.

Carter, B. (2003, May 19). Even as executives scorn the genre, TV networks still rely on reality. *The New York Times,* p. C1; C7.

Cartwright, D. (1979). Contemporary social psychology in historical perspective. *Social Psychology Quarterly, 42,* 82–93.

Cartwright, D., & Zander, A. (Eds.). (1968). *Group dynamics: Research and theory* (3rd ed.). New York: Harper & Row.

Carver, C. S. (2003). Self-awareness. In M. R. Leary & J. P. Tangney (Eds.), *Handbook of self and identity* (pp. 179–196). New York: Guilford Press.

Carver, C. S., De Gregorio, E., & Gillis, R. (1980). Ego-defensive attribution among two categories of observers. *Personality and Social Psychology Bulletin, 6,* 4–50.

Carver, C. S., & Scheier, M. F. (1981). *Attention and self-regulation: A control-theory approach to human behavior.* New York: Springer-Verlag.

Carver, C. S., & Scheier, M. F. (1998). *On the self-regulation of behavior.* New York: Cambridge University Press.

Carver, C. S., & Scheier, M. (2003). Optimism. In S. J. Lopez & C. R. Snyder (Eds.), *Positive psychological assessment: A handbook of models and measures* (pp. 75–89). Washington DC: American Psychological Association.

Caspi, A., & Harbener, E. S. (1990). Continuity and change: Assortive marriage and the consistency of personality in adulthood. *Journal of Personality and Social Psychology, 58,* 250–258.

Catsambis, S. (1999). The path to math: Gender and racial-ethnic differences in mathematics participation from middle school to high school. In L. A. Peplau & S. C. De Bro (Eds.), *Gender, culture, and ethnicity: Current research about women and men* (pp. 102–120). New York: McGraw-Hill.

Cervone, D., & Peake, P. (1986). Anchoring, efficacy, and action: The influence of judgmental heuristics on self-efficacy judgments and behavior. *Journal of Personality and Social Psychology, 50,* 492–501.

Chaiken, S. (1980). Heuristic versus systematic information processing and the use of source versus message cues in persuasion. *Journal of Personality and Social Psychology, 39,* 752–766.

Chaiken, S. (1987). The heuristic model of persuasion. In M. P. Zanna, J. M. Olson, & C. P. Herman (Eds.), *Social influence: The Ontario Symposium* (Vol. 5, pp. 3–39). Hillsdale, NJ: Erlbaum.

Chaiken, S., & Baldwin, M. W. (1981). Affective-cognitive consistency and the effect of salient behavioral information on the self-perception of attitudes. *Journal of Personality and Social Psychology, 41,* 1–12.

Chaiken, S., Wood, W., & Eagly, A. H. (1996). Principles of persuasion. In E. T. Higgins & A. W. Kruglanski (Eds.), *Social psychology: Handbook of basic principles* (pp. 702–742). New York: Guilford Press.

Chang, C., & Chen, J. (1995). Effects of different motivation strategies on reducing social loafing. *Chinese Journal of Psychology, 37,* 71–81.

Chapman, G. B., & Johnson, E. J. (2002). Incorporating the irrelevant: Anchors in judgments of belief and value. In T. Gilovich, D. W. Griffin, & D. Kahneman (Eds.), *Heuristics and biases: The psychology of intuitive judgment* (pp. 120–138). New York: Cambridge University Press.

Chartrand, T. L., & Bargh, J. A. (1996). Automatic activation of impression formation and memorization goals: Nonconscious goal priming reproduces effects of explicit task instructions. *Journal of Personality and Social Psychology, 71,* 464–478.

Chassin, L., Presson, C. G., & Sherman, S. J. (1990). Social psychological contributions to the understanding and prevention of adolescent cigarette smoking. *Personality and Social Psychology Bulletin, 16,* 133–151.

Check, J. V., & Malamuth, N. M. (1983). Sex role stereotyping and reactions to depictions of stranger versus acquaintance rape. *Journal of Personality and Social Psychology, 45,* 344–356.

Chemers, M. M. (2000). Leadership research and theory: A functional integration. *Group Dynamics: Theory, Research, and Practice, 4,* 27–43.

Chemers, M. M., Watson, C. B., & May, S. T. (2000). Dispositional affect and leadership effectiveness: A comparison of self-esteem, optimism, and efficacy. *Personality and Social Psychology Bulletin, 26,* 267–277.

Chen, M., & Bargh, J. A. (1997). Nonconscious behavioral confirmation processes: The self-fulfilling consequences of automatic stereotype activation. *Journal of Experimental Social Psychology, 33,* 541–560.

Chen, N. Y., Shaffer, D. R., & Wu, C. H. (1997). On physical attractiveness stereotyping in Taiwan: A revised sociocultural perspective. *Journal of Social Psychology, 137,* 117–124.

Chen, S., & Andersen, S. M. (1999). Relationships from the past in the present: Significant-other representations and transference in interpersonal life. In M. P. Zanna (Ed.), *Advances in experimental social psychology* (Vol. 31, pp. 123–190). San Diego, CA: Academic Press.

Chen, S., & Chaiken, S. (1999). The heuristic-systematic model in its broader context. In S. Chaiken & Y. Trope (Eds.), *Dual-process theories in social psychology* (pp. 73–96). New York: Guilford Press.

Cheung, F. M., Leung, K., Fang, R. M., Song, W. Z., Zhang, J. X., & Zhang, J. P. (1996). Development of the Chinese Personality Assessment Inventory (CPAI). *Journal of Cross-Cultural Psychology, 27,* 181–199.

Cheung, S. F., Chan, D. K., & Wong, Z. S. (1999). Reexamining the theory of planned behavior in understanding wastepaper recycling. *Environment and Behavior, 31,* 587–612.

Chipman, S. F. (1996). Still far too sexy a topic. *Behavioral and Brain Sciences, 19,* 248–249.

Chiu, C., Morris, M. W., Hong, Y., & Menon, T. (2000). Motivated cultural cognition: The impact of implicit cultural theories on dispositional attribution varies as a function of need for closure. *Journal of Personality and Social Psychology, 78,* 247–259.

Choi, I., Dalal, R., Kim-Prieto, C., & Park, H. (2003). Culture and judgment of causal relevance. *Journal of Personality and Social Psychology, 84,* 46–59.

Choi, I., & Nisbett, R. E. (1998). Situational salience and cultural differences in the correspondence bias and in the actor-observer bias. *Personality and Social Psychology Bulletin, 24,* 949–960.

Choi, I., & Nisbett, R. E. (2000). Cultural psychology of surprise: Holistic theories and recognition of contradiction. *Journal of Personality and Social Psychology, 79,* 890–905.

Choi, I., Nisbett, R. E., & Norenzayan, A. (1999). Causal attribution across cultures: Variation and universality. *Psychological Bulletin, 125,* 47–63.

Christensen, L. (1988). Deception in psychological research: When is its use justified? *Personality and Social Psychology Bulletin, 14,* 664–675.

Christian, J. J. (1963). The pathology of overpopulation. *Military Medicine, 128,* 571–603.

Christianson, S. (1992). Emotional stress and eyewitness memory: A critical review. *Psychological Bulletin, 112,* 284–309.

Cialdini, R. B. (1993). *Influence: Science and practice* (3rd ed.). New York: HarperCollins.

Cialdini, R. B. (2000). *Influence: Science and practice* (4th ed.). Boston: Allyn & Bacon.

Cialdini, R. B., Borden, R. J., Thorne, A., Walker, M. R., Freeman, S., & Sloan, L. R. (1976). Basking in reflected glory: Three (football) field studies. *Journal of Personality and Social Psychology, 34,* 366–375.

Cialdini, R. B., Brown, S. L., Lewis, B. P., Luce, C., & Neuberg, S. L. (1997). Reinterpreting the empathy-altruism relationship: When one into one equals oneness. *Journal of Personality and Social Psychology, 73,* 481–494.

Cialdini, R. B., Cacioppo, J. T., Basset, R., & Miller, J. (1978). Low-ball procedure for producing compliance: Commitment, then cost. *Journal of Personality and Social Psychology, 36,* 463–476.

Cialdini, R. B., Darby, B. L., & Vincent, J. E. (1973). Transgression and altruism: A case for hedonism. *Journal of Experimental Social Psychology, 9,* 502–516.

Cialdini, R. B., & Fultz, J. (1990). Interpreting the negative mood-helping literature via "mega"-analysis: A contrary view. *Psychological Bulletin, 107,* 210–214.

Cialdini, R. B., Kallgren, C. A., & Reno, R. R. (1991). A focus theory of normative conduct: A theoretical refinement and reevaluation of the role of norms in human behavior. In M. P. Zanna (Ed.), *Advances in experimental social psychology* (Vol. 24, pp. 201–234). San Diego, CA: Academic Press.

Cialdini, R. B., Reno, R. R., & Kallgren, C. A. (1990). A focus theory of normative conduct: Recycling the concept of norms to reduce littering in public places. *Journal of Personality and Social Psychology, 58,* 1015–1026.

Cialdini, R. B., Schaller, M., Houlihan, D., Arps, K., Fultz, J., & Beaman, A. L. (1987). Empathy-based helping: Is it selflessly or selfishly motivated? *Journal of Personality and Social Psychology, 52,* 749–758.

Cialdini, R. B., & Trost, M. R. (1998). Social influence: Social norms, conformity, and compliance. In D. T. Gilbert, S. T. Fiske, & G. Lindzey (Eds.), *The handbook of social psychology* (4th ed., Vol. 2, pp. 151–192). New York: McGraw-Hill.

Clark, K., & Clark, M. (1947). Racial identification and preference in Negro children. In T. M. Newcomb & E. L. Hartley (Eds.), *Readings in social psychology* (pp. 169–178). New York: Holt.

Clark, M. S. (1984). Record keeping in two types of relationships. *Journal of Personality and Social Psychology, 47,* 549–577.

Clark, M. S. (1986). Evidence of the effectiveness of manipulations of communal and exchange relationships. *Personality and Social Psychology Bulletin, 12,* 414–425.

Clark, M. S., & Grote, N. K. (1998). Why aren't indices of relationship costs always negatively related to indices of relationship quality? *Personality and Social Psychology Review, 2,* 2–17.

Clark, M. S., & Isen, A. M. (1982). Toward understanding the relationship between feeling states and social behavior. In A. H. Hastorf & A. M. Isen (Eds.), *Cognitive social psychology* (pp. 73–108). New York: Elsevier.

Clark, M. S., & Mills, J. (1979). Interpersonal attraction in exchange and communal relationships. *Journal of Personality and Social Psychology, 37,* 12–24.

Clark, M. S., & Mills, J. (1993). The difference between communal and exchange relationships: What it is and is not. *Personality and Social Psychology Bulletin, 19,* 684–691.

Clark, M. S., Mills, J., & Corcoran, D. M. (1989). Keeping track of needs and inputs of friends and strangers. *Personality and Social Psychology Bulletin, 15,* 533–542.

Clark, M. S., & Waddell, B. (1985). Perception of exploitation in communal and exchange relationships. *Journal of Social and Personal Relationships, 2,* 403–413.

Clark, R., Anderson, N. B., Clark, V. R., & Williams, D. R. (1999). Racism as a stressor for African Americans. *American Psychologist, 54,* 805–816.

Clark, R. D., III, & Maass, A. (1988). The role of social categorization and perceived source credibility in minority influence. *European Journal of Social Psychology, 18,* 347–364.

Clark, R. D., III, & Word, L. E. (1972). Why don't bystanders help? Because of ambiguity? *Journal of Personality and Social Psychology, 24,* 392–400.

Clarke, V. A., Lovegrove, H., Williams, A., & Macpherson, M. (2000). Unrealistic optimism and the Health Belief Model. *Journal of Behavioral Medicine, 23,* 367–376.

Clary, E. G., Snyder, M., Ridge, R. D., Miene, P. K., & Haugen, J. A. (1994). Matching messages to motives in persuasion: A functional approach to promoting volunteerism. *Journal of Applied Social Psychology, 24,* 1129–1149.

Clement, M., & Hales, D. (1997, September 7). How healthy are we? *Parade*, pp. 4–7.

Cline, V. B., Croft, R. G., & Courrier, S. (1973). Desensitization of children to television violence. *Journal of Personality and Social Psychology, 27*, 360–365.

Clore, G. L., Wyer, R. S., Jr., Dienes, B., Gasper, K., Gohm, C., & Isbell, L. (2001). Affective feelings as feedback: Some cognitive consequences. In L. L. Martin & G. L. Clore (Eds.), *Theories of mood and cognition: A user's guidebook* (pp. 27–62). Mahwah, NJ: Erlbaum.

Coats, E. (1998). *Bystander intervention* [E-mail response to G. Mumford, Tobacco update 3/20/98]. Retrieved from http://www.stolaf.edu/cgi-bin/mailarchivesearch.pl?directory=/home/www/people/huff/SPSP&listname=archive98

Cochran, J. L., & Rutten, T. (1998). *Journey to justice*. New York: Ballantine Books.

Cochran, S. D., & Peplau, L. A. (1985). Value orientation in heterosexual relationships. *Psychology of Women Quarterly, 9*, 477–488.

Cohen, A. R. (1962). An experiment on small rewards for discrepant compliance and attitude change. In J. W. Brehm & A. R. Cohen (Eds.), *Explorations in cognitive dissonance* (pp. 73–78). New York: Wiley.

Cohen, D., Nisbett, R. E., Bowdle, B. F., & Schwarz, N. (1996). Insult, aggression, and the southern culture of honor: An "experimental ethnography." *Journal of Personality and Social Psychology, 70*, 945–960.

Cohen, J. (2001, January 18). On the Internet, love really is blind. *New York Times*, pp. E1, E7.

Cohen, S. (1978). Environmental load and the allocation of attention. In A. Baum, J. S. Singer, & S. Valins (Eds.), *Advances in environmental psychology* (Vol. 1, pp. 1–29). Hillsdale, NJ: Erlbaum.

Cohen, S. (2001). Social relationships and susceptibility to the common cold. In C. D. Ryff & B. H. Singer (Eds.), *Emotion, social relationships, and health* (pp. 221–233). New York: Oxford University Press.

Cohen, S., Evans, G. W., Krantz, D. S., Stokols, D., & Kelly, S. (1981). Aircraft noise and children: Longitudinal and cross-sectional evidence on adaptation to noise and the effectiveness of noise abatement. *Journal of Personality and Social Psychology, 40*, 331–345.

Cohen, S., Glass, D. C., & Singer, J. E. (1973). Apartment noise, auditory discrimination, and reading ability in children. *Journal of Experimental Social Psychology, 9*, 407–422.

Cohen, S., Mermelstein, R., Kamarack, T., & Hoberman, H. (1985). Measuring the functional components of social support. In I. G. Sarason & B. R. Sarason (Eds.)., *Social support: Theory, research, and applications* (pp. 73–94). The Hague, Netherlands: Martines Nijhoff.

Cohen, S., Tyrrell, D. A. J., & Smith, A. P. (1991). Psychological stress in humans and susceptibility to the common cold. *New England Journal of Medicine, 325*, 606–612.

Cohen, S., Tyrrell, D. A. J., & Smith, A. P. (1993). Negative life events, perceived stress, negative affect, and susceptibility to the common cold. *Journal of Personality and Social Psychology, 64*, 131–140.

Cohen, S., & Wills, T. A. (1985). Stress, social support, and buffering. *Psychological Bulletin, 98*, 310–357.

Cohn, L. D. & Adler, N. E. (1992). Female and male perceptions of ideal body shapes. *Psychology of Women Quarterly, 16*, 69–79.

Coie, J. D., Cillessen, A. H. N., Dodge, K. A., Hubbard, J. A., Schwartz, D., Lemerise, E. A., & Bateman, H. (1999). It takes two to fight: A test of relational factors and a method for assessing aggressive dyads. *Developmental Psychology, 35*, 1179–1188.

Colligan, M. J., Pennebaker, J. W., & Murphy, L. R. (Eds.). (1982). *Mass psychogenic illness: A social psychological analysis*. Hillsdale, NJ: Erlbaum.

Collins, B. E., & Brief, D. E. (1995). Using person-perception vignette methodologies to uncover the symbolic meanings of teacher behaviors in the Milgram paradigm. *Journal of Social Issues, 51*, 89–106.

Collins, N. L., & Miller, L. C. (1994). Self-disclosure and liking: A meta-analytic review. *Psychological Bulletin, 116*, 457–475.

Collins, W. A., & Sroufe, L. A. (1999). Capacity for intimate relationships: A developmental construction. In W. Furman, C. Feiring, & B. B. Brown (Eds.), *Contemporary perspectives on adolescent romantic relationships*. New York: Cambridge University Press.

Coltrane, S., Archer, D., & Aronson, E. (1986). The social-psychological foundations of successful energy conservation programs. *Energy Policy, 14*, 133–148.

Condon, J. W., & Crano, W. D. (1988). Inferred evaluation and the relation between attitude similarity and interpersonal attraction. *Journal of Personality and Social Psychology, 54*, 789–797.

Cook, S. W. (1984). Cooperative interaction in multiethnic contexts. In N. Miller & M. B. Brewer (Eds.), *Groups in contact: The psychology of desegregation*. New York: Academic Press.

Cook, S. W. (1985). Experimenting on social issues: The case of school desegregation. *American Psychologist, 40*, 452–460.

Cooper, J. (1980). Reducing fears and increasing assertiveness: The role of dissonance reduction. *Journal of Experimental Social Psychology, 47*, 738–748.

Cosmides, L., & Tooby, J. (1992). Cognitive adaptations for social exchange. In J. H. Barkow, L. Cosmides, & J. Tooby (Eds.), *The adapted mind: Evolutionary psychology and the generation of culture* (pp. 163–228). New York: Oxford University Press.

Costanzo, M., & Archer, D. (1989). Interpreting the expressive behavior of others: The interpersonal perceptions task. *Journal of Nonverbal Behavior, 13*, 223–245.

Cottrell, N. B., Wack, K. L., Sekerak, G. J., & Rittle, R. (1968). Social facilitation in dominant responses by the presence of an audience and the mere presence of others. *Journal of Personality and Social Psychology, 9*, 245–250.

Cousins, S. D. (1989). Culture and self-perception in Japan and the United States. *Journal of Personality and Social Psychology, 56*, 124–131.

Cowan, G., & Campbell, R. R. (1994). Racism and sexism in interracial pornography. *Psychology of Women Quarterly, 18*, 323–338.

Crandall, C. S. (1988). Social contagion of binge eating. *Journal of Personality and Social Psychology, 55*, 588–598.

Crandall, C. S., & Greenfield, B. S. (1986). Understanding the conjunction fallacy: A conjunction of effects? *Social Cognition, 4*, 408–419.

Crites, S. L., Jr., Fabrigar, L. R., & Petty, R. E. (1994). Measuring the affective and cognitive properties of attitudes: Conceptual and methodological issues. *Personality and Social Psychology Bulletin, 20*, 619–634.

Crocker, J., & Major, B. (1989). Social stigma and self-esteem: The self-protective properties of stigma. *Psychological Review, 96*, 608–630.

Cropper, C. M. (1998, February 26). Nowhere to hide: Ads crop up in unlikely places. *New York Times on the Web*, http://www.nytimes.com

Crosby, F., Bromley, S., & Saxe, L. (1980). Recent unobtrusive studies of black and white discrimination and prejudice: A literature review. *Psychological Bulletin, 87*, 546–563.

Cross, S. E., Bacon, P. L., & Morris, M. L. (2000). The relational-interdependent self-construal and relationships. *Journal of Personality and Social Psychology, 78*, 791–808.

Cross, S. E., & Gore, J. S. (2003). Cultural models of the self. In M. R. Leary & J. P. Tangney (Eds.), *Handbook of self and identity* (pp. 536–566). New York: Guilford Press.

Cross, S. E., & Madson, L. (1997). Models of the self: Self-construals and gender. *Psychological Bulletin, 122*, 5–37.

Cross, S. E., & Vick, N. V. (2001). The interdependent self-construal and social support: The case of persistence in engineering. *Personality and Social Psychology Bulletin, 27*, 820–832.

Crowley, A. E., & Hoyer, W. D. (1994). An integrative framework for understanding two-sided persuasion. *Journal of Consumer Research, 20*, 561–574.

Croyle, R. T., & Jemmott, J. B., III. (1990). Psychological reactions to risk factor testing. In J. A. Skelton & R. T. Croyle (Eds.), *The mental representation of health and illness* (pp. 121–157). New York: Springer-Verlag.

Crutchfield, R. A. (1955). Conformity and character. *American Psychologist, 10*, 191–198.

Csikszentmihalyi, M., & Figurski, T. J. (1982). Self-awareness and aversive experience in everyday life. *Journal of Personality, 50*, 15–28.

Cunningham, A. J., Phillips, C., Lockwood, G. A., Hedley, D. W., & Edmonds, C. V. I. (2000). Association of involvement in psychological self-regulation with longer survival in patients with metastatic cancer: An exploratory study. *Advances in Mind-Body Medicine, 16,* 276–286.

Cunningham, M. R. (1986). Measuring the physical in physical attractiveness: Quasi-experiments on the sociobiology of female facial beauty. *Journal of Personality and Social Psychology, 50,* 925–935.

Cunningham, M. R., Barbee, A. P., & Pike, C. L. (1990). What do women want? Facialmetric assessment of multiple motives in the perception of male facial physical attractiveness. *Journal of Personality and Social Psychology, 59,* 61–72.

Cunningham, M. R., Roberts, A. R., Barbee, A. P., Druen, P. B., & Wu, C. (1995). "Their ideas of beauty are, on the whole, the same as ours": Consistency and variability in the cross-cultural perception of female physical attractiveness. *Journal of Personality and Social Psychology, 68,* 261–279.

Curtis, R. C., & Miller, K. (1986). Believing another likes or dislikes you: Behaviors making the beliefs come true. *Journal of Personality and Social Psychology, 51,* 284–290.

Curtiss, S. (1977). *Genie: A psycholinguistic study of a modern-day "wild child."* New York: Academic Press.

Cusumano, D. L., & Thompson, J. K. (1997). Body image and body shape ideals in magazines: Exposure, awareness, and internalization. *Sex Roles, 37,* 701–721.

Dabbs, J. M., Jr. (2000). *Heroes, rogues, and lovers.* New York: McGraw-Hill.

Dabbs, J. M., Jr., Carr, T. S., Frady, R. L., & Riad, J. K. (1995). Testosterone, crime, and misbehavior among 692 male prison inmates. *Personality and Individual Differences, 18,* 627–633.

Dabbs, J. M., Jr., Hargrove, M. F., & Heusel, C. (1996). Testosterone differences among college fraternities: Well-behaved vs. rambunctious. *Personality and Individual Differences, 20,* 157–161.

Dabbs, J. M., Jr., Ruback, R. B., Frady, R. L., Hopper, C. H., & Sgoutas, D. S. (1988). Saliva testosterone and criminal violence among women. *Personality and Individual Differences, 7,* 269–275.

Dalbert, C., & Yamauchi, L. A. (1994). Belief in a just world and attitudes toward immigrants and foreign workers: A cultural comparison between Hawaii and Germany. *Journal of Applied Social Psychology, 24,* 1612–1626.

Dallek, R. (2002, December). The medical ordeals of JFK. *Atlantic,* pp. 49–58.

Darley, J. M. (1992). Social organization for the production of evil. *Psychological Inquiry, 3,* 199–218.

Darley, J. M., & Akert, R. M. (1993). *Biographical interpretation: The influence of later events in life on the meaning of and memory for earlier events.* Unpublished manuscript, Princeton University.

Darley, J. M., & Batson, C. D. (1973). From Jerusalem to Jericho: A study of situational and dispositional variables in helping behavior. *Journal of Personality and Social Psychology, 27,* 100–108.

Darwin, C. R. (1859). *The origin of species.* London: Murray.

Darwin, C. R. (1872). *The expression of the emotions in man and animals.* London: Murray.

Davidson, A. R., & Jaccard, J. J. (1979). Variables that moderate the attitude-behavior relation: Results of a longitudinal survey. *Journal of Personality and Social Psychology, 37,* 1364–1376.

Davidson, L., & Duberman, L. (1982). Friendship: Communication and interactional patterns in same-sex dyads. *Sex Roles, 8,* 809–822.

Davidson, R., Putnam, K., & Larson, C. (2000). Dysfunction in the neural circuitry of emotion regulation: A possible prelude to violence. *Science, 289,* 591–594.

Davies, M. F. (1997). Belief persistence after evidential discrediting: The impact of generated versus provided explanations on the likelihood of discredited outcomes. *Journal of Experimental Social Psychology, 33,* 561–578.

Davies, P. G., Spencer, S. J., Quinn, D. M., & Gerhardstein, R. (2002). Consuming images: How television commercials that elicit stereotype threat can restrain women academically and professionally. *Personality and Social Psychology Bulletin, 28,* 1615–1628.

Davis, C. G., Lehman, D. R., Wortman, C. B., Silver, R. C., & Thompson, S. C. (1995). The undoing of traumatic life events. *Personality and Social Psychology Bulletin, 21,* 109–124.

Davis, D. D., & Harless, D. W. (1996). Group versus individual performance in a price-searching experiment. *Organizational Behavior and Human Decision Processes, 66,* 215–227.

Davis, J. H., Kerr, N. L., Atkin, R. S., Holt, R., & Meek, D. (1975). The decision processes of 6- and 12-person mock juries assigned unanimous and two-thirds majority rules. *Journal of Personality and Social Psychology, 32,* 1–14.

Davis, K. E., & Jones, E. E. (1960). Changes in interpersonal perception as a means of reducing cognitive dissonance. *Journal of Abnormal and Social Psychology, 61,* 402–410.

Davis, M. H., & Stephan, W. G. (1980). Attributions for exam performance. *Journal of Applied Social Psychology, 10,* 235–248.

Davitz, J. (1952). The effects of previous training on post-frustration behavior. *Journal of Abnormal and Social Psychology, 47,* 309–315.

Dawes, R. M. (1980). Social dilemmas. *Annual Review of Psychology, 31,* 169–193.

Dawkins, R. (1976). *The selfish gene.* New York: Oxford University Press.

Dean, K. E., & Malamuth, N. M. (1997). Characteristics of men who aggress sexually and of men who imagine aggressing: Risk and moderating variables. *Journal of Personality and Social Psychology, 72,* 449–455.

Deaux, K., & Emsweiler, T. (1974). Explanations of successful performance of sex-linked tasks: What is skill for the male is luck for the female. *Journal of Personality and Social Psychology, 29,* 80–85.

Deaux, K., & La France, M. (1998). Gender. In D. T. Gilbert, S. T. Fiske, & G. Lindzey (Eds.), *The handbook of social psychology* (4th ed., Vol. 1, pp. 788–828). New York: McGraw-Hill.

Deaux, K., & Lewis, L. (1984). Structure of gender stereotypes: Interrelationships among components and gender label. *Journal of Personality and Social Psychology, 46,* 991–1004.

Deaux, K., & Major, B. (1987). Putting gender into context: An interactive model of gender-related behavior. *Psychological Review, 94,* 369–389.

De Bono, K. G., & Snyder, M. (1995). Acting on one's attitudes: The role of a history of choosing situations. *Personality and Social Psychology Bulletin, 21,* 629–636.

Deci, E. L., Koestner, R., & Ryan, R. M. (1999a). A meta-analytic review of experiments examining the effects of extrinsic rewards. *Psychological Bulletin, 125,* 627–668.

Deci, E. L., Koestner, R., & Ryan, R. M. (1999b). The undermining effect is a reality after all—extrinsic rewards, task interest, and self-determination: Reply to Eisenberger, Pierce, and Cameron (1999) and Lepper, Henderlong, and Gingras (1999). *Psychological Bulletin, 125,* 692–700.

Deci, E. L., & Ryan, R. M. (1985). *Intrinsic motivation and self-determination in human behavior.* New York: Plenum.

De Cremer, D. (2002). Respect and cooperation in social dilemmas: The importance of feeling included. *Personality and Social Psychology Bulletin, 28,* 1335–1341.

De Dreu, C. K. W., Weingart, L. R., & Kwon, S. (2000). Influence of social motives on integrative negotiation: A meta-analytic review and test of two theories. *Journal of Personality and Social Psychology, 78,* 889–905.

De Houwer, J., Baeyens, F., & Eelen, P. (1994). Verbal evaluative conditioning with undetected U.S. presentations. *Behavioral Research and Therapy, 32,* 629–633.

De Marco, P. (1994, September 28). "Dear diary." *New York Times,* p. C2.

De Paulo, B. M. (1992). Nonverbal behavior and self-presentation. *Psychological Bulletin, 111,* 203–243.

De Paulo, B. M., Epstein, J. A., & Wyer, M. M. (1993). Sex differences in lying: How women and men deal with the dilemma of deceit. In M. Lewis & C. Saarni (Eds.), *Lying and deception in everyday life* (pp. 126–147). New York: Guilford Press.

De Paulo, B. M., & Friedman, H. S. (1998). Nonverbal communication. In D. T. Gilbert, S. T. Fiske, & G. Lindzey (Eds.), *The handbook of social psychology* (4th ed., Vol. 2, pp. 3–40). New York: McGraw-Hill.

De Paulo, B. M., Kenny, D. A., Hoover, C. W., Webb, W., & Oliver, P. (1987). Accuracy of person perception: Do people know what kinds of impressions they convey? *Journal of Personality and Social Psychology, 52,* 303–315.

De Paulo, B. M., Lassiter, G. D., & Stone, J. I. (1983). Attentional determinants of success at detecting deception and truth. *Personality and Social Psychology Bulletin, 8,* 273–279.

De Paulo, B. M., Stone, J. I., & Lassiter, G. D. (1985). Deceiving and detecting deceit. In B. R. Schlenker (Ed.), *The self and social life* (pp. 323–370). New York: McGraw-Hill.

Deppe, R. K., & Harackiewicz, J. M. (1996). Self-handicapping and intrinsic motivation: Buffering intrinsic motivation from the threat of failure. *Journal of Personality and Social Psychology, 70,* 868–876.

Dershowitz, A. M. (1997). *Reasonable doubts: The criminal justice system and the O. J. Simpson case.* New York: Touchstone.

Derzon, J. H., & Lipsey, M. W. (2002). A meta-analysis of the effectiveness of mass communication for changing substance-use knowledge, attitudes, and behavior. In W. D. Crano & M. Burgoon (Eds.), *Mass media and drug prevention: Classic and contemporary theories and research* (pp. 231–258). Mahwah, NJ: Erlbaum.

Desmond, E. W. (1987, November 30). Out in the open. *Time,* pp. 80–90.

Desportes, J. P., & Lemaine, J. M. (1998). The sizes of human groups: An analysis of their distributions. In D. Canter, J. C. Jesuino, L. Soczka, & G. M. Stephenson (Eds.), *Environmental social psychology* (pp. 57–65). Dordrecht, Netherlands: Kluwer.

Deutsch, M. (1973). *The resolution of conflict: Constructive and destructive processes.* New Haven, CT: Yale University Press.

Deutsch, M. (1990). Cooperation, conflict, and justice. In S. A. Wheelan, E. A. Pepitone, & V. Abt (Eds.), *Advances in field theory* (pp. 149–164). Newbury Park, CA: Sage.

Deutsch, M. (1997, April). *Comments on cooperation and prejudice reduction.* Paper presented at the symposium Reflections on 100 Years of Social Psychology, Yosemite National Park, CA.

Deutsch, M., & Collins, M. E. (1951). *Interracial housing: A psychological evaluation of a social experiment.* Minneapolis: University of Minnesota Press.

Deutsch, M., & Gerard, H. G. (1955). A study of normative and informational social influence upon individual judgment. *Journal of Abnormal and Social Psychology, 51,* 629–636.

Deutsch, M., & Krauss, R. M. (1960). The effect of threat upon interpersonal bargaining. *Journal of Abnormal and Social Psychology, 61,* 181–189.

Deutsch, M., & Krauss, R. M. (1962). Studies of interpersonal bargaining. *Journal of Conflict Resolution, 6,* 52–76.

de Veer, M. W., Gallup, G. G., Jr., Theall, L. A., van den Bos, R., & Povinelli, D. J. (2003). An 8-year longitudinal study of mirror self-recognition in chimpanzees (*Pan troglodytes*). *Neuropsychologia, 41,* 229–234.

Devine, D. J., Clayton, L. D., Dunford, B. B., Seying, R., & Pryce, J. (2001). Jury decision making: 45 years of empirical research on deliberating groups. *Psychology, Public Policy, and Law, 7,* 622–727.

Devine, P. G. (1989a). Automatic and controlled processes in prejudice: The roles of stereotypes and personal beliefs. In A. R. Pratkanis, S. J. Breckler, & A. G. Greenwald (Eds.), *Attitude structure and function* (pp. 181–212). Hillsdale, NJ: Erlbaum.

Devine, P. G. (1989b). Stereotypes and prejudice: Their automatic and controlled components. *Journal of Personality and Social Psychology, 56,* 680–690.

Devine, P. G., & Elliot, A. (1995). Are racial stereotypes really fading? The Princeton trilogy revisited. *Personality and Social Psychology Bulletin, 21,* 1139–1150.

Devine, P. G., & Monteith, M. J. (1999). Automaticity and control in stereotyping. In S. Chaiken & Y. Trope (Eds.), *Dual-process theories in social psychology* (pp. 339–360). New York: Guilford Press.

Devos-Comby, L., & Salovey, P. (2002). Applying persuasion strategies to alter HIV-relevant thoughts and behavior. *Review of General Psychology, 6,* 287–304.

De Waal, F. B. M. (1996). *Good natured: The origins of right and wrong in humans and other animals.* Cambridge, MA: Harvard University Press.

Dickerson, C., Thibodeau, R., Aronson, E., & Miller, D. (1992). Using cognitive dissonance to encourage water conservation. *Journal of Applied Social Psychology, 22,* 841–854.

Diener, E. (1980). Deindividuation: The absence of self-awareness and self-regulation in group members. In P. B. Paulus (Ed.), *Psychology of group influence* (pp. 209–242). Hillsdale, NJ: Erlbaum.

Diener, E., & Wallbom, M. (1976). Effects of self-awareness on antinormative behavior. *Journal of Research in Personality, 10,* 107–111.

Dietz, P. D., & Evans, B. E. (1982). Pornographic imagery and prevalence of paraphilia. *American Journal of Psychiatry, 139,* 1493–1495.

Dijksterhuis, A., & Aarts, H. (2002). *The power of the subliminal: On subliminal persuasion and other potential applications.* Unpublished manuscript.

Dijksterhuis, A., & van Knippenberg, A. (1996). The knife that cuts both ways: Facilitated and inhibited access to traits as a result of stereotype activation. *Journal of Experimental Social Psychology, 32,* 271–288.

Dill, J. C., & Anderson, C. A. (1995). Effects of frustration justification on hostile aggression. *Aggressive Behavior, 21,* 359–369.

Dion, K., Berscheid, E., & Walster, E. (1972). What is beautiful is good. *Journal of Personality and Social Psychology, 24,* 285–290.

Dion, K. K., & Dion, K. L. (1993). Individualistic and collectivistic perspectives on gender and the cultural context of love and intimacy. *Journal of Social Issues, 49,* 53–69.

Dion, K. K., & Dion, K. L. (1996). Cultural perspectives on romantic love. *Personal Relationships, 3,* 5–17.

Dion, K. L. (2000). Group cohesion: From "fields of forces" to multidimensional construct. *Group Dynamics, 4,* 7–26.

Dion, K. L., & Dion, K. K. (1988). Romantic love: Individual and cultural perspectives. In R. J. Sternberg & M. L. Barnes (Eds.), *The psychology of love* (pp. 264–289). New Haven, CT: Yale University Press.

Dion, K. L., & Dion, K. K. (1993). Gender and ethnocultural comparisons in styles of love. *Psychology of Women Quarterly, 17,* 463–473.

Dix, T. (1993). Attributing dispositions to children: An interactional analysis of attribution in socialization. *Personality and Social Psychology Bulletin, 19,* 633–643.

Dodge, K. A., & Schwartz, D. (1997). Social information processing mechanisms in aggressive behavior. In D. M. Stoff & J. Breiling (Eds.), *Handbook of antisocial behavior* (pp. 171–180). New York: Wiley.

Doi, T. (1988). *The anatomy of dependence.* New York: Kodansha International.

Dolinsky, D. (2000). On inferring one's beliefs from one's attempts and consequences for subsequent compliance. *Journal of Personality and Social Psychology, 78,* 260–272.

Dollard, J. (1938). Hostility and fear in social life. *Social Forces, 17,* 15–26.

Dollard, J., Doob, L., Miller, N., Mowrer, O. H., & Sears, R. R. (1939). *Frustration and aggression.* New Haven, CT: Yale University Press.

Domina, T., & Koch, K. (2002). Convenience and frequency of recycling: Implications for including textiles in curbside recycling programs. *Environment and Behavior, 34,* 216–238.

Donnerstein, E. (1980). Aggressive erotica and violence against women. *Journal of Personality and Social Psychology, 39,* 269–277.

Donnerstein, E., & Berkowitz, L. (1981). Victim reactions in aggressive erotic films as a factor in violence against women. *Journal of Personality and Social Psychology, 41,* 710–724.

Donnerstein, E., & Donnerstein, M. (1976). Research in the control of interracial aggression. In R. G. Green & E. C. O'Neal (Eds.), *Perspectives on aggression* (pp. 133–168). New York: Academic Press.

Donnerstein, E., & Linz, D. G. (1994). Sexual violence in the mass media. In M. Costanzo & S. Oskamp (Eds.), *Violence and the law* (pp. 9–36). Thousand Oaks, CA: Sage.

Dougherty, M. R. P., Gettys, C. F., & Ogden, E. E. (1999). MINERVA-DM: A memory process model of judgments of likelihood. *Psychological Review, 106,* 180–209.

Dovidio, J. F. (1984). Helping behavior and altruism: An empirical and conceptual overview. In L. Berkowitz (Ed.), *Advances in experimental social psychology* (Vol. 17, pp. 361–427). New York: Academic Press.

Dovidio, J. F., Evans, N., & Tyler, R. B. (1986). Racial stereotypes: The contents of their cognitive representations. *Journal of Experimental Social Psychology, 22,* 22–37.

Dovidio, J. F., & Gaertner, S. L. (1996). Affirmative action, unintentional racial biases, and intergroup relations. *Journal of Social Issues, 52,* 51–75.

Dovidio, J. F., Kawakami, K., & Gaertner, S. L. (2002). Implicit and explicit prejudice and interracial interaction. *Journal of Personality and Social Psychology, 82,* 62–68.

Dovidio, J. F., Piliavin, J. A., Gaertner, S. L., Schroeder, D. A., & Clark, R. D., III. (1991). The arousal cost-reward model and the process of intervention. In M. S. Clark (Ed.), *Review of personality and social psychology* (Vol. 12, pp. 86–118). Newbury Park, CA: Sage.

Dowd, E. T., Hughes, S., Brockbank, L., Halpain, D., Seibel, C., & Seibel, P. (1988). Compliance-based and defiance-based intervention strategies and psychological reactance in the treatment of free and unfree behavior. *Journal of Counseling Psychology, 35,* 363–369.

Drigotas, S. M., & Rusbult, C. E. (1992). Should I stay or should I go? A dependence model of breakups. *Journal of Personality and Social Psychology, 62,* 62–87.

Driving while black. (1999, March 15). *U.S. News and World Report,* p. 72.

Drummond, T. (1999, June 14). It's not just in New Jersey: Cops across the nation often search people because of their race, a study says. *Time,* p. 61.

Duck, J., Hogg, M., & Terry, D. (1995). Me, us, and them: Political identification and the third-person effect in the 1993 Australian federal election. *European Journal of Social Psychology, 25,* 195–215.

Duck, S. W. (1982). A typography of relationship disengagement and dissolution. In S. W. Duck (Ed.), *Personal relationships 4: Dissolving personal relationships* (pp. 1–32). London: Academic Press.

Duck, S. W. (1994a). *Meaningful relationships: Talking, sense, and relating.* Thousand Oaks, CA: Sage.

Duck, S. W. (1994b). Stratagems, spoils, and a serpent's tooth: On the delights and dilemmas of personal relationships. In B. H. Spitzberg & W. Cupach (Eds.), *The dark side of interpersonal communication* (pp. 3–24). Hillsdale, NJ: Erlbaum.

Duck, S. W., & Pittman, G. (1994). Social and personal relationships. In M. L. Knapp & G. R. Miller (Eds.), *Handbook of interpersonal communication* (2nd ed., pp. 676–695). Thousand Oaks, CA: Sage.

Duke, the ex-Nazi who would be governor. (1991, November 10). *New York Times,* pp. 1, 26.

Dunn, D. S., & Wilson, T. D. (1990). When the stakes are high: A limit to the illusion of control effect. *Social Cognition, 8,* 305–323.

Dunning, D., & Hayes, A. F. (1996). Evidence of egocentric comparison in social judgment. *Journal of Personality and Social Psychology, 71,* 213–229.

Dunning, D., & Stern, L. B. (1994). Distinguishing accurate from inaccurate eyewitness identifications via inquiries about decision processes. *Journal of Personality and Social Psychology, 67,* 818–835.

During blackout, fewer crimes than on a typical NYPD day. (2003, August 16). Retrieved from http://www.wnbc.com/news/2409267/detail.html

Dutton, D. G., & Aron, A. P. (1974). Some evidence for heightened sexual attraction under conditions of high anxiety. *Journal of Personality and Social Psychology, 30,* 510–517.

Duval, T. S., & Silvia, P. J. (2001). *Self-awareness and causal attributions: A dual-systems theory.* Boston: Kluwer Academic.

Duval, T. S., & Silvia, P. J. (2002). Self-awareness, probability of improvement, and the self-serving bias. *Journal of Personality and Social Psychology, 82,* 49–61.

Duval, T. S., & Wicklund, R. A. (1972). *A theory of objective self-awareness.* New York: Academic Press.

Dweck, C. S. (1999). *Self-theories: Their role in motivation, personality, and development.* Philadelphia: Psychology Press.

Dweck, C. S., Chiu, C., & Hong, Y. (1995). Implicit theories and their role in judgments and reactions: A world from two perspectives. *Psychological Inquiry, 6,* 267–285.

Dweck, C. S., Higgins, E. T., & Grant-Pillow, H. (2003). Self-systems give unique meaning to self variables. In M. R. Leary & J. P. Tangney (Eds.), *Handbook of self and identity* (pp. 239–252). New York: Guilford Press.

Eagly, A. H. (1987). *Sex differences in social behavior: A social-role interpretation.* Hillsdale, NJ: Erlbaum.

Eagly, A. H. (1994). On comparing women and men. *Feminism and Psychology, 4,* 513–522.

Eagly, A. H. (1995). The science and politics of comparing women and men. *American Psychologist, 50,* 145–158.

Eagly, A. H. (1996). Differences between women and men: Their magnitude, practical importance, and political meaning. *American Psychologist, 51,* 158–159.

Eagly, A. H., Ashmore, R. D., Makhijani, M. G., & Longo, L. C. (1991). What is beautiful is good, but . . . : A meta-analytic review of research on the physical attractiveness stereotype. *Psychological Bulletin, 110,* 109–128.

Eagly, A. H., & Carli, L. L. (1981). Sex of researchers and sex-typed communications as determinants of sex differences in influenceability: A meta-analysis of social influence studies. *Psychological Bulletin, 90,* 1–20.

Eagly, A. H., & Chaiken, S. (1975). An attribution analysis of communicator characteristics on opinion change: The case of communicator attractiveness. *Journal of Personality and Social Psychology, 32,* 136–244.

Eagly, A. H., & Chaiken, S. (1993). *The psychology of attitudes.* Fort Worth, TX: Harcourt Brace.

Eagly, A. H., & Chaiken, S. (1998). Attitude structure and function. In D. T. Gilbert, S. T. Fiske, & G. Lindzey (Eds.), *The handbook of social psychology* (4th ed., Vol. 1, pp. 269–322). New York: McGraw-Hill.

Eagly, A. H., & Crowley, M. (1986). Gender and helping behavior: A meta-analytic review of the social psychological literature. *Psychological Bulletin, 100,* 283–308.

Eagly, A. H., & Karau, S. J. (2002). Role congruity theory of prejudice toward female leaders. *Psychological Review, 109,* 573–598.

Eagly, A. H., Karau, S. J., & Makhijani, M. G. (1995). Gender and the effectiveness of leaders: A meta-analysis. *Psychological Bulletin, 117,* 125–145.

Eagly, A. H., Makhijani, M. G., & Klonsky, B. G. (1992). Gender and the evaluation of leaders: A meta-analysis. *Psychological Bulletin, 111,* 3–22.

Eagly, A. H., & Steffen, V. J. (1986). Gender and aggressive behavior: A meta-analytic review of the social psychological literature. *Psychological Bulletin, 100,* 309–330.

Eagly, A. H., & Steffen, V. J. (2000). Gender stereotypes stem from the distribution of women and men into social roles. In C. Stangor (Ed.), *Stereotypes and prejudice: Essential readings* (pp. 142–160). Philadelphia: Psychology Press.

Eagly, A. H., & Wood, W. (1991). Explaining sex differences in social behavior: A meta-analytic perspective. *Personality and Social Psychology Bulletin, 17,* 306–315.

Eargle, A., Guerra, N., & Tolan, P. (1994). Preventing aggression in inner-city children: Small group training to change cognitions, social skills, and behavior. *Journal of Child and Adolescent Group Therapy, 4,* 229–242.

Ebbesen, E., Duncan, B., & Konecni, V. (1975). Effects of content of verbal aggression: A field experiment. *Journal of Experimental and Social Psychology, 11,* 192–204.

Educators for Social Responsibility. (2001). *About the Resolving Conflict Creatively Program.* Retrieved from http://www.esrnational.org/about-rccp.html

Edwards, H. (1973, July). The black athletes: 20th-century gladiators in white America. *Psychology Today,* pp. 43–52.

Edwards, K., & Smith, E. (1996). A disconfirmation bias in the evaluation of arguments. *Journal of Personality and Social Psychology, 71,* 5–24.

Eibl-Eibesfeldt, I. (1963). Aggressive behavior and ritualized fighting in animals. In J. H. Masserman (Ed.), *Science and psychoanalysis: Vol. 6. Violence and war* (pp. 8–17). New York: Grune & Stratton.

Eisenberg, N., & Fabes, R. A. (1991). Prosocial behavior and empathy: A multimethod developmental perspective. In M. S. Clark (Ed.), *Review of personality and social psychology* (Vol. 12, pp. 34–61). Newbury Park, CA: Sage.

Eisenberg, N., Guthrie, I. K., Cumberland, A., Murphy, B. C., Shepard, S. A., Zhou, Q., & Carlo, G. (2002). Prosocial development in early adulthood: A longitudinal study. *Journal of Personality and Social Psychology, 82,* 993–1006.

Eisenstat, S. A., & Bancroft, L. (1999). Domestic violence. *New England Journal of Medicine, 341,* 886–892.

Ekman, P. (1965). Communication through nonverbal behavior: A source of information about an interpersonal relationship. In S. S. Tomkins & C. E. Izard (Eds.), *Affect, cognition, and personality* (pp. 390–442). New York: Springer-Verlag.

Ekman, P. (1993). Facial expression and emotion. *American Psychologist, 48,* 384–392.

Ekman, P. (1994). Strong evidence for universals in facial expressions: A reply to Russell's mistaken critique. *Psychological Bulletin, 115,* 268–287.

Ekman, P. (2002). *Telling lies: Clues to deceit in the marketplace, politics, and marriage.* New York: Norton.

Ekman, P., & Davidson, R. J. (Eds.). (1994). *The nature of emotion: Fundamental questions.* New York: Oxford University Press.

Ekman, P., & Friesen, W. V. (1969). The repertoire of nonverbal behavior: Categories, origins, usage, and coding. *Semiotica, 1,* 49–98.

Ekman, P., & Friesen, W. V. (1971). Constants across cultures in the face and emotion. *Journal of Personality and Social Psychology, 17,* 124–129.

Ekman, P., & Friesen, W. V. (1975). *Unmasking the face.* Englewood Cliffs, NJ: Prentice Hall.

Ekman, P., Friesen, W. V., O'Sullivan, M., Chan, A., Diacoyanni-Tarlatzis, I., Heider, K., et al. (1987). Universals and cultural differences in the judgments of facial expressions of emotions. *Journal of Personality and Social Psychology, 53,* 712–717.

Ekman, P., O'Sullivan, M., & Frank, M. G. (1999). A few can catch a liar. *Psychological Science, 10,* 263–266.

Ekman, P., O'Sullivan, M., & Matsumoto, D. (1991). Confusions about content in the judgment of facial expression: A reply to "Contempt and the relativity thesis." *Motivation and Emotion, 15,* 169–176.

Elfenbein, H. A., & Ambady, N. (2002). On the universality and cultural specificity of emotion recognition: A meta-analysis. *Psychological Bulletin, 128,* 203–235.

Ellin, A. (2000, September 17). Dad, do you think I look too fat? *New York Times,* p. 7.

Elliot, J. (1977). The power and pathology of prejudice. In P. Zimbardo & F. Ruch (Eds.), *Psychology and life* (9th ed.). Glenview, IL: Scott, Foresman.

Ellsworth, P. C. (1994). William James and emotion: Is a century of fame worth a century of misunderstanding? *Psychological Review, 101,* 222–229.

Ellsworth, P. C., & Mauro, R. (1998). Psychology and law. In D. T. Gilbert, S. T. Fiske, & G. Lindzey (Eds.), *The handbook of social psychology* (4th ed., Vol. 2, pp. 684–732). New York: McGraw Hill.

Englich, B., & Mussweiler, T. (2001). Sentencing under uncertainty: Anchoring effects in the courtroom. *Journal of Applied Social Psychology, 31,* 1535–1551.

Ennis, M., Kelly, K. S., & Lambert, P. L. (2001). Sex differences in cortisol excretion during anticipation of a psychological stressor: Possible support for the tend-and-befriend hypothesis. *Stress and Health, 17,* 253–261.

Epley, E., & Huff, C. (1998). Suspicion, affective response, and education benefit as a result of deception in psychology research. *Personality and Social Psychology Bulletin, 24,* 759–768.

Epley, N., & Dunning, D. (2000). Feeling "holier than thou": Are self-serving assessments produced by errors in self- or social-prediction?. *Journal of Personality and Social Psychology, 79,* 861–875.

Epley, N., & Gilovich, T. (2001). Putting the adjustment back in the anchoring and adjustment heuristic: Differential processing of self-generated and experimenter-provided anchor. *Psychological Science, 12,* 391–396.

Epley, N., Savitsky, K., & Gilovich, T. (2002). Empathy neglect: Reconciling the spotlight effect and the correspondence bias. *Journal of Personality and Social Psychology, 83,* 300–312.

Eraker, S. A., & Politser, P. (1988). How decisions are reached: Physicians and the patient. In J. Dowie & A. S. Elstein (Eds.), *Professional judgment: A reader in clinical decision making* (pp. 379–394). Cambridge, England: Cambridge University Press.

Erdelyi, M. H. (1984). Hypnotic hypermnesia: The empty set of hypermnesia. *International Journal of Clinical and Experimental Hypnosis, 24,* 379–390.

Eron, L. D. (1982). Parent-child interaction, television violence, and aggression of children. *American Psychologist, 37,* 197–211.

Eron, L. D. (1987). The development of aggressive behavior from the perspective of a developing behaviorism. *American Psychologist, 42,* 425–442.

Eron, L. D. (2001) Seeing is believing: How viewing violence alters attitudes and aggressive behavior. In A. C. Bohart & D. J. Stipek (Eds.), *Constructive and destructive behavior: Implications for family, school, and society* (pp. 49–60). Washington, DC: American Psychological Association.

Eron, L. D., Huesmann, L. R., Lefkowitz, M. M., & Walder, L. O. (1996). Does television violence cause aggression? In D. F. Greenberg (Ed.), *Criminal careers* (Vol. 2, pp. 311–321). Aldershot, England: Dartmouth.

Esser, J. K. (1998). Alive and well after 25 years: A review of groupthink research. *Organizational Behavior and Human Decision Processes, 73,* 116–141.

Esser, J. K., & Lindoerfer, J. S. (1989). Groupthink and the space shuttle *Challenger* accident: Toward a quantitative case analysis. *Journal of Behavioral Decision Making, 2,* 167–177.

Estrada-Hollenbeck, M., & Heatherton, T. F. (1998). Avoiding and alleviating guilt through prosocial behavior. In J. Bybee (Ed.), *Guilt and children* (pp. 215–231). San Diego, CA: Academic Press.

Evans, G. W., Lepore, S. J., & Schroeder, A. (1996). The role of interior design elements in human responses to crowding. *Journal of Personality and Social Psychology, 70,* 41–46.

Evans, W. N., Neville, D., & Graham, J. D. (1991). General deterrence of drunk driving: Evaluation of American policies. *Risk Analysis, 11,* 279–289.

Ewing, G. (2001). Altruistic, egoistic, and normative effects on curbside recycling. *Environment and Behavior, 33,* 733–764.

Fabrigar, L. R., & Petty, R. E. (1999). The role of affective and cognitive bases of attitudes in susceptibility to affectively and cognitively based persuasion. *Personality and Social Psychology Bulletin, 25,* 363–381.

Fabrigar, L. R., Priester, J. R., Petty, R. E., & Wegener, D. T. (1998). The impact of attitude accessibility on elaboration of persuasive messages. *Personality and Social Psychology Bulletin, 24,* 339–352.

Falck, R., & Craig, R. (1988). Classroom-oriented, primary prevention programming for drug abuse. *Journal of Psychoactive Drugs, 20,* 403–408.

Farber, E. W., & Burge-Callaway, K. (1998). Differences in anger, hostility, and interpersonal aggression in Type A and Type B adolescents. *Journal of Clinical Psychology, 54,* 945–952.

Fazio, R. H. (1987). Self-perception theory: A current perspective. In M. P. Zanna, J. M. Olson, & C. P. Herman (Eds.), *Social influence: The Ontario Symposium* (Vol. 5, pp. 129–150). Hillsdale, NJ: Erlbaum.

Fazio, R. H. (1990). Multiple processes by which attitudes guide behavior: The MODE model as an integrative framework. In M. P. Zanna (Ed.), *Advances in experimental social psychology* (Vol. 23, pp. 75–109). San Diego, CA: Academic Press.

Fazio, R. H. (2000). Accessible attitudes as tools for object appraisal: Their costs and benefits. In G. Maio & J. Olson (Eds.), *Why we evaluate: Functions of attitudes* (pp. 1–36). Mahwah, NJ: Erlbaum.

Fazio, R. H., Jackson, J. R., Dunton, B. C., & Williams, C. J. (1995). Variability in automatic activation as an unobtrusive measure of racial attitudes: A bona fide pipeline? *Journal of Personality and Social Psychology, 69,* 1013–1027.

Fazio, R. H., & Olson, M. A. (2003). Implicit measures in social cognition research: Their meaning and uses. *Annual Review of Psychology, 54,* 297–327.

Fazio, R. H., Powell, M. C., & Williams, C. J. (1989). The role of attitude accessibility in the attitude-to-behavior process. *Journal of Consumer Research, 16,* 280–288.

Federal Bureau of Investigation, (2003). *Uniform Crime Reports.*

Feeney, J. A., & Noller, P. (1990). Attachment style as a predictor of adult romantic relationships. *Journal of Personality and Social Psychology, 58,* 281–291.

Feeney, J. A., & Noller, P. (1996). *Adult attachment.* Thousand Oaks, CA: Sage.

Feeney, J. A., Noller, P., & Roberts, N. (2000). Attachment and close relationships. In C. Hendrick & S. S. Hendrick (Eds.), *Close relationships: A sourcebook* (pp. 185–201). Thousand Oaks, CA: Sage.

Fehr, B. (1994). Prototype-based assessment of laypeople's views of love. *Personal Relationships, 1,* 309–331.

Fehr, B. (1996). *Friendship processes.* Thousand Oaks, CA: Sage.

Fehr, B., & Russell, J. A. (1991). The concept of love viewed from a prototype perspective. *Journal of Personality and Social Psychology, 60,* 425–438.

Fein, S. (1996). Effects of suspicion on attributional thinking and the correspondence bias. *Journal of Personality and Social Psychology, 70,* 1164–1184.

Fein, S., McCloskey, A. L., & Tomlinson, T. M. (1997). Can the jury disregard that information? The use of suspicion to reduce the prejudicial effects of pretrial publicity and inadmissable testimony. *Personality and Social Psychology Bulletin, 23,* 1215–1226.

Feingold, A. (1990). Gender differences in effects of physical attractiveness on romantic attraction: A comparison across five research paradigms. *Journal of Personality and Social Psychology, 59,* 981–993.

Feingold, A. (1992a). Gender differences in mate selection preferences: A test of the parental investment model. *Psychological Bulletin, 112,* 125–139.

Feingold, A. (1992b). Good-looking people are not what we think. *Psychological Bulletin, 111,* 304–341.

Feingold, A. (1996). On an evolutionary model of sex differences in mathematics: Do the data support the theory? *Behavioral and Brain Sciences, 19,* 252.

Fejfar, M. C., & Hoyle, R. H. (2000). Effect of private self-awareness on negative affect and self-referent attribution: A quantitative review. *Personality and Social Psychology Review, 4,* 132–142.

Feld, S. L. (1982). Social structural determinants of similarity among associates. *American Sociological Review, 47,* 797–801.

Feldman-Summers, S., & Kiesler, S. B. (1974). Those who are number two try harder: The effect of sex on attributions of causality. *Journal of Personality and Social Psychology, 38,* 846–855.

Femlee, D. H. (1995). Fatal attractions: Affection and disaffection in intimate relationships. *Journal of Social and Personal Relationships, 12,* 295–311.

Femlee, D. H. (1998a). "Be careful what you wish for . . .": A quantitative and qualitative investigation of "fatal attractions." *Personal Relationships, 5,* 235–253.

Femlee, D. H. (1998b). Fatal attractions: Contradictions in intimate relationships. In J. H. Harvey (Ed.), *Perspectives on loss: A sourcebook* (pp. 113–124). Philadelphia: Brunner/Mazel.

Femlee, D. H., Sprecher, S., & Bassin, E. (1990). The dissolution of intimate relationships: A hazard model. *Social Psychology Quarterly, 53,* 13–30.

Fenigstein, A., Scheier, M. F., & Buss, A. H. (1975). Public and private self-consciousness: Assessment and theory. *Journal of Consulting and Clinical Psychology, 43,* 522–527.

Fernald, J. L. (1995). Interpersonal heterosexism. In B. Lott & Maluso, D. (Eds.), *The social psychology of interpersonal discrimination* (pp. 80–117). New York: Guilford Press.

Ferris, T. (1997, April 14). The wrong stuff. *New Yorker,* p. 32.

Feshbach, N. D. (1978, March). *Empathy training: A field study in affective education.* Paper presented at the meetings of the American Educational Research Association, Toronto, Ontario, Canada.

Feshbach, N. D. (1989). Empathy training and prosocial behavior. In J. Groebel & R. A. Hinde (Eds.), *Aggression and war: Their biological and social bases* (pp. 101–111). New York: Cambridge University Press.

Feshbach, N. D. (1997). Empathy—the formative years: Implications for clinical practice. In A. C. Bohart & L. S. Greenberg (Eds.), *Empathy reconsidered: New directions in psychotherapy* (pp. 33–59). Washington, DC: American Psychological Association.

Feshbach, N. D., & Feshbach, S. (1969). The relationship between empathy and aggression in two age groups. *Developmental Psychology, 1,* 102–107.

Feshbach, S. (1971). Dynamics and morality of violence and aggression: Some psychological considerations. *American Psychologist, 26,* 281–292.

Festinger, L. (1954). A theory of social comparison processes. *Human Relations, 7,* 117–140.

Festinger, L. (1957). *A theory of cognitive dissonance.* Stanford, CA: Stanford University Press.

Festinger, L., & Aronson, E. (1960). The arousal and reduction of dissonance in social contexts. In D. Cartwright & A. Zander (Eds.), *Group dynamics* (pp. 214–231). Evanston, IL: Row & Peterson.

Festinger, L., & Carlsmith, J. M. (1959). Cognitive consequences of forced compliance. *Journal of Abnormal and Social Psychology, 58,* 203–211.

Festinger, L., & Maccoby, N. (1964). On resistance to persuasive communications. *Journal of Abnormal and Social Psychology, 68,* 359–366.

Festinger, L., Riecken, H. W., & Schachter, S. (1956). *When prophecy fails.* Minneapolis: University of Minnesota Press.

Festinger, L., Schachter, S., & Back, K. (1950). *Social pressures in informal groups: A study of human factors in housing.* New York: Harper.

Festinger, L., & Thibaut, J. (1951). Interpersonal communication in small groups. *Journal of Abnormal and Social Psychology, 46,* 92–99.

Fiedler, F. (1967). *A theory of leadership effectiveness.* New York: McGraw-Hill.

Fiedler, F. (1978). The contingency model and the dynamics of the leadership process. In L. Berkowitz (Ed.), *Advances in experimental social psychology* (Vol. 11, pp. 59–112). Orlando, FL: Academic Press.

Fiedler, K. (2000). Illusory correlations: A simple associative algorithm provides a convergent account of seemingly divergent paradigms. *Review of General Psychology, 4,* 25–58.

Fiedler, K., Walther, E., & Nickel, S. (1999). Covariation-based attribution: On the ability to assess multiple covariations of an effect. *Personality and Social Psychology Bulletin, 25,* 607–622.

Fincham, F. D., Bradbury, T. N., Arias, I., Byrne, C. A., & Karney, B. R. (1997). Marital violence, marital distress, and attributions. *Journal of Family Psychology, 11,* 367–372.

Fine, G. A., & Elsbach, K. D. (2000). Ethnography and experiment in social psychological theory building: Tactics for integrating qualitative field data with quantitative lab data. *Journal of Experimental Social Psychology, 36,* 51–76.

Fink, B., & Penton-Voak, I. (2002). Evolutionary psychology of facial attractiveness. *Current Directions in Psychological Science, 11,* 154–158.

Finney, P. D. (1987). When consent information refers to risk and deception: Implications for social research. *Journal of Social Behavior and Personality, 2,* 37–48.

Fischhoff, B. (1975). Hindsight foresight: The effect of outcome knowledge on judgment under uncertainty. *Journal of Experimental Psychology: Human Perception and Performance, 1,* 288–299.

Fishbein, M., & Ajzen, I. (1975). *Belief, attitude, intention, and behavior: An introduction to theory and research.* Reading, MA: Addison-Wesley.

Fishbein, M., Chan, D., O'Reilly, K., Schnell, D., Wood, R., Beeker, C., & Cohn, C. (1993). Factors influencing gay men's attitudes, subjective norms, and intentions with respect to performing sexual behaviors. *Journal of Applied Social Psychology, 23,* 417–438.

Fisher, R. P., Brennan, K. H., & McCauley, M. R. (2001). The cognitive interview method to enhance eyewitness recall. In M. L. Eisen (Ed.), *Memory and suggestibility in the forensic interview* (pp. 265–286). Mahwah, NJ: Erlbaum.

Fisher, W. A., & Barak, A. (2001). Internet pornography: A social psychological perspective on Internet sexuality. *Journal of Sex Research, 38,* 312–323.

Fiske, A. P., Kitayama, S., Markus, H. R., & Nisbett, R. E. (1998). The cultural matrix of social psychology. In D. T. Gilbert, S. T. Fiske, & G. Lindzey (Eds.), *The handbook of social psychology* (4th ed., Vol. 2, pp. 915–981). New York: McGraw-Hill.

Fiske, S. T. (1989a). Examining the role of intent: Toward understanding its role in stereotyping and prejudice. In J. S. Uleman & J. A. Bargh (Eds.), *Unintended thought* (pp. 253–283). New York: Guilford Press.

Fiske, S. T. (1989b). *Interdependence and stereotyping: From the laboratory to the Supreme Court (and back).* Address presented at the annual meeting of the American Psychological Association, New Orleans.

Fiske, S. T. (2003). Five core social motives, plus or minus five. In S. J. Spencer, S. Fein, M. P. Zanna, & J. M. Olson (Eds.), *Motivated social perception: The Ontario Symposium* (Vol. 9, pp. 233–246). Mahwah, NJ: Erlbaum.

Fiske, S. T., & Depret, E. (1996). Control, interdependence, and power: Understanding social cognition in its social context. *European Review of Social Psychology, 7*, 31–61.

Fiske, S. T., & Taylor, S. E. (1991). *Social cognition* (2nd ed.). New York: McGraw-Hill.

Flanagan, C. A., Bowes, J. M., Jonsson, B., Csapo, B., & Sheblanova, E. (1998). Ties that bind: Correlates of adolescents' civic commitments in seven countries. *Journal of Social Issues, 54*, 457–475.

Fletcher, G. J. O., Reeder, G. D., & Bull, V. (1990). Bias and accuracy in attitude attribution: The role of attributional complexity. *Journal of Experimental Social Psychology, 26*, 275–288.

Fletcher, G. J. O., & Ward, C. (1988). Attribution theory and processes: A cross-cultural perspective. In M. H. Bond (Ed.), *The cross-cultural challenge to social psychology* (pp. 230–244). Newbury Park, CA: Sage.

Flowers, M. L. (1977). A lab test of some implications of Janis's groupthink hypothesis. *Journal of Personality and Social Psychology, 35*, 888–897.

Folkman, S., & Moskowitz, J. T. (2000). The context matters. *Personality and Social Psychology Bulletin, 26*, 150–151.

Ford, T. E., & Thompson, E. P. (2000). Preconscious and postconscious processes underlying construct accessibility effects: An extended search model. *Personality and Social Psychology Review, 4*, 317–336.

Forgas, J. P. (1995). Mood and judgment: The Affect Infusion Model (AIM). *Psychological Bulletin, 117*, 39–66.

Forgas, J. P., & Bower, G. H. (1987). Mood effects on person-perception judgments. *Journal of Personality and Social Psychology, 53*, 53–60.

Forsterling, F. (1989). Models of covariation and attribution: How do they relate to the analogy of analysis of variance? *Journal of Personality and Social Psychology, 57*, 615–625.

Forsyth, D. R. (2000). One hundred years of group research: Introduction to the special issue. *Group Dynamics, 4*, 3–6.

Fountain, J.W. (1997, May 4). No fare. *Washington Post*, p. F1.

Fouts, G., & Burggraf, K. (1999). Television situation comedies: Female body images and verbal reinforcements. *Sex Roles, 40*, 473–479.

Frager, R. (1970). Conformity and anticonformity in Japan. *Journal of Personality and Social Psychology, 15*, 203–210.

France: An event not hallowed. (2001, November 1). *New York Times*, p. A14.

Frank, J. D. (1978). *Psychotherapy and the human predicament: A psychosocial approach* (P. E. Dietz, Ed.). New York: Schocken Books.

Frank, M. G., & Stennett, J. (2000). The forced-choice paradigm and the perception of facial expressions of emotion. *Journal of Personality and Social Psychology, 80*, 75–85.

Franklin, B. (1900). *The autobiography of Benjamin Franklin* (J. Bigelow, Ed.). Philadelphia: Lippincott. (Originally published 1868)

Frazier, P. A., & Cook, S. W. (1993). Correlates of distress following heterosexual relationship dissolution. *Journal of Social and Personal Relationships, 10*, 55–67.

Fredrickson, B. L., Roberts, T., Noll, S. M., Quinn, D. M., & Twenge, J. M. (1998). That swimsuit becomes you: Sex differences in self-objectification, restrained eating, and math performance. *Journal of Personality and Social Psychology, 75*, 269–284.

Freedman, D., Pisani, R., Purves, R., & Adhikari, A. (1991). *Statistics* (2nd ed.). New York: Norton.

Freedman, J. L. (1965). Long-term behavioral effects of cognitive dissonance. *Journal of Experimental and Social Psychology, 1*, 145–155.

Freud, S. (1930). *Civilization and its discontents* (J. Riviere, Trans.). London: Hogarth Press.

Freud, S. (1933). *New introductory lectures on psychoanalysis.* New York: Norton.

Fried, C., & Aronson, E. (1995). Hypocrisy, misattribution, and dissonance reduction: A demonstration of dissonance in the absence of aversive consequences. *Personality and Social Psychology Bulletin, 21*, 925–933.

Friedman, L. (1977). *Sex-role stereotyping in the mass media: An annotated bibliography.* New York: Garland Press.

Friedman, T. (2002). *Longitudes and attitudes: Exploring the world after September 11.* New York: Farrar, Straus & Giroux.

Frijda, N. H. (1986). *The emotions.* Cambridge, England: Cambridge University Press.

Frodi, A. (1975). The effect of exposure to weapons on aggressive behavior from a cross-cultural perspective. *International Journal of Psychology, 10*, 283–292.

Fry, P. S., & Ghosh, R. (1980). Attributions of success and failure: Comparison of cultural differences between Asian and Caucasian children. *Journal of Cross-Cultural Psychology, 11*, 343–363.

Fulero, S. M. (2002). Afterword: The past, present, and future of applied pretrial publicity research. *Law and Human Behavior, 26*, 127–133.

Fuller, T. D., Edwards, J. N., Vorakitphokatorn, S., & Sermsri, S. (1996). Chronic stress and psychological well-being: Evidence from Thailand on household crowding. *Social Science and Medicine, 42*, 265–280.

Fumento, M. (1997, September 12). Why we need a new war on weight. *USA Weekend*, pp. 4–6.

Funder, D. C. (1995). On the accuracy of personality judgments: A realistic approach. *Psychological Review, 102*, 652–670.

Funder, D. C., & Colvin, C. R. (1988). Friends and strangers: Acquaintanceship, agreement, and the accuracy of personality judgment. *Journal of Personality and Social Psychology, 55*, 149–158.

Furnham, A. (1993). Just world beliefs in twelve societies. *Journal of Social Psychology, 133*, 317–329.

Furnham, A., & Gunter, B. (1984). Just world beliefs and attitudes toward the poor. *British Journal of Social Psychology, 23*, 265–269.

Furnham, A., & Mak, T. (1999). Sex-role stereotyping in television commercials: A review and comparison of fourteen studies done on five continents over 25 years. *Sex Roles, 41*, 413–437.

Furnham, A., & Procter, E. (1989). Beliefs in a just world: Review and critique of the individual difference literature. *British Journal of Social Psychology, 28*, 365–384.

Fury, G., Carlson, E. A., & Sroufe, L. A. (1997). Children's representations of attachment relationships in family drawings. *Child Development, 68*, 1154–1164.

Gabriel, S., & Gardner, W. L. (1999). Are there "his" and "hers" types of interdependence? The implications of gender differences in collective versus relational interdependence for affect, behavior, and cognition. *Journal of Personality and Social Psychology, 77*, 642–655.

Gaertner, S. L., Mann, J. A., Dovidio, J. F., & Murrell, A. J. (1990). How does cooperation reduce intergroup bias? *Journal of Personality and Social Psychology, 59*, 692–704.

Galinsky, A. D., Mussweiler, T., & Medvec, V. H. (2002). Disconnecting outcomes and evaluations: The role of negotiator focus. *Journal of Personality and Social Psychology, 83*, 1131–1140.

Gallup, G. G. (1977). Self-recognition in primates: A comparative approach to the bidirectional properties of consciousness. *American Psychologist, 32*, 329–338.

Gallup, G. G. (1997). On the rise and fall of self-conception in primates. In J. G. Snodgrass & R. L. Thompson (Eds.), *The self across psychology: Self-recognition, self-awareness, and the self-concept* (pp. 73–82). New York: New York Academy of Sciences Press.

Gallup, G. G., & Suarez, S. D. (1986). Self-awareness and the emergence of mind in humans and other primates. In J. Suls & A. G. Greenwald (Eds.), *Psychological perspectives on the self* (Vol. 3, pp. 3–26). Hillsdale, NJ: Erlbaum.

Gangestad, S. W. (1993). Sexual selection and physical attractiveness: Implications for mating dynamics. *Human Nature, 4*, 205–235.

Gangestad, S. W., & Buss, D. M. (1993). Pathogen prevalence and human mate preferences. *Ethology and Sociobiology, 14*, 89–96.

Gao, G. (1993, May). *An investigation of love and intimacy in romantic relationships in China and the United States.* Paper presented at the annual conference of the International Communication Association, Washington, DC.

Gao, G. (1996). Self and other: A Chinese perspective on interpersonal relationships. In W. B. Gudykunst, S. Ting-Toomey, & T.

Nishida (Eds.), *Communication in personal relationships across cultures* (pp. 81–101). Thousand Oaks, CA: Sage.

Gao, G., & Gudykunst, W. B. (1995). Attributional confidence, perceived similarity, and network involvement in Chinese and European American romantic relationships. *Communication Quarterly, 43,* 431–445.

Garcia, L. T., & Milano, L. (1990). A content analysis of erotic videos. *Journal of Psychology and Human Sexuality, 3,* 95–103.

Garcia, S., Stinson, L., Ickes, W. J., Bissonnette, V., & Briggs, S. (1991). Shyness and physical attractiveness in mixed-sex dyads. *Journal of Personality and Social Psychology, 61,* 35–49.

Garcia, S. M., Weaver, K., Moskowitz, G. B., & Darley, J. M. (2002). Crowded minds: The implicit bystander effect. *Journal of Personality and Social Psychology, 83,* 843–853.

Garcia-Marques, L., & Hamilton, D. L. (1996). Resolving the apparent discrepancy between the incongruency effect and the expectancy-based illusory correlation effect: The TRAP model. *Journal of Personality and Social Psychology, 71,* 845–860.

Gardner, W. L., Pickett, C. L., & Brewer, M. B. (2000). Social exclusion and selective memory: How the need to belong influences memory for social events. *Personality and Social Psychology Bulletin, 26,* 486–496.

Garfinkle, H. (1967). *Studies in ethnomethodology.* Englewood Cliffs, NJ: Prentice Hall.

Garner, D. M., Garfinkel, P. E., Schwartz, D., & Thompson, M. (1980). Cultural expectations of thinness in women. *Psychological Reports, 47,* 483–491.

Gates, H. L., Jr. (1995, October 23). Thirteen ways of looking at a black man. *New Yorker,* pp. 56–65.

Gavanski, I., & Hoffman, C. (1987). Awareness of influences on one's own judgments: The roles of covariation detection and attention. *Journal of Personality and Social Psychology, 52,* 453–463.

Gawronski, B. (2003). Implicational schemata and the correspondence bias: On the diagnostic value of situationally constrained behavior. *Journal of Personality and Social Psychology, 84,* 1154–1171.

Geary, D. C. (1996). Sexual selection and sex differences in mathematical abilities. *Behavioral and Brain Sciences, 19,* 229–284.

Geen, R. G. (1989). Alternative conceptions of social facilitation. In P. B. Paulus (Ed.), *Psychology of group influence* (2nd ed., pp. 15–51). Hillsdale, NJ: Erlbaum.

Geen, R. G. (1994). Television and aggression: Recent developments in research and theory. In D. Zillmann, J. Bryant, & A. C. Huston (Eds.), *Media, children, and the family: Social scientific, psychodynamic, and clinical perspectives* (pp. 151–162). Hillsdale, NJ: Erlbaum.

Geen, R. G. (1998). Aggression and antisocial behavior. In D. T. Gilbert, S. T. Fiske, & G. Lindzey (Eds.), *The handbook of social psychology* (4th ed., Vol. 2, pp. 317–356). New York: McGraw-Hill.

Geen, R. G., & Quanty, M. (1977). The catharsis of aggression: An evaluation of a hypothesis. In L. Berkowitz (Ed.), *Advances in experimental social psychology* (Vol. 10, pp. 1–36). New York: Academic Press.

Geen, R. G., Stonner, D., & Shope, G. (1975). The facilitation of aggression by aggression: A study in response inhibition and disinhibition. *Journal of Personality and Social Psychology, 31,* 721–726.

Geiselman, R. E., & Fisher, R. P. (1989). The cognitive interview technique for victims and witnesses of crime. In D. C. Raskin (Ed.), *Psychological methods in criminal investigation and evidence* (pp. 191–215). New York: Springer-Verlag.

Geitemeier, T., & Schulz-Hardt, S. (2003). Preference-consistent evaluation of information in the hidden profile paradigm: Beyond group-level explanations for the dominance of shared information in group decisions. *Journal of Personality and Social Psychology, 84,* 322–339.

Geller, E. S. (2002). The challenge of increasing proenvironmental behavior. In R. B. Bechtel & A. Churchman (Eds.), *Handbook of environmental psychology* (pp. 525–540). New York: Wiley.

Gemmill, G. (1989). The dynamics of scapegoating in small groups. *Small Group Behavior, 20,* 406–418.

George, D. M., Carroll, P., Kersnick, R., & Calderon, K. (1998). Gender-related patterns of helping among friends. *Psychology of Women Quarterly, 22,* 685–704.

George, J. M. (1990). Personality, affect, and behavior in groups. *Journal of Applied Psychology, 75,* 107–116.

Gerard, H. B. (1953). The effect of different dimensions of disagreement on the communication process in small groups. *Human Relations, 6,* 249–271.

Gerard, H. B., & Mathewson, G. C. (1966). The effects of severity of initiation on liking for a group: A replication. *Journal of Experimental Social Psychology, 2,* 278–287.

Gerard, H. B., Wilhelmy, R. A., & Conolley, E. S. (1968). Conformity and group size. *Journal of Personality and Social Psychology, 8,* 79–82.

Gerbner, G., Gross, L., Morgan, M., Signorielli, N., & Shanahan, J. (2002). Growing up with television: Cultivation processes. In J. Bryant & D. Zillmann (Eds.), *Media effects: Advances in theory and research* (pp. 43–67). Mahwah, NJ: Erlbaum.

Gerdes, E. P. (1979). College students' reactions to social psychological experiments involving deception. *Journal of Social Psychology, 107,* 99–110.

Gergen, K. J., Gergen, M. M., & Barton, W. H. (1973, July). Deviance in the dark. *Psychology Today,* pp. 129–130.

Gervey, B. M., Chiu, C., Hong, Y., & Dweck, C. S. (1999). Differential use of person information in decisions about guilt versus innocence: The role of implicit theories. *Personality and Social Psychology Bulletin, 25,* 17–27.

Ghiselin, M. T. (1996). Differences in male and female cognitive abilities: Sexual selection or division of labor? *Behavioral and Brain Sciences, 19,* 254–255.

Gibbons, F. X. (1978). Sexual standards and reactions to pornography: Enhancing behavioral consistency through self-focused attention. *Journal of Personality and Social Psychology, 36,* 976–987.

Gibbons, F. X., Eggleston, T. J., & Benthin, A. C. (1997). Cognitive reactions to smoking relapse: The reciprocal relation between dissonance and self-esteem. *Journal of Personality and Social Psychology, 72,* 184–195.

Gibbons, F. X., Lane, D. J., Gerrard, M., Reis-Bergan, M., Lautrup, C. L., Pexa, N. A., & Blanton, H. (2002). Comparison-level preferences after performance: Is downward comparison theory still useful? *Journal of Personality and Social Psychology, 83,* 865–880.

Gibbs, J. P. (1985). Deterrence theory and research. *Nebraska Symposium on Motivation, 33,* 87–130.

Gibbs, N., & Roche, T. (1999, December 20). The Columbine tapes. *Time,* p. 154.

Gifford, R. (1991). Mapping nonverbal behavior on the interpersonal circle. *Journal of Personality and Social Psychology, 61,* 279–288.

Gifford, R. (1994). A lens-mapping framework for understanding the encoding and decoding of interpersonal dispositions in nonverbal behavior. *Journal of Personality and Social Psychology, 66,* 398–412.

Gigerenzer, G. (2000). *Adaptive thinking: Rationality in the real world.* Oxford, England: Oxford University Press.

Gilbert, B. (1990, April). Earth Day plus 20, and counting. *Smithsonian,* pp. 47–55.

Gilbert, D. T. (1989). Thinking lightly about others: Automatic components of the social inference process. In J. S. Uleman & J. A. Bargh (Eds.), *Unintended thought* (pp. 189–211). New York: Guilford Press.

Gilbert, D. T. (1991). How mental systems believe. *American Psychologist, 46,* 107–119.

Gilbert, D. T. (1993). The assent of man: Mental representation and the control of belief. In D. M. Wegner & J. W. Pennebaker, (Eds.), *The handbook of mental control* (pp. 57–87). Englewood Cliffs, NJ: Prentice Hall.

Gilbert, D. T. (1998a). Ordinary personology. In D. T. Gilbert, S. T. Fiske, & G. Lindzey (Eds.), *The handbook of social psychology* (4th ed., Vol. 2, pp. 89–150). New York: McGraw-Hill.

Gilbert, D. T. (1998b). Speeding with Ned: A personal view of the correspondence bias. In J. M. Darley & J. Cooper (Eds.), *Attribution and social interaction* (pp. 5–36). Washington, DC: American Psychological Association.

Gilbert, D. T., Giesler, R. B., & Morris, K. A. (1995). When comparisons arise. *Journal of Personality and Social Psychology, 69,* 227–236.

Gilbert, D. T., & Hixon, J. G. (1991). The trouble of thinking: Activation and applications of stereotypical beliefs. *Journal of Personality and Social Psychology, 60,* 509–517.

Gilbert, D. T., & Jones, E. E. (1986). Perceiver-induced constraint: Interpretations of self-generated reality. *Journal of Personality and Social Psychology, 50,* 269–280.

Gilbert, D. T., & Malone, P. S. (1995). The correspondence bias. *Psychological Bulletin, 117,* 21–38.

Gilbert, D. T., & Osborne, R. E. (1989). Thinking backward: Some curable and incurable consequences of cognitive busyness. *Journal of Personality and Social Psychology, 57,* 940–949.

Gilbert, D. T., Pelham, B. W., & Krull, D. S. (1988). On cognitive busyness: When person perceivers meet persons perceived. *Journal of Personality and Social Psychology, 54,* 733–740.

Gilbert, G. M. (1951). Stereotype persistence and change among college students. *Journal of Abnormal and Social Psychology, 46,* 245–254.

Gilbert, M. (2000, August 18). Spice of life. *Boston Globe,* pp. D1, D8.

Gilbert, S. J. (1981). Another look at the Milgram obedience studies: The role of the gradated series of shocks. *Personality and Social Psychology Bulletin, 4,* 690–695.

Gilligan, J. (1996). *Violence: Our deadly epidemic and its causes.* New York: Putnam.

Gilovich, T. (1991). *How we know what isn't so: The fallibility of human reasoning in everyday life.* New York: Free Press.

Gilovich, T., & Griffin, D. W. (2002). Introduction: Heuristics and biases, now and then. In T. Gilovich, D. W. Griffin, & D. Kahneman (Eds.), *Heuristics and biases: The psychology of intuitive judgment* (pp. 1–18). New York: Cambridge University Press.

Gilovich, T., Kruger, J., & Medvec, V. H. (2002). the spotlight effect revisited: Overestimating the manifest variability of our actions and appearance. *Journal of Experimental Social Psychology, 38,* 93–99.

Gilovich, T., & Medvec, V. H. (1995a). The experience of regret: What, when, and why. *Psychological Review, 102,* 379–395.

Gilovich, T., & Medvec, V. H. (1995b). Some counterfactual determinants of satisfaction and regret. In N. J. Roese & J. M. Olson (Eds.), *What might have been: The social psychology of counterfactual thinking* (pp. 259–282). Mahwah, NJ: Erlbaum.

Gilovich, T., Medvec, V. H., & Chen, S. (1995). Commission, omission, and dissonance reduction: Coping with regret in the "Monty Hall" problem. *Personality and Social Psychology Bulletin, 21,* 182–190.

Gilovich, T., Medvec, V. H., & Savitsky, K. (2000). The spotlight effect in social judgment: An egocentric bias in estimates of the salience of one's own actions and appearance. *Journal of Personality and Social Psychology, 78,* 211–222.

Gilovich, T., & Savitsky, K. (2002). Like goes with like: The role of representativeness in erroneous and pseudoscientific beliefs. In T. Gilovich, D. W. Griffin, & D. Kahneman (Eds.), *Heuristics and biases: The psychology of intuitive judgment* (pp. 617–624). New York: Cambridge University Press.

Gimlin, D. (1994). The anorexic as overconformist: Toward a reinterpretation of eating disorders. In K. A. Callaghan (Ed.), *Ideals of feminine beauty: Philosophical, social, and cultural dimensions* (pp. 99–111). Westport, CT: Greenwood Press.

Girl born to Japan's princess. (2001, December 1). *New York Times,* p. 8.

Gladwell, M. (1997, May 19). The sports taboo. *New Yorker,* pp. 50–55.

Glass, D. C. (1964). Changes in liking as a means of reducing cognitive discrepancies between self-esteem and aggression. *Journal of Personality, 32,* 531–549.

Glass, D. C., & Singer, J. E. (1972). *Urban stress: Experiments on noise and social stressors.* New York: Academic Press.

Gleick, E. (1997, April 7). Planet Earth about to be recycled. Your only chance to survive—leave with us. *Time,* pp. 28–36.

Glick, P., & Fiske, S (2001). An ambivalent alliance: Hostile and benevolent sexism as complementary justifications for gender inequality. *American Psychologist, 56,* 109–118.

Goethals, G. R., & Darley, J. M. (1977). Social comparison theory: An attributional approach. In J. M. Suls & R. L. Miller (Eds.), *Social comparison processes: Theoretical and empirical perspectives* (pp. 259–278). Washington, DC: Hemisphere/Halsted.

Goffman, E. (1959). *Presentation of self in everyday life.* Garden City, NY: Anchor/Doubleday.

Gold, J. A., Ryckman, R. M., & Mosley, N. R. (1984). Romantic mood induction and attraction to a dissimilar other: Is love blind? *Personality and Social Psychology Bulletin, 10,* 358–368.

Goldberg, P. (1968, April). Are women prejudiced against women? *Trans-Action,* pp. 28–30.

Goldstein, J. H., & Arms, R. L. (1971). Effect of observing athletic contests on hostility. *Sociometry, 34,* 83–90.

Goleman, D. (1982, January). Make-or-break resolutions. *Psychology Today,* p. 19.

Gologor, E. (1977). Group polarization in a non-risk-taking culture. *Journal of Cross-Cultural Psychology, 8,* 331–346.

Gonzales, M. H., Aronson, E., & Costanzo, M. (1988). Using social cognition and persuasion to promote energy conservation: A quasi-experiment. *Journal of Applied Social Psychology, 18,* 1049–1066.

Gonzalez, R., Ellsworth, P. C., & Pembroke, M. (1993). Response biases in lineups and showups. *Journal of Personality and Social Psychology, 64,* 525–537.

Goode, E. (1999, February 9). Arranged marriage gives way to courtship by mail. *New York Times,* p. D3.

Goode, E. (2000, February 15). When women find love is fatal. *New York Times,* pp. F1 ff.

Goodman, N. G. (Ed.). (1945). *A Benjamin Franklin reader.* New York: Crowell.

Goodwin, R. (1999). *Personal relationships across cultures.* New York: Routledge.

Gopaul-McNicol, S. A. A. (1987). A cross-cultural study of the effects of modeling, reinforcement, and color meaning word association on doll color preference of black preschool children and white preschool children in New York and Trinidad. *Dissertation Abstracts International, 48,* 340–341.

Gordon, A. K., & Miller, A. G. (2000). Perspective differences in the construal of lies: Is deception in the eye of the beholder? *Personality and Social Psychology Bulletin, 26,* 46–55.

Gordon, R. A. (1996). Impact of ingratiation on judgments and evaluations: A meta-analytic investigation. *Journal of Personality and Social Psychology, 71,* 54–70.

Gould, S. J. (1997, June 26). Evolution: The pleasures of pluralism. *New York Review of Books,* pp. 47–52.

Granberg, D., & Brown, T. (1989). On affect and cognition in politics. *Social Psychology Quarterly, 52,* 171–182.

Graziano, W. G., Jensen Campbell, L. A., & Finch, J. F. (1997). The self as a mediator between personality and adjustment. *Journal of Personality and Social Psychology, 73,* 392–404.

Graziano, W. G., Jensen-Campbell, L. A., Shebilske, L. J., & Lundgren, S. R. (1993). Social influence, sex differences, and judgments of beauty: Putting the interpersonal back in interpersonal attraction. *Journal of Personality and Social Psychology, 65,* 522–531.

Greenberg, J., & Musham, C. (1981). Avoiding and seeking self-focused attention. *Journal of Research in Personality, 15,* 191–200.

Greenberg, J., & Pyszczynski, T. (1985). The effect of an overheard slur on evaluations of the target: How to spread a social disease. *Journal of Experimental Social Psychology, 21,* 61–72.

Greenberg, J., Pyszczynski, T., & Paisley, C. (1984). The role of extrinsic incentives in the use of test anxiety as an anticipatory attributional defense: Playing it cool when the stakes are high. *Journal of Personality and Social Psychology, 47,* 1136–1145.

Greenberg, J., Pyszczynski, T., & Solomon, S. (1982). The self-serving attributional bias: Beyond self-presentation. *Journal of Experimental Social Psychology, 18,* 56–67.

Greenberg, J., Pyszczynski, T., & Solomon, S. (1986). The causes and consequences of the need for self-esteem: A terror management theory. In R. F. Baumeister (Ed.), *Public self and private self* (pp. 189–212). New York: Springer-Verlag.

Greene, D., Sternberg, B., & Lepper, M. R. (1976). Overjustification in a token economy. *Journal of Personality and Social Psychology, 34,* 1219–1234.

Greenfield, L. A. & Henneberg, M. A. (2001). Alcohol involvement in crime. *Alcohol Research and Health, 25,* 20–32.

Greenglass, E. R. (1991). Type A behavior, career aspirations, and role conflict in professional women. In M. J. Strube (Ed.), *Type A behavior* (pp. 277–292). Newbury Park, CA: Sage.

Greening, L., & Chandler, C. C. (1997). Why it can't happen to me: The base rate matters, but overestimating skill leads to underestimating risk. *Journal of Applied Social Psychology, 27,* 760–780.

Greenwald, A. G., & Banaji, M. R. (1989). The self as a memory system: Powerful but ordinary. *Journal of Personality and Social Psychology, 57,* 41–54.

Greenwald, A. G., & Banaji, M. R. (1995). Implicit social cognition: Attitudes, self-esteem, and stereotypes. *Psychological Review, 102,* 4–27.

Greenwald, A. G., McGhee, D. E., & Schwartz, J. L. K. (1998). Measuring individual differences in implicit cognition: The Implicit Association Test. *Journal of Personality and Social Psychology, 74,* 1464–1480.

Greenwald, A. G., & Nosek, B. A. (2001). Health of the Implicit Association Test at age 3. *Zeitschrift für Experimentelle Psychologie, 48,* 85–93.

Greenwald, A. G., & Ronis, D. L. (1978). Twenty years of cognitive dissonance: Case study of the evolution of a theory. *Psychological Review, 85,* 53–57.

Greenwald, A. G., Spangenberg, E. R., Pratkanis, A. R., & Eskenazi, J. (1991). Double-blind tests of subliminal self-help audiotapes. *Psychological Science, 2,* 119–122.

Greitemeyer, T., & Schulz-Hardt, S. (2003). Preference-consistent evaluation of information in the hidden profileparadigm: Beyond group-level explanations for the dominance of shared information in group decisions. *Journal of Personality and Social Psychology, 84,* 322–339.

Griffin, D. W., Gonzalez, R., & Varey, C. (2001). The heuristics and biases approach to judgment under uncertainty. In A. Tesser & N. Schwarz (Eds.), *Blackwell handbook of social psychology: Intraindividual processes* (pp. 127–133). Oxford, England: Blackwell.

Griffin, D. W., & Ross, L. (1991). Subjective construal, social inference, and human misunderstanding. In L. Berkowitz (Ed.), *Advances in experimental social psychology* (Vol. 24, pp. 319–359). San Diego, CA: Academic Press.

Griffin, D., & Sparks, G. G. (1990). Friends forever: A longitudinal exploration of intimacy in same-sex pairs and platonic pairs. *Journal of Social and Personal Relationships, 7,* 29–46.

Gross, J. J. (1998). Antecedent- and response-focused emotion regulation: Divergent consequences for experience, expression, and physiology. *Journal of Personality and Social Psychology, 74,* 224–237.

Gross, J. J., & Levenson, R. W. (1993). Emotional suppression: Physiology, self-report, and expressive behavior. *Journal of Personality and Social Psychology, 64,* 970–986.

Gross, J. J., & Levenson, R. W. (1997). Hiding feelings: The acute effects of suppressing negative and positive emotion. *Journal of Abnormal Psychology, 106,* 95–103.

Guagnano, G. A., Stern, P. C., & Dietz, T. (1995). Influences on attitude-behavior relationships: A natural experiment with curbside recycling. *Environment and Behavior, 27,* 699–718.

Gudykunst, W. B. (1988). Culture and intergroup processes. In M. H. Bond (Ed.), *The cross-cultural challenge to social psychology* (pp. 165–181). Newbury Park, CA: Sage.

Gudykunst, W. B., Ting-Toomey, S., & Nishida, T. (1996). *Communication in personal relationships across cultures.* Thousand Oaks, CA: Sage.

Guerin, B. (1993). *Social facilitation.* Cambridge, England: Cambridge University Press.

Guimond, S. (1999). Attitude change during college: Normative or informational social influence? *Social Psychology of Education, 2,* 237–261.

Guisinger, S., & Blatt, S. J. (1994). Individuality and relatedness: Evolution of a fundamental dialect. *American Psychologist, 49,* 104–111.

Gully, S. M., Devine, D. J., & Whitney, D. J. (1995). A meta-analysis of cohesion and performance: Effects of level of analysis and task interdependence. *Small Groups Research, 26,* 497–520.

Gump, B. B., & Kulik, J. A. (1997). Stress, affiliation, and emotional contagion. *Journal of Personality and Social Psychology, 72,* 305–319.

Gustafson, R. (1989). Frustration and successful vs. unsuccessful aggression: A test of Berkowitz's completion hypothesis. *Aggressive Behavior, 15,* 5–12.

Hagestad, G. O., & Smyer, M. A. (1982). Dissolving long-term relationships: Patterns of divorcing in middle age. In S. W. Duck (Ed.), *Personal relationships: Vol. 4. Dissolving personal relationships* (pp. 155–188). London: Academic Press.

Haidt, J., & Keltner, D. (1999). Culture and facial expression: Open-ended methods find more faces and a gradient of recognition. *Cognition and Emotion, 13,* 225–266.

Halberstadt, J. B., & Levine, G. L. (1997). *Effects of reasons analysis on the accuracy of predicting basketball games.* Unpublished manuscript, Indiana University.

Halberstadt, J. B., & Rhodes, G. (2000). The attractiveness of nonface averages: Implications for an evolutionary explanation of the attractiveness of average faces. *Psychological Science, 11,* 285–289.

Halberstam, D. (1972). *The best and the brightest.* New York: McGraw-Hill.

Hall, E. T. (1969). *The hidden dimension.* Garden City, NY: Doubleday.

Hall, J. A. (1979). *A cross-national study of gender differences in nonverbal sensitivity.* Unpublished manuscript, Northeastern University.

Hall, J. A. (1984). *Nonverbal sex differences: Communication accuracy and expressive style.* Baltimore: Johns Hopkins University Press.

Hamilton, D. L. (1970). The structure of personality judgments: Comments on Kuusinen's paper and further evidence. *Scandinavian Journal of Psychology, 11,* 261–265.

Hamilton, D. L. (1981). Illusory correlation as a basis for stereotyping. In D. L. Hamilton (Ed.), *Cognitive processes in stereotyping and intergroup behavior* (pp. 563–571). Hillsdale, NJ: Erlbaum.

Hamilton, D. L., & Gifford, R. K. (1976). Illusory correlation in interpersonal perception: A cognitive basis of stereotypic judgments. *Journal of Experimental Social Psychology, 12,* 392–407.

Hamilton, D. L., & Sherman, S. J. (1989). Illusory correlations: Implications for stereotype theory and research. In D. Bar-Tal, C. F. Graumann, A. W. Kruglanski, & W. Stroebe (Eds.), *Stereotypes and prejudice: Changing conceptions* (pp. 59–82). New York: Springer-Verlag.

Hamilton, D. L., Stroessner, S., & Mackie, D. M. (1993). The influence of affect on stereotyping: The case of illusory correlations. In D. M. Mackie & D. L. Hamilton (Eds.), *Affect, cognition, and stereotyping: Interactive processes in group perception* (pp. 39–61). San Diego, CA: Academic Press.

Hamilton, V. L., Sanders, J., & McKearney, S. J. (1995). Orientations toward authority in an authoritarian state: Moscow in 1990. *Personality and Social Psychology Bulletin, 21,* 356–365.

Hamilton, W. D. (1964). The genetical evolution of social behavior. *Journal of Theoretical Biology, 7,* 1–52.

Hammond, J. R., & Fletcher, G. J. O. (1991). Attachment styles and relationship satisfaction in the development of close relationships. *New Zealand Journal of Psychology, 20,* 56–62.

Han, S., & Shavitt, S. (1994). Persuasion and culture: Advertising appeals in individualistic and collectivistic societies. *Journal of Experimental Social Psychology, 30,* 326–350.

Haney, C., Banks, C., & Zimbardo, P. (1973). Interpersonal dynamics in a simulated prison. *International Journal of Criminology and Penology, 1,* 69–97.

Hansen, C. H., & Hansen, R. D. (1988). Finding the face in the crowd: An angry superiority effect. *Journal of Personality and Social Psychology, 54,* 917–924.

Hansen, E. M., Kimble, C. E., & Biers, D. W. (2000). Actors and observers: Divergent attributions of constrained unfriendly behavior. *Social Behavior and Personality, 29,* 87–104.

Hansson, R. O., & Slade, K. M. (1977). Altruism toward a deviant in a city and small town. *Journal of Applied Social Psychology, 7,* 272–279.

Harackiewicz, J. M. (1979). The effects of reward contingency and performance feedback on intrinsic motivation. *Journal of Personality and Social Psychology, 37,* 1352–1363.

Harackiewicz, J. M. (1989). Performance evaluation and intrinsic motivation processes: The effects of achievement orientation and rewards. In D. M. Buss & N. Cantor (Eds.), *Personality psychology: Recent trends and emerging directions* (pp. 128–137). New York: Springer-Verlag.

Harackiewicz, J. M., & Elliot, A. J. (1993). Achievement goals and intrinsic motivation. *Journal of Personality and Social Psychology, 65,* 904–915.

Harackiewicz, J. M., & Elliot, A. J. (1998). The joint effects of target and purpose goals on intrinsic motivation: A mediational analysis. *Personality and Social Psychology Bulletin, 24,* 675–689.

Harackiewicz, J. M., Manderlink, G., & Sansone, C. (1984). Rewarding pinball wizardry: Effects of evaluation and cue value on intrinsic interest. *Journal of Personality and Social Psychology, 47,* 287–300.

Hardin, G. (1968). The tragedy of the commons. *Science, 162,* 1243–1248.

Haritos-Fatouros, M. (1988). The official torturer: A learning model for obedience to the authority of violence. *Journal of Applied Social Psychology, 18,* 1107–1120.

Harkness, A. R., De Bono, K. G., & Borgida, E. (1985). Personal involvement and strategies for making contingency judgments: A stake in the dating game makes a difference. *Journal of Personality and Social Psychology, 49,* 22–32.

Harmon-Jones, E., Brehm, J. W., Greenberg, J., Simon, L., Nelson, D. E. (1996). Evidence that the production of aversive consequences is not necessary to create cognitive dissonance. *Journal of Personality and Social Psychology, 70,* 5–16.

Harries, K. D., & Stadler, S. J. (1988). Heat and violence: New findings from Dallas field data, 1980–1981. *Journal of Applied Social Psychology, 18,* 129–138.

Harrigan, J. A., & O'Connell, D. M. (1996). How do you feel when feeling anxious? Facial displays of anxiety. *Personality and Individual Differences, 21,* 205–212.

Harris, B. (1986). Reviewing 50 years of the psychology of social issues. *Journal of Social Issues, 42,* 1–20.

Harris, M. B. (1974). Mediators between frustration and aggression in a field experiment. *Journal of Experimental and Social Psychology, 10,* 561–571.

Harris, M. B., Benson, S. M., & Hall, C. (1975). The effects of confession on altruism. *Journal of Social Psychology, 96,* 187–192.

Harris, M. B., & Perkins, R. (1995). Effects of distraction on interpersonal expectancy effects: A social interaction test of the cognitive busyness hypothesis. *Social Cognition, 13,* 163–182.

Harris, P. (1996). Sufficient grounds for optimism? The relationship between perceived controllability and optimistic bias. *Journal of Social and Clinical Psychology, 15,* 9–52.

Harris, R. J. (1994). The impact of sexually explicit material. In J. Bryant & D. Zillmann (Eds.), *Media effects: Advances in theory and research* (pp. 247–272). Hillsdale, NJ: Erlbaum.

Harrison, J. A., & Wells, R. B. (1991). Bystander effects on male helping behavior: Social comparison and diffusion of responsibility. *Representative Research in Social Psychology, 19,* 53–63.

Hart, A. J. (1995). Naturally occurring expectation effects. *Journal of Personality and Social Psychology, 68,* 109–115.

Hart, D., & Damon, W. (1986). Developmental trends in self-understanding. *Social Cognition, 4,* 388–407.

Harter, S. (1993). Causes and consequences of low self-esteem in children and adolescents. In R. F. Baumeister (Ed.), *Self-esteem: The puzzle of low self-regard* (pp. 87–116). New York: Plenum.

Harter, S. (2003). The development of self-representations during childhood and adolescence. In M. R. Leary & J. P. Tangney (Eds.), *Handbook of self and identity* (pp. 610–642). New York: Guilford Press.

Hartshorne, H., & May, M. A. (1929). *Studies in the nature of character: Vol. 2. Studies in service and self-control.* New York: Macmillan.

Hartstone, M., & Augoustinos, M. (1995). The minimal group paradigm: Categorization into two versus three groups. *European Journal of Social Psychology, 25,* 179–193.

Hartup, W. W., & Laursen, B. (1999). Relationships as developmental contexts: Retrospective themes and contemporary issues. In W. A. Collins & B. Laursen (Eds.), *Relationships as developmental contexts: Minnesota Symposia on Child Psychology* (Vol. 30, pp. 13–35). Mahwah, NJ: Erlbaum.

Hartup, W. W., & Stevens, N. (1997). Friendships and adaptation in the life course. *Psychological Bulletin, 121,* 355–370.

Harvey, J. H. (1995). *Odyssey of the heart: The search for closeness, intimacy, and love.* New York: Freeman.

Harvey, J. H., Flanary, R., & Morgan, M. (1986). Vivid memories of vivid loves gone by. *Journal of Personal and Social Relationships, 3,* 359–373.

Harvey, J. H., Orbuch, T. L., & Weber, A. L. (1992). The convergence of the attribution and accounts concepts in the study of close relationships. In J. H. Harvey, T. L. Orbuch, & A. L. Weber (Eds.), *Attributions, accounts, and close relationships* (pp. 1–18). New York: Springer-Verlag.

Hassebrauck, M., & Buhl, T. (1996). Three-dimensional love. *Journal of Social Psychology, 136,* 121–122.

Hastie, R., & Pennington, N. (2000). Explanation-based decision making. In T. Connolly & H. R. Arkes (Eds.), *Judgment and decision making: An interdisciplinary reader* (2nd ed., pp. 212–228). New York: Cambridge University Press.

Hastie, R., Penrod, S. D., & Pennington, N. (1983). *Inside the jury.* Cambridge, MA: Harvard University Press.

Hatfield, E. (1988). Passionate and companionate love. In R. J. Sternberg & M. L. Barnes (Eds.), *The psychology of love* (pp. 191–217). New Haven, CT: Yale University Press.

Hatfield, E., Cacioppo, J. T., & Rapson, R. L. (1993). *Emotional contagion.* New York: Cambridge University Press.

Hatfield, E., Greenberger, E., Traupmann, J., & Lambert, P. (1982). Equity and sexual satisfaction in recently married couples. *Journal of Sex Research, 18,* 18–32.

Hatfield, E., & Rapson, R. L. (1993). *Love, sex, and intimacy: Their psychology, biology, and history.* New York: HarperCollins.

Hatfield, E., & Rapson, R. L. (1996). *Love and sex: Cross-cultural perspectives.* Needham Heights, MA: Allyn & Bacon.

Hatfield, E., & Rapson, R. L. (2002). Passionate love and sexual desire: Cultural and historical perspectives. In A. L. Vangelisti, H. T. Reis, & M. A. Fitzpatrick (Eds.), *Stability and change in relationships* (pp. 306–324). New York: Cambridge University Press.

Hatfield, E., & Sprecher, S. (1986). Measuring passionate love in intimate relationships. *Journal of Adolescence, 9,* 383–410.

Hatfield, E., & Sprecher, S. (1995). Men's and women's preferences in marital partners in the United States, Russia, and Japan. *Journal of Cross-Cultural Psychology, 26,* 728–750.

Hatfield, E., & Walster, G. W. (1978). *A new look at love.* Reading, MA: Addison-Wesley.

Haugtvedt, C. P., & Wegener, D. T. (1994). Message order effects in persuasion: An attitude strength perspective. *Journal of Consumer Research, 21,* 205–218.

Hays, C. L. (2003, June 5). Martha Stewart indicted by U.S. on obstruction. *The New York Times,* p. A1; C4.

Hazan, C., & Shaver, P. (1987). Romantic love conceptualized as an attachment process. *Journal of Personality and Social Psychology, 52,* 511–524.

Hazan, C., & Shaver, P. (1994a). Attachment as an organizational framework for research on close relationships. *Psychological Inquiry, 5,* 1–22.

Hazan, C., & Shaver, P. (1994b). Deeper into attachment theory. *Psychological Inquiry, 5,* 68–79.

Hazelwood, J. D., & Olson, J. M. (1986). Covariation information, causal questioning, and interpersonal behavior. *Journal of Experimental Social Psychology, 22,* 276–291.

Hebl, M., Foster, J., Bigazzi, J., Mannix, L., & Dovidio, J. (2002). Formal and interpersonal discrimination: A field study of bias toward homosexual applicants. *Personality and Social Psychology Bulletin, 28,* 815–825.

Heckhausen, J., & Schulz, R. (1995). A life-span theory of control. *Psychological Review, 102,* 284–304.

Hedge, A., & Yousif, Y. H. (1992). Effects of urban size, urgency, and cost on helpfulness. *Journal of Cross-Cultural Psychology, 23,* 107–115.

Hedges, L. V., & Nowell, A. (1995). Sex differences in mental test scores, variability, and numbers of high-scoring individuals. *Science, 269,* 41–45.

Heider, F. (1944). Social perception and phenomenal causality. *Psychological Review, 51,* 358–374.

Heider, F. (1958). *The psychology of interpersonal relations.* New York: Wiley.

Heinberg, L. J., & Thompson, J. K. (1995). Body image and televised images of thinness and attractiveness: A controlled laboratory investigation. *Journal of Social and Clinical Psychology, 14,* 1–14.

Heine, S. J., Kitayama, S., & Lehman, D. R. (2001). Cultural differences in self-evaluation: Japanese readily accept negative self-relevant information. *Journal of Cross-Cultural Psychology, 32*, 434–443.

Heine, S. J., Lehman, D. R., Markus, H. R., & Kitayama, S. (1999). Is there a universal need for positive self-regard? *Psychological Review, 106*, 766–794.

Heine, S. J., Lehman, D. R., Peng, K., & Greenholtz, J. (2002). What's wrong with cross-cultural comparisons of subjective Likert scales?: The reference-group effect. *Journal of Personality and Social Psychology, 82*, 903–918.

Heine, S. J., & Renshaw, K. (2002). Interjudge agreement, self-enhancement, and liking: Cross-cultural divergences. *Personality and Social Psychology Bulletin, 28*, 578–587.

Hejmadi, A., Davidson, R. J., & Rozin, P. (2000). Exploring Hindu Indian emotion expressions: Evidence for accurate recognition by Americans and Indians. *Psychological Science, 11*, 183–187

Helgeson, V. S. (1994). Long-distance romantic relationships: Sex differences in adjustment and breakup. *Personality and Social Psychology Bulletin, 20*, 254–265.

Helgeson, V. S. (2003). Cognitive adaptation, psychological adjustment, and disease progression among angioplasty patents: 4 years later. *Health Psychology, 22*, 30–38.

Helgeson, V. S., & Cohen, S. (1996). Social support and adjustment to cancer: Reconciling descriptive, correlational, and intervention research. *Health Psychology, 15*, 135–148.

Helgeson, V. S., Cohen, S., & Fritz, H. L. (1998). Social ties and cancer. In J. C. Holland (Ed.), *Psycho-Oncology* (pp. 99–109). New York: Oxford University Press.

Helgeson, V. S., & Fritz, H. L. (1999). Cognitive adaptation as a predictor of new coronary events after percutaneous transluminal coronary angioplasty. *Psychosomatic Medicine, 61*, 488–495.

Helgeson, V. S., & Mickelson, K. D. (1995). Motives for social comparison. *Personality and Social Psychology Bulletin, 21*, 1200–1209.

Henderlong, J., & Lepper, M. R. (2002). The effects of praise on children's intrinsic motivation: A review and synthesis. *Psychological Bulletin, 128*, 774–795.

Henderson-King, E., & Nisbett, R. E. (1996). Anti-black prejudice as a function of exposure to the negative behavior of a single black person. *Journal of Personality and Social Psychology, 71*, 654–664.

Henley, N. M. (1977). *Body politics: Power, sex, and nonverbal communication.* Englewood Cliffs, NJ: Prentice Hall.

Henry, R. A. (1995). Using relative confidence judgments to evaluate group effectiveness. *Basic and Applied Social Psychology, 16*, 333–350.

Herrnstein, R. J., & Murray, C. A. (1994). *The bell curve: Intelligence and class structure in American life.* New York: Free Press.

Hersh, S. M. (1970). *My Lai 4: A report on the massacre and its aftermath.* New York: Vintage Books.

Herszenhorn, D. M. (1998, March 4). Likening jingles to roar of a jet, New Jersey town votes to quiet ice-cream trucks. *New York Times on the Web,* http://www.nytimes.com

Heunemann, R. L., Shapiro, L. R., Hampton, M. C., & Mitchell, B. W. (1966). A longitudinal study of gross body composition and body conformation and their association with food and activity in the teenage population. *American Journal of Clinical Nutrition, 18*, 325–338.

Hewitt, J., Alqahtani, M. A. (2003). Differences between Saudi and U.S. students in reaction to same- and mixed-sex intimacy shown by others. *Journal of Social Psychology, 143*, 233–242.

Hewstone, M., & Jaspars, J. (1987). Covariation and causal attribution: A logical model of the intuitive analysis of variance. *Journal of Personality and Social Psychology, 53*, 663–672.

Higgins, E. T. (1987). Self-discrepancy: A theory relating self and affect. *Psychological Review, 94*, 319–340.

Higgins, E. T. (1989). Self-discrepancy theory: What patterns of self-beliefs cause people to suffer? In L. Berkowitz (Ed.), *Advances in experimental social psychology* (Vol. 22, pp. 93–136). New York: Academic Press.

Higgins, E. T. (1996a). Knowledge application: Accessibility, applicability, and salience. In E. T. Higgins & A. R. Kruglanski (Eds.), *Social psychology: Handbook of basic principles* (pp. 133–168). New York: Guilford Press.

Higgins, E. T. (1996b). The "self-digest": Self-knowledge serving self-regulatory functions. *Journal of Personality and Social Psychology, 71*, 1062–1083.

Higgins, E. T. (1998). Promotion and prevention: Regulatory focus as a motivational principle. In M. P. Zanna (Ed.), *Advances in experimental social psychology* (Vol. 30, pp. 1–46). San Diego, CA: Academic Press.

Higgins, E. T. (1999). Self-discrepancy: A theory relating self and affect. In R. F. Baumeister (Ed.), *The self in social psychology* (pp. 150–181). Philadelphia: Psychology Press.

Higgins, E. T., & Bargh, J. A. (1987). Social cognition and social perception. *Annual Review of Psychology, 38*, 369–425.

Higgins, E. T., Bond, R. N., Klein, R., & Strauman, T. (1986). Self-discrepancies and emotional vulnerability: How magnitude, accessibility, and type of discrepancy influence affect. *Journal of Personality and Social Psychology, 51*, 5–15.

Higgins, E. T., & Brendl, C. M. (1995). Accessibility and applicability: Some "activation rules" influencing judgment. *Journal of Experimental Social Psychology, 31*, 218–243.

Higgins, E. T., Klein, R., & Strauman, T. (1987). Self-discrepancies: Distinguishing among self-states, self-state conflicts, and emotional vulnerabilities. In K. M. Yardley & T. M. Honess (Eds.), *Self and identity: Psychosocial perspectives* (pp. 173–186). New York: Wiley.

Higgins, E. T., Rholes, W. S., & Jones, C. R. (1977). Category accessibility and impression formation. *Journal of Experimental Social Psychology, 13*, 141–154.

Hilton, D. J., Smith, R. H., & Kim, S. H. (1995). Process of causal explanation and dispositional attribution. *Journal of Personality and Social Psychology, 68*, 377–387.

Hilton, J. L., Fein, S., & Miller, D. T. (1993). Suspicion and dispositional inference. *Journal of Personality and Social Psychology, 19*, 501–512.

Hinds, M. de C. (1993, October 19). Not like the movie: 3 take a dare and lose. *New York Times*, pp. A1, A22.

Hirt, E. R., Deppe, R. K., & Gordon, L. J. (1991). Self-reported versus behavioral self-handicapping: Empirical evidence for a theoretical distinction. *Journal of Personality and Social Psychology, 61*, 981–991.

Hirt, E. R., & Markman, K. D. (1995). Multiple explanation: A consider-an-alternative strategy for debiasing judgments. *Journal of Personality and Social Psychology, 69*, 1069–1086.

Hirt, E. R., McCrea, S. M., & Boris, H. I. (2003). "I know you self-handicapped last exam": Gender differences in reactions to self-handicapping. *Journal of Personality and Social Psychology, 84*, 177–193.

Hirt, E. R., McDonald, H. E., & Erikson, G. A. (1995). How do I remember thee? The role of encoding set and delay in reconstructive memory processes. *Journal of Experimental Social Psychology, 31*, 379–409.

Hirt, E. R., Melton, J. R., McDonald, H. E., & Harackiewicz, J. M. (1996). Processing goals, task interest, and the mood-performance relationship: A mediational analysis. *Journal of Personality and Social Psychology, 71*, 245–261.

Hitler, A. (1925). *Mein Kampf.* Boston: Houghton Mifflin.

Hobfoll, S. E., & Vaux, A. (1993). Social support: Social resources and social context. In L. Goldberger & S. Breznitz (Eds.), *Handbook of stress: Theoretical and clinical aspects* (2nd ed., pp. 685–705). New York: Free Press.

Hoffman, A. J., Gillespie, J. J., Moore, D. A., Wade-Benzoni, K. A., Thompson, L. L., & Bazerman, M. H. (1999). A mixed-motive perspective on the economics versus environmental debate. *American Behavioral Scientist, 42*, 1254–1276.

Hoffman, C., Lau, I., & Johnson, D. R. (1986). The linguistic relativity of person cognition: An English-Chinese comparison. *Journal of Personality and Social Psychology, 51*, 1097–1105.

Hoffman, H. G., Granhag, P. A., See, S.T.K., & Loftus, E. F. (2001). Social influences on reality-monitoring decisions. *Memory and Cognition, 29*, 394–404.

Hoffman, M. L. (1981). Is altruism a part of human nature? *Journal of Personality and Social Psychology, 40*, 121–137.

Hofstede, G. (1984). *Culture's consequences: International differences in work-related values.* Newbury Park, CA: Sage.

Hofstede, G. (1986). Cultural differences in teaching and learning. *International Journal of Intercultural Relations, 10,* 301–320.

Hogan, R., Curphy, G. J., & Hogan, J. (1994). What we know about leadership effectiveness and personality. *American Psychologist, 49,* 493–504.

Hogg, M. A. (1992). *The social psychology of group cohesiveness: From attraction to social identity.* London: Harvester-Wheatsheaf.

Hogg, M. A. (1993). Group cohesiveness: A critical review and some new directions. In W. Stroebe & M. Hewstone (Eds.), *European review of social psychology* (Vol. 4, pp. 85–111). Chichester, England: Wiley.

Hogg, M. A. (2001). A social identity theory of leadership. *Personality and Social Psychology Review, 5,* 184–200.

Hogg, M. A., & Abrams, D. (1988). *Social identifications.* London: Routledge.

Hogg, M. A., & Hains, S. C. (1998). Friendship and group identification: A new look at the role of cohesiveness in groupthink. *European Journal of Social Psychology, 28,* 323–341.

Holden, G. (1991). The relationship of self-efficacy appraisals to subsequent health related outcomes: A meta-analysis. *Social Work in Health Care, 16,* 53–93.

Hollander, E. P. (1958). Conformity, status, and idiosyncrasy credit. *Psychological Review, 65,* 117–127.

Hollander, E. P. (1960). Competence and conformity in the acceptance of influence. *Journal of Abnormal and Social Psychology, 61,* 361–365.

Hollander, E. P. (1985). Leadership and power. In G. Lindzey & E. Aronson (Eds.), *Handbook of social psychology* (3rd ed., Vol. 2, pp. 485–537). New York: McGraw-Hill.

Holliday, R. E. (2003). Reducing misinformation effects in children with cognitive interviews: Dissociating recollection and familiarity. *Child Development, 74,* 728–751.

Hollingshead, A. B. (2001). Cognitive interdependence and convergent expectations in transactive memory. *Journal of Personality and Social Psychology, 81,* 1080–1089.

Holmes, T. H., & Rahe, R. H. (1967). The Social Readjustment Rating Scale. *Journal of Psychosomatic Research, 11,* 213–218.

Homans, G. C. (1961). *Social behavior: Its elementary forms.* New York: Harcourt Brace.

Hong, G.Y. (1992). *Contributions of "culture-absent" cross-cultural psychology.* Paper presented at the annual meeting of the Society for Cross-Cultural Research, Santa Fe, NM.

Hong, Y., Morris, M. W., Chiu, C., & Benet-Martinez, V. (2000). Multicultural minds: A dynamic constructivist approach to culture and cognition. *American Psychologist, 55,* 709–720.

Honts, C. R. (1994). Psychophysiological detection of deception. *Current Directions in Psychological Science, 3,* 77–82.

Hoose, P. M., (1989). *Necessities: Racial barriers in American sports.* New York: Random House.

Horowitz, I. A., & Bordens, K. S. (2002). The effects of jury size, evidence complexity, and note taking on jury process and performance in a civil trial. *Journal of Applied Psychology, 87,* 121–130.

House, J. S., Robbins, C., & Metzner, H. L. (1982). The association of social relationships and activities with mortality: Prospective evidence from the Tecumseh Community Health Study. *American Journal of Epidemiology, 116,* 123–140.

House, R. J. (1971). A path-goal theory of leadership effectiveness. *Administrative Science Quarterly, 16,* 321–338.

Houts, R. M., Robins, E., & Huston, T. L. (1996). Compatibility and the development of premarital relationships. *Journal of Marriage and the Family, 58,* 7–20.

Hovland, C. I., Janis, I. L., & Kelley, H. H. (1953). *Communication and persuasion: Psychological studies of opinion change.* New Haven, CT: Yale University Press.

Hovland, C. I., & Sears, R. R. (1940). Minor studies in aggression: 6. Correlation of lynchings with economic indices. *Journal of Psychology, 9,* 301–310.

Hovland, C. I., & Weiss, W. (1951). The influence of source credibility on communication effectiveness. *Public Opinion Quarterly, 15,* 635–650.

Howard, J. A., Blumstein, P., & Schwartz, P. (1987). Social or evolutionary theories? Some observations on preferences in human mate selection. *Journal of Personality and Social Psychology, 53,* 194–200.

Hsu, S. S. (1995, April 8). Fredericksburg searches its soul after clerk is beaten as 6 watch. *Washington Post,* pp. A1, A13.

Huesmann, L. R., & Miller, L. S. (1994). Long-term effects of repeated exposure to media violence in childhood. In L. R. Huesmann (Ed.), *Aggressive behavior: Current perspectives* (pp. 153–186). New York: Plenum.

Huffman, K. T., Grossnickle, W. F., Cope, J. G., & Huffman, K. P. (1995). Litter reduction: A review and integration of the literature. *Environment and Behavior, 27,* 153–183.

Huguet, P., Galvaing, M. P., Monteil, J. M., & Dumas, F. (1999). Social presence effects in the Stroop task: Further evidence for an attentional view of social facilitation. *Journal of Personality and Social Psychology, 77,* 1011–1025.

Hui, C. H., & Triandis, H. C. (1986). Individualism-collectivism: A study of cross-cultural researchers. *Journal of Cross-Cultural Psychology, 17,* 225–248.

Hull, J. G. (1981). A self-awareness model of the causes and effects of alcohol consumption. *Journal of Personality and Social Psychology, 40,* 586–600.

Hull, J. G., & Young, R. D. (1983). Self-consciousness, self-esteem, and success-failure as determinants of alcohol consumption in male social drinkers. *Journal of Personality and Social Psychology, 44,* 1097–1109.

Hull, J. G., Young, R. D., & Jouriles, E. (1986). Applications of the self-awareness model of alcohol consumption: Predicting patterns of use and abuse. *Journal of Personality and Social Psychology, 51,* 790–796.

Hunt, G. T. (1940). *The wars of the Iroquois.* Madison: University of Wisconsin Press.

Hurley, D., & Allen, B. P. (1974). The effect of the number of people present in a nonemergency situation. *Journal of Social Psychology, 92,* 27–29.

Huston, A., & Wright, J. (1996). Television and socialization of young children. In T. M. MacBeth (Ed.), *Tuning in to young viewers: Social science perspectives on television* (pp. 37–60). Thousand Oaks, CA: Sage

Hutchinson, R. R. (1983). The pain-aggression relationship and its expression in naturalistic settings. *Aggressive Behavior, 9,* 229–242.

Hyde, J. S. (1997). Mathematics: Is biology the cause of gender differences in performance? In M. R. Walsh (Ed.), *Women, men, and gender: Ongoing debates* (pp. 271–273). New Haven, CT: Yale University Press.

Hygge, S., Evans, G. W., & Bullinger, M. (2002). A prospective study of some effects of aircraft noise on cognitive performance in schoolchildren. *Psychological Science, 13,* 469–474.

Hyman, J.J., & Sheatsley, P. B. (1956). Attitudes toward desegregation. *Scientific American, 195*(6), 35–39.

Iacono, W. G. (2000). The detection of deception. In J. T. Cacioppo & L. G. Tassinary (Eds.), *Handbook of psychophysiology* (2nd ed., pp. 772–793). New York: Cambridge University Press.

Iacono, W. G., & Patrick, C. J. (1999). Polygraph ("lie detector") testing: The state of the art. In A. K. Hess & I. B. Weiner (Eds.), *The handbook of forensic psychology* (2nd ed., pp. 440–473). New York: Wiley.

Ickes, W. J., Patterson, M. L., Rajecki, D. W., & Tanford, S. (1982). Behavioral and cognitive consequences of reciprocal versus compensatory responses to preinteraction expectancies. *Social Cognition, 1,* 160–190.

Impett, E. A., Beals, K. P., & Peplau, L. A. (2001–2002). Testing the investment model of relationship commitment and stability in a longitudinal study of married couples. *Current Psychology, 20,* 312–326.

Imrich, D. J., Mullin, C., & Linz, D. G. (1995). Measuring the extent of prejudicial pretrial publicity in major American newspapers: A content analysis. *Journal of Communication, 45,* 94–117.

Inglehart, M. R. (1991). *Reactions to critical life events: A social psychological analysis.* New York: Praeger.

Insko, C. A., & Schopler, J. (1998). Differential trust of groups and individuals. In C. Sedikides & J. Schopler (Eds.), *Intergroup cognition and intergroup behavior* (pp. 75–107). Mahwah, NJ: Erlbaum.

Insko, C. A., Smith, R. H., Alicke, M. D., Wade, J., & Taylor, S. (1985). Conformity and group size: The concern with being right and the concern with being liked. *Personality and Social Psychology Bulletin, 11,* 41–50.

Isen, A. M. (1987). Positive affect, cognitive processes, and social behavior. In L. Berkowitz (Ed.), *Advances in experimental social psychology* (Vol. 20, pp. 203–253). San Diego, CA: Academic Press.

Isen, A. M. (1999). Positive affect. In T. Dalgleish & M. J. Power (Eds.), *Handbook of cognition and emotion* (pp. 521–539). Chichester, England: Wiley.

Isen, A. M., & Levin, P. A. (1972). Effect of feeling good on helping: Cookies and kindness. *Journal of Personality and Social Psychology, 21,* 384–388.

Isenberg, D. J. (1986). Group polarization: A critical review and meta-analysis. *Journal of Personality and Social Psychology, 50,* 1141–1151.

Izard, C. E. (1994). Innate and universal facial expressions: Evidence from developmental and cross-cultural research. *Psychological Bulletin, 115,* 288–299.

Jackson, J. M., & Williams, K. D. (1985). Social loafing on difficult tasks: Working collectively can improve performance. *Journal of Personality and Social Psychology, 49,* 937–942.

Jackson, J. S., Brown, T. N., Williams, D. R., Torres, M., Sellers, S. L., & Brown, K. (1996). Racism and the physical and mental health status of African Americans: A thirteen-year national panel study. *Ethnicity and Disease, 6,* 132–147.

Jackson, J. S., & Inglehart, M. R. (1995). Reverberation theory: Stress and racism in hierarchically structured communities. In S. E. Hobfoll & M. W. De Vries (Eds.), *Extreme stress and communities: Impact and intervention* (pp. 353–373). Dordrecht, Netherlands: Kluwer.

Jackson, J. W. (1993). Realistic group conflict theory: A review and evaluation of the theoretical and empirical literature. *Psychological Record, 43,* 395–413.

Jackson, L. A. (1992). *Physical appearance and gender: Sociobiological and sociocultural perspectives.* Albany: State University of New York Press.

Jackson, L. A., Hunter, J. E., & Hodge, C. N. (1995). Physical attractiveness and intellectual competence: A meta-analytic review. *Social Psychology Quarterly, 58,* 108–122.

Jacobs, J., & Eccles, J. (1992). The impact of mothers' gender-role stereotypic beliefs on mothers' and children's ability perceptions. *Journal of Personality and Social Psychology, 63,* 932–944.

Jacobs, P., & Landau, S. (1971). *To serve the devil* (Vol. 2). New York: Vintage Books.

Jacowitz, K. E., & Kahneman, D. (1995). Measures of anchoring in estimation tasks. *Personality and Social Psychology Bulletin, 21,* 1161–1166.

Jain, S. P., & Posavac, S. S. (2001). Prepurchase attribute verifiability, source credibility, and persuasion. *Journal of Consumer Psychology, 11,* 169–180

James, C. (2000, August 25). Machiavelli meets TV's reality: Unreal. *New York Times,* p. B28.

James, W. (1890). *The principles of psychology.* New York: Henry Holt.

Janis, I. L. (1972). *Victims of groupthink.* Boston: Houghton Mifflin.

Janis, I. L. (1982). *Groupthink: Psychological studies of policy decisions and fiascoes* (2nd ed.). Boston: Houghton Mifflin.

Janis, I. L., & Feshbach, S. (1953). Effects of fear-arousing communications. *Journal of Abnormal and Social Psychology, 49,* 78–92.

Jankowiak, W. R. (1995). Introduction. In W. R. Jankowiak (Ed.), *Romantic passion: A universal experience?* (pp. 1–19). New York: Columbia University Press.

Jankowiak, W. R., & Fischer, E. F. (1992). A cross-cultural perspective on romantic love. *Ethnology, 31,* 149–155.

Janoff-Bulman, R., & Leggatt, H. K. (2002). Culture and social obligation: When "shoulds" are perceived as "wants." *Journal of Research in Personality, 36,* 260–270.

Janoff-Bulman, R., Timko, C., & Carli, L. L. (1985). Cognitive biases in blaming the victim. *Journal of Experimental Social Psychology, 21,* 161–177.

Jecker, J., & Landy, D. (1969). Liking a person as a function of doing him a favor. *Human Relations, 22,* 371–378.

Jellison, J. M., & Riskind, J. A. (1970). A social comparison of abilities interpretation of risk-taking behavior. *Journal of Personality and Social Psychology, 15,* 375–390.

Jensen-Campbell, L. A., Graziano, W. G., & West, S. G. (1995). Dominance, prosocial orientation, and female preference: Do nice guys really finish last? *Journal of Personality and Social Psychology, 68,* 427–440.

Jet noise. (1991, October 21). *New Yorker,* pp. 30–32.

Johnson, D. M. (1945). The phantom anesthetist of Mattoon: A field study of mass hysteria. *Journal of Abnormal and Social Psychology, 40,* 175–186.

Johnson, D. W., & Johnson, R. T. (1987). *Learning together and alone: Cooperative, competitive, and individualistic learning* (2nd ed.). Englewood Cliffs, NJ: Prentice Hall.

Johnson, F. L., & Arles, E. J. (1983). Conversational patterns among same-sex pairs of late-adolescent close friends. *Journal of Genetic Psychology, 142,* 225–238.

Johnson, J. G., Cohen, P., Smailes, E. M., Kasen, S., & Brook, J. (2002). Television viewing and aggressive behavior during adolescence and adulthood. *Science, 295,* 2468–2471.

Johnson, L. B. (1971). *The vantage point: Perspectives of the presidency, 1963–69.* New York: Holt, Rinehart and Winston.

Johnson, M. K., Hashtroudi, S., & Lindsay, D. S. (1993). Source monitoring. *Psychological Bulletin, 114,* 3–28.

Johnson, M. K., & Raye, C. L. (1981). Reality monitoring. *Psychological Review, 88,* 67–85.

Johnson, M. K., Raye, C. L., Wang, A. Y., & Taylor, T. H. (1979). Fact and fantasy: The roles of accuracy and variability in confusing imaginations with perceptual experiences. *Journal of Experimental Psychology: Human Learning and Memory, 5,* 229–240.

Johnson, R. D., & Downing, R. L. (1979). Deindividuation and valence of cues: Effects of prosocial and antisocial behavior. *Journal of Personality and Social Psychology, 37,* 1532–1538.

Johnson, T. E., & Rule, B. G. (1986). Mitigating circumstance information, censure, and aggression. *Journal of Personality and Social Psychology, 50,* 537–542.

Joiner, T. E., Jr., & Wagner, K. D. (1995). Attributional style and depression in children and adolescents: A meta-analytic review. *Clinical Psychology Review, 15,* 777–798.

Jones, C., & Aronson, E. (1973). Attribution of fault to a rape victim as a function of the respectability of the victim. *Journal of Personality and Social Psychology, 26,* 415–419.

Jones, D., & Hill, K. (1993). Criteria of facial attractiveness in five populations. *Human Nature, 4,* 271–296.

Jones, E. E. (1964). *Ingratiation: A social psychological analysis.* New York: Appleton-Century-Crofts.

Jones, E. E. (1979). The rocky road from acts to dispositions. *American Scientist, 34,* 107–117.

Jones, E. E. (1990). *Interpersonal perception.* New York: Freeman.

Jones, E. E., & Berglas, S. (1978). Control of attributions about the self through self-handicapping strategies: The appeal of alcohol and the role of underachievement. *Personality and Social Psychology Bulletin, 4,* 200–206.

Jones, E. E., & Davis, K. E. (1965). From acts to dispositions: The attribution process in social psychology. In L. Berkowitz (Ed.), *Advances in experimental social psychology* (Vol. 2, pp. 219–266). New York: Academic Press.

Jones, E. E., & Harris, V. A. (1967). The attribution of attitudes. *Journal of Experimental Social Psychology, 3,* 1–24.

Jones, E. E., & Kohler, R. (1959). The effects of plausibility on the learning of controversial statements. *Journal of Abnormal and Social Psychology, 57,* 315–320.

Jones, E. E., & Nisbett, R. E. (1972). The actor and the observer: Divergent perceptions of the causes of behavior. In E. E. Jones, D. E. Kanouse, H. H. Kelley, R. E. Nisbett, S. Valins, & B. Weiner (Eds.), *Attribution: Perceiving the causes of behavior* (pp. 79–94). Morristown, NJ: General Learning Press.

Jones, E. E., & Pittman, T. S. (1982). Toward a general theory of strategic self-presentation. In J. Suls (Ed.), *Psychological perspectives on the self* (pp. 231–262). Hillsdale, NJ: Erlbaum.

Jones, E. E., & Sigall, H. (1971). The bogus pipeline: A new paradigm for measuring affect and attitude. *Psychological Bulletin, 76,* 349–364.

Jones, E. E., & Wortman, C. B. (1973). *Ingratiation: An attributional approach.* Morristown, NJ: General Learning Press.

Jones, L. W., Sinclair, R. W., & Courneya, K. S. (2003). The effects of source credibility and message framing on exercise intentions, behavior and attitudes: An integration of the elaboration likelihood model and prospect theory. *Journal of Applied Social Psychology, 33,* 179–196.

Jones, T. F., Craig, A. S., Hoy, D., Gunter, E. W., Ashley, D. L., Barr, D. B., et al. (2000). Mass psychogenic illness attributed to toxic exposure at a high school. *New England Journal of Medicine, 342,* 96–100.

Jordan, M. (1996, January 15). In Japan, bullying children to death. *Washington Post,* pp. A1, A15.

Jordan, M., & Sullivan, K. (1995, September 8). A matter of saving face: Japanese can rent mourners, relatives, friends, even enemies to buff an image. *Washington Post,* pp. A1, A28.

Josephson, W. D. (1987). Television violence and children's aggression: Testing the priming, social script, and disinhibition prediction. *Journal of Personality and Social Psychology, 53,* 882–890.

Jowett, G. S., & O'Donnell, V. (1999). *Propaganda and persuasion.* Thousand Oaks, CA: Sage.

Judge, T. A., Bono, J. E., Ilies, R., & Gerhardt, M. W. (2002). Personality and leadership: A qualitative and quantitative review. *Journal of Applied Psychology, 87,* 765–780.

Judge rules ACLU discrimination suit against Continental Airlines can go forward. (2002). Retrieved from http://www.aclu.org/RacialEquality/RacialEquality.cfm?ID=10994&c=133

Jürgen-Lohmann, J., Borsch, F., & Giesen, H. (2001). Kooperatives Lernen an der Hochschule: Evaluation des Gruppenpuzzles in Seminaren der Pädagogischen Psychologie. *Zeitschrift für Pädagogische Psychologie, 15,* 74–84.

Jussim, L. (1986). Self-fulfilling prophecies: A theoretical and integrative review. *Psychological Review, 93,* 429–445.

Jussim, L. (1991). Social perception and social reality: A reflection-construction model. *Psychological Review, 98,* 54–73.

Jussim, L., & Eccles, J. S. (1992). Teacher expectations: II. Construction and reflection of student achievement. *Journal of Personality and Social Psychology, 63,* 947–961.

Kahn, J. P. (2003, June 5). Stewart's fans still see a shine under the tarnish. *Boston Globe,* p. D1; D7.

Kahn, J. P. (2003, June 7). How the mighty have fallen. *Boston Globe,* p. D1; D7.

Kahn, M. (1966). The physiology of catharsis. *Journal of Personality and Social Psychology, 3,* 278–298.

Kahneman, D., & Frederick, S. (2002). Representativeness revisited: Attribute substitution in intuitive judgment. In T. Gilovich, D. W. Griffin, & D. Kahneman (Eds). *Heuristics and biases: The psychology of intuitive judgment* (pp. 49–81). New York: Cambridge University Press.

Kahneman, D., & Miller, D. T. (1986). Norm theory: Comparing reality to its alternatives. *Psychological Review, 93,* 136–153.

Kahneman, D., & Tversky, A. (1973). On the psychology of prediction. *Psychological Review, 80,* 237–251.

Kallgren, C. A., Reno, R. R., & Cialdini, R. B. (2000). A focus theory of normative conduct: When norms do and do not affect behavior. *Personality and Social Psychology Bulletin, 26,* 1002–1012.

Kallgren, C. A., & Wood, W. (1986). Access to attitude-relevant information in memory as a determinant of attitude-behavior consistency. *Journal of Experimental Social Psychology, 22,* 328–338.

Kalven, H., Jr., & Zeisel, H. (1966). *The American jury.* Boston: Little, Brown.

Kameda, T., Takezawa, M., & Hastie, R. (2003). The logic of social sharing: An evolutionary game analysis of adaptive norm development. *Personality and Social Psychology Review, 7,* 2–19.

Kappas, A. (1997). The fascination with faces: Are they windows to our soul? *Journal of Nonverbal Behavior, 21,* 157–162.

Karau, S. J., & Williams, K. D. (1993). Social loafing: A meta-analytic review and theoretical integration. *Journal of Personality and Social Psychology, 65,* 681–706.

Karau, S.J., & Williams, K. D. (2001). Understanding individual motivation in groups: The collective effort model. In M. E. Turner (Ed.), *Groups at work—theory and research: Applied social research* (pp. 113–141). Mahwah, NJ: Erlbaum.

Karlins, M., Coffman, T. L., & Walters, G. (1969). On the fading of social stereotypes: Studies in three generations of college students. *Journal of Personality and Social Psychology, 13,* 1–16.

Karney, B. R., & Bradbury, T. N. (2000). Attributions in marriage: State or trait? A growth curve analysis. *Journal of Personality and Social Psychology, 78,* 295–309.

Kashima, Y., Siegel, M., Tanaka, K., & Kashima, E. S. (1992). Do people believe behaviors are consistent with attitudes? Towards a cultural psychology of attribution process. *British Journal of Social Psychology, 31,* 111–124.

Kassarjian, H., & Cohen, J. (1965). Cognitive dissonance and consumer behavior. *California Management Review, 8,* 55–64.

Katz, D. (1960). The functional approach to the study of attitudes. *Public Opinion Quarterly, 24,* 163–204.

Katz, D., & Braly, K. W. (1933). Racial stereotypes of 100 college students. *Journal of Abnormal and Social Psychology, 28,* 280–290.

Kauffman, D. R., & Steiner, I. D. (1968). Conformity as an ingratiation technique. *Journal of Experimental Social Psychology, 4,* 404–414.

Kaya, N., & Erkip, F. (2001). Satisfaction in a dormitory building: The effects of floor height on the perception of room size and crowding. *Environment and Behavior, 33,* 35–53.

Kebbell, M. R., & Wagstaff, G. F. (1998). Hypnotic interviewing: The best way to interview eyewitnesses? *Behavioral Sciences and the Law, 16,* 115–129.

Keelan, J. P. R., Dion, K. L., & Dion, K. K. (1994). Attachment style and hetereosexual relationships among young adults: A short-term panel study. *Journal of Social and Personal Relationships, 11,* 201–214.

Kelley, H. H. (1950). The warm-cold variable in first impressions of persons. *Journal of Personality, 18,* 431–439.

Kelley, H. H. (1955). The two functions of reference groups. In G. E. Swanson, T. M. Newcomb, & E. L. Hartley (Eds.), *Readings in social psychology* (2nd ed., pp. 410–414). New York: Henry Holt.

Kelley, H. H. (1967). Attribution theory in social psychology. In D. Levine (Ed.), *Nebraska Symposium on Motivation* (Vol. 15, pp. 192–238). Lincoln: University of Nebraska Press.

Kelley, H. H. (1972). Attribution in social interaction. In E. E. Jones, D. E. Kanouse, H. H. Kelley, R. E. Nisbett, S. Valins, & B. Weiner (Eds.), *Attribution: Perceiving the causes of behavior* (pp. 1–26). Morristown, NJ: General Learning Press.

Kelley, H. H. (1973). The process of causal attribution. *American Psychologist, 28,* 107–128.

Kelley, H. H. (1983). Love and commitment. In H. H. Kelley, E. Berscheid, A. Christensen, J. H. Harvey, T. L. Huston, G. Levinger, et al. (Eds.), *Close relationships* (pp. 265–314). New York: Freeman.

Kelley, H. H., & Thibaut, J. (1978). *Interpersonal relations: A theory of interdependence.* New York: Wiley.

Kelly, J. R., & Karau, S. J. (1999). Group decision making: The effects of initial preferences and time pressure. *Personality and Social Psychology Bulletin, 25,* 1342–1354.

Keltner, D. (1995). Signs of appeasement: Evidence for the distinct displays of embarrassment, amusement, and shame. *Journal of Personality and Social Psychology, 68,* 441–454.

Keltner, D., & Buswell, B. N. (1996). Evidence for the distinctness of embarrassment, shame, and guilt: A study of recalled antecedents and facial expressions. *Cognition and Emotion, 10,* 155–171.

Keltner, D., & Shiota, M. N. (2003). New displays and new emotions: A commentary on Rozin and Cohen. *Emotion, 3,* 86–91.

Kenny, D. A. (1994a). *Interpersonal perception: A social relations analysis.* New York: Guilford Press.

Kenny, D. A. (1994b). Using the social relations model to understand relationships. In R. Erber & R. Gilmour (Eds.), *Theoretical frameworks for personal relationships* (pp. 111–127). Hillsdale, NJ: Erlbaum.

Kenny, D. A., Albright, L., Malloy, T. E., & Kashy, D. A. (1994). Consensus in interpersonal perception: Acquaintance and the Big Five. *Psychological Bulletin, 116,* 245–258.

Kenny, D. A., & La Voie, L. (1982). Reciprocity of interpersonal attraction: A confirmed hypothesis. *Social Psychology Quarterly, 45,* 54–58.

Kenrick, D. T., & Keefe, R. C. (1992). Age preferences in mate reflect sex differences in human reproductive strategies. *Behavioral and Brain Sciences, 15,* 75–133.

Kenrick, D. T., & MacFarlane, S. W. (1986). Ambient temperature and horn honking: A field study of the heat/aggression relationship. *Environment and Behavior, 18,* 179–191.

Kent, M. V. (1994). The presence of others. In A. P. Hare, H. H. Blumberg, M. F. Davies, & M. V. Kent (Eds.), *Small group research: A handbook* (pp. 81–105). Norwood, NJ: Ablex.

Kerckhoff, A. C., & Back, K. W. (1968). *The June bug: A study of hysterical contagion.* New York: Appleton-Century-Crofts.

Kerr, N. L. (1995). Social psychology in court: The case of the prejudicial pretrial publicity. In G. G. Brannigan & M. R. Merrens (Eds.), *The social psychologists: Research adventures* (pp. 247–262). New York: McGraw-Hill.

Kerr, N. L., & Kaufman-Gilliland, C. M. (1994). Communication, commitment, and cooperation in social dilemmas. *Journal of Personality and Social Psychology, 66,* 513–529.

Kerr, N. L., MacCoun, R. J., & Kramer, G. P. (1996). Bias in judgment: Comparing individuals and groups. *Psychological Review, 103,* 687–719.

Key, W. B. (1973). *Subliminal seduction.* Englewood Cliffs, NJ: Signet Books.

Key, W. B. (1989). *Age of manipulation: The con in confidence and the sin in sincere.* New York: Henry Holt.

Kiesler, C. A., & Kiesler, S. B. (1969). *Conformity.* Reading, MA: Addison-Wesley.

Kihlstrom, J. F. (1987). The cognitive unconscious. *Science, 237,* 1445–1452.

Kihlstrom, J. F. (1996). The trauma-memory argument and recovered memory therapy. In K. Pezdek & W. P. Banks (Eds.), *The recovered memory/false memory debate* (pp. 297–311). San Diego, CA: Academic Press.

Kihlstrom, J. F., Beer, J. S., & Klein, S. B. (2003). Self and identity as memory. In M. R. Leary & J. P. Tangney (Eds.), *Handbook of self and identity* (pp. 68–90). New York: Guilford Press.

Kihlstrom, J. F., & Klein, S. B. (1994). The self as a knowledge structure. In R. S. Wyer & T. K. Srull (Eds.), *Handbook of social cognition: Vol. 1. Basic processes* (pp. 153–206). Hillsdale, NJ: Erlbaum.

Killen, J. D. (1985). Prevention of adolescent tobacco smoking: The social pressure resistance training approach. *Journal of Child Psychology and Psychiatry, 26,* 7–15.

Killen, J. D., Taylor, C. B., Hayward, C., Wilson, D. M., Haydel, K. F., Hammer, L. D., et al. (1994). Pursuit of thinness and onset of eating disorder symptoms in a community sample of adolescent girls: A three-year prospective analysis. *International Journal of Eating Disorders, 16,* 227–238.

Killian, L. M. (1964). Social movements. In R. E. L. Farris (Ed.), *Handbook of modern sociology* (pp. 426–455). Chicago: Rand McNally.

Kim, M. P., & Rosenberg, S. (1980). Comparison of two structural models of implicit personality theory. *Journal of Personality and Social Psychology, 38,* 375–389.

Kim, U., & Berry, J. W. (1993). *Indigenous psychologies: Research and experience in cultural context.* Newbury Park, CA: Sage.

Kim, U., Triandis, H. C., Kagitcibasi, C., Choi, S. C., & Yoon, G. (Eds.). (1994). *Individualism and collectivism: Theory, method, and applications.* Thousand Oaks, CA: Sage.

Kimel, E. (2001, Aug. 2). Students earn cash for summer reading. *Sarasota Herald Tribunem* p. BV2.

Kimura, D. (1987). Are men's and women's brains really different? *Canadian Psychology, 28,* 133–147.

Kinder, D. R., & Sears, D. O. (1981). Prejudice and politics: Symbolic racism versus racial threats to the good life. *Journal of Personality and Social Psychology, 40,* 414–431.

Kindlon, D., & Thompson, M. (2000). *Raising Cain: Protecting the emotional life of boys.* New York: Ballantine Books.

Kirkpatrick, L. A., & Davis, K. E. (1994). Attachment style, gender, and relationship stability: A longitudinal analysis. *Journal of Personality and Social Psychology, 66,* 502–512.

Kirkpatrick, L. A., & Hazan, C. (1994). Attachment styles and close relationships: A four-year prospective study. *Personal Relationships, 1,* 123–142.

Kitayama, S., & Markus, H. R. (1994). Culture and the self: How cultures influence the way we view ourselves. In D. Matsumoto (Ed.), *People: Psychology from a cultural perspective* (pp. 17–37). Pacific Grove, CA: Brooks/Cole.

Kitayama, S., & Masuda, T. (1997). *Cultural psychology of social inference: The correspondence bias in Japan.* Unpublished manuscript, Kyoto University.

Klein, W. M. (1996). Maintaining self-serving social comparisons: Attenuating the perceived significance of risk-increasing behaviors. *Journal of Social and Clinical Psychology, 15,* 120–142.

Kleiner, M. (Ed.). (2002). *Handbook of polygraph testing.* San Diego, CA: Academic Press.

Kleiwer, W., Lepore, S. J., & Evans, G. W. (1990). The costs of Type B behavior: Females at risk in achievement situations. *Journal of Applied Social Psychology, 20,* 1369–1382.

Klenke, K. (1996). *Women and leadership: A contextual perspective.* New York: Springer-Verlag.

Kluger, R. (1996). *Ashes to ashes: America's hundred-year cigarette war, the public health, and the unabashed triumph of Philip Morris.* New York: Knopf.

Knapp, M. L., & Hall, J. A. (1997). *Nonverbal communication in human interaction.* Orlando, FL: Harcourt Brace.

Knopke, H., Norrell, R., & Rogers, R. (1991). *Opening doors: Perspectives on race relations in contemporary America.* Tuscaloosa: University of Alabama Press.

Knowles, E. S., & Sibicky, M. E. (1990). Continuity and diversity in the stream of selves: Metaphorical resolutions of William James's one-in-many-selves paradox. *Personality and Social Psychology Bulletin, 16,* 676–687.

Knox, R., & Inkster, J. (1968). Postdecision dissonance at post time. *Journal of Personality and Social Psychology, 8,* 319–323.

Koehler, J. J. (1993). The base rate fallacy myth. *Psycoloquy, 4,* 49.

Koehler, J. J. (1996). The base rate fallacy reconsidered: Descriptive, normative, and methodological challenges. *Behavioral and Brain Sciences, 19,* 1–53.

Koehnken, G., Malpass, R. S., & Wogalter, M. S. (1996). Forensic applications of line-up research. In S. L. Sporer, R. S. Malpass, & G. Koehnken (Eds.), *Psychological issues in eyewitness identification* (pp. 205–231). Mahwah, NJ: Erlbaum.

Kogan, N., & Wallach, M. A. (1964). *Risk-taking: A study in cognition and personality.* New York: Henry Holt.

Kollack, P., Blumstein, P., & Schwartz, P., (1994). The judgment of equity in intimate relationships. *Social Psychology Quarterly, 57,* 340–351.

Koopman, C., Hermanson, K., Diamond, S., Angell, K., & Spiegel, D. (1998). Social support, life stress, pain and emotional adjustment to advanced breast cancer. *Psycho-Oncology, 7,* 101-111.

Korda, M. (1997, October 6). Prompting the president. *New Yorker,* pp. 88–95.

Koriat, A., Goldsmith, M., & Pansky, A. (2000). Toward a psychology of memory accuracy. *Annual Review of Psychology, 51,* 481–537.

Kortenkamp, K. V., & Moore, C. F. (2001). Ecocentrism and antropocentrism: Moral reasoning about ecological commons dilemmas. *Journal of Environmental Psychology, 21,* 261–272.

Kowert, P. A. (2002). *Groupthink or deadlock: When do leaders learn from their advisors?* Albany: State University of New York Press.

Krakow, A., & Blass, T. (1995). When nurses obey or defy inappropriate physician orders: Attributional differences. *Journal of Social Behavior and Personality, 10,* 585–594.

Kramer, G. P., Kerr, N. L., & Carroll, J. S. (1990). Pretrial publicity, judicial remedies, and jury bias. *Law and Human Behavior, 14,* 409–438.

Krantz, D. S., & McCeney, M. K. (2002). Effects of psychological and social factors on organic disease: A critical assessment of research on coronary heart disease. *Annual Review of Psychology, 53,* 341–369.

Krasner, J. (2003, June 8). Q&A: Michael Houston, marketing professor, on Martha Stewart. *Boston Globe,* p. C2.

Krauss, R. M., & Deutsch, M. (1966). Communication in interpersonal bargaining. *Journal of Personality and Social Psychology, 4,* 572–577.

Krauss, R. M., Freedman, J. L., & Whitcup, M. (1978). Field and laboratory studies of littering. *Journal of Experimental Social Psychology, 14,* 109–122.

Kremer, J. F., & Stephens, L. (1983). Attributions and arousal as mediators of mitigation's effects on retaliation. *Journal of Personality and Social Psychology, 45,* 335–343.

Kressel, K., & Pruitt, D. G. (1989). A research perspective on the mediation of social conflict. In K. Kressel & D. G. Pruitt (Eds.), *Mediation research: The process and effectiveness of third party intervention* (pp. 394–435). San Francisco: Jossey-Bass.

Krosnick, J. A. (1999). Survey research. *Annual Review of Psychology, 50,* 537–567.

Krosnick, J. A., & Alwin, D. F. (1989). Aging and susceptibility to attitude change. *Journal of Personality and Social Psychology, 57,* 416–425.

Krueger, J., Ham, J. J., & Linford, K. (1996). Perceptions of behavioral consistency: Are people aware of the actor-observer effect? *Psychological Science, 7,* 259–264.

Kruglanski, A. W. (1989). *Lay epistemics and human knowledge.* New York: Plenum.

Kruglanski, A. W., & Webster, D. M. (1991). Group members' reactions to opinion deviates and conformists at varying degrees of proximity to decision deadline and of environmental noise. *Journal of Personality and Social Psychology, 61,* 212–225.

Kruglanski, A. W., & Webster, D. M. (1996). Motivated closing of the mind: "Seizing" and "freezing." *Psychological Review, 103,* 263–283.

Krull, D. S. (1993). Does the grist change the mill? The effect of the perceiver's inferential goal on the process of social inference. *Personality and Social Psychology Bulletin, 19,* 340–348.

Krull, D. S., & Dill, J. C. (1996). On thinking first and responding fast: Flexibility in social inference processes. *Personality and Social Psychology Bulletin, 22,* 949–959.

Krull, D. S., Loy, M. H., Lin, J., Wang, C., Chen, S., & Zhao, X. (1999). The fundamental correspondence bias in individualist and collectivist cultures. *Personality and Social Psychology Bulletin, 25,* 1208–1219.

Kubitschek, W. N., & Hallinan, M. T. (1998). Tracking and students' friendships. *Social Psychology Quarterly, 61,* 1–15.

Kuhn, D., Weinstock, M., & Flaton, R. (1994). How well do jurors reason? Competence dimensions of individual variation in a juror reasoning task. *Psychological Science, 5,* 289–296.

Kulik, J. A., & Brown, R. (1979). Frustration, attribution of blame, and aggression. *Journal of Experimental Social Psychology, 15,* 183–194.

Kunda, Z. (1999). *Social cognition: Making sense of people.* Cambridge, MA: MIT Press.

Kunda, Z., Fong, G. T., Sanitioso, R., & Reber, E. (1993). Directional questions about self-conceptions. *Journal of Experimental Social Psychology, 29,* 63–86.

Kunda, Z., & Oleson, K. C. (1997). When exceptions prove the rule: How extremity of deviance determines the impact of deviant examples on stereotypes. *Journal of Personality and Social Psychology, 72,* 965–979.

Kunda, Z., & Schwartz, S. H. (1983). Undermining intrinsic moral motivation: External reward and self-presentation. *Journal of Personality and Social Psychology, 45,* 763–771.

Kunda, Z., Sinclair, L., & Griffin, D. W. (1997). Equal ratings but separate meanings: Stereotypes and the construal of traits. *Journal of Personality and Social Psychology, 72,* 720–734.

Kuo, Z. Y. (1961). *Instinct.* Princeton, NJ: Van Nostrand.

Kurdek, L. A. (1992). Relationship stability and relationship satisfaction in cohabitating gay and lesbian couples: A prospective longitudinal test of the contextual and interdependence models. *Journal of Social and Personal Relationships, 9,* 125–142.

Kuusinen, J. (1969). Factorial invariance of personality ratings. *Scandinavian Journal of Psychology, 10,* 33–44.

Kuykendall, D., & Keating, J. P. (1990). Altering thoughts and judgments through repeated association. *British Journal of Social Psychology, 29,* 79–86.

La France, M., Hecht, M. A., & Paluck, E. L. (2003). The contingent smile: A meta-analysis of sex differences in smiling. *Psychological Bulletin, 129,* 305–334.

Lalancette, M. F., & Standing, L. (1990). Asch fails again. *Social Behavior and Personality, 18,* 7–12.

Lambert, A. J., Burroughs, T., & Nguyen, T. (1999). Perceptions of risk and the buffering hypothesis: The role of just world beliefs and right-wing authoritarianism. *Personality and Social Psychology Bulletin, 25,* 643–656.

Lamm, H., Schaude, E., & Trommsdorff, G. (1971). Risky shift as a function of group members' value of risk and need for approval. *Journal of Personality and Social Psychology, 20,* 430–435.

Lampert, R., Baron, S. J., McPherson, C. A., & Lee, F. A. (2002). Heart rate variability during the week of September 11, 2001. *Journal of the American Medical Association, 288,* 575.

Landman, J. (1993). *Regret: The persistence of the possible.* New York: Oxford University Press.

Langer, E. J., & Rodin, J. (1976). The effects of choice and enhanced personal responsibility for the aged: A field experiment. *Journal of Personality and Social Psychology, 34,* 191–198.

Langlois, J. H., Kalakanis, L., Rubenstein, A. J., Larson, A., Hallam, M., & Smoot, M. (2000). Maxims or myths of beauty? A meta-analytic and theoretical review. *Psychological Bulletin, 126,* 390–423.

Langlois, J. H., Ritter, J. M., Roggman, L. A., & Vaughn, L. S. (1991). Facial diversity and infant preferences for attractive faces. *Developmental Psychology, 27,* 79–84.

Langlois, J. H., & Roggman, L. A. (1990). Attractive faces are only average. *Psychological Science, 1,* 115–121.

Langlois, J. H., Roggman, L. A., Casey, R. J., Ritter, J. M., Rieser-Danner, L. A., & Jenkins, V. Y. (1987). Infant preferences for attractive faces: Rudiments of a stereotype? *Developmental Psychology, 23,* 363–369.

Langlois, J. H., Roggman, L. A., & Musselman, L. (1994). What is average and what is not average about attractive faces? *Psychological Science, 5,* 214–220.

Langlois, J. H., Roggman, L. A., & Rieser-Danner, L. A. (1990). Infants' differential social responses to attractive and unattractive faces. *Developmental Psychology, 26,* 153–159.

La Piere, R. T. (1934). Attitudes vs. actions. *Social Forces, 13,* 230–237.

L'Armand, K., & Pepitone, A. (1975). Helping to reward another person: A cross-cultural analysis. *Journal of Personality and Social Psychology, 31,* 189–198.

Larsen, K. S. (1990). The Asch conformity experiment: Replication and transhistorical comparisons. *Journal of Social Behavior and Personality, 5,* 163–168.

Larson, J. R., Jr., Christensen, C., Franz, T. M., & Abbott, A. S. (1998). Diagnosing groups: The pooling, management, and impact of shared and unshared case information in team-based medical decision making. *Journal of Personality and Social Psychology, 75,* 93–108.

Larson, J. R., Jr., Foster-Fishman, P. G., & Franz, T. M. (1998). Leadership style and the discussion of shared and unshared information in decision-making groups. *Personality and Social Psychology Bulletin, 24,* 482–495.

Latané, B. (1981). The psychology of social impact. *American Psychologist, 36,* 343–356.

Latané, B. (1987). From student to colleague: Retracing a decade. In N. E. Grunberg, R. E. Nisbett, J. Rodin, & J. E. Singer (Eds.), *A distinctive approach to psychological research: The influence of Stanley Schachter* (pp. 66–86). Hillsdale, NJ: Erlbaum.

Latané, B., & Bourgeois, M. J. (2001). Successfully simulating dynamic social impact: Three levels of prediction. In J. P. Forgas & K. D. Williams (Eds.), *Social influence: Direct and indirect processes* (pp. 61–76). Philadelphia: Psychology Press.

Latané, B., & Dabbs, J. M. (1975). Sex, group size, and helping in three cities. *Sociometry, 38,* 108–194.

Latané, B., & Darley, J. M. (1968). Group inhibition of bystander intervention. *Journal of Personality and Social Psychology, 10,* 215–221.

Latané, B., & Darley, J. M. (1970). *The unresponsive bystander: Why doesn't he help?* Englewood Cliffs, NJ: Prentice Hall.

Latané, B., & L'Herrou, T. (1996). Spatial clustering in the conformity game: Dynamic social impact in electronic games. *Journal of Personality and Social Psychology, 70,* 1218–1230.

Latané, B., & Nida, S. (1981). Ten years of research on group size and helping. *Psychological Bulletin, 89,* 308–324.

Lau, R. R., & Russell, D. (1980). Attributions in the sports pages: A field test of some current hypotheses about attribution research. *Journal of Personality and Social Psychology, 39,* 29–38.

Laughlin, P. R. (1980). Social combination processes of cooperative problem-solving groups as verbal intellective tasks. In M.

Fishbein (Ed.), *Progress in social psychology* (Vol. 1, pp. 127–155). Hillsdale, NJ: Erlbaum.

Laursen, B., & Hartup, W. W. (2002). The origins of reciprocity and social exchange in friendships. In L. Brett & W. G. Graziano (Eds.), *Social exchange in development: New directions for child and adolescent development* (pp. 27–40). San Francisco: Jossey-Bass/Pfeiffer.

Lavine, H., Sweeney, D., & Wagner, S. H. (1999). Depicting women as sex objects in television advertising: Effects on body dissatisfaction. *Personality and Social Psychology Bulletin, 25,* 1049–1058.

Lawler, E. J., & Thye, S. R. (1999). Bringing emotions into social exchange theory. *Annual Review of Sociology, 25,* 217–244.

Lazarsfeld, P. (Ed.). (1940). *Radio and the printed page.* New York: Duell, Sloan & Pearce.

Lazarus, R. S. (1966). *Psychological stress and the coping process.* New York: McGraw-Hill.

Lazarus, R. S. (1993). Why we should think of stress as a subset of emotion. In L. Goldberger & S. Breznitz (Eds.), *Handbook of stress: Theoretical and clinical aspects* (2nd ed., pp. 21–39). New York: Free Press.

Lazarus, R. S. (1995). Vexing research problems inherent in cognitive-mediational theories of emotion—and some solutions. *Psychological Inquiry, 6,* 183–196.

Lazarus, R. S. (2000). Toward better research on stress and coping. *American Psychologist, 55,* 665–673.

Lazarus, R. S., & Folkman, S. (1984). *Stress, appraisal, and coping.* New York: Springer-Verlag.

Le, B., & Agnew, C. R. (2003). Commitment and its theorized determinants: A meta-analysis of the investment model. *Personal Relationships, 10,* 37–57.

Lea, M., & Spears, R. (1995). Love at first byte: Building personal relationships over computer networks. In J. T. Wood & S. W. Duck (Eds.), *Understudied relationships: Off the beaten track* (pp. 197–233). Thousand Oaks, CA: Sage.

Lea, M., Spears, R., & de Groot, D. (2001). Knowing me, knowing you: Anonymity effects on social identity processes within groups. *Personality and Social Psychology Bulletin, 27,* 526–537.

Leary, M. R. (1995). *Self-presentation: Impression management and interpersonal behavior.* Madison, WI: Brown & Benchmark.

Leary, M. R., & Tangney, J. P. (2003). The self as an organizing construct in the behavioral and social sciences. In M. R. Leary & J. P. Tangney (Eds.), *Handbook of self and identity* (pp. 3–14). New York: Guilford Press.

Leathers, D. G. (1997). *Successful nonverbal communication: Principles and applications.* Needham Heights, MA: Allyn & Bacon.

Le Bon, G. (1895). *The crowd.* London: Unwin.

Lederman, L. C., Stewart, L. P., Goodheart, F. W., & Laitman, L. (2003). A case against "binge" as a term of choice: Convincing college students to personalize messages about dangerous drinking. *Journal of Health Communication, 8,* 79–91.

Lee, H. (1960). *To kill a mockingbird.* New York: Warner Books.

Lee, R. W. (2001). Citizen heroes. *New American, 17,* 19–32.

Lee, Y., & Seligman, M. E. P. (1997). Are Americans more optimistic than the Chinese? *Personality and Social Psychology Bulletin, 23,* 32–40.

Leeds, J. (2003, March 31). Commercial tie-ins, product promos invade MTV. *Los Angeles Times,* p. C1.

Lehman, D. R., Davis, C. G., De Longis, A., & Wortman, C. B. (1993). Positive and negative life changes following bereavement and their relations to adjustment. *Journal of Social and Clinical Psychology, 12,* 90–112.

Lehman, D. R., Lempert, R. O., & Nisbett, R. E. (1988). The effects of graduate training on reasoning: Formal discipline and thinking about everyday-life events. *American Psychologist, 43,* 431–442.

Leippe, M. R., & Eisenstadt, D. (1994). Generalization of dissonance reduction: Decreasing prejudice through induced compliance. *Journal of Personality and Social Psychology, 67,* 395–413.

Leippe, M. R., & Eisenstadt, D. (1998). A self-accountability model of dissonance reduction: Multiple modes on a continuum of elaboration. In E. Harmon-Jones & J. S. Mills (Eds.),

Cognitive dissonance theory: Revival with revisions and controversies. Washington, DC: American Psychological Association.

Leishman, K. (1988, February). Heterosexuals and AIDS. *Atlantic,* pp. 39–57.

Lemieux, R., & Hale, J. L. (1999). Intimacy, passion, and commitment in young romantic relationships: Successfully measuring the triangular theory of love. *Psychological Reports, 85,* 497–503.

Leor, J., Poole, W. K., & Kloner, R. A. (1996). Sudden cardiac death triggered by an earthquake. *New England Journal of Medicine, 334,* 413–419.

Lepper, M. R. (1995). Theory by numbers? Some concerns about meta-analysis as a theoretical tool. *Applied Cognitive Psychology, 9,* 411–422.

Lepper, M. R. (1996). Intrinsic motivation and extrinsic rewards: A commentary on Cameron and Pierce's meta-analysis. *Review of Educational Research, 66,* 5–32.

Lepper, M. R., Greene, D., & Nisbett, R. E. (1973). Undermining children's intrinsic interest with extrinsic reward: A test of the overjustification hypothesis. *Journal of Personality and Social Psychology, 28,* 129–137.

Lepper, M. R., Henderlong, J., & Gingras, I. (1999). Understanding the effects of extrinsic rewards on intrinsic motivation—uses and abuses of meta-analysis: Comment on Deci, Koestner, and Ryan (1999). *Psychological Bulletin, 125,* 669–676.

Lerner, J. S., & Tetlock, P. E. (1999). Accounting for the effects of accountability. *Psychological Bulletin, 125,* 255–275.

Lerner, M. J. (1980). *The belief in a just world: A fundamental decision.* New York: Plenum.

Lerner, M. J. (1991). The belief in a just world and the "heroic motive": Searching for "constants" in the psychology of religious ideology. *International Journal for the Psychology of Religion, 1,* 27–32.

Lerner, M. J., & Grant, P. R. (1990). The influences of commitment to justice and ethnocentrism on children's allocations of pay. *Social Psychology Quarterly, 53,* 229–238.

Lerner, M. J., & Miller, D. T. (1978). Just world research and the attribution process: Looking back and ahead. *Psychological Bulletin, 85,* 1030–1051.

Leung, K. (1996). Beliefs in Chinese culture. In M. H. Bond (Ed.), *The handbook of Chinese psychology* (pp. 247–262). Hong Kong: Oxford University Press.

Leung, K., & Bond, M. H. (1984). The impact of cultural collectivism on reward allocation. *Journal of Personality and Social Psychology, 47,* 793–804.

Leventhal, H., Watts, J. C., & Pagano, F. (1967). Effects of fear and instructions on how to cope with danger. *Journal of Personality and Social Psychology, 6,* 313–321.

Levi, P. (1986). *"Survival in Auschwitz" and "The Reawakening": Two memoirs.* New York: Summit Books.

Levin, D. T. (2000). Race as a visual feature: Using visual search and perceptual discrimination tasks to understand face categories and the cross-race recognition deficit. *Journal of Experimental Psychology: General, 129,* 559–574.

Levine, G. L., Halberstadt, J. B., & Goldstone, R. (1996). Reasoning and the weighting of attributes in attitude judgments. *Journal of Personality and Social Psychology, 70,* 230–240.

Levine, J. M. (1989). Reaction to opinion deviance in small groups. In P. B. Paulus (Ed.), *Psychology of group influence* (2nd ed., pp. 187–231). Hillsdale, NJ: Erlbaum.

Levine, J. M. (1999). Solomon Asch's legacy for group research. *Personality and Social Psychology Review, 3,* 358–364.

Levine, J. M., Higgins, E. T., & Choi, H.-S. (2000). Development of strategic norms in groups. *Organizational Behavior and Human Decision Processes, 82,* 88–101.

Levine, J. M., & Moreland, R. L. (1990). Progress in small group research. *Annual Review of Psychology, 41,* 585–634.

Levine, J. M., & Moreland, R. L. (1998). Small groups. In D. T. Gilbert, S. T. Fiske, & G. Lindzey (Eds.), *The handbook of social psychology* (4th ed., Vol. 2, pp. 415–469). New York: McGraw-Hill.

Levine, J. M., & Russo, E. M. (1987). Majority and minority influence. In C. Hendrick (Ed.), *Group processes: Review of personality and social psychology* (Vol. 8, pp. 13–54). Newbury Park, CA: Sage.

Levine, J. M., & Thompson, L. (1996). Conflict in groups. In E. T. Higgins & A. W. Kruglanski (Eds.), *Social psychology: Handbook of basic principles* (pp. 745–776). New York: Guilford Press.

Levine, M. P., & Smolak, L. (1996). Media as a context for the development of disordered eating. In L. Smolak, M. P. Levine, & R. Striegel-Moore (Eds.), *Developmental psychopathology of eating disorders: Implications for research, prevention, and treatment* (pp. 235–257). Mahwah, NJ: Erlbaum.

Levine, R., Sato, S., Hashimoto, T., & Verma, J. (1995). Love and marriage in eleven cultures. *Journal of Cross-Cultural Psychology, 26*, 554–571.

Levine, R. A., & Campbell, D. T. (1972). *Ethnocentrism: Theories of conflict, ethnic attitudes, and group behavior.* New York: Wiley.

Levine, R. V., Martinez, T. S., Brase, G., & Sorenson, K. (1994). Helping in 36 U.S. cities. *Journal of Personality and Social Psychology, 67*, 69–82.

Levine, R. V., Norenzayan, A., & Philbrick, K. (2001). Cross-cultural differences in helping strangers. *Journal of Cross-Cultural Psychology, 32*, 543–560.

Levinger, G. (1994). Figure versus ground: Micro and macro perspectives on the social psychology of personal relationships. In R. Erber & R. Gilmour (Eds.), *Theoretical frameworks for personal relationships* (pp. 1–28). Hillsdale, NJ: Erlbaum.

Levy, D. A., & Nail, P. R. (1993). Contagion: A theoretical and empirical review and reconceptualization. *Genetic, Social, and General Psychology Monographs, 119*, 233–284.

Levy, J. S., & Morgan, T. C. (1984). The frequency and seriousness of war: An inverse relationship? *Journal of Conflict Resolution, 28*, 731–749.

Lewin, K. (1943). Defining the "field at a given time." *Psychological Review, 50*, 292–310.

Lewin, K. (1947). Frontiers in group dynamics. *Human Relations, 1*, 5–41.

Lewin, K. (1948). *Resolving social conflicts: Selected papers in group dynamics.* New York: Harper.

Lewin, K. (1951). Problems of research in social psychology. In D. Cartwright (Ed.), *Field theory in social science* (pp. 155–169). New York: Harper.

Lewis, C. C. (1995). *Educating hearts and minds: Reflections on Japanese preschool and elementary education.* Cambridge, England: Cambridge University Press

Lewis, M. (1997). The self in self-conscious emotions. In J. G. Snodgrass & R. L. Thompson (Eds.), *The self across psychology: Self-recognition, self-awareness, and the self-concept* (pp. 119–142). New York: New York Academy of Sciences.

Leyens, J. P., Camino, L., Parke, R. D., & Berkowitz, L. (1975). Effects of movie violence on aggression in a field setting as a function of group dominance and cohesion. *Journal of Personality and Social Psychology, 32*, 346–360.

Liang, D. W., Moreland, R. L., & Argote, L. (1995). Group versus individual training and group performance: The mediating role of transactive memory. *Personality and Social Psychology Bulletin, 21*, 384–393.

Liberman, A., & Chaiken, S. (1992). Defensive processing of personally relevant health messages. *Personality and Social Psychology Bulletin, 18*, 669–679.

Lieberman, M. D., & Rosenthal, R. (2001). Why introverts can't always tell who likes them: Multitasking and nonverbal decoding. *Journal of Personality and Social Psychology, 80*, 294–310.

Liebert, R. M., & Baron, R. A. (1972). Some immediate effects of televised violence on children's behavior. *Developmental Psychology, 6*, 469–475.

Liebert, R. M., & Sprafkin, J. (1988). *The early window* (3rd ed.). New York: Pergamon Press.

Lim, T.-S., & Choi, H.-S. (1996). Interpersonal relationships in Korea. In W. B. Gudykunst, S. Ting-Toomey, & T. Nishida (Eds.), *Communication in personal relationships across cultures* (pp. 122–136). Thousand Oaks, CA: Sage.

Lin, Y. H. W., & Rusbult, C. E. (1995). Commitment to dating relationships and cross-sex friendships in America and China. *Journal of Social and Personal Relationships, 12*, 7–26.

Lindsay, D. S., Read, J. D., & Sharma, K. (1998). Accuracy and confidence in person identification: The relationship is strong when witnessing conditions vary widely. *Psychological Science, 9*, 215–218.

Lindsay, R. C. L., & Wells, G. L. (1985). Improving eyewitness identifications from lineups: Simultaneous versus sequential lineup presentation. *Journal of Applied Psychology, 70*, 556–564.

Lindsay, R. C. L., Wells, G. L., & Rumpel, C. M. (1981). Can people detect eyewitness-identification accuracy within and across situations? *Journal of Applied Psychology, 66*, 79–89.

Linville, P. W., Fischer, G. W., & Salovey, P. (1989). Perceived distributions of characteristics of in-group and out-group members: Empirical evidence and a computer simulation. *Journal of Personality and Social Psychology, 57*, 165–188.

Linz, D. G., Donnerstein, E., & Penrod, S. (1984). The effects of multiple exposures to filmed violence against women. *Journal of Communication, 34*, 130–147.

Little, A. C., & Perrett, D. I. (2002). Putting beauty back in the eye of the beholder. *Psychologist, 15*, 28–32.

Lipkus, I. M., Dalbert, C., & Siegler, I. C. (1996). The importance of distinguishing the belief in a just world for self versus for others: Implications for psychological well-being. *Personality and Social Psychology Bulletin, 22*, 666–677.

Lippmann, W. (1922). *Public opinion.* New York: Free Press.

Lipsey, M. W., Wilson, D. B., Cohen, M. A., & Derzon, J. H. (1997). Is there a causal relationship between alcohol use and violence? A synthesis of evidence. In M Galanter (Ed.), *Recent developments in alcoholism: Vol. 13. Alcohol and violence: Epidemiology, neurobiology, psychology, and family issues* (pp. 245–282). New York: Plenum.

Litt, M. D. (1988). Self-efficacy and perceived control: Cognitive mediators of pain tolerance. *Journal of Personality and Social Psychology, 54*, 149–160.

Livesley, W. J., & Bromley, D. B. (1973). *Person perception in childhood and adolescence.* New York: Wiley.

Lloyd, S. A., & Cate, R. M. (1985). The developmental course of conflict in dissolution of premarital relationships. *Journal of Social and Personal Relationships, 2*, 179–194.

Lockwood, P. (2002). Could it happen to you? Predicting the impact of downward comparisons on the self. *Journal of Personality and Social Psychology, 82*, 343–358.

Lodish, L. M., Abraham, M., Kalmenson, S., Lievelsberger, J., Lubetkin, B., Richardson, B., & Stevens, M. E. (1995). How TV advertising works: A meta analysis of 389 real-world split-cable TV advertising experiments. *Journal of Marketing Research, 32*, 125–139.

Loftus, E. F. (1979). *Eyewitness testimony.* Cambridge, MA: Harvard University Press.

Loftus, E. F. (1993). The reality of repressed memories. *American Psychologist, 48*, 518–537.

Loftus, E. F. (2003). The dangers of memory. In R. J. Sternberg (Ed). *Psychologists defying the crowd: Stories of those who battled the establishment and won* (pp. 105–117). Washington, DC: American Psychological Association.

Loftus, E. F., & Hoffman, H. G. (1989). Misinformation and memory: The creation of new memories. *Journal of Experimental Psychology: General, 118*, 100–104.

Loftus, E. F., Loftus, G. R., & Messo, J. (1987). Some facts about "weapons focus." *Law and Human Behavior, 11*, 55–62.

Loftus, E. F., Miller, D. G., & Burns, H. J. (1978). Semantic integration of verbal information into a visual memory. *Journal of Experimental Psychology: Human Learning and Memory, 4*, 19–31.

Lonner, W., & Berry, J. (Eds.). (1986). *Field methods in cross-cultural research.* Beverly Hills, CA: Sage.

Lord, C. G., Lepper, M. R., & Preston, E. (1984). Considering the opposite: A corrective strategy for social judgment. *Journal of Personality and Social Psychology, 47*, 1231–1243.

Lord, C. G., Scott, K. O., Pugh, M. A., & Desforges, D. M. (1997). Leakage beliefs and the correspondence bias. *Personality and Social Psychology Bulletin, 23*, 824–836.

Lore, R. K., & Schultz, L. A. (1993). Control of human aggression. *American Psychologist, 48*, 16–25.

Lorenz, K. (1966). *On aggression* (M. Wilson, Trans.). New York: Harcourt Brace.

Lott, A. J., & Lott, B. E. (1961). Group cohesiveness, communication level, and conformity. *Journal of Abnormal and Social Psychology, 62,* 408–412.

Lott, A. J., & Lott, B. E. (1974). The role of reward in the formation of positive interpersonal attitudes. In T. L. Huston (Ed.), *Foundations of interpersonal attraction* (pp. 171–189). New York: Academic Press.

Lowry, D. T., Love, G., & Kirby, M. (1981). Sex on the soap operas: Patterns of intimacy. *Journal of Communication, 31,* 90–96.

Ludwig, T. D., Gray, T. W., & Rowell, A. (1998). Increasing recycling in academic buildings: A systematic replication. *Journal of Applied Behavior Analysis, 31,* 683–686.

Lumsdaine, A. A., & Janis, I. L. (1953). Resistance to "counterpropaganda" produced by one-sided and two-sided "propaganda" presentations. *Public Opinion Quarterly, 17,* 311–318.

Lykken, D. T. (1998). *A tremor in the blood: Uses and abuses of the lie detector.* New York: Plenum.

Lynn, M., & Shurgot, B. A. (1984). Responses to lonely hearts advertisements: Effects of reported physical attractiveness, physique, and coloration. *Personality and Social Psychology Bulletin, 10,* 349–357.

Lynn, S. J., Lock, T., Loftus, E., Krackow, E., & Lilienfeld, S. O. (2003). The remembrance of things past: Problematic memory recovery techniques in psychotherapy. In S. O. Lilienfeld & S. J. Lynn (Eds.), *Science and pseudoscience in clinical psychology* (pp. 205–239). New York: Guilford Press.

Lysak, H., Rule, B. G., & Dobbs, A. R. (1989). Conceptions of aggression: Prototype or defining features? *Personality and Social Psychology Bulletin, 15,* 233–243.

Lyubomirsky, S., Caldwell, N. D., & Nolen-Hoeksema, S. (1993). Effects of ruminative and distracting responses to depressed mood on retrieval of autobiographical memories. *Journal of Personality and Social Psychology, 75,* 166–177.

Maass, A., & Clark, R. D., III. (1984). Hidden impact of minorities: Fifteen years of research. *Psychological Bulletin, 95,* 428–450.

Maccoby, E. E., & Jacklin, C. N. (1974). *The psychology of sex differences.* Stanford, CA: Stanford University Press.

MacCoun, R. J. (1989). Experimental research on jury decision-making. *Science, 244,* 1046–1050.

MacDonald, T. K., Zanna, M. P., & Fong, G. T. (1996). Why common sense goes out the window: Effects of alcohol on intentions to use condoms. *Personality and Social Psychology Bulletin, 22,* 763–775.

Mackie, D. M. (1987). Systematic and nonsystematic processing of majority and minority persuasive communications. *Journal of Personality and Social Psychology, 53,* 41–52.

MacKinnon, C. (1993, July-August). Turning rape into pornography: Postmodern genocide. *Ms.,* pp. 24–30.

Maclean, N. (1983). *A river runs through it.* Chicago: University of Chicago Press.

MacNeil, M. K., & Sherif, M. (1976). Norm change over subject generations as a function of arbitrariness of prescribed norms. *Journal of Personality and Social Psychology, 34,* 762–773.

Madaras, G. R., & Bem, D. J. (1968). Risk and conservatism in group decision making. *Journal of Experimental Social Psychology, 4,* 350–366.

Maddux, J. E. (1995). *Self-efficacy, adaptation, and adjustment: Theory, research, and application.* New York: Plenum.

Madon, S., Jussim, L., & Eccles, J. S. (1997). In search of the powerful self-fulfilling prophecy. *Journal of Personality and Social Psychology, 72,* 791–809.

Madon, S., Smith, A., Jussim, L., Russell, D. W., Eccles, J. S., Palumbo, P., & Walkiewicz, M. (2001). Am I as you see me or do you see me as I am? Self-fulfilling prophecies and self-verification. *Personality and Social Psychology Bulletin, 27,* 1214–1224.

Magaro, P. A., & Ashbrook, R. M. (1985). The personality of societal groups. *Journal of Personality and Social Psychology, 48,* 1479–1489.

Magoo, G., & Khanna, R. (1991). Altruism and willingness to donate blood. *Journal of Personality and Clinical Studies, 7,* 21–24.

Maier, N. R. F., & Solem, A. R. (1952). The contribution of a discussion leader to the quality of group thinking: The effective use of minority opinions. *Human Relations, 5,* 277–288.

Main, M., Kaplan, N., & Cassidy, J. (1985). Security in infancy, childhood, and adulthood: A move to the level of representation. In T. Bretherton & E. Waters (Eds.), *Growing points of attachment theory and research. Monographs of the Society for Research on Child Development, 50,* 66–104.

Maio, G. R., & Olson, J. M. (1995). Relations between values, attitudes, and behavioral intentions: The moderating role of attitude function. *Journal of Experimental Social Psychology, 31,* 266–285.

Major, B., & Gramzow, R. H. (1999). Abortion as stigma: Cognitive and emotional implications of concealment. *Journal of Personality and Social Psychology, 77,* 735–745.

Malamuth, N. M. (1981). Rape fantasies as a function of exposure to violent sexual stimuli. *Archives of Sexual Behavior, 10,* 33–47.

Malamuth, N. M., Addison, T., & Koss, M. (2000). Pornography and sexual aggression: Are there reliable effects and can we understand them? *Annual Review of Sex Research, 11,* 26–91.

Malamuth, N. M., Linz, D. G., Heavey, C. L., Barnes, G., & Acker, M. (1995). Using the confluence model of sexual aggression to predict men's conflict with women: A 10-year follow-up study. *Journal of Personality and Social Psychology, 69,* 353–369.

Malle, B. F., & Knobe, J. (1997). Which behaviors do people explain? A basic actor-observer asymmetry. *Journal of Personality and Social Psychology, 72,* 288–304.

Malloy, T. E. (2001). Difference to Inference: Teaching logical and statistical reasoning through on-line interactivity. *Behavior Research Methods, Instruments, and Computers, 33,* 270–273.

Malpass, R. S., & Devine, P. G. (1981). Eyewitness identification: Lineup instructions and the absence of the offender. *Journal of Applied Psychology, 66,* 482–489.

Maner, J. K., Luce, C. L., Neuberg, S. L., Cialdini, R. B., Brown, S., & Sagarin, B. J. (2002). The effects of perspective taking on motivations for helping: Still no evidence for altruism. *Personality and Social Psychology Bulletin, 28,* 1601–1610.

Manstead, A. S. R. (1997). Situations, belongingness, attitudes, and culture: Four lessons learned from social psychology. In G. McGarty & H. S. Haslam (Eds.), *The message of social psychology: Perspectives on mind and society* (pp. 238–251). Oxford, England: Blackwell.

Manza, J., Cook, F. L., & Page, B. I. (Eds.) (2002). *Navigating public opinion: polls, policy, and the future of American democracy.* New York: Oxford University Press.

Marion, R. (1995, August). The girl who mewed. *Discover,* pp. 38–40.

Markey, P. M. (2000). Bystander intervention in computer-mediated communication. *Computers in Human Behavior, 16,* 183–188.

Markoff, J. (1996, December 21). Steven Jobs making move back to Apple. *New York Times,* p. 37.

Markus, H. R. (1977). Self-schemata and processing information about the self. *Journal of Personality and Social Psychology, 35,* 63–78.

Markus, H. R., & Kitayama, S. (1991). Culture and the self: Implications for cognition, emotion, and motivation. *Psychological Review, 98,* 224–253.

Markus, H. R., & Kitayama, S. (2001). The cultural construction of self and emotion: Implications for social behavior. In W. G. Parrott (Ed.), *Emotions in social psychology: Essential readings* (pp. 119–137). Philadelphia: Psychology Press.

Markus, H. R., Kitayama, S., & Heiman, R. J. (1996). Culture and "basic" psychological principles. In E. T. Higgins & A. W. Kruglanski (Eds.), *Social psychology: Handbook of basic principles* (pp. 857–913). New York: Guilford Press.

Markus, H. R., & Zajonc, R. B. (1985). The cognitive perspective in social psychology. In G. Lindzey & E. Aronson (Eds.), *Handbook of social psychology* (3rd ed., Vol. 1, pp. 137–230). New York: McGraw-Hill.

Marlowe, D., & Gergen, K. J. (1970). Personality and social behavior. In K. J. Gergen & D. Marlowe (Eds.), *Personality and social behavior* (pp. 1–75). Reading, MA: Addison-Wesley.

Marques, J., Abrams, D., & Serodio, R. (2001). Being better by being right: Subjective group dynamics and derogation of in-group deviants when generic norms are undermined. *Journal of Personality and Social Psychology, 81,* 436–447.

Martin, A. J., Berenson, K. R., Griffing, S., Sage, R. E., Madry, L., Bingham, L. E., & Primm, B. J. (2000). The process of leaving an abusive relationship: The role of risk assessments and decision certainty. *Journal of Family Violence, 15,* 109–122.

Martin, L. L. (1986). Set/reset: Use and disuse of concepts in impression formation. *Journal of Personality and Social Psychology, 51,* 493–504.

Martin, L. L., Seta, J. J., & Crelia, R. (1990). Assimilation and contrast as a function of people's willingness and ability to expend effort in forming an impression. *Journal of Personality and Social Psychology, 59,* 27–37.

Martin, M. M., & Anderson, C. M. (1995). Roommate similarity: Are roommates who are similar in their communication traits more satisfied? *Communication Research Reports, 12,* 46–52.

Martin, N. G., Eaves, L. J., Heath, A. R., Jardine, R., Feingold, L. M., & Eysenck, H. J. (1986). Transmission of social attitudes. *Proceedings of the National Academy of Science, 83,* 4364–4368.

Masuda, T., & Kitayama, S. (1996). *Correspondence bias in Japan.* Unpublished manuscript, Kyoto University.

Matsumoto, D. (1992). More evidence for the universality of a contempt expression. *Motivation and Emotion, 16,* 363–368.

Matsumoto, D., & Ekman, P. (1989). American-Japanese differences in intensity ratings of facial expressions of emotion. *Motivation and Emotion, 13,* 143–157.

Matsumoto, D., & Kudoh, T. (1993). American-Japanese cultural differences in attributions of personality based on smiles. *Journal of Nonverbal Behavior, 17,* 231–243.

Matthews, K. A. (1988). Coronary heart disease and Type A behaviors: Update on and alternative to the Booth-Kewley and Friedman (1987) quantitative review. *Psychological Bulletin, 101,* 373–380.

Mau, W. & Lynn, A. (2001). Gender differences on the Scholastic Aptitude Test, the American College Test, and college grades. *Educational Psychology, 21,* 133–136.

McAlister, A., Perry, C., Killen, J. D., Slinkard, L. A., & Maccoby, N. (1980). Pilot study of smoking, alcohol, and drug abuse prevention. *American Journal of Public Health, 70,* 719–721.

McAllister, H. A. (1996). Self-serving bias in the classroom: Who shows it? Who knows it? *Journal of Educational Psychology, 88,* 123–131.

McAndrew, F. T. (2002). New evolutionary perspectives on altruism: Multilevel-selection and costly-signaling theories. *Current Directions in Psychological Science, 11,* 79–82.

McArthur, L. Z. (1972). The how and what of why: Some determinants and consequences of causal attribution. *Journal of Personality and Social Psychology, 22,* 171–193.

McArthur, L. Z., & Baron, R. M. (1983). Toward an ecological theory of social perception. *Psychological Review, 90,* 215–238.

McArthur, L. Z., & Berry, D. S. (1987). Cross cultural agreement in perceptions of babyfaced adults. *Journal of Cross-Cultural Psychology, 18,* 165–192.

McArthur, L. Z., & Resko, G. B. (1975). The portrayal of men and women in American television commercials. *Journal of Social Psychology, 97,* 209–220.

McCarthy, J. F., & Kelly, B. R. (1978). Aggressive behavior and its effect on performance over time in ice hockey athletes: An archival study. *International Journal of Sport Psychology, 9,* 90–96.

McCauley, C. (1989). The nature of social influence in groupthink: Compliance and internalization. *Journal of Personality and Social Psychology, 57,* 250–260.

McCloskey, M., & Zaragoza, M. (1985). Misleading postevent information and memory for events: Arguments and evidence against memory impairment hypotheses. *Journal of Experimental Psychology: General, 114,* 1–16.

McConahay, J. B. (1981). Reducing racial prejudice in desegregated schools. In W. D. Hawley (Ed.), *Effective school desegregation.* Beverly Hills, CA: Sage.

McConahay, J. B. (1986). Modern racism, ambivalence, and the Modern Racism Scale. In J. F. Dovidio & S. L. Gaertner (Eds.), *Prejudice, discrimination, and racism: Theory and research* (pp. 91–125). New York: Academic Press.

McDonald, H. E., & Hirt, E. R. (1997). When expectancy meets desire: Motivational effects in reconstructive memory. *Journal of Personality and Social Psychology, 72,* 5–23.

McFadyen-Ketchum, S. A., Bates, J. E., Dodge, K. A., & Pettit, G. S. (1996). Patterns of change in early childhood aggressive-disruptive behavior: Gender differences in predictions from early coercive and affectionate mother-child interactions. *Child Development, 67,* 2417–2433.

McGrath, J. E. (1984). *Groups: Interaction and performance.* Englewood Cliffs, NJ: Prentice Hall.

McGregor, C., Darke, S., Ali, R., & Christie, P. (1998). Experience of non-fatal overdose among heroin users in Adelaide, Australia: Circumstances and risk perceptions. *Addiction, 93,* 701–711.

McGuire, A. M. (1994). Helping behaviors in the natural environment: Dimensions and correlates of helping. *Personality and Social Psychology Bulletin, 20,* 45–56.

McGuire, W. J. (1964). Inducing resistance to persuasion. In L. Berkowitz (Ed.), *Advances in experimental social psychology* (Vol. 1, pp. 192–229). New York: Academic Press.

McGuire, W. J. (1968). Personality and susceptibility to social influence. In E. F. Borgatta & W. W. Lambert (Eds.), *Handbook of personality theory and research* (pp. 1130–1187). Chicago: Rand McNally.

McGuire, W. J. (1985). Attitudes and attitude change. In G. Lindzey & E. Aronson (Eds.), *Handbook of social psychology* (3rd ed., Vol. 2, pp. 233–346). New York: McGraw-Hill.

McHugo, G. J., & Smith, C. A. (1996). The power of faces: A review of John T. Lanzetta's research on facial expression and emotion. *Motivation and Emotion, 21,* 85–120.

McKenna, F. P., & Albery, I. P. (2001). Does unrealistic optimism change following a negative experience? *Journal of Applied Social Psychology, 31,* 1146–1157.

McNally, R. J. (2003). *Remembering trauma.* Cambridge, MA: Harvard University Press.

McNamara, R. S. (1995). *In retrospect: The tragedy and lessons of Vietnam.* New York: Times Books.

McPherson, J. M. (1983). The size of voluntary associations. *American Sociological Review, 61,* 1044–1064.

McPherson, M., Smith-Lovin, L., & Cook, J. M. (2001). Birds of a feather: Homophily in social networks. *Annual Review of Sociology, 27,* 415–444.

Medvec, V. H., Madey, S. F., & Gilovich, T. (1995). When less is more: Counterfactual thinking and satisfaction among Olympic medalists. *Journal of Personality and Social Psychology, 69,* 603–610.

Meertens, R. W., & Pettigrew, T. F. (1997). Is subtle prejudice really prejudice? *Public Opinion Quarterly, 61,* 54–71.

Meeus, W. H. J., & Raaijmakers, Q. A. W. (1995). Obedience in modern society: The Utrecht studies. *Journal of Social Issues, 51,* 155–175.

Mehta, M. D. (2001). Pornography in Usenet: A study of 9,800 randomly selected images. *Cyberpsychology and Behavior, 4,* 695–703.

Meissner, C. A., & Brigham, J. C. (2001a) A meta-analysis of the verbal overshadowing effect in face identification. *Applied Cognitive Psychology, 15,* 603–616.

Meissner, C. A., & Brigham, J. C. (2001b). Thirty years of investigating the own-race bias in memory for faces: A meta-analytic review. *Psychology, Public Policy, and Law, 7,* 3–35.

Melara, R. D., De Witt-Rickards, T. S., & O'Brien, T. P. (1989). Enhancing lineup identification accuracy: Two codes are better than one. *Journal of Applied Psychology, 74,* 706–713.

Menec, V. H., Perry, R. P., Struthers, C. W., Schonwetter, D. J., Hechter, F. J., & Eichholz, B. L. (1994). Assisting at-risk college students with attributional retraining and effective teaching. *Journal of Applied Social Psychology, 24,* 675–701.

Menninger, W. (1948). Recreation and mental health. *Recreation, 42,* 340–346.

Menon, T., Morris, M. W., Chiu, C., & Hong, Y. (1999). Culture and the construal of agency: Attribution to individual versus group dispositions. *Journal of Personality and Social Psychology, 76,* 701–717.

Merikle, P. M. (1988). Subliminal auditory messages: An evaluation. *Psychology and Marketing, 5,* 355–372.

Merton, R. K. (1948). The self-fulfilling prophecy. *Antioch Review, 8,* 193–210.

Messick, D., & Liebrand, W. B. G. (1995). Individual heuristics and the dynamics of cooperation in large groups. *Psychological Review, 102,* 131–145.

Metcalfe, J. (1998). Cognitive optimism: Self-deception or memory-based processing heuristics? *Personality and Social Psychology Review, 2,* 100–110.

Meyer, P. (1999). The sociobiology of human cooperation: The interplay of ultimate and proximate causes. In J. M. G. van der Dennen & D. Smillie (Eds.), *The Darwinian heritage and sociobiology: Human evolution, behavior, and intelligence* (pp. 49–65). Westport, CT: Praeger.

Meyerowitz, B. E., & Chaiken, S. (1987). The effect of message framing on breast self-examination attitudes, intentions, and behavior. *Journal of Personality and Social Psychology, 52,* 500–510.

Middleton, W., Harris, P., & Surman, M. (1996). Give 'em enough rope: Perception of health and safety risks in bungee jumpers. *Journal of Social and Clinical Psychology, 15,* 68–79.

Milgram, S. (1961). Nationality and conformity. *Scientific American, 205,* 45–51.

Milgram, S. (1963). Behavioral study of obedience. *Journal of Abnormal and Social Psychology, 67,* 371–378.

Milgram, S. (1969, March). The lost letter technique. *Psychology Today,* pp. 30–33, 67–68.

Milgram, S. (1970). The experience of living in cities. *Science, 167,* 1461–1468.

Milgram, S. (1974). *Obedience to authority: An experimental view.* New York: Harper & Row.

Milgram, S. (1976). Obedience to criminal orders: The compulsion to do evil. In T. Blass (Ed.), *Contemporary social psychology: Representative readings* (pp. 175–184). Itasca, IL: Peacock.

Milgram, S. (1977). *The individual in a social world.* Reading, MA: Addison-Wesley.

Milgram, S., & Sabini, J. (1978). On maintaining urban norms: A field experiment in the subway. In A. Baum, J. E. Singer, & S. Valins (Eds.), *Advances in environmental psychology* (Vol. 1, pp. 9–40). Hillsdale, NJ: Erlbaum.

Mill, J. S. (1843). *A system of logic ratiocinative and inductive.* London.

Miller, A. G. (1986). *The obedience experiments: A case study of controversy in social science.* New York: Praeger.

Miller, A. G. (1995). Constructions of the obedience experiments: A focus upon domains of relevance. *Journal of Social Issues, 51,* 33–53.

Miller, A. G. (1998). Some thoughts prompted by "Speeding with Ned." In J. M. Darley & J. Cooper (Eds.), *Attribution and social interaction* (pp. 37–51). Washington, DC: American Psychological Association.

Miller, A. G., Ashton, W., & Mishal, M. (1990). Beliefs concerning the features of constrained behavior: A basis for the fundamental attribution error. *Journal of Personality and Social Psychology, 59,* 635–650.

Miller, A. G., Collins, B. E., & Brief, D. E. (1995). Perspectives on obedience to authority: The legacy of the Milgram experiments. *Journal of Social Issues, 51,* 1–19.

Miller, A. G., Jones, E. E., & Hinkle, S. (1981). A robust attribution error in the personality domain. *Journal of Experimental Social Psychology, 17,* 587–600.

Miller, C. E., & Anderson, P. D. (1979). Group decision rules and the rejection of deviates. *Social Psychology Quarterly, 42,* 354–363.

Miller, C. T. (1982). The role of performance-related similarity in social comparison of abilities: A test of the related attributes hypothesis. *Journal of Experimental Social Psychology, 18,* 513–523.

Miller, D. T., & Prentice, D. A. (1996). The construction of social norms and standards. In E. T. Higgins & A. W. Kruglanski (Eds.), *Social psychology: Handbook of basic principles* (pp. 799–829). New York: Guilford Press.

Miller, D. T., & Ross, M. (1975). Self-serving biases in the attribution of causality: Fact or fiction? *Psychological Bulletin, 82,* 213–225.

Miller, D. T., & Taylor, B. R. (2002). Counterfactual thought, regret, and superstition: How to avoid kicking yourself. In T. Gilovich, D. W. Griffin, & D. Kahneman (Eds). *Heuristics and biases: The psychology of intuitive judgment* (pp. 367–378). New York: Cambridge University Press.

Miller, J. G. (1984). Culture and the development of everyday social explanation. *Journal of Personality and Social Psychology, 46,* 961–978.

Miller, J. G., Bersoff, D. M., & Harwood, R. L. (1990). Perceptions of social responsibilities in India and the United States: Moral imperatives or personal decisions? *Journal of Personality and Social Psychology, 58,* 33–47.

Miller, N., & Bugelski, R. (1948). Minor studies in aggression: The influence of frustrations imposed by the in-group on attitudes expressed by the out-group. *Journal of Psychology, 25,* 437–442.

Miller, N., & Campbell, D. T. (1959). Recency and primacy in persuasion as a function of the timing of speeches and measurements. *Journal of Abnormal and Social Psychology, 59,* 1–9.

Miller, P. V. (2002). The authority and limitation of polls. In J. Manza, F. L. Cook, & B. I. Page (Eds.), *Navigating public opinion* (pp. 221–231). New York: Oxford University Press.

Mills, J. (1958). Changes in moral attitudes following temptation. *Journal of Personality, 26,* 517–531.

Mills, J., & Clark, M. S. (1982). Communal and exchange relationships. In L. Wheeler (Ed.), *Review of personality and social psychology* (Vol. 2, pp. 121–144). Beverly Hills, CA: Sage.

Mills, J., & Clark, M. S. (1994). Communal and exchange relationships: Controversies and research. In R. Erber & R. Gilmour (Eds.), *Theoretical frameworks for personal relationships* (pp. 29–42). Hillsdale, NJ: Erlbaum.

Mills, J., & Clark, M. S. (2001). Viewing close romantic relationships as communal relationships: Implications for maintenance and enhancement. In J. Harvey & A. Wenzel (Eds.), *Close romantic relationships: Maintenance and enhancement.* (pp. 13–25). Mahwah, N.J.: Lawrence Erlbaum.

Milton, K. (1971). *Women in policing.* New York: Police Foundation Press.

Minard, R. D. (1952). Race relations in the Pocahontas coal field. *Journal of Social Issues, 8,* 29–44.

Mischel, W. (1968). *Personality and assessment.* New York: Wiley.

Misconceptions about why people obey laws and accept judicial decisions. (1997). *American Psychological Society Observer, 5,* 12–13, 46.

Mitchell, K. J., Johnson, M. K., & Mather, M. (2003). Source monitoring and suggestibility to misinformation: Adult age-related differences. *Applied Cognitive Psychology, 17,* 107–119.

Mitchell, R. W. (2003). Subjectivity and self-recognition in animals. In M. R. Leary & J. P. Tangney (Eds.), *Handbook of self and identity* (pp. 567–593). New York: Guilford Press.

Miyamoto, Y., & Kitayama, S. (2002). Cultural variation in correspondence bias: The critical role of attitude diagnosticity of socially constrained behavior. *Journal of Personality and Social Psychology, 83,* 1239–1248.

Modigliani, A., & Rochat, F. (1995). The role of interaction sequences and the timing of resistance in shaping obedience and defiance to authority. *Journal of Social Issues, 51,* 107–123.

Moghaddam, F. M., Taylor, D. M., & Wright, S. C. (1993). *Social psychology in cross-cultural perspective.* New York: Freeman.

Mohamed, A. A., & Wiebe, F. A. (1996). Toward a process theory of groupthink. *Small Group Research, 27,* 416–430.

Montemayor, R., & Eisen, M. (1977). The development of self-conceptions from childhood to adolescence. *Developmental Psychology, 13,* 314–319.

Moore, J. S., Graziano, W. G., & Millar, M. C. (1987). Physical attractiveness, sex role orientation, and the evaluation of adults and children. *Personality and Social Psychology Bulletin, 13,* 95–102.

Moore, R. L. (1998). Love and limerance with Chinese characteristics: Student romance in the PRC. In V. C. de Munck (Ed.), *Romantic love and sexual behavior* (pp. 251–283). Westport, CT: Praeger.

Moore, T. E. (1982). Subliminal advertising: What you see is what you get. *Journal of Marketing, 46,* 38–47.

Moore, T. E. (1992). Subliminal perception: Facts and fallacies. *Skeptical Inquirer, 16,* 273–281.

Mor, N., & Winquist, J. (2002). Self-focused attention and negative affect: A meta-analysis. *Psychological Bulletin, 128,* 638–662.

Moreland, R. L. (1987). The formation of small groups. In C. Hendrick (Ed.), *Review of personality and social psychology* (Vol. 8, pp. 80–110). Newbury Park, CA: Sage.

Moreland, R. L. (1999). Transactive memory: Learning who knows what in work groups and organizations. In L. L. Thompson & J. M. Levine (Eds.), *Shared cognition in organizations: The management of knowledge* (pp. 3–31). Mahwah, NJ: Erlbaum.

Moreland, R. L., Argote, L., & Krishnan, R. (1996). Socially shared cognition at work: Transactive memory and group performance. In J. L. Nye & A. M. Brower (Eds.), *What's social about social cognition?* (pp. 57–84). Thousand Oaks, CA: Sage.

Moreland, R. L., & Beach, S. R. (1992). Exposure effects in the classroom: The development of affinity among students. *Journal of Experimental Social Psychology, 28,* 255–276.

Moreland, R. L., & Zajonc, R. B. (1982). Exposure effects in person perception: Familiarity, similarity, and attraction. *Journal of Experimental Social Psychology, 18,* 395–415.

Morgan, H. J., & Shaver, P. R. (1999). Attachment processes and commitment to romantic relationships. In J. M. Adams & W. H. Jones, *Handbook of interpersonal commitment and relationship stability* (pp. 109–124). New York: Kluwer.

Morris, E. (Director). (1988). *The thin blue line* [Film]. New York: HBO Videos.

Morris, M. W., & Peng, K. (1994). Culture and cause: American and Chinese attributions for social and physical events. *Journal of Personality and Social Psychology, 67,* 949–971.

Morris, W. N., & Miller, R. S. (1975). The effects of consensus-breaking and consensus-preempting partners on reduction of conformity. *Journal of Experimental Social Psychology, 11,* 215–223.

Morry, M. M., & Staska, S. L. (2001). Magazine exposure: Internalization, self-objectification, eating attitudes, and body satisfaction in male and female university students. *Canadian Journal of Behavioural Science, 33,* 269–279.

Morse, D. R., Martin, J., & Moshonov, J. (1991). Psychosomatically induced death relative to stress, hypnosis, mind control, and voodoo: Review and possible mechanisms. *Stress Medicine, 7,* 213–232.

Moscovici, S. (1985). Social influence and conformity. In G. Lindzey & E. Aronson (Eds.), *Handbook of social psychology* (3rd ed., Vol. 2, pp. 347–412). New York: McGraw-Hill.

Moscovici, S. (1994). Three concepts: Minority, conflict, and behavioral style. In S. Moscovici, A. Mucchi-Faina, & A. Maass (Eds.), *Minority influence* (pp. 233–251). Chicago: Nelson-Hall.

Moscovici, S., Mucchi-Faina, A., & Maass, A. (Eds.). (1994). *Minority influence.* Chicago: Nelson-Hall.

Moscovici, S., & Nemeth, C. (1974). Minority influence. In C. Nemeth (Ed.), *Social psychology: Classic and contemporary integrations* (pp. 217–249). Chicago: Rand McNally.

Moskalenko, S., & Heine, S. J. (2002). Watching your troubles away: Television viewing as a stimulus for subjective self-awareness. *Personality and Social Psychology Bulletin, 29,* 76–85.

Moyer, K. E. (1976). *The psychobiology of aggression.* New York: Harper & Row.

Moyer, K. E. (1983). The physiology of motivation: Aggression as a model. In C. J. Scheier & A. M. Rogers (Eds.), *G. Stanley Hall lecture series* (Vol. 3). Washington, DC: American Psychological Association.

Mukai, T. (1996). Mothers, peers, and perceived pressure to diet among Japanese adolescent girls. *Journal of Research in Adolescence, 6,* 309–324.

Mukai, T., Kambara, A., & Sasaki, Y. (1998). Body dissatisfaction, need for social approval, and eating disturbances among Japanese and American college women. *Sex Roles, 39,* 751–771.

Mullen, B. (1986). Atrocity as a function of lynch mob composition: A self-attention perspective. *Personality and Social Psychology Bulletin, 12,* 187–197.

Mullen, B., Anthony, T., Salas, E., & Driskell, J. E. (1994). Group cohesiveness and quality of decision making: An integration of tests of the groupthink hypothesis. *Small Group Research, 25,* 189–204.

Mullen, B., Brown, R., & Smith, C. (1992). Ingroup bias as a function of salience, relevance, and status: An integration. *European Journal of Social Psychology, 22,* 103–122.

Mullen, B., & Cooper, C. (1994). The relation between group cohesiveness and performance: An integration. *Psychological Bulletin, 115,* 210–227.

Mullen, B., & Johnson, C. (1988). *Distinctiveness-based illusory correlation and stereotyping: A meta-analytic integration.* Unpublished manuscript, Syracuse University.

Mullen, B., Rozell, D., & Johnson, C. (2001). Ethnophaulisms for ethnic immigrant groups: The contributions of group size and familiarity. *European Journal of Social Psychology, 31,* 231–246.

Münsterberg, H. (1908). *On the witness stand: Essays on psychology and crime.* New York: Doubleday.

Muraven, M., Tice, D. M., & Baumeister, R. F. (1998). Self-control as limited resource: Regulatory depletion patterns. *Journal of Personality and Social Psychology, 74,* 774–789.

Murphy, S. T., & Zajonc, R. B. (1993). Affect, cognition, and awareness: Affective priming with optimal and suboptimal stimulus exposures. *Journal of Personality and Social Psychology, 64,* 723–739.

Murr, A., & Smalley, S. (2003, March 17). White power, minus the power. *Newsweek,* pp. 42–45.

Murray, S. L., Holmes, J. G., McDonald, G., & Ellsworth, P. C. (1998). Through the looking glass darkly? When self-doubts turn into relationship insecurities. *Journal of Personality and Social Psychology, 75,* 1459–1480.

Murstein, B. I. (1970). Stimulus value role: A theory of marital choice. *Journal of Marriage and the Family, 32,* 465–481.

Mussweiler, T., & Förster, J. (2000). The sex-aggression link: A perception-behavior dissociation. *Journal of Personality and Social Psychology, 79,* 507–520.

Mussweiler, T., & Strack, F. (1999). Comparing is believing: A selective accessibility model of judgmental anchoring. In W. Stroebe & M. Hewstone (Eds.), *European review of social psychology* (Vol. 10, pp. 135–167). Chichester, England: Wiley.

Mussweiler, T., Strack, F., & Pfeiffer, T. (2000). Overcoming the inevitable anchoring effect: Considering the opposite compensates for selective accessibility. *Personality and Social Psychology Bulletin, 260,* 1142–1150.

Nadler, A. (1991). Help-seeking behavior: Psychological costs and instrumental benefits. In M. S. Clark (Ed.), *Prosocial behavior: Review of personality and social psychology* (Vol. 12, pp. 290–311). Newbury Park, CA: Sage.

Nadler, A., & Fisher, J. D. (1986). The role of threat to self-esteem and perceived control in recipient reactions to help: Theory development and empirical validation. In L. Berkowitz (Ed.), *Advances in experimental social psychology* (Vol. 19, pp. 81–123). New York: Academic Press.

Nail, P. R. (1986). Toward an integration of some models and theories of social response. *Psychological Bulletin, 100,* 190–206.

Nail, P. R., McDonald, G., & Levy, D. A. (2000). Proposal of a four-dimensional model of social response. *Psychological Bulletin, 126,* 454–470.

Nasco, S. A., & Marsh, K. L. (1999). Gaining control through counterfactual thinking. *Personality and Social Psychology Bulletin, 25,* 556–568.

Nathanson, S. (1987). *An eye for an eye? The morality of punishing by death.* Totowa, NJ: Rowman & Littlefield.

National Center for Vital Statistics. (2001). *Crime facts at a glance.* Retrieved from Bureau of Justice Statistics: http://www.ojp.usdoj.gov/bjs/glance/hmrt.htm

Nel, E., Helmreich, R., & Aronson, E. (1969). Opinion change in the advocate as a function of the persuasibility of his audience: A clarification of the meaning of dissonance. *Journal of Personality and Social Psychology, 12,* 117–124.

Nelson, D. E., Bland, S., Powell-Griner, E., Klein, R., Wells, H. E., Hogelin, G., & Marks, J. S. (2002). State trends in health risk factors and receipt of clinical preventive services among US adults during the 1990s. *Journal of the American Medical Association, 287,* 2659–2667.

Nemeroff, C. J., Stein, R. I., Diehl, N. S., & Smilack, K. M. (1995). From the Cleavers to the Clintons: Role choices and body orientation as reflected in magazine article content. *International Journal of Eating Disorders, 16,* 167–176.

Nemeth, C. J., & Chiles, C. (1988). Modeling courage: The role of dissent in fostering independence. *European Journal of Social Psychology, 18,* 275–280.

Neuberg, S. L. (1988). Behavioral implications of information presented outside of awareness: The effect of subliminal presentation of trait information on behavior in the prisoner's dilemma game. *Social Cognition, 6,* 207–230.

Newcomb, T. M. (1961). *The acquaintance process.* New York: Holt, Rinehart and Winston.

Newman, L. S. (1996). Trait impressions as heuristics for predicting future behavior. *Personality and Social Psychology Bulletin, 22,* 395–411.

New York Times Editorial (2003, June 5). Martha Stewart's troubled world. *The New York Times,* p. A34.

Ng, W., & Lindsay, R. C. L. (1994). Cross-racial facial recognition: Failure of the contact hypothesis. *Journal of Cross-Cultural Psychology, 25,* 217–232.

Nichols, J. G. (1975). Casual attributions and other achievement-related cognitions: Effects of task outcome, attainment value, and sex. *Journal of Personality and Social Psychology, 31,* 379–389.

Nicholson, N., Cole, S. G., & Rocklin, T. (1985). Conformity in the Asch situation: A comparison between contemporary British and U.S. university students. *British Journal of Social Psychology, 24,* 59–63.

Niedenthal, P. M., & Kitayama, S. (1994). (Eds.). *The heart's eye: Emotional influences in perception and attention.* San Diego, CA: Academic Press.

Niedenthal, P. M., Tangney, J. P., & Gavanski, I. (1994). "If only I weren't" versus "If only I hadn't": Distinguishing shame and guilt in counterfactual thinking. *Journal of Personality and Social Psychology, 67,* 585–595.

Niederhoffer, K. G., & Pennebaker, J. W. (2002). Sharing one's story: On the benefits of writing or talking about emotional experience. In C. R. Snyder & S. J. Lopez (Eds.), *Handbook of positive psychology* (pp. 573–583). London: Oxford University Press.

Nisbett, R. E. (1993). Violence and U.S. regional culture. *American Psychologist, 48,* 441–449.

Nisbett, R. E. (2003). *The geography of thought: How Asians and Westerners think differently . . . and why.* New York: Free Press.

Nisbett, R. E., Caputo, C., Legant, P., & Marecek, J. (1973). Behavior as seen by the actor and by the observer. *Journal of Personality and Social Psychology, 27,* 154–164.

Nisbett, R. E., & Cohen, D. (1996). *Culture of honor: The psychology of violence in the South.* Boulder, CO: Westview Press.

Nisbett, R. E., Fong, G. T., Lehman, D. R., & Cheng, P. W. (1987). Teaching reasoning. *Science, 238,* 625–631.

Nisbett, R. E., & Ross, L. (1980). *Human inference: Strategies and shortcomings of human judgment.* Englewood Cliffs, NJ: Prentice Hall.

Nisbett, R. E., & Wilson, T. D. (1977). Telling more than we can know: Verbal reports on mental processes. *Psychological Review, 84,* 231–259.

Nixon, R. M. (1990). *In the arena: A memoir of victory, defeat, and renewal.* New York: Simon & Schuster.

Nolen-Hoeksema, S., Girgus, J. S., & Seligman, M. E. P. (1986). Learned helplessness in children: A longitudinal study of depression, achievement, and explanatory style. *Journal of Personality and Social Psychology, 51,* 435–442.

Norenzayan, A., Choi, I., & Nisbett, R. E. (1999). Eastern and Western perceptions of causality for social behavior: Lay theories about personalities and situations. In D. A. Prentice & D. T. Miller (Eds.), *Cultural divides: Understanding and overcoming group conflict* (pp. 239–272). New York: Russell Sage Foundation.

Norris, F. H., & Kaniasty, K. (1996). Received and perceived social support in times of stress: A test of the social support deterioration model. *Journal of Personality and Social Psychology, 71,* 498–511.

Nosek, B. A., Banaji, M. R., & Greenwald, A. G. (2002). Math = male, me = female, therefore math ≠ me. *Journal of Personality and Social Psychology, 83,* 44–59.

Nowak, A., Szamrej, J., & Latané, B. (1990). From private attitude to public opinion: A dynamic theory of social impact. *Psychological Review, 97,* 362–376.

O'Connor, K. M., & Carnevale, P. J. (1997). A nasty but effective negotiation strategy: Misrepresentation of a common-value issue. *Personality and Social Psychology Bulletin, 23,* 504–515.

Ofshe, R., & Watters, E. (1994). *Making monsters: False memories, psychotherapy, and sexual hysteria.* New York: Scribner.

Ogloff, J. R. P., & Vidmar, N. (1994). The impact of pretrial publicity on jurors: A study to compare the relative effects of television and print media in a child sex abuse case. *Law and Human Behavior, 18,* 507–525.

Ohbuchi, K., & Baba, R. (1988). Selection of influence strategies in interpersonal conflicts: Effects of sex, interpersonal relations, and goals. *Tohoku Psychologica Folia, 47,* 63–73.

Ohbuchi, K., Ohno, T., & Mukai, H. (1993). Empathy and aggression: Effects of self-disclosure and fearful appeal. *Journal of Social Psychology, 133,* 243–253.

Ohbuchi, K., & Sato, K. (1994). Children's reactions to mitigating accounts: Apologies, excuses, and intentionality of harm. *Journal of Social Psychology, 134,* 5–17.

Ohtsubo, Y., Masuchi, A., & Nakanishi, D. (2002). Majority influence process in group judgment: Test of the social judgment scheme model in a group polarization context. *Group Processes and Intergroup Relations, 5,* 249–261.

Oishi, S., Wyer, R. S., & Colcombe, S. J. (2000). Cultural variation in the use of current life satisfaction to predict the future. *Journal of Personality and Social Psychology, 78,* 434–445.

O'Leary, A. (1990). Stress, emotion, and human immune function. *Psychological Bulletin, 108,* 363–382.

Olson, J. M., & Zanna, M. P. (1993). Attitudes and attitude change. *Annual Review of Psychology, 44,* 117–154.

Olson, M. A., & Fazio, R. H. (2001). Implicit attitude formation through classical conditioning. *Psychological Science, 12,* 413–417.

Olsson, N. (2000). A comparison of correlation, calibration, and diagnosticity as measures of the confidence-accuracy relationship. *Journal of Applied Psychology, 85,* 504–511.

Olweus, D. (1991). Bully/victim problems among schoolchildren: Basic facts and effects of a school-based intervention program. In D. Pepler & K. Rubin (Eds.), *The development and treatment of childhood aggression* (pp. 411–448). Hillsdale, NJ: Erlbaum.

Olweus, D. (1995a). Bullying or peer abuse at school: Facts and interventions. *Current Directions in Psychological Science, 4,* 196–200.

Olweus, D. (1995b). Bullying or peer abuse in school: Intervention and prevention. In G. Davies, S. Lloyd-Bostock, M. McMurran, & C. Wilson (Eds.), *Psychology, law, and criminal justice: International developments in research and practice* (pp. 248–263). Berlin: de Gruyter.

Olweus, D. (1996). Bullying at school: Knowledge base and an effective intervention program. In C. Ferris & T. Grisso (Eds.), *Understanding aggressive behavior in children* (pp. 265–276). New York: New York Academy of Sciences.

Olweus, D. (1997). Tackling peer victimization with a school-based intervention program. In D. Fry & K. Bjorkqvist (Eds.), *Cultural variation in conflict resolution: Alternatives to violence* (pp. 215–231). Mahwah, NJ: Erlbaum.

Olweus D. (2003). Prevalence estimation of school bullying. *Aggressive Behavior 29,* 239–268.

Omoto, A. M., & Snyder, M. (2002). Considerations of community: The context and process of volunteerism. *American Behavioral Scientist, 45,* 846–867.

Orbell, J. M., van de Kragt, A. J. C., & Dawes, R. M. (1988). Explaining discussion-induced comparison. *Journal of Personality and Social Psychology, 54,* 811–819.

Ortony, A., Clore, G., & Collins, A. (1988). *The cognitive structure of emotions.* Cambridge: Cambridge University Press.

Orvis, B. R., Cunningham, J. D., & Kelley, H. H. (1975). A closer examination of causal inference: The role of consensus, distinctiveness, and consistency information. *Journal of Personality and Social Psychology, 32,* 605–616.

Oskamp, S. (1995). Applying social psychology to avoid ecological disaster. *Journal of Social Issues, 51,* 217–238.

Oskamp, S., Burkhardt, R. I., Schultz, P. W., Hurin, S., & Zelezny, L. (1998). Predicting three dimensions of residential curbside recycling: An observational study. *Journal of Environmental Education, 29,* 37–42.

Ostrom, T., & Sedikides, C. (1992). Out-group homogeneity effects in natural and minimal groups. *Psychological Bulletin, 112,* 536–552.

O'Sullivan, C. S., & Durso, F. T. (1984). Effects of schema-incongruent information on memory for stereotypical attributes. *Journal of Personality and Social Psychology, 47,* 55–70.

Otten, C. A., Penner, L. A., & Waugh, G. (1988). That's what friends are for: The determinants of psychological helping. *Journal of Social and Clinical Psychology, 7,* 34–41.

Ouellette, J. A., & Wood, W. (1998). Habit and intention in everyday life: The multiple processes by which past behavior predicts future behavior. *Psychological Bulletin, 124,* 54–74.

Ovcharchyn, C. A., Johnson, H. H., & Petzel, T. P. (1981). Type A behavior, academic aspirations, and academic success. *Journal of Personality, 49,* 248–256.

Overmier, J. B. (2002). On learned helplessness. *Integrative Physiological and Behavioral Science, 37,* 4–8.

Paik, H., & Comstock, G. (1994). The effects of television violence on antisocial behavior: A meta-analysis. *Communication Research, 21,* 516–546.

Palmgreen, P., Donohew, L., Lorch, E. P., Holye, R., & Stephenson, M. T. (2001). Television campaigns and adolescent marijuana use: Tests of sensation seeking targeting. *American Journal of Public Health, 91,* 292–296.

Pandey, J. (1990). The environment, culture, and behavior. In R. Brislin (Ed.), *Applied cross-cultural psychology* (pp. 254–277). Thousand Oaks, CA: Sage.

Park, B., & Rothbart, M. (1982). Perception of out-group homogeneity and levels of social categorization: Memory for the subordinate attributes of in-group and out-group members. *Journal of Personality and Social Psychology, 42,* 1051–1068.

Parke, R. D., Berkowitz, L., Leyens, J. P., West, S. G., & Sebastian, R. J. (1977). Some effects of violent and nonviolent movies on the behavior of juvenile delinquents. In L. Berkowitz (Ed.), *Advances in experimental social psychology* (Vol. 10, pp. 135–172). New York: Academic Press.

Parks, C. D., & Rumble, A. C. (2001). Elements of reciprocity and social value orientation. *Personality and Social Psychology Bulletin, 27,* 1301–1309.

Patrick, C. J., & Iacono, W. G. (1989). Psychopathy, threat, and polygraph test accuracy. *Journal of Applied Psychology, 74,* 347–355.

Patterson, A. (1974, September). *Hostility catharsis: A naturalistic quasi-experiment.* Paper presented at the annual meeting of the American Psychological Association, New Orleans.

Patton, P. (1989, August 6). Steve Jobs out for revenge. *New York Times Magazine,* pp. 23, 52, 56, 58.

Paulus, P. B. (1998). Developing consensus about groupthink after all these years. *Organizational Behavior and Human Decision Processes, 73,* 362–374.

Paulus, P. B., & Dzindolet, M. T. (1992). The effects of prison confinement. In P. Suedfeld & P. E. Tetlock (Eds.), *Psychology and social policy* (pp. 327–341). New York: Hemisphere.

Paulus, P. B., McCain, G., & Cox, V. (1981). Prison standards: Some pertinent data on crowding. *Federal Probation, 15,* 48–54.

Pavlidis, I., Eberhardt, N. L., & Levine, J. A. (2002). Seeing through the face of deception: Thermal imaging offers a promising hands-off approach to mass security screening. *Nature, 415,* 35.

Pechmann, C., & Knight, S. J. (2002). An experimental investigation of the joint effects of advertising and peers on adolescents' beliefs and intentions about cigarette consumption. *Journal of Consumer Research, 29,* 5–19.

Pedersen, D. M. (1965). The measurement of individual differences in perceived personality-trait relationships and their relation to certain determinants. *Journal of Social Psychology, 65,* 233–258.

Peirce, R. S., Frone, M. R., Russell, M., & Cooper, M. L. (1996). Financial stress, social support, and alcohol involvement: A longitudinal test of the buffering hypothesis in a general population survey. *Health Psychology, 15,* 38–47.

Pennebaker, J. W. (1990). *Opening up: The healing powers of confiding in others.* New York: Morrow.

Pennebaker, J. W. (1997). Writing about emotional experiences as a therapeutic process. *Psychological Science, 8,* 162–166.

Pennebaker, J. W., Barger, S. D., & Tiebout, J. (1989). Disclosure of traumas and health among Holocaust survivors. *Psychosomatic Medicine, 51,* 577–589.

Pennebaker, J. W., & Beale, S. K. (1986). Confronting a traumatic event: Toward an understanding of inhibition and disease. *Journal of Abnormal Psychology, 95,* 274–281.

Pennebaker, J. W., Colder, M., & Sharp, L. K. (1990). Accelerating the coping process. *Journal of Personality and Social Psychology, 58,* 528–537.

Pennebaker, J. W., & Francis, M. E. (1996). Cognitive, emotional, and language processes in disclosure. *Cognition and Emotion, 10,* 601–626.

Pennebaker, J. W., & Sanders, D. Y. (1976). American graffiti: Effects of authority and reactance arousal. *Personality and Social Psychology Bulletin, 2,* 264–267.

Penner, L. A. (2002). Dispositional and organizational influences on sustained volunteerism: An interactionist perspective. *Journal of Social Issues, 58,* 447–467.

Penner, L. A., & Finkelstein, M. A. (1998). Dispositional and structural determinants of volunteerism. *Journal of Personality and Social Psychology, 74,* 525–537.

Penner, L. A., Fritzsche, B. A., Craiger, J. P., & Freifeld, T. S. (1995). Measuring the prosocial personality. In J. Butcher & C. Spielberger (Eds.), *Advances in personality assessment* (Vol. 10, pp. 147–163). Hillsdale, NJ: Erlbaum.

Pennington, J., & Schlenker, B. R. (1999). Accountability for consequential decisions: Justifying ethical judgments to audiences. *Personality and Social Psychology Bulletin, 25,* 1067–1081.

Pennington, N., & Hastie, R. (1988). Explanation-based decision making: Effects of memory structure on judgment. *Journal of Experimental Psychology: Learning, Memory, and Cognition, 14,* 521–533.

Pennington, N., & Hastie, R. (1990). Practical implications of psychological research on juror and jury decision making. *Personality and Social Psychology Bulletin, 16,* 90–105.

Pennington, N., & Hastie, R. (1992). Explaining the evidence: Tests of the story model for juror decision making. *Journal of Personality and Social Psychology, 62,* 189–206.

Penrod, S. D., & Cutler, B. (1999). Preventing mistaken convictions in eyewitness identification trials: The case against traditional safeguards. In R. Roesch, S. D. Hart, & J. R. P. Ogloff (Eds.), *Psychology and law: The state of the discipline* (pp. 89–118). New York: Kluwer.

Peplau, L. A., & Perlman, D. (1982). Perspectives on loneliness. In L. A. Peplau & D. Perlman (Eds.), *Loneliness: A sourcebook of current theory, research, and therapy* (pp. 1–18). New York: Wiley.

Perlstein, L. (1999, November 14). The sweet rewards of learning: Teachers motivate students with tokens for fries and candy. *Washington Post,* pp. A1, A14.

Perrett, D. I., May, K. A., & Yoshikawa, S. (1994). Facial shape and judgments of female attractivenesss. *Nature, 368,* 239–242.

Perrin, S., & Spencer, C. (1981). Independence or conformity in the Asch experiment as a reflection of cultural or situational factors. *British Journal of Social Psychology, 20,* 205–209.

Pertman, A. (1995, February 3). Gestures aren't body of evidence, Ito warns. *Boston Globe,* p. 3.

Peters, L. H., Hartke, D. D., & Pohlmann, J. T. (1985). Fiedler's contingency theory of leadership: An application of the meta-analysis procedures of Schmidt and Hunter. *Psychological Bulletin, 97,* 274–285.

Peterson, C., & Seligman, M. E. P. (1984). Causal explanations as a risk factor for depression: Theory and evidence. *Psychological Review, 91,* 347–374.

Peterson, R. D., & Bailey, W. C. (1988). Murder and capital punishment in the evolving context of the post-Furman era. *Social Forces, 66,* 774–807.

Peterson, R. S., & Nemeth, C. J. (1996). Focus versus flexibility: Majority and minority influence can both improve performance. *Personality and Social Psychology Bulletin, 22,* 14–23.

Petrie, K. J., Booth, R. J., & Pennebaker, J. W. (1998). The immunological effects of thought suppression. *Journal of Personality and Social Psychology, 75,* 1264–1272.

Petrie, T. A., Austin, L. J., Crowley, B. J., Helmcamp, A., Johnson, C. E., Lester, R., et al. (1996). Sociocultural expectations for attractiveness for males. *Sex Roles, 35,* 581–602.

Petroselli, D. M., & Knobler, P. (1998). *Triumph of justice: Closing the book on the Simpson saga.* New York: Crown.

Pettigrew, T. F. (1958). Personality and sociocultural factors and intergroup attitudes: A cross-national comparison. *Journal of Conflict Resolution, 2,* 29–42.

Pettigrew, T. F. (1969). Racially separate or together? *Journal of Social Issues, 25,* 43–69.

Pettigrew, T. F. (1979). The ultimate attribution error: Extending Allport's cognitive analysis of prejudice. *Personality and Social Psychology Bulletin, 5,* 461–476.

Pettigrew, T. F. (1985). New black-white patterns: How best to conceptualize them? *Annual Review of Sociology, 11,* 329–346.

Pettigrew, T. F. (1989). The nature of modern racism in the United States. *Revue Internationale de Psychologie Sociale, 2,* 291–303.

Pettigrew, T. F. (1991). Normative theory in intergroup relations: Explaining both harmony and conflict. *Psychology and Developing Societies, 3,* 3–16.

Pettigrew, T. F. (1998). Reactions toward the new minorities of Western Europe. *Annual Review of Sociology, 24,* 77–103.

Pettigrew, T. F., Jackson, J. S., Brika, J. B., Lemaine, G., Meertens, R. W., Wagner, U., & Zick, A. (1998). Outgroup prejudice in western Europe. *European Review of Social Psychology, 8,* 241–273.

Pettigrew, T. F., & Meertens, R. W. (1995). Subtle and blatant prejudice in western Europe. *European Journal of Social Psychology, 25,* 57–75.

Pettigrew, T. F., & Tropp, L. (2003). *A meta-analytic test and reformulation of intergroup contact theory.* Unpublished manuscript.

Petty, R. E. (1995). Attitude change. In A. Tesser (Ed.), *Advanced social psychology* (pp. 195–255). New York: McGraw-Hill.

Petty, R. E., & Brock, T. C. (1981). Thought disruption and persuasion: Assessing the validity of attitude change experiments. In R. E. Petty, T. M. Ostrom, & T. C. Brock (Eds.), *Cognitive responses in persuasion* (pp. 55–79). Hillsdale, NJ: Erlbaum.

Petty, R. E., & Cacioppo, J. T. (1986). *Communication and persuasion: Central and peripheral routes to attitude change.* New York: Springer-Verlag.

Petty, R. E., Cacioppo, J. T., & Goldman, R. (1981). Personal involvement as a determinant of argument-based persuasion. *Journal of Personality and Social Psychology, 41,* 847–855.

Petty, R. E., Haugtvedt, C. P., & Smith, S. M. (1995). Elaboration as a determinant of attitude strength. In R. E. Petty & J. A. Krosnick (Eds.), *Attitude strength: Antecedents and consequences* (pp. 93–130). Hillsdale, NJ: Erlbaum.

Petty, R. E., Priester, J. R., & Brinol, P. (2002). Mass media attitude change: Implications of the elaboration likelihood model of persuasion. In J. Bryant, & D. Zillmann (Eds.), *Media effects: Advances in theory and research* (2nd ed., pp. 155–198). Mahwah, NJ: Erlbaum.

Petty, R. E., & Wegener, D. T. (1999). The elaboration likelihood model: Current status and controversies. In S. Chaiken & Y. Trope (Eds.), *Dual-process theories in social psychology* (pp. 41–72). New York: Guilford Press.

Petty, R. E., Wegener, D. T., & Fabrigar, L. R. (1997). Attitudes and attitude change. *Annual Review of Psychology, 48,* 609–647.

Petty, R. E., Wells, G. L., & Brock, T. C. (1976). Distraction can enhance or reduce yielding to propaganda: Thought disruption versus effort justification. *Journal of Personality and Social Psychology, 34,* 874–884.

Pezdek, K., & Banks, W. P. (Eds.). (1996). *The recovered memory/false memory debate.* San Diego, CA: Academic Press.

Phillips, D. P. (1983). The impact of mass media violence on U.S. homicides. *American Sociological Review, 48,* 560–568.

Phillips, D. P. (1986). Natural experiments on the effects of mass media violence on fatal aggression: Strengths and weaknesses of a new approach. In L. Berkowitz (Ed.), *Advances in experimental social psychology* (Vol. 19, pp. 207–250). Orlando, FL: Academic Press.

Pickel, K. L. (1998). Unusualness and threat as possible causes of "weapons focus." *Memory, 6,* 277–295.

Pickett, C. L., Silver, M. D., & Brewer, M. B. (2002). The impact of assimilation and differentiation needs on perceived group importance and judgments of ingroup size. *Personality and Social Psychology Bulletin, 28,* 546–558.

Piliavin, I. M., Piliavin, J. A., & Rodin, J. (1975). Costs, diffusion, and the stigmatized victim. *Journal of Personality and Social Psychology, 32,* 429–438.

Piliavin, J. A., & Charng, H. (1990). Altruism: A review of recent theory and research. *Annual Review of Sociology, 16,* 27–65.

Piliavin, J. A., Dovidio, J. F., Gaertner, S. L., & Clark, R. D., III. (1981). *Emergency intervention.* New York: Academic Press.

Piliavin, J. A., & Piliavin, I. M. (1972). The effect of blood on reactions to a victim. *Journal of Personality and Social Psychology, 23,* 253–261.

Pincus, T., & Morley, S. (2001). Cognitive-processing bias in chronic pain: A review and integration. *Psychological Bulletin, 127,* 599–617.

Pinker, S. (2002). *The blank slate: The modern denial of human nature.* New York: Viking.

Pleban, R., & Tesser, A. (1981). The effects of relevance and quality of another's performance on interpersonal closeness. *Social Psychology Quarterly, 44,* 278–285.

PollingReport.com. (2003, July 31). *President Bush: Job ratings.* Retrieved from http://www.pollingreport.com/BushJob.htm

Pope, H. G., Jr., Gruber, A. J., Mangweth, B., Bureau, B., de Col, C., Jouvent, R., & Hudson, J. I. (2000). Body image perception among men in three countries. *American Journal of Psychiatry, 157,* 1297–1301.

Pope, H. G., Jr., Olivardia, R., Gruber, A. J., & Borowiecki, J. (1999). Evolving ideals of male body image as seen through action toys. *International Journal of Eating Disorders, 26,* 65–72.

Pope, H. G., Jr., Phillips, K. A., & Olivardia, R. (2000). *The Adonis complex: The secret crisis of male body obsession.* New York: Freeman.

Porter, J. R. (1971). *Black child, white child: The development of racial attitudes.* Cambridge, MA: Harvard University Press.

Porter, J. R., & Washington, R. E. (1979). Black identity and self-esteem, 1968–1978. *Annual Review of Sociology, 5,* 53–74.

Porter, J. R., & Washington, R. E. (1989). Developments in research on black identity and self-esteem, 1979–1988. *Revue Internationale de Psychologie Sociale, 2,* 339–353.

Postmes, T., & Spears, R. (1998). Deindividuation and antinormative behavior: A meta-analysis. *Psychological Bulletin, 123,* 238–259.

Postmes, T., Spears, R., & Cihangir, S. (2001). Quality of decision making and group norms. *Journal of Personality and Social Psychology, 80,* 918–930.

Povinelli, D. J. (1994). A theory of mind is in the head, not the heart. *Behavioral and Brain Sciences, 17,* 573–574.

Povinelli, D. J., Landau, K. R., & Perilloux, H. K. (1996). Self-recognition in young children using delayed versus live feedback: Evidence of a developmental asynchrony. *Child Development, 67,* 1540–1554.

Powledge, F. (1991). *Free at last? The civil rights movement and the people who made it.* Boston: Little, Brown.

Pratkanis, A. R. (1992). The cargo-cult science of subliminal persuasion. *Skeptical Inquirer, 16,* 260–272.

Prentice, D. A., Miller, D. T., & Lightdale, J. R. (1994). Asymmetries in attachments to groups and to their members: Distinguishing between common-identity and common-bond groups. *Personality and Social Psychology Bulletin, 20,* 484–493.

Pressley, S. A. (2003, July 23). Discord over noise in Rehoboth Beach. *Washington Post,* pp. B1, B4.

Preston, S. D., & De Waal, F.B.M. (2002). Empathy: Its ultimate and proximate bases. *Behavioral and Brain Sciences, 25,* 1–72.

Pronin, E., Lin, D. Y., & Ross, L. (2002). The bias blind spot: Perceptions of bias in self versus others. *Personality and Social Psychology Bulletin, 28,* 369–381.

Pruitt, D. G. (1998). Social conflict. In D. T. Gilbert, S. T. Fiske, & G. Lindzey (Eds.), *The handbook of social psychology* (4th ed., Vol. 2, pp. 470–503). New York: McGraw-Hill.

Pruitt, D. G., & Kimmel, M. J. (1977). Twenty years of experimental gaming: Critique, synthesis, and suggestions for the future. *Annual Review of Psychology, 28,* 363–392.

Purdham, T. S. (1997, March 28). Tapes left by cult suggest comet was the sign to die. *New York Times,* p. A2.

Quattrone, G. A. (1982). Behavioral consequences of attributional bias. *Social Cognition, 1,* 358–378.

Quattrone, G. A. (1986). On the perception of a group's variability. In S. Worchel & W. G. Austin (Eds.), *Psychology of intergroup relations* (2nd ed.). Chicago: Nelson-Hall.

Quattrone, G. A., & Jones, E. E. (1980). The perception of variability within ingroups and outgroups: Implications for the law of small numbers. *Journal of Personality and Social Psychology, 38,* 141–152.

Quinn, A., & Schlenker, B. R. (2002). Can accountability produce independence? Goals as determinants of the impact of accountability on conformity. *Personality and Social Psychology Bulletin, 28,* 472–483.

Raety, H., Vaenskae, J., Kasanen, K., & Kaerkkaeinen, R. (2002). Parents' explanations of their child's performance in mathematics and reading: A replication and extension of Yee and Eccles. *Sex Roles, 46,* 121–128

Rajecki, D. W., Kidd, R. F., & Ivins, B. (1976). Social facilitation in chickens: A different level of analysis. *Journal of Experimental Social Psychology, 12,* 233–246.

Ramsey, S. J. (1981). The kinesics of femininity in Japanese women. *Language Sciences, 3,* 104–123.

Rapoport, A., & Chammah, A. M. (1965). *Prisoner's dilemma: A study in conflict and cooperation.* Ann Arbor: University of Michigan Press.

Raps, C. S., Peterson, C., Jonas, M., & Seligman, M. E. P. (1982). Patient behavior in hospitals: Helplessness, reactance, or both? *Journal of Personality and Social Psychology, 42,* 1036–1041.

Raskin, D. C., Honts, C. R., & Kircher, J. C. (1997). The scientific status of research on polygraph techniques: The case for polygraph tests. In D. L. Faigman, D. H. Kaye, M. J. Saks, & J. Sanders (Eds.), *Modern scientific evidence: The law and science of expert testimony* (pp. 565–582). St. Paul, MN: West.

Reagan, R. (1990). *An American life.* New York: Simon & Schuster.

Rector, M., & Neiva, E. (1996). Communication and personal relations in Brazil. In W. B. Gudykunst, S. Ting-Toomey, & T. Nishida (Eds.), *Communication in personal relationships across cultures* (pp. 156–173). Thousand Oaks, CA: Sage.

Redlawsk, D. P. (2002). Hot cognition or cool consideration? Testing the effects of motivated reasoning on political decision making. *Journal of Politics, 64,* 1021–1044.

Regan, P. C. (1998). Of lust and love: Beliefs about the role of sexual desire in romantic relationships. *Personal Relationships, 5,* 139–157.

Regan, P. C., & Berscheid, E. (1995). Gender differences in beliefs about the causes of male and female sexual desire. *Personal Relationships, 2,* 345–358.

Regan, P. C., & Berscheid, E. (1997). Gender differences in characteristics desired in a potential sexual and marriage partner. *Journal of Psychology and Human Sexuality, 9,* 25–37.

Regan, P. C., & Berscheid, E. (1999). *Lust: What we know about human sexual desire.* Thousand Oaks, CA: Sage.

Regan, P. C., Snyder, M., & Kassin, S. M. (1995). Unrealistic optimism: Self-enhancement or person positivity? *Personality and Social Psychology Bulletin, 21,* 1073–1082.

Rehm, J., Steinleitner, M., & Lilli, W. (1987). Wearing uniforms and aggression: A field experiment. *European Journal of Social Psychology, 17,* 357–360.

Reifman, A. S., Larrick, R. P., Crandall, C. S., & Fein, S. (1996). *Predicting sporting events: Accuracy as a function of reasons analysis, expertise, and task difficulty.* Unpublished manuscript, Research Institute on Addictions, Buffalo, NY.

Reifman, A. S., Larrick, R. P., & Fein, S. (1988). *The heat-aggression relationship in major league baseball.* Paper presented at the annual meeting of the American Psychological Association, San Francisco.

Reis, H. T., & Judd, C. M. (Eds.). (2000). *Handbook of research methods in social and personality psychology.* New York: Cambridge University Press.

Reis, H. T., Nezlek, J., & Wheeler, L. (1980). Physical attractiveness in social interaction. *Journal of Personality and Social Psychology, 38,* 604–617.

Reis, H. T., & Patrick, B. C. (1996). Attachment and intimacy: Component processes. In E. T. Higgins & A. W. Kruglanski (Eds.), *Social psychology: Handbook of basic principles* (pp. 523–563). New York: Guilford Press.

Reis, H. T., Wheeler, L., Speigel, N., Kernis, M. H., Nezlek, J., & Perri, M. (1982). Physical attractiveness in social interaction: 2. Why

does appearance affect social experience? *Journal of Personality and Social Psychology, 43,* 979–996.

Reis, S. M. & Park, S. (2001). Gender differences in high-achieving students in math and science. *Journal for the Education of the Gifted, 25,* 52–73

Reisman, J. M. (1990). Intimacy in same-sex friendships. *Sex Roles, 23,* 65–82.

Reiss, D., & Marino, L. (2001). Mirror self-recognition in the bottlenose dolphin: A case of cognitive convergence. *Proceedings of the National Academy of Sciences, 98,* 5937–5942.

Reiter, S. M., & Samuel, W. (1980). Littering as a function of prior litter and the presence or absence of prohibitive signs. *Journal of Applied Social Psychology, 10,* 45–55.

Reitzes, D. C. (1952). The role of organizational structures: Union versus neighborhood in a tension situation. *Journal of Social Issues, 9,* 37–44.

Renaud, J. M., & McConnell, A. R. (2002). Organization of the self-concept and the suppression of self-relevant thoughts. *Journal of Experimental Social Psychology, 38,* 79–86.

Reno, R. R., Cialdini, R. B., & Kallgren, C. A. (1993). The transsituational influence of social norms. *Journal of Personality and Social Psychology, 64,* 104–112.

Rhodes, G., Yoshikawa, S., Clark, A., Lee, K., McKay, R., & Akamatsu, S. (2001). Attractiveness of facial averageness and symmetry in non-Western cultures: In search of biologically based standards of beauty. *Perception, 30,* 611–625.

Rhodes, N., & Wood, W. (1992). Self-esteem and intelligence affect influenceability: The mediating role of message reception. *Psychological Bulletin, 111,* 156–171.

Rhodes, R. (1995, June 19). The general and World War III. *New Yorker,* pp. 47–59.

Rhodewalt, F., Sanbonmatsu, D. M., Tschanz, B., Feick, D. L., & Waller, A. (1995). Self-handicapping and interpersonal trade-offs: The effects of claimed self-handicaps on observers' performance evaluations and feedback. *Personality and Social Psychology Bulletin, 21,* 1042–1050.

Rholes, W. S., Newman, L. S., & Ruble, D. N. (1990). Understanding self and other: Developmental and motivational aspects of perceiving persons in terms of invariant dispositions. In E. T. Higgins & R. M. Sorrentino (Eds.), *Handbook of motivation and cognition: Foundations of social behavior* (Vol. 2, pp. 369–407). New York: Guilford Press.

Richards, J. M., & Gross, J. J. (1999). Composure at any cost? The cognitive consequences of emotion suppression. *Personality and Social Psychology Bulletin, 25,* 1033–1044.

Richardson, D., Hammock, G., Smith, S., & Gardner, W. (1994). Empathy as a cognitive inhibitor of interpersonal aggression. *Aggressive Behavior, 20,* 275–289.

Richmond, V. P., & McCroskey, J. C. (1995). *Nonverbal behavior in interpersonal relations.* Needham Heights, MA: Allyn & Bacon.

Richter, C. P. (1957). On the phenomenon of sudden death in animals and man. *Psychosomatic Medicine, 19,* 191–198.

Ringelmann, M. (1913). Recherches sur les moteurs animés: Travail de l'homme [Research on driving forces: Human work]. *Annales de l'Institut National Agronomique,* series 2, *12,* 1–40.

Riordan, C. A. (1978). Equal-status interracial contact: A review and revision of a concept. *International Journal of Intercultural Relations, 2,* 161–185.

Robertson, T. (2003, June 8). Cries of gender, celebrity bias over Stewart. *The New York Times,* p. A14.

Robins, R. W., & Beer, J. S. (2001). Positive illusions about the self: Short-term benefits and long-term costs. *Journal of Personality and Social Psychology, 80,* 340–352.

Robins, R. W., Spranca, M. D., & Mendelson, G. A. (1996). The actor-observer effect revisited: Effects of individual differences and repeated social interactions on actor and observer attributions. *Journal of Personality and Social Psychology, 71,* 375–389.

Rodin, J. (1986). Aging and health: Effects of the sense of control. *Science, 233,* 1271–1276.

Rodin, J., & Langer, E. J. (1977). Long-term effects of a control-relevant intervention with the institutional aged. *Journal of Personality and Social Psychology, 35,* 897–902.

Rodrigo, M. F., & Ato, M. (2002). Testing the group polarization hypothesis by using logit models. *European Journal of Social Psychology, 32,* 3–18.

Roesch, S. C., & Amirkhan, J. H. (1997). Boundary conditions for self-serving attributions: Another look at the sports pages. *Journal of Applied Social Psychology, 27,* 245–261.

Roese, N. J. (1997). Counterfactual thinking. *Psychological Bulletin, 121,* 133–148.

Roese, N. J., & Olson, J. M. (1997). Counterfactual thinking: The intersection of affect and function. In M. P. Zanna (Ed.), *Advances in experimental social psychology* (Vol. 29, pp. 1–59). San Diego, CA: Academic Press.

Rogers, P. (1998). The cognitive psychology of lottery gambling: A theoretical review. *Journal of Gambling Studies, 14,* 111–134.

Rogers, R. (1983). Cognitive and physiological processes in fear appeals and attitude change: A revised theory of protection motivation. In J. T. Cacioppo & R. E. Petty (Eds.), *Social psychophysiology: A sourcebook* (pp. 153–176). New York: Guilford Press.

Rogers, R., & Prentice-Dunn, S. (1981). Deindividuation and anger-mediated interracial aggression: Unmasking regressive racism. *Journal of Personality and Social Psychology, 41,* 63–73.

Rogers, T. B., Kuiper, N. A., & Kirker, W. S. (1977). Self-reference and the encoding of personal information. *Journal of Personality and Social Psychology, 35,* 677–688.

Rohan, M., & Zanna, M. P. (1996). Value transmission in families. In C. Seligman, J. M. Olson, & M. P. Zanna (Eds.), *The psychology of values: The Ontario Symposium on personality and social psychology* (Vol. 8, pp. 253–276). Mahwah, NJ: Erlbaum.

Rohrer, J. H., Baron, S. H., Hoffman, E. L., & Swander, D. V. (1954). The stability of autokinetic judgments. *Journal of Abnormal and Social Psychology, 49,* 595–597.

Roiphe, K. (1994). *The morning after: Sex, fear, and feminism.* New York: Little, Brown.

Rosch, E., & Lloyd, B. (Eds.). (1978). *Cognition and categorization.* Hillsdale, NJ: Erlbaum.

Roseman, I. J., & Smith, C. (2001). Appraisal theory: Overview, assumptions, varieties, controversies. In K. Scherer & A. Schorr (Eds.), *Appraisal processes in emotion: Theory, methods, research* (pp. 3–19). New York: Oxford University Press.

Rosen, S., Bergman, M., Plester, D., El-Mofty, A., & Satti, M. (1962). Prebycusis study of a relatively noise-free population in the Sudan. *Annals of Otology, Rhinology, and Laryngology, 71,* 727–743.

Rosenbaum, M. E. (1986). The repulsion hypothesis: On the nondevelopment of relationships. *Journal of Personality and Social Psychology, 51,* 1156–1166.

Rosenberg, L. A. (1961). Group size, prior experience, and conformity. *Journal of Abnormal and Social Psychology, 63,* 436–437.

Rosenberg, M. J., Davidson, A. J., Chen, J., Judson, F. N., & Douglas, J. M. (1992). Barrier contraceptives and sexually transmitted diseases in women: A comparison of female-dependent methods and condoms. *American Journal of Public Health, 82,* 669–674.

Rosenberg, S., Nelson, S., & Vivekananthan, P. S. (1968). A multidimensional approach to the structure of personality impressions. *Journal of Personality and Social Psychology, 9,* 283–294.

Rosenblatt, P. C. (1974). Cross-cultural perspectives on attraction. In T. L. Huston (Ed.), *Foundations of interpersonal attraction* (pp. 79–99). New York: Academic Press.

Rosenman, R. H. (1993). Relationship of the Type A behavior pattern with coronary heart disease. In L. Goldberger & S. Breznitz (Eds.), *Handbook of stress: Theoretical and clinical aspects* (2nd ed., pp. 449–476). New York: Free Press.

Rosenthal, A. M. (1964). *Thirty-eight witnesses.* New York: McGraw-Hill.

Rosenthal, R. (1994). Interpersonal expectancy effects: A 30-year perspective. *Current Directions in Psychological Science, 3,* 176–179.

Rosenthal, R., & De Paulo, B. M. (1979). Sex differences in accommodation in nonverbal communication. In R. Rosenthal (Ed.), *Skill in nonverbal communication: Individual differences* (pp. 68–103). Cambridge, MA: Oelgeschlager, Gunn & Hain.

Rosenthal, R., Hall, J. A., Di Matteo, M. R., Rogers, P. L., & Archer, D. (1979). *Sensitivity to nonverbal communication· The PONS test.* Baltimore: Johns Hopkins University Press.

Rosenthal, R., & Jacobson, L. (1968). *Pygmalion in the classroom: Teacher expectations and student intellectual development.* New York: Holt, Rinehart and Winston.

Ross, L. (1977). The intuitive psychologist and his shortcomings: Distortions in the attribution process. In L. Berkowitz (Ed.), *Advances in experimental social psychology* (Vol. 10, pp. 173–220). Orlando, FL: Academic Press.

Ross, L. (1998). Comment on Gilbert. In J. M. Darley & J. Cooper (Eds.), *Attribution and social interaction* (pp. 53–66). Washington, DC: American Psychological Association.

Ross, L., Amabile, T. M., & Steinmetz, J. L. (1977). Social roles, social control, and biases in social perception. *Journal of Personality and Social Psychology, 35,* 485–494.

Ross, L., Lepper, M. R., & Hubbard, M. (1975). Perseverance in self-perception and social perception: Biased attributional processes in the debriefing paradigm. *Journal of Personality and Social Psychology, 32,* 880–892.

Ross, L., & Nisbett, R. E. (1991). *The person and the situation: Perspectives of social psychology.* New York: McGraw-Hill.

Ross, L., & Ward, A. (1995). Psychological barriers to dispute resolution. In M. P. Zanna (Ed.), *Advances in experimental social psychology* (Vol. 27, pp. 255–304). San Diego, CA: Academic Press.

Ross, L., & Ward, A. (1996). Naive realism: Implications for social conflict and misunderstanding. In T. Brown, E. Reed, & E. Turiel (Eds.), *Values and knowledge* (pp. 103–135). Hillsdale, NJ: Erlbaum.

Ross, M., & Olson, J. M. (1981). An expectancy-attribution model of the effects of placebos. *Psychological Review, 88,* 408–437.

Ross, M., & Wilson, A. E. (2002). It feels like yesterday: Self-esteem, valence of personal past experiences, and judgments of subjective distance. *Journal of Personality and Social Psychology, 82,* 792–803.

Ross, W., & La Croix, J. (1996). Multiple meanings of trust in negotiation theory and research: A literature review and integrative model. *International Journal of Conflict Management, 7,* 314–360.

Rosser, B. S. (1991). The effects of using fear in public AIDS education on the behaviour of homosexually active men. *Journal of Psychology and Human Sexuality, 4,* 123–134.

Rothbaum, F., & Tsang, B. Y.-P. (1998). Lovesongs in the United States and China: On the nature of romantic love. *Journal of Cross-Cultural Psychology, 29,* 306–319.

Rothman, A. J. (2000). Toward a theory-based analysis of behavioral maintenance. *Health Psychology, 19,* 64–69.

Rothman, A. J., & Salovey, P. (1997). Shaping perceptions to motivate healthy behavior: The role of message framing. *Psychological Bulletin, 121,* 3–19.

Rothman, A. J., Salovey, P., Antone, C., Keough, K., & Martin, C. D. (1993). The influence of message framing on intentions to perform health behaviors. *Journal of Experimental Social Psychology, 29,* 408–432.

Rubin, Z. (1970). Measurement of romantic love. *Journal of Personality and Social Psychology, 16,* 265–273.

Rubin, Z., Peplau, L. A., & Hill, C. T. (1981). Loving and leaving: Sex differences in romantic attachments. *Sex Roles, 7,* 821–835.

Rudman, L. A. (1998). Self-promotion as a risk factor for women: The costs and benefits of counterstereotypical impression management. *Journal of Personality and Social Psychology, 74,* 629–645.

Rudman, L. A., & Borgida, E. (1995). The afterglow of construct accessibility: The behavioral consequences of priming men to view women as sexual objects. *Journal of Experimental Social Psychology, 31,* 493–517.

Ruiter, R. A. C., Abraham, C., & Kok, G. (2001). Scary warnings and rational precautions: A review of the psychology of fear appeals. *Psychology and Health, 16,* 613–630.

Rule, B. G., Taylor, B. R., & Dobbs, A. R. (1987). Priming effects of heat on aggressive thoughts. *Social Cognition, 5,* 131–143.

Rusbult, C. E. (1983). A longitudinal test of the investment model: The development (and deterioration) of satisfaction and commitment in heterosexual involvements. *Journal of Personality and Social Psychology, 45,* 101–117.

Rusbult, C. E. (1987). Responses to dissatisfaction in close relationships: The exit-voice-loyalty-neglect model. In D. Perlman & S. W. Duck (Eds.), *Intimate relationships: Development, dynamics, and deterioration* (pp 209–237). Newbury Park, CA: Sage.

Rusbult, C. E. (1991). *Commitment processes in close relationships: The investment model*. Paper presented at the annual meeting of the American Psychological Association, San Francisco.

Rusbult, C. E., & Buunk, B. P. (1993). Commitment processes in close relationships: An interdependence analysis. *Journal of Social and Personal Relationships, 10,* 175–204.

Rusbult, C. E., Johnson, D. J., & Morrow, G. D. (1986). Impact of couple patterns of problem solving on distress and nondistress in dating relationships. *Journal of Personal and Social Psychology, 50,* 744–753.

Rusbult, C. E., & Martz, J. M. (1995). Remaining in an abusive relationship: An investment model analysis of nonvoluntary dependence. *Personality and Social Psychology Bulletin, 21,* 558–571.

Rusbult, C. E., Martz, J. M., & Agnew, C. R. (1998). The investment model scale: Measuring commitment level, satisfaction level, quality of alternatives, and investment size. *Personal Relationships, 5,* 357–391.

Rusbult, C. E., & Van Lange, P. A. M. (1996). Interdependence processes. In E. T. Higgins & A. W. Kruglanski (Eds.), *Social psychology: Handbook of basic principles* (pp. 564–596). New York: Guilford Press.

Rusbult, C. E., Yovetich, N. A., & Verette, J. (1996). An interdependence analysis of accommodation processes. In G. J. O. Fletcher & J. Fitness (Eds.), *Knowledge structures in close relationships: A social psychological approach* (pp. 63–90). Mahwah, NJ: Erlbaum.

Rusbult, C. E., & Zembrodt, I. M. (1983). Responses to dissatisfaction in romantic involvements: A multidimensional scaling analysis. *Journal of Experimental Social Psychology, 19,* 274–293.

Rushton, J. P. (1989). Genetic similarity, human altruism, and group selection. *Behavioral and Brain Sciences, 12,* 503–559.

Russell, D. E. H. (1997). Pornography causes harm to women. In M. R. Walsh (Ed.), *Women, men, and gender: Ongoing debates* (pp. 158–169). New Haven, CT: Yale University Press.

Russell, G. W. (1983). Psychological issues in sports aggression. In J. H. Goldstein (Ed.), *Sports violence* (pp. 157–181). New York: Springer-Verlag.

Russell, J. A. (1994). Is there universal recognition of emotion from facial expression? A review of the cross-cultural studies. *Psychological Bulletin, 115,* 102–141.

Russell, J. A., & Barrett, L. F. (1999). Core effect, prototypical emotional episodes, and other things called emotion: Dissecting the elephant. *Journal of Personality and Social Psychology, 76,* 805–819.

Russo, A. (2001). *Taking back our lives: A call to action for the feminist movement.* New York: Routledge.

Rutter, D. R., Quine, L., & Albery, I. P. (1998). Perceptions of risk in motorcyclists: Unrealistic optimism, relative realism, and predictions of behaviour. *British Journal of Psychology, 89,* 681–696.

Ryan, B., Jr. (1991). *It works! How investment spending in advertising pays off.* New York: American Association of Advertising Agencies.

Ryan, R. M., & Deci, E. L. (2000). Intrinsic and extrinsic rewards: Classic definitions and new directions. *Current Educational Psychology, 25,* 54–67.

Ryff, C. D., & B. H. Singer (Eds.) (2001). *Emotion, social relationships, and health.* New York: Oxford University Press.

Sacks, O. (1987). *The man who mistook his wife for a hat and other clinical tales.* New York: Harper & Row.

Sadik, N. (1991). World population continues to rise. *Futurist, 25,* 9–14.

Sadker, M., & Sadker, D. (1994). *Failing at fairness: How America's schools cheat girls.* New York: Scribner.

Saffer, H. (2002). Alcohol advertising and youth. *Journal of Studies on Alcohol, 14,* 173–181.

Sagarin, B. J., Cialdini, R. B., Rice, W. E., & Serna, S. B. (2002). Dispelling the illusion of invulnerability: The motivations and mechanisms of resistance to persuasion. *Journal of Personality and Social Psychology, 83,* 526–541.

Sakai, H. (1999). A multiplicative power-function model of cognitive dissonance: Toward an integrated theory of cognition, emotion, and behavior after Leon Festinger. In E. Harmon-Jones & J. S. Mills (Eds.), *Cognitive dissonance: Progress on a pivotal theory in social psychology* (pp. 120–138). Washington, DC: American Psychological Association.

Saks, M. J., & Marti, M. W. (1997). A meta-analysis of the effects of jury size. *Law and Human Behavior, 21,* 451–466.

Sakurai, M. M. (1975). Small group cohesiveness and detrimental conformity. *Sociometry, 38,* 340–357.

Salili, F. (1996). Learning and motivation: An Asian perspective. *Psychology and Developing Societies, 8,* 55–81.

Salovey, P., Mayer, J. D., & Rosenhan, D. L. (1991). Mood and helping: Mood as a motivator of helping and helping as a regulator of mood. In M. S. Clark (Ed.), *Prosocial behavior: Review of personality and social psychology* (Vol. 12, pp. 215–237). Newbury Park, CA: Sage.

Salovey, P., & Rodin, J. (1985). Cognitions about the self: Connecting feeling states and social behavior. In P. Shaver (Ed.), *Self, situations, and social behavior: Review of personality and social psychology* (Vol. 6, pp. 143–166). Beverly Hills, CA: Sage.

Salovey, P., Rothman, A. J., Detweiler, J. B., & Steward, W. T. (2000). Emotional states and physical health. *American Psychologist, 55,* 110–121.

Sanders, G. S. (1983). An attentional process model of social facilitation. In A. Hare, H. Bumberg, V. Kent, & M. Davies (Eds.), *Small groups.* London: Wiley.

Sands, E. R., & Wardle, J. (2003). Internalization of ideal body shapes in 9- to 12-year-old girls. *International Journal of Eating Disorders, 33,* 193–204.

Sanger, D. E. (1993, May 30). The career and the kimono. *New York Times Magazine,* pp. 18–19.

Sanna, L. J. (1992). Self-efficacy theory: Implications for social facilitation and social loafing. *Journal of Personality and Social Psychology, 62,* 774–786.

Sanna, L. J., Meier, S., & Wegner, E. A. (2001). Counterfactuals and motivation: Mood as input to affective enjoyment and preparation. *British Journal of Social Psychology, 40,* 235–256.

Sanna, L. J., Schwarz, N., & Stocker, S. L. (2002). When debiasing backfires: Accessible content and accessibility experiences in debiasing hindsight. *Journal of Experimental Psychology: Learning, Memory, and Cognition, 28,* 497–502.

Sansone, C., & Harackiewicz, J. M. (1996). "I don't feel like it": The function of interest in self-regulation. In L. L. Martin & A. Tesser (Eds.), *Striving and feeling: Interactions among goals, affect, and self-regulation* (pp. 203–228). Mahwah, NJ: Erlbaum.

Sansone, C., & Harackiewicz, J. M. (1997) *"Reality" is complicated: Comment on Eisenberger and Cameron.* Unpublished manuscript, University of Utah.

Sarche, J. (2003, June 22). For new female cadets, an Air Force Academy in turmoil. *Boston Globe,* p. A12.

Sargent, J. D., Dalton, M. A., Beach, M. L., Mott, L. A., Tickle, J. J., Ahrens, M. B., & Heatherton, T. F. (2002). Viewing tobacco use in movies: Does it shape attitudes that mediate adolescent smoking? *American Journal of Preventive Medicine, 22,* 137–145.

Sastry, J., & Ross, C. E. (1998). Asian ethnicity and the sense of personal control. *Social Psychology Quarterly, 61,* 101–120.

Savitsky, K. (1998). Embarrassment study [E-mails]. *Society for Personal and Social Psychology e-mail list archive.* Retrieved from http://www.stolaf.edu/cgi-bin/mailarchivesearch.pl?directory=/home/www/people/huff/SPSP&listname=archive98

Savitsky, K., Epley, N., & Gilovich, T. (2001). Do others judge us as harshly as we think? Overestimating the impact of our failures, shortcomings, and mishaps. *Journal of Personality and Social Psychology, 81,* 44–56.

Savitsky, K., Medvec, V. H., Charlton, A. E., & Gilovich, T. (1998). "What, me worry?" Arousal, misattribution, and the effect of temporal distance on confidence. *Personality and Social Psychology Bulletin, 24,* 529–536.

Schachter, S. (1951). Deviation, rejection, and communication. *Journal of Abnormal and Social Psychology, 46,* 190–207.

Schachter, S. (1959). *The psychology of affiliation.* Stanford, CA: Stanford University Press.

Schachter, S. (1964). The interaction of cognitive and physiological determinants of emotional state. In L. Berkowitz (Ed.), *Advances in experimental social psychology* (Vol. 1, pp. 49–80). New York: Academic Press.

Schachter, S., & Singer, J. E. (1962). Cognitive, social, and physiological determinants of emotional states. *Psychological Review, 69,* 379–399.

Schachter, S., & Singer, J. E. (1979). Comments on the Maslach and Marshall-Zimbardo experiments. *Journal of Personality and Social Psychology, 37,* 989–995.

Schacter, D. L. (1996). *Searching for memory: The brain, the mind, and the past.* New York: Basic Books.

Schafer, M., & Crichlow, S. (1996). Antecedents of groupthink: A quantitative study. *Journal of Conflict Resolution, 40,* 415–435.

Schaller, M., Asp, C. H., Rosell, M. C., & Heim, S. J. (1996). Training in statistical reasoning inhibits formation of erroneous group stereotypes. *Personality and Social Psychology Bulletin, 22,* 829–844.

Schama, S. (2003, March 10). The unloved American. *New Yorker,* pp. 34–39.

Scheier, M. F., Carver, C. S., & Bridges, M. W. (1994). Distinguishing optimism from neuroticism (and trait anxiety, self-mastery, and self-esteem): A revision of the Life Orientation Test. *Journal of Personality and Social Psychology, 67,* 1063–1078.

Schemo, D. J. (2003a, July 12). Ex-superintendent of Air Force Academy is demoted in wake of rape scandal. *New York Times,* p. A7.

Schemo, D. J. (2003b, July 24). Study of campus faults some antidrinking drives. *New York Times,* p. A17.

Scherer, K., & Schorr, A. (Eds.). (2001). *Appraisal processes in emotion: Theory, methods, research.* New York: Oxford University Press.

Schiffmann, A., Cohen, S., Nowik, R., & Selinger, D. (1978). Initial diagnostic hypotheses: Factors which distort physicians' judgment. *Organizational Behavior and Human Performance, 21,* 305–315.

Schlenger, W. E., Caddell, J. M., Ebert, L., Jordan, B. K., Rourke, K. M., Wilson, D., et al. (2002). Psychological reactions to terrorist attacks: Findings from the National Study of Americans' Reactions to September 11. *Journal of the American Medical Association, 288,* 581–588.

Schlenker, B. R. (1980). *Impression management: The self-concept, social identity, and interpersonal relations.* Monterey, CA: Brooks/Cole.

Schlenker, B. R., & Weingold, M. F. (1989). Self-identification and accountability. In R. A. Giacalone & P. Rosenfeld (Eds.), *Impression management in the organization* (pp. 21–43). Hillsdale, NJ: Erlbaum.

Schmidt, D. E., & Keating, J. P. (1979). Human crowding and personal control: An integration of the research. *Psychological Bulletin, 86,* 680–700.

Schmitt, B. H., Gilovich, T., Goore, N., & Joseph, L. (1986). Mere presence and social facilitation: One more time. *Journal of Experimental Social Psychology, 22,* 228–241.

Schneider, D. J. (1973). Implicit personality theory: A review. *Psychological Bulletin, 79,* 294–309.

Schneider, D. J., Hastorf, A. H., & Ellsworth, P. C. (1979). *Person perception* (2nd ed.). Reading, MA: Addison-Wesley.

Schneider, M. E., Major, B., Luhtanen, R., & Crocker, J. (1996). Social stigma and the potential costs of assumptive help. *Personality and Social Psychology Bulletin, 22,* 201–209.

Schofield, J. W. (1986). Causes and consequences of the color-blind perspective. In J. F. Dovidio & S. L. Gaertner (Eds.), *Prejudice, discrimination, and racism* (pp. 231–253). Orlando, FL: Academic Press.

Schooler, J. W. (1999). Seeking the core: The issues and evidence surrounding recovered accounts of sexual trauma. In L. M. Williams & V. L. Banyard (Eds.), *Trauma and memory* (pp. 203–216). Thousand Oaks, CA: Sage.

Schooler, J. W., & Eich, E. (2000). Memory for emotional events. In E. Tulving & F. I. M. Craik (Eds.), *The Oxford handbook of memory* (pp. 379–392). Oxford, England: Oxford University Press.

Schooler, J. W., & Engstler-Schooler, T. Y. (1990). Verbal overshadowing of visual memories: Some things are better left unsaid. *Cognitive Psychology, 22,* 36–71.

Schooler, J. W., Fiore, S. M., & Brandimonte, M. A. (1997). At a loss from words: Verbal overshadowing of perceptual memories. *Psychology of Learning and Motivation, 37,* 291–340.

Schopler, J., & Insko, C. A. (1999). The reduction of the interindividual-intergroup discontinuity effect: The role of future consequences. In M. Foddy & M. Smithson (Eds.), *Resolving social dilemmas: Dynamic, structural, and intergroup aspects* (pp. 281–293). Bristol, PA: Taylor & Francis.

Schriesheim, C. A., Tepper, B. J., & Tetrault, L. A. (1994). Least preferred co-worker score, situational control, and leadership effectiveness: A meta-analysis of contingency model performance predictions. *Journal of Applied Psychology, 79,* 561–573.

Schroeder, D. H., & Costa, P. T., Jr. (1984). Influence of life event stress on physical illness: Substantive effects or methodological flaws? *Journal of Personality and Social Psychology, 46,* 853–863.

Schultz, P. W., Oskamp, S., & Mainieri, T. (1995). Who recycles and when? A review of personal and situational factors. *Journal of Environmental Psychology, 15,* 105–121.

Schulz, R. (1976). Effects of control and predictability on the physical and psychological well-being of the institutionalized aged. *Journal of Personality and Social Psychology, 33,* 563–573.

Schulz, R., & Hanusa, B. H. (1978). Long-term effects of control and predictability-enhancing interventions: Findings and ethical issues. *Journal of Personality and Social Psychology, 36,* 1202–1212.

Schuman, H., & Kalton, G. (1985). Survey methods. In G. Lindzey & E. Aronson (Eds.), Handbook of social psychology (3rd ed., Vol. 1, pp. 635–697). New York: McGraw-Hill.

Schwartz, J. (2003, June 7). Shuttle tests seem to back foam theory in accident. *New York Times,* p. A1.

Schwartz, J., & Wald, M. L. (2003, June 7). NASA's failings go beyond foam hitting shuttle, panel says. *New York Times,* p. A1.

Schwartz, S. H. (1992). Universals in the content and structure of values: Theoretical advances and empirical tests in 20 countries. In M. P. Zanna (Ed.), *Advances in experimental social psychology* (Vol. 25, pp. 1–65). San Diego, CA: Academic Press.

Schwartz, S. H., & Gottlieb, A. (1976). Bystander reactions to a violent theft: Crime in Jerusalem. *Journal of Personality and Social Psychology, 34,* 1188–1199.

Schwarz, N., & Bless, H. (1992). Constructing reality and its alternative: An inclusion/exclusion model of assimilation and contrast effects in social judgment. In L. L. Martin & A. Tesser (Eds.), *The construction of social judgment* (pp. 217–245). Hillsdale, NJ: Erlbaum.

Schwarz, N., Bless, H., Strack, F., Klumpp, G., Rittenauer-Schatka, H., & Simmons, A. (1991). Ease of retrieval as information: Another look at the availability heuristic. *Journal of Personality and Social Psychology, 61,* 195–202.

Schwarz, N., & Clore, G. L. (1988). How do I feel about it? Informative functions of affective states. In K. Fiedler & J. Forgas (Eds.), *Affect, cognition, and social behavior* (pp. 44–62). Toronto, Ontario, Canada: Hogrefe.

Schwarz, N., Groves, R. M., & Schuman, H. (1998). Survey methods. In D. T. Gilbert, S. T. Fiske, & G. Lindzey (Eds.), *The handbook of social psychology* (4th ed., Vol. 1, pp. 143–179). New York: McGraw-Hill.

Schwarz, N. & Vaughn, L. A. (2002). The availability heuristic revisited: Ease of recall and content of recall as distinct sources of information. In T. Gilovich, D. W. Griffin, & D. Kahneman (Eds). *Heuristics and biases: The psychology of intuitive judgment* (pp. 103–119). New York: Cambridge University Press.

Schwarzer, R., & Leppin, A. (1991). Social support and health: A theoretical and empirical overview. *Journal of Social and Personal Relationships, 8,* 99–127.

Scoboria, A., Mazzoni, G., Kirsch, I., & Milling, L. S. (2002). Immediate and persisting effects of misleading questions and hypnosis on memory reports. *Journal of Experimental Psychology: Applied, 8,* 26–32.

Scott, J. E., & Cuvelier, S. J. (1993). Violence and sexual violence in pornography: Is it increasing? *Archives of Sexual Behavior, 22,* 357–371.

Scott, J. P. (1958). *Aggression.* Chicago: University of Chicago Press.

Sears, D. O. (1981). Life stage effects on attitude change, especially among the elderly. In S. B. Kiesler, J. N. Morgan, & V. K. Oppenheimer (Eds.), *Aging: Social change* (pp. 183–204). New York: Academic Press.

Secord, P. F., & Backman, C. W. (1964). *Social psychology.* New York: McGraw-Hill.

Sedikides, C., & Anderson, C. A. (1994). Causal perceptions of inter-trait relations: The glue that holds person types together. *Personality and Social Psychology Bulletin, 21,* 294–302.

Sedikides, C., Gaertner, L., & Yoshiyasu, T. (2003). Pancultural self-enhancement. *Journal of Personality and Social Psychology, 84,* 60–79.

Sedikides, C., & Strube, M. J. (1997). Self-evaluation: To thine own self be good, to thine own self be sure, to thine own self be true, and to thine own self be better. In M. P. Zanna (Ed.), *Advances in experimental social psychology* (Vol. 29, pp. 209–269). San Diego, CA: Academic Press.

Seligman, M. E. P. (1975). *Helplessness: On depression, development, and death.* San Francisco: Freeman.

Seligman, M. E. P. (2002). Positive psychology, positive prevention, and positive therapy. In C. R. Snyder & S. J. Lopez (Eds.), *Handbook of positive psychology* (pp. 3–9). New York: Oxford University Press.

Selye, H. (1956). *The stress of life.* New York: McGraw-Hill.

Selye, H. (1976). *Stress in health and disease.* Woburn, MA: Butterworth.

Senchak, M., & Leonard, K. E. (1992). Attachment styles and marital adjustment among newlywed couples. *Journal of Social and Personal Relationships, 9,* 51–64.

Senko, C., & Harackiewicz, J.M. (2002). Peformance goals: The moderating roles of context and achievement orientation. *Journal of Experimental Social Psychology, 38,* 603–610.

Seppa, N. (1997). Children's TV remains steeped in violence. *APA Monitor, 28,* 36.

Sergios, P. A., & Cody, J. (1985). Physical attractiveness and social assertiveness skills in male homosexual dating behavior and partner selection. *Journal of Social Psychology, 125,* 505–514.

Seta, C. E., & Seta, J. J. (1995). When audience presence is enjoyable: The influences of audience awareness of prior success on performance and task interest. *Basic and Applied Social Psychology, 16,* 95–108.

Seta, J. J., Seta, C. E., & Wang, M. A. (1990). Feelings of negativity and stress: An averaging-summation analysis of impressions of negative life experiences. *Personality and Social Psychology Bulletin, 17,* 376–384.

Shackelford, T. K., & Buss, D. M. (1996). Betrayal in mateships, friendships, and coalitions. *Personality and Social Psychology Bulletin, 22,* 1151–1164.

Shapiro, P. N., & Penrod, S. D. (1986). Meta-analysis of facial identification studies. *Psychological Bulletin, 100,* 139–156.

Sharan, S. (1980). Cooperative learning in small groups. *Review of Educational Research, 50,* 241–271.

Sharp, F. C. (1928). *Ethics.* New York: Century.

Sharpe, D., Adair, J. G., & Roese, N. J. (1992). Twenty years of deception research: A decline in subjects' trust? *Personality and Social Psychology Bulletin, 18,* 585–590.

Shaver, P. R., Collins, N., & Clark, C. L. (1996). Attachment styles and internal working models of self and relationship partners. In G. J. O. Fletcher & J. Fitness (Eds.), *Knowledge structures in close relationships: A social psychological approach* (pp. 25–62). Mahwah, NJ: Erlbaum.

Shaver, P. R., Hazan, C., & Bradshaw, D. (1988). Love as attachment: The integration of three behavioral systems. In R. J. Sternberg & M. L. Barnes (Eds.), *The psychology of love* (pp. 68–99). New Haven, CT: Yale University Press.

Shaver, P. R., Wu, S., & Schwartz, J. C. (1992). Cross-cultural similarities and differences in emotion and its representation. In M. S. Clark (Ed.), *Review of personality and social psychology: Vol. 13. Emotion* (pp. 175–212). Newbury Park, CA: Sage.

Shavitt, S. (1989). Operationalizing functional theories of attitude. In A. R. Pratkanis, S. J. Breckler, & A. G. Greenwald (Eds.), *Attitude structure and function* (pp. 311–337). Hillsdale, NJ: Erlbaum.

Shavitt, S. (1990). The role of attitude objects in attitude function. *Journal of Experimental Social Psychology, 26,* 124–148.

Shavitt, S., Sanbonmatsu, D. M., Smittipatana, S., & Posavac, S. S. (1999). Broadening the conditions for illusory correlation formation: Implications for judging minority groups. *Basic and Applied Social Psychology, 21,* 263–279.

Shaw, J. I., & Skolnick, P. (1995). Effects of prohibitive and informative judicial instructions on jury decision making. *Social Behavior and Personality, 23,* 319–325.

Shaw, J. I., & Skolnick, P. (1999). Weapon focus and gender differences in eyewitness accuracy: Arousal versus salience. *Journal of Applied Social Psychology, 29,* 2328–2341.

Sheeran, P., & Taylor, S. (1999). Predicting intentions to use condoms: A meta-analysis and comparison of the theories of reasoned action and planned behavior. *Journal of Applied Social Psychology, 29,* 1624–1675.

Sheldon, K. M. (1999). Learning the lessons of tit-for-tat: Even competitors can get the message. *Journal of Personality and Social Psychology, 77,* 1245–1253.

Shepperd, J. A., & Taylor, K. M. (1999). Social loafing and expectancy-value theory. *Personality and Social Psychology Bulletin, 25,* 1147–1158.

Sherif, M. (1936). *The psychology of social norms.* New York: Harper.

Sherif, M. (1966). *In common predicament: Social psychology of intergroup conflict and cooperation.* Boston: Houghton Mifflin.

Sherif, M., Harvey, O. J., White, J., Hood, W., & Sherif, C. W. (1961). *Intergroup conflict and cooperation: The robber's cave experiment.* Norman: Institute of Intergroup Relations, University of Oklahoma.

Sherman, D. K., & Kim, H. S. (2002). Affective perseverance: The resistance of affect to cognitive invalidation. *Personality and Social Psychology Bulletin, 28,* 224–237.

Sherrod, D. R. (1974). Crowding, perceived control, and behavioral aftereffects. *Journal of Applied Social Psychology, 4,* 171–186.

Sherrod, D. R., & Cohen, S. (1979). Density, personal control, and design. In A. Baum & J. R. Aiello (Eds.), *Residential crowding and design* (pp. 217–227). New York: Plenum.

Shotland, R. L., & Straw, M. K. (1976). Bystander response to an assault: When a man attacks a woman. *Journal of Personality and Social Psychology, 34,* 990–999.

Showers, C., & Zeigler-Hill, V. (2003). Organization of self-knowledge: Features, functions, and flexibility. In M. R. Leary & J. P. Tangney (Eds.), *Handbook of self and identity* (pp. 47–67). New York: Guilford Press.

Shupe, L. M. (1954). Alcohol and crimes: A study of the urine alcohol concentration found in 882 persons arrested during or immediately after the commission of a felony. *Journal of Criminal Law and Criminology, 33,* 661–665.

Sibley, C. G., & Lui, J. H. (2003). Differentiating active and passive littering: A two-stage process model of littering behavior in public spaces. *Environment and Behavior, 35,* 415–433.

Siero, F. W., Bakker, A. B., Dekker, G. B., & Van Den Burg, M. T. C. (1996). Changing organizational energy consumption behavior through comparative feedback. *Journal of Environmental Psychology, 16,* 235–246.

Sigall, H., & Page, R. (1971). Current stereotypes: A little fading, a little faking. *Journal of Personality and Social Psychology, 18,* 247–255.

Signorielli, N., Gerbner, G., & Morgan, M. (1995). Violence on television: The Cultural Indicators Project. *Journal of Broadcasting and Electronic Media, 39,* 278–283.

Silver, L. B., Dublin, C. C., & Lourie, R. S. (1969). Does violence breed violence? Contributions from a study of the child abuse syndrome. *American Journal of Psychiatry, 126,* 404–407.

Silver, R., Holman, E., A., McIntosh, D. N., Poulin, M., & Gil-Rivas, V. (2002). Nationwide longitudinal study of psychological responses to September 11. *Journal of the American Medical Association, 288,* 1235–1244.

Silvera, D. H. (2000). The effects of cognitive load on strategic self-handicapping. *British Journal of Social Psychology, 39,* 65–72.

Silverstein, B., Perdue, L., Peterson, B., & Kelly, E. (1986). The role of the mass media in promoting a thin standard of bodily attractiveness for women. *Sex Roles, 14,* 519–532.

Silverstein, B., Peterson, B., & Perdue, L. (1986). Some correlates of the thin standard of bodily attractiveness for women. *International Journal of Eating Disorders, 5,* 895–906.

Silvia, P. J., & Abele, A. E. (2002). Can positive affect induce self-focused attention? Methodological and measurement issues. *Cognition and Emotion, 16,* 845–853.

Sime, J. D. (1983). Affiliative behavior during escape to building exits. *Journal of Environmental Psychology, 3,* 21–41.

Simms, L. J. (2002). The application of attachment theory to individual behavior and functioning in close relationships: Theory, research, and practical applications. In J. H. Harvey & A. Wenzel (Eds.), *A clinician's guide to maintaining and enhancing close relationships* (pp. 63–80). Mahwah, NJ: Erlbaum.

Simon, H. A. (1990). A mechanism for social selection and successful altruism. *Science, 250,* 1665–1668.

Simonton, D. K. (1984). *Genius, creativity, and leadership: Historiometric inquiries.* Cambridge, MA: Harvard University Press.

Simonton, D. K. (1985). Intelligence and personal influence in groups: Four nonlinear models. *Psychological Review, 92,* 532–547.

Simonton, D. K. (1987). *Why presidents succeed: A political psychology of leadership.* New Haven, CT: Yale University Press.

Simonton, D. K. (1998). Historiometric methods in social psychology. *European Review of Social Psychology, 9,* 267–293.

Simonton, D. K. (2001). Predicting presidential performance in the United States: Equation replication on recent survey results. *Journal of Social Psychology, 141,* 293–307.

Simpson, J. A. (1987). The dissolution of romantic relationships: Factors involved in relationship stability and emotional distress. *Journal of Personality and Social Psychology, 53,* 683–692.

Simpson, J. A., & Gangestad, S. W. (1992). Sociosexuality and romantic partner choice. *Journal of Personality, 60,* 31–51.

Simpson, J. A., & Rholes, W. S. (1994). Stress and secure base relationships in adulthood. In K. Bartholomew & D. Perlman (Eds.), *Advances in personal relationships: Vol. 5. Attachment processes in adulthood* (pp. 181–204). Bristol, PA: Kingsley.

Simpson, J. A., Rholes, W. S., & Nelligan, J. S. (1992). Support seeking and support giving within couples in an anxiety-provoking situation: The role of attachment styles. *Journal of Personality and Social Psychology, 62,* 434–446.

Sinclair, R. C., Hoffman, C., Mark, M. M., Martin, L. L., & Pickering, T. L. (1994). Construct accessibility and the misattribution of arousal: Schachter and Singer revisited. *Psychological Science, 5,* 15–19.

Singelis, T. M. (1994). The measurement of independent and interdependent self-construals. *Personality and Social Psychology Bulletin, 20,* 580–591.

Singer, J. E., Baum, C. S., Baum, A., & Thew, B. D. (1982). Mass psychogenic illness: The case for social comparison. In M. J. Colligan, J. W. Pennebaker, & L. R. Murphy (Eds.), *Mass psychogenic illness: A social psychological analysis* (pp. 155–169). Hillsdale, NJ: Erlbaum.

Singer, M. (1990, January 29). Talk of the town. *New Yorker,* pp. 25–26.

Singer, M. (2002, May 20). A year of trouble. *New Yorker,* pp. 42–46.

Sirois, F. (1982). Perspectives on epidemic hysteria. In M. J. Colligan, J. W. Pennebaker, & L. R. Murphy (Eds.), *Mass psychogenic illness: A social psychological analysis* (pp. 217–236). Hillsdale, NJ: Erlbaum.

Skinner, E. A. (1995). *Perceived control, motivation, and coping.* Thousand Oaks, CA: Sage.

Skinner, E. A. (1996). A guide to constructs of control. *Journal of Personality and Social Psychology, 71,* 549–570.

Slavin, R. E. (1996). Cooperative learning in middle and secondary schools. (Special section: Young adolescents at risk.) *Clearing House, 69,* 200–205.

Slavin, R. E., & Cooper, R. (1999). Improving intergroup relations: Lessons learned from cooperative learning programs. *Journal of Social Issues, 55,* 647–663.

Sloan, J. H., Kellerman, A. L., Reay, D. T., Ferris, J. A., Koepsell, T., Rivara, F. P., et al. (1988). Handgun regulations, crime, assaults, and homicide: A tale of two cities. *New England Journal of Medicine, 319,* 1256–1261.

Sloman, S. A. (1996). The empirical case for two systems of reasoning. *Psychological Bulletin, 119,* 3–22.

Slovic, P., Fischhoff, B., & Lichtenstein, S. (1976). Cognitive processes and societal risk taking. In J. S. Carroll & J. Payne (Eds.), *Cognition and social behavior* (pp. 165–184). Hillsdale, NJ: Erlbaum.

Slovic, P., & Lichtenstein, S. (1971). Comparison of Bayesian and regression approaches to the study of information processing in judgment. *Organizational Behavior and Human Performance, 6,* 649–744.

Slusher, M. P., & Anderson, C. A. (1989). Belief perseverance and self-defeating behavior. In R. Curtis (Ed.), *Self-defeating behaviors:*

Experimental research, clinical impressions, and practical implications (pp. 11–40). New York: Plenum.

Smith, A. E., Jussim, L., & Eccles, J. S. (1999). Do self-fulfilling prophecies accumulate, dissipate, or remain stable over time? *Journal of Personality and Social Psychology, 77,* 548–565.

Smith, C. M., Tindale, R. S., & Dugoni, B. L. (1996). Minority and majority influence in freely interacting groups: Qualitative versus quantitative differences. *British Journal of Social Psychology, 35,* 137–149.

Smith, D. D. (1976). The social content of pornography. *Journal of Communication, 26,* 16–24.

Smith, E. R., & De Coster, J. (1999). Associative and rule-based processing: A connectionist interpretation of dual-process models. In S. Chaiken & Y. Trope (Eds.), *Dual-process theories in social psychology* (pp. 323–336). New York: Guilford Press.

Smith, M. B., Bruner, J., & White, R. W. (1956). *Opinions and personality.* New York: Wiley.

Smith, P. B., & Bond, M. H. (1999). *Social psychology across cultures* (2nd ed.). Needham Heights, MA: Allyn & Bacon.

Smith, R. E., Wheeler, G., & Diener, E. (1975). Faith without works: Jesus people, resistance to temptation, and altruism. *Journal of Applied Psychology, 5,* 320–330.

Smith, S. S., & Richardson, D. (1983). Amelioration of deception and harm in psychological research: The important role of debriefing. *Journal of Personality and Social Psychology, 44,* 1075–1082.

Smith, V. L. (1991). Prototypes in the courtroom: Lay representation of legal concepts. *Journal of Personality and Social Psychology, 61,* 857–872.

Smith, V. L., & Ellsworth, P. C. (1987). The social psychology of eyewitness accuracy: Misleading questions and communicator expertise. *Journal of Applied Psychology, 72,* 294–300.

Smith, V. L., Kassin, S. M., & Ellsworth, P. C. (1989). Eyewitness accuracy and confidence: Within- versus between-subjects correlations. *Journal of Applied Psychology, 74,* 356–359.

Smyth, J. M. (1998). Written emotional expression: Effect sizes, outcome types, and moderating variables. *Journal of Consulting and Clinical Psychology, 66,* 174–184.

Snyder, C. R., & Higgins, R. L. (1988). Excuses: Their effective role in the negotiation of reality. *Psychological Bulletin, 104,* 23–35.

Snyder, C. R., Irving, L. M., & Anderson, J. R. (1991). Hope and health. In C. R. Snyder & D. R. Forsyth (Eds.), *Handbook of clinical and social psychology* (pp. 285–305). New York: Pergamon.

Snyder, C. R., & Lopez, S. J. (Eds.). (2002). *Handbook of positive psychology.* New York: Oxford University Press.

Snyder, M. (1984). When belief creates reality. In L. Berkowitz (Ed.), *Advances in experimental social psychology* (Vol. 18, pp. 247–305). Orlando, FL: Academic Press.

Snyder, M. (1993). Basic research and practical problems: The promise of a "functional" personality and social psychology. *Personality and Social Psychology Bulletin, 19,* 251–264.

Snyder, M., & De Bono, K. G. (1989). Understanding the functions of attitudes: Lessons for personality and social behavior. In A. R. Pratkanis, S. J. Breckler, & A. G. Greenwald (Eds.), *Attitude structure and function* (pp. 339–359). Hillsdale, NJ: Erlbaum.

Snyder, M., & Ickes, W. J. (1985). Personality and social behavior. In G. Lindzey & E. Aronson (Eds.), *Handbook of social psychology* (3rd ed., pp. 883–947). New York: McGraw-Hill.

Snyder, M., Tanke, E. D., & Berscheid, E. (1977). Social perception and interpersonal behavior: On the self-fulfilling nature of social stereotypes. *Journal of Personality and Social Psychology, 35,* 656–666.

Soames, R. F. (1988). Effective and ineffective use of fear in health promotion campaigns. *American Journal of Public Health, 78,* 163–167.

Solomon, L. Z., Solomon, H., & Stone, R. (1978). Helping as a function of number of bystanders and ambiguity of emergency. *Personality and Social Psychology Bulletin, 4,* 318–321.

Somerfield, M. R., & McCrae, R. R. (2000). Stress and coping research. *American Psychologist, 55,* 620–625.

Sontag, S. (1978). *Illness as metaphor.* New York: Farrar, Straus & Giroux.

Sontag, S. (1988). *AIDS and its metaphors.* New York: Farrar, Straus & Giroux.

Sorensen, J., Wrinkle, R. Brewer, V., & Marquart, J. (1999). Capital punishment and deterrence: Examining the effect of executions on murder in Texas. *Crime and Delinquency, 45,* 481–493.

Sorenson, T. C. (1966). *Kennedy.* New York: Bantam Books.

Sorkin, A. R. (2003, June 5). Despite shuffle, Stewart still in charge. *The New York Times,* p. C1; C5.

Sorkin, R. D., Hays, C. J., & West, R. (2001). Signal-detection analysis of group decision making. *Psychological Review, 108,* 183–203.

Spalding, L. R., & Hardin, C. D. (1999). Unconscious unease and self-handicapping: Behavioral consequences of individual differences in implicit and explicit self-esteem. *Psychological Science, 10,* 535–539.

Spain, J. S., Eaton, L. G., & Funder, D. C. (2000). Perspectives on personality: The relative accuracy of self versus others for the prediction of emotion and behavior. *Journal of Personality, 68,* 837–867.

Spanier, G. B. (1992). Divorce: A comment about the future. In T. L. Orbuch (Ed.), *Close relationship loss: Theoretical approaches* (pp. 207–212). New York: Springer-Verlag.

Speed, A., & Gangestad, S. W. (1997). Romantic popularity and mate preferences: A peer-nomination study. *Personality and Social Psychology Bulletin, 23,* 928–935.

Spencer, S, J., Fein, S., Zanna, M. P., & Olson, J. M. (Eds.). (2003). *Motivated social perception: The Ontario Symposium* (Vol. 9). Mahwah, NJ: Erlbaum.

Spencer, S. J., Steele, C. M., & Quinn, D. M. (1999). Stereotype threat and women's math performance. *Journal of Experimental Social Psychology, 35,* 4–28.

Spiegel, D., Bloom, J. R., Kraemer, H. C., & Gottheil, E. (1989). Psychological support for cancer patients. *Lancet, 2,* 1447.

Spiegel, H., & Spiegel, D. (1987). *Trance and treatment: Clinical uses of hypnosis.* Washington, DC: American Psychiatric Press. (Original work published 1978)

Sporer, S. L., Koehnken, G., & Malpass, R. S. (1996). Introduction: 200 years of mistaken identification. In S. L. Sporer, R. S. Malpass, & G. Koehnken (Eds.), *Psychological issues in eyewitness identification* (pp. 1–6). Mahwah, NJ: Erlbaum.

Sprecher, S., Aron, A., Hatfield, E., Cortese, A., Potapova, E., & Levitskaya, A. (1994). Love: American style, Russian style, and Japanese style. *Personal Relationships, 1,* 349–369.

Sprecher, S., & Schwartz, P. (1994). Equity and balance in the exchange of contributions in close relationships. In M. J. Lerner & G. Mikula (Eds.), *Entitlement and the affectional bond: Justice in close relationships* (pp. 11–42). New York: Plenum.

Sprecher, S., Sullivan, Q., & Hatfield, E. (1994). Mate selection preference: Gender differences examined in a national sample. *Journal of Personality and Social Psychology, 66,* 1074–1080.

Sprink, K. S., & Carron, A. V. (1994). Group cohesion effects in exercise classes. *Small Group Research, 25,* 26–42.

Squire, C. (2000). *Culture in psychology.* Bristol, PA: Taylor & Francis.

Stangor, C., & McMillan, D. (1992). Memory for expectancy-congruent and expectancy-incongruent information: A review of the social and social developmental literatures. *Psychological Bulletin, 111,* 42–61.

Stapel, D. A., Koomen, W. (2000). How far do we go beyond the information given? The impact of knowledge activation on interpretation and inference. *Journal of Personality and Social Psychology, 78,* 19–37.

Stasser, G. (2000). Information distribution, participation, and group decision: Explorations with the DISCUSS and SPEAK models. In D. R. Ilgen & C. L. Hulin (Eds.), *Computational modeling of behavior in organizations: The third scientific discipline* (pp. 135–161). Washington, DC: American Psychological Association.

Stasser, G., Stewart, D. D., & Wittenbaum, G. M. (1995). Expert roles and information exchange during discussion: The importance of knowing who knows what. *Journal of Experimental and Social Psychology, 31,* 244–265.

Stasser, G., & Titus, W. (1985). Pooling of unshared information in group decision making: Biased information sampling during discussion. *Journal of Personality and Social Psychology, 48,* 1467–1478.

Staub, E. (1974). Helping a distressed person: Social, personality, and stimulus determinants. In L. Berkowitz (Ed.), *Advances in experimental social psychology* (Vol. 7, pp. 293–341). New York: Academic Press.

Staub, E. (1989). *The roots of evil: The origins of genocide and other group violence.* Cambridge, England: Cambridge University Press.

Steblay, N. M. (1987). Helping behavior in rural and urban environments: A meta-analysis. *Psychological Bulletin, 102,* 346–356.

Steblay, N. M. (1997). Social influence in eyewitness recall: A meta-analytic review of lineup instruction effects. *Law and Human Behavior, 21,* 283–297.

Steblay, N. M., Besirevic, J., Fulero, S. M., & Jimenez-Lorente, B. (1999). The effects of pretrial publicity on juror verdicts: A meta-analytic review. *Law and Human Behavior, 23,* 219–235.

Steblay, N. M., Dysart, J., Fulero, S. M., & Lindsay, R.C.L. (2001). Eyewitness accuracy rates in sequential and simultaneous lineup presentations: A meta-analytic comparison. *Law and Human Behavior, 25,* 459–473.

Steele, C. M. (1988). The psychology of self-affirmation: Sustaining the integrity of the self. In L. Berkowitz (Ed.), *Advances in experimental social psychology* (Vol. 21, pp. 261–302). New York: Academic Press.

Steele, C. M. (1992, April). Race and the schooling of black Americans. *Atlantic,* pp. 68–78.

Steele, C. M. (1997). A threat in the air: How stereotypes shape intellectual ability and performance. *American Psychologist, 52,* 613–629.

Steele, C. M., & Aronson, J. M. (1995a). Stereotype threat and the intellectual test performance of African-Americans. *Journal of Personality and Social Psychology, 69,* 797–811.

Steele, C. M., & Aronson, J. M. (1995b). Stereotype vulnerability and intellectual performance. In E. Aronson, (Ed,), *Readings about the social animal* (7th ed.). New York: Freeman.

Steele, C. M., Hoppe, H., & Gonzales, J. (1986). *Dissonance and the lab coat: Self-affirmation and the free-choice paradigm.* Unpublished manuscript, University of Washington.

Steele, C. M., Spencer, S. J., & Aronson, J. M. (2002). Contending with group image: The psychology of stereotype and social identity threat. In M. P. Zanna (Ed.), *Advances in experimental social psychology* (Vol. 34, pp. 379–440). San Diego, CA: Academic Press.

Steele, C. M., Spencer, S. J., & Josephs, R. A. (1992). *Seeking self-relevant information: The effects of self-esteem and stability of the information.* Unpublished manuscript, University of Michigan.

Steiner, I. D. (1972). *Group process and productivity.* New York: Academic Press.

Stephan, W. G. (1978). School desegregation: An evaluation of predictions made in *Brown* v. *Board of Education. Psychological Bulletin, 85,* 217–238.

Stephan, W. G. (1985). Intergroup relations. In G. Lindzey & E. Aronson (Eds.), *Handbook of social psychology* (3rd ed., Vol. 2, pp. 599–658). New York: McGraw-Hill.

Stern, L. B., & Dunning, D. (1994). Distinguishing accurate from inaccurate eyewitness identifications: A reality monitoring approach. In D. F. Ross, J. D. Read, & M. P. Toglia (Eds.), *Adult eyewitness testimony: Current trends and developments* (pp. 273–299). New York: Cambridge University Press.

Stern, P. C., & Aronson, E. (1984). *Energy use: The human dimension.* New York: Freeman.

Sternberg, R. J. (1986). A triangular theory of love. *Psychological Review, 93,* 119–135.

Sternberg, R. J. (1988). *The triangle of love.* New York: Basic Books.

Sternberg, R. J. (1997). Construct validation of a triangular love scale. *European Journal of Social Psychology, 27,* 313–335.

Sternberg, R. J., & Beall, A. E. (1991). How can we know what love is? An epistemological analysis. In G. J. O. Fletcher & F. D. Fincham (Eds.), *Cognition in close relationships* (pp. 257–280). Hillsdale, NJ: Erlbaum.

Sternberg, R. J., & Vroom, V. (2002). The person versus the situation in leadership. *Leadership Quarterly, 13,* 301–323.

Stewart, D. D., & Stasser, G. (1995). Expert role assignment and information sampling during collective recall and decision making. *Journal of Personality and Social Psychology, 69,* 619–628.

Stewart, J. B. (2002). *Heart of a soldier.* New York: Simon & Schuster.

Stice, E., & Shaw, H. E. (1994). Adverse effects of the media-portrayed thin ideal on women and linkages to bulimic symptomology. *Journal of Social and Clinical Psychology, 13,* 288–308.

Stipek, D., & Gralinski, J. H. (1991). Gender differences in children's achievement-related beliefs and emotional responses to success and failure in mathematics. *Journal of Educational Psychology, 83,* 361–371.

Stoff, D. M., & Cairns, R. B. (Eds.). (1997). *Aggression and violence: Genetic, neurobiological, and biosocial perspectives.* Mahwah, NJ: Erlbaum.

Stone, A. A., Bovbjerg, D. H., Neale, J. M., Napoli, A., Valdimarsdottir, H., Cox, D., et al. (1993). Development of common cold symptoms following experimental rhinovirus infection is related to prior stressful life events. *Behavioral Medicine, 8,* 115–120.

Stone, J., Aronson, E., Crain, A. L., Winslow, M. P., & Fried, C. (1994). Inducing hypocrisy as a means of encouraging young adults to use condoms. *Personality and Social Psychology Bulletin, 20,* 116–128.

Stone, J., Lynch, C. I., Sjomeling, M., & Darley, J. M. (1999). Stereotype threat effects on black and white athletic performance. *Journal of Personality and Social Psychology, 77,* 1213–1227.

Stone, J., Perry, Z., & Darley, J. (1997). "White men can't jump": Evidence for perceptual confirmation of racial stereotypes following a basketball game. *Basic and Applied Social Psychology, 19,* 291–306.

Stormo, K. J., Lang, A. R., & Stritzke, W. G. K. (1997). Attributions about acquaintance rape: The role of alcohol and individual differences. *Journal of Applied Social Psychology, 27,* 279–305.

Storms, M. D. (1973). Videotape and the attribution process: Reversing actors' and observers' points of view. *Journal of Personality and Social Psychology, 27,* 165–175.

Stouffer, S. A., Suchman, E. A., De Vinney, L. C., Star, S. A., & Williams, R. M., Jr. (1949). *The American soldier: Adjustment during army life* (Vol. 1). Princeton, NJ: Princeton University Press.

Strack, F., & Hannover, B. (1996). Awareness of influence as a precondition for implementing correctional goals. In P. M. Gollwitzer & J. A. Bargh (Eds.), *The psychology of action: Linking cognition and motivation to behavior* (pp. 579–596). New York: Guilford Press.

Strahan, E. J., Spencer, S. J., & Zanna, M. P. (2002). Subliminal priming and persuasion: Striking while the iron is hot. *Journal of Experimental Social Psychology, 38,* 556–568.

Strauss, M. A., & Gelles, R. J. (1980). *Behind closed doors: Violence in the American family.* Garden City, NY: Anchor/Doubleday.

Stroebe, W., & Stroebe, M. (1996). The social psychology of social support. In E. T. Higgins & A. W. Kruglanski (Eds.), *Social psychology: Handbook of basic principles* (pp. 597–621). New York: Guilford Press.

Strossen, N. (1997). Why censoring pornography would not reduce discrimination or violence against women. In M. R. Walsh (Ed.), *Women, men, and gender: Ongoing debates* (pp. 170–179). New Haven, CT: Yale University Press.

Studer, J. (1996). Understanding and preventing aggressive responses in youth. *Elementary School Guidance and Counseling, 30,* 194–203.

Stukas, A. A., Snyder, M., & Clary, E. G. (1999). The effects of "mandatory volunteerism" on intentions to volunteer. *Psychological Science, 10,* 59–64.

Stumpf, H., & Stanley, J. C. (1998). Stability and change in gender-related differences on the college board advanced placement and achievement tests. *Current Directions in Psychological Science, 7,* 192–196.

Stuster, J. W., & Blowers, M. A. (1995). *Experimental evaluation of sobriety checkpoint programs.* Washington, DC: National Highway Safety Administration.

Suls, J. M., & Fletcher, B. (1983). Social comparison in the social and physical sciences: An archival study. *Journal of Personality and Social Psychology, 44,* 575–580.

Suls, J. M., Martin, R., & Wheeler, L. (2000). Three kinds of opinion comparison: The triadic model. *Personality and Social Psychology Review, 4,* 219–237.

Suls, J. M., & Miller, R. L. (Eds.). (1977). *Social comparison processes: Theoretical and empirical perspectives.* Washington, DC: Hemisphere/Halstead.

Suls, J. M., & Wheeler, L. (Eds.). (2000). *Handbook of social comparison: Theory and research.* New York: Kluwer/Plenum.

Summers, G., & Feldman, N. S. (1984). Blaming the victim versus blaming the perpetrator: An attributional analysis of spouse abuse. *Journal of Social and Clinical Psychology, 2,* 339–347.

Sundstrom, E., Bell, P. A., Busby, P. L., & Asmus, C. (1996). Environmental psychology. *Annual Review of Psychology, 47,* 485–512.

Swann, W. B., Jr. (1990). To be adored or to be known? The interplay of self-enhancement and self-verification. In E. T. Higgins & R. M. Sorrentino (Eds.), *Handbook of motivation and cognition* (Vol. 2, pp. 404–448). New York: Guilford Press.

Swann, W. B., Jr. (1992). Seeking "truth," finding despair: Some unhappy consequences of a negative self-concept. *Psychological Science, 1,* 15–17.

Swann, W. B., Jr. (1996). *Self-traps: The elusive quest for higher self-esteem.* New York: Freeman.

Swann, W. B., Jr., & Pelham, B. W. (1988). *The social construction of identity: Self-verification through friend and intimate selection.* Unpublished manuscript, University of Texas, Austin.

Swann, W. B., Jr., Stein-Seroussi, A., & McNulty, S. E. (1992). Outcasts in a white-lie society: The enigmatic worlds of people with negative self-concepts. *Journal of Personality and Social Psychology, 62,* 618–624.

Swap, W. C. (1977). Interpersonal attraction and repeated exposure to rewarders and punishers. *Personality and Social Psychology Bulletin, 3,* 248–251.

Sweeney, P. D., Anderson, K., & Bailey, S. (1986). Attributional style in depression: A meta-analytic review. *Journal of Personality and Social Psychology, 50,* 974–991.

Swim, J. K. (1994). Perceived versus meta-analytic effect sizes: An assessment of the accuracy of gender stereotypes. *Journal of Personality and Social Psychology, 66,* 21–36.

Swim, J. K., Borgida, E., Maruyama, G., & Myers, D. G. (1989). Joan McKay vs. John McKay: Do gender stereotypes bias evaluations? *Psychological Bulletin, 105,* 409–429.

Swim, J. K., & Sanna, L. (1996). He's skilled, she's lucky: A meta-analysis of observers' attributions for women's and men's successes and failures. *Personality and Social Psychology Bulletin, 22,* 507–519.

Symons, C. S., & Johnson, B. T. (1997). The self-reference effect in memory: A meta-analysis. *Psychological Bulletin, 121,* 371–394.

Symons, D. (1979). *The evolution of human sexuality.* New York: Oxford University Press.

Tajfel, H. (1982a). *Social identity and intergroup relations.* Cambridge, England: Cambridge University Press.

Tajfel, H. (1982b). Social psychology of intergroup relations. *Annual Review of Psychology, 33,* 1–39.

Tajfel, H., & Billig, M. (1974). Familiarity and categorization in intergroup behavior. *Journal of Experimental Social Psychology, 10,* 159–170.

Tajfel, H., & Turner, J. C. (1979). An integrative theory of social contact. In W. Austin & S. Worchel (Eds.), *The social psychology of intergroup relations* (pp. 162–173). Monterey, CA: Brooks/Cole.

Tamres, L. K., Janicki, D., & Helgeson, V. S. (2002). Sex differences in coping behavior: A meta-analytic review. *Personality and Social Psychology Review, 6,* 2–30.

Tan, D. T. Y., & Singh, R. (1995). Attitudes and attraction: A developmental study of the similarity-attraction and dissimilarity-repulsion hypotheses. *Personality and Social Psychology Bulletin, 21,* 975–986.

Tanford, S., & Penrod, S. D. (1984). Social influence model: A formal integration of research on majority and minority influence processes. *Psychological Bulletin, 95,* 189–225.

Tang, S., & Hall, V. C. (1995). The overjustification effect: A meta-analysis. *Applied Cognitive Psychology, 9,* 365–404.

Taylor, S. E. (1981). A categorization approach to stereotyping. In D. L. Hamilton (Ed.), *Cognitive processes in stereotyping and intergroup relations* (pp. 418–429). Hillsdale, NJ: Erlbaum.

Taylor, S. E. (1989). *Positive illusions: Creative self-deception and the healthy mind.* New York: Basic Books.

Taylor, S. E., & Armor, D. (1996). Positive illusions and coping with adversity. *Journal of Personality, 64,* 873–898.

Taylor, S. E., & Aspinwall, L. G. (1993). Coping with chronic illness. In L. Goldberger & S. Breznitz (Eds.), *Handbook of stress:*

Theoretical and clinical aspects (2nd ed., pp. 511–531). New York: Free Press.

Taylor, S. E., & Brown, J. D. (1988). Illusion and well-being: A social psychological perspective on mental health. *Psychological Bulletin, 103,* 193–210.

Taylor, S. E., & Brown, J. D. (1994). Positive illusions and well-being revisited: Separating fact from fiction. *Psychological Bulletin, 116,* 21–27.

Taylor, S. E., & Crocker, J. (1981). Schematic bases of social information processing. In E. T. Higgins, C. P. Herman, & M. P. Zanna (Eds.), *Social cognition: The Ontario Symposium* (Vol. 1, pp. 89–134). Hillsdale, NJ: Erlbaum.

Taylor, S. E., & Fiske, S. T. (1975). Point of view and perceptions of causality. *Journal of Personality and Social Psychology, 32,* 439–445.

Taylor, S. E., & Gollwitzer, P. (1995). Effects of mindset on positive illusions. *Journal of Personality and Social Psychology, 69,* 213–226.

Taylor, S. E., Klein, L. C., Lewis, B. P., Gruenewald, T. L., Gurung, R. A. R., & Updegraff, J. A. (2000). Biobehavioral responses to stress in females: Tend-and-befriend, not fight-or-flight. *Psychological Review, 107,* 411–429.

Taylor, S. E., Lichtman, R. R., & Wood, J. V. (1984). Attributions, beliefs about control, and adjustment to breast cancer. *Journal of Personality and Social Psychology, 46,* 489–502.

Taylor, S. E., Repetti, R. L., & Seeman, T. (1997). Health psychology: What is an unhealthy environment and how does it get under the skin? *Annual Review of Psychology, 48,* 411–447.

Taylor, S. P., & Leonard, K. E. (1983). Alcohol and human physical aggression. In R. G. Geen & E. Donnerstein (Eds.), *Aggression: Theoretical and empirical reviews* (pp. 77–101). New York: Academic Press.

Teger, A. L., & Pruitt, D. G. (1967). Components of group risk taking. *Journal of Experimental Social Psychology, 3,* 189–205.

Tesser, A. (1988). Toward a self-evaluation maintenance model of social behavior. In L. Berkowitz (Ed.), *Advances in experimental social psychology* (Vol. 21, pp. 181–227). Orlando, FL: Academic Press.

Tesser, A. (1991). Emotion in social comparison and reflection processes. In J. M. Suls & T. A. Wills (Eds.), *Social comparison: Contemporary theory and research* (pp. 117–148). Hillsdale, NJ: Erlbaum.

Tesser, A. (1993). The importance of heritability in psychological research: The case of attitudes. *Psychological Review, 100,* 129–142.

Tesser, A. (2003). Self-evaluation. In M. R. Leary & J. P. Tangney (Eds.), *Handbook of self and identity* (pp. 275–290). New York: Guilford Press.

Tesser, A., & Beach, S. R. H. (1998). Life events, relationship quality, and depression: An investigation of judgment discontinuity in vivo. *Journal of Personality and Social Psychology, 74,* 36–52.

Tesser, A., Campbell, J. D., & Mickler, S. (1983). The role of social pressure, attention to the stimulus, and self-doubt in conformity. *European Journal of Social Psychology, 13,* 217–233.

Tesser, A., & Paulus, D. (1983). The definition of self: Private and public self-evaluation management strategies. *Journal of Personality and Social Psychology, 44,* 672–682.

Tesser, A., & Smith, J. (1980). Some effects of friendship and task relevance on helping: You don't always help the one you like. *Journal of Experimental Social Psychology, 16,* 582–590.

Tetlock, P. E. (1981). The influence of self-presentational goals on attributional reports. *Social Psychology Quarterly, 44,* 300–311.

Tetlock, P. E. (1992). The impact of accountability on judgment and choice: Toward a social contingency model. In M. P. Zanna (Ed.), *Advances in experimental social psychology* (Vol. 25, pp. 331–376). San Diego, CA: Academic Press.

Tetlock, P. E. (2002). Theory-driven reasoning about plausible pasts and probable futures in world politics. In T. Gilovich, D. W. Griffin, & D. Kahneman (Eds.), *Heuristics and biases: The psychology of intuitive judgment* (pp. 749–762). New York: Cambridge University Press.

Tetlock, P. E., Peterson, R. S., McGuire, C., Chang, S., & Field, P. (1992). Assessing political group dynamics: A test of the groupthink model. *Journal of Personality and Social Psychology, 63,* 403–425.

Theus, K. T. (1994). Subliminal advertising and the psychology of processing unconscious stimuli: A review. *Psychology and Marketing, 11,* 271–290.

Teves, O. (2002, May 28). WHO warns Asia 25% of youth will die from smoking without curbed advertising. Associated Press.

Thernstrom, M. (2003, August 24). Untying the knot. *New York Times Magazine,* p. 38.

Thibaut, J. W., & Kelley, H. H. (1959). *The social psychology of groups.* New York: Wiley.

Thill, E. E., & Curry, F. (2000). Learning to play golf under different goal conditions: Their effects on irrelevant thoughts and on subsequent control strategies. *European Journal of Social Psychology, 30,* 101–122.

Thomas, J. (1997, January 30). Suspect's sketch in Oklahoma case called an error. *New York Times,* pp. 1–2.

Thomas, M. H. (1982). Physiological arousal, exposure to a relatively lengthy aggressive film, and aggressive behavior. *Journal of Research in Personality, 16,* 72–81.

Thomas, M. H., Horton, R., Lippincott, E., & Drabman, R. (1977). Desensitization to portrayals of real-life aggression as a function of exposure to television violence. *Journal of Personality and Social Psychology, 35,* 450–458.

Thomas, S. L., Skitka, L. J., Christen, S., & Jurgena, M. (2002). Social facilitation and impression formation. *Basic and Applied Social Psychology, 242,* 67–70.

Thomas, W. I. (1928). *The child in America.* New York: Knopf.

Thompson, J. (2000, June 18). "I was certain, but I was wrong." *New York Times,* p. D15.

Thompson, J. K., & Heinberg, L. J. (1999). The media's influence on body image disturbance and eating disorders: We've reviled them, now can we rehabilitate them? *Journal of Social Issues, 55,* 339–353.

Thompson, L. (1995). They saw a negotiation: Partisanship and involvement. *Journal of Personality and Social Psychology, 68,* 839–853.

Thompson, L. (1997). *The mind and heart of the negotiator.* Upper Saddle River, NJ: Prentice Hall.

Thompson, S. C. (1999). Illusions of control: How we overestimate our personal influence. *Current Directions in Psychological Science, 8,* 187–190.

Thompson, S. C. (2002). The role of personal control in adaptive functioning. In C. R. Snyder & S. J. Lopez (Eds.), *Handbook of positive psychology* (pp. 202–213). London: Oxford University Press.

Thompson, S. C., Nanni, C., & Levine, A. (1994). Primary versus secondary and central versus consequence-related control in HIV-positive men. *Journal of Personality and Social Psychology, 67,* 540–547.

Thornton, D., & Arrowood, A. J. (1966). Self-evaluation, self-enhancement, and the locus of social comparison. *Journal of Experimental Social Psychology, 1*(Suppl.), 40–48.

Timaeus, E. (1968). Untersuchungen zum sogenannten konformen Verhalten [Research into so-called conforming behavior]. *Zeitschrift für Experimentelle und Angewandte Psychologie, 15,* 176–194.

Tindale, R. S. (1993). Decision errors made by individuals and groups. In N. J. Castellan Jr. (Ed.), *Individual and group decision making* (pp. 109–124). Hillsdale, NJ: Erlbaum.

Tindale, R. S., Munier, C., Wasserman, M., & Smith, C. M. (2002). Group processes and the Holocaust. In L. S. Newman & R. Erber (Eds.), *Understanding genocide: The social psychology of the Holocaust* (pp. 143–161). New York: Oxford University Press.

Ting, J., & Piliavin, J. A. (2000). Altruism in comparative international perspective. In J. Phillips, B. Chapman, & D. Stevens (Eds.), *Between state and market: Essays on charities law and policy in Canada* (pp. 51–105). Montreal and Kingston, Ontario, Canada: McGill-Queens University Press.

Ting-Toomey, S., & Chung, L. (1996). Cross-cultural interpersonal communication: Theoretical trends and research directions. In W. B. Gudykunst, S. Ting-Toomey, & T. Nishida (Eds.), *Communication in personal relationships across cultures* (pp. 237–261). Thousand Oaks, CA: Sage.

Toch, H. (1980). *Violent men* (Rev. ed.). Cambridge, MA: Schenkman.

Todorov, A., & Bargh, J. A. (2002). Automatic sources of aggression. *Aggression and Violent Behavior, 7,* 53–68.

Toi, M., & Batson, C. D. (1982). More evidence that empathy is a source of altruistic motivation. *Journal of Personality and Social Psychology, 43,* 281–292.

Tollestrup, P. A., Turtle, J. W., & Yuille, J. C. (1994). Expectations of eyewitness performance: Jurors' verdicts do not follow from their beliefs. In D. F. Ross, J. D. Read, & M. P. Toglia (Eds.), *Adult eyewitness testimony: Current trends and developments* (pp. 144–162). New York: Cambridge University Press.

Toobin, J. (1995, October 23). A horrible human event. *New Yorker,* pp. 40–49.

Tourangeau, R., Smith, T., & Rasinski, K. (1997). Motivation to report sensitive behaviors on surveys: Evidence from a bogus pipeline experiment. *Journal of Applied Social Psychology, 27,* 209–222.

Trafimow, D., & Finlay, K. A. (1996). The importance of subjective norms for a minority of people: Between-subjects and within-subjects analyses. *Personality and Social Psychology Bulletin, 22,* 820–828.

Trappey, C. (1996). A meta-analysis of consumer choice and subliminal advertising. *Psychology and Marketing, 13,* 517–530.

Travis, C. B., & Yeager, C. P. (1991). Sexual selection, parental investment, and sexism. *Journal of Social Issues, 47,* 117–129.

Trends in cigarette smoking among high school students: United States, 1991–2002. (2002). *Centers for Disease Control, Morbidity and Mortality Weekly Report, 51,* 409–412.

Triandis, H. C. (1989). The self and social behavior in differing cultural contexts. *Psychological Review, 96,* 506–520.

Triandis, H. C. (1990). Cross-cultural studies of individualism and collectivism. In J. J. Berman (Ed.), *Nebraska Symposium on Motivation, 1989* (pp. 41–133). Lincoln: University of Nebraska Press.

Triandis, H. C. (1994). *Culture and social behavior.* New York: McGraw-Hill.

Triandis, H. C. (1995). *Individualism and collectivism.* Boulder, CO: Westview Press.

Triandis, H. C. (2001). Individualism-collectivism and personality. *Journal of Personality, 69,* 907–924.

Triplett, N. (1898). The dynamogenic factors in pace making and competition. *American Journal of Psychology, 9,* 507–533.

Trivers, R. L. (1971). The evolution of reciprocal altruism. *Quarterly Review of Biology, 46,* 35–57.

Trivers, R. L. (1985). *Social evolution.* Menlo Park, CA: Benjamin-Cummings.

Trope, Y., & Lieberman, A. (1996). Social hypothesis testing: Cognitive and motivational mechanisms. In E. T. Higgins & A. W. Kruglanski (Eds.), *Social psychology: Handbook of basic principles* (pp. 239–270). New York: Guilford Press.

Tseëlon, E. (1995). *The presentation of woman in everyday life.* Thousand Oaks, CA: Sage.

Turner, C., & Leyens, J. (1992). The weapons effect revisited: The effects of firearms on aggressive behavior. In P. Suedfeld & P. E. Tetlock (Eds.), *Psychology and social policy* (pp. 201–221). New York: Hemisphere.

Turner, C., Simons, L., Berkowitz, L., & Frodi, A. (1977). The stimulating and inhibiting effects of weapons on aggressive behavior. *Aggressive Behavior, 3,* 355–378.

Turner, F. J. (1932). *The significance of sections in American history.* New York: Henry Holt.

Turner, M. E., & Horvitz, T. (2001). The dilemma of threat: Group effectiveness and ineffectiveness under adversity. In M. E. Turner (Ed.), *Groups at work: Theory and research* (pp. 445–470). Mahwah, NJ: Erlbaum.

Turner, M. E., Pratkanis, A. R., Probasco, P., & Leve, C. (1992). Threat, cohesion, and group effectiveness: Testing a social identity maintenance perspective on groupthink. *Journal of Personality and Social Psychology, 63,* 781–796.

Tversky, A., & Kahneman, D. (1973). Availability: A heuristic for judging frequency and probability. *Cognitive Psychology, 5,* 207–232.

Tversky, A., & Kahneman, D. (1974). Judgment under uncertainty: Heuristics and biases. *Science, 185,* 1124–1131.

Twenge, J. M. (1997). Attitudes toward women, 1970–1995: A meta-analysis. *Psychology of Women Quarterly, 21,* 35–51.

Twenge, J. M. (2001). Changes in women's assertiveness in response to status and roles: A cross-temporal meta-analysis, 1931–1993. *Journal of Personality and Social Psychology, 81,* 133–145.

Tyler, T. R. (1990). *Why people obey the law.* New Haven, CT: Yale University Press.

Uchino, B. N., Cacioppo, J. T., & Keicolt-Glaser, J. K. (1996). The relationship between social support and physiological processes: A review with emphasis on underlying mechanisms and implications for health. *Psychological Bulletin, 119,* 488–531.

U.S. Department of Justice. (2000). *Violence by intimates.* Washington, DC: Bureau of Justice Statistics.

U.S. Environmental Protection Agency. (2001). *Improve energy efficiency this winter.* Retrieved from http://www.epa.gov/epa-home/headline_113001.htm

Uzzell, D. (2000). Ethnographic and action research. In G. M. Breakwell, S. Hammond, & C. Fife-Schaw (Eds.), *Research methods in psychology* (2nd ed., pp. 326–337). Thousand Oaks, CA: Sage.

Vallone, R. P., Griffin, D. W., Lin, S., & Ross, L. (1990). The overconfident prediction of future actions and outcomes by self and others. *Journal of Personality and Social Psychology, 58,* 582–592.

Van Boven, L., Kamada, A., & Gilovich, T. (1999). The perceiver as perceived: Everyday intuitions about the correspondence bias. *Journal of Personality and Social Psychology, 77,* 1188–1199.

Vance, C. S. (1986, August 2). The Meese Commission on the road. *Nation,* pp. 65, 76.

van de Vijver, F., & Leung, K. (1997). *Methods and data analyses for cross-cultural research.* Thousand Oaks, CA: Sage.

Van Lange, P. A. M., Ouwerkerk, J. W., & Tazelaar, M. J. A. (2002). How to overcome the detrimental effects of noise in social interaction: The benefits of generosity. *Journal of Personality and Social Psychology, 82,* 768–780.

Van Lange, P. A. M., Rusbult, C. E., Drigotas, S. M., Arriaga, X. B., Witcher, B. S., & Cox, C. L. (1997). Willingness to sacrifice in close relationships. *Journal of Personality and Social Psychology, 72,* 1373–1395.

Van Overwalle, F., & De Metsenaere, M. (1990). The effects of attribution-based intervention and study strategy training on academic achievement in college freshmen. *British Journal of Educational Psychology, 60,* 299–311.

Van Vugt, M. (2001). Community identification moderating the impact of financial incentives in a natural social dilemma: Water conservation. *Personality and Social Psychology Bulletin, 27,* 1440–1449.

Van Vugt, M., & De Cremer, D. C. (1999). Leadership in social dilemmas: The effects of group identification on collective actions to provide public goods. *Journal of Personality and Social Psychology, 76,* 587–599.

Van Vugt, M., & Samuelson, C. (1999). The impact of personal metering in the management of a natural resource crisis: A social dilemma analysis. *Personality and Social Psychology Bulletin, 25,* 731–745.

Van Yperen, N. W., & Buunk, B. P. (1990). A longitudinal study of equity in intimate relationships. *European Journal of Social Psychology, 20,* 287–309.

Vargas Llosa, M. (1986, February 16). My son the Rastafarian. *New York Times Magazine,* pp. 20–30, 41–43, 67.

Vidyasagar, P., & Mishra, H. (1993). Effect of modelling on aggression. *Indian Journal of Clinical Psychology, 20,* 50–52.

Vining, J., & Ebreo, A. (2002). Emerging theoretical and methodological perspectives on conservation behavior. In R. B. Bechtel & A. Churchman (Eds.), *Handbook of environmental psychology* (pp. 541–558). New York: Wiley.

Visscher, T. L. S., & Seidell, J. C. (2001). The public health impact of obesity. *Annual Review of Public Health, 22,* 355–375.

Vissing, Y., Straus, M., Gelles, R., & Harrop, J. (1991). Verbal aggression by parents and psychosocial problems of children. *Child Abuse and Neglect, 15,* 223–238.

Viswesvaran, C., & Deshpande, S. P. (1996). Ethics, success, and job satisfaction: A test of dissonance theory in India. *Journal of Business Ethics, 10,* 487–501.

Voas, R. B., Holder, H. D., & Gruenewald, P. J. (1999). The effect of drinking and driving interventions on alcohol-related traffic crashes within a comprehensive community trial. *Addiction, 92,* S221–S236.

Vohs, K. D., & Heatherton, T. F. (2000). Self-regulatory failure: A resource-depletion approach. *Psychological Science, 11,* 249–254.

von Hippel, W., Hawkins, C., & Schooler, J. W. (2001). Stereotype distinctiveness: How counterstereotypic behavior shapes the self-concept. *Journal of Personality and Social Psychology, 81,* 193–205.

Vonk, R. (1995). Effects of inconsistent behaviors on person perception: A multidimensional study. *Personality and Social Psychology Bulletin, 21,* 674–685.

Vonk, R. (1999). Effects of outcome dependency on correspondence bias. *Personality and Social Psychology Bulletin, 25,* 382–389.

Vonk, R. (2002). Self-serving interpretations of flattery: Why ingratiation works. *Journal of Personality and Social Psychology, 82,* 515–526.

Vonnegut, K., Jr. (1963). *Cat's cradle.* New York: Delacorte Press.

Vrijheid, M., Dolk, H., Armstrong, B., Abramsky, L., Bianchi, F., Fazarinc, I., et al. (2002). Chromosomal congenital anomalies and residence near hazardous waste landfill sites. *Lancet, 359,* 320–322.

Wagner, A. W., Roemer, L., Orsillo, S. M., & Litz, B. T. (2003). Emotional experiencing in women with posttraumatic stress disorder: Congruence between facial expressivity and self-report. *Journal of Traumatic Stress, 16,* 67–75.

Wagner, M., & Armstrong, N. (2003). *Field guide to gestures.* Philadelphia: Quirk Books.

Wagstaff, G. (1982). Attitudes to rape: The "just world" strikes again? *Bulletin of the British Psychological Society, 35,* 277–279.

Walker, I., & Crogan, M. (1998). Academic performance, prejudice, and the jigsaw classroom: New pieces to the puzzle. *Journal of Community and Applied Social Psychology, 8,* 381–393.

Walker, L. G., Heys, S. D., & Eremin, O. (1999). Surviving cancer: Do psychosocial factors count? *Journal of Psychosomatic Research, 47,* 497–503.

Wallach, M. A., Kogan, N., & Bem, D. J. (1962). Group influences on individual risk taking. *Journal of Abnormal and Social Psychology, 65,* 75–86.

Walster, E. (1966). Assignment of responsibility for an accident. *Journal of Personality and Social Psychology, 3,* 73–79.

Walster, E., Aronson, V., Abrahams, D., & Rottman, L. (1966). Importance of physical attractiveness in dating behavior. *Journal of Personality and Social Psychology, 5,* 508–516.

Walster, E., & Festinger, L. (1962). The effectiveness of "overheard" persuasive communication. *Journal of Abnormal and Social Psychology, 65,* 395–402.

Walster, E., Walster, G. W., & Berscheid, E. (1978). *Equity: Theory and research.* Needham Heights, MA: Allyn & Bacon.

Walther, E. (2002). Guilty by mere association: Evaluative conditioning and the spreading attitude effect. *Journal of Personality and Social Psychology, 82,* 919–934.

Walther, J., Anderson, J. F., & Park, D. W. (1994). Interpersonal effects in computer mediated interaction: A meta-analysis of social and antisocial communication. *Communication Research, 21,* 460–487.

Wann, D. L., & Schrader, M. P. (2000). Controllability and stability in the self-serving attributions of sport specators. *Journal of Social Psychology, 140,* 160–168.

Watson, D. (1982). The actor and the observer: How are their perceptions of causality divergent? *Psychological Bulletin, 92,* 682–700.

Watson, D., & Pennebaker, J. W. (1989). Health complaints, stress, and distress: Exploring the central role of negative affectivity. *Psychological Review, 96,* 234–254.

Watson, J. (1950). Some social and psychological situations related to change in attitude. *Human Relations, 3,* 15–56.

Watson, R. I. (1973). Investigation into deindividuation using a cross-cultural survey technique. *Journal of Personality and Social Psychology, 25,* 342–345.

Watson, W. E., Johnson, L., Kumar, K., & Critelli, J. (1998). Process gain and process loss: Comparing interpersonal processes and performance of culturally diverse and non-diverse teams across time. *International Journal of Intercultural Relations, 22,* 409–430.

Wattenberg, M. P. (1987). The hollow realignment: Partisan change in a candidate-centered era. *Public Opinion Quarterly, 51,* 58–74.

Weary, G., & Arkin, R. C. (1981). Attributional self-presentation. In J. H. Harvey, W. J. Ickes, & R. F. Kidd (Eds.), *New directions in attribution research* (Vol. 3, pp. 223–246). Hillsdale, NJ: Erlbaum.

Webber, R., & Crocker, J. (1983). Cognitive processes in the revision of stereotypic beliefs. *Journal of Personality and Social Psychology, 45,* 961–977.

Weber, E. U., Bockenholt, U., Hilton, D. J., & Wallace, B. (1993). Determinants of diagnostic hypothesis generation: Effects of information, base rates, and experience. *Journal of Experimental Psychology: Learning, Memory, and Cognition, 19,* 1151–1164.

Webster, D. M. (1993). Motivated augmentation and reduction of the overattributional bias. *Journal of Personality and Social Psychology, 65,* 261–271.

Wechsler, H., Lee, J. E., Kuo, M., Siebring, M., Nelson, T. F., & Lee, H. (2002). Trends in college binge drinking during a period of increased prevention efforts: Findings from 4 Harvard School of Public Health college alcohol study surveys, 1993–2001. *Journal of American College Health, 50,* 203–217.

Wegener, D. T., & Petty, R. E. (1994). Mood management across affective states: The hedonic contingency hypothesis. *Journal of Personality and Social Psychology, 66,* 1034–1048.

Wegener, D. T., & Petty, R. E. (1995). Flexible correction processes in social judgment: The role of naive theories in corrections for perceived bias. *Journal of Personality and Social Psychology, 68,* 36–51.

Wegener, D. T., & Petty, R. E. (1997). The flexible correction model: The role of naive theories of bias in bias correction. In M. P. Zanna (Ed.), *Advances in experimental social psychology* (Vol. 29, pp. 141–208). San Diego, CA: Academic Press.

Wegner, D. M. (1986). Transactive memory: A contemporary analysis of the group mind. In B. Mullen & G. R. Goethals (Eds.), *Theories of group behavior* (pp. 185–208). New York: Springer-Verlag.

Wegner, D. M. (1989). *White bears and other unwanted thoughts: Suppression, obsession, and the psychology of mental control.* New York: Viking.

Wegner, D. M. (1992). You can't always think what you want: Problems in the suppression of unwanted thoughts. In M. P. Zanna (Ed.), *Advances in experimental social psychology* (Vol. 25, pp. 193–225). San Diego, CA: Academic Press.

Wegner, D. M. (1994). Ironic processes of mental control. *Psychological Review, 101,* 34–52.

Wegner, D. M. (1995). A computer network model of human transactive memory. *Social Cognition, 13,* 319–339.

Wegner, D. M. (2002). *The illusion of conscious will.* Cambridge, MA: MIT Press.

Wegner, D. M., Ansfield, M., & Pilloff, D. (1998). The putt and the pendulum: Ironic effects of the mental control of action. *Psychological Science, 9,* 196–199.

Wegner, D. M., & Bargh, J. A. (1998). Control and automaticity in social life. In D. T. Gilbert, S. T. Fiske, & G. Lindzey (Eds.), *The handbook of social psychology* (4th ed., Vol. 1, pp. 446–498). New York: McGraw-Hill.

Wegner, D. M., Erber, R., & Raymond, P. (1991). Transactive memory in close relationships. *Journal of Personality and Social Psychology, 61,* 923–929.

Wegner, D. M., Fuller, V. A., & Sparrow, B. (2003). Clever hands: Uncontrolled intelligence in facilitated communication. *Journal of Personality and Social Psychology, 85,* 5–19.

Wegner, D. M., Quillian, F., & Houston, C. E. (1996). Memories out of order: Thought suppression and the disturbance of sequence memory. *Journal of Personality and Social Psychology, 71,* 680–691.

Wegner, D. M., Wenzlaff, R., Kerker, M., & Beattie, A. E. (1981). Incrimination through innuendo: Can media questions become public answers? *Journal of Personality and Social Psychology, 40,* 822–832.

Wehrle, T., Kaiser, S., Schmidt, S., & Scherer, K. R. (2000). Studying the dynamics of emotional expression using synthesized facial muscle movements. *Journal of Personality and Social Psychology, 78,* 105–119.

Weiner, B. (1985). "Spontaneous" causal thinking. *Psychological Bulletin, 97*, 74–84.

Weiner, B., Amirkhan, J., Folkes, V. S., & Verette, J. A. (1987). An attributional analysis of excuse giving: Studies of a naive theory of emotion. *Journal of Personality and Social Psychology, 52*, 316–324.

Weinstein, N. D. (1980). Unrealistic optimism about future life events. *Journal of Personality and Social Psychology, 39*, 806–820.

Weinstein, N. D., & Klein, W. M. (1996). Unrealistic optimism: Present and future. *Journal of Social and Clinical Psychology, 15*, 1–8.

Weir, W. (1984, October 15). Another look at subliminal "facts." *Advertising Age*, p. 46.

Weiss, S. (2003, April 1). Scream cuisine: The noise squad dines out. *Washington Post*, p. F1.

Wells, G. L. (1984). The psychology of lineup identifications. *Journal of Applied Social Psychology, 14*, 89–103.

Wells, G. L. (1993). What do we know about eyewitness identification? *American Psychologist, 48*, 553–571.

Wells, G. L., & Bradfield, A. L. (1998). "Good, you identified the suspect": Feedback to eyewitness reports distorts their reports of the witnessing experience. *Journal of Applied Social Psychology, 83*, 360–376.

Wells, G. L., & Luus, C. A. E. (1990). Police lineups as experiments: Social methodology as a framework for properly conducted lineups. *Personality and Social Psychology Bulletin, 16*, 106–117.

Wells, G. L., Malpass, R. S., Lindsay, R. C. L., Fisher, R. P., Turtle, J. W., & Fulero, S. M. (2000). From the lab to the police station. *American Psychologist, 55*, 581–598.

Wells, G. L., & Olson, E. A. (2003). Eyewitness testimony. *Annual Review of Psychology, 54*, 277–295.

Wells, G. L., Olson, E. A., & Charman, S. D. (2002). The confidence of eyewitnesses in their identifications from lineups. *Current Directions in Psychological Science, 11*, 151–154.

Wells, G. L., Small, M., Penrod, S. D., Malpass, R. S., Fulero, S. M., & Brimacombe, C. A. E. (1998). Eyewitness identification procedures: Recommendations for lineups and photospreads. *Law and Human Behavior, 22*, 603–645.

Wells, G. L., Wright, E. F., & Bradfield, A. L. (1999) Witnesses to crime: Social and cognitive factors governing the validity of people's reports. In R. Roesch, S. D. Hart, & J. R. P. Ogloff (Eds.), *Psychology and law: The state of the discipline* (pp. 53–88). New York: Kluwer.

Wells, W. D. (Ed.). (1997). *Measuring advertising effectiveness*. Mahwah, NJ: Erlbaum.

Wenzel, M. (2000). Justice and identity: The significance of inclusion for perceptions of entitlement and the justice motive. *Personality and Social Psychology Bulletin, 26*, 157–176.

Wenzlaff, R. M., & Bates, D. E. (2000). The relative efficacy of concentration and suppression strategies of mental control. *Personality and Social Psychology Bulletin, 26*, 1200–1212.

Wenzlaff, R. M., & Wegner, D. M. (2000). Thought suppression. *Annual Review of Psychology, 51*, 59–91.

Werth, L., & Foerster, J. (2002). Implicit person theories influence memory judgments: The circumstances under which metacognitive knowledge is used. *European Journal of Social Psychology, 32*, 353–362.

Werth, L., Strack, F., & Foerster, J. (2002). Certainty and uncertainty: The two faces of the hindsight bias. *Organizational Behavior and Human Decision Processes, 87*, 323–341.

Weyant, J. M. (1996). Application of compliance techniques to direct-mail requests for charitable donations. *Psychology and Marketing, 13*, 157–170.

Wheeler, D. L., Jacobson, J. W., Paglieri, R. A., & Schwartz, A. A. (1993). An experimental assessment of facilitated communication. *Mental Retardation, 31*, 49–59.

Wheeler, L., & Kim, Y. (1997). What is beautiful is culturally good: The physical attractiveness stereotype has different content in collectivistic cultures. *Personality and Social Psychology Bulletin, 23*, 795–800.

Wheeler, L., Koestner, R., & Driver, R. (1982). Related attributes in the choice of comparison others: It's there, but it isn't all there is. *Journal of Experimental Social Psychology, 18*, 489–500.

White, H. (1997). Longitudinal perspective on alcohol and aggression during adolescence. In M. Galanter (Ed.), *Recent developments in alcoholism: Vol. 13. Alcohol and violence: Epidemiology, neurobiology, psychology, and family issues* (pp. 81–103). New York: Plenum.

White, J. W., Donat, P. L. N., & Humphrey, J. A. (1995). An examination of the attitudes underlying sexual coercion among acquaintances. *Journal of Psychology and Human Sexuality, 8*, 27–47.

White, P. A. (2002). Causal attribution from covariation information: The evidential evaluation model. *European Journal of Social Psychology, 32*, 667–684.

White, R. K. (1977). Misperception in the Arab-Israeli conflict. *Journal of Social Issues, 33*, 190–221.

Whittaker, J. O., & Meade, R. D. (1967). Social pressure in the modification and distortion of judgment: A cross-cultural study. *International Journal of Psychology, 2*, 109–113.

Whorf, B. L. (1956). *Language, thought, and reality*. New York: Wiley.

Wicker, A. W. (1969). Attitudes versus actions: The relationship between verbal and overt behavioral responses to attitude objects. *Journal of Social Issues, 25*, 41–78.

Wicklund, R. A., & Brehm, J. W. (1998). Resistance to change: The cornerstone of cognitive dissonance theory. In E. Harmon-Jones & J. S. Mills (Eds.), *Cognitive dissonance theory: Revival with revisions and controversies* (pp. 310–322). Washington, DC: American Psychological Association.

Wiedenfeld, S. A., O'Leary, A., Bandura, A., Brown, S., Levine, S., & Raska, K. (1990). Impact of perceived self-efficacy in coping with stressors on components of the immune system. *Journal of Personality and Social Psychology, 59*, 1082–1094.

Wilder, D. A. (1981). Perceiving persons as a group: Categorization and intergroup relations. In D. L. Hamilton (Ed.), *Cognitive processes in stereotyping and intergroup behavior* (pp. 213–257). Hillsdale, NJ: Erlbaum.

Wilder, D. A. (1984). Intergroup contact: The typical member and the exception to the rule. *Journal of Experimental Psychology, 20*, 177–194.

Wilder, D. A. (1986). Social categorization: Implications for creation and reduction of intergroup bias. In L. Berkowitz (Ed.), *Advances in experimental social psychology* (Vol. 19, pp. 291–355). New York: Academic Press.

Wilder, D. A., & Shapiro, P. N. (1989). Role of competition-induced anxiety in limiting the beneficial impact of positive behavior by an out-group member. *Journal of Personality and Social Psychology, 56*, 60–69.

Williams, J. (1998). *Thurgood Marshall: American revolutionary*. New York: Times Books.

Williams, K. R., & Hawkins, R. (1986). Perceptual research on general deterrence: A critical review. *Law and Society Review, 20*, 545–572.

Williams, R. B. (2002). Hostility, neuroendocrine changes, and health outcomes. In H. G. Koenig & H. J. Cohen (Eds.), *The link between religion and health: Psychoneuroimmunology and the faith factor* (pp. 160–173). London: Oxford University Press.

Williams, R. H., & Ross, M. H. (1980, March-April). Drilling for oil and gas in our houses. *Technology Review*, pp. 24–36.

Williams, T. P., & Sogon, S. (1984). Group composition and conforming behavior in Japanese students. *Japanese Psychological Research, 26*, 231–234.

Williamson, G. M., & Clark, M. S. (1989). Providing help and desired relationship type as determinants of changes in moods and self-evaluations. *Journal of Personality and Social Psychology, 56*, 722–734.

Williamson, G. M., & Clark, M. S. (1992). Impact of desired relationship type on affective reactions to choosing and being required to help. *Personality and Social Psychology Bulletin, 18*, 10–18.

Williamson, G. M., Clark, M. S., Pegalis, L. J., & Behan, A. (1996). Affective consequences of refusing to help in communal and exchange relationships. *Personality and Social Psychology Bulletin, 22*, 34–47.

Wilson, A. E., & Ross, M. (2000). The frequency of temporal-self and social comparisons in people's personal appraisals. *Journal of Personality and Social Psychology, 78*, 928–942.

Wilson, D. K., Purdon, S. E., & Wallston, K. A. (1988). Compliance in health recommendations: A theoretical overview of message framing. *Health Education Research, 3,* 161–171.

Wilson, D. S. (1997). Atruism and organism: Disentangling the themes of multilevel selection theory. *American Naturalist, 150,* S122–S134.

Wilson, E. O. (1975). *Sociobiology: The new synthesis.* Cambridge, MA: Belknap Press.

Wilson, J. Q., & Hernstein, R. J. (1985). *Crime and human nature.* New York: Simon & Schuster.

Wilson, T. D. (1990). Self-persuasion via self-reflection. In J. M. Olson & M. P. Zanna (Eds.), *Self-inference: The Ontario Symposium* (Vol. 6, pp. 43–67). Hillsdale, NJ: Erlbaum.

Wilson, T. D. (2002). *Strangers to ourselves: Discovering the adaptive unconscious.* Cambridge, MA: Harvard University Press.

Wilson, T. D., & Brekke, N. C. (1994). Mental contamination and mental correction: Unwanted influences on judgments and evaluations. *Psychological Bulletin, 116,* 117–142.

Wilson, T. D., Centerbar, D. B., & Brekke, N. (2002). Mental contamination and the debiasing problem. In T. Gilovich, D. W. Griffin, & D. Kahneman (Eds.), *Heuristics and biases: The psychology of intuitive judgment* (pp. 185–200). New York: Cambridge University Press.

Wilson, T. D., Damiani, M., & Shelton, N. (2002). Improving the academic performance of college students with brief attributional interventions. In J. Aronson (Eds.), *Improving academic achievement: Impact of psychological factors on education* (pp. 88–108). San Diego, CA: Academic Press.

Wilson, T. D., Dunn, D. S., Bybee, J. A., Hyman, D. B., & Rotondo, J. A. (1984). Effects of analyzing reasons on attitude-behavior consistency. *Journal of Personality and Social Psychology, 47,* 5–16.

Wilson, T. D., Dunn, D. S., Kraft, D., & Lisle, D. J. (1989). Introspection, attitude change, and attitude-behavior consistency: The disruptive effects of explaining why we feel the way we do. In L. Berkowitz (Ed.), *Advances in experimental social psychology* (Vol. 19, pp. 123–205). Orlando, FL: Academic Press.

Wilson, T. D., Gilbert, D. T., & Wheatley, T. (1998). Protecting our minds: The role of lay beliefs. In V. Yzerbyt, G. Lories, & B. Dardenne (Eds.), *Metacognition: Cognitive and social dimensions* (pp. 171–201). New York: Russell Sage Foundation.

Wilson, T. D., Hodges, S. D., & La Fleur, S. J. (1995). Effects of introspecting about reasons: Inferring attitudes from accessible thoughts. *Journal of Personality and Social Psychology, 69,* 16–28.

Wilson, T. D., Houston, C. E., Etling, K. M., & Brekke, N. C. (1996). A new look at anchoring effects: Basic anchoring and its antecedents. *Journal of Experimental Psychology: General, 125,* 387–402.

Wilson, T. D., Houston, C. E., & Meyers, J. M. (1998). Choose your poison: Effects of lay beliefs about mental processes on attitude change. *Social Cognition, 16,* 114–132.

Wilson, T. D., & Kraft, D. (1993). Why do I love thee? Effects of repeated introspections about a dating relationship on attitudes toward the relationship. *Personality and Social Psychology Bulletin, 19,* 409–418.

Wilson, T. D., & La Fleur, S. J. (1995). Knowing what you'll do: Effects of analyzing reasons on self-prediction. *Journal of Personality and Social Psychology, 68,* 21–35.

Wilson, T. D., Laser, P. S., & Stone, J. I. (1982). Judging the predictors of one's own mood: Accuracy and the use of shared theories. *Journal of Experimental Social Psychology, 18,* 537–556.

Wilson, T. D., Lindsey, S., & Schooler, T. Y. (2000). A model of dual attitudes. *Psychological Review, 107,* 101–126.

Wilson, T. D., & Linville, P. W. (1982). Improving the academic performance of college freshmen: Attribution therapy revisited. *Journal of Personality and Social Psychology, 42,* 367–376.

Wilson, T. D., & Linville, P. W. (1985). Improving the performance of college freshmen using attributional techniques. *Journal of Personality and Social Psychology, 49,* 287–293.

Wilson, T. D., Lisle, D., Schooler, J. W., Hodges, S. D., Klaaren, K. J., & La Fleur, S. J. (1993). Introspecting about reasons can reduce post-choice satisfaction. *Personality and Social Psychology Bulletin, 19,* 331–339.

Winslow, R. W., Franzini, L. R., & Hwang, J. (1992). Perceived peer norms, casual sex, and AIDS risk prevention. *Journal of Applied Social Psychology, 22,* 1809–1827.

Wiseman, C. V., Gray, J. J., Mosimann, J. E., & Ahrens, A. H. (1992). Cultural expectations of thinness in women: An update. *International Journal of Eating Disorders, 11,* 85–89.

Witelson, S. F. (1992). Cognitive neuroanatomy: A new era. *Neurology, 42,* 709–713.

Wolf, S. (1985). Manifest and latent influence of majorities and minorities. *Journal of Personality and Social Psychology, 48,* 899–908.

Wolfe, C., & Spencer, S. (1996). Stereotypes and prejudice: Their overt and subtle influence in the classroom. *American Behavioral Scientist, 40,* 176–185.

Woll, S. (1986). So many to choose from: Decision strategies in video-dating. *Journal of Social and Personal Relationships, 3,* 43–52.

Wollenberg, S. (2000, June 19). Mobile ads to hit the streets soon. *Charlottesville Daily Progress,* p. A1.

Wood, J. V. (1996). What is social comparison and how should we study it? *Personality and Social Psychology Bulletin, 22,* 520–537.

Wood, J. V., Taylor, S. E., & Lichtman, R. R. (1985). Social comparison in adjustment to breast cancer. *Journal of Personality and Social Psychology, 49,* 1169–1183.

Wood, W. (1982). Retrieval of attitude-relevant information from memory: Effects on susceptibility to persuasion and on intrinsic motivation. *Journal of Personality and Social Psychology, 42,* 798–810.

Wood, W. (1987). Meta-analytic review of sex differences in group performance. *Psychological Bulletin, 102,* 53–71.

Wood, W., Christensen, P. N., Hebl, M. R., & Rothgerber, H. (1997). Conformity to sex-typed norms, affect, and the self-concept. *Journal of Personality and Social Psychology, 73,* 523–535.

Wood, W., & Eagly, A. H. (2002). A cross-cultural analysis of the behavior of women and men: Implications for the origins of sex differences. *Psychological Bulletin, 128,* 699–727.

Wood, W., Lundgren, S., Ouellette, J. A., Busceme, S., & Blackstone, T. (1994). Minority influence: A meta-analytic review of social influence processes. *Psychological Bulletin, 115,* 323–345.

Wood, W., Pool, G. J., Leck, K., & Purvis, D. (1996). Self-definition, defensive processing, and influence: The normative impact of majority and minority groups. *Journal of Personality and Social Psychology, 71,* 1181–1193.

Wood, W., & Quinn, J. M. (2003). Forewarned and forearmed? Two meta-analytic syntheses of forewarnings of influence appeals. *Psychological Bulletin, 129,* 119–138.

Word, C. O., Zanna, M. P., & Cooper, J. (1974). The nonverbal mediation of self-fulfilling prophecies in interracial interaction. *Journal of Experimental Social Psychology, 10,* 109–120.

Wortman, C. B., & Brehm, J. W. (1975). Response to uncontrollable outcomes: An integration of reactance theory and the learned helplessness model. In L. Berkowitz (Ed.), *Advances in experimental social psychology* (Vol. 8, pp. 277–336). New York: Academic Press.

Wright, D. B., & Stroud, J. N. (2002). Age differences in lineup identification accuracy: People are better with their own age. *Law and Human Behavior, 26,* 641–654.

Wright, E. F., Luus, C. A. E., & Christie, S. D. (1990). Does group discussion facilitate the use of consensus information in making causal attributions? *Journal of Personality and Social Psychology, 59,* 261–269.

Wright, L. (1994). *Remembering Satan.* New York: Knopf.

Wyer, R. S., Jr. (1988). Social memory and social judgment. In P. R. Solomon, G. R. Goethals, C. M. Kelley, & B. R. Stephens (Eds.), *Perspectives on memory research.* New York: Springer-Verlag.

Wyer, R. S., Jr., & Srull, T. K. (1989). *Memory and cognition in its social context.* Hillsdale, NJ: Erlbaum.

Wylie, L. W. (1977). *Beaux gestes: A guide to French body talk.* New York: Cambridge University Press.

Yamaguchi, K., & Kandel, D. B. (1984). Patterns of drug use from adolescence to young adulthood: III. Predictors of progression. *American Journal of Public Health, 74,* 673–681.

Yang, A. S. (1997). Poll trends: Attitudes toward homosexuality. *Public Opinion Quarterly, 61,* 477–507.

Yee, D., & Eccles, J. S. (1988). Parent perceptions and attributions for children's math achievement. *Sex Roles, 19,* 317–333.

York, A. (2001, April 26). The product placement monster that E.T. spawned. *Salon* [Online journal.] Retrieved from http://archive.salon.com/tech/feature/2001/04/26/product_placement/print.html

Yudko, E., Blanchard, D., Henne, J., & Blanchard, R. (1997). Emerging themes in preclinical research on alcohol and aggression. In M. Galanter (Ed.), *Recent developments in alcoholism: Vol. 13. Alcohol and violence: Epidemiology, neurobiology, psychology, and family issues* (pp. 123–138). New York: Plenum.

Zajonc, R. B. (1965). Social facilitation. *Science, 149,* 269–274.

Zajonc, R. B. (1968). Attitudinal effects of mere exposure. *Journal of Personality and Social Psychology, 9*(Monograph Suppl. 2, pt. 2).

Zajonc, R. B. (1980). Compresence. In P. B. Paulus (Ed.), *Psychology of group influence* (pp. 35–60). Hillsdale, NJ: Erlbaum.

Zajonc, R. B., Heingartner, A., & Herman, E. M. (1969). Social enhancement and impairment of performance in the cockroach. *Journal of Personality and Social Psychology, 13,* 83–92.

Zanna, M. P., & Fazio, R. H. (1982). The attitude-behavior relation: Moving toward a third generation of research. In M. P. Zanna, E. T. Higgins, & C. P. Herman (Eds.), *Consistency in social behavior: The Ontario Symposium* (Vol. 2, pp. 283–301). Hillsdale, NJ: Erlbaum.

Zanna, M. P., Goethals, G. R., & Hill, J. (1975). Evaluating a sex-related ability: Social comparison with similar others and standard setters. *Journal of Experimental Social Psychology, 11,* 86–93.

Zanna, M. P., & Rempel, J. K. (1988). Attitudes: A new look at an old concept. In D. Bar-Tal & A. W. Kruglanski (Eds.), *The social psychology of attitudes* (pp. 315–334). New York: Cambridge University Press.

Zanot, E. J., Pincus, J. D., & Lamp, E. J. (1983). Public perceptions of subliminal advertising. *Journal of Advertising, 12,* 39–45.

Zebrowitz, L. A. (1997). *Reading faces: Window to the soul?* Boulder, CO: Westview Press.

Zebrowitz, L. A., & Montepare, J. M. (1992). Impressions of baby-faced individuals across the life-span. *Developmental Psychology, 28,* 1143–1152.

Zeman, Z. A. B. (1995). The state and propaganda. In R. Jackall (Ed.), *Propaganda* (pp. 174–189). New York: New York University Press.

Zillmann, D. (1978). Attribution and misattribution of excitatory reactions. In J. H. Harvey, W. J. Ickes, & R. F. Kidd (Eds.), *New directions in attribution research* (Vol. 2, pp. 335–370). Hillsdale, NJ: Erlbaum.

Zimbardo, P. G. (1970). The human choice: Individuation, reason, and order versus deindividuation, impulse, and chaos. In W. J. Arnold & D. Levine (Eds.), *Nebraska Symposium on Motivation, 1969* (Vol. 17, pp. 237–307). Lincoln: University of Nebraska Press.

Zimbardo, P. G., & Andersen, S. (1993). Understanding mind control: Exotic and mundane mental manipulations. In M. D. Langone (Ed.), *Recovery from cults* (pp. 104–125). New York: Norton.

Zimbardo, P. G., Weisenberg, M., Firestone, I., & Levy, B. (1965). Communicator effectiveness in producing public conformity and private attitude change. *Journal of Personality, 33,* 233–255.

Zubek, J. P. (Ed.). (1969). *Sensory deprivation: Fifteen years of research.* New York: Appleton-Century-Crofts.

Zuber, J. A., Crott, H. W., & Werner, J. (1992). Choice shift and group polarization: An analysis of the status of arguments and social decision schemes. *Journal of Personality and Social Psychology, 62,* 50–61.

Zuwerink, J., Monteith, M., Devine, P. G., & Cook, D. (1996). Prejudice toward blacks: With and without compunction? *Basic and Applied Social Psychology, 18,* 131–150.

CREDITS

CHAPTER 1

Text and Art: **p. 16:** Figure 1.1 adapted from L. Ross and S.M. Samuels. *The predictive power of personal reputation versus labels and construal in the Prisoner's Dilemma Game.* Unpublished manuscript. Stanford University. Copyright © 1993. Reprinted by permission of Dr. Lee Ross.
Photos and Cartoons: **p. 2:** Melissa Farlow/Aurora Photos; **p. 7:** Copyright © Michael J. Doolittle/The Image Works; **p. 8:** Roger Lemoyne/Getty Images, Inc – Liaison; **p. 10:** AP/Wide World Photos; **p. 13:** Paul Chesley/National Geographic Image Collection; **p. 15:** B. Seitz/Photo Researchers, Inc.; **p. 17:** Getty Images Inc. - Hulton Archive Photos; **p. 19:** Photograph courtesy of Trudy Festinger. Reprinted by permission; **p. 20:** AP/Wide World Photos; **p. 24:** Rick Kopstein.

CHAPTER 2

Text and Art: **p. 52:** Figure 2.3 adapted from "Ethical principles of psychologists and code of conduct," *American Psychologist, 2002, 57,* pp. 1060–1073. Copyright © 2002 by the American Psychological Association. Adapted by permission of the APA.
Photos and Cartoons: **p. 26:** AP/Wide World Photos; **p. 31:** AP/Wide World Photos; **p. 33:** Copyright © Felicia Martinez/PhotoEdit, Inc; **p. 37:** Courtesy of the Library of Congress; **p. 38:** Myrleen Ferguson/PhotoEdit; **p. 45:** John Gaps III/AP/Wide World Photos; **p. 48 (left):** REUTERS/Reuters TV/CORBIS BETTMANN; **p. 48 (right):** David Austen/Stock Boston.

CHAPTER 3

Text and Art: **p. 61:** Figure 3.1 adapted from Correll, Joshua; Park, Bernadette; Judd, Charles M; Wittenbrink, Bernd. The police officer's dilemma: Using ethnicity to disambiguate potentially threatening individuals. *Journal of Personality & Social Psychology.* Vol 83 (6) Dec 2002, 1314–1329. Copyright © 2002 by the American Psychological Association; **p. 66:** Figure 3.3 from "Category Accessibility and Impressing Formation," by Higgins et al., in *Journal of Experimental Psychology, vol. 13,* pp. 141–154. Copyright © 1977. Reprinted with permission of Elsevier; **p. 68:** Figure 3.4 adapted from L. Ross, M.R. Lepper and M. Hubbard. "Perseverance in self-perception and social perception: Biased attributional processes in the debriefing paradigm." *Journal of Personality and Social Psychology, vol. 32,* pp. 880–892. Copyright © 1975 by the American Psychological Association. Table 1, p. 883 adapted with permission of the APA & the author; **p. 76:** Figure 3.7 adapted from N. Schwartz et al. "Ease of retrieval as information: Another look at the availability heuristic." *Journal of Personality and Social Psychology, vol. 61,* pp. 195–202. Copyright © 1991 by the American Psychological Association. Table 1, p. 197 adapted with permission of the APA and the author; **p. 89:** Figure 3.09 reprinted with permission from Nisbett et al., "Teaching Reason," *Science, vol. 239,* pp. 625–631. Copyright © 1987 American Association for the Advancement of Science. Reprinted by permission of the AAAS and the author.
Photos and Cartoons: **p. 56:** Wally Skalij/The Daily Breeze; **p. 59:** Gala/SuperStock, Inc; **p. 60:** Joshua Correll/Courtesy Charles Judd, University of Colorado at Boulder; **p. 62:** National Archives and Records Administration; **p. 64:** AP/Wide World Photos; **p. 70:** Mary Kate Denny/PhotoEdit; **p. 73:** Irven De Vore/Anthro-Photo File; **p. 75:** Charles Thatcher/Getty Images, Inc. - Stone Allstock; **p. 77:** Yellow Dog Productions/Getty Images Inc. - Image Bank; **p. 82:** Copyright © Eric Fowke/PhotoEdit, Inc; **p. 86:** Bill Frakes/Sports Illustrated.

CHAPTER 4

Text and Art: **p. 93:** Excerpt from P. DeMarco, "Dear Diary." *New York Times,* September 28th, 1994. Copyright © 1994 The New York Times Company. Reprinted by permission; **p. 101:** Figure 4.1 based on Archer, 1991, 1997a, 1997b; Gudykunst, Ting-Toomey, & Nishida, 1996; Hewitt & Alquahtani, 2003; Knapp & Hall, 1997; Richmond & McCroskey, 1995; **p. 106:** Figure 4.2 adapted from C. Hoffman, I. Lau, and D.R. Johnson, "The linguistic relativity of person cognition: An English-Chinese comparison." *Journal of Personality and Social Psychology, vol. 51,* pp. 1097–1105. Copyright © 1986 by the American Psychological Association. Table 5, p. 1103 adapted with permission of the APA and the author; **p. 112:** Figure 4.4 from "The attribution of attitudes," by E.E. Jones and V.V. Harris in *Journal of Experimental Social Psychology, Vol. 28,* pp. 255–276. Copyright © 1992. Reprinted with permission from Elsevier; **p. 114 (top):** Figure 4.5 adapted from S.E. Taylor and S.T. Fiske, "Point of view and perceptions of causality." *Journal of Personality and Social Psychology, vol. 32,* pp. 439–445. Copyright © 1975 by the American Psychological Association. Reprinted by permission of the APA and the author; **p. 114 (bottom):** Figure 4.5 adapted from S.E. Taylor and S.T. Fiske, "Point of view and perceptions of causality." *Journal of Personality and Social Psychology, vol. 32,* pp. 439–445. Copyright © 1975 by the American Psychological Association. Table 1, p. 441 reprinted by permission of the APA and the author.
Photos and Cartoons: **p. 92:** Rainer Grosskopf/Getty Images Inc. - Stone Allstock; **p. 97 (top left):** David Cooper/Getty Images, Inc – Liaison; **p. 97 (top center):** Alan Weiner/Getty Images, Inc – Liaison; **p. 97 (top right):** Lynn McLaren/Index Stock Imagery, Inc; **p. 97 (bottom left):** Copyright © Guido Alberto Rossi/TIPS Images; **p. 97 (bottom center):** Richard Pan/StockPhotos Inc./Globe Photos, Inc; **p. 97 (bottom right):** Costa Manos/Magnum Photos, Inc; **p. 99:** Paul Ekman, Ph.D., Professor of Psychology/Human Interaction Laboratory; **p. 101 (left):** Copyright © SETBOUN/CORBIS; **p. 101 (top center):** Copyright © Carol Beckwith & Angela Fisher /HAGA/The Image Works; **p. 101 (bottom center):** Sundberg, Dag/Getty Images Inc. - Image Bank; **p. 101 (top right):** Bill Bachmann/Photo Researchers, Inc; **p. 101 (bottom right):** Sisse Brimberg/National Geographic Image Collection; **p. 102:** Rick Stafford; **p. 105 (left):** Darlene Hammond/Getty Images Inc. - Hulton Archive Photos; **p. 105 (right):** Copyright © Yang Liu/CORBIS; **p. 108:** Hartmut Schwarzbach/Peter Arnold, Inc; **p. 111 (left):** Copyright © John Dominis/Time Life Pictures/Getty Images, Inc; **p. 111 (right):** AP/Wide World Photos; **p. 118:** Creators Syndicate; **p. 119:** Shaun Botterill/Getty Images, Inc. - Allsport Photography; **p. 126:** David Turnley/CORBIS BETTMANN.

CHAPTER 5

Text and Art: **p. 131:** Reuse of excerpt from Goodman, "A Benjamin Franklin Reader" 1945, p. 746; **p. 133:** Excerpt from R. Montemayor and M. Eisen, "The development of self-conceptions from childhood to adolescence." *Developmental Psychology, vol. 13,* pp. 314–319. Copyright © 1977 by the American Psychological Association. Reprinted by permission of the APA and the author; **p. 136:** Try It! From Ted Singelis, "The measurement of independent and interdependent self-construals." *Personality and Social Psychology Bulletin, vol. 20,* p. 580 and 585. Copyright © 1994. Reprinted by permission of the author; **p. 137:** Figure 5.1 from S. Gabriel and W.L. Gardner, "Are there "his" and "hers" types of interdependence? The implications of gender difference in collective versus relational interdependence of affect, behavior and cognition." *Journal of Personality and Social Psychology, vol. 77,* pp. 642–655. Copyright © 1999 by the American Psychological Association. Figure 3, p. 648 reprinted with permission of the APA; **p. 138:** Excerpt from S.E. Cross, P.L. Bacon and M.L. Morris, "The relational -

CHAPTER 6

CHAPTER 7

CHAPTER 8

CHAPTER 9

CHAPTER 10

The development (and deterioration) of satisfaction and commitment in heterosexual involvements." *Journal of Personality and Social Psychology, vol. 45*, pp. 101–117. Copyright © 1983 by the American Psychological Association. Adapted with permission of the APA and the author; **p. 350:** Figure 10.7 from "A typography of relationship disengagement and dissolution," by S. Duck in *Personal Relationships 4: Dissolving Personal Relationships.* Copyright © 1982. Reprinted with permission from Elsevier.

Photos and Cartoons: **p. 316:** Jonathan Player/The New York Times; **p. 319:** Michael Newman/PhotoEdit; **p. 323:** Willie J. Allen Jr./The New York Times; **p. 326 (top left):** Evan Agostini/Getty Images, Inc – Liaison; **p. 326 (top center):** Getty Images Inc. - Hulton Archive Photos; **p. 326 (top right):** Mike Grey/Getty Images Inc. - Hulton Archive Photos; **p. 326 (bottom left):** Jeff Manzetti/AP/Wide World Photos; **p. 326 (bottom center):** AP/Wide World Photos; **p. 326 (bottom right):** Aaron Rapoport/Fox/Picture Desk, Inc./Kobal Collection; **p. 328:** Courtesy of Judith H. Langlois/Dept. of Psychology/University of Texas; **p. 329:** Buddy Mays/ImageState/International Stock Photography Ltd; **p. 332:** Copyright © Esbin-Anderson/The Image Works; **p. 334:** Sidney Harris; **p. 335:** Anita Weber/SIPA Press; **p. 340:** Bruce Dale/National Geographic Image Collection; **p. 342:** Copyright © Elizabeth Crews/The Image Works; **p. 348 (left):** David Hanover/Getty Images Inc. - Stone Allstock; **p. 348 (right):** GARY BUSS/Getty Images, Inc. – Taxi; **p. 352:** Copyright © Jeff Greenberg/The Image Works.

CHAPTER 11

Text and Art: **p. 364:** Figure 11.2 adapted from M. Toi and C.D. Batson, "More evidence that empathy is a source of altruistic motivation." *Journal of Personality and Social Psychology, 43*, pp. 281–292. Copyright © 1982 by the American Psychological Association; **p. 375:** Figure 11.3 adapted from Darley et al. "Bystander Intervention in emergencies: Diffusion and responsibility," in *Journal of Personality and Social Psychology, vol. 8*, pp. 377–383. Copyright © 1968 by the American Psychological Association. Figure 1, p. 380 adapted with permission of the APA and the author; **p. 376:** Adapted from "The Unresponsive Bystander, Why Doesn't He Help?" by Latane/Darley. Copyright © 1970. Adapted by permission of Pearson Education. Upper Saddle River, NJ.

Photos and Cartoons: **p. 356:** Allan Tannenbaum/The Image Works; **p. 359:** Steve Mason/Getty Images, Inc.- Photodisc; **p. 365:** UPI/CORBIS BETTMANN; **p. 366:** Robert Allison/Contact Press Images Inc; **p. 367:** PhotoEdit; **p. 368:** Elena Rooraid/PhotoEdit; **p. 372 (left):** Frank Siteman/PhotoEdit; **p. 372 (right):** Kindra Clineff/Index Stock Imagery, Inc; **p. 374:** New York Times Pictures; **p. 377:** Steve McCurry/Magnum Photos, Inc; **p. 380:** Charles Gupton/Stock Boston; **p. 382:** Ryan McVay/Getty Images, Inc.- Photodisc; **p. 383:** Myrleen Ferguson/PhotoEdit.

CHAPTER 12

Text and Art: **p. 398:** Figure 12.1 adapted from J.M. Carlsmith and C.A. Anderson, "Ambient temperature and the occurrence of collective violence: A new analysis." *Journal of Personality and Social Psychology, vol. 37*, pp. 337–344. Copyright © 1979 by the American Psychological Association. Figure 3, p. 341 adapted with permission; **p. 402:** Figure 12.2 adapted from L. Berkowitz and A. LePage, "Weapons as aggression - eliciting stimuli." *Journal of Personality and Social Psychology, vol. 7*, pp. 202–207. Copyright © 1967 by the American Psychological Association; **p. 406:** Figure 12.3 adapted from R.M. Liebert and R.A. Baron, "Some immediate effects of televised violence on children's behavior." *Developmental Psychology, vol. 6*, pp. 469–475. Copyright © 1972 by the American Psychological Association. Adapted with permission of the APA and the author; **p. 418:** Figure 12.5 adapted from D. Archer and R. Gartner, "Violence and Crime in Cross-National Perspective." Copyright © 1984. Used with permission of Yale University Press.

Photos and Cartoons: **p. 388:** Copyright © Robert Trippett/SIPA Press; **P. 392:** Catherine Ursillo/Photo Researchers, Inc; **p. 393:** Anthro-Photo File; **p. 396:** Copyright © Eastcott/Momatiuk/The Image Works; **p. 400:** Yellow Dog Productions/Getty Images Inc. - Image Bank; **p. 403:** Chris Martinez/Getty Images, Inc – Liaison; **p. 404:** Albert Bandura, Stanford University/Albert Bandura, D. Ross & S.A. Ross, Imitation of film-mediated aggressive models. "Journal of Abnormal and Social Psychology", 1963, 66. P. 8; **p. 407:** Joe Raedle/Getty Images, Inc – Liaison; **p. 409:** Sidney Baldwin/Warner Bros. ProductionsLtd./Regency Enterprises/Picture Desk, Inc./Kobal Collection; **p. 413:** Copyright © Jennie Woodcock/CORBIS; **p. 416:** Photo Researchers, Inc; **p. 417 (left):** National Archives and Records Administration; **p. 417 (right):** U. S.

Army Photograph; **p. 421:** Charles Moore/Black Star; **p. 423:** Jonathan Nourok/PhotoEdit.

CHAPTER 13

Text and Art: **p. 437:** Figure 13.1 adapted from C. Bond and C. DiCandia. *Personality and Social Psychology Bulletin, vol. 14*, 1988, pp. 448–458. Copyright © 1988 by Society for Personality and Social Psychology. Reprinted by permission of Sage Publication, Inc; **p. 443:** Figure 13.2 adapted from G.A. Quattrone and E.E. Jones, "The perception of variability within ingroups and outgroups: Implications for the law of small numbers." *Journal of Personality and Social Psychology, vol. 38*, pp. 141–152. Copyright © 1980 by the American Psychological Association. Adapted from table 3, p. 147 by permission of the APA; **p. 443, 465:** Excerpt from *The Nature of Prejudice* by Gordon Allport, p. 281. Copyright © 1979, 1958, 1954. Reprinted by permission of Perseus Books, LLC; **p. 446:** Figure 13.3 adapted from Greenberg, J. and Pyszczynski, T. "The effect of an overheard slur on evaluations of the target: How to spread a social disease." *Journal of Experimental Social Psychology, vol. 21*, 1985, pp. 61–72. Copyright © 1985. Reprinted with permission from Elsevier; **p. 458:** Excerpt from J. Dollard, "Hostility and Fear in Social Life." *Social Forces, 17*, 1938. Reprinted by permission of North Carolina University Press; **p. 460:** Figure 13.6 adapted from R. Rogers and S. Prentice-Dunn, "Deindividuation and anger-mediated interracial aggression: Unmasking regressive racism." *Journal of Personality and Social Psychology, vol. 41*, pp. 63–73. Copyright © 1987 by the American Psychological Association. Figure 1, p. 68 adapted with permission of the APA and the author; **p. 466:** Figure 13.7 adapted from Sherif, "Intergroup conflict and cooperation: The Robber's Cave Experiment. Copyright © 1961. Reprinted by permission of O.J. Harvey.

Photos and Cartoons: **p. 428:** Jack Delano/Courtesy of the Library of Congress; **p. 430:** Marty Lederhandler/AP/Wide World Photos; **p. 432:** Laura Dwight/PhotoEdit; **p. 433:** Copyright © Larry Fisher, Quad City Times/The Boston Globe c/o Copyright © Clearance Center/The New York Times Agency; **p. 434:** Christoph Wilhelm/Getty Images, Inc. – Taxi; **p. 439:** Ross Taylor/AP/Wide World Photos; **p. 441:** David Young-Wolff/PhotoEdit; **p. 448:** Michael Jang/Getty Images Inc. Stone Allstock; **p. 450:** Suzanne Hanover/Picture Desk, Inc./Kobal Collection; **p. 451:** AP/Wide World Photos; **p. 454:** David Young-Wolff/PhotoEdit; **p. 458:** Jeff Greenberg/PhotoEdit; **p. 463 (left):** CORBIS BETTMANN; **p. 463 (right):** Courtesy of W.S. Hoole Special Collections Library, University of Alabama; **p. 467:** Jonathan Nourok/PhotoEdit; **p. 470:** Tom Watson/Merrill Education.

SOCIAL PSYCHOLOGY IN ACTION 1

Text and Art: **p. 478:** Table SPA 1.01 reprinted from *Journal of Psychosomatic Research, vol. 11.* T.H. Holmes and R.H. Rahe, "The social readjustment rating scale." Copyright © 1967. Reprinted with permission from Elsevier; **p. 481:** Figure SPA 1.01 adapted from S. Cohen,, D. Tyrrell and A.P. Smith, "Psychological Stress and Susceptibility to the Common Cold." *The New England Journal of Medicine, vol. 325*, 1991, pp. 606–612; **p. 483:** Figure SPA 1.02 from Langer et al. "The effects of choice and enhanced personal responsibility for the aged: A field experiment." *Journal of Personality and Social Psychology, 31*. Copyright © 1976 by the American Psychological Association. Reprinted by permission of the APA and Ellen Langer (Professor of Psychology at Harvard University).

Photos and Cartoons: **p. 474:** Landov LLC; **p. 479 (top left):** Robert Brenner/PhotoEdit; **p. 479 (top right):** Ryan McVay/Getty Images, Inc.-Photodisc; **p. 479 (bottom left):** Thomas Hoepker/Magnum Photos, Inc; **p. 479 (bottom right):** Elena Rooraid/PhotoEdit; **p. 483:** Telegraph Colour Library/Getty Images, Inc. – Taxi; **p. 488:** Mark Lewis/Getty Images Inc. - Stone Allstock; **p. 492:** SuperStock, Inc; **p. 496:** Bob Daemmrich/Stock Boston; **p. 497:** Bruce Ayres/Getty Images Inc. - Stone Allstock; **p. 500 (left):** Donna Day/Getty Images Inc. - Stone Allstock; **p. 500 (right):** Billy E. Barnes/PhotoEdit.

SOCIAL PSYCHOLOGY IN ACTION 2

Text and Art: **p. 508:** Figure SPA 2.01 adapted from D.R. Sherrod, "Crowding, perceived control, and behavioral after effects." Reprinted with permission from the *Journal of Applied Social Psychology, vol. 4*, pp. 171–186. Copyright © V.H. Winston & Sons, 360 South Ocean Boulevard, Palm Beach, FL 33480. All rights reserved; **p. 511:** Figure SPA 2.02 adapted from D.C. Glass and J.E. Singer,

"Urban Stress: Experiments on noise and social stressors." Copyright © 1972. Reprinted by permission of the author; **p. 521:** Figure SPA 2.04 adapted from R.B. Cialdini, R.R. Reno and C.A. Kallgren, "A focus theory of normative conduct: Recycling the concept of norms to reduce littering in public places." *Journal of Personality and Social Psychology, vol. 58,* pp. 1015–1026. Copyright © 1990 by the American Psychological Association. Figure 4, pg. 1020 adapted with permission of the APA and the author.

Photos and Cartoons: **p. 504:** AP/Wide World Photos; **p. 507:** Figaro Magazine/Getty Images, Inc – Liaison; **p. 510:** Copyright © Cameramann/The Image Works; **p. 512:** David Young-Wolff/PhotoEdit; **p. 517:** Copyright © Pedrick/The Image Works; **p. 521:** Pearson Education/PH College; **p. 522:** Bonnie Kamin/PhotoEdit.

SOCIAL PSYCHOLOGY IN ACTION 3

Text and Art: **p. 530:** Figure SPA 3.01 adapted from Lindsay et al., "Can people detect eyewitness identification." *Journal of Applied Psychology, vol. 66,* pp. 79–89. Copyright © 1981 by the American Psychological Association. Figure 1, p. 85 adapted with permission of the APA and the author.

Photos and Cartoons: **p. 526:** Bryan Singer/Picture Desk, Inc./Kobal Collection/ POLYGRAM/SPELLING; **p. 528:** Dallas Morning News; **p. 532:** James Schnepf/Getty Images, Inc – Liaison; **p. 534:** Loftus EF, Miller DG, Burns HJ, (1978). Semantic integration of verbal information into a visual memory. *"Journal of Experimental Psychology";* Human Learning and Memory, 4, 19–31; **p. 536:** Getty Images, Inc – Liaison; **p. 542:** Mark C. Burnett/Photo Researchers, Inc; **p. 545:** Steve Bloom; **p. 549:** Photofest; **p. 551:** DALLAL/SIPA Press; **p. 552:** Spencer Grant/PhotoEdit.

NAME INDEX

SUBJECT INDEX